A Practical Guide To Drafting Irrevocable Life Insurance Trusts

(With Sample Forms And Checklists)

Second Edition

ALI ABA

American Law Institute | American Bar Association

Continuing Leadership in Professional Education

Related ALI-ABA Publications

A Practical Guide To Drafting Marital Deduction Trusts (With Sample Forms And Checklists, And 2006 CD-ROM Supplement)
Sebastian V. Grassi, Jr.
Hardcover with CD; 687 pp. (2006). $149 plus free shipping. Order Code No. BK36K

A Practical Guide To Drafting Irrevocable Life Insurance Trusts (With Sample Forms And Checklists)
Sebastian V. Grassi, Jr.
Hardcover with CD; 390 pp. (2003). $149 plus free shipping. Order Code No. BK28

Pre-Mortem Estate Planning Checklist, Second Edition
Edward S. Schlesinger and Robert D. Howard
Looseleaf; 484 pp. (2003). $137.50 plus free shipping. Order Code No. BK19

A Practical Guide To Drafting Irrevocable Life Insurance Trusts

(With Sample Forms And Checklists)

Second Edition

Sebastian V. Grassi, Jr.

ALI ABA

Library of Congress Control Number: 2007932260

First Edition 2007

Printed in the United States of America

Third Printing 2009

ISBN: 978-0-8318-0007-9

John B. Spitzer of the ALI-ABA staff supervised the production of this book.

ALI-ABA has a history of outreach to underrepresented groups in the legal community and is firmly committed to providing a welcoming environment and ensuring that the attorneys who speak and write for our organization represent the increasing diversity of our profession. We welcome suggestions for new speakers and authors, especially from underrepresented groups in the legal community, to support the full participation of all of the talent in our profession.

Nothing in this publication should be considered as the rendering of legal advice. Non-lawyers should seek the advice of a licensed attorney in all legal matters. Readers should assure themselves that the material in this publication is still current and applicable at the time it is read. Neither ALI-ABA nor the author can warrant that the material will continue to be accurate, nor do they warrant it to be completely free of errors when published. Readers should verify statements before relying on them. The materials in this publication reflect the viewpoints of the author and do not necessarily express the opinions of ALI-ABA Continuing Professional Education or its sponsors.

Dedication

This book is dedicated to my wife Elizabeth A. Grassi (Proverbs 18:22 and 31:28-29), and to my children, Laura, Stephen, and Carolyn (Proverbs 17:6 and Psalms 127:3).

Foreword

This second edition of *A Practical Guide to Drafting Irrevocable Life Insurance Trusts (with Sample Forms and Checklists)* will become a key resource to estate planning lawyers. The author, Sebastian V. Grassi, Jr. is a nationally recognized estate planning practitioner. He has written numerous articles and has lectured extensively on the subject of irrevocable life insurance trusts (ILITs). Throughout the book, he incorporates and shares his years of experience and understanding of the issues surrounding ILITs. Mr. Grassi has given special care and attention to the drafting issues that face estate planners and their clients.

Full of practical guidance, this book gives the reader an in-depth analysis of the rules, regulations and case law governing ILITs; useful applications, tips and warnings that clarify and illustrate each topic; plus sample ILIT documents. This is the book that estate planners will turn to when designing and drafting ILITs. Written as a drafting guide rather than a treatise, this book covers all of the tax principles an estate planner must consider to ensure that the ILIT is complete in every way.

The book is divided into 17 chapters. Chapter 1 examines the numerous tax and non-tax advantages of an ILIT. Subsequent chapters deal with the income tax consequences of ILITs, including the transfer-for-value rule, a discussion on viatical and life settlements, and a discussion of the grantor trust rules (Chapter 2); the gift tax consequences of ILITs, including a close look at *Crummey* withdrawal powers and the new rules on grantor trusts (Chapter 3); the estate tax issues surrounding ILITs and the tax traps to be avoided under Internal Revenue Code sections 2035, 2036 and 2038 (Chapter 4); an expansive look at the generation skipping transfer (GST) tax issues in drafting ILITs, along with an invaluable checklist of 25 key rules for GST planning with ILITs (Chapter 5); a review of the 2001 Tax Act's liberalization of the GST rules, including the new qualified severance rules (Chapter 6); a summary of the key changes made to transfer taxes by the 2001 Tax Act (Chapter 7); a detailed analysis of the income, gift and estate tax consequences when a beneficiary serves as a trustee of an ILIT (Chapter 8); a new chapter on the many issues to be considered (both tax and non-tax) when selecting a trustee (Chapter 9); a copious checklist of 26 issues that must be addressed in designing and drafting an ILIT (Chapter 10); an expansive look at ways to draft an ILIT to adapt to changing circumstances (Chapter 11); another checklist for administering an ILIT, including a discussion of the often overlooked issue as to how to handle multiple *Crummey* withdrawal rights, and how to deal with the insurable interest rule requirement where an ILIT is the initial policy owner on the life of the insured-grantor (Chapter 12); proper coordination of an ILIT with the grantor's revocable living trust and general durable power of attorney for financial affairs, including a look at tax apportionment issues, and HIPAA issues relating to an ILIT (Chapter 13); a detailed discussion of 15 advanced estate planning strategies which provide practical, unique and creative ways to fund ILITs (Chapter 14); a discussion of typical problems that may afflict an ILIT and suggested "fixes" to remedy such problems (Chapter 15); a very useful overview of the various types of life insurance policies and helpful suggestions for managing trust owned life insurance (Chapter 16); and finally, updated sample ILIT documents (for both single and survivorship policies) and related forms which are provided on CD-ROM (Chapter 17).

The Appendixes include sample forms for making (or opting out of) GST allocations; a detailed summary of the income tax reporting requirements for grantor trusts; and a practical letter of instructions to grantors, trustees and beneficiaries.

The first edition of this book was widely accepted nationwide. I expect that this book—with its expansive coverage and updates for recent changes in the tax laws—will be an even more valuable and timely resource for attorneys, accountants, life insurance advisors, financial planners and trust officers alike. In a field as dynamic as ILITs, planners need the very best, concise, practical and most timely information available. No one delivers this better than Sebastian V. Grassi, Jr.

Julius H. Giarmarco, Esq.
Giarmarco, Mullins & Horton, P.C.
Troy, Michigan

Acknowledgments

The second edition of this book is the collaborative effort of many people across the United States—some directly, some indirectly, and some remotely.[1] Although it is impossible to identify all the people who have had some connection with this book, I would like to acknowledge and express my gratitude to the following people: My family, especially my wife who graciously allowed me to spend many early morning and late evening hours at the computer keyboard, and who from time to time assisted me in editing my manuscript. My parents Sebastian V. Grassi, Sr. (1924-1990) and Hortense T. Grassi (Proverbs 23: 22-25). My grandfather, a Boston area banker who had the foresight to establish a dynasty trust for the benefit of his descendants long before the generation-skipping transfer tax was even conceived (Proverbs 13:22a). My partner and close friend, Douglas L. Toering, Esq. (Ecclesiastes 4:9-10). My friend and estate planning colleague, Julius H. Giarmarco, Esq., of Giarmarco, Mullins & Horton, P.C. of Troy, Michigan, who throughout the years, has generously shared with me (and ultimately the readers of this book) his thoughts on estate planning and life insurance matters. Julius also spent many hours reviewing and editing my manuscript drafts and is the principal author of Chapter 14. Laura H. Peebles, CPA, PFS who reviewed numerous drafts of my manuscript and shared many practical ideas based on her years of experience. Laura is the Director of Estate, Gift and Trust Services of the national office of Deloitte & Touche, LLP in Washington, DC. Gary R. Lee, Esq., LLM (Tax), CPA, CFP of Boston, Massachusetts, who is the National Director of Insurance Consulting Services for Deloitte & Touche, LLP. Gary, an expert

[1] Like mountain climbing, no person climbs the "ladder of success" without the help: (i) of those who have gone before him/her and have placed the rungs, (ii) those who come behind him/her and provide the shoulders on which he/she stands, (iii) support from base camp, and (iv) the good Lord above who reaches down from on high, steadies the ladder and helps the climber from losing his or her balance. "To many is owed much."

and author on life insurance matters, also reviewed my manuscript and provided many helpful comments and suggestions, particularly concerning Chapter 16. Jane A. Hays, Esq., CLU of The Downey Group, Inc. of Champaign, Illinois also helped in the writing and editing of Chapter 16. Jon J. Gallo, Esq., of Greenberg, Glusker, Fields, Claman, Machtinger & Kinsella, L.L.P. of Los Angeles, California, and Dennis M. Mitzel, Esq. of Berry Moorman, P.C. of Detroit, Michigan whose contributions to the chapter on GST tax issues were of great value. Many of Jon's thoughts on life insurance and ILITs are also scattered through out the book. Jon was also generous in sharing with the readers his article on life insurance selection, which serves as the basis for Chapter 16. Mary Ann Mancini, Esq. of Bryan Cave of Washington, DC whose insight on donor retained interests was very helpful in the writing of Chapter 4, and who contributed to the discussion of the insurable interest rule in Chapter 12. Ellen K. Harrison, Esq. of Pillsbury, Winthrop, Shaw, Pittman, LLP of Washington, DC who assisted me in the discussion of grantor trust issues. Santo ("Sandy") Bisignano, Jr., Esq. of Bisignano & Harrison, LLP of Dallas, Texas and Stephanie E. Donaho, Esq. of Locke Liddell & Sapp, LLP of Houston, Texas, both of whom were significant contributors to Chapter 15 concerning "damaged" ILITs. The many other Fellows of the American College of Trust and Estate Counsel who directly or indirectly lent a helping hand and a perceptive eye in the writing of this book (including those ACTEC Fellows who are personally acknowledged in this book and those ACTEC Fellows who have authored treatises, articles, and CLE materials that are referenced in this book). A hearty thanks to all of you and to all the other authors whose articles and CLE outlines are referenced in this book. I could not have done it without you having first blazed the trail—you made my job all the more easier and enjoyable. Thanks are also extended to Adam Slonim, Esq. of San Diego, California for his suggested edits/clarifications to the sample ILIT trust forms.

Special recognition goes to Lawrence Brody, Esq. of Bryan Cave, LLP of St. Louis, Missouri, who served as the reviewing editor of the first draft of my manuscript (which initially appeared as an article in the *ACTEC Journal*). If it were not for Larry's detailed comments (about 30 pages worth), this book might not have been written.

I would also like to thank my editor, John B. Spitzer, Esq. of ALI-ABA. He is the (forbearing) person behind the scenes who is responsible for the final editing of my manuscript and turning it into a book—no small task. Thanks are also, and appropriately, extended to Mark T. Carroll, Esq. of ALI-ABA, who also had a significant behind the scenes role in the production of this book. Thanks guys.

Finally, and most importantly, I would like to acknowledge the hand of the good Lord above, who has put it in my heart to write this book, and who has brought these (and many other) fine people into my life (Proverbs 13:20a). I am most blessed indeed. May you and your practice be enriched by this book and the prayers that accompany it (Numbers 6: 24-26).

Sebastian V. Grassi, Jr.
(1 Corinthians 10:31)

Contents

CHAPTER 3
GIFT TAX ISSUES

CHAPTER 4
ESTATE TAX ISSUES

CHAPTER 5
GENERATION-SKIPPING TRANSFER TAX ISSUES

CHAPTER 6
2001 TAX ACT AND LIBERALIZED GST RULES

CHAPTER 7
KEY CHANGES AFFECTING TRANSFER TAXES UNDER THE 2001 TAX ACT

CHAPTER 8
TAX-SENSITIVE POWERS REGARDING THE BENEFICIARY-TRUSTEE

CHAPTER 9
TRUSTEE SELECTION

CHAPTER 10
CHECKLIST OF ISSUES FOR DRAFTING AN ILIT

CHAPTER 11
DRAFTING AN ILIT FOR FLEXIBILITY AND CHANGING CIRCUMSTANCES

CHAPTER 12
ILIT ADMINISTRATION CHECKLIST

CHAPTER 13
COORDINATION OF ILIT WITH INSURED'S OTHER ESTATE PLANNING DOCUMENTS

CHAPTER 14
ADVANCED PLANNING OPPORTUNITIES AND TECHNIQUES FOR ILITS

CHAPTER 15
FIXING A DAMAGED ILIT

CHAPTER 16
GENERAL OVERVIEW OF LIFE INSURANCE POLICIES

CHAPTER 17
SAMPLE IRREVOCABLE LIFE INSURANCE TRUST FORMS (AND OTHER RELATED ITEMS)

APPENDIXES

1

Benefits Of An Irrevocable Life Insurance Trust

CHAPTER OVERVIEW

Life insurance is the only asset that Congress has bestowed with "most favored tax" status.[1] No other investment provides the potential benefit that life insurance provides. Life insurance is unique[2] and enjoys favorable tax status because of the important role it plays in protecting families. As a matter of policy, Congress has decided that life insurance is critical to protecting America's families and businesses, and it is hoped that status will not change.[3] For a "few dollars" of premium an insured can obtain thousands of dollars of life insurance coverage. No other investment provides a "payoff"

---

[1] Life insurance is the only tax-free investment under the Internal Revenue Code. All other investments are potentially subject to income (or capital gains) tax. For example, municipal bonds are essentially "pre-taxed" because their lower rates of return reflect their income tax free feature, and qualified retirement plans and annuities are tax deferred—not tax free. Only with a life insurance policy does the event of death eliminate the income tax. If estate taxes are permanently repealed, the loss of a complete step-up in basis will make life insurance even more attractive.

[2] "Life insurance is a unique form of property. There is no other investment vehicle that can as effectively guarantee the delivery of a specific amount of cash at the precise, but unpredictable, moment cash is needed, namely, at death." Brody, Richey, and Baier, 828 T.M., *Compensating Employees with Insurance,* section II, B, 2, a (Bureau of National Affairs, Washington, DC).

[3] *See,* Jeffrey A. Baskies, "Could Abuses in the Life Insurance Industry Lead to Penalties?," 33 *Estate Planning* 22 (February 2006).

like life insurance. Pay the first year's premium, die several months later, and the insured's beneficiaries receive thousands (possibly millions) of dollars of death benefits—income tax free. Not only does life insurance enjoy special income tax treatment, but when life insurance is owned by an irrevocable life insurance trust ("ILIT"), the death benefits can also be received free of death taxes and generation-skipping transfer taxes, and be used to benefit the insured's love ones for generations to come. This chapter highlights 22 reasons/benefits[4] of using an ILIT.[5] ILITs can play an important role if the grantor is the owner of a closely held business, particularly one that is family owned. As will be seen, an ILIT can be structured to accomplish a multitude of objectives, limited only by the grantor's imagination and cash flow, and the Internal Revenue Code.

§1.1 AVOID INCLUSION OF LIFE INSURANCE PROCEEDS IN INSURED'S GROSS ESTATE

The principal goal of an ILIT is to remove the life insurance proceeds from the insured-grantor's gross estate for federal estate tax purposes.[6] For a grantor to successfully remove transferred property

---

[4] Some of the disadvantages of using an ILIT might be (i) the cost of establishing the ILIT, (ii) the complexity of making gifts to an ILIT because of the need for *Crummey* withdrawal rights or the use of the grantor's gift tax applicable exclusion amount (currently $1 million), (iii) the ongoing expense of trust administration, including annual *Crummey* withdrawal right notices, (iv) the possible income tax disadvantages if the ILIT is taxed as a separate taxpayer (and is not taxed as a grantor trust in its entirety), (v) the "irrevocability" of the ILIT and inability to change beneficiaries, (vi) the insured's lack of control over the life insurance policy, its cash value, and lack of control over the other ILIT assets, and (vii) the potential of IRC section 2035 applying to a policy transferred within 3 years of the insured's death and the loss of the federal estate tax marital deduction if the ILIT is not drafted carefully. However, by drafting a flexible ILIT, the grantor can maintain some indirect control over the policy. *See*, Chapter 11, below.

[5] *See*, Giarmarco & Mittra, *Estate Planning with Insurance*, Mittra & Associates, Rochester Hills, MI (which can be purchased at Amazon.com) for an overview of the many different ways life insurance can be used in planning a client's estate.

[6] "After bypass trusts, life insurance trusts are probably the most frequently used estate planning device. The reason for their popularity is simple: enormous transfer tax savings." Bradley E.S. Fogel, "Life Insurance and Life Insurance Trusts: Basics and Beyond," 16 *Probate & Property* 8 (January/February 2002).

(such as an existing life insurance policy or cash to fund an ILIT) from his or her gross estate, the grantor must:

(1) Make a completed gift of the property transferred to the ILIT. Treas. Reg. §§25.2511-2(b) and (c).[7] *See*, section 3.5, below.

(2) Survive three years after making a gratuitous transfer of the property if the transferred property would otherwise be in-

---

Life insurance owned by a nonresident alien is not subject to federal estate taxes, even if the life insurance proceeds are payable to the nonresident alien's estate. IRC section 2105(a). Life insurance owned by a resident alien is, however, subject to federal estate tax, and an ILIT is an appropriate estate planning tool for keeping the proceeds out of his or her gross estate. IRC sections 2001 and 2031.

[7] Treas. Reg. §25.2511-2(b) provides that a gift is complete as to any property with respect to which the donor has so parted with dominion and control as to leave the donor with no power to change the disposition of the property, whether for the donor's own benefit, or for the benefit of another. But if upon a transfer of property (whether in trust or otherwise) the donor reserves any power over its disposition, the gift may be wholly incomplete, or may be partially complete and partially incomplete, depending upon all the facts in the particular case. An example of a reserved power that causes an incomplete gift is where the donor transfers property in trust to pay the income to the donor, or accumulate income in the discretion of the trustee, and the donor retains a testamentary power to appoint the remainder among the donor's descendants. However, if the donor does not retain a testamentary power of appointment, but instead provides that the remainder should go to a third party or to the donor's heirs, the entire transfer would be a completed gift.

Special rules apply concerning the donor's parting of dominion and control regarding negotiable securities. Treas. Reg. §25.2511-2(h).

Treas. Reg. §25.2511-2(c) states that a gift is incomplete in every instance in which a donor reserves the power to revest the beneficial title in himself or herself. The power to revest can be direct or indirect, such as through distributions to the donor subject to a fixed or an enforceable ascertainable standard. *See*, Treas. Reg. §25.2511-1(g)(2) concerning fixed or ascertainable standards. Under Treas. Reg. §25.2511-2(e), a donor is considered as possessing a reserved power if it is exercisable by the donor in conjunction with any person not having a substantial adverse interest in the disposition of the transferred property. *See*, Rev. Rul. 79-63, 1979-1 C.B. 302 where the IRS ruled that a joint powerholder did not have a substantial adverse interest in the exercise of an inter-vivos general power of appointment (even though the joint powerholder was a permissible appointee under the inter-vivos general power of appointment) since the joint powerholder was not a taker in default upon the non-exercise of the inter-vivos general power of appointment.

Also, Treas. Reg. §25.2511-2(f) provides that the relinquishment or termination of a reserved power to change the beneficiaries of transferred property, occurring otherwise than by death of the donor, is regarded as the event that completes the gift

cludable in the grantor's gross estate under IRC sections 2036, 2037, 2038, and 2042 or if the grantor relinquishes a power over the transferred property. IRC section 2035. *See,* sections 1.4 and 4.1, below.

(3) Not retain any interest beneficial interest in the transferred property or in the ILIT. IRC section 2036. *See,* section 4.2, below.

(4) Not provide that the possession or enjoyment of the transferred property can be obtained only by surviving the grantor, and not retain a reversionary interest in the transferred property or in the ILIT that is greater than 5% at the time of the grantor's death. IRC section 2037.

---

and causes the gift tax to apply. A gift is also incomplete to the extent that the donor has the power to add or remove beneficiaries or to change the interests of the beneficiaries as between themselves (such as a sprinkling power or power to accumulate) unless the power is a fiduciary power limited by a fixed or ascertainable standard, such as health, education, support and maintenance, or the donor possess the fiduciary power in conjunction with another person who has a substantial adverse interest in the transferred property. Treas. Reg. §§25.2511-2(c) and (e). If the donor possesses a fiduciary power not limited by an ascertainable standard, the property may be includable in the donor' s gross estate pursuant to IRC sections 2038 and 2041.

If a donor retains a purely discretionary interest in a trust and is not the trustee, but the donor's creditors can reach the transferred property, the gift is incomplete. Rev. Rul. 76-103, 1976-1 C.B. 293. In such instances, the gift becomes complete when the donor dies or when the trust moves to a jurisdiction where the donor's creditors cannot reach the transferred property.

If the grantor retains an interest under IRC section 2036 in the transferred property, the transfer of the property will not be a completed gift. Rev. Rul. 76-103, 1976-1 C.B. 293. A typical situation would be where the grantor has retained a discretionary interest in the trust, and the retention of the discretionary interest is subject to the claims of the grantor's creditors. IRC section 2036 will apply in such instance even if the trustee is an independent trustee with the sole, absolute, and uncontrolled power to make distributions. The reason being is that the focus is on the grantor's transfer (not the trustee's discretionary power) that typically gives rise to a creditor's ability to reach the trust assets. *See,* section 4.2(d), below.

In TAM 9533001, the IRS ruled that a provision in an ILIT that required life insurance proceeds includable in the insured's gross estate to be paid to the insured's revocable living trust did not cause the gift of the policies to the ILIT to be incomplete. In this instance, both the ILIT and the revocable living trust were established by the insured's conservator pursuant to a court order, after the insured became incompetent.

(5) Not retain the power to alter, amend, revoke, or control the beneficial enjoyment of the transferred property, or the power to alter, amend, or revoke the ILIT. IRC section 2038. *See,* section 4.3, below.

(6) Not hold a power of appointment over the transferred property or the ILIT. IRC sections 2514 and 2041. *See,* section 10.15, below.

(7) Not possess any incidents of ownership in any life insurance policies transferred to the ILIT or owned by the ILIT. IRC section 2042. *See,* section 4.8, below.

(8) Not possess or exercise any powers over the ILIT. *See,* section 10.15, below.

(9) Not serve as a trustee of the ILIT. *See,* section 10.16, below.

(10) Not use community property funds to pay for a single life policy. *See,* section 12.4, below.

See, Paragraphs 1.1 and 2.1 of Sample ILIT. [8]

> **Caution:** To avoid the three year rule of IRC section 2035, a life insurance policy should not be purchased by the ILIT trustee until the ILIT has been executed and funded. *See,* section 4.12, below, concerning an insured's "test application" for a life insurance policy. *See also*, section 12.10, below.

§1.2 INCUR LITTLE OR NO GIFT TAX UPON CREATION OF THE ILIT AND PAYMENT OF SUBSEQUENT PREMIUMS

A *Crummey* withdrawal right granted to each beneficiary, when used in conjunction with the gift tax annual exclusion amount under IRC section 2503(b) and gift splitting under IRC section 2513 (for married persons), allows the grantor's payment of premiums to be gift tax free. *See,* sections 3.5 and 3.10, below.

Although a *Crummey* withdrawal provision may turn a gift of a future interest into a gift of a present interest qualifying for the gift tax annual exclusion under IRC section 2503, a transfer to a trust that qualifies for the gift tax annual exclusion does not automatically qualify for the GST tax exemption purposes. Under the GST rules, a transfer that qualifies for the gift tax annual exclusion constitutes a

[8] The Sample ILIT referenced throughout this book is set forth in Appendix 1.

transfer to a trust (and not a transfer to a beneficiary—even though the beneficiary can withdraw the transfer because of the *Crummey* withdrawal right). Treas. Reg. §26.2642-1(c)(3). Thus, unless the ILIT is a skip-person trust under IRC sections 2642(c) or 2503(c) (e.g., a trust for a *single* beneficiary and if the beneficiary dies before the trust terminates, the trust assets must be includable in the beneficiary's gross estate), the transfer of cash or other property to the trust by the grantor will not be GST exempt and GST tax exemption will have to be allocated to the trust to obtain a zero inclusion ratio. *See,* section 5.7, below.

Additionally, assuming the ILIT is not an IRC section 2642(c) or 2503(c) trust, the *Crummey* withdrawal right should be limited to a five-by-five power under IRC section 2514(e), unless separate trust shares with testamentary limited powers of appointment exist for each beneficiary or hanging *Crummey* powers are used. *See,* sections 3.12 and 3.13, below. Otherwise, the lapse of a withdrawal right greater than five-by-five will cause the excess to be considered as being transferred by the beneficiary. *See,* section 3.11, below. As a result, the beneficiary becomes the (new) transferor for GST purposes with regard to the excess lapse amount. Treas. Reg. §26.2652-1(a)(5), Example 5. *See,* sections 5.20 and 5.21, below.

> **Practice Point:** If the grantor's spouse has a *Crummey* withdrawal right in excess of five-by-five or is granted a withdrawal right for greater than 60 days from the date of the transfer into the trust, then the grantor will not be able to allocate his or her GST tax exemption because of the estate tax inclusion period ("ETIP") rules and the spouse's holding of an impermissible withdrawal right for GST purposes. IRC section 2642(f); Treas. Reg. §26.2632-1(c)(2)(ii). *See,* section 5.17, below.

§1.3 REMOVE AN EXISTING LIFE INSURANCE POLICY FROM THE INSURED'S GROSS ESTATE AT LITTLE OR NO GIFT TAX COST

The transfer of an existing life insurance policy to an ILIT can generally be accomplished with little or no gift tax having to be paid. This is because the gift tax value of an existing life insurance policy is generally a fraction of its face (i.e., death benefit) value. *See,* section 3.1, below, concerning the valuation of life insurance policies.

Thus, tremendous leveraging occurs when the policy is valued at a fraction of its face value and gift tax annual exclusion *Crummey* withdrawal rights are used in conjunction with the transfer of the policy to the ILIT. *See,* section 3.5 below. For example, a married grantor using gift splitting and hanging *Crummey* withdrawal rights, can gift up to $24,000 per year (in calendar year 2006) per ILIT beneficiary (other than to the grantor's spouse). *See,* sections 3.5 and 3.10, below. If the life insurance policy has a low gift tax value at the date of its transfer to the ILIT, and there are enough *Crummey* withdrawal right beneficiaries available to "absorb" the policy's gift tax value, no gift tax will be incurred on the transfer of the policy to the ILIT.

§1.4 MINIMIZE THE ADVERSE TAX CONSEQUENCES OF THE THREE-YEAR RULE OF IRC SECTION 2035

If a life insurance policy that a married grantor transfers to the ILIT is included in the grantor's gross estate under IRC section 2035 because the grantor dies within three years of the transfer, the ILIT can, under certain circumstances, defer, minimize, or even eliminate the payment of federal estate taxes by the grantor's estate. *See,* section 4.1, below. The ILIT trustee could pay or hold the life insurance proceeds in a manner that qualifies for the federal estate tax marital deduction (or qualifies for the charitable estate tax deduction). *See,* section 11.3, below. *See,* Paragraph 5.1 of Sample ILIT.

If the marital deduction trust is a general power of appointment trust under IRC section 2056(b)(5), the surviving spouse could be granted the power to withdraw principal and use it to make gifts to the grantor's descendants. *See,* section 4.13, below. This power of withdrawal would, of course, exist only if the grantor died within three years of the transfer of the life insurance policy to the ILIT. Similarly, a QTIP trustee who is an independent trustee could be granted the power to make discretionary distributions of principal to the surviving spouse, who could then also make gifts. Note however, that under IRC section 2056(b)(7), no one, not even the surviving spouse, can be granted a lifetime power to appoint the QTIP property to anyone but the spouse. This means that there should be no provision allowing the QTIP trustee to make distributions for the purpose of allowing the surviving spouse to make gifts. *See,* section 4.14, below. Such authority may run afoul of the aforementioned restriction. The surviving spouse could, however, be granted an annual five-by-five withdrawal right over the QTIP trust, and the withdrawals could then be gifted by the spouse. *See*, Paragraph 5.1(A)(2)(a) of Sample ILIT.

A contingent marital deduction trust should not be used in conjunction with a second-to-die policy insuring the lives of both spouses. If both spouses die within three years of transferring the policy into the ILIT, absent a bequest of the policy proceeds that qualifies for the charitable estate tax deduction (with a corresponding waiver in the spouses' will of the estate tax apportionment provisions of IRC section 2206)[9] the proceeds will be includable in the gross estate of the surviving spouse.

If the life insurance proceeds do not qualify for a marital or charitable deduction, consider who should be responsible for the payment of the federal estate taxes attributable to the proceeds that are held by the ILIT. The executor of an insured's estate is entitled to recover federal estate taxes paid by the estate that are attributable to life insurance proceeds included in the insured's gross estate. IRC section 2206. *See*, section 4.15, below. The executor's right of apportionment/recovery is on a pro rata basis. A decedent can opt out of the recovery/apportionment provisions of IRC section 2206 by stating so in his or her will. A general provision in the decedent's will to pay all taxes from residue will be sufficient to opt out of the IRC section 2206 apportionment/recovery scheme. To the extent the insured's estate has other assets sufficient to pay the death taxes attributable to the ILIT proceeds, it may be advantageous for the burden of payment to be shifted from the ILIT to the insured's estate without any right of apportionment or recovery from the ILIT. This is true particularly if the ILIT has a zero inclusion ratio for GST tax purposes. By doing so, the previously allocated GST tax exemption (and GST-tax-exempt ILIT property) will remain intact and undiminished by the federal estate tax burden assumed by the decedent's estate. However, burdening the residue of the insured's estate may not be appropriate when the residuary beneficiaries are different than the ILIT beneficiaries.

---

[9] In the case of life insurance proceeds that are qualified and elected for the marital deduction provisions of IRC section 2056, the apportionment and recovery rules of IRC section 2206 do not apply with respect to the qualified and elected amount. However, IRC section 2206 has no similar exoneration for charitable bequests of life insurance proceeds.

Drafting Example For Decedent's Will:

If generation-skipping tax exemption has been allocated to a trust or property that is included in my gross estate for federal estate tax purposes, I direct that any federal estate taxes attributable to such property be paid from the trust or property that does not have an inclusion ratio of zero (0), and if the federal estate taxes exceed the trust or property that does not have an inclusion ratio of zero (0), it is my desire that the balance of the federal estate taxes otherwise apportioned against such trust or property be paid instead from the residue of my estate which is not included in a gift qualifying for the marital or charitable deduction and is so elected/deducted; and if practicable, such payment from the residue shall be with no right of recovery, reimbursement, or contribution (but only to the extent of such payment), it being my desire to preserve the full value of the zero (0) inclusion ratio property, if possible.

§1.4(a) Effect Of The Deemed Transfer Rule

Effective January 1, 1982, the three-year look back rule concerning "gifts in contemplation of death" was repealed pursuant to the Economic Recovery Tax Act of 1981. However, there was some uncertainty if the repeal of that rule also repealed the "deemed transfer" rule.[10] Subsequent court decisions have struck down the "deemed transfer" rule, and in 1991 the IRS acquiesced in the courts' abolishment of the rule. *See, Estate of Frank Martin Perry, Sr. v. Commissioner*, 927 F.2d 209 (5th Cir. 1991); *Estate of Eddie L. Headrick v. Commissioner*, 93 T.C. 171 (1989), *aff'd*, 918 F.2d 1236 (6th Cir. 1990); *acq.* AOD 1991-12 (7/3/1991); *Estate of Joseph Leder v. Commissioner*, 89 T.C. 235 (1987), *aff'd*, 893 F.2d 237 (10th Cir. 1989). However, caution may still be advised so as to avoid the imputation that the trustee is merely the agent of the insured/grantor. Thus, do not identify the trust as the "John Doe Irrevocable *Life*

[10] The deemed transfer rule (aka the "beamed transfer rule") was an argument that the IRS asserted in order to impute incidents of ownership to an insured where a third party (such as an ILIT, the insured's spouse, or the insured's children) owned the life insurance policy and the insured paid the premiums directly to the insurance company. The IRS argued that the third-party owner (such as an ILIT, spouse or child) was acting an agent of the insured, and that actions of the agent should be

Insurance Trust," but simply the "John Doe Irrevocable Trust." Query whether this is merely form over substance.

Do not require the trustee to purchase life insurance, but do give the trustee broad discretion with regard to life insurance matters, including the right to indemnification under certain circumstances. *See,* sections 10.19 and 10.20, below. *See,* Paragraph 7.1(D) of Sample ILIT. The trustee's right to indemnification should not give rise to the trustee being an agent of the grantor. Grantors often indemnify trustees with respect to high-risk assets such as closely held businesses and real estate. In fact, many trustees will not serve as trustee of an ILIT without indemnification or some other mechanism of protection, which may be even more costly than the risk of indemnification. The indemnification of the ILIT trustee should not cause the insured to be deemed to have any incidents of ownership over the life insurance policy, since the insured cannot exercise any rights over the policy.

§1.5 PROVIDE THE INSURED WITH GREATER CONTROL OVER THE POLICY AND OVER THE DISPOSITION OF THE LIFE INSURANCE PROCEEDS

The transfer of a life insurance policy to an ILIT gives the insured more control over the policy than if it were gifted outright, and an

---

imputed to (i.e., "deemed to be made by") the insured. Another variation of rule was the argument that the direct payment of premiums by the insured was a "beaming" of the policy to the third party, and constituted a transfer of the policy. Thus, if an ILIT was the initial and original owner of a life insurance policy, the insured paid the premiums directly to the life insurance company, and the insured died within 3 years of the establishment of the ILIT, the IRS would argue that the proceeds should be included in the insured's gross estate. *See, First National Bank of Oregon v. United States,* 488 F.2d 575 (9th Cir. 1973) where the court held, "We agree with *Detroit Bank and Trust Co. v. United States,* 467 F.2d 964 (6th Cir. 1972), *cert. denied,* 410 U. S. 929 (1973), and *Bel v. United States,* 452 F.2d 683 (5th Cir. 1971), *cert. denied,* 406 U. S. 919 (1972), that where life insurance policies are procured at the instance of the decedent within the presumptive [three-year period] period and where the premiums are paid by the deceased, the gross estate includes the proceeds of the policies." *Id.* at 576. The courts have now rejected the deemed transfer rule as a result of the 1982 addition of IRC section 2035(d). IRC section 2035(d) requires the insured to have relinquished incidents of ownership within three years of death in order for the life insurance proceeds to be includable in the insured's gross estate. If the insured never possesses any incidents of ownership in the life insurance policy, the three year rule of IRC section 2035 is not applicable.

ILIT provides the insured with more control over the ultimate disposition of the life insurance proceeds than if the insured named an individual beneficiary. An ILIT provides a solution to the following concerns: (i) how the life insurance death benefit should be paid out by the life insurance company—the trustee will decide which settlement option is suitable,[11] (ii) who should share in the life insurance proceeds if the primary beneficiary predeceases the insured (or dies simultaneous with the insured), (iii) how will the proceeds be invested, and by whom, (iv) when should the proceeds be distributed to a beneficiary, and under what circumstances or criteria, (v) how long should the proceeds benefit the insured's loved ones—years, decades, multiple generations, etc. An ILIT provides the insured with a certain amount of "control from the grave." Of course, an ILIT should also be drafted with sufficient flexibility to deal with changing and unforeseeable circumstances. *See,* Chapter 11, below.

§1.6 PROVIDE COORDINATION OF THE INSURED'S ESTATE PLAN

An ILIT can be used to coordinate the disposition of the policy proceeds and the grantor's other assets and estate planning documents. Coordination through an ILIT (rather than relying on a policy beneficiary designation) ensures that the life insurance proceeds inure to the benefit of the right beneficiaries, regardless of who does not survive the insured. *See,* Chapter 13, below.

§1.7 INSULATE LIFE INSURANCE PROCEEDS FROM PROBATE AND SUCCESSIVE TAXATION AT MULTIPLE GENERATIONS

With proper planning, life insurance proceeds can benefit successive generations without being subject to probate and without being included in the gross estates of the spouse and other beneficiaries.[12]

---

[11] See, Figure 5.1 of Leimberg and Doyle, *Tools & Techniques of Life Insurance Planning—3d Edition,* 103, The National Underwriter Company, Cincinnati, Ohio (2004), www.nuco.com for a comparison of settlement options available to trustees.

[12] *See,* Robert I. Ury and Thomas F. McGuire, "An Analysis of the Tax and Non-Tax Factors for Long-Term Trusts," 28 *Tax Management Estates Gifts and Trusts Journal* 87 (March 13, 2003).

The use of an ILIT to hold the life insurance proceeds will avoid the proceeds being subject to probate when the insured dies and/or when trust beneficiaries die. This means that the life insurance proceeds may not be subject to a surviving spouse's elective share or be part of the decedent's augmented estate, depending on state law. Also, the ILIT can avoid the imposition of death taxes on the trust property when the beneficiaries die. However, to avoid death taxes when a trust beneficiary dies, the practitioner must carefully draft the ILIT.

It has been suggested that to avoid potential GST tax problems, the long-term trust should be established in a jurisdiction that has completely repealed the rule against perpetuities (i.e., there is no perpetuity period) and the exercise of a limited power of appointment under that jurisdiction's laws will not create a "Delaware tax trap" under IRC sections 2041(a)(3) and 2514(d). Only a few jurisdictions meet this criteria: (i) South Dakota (which does not impose a state income tax on trusts, permits trust protectors and domestic asset protection trusts); (ii) Delaware— except for real estate (does not impose a state income tax on non-residents, and permits trust protectors and domestic asset protection trusts); (iii) Alaska (which limits powers of appointment to 1,000 years, does not impose a state income tax on trusts, and permits trust protectors and domestic asset protection trusts); (iv) New Hampshire (which imposes a special "income" tax on residents with regard to dividends and interest, and permits trust protectors); (v) Idaho (which imposes a state income tax on all trusts, and permits trust protectors); (vi) Missouri (which imposes a state income tax on all trusts, and permits domestic asset protection trusts); (vii) Wisconsin (which imposes a state income tax on residents only); and (viii) New Jersey (which imposes a state income tax on all trusts). *See,* Daniel G. Worthington, "Perpetual Trust States—The Latest Rankings," 146 *Trust & Estates* 59 (January 2007). Mr. Worthington's top four jurisdictions for establishing a perpetual GST dynasty trust are South Dakota (first place), Delaware (second place), Alaska, and New Hampshire (both tied for third place). Mr. Worthington, does, however, express concern that the IRS may not respect Alaska's 1,000-year period of vesting for GST tax purposes (in contrast to jurisdictions that have completely repealed the rule against perpetuities and have not just extended the time for vesting). *Id.* at 59 and 61. *See also,* Daniel G. Worthington, "The Problems and Promise Of Perpetual Trust Laws," 143 *Trust & Estates* 15 (December 2004); and Richard W. Nenno, "Choosing and Rechoosing the Jurisdiction for a Trust," 40 *Heckerling Institute on Estate Planning,* Chapter 4 (Matthew Bender/Lexis-Nexis, Newark, NJ 2006).

See, Elizabeth Carrott Minnigh, "Utilizing Trust Protectors in Domestic Estate Planning," 48 *Tax Management Memorandum* 3 (January 8, 2007) ("Minnigh"); Alexander A. Bove, Jr., "Trust Protectors," 144 *Trusts & Estates* 28 (November 2005); and Alexander A. Bove, Jr., "The Trust Protector: Trust(y) Watchdog or Expensive Exotic Pet?," 30 *Estate Planning* 390 (August 2003) concerning the use of a trust protector.

Also, be careful that the spouse and other beneficiaries are not deemed to hold a retained interest (because of a taxable release of a *Crummey* withdrawal right). *See*, sections 4.2 and 4.6, below. Also be careful when drafting the ILIT that the spouse and beneficiaries do not hold any general powers of appointment over the trust assets, either as a beneficiary or as a trustee. *See*, Chapter 8, below.

If a spouse or beneficiary serves as a trustee or co-trustee, that person's powers (as trustee) must be limited to ascertainable standards such as "health, education, support, and maintenance," as permitted under Treas. Reg. §§25.2511-1(g)(2), 25.2514-1(c)(2), and 20.2041-1(c)(2). Typically, a clause limiting the trustee's ability to make distributions that can result in the trustee possessing a general power of appointment over the trust property is used to accomplish this purpose. A clause that prohibits a trustee from using the trust property to discharge his or her personal legal obligations (including the obligation of support) is typically referred to as an "Upjohn" clause, and is named after the case where the clause was used and discussed by the court. *See*, *William John Upjohn v. United States*, 72-2 U.S.T.C. ¶12,888 (W.D. Mich. 1972). *See*, Paragraph 7.1(C)(4) of Sample ILIT. *See*, Chapters 8 and 9, below.

Make sure that the grantor's spouse or a beneficiary does not hold any powers as a beneficiary that constitute a general power of appointment, such as the beneficiary's unrestricted right to remove and replace a trustee with a related or subordinate party (as defined in IRC section 672(c)). *See*, section 9.1 (a), below. *See*, Paragraph 6.21 of Sample ILIT, which is modeled after Priv. Letter Rul. 9303018 and which sets forth a comprehensive list of IRS-approved reasons for a trustee's removal for "reasonable cause" by a beneficiary.

In 1995, the IRS reversed its position taken in Rev. Rul. 79-353, and held that a grantor's reservation of an unqualified power to remove an existing trustee and appoint a replacement trustee who is not related or subordinate to the grantor (within the meaning of IRC section 672(c)) is not a reservation by the grantor of the trustee's discretionary powers of distribution that might cause trust corpus to be included in the grantor's estate under IRC sections 2036(a) and 2038(a)(1) (concerning retained interests or the ability to affect the beneficial enjoyment of gifted property) and IRC section 2511 (for gift tax purposes, as an incomplete gift). Rev. Rul. 95-58, 1995-2 C.B. 191. The holding of Rev. Rul. 95-58 is as follows:

> Rev. Rul. 77-182 concludes that a decedent's power to appoint a successor corporate trustee only in the event of the resignation or removal by judicial process of the original trustee did not amount to a power to remove the original trustee that would have endowed the decedent with the trustee's discretionary control over trust income....Rev. Rul. 79-353 and Rev. Rul. 81-51 are revoked. Rev. Rul. 77-182 is modified to hold that even if the decedent had possessed the power to remove the trustee and appoint an individual or corporate successor trustee that was not related or subordinate to the decedent (within the meaning of section 672(c)), the decedent would not have retained a trustee's discretionary control over trust income.

In Priv. Letter Ruls. 9746007, 9735025, and 9607008, the IRS extended its holding in Rev. Rul. 95-58 to beneficiaries who were given the unqualified power to remove an existing trustee and appoint a replacement trustee who is not related or subordinate to the beneficiaries (within the meaning of IRC section 672(c)).

If a beneficiary can appoint him or herself as trustee or as a co-trustee (unless the other co-trustee has a substantially adverse interest in the trust), the beneficiary will be treated as possessing the powers of the trustee, which may result in the beneficiary holding a general power of appointment. Treas. Reg. §20.2041-1(b)(1). *See*, section 8.1(d), below, concerning "substantial and adverse interest." Depending on the powers and assets held by the removed trustee, this could mean that the removing party will hold a general power of appointment over the trust assets (or possibly an incident of ownership with regard to life insurance policies held by the trustee insuring the life of the removing party), which will result in the trust property being included in the removing party's estate under IRC section 2041 (or IRC section 2042 with regard to any life insurance policies). If the beneficiary holds a general power of appointment, he or she will be the (new) transferor for GST purposes and any GST tax exemption previously allocated by the grantor will be wasted. Limiting a beneficiary's right to remove a trustee for reasonable cause will obviate this problem and provide flexibility concerning the choice of the successor trustee. Limiting the trustee's powers of invasion to an ascertainable standard relating to the beneficiaries' health, education, support and maintenance will also resolve this issue.

Do not give the spouse or other beneficiaries an annual withdrawal right in excess of the greater of $5,000 or 5 percent of the trust corpus (often referred to as a "5X5" or "five-by-five" power) (or, if a hanging power (which is discussed in section 3.13, below) is granted to a beneficiary other than the grantor's spouse, make sure the hanging power is limited to the annual gift tax exclusion amount under IRC section 2503(b) and lapses each calendar year within the five-by-five safe harbor rules). Otherwise, the lapse in excess of five-by-five, in conjunction with an income/principal interest in the trust, will constitute a retained interest in the spouse's (or other beneficiaries') share of the excess property, which will be included in the spouse's (or other beneficiaries') estate as a retained interest (following the release of a general power of appointment). IRC sections 2036(a) and 2041(a)(2). *See*, section 4.2, below. Furthermore, there may be gift tax consequences to a lapse in excess of five-by-five. *See*, section 3.11, below. *See*, Paragraphs 3.1(A)(1) and 3.2(D) of Sample ILIT.

Also be careful about the powers and rights the beneficiaries may have over any policies of insurance on their lives held by the ILIT trustee. An insured beneficiary should: (1) not be permitted to serve as trustee of the trust that holds the insurance on his or her life (unless a co-trustee is granted exclusive ownership rights and control over the policy); (2) not hold any incidents of ownership over the life insurance policy; and (3) not hold a power of appointment over the policy. IRC sections 2042 and 2041. *See*, sections 4.8, 4.10 and 14.4, below. *See*, Paragraph 7.1(C)(3) of Sample ILIT.

Depending on the type of policy that the ILIT owns, the ILIT can also accomplish income free investing for the benefit of the insured's beneficiaries. *See,* Chapter 16, below for a general discussion of life insurance policies, and how certain policies can be structured to pay for life insurance premiums income tax free and can be used to purchase mutual fund type investments without having to pay any income tax on capital gains, dividends, or interest received on those investments. Thus, with the right policy and with good investments contained within the policy, an ILIT can become a financial fortress that protects future generations of the insured's family.

§1.8 REDUCE INCOME TAXES

An ILIT can reduce income taxes—federal, state, and local, if the ILIT is a separate taxpayer and is administered in a jurisdiction that does not impose a state income tax on the trust itself, and the ILIT trustee is able to either accumulate income and/or sprinkle income among the grantor's descendants, who are in lower income tax brackets. An ILIT can also be structured so that the grantor is responsible for paying all the income taxes on the trust's income, dividends, and capital gains. *See,* section 2.7, below. This will eliminate the ILIT having to pay income taxes during the grantor's lifetime and will help "preserve" the ILIT income and corpus for the beneficiaries and increase the ILIT's net cash flow while reducing the grantor's taxable estate. The grantor's payment of the ILIT's income taxes is the equivalent of a tax-free gift to the beneficiaries. *See,* section 3.18, below.

§1.9 MAKE IT EASIER FOR THE INSURED'S ESTATE TO QUALIFY FOR SPECIAL TAX TREATMENT

By removing an existing life insurance policy from the insured-grantor's gross estate, it may be easier for the insured's estate to meet the percentage requirements necessary to obtain special tax treatment under IRC sections 303, 2032A, 2057, and 6166.[13]

§1.10 LEVERAGE THE INSURED'S GST TAX EXEMPTION

Use of an ILIT as a generation-skipping trust, or so-called dynasty trust, is an extremely efficient technique to leverage the transferor's GST tax exemption and applicable exclusion amounts.[14] The dynasty trust can be established with no withdrawal rights being granted. Although the grantor's transfer of property to the ILIT will be that of a future interest and, therefore, will not qualify for the annu-

---

[13] *See,* Section III, C of Mezzullo, 809-2d T.M., *Estate Planning for Owners of Closely Held Business Interests*; Gopman and McCawley, 832 T.M., *Estate Tax Payments and Liabilities*; Zumbach, Reames, and Tausner, 833-2d T.M., *Section 2032A - Special Use Valuation;* Harl and McEowen, 829-2d T.M., *The Family-Owned Business Deduction-Section 2057*; Section VII *of* Acker, 855 T.M., *Estate and Trust Administration - Tax Planning*; Robert M. Bellatti, *Estate Planning for Farms and Other Family-Owned Businesses,* (Warren, Gorham & Lamont, Boston, Massachusetts, Supp. 2006); and Pennell & Danforth, 834 T.M., *Transfer Tax Payment and Apportionment* for a discussion of IRC sections 303, 2032A, 2057 and 6166.

[14] *See,* chapter 5, below, for a discussion of the GST tax. *See also,* Kevin W. Blanton and Rachna D. Balakrishna, "Dynasty Trusts and Life Insurance: New Opportunities for Leverage," 30 *Estate Planning* 407 (August 2003); Vincent M. Toscano,

al gift tax exclusion, and the grantor will have to allocate his or her gift tax applicable exclusion amount and GST tax exemption to the transfer, the result will be a guaranteed insulation of the transfer and subsequent proceeds from successive generational tax.

If the ILIT is designed as a generation-skipping trust, the following steps must be undertaken:

(1) If the ILIT is not a "GST trust" as defined in IRC section 2632(c)(3)(B), the transferor's GST tax exemption must be allocated on a timely filed U.S. Gift Tax Return (IRS Form 709). *See*, section 5.32, below.

(2) The ILIT must be drafted to avoid creating general powers of appointment in the beneficiaries so as to prevent inclusion in their gross estates. If trust property is included in a beneficiary's estate, that beneficiary becomes the (new) transferor for GST purposes and the original transferor's previously allocated GST tax exemption will be wasted. *See,* section 5.10, below.

(3) The ILIT must be drafted to avoid the possibility of a taxable release of a *Crummey* withdrawal right. This can be accomplished by limiting the annual noncumulative withdrawal right amount to the lesser of either the gift contribution amount or the \$5,000 × 5% amount specified in IRC section 2514(e). Alternatively, the grantor could not grant any *Crummey* withdrawal rights and instead use part of his or her applicable exclusion amount. Another approach, which is a bit more risky, is to use a hanging *Crummey* power. *See,* section 3.13, below. The risk of a power holder dying before the hanging power fully lapses may be the appropriate

---

"How To Use Life Insurance to Enhance the Benefits of a Dynasty Trust," 141 *Trust & Estates* 12 (May 2002); Charles E. Hodges, II, "Issues to Consider in Drafting Generation-Skipping Insurance Trusts," 26 *Estate Planning* 77 (February 1999); Alexander A. Bove, "The No-Tax Dynasty Trust," 145 *Trusts & Estates* 30 (March 2006), where the author suggests that after the insured-grantor dies, the ILIT trustee should use some of the life insurance proceeds to purchase a single premium life insurance policy on the life of the youngest beneficiary of the succeeding generation, and so forth (assuming the trustee has an insurable interest in the beneficiary). Thus, the dynastic GST tax exempt ILIT becomes a perpetual cascading life insurance trust that provides increasing wealth for multiple generations of the grantor's descendants.

trade-off for the increased amount of annual gift tax exclusion provided to the grantor.

(4) The ILIT must be drafted to avoid creating an estate tax inclusion period ("ETIP"). *See*, section 5.17, below. An ETIP prevents a transferor from currently allocating his or her GST tax exemption until the close of the ETIP (when the ILIT's value for GST-tax-exemption allocation purposes may be even greater than the value of the transferor's cumulative gifts to the ILIT).

(5) The ILIT's term should be for the maximum length of time permitted by the state's rule against perpetuities. Alternatively, the ILIT could be established in a jurisdiction that has abolished the rule against perpetuities and where the exercise of a non-general power of appointment will not result in the application of the "Delaware tax trap" under IRC sections 2041(a)(3) and 2514(d).[15] Even if the grantor is not a resident of a state that has abolished the rule against perpetuities, the grantor can choose the governing law of that state, provided there is a sufficient "nexus" between the ILIT and that state, such as having a co-trustee who is located in that state.

But note this caveat: Professor Ira Mark Bloom of Albany Law School argues that the states, in a blind race to facilitate the exploitation of the GST tax exemption by perpetual dynasty trusts, have overlooked important non-tax societal reasons for the rule against perpetuities, which serves to limit "dead hand control." He asserts that, over time, the administration of such trusts is likely to become unwieldy and very costly, noting that the average grantor will have more than 100 descendants in 150 years, 2,500 beneficiaries in 250 years, and 45,000 beneficiaries in 350 years.

Subject to the foregoing, typical provisions of a generation skipping trust can include:

---

[15] Such states include, South Dakota, Delaware, New Hampshire, Idaho, Missouri, Wisconsin, and New Jersey. *See, See,* Daniel G. Worthington, "Perpetual Trust States—The Latest Rankings," 146 *Trust & Estates* 59 (January 2007); and Stephen E. Greer, "The Delaware Tax Trap and the Abolition of the Rule Against Perpetuities," 28 *Estate Planning* 68 (February 2001).

• Separate shares for each child (rather than a single "pot" trust). *See,* Alternate 1 to Paragraph 5.3 of Sample Second To Die ILIT in Appendix 2.

• A lifetime income interest for the children.

• Principal invasion for the children that is subject to an ascertainable standard.

• A five-by-five annual withdrawal power held by each child.

• An inter-vivos limited power of appointment in favor of the children, issue or their spouses (provided the exercise of the power does not create a "Delaware tax trap," which is discussed in section 3.16, below).

• A testamentary limited power of appointment by each child over his or her share (provided the exercise of the power does not create a "Delaware tax trap," which is discussed in sections 3.16, 4.7, and 5.26, below).

• An option to provide for a child's surviving spouse (typically a life estate).

• The child can be trustee or co-trustee (if trust provisions are properly and carefully drafted). *See,* Chapter 8, below.

• Trustee removal provisions. *See,* section 11.9, below.

• Change of situs provisions (for portability). *See,* section 11.6, below.

• An independent trustee's ability to make discretionary income and principal distributions. *See,* section 9.7, below.

• A special powerholder or trust protector. *See,* section 11.1., below.

§1.11 CREATE LIQUIDITY FOR THE INSURED'S ESTATE

If the life insurance proceeds are needed to provide liquidity (i.e., cash) to the insured's estate, the trustee can be authorized (but not be required) to buy assets from the insured's estate or loan[16] funds to the estate. *See,* section 10.25, below. The trustee can also be author-

---

[16] In certain instances, the estimated future loan interest may be deductible as an up front estate tax deduction under IRC section 2503, thus reducing the overall federal estate tax liability. *Estate of Howard Gilman v. Commissioner,* T.C. Memo 2004-286; *Estate of Cecil Graegin,* T.C. Memo 1988-477; TAM 200513028 (interest expense non-deductible because loan from the family-limited partnership was

ized (but not required) to loan money to the insured's estate, spouse, and descendants. Loans from the ILIT will help preserve the estate's assets since they will not have to be liquidated, subject to a "forced" sale, or be sold to an "outsider." This is particularly important where the estate assets may not be readily marketable, such as a closely held business. The estate can use the sales proceeds (or loans) to pay the insured's debts, death taxes, and estate administration expenses. The trustee must not be required to purchase estate assets or loan

---

not necessary to the estate's administration—estate could have liquidated the FLP (which held a substantial amount of marketable securities) and have obtained the liquid assets to pay the estate tax); Priv. Letter Ruls. 200449031, 200020011, 199952039, and 199903038. The U.S. Court of Appeals for the Sixth Circuit has plainly held that the question of allowing an expense under IRC section 2053 is solely a matter of state law. If the expense was allowed in the probate proceeding, then it must be allowed as an administrative expense deduction. *Estate of Park v. Commissioner*, 475 F.2d 673 (6th Cir. 1973). *See*, Dennis I. Belcher, "Paying the Estate Tax Attributable to a Private Business Using IRC Section 6166, IRC Section 303, and *Graegin*-Style Promissory Notes," 39 *Heckerling Institute on Estate Planning*, Chapter 6 (Matthew Bender/LexisNexis, Newark, NJ 2005).

In *Graegin*, a related corporation loaned money to the estate to pay estate tax, because the estate did not have sufficient liquidity to pay estate tax. The loan was approved by the local probate court, and a guardian ad litem was appointed to represent the minor beneficiaries. The loan was an unsecured 15-year balloon note. No payments of interest or principal were due until the expiration of the note's term. Neither interest nor principal could be pre-paid. At the end of 15 years (which coincided with the surviving spouse's life expectancy), the principal amount plus 15 years of accrued interest was to be paid. The Tax Court allowed the estate to deduct on the federal estate tax return the entire amount of the 15 years of interest, which was payable at 15% per year (which was the prime rate amount at the time of the loan, as published in the *Wall Street Journal*).

In Rev. Rul. 84-75, 1984-1 C.B. 193, the IRS ruled that if a loan is obtained to avoid a forced sale of the estate's assets, the loan is reasonably and necessarily incurred in administering the estate. Therefore, the estimated future interest to be incurred on the loan is deductible on the federal estate tax return as an expense of administration under IRC section 2053(a)(2). However, in situations where the loan permits pre-payment without penalty at the option of the estate, the amount of future interest that will be paid by the estate on the loan amount is indefinite (because pre-payment of the loan amount will stop the accrual of interest). Therefore, for purposes of IRC section 2053, a deduction is not allowed for the estimated amount of interest that will accrue upon funds borrowed by the estate to pay the federal estate tax if repayment of the loan could be accelerated at the option of the estate without penalty. In such instance, the interest is deductible as an administrative expense only as it accrues. However, in those situations where an estate tax deduction is sought for interest that has accrued after the federal estate tax liability

monies, otherwise such requirements may be tantamount to "proceeds being receivable by an executor" and, therefore, taxable in the insured's gross estate. Treas. Reg. §20.2042-1(b). *See*, section 4.9, below. *See*, Paragraph 5.2 of Sample ILIT.

§1.12 CREATE WEALTH AND INCOME REPLACEMENT FOR THE INSURED'S ESTATE

Besides creating liquidity for the insured's estate, an ILIT can be used to create "instant" wealth upon the death of the insured, and can also be used to replace wealth that is either consumed during the insured's life or will be consumed upon the insured's death by estate taxes, income taxes, and estate administration expenses.

It is estimated that Generation X, Generation Y, and the Millennium Kids (to wit, the children of the baby boomer generation) may not receive much of an inheritance. This is because of their parents living longer and consuming more wealth to pay for their retirement expenses, home equity loans, rising health care costs, nursing home expenses, etc.[17] A way to ensure that a baby boomer's

---

has been paid, a refund of the estate tax may be requested by filing a claim for refund of tax within the applicable period of limitation set forth in IRC section 6511.

According to IRS Litigation Guideline Memorandum TM-65 (March 14, 1989), "Indebtedness incurred to avoid a sacrifice sale of non-liquid estate assets is a necessary step in the administration of an estate. Interest on such indebtedness is therefore a deductible administrative expense. Where such interest is uncertain in amount because of fluctuations in rate or the possibility of accelerated repayment, however, it may not be deducted until accrued or paid. If, in a balloon payment loan, the rate is fixed and the length of the loan is not subject to acceleration, the interest amount may be accrued and deducted on the estate tax return even though it will not be paid for a number of years. This was the situation in *Estate of Graegin.* Challenges can still be raised to such balloon payment structures where the underlying indebtedness is not bona fide, on the grounds that the interest will not actually be paid. In the case of a transaction between related parties, where the interest obligation is far greater than it would have been had a loan been obtained from an arms'-length lender, if it can be demonstrated that such a loan [such as a loan from a commercial lending institution] would have been available to the party in question, it can also be argued that the amount of the obligation is greater than necessary, and the deduction can be disallowed in full or in part. Consistent or inconsistent treatment of the interest by the lender will contribute to the analysis of any such transaction."

[17] Mary Deibel, "Retirement Worries for Gen X," *Scripps Howard News Service* (June 15, 2006), http://www.shns.com/shns/g_index2.cfm?action=detail&pk=WALLETWATCH-06-15-06.

heirs will receive an inheritance is for the boomer to establish an ILIT and fund it with a limited pay permanent life insurance product. *See*, Chapter 16, below. The premium payments should be structured so that the policy is paid in full before the insured-boomer needs Medicaid assistance. In most states, the ILIT and the life insurance policy will be exempt from the claims of creditors, including Medicaid (assuming all transfers to the ILIT by the insured are more than 60 months prior to applying for Medicaid assistance).

The ILIT can also be used to provide income for the insured's family, such as the surviving spouse, minor or disabled children, or other family members who may have no means or ability to be self-supporting.

An ILIT can serve as a wealth replacement vehicle concerning charitable giving. Many donors desire to make lifetime or testamentary charitable gifts if they can be assured that their family's overall wealth will not be diminished because of the charitable gift. An ILIT can serve to alleviate that concern. For example, a lifetime gift of appreciated assets (such a closely held C corporation stock) to an inter-vivos charitable remainder trust ("CRT") will avoid capital gains tax being paid by the donor when the assets are sold by the CRT (which is tax exempt), and the CRT will pay the donor an annuity (or unitrust) amount. IRC section 664(c). The donor will also get an immediate income and gift tax deduction equal to the present value of the remainder interest that will pass to the charity. IRC section 170(c)(2)(A). Because the CRT is tax exempt and pays no income or capital gains tax, the CRT will be able to sell the appreciated assets tax free. This will result in the full value of the assets being available to pay a larger annuity (or unitrust) amount to the donor (rather than had the donor sold the appreciated assets and paid the capital gains tax). This "larger" annuity (or unitrust) amount (i.e., the income and capital gains tax savings amount) and the amount of the income tax savings from the charitable income tax deduction taken when assets were contributed to the inter-vivos CRT can be used to fund an ILIT. The ILIT can then purchase life insurance equal to or greater than the value of the contributed assets, thereby replacing (or increasing) the value of the assets that were transferred to the CRT. In many instances, the family's overall wealth will actually increase because the ILIT proceeds will be free of income tax and estate tax. *See*, section 14.11, below.

§1.13 PROVIDE PROFESSIONAL MANAGEMENT OF THE LIFE INSURANCE PROCEEDS

An ILIT provides a vehicle for the management of the insured's life insurance policy and subsequent proceeds. The ILIT protects beneficiaries who are inexperienced in the management and investment of money. If a beneficiary is a minor or under some other disability that prevents the beneficiary from properly managing and investing the proceeds, the ILIT protects that beneficiary. In these situations, the ILIT can provide for proper management, investment, and conservation of the life insurance proceeds for the continued benefit of the beneficiaries. *See,* sections 11.10, 11.11, and 11.12, below. *See,* Paragraph 1.6 of Sample ILIT.

§1.14 PROVIDE CREDITOR AND DIVORCE PROTECTION TO THE BENEFICIARIES

An ILIT can also insure that the grantor's beneficiaries are protected from their inabilities, disabilities, predators, and creditors, including potential ex-spouses (in some instances).[18] An outright transfer of an insurance policy to beneficiaries cannot provide such protection nor provide the control that the grantor may desire. Maximum flexibility and creditor protection can be achieved through the use of a disinterested or independent trustee with broad discretionary powers over the trust, a spendthrift provision, and the non-insured surviving spouse having a testamentary limited power of appointment over the ILIT (after the death of the grantor-insured).[19] Additionally, flexibility can be provided by allowing the trustee to permit a beneficiary to use trust assets, such as a house, free of rent, and by permitting the trustee to move trust assets to a less creditor-friendly jurisdiction by changing the situs of trust administration.[20] *See,* section 14.2, below. *See,* Paragraphs

---

[18] *See,* ¶13.16 of Spero, *Asset Protection: Legal Planning, Strategies and Forms* (Warren, Gorham & Lamont, Boston, Massachussetts) for an asset protection planning checklist concerning an ILIT.

[19] *See, Steve Leimberg's Asset Protection Planning Newsletter 82* (April 26, 2006) at http://www.leimbergservices.com for a discussion of 12 key issues to consider when drafting a third-party-created discretionary spendthrift trust or third-party-created asset protection trust.

[20] *See,* Philip J. Michaels and Laura M. Twomey, "How, Why, and When to Transfer the Situs of a Trust," 31 *Estate Planning* 28 (January 2004). *See also,* section 11.6, below.

1.6, 4.1(A), 5.1(A)(2), 5.4(A) (alternate 2), 5.4(B) (alternate 2), 5.4(C) (alternate 2), 5.5(A), 7.1(A)(15), 7.2, 7.3, and 8.3(A) of Sample ILIT.

§1.15 PROVIDE INCENTIVES TO BENEFICIARIES

The ILIT can contain provisions that seek to affect a beneficiary's behavior by conditioning a distribution from the ILIT on the beneficiary's adoption (or rejection) of certain types of behavior or characteristics, or the beneficiary achieving certain goals deemed desirable by the grantor, provided the goals are not illegal or against public policy. The grantor can attempt to influence the beneficiary's behavior by setting forth the grantor's philosophy concerning who, when, how, and why the ILIT trustee is to make distributions, or the grantor can set forth explicit objective criteria in the ILIT for the trustee to follow.[21]

§1.16 PROVIDE FLEXIBILITY IN AN UNCERTAIN AND CHANGING ENVIRONMENT

The use of certain trust provisions, along with an independent trustee, coupled with a special powerholder (or trust protector) can provide significant flexibility, thus enabling the ILIT to be "flexible" and to adapt to changing circumstances, if that is what the grantor desires. *See*, Chapter 11, below.

---

[21] *See*, Joshua C. Tate, "Conditional Love: Incentive Trusts And The Inflexibility Problem," 41 *Real Property, Probate and Trust Journal* 445 (Fall 2006); James E. McNair, Gregory J. Rupert and Cynthia L. Gausvik, "Get FIT," 145 *Trusts & Estates* 36 (February 2006); Marjorie J. Stephens, "Incentive Trusts: Considerations, Uses and Alternatives," 29 *ACTEC Journal* 5 (Summer 2003); Paul A. Meints, "Using Trusts To Provide Incentives, Rewards, Remembrances, and Other Benefits To Chosen Beneficiaries: A Checklist," 15 *The Practical Tax Lawyer* 25 (Winter 2001); Ellen Evans Whiting, "Controlling Behavior by Controlling the Inheritance: Considerations in Drafting Incentive Provisions," 15 *Probate & Property* 6 (September/October 2001); Nancy G. Henderson, "Managing the Benefits and Burdens of New Wealth with Incentive Trusts (With Sample Provisions)," 47 *The Practical Lawyer* 51 (September 2001) (Part 1); 47 *The Practical Lawyer* 11-26 (October 2001) (Part 2); David R. Hodgman and Debra L. Stetter, "Can Incentive Trusts Encourage Children to Behave Responsibly?," 27 *Estate Planning* 459 (December 2000) for more information about incentive trusts.

§1.17 PROVIDE/EQUALIZE INHERITANCE FOR CHILDREN WHO ARE NOT ACTIVE IN THE FAMILY OWNED BUSINESS

If the grantor owns a business where some of the children are active in that business and will eventually inherit the business from grantor, life insurance owned by an ILIT can be an inexpensive way to provide an inheritance for the inactive children, or to "equalize" the inheritance between the active and inactive children, so that the inactive children are treated fairly.[22] For example, the ILIT can be for the sole benefit of the inactive children and their descendants. Or, the ILIT can provide for an adjustment (i.e., increase) of the inactive children's beneficial share in the ILIT (after the grantor's death) based on a formula tied to the value of the business inherited by the other children. The ILIT can also provide a source of liquidity to pay the death taxes attributable to the closely held business by making loans to the business or to the children who inherit the business. *See,* section 10.25, below. Leaving the business to the active children and life insurance to the inactive children not only equalizes the inheritances among the children but also avoids the need for the active children to purchase the interests of the inactive children—perhaps at a time when the business may be unable to afford it.

§1.18 CREATE A FAMILY BANK FOR THE ACTIVE AND INACTIVE CHILDREN IN THE FAMILY-OWNED BUSINESS

When the decision is made to leave the business to both active and inactive children, it is usually advisable to leave only the active children with voting interests in the business. In addition, "put" and "call" options-agreements should be entered into. Usually, a put option requires the business to purchase all or a portion of the inactive children's interest in the business upon a set price and terms. Without a put option, there may be no practical way for an inactive

---

[22] *See,* Jon J. Gallo and David A. Hjorth, "Using a Crummey Trust and a Defective Trust as Part of an Estate Plan," 33 *Estate Planning* 31 (April 2006), where the authors discuss recapitalizing an S corporation, having the owners sell all their non-voting shares of the recapitalized S corporation to an intentionally defective grantor trust for the benefit of the active children in the business, and using the installment note payments from the intentionally defective grantor trust to fund an ILIT for the benefit of the inactive children.

child to benefit from owning the business interest unless the business is sold.

On the other hand, a call option allows the active children (or the business itself) to purchase the business interests of the inactive children upon a set price and terms. Without a call option, there may be no effective way for the active children to avoid conflicts that can occur between the active children who are receiving salaries and bonuses, and the inactive children who are not. By having the active children own life insurance on a senior family member's life, a "bank" is created to provide the funds to satisfy any such puts and calls. Usually, the policy will be owned outside of the business entity, such as in a trust for the benefit of the active children, or by a limited liability company owned by the active children.

§1.19 PROVIDE/EQUALIZE INHERITANCE FOR CHILDREN FROM A PRIOR MARRIAGE

Another common equalization technique involves families where the children from the first marriage are significantly older than the children from the second marriage or the children from the first marriage are significantly older than their step-parent. Rather than having the older children wait for their inheritance until their step-parent dies or until their step-siblings come of age, an ILIT can be used to either provide an immediate inheritance for the older children without endangering the financial security of the step-parent and/or younger step-siblings.[23]

§1.20 PROVIDE CREDITOR PROTECTION TO THE INSURED

An ILIT can provide creditor protection to the insured-grantor. If the insured were to own an equity-building life insurance policy in his or her own name, the equity may, depending on state law, be subject to the claims of the insured's creditors. Also, if the life insurance proceeds are payable to the insured's probate estate, revocable living trust or to a testamentary trust to be established under the

---

[23] *See,* Section 12.13 of Sebastian V. Grassi, Jr., *A Practical Guide to Drafting Marital Deduction Trusts (with Sample Forms and Checklists),* ALI-ABA, Philadelphia, PA (2004, Supp. 2006) (800) 253-6397, http://www.ali-aba.org/ali-aba/bk36.asp for a discussion of drafting the marital deduction trust in a second marriage situation.

insured's will, the proceeds may be subject to the claims of the insured's creditors and the creditors of the insured's estate, depending on state law. However, if an ILIT owns the life insurance policy, and the insured makes annual gift contributions to the ILIT that are not fraudulent conveyances (and the insured has not retained a beneficial interest in the ILIT[24]), the life insurance policy and its equity should be insulated from the claims of the insured's creditors. Additionally, through the use of loans by the ILIT trustee, the ILIT's equity could be indirectly "made available" to the insured-grantor. *See*, section 14.13, below, for a discussion of trustee loans to a non-grantor insured spouse.

§1.21 PROVIDE A HEDGE AGAINST REPEAL OF THE FEDERAL ESTATE TAX

Regardless of how the federal estate tax situation evolves, the characteristics of life insurance make an ILIT a unique hedge against both the uncertainty of the tax law and the certainty of mortality. An ILIT

---

[24] Certain jurisdictions (e.g., Alaska, Delaware, Nevada, Rhode Island, Utah, Colorado, etc.) permit a grantor to retain a discretionary beneficial interest in a self-settled irrevocable trust. Under these states' law, the grantor's discretionary interest is not subject to the claims of the grantor's creditors. However, this type of trust (commonly referred to as "domestic asset protection trust") is still in the infancy stage, and great care should be taken when establishing a domestic asset protection trust for a grantor who is not a resident of such a state. Additionally, care should also be taken to avoid the insured-grantor retaining an interest in the ILIT that would cause the life insurance proceeds to be included in his or her gross estate for federal estate tax purposes. *See*, Erin C. V. Bailey, "Asset Protection Trusts Protect The Assets: But What About the Trustees?," 21 *Probate & Property* 58 (January/February 2007) - only four states specifically protect the trustees, Alaska, Delaware, South Dakota and Utah; Richard W. Nenno, "Planning With Domestic Asset-Protection Trusts: Part II," 40 *Real Property, Probate and Trust Journal* 477 (Fall 2005); Richard W. Nenno, "Planning With Domestic Asset-Protection Trusts: Part I," 40 *Real Property, Probate and Trust Journal* 263 (Summer 2005); F. Peter Conaty, Jr. and William H. Lunger, "Practical Considerations in Drafting a Delaware Asset-Protection Trust," 30 *Tax Management Estates, Gifts and Trusts Journal* 117 (March 10, 2005); Jeffrey A. Zaluda, "Asset Protection for Professionals and Business Executives," 30 *Tax Management Estates, Gifts and Trusts Journal* 125 (March 10, 2005); Charles D. Fox IV and Michael J. Huft, "Asset Protection and Dynasty Trusts," 37 *Real Property, Probate and Trust Journal* 287 (Summer 2002); Henry J. Lischer, Jr., "Domestic Asset Protection Trusts: Pallbearers to Liability?," 35 *Real Property, Probate and Trust Journal* 479 (Fall 2000).

ensures predictable results whether the estate tax is repealed or not, whether transferred assets are treated as having a stepped-up or carry-over income tax basis, and whether the insured lives for one year or twenty-five years; with an ILIT, the insured wins either way.

§1.22 PROVIDE A HEDGE AGAINST THE PREMATURE DEATH OF AN ANNUITANT

A grantor-retained annuity trust ("GRAT") is an irrevocable trust to which the grantor transfers a rapidly appreciating asset, (i.e., appreciating greater that the IRC section 7520 rate that is used to value the gifted remainder interest in the GRAT), such as a closely held business interest, while retaining the right to receive a fixed annuity from the trust for a stated term of years. The longer the stated term and the larger the annuity, the smaller the taxable gift. At the end of the GRAT's stated term, the trust property passes gift tax free to remainder beneficiaries. The risk of a GRAT is that if the grantor dies during the annuity term of the GRAT, the IRS has taken the position that the grantor's retained annuity interest causes some or all of the value of the GRAT to be included in the grantor's gross estate for federal estate tax purposes pursuant to IRC sections 2036 and 2039.[25] IRC sections 2036 and 2039; TAM 200210009. By funding an ILIT for the benefit of the GRAT's remainder beneficiaries, however, the grantor can leave the assets to the GRAT's remainder beneficiaries, who will then use the life insurance proceeds to pay the federal estate taxes due. Alternatively, a married grantor might qualify the assets in the GRAT for the marital deduction and have an ILIT (for the benefit of the GRAT's remainder beneficiaries) use the life insurance proceeds to purchase the assets from the grantor's estate. *See also,* section 14.3, below.

---

[25] *See*, Michael D. Whitty, "Heresy or Prophecy: The Case For Limiting Estate Tax Inclusion of GRATs To The Annuity Payment Right," 41 *Real Property, Probate and Trust Journal* 381 (Summer 2006). The author suggests that the GRAT *not* require the annuity to be paid from the trust's net income (and then principal if the net income is insufficient). Rather, the author suggests that the trust instrument be silent about the annuity amount being payable from income. Consequently, it is the author's opinion that the amount includable in the grantor's gross estate is the value of the remaining unpaid annuity payments. *See also*, Michael D. Whitty, "Repercussions of Walton—Estate Tax Inclusion of GRAT Remainders," 19 *Probate & Property* 13 (May/June 2005).

An ILIT can also be useful where the grantor has sold an asset in exchange for a private annuity.[26] In a private annuity transaction, the purchaser is obligated to pay the annuity amount for the lifetime of the grantor-annuitant. When the annuitant dies, the payments under the annuity cease, and the value of the "unpaid" annuity is not included in the annuitant's gross estate for federal estate tax purposes. When utilizing a private annuity arrangement, the purchaser, who is personally obligated to pay the annuity, can fund an ILIT for the benefit of the purchaser's family so that they will have the cash to continue to pay the private annuity amount should the purchaser predecease the annuitant. Conversely, the annuitant can fund an ILIT for the benefit of his or her family as a hedge against the annuitant's premature death. In either case, the amount of life insurance needed would be based on the present value of the future annuity payments. *See also,* section 14.8, below.

A variation on the same theme involves the grantor's sale of an asset in exchange for a self-cancelling installment note ("SCIN"). With a SCIN, upon the grantor-seller's death, all remaining payments under the promissory note are canceled, similar to a private annuity. The purchaser must pay a "premium" for this cancellation feature, either by a higher interest rate or by a higher purchase price. Like a private annuity, upon the seller's death, the value of the "unpaid" SCIN is not included in the seller's gross estate for federal estate tax purposes. When using a SCIN, just as with a private annuity, the seller can fund an ILIT for the benefit of his or her family as a hedge against the seller's premature death. Conversely, the purchaser in a SCIN transaction can fund an ILIT for the benefit of his or her family so that they will have the cash to continue to pay the SCIN should the purchaser predecease the seller.

---

[26] *See,* Stephan R. Leimberg, Kevin J. McGrath and Howard M. Zaritsky, "Deferral of Gain Eliminated In Sales of Appreciated Property for a Private Annuity," 34 *Estate Planning*

2

Income Tax Issues

CHAPTER OVERVIEW

This chapter discusses selected key income tax issues concerning life insurance and ILITs.[1] Recent changes in the Internal Revenue Code now permit an insured to receive life insurance proceeds income tax free under certain conditions, such as during a terminal or chronic illness. An ILIT drafted with sufficient flexibility can take advantage of these special benefits. The income tax aspects of life insurance must be understood if the death benefit is to be received income tax free. Thus, the transfer for value rule is extremely important and is an income tax trap for the unwary. This special rule, which can cause life insurance proceeds to be subject to income taxation is also important for understanding how to fix a "damaged" ILIT. *See,* Chapter 15, below. The grantor trust rules, among other things, provide tremendous flexibility, especially if the grantor wants to make additional "tax-free" gifts to the ILIT that are in excess of the grantor's gift tax annual exclusion amount, or if the grantor wants to transact with the ILIT on an income tax free basis. The grantor trust rules also provide flexibility in fixing a damaged ILIT. This chapter also contains a brief discussion of the "tax-free"

---

[1] *See,* Norman H. Lane & Howard M. Zaritsky, *Federal Income Taxation of Estates and Trusts* (Warren, Gorham & Lamont of RIA, 3d ed. 2003 & Supp. 2007); and Alan S. Acker, 852-2nd T.M., *Income Taxation of Trusts and Estates,* Bureau of National Affairs, Washington, DC, for an overview of the income taxation of estates, trusts, and beneficiaries. *See also,* Chapter 2 of Howard M. Zaritsky & Stephan R. Leimberg, *Tax Planning With Life Insurance: Analysis With Forms—2d Edition,* Warren, Gorham & Lamont, Boston, Massachusetts (Supp. 2007) for an overview of the income taxation of life insurance.

exchange of a life insurance policy; the income taxation of policy dividends and loans; the income taxation upon the surrender, cancellation, or lapse of a policy; and the income taxation upon the sale of a policy.

§2.1 LIFE INSURANCE PROCEEDS RECEIVED INCOME TAX FREE

Generally, proceeds paid under a life insurance contract (as defined in IRC section 7702 concerning policies issued after December 31, 1984; and as defined in *Helvering v. LeGierse*, 312 U.S. 531 (1941) for policies issued before January 1, 1985) by reason of the insured's death[2] are not subject to income tax.[3] IRC section 101(a)(1). There is

---

[2] Payment of life insurance proceeds due to an insured member of the uniformed services who is declared Missing In Action constitutes a payment by reason of the insured's death. Rev. Rul. 78-372, 1978-2 C.B. 93. However, payment of life insurance proceeds to a creditor to discharge an indebtedness of the insured where the creditor is the policy owner, beneficiary, and makes all the premium payments, is not income tax free to the creditor; rather, the payment of the life insurance proceeds is a collection of the unpaid amount owed the creditor. In such an instance, the creditor's payment of premiums is typically deductible as a business expense. Rev. Rul. 70-254, 1970-1 C.B. 31. *See also*, *Landfield Finance Company v. United States*, 418 F.2d 172 (7th Cir. 1969) (proceeds payable to a creditor in satisfaction of a debt owed to the creditor are not excludable from the creditor's gross income).

[3] An exception to the income tax free receipt of life insurance proceeds applies to certain employer-owned life insurance ("EOLI") contracts issued (or materially modified) after August 17, 2006. IRC sections 101(j) and 6039I. These Code sections were added by section 863 of the Pension Protection Act of 2006 (8/17/2006) and may affect life insurance funded buy-sell agreements (redemption and cross-purchase), deferred compensation agreements, and any other type of EOLI. Generally, under IRC section 101(j), when an employer (or an employer-related person) receives death proceeds from an EOLI policy, the proceeds will be ordinary income–except to the extent of premiums and other amounts paid by the employer (or an employer-related person) for the life insurance contract. The new rules were added in an attempt to put an end to so called "janitor life insurance," where employers (such as Winn-Dixie Stores, Inc.) were purchasing life insurance as an investment on its rank and file employees without the knowledge or consent of the insured-employee, and collect the death proceeds many years later—typically after the insured was no longer an employee.

Who constitutes an "employee" is rather broad under the under the new law, and may include common law employees, the self-employed, and independent contractors. *See*, Temporary Treas. Reg. §414(q), Q&A 7. Until Treasury Regulations for IRC section 101(j) are issued clarifying the definition of an "employee" or providing exemptions, it is suggested that the cautious-conservative advisor have his or her client operate under the broad definition of an "employee."

no limitation on the amount of life insurance proceeds that a beneficiary can receive income tax free. IRC section 101(a)(1) is an exception to the definition of gross income under IRC section 61(a)(10).

Also, the "related person" definition in IRC section 101(j)(3)(A)(i) may be a trap for the unwary. In the absence of clarifying regulations (or technical amendments to IRC section 101(j)), the definition of a related person may be interpreted to include a relative (as defined in IRC section 267(b)) of the employer or a 50% or more owner of the employer, such as a co-shareholder, partner, member, or a trust controlled by the employer. Thus, a life insurance policy that is owned by or payable to an employer-related person, may be treated by the IRS as being owned by the employer and be subject to the new rules. Therefore, life insurance-funded cross-purchase agreements may come within the ambit of IRC section 101(j), as may certain split-dollar plans, VEBAs, life insurance funded non-qualified deferred compensation plans, life insurance-funded rabbi and secular trusts, and life insurance contained in a qualified retirement plan. Consequently, the employee-notice and consent requirements ***and*** the IRS reporting requirements (discussed below) should be complied with when an employer-related person is the owner or beneficiary of the insurance policy on the employee's life. *See, Steve Leimberg's Estate Planning Newsletter # 1044* (October 27, 2006) at http://www.leimbergservices.com.

In order for the EOLI to be excluded from income pursuant to IRC section 101(a), the following three employee-notice and consent requirements must be met: (1) before the issuance of the EOLI policy, the employee must be notified in writing that the employer (or an employer-related person) intends to insure the employee's life and the maximum face amount of life insurance that the employer (or the employer-related person) might take out on the employee's life; (2) before the issuance of the EOLI policy, the employee provides written consent to being insured under the policy and consents that the coverage may continue after the insured terminates employment; and (3) before the issuance of the EOLI policy, the employee is informed in writing that the employer (or the employer-related person) will be a beneficiary of any proceeds payable upon the death of the employee. If it is subsequently determined that all three employee-notice and consent requirements were not met when the policy was issued, the problem can be corrected by cancelling the non-compliant policy and re-issuing a new EOLI policy that is employee-notice and consent compliant.

If all three employee-notice and consent requirements are met, the EOLI death benefit proceeds will be excludable from the employer's (or the employer-related person's) income pursuant to IRC section 101(a) if any one or more of the following four exceptions exist: (1) the insured was an employee within 12 months of his or her death; (2) the policy proceeds are paid to a member of the insured's family (within the meaning of IRC section 267(c)(4)), any individual who is the designated beneficiary of the insured under the policy (other than the employer (or possibly an employer-related person)), a trust established for the benefit of any such member of the insured's family or designated beneficiary, or to the insured's estate; (3) the policy proceeds are used by the employer (or possibly an employer-related person) to redeem-purchase an

Caution: Interest paid by the life insurance company because of a delay in payment of the life insurance pro-

---

equity (or partnership capital or profits) interest in the employer owned by the insured, a member of the insured's family (within the meaning of IRC section 267(c)(4)), any individual who is the designated beneficiary of the insured under the policy (other than the employer (or possibly an employer-related person)), a trust established for the benefit of any such member of the insured's family or designated beneficiary, or by the insured's estate (and according to the Report of the Joint Committee on Taxation, it is intended that "such amounts be so paid or used by" the due date of the employer's income tax return for the year in which the life insurance proceeds are received); or (4) the insured was a director or highly compensated employee at the time the policy was issued. A "highly compensated employee" is a person who: (i) is a 5% or more owner of the business, (ii) is a director or officer of key management of the business, (iii) received in the prior year compensation in excess of $100,000 (for 2006), or (iv) anyone else within the top 35% of employees ranked by pay.

Additionally, IRC section 6039I requires an employer (or an employer-related person) who owns one or more EOLI policies issued after August 17, 2006, to file an annual information report with the IRS. The report must state: (1) the number of employees of the employer (or possibly an employer-related person) at the end of the year; (2) the number of those employees insured under post-August 17, 2006 EOLI contracts at the end of the year; (3) the total amount of insurance in force under the post-August 17, 2006 EOLI contracts at the end of the year; (4) the employer's (or possibly an employer-related person's) name, address, taxpayer identification number, and the employer's (or possibly an employer-related person's) type of business; and (5) that the employer (or possibly an employer-related person) has a valid consent for each insured-employee, and the number of insured-employees for whom such consent was not obtained. Employers (or an employer-related person) owning life insurance policies that are subject to the new IRC section 101(j) rules must also maintain records necessary to determine whether the IRC section 101(j) requirements are met. The information-filing rules do not apply to an EOLI policy issued after August 17, 2006, pursuant to an IRC section 1035 exchange for an employer-owned policy that was issued before August 17, 2006. However, certain material increases in the death benefit or other material changes in an EOLI policy will cause a grandfathered policy to be treated as a new policy issued after August 17, 2006, and be subject to the new rules of IRC sections 101(j) and 6039I. But increases in the death benefit that occur as a result of the operation of IRC section 7702 (corridor or cash value tests) or the terms and normal operation of the existing policy (e.g., paid-up additions or as the result of market performance or policy design), if the insurer's consent to the increase is not required, will not cause a grandfathered policy to be treated as a new policy.

See, Sebastian V. Grassi, Jr., "New Rules Concerning Employer-Owned Life Insurance Affect Buy-Sell Agreements (With Sample Drafting Language)," 21 *Practical Tax Lawyer* 7 (Winter 2007); and James Magner and Stephan R. Leimberg, "Pension Protection Act Adopts Far-reaching New Rules for COLI," 33 *Estate Planning* 3 (October 2006).

ceeds is subject to income tax.[4] IRC sections 101(c) and (d). Interest or dividends paid by the Veterans Administration on a United States Government Life Insurance policy or on a National Service Life Insurance contract (i.e., a U.S. military government life insurance policy) are however income tax free. 38 U.S.C. section 38 U.S.C. §5301(a)(1).; Rev. Rul. 91-14, 1991-1 C.B. 18; Rev. Rul. 71-306, 1971-2 C.B. 76.

§2.2 ACCELERATED DEATH BENEFITS AND VIATICAL SETTLEMENT PROCEEDS RECEIVED INCOME-TAX FREE

§2.2(a) Accelerated Death Benefits

Accelerated death benefits paid under a life insurance policy because of the insured being either terminally ill (i.e., death is reasonably expected to occur within 24 months) or chronically ill (i.e., meets the criteria established under IRC section 7702B(c)(2)) are generally not subject to income tax. IRC sections 101(g)(1) and (4).

§2.2(b) Viatical Settlements

Similarly, proceeds from the sale or assignment of any portion of the death benefit of a life insurance policy on a terminally ill (i.e., death is reasonably expected to occur within 24 months) or chronically ill insured paid by a viatical settlement provider (defined in IRC section 101(g)(2)(B)) are generally not subject to income tax.[5] IRC section 101(g)(2).

---

[4] Typically a life insurance policy contains several death benefit payment options available to the beneficiary, such as: (i) lump sum payment, (ii) annuity for life payments, (iii) interest-only payments, (iv) income for life payments, and (v) installment payments. Each payment option may generate taxable interest that is earned on the delayed payment of the payment of the policy's death benefit. IRC section 101(c) and (d). Additionally, each payment option may qualify for the federal estate tax marital deduction if certain conditions are met. *See, e.g.*, IRC section 2056(b)(6).

[5] On December 11, 2006, the National Association of Insurance Commissioners ("NAIC") took a major step toward ending investor-initiated life insurance purchases. NAIC's Life Insurance and Annuities Committee adopted amendments to its Viatical Settlements Model that would impose a five-year ban on an insurance policy that is financed with the specific intent to be sold to investors (typically hedge funds). The

Practice Point: A viatical settlement will provide the ILIT with cash that can be distributed to the beneficiaries, such as the insured's spouse. The beneficiaries can then use the money (if they choose) to assist in the care and comfort of the dying grantor–their loved one. In this regard, make sure the ILIT trustee has the authority to make discretionary distributions to the beneficiaries (but not to the grantor-insured) during the grantor-insured's lifetime. Also make sure the trustee can change the governing law or situs of the trust to a jurisdiction that has favorable laws governing vitaical settlements and/or life settlements. *See*, Paragraphs 4.1 and 8.3(A) of Sample ILIT.

Practice Point: IRC section 101(g)(3) limits the amount that a *chronically* ill person may receive income tax free under a viatical settlement. The amount is $63,875 (adjusted for inflation) per calendar year. Thus, viatical settlements for a chronically ill insured should be paid in installments if the settlement amount is greater than $63,875. However, for the proceeds from a chronically ill viatical settlement to be income tax free, the viatical payments must be for the reimbursement of the actual cost of qualified long-term care services (as defined under IRC section 7702B) that were actually incurred by the chronically ill insured. The prohibition on receipt of settlement proceeds for expenses reimbursable under Medicare may result in many individuals not being able to satisfy the

---

amendments were proposed to attack the life insurance practice known as "stranger-owned life insurance ("SOLI") aka "investor initiated life insurance" ("IILI") or "investor-owned life insurance" ("IOLI") *See*, section 12.9 below. SOLI policies are life insurance policies that are financed and purchased with the intent of selling them for life settlements. Certain policy owners who are able to satisfy specified exceptions would be excluded from this ban. By way of example, this five-year ban would not apply if during the first two years after the issuance of the policy, the insured, a family member, or employer of the insured, put up his/her/or its own money or collateral to fund the premiums. The amendment prohibits entry into a viatical settlement contract at any time before the application or issuance of a policy which is the subject of a viatical settlement contract within five years after the issuance of an insurance policy unless there are circumstances including (i) terminal or chronic illness from a viator or insured; (ii) the death or divorce of a viator's spouse; or (iii) the viator's retirement from full-time employment. Many states have already adopted the Viatical Settlements Model, but it is uncertain how many will adopt these changes.

requirements for a chronically ill viatical settlement. Payments for a chronically ill viatical settlement are income tax free only within the limits allowed under long-term care insurance contracts pursuant to IRC section 7702B. A viatical settlement for a chronically ill grantor-insured will not be income tax free because the viatical proceeds will be paid to the ILIT and not to the insured. However, the viatical proceeds should be income tax free if the ILIT were an intentionally defective grantor trust for income tax purposes. Regardless of the income tax consequences of a viatical settlement for a chronically ill insured, a chronically ill insured-grantor cannot be a beneficiary of an ILIT without running afoul of IRC section 2036. *See,* section 4.2, below.

§2.3 ACCELERATED DEATH BENEFITS AND VIATICAL SETTLEMENT PROCEEDS SUBJECT TO INCOME TAX

If a life insurance policy is owned by a business in which the insured has a financial interest, or if the policy is owned by a business in which the insured is an officer, director, or employee, the viatical settlement proceeds and the accelerated death benefits payable as a result of the insured being either chronically ill or terminally ill are subject to income tax if they are not paid directly to the insured. IRC section 101(g)(5).

§2.4 INCOME TAXATION OF A LIFE SETTLEMENT

A "life settlement" is the sale to a third party (such as a hedge fund or an institutional investor) of a life insurance policy (including term life insurance) of an elderly (but not chronically or terminally ill) insured (usually age 65 or older) who has an abbreviated life expectancy (generally between 2 to 12 years), has a policy(ies) with an aggregate death benefit of $250,000 or more, and the insured has owned the policy(ies) for at least two years. The proceeds from a life settlement (which are typically more than the cash surrender value but less than the face amount of the policy(ies)), are not exempt from income taxation under IRC section101, and are subject to the general rules of taxation. There are two unresolved issues concerning the income taxation of life settlements: (i) how to compute the policy owner's basis in the policy, and (ii) if there is gain on the sale of the policy, is the gain capital gain or ordinary income?[6] *See*, IRS Internal Legal Memorandum 200501004 and Priv. Letter Rul. 9443020, concerning the income tax basis issue in a life settlement. *See also*, footnote to section 2.5(b), below, concerning how to determine "basis."

> **Practice Point:** Life settlements concerning variable life insurance policies and variable universal life insurance policies are also subject to rules promulgated by the National Association of Securities Dealers.[7] However, many states do not require licensing of life settlement brokers or disclosure of compensation practices, and so these transactions largely occur without regulatory oversight. The lack of regulatory oversight and lack of disclosure to the policy owner has led to abuses in the industry, including alleged schemes of broad and pervasive fraud.[8]

---

[6] *See*, James C. Magner and Stephan R. Leimberg, "Life Settlement Transactions: Important Tax and Legal Issues to Consider," 34 Estate Planning 3 (April 2007); Allan Goldstein, Leigh Harter, and David Holaday, "Sell Your Policy?," 145 *Trust & Estates* 24 (September 2006); Stephan R. Leimberg, E. Randolph Whitelaw, Richard M. Weber, and Liz Colosimo, "Life Settlements: Tax, Accounting, and Securities Law Issues," 33 *Estate Planning* 3 (September 2006); Stephan R. Leimberg, E. Randolph Whitelaw, Richard M. Weber, and Liz Colosimo, "Life Settlements: Risk Management Guidance for Advisors and Fiduciaries," 33 *Estate Planning* 3 (August 2006); Charles Ratner, "Cash Out or Cash In?," 144 *Trusts and Estates* 49 (May 2005); Andrew H. Hook and Thomas D. Begley, Jr., "Lawyering for Older Clients: A New Paradigm—Part 1," 32 *Estate Planning* 48 (April 2005); Damien Rios, "An Introduction to the Use of Viatical and Life Settlements," 31 *Estate Planning* 533 (November 2004); Michael I. Frankel, "Life Settlements: Sale of Life Insurance Policies in the Open Market," 39 *Heckerling Institute on Estate Planning*, Chapter 9 (Matthew Bender/Lexis-Nexis, Newark, NJ 2005); Stephan R. Leimberg and Albert Gibbons, "Life Settlements and the Planning Opportunities They Offer," 30 *Estate Planning* 517 (October 2003); Morton P. Greenberg and John E. Mayer, "Extracting Hidden Value From Unwanted Life Insurance Policies," 28 *Estate Planning* 434 (September 2001); Bernard Eizen and Victor S. Levy, "New and Expanded Uses of Viatical Settlements in Insurance Planning," 26 *Estate Planning* 475 (December 1999).

[7] *See*, http://www.nasd.com/web/groups/rules_regs/documents/notice_to_members/nasdw_017131.pdf.

[8] In October 2006, the New York Attorney General filed suit against Coventry First, a major life settlement company. The suit alleges collusion among the company and life insurance advisors who represent policy owners. The suit alleges that Coventry First paid undisclosed co-commission fees to advisors in order to encourage them to not provide (or solicit) competitive life settlement bids from other companies and to

Practice Point: A life settlement involving an ILIT that is a grantor trust for income tax purposes will result in the grantor being taxed on the portion of the life settlement proceeds that are subject to income or capital gains tax. If the ILIT does not contain a reimbursement provision for the grantor's payment of income/capital gains tax, the grantor has in effect made a tax-free gift (of the amount of the income/capital gains tax paid by the grantor) to the ILIT beneficiaries, and has done so without having to use any of the grantor's gift tax annual exclusion amount or lifetime gift tax applicable exclusion amount. *See*, section 3.18, below.

Practice Point: A life settlement may be an alternative to surrendering or terminating a policy that is no longer needed, no longer suitable, no longer affordable, or is under-performing. When undertaking a life settlement, a trustee may want to obtain several life settlement quotes.

§2.5 TRANSFER FOR VALUE RULE AND INCOME TAXATION OF LIFE INSURANCE PROCEEDS

A major exception[9] to the income-tax free receipt of life insurance proceeds is if there has been a "transfer for value" of an interest in a life insurance policy. IRC section 101(a)(2). If a life insurance policy (or any interest in an existing life insurance policy) is transferred for valuable consideration (of any form, such as cash, mutuality of promises, etc.), then the income tax exclusion under IRC section 101(a)(1) is not available and the regular income tax rules apply (concerning the

---

provide the policy owner with only one bid—that of First Coventry, which was typically a low bid (i.e., a low purchase price) for the policy. As a result of the alleged abuse, Stephan R. Leimberg suggests the following: "(1) the absolute 'must' of using a process of 'due care' in selecting a life settlement broker; (2) the importance of a Request for Proposal process among pre-screened and approved institutional funders; and (3) insistence on a broker full disclosure of *all* offers [including the amount of the broker's compensation and any otherwise undisclosed co-commissions]." *Steve Leimberg's Estate Planning Newsletter # 1045* (October 30, 2006) at http://www.leimbergservices.com.

[9] Another exception is the alternative minimum tax on certain C corporation-owned life insurance policies concerning the policy's inside build up of cash value, and the C corporation's receipt of death benefit proceeds. IRC section 55.

income taxation of the life insurance proceeds).[10] The result is that the consideration paid to acquire the policy (or an interest in the policy) plus any future premiums paid by the transferee (i.e., the transferee's basis in the contract) are received income tax free, but the remaining proceeds are taxed as ordinary income. Treas. Reg. §1.101-1(b)(3)(i).

---

[10] *See*, Lawrence Brody and Stephan R. Leimberg, "Avoiding the Tax Trap of the Transfer for Value Rule," 32 *Estate Planning* 3 (October 2005); Lawrence Brody and Lucinda A. Althauser, "Typical Life Insurance Planning Mistakes and Some Suggested Solutions," 28 *Estate Planning* 51 (February 2001); George D. Brenner, "Avoiding Common Mistakes in the Use of Life Insurance," 23 *Estate Planning* 320 (September 1996); Diana S.C. Zeydel, "The Transfer For Value Rule: Developments And Clarifications," 134 *Trusts & Estates* 75, 77 (April 1995).

Other tax traps involving life insurance include (i) the *Goodman v. Commissioner*, 156 F.2d 218 (2d Cir. 1946) and Rev. Rul. 77-48, 1977-1 C.B. 292 triangle where the insured, the owner, and the named beneficiary of the policy are three different persons (i.e., upon the insured's death, the owner will be deemed to have made a gift of the life insurance proceeds to the named beneficiary); (ii) the insured's payment of premiums for life insurance not owned by the insured (i.e., the payment of premiums constitutes a gift); (iii) the insured's payment of premiums for a life insurance policy co-owned by two or more other persons (i.e., the payment of premiums is a gift of a future interest since the co-owners must act jointly to exercise incidents of ownership over the policy); (iv) life insurance on the surviving spouse's life that is held in a credit shelter trust (i.e., unless credit shelter trust is carefully drafted, the surviving spouse may have incidents of ownership over the policy that result in the life insurance proceeds being includable in the surviving spouse's gross estate for federal estate tax purposes); (v) corporate-owned life insurance payable or distributed to co-shareholders (*see*, Rev. Rul. 71-79, 1971-1 C.B. 112—distribution of proceeds to co-shareholders treated as a dividend to the extent of the corporation's earnings and profits) or payable to the insured's spouse (or other family member) (i.e., the corporation will be deemed to have received the proceeds (because it is the legal owner of the policy and is entitled to the proceeds) and the insured (now deceased), will be deemed to have received a dividend or taxable compensation from the corporation in the amount of the death proceeds; (vi) the transfer of life insurance policies among shareholders as part of a buy-sell restructuring, such as when the corporation switches from a redemption buy-sell agreement to a cross-purchase buy-sell agreement (i.e., the life insurance proceeds received by the shareholder (who is not the insured under the policy) will be subject to the transfer for value rule if the shareholder is not one of the protected party exceptions); (vii) the insured's gift of a life insurance policy with an outstanding loan amount greater than the insured's basis in the policy (i.e., the transferor's basis exception to the transfer for value rule will not be available, the insured will recognize gain on the amount of the loan that exceeds the insured's basis in the policy, and the life insurance proceeds will be includable in the insured's gross estate for federal estate tax purposes if the insured dies within three years of the gift of the policy); (viii) the collateral assignment of a modified endow-

To invoke the transfer for value rule, there must be a transfer of the policy (or an interest in the policy) and valuable consideration must have been given in exchange for the transfer.

A transfer for value is any absolute transfer for value of a right to receive all or any part of a life insurance policy. Treas. Reg. §1.101-1(b)(4). Even term life insurance policies that have no cash value are subject to the transfer for value rule. *See, e.g.,* Priv. Letter Rul. 7734048. The transfer does not have to be of the policy itself. A transfer of some or all of any of the underlying interests in the policy (such as the death benefit proceeds) is sufficient to invoke the rule, which is broadly defined. For example, the creation, for value, of an enforceable contractual right to receive all or a part of the proceeds of a life insurance policy may constitute a transfer for a valuable consideration, as would be the case when an insured shareholder owning a policy on his life is contractually bound under a buy-sell agreement to name a fellow shareholder as the beneficiary of the policy. Another example of a transfer for value would be to name a particular person as a beneficiary of the policy in exchange for valuable consideration. A reciprocal

---

ment contract ("MEC") life insurance policy or using the MEC to secure a loan (i.e., the assignment or pledging of the MEC as security may be treated as a distribution from the MEC, which would cause the annual growth in policy cash values to be currently taxed as ordinary income—MECs are subject to special (onerous) income tax rules, and great care needs to be taken when dealing with a MEC in order to avoid the potential income tax traps); (ix) an IRC section 1035 exchange of a life insurance policy with an outstanding loan amount for a new policy with no loan (i.e., the loan amount is extinguished by the insurance company, the extinguished amount of the loan constitutes receipt of "boot" by the insured, and the "boot" is taxable to the insured to the extent of the amount of the gain in the policy at the time of the 1035 exchange); (x) using group term life insurance to fund a shareholder cross-purchase agreement (i.e., by naming the non-insured shareholder as the beneficiary of the insured shareholder's interest in the group term policy, there has been a transfer for value); and (xi) the alternative minimum tax trap on certain C corporation-owned life insurance policies concerning the policy's inside build up of cash value, and the C corporation's receipt of death benefit proceeds. *See, Steve Leimberg's Estate Planning Newsletter # 875* (September 27, 2005) at http://www.leimbergservices.com for a more detailed discussion of these tax traps and how to avoid them.

When a person transfers a life insurance policy for valuable consideration, the sales proceeds (for purposes of determining the amount of gain) include: (i) cash, (ii) the fair market value of any property received (other than cash), and (iii) the amount of any policy loan that the transferor is relieved from paying. IRC sections 1001(a) and (b); Treas. Reg. §1.1001-2(a)(1).

promise can also constitute valuable consideration. For example, if several insured co-shareholders agree to "gift" their policies to one another to fund a cross-purchase arrangement, the reciprocal gifting constitutes valuable consideration. Also, if the co-shareholders agree to continue paying premiums on the "gifted" policies (to fund the cross-purchase agreement), this, too, constitutes valuable consideration. However, if the co-shareholders are all partners, then the transaction may be exempt from the transfer for value rule under the partner-protected party exception, which is discussed below. *See*, *J.R. Monroe v. Patterson,* 197 F. Supp. 146 (N.D. Ala. 1961); Priv. Letter Rul. 1999-03020. On the other hand, the pledging or assignment of a life insurance policy as collateral security for a loan or other obligation owed by the policy owner is not a transfer for a valuable consideration of the policy or an interest therein. IRC section 101(a)(2) is not applicable to any amounts received by the pledgee or assignee (which amounts are treated as a repayment of capital and are therefore generally income tax free to the extent of the outstanding debt amount; however, insurance proceeds representing interest on the debt are taxed as ordinary income to the creditor). Treas. Reg. §1.101-1(b)(4).

> **Practice Point**: There are two income tax issues that must be considered when selling/transferring a life insurance policy for valuable consideration: (1) the transfer for value rule, and (2) the income tax consequences to the seller of the policy. *See*, section 2.19, below.

§2.5(a) Five Statutory Exceptions To Transfer For Value Rule

There are five statutory exceptions to the transfer for value income tax rule. Under these five exceptions, life insurance proceeds are received income-tax free even if there has been a transfer for valuable consideration of a policy or an interest in the policy.[11] IRC section 101(a)(2)(A) and (B).

§2.5(b) Transferor's Basis Exception

The first exception to the transfer for value rule is if the transferee's basis in the life insurance policy is determined in whole or in part

---

[11] *See*, Treas. Reg. §1.101-1(b) concerning the amount that is received income "tax free" under the five exceptions. *See, also,* Lawrence Brody and Stephan R. Leimberg, "Avoiding the Tax Trap of the Transfer for Value Rule," 32 *Estate Planning* 3 (October 2005).

by reference to the original transferor's basis in the policy.[12] IRC sections 1015(a), 101(a)(2)(A), 72(c)(1) and 72(e)(6); Treas. Reg. §1.101-1(b)(1); *James F. Waters, Inc. v. Commissioner*, 160 F. 2d 596

---

[12] Generally, an insured's basis in the contract is "the net premiums he has paid less any policy dividends received as a return of basis, *perhaps* reduced by the mortality costs incurred. *See*, Ltr. Rul. 9443020 and ILM [IRS Internal Legal Memorandum] 200501004, both taking the position, without citing any authority, that basis in a policy is reduced by the cost of the insurance protection 'consumed' by the owner, which, according to the letter ruling, can be approximated by the difference between the premiums paid and the policy's cash value. *But see*, Section 72(e) (dealing with investment in the contract) and, e.g., *Gallun v. Commissioner*, 13 AFTR 2d 660, 327 F.2d 809, 64-1 USTC ¶9253 (7th Cir. 1964), not requiring such a reduction in basis." Lawrence Brody and Stephen R. Leimberg, "Avoiding the Tax Trap of the Transfer for Value Rule," 32 *Estate Planning* 3, 6 (October 2005). As evidenced from the above quote, some commentators are of the opinion that IRC section 72(e)(6) (and not ILM 200501004 and Priv. Letter Rul. 9443020) defines basis (i.e., investment in the contract) as the "aggregate amount of premiums or other consideration paid for the contract before such date, minus the aggregate amount received under the contract before such date, to the extent that such amount was excludable from gross income under this subtitle or prior income tax laws." *See*, Stephan R. Leimberg and Albert Gibbons, "Life Settlements and the Planning Opportunities They Offer," 30 *Estate Planning* 517 (October 2003); Bernard Eizen and Victor S. Levy, "New and Expanded Uses of Viatical Settlements in Insurance Planning," 26 *Estate Planning* 475 (December 1999). The issue of basis may not be resolved absent litigation with the IRS.

However, depending on the circumstances, some commentators do not "disagree" with the IRS's determination of basis. "Generally, an insured's basis in the contract is the total premiums the insured had paid, reduced by the 'cost of insurance protection' provided throughout the date of the sale, and nontaxable dividends the insured has received under the contract. [Rev. Rul. 70-38, 1970-1 C.B. 11.] The premiums paid, less the 'cost of insurance protection,' are equal to those portions of the premiums paid that increase the cash surrender value of the policy. [Citations omitted.]...[With regard to ILM 200501004] [s]ection 72(e), however, does not actually establish the standard by which one determines either a taxpayer's basis in a life insurance contract or the portion of a damage award relating to the policy that should be tax free. Section 72(e) governs the taxation of amounts received under an annuity, endowment, or life insurance contract (and not received as an annuity). It governs the taxation of withdrawals and distributions from the policy [and not the income taxation of the sale or surrender of the policy]." ¶2.11[1] of Howard M. Zaritsky & Stephan R. Leimberg, *Tax Planning With Life Insurance: Analysis With Forms—2d Edition,* Warren, Gorham & Lamont, Boston, Massachusetts (Supp. 2007).

"A taxpayer's basis in a life insurance contract or policy equals the sum of the premiums paid *to the extent that the premiums created a right to a cash surrender value.* [*See*, *London Shoe Co., Inc. v. Commissioner*, 80 F.2d 230 (2nd Cir. 1935) where the court of appeals held: "The holding of the Third Circuit [in *Century Wood Preserving Co. v.*

(9th Cir. 1947), *cert. denied,* 332 U.S. 767 (1947). This exception is commonly referred to as the "transferor's basis exception," and applies to transfers if the transferee takes a carryover income tax basis in the policy from the original transferor.

Commissioner] that cost [i.e., the taxpayer's basis in the life insurance policy] is approximately reflected in the cash surrender value of a policy, and consequently that there could be no loss [when the policy was cashed in for an amount less than the aggregate premiums paid] though the [aggregate] premiums [paid by the taxpayer] exceeded the [cash surrender] value, seems to us correct and applicable to the facts before us....We can see no escape from the conclusion reached by the Board [of Tax Appeals] that no loss was established in this case, for the reason that the [taxpayer's] cost [in the life insurance policy] was approximately reflected in the [policy's] cash surrender value. The portion of the premiums not used to build up the [cash] reserve was paid to obtain the insurance protection which was for many years afforded [to the taxpayer]. *Century Wood Preserving Co. v. Commissioner of Internal Revenue* (C.C.A.) 69 F.(2d) 967; *Keystone Consolidated Publishing Co. v. Commissioner of Internal Revenue,* 26 B.T.A. 1210; *Appeal of Standard Brewing Co.*, 6 B.T.A. 980." *See also,* Priv. Letter Rul. 9443020.] The remainder of the premium constitutes the expense of obtaining annual insurance protection. For example, if a $1,000 premium payment is accompanied by a $350 increase in the policy's cash value, the taxpayer's basis in the policy will increase by that $350 and the taxpayer would have $650 of insurance expense. In the case of a term life insurance policy the only basis would be the unearned premium (i.e., the prepaid expense)." William D. Klein, "Life Insurance Funding of S Corporation Buy-Sell Agreements," 45 *Tax Management Memorandum* 461-62 (November 15, 2004).

"Whether or not the I.R.S. is correct in its position [under Priv. Ltr. Rul. 9443020 and ILM [IRS Internal Legal Memorandum] 200501004], caution dictates making the additional subtraction for cost of insurance protection to determine whether a transferor has received consideration in excess of basis for purposes of the part sale/part gift exception. In the absence of proof to the contrary, the cost of insurance protection may be approximated by using the difference between (i) the aggregate premiums paid, and (ii) the cash value of the contract with regard to surrender charges." Diana S.C. Zeydel, "The Transfer For Value Rule: Developments And Clarifications," 134 *Trusts & Estates* 75, 77 (April 1995).

"Of course, an insured's basis in the policy may be determined by other factors, if the policy is not acquired from the insurance company. The initial basis in a policy purchased from a prior policy owner should be the amount paid for the policy (including debt assumed). [Citations omitted.] The initial basis in a policy acquired by gift should be the transferor's basis, increased by any gift tax imposed on the net appreciation. [Citations omitted.] The initial basis in a policy acquired from a decedent should be the fair market value of the policy on the date of death (or alternate valuation date, if elected.) [Citations omitted.]" ¶2.11[1] of Howard M. Zaritsky & Stephan R. Leimberg, *Tax Planning With Life Insurance: Analysis With Forms—2d Edition,* Warren, Gorham & Lamont, Boston, Massachusetts (Supp. 2007).

§2.5(b)(1) Gift, Or Part Sale And Part Gift Of Policy

The most common example of the transferor's basis exception is a gift (or a part sale and part gift) by the original transferor.[13] To qualify under the part sale and part gift exception, the transferee's consideration for the policy[14] must be: (i) less than the policy's fair market value (*see*, section 3.1, below concerning valuation of life insurance policies), *and* (ii) less than the original transferor's basis in the policy. Thus, if: (i) the amount of the transferee's consideration exceeds the original transferor's basis in the policy, *or* (ii) the policy is subject to an outstanding loan amount that exceeds the original transferor's basis in the policy, the transfer will be subject to the transfer for value rule (unless another exception to the transfer for value rule applies).

§2.5(b)(2) Problems Caused By Policy Loans

If there is an outstanding policy loan[15] and the policy loan amount exceeds the original transferor's basis in the policy, the transferee's basis in the policy is not the transferor's basis but the amount of the loan (debt) assumed by the transferee (unless the transferee is an intentionally defective grantor trust with regard to the transferor). In such a case, the transfer for value rule is triggered because the assumption of the loan amount is considered to be both valuable consideration to the transferor and "the amount paid by the transferee for the

---

[13] Where a transfer of property is in part a sale and in part a gift, the unadjusted basis of the property in the hands of the transferee is the sum of: (1) whichever of the following is the greater: [(i) the amount paid by the transferee for the property, or (ii) the transferor's adjusted basis for the property at the time of the transfer], ***and*** (2) the amount of increase, if any, in basis authorized by IRC section 1015(d) for gift tax paid. Treas. Reg. §1.1015-4. A special rule, however, applies to transfers or sales between spouses. *See,* IRC section 1041, which is discussed in section 2.5(b)(5), below.

[14] The consideration for the transfer of a life insurance policy is the sum of: (i) the outstanding policy loan, and (ii) any other consideration supplied by the transferee. As discussed in section 2.5(b)(2), below, policy loans can trigger the transfer for value rule.

[15] For purposes of this discussion, it is assumed that policy loans are non-recourse to the policy owner. If a policy owner takes out a loan and the loan remains unpaid at the insured's death, the outstanding loan amount is deducted from the face value amount payable by the life insurance company to the beneficiary.

property" under Treas. Reg. §1.1015-4(a)(1)(i).[16] *See, e.g.*, Rev. Rul. 69-187, 1969-1 C.B. 45; Treas. Reg. §1.1001-2(a)(4)(i); Pvt. Letter Ruls. 8951056 and 7724048. Thus, the assumption of the loan amount by the transferee is treated as a sale by the transferor to the transferee of the policy for the amount of the outstanding loan. Consequently, the transferor will be required to recognize gain on the transfer of the policy because the transferor's loan has been effectively discharged. The amount of the assumed (i.e., discharged) loan will be treated as the amount realized by the transferor for gain purposes, and the transferor will report the amount of gain that exceeds his or her basis in the policy. The gain will be taxed as ordinary income (and not as capital gain). *Edwin A. Gallun v. Commissioner*, 327 F.2d 809 (7th Cir. 1964); *Simon v. Commissioner*, 285 F.2d 422 (3d Cir. 1960); *Commissioner v. Percy W. Phillips*, 275 F.2d 33 (4th Cir. 1960); *Abram Nesbitt 2d v. Commissioner*, 43 T.C. 629 (1965).

On the other hand, if the assumed loan amount does not exceed the original transferor's basis in the policy, the transferee's basis in the policy will be determined in part by reference to the original transferor's basis; the transfer for value rule will not be triggered and the transferor will not recognize any gain on the transfer of the policy. Also, even if the loan amount exceeds the original transferor's basis in the policy, if the transferee is an intentionally defective grantor trust with regard to the original transferor, the trust will receive the original transferor's carryover basis in the transferred policy and the transfer for value rule will not be triggered (nor will the transferor recognize any gain on the transfer of the policy). *See,* Rev. Rul. 85-13, 1985-1 C.B. 184.[17]

---

[16] In addition to the transfer for value rule being invoked upon the transfer of the policy, the transferor will realize ordinary income in the amount of the difference between the policy loan amount and the transferor's basis in the policy. Another common income tax trap involving policy loans concerns the surrender (or lapse) of a policy with an outstanding loan amount greater than the owner's basis in the policy. In such an instance, phantom income will be triggered on the amount of the difference between the loan amount (plus accrued interest) and the owner's basis in the policy.

[17] Rev. Rul. 85-13, 1985-1 C.B. 184 provides that, if a grantor is treated as the owner of an entire trust for income tax purposes, the grantor is considered to be the owner of the trust's assets for federal income tax purposes. Therefore, a transaction between the grantor and his or her grantor trust will not be recognized as a sale or exchange for federal income tax purposes since the same person (to wit, the grantor) is treated as

Practice Point: In order for a transfer of a life insurance policy to come within the transferor's basis exception under a part sale part gift transfer, the amount of the consideration given for the transfer of the policy (which amount includes the policy loan amounts assumed by the transferee) must be (i) less than the policy's fair market value, ***and*** (ii) less than the original transferor's basis in the policy.

Caution: Generally speaking, in order to come within the transferor's basis exception, do not transfer a life insurance policy with a loan amount in excess of the transferor's basis. Instead, before making the transfer, repay all or a portion of the loan so that the outstanding loan amount is less than the amount of the transferor's basis in the policy.

§2.5(b)(3) Tax-Free Reorganization

Another common example of the transferor's basis exception is when the life insurance policy is transferred from one company to another company pursuant to a tax-free reorganization (assuming the policy is not already tainted because of a prior transfer for value). Because the tax basis for the insurance policy does not change under the tax-free reorganization rules, the transfer for value rule is not invoked. Corporate tax-free reorganizations under IRC section 368 include mergers, consolidations, and the transfer of substantially all of one corporation's property solely in exchange for the voting stock of another corporation. Also included in the transferor's basis exception is the transfer of a life insurance policy to a corporation in a manner that qualifies as a tax-free transfer of property in exchange for stock under IRC section 351. Treas. Reg. §1.101-1(b)(5), Example 2.

owning the purported consideration both before and after the transaction. Because the transfer of the life insurance policy to the trust is disregarded and not recognized for income tax purposes, the transfer for value rule is not applicable since there has been no transfer for valuable consideration by the transferor-grantor. This conclusion was recently confirmed by the IRS in Rev. Rul. 2007-13, 2007-11 I.R.B. 684 (3/12/2007), which cites Rev. Rul. 85-13 as the basis for its conclusion.

Rev. Rul. 85-13 has also been relied upon by the IRS in other public rulings. *See,* Rev. Rul. 2004-86, 2004-2 C.B. 191; Rev. Rul. 90-7, 1990-1 C.B. 153; Rev. Rul. 88-103, 1988-2 C.B. 304; Rev. Rul. 87-61, 1987-2 C.B. 219; Notice 97-34, 1997-1 C.B. 422; Notice 97-24, 1997-1 C.B. 409.

A corporation's purchase of another company's assets is not a tax-free reorganization, and therefore, if the assets purchased include a life insurance policy owned by the selling company, the transfer for value rule will come into play (unless another exception to the transfer for value rule applies, such as the insured is an officer or shareholder of the purchaser corporation). *See*, *Spokane Dry Goods Co.*, T.C.M. (PH) ¶43182, [pg. 43-559], 1 T.C.M. (CCH) 921 (1943).

> **Practice Point:** When a life insurance policy is acquired in the acquisition of a business, care must be taken that the policy is not transferred for value (directly or indirectly) when the business is acquired. If possible, the purchaser of the policy should attempt to structure the acquisition so that the policy comes within an exception to the transfer for value rule, such as the original transferor's basis exception. If this is not possible, allocate as much of the purchase price (as is reasonable) to the consideration paid for the policy. This will provide a higher cost basis for the purchaser and will minimize the subsequent income taxation of the death proceeds.

§2.5(b)(4) *Sale Of Life Insurance Policy By Insured To A Grantor Trust*

Another example of the transferor's basis exception is a sale between the same taxpayer (or a sale between the insured and the insured's grantor trust, which is discussed in section 2.5(b)(7), below).

§2.5(b)(5) *Transfer Of Life Insurance Policy To Insured's Spouse Or Incident To A Divorce*

Under the carryover basis rule of IRC section 1041(b), certain transfers (including sales) between an insured and his or her spouse (or ex-spouse pursuant to a divorce, if certain criteria are met) are *not* treated as "sales," and therefore come within the transferor's basis exception to the transfer for value rule. (Special rules apply for intra-spousal transfers of life insurance policies issued before July 18, 1984.) Even if at the time of the transfer (or sale) the fair market value of the policy is less than, equal to, or greater than the transferor-spouse's basis in the policy, the carryover basis rule under IRC section 1041(b) applies (because the transfer is treated as a gift, and not as a "transfer for valuable consideration"). For purposes of the transfer for value rule, the transferee spouse's (or ex-spouse's) basis in the transferred policy is the same as the transferor spouse's basis in the policy, even if the policy has an outstanding loan amount that is in excess of the transferor's basis in the policy. The rules of IRC section 1041 provide a special form of protection under the transferor's basis exception to the transfer for value rule. The intra-spousal transfer basis rule under IRC section 1041 is an exception to the general rule concerning the determination of the basis of gifted property under IRC section 1015.[18] Consequently, Example 6 of Treas. Reg. §1.101-1(b)(5) appears to be obsolete because the wife would receive a carryover basis in the policy from her insured husband, and the subsequent transfer of the policy by the wife to their son would come within the transferor's basis exception.

> **Caution:** Transfers to a trust for the benefit of a spouse (or ex-spouse) do not come within the purview of IRC section 1041(b). IRC section 1041(e). This is a potential trap concerning the transfer of a life insurance policy to a trust for the benefit of the insured's spouse (or ex-spouse) if the transferor's basis in the policy is subject to an outstanding loan amount that exceeds the transferor's basis in the policy. A way to avoid this potential trap is for the spouse (or ex-spouse) to be treated as the grantor of the trust under IRC sections 671-677. Pvt. Letter Rul. 200120007. Transfers from a corporation to the insured's spouse for valuable consideration also do not come within the purview of IRC section 1041(b) and constitute a transfer of value, even though the spouse may pay less than fair market value for the policy. *Estate of B. Joseph Rath v. U.S.*, 608 F. 2d 254 (6th Cir. 1979). IRC section 1041 does not apply to transfers to nonresident alien spouses or nonresident alien ex-spouses. IRC section 1041(d). Furthermore, IRC section 1041(b) does not apply to a "future spouse" that the insured plans to marry. Consequently, IRC section 1041(b) does not apply to the transfer of a life insurance policy pursuant to a premarital agreement.

---

[18] Under IRC section 1015, if the total consideration paid for the transfer of a life insurance policy (i.e., the amount of the outstanding policy loan and any other "cash type" consideration (or "boot") supplied by the transferee) exceeds the transferor's basis in the policy at the time of the loan, the transferee does not receive a carryover basis in the policy and is therefore not eligible for the transferor's basis exception to the transfer for value rule.

If an ILIT that is a grantor trust as to the insured transfers an existing life insurance policy to the non-insured spouse, the non-insured spouse can then transfer the policy to a new ILIT. The original transferor's basis exception to the transfer for value rule should apply (because the spouse takes the insured-spouse's basis in the policy under IRC section 1041(b)). Although IRC section 2035 will not apply to the transfer of the policy by the spouse to the new ILIT (because IRC section 2035 applies to an insured), IRC section 2036 will apply to the non-insured spouse if the spouse is a beneficiary of the new ILIT. IRC sections 2037, 2038, and 2041 may also apply to the non-insured spouse's retained beneficial interest in the new ILIT. When a donor transfers property into a trust in which he or she retains a beneficial interest, state law may permit the donor's creditors to reach the donor's retained interest in the trust, particularly if the donor is serving as a trustee. *See, Restatement (Third) of Trusts* §58(2).[19]

A way to avoid IRC sections 2036, 2037, and 2038 is for the non-insured spouse to sell, for full and adequate consideration, the policy to the new ILIT, of which the non-insured spouse is treated as the grantor under IRC sections 671-677. (IRC sections 2035, 2036, 2037, and 2038 do not apply to a bonafide sale for full and adequate consideration in money or money's worth.) *See*, section 3.1, below, concerning the valuation of a life insurance policy. The sale of the policy to the new ILIT should be a non-event for income tax purposes under Rev. Rul. 85-13, 1985-1 C.B. 184, and the sale of the life insurance policy should come within the original transferor's basis exception to the transfer for value rule. For the more cautious practitioner, consider having the new ILIT also be a partner with the insured in a bonafide partnership or limited liability company. *See*, section 2.5(c),

---

[19] *Restatement (Third) of Trusts* (ALI, Philadelphia, 2003) §58(2) provides, "[a] restraint on the voluntary and involuntary alienation of a beneficial interest retained by the settlor of a trust is invalid." For purposes of the *Restatement*, a transferor of property to a trust is a settlor with respect to the transferred property. *Restatement (Third) of Trusts* §58 (comment f). *See also, Restatement (Second) of Trusts* (ALI, Philadelphia, 1959) §156, which provides, "Where a person creates for his own benefit a trust with a provision restraining the voluntary or involuntary transfer of his interest, his transferee or creditors can reach his interest. Where a person creates for his own benefit a trust for support or a discretionary trust, his transferee or creditors can reach the maximum amount which the trustee under the terms of the trust could pay to him or apply for his benefit."

below. However, if under applicable state law the non-insured spouse's creditors can reach the assets of the new ILIT (because of the non-insured spouse's beneficial interest in the new ILIT), the spouse may have a general power of appointment under IRC section 2041. Unlike IRC sections 2035-2038, IRC section 2041 does not have an exception for transfers for "full and adequate consideration in money or money's worth." The more cautious approach is for the non-insured spouse not to be a beneficiary of the new ILIT if under applicable state law a creditor of the non-insured spouse can reach the trust's assets.[20]

§2.5(b)(6) Sale Of Life Insurance Policy To Insured's Spouse

A method of using the transferor's basis exception and having the insured avoid the three-year inclusion rule of IRC section 2035 is by having the insured sell the existing life insurance policy to his or her non-insured spouse for full and adequate consideration in money or money's worth (with the spouse using his or her own separate funds to purchase the policy).[21] Treas. Reg. §20.2043-1(a). *See,* section 3.1, below, concerning the valuation of a life insurance policy. Under IRC section 1041, the spouse would have the same basis in the policy as the insured, and there would be no transfer for value under IRC section 101(a)(2).[22] Because the spouse has paid full and adequate consideration for the policy, the three-year inclusion rule of IRC section 2035 would not apply to the transfer of the policy by the insured. IRC section 2035(d). The

---

[20] *See,* Mitchell Gans and Jonathan G. Blattmachr, "Life Insurance and Some Common 2035/2036 Problems: A Suggested Remedy," 139 *Trust & Estates* 58 (May 2000) for an discussion of a non-insured spouse transferring a life insurance policy to a new trust.

[21] In order to reduce the purchase price, the policy owner could borrow most of the cash value from the policy. However, this may result in taxable income to policy owner if loan balance exceeds basis. In addition, the policy may require sufficient cash value to sustain itself. In order to sustain the policy, the loan may have to be repaid, and this may necessitate a substantial gift or loan of that amount (plus interest) to the new policy owner, such as a new ILIT (if the policy is transferred to a new ILIT). Also, consider the effect a policy loan may have on the transferor's basis under the transfer for value rule. *See,* section 2.5(b)(2), above.

[22] As previously mentioned, IRC section 1041 protection does not apply to transfers to nonresident alien spouses or nonresident alien ex-spouses, nor does it apply to "future spouses" incident to an upcoming marriage. It also does not apply to a transfer of a life insurance policy to a trust for the benefit of the spouse or ex-spouse when the policy is subject to an outstanding loan amount in excess of the owner's basis and the trust is a not a grantor trust as to the spouse.

spouse could then gift the policy to an ILIT for the benefit of the insured's descendants. Because of retained interest rules of IRC section 2036-2038, the non-insured spouse should not be a beneficiary of the new ILIT that holds the gifted policy. IRC section 2035 would not apply to the spouse's gift of the existing policy to the ILIT because the three-year inclusion rule only applies to transfers by the insured.

§2.5(b)(7) Use Of An Intentionally Defective Grantor Trust

Another method of using the transferor's basis exception is by creating an intentionally defective irrevocable trust (i.e., a grantor trust) under IRC sections 671-677. Grantor trust status means that the insured-grantor is treated as the owner of the trust for income tax purposes (but not for federal estate tax purposes). Thus, a transfer from the insured-transferor to the transferor's grantor trust is disregarded for income tax purposes, and the basis in the life insurance policy remains the same, whether the policy is gifted or sold to the trust. Because the transfer or sale between the grantor and his or her grantor trust is disregarded for income tax purposes, if the policy has an outstanding loan amount greater than the transferor's basis in the policy, there is no recognition of gain on the sale or transfer of the policy to the trust. Also, because the transfer or sale between the grantor and his or her grantor trust is disregarded for income tax purposes, there is no transfer for value issue since there has been no "transfer for valuable consideration" between the transferor and his or her grantor trust. Rev. Rul. 2007-13, 2007-11 I.R.B. 684 (3/12/2007); Rev. Rul. 85-13, 1985-1 C.B. 184; Pvt. Letter Ruls. 200636086 (sale of policy by insured to an ILIT for the benefit of his children if the ILIT is a grantor trust and the grantor's spouse is the trustee and has the power to make discretionary distributions of income and principal to the grantor's descendants), 200606027, 200518061, 200514001, 200514002, and 200228019 (concerning the sale-transfer of a second to die life insurance policy between two intentionally defective grantor trusts involving the same grantor). *See,* Pvt. Letter Rul. 200247006 (concerning transfer of individual and second-to-die life insurance policies). *See also,* Rev. Proc. 2007-3, 2007-1 I.R.B. 108, section 3.01(7).[23] Furthermore, the insured's sale of an existing life insurance

---

[23] According to this Revenue Procedure the IRS will not issue a private letter ruling concerning: "Whether there has been a transfer for value for purposes of section 101(a)

policy for full and adequate consideration (*see,* section 3.1, below for the valuation of life insurance policies) to an intentionally defective grantor trust will avoid both the three-year inclusion rule of IRC section 2035 and the transfer for value rule. Priv. Letter Rul 9413045. (*See,* section 2.7, below, for a discussion of IRC sections 671-677 concerning the grantor trust rules.)

> **Practice Point:** If an existing ILIT, which is a grantor trust for income tax purposes,[24] contains a provision that would

---

in situations involving a grantor and a trust when (i) substantially all of the trust corpus consists or will consist of insurance policies on the life of the grantor or the grantor's spouse, (ii) the trustee or any other person has a power to apply the trust's income or corpus to the payment of premiums on policies of insurance on the life of the grantor or the grantor's spouse, (iii) the trustee or any other person has a power to use the trust's assets to make loans to the grantor's estate or to purchase assets from the grantor's estate, and (iv) there is a right or power in any person that would cause the grantor to be treated as the owner of all or a portion of the trust under sections 673 to 677." However, the IRS has provided guidance concerning the transfer for value rule and grantor trusts in Rev. Rul. 2007-13, 2007-11 I.R.B. 684 (3/12/2007).

[24] If the existing ILIT is not a grantor trust for income tax purposes, consider merging the existing trust into a newly created trust that does not contain the offending provisions and/or provides the flexibility desired by the grantor. A merger of two trusts must be permitted and accomplished in accordance with applicable state law. *But see,* section 2.7(e), below concerning "turning on" grantor trust status by having the grantor borrow income and corpus from the ILIT.

"One commentator has correctly suggested that a trustee-to-trustee transfer of life insurance is most appropriate if (1) the old trust has shortcomings that make it undesirable for tax or other reasons (e.g., the trust is not set up to handle cash gifts large enough to permit the payment of the premiums required to keep both old and new policies in force when coverage is increased or the trust will not qualify under S corporation rules to hold such stock); (2) the old trust's terms do not adequately address the special needs or situation of a particular beneficiary; or (3) the old trust does not adequately address changes in the grantor objectives (e.g., the grantor wants to eliminate or cut down or increase the interest of a beneficiary or class of beneficiaries or wants to change the shares of beneficiaries or the timing of when they receive their money). [Citation omitted.] This same commentator also wisely suggests that the trustee of the old trust obtain releases from the beneficiaries (both of current and future interests), and allow them to review the new trust or examine a summary of its terms. The beneficiaries also should be given a fair comparison of what the terms of the new trust will mean to them, distinguishing the terms of the new trust from those of the old trust. Obviously, this procedure may render the trustee-to-trustee approach impractical for some trusts, but such disclosure and release are probably essential to protect the trustee from possible future liability." Howard M. Zaritsky & Stephan R. Leimberg, *Tax Planning With Life Insurance: Analysis With Forms—2d Edition,* Warren, Gorham & Lamont, Boston, Massachusetts (Supp. 2007).

result in the life insurance proceeds being included in the insured's gross estate (or if the insured wants to "move" the policy to a new ILIT with more desirable provisions or different beneficiaries), consider having the existing ILIT sell for fair market value (or transfer) the life insurance policy to a new ILIT that is also a grantor trust for income tax purposes. *See,* Rev. Rul. 2007-13, 2007-11 I.R.B. 684 (3/12/2007); Pvt. Letter Ruls. 200606027, 200518061, 200514001, and 200514002. If the policy is sold, the new ILIT comes within the transfer for value exception concerning transfers of a life insurance policy to the insured (which is discussed immediately below)[25] and also avoids the three-year inclusion rule of IRC section 2035. Pvt. Letter Ruls. 200518061, 200514001, and 200514002. If the policy is transferred (and not sold), the new ILIT also comes within the transfer for value exception because it acquires the transferor's basis in the policy. However, there must be provisions in the existing ILIT that would permit such a transfer. *See,* Paragraph 7.1(D)(4) of Sample ILIT.

---

[25] Besides avoiding the transfer for value rule, other factors must be considered before having a new ILIT purchase a life insurance policy from an existing ILIT. First, does the existing ILIT permit the trustee to sell the policy? Second, if the beneficiaries of the new ILIT are different than the existing ILIT, will the trustee of the existing ILIT face some challenge for selling the policy? If so, this challenge can be minimized if the grantor informs the trustee in writing that he or she will no longer be making gifts to the existing ILIT (with which to pay premiums) and the policy's cash value in insufficient to sustain the policy. Third, in determining the fair market value of the policy being sold, the trustee of the existing ILIT should take into account the insured's age and health. In fact, the trustee might be well advised to shop the policy with two or three life settlement companies before agreeing to a sales price. Fourth, the grantor must be willing to fund the new ILIT with sufficient cash to purchase the policy from the existing ILIT. Moreover, this gift will use up some of the grantor's gift tax applicable exclusion amount (or will be subject to gift tax if there is no applicable exclusion amount available). For the more cautious practitioner who wants to be assured of complete grantor trust status, it is generally advisable to not grant *Crummey* withdrawal rights when the new ILIT is initially funded. However, if it is clear that the "tie-breaker" rule of IRC section 678(b) will clearly create grantor status with respect to the insured (*see,* section 2.13, below), then *Crummey* withdrawal rights can be granted, and the insured will be treated as the grantor of the trust. Finally, the grantor must understand that the existing ILIT will continue after it sells the policy; however, the existing ILIT's only asset will (presumably) be the cash it received from the sale of the life insurance policy to the new ILIT.

Caution: Once a policy is tainted by the transfer for value rule, a subsequent transfer under the transferor's basis exception will not eliminate the taint, and the proceeds will be subject to income taxation. Treas. Reg. §§1.101-1(b)(3); 1.101-1(b)(5) Example 6. *See also, James F. Waters, Inc. v. Commissioner*, 160 F. 2d 596 (9th Cir. 1947), *cert. denied,* 332 U.S. 767 (1947). However, if the policy is transferred to one of the four "protected party exceptions" (discussed below), the prior taint is removed. Treas. Reg. §1.101-1(b)(3)(ii). If however, the protected party subsequently transfers the policy (or an interest in the policy) for valuable consideration, the transfer for value rule will (once again) be applicable unless the transfer by the protected party comes within the transferor's basis exception or is to another protected party.

§2.5(c) Protected Party Exceptions

The next four exceptions, which are contained in IRC section 101(a)(2)(B) and Treas. Reg. §1.101-1(b)(1), are commonly referred to as the "protected party exceptions":

§2.5(c)(1) Transfer To The Insured

The first protected party exception is the transfer of the life insurance policy to the insured[26] (*W. Clarke Swanson, Jr. Trust v. Commissioner*, 518 F.2d 59 (8th Cir. 1975) *aff'g* T.C Memo 1974-61

---

[26] *See,* Priv. Letter Rul. 8951056 where the insured terminated contributions to an existing ILIT that was for the benefit of his wife and four children, purchased the policies on his life that were owned by the existing ILIT, created a new ILIT for the sole benefit of his four children, and then gifted the policies to the new ILIT. The existing ILIT was then terminated and distributed its assets (presumably cash) to the beneficiaries. The IRS ruled that existing ILIT's sale of the policy to the insured was not a transfer for value (since the insured is an excepted party), and that the insured's transfer of the policies to the new ILIT was not a transfer for value because the new ILIT received the insured-transferor's carryover basis in the policies. The ruling did not mention the application of IRC section 2035, which would apply if the insured died within three years of the transfer of the policies to the new ILIT. *See,* section 4.1, below concerning IRC section 2035.

(1974))[27] or the transfer of the life insurance policy to a grantor trust created by the insured (or the transfer of the life insurance policy from one grantor trust to another grantor trust, involving the same insured-grantor) (Rev. Rul. 2007-13, 2007-11 I.R.B. 684 (3/12/2007)[28]; Pvt. Letter Ruls. 200606027, 200514001, and 200247006)[29];

---

[27] The IRS's Action On Decision concerning the *Swanson* case (7/23/1975), in which the IRS disagreed with the Tax Court and the Eighth Circuit Court of Appeals, has, for all practical purposes, been superseded by Rev. Rul. 2007-13, 2007-11 I.R.B. 684 (3/12/2007); Rev. Rul. 85-13, 1985-1 C.B. 184 and the subsequent private letter rulings that permit the transfer of a life insurance policy between a grantor and a grantor trust without invoking the transfer for value rule. In such an instance, the transfer is disregarded for income tax purposes. In *Swanson,* both the Tax Court and the Eighth Circuit Court of Appeals held that partial (91%) grantor trust status for income tax purposes (in contrast to full (100%) grantor trust status for income tax purposes) was sufficient for life insurance policies transferred to the trusts to be treated as a transfer to the insured himself.

[28] Rev. Rul. 2007-13 holds:

(1) That a grantor who is treated for federal income tax purposes as the owner of a trust that owns a life insurance policy on the grantor's life is treated as the owner of the life insurance contract for purposes of applying the transfer for value rule of IRC section 101(a)(2).

(2) That the transfer of a life insurance policy on the life of the grantor between two grantor trusts that are treated as *wholly owned* by the same insured-grantor is not a transfer for a valuable consideration within the meaning of IRC section 101(a)(2), i.e., the transfer of the policy between the two grantor trusts is a non-event for income tax purposes.

(3) That the transfer of a life insurance policy from a non-grantor trust to a grantor trust that is treated as *wholly owned* by the insured-grantor is deemed to be a transfer to the insured within the meaning of IRC section 101(a)(2)(B)—i.e., a transfer that comes within the protected party exception, to wit, a transfer to the insured.

> **Caution:** The IRS will not issue a private letter ruling on the grantor trust status of an ILIT. Rev. Proc. 2007-3, 2007-1 I.R.B. 108, section 3.01(47). Therefore, a cautious practitioner may also want to rely on the "partner of the insured" protected party exception by making each trust and the insured a partner of one another prior to the transfer of the policy.

[29] There is a difference between the transfer of a life policy that comes within the scope of Rev. Rul. 85-13 (concerning transactions between a grantor and a grantor trust) and the transfer of a life insurance policy that comes within the scope of *Swanson.* In *Swanson,* there was a transfer for value, but the transfer came within one of the protected party exceptions—a transfer to the insured. Under Rev. Rul. 85-13, because the transfer is disregarded for income tax purposes, there is no transfer for valuable con-

§2.5(c)(2) Transfer To A Partner Of The Insured

The second protected party exception is the transfer of the life insurance policy to a bona fide partner[30] (or member of a limited liability company that is being taxed as a partnership) of the insured (Pvt. Letter Ruls. 200228019, 199905010, and 9347016);

§2.5(c)(3) Transfer To A Partnership

The third protected party exception is the transfer of the life insurance policy to a bona fide partnership (or limited liability company that is being taxed as a partnership) in which the insured is a general or limited partner (or a member)[31] at the time of the transfer (Pvt. Letter Ruls. 200111038, 9843024, and 9625013).

§2.5(c)(3)(A) Create A Partnership Between The Insured And The ILIT. A popular method of using the protected party exception is to create a partnership between the insured (or insureds in the case of a second-to-die policy) and the ILIT.[32] It appears that a limited liability

---

sideration in the first instance. For all practical purposes, a transfer that comes within the scope of Rev. Rul. 85-13 is really a transfer to the insured. It's as if the insured shifted ownership of the policy to him or herself. Rev. Rul. 2007-13, 2007-11 I.R.B. 684 (3/12/2007) validates both propositions.

[30] The transferor and the transferee can become bonafide partners by owning limited partnership units in the same publicly traded partnership. For example, the following publicly traded partnerships are listed on the New York Stock Exchange (NYSE): Alliance Bernstein Holding Limited Partners (Symbol: AB); Atlas Pipeline Partners, L.P. (Symbol: APL); Buckeye Partners (Symbol: BPL); Natural Resources Partners, L.P. (Symbol: NRP); Northern Border Partners Limited Partnership (Symbol: NBP); Penn Virginia Resource Partners Limited Partnership (Symbol: PVR); Plains All American Pipeline Limited Partnership (Symbol: PAA); Suburban Propane Partners Limited Partnership (Symbol: SPH); Teppco Partners Limited Partnership (Symbol: TPP); Terra Nitrogen Company Limited Partnership (Symbol: TNH); US Shipping Partners Limited Partnership (Symbol: USS).

[31] *See,* David T. Lewis and Christopher J. C. Jones, "Limited Liability Companies as Trust Substitutes, Part 2," 18 *Probate & Property* 52 (January/February 2004).

[32] If the only partners (or members in the case of a limited liability company) are the insured and his or her intentionally defective grantor trust, the partnership (or limited liability company) may not be recognized for income tax purposes because the IRS will "look through" the intentionally defective grantor trust and treat the insured as the owner of the trust's partnership interest (or membership interest). Thus, what may appear to be a partnership of two persons may in fact be a sole proprietorship. Treas. Reg. §1.1001-2(c), Example 5; Rev. Rul. 77-402, 1977-2 C.B. 222. *Cf.*, Rev. Rul.

company (that is being taxed as a partnership[33]), with the insured(s) and the ILIT as members, not only will work but may be a preferable manner of using this exception. *See, e.g.*, Pvt. Letter Ruls. 200120007 and 9625013. The partnership should exist for reasons other than solely to avoid the transfer for value rule. In other words, the partnership should carry on a trade or business for profit and own some assets, with an incidental purpose being the avoidance of the transfer for value rule.[34] *See, e.g.*, Pvt. Letter Ruls. 199905010, 9843024, and 9347016. *See also*, IRC sections 761(a) and 7701(a) (2) for the definition of a "partnership."

2004-77, 2004-2 C.B. 119; Chief Counsel Memo 200501001 (January 7, 2005). Consequently, the partnership (or limited liability company) may need to be composed of more than just the insured and his or her intentionally defective grantor trust. Furthermore, if grantor trust status ceases during the grantor's life time, the grantor will be treated as having transferred the partnership interest (or membership interest) and the other trust assets to the trust. Under certain conditions, the transfer may result in the grantor having to recognize income. *See*, Rev. Rul. 77-402, 1977-2 C.B. 222; *Bernard and Joyce Madorin v. Commissioner*, 84 T.C. 667 (1985); Treas. Reg. §1.1001-2(c), Example 5; TAMs 200011005, 200010011, and 200010010.

[33] IRC sections 761(a) and 7701(a)(2) provide that the term "partnership" means a business entity that has at least two members. *See*, Treas. Reg. §301.7701-2(c)(1). A partnership includes a syndicate, group, pool, joint venture, or other unincorporated organization, through or by means of which any business, financial operation, or venture is carried on, and which is not, within the meaning of the Internal Revenue Code, a trust, estate, or corporation. The term "partner" means a member of a partnership. IRC sections 761(b) and 7701(a)(2). Unless it elects otherwise, a domestic eligible entity formed after January 1, 1997, with two or more members is treated as a partnership for federal tax purposes. Treas. Reg. §301.7701-3(b)(1).

[34] "[C]ommentators are generally uncomfortable with a situation where 'substantially all of the organization's assets consist or will consist of life insurance on the lives of members'—in spite of a ruling [Pvt. Letter Rul. 9309021] that has been widely (but mistakenly in the view of many commentators) touted to mean that a 'life insurance only' partnership would per se qualify under one of the two partnership safe harbors. It may be helpful in establishing the bona fides of the partnership to show that the cash values of insurance owned by and payable to the partnership in question comprise less than 50% of the partnership's assets and to specifically authorize the carrying on, investment, and reinvestment of other businesses and investments. [*See*, Pvt. Letter Ruls. 9725007, 9725008, and 9725009.] Prudent planners will accumulate evidence supporting the fact that the partnership has purposes beyond the mere ownership and management of life insurance contracts and is therefore a bona fide entity serving purposes that range beyond mere 'investment in life insurance.' [*See*, Pvt. Letter Rul. 200017051.]" Lawrence Brody and Stephan R. Leimberg, "Avoiding the Tax Trap of the Transfer for Value Rule," 32 *Estate Planning* 3, 10 (October 2005) (citation omitted).

Note that the IRS will not rule whether, in connection with the transfer of a life insurance policy to an unincorporated organization (such as a partnership or limited liability company) (1) the organization will be treated as a partnership under IRC sections 761 and 7701; or (2) the transfer of the life insurance policy to the organization will be exempt from the transfer for value rule of IRC section 101, when substantially all of the organization's assets consist or will consist of life insurance policies on the lives of the members. Rev. Proc. 2007-3, 2007-1 I.R.B. 108, section 3.01(8).

> **Practice Point:** If an existing ILIT, which is ***not*** a grantor trust for income tax purposes, contains a provision that would result in the life insurance proceeds being included in the insured's gross estate (or if the insured wants to "move" the policy to a new ILIT), the insured can establish a new ILIT that is a grantor trust and have the existing ILIT transfer or sell the policy to the new ILIT. The transfer or sale from the existing ILIT to the new ILIT will be treated as a transfer to the insured—one of the protected party exceptions. Another alternative is for the existing ILIT to sell for fair market value (or transfer) the life insurance policy to a new ILIT (that does not have to be a grantor trust) that is a partner with the insured in a bonafide partnership (or member in the case of a limited liability company being taxed as a partnership). This would make the transferee ILIT a partner of the insured at the time of the policy's transfer. Thus, the purchase of the existing policy from the "old" ILIT by the new ILIT would come within the safe harbor for a transfer to a partner of the insured. *See,* Pvt. Letter Ruls. 199903020 (real estate investment partnership) and 9347016 (investment partnership holding a working interest in an oil and gas well, futures contracts, and various shares of stock). In addition, such a sale avoids the three-year rule of IRC section 2035 because that section does not apply to transfers made for full and adequate consideration in money or money's worth.

> **Caution:** Although the transfer may be "exempt" from the transfer for value rule (and the life insurance proceeds will not be subject to income taxation), the sale or transfer of a policy from the existing non-grantor ILIT to the new ILIT

may still result in the selling ILIT realizing income/gain if the consideration for the transfer of the policy exceeds the selling ILIT's basis in the policy. *See,* section 2.19, below.

§2.5(c)(4) Transfer To A Corporation

The fourth protected party exception is the transfer of the transfer of the life insurance policy to a corporation in which the insured is either a shareholder or bona fide officer at the time of the transfer. However, if the insured is an employee or a director and is not an officer or a shareholder of the corporation, the exception does not apply and the policy will be subject to the transfer for value rule.

Practice Point: To come within the bona fide officer exception, consider whether the board of directors should appoint the shareholder as an officer of the corporation *before* the transfer of the policy.

§2.5(c)(4)(A) Transfer To A Co-Shareholder. Note that the transfer of a life insurance policy to a co-shareholder of the insured does not fall within the statutory exceptions, nor does a corporation's transfer of a life insurance policy to a shareholder, employee, director, or officer who is not the insured. *See J.R. Monroe v. Patterson,* 197 F. Supp. 146 (N.D. Ala. 1961). This is a potential trap for buy-sell agreements that permit a co-shareholder to buy a policy on the life of another shareholder from a deceased shareholder's estate, or from the corporation.[35] *See also,* Priv. Letter Rul 7734048.

---

[35] *See,* Stephen R. Akers and Myron E. Sildon, *A Practical Guide to Buy-Sell Agreements* (ALI-ABA, Philadelphia 2002) for a comprehensive discussion of buy-sell agreements. *See, Id.* §7.04; ¶2.07 of Howard M. Zaritsky & Stephan R. Leimberg, *Tax Planning With Life Insurance: Analysis With Forms—2d Edition,* Warren, Gorham & Lamont, Boston, Massachusetts (Supp. 2007); ¶8.02[1] of Howard M. Zaritsky, *Structuring Buy-Sell Agreements: Analysis With Forms* (Warren, Gorham & Lamont, Supp. 2007); and Section II, F, 5 of Brody, Richey, and Baier, 828 T.M., *Compensating Employees with Insurance* concerning the transfer for value issues regarding buy-sell agreements. *See also,* Lawrence Brody and Stephan R. Leimberg, "Using a Transactional Analysis to Avoid the Transfer for Value Rule," 32 *Estate Planning* 3 (November 2005). Other common transfer for value traps are (i) an uninsurable shareholder sells his or her policy to a co-shareholder to help fund a cross-purchase agreement, (ii) a corporation sells or transfers a policy to a co-shareholder who is not the insured, (iii) a corporation sells its policies to its insured shareholders who then make a gift of the policies to one

In *Estate of B. Joseph Rath v. United States*, 608 F.2d 254 (6th Cir. 1979), the insured had the option to name a purchaser for (or to personally purchase) a corporate-owned policy on his life that was no longer needed by the corporation. Instead, the insured named his wife as the purchaser of the policy and directed the corporation to name her as the new owner. The wife's purchase of the policy from the corporation resulted in a transfer for value. Had the insured purchased the policy from the corporation and gifted the policy to his wife, there would have been no transfer for value.

Another potential trap arises when an insured-shareholder names his or her co-shareholders as the beneficiary of the insured's policy to fund a cross-purchase of the insured's shares of stock upon his or her demise, and the other shareholders do the same for one another with regard to their life insurance policies. If there is no valid partnership between the shareholders, a transfer (i.e., the transfer of the death proceeds) for value occurs. The consideration (i.e., value) is the mutual naming of the co-shareholders as beneficiaries in return for their naming the insured as a beneficiary of their policy and for the parties' mutual obligation to use the death proceeds to fund the cross-purchase arrangement. *See*, *J.R. Monroe v. Patterson,* 197 F. Supp. 146 (N.D. Ala. 1961). Furthermore, the life insurance proceeds payable to the co-shareholders would be includable in the insured's gross estate under IRC section 2042 (concerning incidents of ownership)—a disastrous result!

§2.5(c)(5) Protected Party Exceptions Do Not Avoid Gain

The protected party exceptions applies solely for purposes of IRC sections 61 and 101, and do not apply for purposes of determining the transferor's gain or loss under IRC section 1001. Thus, if the policy has an outstanding loan in excess of the transferor's basis in the

---

another in order to fund a cross-purchase agreement (the transfer for value is the reciprocal promise to transfer the policies to one another in order to fund the cross-purchase agreement), (iv) a buy-sell agreement permits the remaining shareholders to purchase life insurance policies owned by a deceased shareholder on the lives of the other co-shareholders, and (v) an ILIT sells a life insurance policy on the grantor's life to his or her children, who continue to make the premium payments of the policy. *See*, Appendix G of Stephan R. Leimberg and Robert J. Doyle, *Tools and Techniques of Life Insurance Planning (3d ed 2004)*, The National Underwriter Company, Erlanger, KY, www.NUCO.com.

policy, the transferor may have taxable gain upon the transfer of the policy to one of the protected parties. *See,* section 2.5(b)(2), above.

§2.5(d) Final Transferee Of The Policy

Once the insured (or one of the other three protected parties described above) becomes the final transferee of the policy, all prior transfer for value taint is eliminated and the proceeds once again become income tax free. Treas. Reg. §§1.101-1(b)(3)(ii); 1.101-1(b)(5), Examples 5 and 7.

§2.5(e) Summary Of Transfer For Value Rule Exceptions

The exceptions to the transfer for value rule can be generally summarized as follows (regardless of the identity of the transferor):

Transferee For Value	**Income Taxation Of Death Benefit**
Anyone whose basis is determined by reference to original transferor's basis	Not taxable
Insured	Not taxable
Insured's spouse (or ex-spouse—if incident to a divorce and meets the IRC section 1041 tests)	Not taxable
Partner of insured	Not taxable
Partnership in which insured is a partner	Not taxable
Corporation in which insured is a shareholder or officer	Not taxable
Assignee or pledgee to secure policy owner's debt	Not taxable
Co-stockholder of insured	**Taxable**[36]
Anyone else	**Taxable**[37]

---

[36] If the original transferor's basis exception applies, the transfer for value rule will not apply, and the life insurance proceeds will not be subject to income tax under the transfer for value rule.

[37] *Id.*

§2.6 RELATED OR SUBORDINATE PARTY DEFINITION

In Rev. Rul. 95-58, 1995-2 C.B. 191, the IRS adopted the related or subordinate party definition of IRC section 672(c). The 1995 ruling (which revoked Rev. Ruls. 81-51, 1981-1 C.B. 458 and 79-353,1979-2 C.B. 325, and modified Rev. Rul. 77-182, 1977-1 C.B. 273) holds that a grantor's reservation of an unqualified power to remove an existing trustee and appoint a replacement trustee who is not related or subordinate to the grantor (within the meaning of IRC section 672(c)) is not a reservation of the trustee's discretionary powers of distribution that might cause trust corpus to be included in the grantor's estate under IRC sections 2036(a) and 2038(a)(1) (concerning retained interests or the ability to affect the beneficial enjoyment of gifted property). *See*, sections 4.3(a) and 11.9, below, for further discussion of the power to remove a trustee.

> **Caution:** The following individuals, if they ***are*** a non-adverse party,[38] are treated as related and subordinate to the power holder: (1) the power holder's spouse if living with the power holder; (2) the power holder's father, mother, issue, brother, or sister; (3) a corporation, or any employee of a corporation, in which the power holder's voting control is significant; and (4) a subordinate employee of a corporation in which the power holder is an executive. In the absence of a preponderance of the evidence to the contrary,

---

[38] A "non-adverse party" is a person who is not an "adverse party." IRC section 672(b). An "adverse party" is any person: (i) who has a beneficial interest in a trust, (ii) the beneficial interest is substantial, and (iii) the person's beneficial interest would be adversely affected by the exercise or non-exercise of a power held by the grantor or another person. A trustee is not an adverse party merely because of his interest as trustee. A person having a general power of appointment over the trust property is deemed to have a beneficial interest in the trust. An interest is a substantial interest if its value in relation to the total value of the property subject to the power is not insignificant. A contingent beneficiary may have a substantial interest in a trust. Treas. Reg. §1.672(a)-1(c). Ordinarily, a beneficiary will be an adverse party, but if his right to share in the income or corpus of a trust is limited to only a part, he may be an adverse party only as to that part. The interest of an ordinary income beneficiary of a trust may or may not be adverse with respect to the exercise of a power over corpus. The interest of a remainder beneficiary is adverse to the exercise of any power over the corpus of a trust, but not to the exercise of a power over any income interest preceding the beneficiary's remainder interest. Thus, an interest may be adverse as to income or corpus or both. IRC section 672(a); Treas. Reg. §1.672(a)-1.

a related and subordinate party is presumed for purposes of IRC section 672(f), 674, and 675, to be subservient to the wishes of the grantor with regard to the exercise or non-exercise of a power. However, the following individuals are ***not*** related or subordinate parties under IRC section 672(c), as concerns the power holder: (1) the power holder's nieces and nephews, (2) the power holder's grandparents; (3) spouses of the power holder's children, grandchildren, brothers, or sisters; and (4) partners of the power holder. Treas. Reg. §1.672(c)-1.

§2.7 INCOME TAXATION OF ILIT AND THE GRANTOR (THE GRANTOR TRUST RULES)[39]

An ILIT is a separate taxpayer (IRC section 641) unless the ILIT is (1) a grantor trust under sections 671-677[40] (in which case the income,

---

[39] The author gratefully acknowledges the contributions of Ellen K. Harrison, Esq. of Pillsbury, Winthrop, Shaw, Pittman, LLP of Washington, DC and Virginia F. Coleman, Esq. of Ropes & Gray, LLP of Boston, Massachusetts in the writing of this section.

[40] A detailed discussion of the grantor trust rules and how to establish an intentionally defective grantor trust (including a sale to an intentionally defective grantor trust) is beyond the scope of this book. *See,* Pvt. Letter Rul. 9535026, which provides a roadmap for an installment sale to an intentionally defective grantor trust. *See also,* Pvt. Letter Rul. 200432012. The term "defective grantor trust" refers to a completed gift of assets to a trust where the grantor is treated as the owner of the trust for income tax purposes but not for estate tax purposes. *See,* Zaritsky, 858-2nd T.M., *Grantor Trusts: Sections 671-679* (Bureau of National Affairs, Washington, DC), for a general discussion of the grantor trust rules (including sample grantor trust language) and the use of inter-vivos trusts (such as ILITs) in estate planning; ¶30.10 of Henkel, *Estate Planning and Wealth Preservation: Strategies and Solutions* (Warren, Gorham & Lamont, Boston, Massachusetts, Supp. 2007); ¶12.07 of Zaritsky, *Tax Planning for Family Wealth Transfers: Analysis With Forms* (Warren, Gorham & Lamont, Supp. 2007); Samuel A. Donaldson, "Understanding Grantor Trusts," 40 *Heckerling Institute on Estate Planning,* Chapter 3 (Matthew Bender/Lexis-Nexis, Newark, NJ 2006); Michael D. Mulligan, "How To Use an Intentionally Defective Irrevocable Trust To Freeze an Estate," 8 *ALI-ABA Estate Planning Course Materials Journal* 5 (April 2002); Carmen Irizarry-Diaz, "How Defective is Your Trust? Suggestions on Structuring an Intentionally Defective Grantor Trust," 41 *Tax Management Memorandum* 231 (June 19, 2000); Virginia Coleman, "The Grantor Trust: Yesterday's Disaster, Today's Delight, Tomorrow's What?" 6 *ALI-ABA Course Materials Journal* 15 (February 2000); Richard A. Oshins and Steven J. Oshins, "Protecting & Preserving Wealth Into The

credits, and deductions of the ILIT are attributed to the grantor[41] and are included in determining the grantor's income tax liability under IRC section 671—regardless of who actually receives the cash distributions)[42]; (2) a foreign trust under IRC section 679 that has both a

---

Next Millennium (Part 2)," 137 *Trusts & Estates* 68, 82-90 (October 1998); Michael D. Mulligan "Sale to a Defective Grantor Trust: An Alternative to a GRAT," 23 *Estate Planning* 3 (January 1996); and Michael D. Mulligan, "Defective Grantor Trusts Offer Many Tax Advantages," 19 *Estate Planning* 131 (May/June 1992). *See also*, Robert S. Kebler and Peter J. Melcher, "Structuring IDGT Sales to Avoid Sections 2701, 2702, and 2036," 32 *Estate Planning* 19 (October 2005); Michael D. Mulligan, "The Reinvigorated GRAT: Is a Sale to a Defective Trust Still Superior?," 29 *Estate Planning* 379 (August 2002); Robert T. Danforth, "The Use of Grantor Trusts in Estate Planning," 31 *Tax Management Estates, Gifts and Trusts Journal* 103 (March 9, 2006); John Huffaker and Edward Kessel, "How the Disconnect Between the Income and Estate Tax Rules Created Planning for Grantor Trusts," 100 *Journal of Taxation* 206 (April 2004); Domingo P. Such, III, "Fix-Ups Of Estate Plans After They Have Become Irrevocable (With Sample Language) (Part 1)," 12 *ALI-ABA Estate Planning Course Materials Journal* 45 (February 2006).

[41] For transfers to a trust or transfers of an interest in a trust that occur on or after August 10, 1999, a "grantor" for income tax purposes includes any person to the extent such person either creates a trust, or directly or indirectly makes a gratuitous transfer of property to a trust. Treas. Reg. §§1.671-2(e)(1) and 1.671-2(e)(7) A trust, all of which is treated as owned by a husband and wife as grantors, and who file a single joint income tax return, is considered to be owned by one grantor for purposes of Treas. Reg. §1.671-4(b). Treas. Reg. §1.671-4(b)(8). A person who makes a contribution to a trust on behalf of another person and is reimbursed for such contribution within a reasonable period of time is treated as an "accommodation grantor" and is not treated as the owner of any portion of the trust under the grantor trust rules. Treas. Reg. §1.671-2(e)(1).

For transfers to a trust or transfers of an interest in a trust that arise before August 10, 1999, a "grantor" for income tax purposes is determined by case law, and is generally defined as the person whose economic contributions created the trust. Treas. Reg. §1.671-2(e)(7). *But see*, Treasury Decision 8890, 65 Fed. Reg. 41332 (7/5/2000) (concerning the July 5, 2000 effective date of the section 671 Treasury Regulations).

[42] The IRS will not issue a private letter ruling on the grantor trust status of an ILIT. Rev. Proc. 2007-3, 2007-1 I.R.B. 108, section 3.01(47). Grantor trust status can exist over all or some of the: (i) trust income; (ii) trust corpus; or (iii) both trust income and corpus. When a grantor is taxable on all the trust's income and corpus, the grantor has "full" grantor trust status over the trust. *See*, Treas. Reg. §§1.671-2(b) and 1.671-3. *See*, Jonathan G. Blattmachr and Bridget J. Crawford, "Grantor Trusts and Income Tax Reporting Requirements: A Primer," 16 *ABA Probate and Property* 18 (March/April 2002); and Kathleen M. Weiden and Charles A. Barragato, "Get A Handle On Grantor Trust Tax Rules and Strategies," 74 *Practical Tax Strategies* 87 (February 2005). *See*, Exhibit 1 contained in Appendix 5 for a summary of the IRC reporting requirements for a grantor trust.

U.S. grantor and at least one U.S. beneficiary (in which case the grantor will be taxed on the ILIT's income),[43] or (3) a nongrantor (such as a beneficiary) is treated as the owner of the trust for income tax purposes under IRC section 678 (in which case the non-grantor will be taxed on the trust's income[44]). Grantor trust status may be par-

---

[43] A trust with virtually any possibility of U.S. beneficiaries will be treated as having a U.S. beneficiary. IRC section 679(b). Thus, section 679 is a way to create grantor trust status during the grantor's lifetime where an existing trust does not have other grounds or means for becoming a grantor trust. However, foreign trust status creates special tax reporting requirements during the grantor's life time. Foreign trust status could be obtained by having a foreign (e.g., a Canadian) person hold certain trust administration powers. Since 1997, it has been remarkably easy to create a foreign trust, even if the trust is administered in the United States by a U.S. trustee and has a U.S. grantor and beneficiaries. *See*, IRC section 7701(a)(31). Any trust with a single foreign trustee or that requires the trustees to act unanimously, will be a foreign trust; similarly a foreign trust protector, or a foreign person with power to appoint successor trustees, will cause a trust to be a foreign trust. Because of the new definition of a foreign trust, it is not only easier to create one but also easier to cause the trust to cease to be a foreign trust, and thus to cease to be a grantor trust. One need only substitute a U.S. person for the foreign person who has the power that triggers grantor trust status. The primary drawback to the technique, and it is a major one, is the tax consequence of termination of grantor trust status if the trust thereafter remains a foreign trust. Therefore, in order to avoid a deemed disposition of the trust assets at the grantor's death (and an income tax to pay), foreign trust status should be toggled off prior to the grantor's death by giving a trust protector the ability to remove the foreign trustee and replace the removed foreign trustee with a U.S. trustee. If a foreign trust ceases to be a grantor trust during the grantor's lifetime, a tax will be imposed on all the appreciation in the trust assets (without any offset for the loss on depreciated trust assets) if it is still a foreign trust. IRC section 684; Treas. Reg. §1.684-2(e). This rule will not apply if grantor trust status terminates because of the grantor's death and the assets are includable in the grantor's gross estate and receive a new basis under IRC section 1014. Treas. Reg. §1.684-3(c).

[44] *See, Mallinckrodt v. Nunan*, 146 F.2d 1 (8th Cir. 1945), *aff'g* 2 T.C. 1128 (1943), *cert. denied*, 324 U.S. 871 (1945); Rev. Rul. 81-6, 1981-1 C.B. 38; Rev. Rul. 67-241, 1967-2 C.B. 225; Priv. Letter Ruls. 200104005 and 9034004. Such a trust is referred to as a "beneficiary-owned" trust, or a *"Mallinckrodt"* trust.

A person who is neither a beneficiary nor a grantor of a trust can, under certain circumstances be taxed on the trust's income. The Internal Revenue Code and Treasury Regulations provide that any one of the following situations will result in a non-grantor non-beneficiary being taxed on all or a portion of a trust: (i) the trust requires the trustee to use trust income to discharge a legal obligation of the non-grantor non-beneficiary, including that person's obligation of support (Treas. Reg. §1.662(a)-4); (ii) the non-grantor non-beneficiary has the power exercisable solely by

tial or full, depending on the powers held by the grantor (or beneficiary in the case of IRC section 678(a)).[45] Application of the grantor trust rules is not elective—the grantor (or beneficiary as the case may be under section 678) cannot elect out of the grantor trust rules if they otherwise apply (the grantor may, however, be able to relinquish grantor trust status by releasing the power that triggers grantor trust status).

One of the key transfer tax benefits of grantor trust status is that the payment of the trust's income taxes by the grantor permits the trust to grow "income tax free." The income taxes paid by the grantor on behalf of the trust is gift tax free, and removes that amount from the grantor's gross estate for federal estate tax purposes. *See*, sections 3.18 and 4.2(b), below, for further discussion on the gift and estate tax consequences of the grantor's payment of the trust's income taxes.

---

him or herself, in any capacity other than that of a trustee, to apply trust income in discharge of the non-grantor non-beneficiary's obligation of support or maintenance (Treas. Reg. section 1.678(c)-1(b); or (iii) the non-grantor non-beneficiary is a trustee or co-trustee who has the sole authority (*and* exercises that authority) to apply trust income for the support or maintenance of a person the trustee has the obligation to support or maintain (IRC section 678(c); Treas. Reg. §1.678(c)-1(a)).

[45] A grantor may be treated as the owner of any portion of a trust, including (i) some or all of the income, or (ii) some or all of the corpus, or (iii) a fractional or pecuniary share, or (iv) a specific asset, or (v) all of the income and corpus (in which case the grantor (or beneficiary in the case of IRC section 678(a)) has "full" grantor trust status over the trust because of his or her "ownership" over all of the income and corpus). Treas. Reg. §1.671-3. If a grantor is treated as the owner of a portion of a trust consisting of specific trust property and its income, the grantor is considered to be the owner of that specific trust property for federal income tax purposes.

The portion rules of Treas. Reg. §1.671-3 provide, for example, that if the grantor has the right to receive fiduciary accounting income (i.e., ordinary income) and not income allocable to principal (such as capital gains), in general the grantor will be treated as the owner of income allocated to the fiduciary income account and not capital gains, to the extent gains are allocated to principal. Conversely, if all fiduciary accounting income is required to be distributed to another person and the grantor has a reversion of principal, the grantor may only be taxable on the capital gains accruing to the trust that are allocated to principal. The application of the portion rules to certain of the grantor trust rules is unclear.

A trust can have more than one grantor, with different persons being treated as owners of different portions of the same trust. Treas. Reg. §1.671-2(e)(6), Example 1. If a trust has more than one grantor, and the grantors have "full" grantor trust status over the trust, the trustee may report the income, credits and deductions pursuant to Treas. Reg. §1.671-4(b). *See*, Exhibit 1 contained in Appendix 5 for a summary of the IRC reporting requirements for a grantor trust.

Caution: Not all states follow the federal grantor trust rules concerning the state income taxation of trusts.

§2.7(a) Power Or Interest Held By Grantor's Spouse Attributable To Grantor

For transfers in trust after March 1, 1986, the grantor of an irrevocable trust is treated as having any power or interest of the grantor's spouse. IRC section 672(e)(1). Therefore, if the spouse is the trustee or beneficiary of the trust, the trust should be treated as a grantor trust for income tax purposes, and the trust's income will be taxed to the grantor. If the spouse is not a trustee, beneficiary, or grantor of the trust, but the spouse holds the power to substitute trust assets under IRC section 675(4)(C) or the power to borrow the trust corpus or income for adequate interest but without any security under IRC section 675(2), the trust should be treated as a grantor trust under IRC section 672(e) for income tax purposes, and the trust's income will be taxed to the grantor. However, the attribution to the grantor of the spouse's power and interest over the trust property does not apply to transfers made to the trust when (i) the parties are married but legally separated, (ii) the parties are legally divorced. In such an instance, grantor trust status may be "partial" to the grantor (concerning transfers that occurred before the legal separation or divorce (*see* IRC section 672(e)(1)(A)), or (iii) the spouse resigns as a trustee and the successor trustee is not a related or subordinate person, and the trust may be a separate taxpayer with regard to transfers occurring after the separation, divorce, or resignation of the spouse-trustee. However, the death of the grantor's spouse (but not their divorce,) will end the spouse's powers and interests being attributed to the grantor, and grantor trust status because of the spousal attribution rules will terminate at that time.[46] IRC section 672(e)(2).

---

[46] "It should be noted that if parties were married and not legally separated on the date of a trust transfer, a subsequent divorce does not terminate the imputation [of the spouse's powers to the grantor under IRC section 672(e)]. The death of the grantor or grantor's spouse, however, will end the trust's grantor trust status [under the spousal attribution rules of IRC section 672(e)]." ¶7.10[2] of Howard M. Zaritsky & Stephan R. Leimberg, *Tax Planning With Life Insurance: Analysis With Forms—2d Edition,* Warren, Gorham & Lamont, Boston, Massachusetts (Supp. 2007).

§2.7(b) Power To Control The Beneficial Enjoyment Of The Trust Property

A grantor's power to control the beneficial enjoyment of the trust property (for income tax purposes) includes the power of a non-adverse party (as defined under IRC section 672(b), i.e., someone other than the grantor, the grantor' spouse, a trust beneficiary or a holder of a general power of appointment over the trust property) to add additional trust beneficiaries (other than after-born or adopted children), such as spouses of beneficiaries, the grantor's nieces and nephew, and/or charities. IRC sections 674(a),(c), and (d). Treas. Reg. §1.674(d)-2(b).

A common method of creating full grantor trust status is by permitting an independent trustee,[47] who is a non-adverse party, to add or remove charitable beneficiaries and the spouses of the grantor's descendants during the grantor's lifetime and to make discretionary distributions to such beneficiaries.[48] *Bernard and Joyce Madorin v. Commissioner of Internal Revenue*, 84 T.C. 667 (1985); (non-adverse, independent trustee's power to add charitable beneficiaries held to cause grantor trust status); Pvt. Letter Ruls. 200030018, 199936031, 9709001, 9010065. *See also*, Priv. Letter Ruls. 9838017 (power of independent trustee to add and make distributions to charitable beneficiaries and spouses of grantor's issue after a trust ceased to be a GRAT), and 199936031 (power to add charitable beneficiaries after the termination of a charitable lead annuity trust was effective to make the lead trust a grantor trust).

This grantor trust power can be relinquished[49] by the holder of the power. Because of the adverse estate tax consequences triggered by IRC sections 2036 and 2038, neither the grantor nor a donor of

---

[47] An independent trustee is a trustee who is not related or subordinate (within the meaning of IRC section 672(c)) to the grantor. *See also*, IRC section 674(c).

[48] Care must be taken to limit the number or class of beneficiaries if the ILIT is a "grantor" trust and later becomes an Electing Small Business Trust under IRC section 1361(c)(2)(A)(v). In such an instance, the trustee should not be permitted to add as a beneficiary any person who is not a permissible S corporation shareholder and the trustee should be prohibited from expanding the class of additional beneficiaries beyond the permissible number of persons who can be S corporation shareholders (including "potential current beneficiaries"). IRC section 1361(e)(2).

[49] If the grantor trust status is no longer desired, e.g., the grantor does not want to pay the trust's income taxes, or the grantor wants to sell assets to the trust and the trustee wants a cost basis in the assets (rather than the grantor's carryover basis), the holder of

property to the trust should be given the power to add beneficiaries. Also, if the grantor or donor holds the power to add beneficiaries, any gifts to the trust will be incomplete for gift tax purposes. Treas. Reg. §25.2511-2(c); Priv. Letter Rul. 200612002.

> **Practice Point:** To avoid creating a general power of appointment in the person who holds the power to add beneficiaries, the power holder should not be able to add him or herself, his or her estate or the creditors of either as a beneficiary. *See,* IRC sections 2041 and 2514.

> **Practice Point:** Another way to create grantor trust status under ITC section 674(a) is to permit a related trustee, such as the grantor's spouse (*see,* section 2.6, above for the definition of a "related" person) the power to distribute income and principal among the grantor's descendants, without limiting this power to an ascertainable standard.

§2.7(c) Power Of Independent Third Party To Affect Beneficial Enjoyment Of Trust Property

If the grantor appoints a special power holder (who is not an adverse party or a trustee) with the discretionary power to appoint the trust assets during the grantor's lifetime to two or more trust beneficiaries without any fiduciary requirement, without any ascertainable standard, without the appointed property being chargeable against the proportionate share of corpus held in trust for the payment of income to the beneficiary as if the corpus constituted a separate trust *(see,* IRC section 674((b)(5)(B)), and without any requirement to make compensating adjustments between beneficiaries who do not receive the appointed property, IRC section 674(a) will cause the grantor to have full grantor trust status over the trust property that is subject to the special power holder's discretionary non-fiduciary power of appointment. *See,* section 11.1, below concerning the appointment of a special power holder.

---

the grantor trust power may be able to relinquish (i.e., "turn off") the grantor trust power. *See,* Section 319 of Akers, "Selection of Trustees: A Detailed Review of Gift, Estate and Income Tax Effects and Non-Tax Effects," 38 *Heckerling Institute on Estate Planning,* Chapter 3 (Matthew Bender/Lexis-Nexis, Newark, NJ 2004). However, it may be somewhat problematical (and difficult) to "turn off" a grantor trust power that is attributable to the grantor solely because of the spouse's interest or power over the trust property under IRC section 672(e)(1).

§2.7(d) Power To Substitute Property Of Equal Value

A common method of creating full grantor trust status is by including a power in the trust instrument allowing the grantor, the grantor's spouse, or a non-adverse party (as defined under IRC section 672(b)), acting in a non-fiduciary capacity and without the approval or consent of any person acting in a fiduciary capacity, to substitute trust property with other property of an equivalent value. IRC section 675(4)(C); Treas. Reg. §1.675-1(b)(4). Because the power to substitute trust property must be held in a "non-fiduciary capacity" and must not require the consent of a fiduciary, this power should not be given to a trustee. This grantor trust power can be relinquished by the holder of the power.

The power of substitution, if held by the grantor, does not prevent a gift to the trust from being a completed gift under IRC section 2511. Priv. Letter Ruls. 9415012, and 9227013.

This power, held in a nonfiduciary capacity, should not result in the trust property being included in the grantor's gross estate, and will cause the trust's income and capital gains to be taxed to the grantor.[50] *Estate of Anders Jordahl v. Commissioner*, 65 T.C. 92 (1975), *acq*. 1977-2 C.B. 1 (where grantor-insured's power to substitute life insurance policies was expressly held in a fiduciary capacity).[51] *See*, Rev. Rul. 82-

---

[50] Even if the grantor holds the power of substitution (whether in a fiduciary or non-fiduciary capacity), IRC section 2036 should not apply to the grantor because the power of substitution "does not include a power over the transferred property itself which...[would] affect the enjoyment of the income received or earned during the decedent's life." Treas. Reg. §20.2036-1(b)(3). Nor should IRC section 2038 apply to the grantor because the power of substitution is not "a power by the decedent to alter, amend, revoke or terminate" the trust. Treas. Reg. 20.2038-1(a).

[51] In Priv. Letter Rul. 9413045 the IRS ruled that the insured-grantor's right, in a non-fiduciary capacity, to substitute comparable assets for a trust owned life insurance policy did not constitute an incident of ownership in the life insurance policy owned by the ILIT. In its ruling, the IRS stated, "[T]he court in *Estate of Jordahl* held that the ability of an individual to substitute an insurance policy in a trust for assets of equivalent value cannot be seen as a right to the economic benefits of that insurance policy. The court held that in the case of an insurance policy the only asset that should be of equal value would be another insurance policy with 'equal cash surrender and face value, comparable premiums, and a similar form of policy.' *Estate of Jordahl v. Commissioner*, supra at 99. Thus, an insured does not possess incidents of ownership for purposes of section 2042 in an insurance policy held in a trust solely because the insured has the right to substitute assets of similar value for those policies." *See also*, Priv. Letter Ruls. 9548013 and 9227013.

5, 1982-1 C.B. 131; Pvt. Letter Ruls. 200434012, 200001015, 200001013, 199922007, 9843024, 9713017, 9548013, 9413045, and 9227013. The power of substitution can also be held by a non-

---

"The Service has ruled that the retention of the power of substitution by the grantor does not preclude a transfer from being a completed gift at the time of the transfer for purposes of §2511. [Priv. Letter Ruls. 9415012 and 9227013.] It has reasoned that the power of substitution does not affect the disposition of the corpus of the trust nor the value of the corpus of the trust at the time of the substitution. The power of substitution in §675(4)(C) does not cause inclusion of the trust property in the grantor's estate. In *Jordahl Est. v. Comm'r*, [65 T.C. 92 (1975)] the court held that a power of substitution held by a grantor as co-trustee did not cause inclusion of the property of the trust in the grantor's estate for federal estate-tax purposes under §§2038(a)(2) and 2042(a)(2). The court reasoned that the power of substitution did not constitute a power to 'alter, amend or revoke' under §2038(a)(2) the trust as the trust agreement specifically provided that any property substituted should be "of equal value" and thus prevented the grantor from depleting the trust corpus. It found that the power to substitute property 'of equal value' is akin to the retention by the settlor of the power to direct trustees as to investments, which generally do not cause estate tax inclusion. The court also held that the power of substitution did not constitute the retention of any 'incidents of ownership' that would have required inclusion of the insurance proceeds under §2042(2). The court reasoned that the grantor would have had to substitute an almost identical policy for the reacquired policy. The power of substitution held by the grantor in *Jordahl* was held in a fiduciary capacity. ***The result should have been the same, however, had the power not been held in a fiduciary capacity, given the requirement that the property substituted be of equivalent value to that of the reacquired property.*** The holding of *Jordahl* should also apply for purposes of §2036(a)(2), given the court's holding with regard to §2042(a)(2). In that regard, note that there is no recognized exception to the estate-inclusion rule in §2042(a)(2) for powers subject to a definite external standard as there is for §§2036-2038. [*See, Jennings v. Smith*, 161 F.2d 74 (2d Cir. 1947).] Thus, it seems that if the power of substitution in §675(4)(C) satisfies the more stringent threshold of §2042(a)(2), it should satisfy §2036(a)(2) as well. The Service has also ruled that the power of substitution does not trigger inclusion of trust assets in the estate of the grantor for federal estate-tax purposes. [See, Priv. Letter Ruls. 9548013 (grantor's power of substitution and to designate a successor powerholder does not constitute a power to alter, amend, or revoke under §2038(a)); 9413045 (grantors' power of substitution will not cause inclusion of trust corpus in the estate of either grantor under §§2036 and 2038); 9247024 (no inclusion of trust property in grantor's gross estate under §§2033, 2035, 2037, 2038, 2041, or 2042; power of substitution held by nonadverse party); 9227013 (grantors' power of substitution does not constitute a power to alter, amend, or revoke under §2038(a)); 9037011 (power of substitution of nonadverse trustees exercisable in nonfiduciary capacity will not cause inclusion of trust property in the estate of either grantor for federal estate tax purposes); 9011052 (power of substitution of nonadverse parties will not cause estate tax inclusion).]" Carmen Irizarry-Diaz, "How Defective is Your Trust? Suggestions on Structuring an Intentionally Defective Grantor Trust," 41 *Tax Management Memorandum* 231, 237-238 (June 19, 2000). (Emphasis added.)

adverse third party. Pvt. Letter Ruls. 200434012 (grantor's father held power of substitution), 199908002 (grantor's brother held power of substitution), 9810019 (the *Karmazin* ruling, where a disinterested party held the power of substitution), 9037011 (co-trustee held power of substitution, and 9026036 (grantor's spouse held power of substitution). *See also*, Pvt. Letter Ruls. 9713017, 9642039, 9227013, and 9247024. If a third party holds the power to substitute assets, there is less risk of the IRS attempting to include the trust assets in the grantor's gross estate under IRC sections 2036, 2038, or 2042. However, when a third party holds the power of substitution, the grantor trust power under IRC section 675(4)(C) will terminate upon the third party's death or resignation, unless a new non-adverse third party is appointed before the death or resignation of the current third party holder of the power of substitution. Priv. Letter Ruls. 199908002 (trust instrument appointed a successor to the non-adverse party powerholder), and 9548013 (grantor/powerholder retained the power to appoint a successor powerholder).

> **Practice Point:** The determination of whether the power of substitution is exercisable in a fiduciary or a nonfiduciary capacity depends on all the terms of the trust and the circumstances surrounding its creation and administration. Treas. Reg. §1.675-1(b)(4); Pvt. Letter Ruls. 9713017, 9437023, and 9437022. Because of the facts and circumstances test that must be employed to determine if the power is held in a non-fiduciary capacity, it may be wise to rely on other grantor trust powers, or to bundle the power of substitution with other grantor trust powers to ensure grantor trust treatment. Pvt. Letter Rul. 9413045. *See*, Rev. Proc. 2007-3, 2007-1 I.R.B. 108, section 3.01(47).[52] *See also*, Treas. Reg. §1.675-1(a), which states as a general

[52] According to this Rev. Proc., the IRS will not issue a private letter ruling concerning: "Whether the grantor will be considered the owner of any portion of a trust when (i) substantially all of the trust corpus consists or will consist of insurance policies on the life of the grantor or the grantor's spouse, (ii) the trustee or any other person has a power to apply the trust's income or corpus to the payment of premiums on policies of insurance on the life of the grantor or the grantor's spouse, (iii) the trustee or any other person has a power to use the trust's assets to make loans to the grantor's estate or to purchase assets from the grantor's estate, and (iv) there is a right or power in any person that would cause the grantor to be treated as the owner of all or a portion of the trust under sections 673 to 677."

rule, "Section 675 provides in effect that the grantor is treated as the owner of any portion of a trust if under the terms of the trust instrument or circumstances attendant on its operation administrative control is exercisable primarily for the benefit of the grantor rather than the beneficiaries of the trust."

Practice Point: If the grantor's power to substitute assets does not extend to all of the trust assets (e.g., the trust instrument prohibits the grantor's substitution of IRC section 2036(b) stock and/or life insurance policies on the grantor's life), the grantor will not have grantor trust status over the assets that are "excluded" from the power of substitution. Consequently, it will be necessary to rely on other grantor trust powers to achieve grantor trust status over the "excluded" assets. In Pvt. Letter Ruls. 200514001 and 200514002, the grantor had the power to substitute trust assets other than IRC section 2036(b) stock, the trust held 2036(b) stock and other substantial assets, the grantor proposed to sell a life insurance policy to the trust for full an adequate consideration, and the trust proposed to pay for the policy using trust assets other than the 2036(b) stock. The IRS ruled that that the sale of the policy to the trust was not a transfer for value but a transfer to the insured because the trust assets that were to be used to purchase the policy were taxable (for income tax purposes) to the insured-grantor and, therefore, the insured-grantor was treated as owning the purported consideration both before and after the transaction pursuant to Rev. Rul. 85-13, 1985-1 C.B. 184.

Practice Point: In addition to creating grantor trust status, an advantage of using the power of substitution is that it provides the grantor with the opportunity to substitute low basis assets in the trust with high basis assets or cash. As such, if the low basis assets remain in the grantor's estate, they will obtain a stepped-up basis at the grantor's death. In Priv. Letter Rul. 200603040, the IRS ruled that neither the grantor nor the trust would recognize any income or loss upon the grantor's exercise of the power of substitution, nor would the exercise of the power be treated as a gift to the trust by the grantor.

Caution: If the grantor transfers pre-IPO stock or publicly traded corporate securities to the trust, be mindful of the insider trading rules under section 10(b) of the Securities and Exchange Act of 1934, and Rules 10b-5 and 10b5-1. The ability to reacquire the securities may be construed as an option, and the reacquisition of the securities may give rise to a charge by the U.S. Securities and Exchange Commission of insider trading. Therefore, in such situations, do not use the power of substitution to create grantor trust status, and do not use a trustee who is a corporate insider with respect to the shares of stock. Also, if the trust makes an in kind distribution of restricted stock to the grantor, the grantor may be able to tack on the trust's holding period for purposes of Rule 144.[53]

§2.7(e) Power To Borrow Money From The Trust For Adequate Interest But Without Any Security

Another common method of creating full grantor trust status is by giving the grantor, the grantor's spouse, or a non-adverse party (as defined under IRC section 672(b)) the ***power to borrow*** the trust corpus or income for adequate interest but without any security, provided the trustee does not have the power under a general lending provision to make loans to any person without adequate interest or security. IRC section 675(2). Pvt. Letter Ruls. 199942017, 9645013, and 9525032. This grantor trust power is typically triggered by giving an independent trustee (as defined under IRC section 672(c)) the power to make loans to the grantor (or the grantor's spouse) without any security but with an adequate rate of interest; provided loans during the grantor's lifetime to all other persons must bear an adequate rate of interest and be adequately secured. This grantor trust power can be relinquished by the holder of the power.

Caution: The ability of the grantor to borrow trust funds without adequate interest may result in the inclusion of the

---

[53] *See*, Diana Hastings Temple and Nicholas Unkovic, "Federal Securities Laws and Administration of the Grantor Retained Annuity Trust," 29 *ACTEC Journal* 299 (Spring 2004); and Charles E. Muller II and Brian A. Lebensburger, "Estate Planning Meets Business Law," 26 *Tax Management Estates, Gifts and Trusts Journal* 209 (September 14, 2001) for a discussion of the securities law aspects of restricted stock held by a GRAT.

trust property in the grantor's gross estate under IRC sections 2036 and 2038. Furthermore, if the grantor has the power to borrow trust assets for less than full and adequate consideration, this, too, may risk the trust property being included in the grantor's gross estate under IRC sections 2036 and 2038.

Practice Point: Any amounts actually borrowed by the grantor or the grantor's spouse should be evidenced by a promissory note bearing adequate interest but without any security.[54] This means the note must bear the minimum interest rate under IRC section 1274 to avoid a deemed gift of forgone interest under IRC section 7872. If the grantor desires to maximize the amount that he or she can transfer to the trust "gift tax free," consider a higher rate of interest, similar to what a bank might charge for an unsecured loan, e.g., the interest rate charged by a credit card company (typically 18% to 24%). However, do not charge of rate of interest that is usurious. Because the trust will be a grantor trust, the grantor's payment of interest on the promissory note should be ignored for income tax purposes, i.e., the grantor will not be entitled to an interest expense deduction and the interest received by the trust will not be subject to income taxation, since the payments and receipts are transactions between the grantor and his or her grantor trust. Rev. Rul. 85-13, 1985-1 C.B. 184.

§2.7(f) Actual Borrowing Of Money From The Trust For Adequate Interest But Without Any Security

A supplement to the IRC section 675(2) power to borrow rules, and a way to create full grantor trust status if an existing trust does not have other grounds or means for becoming a grantor trust, is for the grantor or the grantor's spouse to ***actually borrow*** income and/or corpus (directly or indirectly) from the trust and not fully repay the loan before the beginning of the trust's taxable year in which the loan is

---

[54] Security refers to a secured loan, such as a UCC security interest in the grantor's property or a pledge of collateral by the grantor. When a loan to a grantor is unsecured, the trustee in fulfilling its fiduciary duty to the trust beneficiaries, may need to charge the grantor a higher rate of interest than the applicable federal rate.

made. IRC section 675(3). Thus, any loan made to the grantor (or the grantor's spouse) after the beginning of the trust's taxable year (e.g., a loan made on or after January 1, 2007) will result in grantor trust status for the entire tax year, even if the loan is repaid before the close of the trust's taxable year (e.g., the grantor repays the loan in full on March 3, 2007).[55] This grantor trust power can be relinquished or "turned off" by not borrowing for any day during the tax year in question. The loan can be made by an independent trustee (in which case an adequate rate of interest must be charged, but ***no*** security must be given), or the loan can be made by a trustee who is related or subordinate to the grantor (in which case the subordinate or related trustee can charge interest ***and*** obtain security for the loan, or not charge any interest and/or not obtain any security). However, to avoid potential gift tax implications under IRC section 7872 and to avoid estate tax inclusion under IRC sections 2036 and 2038, it is best for the grantor to pay an adequate rate of interest under IRC section 1274 but provide no security for the loan, regardless of the identity of the trustee.

In *William K. M. Mau v. United States*, 355 F. Supp. 909 (D. Haw. 1973), the court held that the actual borrowing of trust corpus or income by a grantor at any time during a taxable year would result in the grantor being taxed on trust income for that entire year under IRC section 675(3). *See also*, Rev. Rul. 86-82, 1986-1 C.B. 253, where the IRS ruled that a grantor-trustee who had both borrowed the entire trust corpus and repaid the borrowed funds plus interest in the same year would be treated for federal income tax purposes as the owner of the entire trust for that year. The ruling stands for the proposition that if the grantor of a trust borrows trust corpus or income at any time during the trust's taxable year, the grantor is taxed on the trust income for the entire year under IRC section 675(3).[56] Once the loan is repaid in full, grantor trust status ceases under IRC section 675(3) for the taxable year succeeding the year in which the loan is repaid (e.g., if a loan is made January 2, 2006 and repaid January 3, 2007, the grantor is treated as the owner of the trust for tax years 2006 and 2007, but not for succeeding tax years in which there is no borrowing).

---

[55] Logically speaking, because the loan is made during the taxable year, it cannot be repaid before the beginning of the same taxable year.

[56] For example, if a loan is made on January 1 and repaid on January 2 of a given year, all the income for that year is within the reach of IRC section 675(3) and is taxable to the grantor.

In *Larry W. Benson v. Commissioner*, 76 T.C. 1040 (1981), the grantor borrowed *all* the trust income, which consisted of rental income, but did not borrow any of the trust corpus, which consisted of a commercial building (hence the rental income), and the court ruled that the grantor "borrowed all the trust income and that income was derived from the entire trust corpus. Thus, it is clear that ...[the grantor] should be treated as owner of the entire trust."[57]

If the grantor borrows less than all of the trust's income or corpus, the authorities are unclear regarding the portion of the trust the grantor is treated as owning under IRC section 675(2). The Code says that the grantor is treated as the owner of "any portion of a trust in respect of which" he has borrowed the corpus or the income. What is the "portion" where the grantor has borrowed less than all of the trust assets?

In *O'Neil Bennett v. Commissioner,* 79 T.C. 470 (1982), the grantor borrowed *less than all of the income* of the trust. The Tax Court held that the grantor should be taxed on that fraction of the current year's trust income the numerator of which equaled the total unpaid loans at the beginning of the taxable year and the denominator of which equaled the sum of the income of the trust for prior years plus the income of the trust for the current year.

In the *Estate of Jonathan Holdeen v. Commissioner*, 34 T.C.M. (CCH) 129 (1975), the grantor, Jonathan Holdeen, *borrowed less than all of the trust corpus* (to wit, approximately 28% of the total trust corpus) for the period of 1951 to 1953, and the Tax Court (applying the 1939 Internal Revenue Code, and interpreting the "portion" issue under IRC section 675(3) of the 1954 Internal Revenue Code) ruled:

> It is clear that the loan, including interest, was not completely repaid before the beginning of the taxable year 1951 or 1952 or 1953. The question remains whether

[57] In dealing with the grantor's contention that he should be taxed on only a portion of the trust's income, the court stated, "[W]e reject...[the grantor's] contention that 'portion' refers to the amount borrowed in comparison to the entire trust. [The grantor]...would have us calculate a fraction arrived at by dividing the amount borrowed by the trust corpus, and treat that fraction as the trust 'portion' owned by the grantor. If such were the case, a trust grantor could borrow the entire trust income derived from the entire trust corpus but only be treated as owning a fraction of the trust, even though his borrowing evidences dominion and control over the entire trust. We find such a result patently unreasonable and unsupported by the statutory language or any other authority." *Id.* at 1047.

> under the regulations the entire income of Trust 45-10 or only the income from $80,000 of the assets of Trust 45-10 is taxable to Holdeen. The regulations [to the 1939 Internal Revenue Code] do not specifically limit the taxable amount to the income of the "portion" of the trust, as do the provisions of the 1954 Code, section 675(3), supra, which are in pari materia. A court may properly look to subsequent legislation as an aid to statutory construction. [Citations omitted.] The administrative control referred to in the regulations [pertaining to the 1939 Code provision in question] was exercised primarily for the benefit of the grantor only with respect to the $80,000 loan and not with respect to the total assets of the trust, which amounted to $278,000 in 1948 and $696,000 in 1954. We hold that the income from $80,000 of the trust's assets is taxable to Holdeen rather than the entire income of Trust 45-10 in the years 1951, 1952 and 1953." *Id.* at 193.[58]

In *Richard L. Patsey v. United States*, 84-1 U.S. Tax Cas. (CCH) 9304 (N.D. Cal. 1984), the grantor borrowed more than 50% of the trust corpus and nearly all of the trust's income. The court held that all of the trust's income was taxable to the grantor. In its opinion, the court stated:

> Patsey borrowed the trust funds without security, and had not made any principal or interest payments on the loans before the beginning of 1974 or the beginning of 1975, the taxable years at issue here. Thus, under §675(3), the 'portion of [the] trust in respect of which' Patsey borrowed is treated as being owned by him. In 1973 Patsey received an unsecured loan $97,000, of which $90,000 was corpus and $7,000 was interest. These figures represent approxi-

[58] In *Holdeen*, "We [the Tax Court] held that the grantor-taxpayer indirectly borrowed $80,000 from the trust which he repaid when he transferred the mortgaged property to the trust. We held further that the grantor-taxpayer was to be treated under sec. 675(3) as owner of an $80,000 'portion' of the trust during the years between the loan and the repayment. It might seem that *Holdeen* stands for the proposition that 'portion' means the amount actually borrowed. However, such does not follow from a careful reading of that case. The $80,000 borrowed in *Holdeen* was corpus and we, in effect held that $80,000 of the corpus was the 'portion of [the] trust in respect of which' the grantor-taxpayer borrowed. Furthermore, it is unclear whether any more could have been borrowed." *Larry W. Benson v. Commissioner*, 76 T.C. 1040, 1047 (1981).

mately 60% of the trust's total corpus (assuming it is $152,000), and nearly 100% of its 1973 income (the trust had total interest income of $7,117.08). In 1974 Patsey received an additional $53,300, of which $40,000 was corpus and $13,300 interest. By the end of 1974, then, Patsey had over 85% of the trust's corpus ($130,000 out of $152,000) and borrowed over 90% of its 1974 income (out of $13,903.44). These figures clearly show that by the beginning of the 1974 and 1975 tax years, Patsey had evidenced control and dominion over the entire trust, and all of the trust's income is taxable to him. *See, Benson v. Commissioner*, 76 T.C. 1040 (1981). *Id.* at 83,667

Thus, we can conclude the following:

- If the grantor borrows *all of the trust corpus*, the grantor is taxed on all of the trust's income for the tax years that any part of the loan remains unpaid. IRC section 675(3); Rev. Rul. 86-82, 1986-1 C.B. 253; *Mau, supra.*
- If the grantor borrows *all of the trust's income,* the grantor is taxed on all of the trust's income for the tax years that any part of the loan remains unpaid. *Benson, supra.*
- If the grantor borrows *some of the trust's income,* the grantor is taxed on a proportionate share of the trust's income for the tax years that any part of the loan remains unpaid. *Bennett, supra.*
- If the grantor borrows *some of the trust's corpus,* the grantor is taxed on a proportionate share of the trust's income for the tax years that any part of the loan remains unpaid. *Holdeen, supra.*
- If the grantor borrows a *significant portion of the trust corpus* (i.e., more than 50%) and/or borrows a *significant portion of the trust's income,* the grantor is taxed on all of the of the trust's income for the tax years that any part of the loan remains unpaid. *Patsey, supra.*

Practice Point: Any amounts actually borrowed by the grantor or the grantor's spouse should be evidenced by a promissory note bearing adequate interest but without any security.[59] This means the note must bear the mini-

---

[59] Security refers to a secured loan, such as a UCC security interest in the grantor's property or a pledge of collateral by the grantor. When a loan to a grantor is unsecured, the trustee in fulfilling its fiduciary duty to the trust beneficiaries, may need to charge the grantor a higher rate of interest than the applicable federal rate.

mum interest rate under IRC section 1274 to avoid a deemed gift of forgone interest under IRC section 7872. If the grantor desires to maximize the amount that he or she can transfer to the trust "gift tax free," consider a higher rate of interest, similar to what a bank might charge for an unsecured loan, e.g., the interest rate charged by a credit card company (typically 18% to 24%). However, do not charge of rate of interest that is usurious. Because the trust will be a grantor trust, the grantor's payment of interest on the promissory note should be ignored for income tax purposes, i.e., the grantor will not be entitled to an interest expense deduction and the interest received by the trust will not be subject to income taxation, because the payments and receipts are transactions between the grantor and his or her grantor trust. Rev. Rul. 85-13, 1985-1 C.B. 184.

Practice Point: Grantor trust status under IRC section 675(3) may be difficult to achieve where the only asset of the trust is a life insurance policy that has no cash surrender value. But, if the ILIT contains other assets, such as cash (including cash received as a withdrawal or loan from the policy) and the grantor actually borrows all the trust's cash (i.e., trust corpus) and all the trust's income (i.e., trust income), grantor trust status should arguably apply for the tax years in question. Creating grantor trust status is important concerning the transfer for value rule, which is discussed in section 2.5, above, and special care must be taken when there are outstanding policy loans. *See,* section 2.5(b)(2), above, concerning policy loans.

Practice Point: Actual borrowing from an irrevocable trust is to obtain grantor trust status incongruent with the notion of an installment sale to the trust.

§2.7(g) Payment Of Income To Spouse Or Payment Of Premiums Of Life Insurance On Life Of Grantor Or Spouse

If a non-adverse trustee is required (or has the discretion) to distribute (or can hold and accumulate for future distribution) income from the ILIT to or for the benefit of the grantor's spouse,[60] grantor trust status will be triggered, and the trust's income will be taxed to the grantor under IRC sections 677(a)(1) and (2). Treas. Reg. §§1.677(a)-1(b)(2) and 1.677(a)-1(g), Example 1.[61] Grantor trust status under IRC section 677(a) will end when the spouse dies or becomes divorced

---

[60] When using this grantor trust power care must betaken to avoid the spouse becoming a grantor of the trust by contributing community property or by allowing a *Crummey* withdrawal right to lapse in an amount greater than 5x5. In such instance, the assets will be includable in the spouse's gross estate when the spouse dies. IRC section 2036(a)(1).

[61] *See, e.g.*, Treas. Reg. §1.677(a)-1(f) & (g), Ex. 2; Priv. Letter Ruls. 9543049, 9535026 and 9501004, all of which apply IRC section 677 to make a trust a grantor trust as to capital gains allocated to principal. Treas. Reg. §1.677(a)-1(g), Example 1 seems to indicates that if the spouse has an income only interest in the trust then the grantor will be taxed only on the trust's ordinary income and not its corpus, and that the trust will pay the capital gains tax. *See, Larry W. Benson v. Commissioner*, 76 T.C. 1040 (1981), where the court stated in dicta, "In most cases, it is fairly simple to tell over what part of a trust a power extends; therefore, the meaning of "portion" is easily decided. For example, if a grantor has the power to distribute the entire trust to his spouse, the entire trust is treated as his even if only part of the trust is actually so distributed. *See* sec. 677(a)(1). On the other hand, if a grantor has the power to distribute only current income to his spouse, he is treated as owning only the current income interest in the trust. In the latter case, "portion" means only the current income interest, because that is the only trust segment over which the grantor has any power." *But see,* Treas. Reg. §1.671-3(b) (concerning what "portion" of a trust (income and/or corpus) is taxable to a grantor). *See also,* Treas. Reg. §1.671-2(b) which provides that "income" used in subpart E of Sub Chapter J means *taxable* income (i.e., income and capital gains) and not fiduciary accounting income (which by definition does not include capital gains). By contrast, IRC section 643(b) defines "income" as fiduciary accounting income for purposes of subparts B, C, and D, *but not for purposes of subpart E.* Therefore, the grantor will be treated as the owner of fiduciary accounting income if fiduciary accounting income may be paid to the grantor or to the grantor's spouse, and the grantor will be treated as the owner of income allocable to principal if capital gains may be paid to the grantor or the grantor's spouse. This is consistent with Treas. Reg. §1.1361-1(k)(1), Example 10(iii), which states that if the terms of the inter-vivos QTIP trust do not permit corpus to be distributed to the spouse, the grantor is treated as the owner of the trust's income only (and is not treated as the owner of the trust's corpus). As a result of the *Benson* case and these Examples in the Regulations, one can safely conclude that (i) an income-only interest given by the grantor to his or her spouse (where the income does not include capital gains) results in partial grantor trust status as concerns the grantor, who will be taxed on the trust's ordinary income only, and (ii) an income interest given to the spouse along with a mandatory or discretionary right to receive trust principal results in full grantor trust status as concerns the grantor, who will be taxed on the trust's ordinary income and

(IRC section 682) or legally separated from the grantor. Treas. Reg. §1.677(a)-1(b)(2). This grantor trust power is more difficult to relinquish by the holder of the power because it is typically part of the ILIT's dispositive provisions, whereas the other grantor trust powers (discussed above) are typically administrative powers. Also, if a non-adverse trustee can use income from the ILIT for the payment of premiums on the life of the insured grantor or the grantor's spouse, grantor trust status will be triggered, and the trust's income will be taxed to the grantor. IRC section 677(a)(3). Grantor trust status is not triggered if the life insurance is irrevocably payable for a charitable purpose described in IRC section 170(c). This grantor trust power terminates: (i) if the spouse predeceases the grantor, (ii) the grantor and the spouse become legally separated or divorced (*see*, Paragraph 10.1 of Sample ILIT), (iii) the spouse makes a qualified disclaimer of his or her beneficial interest within 9 months of the creation of the ILIT, or (iv) the spouse makes a non-qualified disclaimer of his or her beneficial interest in the ILIT—in which case the spouse may be treated as making a taxable gift to the other ILIT beneficiaries of the spouse's disclaimed interest in the ILIT. This grantor trust power is difficult to relinquish, and may require a court proceeding to remove the spouse as a beneficiary of the ILIT.

> **Practice Point:** If a non-adverse trustee can distribute *both income and principal* to the grantor's spouse, the IRS has ruled that full grantor trust status will exist as to the grantor, even if the trustee's power is discretionary (Priv. Letter Rul. 200606006) and the trustee can also distribute income and principal to other trust beneficiaries (Priv. Letter Rul. 200603040). However, when the spouse dies or becomes divorced or legally separated from the grantor, full grantor trust status will cease under this Code section. Treas. Reg. §1.677(a)-1(b)(2). Lost of grantor trust status could result in recognition of gain, if the trust property is subject to debt in excess of the property's basis. Treas. Reg. §1.677(a)-1(b)(2).

---

capital gains. Several Private Letter Rulings affirm this conclusion. Pvt. Letter Ruls. 200606006 and 200603040 (spouse's discretionary income and principal interest in a trust was sufficient to confer full grantor trust status on the grantor) and 9321050 (spouse's mandatory income interest coupled with the spouse's 30-day inter-vivos general power of appointment and the right to substitute trust property of equivalent value, was sufficient to confer full grantor trust status on the grantor). *Id.* at 1045.

Practice Point: If the grantor's spouse holds an inter-vivos limited power of appointment over trust corpus, the grantor will be deemed to own the corpus for income tax purposes. IRC sections 674(a) (concerning power of disposition over corpus exercisable by the grantor) and 672(e) (grantor is treated as holding any power or interest held by any individual who was the spouse of the grantor at the time of the creation of the power or interest). Thus, the spouse's power of disposition over corpus is attributed to the grantor for income tax purposes. *See,* Priv. Letter Rul. 9141027.

Practice Point: Do not overlook the need to have a non-adverse trustee if relying on this grantor trust provision. Many family trustees are adverse parties. *See,* footnotes to section 2.6, above, for a definition of "non-adverse party."

Practice Point: Do not permit the trustee to use the income or principal to discharge the grantor's legal obligations, such as the legal obligation to support the grantor's spouse or children, because this will cause the trust property to be included in the grantor's gross estate for federal estate tax purposes. *See,* section 4.2(a), below.

Practice Point: Cases concerning life insurance premium payments triggering grantor trust status (which were decided under the predecessor to IRC section 677(a)(3)) held that grantor trust status applies only if trust income is actually used to pay the life insurance premiums. *Lorenz Iversen v. Commissioner,* 3 T.C. 756 (1944); *Joseph Weil v. Commissioner,* 3 T.C. 579 (1944), *acq.,* 1944 C.B. 29; *Frank C. Rand v. Commissioner,* 40 B.T.A. 233 (1939), *acq.,* 1939-2 C.B. 30, *aff'd,* 116 F.2d 929 (8th Cir. 1941), *cert. denied,* 313 U.S. 594 (1941); and *Genevieve F. Moore v. Commissioner,* 39 B.T.A. 808 (1939), *acq.,* 1939-2 C.B. 25. *See also, Corning v. Commissioner,* 104 F.2d 329 (6th Cir. 1939); Rev. Rul. 66-313, 1966-2 C.B. 245. Also, the IRS will not issue a private letter ruling on grantor trust status where an ILIT trustee can use income to pay life insurance premiums.[62] Consequently, this grantor trust

---

[62] In Rev. Proc. 2007-3, 2007-1 I.R.B. 108, section 3.01(47) the IRS states that it will not issue a private letter ruling "[w]hether the grantor will be considered the owner of

power should be used in conjunction with another grantor trust power, particularly if the grantor wants to be assured of being treated as the grantor of both the trust's income and corpus for income tax purposes.[63]

Caution: The grantor of an ILIT should not retain the following grantor trust powers: (1) the power to control the beneficial enjoyment of the trust property (IRC section 674), since this will result in the ILIT property being includable in the grantor's gross estate under IRC section 2038; (2) the power to revoke the trust (IRC section 676), because this will result in the ILIT property being includ-

---

any portion of a trust when (i) substantially all of the trust corpus consists or will consist of insurance policies on the life of the grantor or the grantor's spouse, (ii) ***the trustee or any other person has a power to apply the trust's income or corpus to the payment of premiums on policies of insurance on the life of the grantor or the grantor's spouse,*** (iii) the trustee or any other person has a power to use the trust's assets to make loans to the grantor's estate or to purchase assets from the grantor's estate, and (iv) there is a right or power in any person that would cause the grantor to be treated as the owner of all or a portion of the trust under sections 673 to 677. (Emphasis added.)

[63] *See,* Laura H. Peebles, "Tax Aspects of Choice of Trustee," 31 *Estate Planning* 43 (January 2004). *But see,* Field Attorney Advisory 20062701F (July 7, 2006) issued by the IRS Office of Chief Counsel (cannot be cited as precedent) that held "Section 677(a)(3) of the Code provides that the grantor shall be treated as the owner of any portion of a trust whose income without the approval or consent of an adverse party is, or, in the discretion of the grantor or a nonadverse party, or both, may be applied to the payment of premiums on policies of insurance on the life of the grantor or the grantor's spouse. Article II of B Trust Agreement *authorizes* the trustee to purchase life insurance on taxpayer. There does not appear to be any limit on the amount the trustee may apply to the payment of premiums. *Therefore, pursuant to section 677(a)(3), taxpayer is treated as the owner of [Trust] B. Because taxpayer is the grantor and the owner of [Trust] B, B is a grantor trust, which is generally disregarded for Federal income tax purposes.* See Revenue Ruling 85-13, 1985-1 C.B. 184 (providing that, if a grantor is treated as the owner of an entire trust, the grantor is considered to be the owner of the trust's assets for Federal income tax purposes)." (Emphasis added.) Although FAA 20062701F is consistent with Priv. Letter Rul. 8852003 (trustee's mere power to pay life insurance premiums from income is sufficient to cause grantor trust status thereby permitting trust to own S corporation stock), the position taken in the FAA with respect to IRC section 677(a)(3) in all likelihood does not represent a shift in the IRS's litigation position but is explainable by the unusual facts of the case. *See also,* Priv. Letter Ruls. 8126047, 8118051, 8014078 (requirement that trustee pay premiums from trust income resulted in grantor trust status), and 8103074 (trustee's discretionary power to pay premiums from trust income resulted in grantor trust status).

able in the grantor's gross estate under IRC section 2038; (3) the power to borrow trust assets without adequate security (IRC section 675(2))—as concerns life insurance policies or shares of stock described in IRC section 2036(b), because this may result in the ILIT property being includable in the grantor's gross estate under IRC section 2036 and 2042; (4) the right to the trust's income (IRC section 677), because this will result in the ILIT property being includable in the grantor's gross estate under IRC section 2036; or (5) the power to substitute trust property in a non-fiduciary capacity (IRC section 675(4)(C); Priv. Letter Rul. 200408015)—as concerns life insurance policies or shares of stock described in IRC section 2036(b), because this may result in the life insurance proceeds or IRC 2036(b) stock being includable in the grantor's gross estate under IRC sections 2036 and 2042.

§2.7(h) Transfers Between A Grantor And A Grantor Trust

As previously mentioned, transfers between a grantor and a grantor trust (or transfers between a grantor trust and another grantor trust concerning the same grantor) are not recognized for income tax purposes. Rev. Rul. 85-13, 1985-1 C.B. 184; Rev. Rul. 2007-13, 2007-11 I.R.B. 684 (3/12/2007). *See also*, Pvt. Letter Ruls. 8718046 and 8636053. Grantor trust status provides potential planning opportunities if the ILIT trustee desires to subsequently sell the life insurance policies for full and adequate consideration to another grantor trust under the transfer for value rule exception of IRC section 101(a)(2). Pvt. Letter Rul. 9413045. Grantor trust status also permits the grantor to sell assets to the ILIT without gain being recognized by the grantor. *See,* Rev. Rul. 85-13, 1985-1 C.B. 184 and Pvt. Letter Ruls. 8718046 and 8636053. Another area of flexibility provided by the grantor trust rules concerns loans made by the grantor to the ILIT. Such loans may be made because the grantor does not desire to make gifts to the ILIT, or desires to provide additional funds to the ILIT above the annual gift tax exclusion amount. Provided such loans are properly documented and contain the rate of interest required by IRC sections 7872 and 1274 (or, for the more conservative and cautious, the IRC 7520 rate), the interest paid by the ILIT on the funds it borrows from the grantor should not result in any taxable income to the grantor during the grantor's life, and should not result in a gift of foregone interest being made by the grantor to the ILIT. (However, after the grantor's death, the ILIT will cease to be a grantor trust for income tax purposes and any payment of loan interest by the ILIT to the grantor's estate will result in taxable income to the grantor's estate.) The grantor's lending of money to the ILIT to pay premiums does not constitute a retained interest in the ILIT or an incident of ownership in the underlying life insurance policies for estate tax purposes, provided the loan is not secured by a collateral assignment of the policy on the grantor's life and the ILIT has some "independent equity" to pay the loans (other than the loaned amounts). Pvt. Letter Rul. 9809032.[64] However, depending on how long the grantor lives, the ILIT's indebtedness on annual loans used to pay premiums may eventually exceed the policy's death benefit. If this happens, the ILIT trustee may be liable for breach of its fiduciary

[64] *But see*, Pvt. Letter Rul. 9745019 where the IRS ruled that the insured's limited collateral assignment in a second-to-die policy owned by their ILIT under a private split-dollar arrangement did not constitute an incident of ownership under IRC section 2042 for federal estate tax purposes, and their payment of premiums under the split-dollar arrangement did not constitute a gift to the ILIT. *See, also*, Pvt. Letter Rul. 9636033 (issued before the final split dollar regulations) where the IRS ruled that there was no gift where the non-insured spouse made premium payments under a private split-dollar arrangement to her husband's ILIT and had a right to be reimbursed by the ILIT for those premium payments. If the only asset of the ILIT is the life insurance policy, at least one commentator is of the opinion that Treas. Reg. §1.61-22(b)(1)(ii) (concerning the definition of a split dollar loan arrangement) may require the insured-lender either (i) to obtain a bare bones limited collateral assignment in the policy's cash surrender value in case the split-dollar arrangement terminates during the insured's lifetime, or from the death proceeds if the split dollar arrangement terminates with the insured's death (the bare bones collateral assignment should be equal to the amount of the insured-lender's outstanding loans), or (ii) in the absence of the ILIT having "seed money" of at least 10% of the value of the loan, to obtain a guaranty from the ILIT beneficiaries (and the ILIT beneficiaries may have to be paid by the ILIT for giving their personal guaranty in order to avoid the guaranty being treated as a gift by the beneficiaries to the ILIT, which could have adverse gift and estate tax consequences to the beneficiaries). *See*, Lawrence Brody and Charles L. Ratner, "Today's Split Dollar," 146 Trusts & Estates 38 (2007); Donald O. Jansen, "Financed Life Insurance is Back! Premium Loans to ILITS," *30th Annual Notre Dame Tax & Estate Planning Institute* (October 2004). *See*, also, Donald O. Jansen, "Split Dollar Has Split—So How Do We Finance Premiums Now?," 38 *Heckerling Institute on Estate Planning*, Chapter 13 (Matthew Bender/Lexis-Nexis, Newark, NJ 2004); and Donald O. Jansen, "Private/Family Split Dollar Plans," 25 *ACTEC Notes* 68 (Summer 1999).

duty[65] Also, under the final split dollar regulations issued in 2003, the grantor's lending of money to the ILIT (particularly if the only asset of the ILIT is a life insurance policy) may constitute a private split-dollar arrangement[66] that must comply with the regulation's "loan regime" rules where each payment of the premium (or loan of money) by the grantor is treated as a separate loan[67] for federal tax purposes.

---

[65] If possible, the lender and the ILIT should have an "exit strategy" to pay off the loan before the insured's life expectancy. This might be accomplished using income or growth from other assets transferred to the ILIT, particularly assets that have been transferred to the ILIT at a valuation discount, such as family limited partnership interests. *See*, Lawrence Brody and Charles L. Ratner, "Today's Split Dollar," 146 Trusts & Estates 38, 42 (2007).

[66] See, Lawrence Brody and Charles L. Ratner, "Today's Split Dollar," 146 Trusts & Estates 38 (2007); Charles Ratner and Stephan Leimberg, "A Planner's Guide to Split-Dollar After the Final Regulations," 31 *Estate Planning* 3 (January 2004); Donald Jansen, "Taxation of Split Dollar Life Insurance Arrangements Under the Final Regulations," 29 *ACTEC Journal* 285 (Spring 2004); Donald Jansen, "Financed Life Insurance is Back! Premium Loans to ILITS," *30th Annual Notre Dame Tax & Estate Planning Institute* (October 2004); Charles Ratner, "The Post Split Dollar World," 142 *Trusts and Estates*, 18 (December 2003); and Gary Lee and Deborah Walker, "A Practical Guide To The Final Regs. Governing Split-Dollar Life Insurance," 99 *Journal of Taxation* 282 (November 2003). According to the Preamble to the final split-dollar regulations, "These final [split dollar] regulations...apply for purposes of Federal income, employment, self-employment, and gift taxes....If a split-dollar loan does not provide for sufficient interest, the loan is a below-market split-dollar loan subject to [IRC] section 7872 and [Treas. Reg.] §1.7872-15. If the split-dollar loan provides for sufficient interest, then, except as provided in [Treas. Reg.] §1.7872-15, the loan is subject to the general rules for debt instruments (including the rules for...[original issue discount under IRC section 1271 - 1275])....The final [split dollar] regulations apply for gift tax purposes, including private split-dollar life insurance arrangements. Thus, if an irrevocable life insurance trust is the owner of the life insurance contract underlying the split-dollar life insurance arrangement, and a reasonable person would expect that the donor, or the donor's estate, will recover an amount equal to the donor's premium payments, those premium payments are treated as loans made by the donor to the trust and are subject to [Treas. Reg.] §1.7872-15. In such a case, payment of a premium by the donor is treated as a split-dollar loan to the trust in the amount of the premium payment." See 68 Fed. Reg. 54,336-343 (Sept. 17, 2003).

[67] The split-dollar loan can be structured as either a term loan or a demand loan. Each type of loan has potentially different tax consequences. *See*, Robert M. Hartley, "Working Within the Final Split-Dollar Life Insurance Regulations," 29 *Michigan Tax Lawyer* 9 (Fall 2003). Generally speaking, a split-dollar arrangement is where one party (such as an ILIT) owns all the incidents of ownership in a life insurance policy and another party (such as an employer) pays the premiums and has a security interest in the policy's cash surrender value or the policy's death benefit. The security interest permits the noninsured party to recover the policy premiums it has paid.

See, Treas. Reg. §§1.61-22 (split dollar generally, and the "economic benefit regime" rules); 1.61-22(b) (definition of split-dollar life insurance arrangement); 1.61-22(b)(3) (application of split-dollar loan rules); 1.7872-15 (split-dollar loan rules generally, and the "loan regime" rules)); 1.7872-15(a)(2) (definition of split-dollar loan); 1.7872-15(a)(4) (payment of split-dollar loan interest by insured-donor may be disregarded and treated as an additional loan without adequate interest)[68]; 1.7872-15(b) (definition of split-dollar life insurance arrangement and split-dollar loan); 1.7872-15(d)(2) and 1.7872-15(j)(2)(ii) (special one-time written representation by the insured-donor and the ILIT that must accompany their income tax returns concerning a non-recourse split-dollar loan—to keep the loan from being treated as a "contingent" payment that is subject to unfavorable assumptions when testing the loan for adequate stated interest). It is recommended that loans by the insured or other family members to the ILIT require that interest be paid annually, rather than accumulated.[69]

The payment of a defective grantor trust's income tax liability by the grantor does not result in the grantor making an additional gift to the trust beneficiaries. Rev. Rul. 2004-64, 2004-2 C.B. 7. However, the grantor's right to be reimbursed by the trust for the payment of the incomes taxes may have adverse estate tax consequences to the grantor. *See,* section 4.2(b), below.

§2.8 BENEFITS OF FULL GRANTOR TRUST STATUS

§2.8(a) Grantor Pays Trust's Income Taxes

The most obvious advantage of grantor trust status is the grantor being taxed on the trust's income. The income tax imposed as a result

---

[68] This provision of the final split dollar regulations is a potential impediment to the donor-insured making annual *Crummey* gifts to the ILIT in order to provide the ILIT with sufficient money to pay the interest owed to the donor-insured under the split-dollar loan arrangement. It is suggested that the annual *Crummey* gifts be greater than the amount of the annual interest payment owed to the donor-insured, and that the *Crummey* gifts be made in advance of the annual interest payment from the ILIT to the donor-insured.

[69] Donald Jansen, "Financed Life Insurance is Back! Premium Loans to ILITS," *30th Annual Notre Dame Tax & Estate Planning Institute* (October 2004); *See,* Lawrence Brody and Charles L. Ratner, "Today's Split Dollar," 146 Trusts & Estates 38, 40-44 (2007).

of the application of the grantor trust rules may be less than the tax that would be imposed at the trust's bracket. Because of the compressed rates applicable to trusts, a trust almost always will be in the highest bracket. More significant, however, are the collateral effects of grantor trust status: (i) the grantor's payment of income tax on income accruing to the trust allows the grantor to transfer wealth without incurring gift or estate tax, and (ii) transactions between the grantor and a grantor trust do not have income tax consequences.

§2.8(b) Certain Transactions Are Disregarded For Income Tax Purposes

In addition to the advantage of having the grantor (rather than the beneficiaries or the trust) pay taxes on income accruing to the trust, transactions between the grantor and a grantor trust are disregarded for income tax purposes, including:

§2.8(b)(1) Sales

The IRS has consistently taken the position that income and deductions of a grantor trust will be treated as realized by the grantor directly; thus, a transaction between the grantor and a grantor trust cannot give rise to any taxable income because it is treated as a transaction between the grantor and him or herself. Rev. Rul. 85-13, 1985-1 C.B. 184; Priv. Letter Ruls. 9535026, 9525032, 9519029, 9508007, and 9345035 (all concluding that no gain or loss is realized on the transfer of (appreciated) property by a grantor to a grantor trust; the transfer is disregarded for income tax purposes). *But see, Rothstein v. United States*, 735 F. 2d 704 (2d Cir. 1984), which held that a grantor acquired a new cost basis for property purchased from a grantor trust. Revenue Ruling 85-13 was critical of, and announced the IRS' non-acquiescence in, the *Rothstein* decision. Sales by a grantor to a grantor trust and purchases by a grantor from a grantor trust will be ignored for income tax purposes.[70] This decision allows the grantor to sell assets to a grantor trust for fair market value to transfer future appreciation

---

[70] Note, however, that the fact that a sale is disregarded for income tax purposes does not mean that the sale will be disregarded for other purposes, such as for purposes of the short-swing profits rule of section 16(b) of the Securities and Exchange Act of 1934 (codified as amended at 15 U.S.C. section 78p(b)).

to the beneficiaries without incurring income or gift tax.[71] This decision also allows a grantor to reacquire low-basis assets owned by a grantor trust so that the low-basis assets will acquire a new (stepped-up) basis at the grantor's death.[72] It also permits a grantor to reacquire trust assets income tax free in order to enable the grantor's estate to qualify for redemption of stock to pay estate tax under IRC section 303, installment payment of tax under IRC section 6166 or special use valuation under IRC section 2032A.

> **Practice Point:** A grantor trust can distribute appreciated property in kind to a grantor in satisfaction of the trust's installment obligation, and no gain will be realized by the trust on the distribution of the appreciated asset.
>
> **Practice Point:** Because there is no income tax between a grantor and a grantor trust, there is no concern about the

---

[71] *See,* Jonathan G. Blattmachr and Diana S. C. Zeydel, "Evaluating the Potential Success of a GRAT Against Competing Strategies to Transfer Wealth," 31 *Tax Management Estates, Gifts and Trusts Journal* 115 (May 11, 2006), which compares and contrasts a GRAT and an installment sale to a grantor trust; Michael D. Mulligan, "How To Use an Intentionally Defective Irrevocable Trust To Freeze an Estate," 8 *ALI-ABA Estate Planning Course Materials Journal* 5 (April 2002); Richard A. Oshins and Steven J. Oshins, "Protecting & Preserving Wealth Into The Next Millennium (Part 2)," 137 *Trusts & Estates* 68 (October 1998); Michael D. Mulligan "Sale to a Defective Grantor Trust: An Alternative to a GRAT," 23 *Estate Planning* 3 (January 1996); and Michael D. Mulligan, "Defective Grantor Trusts Offer Many Tax Advantages," 19 *Estate Planning* 131 (May/June 1992). *See also,* Robert S. Keebler and Peter J. Melcher, "Structuring IDGT Sales to Avoid Sections 2701, 2702, and 2036," 32 *Estate Planning* 19 (October 2005); Michael D. Mulligan, "The Reinvigorated GRAT: Is a Sale to a Defective Trust Still Superior?," 29 *Estate Planning* 379 (August 2002).

[72] *See,* David A. Handler, "The Power of Grantor Trusts," 145 *Trusts & Estates* 24 (March 2006) for numerous illustrations of the benefits of a grantor trust, and for a discussion of what a trustee or grantor should consider when the grantor is on his or her death bed (such as purchasing low-basis assets from the trust for cash in order to obtain a stepped-up basis for those assets at death, or swapping loss stock for trust assets—in order to avoid a step down at basis on the loss assets at the grantor's death). If the grantor does not have enough cash to purchase the low-basis assets from the trust consider having the grantor obtain a bank loan. Another alternative is for the grantor to issue a promissory note with appropriate interest to the trust. The grantor's payment of interest to the trust would be a non-event for income tax purposes and would be a "tax free gift" to the trust. When the grantor dies, the grantor's estate would get an estate tax deduction for the outstanding loan amount, and the reacquired assets would get a stepped-up basis, and those assets could be sold (without incurring gain) to pay off the loan.

additional interest under IRC section 453A regarding deferred tax liability that exceeds $5 million. IRC section 453A(b)(2)(B).

§2.8(b)(2) Interest

Interest payments on loans between the grantor and a grantor trust are not taxable to the payee or deductible by the payor. Rev. Rul. 85-13, 1985-1 C.B. 184; TAM 9604005; Priv. Letter Rul. 9535026. However, the loans are not entirely disregarded. A below-market interest rate loan between a grantor and a grantor trust will have no income tax consequences, but the loan will have gift tax consequences.[73] The foregone interest will be a gift in accordance with the rules of IRC section 7872. Also, if the grantor trust makes in kind distribution to the grantor to satisfy an obligation that the trust owes to the grantor (such payment on a promissory note issued by the trust to the grantor) the in kind distribution of assets from the trust to the grantor will not constitute a taxable event. Priv. Letter Ruls. 9838017, 976028, 9625021, and 9415012.

§2.8(b)(3) Liabilities In Excess Of Basis

A grantor's transfer to a grantor trust of assets subject to liabilities in excess of the grantor's basis will not result in the realization of gain. *Bernard and Joyce Madorin v. Commissioner*, 84 T.C. 667 (1985).[74]

---

[73] In the GRAT context, *see,* TAM 9604005, which advised that interest free notes used by a GRAT did not satisfy the trust's obligation to make annuity payments). Treas. Reg. §25.2702-3(b)(1)(i) prohibits the use of notes to pay the GRAT's annuity obligation even if the note bears adequate interest.

[74] In *Madorin*, the court held (a) the grantor of a grantor trust is treated as owning partnership interest held in the trust for income tax purposes, not owning "items of income, deductions, and credits only"; (b) trustee's relinquishment of power to add charitable beneficiaries resulted in termination of grantor trust status; (c) such termination is a deemed disposition of the partnership interests by the grantor to the now-separate trust; and (d) on disposition of the partnership interests, liabilities in excess of basis will result in gain to the grantor, and unrealized receivables will result in ordinary income to the grantor. At issue in *Madorin* was the validity of Treas. Reg. §1.1001-2(c), Ex. 5, which presents substantially identical facts, and which the case upholds. *See also,* Rev. Rul. 77-402, 1977-2 C.B. 222 (reaching the same conclusions with respect to grantor trust rules and liabilities in excess of basis).

§2.8(b)(4) Transfers Of Installment Obligations And Annuities

Grantor trust status permits the grantor to transfer an installment note to the trust without triggering the realization of deferred gain under IRC section 453. *See,* Rev. Rul. 74-613, 1974-2 C.B. 153; Rev. Rul. 76-100, 1976-1 C.B. 123. Also, a grantor's transfer of an annuity to the trust will not be a taxable disposition for purposes of IRC section 72(e).

§2.8(b)(5) Sale Of Life Insurance

The sale of a life insurance policy from the grantor to a grantor trust should not be treated as a transfer for value. *See,* section 2.5(b)(7), above.

§2.8(b)(6) Rent

Rent payments between a grantor and a grantor trust will not be taxable because the grantor is treated as paying rent to him or herself. This is useful for situations where the grantor wishes to rent a residence after the term interest expires in a qualified personal residence trust ("QPRT") and the QPRT continues to be fully a grantor trust. In addition, if the leased residence is sold by the trust, the exclusion under IRC section 121 will be available to the grantor (*see,* section 2.8(c), below), and any real estate taxes paid by the trust on the leased residence will also be deductible by the grantor. IRC section 164(a)(1).

A repurchase of the residence from a QPRT while it is a grantor trust has been prohibited by IRS regulations, at least for trusts established after May 16, 1996.[75] *See,* section 14.1, below, concerning the use of an ILIT in conjunction with a QPRT.

---

[75] Treas. Reg. §25.2702-5(c)(5)(ii)(C) adds as a governing instrument requirement a prohibition on the sale to the grantor or to the grantor's spouse not only during the term of the grantor's retained interest but so long thereafter as the trust continues as a grantor trust. Furthermore, the explanation to the regulation states "Notwithstanding the proposed effective date, if the IRS examines a pre-effective date trust and finds it inconsistent with the purposes of section 2702 or the regulations thereunder, the IRS, by using established legal doctrines such as the substance over form doctrine, may treat the trust as not qualifying under section 2702. Thus, for example, if the grantor actually purchases the residence from the trust pursuant to a right or option to purchase that is stated in the trust instrument or a collateral document, the IRS may not treat the trust as a qualified personal residence trust." A sale to the grantor from a pre-effective date trust where there is no "right or option" should not raise a question. It is questionable whether this regulation is valid, particularly as it applies to the period after the trust ceases to be a QPRT.

§2.8(b)(7) *Partnership Deemed Sale Rules*

The deemed sale rules upon distributions of partnership assets to a partner also will not be applicable. For example, IRC section 704(c)(1)(B) provides that if a partner contributes appreciated property to a partnership and within seven years, such property is contributed to another partner, the contributing partner is taxed on the "pre-contribution" gain as if it had been sold. This deemed sale should not occur where the "other partner" is a grantor trust and receives property contributed by the grantor. Similarly, IRC section 731(c) imposes gain where marketable securities are distributed to a partner other than the partner who contributed the securities. An exception applies for investment partnerships. If marketable securities contributed to the partnership by the grantor are distributed to a grantor trust partner, the distribution should not incur tax.

§2.8(c) Residence Sale Exclusion

A sale of a residence owned by a grantor trust, such a QPRT's sale of a residence, will qualify for the exclusion from gain allowed under IRC section 121, to the same extent it would have so qualified if the grantor owned the residence directly. Treas. Reg. §1.121-1(c)(3); Pvt. Letter Rul. 199912026 ("The reasoning of Rev. Rul. 85-45 is still valid even though section 121 has been substantially amended. In the present case, because Taxpayer will be considered the owner of the entire Trust (including the Residence) under sections 676(a) and 671, Taxpayer will be treated as the owner of the Residence for purposes of satisfying the ownership requirements of section 121 of the Code." *Id.*); Pvt. Letter Rul. 9118017 (decided under predecessor to IRC section 121). *See,* Rev. Rul. 85-45, 1985-1 C.B. 183 (holding that the former IRC section 121 gain exclusion of $125,000 was available to the grantor of a grantor trust which owned the grantor's personal residence; "Since W is treated as the owner of the entire trust under sections 678 and 671 of the Code, the sale by the trust will be treated for federal income tax purposes as if made by W."). *See also,* Priv. Letter Rul. 8007050 (reaching the same conclusion); Rev. Rul. 66-159, 1966-1 C.B. 162. (gain realized from the sale of grantor trust-titled property used by the grantor as principal residence qualifies for former IRC section 1034 rollover of gain because grantor treated as the owner of the entire trust, thus sale treated as made by grantor). *See,* section 14.1, below, concerning the use of an ILIT in conjunction with a QPRT.

§2.8(d) Mortgage Interest Deduction

Similarly, any home mortgage interest deduction available pursuant to IRC section 163(h)(3) should flow through to the grantor. *See, e.g.*, Priv. Letter Rul. 9516026.

§2.8(e) S Corporation Shareholder

A grantor trust qualifies as an S corporation shareholder (provided that it is not a foreign grantor trust, and provided the grantor is a permitted S corporation shareholder). IRC sections 1361(c)(2)(A)(i), 1361(d)(1), and 1361(d)(3)(B); Pvt. Letter Rul. 200001015. A grantor trust provides more flexibility than a qualified Subchapter S trust ("QSST"), which is required to distribute all of its income currently. A grantor trust also has the potential for a lower income tax rate on the Subchapter S income than does an electing small business trust ("ESBT"), which is taxable at the highest rates applicable to individuals. IRC section 641(c)(2).

> **Practice Point:** Dividends from S corporation stock held by an ILIT that is a grantor trust can be used by the trustee to pay life insurance premiums.

§2.8(f) Preserve Non-MEC Status For Life Insurance

Grantor trust status can preserve the grandfathered status of a life insurance policy that would now be classified as a modified endowment contract ("MEC") under section 7702, if the policy was issued before January 1, 1988. Pvt. Letter Rul. 9033023.

§2.8(g) Flow Through Of Tax Incidents

Grantor trust status allows for the pass through of tax incidents with partnerships, and limited liability companies that are taxed as a partnership. Grantor trust status also allows the trust's net operating losses to be passed through to the grantor and be taken on his or her IRS Form 1040 rather than on the trust's income tax return.

§2.8(h) Sales Between Spouses And A Grantor Trust

Sales between spouses are generally ignored for income tax purposes under IRC section 1041. Therefore, it logically follows that a sale from the grantor's spouse to the grantor's grantor trust, or vice versa, should have the same tax consequences, that is, no income tax consequences.

§2.8(h)(1) Potential Gift And Estate Tax Consequences For Spouse

If the grantor's spouse sells assets to the grantor trust on a bargain sale basis and the spouse is a beneficiary of the trust, the gift portion of the sale is likely to be included in the spouse's estate as a retained interest under IRC section 2036.

§2.8(h)(2) Avoiding A Gift Tax Deficiency On A Sale To A Grantor Trust

If the grantor's spouse sells assets to the trust and the spouse has a power of appointment over the trust assets, any gift made by the spouse (i.e., a bargain sale) to the trust would be incomplete because of the spouse's retained power of appointment. Treas. Reg. §25.2511-2(b). This provides the same protection against the imposition of a gift tax as is afforded by a defined value formula gift, assuming such formulas are effective.

§2.8(h)(3) Interest Payments Are Not Disregarded

However, IRC section 1041 does not apply to interest paid from spouse to spouse and therefore, interest payments between a spouse and the grantor trust will *not* be disregarded for income tax purposes because IRC section 1041 provides for the non-recognition of gain or loss under certain circumstances—it does not provide for the exclusion of income. *Cf., Gibbs v. Commissioner*, 73 T.C.M. (CCH) 2669, involved payments from a divorced husband to his former wife as part of a marital settlement in which the husband received a convenience store owned by them jointly, and became obligated to make periodic payments to the wife at a stated interest rate. The wife did not include any of the payments in income, relying on IRC section 1041. The IRS claimed that the interest portion of the payments should be included in gross income. The court agreed with the IRS, holding:

> [S]ection 1041 does not provide for the exclusion of income; it provides for the nonrecognition of gain or loss under the circumstances described therein. As in the case of other nonrecognition sections, the Federal income tax consequences of a transaction described in section 1041 are deferred. Also similar to other nonrecognition sections, the tax deferral is effectuated through the treatment of the basis of the

property involved in the underlying transaction. *Id.* at 2671.

§2.8(i) Transactions Between Beneficiary-Owner And Trust

Sales between a trust that is treated as owned by a beneficiary under IRC section 678 (a "section 678 trust") and the beneficiary who is treated as the owner (or such beneficiary's spouse) will be disregarded for income tax purposes to the same extent as sales between a grantor and a grantor trust. *See,* section 2.8(b)(1), above.

§2.8(i)(1) Avoiding A Gift Tax Deficiency On A Sale To The Trust

A section 678 trust may be used to avoid gift tax. For example, suppose the beneficiary's parent establishes a trust for the beneficiary's benefit and transfers $50,000 to the trust. The trust gives the beneficiary the power to withdraw any part or all of trust income or principal at any time. Each year, the withdrawal right lapses to the maximum extent it can without the lapse being treated as a release of a general power of appointment. IRC section 2514(e). If the trust is not a grantor trust with respect to the parent, the beneficiary will be treated as the owner of the trust under IRC section 678. If the beneficiary sells assets to the trust in exchange for a promissory note from the trust, the sale will be disregarded for income tax purposes. If the beneficiary has a limited testamentary power of appointment, any gift the beneficiary is deemed to have made because of the insufficiency of the amount paid by the trust (i.e., a bargain sale) is an incomplete gift. Treas. Reg. §25.2514-3(c).

§2.9 BURDENS OF FULL GRANTOR TRUST STATUS

§2.9(a) Grantor Does Not Desire To Pay Tax On Trust's Income

Grantor trust status is not desirable where the grantor does not want to pay the tax on the trust's income. In other words, grantor trust status is not for someone who does not want (or have the ability) to pay the trust's income taxes (although most ILITs do not generate significant income tax liability if the only asset is a life insurance policy).

§2.9(b) Tax Benefits Would Be Denied

Grantor trust status is not desirable where a tax benefit would be denied. For example, under IRC section 664, a grantor trust cannot be a qualified charitable remainder trust.

§2.9(c) Grantor Subject To Income Tax Where Trust Is Not

Grantor trust status may not be desirable where the trust has a tax situs in a state that does not impose state income tax on the trust's income, but the grantor or beneficiaries reside in a state that does impose an income tax. However, some states treat a trust as resident in the state based on the residence of the grantor even if the trust has no other connection with the state.

§2.9(d) Grantor Subject To Higher Income Tax Rate Than Trust

If the grantor is in a higher marginal tax bracket than the trust,[76] grantor trust status may not be desirable. Furthermore, having the trust's income taxed to the grantor may result in a phase out of the grantor's itemized deductions.

§2.9(e) Lack Of Basis Adjustment

Because the assets in the grantor trust are treated as owned by the grantor, the trust does not enjoy a basis adjustment for sales to the trust, and receives the grantor's carryover basis in the purchased assets. For the same reason, a basis adjustment may not be allowed for gift tax paid on the transfer to the trust.

§2.9(f) Liabilities In Excess Of Basis

If the grantor trust assets include an asset (such as a partnership interest) with nonrecourse liabilities in excess of basis, upon cessation of grantor trust status during the grantor's lifetime, the asset will be deemed to have been transferred to a new entity (the non-grantor trust), and the grantor will realize income equal to the excess of liabilities over basis.[77]

---

[76] A trust is subject to compressed income tax rates, and reaches the maximum income tax rate of 35% at $10,050 of taxable income in 2006. An unmarried individual reaches the maximum income tax rate of 35% at $326,450 of taxable income in 2006.

[77] Treas. Reg. §1.1001-2(c), Ex. 5; *Bernard and Joyce Madorin v. Commissioner*, 84 T.C. 667 (1985) (upholding Example 5 and applying it retroactively); Rev. Rul. 77-402, 1977-2 C.B. 222.

§2.9(g) Potential "Whipsaw"

If the wrong taxpayer pays the tax, there could be a substantial resulting loss even if the tax payable by the trust was no more than the grantor paid. The statute of limitations may bar a refund by the grantor for a year for which the trust remained subject to assessment. In addition, the rate of interest paid on refunds is 1% less than that payable on deficiencies, and interest payable on deficiencies is not deductible.

§2.10 INCOME TAX CONSEQUENCES OF TERMINATION OF GRANTOR TRUST STATUS DURING GRANTOR'S LIFETIME

§2.10(a) Foreign Trust Taxation

The termination of grantor trust status during the lifetime of the grantor could cause income to be recognized if the trust is foreign or if there are outstanding liabilities. IRC section 684; Treas. Reg. §1.684-2(e).

§2.10(b) Loss Of S Corporation Status

Termination of grantor trust status could also cause the trust to cease to qualify as an S corporation shareholder. If the ILIT, which is a grantor trust, holds S corporation stock and grantor trust status ceases during the grantor's lifetime, there is no grace period during which the successor trust may continue to hold S stock even though it does not meet the ESBT or QSST requirements. If grantor trust status ends at death, however, there is a two-year grace period to qualify the trust as a sub Chapter S shareholder. *See,* IRC section 1361(c)(2)(A)(ii) allowing a two-year grace period for a trust to qualify as QSST or ESBT where a trust ceases to be a grantor trust because the grantor has died.

> **Caution:** A foreign grantor trust cannot be an S corporation shareholder. IRC section 1361(c)(2)(A)(i).

§2.10(c) Income Taxation Of Outstanding Trust Liabilities[78]

Termination of grantor trusts status during the grantor's lifetime may result in the following: (i) the grantor is deemed to have trans-

---

[78] *See,* Deborah V. Dunn and Lucy K. Park, "Basis Boosting," 146 *Trusts & Estates* 22, 23 (February 2007); Deborah V. Dunn and David A. Handler, "Tax Consequences of Outstanding Trust Liabilities When Grantor Status Terminates," 95 *Journal of Taxation* 49 (July 2001).

ferred to the trust (which is now a separate taxpayer), for income tax purposes only, the assets then held by the trust, and (ii) the grantor is deemed to have transferred to the trust, for income tax purposes only, the current liabilities of the trust. The deemed transfer of liabilities to the trust relieves the grantor of a debt obligation, and the trust assumes the responsibility to pay the amount of the debt. If the amount of debt assumed by the trust exceeds the grantor's basis in the trust assets, the grantor realizes capital gain on the difference between the amount of the debt assumed by the trust and the grantor's basis in the trust assets. The gain realized by the grantor will result in the trust receiving a stepped-up basis in the trust assets equal to the amount of such gain. Also, if there is an outstanding installment note issued to the grantor by his or her grantor trust (as a result of a sale of assets to the trust), cessation of grantor trust status during the grantor's lifetime while the note is still unpaid will also result in the capital gain being accelerated and taxed to the grantor. Treas. Reg. §1.1001-2(c), Example 5; *Bernard and Joyce Madorin v. Commissioner of Internal Revenue*, 84 T.C. 667 (1985); Rev. Rul. 77-402, 1977-2 C.B. 222; TAM 200011005. *See,* section 2.11(b), below, for a more detailed analysis of this issue.

§2.10(c)(1) *Income Taxation Of Crummey Withdrawal Right Beneficiary*

Once grantor trust status terminates during the grantor's lifetime, future unexercised *Crummey* withdrawal rights produce significant income tax complications by creating partial grantor trust status under IRC section 678(a) with regard to the withdrawal right beneficiary. Furthermore, if unexercised withdrawal rights accumulate over the years, more of the trust income and corpus will be taxable (for income tax purposes) to the withdrawal right beneficiary. Rev. Rul. 67-241, 1967-2 C.B. 225; Pvt. Letter Ruls. 200022035 and 9034004. *See*, Priv. Letter Rul. 200104005, which refers to the formula for calculating the portion taxable to the withdrawal right beneficiary. *See also*, sections 2.12 and 2.13, below.

§2.11 INCOME TAX CONSEQUENCES OF TERMINATION OF GRANTOR TRUST STATUS AT GRANTOR'S DEATH

There is no authority addressing a situation in which grantor trust status ceases because of the grantor's death. Traditionally, death has not been an income recognition event. However, if the trust (which is now a separate taxpayer as a result of the grantor's death) has an outstanding liability such as a promissory note that the trust issued to the grantor in exchange for the sale of assets to the trust, the following income tax consequences may occur.[79]

---

[79] "The income tax consequences of the grantor's death are more uncertain. According to certain commentators, the change of the grantor owned status of the trust results in a realization of gain by the grantor. See *Madorin v. Commissioner*, 84 T.C. 667 (1985). However, *Madorin* was based on Treas. Reg. §1.1001-2(c), Example 5, which is a discharge-of-liabilities provision, not a grantor trust regulation. Further, Madorin involved a negative basis partnership issue. It is not a garden variety grantor trust type issue, which would rarely be present in the installment sale context. In short, the application of *Madorin* to recognition of income in most grantor trust planning is questionable. Other commentators believe that at death there would be a realization of gain only in proportion to the unpaid portion of the installment note, and still others believe that there is no recognition of gain." Chapter 12.31 of Susan T. Bart, *Estate Planning Forms and Commentary 2005 Edition* (Illinois Institute for Continuing Education, Springfield, Illinois 2005).

"Practitioners argue about what the income tax consequences are if the seller in an IDIT transaction (Installment Sale to an Intentionally Defective Grantor Irrevocable Trust) dies before the note is paid off. Some commentators believe that this area is terra incognita, and all answers must be determined by analogy. Others, myself included, believe that existing rules are equal to the task, even though they were not created with IDITs in mind. The theories so far have fallen generally into two camps regarding collections on the note by the heirs: One says that the note is Income in Respect of Decedent (IRD) property under Internal Revenue Code (IRC) Section 691 and therefore the heirs must report taxable income as collections are received on the note [*see, e.g.,* Deborah V. Dunn and David A. Handler, "Tax Consequences of Outstanding Trust Liabilities When Grantor Status Terminates," 95 *Journal of Taxation* 49 (July 2001)]; the other says that because the decedent would not have paid income tax on payments received from a grantor trust, Section 691 does not apply, so the heirs don't pay income tax on the post-mortem collections on the inherited note [*see, e.g.*, Jonathan G. Blattmachr, Mitchell M. Gans and Hugh H. Jacobson, "Income Tax Effects of Termination of Grantor Trust Status by Reason of the Grantor's Death," 97 *Journal of Taxation* 149 (September 2002); and Jerome M. Hesch, "Installment Sale, SCIN and Private Annuity Sales to a Grantor Trust: Income Tax and Transfer Tax Elements," 23 *Tax Management Estates, Gifts and Trusts Journal* 114 (May 14, 1998)]. There is, however, a third position: There is no gain reportable by the noteholders as payments are collected [after the seller's death], and the property purchased has the seller's basis as of the moment before death." Laura H. Peebles, "Death of an IDIT Noteholder," 144 *Trusts & Estates* 28 (August 2005). (Footnotes omitted.)

See, Joy Elizabeth Hodge, "On the Death of Dr. Jekyll—The Disposition of Mr. Hyde: The Proper Treatment of an Intentionally Defective Grantor Trust at the Grantor's Death," 29 *Tax Management Estates, Gifts and Trusts Journal* 275 (November 11, 2004); Jonathan G. Blattmachr, Mitchell M. Gans and Hugh H. Jacobson,

§2.11(a) Is Gain Realized By The Grantor's Estate?

Where grantor trust status terminates on death, there may be a deemed installment sale of the property to the trust immediately prior to the grantor's death for the outstanding amount of the promissory note.[80] However, it would be inconsistent with Rev. Rul. 85-13 for any gain realized by reason of a deemed installment sale at death to be reported on the grantor's final income tax return (IRS Form 1040). If there is any gain as a result of a deemed installment sale of the assets to the trust at the grantor's death (and all of the commentators cited in the above referenced footnote are of the opinion that there is no gain) the gain would be reportable on the first income tax return of the grantor's estate (IRS Form 1041).

"Income Tax Effects of Termination of Grantor Trust Status by Reason of the Grantor's Death," 97 *Journal of Taxation* 149 (September 2002); Deborah V. Dunn and David A. Handler, "Tax Consequences of Outstanding Trust Liabilities When Grantor Trust Status Terminates," 95 *Journal of Taxation* 49 (July 2001); Elliott Manning and Jerome M. Hesch, "Deferred Payment Sales to Grantor Trusts, GRATs, and Net Gifts: Income and Transfer Tax Elements," 24 *Tax Management Estates, Gifts and Trusts Journal* 3 (January-February 1999); Jerome M. Hesch, "Installment Sale, SCIN and Private Annuity Sales to a Grantor Trust: Income Tax and Transfer Tax Elements," 23 *Tax Management Estates, Gifts and Trusts Journal* 114 (May 14, 1998); and Richard A. Oshins and Steven J. Oshins, "Protecting & Preserving Wealth Into The Next Millennium (Part 2)," 137 *Trusts & Estates* 68, 82-90 (October 1998), for a thorough presentation of these arguments. To avoid the uncertainties associated with an outstanding trust liability at the grantor's death, the best strategy is for the trust to pay off the liability before the grantor dies. This can be accomplished by having the note's term be for a period less than the grantor's life expectancy, by permitting the payor of the promissory note (to wit, the grantor trust) to prepay the note without penalty, and by permitting the payor to be able to make note payments in cash and/or in kind. If the grantor trust distributes low-basis assets to a dying grantor in satisfaction of the note, those assets will be included in the grantor's gross estate for federal estate tax purposes and will receive a new (stepped up) basis at the grantor's death.

Another suggested method (by the late Professor Jerry A. Kasner) to avoid gain at the seller's death is to have the seller elect out-of-installment reporting under IRC section 453(d) and report all the gain in the year of sale. However, because the sale is not recognized for income tax purposes, there is no taxable gain and there is no installment reporting! Richard A. Oshins and Steven J. Oshins, "Protecting & Preserving Wealth Into The Next Millennium (Part 2)," 137 *Trusts & Estates* 68, 87 (October 1998).

[80] "There is some debate, however, as to whether the grantor, or the grantor's estate, must recognize gain from the installment sale upon the grantor's death (and the resulting termination of grantor trust status). Compare Dunn & Handler, "Tax Conse-

§2.11(b) Do The Trust's Post Death Payments On The Promissory Note To The Grantor's Estate Or Beneficiaries Constitute IRD?

By definition, no "sale" to the grantor trust could occur for income tax purposes while the grantor was alive, thus a promissory note held in the grantor's estate that was issued by the trust should not be income in respect of a decedent ("IRD"), and therefore, the promissory note issued by the trust should qualify for a stepped up basis under IRC section 1014. However, if there is any gain realized by the grantor's estate (and all of the commentators cited in the above referenced footnote are of the opinion that there is no gain), the deferred gain on the sale to the trust would ultimately be recognized either by the grantor's estate or by the beneficiaries. *See,* IRC section 691.

§2.11(c) What Is The Income Tax Basis Of The Trust's Assets?

The basis of the assets sold by the grantor to the trust in exchange for the promissory note is carryover basis because the trust's purchase of the assets when the grantor was alive is not treated as a sale or exchange. The argument could be made that because IRC section 1014 is an income tax provision, and because for income tax purposes the grantor was treated as the owner of trust assets at his or her death, the assets held by the trust also are entitled to a new basis under IRC section 1014. However, if there is any gain realized by the grantor's estate (and all of the commentators cited in the above referenced footnote are of the opin-

---

quences of Outstanding Trust Liabilities When Grantor Trust Status Terminates," *J. Tax'n* 49 (2001) (arguing that gain will be recognized by the grantor's estate if the note is outstanding at death) with Blattmachr, Gans, & Jacobson, "Income Tax Effects of Termination of Grantor Trust Status by Reason of the Grantor's Death," *J. Tax'n* 149 (Sept. 2002), Kwon, McCaffrey, and Hesch, "Deciding Upon the Appropriate Estate Freeze Technique," [Section of Real Property, Probate and Trust Law, American Bar Association (April 29, 2005)]; and Hesch, "Installment Sale, SCIN and Private Annuity Sales to a Grantor Trust: Income Taxes and Transfer Tax Elements," 23 *Tax Mgmt. Est., Gifts & Tr. J.* 114 (May/June 1998) (arguing that the death of the grantor is not a realization event, so gain is not recognized by the grantor or the grantor's estate). See also Peebles, "Death of an IDIT Noteholder," 144 *Trusts & Estates* 28 (Aug. 2005) (adding a third position that carryover basis applies under Regs. §1.1015-2(a)(1) upon the sale to the grantor trust and no gain is reportable by the noteholder under §691 when post-mortem payments are received on the note)." Todd Steinberg, Jerome M. Hesch, and Jennifer M. Smith, "Grantor Trusts: Supercharging Your Estate Plan," 32 *Tax Management Estates, Gifts and Trusts Journal* 66, 72 (footnote 24) (January 11, 2007).

ion that there is no gain), the trust's basis in the assets deemed sold by the grantor to the trust immediately before the grantor's death should be equal to the sales price. Similarly, a beneficiary who acquires the property from the trust should receive a basis in the trusts assets equal to the sales price.

§2.12 INCOME TAXATION OF ILIT AND THE *CRUMMEY* WITHDRAWAL RIGHT BENEFICIARY

Under IRC section 678, a person other than the grantor is treated as the owner (for income tax purposes) of any portion of a trust with respect to which such person (such as an ILIT beneficiary) either

(1) Has a power exercisable solely by him or herself to vest the corpus or the income from the corpus in him or herself (such as a beneficiary with a *Crummey* withdrawal right); or

(2) Such a person has previously partially released or modified such a power and afterward retains sufficient control that would make the person taxable as an owner of the trust under one of the grantor trust rules. *See*, Rev. Rul. 67-241, 1967-2 C.B. 225 concerning income taxation of a beneficiary's annual non-cumulative $5,000 or 5%.

§2.13 GRANTOR TRUMPS *CRUMMEY* WITHDRAWAL RIGHT BENEFICIARY FOR INCOME TAX PURPOSES

If the grantor holds a power under IRC sections 673 through 677 and the beneficiary holds an IRC section 678 power (such as a *Crummey* withdrawal right) over the same income, the beneficiary's power is disregarded, and the grantor is taxed as the owner of the trust income. IRC section 678(b). Note, however, that it is unclear whether the grantor will be taxed as the owner of the corpus, because IRC section 678(b) refers only to "income," whereas IRC section 678(a)(1) refers to a beneficiary's power to vest "corpus or the income therefrom."

Several commentators are of the opinion that this incongruency is a legislative drafting error, and that the grantor trumps the beneficiary as to both income and corpus.[81] In several private letter rulings the IRS has

---

[81] "Over the years, there have been a number of questions regarding the wording of IRC Section 678, specifically the difference between Section 678(a), which refers to the right 'to the corpus or the income therefrom,' and Section 678(b), which refers to a 'power over income.' This difference matters when the settlor might be taxed on trust

taken the position that the grantor is treated as the owner of the corpus (whenever possible) despite the existence of an IRC section 678 power

---

income under IRC Section 678(b): Would he be taxed on all of the trust income, or only that taxable income allocable to trust accounting income, causing the *Crummey* powerholder to be taxed on the corpus gains and losses? To find out, [our first stop is] the definitions in IRC Section 643(b), which tells us that the word 'income' in subchapter J, unless preceded by another adjective, refers to trust accounting income. However, that definition does not apply to subpart E of Subchapter J, which is the grantor trust section. In the regulations for subpart E [Treas. Reg. §1.671-2(b)], we are told that 'income' in the subpart E regulations refers to taxable income [i.e., ordinary income and capital gains] rather than to trust [accounting] income. Although this reference appears in the regulations rather than in the statute, it is a strong indication that the [reference to] 'income' in Section 678(b) refers to taxable, not trust accounting, income. The Section 678 regulations are consistent with this interpretation: Treasury Regulations Section 1.678(a)-1(a) clearly contemplates that the settlor could be taxed on both trust accounting income and corpus transactions [under the IRC section 678(b) tie-breaker rules]." Laura H. Peebles, "*Crummey* Powers Can Increase Your Income Tax," 145 *Trust & Estates* 35, 37 (November 2006).

See, Jonathan E. Gopman, "*Crummey,* The Saga Continues," 25 *Tax Management Estates, Gifts and Trusts Journal* 194, 231 (July 13, 2000); and James C. Davis, "Interaction of the Grantor Trust Rules and Life Insurance," 26 *Estate Planning* 418 (November 1999). "Section 678(b) states that 678(a) does not apply—i.e., the powerholder will not be treated as the grantor 'with respect to a power over income as originally granted or thereafter modified'—if the grantor is otherwise treated as the owner. Does the statute's use of the word 'income,' rather than 'portion,' prevent the grantor from replacing the powerholder as the taxpayer for some types of gains or losses? The author believes the answer is 'no.' Because of the way 'income' is defined in Reg. 1.671-2(b), it is logical to read the phrase 'power over income' as 'power over any portion of a trust.' Several commentators, and perhaps even the IRS, believe this is the proper interpretation, and that the use of the word 'income' was actually a drafting error. The original enactment of Sections 678(a) and 678(b) dates back to 1954, and Congress intended to use the word 'income' because the new Section 678(b) was intended to mirror the language of Section 677(b), which also used (and still uses) the word 'income.' The use of the word 'income' in Section 677 and its predecessors can be traced back to the beginning in 1924; the word 'portion' does not appear in Section 677 until 1954. A good argument can be made that in both Sections 677(b) and 678(b), the use of the word 'income' is simply an oversight and the statutory language has not been modernized to use the word 'portion.' Reg. 1.677(b)-1 (relating to Section 677(b)) clearly creates the possibility that any type of income of the trust may become taxable to the grantor." *Id.* at 419-20. (Citations omitted.) *See also,* the articles cited in Jonathan E. Gopman, "The Income Tax Consequences of an Irrevocable Life Insurance Trust," 22 *Tax Management Estates, Gifts and Trusts Journal* 211, 217 n.53 (September-October 1977).

(of withdrawal) held by a beneficiary.[82] Pvt. Letter Ruls. 200606006, 200604028, 200603040, 200011054, 9321050, 9309023, 9226037, 9141027, 8701007, 8535076, 8521060, 8308033, 8326074, 8308033, 8142061, 8103074, and 7909031.

An additional incongruence is found in the language of IRC section 678(a)(2) itself, which refers to a beneficiary who has "previously partially *released* or otherwise modified such a power and after the *release* or modification retains such control as would, within the principles of IRC sections 671 to 677, inclusive, subject the grantor of a trust to treatment as the owner thereof." (Emphasis added.) Note that the Code refers to a "release." A release connotes an affirmative act on the part of the power holder. A lapse, on the other hand, requires no action by the power holder. Interestingly, Congress found it necessary to expressly state that a lapse of a general power of appointment is a "release" for estate and gift tax purposes. However, the failure of Congress to make a similar statement for income tax purposes appears to be an indication that Congress did not intend to equate a lapse with a release for the grantor trust rules.

> **Practice Point:** If grantor trust status terminates during the grantor's lifetime, the *Crummey* withdrawal right beneficiary may be treated, for income tax purposes, as a grantor

---

[82] For example, in Priv. Letter Rul. 200606006, the IRS ruled:

> Section 678(b) provides that §678(a) shall not apply with respect to a power over income, as originally granted or thereafter modified, if the grantor of the trust or a transferor (to whom §679 applies) is otherwise treated as the owner under the provisions of subpart E other than §678. Rev. Rul. 85-13, 1985-1 C.B. 184, provides that if a grantor is treated as the owner of the entire trust, the grantor is considered to be the owner of the trust assets for federal income tax purposes. The power granted to Spouse to withdraw amounts contributed to Trust will result in Spouse being treated as the owner of the portion of Trust subject to her withdrawal power, unless as provided in §678(b), Grantor is treated as the owner. Under the terms of Trust, both income and corpus are payable to Spouse during Grantor's life. Accordingly, Grantor is treated as the owner of Trust under §677(a). Because Trust is a grantor trust under §677 with respect to Grantor, it is a grantor trust in its entirety with respect to Grantor notwithstanding the powers of withdrawal held by Spouse that would otherwise make her an owner under §678. Accordingly, all items of income, deductions, and credits against tax of Trust are included in computing the Grantor's taxable income and credits.

of part of the ILIT. *See,* section 2.10(c)(1), above. Also, when the grantor dies, partial grantor trust status may also exist with regard to a *Crummey* withdrawal right beneficiary's unlapsed withdrawal rights. *See,* section 2.11(a), above. It should be noted that the IRS has changed its position on the partial grantor trust status issue at least once. In Priv. Letter Rul. 9026036 the IRS ruled that the withdrawal right holder would be deemed the grantor after the death of the original grantor; however, in Priv. Letter Rul. 9321050 the IRS reversed itself, and withdrew the earlier ruling without providing any analysis for its action.[83] Thus, as a result of these rulings, we can conclude that when the original grantor is the owner of the trust under the grantor trust rules, the *Crummey* powerholder is not treated as the owner of the trust under IRC section 678(a), either before or after the grantor's death (assuming the *Crummey* withdrawal right ceases at the grantor's death). However, the result may be different if the beneficiary possesses a *Crummey* withdrawal right that is exercisable after the grantor's death. *See,* section 8.3, below.

§2.14 NON-RECOGNITION OF GAIN OR LOSS ON CERTAIN EXCHANGES OF LIFE INSURANCE POLICIES

If an existing policy of life insurance is no longer suitable and must be replaced, or if the insurance carrier is suffering financial weakness,[84] the existing policy may be exchanged for a new policy.[85]

---

[83] "[I]n PLR 9321050, the IRS reconsidered the issues in PLR 9026036 and revised its ruling to conclude that, after the death of the wife, the husband would not be treated as the owner for federal income tax purposes of the income of the trust. The only change in the IRS's analysis is a deletion of the discussion of legislative history to §678. Thus, it appears that after a trust ceases to be treated as a grantor trust with respect to the grantor, the trust will be treated as a separate taxpayer for income tax purposes and the powerholders will not be treated as the owner of the income of the trust for federal income tax purposes." Georgiana J. Slade, "Life After Execution of an Insurance Trust," 40 *Tax Management Memorandum* 375, 389 (October 25, 1999).

[84] See, Rev. Proc. 92-44, 1992-1 C.B. 875 and Rev. Proc. 92-44A, 1992-1 C.B. 876 concerning non-recognition of income when the policy to be exchanged was issued by a life insurance company that is experiencing financial distress and is subject to conservatorship, receivership, or similar state regulatory proceedings.

[85] *See,* ¶2.17 Zaritsky & Lane, *Federal Income Taxation of Estates and Trusts (3d Edition)* (Supp. 2007) Warren, Gorham & Lamont, Boston, Massachusetts; and section II, D

Caution: To qualify as an IRC section 1035 exchange, the policy can not be surrendered and the proceeds rolled over into a new policy. Do not take "short cuts"!

---

of Brody, Richey, and Baier, 828 T.M., *Compensating Employees with Insurance*, (Bureau of National Affairs, Washington, DC) ("Brody, Richey and Baier") for a summary of the section 1035 exchange rules. A rollover of a policy is not a 1035 exchange. A rollover involves the surrender of the policy and using the cash surrender value to acquire a new policy. *See*, section 2.18, below concerning the income tax consequences of surrendering a life insurance policy.

There are two types of 1035 exchanges—an "inside exchange" and an "outside exchange." An inside exchange involves the exchange of a policy within the same life insurance company, i.e., the policy owner might exchange a whole life policy for a universal life policy issued by the same carrier. An outside exchange is where the policy owner moves the business to a new life insurance company. When contemplating an exchange, the policy owner should find out if the existing carrier offers an inside exchange program, which may be more advantageous than an outside exchange. The policy owner might find that the inside exchange can be done without full medical underwriting, the commission on the new product reduced or eliminated, and the sales loads and other policy costs reduced or eliminated. In all cases, the policy owner must understand how any proposed replacement policy works, what values and benefits are guaranteed and what are not, the premium structure, amount and duration and the respective tax characteristics of the existing and new policies. In some instances, the existing policy may not need to be exchanged—the policy may only need some attention or some more premium.

"When evaluating whether to replace an existing policy, insureds and planners should return to the original admonition, "MATCH THE PRODUCT TO THE PROBLEM." Often, when an insured's objectives change and an existing policy is not entirely suitable for the revised objectives, it may be best to keep the existing policy in place and to purchase additional coverage with the flexibility and features one needs. Sometimes it may be wise to keep an existing policy in place and to use borrowing from the cash value to pay premiums on new supplemental coverage, rather than to exchange the old policy for a new policy. In almost all replacement cases where the old policy is just not suitable and must be replaced (or where replacement is being considered because of the financial weakness of the company that issued the old policy), the insured should consider using the provisions of IRC Section 1035 to ensure that the exchange is treated as a nontaxable event. If the insured surrenders the old policy and uses the cash surrender value to help finance the new policy, two adverse tax consequences could ensue. First, to the extent of gain in the policy (that the cash value exceeds the net premiums paid), the surrender value will be subject to income tax at the policy owner's ordinary tax rate. Second, if a large after-tax surrender value is placed in the new policy, the new policy could be treated as a modified endowment contract (MEC) with very adverse tax consequences with respect to any lifetime withdrawals or loans. Even if the policy is not treated as a MEC, the insured may be subject to the 15-year rule with respect to withdrawals, where amounts withdrawn with-

Under IRC section 1035, no gain or loss is recognized (i.e., the gain or loss is deferred) on the exchange of:

(1) A life insurance policy for another life insurance policy or for an endowment or annuity contract; or

(2) A contract of endowment insurance for (a) another contract of endowment insurance which provides for regular payments beginning at a date not later than the date payments would have begun under the contract exchanged, or (b) an annuity contract; or

(3) An annuity contract for an annuity contract (but not for an endowment contract or a life insurance policy).

IRC section 1035 applies only if the policy exchanged relates to the same insured[86] (although the life insurance company issuing the new policy can be different from the company that issued the policy that is being replaced). Treas. Reg. §1.1035-1(c). In Pvt. Letter Rul. 9542037, the IRS stated that IRC section 1035 treatment was not available to an insured who proposed to exchange a policy on his life for a second-to-die policy on his life and that of his spouse, since the exchange did not relate solely to the same insured. However, in Pvt. Letter Rul. 9330040 the IRS permitted the tax free exchange of a second to die policy (following the death of one insured) for a single life policy on the surviving insured. The exchange may not be completely tax free if the policy has an outstanding loan. In such instance, the owner of the policy may be taxable on the amount of the loan that is extinguished in the 1035 exchange. Treas. Reg. §1.1031(d)-2.The IRS has, however, ruled that if the new policy is subject to the same indebtedness as the old policy, there is no taxable extinguishment of the

---

in the first 15 years may be taxed on the interest-first rule rather than the cost-first rule. Finally, whenever an old policy is exchanged for a new policy, the insured surrenders certain rights. For example, the new policy generally is issued with a new suicide period and a new incontestable period, even if the old policy had long surpassed the reach of those provisions. In addition, the insured may forfeit more favorable guarantees as to minimum rates credited to the cash values, and more favorable provisions and rates for policy loans." (Citations omitted). Stephen R. Leimberg and Robert J. Doyle, *Tools & Techniques of Life Insurance Planning (3d ed. 2004),* 83 and 85, The National Underwriter Company, Cincinnati, Ohio (2004), www.nuco.com.

[86] In Rev. Rul. 90-109, 1990-2 C.B. 191, the IRS ruled that a corporation's attempt to change the insured on a key person life insurance policy (pursuant to a policy rider) constituted a sale or other disposition of the policy under IRC section 1001, and did not qualify as a tax free exchange under IRC section 1035.

indebtedness.[87] Pvt. Letter Ruls. 8816015, 8806058, and 8604033. Also, if the transfer does not qualify as a tax-free exchange under IRC section 1035, the owner of the policy will have to recognize as income the amount of the cash surrender value that exceeds the owner's basis[88] in the transferred policy. Treas. Reg. §1.1035-1(c); Rev. Rul. 54-264, 1954-2 C.B. 57; *W. Stanley Barrett v. Commissioner*, 348 F.2d 916 (1st Cir. 1965), aff'g, 42 T.C. 993 (1964).

> **Practice Point:** The three-year rule of IRC section 2035 is not applicable to a 1035 exchange if the policy to be exchanged was initially purchased by the ILIT trustee. If the policy to be exchanged was purchased by the insured and gifted to an ILIT, a 1035 exchange more than three years after the policy's transfer to the ILIT should not be subject to IRC section 2035. Priv. Letter Rul. 8819001. However, if an a 1035 exchange is made by the ILIT trustee during the initial three-year period in which the original policy was gifted to the ILIT by the insured, IRC section 2035 may apply starting from the date of the initial gift of the original policy to the ILIT by the insured.

> **Practice Point:** If an existing policy has little or no cash value but a positive cost basis and the owner wants to replace the old policy with a new policy, consider a 1035 exchange rather than the cancellation of the old policy. A 1035 exchange will permit the old policy's cost basis to be carried over into the new policy. Treas. Reg. §1.101-1(b)(3)(iii). A carryover basis will permit the owner to withdraw more money tax-free from the new policy's cash value, and will reduce the owner's gain if the new policy is subsequently sold.

> **Caution:** An IRC section 1035 exchange of a policy that is grandfathered from MEC status (i.e., the life insurance policy was issued before June 21, 1988) may result in the new policy being subject to a special "adjusted

---

[87] If the life insurance company will not issue a new policy subject to same indebtedness as the old policy, the owner can avoid being taxed on the loan by paying off the existing loan prior to obtaining the new policy, and after the new policy is issued, borrow from the new policy.

[88] *See,* footnote to section 2.5(b), above, concerning how to determine "basis."

seven-pay" MEC status test. IRC section 7702A(c)(3)(A). *See*, Priv. Letter Rul. 9044022.

§2.15 INCOME TAXATION OF LIFE INSURANCE POLICY DIVIDENDS

An important feature of life insurance is the tax-deferred build up of cash value within the policy. The earnings on the cash value in the policy build up income tax free (i.e., are tax deferred) until the policy owner receives the cash value by surrender, a withdrawal in excess of the owner's investment in the contract, or by other means. IRC section 7702(g); *Abram Nesbitt 2d v. Commissioner*, 43 T.C. 629 (1965); *Theodore H. Cohen v. Commissioner*, 39 T.C. 1055 (1963), *acq.* 1964-2 C.B. 4. As a general rule, dividends paid on a participating policy issued by a mutual life insurance company (as opposed to a stock company), are considered a partial refund of paid premiums. Dividends are income tax free until the amount of the dividends exceed the owner's investment in the contract,[89] at which time they are taxed as ordinary income.[90] In other words, once a policy owner has recovered his or her investment in the contract, dividends and other distributions during the policy owner's lifetime are taxable as ordinary income. IRC sections 72(e)(5)(A) and 72(e)(5)(C); Treas. Reg. §1.72-11(b)(1). However, dividends paid by a life insurance company that are not includable in the policy owner's income (i.e., "income tax free" dividends) reduce the owner's basis in policy (because, as previously mentioned, these dividends represent a return of the paid premium and hence reduce the owner's investment in the contract). *Steven H. and Anna J. Jensen v. Commissioner*, T.C. Summary Opinion 2004-75 (2004).

---

[89] IRC section 72(e)(6) states " the investment in the contract as of any date is: (A) the aggregate amount of premiums or other consideration paid for the contract before such date, minus (B) the aggregate amount received under the contract before such date, to the extent that such amount was excludable from gross income under this subtitle or prior income tax laws." In other words, "investment in the contract" is the accumulated premiums and other consideration paid for the policy, reduced by the aggregate of any tax-free distributions the policy owner has received, such as dividends that reduce basis, un-repaid loans, and tax-free withdrawals. Treas. Reg. §1.72-6(9)(i). *See also*, footnote to section 2.5(b), above, concerning how to determine "basis."

[90] *See*, section II, C of Brody, Richey, and Baier for a summary of the taxation of policy dividends, and the special rules concerning modified endowment contracts ("MECs") and dividends.

If the dividends are left with the insurance company to accumulate with interest, the interest paid or credited on the dividends will be subject to income taxation in the year that the owner of the policy has an unrestricted right to withdraw the interest. Treas. Reg. §§1.451-2(b) and 1.61-7(d); *Theodore H. Cohen v. Commissioner*, 39 T.C. 1055 (1963), *acq.* 1964-2 C.B. 4. Dividends that are retained by the life insurance company as a premium or as other consideration paid for the life insurance contract are not included in the policy owner's gross income. IRC section 72(e)(4)(B). For example, dividends used to pay current premium costs, purchase paid up additional insurance, or to purchase one-year term coverage, are considered additional premiums to acquire additional death benefits, and are not considered taxable income. Nor do such dividends reduce the owner's basis in the policy. In such an instance, there is no taxable income until the policy is surrendered (in whole or part) and the amount received by the policy owner is in excess of their investment in the contract.

Practice Point: Dividends can generally be (i) received in cash, (ii) used to pay current premium costs, (iii) left with the insurance company to accumulate with interest, (iv) used to purchase additional paid up insurance, (v) used to purchase one-year term insurance equal to the cash value of the policy. Rather than using dividends to pay the existing premium costs, the owner of the policy should, if possible, use the dividends to buy additional paid up insurance or to purchase one-year term coverage. This will help to maintain the real value of the policy, and provide a larger death benefit.

Practice Point: Dividends paid by the Veterans Administration on a United States Government Life Insurance policy or on a National Service Life Insurance contract (i.e., a U.S. military government life insurance policy) are income tax free and the exemption continues even after the policy owner has recovered his or her investment in the contract. Even the interest on dividends paid on government life insurance is income tax free. Also, when the policy is surrendered or if the policy matures during the insured's lifetime, there is no income tax on the gain. 38 U.S.C. section 5301(a)(1); Rev. Rul. 91-14, 1991-1 C.B. 18; Rev. Rul. 72-604, 1972-2 C.B. 35; Rev. Rul. 71-306, 1971-2 C.B. 76.

Caution: Variable life insurance policies (*see*, section 16.3, below) are subject to investment diversification requirements. IRC sections 817(h) and 851(b)(3). If those requirements are violated the policy is not treated as a life insurance policy under IRC 7702, and annual increases in the cash value of the variable life insurance policy will be taxed to the policy owner as ordinary income for those years in which the policy violates the diversification requirements. IRC section 7702(g) and (h).

§2.16 INCOME TAXATION OF LIFE INSURANCE POLICY LOANS

The owner of the policy can borrow the built up cash value, including the profit element or, if the policy permits, withdraw the built-up cash value (within certain limits). Generally, borrowing the cash value[91] (or using the cash value to reduce premiums[92]) does not result in the recognition of income by the policy owner if the policy is not a MEC.[93] IRC sections 72(e)(5)(A)(i) and 72(e)(5)(C). A loan is not a withdrawal from the policy. Because a loan is secured by the policy itself, the loan is non-recourse to the policy owner. If there is an outstanding loan balance when the insured dies, the loan amount is deducted from the death benefit, and in almost all cases, there is no recognition of income as a result of the loan being discharged. IRC section 101(a)(1).

Caution: As previously mentioned in section 2.5(b)(2), above, policy loans can create adverse income tax consequences if the policy is transferred (sold or gifted) with an outstanding loan balance, or if the policy owner has an outstanding loan balance and uses the existing policy's cash value to purchase a single premium permanent policy with a lower death benefit and the outstanding loan balance is reduced as a result of the purchase of the new policy.

---

[91] The policy owner does not actually borrow the cash value; rather, the life insurance company lends the money and secures the loan against the policy.

[92] *See,* Chapter 16, below.

[93] *See,* IRC sections 72(e)(10) and 72(v) concerning MEC policy loans.

§2.17 INCOME TAXATION OF POLICY WITHDRAWALS

A withdrawal from a life insurance policy (such as a flexible premium policy) is a partial surrender of the policy. Because a withdrawal is made from the policy's cash value account, there is a corresponding reduction in the policy's cash value amount. However, because a withdrawal is not a loan, the policy owner incurs no interest charge on the withdrawn amount. Generally, withdrawals of the policy's cash value are income tax free until the withdrawals (and other tax free distributions from the policy such as dividends) exceed the owner's investment in the contract. This is known as the "premium first" rule. Under the "premium first" rule, withdrawals are treated first as a tax-free return of the owner's investment in the contract. Once the cumulative withdrawals exceed the owner's investment in the contract, future withdrawals are treated as gain in the contract and are taxed as ordinary income. IRC sections 72(e)(5)(A) and (C). However, the owner of a post-1984 flexible premium policy (such as adjustable whole life, universal life or variable universal life) is subject to special income tax rules and can be taxed more quickly on withdrawals that are made during the first 15 years of the policy's issuance if a withdrawal results in a corresponding reduction in the policy's contractual death benefits. In such an instance, the transaction has to be tested under IRC section 7702(f)(7) to ensure the amount of money in the cash value account (after the reduction in the policy's contractual death benefit amount) is not excessive in relation to the reduced death benefit, otherwise some or all of the cash value (subject to a statutory ceiling) will be treated as taxable income to the extent of gain accumulated in the policy. IRC section 72(e)(10). Upon the expiration of the fifteen year period, no immediate taxation will occur on a withdrawal.

If a life insurance policy is classified as a modified endowment contract ("MEC") under IRC section 7702A,[94] special income tax

---

[94] An MEC is a life insurance contract that meets the requirements of IRC section 7702 (concerning the definition of life insurance), but fails the "seven-pay" test. "[A] contract fails to meet the 7-pay test...if the accumulated amount paid under the contract at any time during the 1st 7 contract years exceeds the sum of the net level premiums which would have been paid on or before such time if the contract provided for paid-up future benefits after the payment of 7 level annual premiums" IRC section 7702A(b). The purpose of the seven-pay test is to discourage the use of investment-oriented life insurance that is more "investment" than "insurance."

rules apply concerning withdrawals.[95] In such an instance, lifetime withdrawals are deemed to be of taxable interest first (to the extent of gain accumulated in the policy) and principal (basis) last. This is known as the "income first" rule.[96] In addition, a 10% excise tax generally applies on withdrawals from a MEC unless certain conditions are met. IRC sections 72(e)(10), and 72(q). If the MEC is assigned as collateral security, the assignment is treated as a distribution under the MEC and is taxable to the extent of gain. IRC section 72(e)(4)(A).

> **Practice Point:** The 15-year rule does not apply to the withdrawal of cash from a flexible premium life insurance policy issued before 1985. The 15-year rule also does not apply to policy loans—just to withdrawals from a flexible premium policy issued after 1984.
>
> **Caution:** A withdrawal reduces the policy's cash value. A withdrawal from a universal life product with an Option B/Option 2 payout will reduce the death benefit. However, a withdrawal will not decrease the face amount of the policy unless the policy's cash value account is insufficient to bear the mortality and expense charges on the policy's face amount. Life insurance companies do not charge interest on policy withdrawals.

§2.18 INCOME TAXATION UPON THE SURRENDER, CANCELLATION OR LAPSE OF A LIFE INSURANCE POLICY

When a life insurance policy is surrendered, cancelled, or lapses while the insured is alive and there is an outstanding loan or withdrawal in excess of the owner's investment in the contract, ordinary income will have to be recognized on the amount of the loan (plus accrued but

---

[95] Single premium life insurance policies issued before June 21, 1988 are grandfathered from the MEC rules. However, under certain circumstances a grandfathered policy can lose its favorable tax status and become a MEC.

[96] The "income-first" rule is the reverse of the "premium-first" rule of IRC section 72(e)(5). As previously mentioned, under the "premium first" rule, all withdrawals are income tax free until the withdrawals exceed the policy owner's investment in the contract.

unpaid interest) that exceeds the investment in the contract.[97] Also, if the policy is completely surrendered (and not converted into an annuity, *see*, below) or matures (other than by reason of the insured's death) and the accumulated value of the policy exceeds the owner's investment in the contract, the excess amount (i.e., gain) will be taxed as ordinary income to the owner, and not as capital gain.[98] IRC sections 72(e)(1)(A), 72(e)(2)(B), 72(e)(5)(A) and 72(e)(5)(E); Treas. Reg. §1.72-11(d)(1); *Julie J. Revolinski and Kenneth T. White v. Commissioner*, T.C. Summary Opinion 2005-26 (2005); *Steven H. and Anna J. Jensen v. Commissioner*, T.C. Summary Opinion 2004-75 (2004); *Stephen L. Atwood v. Commissioner*, T.C. Memo 1999-61 (1999); *Minnis v. Commissioner*, 71 T.C. 1049, 1056 (1979); *Blum v. Higgins*, 150 F.2d 471 (2d Cir. 1945); *Perkins v. United States*, 125 F.2d 150 (6th Cir. 1942); *Avery v. Commissioner*, 111 F.2d 19 (9th Cir. 1940). However, if the policy owner elects within 60 days of the policy's surrender to receive an annuity payout rather than a lump sum cash payout, the gain is deferred and taxable income is recognized only as annuity payments are received. IRC section 72(h).

> **Practice Point:** Rather than surrendering a policy for its cash surrender value, a policy owner can purchase a paid-up policy with an equal death benefit for a limited number of years, or purchase a paid-up policy with a reduced death benefit.

§2.19 INCOME TAXATION UPON THE SALE OF A LIFE INSURANCE POLICY

When a life insurance policy is sold by its owner, the gain on the sale is taxed as ordinary income. *Edwin A. Gallun v. Commissioner*, 327 F.2d 809 (7th Cir. 1964); *Simon v. Commissioner*, 285 F.2d 422 (3d Cir. 1960); *Commissioner v. Percy W. Phillips*, 275 F.2d 33 (4th Cir. 1960); *Abram Nesbitt 2d v. Commissioner*, 43 T.C. 629 (1965). Gain is deter-

---

[97] IRC section 72(e)(6) defines investment in the contract as "the aggregate amount of premiums or other consideration paid for the contract...***minus*** the aggregate amount received under the contract...to the extent that such amount was excludable from gross income [such as dividends received in cash, dividends used to reduce premiums or dividends used to buy term insurance]...."

[98] *See*, George D. Brenner, "Avoiding Common Mistakes in the Use of Life Insurance," 23 *Estate Planning* 320 (August/September 1996).

mined as if the life insurance policy had been surrendered by the owner, i.e., gain is equal to the difference between the policy's sales price (including any outstanding policy loan) and the taxpayer's basis in the policy.[99] *See,* section 2.18, above. However, because none of these cases dealt with the sale of a life insurance policy for greater than its cash surrender value, it is uncertain how gain in excess of the cash surrender value is taxed, particularly with regard to life settlements. Many commentators are of the opinion that gain in excess of the policy's cash surrender value should be taxed as capital gain, and not as ordinary income. *See,* section 2.4, above and its accompanying footnote.

> **Practice Point:** A policy owner is not permitted to recognize a loss upon the sale, transfer or surrender of a life insurance policy. *See, London Shoe Co. v. Commissioner,* 80 F.2d 230 (2d Cir. 1935); *Keystone Consolidated Publishing Company. v. Commissioner,* 26 B.T.A. 1210 (1932).

> **Practice Point:** The sale of a life insurance policy from one grantor trust to another grantor trust (concerning the same grantor) will not result in the realization of income/gain, because the sale is treated as a non-event and is "disregarded" for income tax purposes. Rev. Rul. 85-13, 1985-1 C.B. 184. Consequently, the purchasing trust will receive a carryover basis in the policy. However, a sale/transfer for valuable consideration from a non-grantor trust to a grantor trust (involving the insured-grantor) may result in the realization of income/gain if the fair market value of the life insurance policy exceeds the selling trust's basis in the policy.

---

[99] *See also,* section 2.5, above concerning the transfer for value rule.

3

Gift Tax Issues

CHAPTER OVERVIEW

This chapter discusses selected key gift tax issues concerning life insurance, including the gifting of an existing policy to an ILIT, and the payment of life insurance premiums.[1] The starting point for gifts and life insurance is to determine the value of the policy that the insured wants to transfer either outright or in trust. Once a gift of a policy has been made (or if the grantor's ILIT has acquired a policy), the grantor has to determine how to pay the life insurance premiums in a tax-efficient manner.

An ILIT can be funded or unfunded. A funded ILIT is where the trust owns a life insurance policy and the grantor transfers income producing assets (preferably rapidly appreciating income producing assets), such as a large amount of cash, marketable securities or a limited liability company that owns rental property, and the income from the transferred asset (such as the interest, dividends, or rental income from the limited liability company, etc.) is used by the trustee to pay some or all of life insurance premiums. *See*, Chapter 14, below, for additional ways to fund an ILIT. Also, if the ILIT is an intentionally defective grantor trust, the ILIT will not have to pay any income tax on the income earned by the income-producing assets; instead, the income tax will be paid by the

---

[1] *See,* Chapter 3 of Howard M. Zaritsky & Stephan R. Leimberg, *Tax Planning With Life Insurance: Analysis With Forms—2d Edition*, Warren, Gorham & Lamont, Boston, Massachusetts (Supp. 2007) for an overview of the gift taxation of life insurance. *See also,* Lischer, 845-2d T.M., *Gifts,* Bureau of National Affairs, Washington, DC, for a general overview of gifts.

grantor. Consequently, the ILIT trustee will have more "tax-free" income available for life insurance premium payments. *See*, section 2.7, above.

An unfunded ILIT is where the trust holds only a life insurance policy, the insured makes annual gifts (typically cash gifts) to the ILIT, and the trustee uses the annual gifts to pay the life insurance premiums. The most efficient way for most insured-grantors to pay the ILIT life insurance premiums each year is to use their gift tax annual exclusion amount. Thus, a fundamental gift tax issue concerning the use of an ILIT is: When does a grantor's gift to an ILIT constitute a gift of a present interest that is eligible for the gift tax annual exclusion? If the gift to the ILIT is not a gift of a present interest, then the gift is classified as a gift of a future interest and the grantor will have to apply some or all of his or her lifetime gift tax applicable exclusion amount (currently $1 million) to the future interest gifts. A closely related issue to qualifying a gift to an ILIT for the gift tax annual exclusion is how to structure the beneficiary's right to the gift amount so that the ILIT trustee can use the gift amount to pay premiums and do so without the beneficiary creating an adverse gift, estate, or GST tax issue for him or herself. Granting the beneficiary a *Crummey* withdrawal right over the gift amount and allowing the gift amount to "lapse" within amounts specified by the Internal Revenue Code helps to solve this dilemma.

This chapter will also help practitioners draft an ILIT that avoids adverse gift tax consequences for both the grantor and the ILIT beneficiaries.

§3.1 VALUATION OF LIFE INSURANCE POLICIES

The gift tax value of a life insurance policy is the replacement cost of the policy at the time of the gift. Treas. Reg. §25.2512-6(a). The manner by which the replacement cost is determined, however, varies depending on the nature of the policy.[2] Generally, the replacement cost is established through the sale of the particular policy by the insurance company or through the sale by the insurance company of comparable policies. Because valuation of an insurance policy through sale of comparable policies is not possible when the gift

[2] *See*, Leimberg, "Policies for Valuation of Life Insurance," 139 *Trusts & Estates* 46 (March 2000).

is of an existing policy that has been in force for some time and on which further premium payments are to be made, the value of an existing policy is its interpolated terminal reserve at the date of the gift plus the unused portion of the last-paid premium. A policy's interpolated terminal reserve value is available from the life insurance company by requesting IRS Form 712. The policy's interpolated terminal reserve value is generally greater than the policy's cash surrender value.

For annual renewable term insurance or group term insurance, the gift tax value is the unused portion of the last-paid premium. The gift of a group term policy on the day before its premium due date has no ascertainable value. Rev. Rul. 76-490, 1976-2 C.B. 300. *See also*, Treas. Reg. §1.79-3(d)(2). Thus, the transfer of a group term policy (to the extent the transfer is not prohibited by the master policy or by state law) or an annual renewable term policy on the day before its premium due date should result in the policy being valued at zero for gift tax purposes. *See*, Rev. Rul. 84-147, 1984-2 C.B. 201 concerning the valuation of a group term policy.

For level premium term insurance (where the premium is level for a fixed term of years), the gift tax value may be the policy's replacement cost. In the early years, the replacement cost for level term life insurance should be less than the annual premium. However, after approximately 40% to 50% of the policy's term has expired, the replacement cost will probably be greater than the annual premium.

Near the end of the term, if the insured is no longer in good health, the replacement cost may be significantly higher. Because a level term policy has no cash value, a gift of as level premium term policy on the premium due date should result in the policy being valued at zero for gift tax purposes. However, if the insured is terminally ill, the gift tax value, even on its premium due date, may need to be determined by soliciting viatical or life settlement offers. These may be the best indication of the policy's fair market value.

For permanent (or cash value) life insurance (other than a single premium policy or paid-up policy) the gift tax value is the policy's interpolated terminal reserve at the date of the gift plus the unused portion of the last-paid premium, plus accumulated dividends, less any outstanding loans amounts against the policy. Treas. Reg. §25.2512-6(a), Example 4. (In many cases, however, the value of the policy can be reduced or even eliminated by loans against the policy, and by gifting the policy as close to the premium due date so as to reduce the amount of the unearned premium.)

> **Caution:** If the loan amount exceeds the donor's basis in the policy, the donee's basis in the policy is not the donor's basis, but rather the amount of the loan assumed by the donee, in which case the transfer for value rule under IRC section 101(a)(2) may be triggered. *See*, section 2.5, above.

For a universal or variable policy where the owner is no longer paying premiums and for a whole life policy where the premium are offset by policy dividends, the value of the policy is its interpolated terminal reserve at the date of the gift.

For a single premium policy or paid-up cash value policy, the policy's gift tax value is the amount that the insurance company would charge for the same policy on the life of a person the same age as the insured at the date of the gift. Treas. Reg. §25.2512-6(a) Example 3. When the policy has been in existence for some time, it may not be possible to use the replacement cost method just described. Instead, the policy is usually valued at its interpolated terminal reserve. Rev. Rul. 78-137, 1978-1 C.B. 280. Generally, policies that have a large cash value are not good candidates for transfers to an ILIT because the death benefit may be not much greater than the gift tax value of the policy. Furthermore, the donor will be giving up direct access to the policy's (significant) cash value.

For a newly purchased cash value policy (presumably less than one or two years old), the gift tax value is its cost, i.e., actual premiums paid. Treas. Reg. §25.2512-6(a), Example 1.

Split-dollar insurance arrangements entered into before September 18, 2003 (and not materially modified after September 17, 2003) are valued in the same manner as cash value life insurance policies (discussed immediately above) less the employer's ownership interest in the policy at the date of transfer. Rev. Rul. 81-198, 1981-2 C.B. 188.[3]

---

[3] "For split-dollar arrangements entered into or materially modified after September 17, 2003, the economic benefit regime applies if the employer, donor, or other person is the owner (with an endorsement of the death benefit to the trustee of the

Practice Point: Rev. Proc. 2005-25, 2005-17 I.R.B. 962 provides guidance on how to determine the fair market value of a life insurance contract, retirement income contract, endowment contract, or other contract providing life insurance protection for purposes of applying the rules of IRC sections 79 (employer provided group term life insurance), 83 (property transferred to a person in connection with the performance of services), and 402 (distributions from qualified retirement plans).[4] Presumably, the IRS would allow this guidance to apply to other situations as well, although the purpose of this guidance was to prohibit the perceived abuses of purchasing life insurance policies with so-called "springing" cash values; and to put an end to so-called "pension rescue" plans,[5] which use artificially depressed values of a life insurance policy to take assets out of a taxable account on a favorable basis. Thus, the guidance generally results in higher values for the policy.

---

irrevocable trust). The loan regime applies if the trustee is the owner (and the employer or corporation has a collateral assignment). [*See,* Treas. Reg. §§1.6122(d) - (g); 1.787215(b)(1).] Although the final regulations do not discuss expressly the gift tax consequences of a policy transfer under the economic benefit regime or the loan regime, the preamble to the final regulations states that the 'gift tax consequences of the transfer of an interest in a life insurance contract to a third party will continue to be determined under established gift tax principles notwithstanding who is treated as the owner of the life insurance contract under the final regulations.' [T.D. 9092, 2003-2 C.B. 1055, 1063.] The preamble cites Revenue Ruling 81-198 [19812 C.B. 188] for this proposition. Consequently, new split-dollar arrangements will continue to be valued for gift tax purposes in the same manner as a brand new policy or an existing policy, less the employer's, donor's, or other person's ownership or collateral assignment interest in the policy at the date of transfer." Donald O. Jansen, "Giving Birth To, Caring For, And Feeding The Irrevocable Life Insurance Trust," 41 *Real Property, Probate and Trust Journal* 571, 590 (Fall 2006). *See also,* Lawrence Brody and Charles L. Ratner, "Today's Split Dollar," 146 Trusts & Estates 38 (May 2007).

[4] *See,* Stephan R. Leimberg and Charles L. Ratner, "Valuation of Life Insurance: Rev. Proc. 2005-25 Provides New Guidance," 32 *Estate Planning* 13 (August 2005).

[5] *See,* J. Maxey Sanderson, "Pension Rescue," 142 *Trusts & Estates* 46 (May 2003); Natalie B. Choate, "Life Insurance In The Retirement Plan," 142 *Trusts & Estates* 50 (May 2003).

§3.1(a) Insured Terminally Ill

If the insured has become uninsurable or is terminally ill at the time of the gift, the fair market value of the life insurance policy may be significantly higher than the amount computable under the Regulations. In some instances, the fair market value may be the discounted amount of the death proceeds. The valuation of the policy will depend on the facts and circumstances. Treas. Reg. §25.2512-1 indicates that "[a]ll relevant facts and elements of value as of the time of the gift [of the policy] shall be considered," which may include the value of the policy in the secondary markets, such as viatical settlement companies. *See, e.g.*, *Estate of Pritchard v. Commissioner*, 4 T.C. 204 (1944); *United States v. Ryerson*, 312 US 260 (1941); Priv. Letter Rul. 9413045; TAM 9127007.[6] Arguably, the value of such a policy will be its value in the life settlement market.[7]

> **Caution:** When death is imminent, it may not be efficacious for the terminally ill insured to make a gift of the life insurance policy, because the proceeds will most likely be included in the insured's gross estate because of the three-year inclusion rule of IRC section 2035(d).

> **Caution:** An Estate Tax Inclusion Period ("ETIP") (*see,* section 5.17, below) will prevent the effective allocation of a transferor's GST tax exemption to an ILIT. The allocation will be deemed to have occurred at the close of the ETIP, and at that time, the transferor's previously allocated GST tax exemption will be applied against the

---

[6] In *Ryerson*, the Supreme Court held that a life insurance policy has both an insurance and an investment value. The Court held that the cost of duplicating the policy at the date of the gift is, in the absence of more cogent evidence, one criterion that reflects both the insurance and investment value to the owner at the time of the transfer. In *Estate of Pritchard*, the Tax Court held that the cost of replacement value at the date of transfer is authoritatively recognized as the value of the policy for gift tax purposes. When death is imminent, however, the court held that the value of the policy being transferred must be based on the proceeds that will be received at the insured's death.

[7] *See,* Michael I. Frankel, "Life Settlements: Sale of Life Insurance Policies in the Open Market," 39 *Heckerling Institute on Estate Planning*, ¶905.1 (Matthew Bender/Lexis-Nexis, Newark, NJ 2005); Neil Alexander and Jon J. Gallo, "The Effect of the Secondary Market on the Valuation of Life Insurance Contracts," 15 *Probate & Property* 53 (July/August 2001).

fair market value of the trust property (at the close of the ETIP). If the insured is terminally ill, uninsurable, or the policy has "matured," the previously allocated GST tax emption may not be sufficient to cause the ILIT to be GST tax exempt.

Practice Point: When selling a life insurance policy for full and adequate consideration in money or money's worth to avoid the three-year rule of IRC section 2035, consider soliciting quotes from viatical or life settlement companies regarding the value of the policy, and document the file. The secondary market's value may be a good indication of the policy's fair market value under the willing buyer/willing seller test of Treas. Reg. §25.2512-1.

§3.2 GIFT TAX CONSEQUENCES OF THIRD-PARTY PAYMENTS OF LIFE INSURANCE PREMIUMS

The payment (directly or indirectly) of life insurance premiums by someone other than the owner of the policy is a taxable gift. Treas. Reg. §25.2511-1(h)(8). Thus, direct payment of life insurance premiums by the insured (where the ILIT owns the life insurance policy) is a taxable gift to the beneficiaries of the ILIT. Treas. Reg. §25.2503-3(c), Example 6. Direct payment of premiums by the insured where the policy is owned outright (i.e., free of trust) by another person is a gift of a present interest. *Id.* Similarly, for split-dollar insurance arrangements entered into before September 18, 2003 (and not materially modified after September 17, 2003) employer premium payments (and employee premium payments under a contributory split-dollar arrangement) are an imputed gift by the employee to the ILIT.[8]

---

[8] "For split-dollar arrangements entered into or materially modified on or after September 18, 2003, when the employer, corporation, or donor owns the policy with an endorsement of insurance coverage to the life insurance trust (or when the trustee owns a non-equity policy with a collateral assignment of the entire cash value to the employer, corporation, or donor), Treasury Regulation section 1.6122 treats any economic benefit from the split-dollar arrangement as provided by the owner to the non-owner (for example, a life insurance trust). [*See,* Treas. Reg. §1.6122(d)(1).] The tax treatment of the economic benefit will depend upon the relationship between the owner and the non-owner-employee (compensation), shareholder (dividend), or private split-dollar (gift). If a third party is involved, two

§3.3 GIFT TAX CONSEQUENCES OF EMPLOYER-PAID GROUP TERM PREMIUMS

Payment of group term insurance premiums by an employer is an indirect gift from the employee to the transferee of the policy (such as an ILIT). Rev. Rul. 76-490, 1976-2 C.B. 300; Rev. Rul. 79-47, 1979-1 C.B. 312. The value of the gift is the lower of: (i) the actual cost of the group term coverage; or (ii) the Table I value without the $50,000 coverage exclusion (set out in Treas. Reg. §1.79-3(d)(2)), provided the group term policy is nondiscriminatory and qualifies under section 79. If the plan discriminates, the value of the gift is the actual cost of coverage to the employer. Rev. Rul. 84-147,

---

tax consequences could result with regard to a split-dollar arrangement between an employer and a life insurance trust: the economic benefit would be treated as compensation to the employee, followed by the employee's gift to the trust.

Three possible economic benefits to the non-owner exist under the economic benefit regime pursuant to Treasury Regulation section 1.6122(d)(2): (1)The cost of current life insurance protection (Table 2001 or the term premium of the insurance carrier if lower). [*See*, I.R.S. Notice 20028, 20021 C.B. 398.] (2) The amount of policy cash value to which the non-owner has current access (to the extent that such amount has not been taxed to the non-owner in a prior taxable year). Thus, any equity buildup in the insurance policy will be taxed currently to the employee and will be a gift from the employee to the trust if the trust has current access to the equity cash value. (3) The value of any other economic benefit to the extent not taken into account by the non-owner in a prior year—amounts actually received as dividends, withdrawals, partial surrenders, and specified policy loans. [See Treas. Reg. §1.6122(e)(1).]

For split-dollar arrangements entered into or materially modified on or after September 18, 2003, when the trustee owns the policy and the employer, corporation, or donor loans the premiums to the trust with a collateral assignment against the policy, the income and gift tax rules of section 7872 apply. [*See*, Treas. Reg. §1.787215(e)(1).] There are two ways in which the interest on the premium loan may result in gifts: (1) If the trust does not pay the applicable federal interest rate, the foregone interest would be a gift from the donor or employee to the trust with income tax consequences to the donor or employee. The amount of the income and gift depends on whether the loan is a demand loan, a term loan, or a hybrid loan under the regulations. (2) If the trustee pays the applicable federal interest rate without gift tax consequences under section 7872 the donor may have to give the interest to the trustee to make the payment, unless the trustee has other funds in the trust." Donald O. Jansen, "Giving Birth To, Caring For, And Feeding The Irrevocable Life Insurance Trust," 41 *Real Property, Probate and Trust Journal* 571, 594-595 (Fall 2006). *See also*, Lawrence Brody and Charles L. Ratner, "Today's Split Dollar," 146 *Trusts & Estates* 38 (May 2007).

1984-2 C.B. 201. *See also*, Rev. Rul. 78-420, 1978-2 C.B. 67, applying the same principles to split-dollar arrangements.

An employer's payment of premiums (for a group term policy that the employee irrevocably assigned to an ILIT) constitutes a gift of a present interest by the employee-insured to the ILIT beneficiaries who hold *Crummey* withdrawal rights. Rev. Ruls. 79-47, 1979-1 C.B. and 76-490, 1976-2 C.B. 300; Priv. Letter Ruls. 8138102, 8111123, 8103074, 8021058, and 8006109.

> **Practice Point:** State law and the master group policy, which govern the ability of an employee to assign his or her group term coverage to an ILIT, should be consulted to determine if the group term coverage is assignable. Do not rely on the employee's certificate of insurance coverage. If possible, try to obtain written confirmation from the life insurance carrier of the date that it irrevocably assigned the group term policy to the ILIT.

§3.4 TRANSFER OF LIFE INSURANCE POLICY TO CO-OWNERS IS NOT ELIGIBLE FOR THE GIFT TAX ANNUAL EXCLUSION

An outright transfer of a life insurance policy to an individual donee is a gift of a present interest in the policy, even if the policy has no cash value. Treas. Reg. §25.2503-3(a); Rev. Rul. 55-408, 1955-1 C.B. 113. However, the transfer of a single policy to two or more co-owners when no one co-owner can exercise rights of ownership without consent of the other co-owners constitutes a gift of a future interest.[9] *Ryerson v. United States*, 312 U.S. 405 (1940). *See also*, *Skouras v. Commissioner*, 188 F.2d 831 (2d Cir. 1951).

> **Practice Point:** If each co-owner has the immediate and individual power to sever the joint ownership of the policy and immediately obtain his or her share of policy

---

[9] A gift of property to a beneficiary is a gift of a "future interest" if the beneficiary's enjoyment of the property is limited to commence in use, possession, or enjoyment at some future date or time. Treas. Reg. §25.2503-3(a); *Fondren v. Commissioner,* 324 U.S. 18 (1945); *Commissioner v. Disston,* 325 U.S. 442 (1945) *See also*, Rev. Rul. 83-108, 1983-1 C.B. 14 where the IRS states that if a trustee has discretion to accumulate the trust income even for a brief period, the gift of an income interest is a gift of a future interest.

cash values and other rights, the gift to each transfer should be considered a present interest. As a practical matter, it is far better planning to have the insurance company divide the policy into two (or more) parts, i.e. reissue as two policies, than to use joint ownership—which can get very messy if one co-owner dies, divorces, goes bankrupt, etc. *See,* Priv. Letter Ruls. 200652043 (concerning the splitting of a parent corporation's master life insurance policy into two separate (but otherwise identical) policies for the benefit of two of the parent corporation's subsidiaries, where the IRS ruled there was no transfer for value because the subsidiary-transferees received the original parent-transferor's basis in the policy, and there was no sale or exchange under the *Cottage Savings Association v. Commissioner*, 499 U.S. 554 (1991)[10] interpretation of IRC section 1001) and 9852041 concerning the splitting of a jointly owned policy into two separate policies where an ILIT terminated and distributed a life insurance policy jointly to the two trust beneficiaries and the beneficiaries sought to split the single policy into two separate policies, each separate policy to be equal to 50% of the jointly owned policy. The IRS ruled that there was no transfer for value under IRC section 101(a)(2) upon the splitting of the jointly owned policy.

§3.5 GIFT TAX ANNUAL EXCLUSION AND THE *CRUMMEY* WITHDRAWAL RIGHT

An outright transfer of a life insurance policy to an individual donee is a completed gift,[11] and is a gift of a present interest in the policy,

---

[10] *See,* section 15.7(d), below, for a discussion of the *Cottage Savings* doctrine.

[11] Treas. Reg. §25.2511-2(b) provides that a gift is complete as to any property with respect to which the donor has so parted with dominion and control as to leave the donor with no power to change the disposition of the property, whether for the donor's own benefit, or for the benefit of another. But if upon a transfer of property (whether in trust or otherwise) the donor reserves any power over its disposition, the gift may be wholly incomplete, or may be partially complete and partially incomplete, depending upon all the facts in the particular case.

even if the policy has no cash value. Treas. Reg. §25.2503-3(a); Rev. Rul. 55-408, 1955-1 C.B. 113. However, a gift or transfer of money (or other property, such as cash or an existing life insurance policy) to an ILIT is a gift of a future interest and not a gift of a present interest. A gift of a future interest does not qualify for the gift tax annual exclusion under IRC section 2503(b)(1), and the gift is subject to gift tax under IRC section 2501. For a gift to qualify as a gift of a "present interest" that is eligible for the gift tax annual exclusion, the donee (i.e., the ILIT beneficiary) must have the unrestricted right to the immediate use, possession, or enjoyment of the gift property or the income[12] from the gift property. IRC section 2503(b); Treas. Reg. §25.2503-3(b). An ILIT does not, in and of itself, give a donee the unrestricted right to the ILIT property or gifts made to the ILIT; in fact, the gifts to the ILIT are purposely designed to be "restricted" to ensure that the gifted property remains in the ILIT for use by the trustee for the benefit of the beneficiaries, including the payment of life insurance premiums. Therefore, if the grantor wants to have gifts to the ILIT qualify for the gift tax annual exclusion, the ILIT must be designed to provide the donee with a limited opportunity to withdraw the gifted

---

Treas. Reg. §25.2511-2(c) provides that a gift is incomplete in every instance in which a donor reserves the power to revest the beneficial title in himself or herself. A gift is also incomplete if and to the extent that a reserved power gives the donor the power to name new beneficiaries or to change the interests of the beneficiaries as between themselves unless the power is a fiduciary power limited by a fixed or ascertainable standard. Under Treas. Reg. §25.2511-2(e), a donor is considered as possessing a reserved power if it is exercisable by the donor in conjunction with any person not having a substantial adverse interest in the disposition of the transferred property. Also, Treas. Reg. §25.2511-2(f) provides that the relinquishment or termination of a reserved power to change the beneficiaries of transferred property, occurring otherwise than by death of the donor, is regarded as the event which completes the gift and causes the gift tax to apply.

[12] "[A] requirement that the beneficiary receive, at least annually, all the net income of a trust holding a life insurance policy will be treated in its entirety as a "future interest" because the policy is a non-income-producing asset. *See*, *Jesse S. Phillips*, 12 T.C. 216 (1949); *see also*, Treas. Reg. §25.2503-3(c), Example 2 (income distributions that begin after insurance policy matures are a gift of a future interest)." Diana S. C. Zeydel, "How to Create and Administer a Successful Irrevocable Life Insurance Trust," 34 *Estate Planning* 3, 9 (June 2007).

amount. This is accomplished by giving the donee a *Crummey* withdrawal right over property that is gifted to the ILIT.[13]

A *Crummey* withdrawal right over a gift to an ILIT constitutes an unrestricted right to the immediate use, possession, or enjoyment of the gifted property and converts what would otherwise be a gift of a future interest into a gift of a present interest that qualifies for the gift tax annual exclusion under IRC section 2503(b). A *Crummey* withdrawal right permits a beneficiary to make a one-time demand for the trustee to distribute to the beneficiary either the gifted property or other trust assets of equivalent value subject to the limitations of IRC sections 2503(b) (concerning the gift tax annual exclusion amount) and 2513 (concerning twice the gift tax annual exclusion amount if there is gift splitting).[14] The beneficiary's right to demand distribution of the gifted property (or other trust assets) is typically of limited duration, such as 30 or 60 days. If the beneficiary does not exercise his or her *Crummey* withdrawal right within the specified time period, the withdrawal right lapses, and the beneficiary cannot make another demand on the trustee as concerns the lapsed amount. The beneficiary's one-time right of withdrawal with respect to the gift amount is known as a "non-cumulative right of withdrawal." If the amount of the *Crummey* withdrawal right exceeds $5,000 or 5% of the value of the trust assets, the lapse of a *Crummey* withdrawal right may, if not handled correctly, create transfer tax problems for the beneficiary. *D.C. Clifford Crummey v. Commissioner*, 397 F.2d 82

---

[13] *See*, Hannah W. Mensch, "A 'Gift' From the IRS: A Guide to the Gift Tax Annual Exclusion," 33 *Estate Planning* 16 (December 2006).

[14] A gift to an ILIT in excess of the gift tax annual exclusion amount (or twice that amount if there is gift splitting) per *Crummey* withdrawal right beneficiary does not qualify for the gift tax annual exclusion because it will exceed the amount permitted under IRC section 2503(b). For example, if a married grantor gifts $60,000 to an ILIT in 2007 and his two children have *Crummey* withdrawal rights over their pro-rata share of the $60,000 gift, only $48,000 ($24,000/child) will be eligible for the gift tax annual exclusion (assuming gift splitting). The remaining $12,000 will be subject to gift tax, and be a gift of a future interest. If the children have a hanging *Crummey* power, each child's $24,000 withdrawal right will be eligible for the gift tax annual exclusion and will lapse at the rate of $5,000 per year. *See*, section 3.13, below, concerning hanging *Crummey* powers.

(9th Cir. 1968)[15]; Rev. Rul. 73-405, 1973-2 C.B. 321. *See also, Gilmore v. Commissioner,* 213 F.2d 520 (6th Cir. 1954); *Kieckhefer v. Commissioner,* 189 F.2d 118 (7th Cir. 1951). *See,* Paragraph 3.1 of Sample ILIT. *See,* sections 3.11, 3.12, 3.13, 3.14, 3.15, 3.17, 4.4, 4.5, 4.6, 5.19, 5.20, and 5.21, below, concerning the transfer tax issues regarding the lapse of a *Crummey* withdrawal right in excess of $5,000 or 5% of the value of the trust assets.

> **Practice Point:** There are numerous other tax issues and technical requirements concerning *Crummey* withdrawal rights, many of which are discussed in this Chapter and in Chapters 2, 4, 5, 10, 11, 12, and 15.

Since 1973, the IRS has recognized the validity of a *Crummey* withdrawal right to create a gift of a present interest that is eligible for the gift tax annual exclusion. Rev. Rul. 73-405, 1973-2 C.B. 321. However, over the years, the IRS has attempted to place limits on the expansion of the class of beneficiaries eligible to hold *Crummey* withdrawal rights. Fortunately, the courts have resisted many of those changes.

Generally, the IRS officially recognizes only *Crummey* withdrawal right beneficiaries who hold a current income interest or vested remainder interest in the trust, provided there is no preexisting understanding between the grantor and the beneficiaries concerning the nonexercise of their withdrawal rights. TAM 9731004;

---

[15] In *Crummey v. Commissioner,* the court held that a gift of property in trust for a minor child is a gift of a present interest in property where the minor has a legally unrestricted present right to demand that the trustee distribute the property to him free and clear. The donor created a trust for his four children, two of whom were minors. Contributions were made approximately two weeks before the close of the year. Each beneficiary had the right to demand a distribution of contributions made to the trust during the year. The right was exercisable at any time before the end of the year. The court held that each beneficiary was legally and technically capable of immediately enjoying the property. The transfers were, thus, gifts of a present interest regardless of the fact that the minors would need a guardian to make the demand, that no guardians had officially been appointed for the years when the gifts under scrutiny were made, and in fact, there could be no demand made by the minors. The court also noted that it was unlikely that the minor beneficiaries knew (or would ever know) about the gifts. *See,* Marc A. Chorney, "Transfer Tax Issues Raised by *Crummey* Powers," 33 *Real Property, Probate and Trust Journal* 755 (Winter 1999). *See,* sections 15.3 and 15.4, below for a detailed history of *Crummey,* and the evolution of the *Crummey* doctrine.

Priv. Letter Rul. 9030005; Rev. Rul. 85-24, 1985-1 C.B. 329; Rev. Rul. 81-7, 1981-1 C.B. 474. *But see, Estate of Maria Cristofani v. Commissioner*, 97 T.C. 74 (1991), AOD 1996-010; *Estate of Lieselotte Kohlsaat v. Commissioner*, T.C. Memo 1997-212 (1997); *Estate of Carolyn W. Holland v. Commissioner*, T.C. Memo 1997-302 (1997) (where the Tax Court rejected the IRS's "prearranged understanding" test, and permitted *Crummey* withdrawal rights to qualify for the gift tax annual exclusion when the beneficiaries had discussed in detail the purpose of the trust and their desire to not exercise their right of withdrawal). *See,* Chapter 15, below for a more comprehensive discussion of the *Crummey* case and its evolution. *See,* sections 10.1 through 10.10, 10.12, 11.2, 11.5, 12.2, and 12.6, below, concerning the administration of a *Crummey* withdrawal right.

The IRS generally will not issue advance rulings concerning the availability of the gift tax annual exclusion involving ILITs with *Crummey* withdrawal rights. *See,* Rev. Proc. 2007-3, 2007-1 I.R.B. 108, section 4.01(45).[16]

> **Caution:** A *Crummey* withdrawal right does not constitute a present interest gift if the trustee can defeat or impair the beneficiary's right to withdraw the property. Rev. Rul. 83-108, 1983-2 CB 167; TAM 8107009; Priv. Letter Rul. 8121051. Therefore, all discretionary powers held by the trustee or a special powerholder should be expressly limited to prevent the trustee or special powerholder from defeating or impairing a beneficiary's unlapsed power of withdrawal. *See,* Paragraphs 3.2(F),

---

[16] According to this Rev. Proc., the IRS will ordinarily not issue a private letter ruling concerning: "Whether the transfer of property to a trust will be a gift of a present interest in property when (i) the trust corpus consists or will consist substantially of insurance policies on the life of the grantor or the grantor's spouse, (ii) the trustee or any other person has a power to apply the trust's income or corpus to the payment of premiums on policies of insurance on the life of the grantor or the grantor's spouse, (iii) the trustee or any other person has a power to use the trust's assets to make loans to the grantor's estate or to purchase assets from the grantor's estate, (iv) the trust beneficiaries have the power to withdraw, on demand, any additional transfers made to the trust, and (v) there is a right or power in any person that would cause the grantor to be treated as the owner of all or a portion of the trust under sections 673 to 677."

3.2(J), 4.1(B), 4.2, 7.1(D)(3), 7.2, 7.3, 7.6, 7.10, and 8.2(C) of Sample ILIT.

Practice Point: Unless the trust qualifies as a skip person under IRC section 2642(c)(2), a gift to a trust that has *Crummey* withdrawal rights is not considered a gift to the individual donees; rather, it is considered a transfer to the trust itself. Treas. Reg. §26.2642-1(b)(3). *See also*, Treas. Reg. §26.2612-1(d)(2) concerning trusts that are skip persons. This means that the *Crummey* withdrawal right is not automatically GST tax exempt, and GST tax exemption will have to be allocated to the annual gifts to the ILIT in order for the ILIT to be GST tax exempt. *See*, section 5.29, below.

Practice Point: IRC section 6039F requires a donee to report to the IRS gifts that the donee receives (other than the donor's direct payment of medical expenses or tuition under IRC section 2503(e)(2)) from certain foreign persons if the aggregate value of the gifts received in a taxable year gift exceeds $10,000 (adjusted for inflation). The 2007 threshold amount is $13,258.

§3.6 GIFT TAX MARITAL DEDUCTION AND THE *CRUMMEY* WITHDRAWAL RIGHT

A *Crummey* withdrawal right granted to a spouse is a nondeductible terminable interest (because it lapses and other beneficiaries succeed to a right in the property) and therefore does not qualify for the gift tax marital deduction (although the withdrawal right may qualify for the gift tax annual exclusion under IRC section 2503(b)). IRC section 2523(b).

Practice Point: There is no gift tax marital deduction if the spouse is not a U.S. citizen. If the donee-spouse is not a U.S. citizen the annual gift tax exclusion amount available to the donor-spouse concerning present interest gifts to a non-U.S. citizen donee-spouse is, however, increased to $100,000 (indexed for inflation after 1998) per calendar year. IRC section 2513(i). In 2007, the amount is $125,000. Rev. Proc. 2006-53, 2006-48 I.R.B. 996 (11/27/2006). However, as previously mentioned, a gift to an ILIT where the non-U.S. citizen spouse has a *Crummey* withdrawal right is limited to the gift tax annual exclusion amount of $10,000 (indexed for inflation) under IRC section 2503(b). In 2007, the gift tax annual exclusion amount is $12,000. *Id.*

§3.7 DATE OF COMPLETED GIFT TO ILIT

A grantor's irrevocable contribution to an ILIT on December 31 is a completed gift as of that date (for gift tax purposes), even though the beneficiary does not receive notice of the contribution until several days later and the beneficiary's *Crummey* withdrawal right does not expire until 30 days thereafter. Rev. Rul. 83-108, 1983-2 C.B. 167.

If the grantor dies shortly after delivery of a gift check to the ILIT trustee, the gift check will be considered a completed gift in the calendar year for which completed gift treatment is sought, if certain conditions are met.[17]

According to Rev. Rul. 96-56, 1996-2 C.B. 16 (*modifying* Rev. Rul. 67-396, 1967-2 C.B. 351), the delivery of a check to a noncharitable donee will be deemed to be a completed gift for federal gift and estate tax purposes on the earlier of (i) the date on which the donor has so parted with dominion and control under local law as to leave in the donor no power to change its disposition, or (ii) the date on which the donee deposits the check (or cashes the check against available funds of the donee) or presents the check for payment, if it is established that (1) the check was paid by the drawee bank when first presented to the drawee bank for payment; (2) the donor was alive when the check was paid by the drawee bank; (3) the donor intended to make a gift; (4) delivery of the check by the donor was unconditional; and (5) the check was deposited, cashed, or presented in the calendar year for which completed gift treatment is sought and within a reasonable time of issuance. *See also*, *John A. Metzger v. Commissioner,* 100 T.C. 204 (1993), *aff'd*, 38 F.3d 1181 (4th Cir. 1994).

Practice Point: To be assured of completed gift treatment for the calendar year in which the check is written, a year end gift check by the grantor to the ILIT trustee should

---

[17] *See*, Frank S. Berall, "The Relation Back Doctrine and Noncharitable Gifts by Check," 15 *The Practical Tax Lawyer* 53 (Spring 2001).

be immediately deposited, or the grantor should issue a certified check, a bank money order, or a bank cashier's check to the ILIT trustee in lieu of a regular check.

§3.8 GIFT TAX ANNUAL EXCLUSION FOR IRC SECTION 2503(C) MINOR'S TRUST

A gift to a trust for the sole benefit of the individual who is under 21 on the date of the gift, is considered a gift of a present interest in the property for purposes of IRC section 2503(b), provided:

(1) The gift/property and the income therefrom may be expended by, or for the benefit of, the donee before attaining age 21; and

(2) The trust property will either pass to the donee upon attaining age 21,[18] or if the donee dies before age 21, the trust property is either payable to the donee's estate or as the donee may appoint under a testamentary general power of appointment. IRC section 2503(c).[19]

Thus, a gift to an IRC section 2503(c) trust that owns (or is authorized to own) life insurance qualifies for the annual gift tax exclusion without giving the donee a *Crummey* withdrawal right over the gift contribution. *John A. Duncan v. U.S.*, 368 F.2d 98 (5th Cir. 1966). However, IRC section 2503(c) trusts are generally not desirable to hold life insurance on the grantor's life because of the

---

[18] "[A] gift to a minor in [an IRC section 2503(c)] trust, with the provision that the beneficiary has, upon reaching age 21, either (1) a continuing right to compel immediate distribution of the trust corpus by giving written notice to the trustee, or to permit the trust to continue by its own terms, or (2) a right during a limited period to compel immediate distribution of the trust corpus by given written notice to the trustee which if not exercised will permit the trust to continue by its own terms, will not be considered to be the gift of a future interest as the gift satisfies the requirements of section 2503(c) of the Code, and the exclusion provided for in section 2503(b) is allowable." Rev. Rul. 74-43, 1974-1 C.B. 285.

[19] *See,* Hannah W. Mensch, "A 'Gift' From the IRS: A Guide to the Gift Tax Annual Exclusion," 33 *Estate Planning* 16 (December 2006); and Bradley E.S. Fogel, "Billion Dollar Babies: Annual Exclusion Gifts to Minors," 13 *Probate & Property* 6 (September/October 1998).

age 21 payout requirement.[20] *See*, section 5.7(c) concerning GST issues and IRC section 2503(c) trusts.

> **Practice Point:** A gift of a life insurance policy to a non-IRC section 2503(c) trust that is required to pay all of its income at least annually to the beneficiary will not qualify as a gift of a present interest if the life insurance policy does not pay income until the insured's death. Treas. Reg. §25.2503-3(c), Example 2; *Jesse S. Phillips v. Commissioner*, 12 T.C. 216 (1949).[21]

§3.9 ILIT BENEFICIARY'S EXERCISE OF INTER-VIVOS LIMITED POWER OF APPOINTMENT MAY BE SUBJECT TO GIFT TAX

Limited powers of appointment are often included in ILITs to provide some flexibility in what is otherwise an irrevocable transaction. However, the lifetime exercise of a limited power of appointment over the trust corpus by the trust's income beneficiary is a gift equal to the

---

[20] "Typically, a Section 2503(c) trust confers on its beneficiary the right, upon attaining age 21 and for a limited time, to withdraw all the assets of the trust. If the Section 2503(c) trust were an ILIT, this would mean that the beneficiary would have the right to withdraw and retain the insurance policy. In addition, unless the beneficiary's power of withdrawal continues after age 21, subsequent contributions to the trust may not qualify for the [gift tax] annual exclusion because the beneficiary may have no present right to receive those contributions. Although it might not often be used, a Section 2503(c) trust should not be ruled out as a possible form of ILIT because it will avoid an annual power of withdrawal and the need for the annual notices required in a so-called *Crummey* power ILIT....And if the policy becomes paid up during the period before the beneficiary attains age 21, no further contributions to pay premiums would be required." Diana S. C. Zeydel, "How to Create and Administer a Successful Irrevocable Life Insurance Trust," 34 *Estate Planning* 3, 9 (June 2007).

[21] "In *Commissioner v. Boeing* (CCA-9), 123 Fed. (2d) 86, taxpayer irrevocably transferred to a trustee six insurance policies on his own life. Under the trust agreement the net income was payable one-half to his wife and son, the immediate beneficiaries, during their respective lives, or to the survivor thereof. The court therein stated: 'Clearly, the beneficiaries have no right to the present enjoyment of the policy proceeds, and they will never have that right unless they survive the trustor, or, in any event, unless they survive the possible lapse of the policies. Their use and enjoyment are 'postponed to the happening of a future uncertain event [and therefore the transfer of the policies to the trust are gifts of a future interest]....'" *Id.* at 223.

present value of the beneficiary's income interest. IRC section 2511. The beneficiary's exercise of the power over the corpus does not terminate the income interest; rather, when trust corpus is transferred, income generated by the transferred corpus is also (gratuitously) transferred to the transferee of the corpus, thus resulting in a gift of the beneficiary's transferred income interest. *Estate of Ruth B. Regester v. Commissioner*, 83 T.C. 1 (1984). This rule is of importance where the ILIT beneficiary (such as the grantor's spouse) holds an inter-vivos limited power of appointment over the trust corpus during the grantor's lifetime, with the ability to appoint the ILIT corpus (including insurance policies held by the ILIT on the grantor's life) to another person (including the insured-grantor, but excluding the appointing beneficiary, the appointing beneficiary's estate, or the creditors of either). Any such appointment may result in a gift being made by the appointing beneficiary, who will then become the "new" transferor for GST tax purposes of the appointed property. Rev. Rul. 79-327, 1979-2 C.B. 342; Treas. Reg. §§25.2514-1(b)(2); 25.2514-3(e), Examples 1 and 3; 26.2652-1(a)(2).

If the appointing beneficiary's interest in the trust is purely discretionary or subject to an ascertainable standard, the beneficiary's exercise of an inter-vivos limited power of appointment may still result in a gift being made by the appointing beneficiary. Priv. Letter Ruls. 200243026, 9451049, 9419007, and 8535020.

> **Practice Point:** The ILIT can give the grantor-insured's spouse (unless the ILIT owns a survivorship policy), the insured's child, or another trusted individual a limited power of appointment, during the grantor-insured's lifetime, to appoint trust income and principal to anyone other than the powerholder, the powerholder's estate, or the creditors of either. With such a provision, the powerholder could appoint the policy back to the grantor-insured or directly to a new ILIT with revised terms. If the policy is returned to the grantor-insured, the death proceeds will be included in his or her gross estate if the policy is still owned at death. However, the mere existence of this form of limited power of appointment in the ILIT, whether or not exercised, will not cause the property still in the trust to be included in the grantor-insured's gross estate. Because the power to distribute the policy is exercisable only in the absolute discretion of the

powerholder, the value of the reversionary interest is less than 5%. IRC section 2042(2). Because the limited power of appointment is not exercisable by the grantor-insured, it is not a general power of appointment. IRC section 2041(a)(2). Because the limited power of appointment is not exercisable by the grantor-insured, the insured does not have the power to alter, amend, revoke, or terminate the transfer. IRC section 2038(a)(1). If there was no understanding, express or implied, between the grantor-insured and the powerholder that the powerholder would later distribute trust income or principal to the grantor-insured, then the grantor-insured will not be treated as having retained the right to possess or enjoy the trust property. IRC section 2036(a)(1). *See,* Paragraph 4.2 of Sample ILIT.

§3.10 GIFT SPLITTING AND LARGE GIFT CONTRIBUTIONS TO ILIT

Gift splitting used in conjunction with a hanging *Crummey* withdrawal right, or with trust beneficiaries having separate trust shares coupled with testamentary powers of appointment, permits the grantor to make annual gifts to the ILIT that are twice the amount of the grantor's available annual gift tax exclusion amount. Gift splitting is available to the grantor if:

(1) Each spouse is a resident of the United States or a U.S. citizen;

(2) The spouse is married to the grantor at the time of the gift;

(3) The spouse is alive at the time of the gift; and

(4) The spouse does not remarry during the remainder of the calendar year. IRC section 2513; Treas. Reg. §25.2513-1(b)(1); Rev. Rul. 55-506, 1955-2 C. B 609; Priv. Letter Rul. 200408014 (gifts made by a surviving spouse after the other spouse's death cannot be gift split with the deceased spouse).

Gift splitting is particularly helpful in large premium cases. However, a donor cannot elect gift splitting with respect to gifts to his or her spouse (i.e., a donee spouse cannot elect to split gifts to himself or herself). IRC section 2513(a)(1) (first sentence). Nor can the donor elect to split gifts with his or her spouse concerning a gift to a third party if the consenting spouse holds a general power of appointment ("GPOA") over the gifted property. IRC section 2513(a)(1) (second sentence). This is because the consenting spouse's GPOA over the property gifted to the third party is the equivalent of the consenting spouse receiving outright ownership of the property; and as previously mentioned, a spouse cannot elect to split gifts to himself or herself. A consenting spouse can, however, hold a testamentary limited power of appointment over property that is gifted to third parties and is elected for gift splitting. For example, the IRS allowed gift splitting where a wife transferred assets to a trust for the benefit of her children and husband (each of whom had *Crummey* withdrawal rights over the gifts), and the husband also had a testamentary limited power to appoint the trust assets to one or more of his wife's descendants. Priv. Letter Rul. 200130030.[22] This ruling suggests that a donee (consenting) spouse's limited power of appointment over property transferred by a donor will not preclude gift splitting; otherwise, the donee (consenting) spouse's election to split gifts would render the gift incomplete and the issue of gift splitting would be moot because there would be no completed gift. *See also*, Priv. Letter Rul. 200213013 where the IRS ruled that a split gift to an irrevocable GST tax exempt dynasty trust (where there were no *Crummey* withdrawal rights) was complete and that the gifted property would not be includable in either the donor's estate or the consenting spouse's gross estate, even though the consenting spouse was given a contin-

---

[22] In Priv. Letter Rul. 200130030, the IRS ruled: "In the present case, it is represented that only Wife will transfer property to Trust. Although Wife and Husband will consent under §2513 to treat the gifts to Trust made by Wife as if made one-half by Wife and one-half by Husband, Wife will be treated as the transferor of the entire value of the gifts to Trust for purposes of §§2036 through 2038. Sections 2036 through 2038 do not apply to property interests that the decedent [to wit, Husband] did not actually own and thus did not transfer. Accordingly, assuming only Wife makes transfers to Trust, Husband [who, along with his children are beneficiaries the trust (with distributions being subject to an ascertainable standard), and who holds a testamentary limited power of appointment over the trust to appoint the trust to any of the Wife's descendants, and if the testamentary limited power of appointment is not exercised, the trust is payable to the Wife's children] will not be the transferor of property to Trust for purposes of §§2036 through 2038. Therefore, no portion of the value of Trust will be includible in Husband's gross estate under §§2036 through 2038. See Rev. Rul. 82-198, 1982-2 C.B. 206; Rev. Rul. 74-556, 1974-2 C.B. 300; Rev. Rul. 54-246, 1954-1 C.B. 179."

gent remainder interest in the trust property (subject to an ascertainable standard) and was given a testamentary limited power of appointment over her contingent remainder interest to appoint the trust property to anyone other than her estate or her creditors. Said the IRS, "[A]lthough Spouse will consent under § 2513 to treat the gift to Trust made by Settlor as if made one-half by Spouse, §2035(a) and §§2036 through 2038 do not apply to property interests that the decedent [consenting Spouse] did not actually own and thus did not transfer. Accordingly, assuming only Settlor makes transfers to Trust, [consenting] Spouse will not be the transferor of property to Trust for purposes of §2035(a), and §§2036 through 2038. See Rev. Rul. 82-198, 1982-2 C.B. 206; Rev. Rul. 74-556,1974-2 C.B. 300; Rev. Rul. 54-246, 1954-1 C.B. 179." Another interesting aspect of Priv. Letter Rul. 200213013 is that the irrevocable GST tax-exempt dynasty trust stated that if any of the trust property was includable in the donor-husband's gross estate, the trustee of the irrevocable GST tax-exempt dynasty trust was to distribute the property either to the donor-husband's estate or to any revocable trust the donor-husband had established before his death. In this regard, the IRS ruled: "Under the terms of Trust, Trust is irrevocable and Settlor [donor-husband] will have no right, title or interest in or power over, privilege or incident of ownership in regard to any trust property. Settlor has retained no beneficial interest in the trust and has not retained any right to alter, amend, revoke, or terminate the Trust within the meaning of §2038, or the right to designate the persons who will possess or enjoy the property or the income therefrom within the meaning of §2036." This ruling suggests that a gift to an irrevocable trust can be complete and irrevocable, despite that fact that any trust property that is includable in the donor's gross estate is to be distributed to the donor's estate or the donor's ***revocable*** trust. This should be of comfort to practitioners who have drafted ILITs that require ILIT property which is includable in the grantor's gross estate to be distributed to the grantor's revocable trust.

If a donor transfers property in part to the donee-spouse and in part to third parties, the election to split such a gift by the donee-spouse is effective, but only *"with respect to the interest transferred to third parties only insofar as such interest is ascertainable at the time of the gift and hence severable from the interest transferred to [the donee] spouse."* Treas. Reg. §25.2513-1(b)(4) (emphasis added). *See,* Paragraph 3.1(A)(1) of Sample ILIT which further defines "contribution" by excluding any amount that has been gift split by the donee-spouse.

If the donee (consenting) spouse has an annuity, life estate, remainder interest, or other determinable or ascertainable interest, the third parties' interests would be ascertainable and would be eligible for gift splitting.[23]

When the donee (consenting) spouse and other beneficiaries have *Crummey* withdrawal rights over the gifted property, the amount subject to withdrawal by the other beneficiaries would be ascertainable and thus eligible for gift splitting (assuming the rights of the income and corpus beneficiaries are subordinate to any unlapsed *Crummey* withdrawal rights). *See,* Priv. Letter Ruls. 200422051, 8044080, 8112087, 8138171, 8138170, 8143045, and 200130030. *See,* Paragraph 3.1(A)(1) of Sample ILIT. However, the amount subject to withdrawal by the donee (consenting) spouse would not be eligible for gift splitting. If the donee (consenting) spouse does not have a *Crummey* withdrawal right over the gift property but does have a general power of appointment over all the gift property, the gift cannot be split. Treas. Reg. §25.2513-1(b)(3).

If the gift is not subject to withdrawal rights and the trust is a common "pot" trust from which the donee (consenting) spouse and the other beneficiaries may receive discretionary distributions, the gift cannot be split because there are no readily ascertainable interests. *See*, Rev. Rul. 56-439, 1956-2 C.B. 605; *Max Kass v. Commissioner*, T.C. Memo 1957-227 (1957); and *Stanley L. Wang v. Commissioner*, T.C. Memo 1972-143 (1972). *See also*, Priv. Letter Rul. 200551009. This is because the donee spouse's and the other beneficiaries' interests cannot be ascertained. However, if the trustee is directed (i.e., "shall" in contrast to "may") to make distributions pursuant to an ascertainable standard (*e.g.*, for the donee spouse's health, education, support, and maintenance), the value of the third-party (nonspouse) beneficiaries' interests should be ascertainable. *See*, TAM 9419007; *Estate of Ruth B. Regester v. Commissioner*,

---

[23] *See,* Diana S.C. Zeydel, "Gift-Splitting - A Boondoggle or a Bad Idea? A Comprehensive Look at the Rules," 106 *Journal of Taxation* 334 (June 2007); Laura H. Peebles, "Gift Splitting Made Easy," 143 *Trusts & Estates* 24 (August 2004); and Carmen Irizarry-Diaz, "Effective Use of the Election to Split Gifts," 26 *Tax Management Estates, Gifts and Trusts Journal* 247 (November 8, 2001) ("Irizarry-Diaz").

83 T.C. 1 (1984); Rev. Rul. 79-327, 1979-2 C.B. 342 (which relate to taxable gifts upon the exercise of a limited power of appointment over a trust with ascertainable standards). In such an instance, that portion of the gift could be split with the donee (consenting) spouse. If the donee (consenting) spouse does not have a *Crummey* withdrawal right but the other beneficiaries have *Crummey* withdrawal rights over the gifted property, the amount subject to withdrawal by the other beneficiaries would be ascertainable and eligible for gift splitting. Treas. Reg. §25.2513-1(b)(4).

The amount of the gift that may be split is the value of the property transferred by the donor less the donee (consenting) spouse's ascertainable interest in the property, which is a factual determination. *See*, *Sands G. Falk v. Commissioner*, T.C. Memo 1965-22 (1965).

Merely consenting to split gifts made in trust with the donor spouse does not make the donee (consenting) spouse, who is also a trust beneficiary, a transferor for purposes of the retained interest rules of IRC sections 2035–2038, nor does it make the donee (consenting) spouse a "grantor" for income tax purposes under IRC sections 673-677. IRC section 2513(a)(1); Priv. Letter Rul. 200130030. *See*, Rev. Rul. 82-198, 1982-2 C.B. 206; Rev. Rul. 74-556, 1974-2 C.B. 300; Rev. Rul. 54-246, 1954-1 C.B. 179. However, gift splitting does make the donee spouse a transferor for GST tax purposes as to the one-half of the entire gift amount without regard to the consenting spouse's ascertainable interest in the gift, and the consenting spouse must allocate his or GST tax exemption to the gift amount. *See*, section 5.22, below.

> **Caution:** To avoid the IRC section 2036 trap inherent when an ILIT income beneficiary transfers assets to an ILIT (such as transfers by the grantor and the grantor's spouse, where the spouse is also an ILIT beneficiary), only the grantor should make gifts to the ILIT, and any gifts of the grantor in excess of the IRC section 2503(b) amount should be split with the spouse under IRC section 2513.

> **Practice Point:** Do not split gifts when transferring an existing life insurance policy into generation-skipping ILIT. If the transferor-grantor dies within three years of the transfer, the policy proceeds will be included in his or her estate under IRC section 2035 (thus changing the identity of the transferor for

GST tax purposes) and the consenting spouse's previously allocated GST tax exemption will be lost and wasted, resulting in an inclusion ratio of .50 (instead of 0). The better approach is to not split gifts, but instead have the transferor-grantor allocate his or her GST tax exemption to the trust at the time of the initial transfer of the life insurance policy. Also, although the portion of the gifted property includable in the grantor's gross estate under IRC section 2035 is not included in the consenting spouse's adjustable taxable gifts for purposes of IRC section 2001(b)(i)(B)(b), all future tax liability is determined with regard to the split gifts and the gift tax rate will be based on the prior split gifts.[24]

Practice Point: In describing the amount available for withdrawal by a beneficiary, do not condition the amount on the donor spouse's election to split the gift. Priv. Letter Rul. 8022048. The reason is that the IRS has ruled that the annual exclusion is not available for the spouse's portion of the split gift if the amount of the withdrawal power is conditioned upon the election being made. Priv. Letter Rul. 8044080. Therefore, state that the amount available for withdrawal is based on the assumption that a married donor's spouse will elect to split the gift amount, whether or not the election is made. *See,* Paragraph 3.1(A)(3) of Sample ILIT.

Caution: Once elected, gift splitting applies to all gifts made by either spouse during the calendar year in question. IRC section 2513(a)(2). Also, gift splitting makes both spouses jointly and severally liable for the gift tax. IRC section 2513(d).

§3.11 GIFT TAX CONSEQUENCES OF LAPSE OF A *CRUMMEY* WITHDRAWAL RIGHT

Most ILITs use *Crummey* withdrawal rights to convert a future interest gift into a present interest gift that qualifies for the gift tax annual exclusion under IRC section 2503(b). *See,* section 3.5, above. A *Crummey* withdrawal right is a general power of appointment. IRC sections 2514 and 2041. Be very careful when inserting *Crummey* withdrawal rights in an amount greater than $5,000 or

---

[24] *See,* Irizarry-Diaz at 254-255.

5% of the value of the trust assets. IRC section 2514(b) indicates that the exercise or release of a general power of appointment will be treated as a transfer by the individual who released the power. Under IRC section 2514(e), a *lapse* of a power of appointment is considered a release. A specific exception to this rule is set forth under IRC sections 2514(e)(1) and (2), which state that the *lapse* of a power (in contrast to a *release* or a *waiver* of the power) not exceeding $5,000 or 5% of the value of the assets out of which the power can be satisfied, will not be treated as a transfer. What this means is that a lapse of a *Crummey* withdrawal right in excess of the five-by-five limits will be treated as a transfer to the other trust beneficiaries by the *Crummey* withdrawal beneficiary. Furthermore, if the lapse of the excess amount is a completed gift, the withdrawal right beneficiary's retained interest in the excess amount will be valued at $0 for gift tax purposes if the remainder beneficiaries/donees of the excess amount are members of the withdrawal right beneficiary's family. IRC section 2702(a)(2). Priv. Letter Rul. 9804047. A lapsed withdrawal right within the five-by-five limits will continue to be treated as a transfer by the donor.

A lapse in excess of the five-by-five statutory protection amount can cause disastrous estate, gift, and GST tax consequences. For example, if a trust was established with an initial gift contribution of $11,000, and the spouse was the only *Crummey* withdrawal right beneficiary and was given an $11,000 withdrawal right that lapsed, the spouse would be deemed to be the transferor (for gift tax purposes) of the amount of the withdrawal right in excess of $5,000, to wit, $6,000. In this example the spouse would be the deemed transferor of 55% of the trust assets ($6,000 excess ÷ $11,000 trust value) and because the spouse held a life interest in the trust, 55% of the trust assets would be includable in the spouse's estate for federal estate tax purposes. Treas. Reg. §20.2041-3(d)(4). Furthermore, the spouse would also be a transferor for GST purposes over the $6,000 and the grantor's previously allocated GST tax exemption would be lost and wasted. This would require the spouse to allocate his or her GST tax exemption to maintain a zero inclusion ratio. Treas. Reg. §26.2652-1(a)(5) Example 5. Because of the ETIP rules contained in Treas. Reg. §26.2632-1(c)(2) (*see*, section 5.17, below), the spouse cannot effectively allocate GST tax exemption until the close of the ETIP. This may result in a larger amount of GST tax exemption having to be allocated, especially if the ETIP ends on the insured's death (and the life insurance policy "matures"). Another potential problem because of the ETIP rules, is that the grantor's GST tax exemption may not be allocated effectively until the close of the spouse's ETIP. These potential GST and estate tax issues underscore the need for making sure that *Crummey* withdrawal rights lapse within the annual five-by-five safe harbor amounts.

§3.11(a) Apply The Five-By-Five Safe Harbor Lapse Amount Against The Entire ILIT Trust Estate

The 5% portion of the five-by-five safe harbor lapse amount under IRC section 2514 is measured against "the aggregate value of the assets out of which, or the proceeds of which, the exercise of the lapse power could be satisfied." IRC section 2514(e)(2). Thus, to obtain the largest 5% lapse protection amount, the 5% should be measured against the entire trust estate, and not against the amount of the periodic gift contribution. *See*, Paragraph 3.2(L) of Sample ILIT. *See*, section 3.17, below, concerning the aggregation of multiple *Crummey* withdrawal rights held by a beneficiary.

§3.11(b) Limiting The Beneficiary's *Crummey* Withdrawal Right

Because a lapse in excess of five-by-five constitutes a taxable release by the powerholder, it is usually best to limit a beneficiary's *Crummey* withdrawal right amount to the lesser of: (1) the gift contribution amount; or (2) the greater of five-by-five. This will ensure that when the withdrawal right lapses it will fall within the safe harbor amount of IRC section 2514(e).[25] Without such a limitation on

---

[25] According to Rev. Proc. 2007-3, 2007-1 I.R.B. 108, section 4.01(46), the IRS will ordinarily not issue a private letter ruling concerning: "If the beneficiaries of a trust permit a power of withdrawal to lapse, whether section 2514(e) will be applicable to each beneficiary in regard to the power when (i) the trust corpus consists or will consist substantially of insurance policies on the life of the grantor or the grantor's spouse, (ii) the trustee or any other person has a power to apply the trust's income or corpus to the payment of premiums on policies of insurance on the life of the grantor or the grantor's spouse, (iii) the trustee or any other person has a power to use the trust's assets to make loans to the grantor's estate or to purchase assets from the grantor's estate, (iv) the trust beneficiaries have the power to withdraw, on demand, any additional transfers made to the trust, and (v) there is a right or power in any person that would cause the grantor to be treated as the owner of all or a portion of the trust under sections 673 to 677."

the amount of the *Crummey* withdrawal right, the lapse of the withdrawal right in excess of five-by-five (absent a hanging *Crummey* power (*see*, section 3.13, below) or the beneficiary having a separate trust share and holding a testamentary power of appointment over the amount of the withdrawal right in excess of five-by-five (*see*, section 3.12, below))[26] will constitute both a taxable release under IRC section 2514(b) and an immediate gift of a future interest to the other ILIT beneficiaries by the powerholder.

§3.12 AVOID TAXABLE RELEASE OF A *CRUMMEY* WITHDRAWAL RIGHT BY CREATING SEPARATE TRUST SHARES WITH TESTAMENTARY CONTROLS

One way to deal with a *Crummey* withdrawal right beneficiary's potential taxable release and a completed gift of a future interest to other ILIT beneficiaries problem (*see*, section 3.11, above) is to initially establish separate trust shares for each ILIT beneficiary and give the beneficiary a testamentary limited power of appointment over his or her trust share for the amount in excess of the five-by-five safe harbor amount. This will prevent the lapsed amount in excess of five-by-five from being a completed gift to the other trust beneficiaries. Treas. Reg. §25.2511-2(b); Priv. Letter Ruls. 9030005, 8517052, 8229097, 8142061, and 8011123. However, the separate-trust share coupled with a testamentary limited power of appointment will not avoid the taxable release problem of IRC section 2514(e). Consequently, when the beneficiary dies, the assets over which the beneficiary retained a testamentary limited power of appointment (i.e., the amounts in excess of five-by-five) will be included in the beneficiary's gross estate under IRC section 2041(a)(2). Additionally, because the beneficiary has a retained interest in the separate trust share, all or a portion of the value of the trust share will be included in the beneficiary's gross estate upon his or her death. IRC section 2036(a); Treas. Reg. §20.2041-3(d)(4).

---

[26] Treas. Reg. §25.2511-2(b) and Priv. Letter Rul. 9030005. When the beneficiary dies, however, the assets subject to the taxable release over which the beneficiary retained a power of appointment (even a testamentary limited power of appointment) will be includable in the beneficiary's gross estate. IRC sections 2038 and 2041(a)(2).

The effect of cumulative taxable releases with a retained interest by the beneficiary may result in all (or a significant portion) of the beneficiary's separate trust share being included in his or her gross estate. Treas. Reg. §20.2041-3(d)(5). Furthermore, the beneficiary will become the (new) transferor for GST tax purposes of the trust share that is includable in his or her gross estate, thus wasting any GST tax exemption that was previously allocated to the trust share. IRC section 2652(a)(1); Treas. Reg. §26.2652-1(a)(2). *See*, section 5.10, below. Generally, the testamentary limited power of appointment approach will work best in ILITs where:

(1) The grantor's spouse is not a beneficiary;

(2) The ILIT is not designed to be a long-term generation skipping dynasty trust;

(3) There is a single trust with a single beneficiary (or there are separate trust shares for each beneficiary who possess a *Crummey* withdrawal right); and

(4) The beneficiary's estate would most likely incur little or no federal estate tax (because of its modest size) if the beneficiary were to die before the termination of his or her interest in the ILIT.

Practice Point: An alternative to separate trust shares with testamentary limited powers of appointment, is to use a vested trust for the benefit of a sole beneficiary and have all of the trust property be includable in the beneficiary's gross estate when he or she dies. This can be accomplished by granting a testamentary general power of appointment to the beneficiary over his or her trust share or by having the trust share be paid to the beneficiary's estate. *See,* Priv. Letter Ruls. 8545076 and 8517052 (testamentary general power of appointment granted to beneficiary over his trust share). In Priv. Letter Rul. 8142061, the IRS ruled "where the trust instrument provides that the sole-beneficiary or his estate will receive the trust-corpus, the lapse of the annual demand right (or its release) will not result in a taxable gift as a result of the lapse (or release) of such general power of appointment." However, if the insured's desire is to avoid the policy's inclusion in the beneficiary's gross estate, this arrangement will not be viable.

§3.13 AVOID TAXABLE RELEASE OF A *CRUMMEY* WITHDRAWAL RIGHT BY USING A HANGING *CRUMMEY* POWER

Another way to deal with a *Crummey* withdrawal right beneficiary's potential taxable release and completed gift of a future interest to other ILIT beneficiaries problem (*see*, section 3.11, above) is to allow the beneficiary's *Crummey* withdrawal right to continue with regard to any amount in excess of the five-by-five safe harbor amount, and allow the excess amount to annually lapse within the five-by-five safe harbor amount.[27] This is known as a hanging

[27] A *Crummey* withdrawal right converts a gift of a future interest to an ILIT into a gift of a present interest that is eligible for the gift tax annual exclusion under IRC section 2503(b). The beneficiary's right to withdraw the gift amount is non-cumulative and completely lapses at the end of the specified time period (typically 30 days after the gift is made to the ILIT). In order for the withdrawal right to lapse completely, the *Crummey* withdrawal right amount granted to the beneficiary has to be limited to the greater of $5,000 or 5% of the value of the trust's assets ("five-by-five"). This is in contrast to a hanging *Crummey* power, which permits annual exclusion gifts greater than the five-by-five amount. Under a hanging *Crummey* power, the (larger) gift amount lapses annually at the rate of five-by-five, and the beneficiary has a continuing (i.e., cumulative) right to withdraw the gift amount that is in excess of the five-by-five lapse amount. A hanging *Crummey* power provides for the gift amount in excess of five-by-five to lapse annually within the safe harbor amounts under IRC section 2514. The beneficiary's continuing right of withdrawal ends when the gift amount completely lapses—typically several years or more after the gift is made. For example, if a married grantor gifts $60,000 to an ILIT in 2007 (and makes no further gifts to the ILIT) and his two children have *Crummey* withdrawal rights over their pro-rata share of the $60,000 gift, only $48,000 ($24,000/child) will be eligible for the gift tax annual exclusion (assuming gift splitting under IRC section 2513). The remaining $12,000 (which is the amount that exceeds the gift tax annual exclusion amount available to the grantor under gift splitting) will be subject to gift tax, and will not be subject to a *Crummey* withdrawal right or a hanging *Crummey* power. If the children have a hanging *Crummey* power, the $24,000 gift amount allocable to the child will be eligible for the gift tax annual exclusion under IRC sections 2503(b) and 2513. As a result of the hanging *Crummey* power, each child will have the right to withdraw the full $24,000 amount in 2007. If not withdrawn, the $24,000 gift amount will lapse annually at the rate of five-by-five. Thus, in 2007, $5,000 of the $24,000 amount per child will lapse, and each child will have a continuing right to withdraw $19,000. In 2008, an additional $5,000 will lapse and each child will have the continuing right to withdraw $14,000. In 2009, an additional $5,000 will lapse and each child will have the continuing right to withdraw $9,000, etc. In 2011, the initial $24,000 gift amount will have completely lapsed and each child's continuing right of withdraw will cease.

Crummey withdrawal right (or a hanging *Crummey* power).[28] *See,* Paragraph 3.2 (D) (alternative 2) of Sample ILIT. A hanging *Crummey* withdrawal right allows the beneficiary to withdraw up to the gift tax annual exclusion amount (or twice that amount if there is gift splitting under IRC section 2513). Under a hanging *Crummey* power, the beneficiary has a continuing right to withdraw the amount of the gift that has not lapsed.[29] In some instances, the beneficiary may have a continuing right of withdrawal that will last for several years. Under a hanging *Crummey* power, any amount that is not withdrawn each year by the beneficiary will automatically lapse (typically on January 31 or December 31 of the year in question) within the safe harbor amounts of 5% or $5,000, per IRC section 2514(e).

Although the IRS has not favorably ruled on the use of hanging *Crummey* powers, the one ruling on this issue seems to suggest that if the hanging power is not drafted as a condition subsequent, it should be effective. Priv. Letter Rul. 8901004. A spouse should never be given a hanging *Crummey* power in a generation-skipping trust, because the spouse's power may be deemed to create an Estate Tax Inclusion Period ("ETIP") under IRC section 2642(f), which will prevent the grantor from allocating his or her GST tax exemption to the ILIT until the close of the ETIP. *See,* section 5.17, below.

The purpose of a hanging *Crummey* power is twofold. First, a hanging *Crummey* power permits larger ILIT contribution amounts that qualify for the gift tax exclusion annual amount. Second, a hanging *Crummey* power avoids adverse estate and gift tax consequences under IRC sections 2514(b) and 2036(a) to the ILIT beneficiaries who hold *Crummey* withdrawal rights. This is achieved by having the beneficiary's withdrawal right be a cumulative power of withdrawal that lapses every calendar year in the amount specified in IRC sections 2514(e)(1) and (2).

There are two disadvantages to using a hanging *Crummey* power. First, the beneficiary has a continuing right of withdrawal that he or she can exercise at any time (even though the gift amount that

---

[28] *See,* footnote to section 10.2, below, for a discussion of Circular 230 and hanging *Crummey* powers.

[29] The beneficiary's continuing right of withdrawal with respect to the gift amount is known as a "cumulative right of withdrawal."

is subject to the continuing right of withdrawal has been used by the trustee to pay life insurance premiums). This potential issue can be mitigated by requiring a disinterested or independent trustee (who is not an adverse party or the creator of the power) to consent to the beneficiary's exercise of his or her continuing right of withdrawal.[30] *See*, Paragraph 3.2(D) (alternate 2) of Sample ILIT. The consent of a disinterested or independent trustee over the unlapsed portion of the gift amount does not cause the gift to be a gift of a future interest. This is because beneficiary could have withdrawn the full gift amount in the year of the gift. Also, the consent of the disinterested or independent trustee does not cause the beneficiary's right of withdrawal to be illusory or to be treated as a non-general power of appointment. *See*, IRC section 2514(c)(3). Second, if a beneficiary dies while possessing a hanging power that has not fully lapsed, the value of the unlapsed hanging power will be included in the beneficiary's gross estate. IRC section 2041(a)(2). The beneficiary will also become the (new) transferor for GST purposes of the ILIT amount included in his or her estate, and the beneficiary's executor may need to allocate GST tax exemption to the included amount.

A hanging *Crummey* withdrawal right works best where:

(1) The ILIT holds sufficient assets to absorb the hanging (unlapsed) amount, i.e., either the 5% of the five-by-five safe harbor lapse amount is increasing each year;

---

[30] "Although it may not be the intention that any beneficiary actually exercise the [*Crummey*] power (no implied understanding, please), the occasional beneficiary will give it a whirl. One suggested way to cope with this possibility is to require the consent of another person (such as the trustee) with respect to the portion that hangs beyond the original *Crummey* withdrawal period. If the consenter is a person who is not the creator of the trust and who has no substantial interest in the trust adverse to the exercise of the hanging power, the power should continue to be a general power of appointment with respect to the powerholder. [IRC section 2041(b)(1)(C); *see*, Rev. Rul. 82-156, 1982-2 C.B. 216.] Accordingly, no lapse of a general power of appointment should occur by requiring consent to the exercise of the hanging power. Consent may not be required for purposes of exercising the original *Crummey* power without violating the present interest rule. [*See*, Treas. Reg. §25.2503-3(b) (only an unrestricted right to immediate use, possession, or enjoyment of property is a present interest).] However, after the initial withdrawal period, the continuing withdrawal right that avoids the lapse of a general power could require consent for its exercise." Diana S. C. Zeydel, "How to Create and Administer a Successful Irrevocable Life Insurance Trust," 34 *Estate Planning* 3, 12-13 (June 2007).

(2) The ILIT holds a quick (or limited) pay life insurance policy or a "vanishing premium" policy,[31] neither of which require continuing premium payments during the insured's lifetime[32]; or

(3) The ILIT continues for a substantial time after the insured's death so that the handing power amount can lapse. *See*, Paragraph 3.2(E) of Sample ILIT.

§3.14 GIFT TAX CONSEQUENCES OF AN UNLAPSED *CRUMMEY* WITHDRAWAL RIGHT

There are no gift tax consequences to a beneficiary while he or she holds a *Crummey* withdrawal right that has not yet lapsed.

§3.15 GIFT TAX CONSEQUENCES OF WAIVER OR RELEASE OF A *CRUMMEY* WITHDRAWAL RIGHT

Because a *Crummey* withdrawal right is a general power of appointment, a beneficiary's waiver of the right of withdrawal constitutes a taxable release (and not a lapse) of a general power of appointment and constitutes a taxable gift of a future interest to the other trust beneficiaries. IRC section 2514(b). To avoid this adverse tax consequence, the beneficiary should not waive the right to withdraw the ILIT contribution. Instead, the beneficiary should merely permit the right of withdrawal to lapse. Also, a lapse of a beneficiary's *Crummey* withdrawal right in excess of five-by-five constitutes a taxable release of a general power of appointment and constitutes a taxable gift of a future interest to the other trust beneficiaries. To avoid *this* adverse tax consequence, the beneficiary's right of withdrawal should either be limited to five-by-five (*See*, Alternative 1 to Paragraph 3.2(D) of Sample ILIT) or be subject to continuing lapse under a hanging

---

[31] *See*, section 16.1(b), below, concerning limited pay policies and "vanishing premium" policies.

[32] The use of more *Crummey* withdrawal right beneficiaries and/or larger gifts to the ILIT makes the 5% safe harbor amount increase more with respect to each beneficiary's hanging *Crummey* withdrawal right. Substantial funding of the ILIT will also increase the 5% safe harbor lapse amount. For example, if the trust estate has a value of $300,000, the 5% lapse amount is $15,000 (which, in 2006 is $3,000 greater than the annual gift tax exclusion amount). If the trust estate has a value of $1,000,000 the 5% lapse amount is $50,000, etc. Thus, "super funding" the ILIT will permit larger amounts of annual gifts to lapse within the five-by-five safe harbor.

power of withdrawal that lapses annually at the rate of five-by-five (*See*, Alternative 2 to Paragraph 3.2(D) of Sample ILIT).

§3.16 GIFT TAX CONSEQUENCES OF THE DELAWARE TAX TRAP

If in exercising an inter-vivos non-general power of appointment created after October 21, 1942, another power of appointment (general or non-general) is created, which under applicable local law can be validly exercised so as to postpone the vesting of the appointed property or suspend the absolute ownership or power of alienation of such property, for a period ascertainable without regard to the date of the creation of the first power (i.e., extend the original perpetuities period with respect to the appointed property), the exercise of the inter-vivos non-general power of appointment will be treated as the exercise of an inter-vivos general power of appointment by the donee, and will result in a taxable gift being made by the donee. IRC section 2514(d). (The donee will also become the (new) transferor of the appointed property for GST tax purposes).[33] *See*, Paragraph 8.1(A) of Sample ILIT, which negates the occurrence of the trap.

---

[33] *See*, Stephen E. Greer, "The Delaware Tax Trap and the Abolition of the Rule Against Perpetuities," 28 *Estate Planning* 68 (February 2001); and Jesse Dukeminier, "The Uniform Statutory Rule Against Perpetuities And The GST Tax: New Perils For Practitioners And New Opportunities," 30 *Real Property, Probate and Trust Journal* 185 (Summer 1995). Mr. Greer posits that the Delaware Tax Trap may be applicable in states that have abolished the rule against perpetuities but have no rule against the suspension of the power of alienation. This is in contrast to states that have merely extended the length of time for vesting from a life in being plus 21 years to a longer period of time, such as 360 years (Florida) or states that have "repealed the Perpetuities Rule and have adopted instead a rule against the suspension of the power of alienation, but specify that the power of alienation is not suspended if the trustee has a power of sale, e.g., Idaho, South Dakota, Wisconsin, Delaware, Missouri, New Hampshire and New Jersey. In a jurisdiction that abolished the rule against perpetuities and has no rule against the suspension of the power of alienation, there is no stated period of time within which a property interest must vest. When a power of appointment is exercised to create a successive nongeneral power of appointment, the property subject to this power will have its vesting postponed for a period of time that can not be ascertained by referring back to the date of the instrument creating the first power of appointment....Thus, if trust property is subject to the exercise of a nongeneral power of appointment, the exercise of that power to create a trust giving the beneficiaries nongeneral powers of appointment renders

§3.17 LIMIT ON ANNUAL FIVE-BY-FIVE SAFE HARBOR LAPSE AMOUNT FOR A BENEFICIARY WITH MULTIPLE *CRUMMEY* WITHDRAWAL RIGHTS

Rev. Rul. 85-88, 1985-2 C.B. 201, holds that only one five-by-five safe harbor lapse is permitted per calendar year per donee for all powers of withdrawal (granted under all trusts) available to that donee during the year. Multiple withdrawal rights held by the same donee over the same or different trusts that are also subject to a five-by-five lapse must be aggregated to determine whether they violate the five-by-five safe harbor amount.[34] *See also*, G.C.M. 39371 (1985). In this regard the ILIT can contain an ordering rule for a donee who holds multiple withdrawal rights that are subject to a five-by-five lapse.[35] The ILIT can provide that the donee's unexer-

---

that property subject to estate tax or gift tax [under the Delaware Tax Trap]. The solution for states that have this problem is to introduce an Alienation statute or, alternatively, to merely extend the permissible period when non-vested interests must vest and the time in which nongeneral and general testamentary powers of appointment may be exercised. It is this latter course of action that Alaska and Florida have chosen. Alaska extended its perpetuities period to 1,000 years but only in the limited circumstance of the time in which a nongeneral and general testamentary power of appointment must be exercised and the time in which property subject to the exercise of these powers must vest. Florida amended its USRAP provisions by extending the permissible 'wait and see' period to 360 years." *Id.* (Citations omitted). *See also*, sections 1.7 and 1.10, above.

[34] "For example, suppose B has the power to withdraw $20,000 from the corpus of one trust, and the power lapses on June 1, when the trust corpus is worth $300,000. If B has a second non-cumulative power to withdraw $20,000 from the corpus of the same trust, and such power lapses on December 1, when the value of the trust corpus has appreciated to $400,000, then the maximum amount of trust assets subject to B's withdrawal power at the time of any lapse during the calendar year would be $400,000, and the amount of B's 5-and-5 exemption for the year would be $20,000 (5% x $400,000). On the other hand, ***if B's second withdrawal power in the example is exercisable only with respect to a second, separate trust, B's 5-and-5 exemption for the year would be $35,000 (4% x $700,000).***" Rev. Rul. 85-88, 1985-2 C.B. 201. (Emphasis added.)

[35] Not all *Crummey* withdrawal rights are subject to a five-by-five lapse. For example, a *Crummey* withdrawal right in an IRC section 2642(c) trust does not need to contain a five-by-five lapse provision concerning the primary beneficiary because the amount subject to withdrawal by the primary beneficiary will be includable in his or her gross estate when he or she dies, either through a testamentary general power of appointment that is given to the primary beneficiary, or by requiring the trust residue to be paid to the primary beneficiary's estate upon his or her death. IRC section 2642(c)(2)(B).

cised withdrawal right in the ILIT property shall lapse after all other unexercised withdrawal rights previously granted to the donee (whether under the ILIT or another instrument) have lapsed. Alternatively, the ILIT can provide that all unexercised withdrawal rights held by the donee shall be aggregated to determine the maximum amount that can lapse within the five-by-five safe harbor provisions of IRC sections 2514(e)(1) and (2).[36] *See*, Paragraph 3.2(L) of Sample ILIT.

§3.18 GIFT TAX CONSEQUENCES OF GRANTOR'S PAYMENT OF ILIT'S INCOME TAXES

The payment of a defective grantor trust's income tax liability by the grantor does not result in the grantor making an additional gift to the trust beneficiaries. Rev. Rul. 2004-64, 2004-27 I.R.B. 7. However, the grantor's right to be reimbursed by the trust for the payment of the incomes taxes (including a discretionary right to reimbursement), may have adverse estate tax consequences to the grantor. *See*, section 4.2(b), below.

---

[36] David A. Handler, Esq. of Kirkland and Ellis recommends granting beneficiaries of other irrevocable trusts "nominal" annual withdrawal rights that can be aggregated with the same beneficiaries' withdrawal rights under the ILIT. According to David, "The IRS has ruled that in applying the '5 and 5 rule' of Section 2514, the 5% is the total amount out of which the beneficiary's withdrawal rights under all trusts can be satisfied. Rev. Rul. 85-88, 1985-2 C.B. 201 (Jan. 1, 1985). So, if a $22,000 initial gift is made to a trust [such as an ILIT] that gives the beneficiary a withdrawal right, it can lapse by $5,000 per year. However, if another trust with $2 million [such as an irrevocable inter-vivos dynasty trust] gives the same beneficiary the right to withdraw $1,000 per year with such right lapsing each year, then the total amount out of which the beneficiary's withdrawal rights can be satisfied from both trusts is $2,022,000. Five percent of that amount is $101,100, so that the total amount of withdrawal rights that can lapse for the beneficiary under the 5 and 5 rule is $101,100. By giving the beneficiary the right to withdraw $1,000 from a large trust under this provision, it allows his larger withdrawal right from a smaller trust to fully lapse after 30 days under the '5 and 5' rule. The lapse will not be a deemed gift nor mess up GST exemption allocations. This [technique] could eliminate hanging [*Crummey*] withdrawal rights." David A. Handler and Deborah V. Dunn, *Drafting the Estate Plan: Law and Forms,* (CCH), tax.cchgroup.com, 800-248-3248.

David suggests the following sample language for the large trust (which has been adapted by the author, and needs to be appropriately adapted by the practitioner):

§3.19 GIFT TAX CONSEQUENCES OF LIFE INSURANCE PROCEEDS PAID TO NON-OWNER

If the beneficiary of the life insurance policy is not the owner of the policy, the owner will be deemed to have made a gift of the life insurance proceeds to the beneficiary to the extent of any interest not retained by the owner. If the policy owner's spouse is the beneficiary of the policy, the proceeds may qualify for the unlimited marital deduction pursuant to IRC section 2056. *Adele F. Goodman v. Commissioner*, 4 T.C. 191 (1944), *aff'd*, 156 F.2d 218 (2d Cir. 1946); Rev. Rul. 81-166, 1981-1 C.B. 477; Rev. Rul. 77-48, 1977-1 C.B. 292. Thus, if an ILIT is the owner of the life insurance policy, the ILIT should be the beneficiary of the policy.

---

*"**Special Withdrawal Rights.** If (1) a contribution (as hereinafter defined) is made to another trust (i.e., to a trust not established under this Agreement) of which a beneficiary of this Agreement is also a beneficiary of the other trust, and (2) as a result of such contribution to the other trust, the beneficiary is granted the right to withdraw all or a portion of such contribution from the other trust, and (3) this Agreement does not, in the first instance, otherwise grant the beneficiary a right to withdraw property from the initial trust established under this Agreement, then and in that event, commencing with the date such contribution is made to the other trust, the beneficiary shall have the non-cumulative right to withdraw One Thousand Dollars ($1,000) of property from the initial trust under this Agreement. The beneficiary's right to withdraw the $1,000, if not exercised within 45 days from the date of the contribution to the other trust, shall thereafter lapse. The beneficiary may exercise his or her $1,000 withdrawal right by delivering written notice of such exercise to the trustee of the initial trust within the aforesaid 45 days."*

4

Estate Tax Issues[1]

CHAPTER OVERVIEW

One of the primary reasons for creating an ILIT is to keep life insurance proceeds out of the insured's gross estate for federal estate tax purposes. *See,* section 1.1, above. This chapter discusses the many ways an ILIT can fail to accomplish that purpose, and how to avoid those types of issues. The chapter also discusses selected key estate tax issues concerning life insurance.[2]

There are numerous estate tax "retained" interest traps, as well as incidents of ownership and general powers of appointment issues that must be examined when drafting an ILIT.[3] If the grantor-

---

[1] The author gratefully acknowledges the contribution of Mary Ann Mancini, Esq. of Bryan Cave, LLP of Washington, DC in the writing of this chapter.

The chapter does not discuss all of the estate tax aspects of life insurance, only selected aspects. For example, if the decedent owns an insurance policy on the life of another person, the value of the policy is includable in the decedent's gross estate under IRC section 2033.

[2] *See,* Chapter 3 of Howard M. Zaritsky & Stephan R. Leimberg, *Tax Planning With Life Insurance: Analysis With Forms—2d Edition,* Warren, Gorham & Lamont, Boston, Massachusetts (Supp. 2007) for an overview of the estate taxation of life insurance.

[3] *See,* Dodge, 50-5th T.M., *Transfers with Retained Interests and Powers,* Bureau of National Affairs, Washington, DC, for a detailed discussion of retained interests under IRC section 2036 - 2038.

IRC sections 2036 and 2038 are valuation sections and do not physically return the asset to the grantor's estate. Thus, the grantor's estate cannot claim a marital deduction for the increased value unless the interest subject to IRC sections 2036 or 2038 went to the surviving spouse in a manner that qualifies for the marital deduction.

insured is married and is the sole insured, certain "safety nets" can be placed in the ILIT to minimize adverse estate tax consequences, particularly if the grantor dies within three years of transferring an existing policy to the ILIT. Also, gifts made to an ILIT by the grantor can create income, estate, gift, and GST tax problems for the trust beneficiary if the beneficiary dies or if the right of withdrawal is not properly drafted. This chapter discusses the estate tax implications of these issues.

§4.1 ESTATE TAX CONSEQUENCES OF INSURED'S TRANSFER OF LIFE INSURANCE WITHIN THREE YEARS OF DEATH

Although the "deemed transfer" rule[4] and the three-year "transfer in contemplation of death" rule[5] has, since 1981, been eliminated with respect to most gifts, the insured's transfer of an incident of ownership in a life insurance policy within three years of the insured's death for less than full and adequate consideration will result in some or all[6] of the life insurance policy being includable in the

---

[4] *See,* section 1.4(a), above, concerning the abolition of the deemed transfer rule.

[5] *See,* Brody, Althauser, and English, 818 T.M., *Section 2035 Transfers,* Bureau of National Affairs, Washington, DC for a detailed discussion of IRC section 2035.

Prior to 1977, gifts made within three years of death were includible in the gross estate if they were made in contemplation of death. This resulted in the grantor's estate and the IRS having to ascertain the (now deceased) grantor's subjective intent at the time of the gift.

[6] *See, Estate of Morris R. Silverman v. Commissioner,* 61 T.C. 338 (1973), *aff'd on other grounds,* 521 F.2d 574 (2d Cir. 1975), *acq.,* 1978-1 C.B. 2 for determining the percentage of policy proceeds that are includable in the insured's gross estate after a policy has been transferred and the transferee pays the premiums with his or her own money (and not with money supplied by the insured). *See also,* TAM 9128008; Priv. Letter Rul. 8724014; *Estate of Sidney M. Friedberg v. Commissioner,* T.C. Memo 1992-310; GCM 38110 (9/25/79); GCM 37695 (9/27/78) (concerning transfer of policy subject to Texas community property law).

Under the *Silverman* rule, a cautious insured will have the transferee of the policy pay the premiums for the first three years after the insured transfers the policy (for less than full and adequate consideration) to the transferee. This will minimize the amount of the life insurance proceeds that are includable in the insured's gross estate if the insured dies within three years of the policy's transfer.

insured's gross estate.[7] IRC section 2035(a); Priv. Letter Rul. 200432015. *See also*, IRC section 2043. If a grantor gratuitously transfers an interest in property or relinquishes a power in property (including the relinquishment of a general power of appointment) for less than full and adequate consideration within three years of his or her death, (which power or interest would have been included in the grantor's gross estate under IRC sections 2036, 2037, 2038 or 2042 but for the grantor's disposition or relinquishment of that interest or power), IRC section 2035 will cause the federal estate tax value of the property (or interest therein) to be includable in the grantor's gross estate.[8] *Estate of Helen Ward DeWitt*, T.C. Memo

---

[7] If the insured gratuitously transfers the policy and lives for more than three years, the policy proceeds will not be includable in the insured's gross estate under IRC section 2035. Therefore, when transferring an existing policy, the insured should make sure that the life insurance company actually transfers the policy and follows the insured's instructions. There have been several instances where it was discovered shortly before the insured's death (but more than three years after the initial request for the policy transfer) that the carrier had not completed the paperwork and still showed the insured as the owner. To successfully avoid the application of IRC section 2042 (incidents of ownership) and IRC section 2035 to the insured's estate, the insured's estate's (or the IRS) have requested private rulings, which have been granted. *See*, TAM 9651004 where the IRS ruled that the provisions of the life insurance policy (the "policy facts") were rebutted by documentary evidence that corroborated the insured's intent (the "intent facts") to transfer the policy's ownership and change the beneficiary designation more than three years prior to the insured's death. In Priv. Letter Rul. 200603002 the IRS ruled that the "intent facts" rebutted the "policy facts," and recognized the insureds' reformation of a second to die life insurance policy to reflect their ILIT as the policy owner. The IRS ruled that the reformation and assignment would not be a transfer subject to gift tax, and that if the insureds died within three years of the policy's reformation and assignment to their ILIT, the life insurance proceeds would not be includable in their gross estates under IRC section 2035. In Priv. Letter Rul. 8610068 the IRS ruled that the "intent facts" showed that the decedent's corporation (and not the decedent) was supposed to be the named beneficiary of the policy, and therefore the proceeds were not includable in the decedent's gross estate under IRC section 2042. *See*, section I,C,4 of Budin, 826 T.M., *Life Insurance*, Bureau of National Affairs, Washington, DC for a discussion of the "policy facts" doctrine and its exceptions.

[8] The three-year rule of IRC section 2035(a) concerning the grantor's disposition of an interest under IRC section 2036, 2037, and 2038 is not applicable to the grantor's original "retained" interest per se (since the grantor's retention of an interest in the property is already subject to inclusion in the grantor's gross estate under IRC sections 2036, 2037, 2038). Rather, IRC section 2035(a) is applicable to the

1994-552 (1994). *See, also,* Treas. Reg. §20.2041-3(d). Also, any gift taxes paid by the grantor (or by the donee under the terms of a net gift) within three years of death are includable in the grantor's gross estate. IRC section 2035(b). *Estate of Samuel C. Sach v. Commissioner of Internal Revenue,* 88 T.C .769 (1987), *aff'd on this issue,* 856 F.2d 1158 (8th Cir. 1988). *See,* TAM 200432106 (which held that the three-year rule starts on the date of the transfer, rather than the first day after the transfer).

If the life insurance policy is initially acquired directly by a third party (such as an ILIT), without any incidents of ownership in the insured, the proceeds will not be included in the insured's estate, even if the insured pays all of the premiums and dies within three years of the acquisition of the policy.[9]

IRC section 2035(d) provides that life insurance transferred for full and adequate consideration in money or money's worth is not includable under the three-year rule. If new insurance cannot be obtained, the transfer of cash to an ILIT that contains grantor trust provisions and the purchase of the existing policy by that ILIT for

---

grantor's subsequent divestment or relinquishment of the "retained" interest within three years prior to the grantor's death for less than full and adequate consideration. Thus, a "lapse" or "cessation" of the grantor's retained interest, such as the expiration of the grantor's interest in a grantor retained annuity trust (GRAT) or a qualified personal residence trust (QPRT) at the end of the GRAT or QPRT's term (as specified in the trust agreement), is not subject to the three-year rule of IRC section 2035(a). Note, however, that IRC section 2036(b)(3) has its own special three-year rule concerning the termination of the grantor's retained voting rights in a controlled corporation, including voting rights held by the grantor as a trustee. Under IRC section 2036(b)(3) a "lapse," "cessation," or "expiration" of the grantor's voting rights in a controlled corporation is subject to the three-year rule of IRC section 2035(a). Therefore, to avoid inclusion under IRC section 2035(a) and 2036(b), any voting rights retained by the grantor in a controlled corporation must be relinquished more than three years prior to the grantor's death. Thus, if the grantor of a GRAT has the right, as a trustee or co-trustee, to vote IRC section 2036(b) stock held by the GRAT, the grantor would have to cease serving as trustee at least three years before his or her death to avoid the value of the stock's inclusion in his or her gross estate. The termination of the GRAT's term does not in and of itself cause the special three-year rule of IRC section 2036(b)(3) to cease.

[9] *See,* section 12.9, below, for a discussion of whether a trust can have an insurable interest in the life of the another person, such as the grantor of the ILIT, and the unresolved issues created by *Chawla v. Transamerica Occidental Life* Ins. Co., 440 F.3d 639 (4th Cir. 2006), *aff'g in part, vac'g in part,* 2005 WL 405405 (E.D. Va. Feb. 3, 2005).

the policy's fair market value should avoid the three-year rule and transfer for value rule.[10] Pvt. Letter Rul. 9413045. (*See,* transfer for value discussion under section 2.1(a)(2), above.)

Transfer of a life insurance policy to an ILIT may be a completed gift for gift tax purposes, even though the policy ultimately is included in the grantor's gross estate under IRC section 2035. Furthermore, the possibility that the policy proceeds might be payable to the deceased grantor's revocable trust if the proceeds are determined to be includable in the grantor's gross estate is not sufficient retention of dominion and control by the grantor such that the initial gift of the life insurance policy to the ILIT will be considered as incomplete for gift tax purposes. TAM 9533001.

> **Practice Point:** If the insured transfers a policy to an ILIT, the consequences of IRC section 2035 can be mitigated by having the ILIT buy term insurance for a three-year period in an amount equal to the potential federal estate tax liability. Once the IRC section 2035 period has ended, the ILIT can cancel the term insurance.
>
> **Practice Point:** If the ILIT insures only the grantor (and not the grantor's spouse) and the grantor's spouse is a beneficiary of the ILIT, a contingent marital deduction trust contained in the ILIT can also be used to mitigate the effects of IRC section 2035. *See,* section 11.3, below.
>
> **Practice Point:** The gratuitous transfer of an employer provided group term life insurance policy to an ILIT is subject to IRC section 2035. Rev. Rul. 82-15, 1982-1 C.B. 132.
>
> **Practice Point:** The gratuitous transfer of a life insurance policy to an insured's limited liability company is subject to IRC section 2035. TAM 200432015.
>
> **Practice Point:** The gratuitous transfer of a life insurance policy by an insured's closely held corporation may be subject to IRC section 2035. Treas. Reg. §20.2042-1(c)(6); Rev. Rul. 82-141, 1982-2 C.B. 209.

---

[10] *See,* Lawrence I. Richman, "Sidestepping 2035," 146 *Trusts & Estates* 32 (April 2007). The author recommends that the ILIT purchase the existing policy for cash. If a promissory note is used to purchase the policy, the author suggests that the note be paid in full prior to the insured's death. *Id.* at 34.

Practice Point: IRC section 2042 (and thus the three-year rule of IRC section 2035) applies only to "proceeds of insurance on the decedent's life." Treas. Reg. §20.2042-1(a)(1). Thus, if an insured transfers a second to die policy to an ILIT within three years of his or her death and the other insured is still living and does not die within three years of the transfer, the three-year rule of IRC section 2035 does not apply with regard to the transferred policy and no value attributable to the second to die policy should be includable in the insured's gross estate under IRC section 2035.[11] However, if the surviving insured dies within three years of the policy's transfer to the ILIT and the surviving insured had an incident of ownership in the policy at the time of the transfer, then IRC section 2035 would apply as to the surviving insured.

Practice Point: If an insured dies within three years of the transfer of a second to die life insurance policy and the other insured under the policy dies within six months after the first insured's death, do ***not*** elect alternate valuation under IRC section 2032 with regard to the first insured's estate. Alternate valuation will result in the full amount of the life insurance proceeds being included in the first insured's estate due to the death of the second insured within the six month alternate valuation period.

Practice Point: Life insurance transferred by a decedent who is not the insured does not come within the purview of IRC section 2035 vis-à-vis IRC section 2042. Treas. Reg. §20.2042-2(a)(2).

Practice Point: If the insured has incidents of ownership in a life insurance policy and wants to avoid the three-year rule of IRC section 2035, the insured should sell (rather than gift) the policy for its fair market value to an

---

[11] If the deceased-insured owned the second to die policy outright (and had not transferred it to an ILIT) and the other insured survives the deceased-insured , the deceased-insured's estate would include the value of the policy in his or her estate under IRC section 2033. *See*, section 3.1, above, concerning the valuation of an un-matured life insurance policy.

ILIT that is structured as a grantor trust (to avoid the transfer for value rule under IRC section 101(a)(2) and to avoid the recognition of any gain on the sale of the policy). IRC section 2035 does not apply to bonafide sales of life insurance policies for full and adequate consideration in money or money's worth. *See,* Priv. Letter Rul 9413045. If the new ILIT, is structured as a grantor trust with respect to the insured and the new ILIT issues (an unsecured) promissory note for the purchase of the life insurance policy, the insured will not be taxable on any interest paid under the note; nor will the insured be required to recognize any imputed income under IRC section 7872 if the promissory note does not pay an adequate rate of interest. Rev. Rul 85-13, 1985-1 C.B. 184.[12] *See,* sections 2.5 (transfers for value) and 3.1 (valuation of life insurance policies), above.

§4.1(a) Gift Splitting Does Not Invoke IRC Section 2035

Merely consenting to split gifts made in trust with the donor spouse does not make the donee (consenting) spouse, who is also a trust beneficiary, a transferor for purposes of the three-year rule of IRC sections 2035. IRC section 2513(a)(1); Pvt. Letter Rul. 200130030. *See,* Rev. Rul. 82-198, 1982-2 C.B. 206; Rev. Rul. 74-556,1974-2 C.B. 300; Rev. Rul. 54-246, 1954-1 C.B. 179. However, gift splitting does make the donee spouse a transferor for GST tax purposes as to the one-half of the entire gift amount without regard to the consenting spouse's ascertainable interest in the gift, and the consenting spouse must allocate his or GST tax exemption to the gift amount. *See,* section 5.22, below.

§4.2 ESTATE TAX CONSEQUENCES OF TRANSFER OF PROPERTY TO ILIT WITH A RETAINED INTEREST BY GRANTOR

The grantor's retained interest in property gifted to an ILIT may result in that property being included in his or her gross estate.

---

[12] *See,* Mitchell Gans and Jonathan G. Blattmachr, "Life Insurance and Some Common 2035/2036 Problems: A Suggested Remedy," 139 *Trust & Estates* 58 (May 2000) for a discussion of an insured transferring a life insurance policy to avoid IRC section 2035.

IRC section 2036; Treas. Reg. §20.2036-1(a)(1). IRC section 2036(a)(1) includes in a decedent's gross estate the date of death (or the alternate valuation date) value of property previously transferred (for less than full and adequate consideration in money or money's worth) during the decedent's lifetime in which the decedent retains the use, possession, right to income, or other enjoyment of the gratuitously transferred property[13] (i) for his or her lifetime, or (ii) for a period of time ascertainable without reference to the decedent's death (such as a retained beneficial interest in a trust (e.g., a grantor retained annuity trust, a grantor retained unitrust or a qualified personal residence trust) for a specified period of time and the decedent dies prior to the expiration of the retained beneficial interest[14]), or (iii) for a period of time measured from the decedent's death, such as "the grantor's right to income from this trust shall expire 60 days before the grantor's death"). Therefore, the grantor of the ILIT should not be a beneficiary of the ILIT. The rules of IRC section 2036 apply both to the grantor and the ILIT beneficiaries. For example, if there is a taxable release of a *Crummey* withdrawal right (such as a lapse of a *Crummey* withdrawal right in excess of the five-by-five safe harbor amount) and the beneficiary causing the release retains an income interest for life in the ILIT (or an interest in the ILIT that is otherwise ascertainable), the beneficiary has transferred property to the ILIT (to wit, the property subject to the taxable release) and has retained an interest in the released property for purposes of IRC section 2036(a). In this instance, the beneficiary is also a "grantor" of the ILIT and a portion (if not all) of the trust estate may be included in the beneficiary's gross estate. *See*, Treas. Reg. §20.2041-3(d)(4). If the grantor's spouse is a beneficiary of the ILIT, it is important that the spouse not make gift contributions to the ILIT (other than consenting to the splitting of gifts made by the grantor). *See*, Paragraph 1.3 of Sample ILIT, which defines "donor"

---

[13] *See also*, the special valuation rules of IRC section 2702 concerning a grantor's retained interest in trust property where certain family members are also beneficiaries of the trust. Generally speaking, if the grantor's retained interest is not a "qualified interest" under IRC section 2702(b), the value of the grantor's retained interest is zero for gift tax purposes.

[14] However, if the grantor survives the specified period of time by one day, the property is not includable in his or her gross estate under IRC section 2036(a)(1), nor is it includable under IRC section 2035.

to include not only the grantor but other persons who make certain types of gift contributions to the ILIT.

> **Caution:** If an existing ILIT distributes a life insurance policy to the non-insured spouse, who is a beneficiary of the ILIT, the non-insured spouse can contribute the life insurance policy to a new trust (assuming there is no transfer for value issue (*see,* section 2.5, above)). Although IRC section 2035 will not apply to the transfer by the non-insured spouse to the new ILIT (since IRC section 2035 applies to an insured), IRC section 2036 may apply to the non-insured spouse if he or she is a beneficiary of the new ILIT. IRC sections 2038 and 2041 may also apply to the spouse's retained beneficial interest in the new ILIT.[15]

§4.2(a) Discharging Grantor's Legal Obligations

Another form of a grantor's retained interest in gifted property is the trustee's use of ILIT property to discharge the grantor's legal obligations (e.g., support of a spouse or a dependent, or trustee's use of ILIT property for the grantor's pecuniary benefit, such as the payment of the grantor's debts or living expenses). Treas. Reg. §20.2036-1(b)(2). Therefore, trust distributions to beneficiaries during the grantor's lifetime should be made on a discretionary basis limited to an ascertainable standard for health, education, support, and maintenance, rather than as mandatory distributions (which may have the effect of discharging the grantor's legal obligation of support to his or her spouse or minor children). Causing discretionary distributions to be capped by an ascertainable standard should not be construed as creating a floor that mandates distribution. *See,* Paragraph 8.3(G) of Sample ILIT. Furthermore, when making a discretionary distribution limited to matters pertaining to an ascertainable standard, the trustee should be required to consider all other resources available to the beneficiary, including any legal obligation of support that another person (such as the grantor) may

---

[15] *See,* Mitchell Gans and Jonathan G. Blattmachr, "Life Insurance and Some Common 2035/2036 Problems: A Suggested Remedy," 139 *Trust & Estates* 58 (May 2000) for an discussion of a non-insured spouse transferring a life insurance policy to a new trust.

owe to such beneficiary; and the trustee should also be prohibited from making a distribution that would have the effect of discharging the grantor's legal obligations, including the obligation of support. *See*, Paragraphs 1.1(B) and 7.11 of Sample ILIT. These two requirements should negate the application of IRC section 2036(a)(1). Pvt. Letter Rul. 8504011; *Restatement Third (Trusts)* section 50 (comment e (3)). *See*, Paragraphs 4.1(A), (B) and 4.2 of Sample ILIT.

§4.2(b) Reimbursement Of Grantor For Income Taxes Attributable To Trust Property

If the ILIT is a defective grantor trust created on or after October 4, 2004, the grantor's right (under state law or the governing instrument) to be reimbursed by the trustee for income taxes borne by the grantor is a retained interest in the transferred property under IRC section 2036, and the ILIT property will be included in the grantor's gross estate. The right of reimbursement constitutes a discharge of the grantor's legal obligation to pay income taxes. If neither state law nor the governing instrument requires the trustee to reimburse the grantor, there is no retained interest. However, if the trustee has the discretion (under state law or the governing instrument) to reimburse the grantor and the trustee exercises that discretion, the grantor may have a retained interest in the ILIT under IRC section 2036 if there is an express or implied "understanding" or "arrangement' between the trustee and the grantor concerning the exercise of the trustee's discretion.[16] Specifically negating the grantor's right to be reimbursed by the ILIT trustee for any income and capital gains tax imposed on the grantor (because of defective grantor trust status) should be sufficient to avoid the application of IRC section 2036. Therefore, consider including the following language in the defective grantor trust: "*The grantor hereby waives any right that the grantor would or might otherwise have to be reimbursed from the trust (or its beneficiaries) for any income tax (including capital gains tax) concerning trust property (or a transaction*

---

[16] *See*, William S. Forsberg and James C. Worthington, "Income Tax Reimbursement Clauses in Irrevocable Trusts—When to Use Them and When Not To," 19 *Probate & Property* 36 (May/June 2005).

by the trust) that is taxable to the grantor under the IRC sections 671-679 and/or applicable local law."

ILIT assets could also be included in the grantor's estate under IRC section 2036 if the trustee has the discretion to reimburse the grantor and the grantor has the right to remove the trustee and appoint him or herself as successor trustee (or to remove a trustee and appoint a successor who is related or subordinate to the grantor within the meaning of IRC section 672(c)), or if state law subjects the trust's assets to the claims of the grantor's creditors. Furthermore, if the grantor dies before the gift becomes a completed gift, the date of death value of the trust corpus will be includible in the grantor's gross estate, for federal estate tax purposes, under IRC section 2038 because of the grantor's retained power to, in effect, terminate the trust by relegating the grantor's creditors to the entire property of the trust. Rev. Rul. 76-103, 1976-1 C.B. 293.[17] Consequently, caution dictates that any discretionary right to reimbursement should be vested exclusively in an independent trustee who is not related or subordinate to the grantor within the meaning of IRC section 672(c),[18] provided the discretionary right to reim-

---

[17] In that Revenue Ruling, the IRS held, "the transfer of property to an irrevocable inter vivos trust created in, and administered under the laws of a state in which the trust is deemed a 'discretionary trust' whose assets are subject to claims of the grantor's creditors does not constitute a completed gift...If and when the grantor's dominion and control of the trust assets ceases, such as by the trustee's decision to move the situs of the trust to a State where the grantor's creditors cannot reach the trust assets, then the gift is complete for Federal gift tax purposes under the rules set forth in section 25.2511-2 of the regulations....Furthermore, if the grantor dies before the gift becomes complete, the date of death value of the trust corpus will be includible in the grantor's gross estate, for Federal estate tax purposes, under section 2038 of the Code because of the grantor's retained power to, in effect, terminate the trust by relegating the grantor's creditors to the entire property of the trust."

[18] Within the definition of an "independent trustee," the following individuals are ***not*** related or subordinate parties under IRC section 672(c), as concerns the powerholder, to wit, the powerholder's nieces, nephews, grandparents, spouses of children, spouses of grandchildren, spouses of brothers and sisters, and partners of the power holder. However, the following individuals, if they ***are*** a non-adverse party, are treated as a related and subordinate to the powerholder, to wit, the powerholder's spouse if living with the powerholder, the powerholder's father, mother, issue, brother or sister, and certain employees of the powerholder or his or her business. Treas. Reg. §1.672(c)-1.

bursement will ***not*** subject the trust assets to the claims of the grantor's creditors, as is the case under the laws of certain jurisdictions (e.g., Alaska, Delaware, Nevada, Missouri, Rhode Island, Utah, Oklahoma, and South Dakota) that permit a grantor to retain a discretionary beneficial interest in a self-settled irrevocable trust (which is also commonly referred to as a "domestic asset protection trust"). In any event, the grantor's payment of the incomes taxes attributable to defective grantor trust status (whether the grantor receives reimbursement from the ILIT or not) does not constitute a gift being made by the grantor to the ILIT beneficiaries, because the grantor is legally liable for the income taxes. Rev. Rul. 2004-64, 2004-27 I.R.B. 7.

> **Practice Point:** According to Rev. Rul. 2004-64, pre-October 4, 2004 defective grantor trusts that ***require*** reimbursement of the grantor's income tax liability do not constitute a retained interest under IRC section 2036, and the trusts are grandfathered from the rules set forth in the Revenue Ruling. However, to not disturb the grandfathered status of these grantor trust, it may be advisable to not make any additions to the trusts after October 3, 2004.

> **Caution:** Pre-October 4, 2004 defective grantor trusts that contain ***discretionary*** reimbursement clauses are subject to the rules set forth in Rev. Rul. 2004-64; such trusts are not grandfathered from Rev. Rul. 2004-64.

§4.2(c) Danger Of Using Illiquid Assets

A grantor's retained interest in property transferred to an irrevocable trust will be included in the grantor's gross estate. In *Estate of Eleanor T.R. Trotter v. Commissioner*, T.C. Memo 2001-250 (2001), the Tax Court held that *Crummey* withdrawal rights held by the trust beneficiaries were not sufficient to negate the grantor's retained power over the transferred property, and that the transferred property (a condominium that the grantor continued to live in without paying rent after transferring it to the trust) was includable in the grantor's gross estate under IRC section 2036(a)(1). The grantor's estate argued that IRC section 2036(a)(1) did not apply because the beneficiaries' *Crummey* withdrawal rights defeated all other rights. The disturbing part of the Tax Court's opinion is not the IRC section 2036 retained interest holding, but how it disposed of the estate's argument that the beneficiaries' *Crummey* withdrawal rights precluded application of IRC section 2036(a)(1). In that regard, the Tax Court stated:

> "Moreover, we are satisfied that the logical conclusion to be drawn [from the terms of the trust itself] is not negated by the withdrawal provisions upon which the estate so heavily relies. The numerous indicia discussed above [concerning the terms of the trust itself, section 2036, and the retained interest in the transferred condominium] are equally supportive of an implied understanding that the withdrawal rights would not be exercised, an interpretation buttressed by the awareness that the beneficiaries were the decedent's grandchildren (and three of the five were minors). *We cannot blind ourselves to the reality of the family relationships involved, and the estate has failed to show that the withdrawal rights were anything more than a paper formality without intended economic substance. In addition, such construction is strengthened still further by the fact that the trust's having been funded solely with a single piece of real estate would have made any attempt to effectuate a withdrawal complex and burdensome at best. While it is not entirely clear from the document how the [withdrawal] provision would operate in this circumstance, we doubt that any beneficiary would have seriously contemplated forcing the trustee to sell the home so that he or she could collect $10,000."*

Id. at 637 (emphasis added).

This comment by the Tax Court emphasizes the need to try to fund the ILIT with liquid assets (such as premium contributions or liquid seed money), if possible, and that the beneficiaries need to be granted sufficient time to exercise their right of withdrawal over the liquid assets.[19] This comment should not cause concern regarding group term life insurance policies held by an ILIT where the premiums are paid by the grantor's employer, provided the beneficiaries receive timely notice from the donor or trustee of the schedule of pre-

---

[19] *See*, Andrew J. Willms, "What's Up With Those *Crummey* Powers?," 16 *The Practical Tax Lawyer* 55 (Winter 2002).

mium payments by the employer, and have a right to withdraw the value of the premium payments, usually in the form of a fractional interest in the life insurance policy itself or from a side fund of cash or liquid assets. *See*, section 12.3, below. Furthermore, the Tax Court's concern about the difficulty of dividing a house into $10,000 parcels is less problematic for an ILIT when the trustee has the power to borrow funds or can transfer the policy to the beneficiaries.

§4.2(d) Other IRC Section 2036 Issues

The retained interest rule of IRC section 2036 also includes (1) the value of transferred property that is subject to the claims of the grantor's creditors[20] (*Commissioner v. Sarah Gilkey Vander Weele*, 254 F.2d 895 (6th Cir. 1958); *Estate of Estelle E. German v. United States*, 7 CL. Ct. 641(1985); *Estate of Floyd G. Paxton*, 86 T.C. 785 (1986); *Mary M. Outwin v. Commissioner*, 76 T.C. 153 (1981) *acq.* 1981-2 C.B. 2; *Alice S. Paolozzi v. Commissioner*, 23 T.C. 182

---

[20] In such an instance, the grantor's transfer of the property will not be a completed gift. Treas. Reg. §25.2511-2(c) provides that a gift is incomplete in every instance in which a donor reserves the power to revest the beneficial title in himself or herself. A gift is also incomplete if and to the extent that a reserved power gives the donor the power to name new beneficiaries or to change the interests of the beneficiaries as between themselves unless the power is a fiduciary power limited by a fixed or ascertainable standard, such as health, education, support, and maintenance. Under Treas. Reg. §25.2511-2(e), a donor is considered as possessing a reserved power if it is exercisable by the donor in conjunction with any person not having a substantial adverse interest in the disposition of the transferred property. Also, Treas. Reg. §25.2511-2(f) provides that the relinquishment or termination of a reserved power to change the beneficiaries of transferred property, occurring otherwise than by death of the donor, is regarded as the event which completes the gift and causes the gift tax to apply.

If the grantor retains an interest under IRC section 2036 in the transferred property, the transfer of the property will not be a completed gift. Rev. Rul. 76-103, 1976-1 C.B. 293. A typical situation would be where the grantor has retained a discretionary interest in the trust, and the retention of the discretionary interest is subject to the claims of the grantor's creditors. IRC section 2036 will apply in such instance even if the trustee is an independent trustee with the sole, absolute, and uncontrolled power to make distributions. The reason being, is that the focus is on the grantor's transfer (not the trustee's discretionary power) that typically gives rise to a creditor's ability to reach the trust assets.

(1954) *aff'd* in an unpublished decision, *acq.* 1962-1 C.B. 4[21]; *Estate of Edgar M. Uhl v. Commissioner*, 25 T.C. 22 (1955), *rev'd in part* 241 F.2d 867 (7th Cir. 1957); Rev. Rul. 77-378, 1977-2 C.B. 347; Rev. Rul. 76-103, 1976-1 CB 293; Pvt. Letter. Ruls. 200223013, 200223014, 200123002, 199917001, 9332006, and 8752064; G.C.M. 35112 (11/13/1972)), (2) the grantor's right to remove a trustee and replace a trustee (Treas. Reg. §20.2036-1(b)(3)), (3) the grantor's right to vote (directly or indirectly, as a trustee, general partner, manager, or otherwise) shares of a controlled corporation that the grantor has gifted to a trust or transferred to a partnership or limited liability company[22] (IRC section 2036(b)), (4) the

---

[21] "In *Paolozzi v. Commissioner*, 23 T.C. 182 (1954), the taxpayer created a trust under the terms of which the trustees were authorized to pay her so much of the trust income as they in their absolute discretion determined to be in her best interest. Upon her death, the trust assets were to be distributed to her issue. She reported a taxable gift when the trust was established in an amount equal to the value of the assets transferred reduced by the value of a life estate for an individual her age. Respondent [IRS] determined that the amount of the gift should be undiminished by the value of the life estate since her interest in the trust income was at best an expectancy, and not susceptible of valuation by actuarial methods. This Court rejected respondent's determination on the ground that, under Massachusetts law, the creditors of a settlor-beneficiary of a discretionary trust could reach for satisfaction of claims the maximum amount that the trustee could pay to the settlor or apply for her benefit. Thus, we concluded that the taxpayer could at any time obtain the economic benefit of the trust income simply by borrowing [from third parties] and then forcing her creditors to look to her interest in the trust income for a source of repayment. On this basis, we held that the gift was incomplete to the extent of the value of her life estate. Accord, *Vander Weele v. Commissioner*, 27 T.C. 340, 343-344 (1956), *aff'd*, 254 F.2d 895 (6th Cir. 1958) (involving Michigan law). See also *Estate of Holtz v. Commissioner* , 38 T.C. 37, 42 n. 3 (1962); *Herzog v. Commissioner*, 116 F.2d 591 (2d Cir. 1941) (reaching a contrary result under New York law); Rev. Rul. 76-103, 1976-1 C.B. 293. Cf. *Hambleton v. Commissioner*, 60 T.C. 558, 565-566 (1973)." *Mary M. Outwin v. Commissioner*, 76 T.C. 153, 162-163(1981), *acq.*, 1981-2 C.B. 1.

[22] Under IRC section 2036(b)(3) a "lapse," "cessation," or "expiration" of the grantor's voting rights in a controlled corporation is subject to the three-year rule of IRC section 2035(a). Therefore, to avoid inclusion under IRC section 2035(a) and 2036(b), any voting rights retained by the grantor (whether individually, as a trustee, as a general partner or as a member/manager) in a controlled corporation must be relinquished more than three years prior to the grantor's death. For example, if a grantor retains the right (as trustee) to vote controlled corporation stock until the expiration of a GRAT's term, the grantor must survive an additional three years after the expiration of the GRAT's term.

grantor's power to distribute trust income or principal, where the power is not limited by an ascertainable standard, and (5) the grantor's right, either alone or in conjunction with another person (including a co-trustee, beneficiary, or a person having an adverse interest in the exercise of the grantor's right/power) to designate which beneficiaries shall possess or enjoy the trust property or its income, including the ability to control the timing and manner of a beneficiary's enjoyment of the trust property, (IRC section 2036(a)(2); Treas. Reg. §20.2036-1(b)(3)). If the grantor serves as a trustee or co-trustee of the gifted property, IRC section 2036(a)(2) could cause that property to be included in the grantor's gross estate.[23] Therefore, the grantor of an ILIT should not serve as a trustee of the gifted property.

> **Caution:** Powers retained by the grantor that are subject to a contingency may also result in the property's inclusion in the grantor's gross estate under IRC section 2036(a)(2), even though the contingency is outside of the grantor's control or did not in fact occur prior to the grantor's death. Treas. Reg. §20.2036-1(b)(3).

§4.2(e) Family And Entity Attribution Rules Apply For Controlled Corporations

Unlike IRC section 672 of the grantor trust rules, IRC section 2036(a) does not contain a spousal attribution rule. However, the attribution rules of IRC section 318 do apply to controlled corporations. IRC section 2036(b). A "controlled corporation is one in which the grantor and related parties (using the IRC section 318 attribution rules) own 20% or more of the voting stock. Even where there is no application of the attribution rule, if the reciprocal trust doctrine applies to the grantor, the uncrossing of the reciprocal trusts or reciprocal powers of appointment could result in the grantor holding a retained interest under IRC section 2036. *See*, Chapter 10, below, for a discussion of the reciprocal trust and reciprocal power of appointment doctrines.

---

[23] *See*, Stuart B. Dorsett, "Having Your Cake and Eating It, Too—Parental Control Over Irrevocable Trusts For Children," 16 *Probate & Property* 58 (November/December 2002).

§4.2(f) Non-Gratuitous Transfers Or Ascertainable Standards

IRC section 2036 does not apply to transfers made for full and adequate consideration in money or money's worth. IRC section 2036(a). *See also*, IRC section 2043. Also, IRC section 2036(a)(2) does not apply to non-discretionary powers held by the grantor that are limited by an enforceable ascertainable standard, such as the beneficiary's health, education, support, and maintenance. *Oliver Gould Jennings v. Smith*, 161 F.2d 74 (2d Cir. 1947); *Estate of Walter E. Frew v. Commissioner*, 8 T.C. 1240 (1947), acq. 1947-2 C.B. 2; *Estate of Ralph Budd, Petitioner v. Commissioner*, 49 T.C. 468 (1968), acq. 1973-2 C.B. 1; *Estate of Marvin L. Pardee v. Commissioner*, 49 T.C. 140 (1967) (applying Michigan law), acq. 1973-2 C.B. 3; Rev. Rul. 73-143, 1973-1 C.B. 407; Pvt. Letter Ruls. 200419011, 200213013, 200123034, 199903025, and 8916032. *Cf.*, Treas. Reg. §25.2511-2(g).[24]

§4.2(g) Gift Splitting Does Not Invoke IRC Section 2036

Merely consenting to split gifts made in trust with the donor spouse does not make the donee (consenting) spouse, who is also a trust beneficiary, a transferor for purposes of the retained interest rules of IRC section 2036. IRC section 2513(a)(1); Pvt. Letter Rul. 200130030. *See*, Rev. Rul. 82-198, 1982-2 C.B. 206; Rev. Rul. 74-556,1974-2 C.B. 300; Rev. Rul. 54-246, 1954-1 C.B. 179.

> **Practice Point:** To avoid the IRC section 2036 trap inherent when an ILIT income beneficiary transfers assets to an ILIT (such as transfers by the grantor and the grantor's spouse, where the spouse is also an ILIT beneficiary), only the grantor should make gifts to the ILIT, and any gifts of the grantor in excess of the IRC section 2503(b) amount should be split with the spouse under IRC section 2513. Accordingly, where the grantor's spouse is a beneficiary of the ILIT, it is preferable for the grantor to use his or her separate property when making contributions to the ILIT; and, to avoid using joint assets. *See*, sec-

[24] The non-discretionary ascertainable standard exception does not apply to an IRC section 2036(a)(1) interest retained by a grantor.

tion 12.7, below for a discussion of using a joint bank account to pay life insurance premiums.

§4.3 ESTATE TAX CONSEQUENCES OF TRANSFER OF PROPERTY TO ILIT WITH GRANTOR'S POWER TO CONTROL BENEFICIAL ENJOYMENT OF ILIT PROPERTY (INCLUDING POWER TO REMOVE A TRUSTEE)

The rules of IRC section 2038 (concerning the power (held by the grantor at his or her death) to control the beneficial enjoyment of trust property that has been gratuitously transferred by the grantor during his or her lifetime) are similar to the rules of IRC section 2036(a)(2), and apply both to the grantor and the ILIT beneficiaries.[25] For example, if there is a taxable release of a *Crummey* withdrawal right (such as a lapse in excess of the five-by-five safe harbor amount) and the beneficiary causing the release has discretionary power over the released property (either as a beneficiary or as a trustee), the beneficiary is deemed to be a "grantor" of the released property and a portion (if not all) of the value of the trust estate may be included in the beneficiary's gross estate because of the beneficiary's power to control the distribution or devolution of the released property. IRC section 2038(a); Treas. Reg. §20.2038-1(a).

A grantor does not retain the power to control the beneficial enjoyment of ILIT property if the grantor subsequently gets divorced, has more children, or adopts children. These are acts of independent significance and are considered beyond the grantor's control. TAM 8819001. Similarly, such acts do not constitute an incident of ownership over the life insurance held by an ILIT.

§4.3(a) Removing The Trustee

Both IRC sections 2036 and 2038 include the grantor's ability to remove and replace a trustee. Treas. Reg. §§20.2036-1(b)(3) and 20.2038-1(a)(3). Fortunately, in 1995, the IRS reversed its position taken in Rev. Rul. 79-353, and held that a grantor's reservation of an unqualified power to remove an existing trustee and appoint a replacement trustee who is not related or subordinate to the grantor

[25] IRC section 2038 also overlaps with IRC section 2037 concerning the taxation of transfers taking effect at death.

(within the meaning of IRC section 672(c)) is not a reservation of the trustee's discretionary powers of distribution that might cause trust corpus to be included in the grantor's estate under IRC sections 2036(a) and 2038(a)(1). Rev. Rul. 95-58, 1995-2 C.B. 191.

The holding of Rev. Rul. 95-58 is as follows:

> Rev. Rul. 77-182 concludes that a decedent's power to appoint a successor corporate trustee only in the event of the resignation or removal by judicial process of the original trustee did not amount to a power to remove the original trustee that would have endowed the decedent with the trustee's discretionary control over trust income....Rev. Rul. 79-353 and Rev. Rul. 81-51 are revoked. Rev. Rul. 77-182 is *modified* to hold that even if the decedent had possessed the power to remove the trustee and appoint an individual or corporate successor trustee that was not related or subordinate to the decedent (within the meaning of IRC section 672(c)), the decedent would not have retained a trustee's discretionary control over trust income. (Emphasis added.)

In Pvt. Letter Ruls. 9746007, 9735025, and 9607008, the IRS extended its holding in Rev. Rul. 95-58 to beneficiaries who were given the unqualified power to remove an existing trustee and appoint a replacement trustee who is not related or subordinate to the beneficiaries (within the meaning of IRC section 672(c)). Pvt. Letter Rul. 9832039 clarifies Rev. Rul. 95-58 by holding that the removal and replacement of a trustee by a grantor does not have to be limited to "cause," as long as the replacement trustee is not related or subordinate to the grantor (within the meaning of IRC section 672(c)). Pvt. Letter Rul. 9832039 also clarifies Rev. Rul. 95-58 by holding that the insured's ability to remove a trustee for "cause" and replace that trustee with someone other than the insured does not constitute the insured holding an incident of ownership over the insurance policy held by the ILIT on the insured's life. Thus, a grantor can remove an ILIT trustee at anytime for no cause as long as the grantor cannot name a replacement trustee (in contrast to a successor trustee already named in the ILIT) who is the grantor, an insured, or a person who is "related or subordinate" to the grantor within the meaning of IRC section 672(c).

In Pvt. Letter Rul. 200314009, the IRS extended its holding in Rev. Rul. 95-58 to the insured. In Pvt. Letter Rul. 200314009 the IRS permitted the reformation of an ILIT to correct a scrivener's error concerning a patent ambiguity concerning the office of trustee and Rev. Rul. 95-58. The reformation added a provision to the ILIT that precluded the grantor and any person related or subordinate to the grantor (within the meaning of IRC section 672(c)) from serving as a trustee of the ILIT. Prior to the reformation, the grantor could, as a result of the ambiguity, have been appointed as a successor trustee. The ruling held that the reformation (which clarified the trustee ambiguity) did not result in a release or transfer of the trust property under the three-year rule of IRC section 2035, nor would the proceeds of the life insurance policies be includable in the grantor's gross estate under IRC section 2042(2).

A grantor or beneficiary who has the unrestricted right to remove a trustee and appoint a related or subordinate person as successor trustee is deemed to hold the powers of the removed trustee. Treas. Reg. §20.2041-1(b). Depending on the powers and assets held by the removed trustee, this generally means that the removing party will hold a general power of appointment over the trust assets (or possibly an incident of ownership with regard to life insurance policies held by the trustee insuring the life of the removing party), which will result in the trust property being included in the removing party's gross estate under IRC section 2041 (or IRC section 2042 with regard to any life insurance policies). If a beneficiary ends up holding a general power of appointment, he or she will be the (new) transferor for GST purposes and any GST tax exemption previously allocated by the grantor will be wasted. Limiting a beneficiary's right to remove a trustee for reasonable cause will obviate this problem and provide flexibility concerning the choice of the successor trustee (which of course should never be the grantor). *See*, Paragraph 6.21 of Sample ILIT.

§4.3(b) Other IRC Section 2038 Issues

A grantor's right or power to alter, amend, revoke,[26] or terminate a gratuitous transfer previously made by the grantor, consti-

---

[26] Needless to say an ILIT must be irrevocable to avoid the application of IRC section 2038. Also, gifts made by an agent under a durable power of attorney where

tutes a prohibited power under IRC section 2038, and could cause the gratuitous transfer to be partially or wholly incomplete for gift tax purposes. Treas. Reg. §§25.2511-2(b) and (c).[27] If the grantor relinquishes the prohibited power within three years of his or her death or holds the prohibited power at his or her death, the value of the property over which the grantor held (or holds) the prohibited power is included in the grantor's gross estate. IRC section 2038(a); Treas. Reg. §20.2038-1(a). Consequently, the grantor's right under state law or the trust instrument to amend or terminate an ILIT (in conjunction with the ILIT beneficiaries or the trustee) should be

---

neither state law nor the durable power of attorney expressly permit the making of gifts will cause the gifts to be "revocable" and includable in the principal's gross estate under IRC section 2038. *Estate of Casey v. Commissioner*, 948 F.2d 895 (4th Cir. 1991); *Estate of Mary C. IX Gaynor v. Commissioner*, T.C.M. 2001-206 (2001); TAMs 9342003, 9736004. Consequently, the grantor's durable power of attorney should expressly permit the making of gifts, including gifts to the ILIT. *See*, section 13.2, below.

[27] For this reason, a grantor generally should not serve as custodian of an UGMA or UTMA account that he or she establishes. Rev. Rul. 57-366, 1957-2 C.B. 618. Nor should the grantor be the trustee of an IRC section 2503(c) trust, since the requirements for such a trust preclude the use of an ascertainable standard for distributions and would result in the trust property being included in the grantor's gross estate under IRC sections 2036 and 2038 if the grantor dies prior to the termination of the trust or resigns as trustee within three years of death. Treas. Reg. §25.2503-4(b); Rev. Rul. 67-270, 1967-2 C.B. 349. Furthermore, the grantor's spouse should not serve as trustee of an IRC section 2503(c) trust for the benefit of a dependent child, since to do so would cause the trust property to be includable in the spouse's gross estate (as a general power of appointment) if the spouse were to die prior to the termination of the trust or the spouse resigning as trustee. *See*, IRC sections 2041 and 2514; Treas. Reg. §§20.2041-1(c) and 25.2514-1(c), concerning a trustee's use of trust property to discharge a legal obligation (of support).

Treas. Reg. §25.2511-2(c) provides that a gift is incomplete in every instance in which a donor reserves the power to revest the beneficial title in himself or herself. A gift is also incomplete if and to the extent that a reserved power gives the donor the power to name new beneficiaries or to change the interests of the beneficiaries as between themselves unless the power is a fiduciary power limited by a fixed or ascertainable standard, such as health, education, support, and maintenance. Under Treas. Reg. §25.2511-2(e), a donor is considered as possessing a reserved power if it is exercisable by the donor in conjunction with any person not having a substantial adverse interest in the disposition of the transferred property. Also, Treas. Reg. §25.2511-2(f) provides that the relinquishment or termination of a reserved power to change the beneficiaries of transferred property, occurring otherwise than by death of the donor.

expressly negated by stating in the ILIT that the trust agreement is irrevocable and that the grantor retains no rights under IRC sections 2036(a) or 2038. *But see*, Treas. Reg. §20.2038-1(a)(2), which states that "[i]f the decedent's power [to terminate the trust] could be exercised only with the consent of all parties having an interest (vested or contingent) in the transferred property, and if the power [to terminate the trust] adds nothing to the rights of the parties under local law" then IRC section 2038 does not apply.[28] *See*, Paragraphs 1.1(A) and 2.1 of Sample ILIT.

Other examples of powers held by the grantor that could cause the transferred property to be included in the grantor's gross estate under IRC section 2038, include (1) the power to change or add beneficiaries[29]; (2) the power to accumulate or distribute income or corpus to a beneficiary (even if the accumulated income and corpus is vested in the beneficiary or the beneficiary's estate and no other

[28] However, in Rev. Rul. 70-513, 1970-2 CB 194, the IRS ruled that IRC section 2038 applied if the grantor had to acquiesce in a trustee's decision to terminate an inter-vivos irrevocable trust established by the grantor for the benefit of his son. The IRS deemed the grantor's power of acquiescence akin to the power to "veto" a trustee's decision concerning the beneficial enjoyment of the trust property with regard to the disposition of the terminated trust property, i.e., the disposition of the trust's remainder interest. Said the IRS, "The fact that the [grantor's] power [to acquiesce to the trust's termination during the grantor's lifetime] could be exercised only after the trustees had taken action [i.e., decided to terminate the trust] does not alter its basic nature as a joint power exercisable by the decedent in conjunction with other persons within the meaning of section 2038 of the Code. In disposing of a similar issue, the court in *Estate of Carrie Grossman v. Commissioner*, 27 T.C. 707 (1957), noted 'it is irrelevant whether the decedent's participation initiates the termination, or, as here, is in the nature of a consent after others have set the machinery in motion, it being sufficient under the statute merely that she act 'in conjunction' with the others...,' citing *Thorp's Estate v. Commissioner*,164 F.2d 966 (1947), *cert. denied*, 333 U.S. 843; and *Du Charme's Estate v. Commissioner*, 164 F.2d 959 (1947)."

[29] The grantor's power to exclude certain ILIT beneficiaries from exercising their *Crummey* withdrawal right as concerns a concurrent or future contribution to the ILIT by the grantor does not constitute an IRC section 2038 interest. *See*, section 11.2, below. A grantor does not retain the power to control the beneficial enjoyment of ILIT property if the grantor subsequently gets divorced, has more children, or adopts children. These are acts of independent significance and are considered beyond the grantor's control. TAM 8819001.

person has a beneficial interest in the trust)[30]; (3) the power to appoint the gratuitously transferred property by will or to subsequently affect a beneficiary's interest by will; (4) the power to manage the gratuitously transferred property in a manner that will affect a beneficiary's rights, including the power to control the timing and manner of a beneficiary's enjoyment of the trust property; (6) the power to change beneficial interests that are not subject to an ascertainable standard; (7) the power to revest title to the trust property in the grantor; (8) the power to purchase, sell, or reacquire trust property for less than full and adequate consideration (this is tantamount to having the power to revoke the trust); and (9) the power to distribute trust income or principal, where the power is not limited by an ascertainable standard. None of these powers should be retained by the grantor of an ILIT.

> **Practice Point:** Unlike IRC section 2036(a)(2), IRC section 2038 does not require the grantor to have retained the prohibited power at the time of the gratuitous transfer. IRC section 2038 applies to a grantor's right or power regardless of how the power was acquired (whether expressly stated in the governing instrument, granted by state law, held as a fiduciary or as an individual, or given to the grantor through a person exercising a power of appointment) and regardless of whether the power to alter, amend, revoke, or terminate is exercisable alone or

---

[30] "For example, section 2038 is applicable to a power reserved by the grantor of a trust to accumulate income or distribute it to A, and to distribute corpus to A, even though the remainder is vested in A or his estate, and no other person has any beneficial interest in the trust." Treas. Reg. §20.2038-1(a). *See also*, Pvt. Letter Rul. 200419011, where the trustee of an irrevocable trust had absolute and sole discretion to distribute the trust's principal, subject to the unanimous approval of an advisory committee of which the grantor was a member. If the committee did not approve or disapprove of the distribution within 30 days, the trustee could make the distribution. The IRS ruled that the grantor's power to veto or approve trust distributions not limited to an ascertainable standard causes the trust property to be included in the grantor's gross estate under IRC section 2038. Furthermore, the grantor's allocation of GST exemption was subject to an ETIP (because of IRC section 2038) and the ETIP would end only upon the earlier of the grantor's death or resignation from the advisory committee.

in conjunction with someone else.[31] If the grantor holds the prohibited power at the time of the grantor's death (or has relinquished the power within three years of the grantor's death), IRC section 2038 applies.

§4.3(c) No Family Attribution Rule

Unlike IRC section 672 of the grantor trust rules, IRC section 2038 does not contain a spousal attribution rule. However, if the reciprocal trust doctrine applies to the grantor, the uncrossing of the reciprocal trusts or reciprocal powers of appointment could result in the grantor holding a retained interest under IRC section 2038. *See*, Chapter 10 for a discussion of the reciprocal trust and reciprocal power of appointment doctrines.

§4.3(d) Non-Gratuitous Transfers Or Ascertainable Standards

IRC section 2038 does not apply to transfers made for full and adequate consideration in money or money's worth. IRC sections 2038(a)(1) and (2). *See also*, IRC section 2043. Also, IRC sections 2038 does not apply to non-discretionary powers held by the grantor that are limited by an enforceable ascertainable standard, such as the beneficiary's health, education, support, and maintenance. *Oliver Gould Jennings v. Smith*, 161 F.2d 74 (2d Cir. 1947); *Estate of Walter E. Frew v. Commissioner*, 8 T.C. 1240 (1947), acq. 1947-2 C.B. 2; *Estate of Ralph Budd, Petitioner v. Commissioner*, 49 T.C. 468 (1968), acq. 1973-2 C.B. 1; *Estate of Marvin L. Pardee v. Commissioner*, 49 T.C. 140 (1967) (applying Michigan law), acq. 1973-2 C.B. 3; Rev. Rul. 73-143, 1973-1 C.B. 407; Pvt. Letter Ruls. 200419011, 200213013, 200123034, 199903025, and 8916032. *Cf.*, Treas. Reg. §25.2511-2(g).

§4.3(e) Gift Splitting Does Not Invoke IRC Section 2038

Merely consenting to split gifts made in trust with the donor spouse does not make the donee (consenting) spouse, who is also a

---

[31] *See*, Treas. Reg. §20.2036-1(b)(3). Individual and joint powers are subject to IRC section 2038. It is irrelevant that the co-holder of a joint power is an adverse party or an independent trustee.

trust beneficiary, a transferor for purposes of the retained interest rules of IRC section 2038. IRC section 2513(a)(1); Pvt. Letter Rul. 200130030. *See,* Rev. Rul. 82-198, 1982-2 C.B. 206; Rev. Rul. 74-556,1974-2 C.B. 300; Rev. Rul. 54-246, 1954-1 C.B. 179.

§4.4 ESTATE TAX CONSEQUENCES OF LAPSE OF A CRUMMEY WITHDRAWAL RIGHT

If a beneficiary dies after his or her *Crummey* withdrawal right has lapsed within the five-by-five limits imposed by IRC sections 2514(e) and 2041(b)(2), the lapsed amount is not included in the beneficiary's gross estate because the lapse does not constitute a taxable release of the power. IRC section 2041(a)(2), (b)(2).

§4.5 ESTATE TAX CONSEQUENCES OF AN UNLAPSED *CRUMMEY* WITHDRAWAL RIGHT

A *Crummey* withdrawal right is a general power of appointment. IRC sections 2514 and 2041. Its termination during the powerholder's lifetime may not be a taxable release if the right of withdrawal (or rate of lapse under a hanging right of withdrawal) is limited under the five-by-five safe harbor rules of IRC sections 2514(e) and 2041(b)(2). However, if the powerholder dies before the termination (i.e., lapse) of the (single or hanging) withdrawal right, the amount of the unlapsed right of withdrawal for the year of death will be included in the powerholder's gross estate. IRC section 2041(a)(2). Additionally, the powerholder will become the (new) transferor of the unlapsed power for GST tax purposes, and the GST tax exemption previously allocated by the grantor will be lost and wasted. Treas. Reg. §26.2652-1(a)(2). However, this is usually of minor concern where the ILIT beneficiaries are younger than the grantor.

§4.6 ESTATE TAX CONSEQUENCES OF WAIVER OR RELEASE OF A *CRUMMEY* WITHDRAWAL RIGHT

The gross estate of a decedent includes the value of property subject to a general power of appointment that was released or exercised before the decedent's death if the result of the release or exercise is the creation of a retained interest described in IRC sections 2035, 2036, 2037, or 2038. IRC section 2041(a)(2). If a beneficiary waives his or her *Crummey* withdrawal right or allows his or her *Crummey* withdrawal right (which, as previously mentioned, is a general power of appointment under IRC sections 2514 and 2041) to lapse in an amount greater than the five-by-five safe harbor amount described in IRC sections 2514(e) and 2041(b)(2), the waiver or lapse in excess of five-by-five will be treated as a taxable release of a general power of appointment for transfer tax purposes. Additionally, the power-holder will become the (new) transferor of the released power for GST tax purposes. Treas. Reg. §26.2652-1(a)(2).[32]

However, by using a hanging *Crummey* withdrawal right, you may be able to avoid a taxable release. *See,* section 3.13, above.

If the ILIT provides the beneficiary with a lifetime income interest in the trust, an estate tax problem arises because the beneficiary has made a transfer (i.e., a transfer of the amount of the taxable release) with a retained life income interest in the ILIT property. IRC section 2036(a). When the beneficiary dies, a percentage of the ILIT will be included in his or her gross estate. The percentage included will be based on a fraction—the numerator is the amount of the release and the denominator is the amount of the value of the ILIT at the time of the release. Treas. Reg. §20.2041-3(d)(4). Multiple or cumulative taxable releases are aggregated. Treas. Reg. §20.2041-3(d)(5).

§4.7 ESTATE TAX CONSEQUENCES OF THE DELAWARE TAX TRAP

If in exercising a testamentary non-general power of appointment created after October 21, 1942, another power of appointment (general or non-general) is created, which under applicable local law can be validly exercised so as to postpone the vesting of the appointed property or suspend the absolute ownership or power of alienation of such property, for a period ascertainable without regard to the date of the creation of the first power (i.e., extend the original perpetuities period with respect to the appointed property), the exercise of the testamentary non-general power of appointment by

[32] The fact that the beneficiary holds a testamentary limited power of appointment over the property subject to the taxable release will not avoid inclusion of that property in the beneficiary's gross estate. IRC section 2041(a)(2). The testamentary limited power of appointment over the released property will, however, prevent the taxable release from being a completed gift (to the other ILIT beneficiaries) at the time of its release under IRC section 2514(b). Treas. Reg. §25.2511-2(b).

the donee will be treated as the exercise of a testamentary general power of appointment, and will result in the appointed property being included in the donee's gross estate. (The donee will also become the (new) transferor of the appointed property for GST tax purposes.)[33] IRC sections 2041(a)(3) and 2514(d). *See*, Paragraph 8.1(A) of Sample ILIT, which negates the occurrence of the trap.

§4.8 INCLUSION OF LIFE INSURANCE PROCEEDS IN INSURED'S GROSS ESTATE

Inclusion of life insurance proceeds in the decedent's gross estate under IRC section 2042 applies only if the proceeds are payable to

---

[33] *See*, Stephen E. Greer, "The Delaware Tax Trap and the Abolition of the Rule Against Perpetuities," 28 *Estate Planning* 68 (February 2001); and Jesse Dukeminier, "The Uniform Statutory Rule Against Perpetuities And The GST Tax: New Perils For Practitioners And New Opportunities," 30 *Real Property, Probate and Trust Journal* 185 (Summer 1995). Mr. Greer posits that the Delaware Tax Trap may be applicable in states that have abolished the rule against perpetuities but have no rule against the suspension of the power of alienation. This is in contrast to states that have merely extended the length of time for vesting from a life in being plus 21 years to a longer period of time, such as 360 years (Florida) or states that have "repealed the Perpetuities Rule and have adopted instead a rule against the suspension of the power of alienation, but specify that the power of alienation is not suspended if the trustee has a power of sale, e.g., Idaho, South Dakota, Wisconsin, Delaware, Missouri, New Hampshire and New Jersey. In a jurisdiction that abolished the rule against perpetuities and has no rule against the suspension of the power of alienation, there is no stated period of time within which a property interest must vest. When a power of appointment is exercised to create a successive nongeneral power of appointment, the property subject to this power will have its vesting postponed for a period of time that cannot be ascertained by referring back to the date of the instrument creating the first power of appointment....Thus, if trust property is subject to the exercise of a nongeneral power of appointment, the exercise of that power to create a trust giving the beneficiaries nongeneral powers of appointment renders that property subject to estate tax or gift tax [under the Delaware Tax Trap]. The solution for states that have this problem is to introduce an Alienation statute or, alternatively, to merely extend the permissible period when non-vested interests must vest and the time in which nongeneral and general testamentary powers of appointment may be exercised. It is this latter course of action that Alaska and Florida have chosen. Alaska extended its perpetuities period to 1,000 years but only in the limited circumstance of the time in which a nongeneral and general testamentary power of appointment must be exercised and the time in which property subject to the exercise of these powers must vest. Florida amended its USRAP provisions by extending the permissible 'wait and see' period to 360 years." *Id.* (Citations omitted).

or for the benefit of the insured's estate, or if the insured possessed any of the incidents of ownership in the policy exercisable alone or in conjunction with any other person. If life insurance policies are transferred to another individual or to an ILIT, the death proceeds may be excluded from the gross estate if the insured lives for more than three years after the transfer. *See*, IRC section 2035. However, if the decedent is a trustee of an ILIT that holds insurance on the life of the decedent, the life insurance proceeds will be includable in the decedent's gross estate because the trustee, as the legal owner of the policy, will have incidents of ownership in the policy. IRC section 2042. Thus, an insured should never serve as trustee of an ILIT. *See*, Paragraphs 1.1(A), 6.1(E), and 7.1(C)(3) of Sample ILIT.

If the non-insured owner of the life insurance policy predeceases the insured, the value of the policy will be includable in the non-insured owner's gross estate pursuant to IRC section 2033. The amount that is includable is similar to the valuation of a policy for gift tax purposes. *See*, section 3.1, above.

§4.9 ESTATE TAX CONSEQUENCES OF LIFE INSURANCE PROCEEDS RECEIVABLE BY THE EXECUTOR

Treasury Regulations indicate that life insurance proceeds subject to a legally binding obligation to pay taxes, debts, or other charges of the insured-decedent will be deemed payable to the insured's estate (to the extent of the obligation) and will be includable in the insured's gross estate for federal estate tax purposes. Treas. Reg. §20.2042-1(b)(1). If the life insurance proceeds are community property, and under applicable local law one-half of the proceeds belongs to the decedent's surviving spouse, then only one-half of the proceeds are deemed to be receivable by the decedent's executor. Treas. Reg. §20.2042-1(b)(2). If the insured purchased an insurance policy payable to another person as collateral security for a loan of the insured (e.g., credit life insurance), the proceeds would be includable in the gross estate. However, the amount of the loan will be deductible in determining the taxable estate. This example in the Regulation appears inconsistent with the statement of inclusion of the life insurance proceeds "to the extent of the...obligation."

Proceeds from a second-to-die insurance policy transferred to an ILIT are not includable in the gross estate of the surviving spouse if the trustee only has discretionary power to use the life insurance proceeds to pay the federal estate tax of the surviving spouse. As such, the proceeds are not received by the trustee subject to an obligation, legally binding upon the trustee, to pay taxes, debts, or other charges enforceable against the estate of the surviving spouse under Treas. Reg. §20.2042-1(b)(1). Pvt. Letter Rul. 200147039. *Cf.*, Rev. Rul. 77-157, 1977-1 C.B. 279. The private letter ruling does not, however, address the issue of what the estate tax consequences would be if the trustee had in fact used the life insurance proceeds to pay the taxes, claims, and other obligations of the surviving spouse. Presumably the proceeds so used would be includable in the gross estate of the surviving spouse. *See also*, *Estate of Charles Howard Wade v. Commissioner*, 47 B.T.A. 21 (1942), acq. 1944 C.B. 29; *Old Colony Trust Company v. Commissioner*, 39 B.T.A. 871 (1939), acq. 1939-2 C.B. 27 where the court held that the trustee's mere power to pay taxes, debts and expenses of the insured was not sufficient to result in the life insurance proceeds being includable in the insured's gross estate, when the power is not so exercised.

> **Practice Point:** Do not direct the ILIT trustee to pay the insured's death taxes, debts or costs of estate administration. Rather, give the trustee the authority to make loans to the insured's estate or to purchase assets from the insured's estate. This is how the ILIT can provide liquidity to the insured's estate without the ILIT assets being subject to inclusion in the insured's gross estate. *See,* Paragraph 5.2 of Sample ILIT.

§4.10 ESTATE TAX CONSEQUENCES OF THE INSURED'S INCIDENTS OF OWNERSHIP IN LIFE INSURANCE

Even if a life insurance policy is transferred more than three years before the insured's death, the insured's retention of certain incidents of ownership (exercisable either alone or in conjunction with any other person) will cause inclusion of the life insurance in the insured's gross estate, regardless of who receives the proceeds upon the insured's death. IRC section 2042; Treas. Reg. §§20.2042-1(c)(2), (3), (4). "Incidents of ownership" is not limited in its meaning to ownership of the policy in the technical legal sense. Generally speaking, the "incidents of ownership" refers to the right of the insured or the insured's estate to the economic benefits of the policy. Thus, "incidents of ownership" includes the power to change the beneficiary, to surrender or cancel the policy, to assign the policy, to revoke an assignment, to pledge the policy for a loan, to obtain from the insurer a loan against the surrender value of the policy, etc.[34] In the ILIT context, incidents of ownership problems arise when the insured possess an indirect incident of ownership in the policy that is owned by the ILIT.

§4.10(a) Examples Of Incidents Of Ownership For Estate Tax Purposes

Incidents of ownership in a life insurance policy include the following:

(1) A reversionary interest greater than 5%. IRC section 2042(2) states that the term "incidents of ownership" includes a reversionary interest (if the value of such interest exceeds 5% of the value of the policy immediately before death), which includes a possibility that the policy or the proceeds may return to the decedent or be subject to a power of disposition by him or her. *See,* section 11.1, below concerning the 5% reversionary rule where a special power holder can appoint the policy to a class of appointees that includes the insured.

Practice Point: The fact that the insured may, at a later date, receive the policy or its proceeds by inheritance through the estate of another person, or as a surviving spouse under a statutory right of election or a similar right does not constitute a reversionary interest in the policy or an incident of ownership in the policy. Treas. Reg. §20.2042-1(c)(3).

(2) Power to change beneficiary (or to veto a change of beneficiary). *See,* Treas. Reg. §20.2042-1(c)(2); *Eleanor M. Schwager v. Commissioner,* 64 T.C. 781 (1975) (power of insured to veto a change of beneficiary by the policy owner also constitutes an incident of ownership).

(3) Power to surrender or cancel the policy (or to prevent or veto a cancellation). *See,* Treas. Reg. §20.2042-1(c)(2).

---

[34] *See,* Donald O. Jansen, "Section 2042 From Soup To Nuts," 22 *ACTEC Notes* 24 (1996). Incidents of ownership can occur even though the decedent was physically unable to exercise any power over the policy at the time of death. Rev. Rul. 61-123, 1961-2 C.B. 151.

(4) Power to assign the policy. *See,* Treas. Reg. §20.2042-1(c)(2).

(5) Power to revoke an assignment of the policy. *See,* Treas. Reg. §20.2042-1(c)(2).

(6) Power to pledge the policy for a loan. *See,* Treas. Reg. §20.2042-1(c)(2).

(7) Power to obtain a loan from the insurer against the policy's surrender value. *See,* Treas. Reg. §20.2042-1(c)(2). The term "incidents of ownership" includes legal ownership of the policy, the power to change the beneficiary, to surrender or cancel the policy, to assign the policy, to revoke an assignment, to pledge the policy for a loan, to obtain from the insurer a loan against the surrender value of the policy, etc.

Practice Point: One method of reducing the current value of a life insurance policy for gifting purposes may be to take out a loan against the policy. The burdened policy may then be transferred as a gift in one year. Cash may be transferred to the ILIT in the following year, which is then used to pay off the loan. If attempting this strategy, be careful not to violate the transfer for value rule. If the ILIT is deemed to have relieved the taxpayer of an existing liability (i.e., the loan amount) greater than the taxpayer's basis in the life insurance policy, then the transfer of the burdened policy may inadvertently trigger the transfer for value rule, causing the proceeds of the policy to be subject to income tax in the hands of the ILIT trustee. *See,* section 2.5(b)(6), above, for a possible solution to this problem.

(8) Power to change the beneficial ownership (either alone or with another). *See,* Treas. Reg. §20.2042-1(c)(4). An insured decedent is considered to have an incident of ownership in an insurance policy on his or her life held in trust if, under the terms of the policy, the decedent (either alone or in conjunction with another person or persons) has the power (*as trustee or otherwise*) to change the beneficial ownership in the policy or its proceeds. Therefore, the insured should not serve as trustee of the ILIT or be permitted to be appointed as a co-trustee or successor trustee. Nor should the insured have a power of appointment (general or limited) over the ILIT property. *See*, Paragraphs 1.1(A), 2.1, 6.1(E) and 7.1(C)(3) of Sample ILIT.

(9) Power to change the time or manner of enjoyment even though decedent has no beneficial interest. *See*, Treas. Reg. §20.2042-1(c)(4). A deceased grantor-insured is considered to have an incident of ownership in an insurance policy on his or her life held in trust if, under the terms of the policy, the decedent (either alone or in conjunction with another person or persons) has the power (*as trustee or otherwise*) to change the time or manner of enjoyment of the insurance proceeds, even though the insured decedent has no beneficial interest in the trust. *See*, Paragraphs 1.1(A), 2.1, 6.1(E) and 7.1(C)(3) of Sample ILIT.

Caution: The insured should not hold the power, whether alone or in conjunction with others, to modify or terminate the ILIT, or to veto or approve decisions concerning the life insurance policy owned by the ILIT on the insured's life. Rev. Rul. 75-70, 1975-1C.B. 301. Even if the insured cannot initiate the acts associated with the incidents of ownership but can only consent to or veto the exercise of the incidents of ownership by another, the courts and IRS have held that the veto or consent power itself constitutes an incident of ownership over the policy. *Eleanor M. Schwager v. Commissioner,* 64 T.C. 781 (1975) (concerning insured's power to veto a change in beneficiary designation by the owner of the policy); TAM 7406240100A (concerning insured's consent to change beneficiaries or to assign the policy). The Second Circuit held that where the insured must consent to the actions of others in altering or amending a revocable trust which included an insurance policy on the insured's life, the insured had incidents of ownership in the policy. *Estate of Miran Karagheusian*, 233 F.2d 197 (2d Cir. 1956). Similarly, the Court of Claims held that where the beneficiary/owner of the life insurance policy had the power to change the beneficiary but the power could be exercised only with the consent of the insured, the insured held incidents of ownership in the policy for federal estate tax purposes. *Goldstein's Estate v. United States*, 122 F. Supp. 677 (Ct. Cl. 1954). *See also*, Rev.

Rul 79-46, 1979-1 C.B. 303, in which the IRS ruled that the insured had a reversionary interest in the life insurance policy because of his right to purchase the policy owned by his corporate employer (but made payable to the insured's wife) if the corporation ceased paying premiums or wished to surrender and terminate the policy. The IRS concluded that the insured's right to purchase the policy was the equivalent of the right to veto the employer's incident of ownership in surrendering the policy. *But see, Estate of John Smith v. Commissioner,* 73 T.C. 307 (1979), *acq. in result only*, AOD 1981-066 (01/12/1981), which involved almost identical facts with those of Rev. Rul. 79-46, except that the corporation was both the owner and beneficiary of the policy. Said the court, "At his death, Smith could neither have initiated changes in the two [key man life insurance] policies [owned by and payable to the publicly traded company that employed Smith] nor consented to them; the company [in which Smith owned only a few shares of stock and was not a controlling shareholder] alone maintained full control over the policies." The Service's acquiescence in *Smith* implies that the IRS will not consider the right to purchase a life insurance policy owned and made payable to a corporation as an incident of ownership (in contrast to a policy owned by a corporation but made payable to a third party, such as the insured's spouse, as was the case in Rev. Rul 79-46). *See also*, Priv. Letter Rul. 8049002.

(10) Controlled ownership or control through entity. If an insurance policy, or any of its benefits, is owned by a corporation or other entity that is controlled by the insured, that control through the entity may cause the life insurance proceeds to be included in the insured's gross estate. Treas. Reg. §20.2042-1(c)(6) states that life insurance owned by and payable to a corporation in which the insured is a majority shareholder[35] will not result in the proceeds being included in

[35] A majority stockholder is one who owns, at death, stock possessing more than fifty percent of the total combined voting power of a corporation. "The decedent will not be deemed to be the controlling stockholder unless, at the time of death,

the insured's gross estate (because the proceeds would be taken into account when valuing the insured's stock holdings). However, if the life insurance proceeds are payable to a third party for non-business purposes, the incidents of ownership held by the insured's corporation (where the insured is the sole or majority shareholder) will be attributed to the insured through his or her stock ownership and the proceeds will be included in the insured's gross estate under IRC section 2042. Rev. Rul. 82-145, 1982-2 C.B. 213; Rev. Rul. 76-274, 1976-2 C.B. 278, situation 1; *Estate of Milton Levy v. Commissioner,* 70 T.C. 873 (1978).

Life insurance owned by and payable to a partnership or limited liability company in which the insured is a partner or member will not result in the proceeds being included in the insured's gross estate under IRC section 2042 (because the proceeds would be taken into account when valuing the partner's/member's interest in the entity). *Estate of Frank H. Knipp v. Commissioner*, 25 T.C. 153 (1955), *acq. in result,* 1959-1 C.B. 4, *aff'd on another issue,* 244 F.2d 436 (4th Cir.), *cert. denied,* 355 U.S. 827 (1957). *See*, Pvt. Letter Ruls. 200214028 and 200111038. Nevertheless, it is advisable to provide in the partnership agreement or limited liability operating agreement that the insured partner or insured member shall have no rights over a policy insuring his or her life that is owned by the entity. Instead, any such rights should be held exclusively by the other partners or members. *See,* Priv. Letter Rul. 200017051 (general partner prohibited from participating in decisions regarding insur-

---

the decedent owned stock possessing more than 50% of the total combined voting power of the corporation. The decedent is considered to own (1) the stock to which the decedent had legal title, (2) the stock in which the decedent had a beneficial interest through a voting trust, and (3) the stock held in any other trust with respect to which the decedent was treated as the owner under the income tax grantor trust rules immediately prior to death. Thus, if estate planning with the stock of a closely held corporation using grantor trusts has been implemented, and the proceeds of an insurance policy owned by the corporation are not payable to the corporation, stock ownership must be carefully tallied. Jointly owned stock is counted to the extent of the proportionate consideration furnished by the decedent. However, in the case of group term insurance under Section 79, the power to surrender or cancel the policy by a corporation is not attributed to any decedent through the decedent's stock ownership." Diana S. C. Zeydel, "How to Create and Administer a Successful Irrevocable Life Insurance Trust," 34 *Estate Planning* 3, 8 (June 2007).

ance on his own life). However, if the life insurance is owned by a general partnership or a limited liability company, and is not payable to or for the benefit of the partnership or limited liability company, the insured general partner/member (even if the insured general partner/member does not own a controlling interest in the partnership/limited liability company) will be deemed to possess incidents of ownership in the policy and the proceeds will be includable in the insured general partner/member's gross estate. Rev. Rul. 83-147, 1983-2 C.B. 158.

Caution: If a majority shareholder permits the corporation to transfer the life insurance policy on his or her life to a third party within three years of the majority shareholder's death, the policy proceeds may be includable in that shareholder's gross estate under the three-year rule of IRC section 2035, unless: (i) the majority shareholder transfers his or her controlling interest in corporation more than three years before his or her death, or (ii) the transfer of the life insurance policy by the corporation to the third party constitutes a bonafide sale for adequate and full consideration in money or money's worth. Rev. Rul. 90-21, 1990-1 C.B. 172; Pvt. Letter Rul. 199905-010. *See,* section 3.1, above, for a discussion on how to value the policy in such a case.

(11) Power to select settlement option. According to the U.S. Fifth Circuit Court of Appeals, the decedent's right to select a settlement option is an incident of ownership. *Estate of James H. Lumpkin, Jr. v. Commissioner,* 474 F.2d 1092 (5th Cir. 1973), *rev'g.* 56 T.C. 815 (1971). *But see, Estate of John J. Connelly, Sr. v. Commissioner,* 551 F.2d 545 (3d Cir. 1977), which held that the decedent's right to select a settlement option was not an incident of ownership.

§4.10(b) What Doesn't Constitute Incidents Of Ownership For Estate Tax Purposes

Examples of what does not constitute incidents of ownership in a life insurance policy include the following:

(1) Loans To ILIT By The Insured. A grantor's loan of money to an ILIT trustee to pay life insurance premiums does not, in and of itself, constitute an incident of ownership. Pvt. Letter Rul. 9809032.

(2) Direct Payment Of Premiums By The Insured. Although direct payment of ILIT premiums by the grantor should be avoided (to provide efficacy to the *Crummey* withdrawal rights granted the ILIT beneficiaries), such action by the grantor will not, in and of itself, constitute an incident of ownership in the ILIT's life insurance policy. *Estate of Frank Martin Perry, Sr. v. Commissioner*, 927 F.2d 209 (5th Cir. 1991); *Estate of Eddie L. Headrick v. Commissioner*, 93 T.C. 171 (1989), *aff'd*, 918 F.2d 1263 (6th Cir. 1990), AOD 1991-012 (7/3/1991); *Estate of Joseph Leder v. Commissioner*, 89 T.C. 235 (1987), *aff'd*, 893 F.2d 237 (10th Cir. 1989). Infrequent direct payments of ILIT premiums by the grantor should not cause the trustee to be treated as an agent of the grantor, with the grantor being a de facto trustee. An occasional (inadvertent) direct payment with proper notice to the beneficiaries who hold withdrawal rights is no different than employer-paid group term or split-dollar premiums. *See*, sections 1.4(a), above and 10.7, below.

(3) Direct Payment Of Premiums By The Insured's Employer. Direct payment of premiums by the insured's employer under a split-dollar plan or under a group term life plan will not, in and of itself, constitute an incident of ownership in the ILIT's life insurance policy. *See*, section 3.2 and 3.3, above.

Practice Point: To ensure that direct payment of premiums by the insured or the insured's employer constitutes a gift of a present interest, the ILIT should contain special language concerning such direct payments, the ILIT should specify how notice is to be given to the *Crummey* withdrawal right beneficiaries when such premium payments are made, and the ILIT should specify how a *Crummey* withdrawal right is to be satisfied when premiums are paid directly by the insured or the insured's employer. *See*, Paragraphs 3.2(A), (F) and (G) of Sample ILIT.

(4) Use Of Non-Community Property Joint Account To Pay Premiums. A joint tenant's use of funds from a joint bank account does not, in and of itself, constitute the payment of premiums (and hence a possible incident of ownership) by the non-withdrawing joint tenant who contributed some or all of the funds to the joint bank account. Joint bank accounts are frequently used by husbands and wives. *See, Estate of Lee J. Clay v. Commissioner*, 86 T.C. 1266 (1986), where the Tax Court held, "[W]e assume, as the parties do, that each tenant to this joint account had the power to withdraw the whole or any part of funds in the account, even though...the funds belonged to them in proportion to their net contributions....The withdrawal of funds with decedent's knowledge and consent constituted a transfer of those funds by decedent to...[the joint account tenant], terminating...[the decedent's] interest therein. Therefore, under the circumstances of this case, we reject...[the IRS'] tracing analysis and hold that, in the absence of an agency relationship, the mere payment of premiums with funds withdrawn from a joint account does not constitute payment by the nonwithdrawing tenant." Id. at 1274.

(5) Insured's Ability To Convert Group Term Policy To Ordinary Insurance. An insured's ability to convert a group term policy owned by a third party (such as an ILIT) into individual coverage upon termination of the insured's employment does not constitute an incident of ownership by the insured. *Estate of James Smead v. Commissioner*, 78 T.C. 43 (1975); Rev. Rul. 84-130, 1984-2 C.B. 194. Also, where the power to cancel an insurance policy is exercisable only by the insured terminating his or her employment, the insured is not deemed to have an incident of ownership in the policy. Thus, the cancellation of a group term policy upon termination of the insured's employment does not constitute an incident of ownership by the insured. Rev. Rul. 72-30, 1972-1 C.B. 307. The termination of an insured's employment is considered to be collateral consequence of an act of independent significance.

(6) Divorce Of Spouse-Beneficiary. The IRS has also ruled that divorcing one's spouse is an act of independent significance and not a power to change the beneficial enjoyment of insurance proceeds, and therefore is not an incident of ownership in a life insurance policy. TAM 8819001. In reaching its decision the IRS quoted the court from the *Estate of Edward A. Tully, Sr. v. United States*, 528 F. 2d 1401 (Ct. Cl. 1976), "In reality, a man might divorce his wife, but to assume that he would fight through an entire divorce process merely to alter employee death benefits approaches the absurd." In that same private letter ruling the IRS also ruled that an IRC section 1035 exchange did not trigger a new three-year period under IRC section 2035 where the life insurance policy was owned by an ILIT and the transfer of the policy to the ILIT had occurred more than three years prior to the IRC section 1035 exchange.

(7) Errors Caused By Life Insurance Agent In Processing Of Application. The courts and the IRS have ruled that a life insurance agent's errors in completing a life insurance application did not result in the insured having incidents of ownership in the policy, where the policy was supposed to be owned by an ILIT. *Estate of Bert L. Fuchs* v. *Commissioner*, 47 T.C. 199 (1966), *acq.*, 1967-1 C.B. 2. Priv. Letter Rul. 200603002.[36]

(8) Insured's Right To Substitute Policy For Property Of Equal Value. In Priv. Letter Rul. 9413045 the IRS ruled that the insured-grantor's right, in a non-fiduciary capacity, to substitute comparable assets for a trust-owned life insurance policy did not constitute an incident of ownership in the life insurance policy owned by the ILIT. In its ruling, the IRS stated, "[T]he court in *Estate of Jordahl* held that the ability of an

[36] Generally, ownership of a life insurance policy for estate and gift tax purposes is presumed to be determined from the terms of the policy itself. This is referred to as "policy facts." *See, Commissioner v. Estate of Noel*, 380 U.S. 678 (1965). In Priv. Letter Rul. 200603002 the IRS noted that the parties have a heavy burden to overcome this presumption. However, several Tax Court cases have held that the estate tax treatment of life insurance policies that were mistakenly drawn up in a manner that did not reflect the intent of the parties should be read in light of the parties' intent ("intent facts"), rather than the policy facts. *See, Watson v. Commissioner*, 36 T.C.M 1084 (1977); *Estate of Fuchs v. Commissioner*, 47 T.C. 199 (1966); *National Metropolitan Bank v. United States*, 87 F. Supp. 773 (Ct. Cl. 1950). In Priv. Letter Rul. 200603002 the IRS stated that the intent facts, rather than the policy facts, should determine whether the assignment of the joint and survivor policy to the ILIT would constitute a transfer subject to gift tax, or cause the proceeds to be includible in the estates of husband and wife if either died within three years of the assignment. In ruling in favor of the taxpayers, the IRS considered relevant the fact that the intent of the parties had been set forth in several contemporaneous documents at the time that the survivorship policy was purchased and issued. *See also*, Priv. Letter Rul. 8610068.

individual to substitute an insurance policy in a trust for assets of equivalent value cannot be seen as a right to the economic benefits of that insurance policy. The court held that in the case of an insurance policy the only asset that should be of equal value would be another insurance policy with 'equal cash surrender and face value, comparable premiums, and a similar form of policy.' *Estate of Jordahl v. Commissioner, supra* at 99. Thus, an insured does not possess incidents of ownership for purposes of section 2042 in an insurance policy held in a trust solely because the insured has the right to substitute assets of similar value for those policies." *See also,* Priv. Letter Ruls. 9548013 and 9227013.

Practice Point: Although the *Jordhal* decision involved the power of substitution held in a fiduciary capacity, that fact should make no difference.[37] However, a cautious practitioner may want to consider excluding the insured from having the power to substitute (in a non-

---

[37] "The Service has ruled that the retention of the power of substitution by the grantor does not preclude a transfer from being a completed gift at the time of the transfer for purposes of §2511. [Priv. Letter Ruls. 9415012 and 9227013.] It has reasoned that the power of substitution does not affect the disposition of the corpus of the trust nor the value of the corpus of the trust at the time of the substitution. The power of substitution in §675(4)(C) does not cause inclusion of the trust property in the grantor's estate. In *Jordahl Est. v. Comr.*, [65 T.C. 92 (1975)] the court held that a power of substitution held by a grantor as co-trustee did not cause inclusion of the property of the trust in the grantor's estate for federal estate-tax purposes under §§2038(a)(2) and 2042(a)(2). The court reasoned that the power of substitution did not constitute a power to 'alter, amend or revoke' under §2038(a)(2) the trust as the trust agreement specifically provided that any property substituted should be "of equal value" and thus prevented the grantor from depleting the trust corpus. It found that the power to substitute property 'of equal value' is akin to the retention by the settlor of the power to direct trustees as to investments, which generally do not cause estate tax inclusion. The court also held that the power of substitution did not constitute the retention of any 'incidents of ownership' that would have required inclusion of the insurance proceeds under §2042(2). The court reasoned that the grantor would have had to substitute an almost identical policy for the reacquired policy. The power of substitution held by the grantor in *Jordahl* was held in a fiduciary capacity. ***The result should have been the same, however, had the power not been held in a fiduciary capacity, given the requirement that the property substituted be of equivalent value to that of the reacquired property.*** The holding of *Jordahl* should also apply for purposes of §2036(a)(2), given the court's holding with regard to §2042(a)(2). In that regard,

fiduciary capacity) any policy that insures his or her life that is owned by the ILIT. Similarly, a cautious practitioner may also want to prohibit a grantor who has contributed IRC section 2036(b) controlled corporation stock to a trust from substituting other property for the stock. *See*, section 4.2, above. However, if such property is excluded from the power of substitution, the grantor may not have full grantor trust status over the ILIT, and other grantor trust powers will have to be used to obtain full grantor trust status for income tax purposes.

(9) Insured's Ability To Apply For Life Insurance. An insured's ability to apply for life insurance does not constitute an incident of ownership. *See*, section 4.12, below.

(10) Insured's Ability To Purchase Employer-Owned Policy. If an insured-shareholder or insured-employee has the right to purchase life insurance policies owned by his or her employer upon termination of the insured's employment or termination of the insured's ownership interest in the corporation (or such other acts of independent significance), the insured is not deemed to have an incident of ownership in the employer-owned policy. Priv. Letter Rul. 8049002. However,

---

note that there is no recognized exception to the estate-inclusion rule in §2042(a)(2) for powers subject to a definite external standard as there is for §§2036 - 2038.[*See, Jennings v. Smith*, 161 F.2d 74 (2d Cir. 1947).] Thus, it seems that if the power of substitution in §675(4)(C) satisfies the more stringent threshold of §2042(a)(2), it should satisfy §2036(a)(2) as well. The Service has also ruled that the power of substitution does not trigger inclusion of trust assets in the estate of the grantor for federal estate-tax purposes. [See, Priv. Letter Ruls. 9548013 (grantor's power of substitution and to designate a successor powerholder does not constitute a power to alter, amend, or revoke under §2038(a)); 9413045 (grantors' power of substitution will not cause inclusion of trust corpus in the estate of either grantor under §§2036 and 2038); 9247024 (no inclusion of trust property in grantor's gross estate under §§2033, 2035, 2037, 2038, 2041, or 2042; power of substitution held by nonadverse party); 9227013 (grantors' power of substitution does not constitute a power to alter, amend, or revoke under §2038(a)); 9037011 (power of substitution of nonadverse trustees exercisable in nonfiduciary capacity will not cause inclusion of trust property in the estate of either grantor for federal estate tax purposes); 9011052 (power of substitution of nonadverse parties will not cause estate tax inclusion).]" Carmen Irizarry-Diaz, "How Defective is Your Trust? Suggestions on Structuring an Intentionally Defective Grantor Trust," 41 *Tax Management Memorandum* 231, 238-239 (June 19, 2000). (Emphasis added.)

as previously stated above, if the insured's right to purchase the policy is in his or her sole discretion (i.e., the right to purchase is not subject to a preceding act of independent significance), then the insured will be deemed to have incidents of ownership in the employer-owned policy. *See*, Rev. Rul 79-46, 1979-1 C.B. 303.

(11) Insured's Ability To Expand Class Of ILIT Beneficiaries By Having More Children. The insured's act of bearing or adopting children is an act of independent significance, the incidental and collateral consequence of which is to add the child as beneficiary to the ILIT. Although the insured's act of bearing or adopting children will automatically result in adding the child as beneficiary to the ILIT, such result is merely a collateral consequence of the bearing or adopting children. Rev. Rul. 80-255, 1980-2 C.B. 272.

§4.10(c) Estate Tax Consequences Of ILIT Paying Death Taxes And Expenses

A provision within an ILIT or other governing instrument requiring the ILIT trustee to pay the deceased insured's death taxes (or other expenses) will cause inclusion of the ILIT in the insured's estate. Treas. Reg. §20.2042-1(b)(1). Instead of directing payment, an authorization in the ILIT permitting the trustee to purchase assets at fair market value from the decedent's estate or trust or to loan funds to the decedent's estate (for adequate interest and security) will not cause the proceeds to be includable in the insured's estate as "proceeds receivable by an executor." Authorizing the ILIT trustee to make loans and purchase assets will provide the liquidity necessary to pay the insured's death taxes and expenses. *See*, Paragraph 5.2 of Sample ILIT.

Proceeds from a second-to-die insurance policy transferred to an ILIT are not includable in the gross estate of the surviving spouse if the trustee only has *discretionary* power (in contrast to a *duty*) to use the life insurance proceeds to pay the federal estate tax of the surviving spouse. As such, the proceeds are not received by the trustee subject to an obligation, legally binding upon the trustee, to pay taxes, debts, or other charges enforceable against the estate of the surviving spouse under Treas. Reg. §20.2042-1(b). Pvt. Letter Rul. 200147039. The private letter ruling does not, however, address the issue of what the estate tax consequences would be if the trustee had in fact used the life insurance proceeds to pay the taxes, claims, and other obligations of the surviving spouse. Presumably the proceeds so used would be includable in the gross estate of the surviving spouse. *See also*, *Estate of Charles Howard Wade v. Commissioner*, 47 B.T.A. 21 (1942), acq. 1944 C.B. 29; *Old Colony Trust Company v. Commissioner*, 39 B.T.A. 871 (1939), acq. 1939-2 C.B. 27 where the court held that the trustee's mere power to pay taxes, debts, and expenses of the insured was not sufficient to result in the life insurance proceeds being includable in the insured's gross estate, when the power is not so exercised.

§4.11 INSURED-TRUSTEE NOT DEEMED TO HOLD INCIDENTS OF OWNERSHIP IN LIFE INSURANCE UNDER LIMITED CIRCUMSTANCES

An insured-trustee will not be deemed to hold incidents of ownership in policies of insurance held by the trust on the trustee's life, if:

(1) The insured does not retain any incidents of ownership at the time of the initial transfer, assuming the insured originally owned the policy;

(2) The insured did not transfer the policy to the trust;

(3) The insured does not provide (directly or indirectly) any assets to purchase or maintain the policy (including permitting a trustee to pay premiums from trust income or corpus that is required to be distributed to the insured[38]);

(4) The devolution of the trustee powers on insured was not part of a prearranged plan involving the participation of insured; and

---

[38] For example, if trust income is ***required*** to be distributed to the insured-beneficiary, the premiums must be paid from the trust principal and not out of income otherwise payable to the insured-beneficiary. The same holds true for mandatory distributions of trust principal to the insured-beneficiary. However, if trust principal ***may*** be paid to the insured-beneficiary to provide for the insured-beneficiary's health, education, support, and maintenance in accordance with the insured-beneficiary's accustomed standard of living, principal can be safely used to pay the premiums on the life insurance policy, because the distribution of principal is not mandatory. Priv. Letter. Rul. 9748020.

(5) The insured cannot exercise any powers (including trustee powers) over the policy for the insured's own personal benefit. Rev. Rul. 84-179, 1984-2 C.B. 195; Priv. Letter Ruls. 200617008, 200518005, and 9748020.

The criteria set forth in this ruling is an exception to the general rule of an insured-trustee possessing "incidents of ownership" under IRC section 2042. However, the ruling will never be applicable to a traditional ILIT, especially when the insured is making annual gifts to the ILIT; and the ruling should not be relied upon as authority for permitting an insured to serve as trustee of his or her ILIT. *See also, Estate of Hector R. Skifter v. Commissioner,* 468 F.2d 699 (2nd Cir. 1972); *Estate of Harry R. Fruehauf v. Commissioner,* 427 F.2d 80 (6th Cir. 1970), which describes several situations in which holding powers in a fiduciary capacity over a policy on the trustee's life will not cause the proceeds to be included in the trustee's estate upon his death. But if the trustee is also the income beneficiary (the *Fruehauf* situation), the proceeds are included.

§4.12 INSURED'S NON-BINDING TEST APPLICATION FOR LIFE INSURANCE IS NOT AN INCIDENT OF OWNERSHIP IN THE LIFE INSURANCE POLICY

TAM 9323002 holds that an application for life insurance when the insured did not sign as the policy "owner" but only as the "insured," and for which no premium payment accompanied the application did not create an incident of ownership in the insured since the application clearly stated that the policy would not be issued until the premium was paid. Thus a non-binding "test" application for life insurance showing "an ILIT to be created" as the potential owner should not result in the insured possessing an incident of ownership in the policy when it is finally issued to the ILIT trustee. Nor, should the non-binding "test" application result in the application of the IRC section 2035 three-year rule to the insured. *See,* section 4.1, above. Also, an insured's ability to apply for life insurance coverage does not create an incidents of ownership. Rev. Rul. 76-421, 1976-2 C.B. 280.[39]

---

[39] In Rev. Rul. 76-421, 1976-2 C.B. 280, the IRS ruled, "In the event that the insurance on the decedent's life terminates as a result of the cessation of the applicant owner's eligibility to own such insurance, the decedent is again eligible or

§4.13 GENERAL POWER OF APPOINTMENT MARITAL DEDUCTION

If the insured is married and the ILIT does not hold a second to die policy on the insured and his or her spouse, consider including a contingent marital deduction trust in the ILIT. If the ILIT proceeds are includable in the insured's gross estate, the contingent marital deduction provisions can eliminate any federal estate tax due upon the insured's death. A marital deduction may be accomplished by requiring the ILIT trustee to distribute the death benefit proceeds to the surviving spouse, either outright or through a marital deduction trust, such as a life estate with a general power of appointment (which is discussed immediately below), or a qualified terminable interest property ("QTIP") arrangement (which is discussed in section 4.14, below).

For a life estate with a general power of appointment to qualify for the estate tax marital deduction, three requirements must be met (which are in addition to the six preliminary requirements for the marital deduction).[40] IRC section 2056(b)(5). These three requirements are:

---

again has the right to enroll for insurance coverage. What reverts to the decedent, in such instance, is not insurance or the proceeds of insurance as required by the Code, but rather the right to enroll for insurance coverage provided the decedent takes affirmative action by submitting a new enrollment election form. The possession by the decedent of such right to enroll for insurance on the decedent's life, or the possibility of reversion of such right is not an 'incident of ownership,' as that term is defined in sections 20.2042-1(c)(2) and 20.2042-1(c)(3) [concerning 5% reversionary interest in policy or its proceeds] of the regulations."

[40] The six (6) preliminary requirements that must be met for an interest to qualify for the federal estate tax marital deduction are: (i) the decedent must be legally married at the time of his or her death; (ii) the person to whom the decedent is legally married to at the time of his or her death must survive the decedent; (iii) the surviving spouse must be a U.S. citizen; (iv) the interest passing to the surviving spouse must be includable in the decedent's U.S. gross estate; (v) the interest must "pass" to the surviving spouse; and (vi) the interest received by the surviving spouse cannot be a nondeductible terminable interest. If the surviving spouse is not a U.S. citizen, the marital deduction is available only if the property is held in a qualifying domestic trust under IRC section 2056A. *See*, Sebastian V. Grassi, Jr., *A Practical Guide to Drafting Marital Deduction Trusts (with Sample Forms and Checklists)*, (ALI-ABA, Philadelphia 2004, Supp. 2006) (800) 253-6397, www.ali-aba.org/aliaba/bk36.asp, for a discussion of the estate tax marital deduction.

(1) The surviving spouse must have a lifetime right to all of the income from the entire interest, or a specific portion of the entire interest;

(2) The income must be payable to the surviving spouse annually or more often; and

(3) The surviving spouse must have the power to appoint the entire interest or the specific portion to him/herself or to his or her estate. IRC section 2056(b)(5); Treas. Reg. §20.2056(b)-5(a).

§4.14 QUALIFIED TERMINABLE INTEREST PROPERTY MARITAL DEDUCTION

The qualified terminable interest property ("QTIP") devise is a statutory exception to the definition of "nondeductible terminable interest" for federal estate tax marital deduction purposes. Under this exception, the federal estate tax marital deduction is allowed for property given to a QTIP trust for the benefit of the decedent's surviving spouse, provided:

(1) The surviving spouse has a lifetime right to all of the income from the trust;

(2) All trust income is payable to the surviving spouse annually or more often;

(3) During the lifetime of the surviving spouse, no person, (including the surviving spouse or trustee) may possess the power to appoint QTIP marital deduction trust property to any person other than to the surviving spouse; and

(4) The decedent's executor makes an election to treat all or a specific portion of the trust property as qualified terminable interest property. IRC section 2056(b)(7).

§4.15 LIABILITY OF ILIT OR BENEFICIARY FOR ESTATE TAX ON LIFE INSURANCE PROCEEDS

The executor of a decedent's estate is entitled to recover federal estate taxes paid by the estate that are attributable to life insurance proceeds included in the insured's gross estate. IRC section 2206. If the life insurance proceeds are qualified and elected for the marital deduction, the executor is not entitled to apportionment or recovery under IRC section 2206. This special rule of exoneration is not, however, available for bequests of life insurance proceeds that qualify for the estate tax charitable deduction. Consequently, if life insurance proceeds are to be paid to a charity, the insured's will must waive the right of apportionment or recovery under IRC section 2206. In the absence of a waiver, the executor's right of apportionment/recovery for federal estate taxes attributable to life insurance proceeds includable in the insured's gross estate is on a pro rata basis. An insured can opt out of the recovery/apportionment provisions of IRC section 2206 by stating so in his or her will. A general provision in the insured's will to pay all taxes from residue will be sufficient to opt out of the Code's apportionment/recovery scheme. However, if the estate tax on the ILIT proceeds could be substantial, it may not be desirable to waive the right to recovery in all instances, particularly where the residuary beneficiaries and the ILIT beneficiaries differ significantly.

Life insurance proceeds received by the ILIT may be included in the insured's gross estate because of the three-year inclusion rule of IRC section 2035.

§4.16 EXECUTOR'S RIGHT TO RECOVER ESTATE TAX ATTRIBUTABLE TO GENERAL POWER OF APPOINTMENT

The executor of a decedent's estate is entitled to recover federal estate taxes paid by the estate that are attributable to property over which the decedent held a general power of appointment, and which property is included in the decedent's gross estate. IRC section 2207. The executor's right of apportionment/recovery is on a pro rata basis. A decedent can opt out of the recovery/apportionment provisions of IRC section 2207 by stating so in his or her will. A general provision in the decedent's will to pay all taxes from residue will be sufficient to opt out of the Code's apportionment/recovery scheme.

As previously mentioned, a *Crummey* withdrawal right is a general power of appointment and may be included in a beneficiary's estate under IRC section 2041. Who should be responsible for the federal estate taxes in such instance? Moreover, is it the drafting attorney's responsibility to notify the beneficiaries regarding this issue? The ILIT may be illiquid and unable to reimburse the beneficiary's estate under the recovery rules of IRC section 2207. The

ILIT may be illiquid and also unable to reimburse the beneficiary's estate under the recovery rules of IRC section 2207B.

§4.17 EXECUTOR'S RIGHT TO RECOVER ESTATE TAX ATTRIBUTABLE TO QTIP TRUST PROPERTY

The executor of a decedent's estate is entitled to recover federal estate taxes paid by the estate that are attributable to QTIP property included in the decedent's gross estate under IRC section 2044. IRC section 2207A. The executor's right of apportionment/recovery is on a marginal or incremental basis. A decedent can opt out of the recovery/apportionment provisions of IRC section 2207A by stating so in his or her will or revocable living trust. However, specific reference to IRC section 2207A (or its provisions) in the decedent's will or revocable living trust is required to opt out of the Code's apportionment/recovery scheme. If the surviving spouse waives the right to be reimbursed for estate taxes attributable to reverse QTIP property, the waiver (and payment of the estate taxes by the surviving spouse's estate) does not constitute a constructive addition to the reverse QTIP trust. Treas. Reg. §26.2652-1(a)(5), Example 8. If the ILIT contains a QTIP marital deduction trust to hold proceeds that are determined to be includable in the grantor's gross estate, should the surviving spouse waive the right to reimbursement? What if the beneficiaries of the surviving spouse's estate are different from the beneficiaries of the ILIT, which often occurs in a second marriage situation?

§4.18 EXECUTOR'S RIGHT TO RECOVER ESTATE TAX ATTRIBUTABLE TO GRANTOR'S RETAINED INTEREST

The executor of a decedent's estate is entitled to recover federal estate taxes paid by the estate that are attributable to property or interests in property that are included in the decedent's gross estate under the retained interest rules of IRC section 2036. IRC section 2207B. The executor's right of apportionment/recovery is on a marginal or incremental basis. A decedent can opt out of the recovery/apportionment provisions of IRC section 2207B by stating so in his or her will or revocable living trust. However, specific reference to IRC section 2207B (or its provisions) in the decedent's will or revocable living trust is required to opt out of the Code's apportionment/recovery scheme.

As previously mentioned, a *Crummey* withdrawal right is a general power of appointment. If the beneficiary releases the power and retains an interest in the ILIT that is included in the beneficiary's estate under IRC section 2036, who should be responsible for the federal estate taxes in such instance? The ILIT may be illiquid and unable to reimburse the beneficiary's estate under the recovery rules of IRC section 2207B.

ILIT property may be included in the grantor's gross estate because the grantor retained the right to vote shares of stock described in IRC section 2036(b).

Query, which section of the Code applies for apportionment/recovery when the retained interest results in the life insurance proceeds being included in the grantor's gross estate? IRC section 2206 calls for pro rata reimbursement whereas IRC section 2207B calls for incremental reimbursement. A possible solution may be for the grantor's will to require all apportionment/reimbursement under IRC sections 2206-2207B to be on an incremental basis.

5

Generation-Skipping Transfer Tax Issues

OVERVIEW OF CHAPTER

This chapter[1] discusses selected key generation-skipping transfer (GST) tax issues concerning life insurance.[2]

The GST tax is one of the most complicated provisions of the federal transfer tax system, and probably one of the least understood by practitioners who do not practice in the GST tax area on a frequent basis. The application of the GST tax exemption to an ILIT is important because of the insured's ability to leverage the transferor's GST

---

[1] The author gratefully acknowledges the contributions of Jon J. Gallo, Esq., of Greenberg, Glusker, Fields, Claman, Machtinger & Kinsella, LLP of Los Angeles, California, and Dennis M. Mitzel, Esq. of Berry Moorman, PC of Detroit, Michigan in the writing of this Chapter.

[2] *See,* Chapter 3 Howard M. Zaritsky & Stephan R. Leimberg, *Tax Planning With Life Insurance: Analysis With Forms—2d Edition,* Warren Gorham & Lamont, Boston, Massachusetts (Supp. 2007) for an overview of the GST taxation of life insurance. *See also,* Chapter 10 of Antonucci and Whitman, *After Death Tax Planning: Minimizing Tax Liabilities* (ALI-ABA, Philadelphia, 3d ed. 2004), www.ali-aba.org/aliaba/BK32/; Carol A. Harrington and Frederick G. Acker, 850 T.M., *Generation-Skipping Tax* (BNA Inc., Washington, DC); Carol A. Harrington, Lloyd Leva Plaine & Howard M. Zaritsky, *Generation-Skipping Transfer Tax Analysis With Forms,* (Warren, Gorham & Lamont, RIA, 2d ed. 2001 & 2006 Supp.); Jon J. Gallo, "The Use of Life Insurance in Estate Planning: A Guide To Planning and Drafting—Part 1," 33 *Real Property, Probate and Trust Journal* 685 (Winter 1999); Jon J. Gallo, "The Use of Life Insurance in Estate Planning: A Guide To Planning and Drafting—Part II," 34 *Real Property, Probate and Trust Journal* 55 (Spring 1999); and Jon J. Gallo, "Estate Planning and the Generation-Skipping Tax," 33 *Real Property, Probate and Trust Journal* 457 (Fall 1998).

exemption through the use of life insurance. The amount of GST tax exemption that generally needs to be allocated to an ILIT is small in comparison to the huge reward that is reaped when the insured dies and the ILIT receives the policy death benefits. This makes the ILIT an attractive candidate for dynasty trust treatment. The GST tax also impacts a beneficiary's right to withdraw gifts that are made to the ILIT. For example, if the beneficiary dies before the withdrawal right lapses, there may be a GST tax event, which could cause a conflict with the grantor's structure of the trust for transfer tax purpose. This chapter discusses these potential beneficiary-caused GST tax traps and how to avoid them.

In the ILIT context, there are several key GST tax issues that the advisor should note:

• The fact that a *Crummey* withdrawal right gift may qualify for the gift tax annual exclusion does not mean that the gift is automatically GST tax exempt. Because there is a disconnect between the gift tax annual exclusion under IRC section 2503(b) and the GST rules, GST tax exemption may still need to be allocated to the ILIT.

• If the spouse is a beneficiary of an ILIT, the spouse's *Crummey* withdrawal right should be limited to the five-by-five safe harbor amounts of IRC section 2514 and 2041, and the right of withdrawal must lapse no later than 60 days after the date of the transfer that creates the withdrawal right.

• Every ILIT is possibly subject to the indirect skip rules that came into existence under the 2001 Tax Act. A decision must be made to either opt in or opt out of those rules.

§5.1 BRIEF OVERVIEW OF THE GST TAX

Before the existence of the GST tax, many wealthy families transferred property to their descendants in trust rather than outright. At each subsequent death, the beneficiary's life estate was not includable in the beneficiary's gross estate, and for succeeding generations, the family's wealth went untaxed. The GST tax was designed to stop this tax-free transmission of wealth. The GST tax was initially adopted in 1976 and then replaced in its entirety with a new set of GST tax rules in 1986. The 1976 version of the GST tax was overly complicated. A lack of understanding, inability by the IRS to devise appropriate GST tax reporting forms, and scattered compliance all led to the demise of the original version of the GST tax. The 1986 version of the GST tax (as amended) is still in effect at this time (but will be repealed for calendar year 2010, and then reinstated on January 1, 2011). The GST tax is set forth in Chapter 13 of the Internal Revenue Code of 1986 (as amended), and is structured on a series of defined terms, many of which are discussed below. The purpose of the GST tax is to prevent the dynastic accumulation of inherited wealth that can occur when multiple generations of a transferor's family are benefited by property transfers that are not subject to additional estate taxation at each succeeding generation. Simply put, Congress wants to ensure that significant wealth transferred to a person's descendants (or transferees) is eventually taxed, even though the transferred wealth is insulated from successive estate or gift taxation. The imposition of the GST tax occurs at generations that are two or more below that of the transferor, such as the transferor's grandchildren or more remote descendants.

> **Example:** An individual dies leaving a credit shelter trust for the surviving spouse. After the death of the surviving spouse, the balance of the credit shelter trust, which is not GST tax exempt, is payable outright to the transferor's descendants, per stirpes. Six months after the transferor's death, the transferor's son dies leaving surviving issue. Upon the death of the transferor's surviving spouse, the trust distribution to the deceased son's issue will be subject to the GST tax, as a taxable termination.

> **Example:** After the surviving spouse's death, the balance of the credit shelter trust, which is not GST tax exempt, remains in trust for the benefit of the transferor's descendants for as long as is permitted under the rule against perpetuities. At the death of each descendant, as his or her interest passes to the next generation, that interest in the trust generally escapes estate tax, but is instead subject to the GST tax.

§5.2 GENERATION-SKIPPING TRANSFER DEFINED

The following events constitute a generation-skipping transfer: (1) a taxable termination; (2) a taxable distribution; or (3) a direct skip. IRC section 2611(a). An outright transfer to an individual who is a skip person that qualifies for the gift tax annual exclusion under IRC section 2503(b) does not constitute a GST event. Also, a transfer under IRC section 2503(e) (concerning direct payment of medical expenses and tuition) does not constitute a GST event; nor does any transfer: (1) to the extent the property transferred was subject to a prior GST tax; (2) the transferee in the prior transfer was assigned to the same generation as (or a lower generation than) the generation assignment of the transferee in the current transfer; and (3) the current transfer does not have the effect of avoiding the GST tax with respect to any transfer. IRC section 2611(b).

> **Practice Point:** Certain transfers from trusts or wills that were executed before a certain date are not subject to the GST tax. Treas. Reg. §26.2601-1. *See,* section 5.24, below. However, a modification of such instrument or an addition (including a constructive addition) to such trust may cause the trust to lose its GST grandfathered status. *See,* section 5.25, below.

§5.3 TAXABLE TERMINATION DEFINED

A taxable termination is the termination (by death, lapse of time, release of a power, or otherwise) of a beneficiary's interest in property held in a trust[3] (such as a life estate) where immediately after the termination, there is no person who has an interest[4] in the trust property

---

[3] For GST tax purposes, "[t]he term 'trust' includes any arrangement (other than...[a probate] estate) which, although not a trust, has substantially the same effect as a trust." IRC section 2652(b). For example, life insurance proceeds that are payable over time by the life insurance company constitute a trust arrangement. Treas. Reg. §26.2652-1(b)(1). Property held in a custodial arrangement (such as an UGMA or UTMA account) for the benefit of a skip person is a trust arrangement. Treas. Reg. §26.2652-1(b)(2), Example 1.

[4] IRC section 2652(c) defines what constitutes an "interest" in trust property for GST tax purposes. It is important to know who holds an "interest" in a trust for purposes of determining whether the trust is a skip person, and for purposes of determining if a taxable termination has occurred. A taxable termination may be postponed if a non-skip person has an "interest" in the trust as long as possible. However, certain "interests" are disregarded for GST purposes, including certain discretionary interests of charitable beneficiaries, and interests that are used primarily to postpone or avoid the GST tax. IRC sections 2652(c).

A person has an interest in property held in trust (i) if the person has a present legal right to receive income or corpus from the trust, or (ii) if the person is a permissible current non-charitable recipient of income or corpus of a trust. IRC section 2652(c). IRC section 2651(f)(2) provides a "look through" rule where an estate, trust or other entity has an interest in the property.

other than a skip person, or after the termination, no distribution may be made from the trust to a non-skip person. IRC section 2612(a). A taxable termination does not occur if, at the time of the termination of the beneficiary's interest, a transfer of the trust property occurs and that transfer is subject to estate or gift tax (such as the trust property's being includable in the beneficiary's gross estate because he or she has been granted a testamentary general power of appointment over the non-GST tax-exempt trust property). A taxable termination can occur only from a trust (or a trust arrangement). A taxable termination cannot occur from a probate estate.[5] Thus, a taxable termination of a trust is when all interests of non-skip persons come to an end. Because the GST tax is levied on the termination of any interest in trust property, a taxable termination can occur on more than one occasion.

For example, if T creates a trust to pay income for life to T's child (C) for life, then to T's grandchild (GC) for life, with distribution of the remainder to T's great grandchild (GGC), two taxable terminations will occur—one when C dies, and one when GC dies. The severity of taxable terminations underscores the need for transferors to allocate GST tax exemption to trusts that are intended to benefit skip persons.

> **Practice Point:** A non-skip person's interest in a trust that is used primarily to postpone or avoid any GST tax is disregarded for GST tax purposes. IRC section 2652(c)(2). An interest is considered so used if a significant purpose for the creation of the interest is to postpone or avoid the GST tax. Treas. Reg. §26.2612-1(e)(2)(ii). The interest to be disregarded does not have to be nominal.

> **Practice Point:** A charity's interest in a trust will not avoid a taxable termination if (i) the charity's interest is discretionary, or (ii) the charity's interest is a separate share that existed at all times from the creation of the trust (or results from a qualified severance), or (iii) the charity's interest is used primarily to postpone or avoid the GST tax. Treas.

[5] *But see*, Treas. Reg. §26.2652-1(b)(2), Example 3, which takes the position that a bequest payable under a transferor's will is treated as a "transfer in trust" if the identity of the transferee is contingent upon the occurrence of an event (such as the transferee's survival) that will not necessarily occur within six months of the transferor's death.

Reg. §§26.2612-1(e)(1)(ii), 26.2612-1(e)(2)(ii), and 26.2654-1(a).

§5.3(a) Amount Of GST Tax Attributable To A Taxable Termination

The amount of the taxable termination that is subject to GST tax is described in IRC section 2622. Since the GST tax is paid from the property giving rise to the taxable termination, the tax is similar to the tax-inclusive nature of the estate tax, i.e., the dollars used to pay the GST tax are subject to the GST tax. Because, the GST tax is calculated on a tax-inclusive basis, this has the effect of approximating the result of the property being subject to estate tax in the estate of the skipped person. The trustee of the trust is liable for paying the GST tax, which is paid from the assets giving rise to the taxable termination. IRC section 2603(a)(2); Treas. Reg. §26.2662-1(c)(1)(ii).

§5.3(a)(1) Meaning Of Tax-Inclusive Basis

Being on a "tax-inclusive" basis means that GST tax is paid not only on the transfer giving rise to the GST tax but also on the GST tax actually paid as a result of the transfer—a tax on a tax. In other words, the dollars used to pay the GST tax are subject to the GST tax and are part of the transferred property's tax base. At the 50% tax rate, the cost in transfer taxes (gift tax and GST tax) for an inter-vivos direct skip is "only" 125% of the amount actually received by the skip person, which is the least costly method of making taxable GSTs (see, example below). This is because an inter-vivos direct skip is taxed on a tax-exclusive basis, with the transferor responsible for paying the tax. Being on a tax-exclusive basis means that the GST tax is paid only on the transferred property and not on the dollars used to pay the GST tax. However, because of the tax-inclusive nature of the federal estate tax, direct skips at the transferor's death, direct skips from a trust, taxable distributions, and taxable terminations from trusts created during the transferor's lifetime generally result in transfer taxes of 200% of the amount actually received by the skip person. The most expensive forms of GST transfers are taxable terminations or taxable distributions occurring from trusts established at the transferor's death that are subject to federal estate tax. In those instances, the total transfer tax cost (at a 50% GST and 50% federal estate tax rate) to transfer $1 million to a skip person is 300% of the amount actually received by the skip person, to wit, \$4 million devise × .50 (FET Rate) = \$2 million × .50 (GST Rate) = \$1 million net to skip person.

Example (Direct Skip During Transferor's Lifetime): Grandfather makes an inter vivos transfer gift of \$1 million to his grandchild. No applicable exclusion amount credit and no GST tax exemption are available for allocation to the gift. The total cost of the transfer will be \$2.25 million. Transfer taxes will total \$1.25 million, computed as follows:

Gift tax on \$1 million gift =	\$500,000 (Paid by grandfather)
GST tax on \$1 million gift =	\$500,000 (Paid by grandfather)
Gift tax on \$500,000 GST tax =	\$250,000 (Paid by grandfather)
Total transfer taxes =	\$1,250,000

Total transfer taxes (\$1.25 million) amount to 125% of the amount (\$1 million) gifted to the skip person. Thus, it will take \$2.25 million to transfer \$1 million to the grandchild. (The GST tax paid by grandfather will be removed from the grandfather's death-time taxable estate, as will the gift tax paid by the grandfather [assuming he lives for more than 3 years after the gift (IRC section 2035(b))], ultimately saving 50% of the lifetime transfer taxes paid.)

Example (Direct Skip At Transferor's Death): Grandfather devises \$1 million to his grandchild. No applicable exclusion amount credit and no GST tax exemption is available for allocation to the devise. The total cost of the transfer will be \$3 million. The formula is: [\$1 million (devise) + \$500,000 (GST tax)]/1-.50 (where .50 is the applicable federal estate tax rate) = \$3 million (in other words, to be able to pay \$1 million plus the \$500,00 GST tax (\$1.5 million), it is necessary to start with twice that amount because of the 50% estate tax). Transfer taxes (estate and GST taxes) will total \$2 million, which amounts to 200% of the amount (\$1 million) transferred to the grandchild. Thus, it will take \$3 million to transfer \$1 million to the grandchild.

Example (Taxable Termination From Trust Established During Transferor's Lifetime): Grandfather gifts \$2 million in trust with income only to his only son and remainder to his sole grandchild. The grandfather desires the grandchild to receive $1 million net of all transfer taxes. No applicable exclusion amount credit and no GST tax exemption are available for allocation to the inter-vivos gift. The total cost of the transfer taxes will be 200% of the $1 million amount received by the grandchild. The total cost of the transfer will be $3 million. Transfer taxes will total $2 million, computed as follows:

Gift tax on $2 million gift =	$1,000,000 (Paid by grandfather)
GST tax on $2 million termination =	$1,000,000 (Paid from the gifted funds)
Total transfer taxes =	$ 2,000,000

Total transfer taxes ($2 million) amount to 200% of the amount ($1 million) received by the skip person. Thus, it will take $3 million to transfer $1 million to the grandchild. (The gift tax paid by the grandfather (assuming he lives for more than 3 years after the gift [IRC section 2035(b))], will be also removed from the death-time taxable estate, ultimately saving 50% of the gift tax paid.)

Example (Taxable Termination From Trust Established At Transferor's Death): Grandfather devises $2 million in trust with income only to his only son and remainder to his sole grandchild. No applicable exclusion amount credit and no GST tax exemption are available for allocation to the devise. Estate tax of $2 million will be paid at death on the $4 million needed to pay the tax, leaving a $2 million bequest. Another 50% GST tax ($1 million) is due at the taxable termination, leaving $1 million to the grandchild. The total cost of the transfer taxes will be 300% of the remaining amount received by the grandchild. The formula is: [$1 million (remaining devise) + $1 million (GST tax)]/1-.50 (where .50 is the applicable federal estate tax rate) = $4 million. Transfer taxes (estate and GST taxes) will total $3 million, which amount to 300% of the amount ($1 million) transferred to the skip person. The total amount transferred is $4 million for a $1 million distribution to the grandchild.

§5.3(b) Simultaneous Terminations

Simultaneous termination of two or more interests creates only one taxable termination. Treas. Reg. §26.2612-1(b)(3), (f), Example 8.

§5.3(c) Change In Identity Of Transferor

Because the estate tax and gift tax supersede the GST tax and determine the identity of the transferor, a transfer from a trust that would otherwise be a taxable termination is not subject to GST tax if the transfer is subject to estate or gift tax. Treas. Reg. §26.2612-1(b)(1)(i).

§5.3(d) Death Of A Lineal Descendant

If a portion of a trust is distributed outright to a skip person because of the death of a lineal descendant of the transferor, the distribution to the skip person is a taxable termination (and not a taxable distribution) because there has been a termination of a portion of the trust estate. IRC section 2612(a)(2); Treas. Reg. §26.2612-1(b)(2), (f), Example 9.

§5.3(e) IRS Reporting Requirements For A Taxable Termination

Taxable terminations must be reported by the trustee, even if the taxable termination has an inclusion ratio of zero and does not generate any GST tax. The trustee must file IRS Form 706-GS(T) (Generation-Skipping Transfer Tax Return For Terminations) and pay any GST tax that may be owed. Treas. Reg. §26.2662-1(b)(2).

§5.4 BASIS ADJUSTMENT FOR GST TAX PAID

The basis of property for which a GST tax has been paid is increased (but not above fair market value). IRC section 2654(a). The property's basis is increased by the amount of the GST tax paid (computed without regard to the IRC section 2604 credit for state GST taxes[6]) on the

[6] As a result of the 2001 Tax Act, the credit for state GST tax expired on December 31, 2004 and is automatically reinstated when the provisions of the 2001 Tax Act expire on December 31, 2010. IRC section 2604 (c).

property's unrealized gain, and the adjustment is made after any basis adjustment to the property is made under IRC section 1015 (concerning gift tax paid). The property's unrealized gain is the excess of the property's fair market value over its adjusted basis immediately before the transfer that gives rise to the GST tax. Thus, an inter-vivos direct skip with an increase in basis for gift tax paid and an increase in basis for GST tax paid may result in a basis increase close to the transferred property's fair market value. This will not be the case in a taxable distribution or a taxable termination. However, if the property is transferred in a taxable termination that occurs at the same time and as a result of the death of an individual, the basis of such property is adjusted as provided under IRC section 1014(a) (concerning basis of property acquired from a decedent); except that, if the inclusion ratio of the transferred property is less than one, any increase or decrease in basis is limited by multiplying such increase or decrease (as the case may be) by the inclusion ratio. IRC section 2654(a). Property transferred in a direct skip at death has a basis equal to its federal estate tax value–no basis adjustment for the GST tax is made.

§5.5 TAXABLE DISTRIBUTION DEFINED

A taxable distribution is any distribution from a trust (other than a direct skip or taxable termination) to a skip person when non-skip persons are also beneficiaries of the trust. IRC section 2612(b). A taxable distribution can occur only from a trust (or a trust arrangement). A taxable distribution cannot occur from a probate estate.[7] If the distribution is of taxable income, the GST tax paid is deductible for income tax purposes. IRC section 164(a)(4). Taxable distributions do not include distributions described under IRC section 2503(e) (concerning direct payment of medical expenses and tuition). IRC section 2611(b)(1); Pvt. Letter Rul. 9823006. For example, in a spray trust from which income or principal can be paid to the grantor's children and more remote descendants, any distribution to a grandchild (who is a skip person) is a taxable distribution. However, if the trustee pays the grandchild's

---

[7] *But see*, Treas. Reg. §26.2652-1(b)(2), Example 3, which takes the position that a bequest payable under a transferor's will is treated as a "transfer in trust" if the identity of the transferee is contingent upon the occurrence of an event (such as the transferee's survival) that will not necessarily occur within six months of the transferor's death.

tuition or medical expenses directly from the trust (rather than reimbursing the grandchild), there is no taxable distribution. Taxable distributions do not include distributions that meet the definitional requirements of taxable terminations or direct skips. IRC section 2612(b). A skip person's exercise of a power of withdrawal (such as a five-by-five power or a *Crummey* withdrawal right) in a trust that does not have a zero inclusion ratio (i.e., a non-GST tax exempt trust or a non-IRC section 2642(c)(2) trust[8]), is a taxable distribution if the beneficiary has a continuing interest in the trust. Treas. Reg. §26.2612-1(f), Example 13. When a GST transfer meets the definitional requirements of both a taxable distribution and taxable termination, IRC section 2612 provides that the GST transfer is classified as a taxable termination.

§5.5(a) Amount Of GST Tax Attributable To A Taxable Distribution

The amount of the taxable distribution that is subject to GST tax is described in IRC section 2621(a). The distributee is liable for paying the GST tax, which causes the GST tax to be calculated on a tax-inclusive basis because the distributee pays the GST tax out of the distributed property. IRC section 2603(a)(1); Treas. Reg. §26.2662-1(c)(1)(i). This has the effect of approximating the result of the property being subject to estate tax in the estate of the skipped person.

§5.5(b) Payment Of GST Tax By Trustee

If the trustee pays the GST tax on the taxable distribution, the trustee's payment constitutes an additional taxable distribution to the skip person, for which GST tax must be paid. IRC section 2621(b).

---

[8] Under IRC section 2642(c), the amount of the gift to the trust must be a non-taxable gift (i.e., not exceed the annual gift tax exclusion amount available to the donor as concerns the skip-person-beneficiary), the trust must have only one beneficiary, distributions can be made only to or for the benefit of the skip-person-beneficiary, the assets must be includable in the skip-person-beneficiary's gross estate if the beneficiary dies before the trust terminates, and if the trust terminates before the beneficiary dies, the trust assets must be distributed to the ski-person-beneficiary. If the gift is an interest in a family-limited partnership or closely held business, which is hard to value, the transferor should, as a matter of caution, consider filing a "*Notice of Allocation of GST Tax Exemption to Trust*" (*see*, Appendix 4) in order to be assured that the trust is GST tax exempt if the IRS determines that the trust is not an IRC section 2642(c) trust because of a change (i.e., increase) in the value of the transferred assets.

§5.5(c) Multiple Simultaneous Skips

Taxable distributions are subject to GST tax only once, even though multiple generations may be simultaneously skipped. For example, a non-GST-tax-exempt trust makes a distribution to great-grandchild (skipping a grandchild). The distribution to the great-grandchild is taxed only once, even though the grandchild's generation was skipped.

§5.5(d) IRS Reporting Requirements For A Taxable Distribution

Taxable distributions must be reported by the trustee, even if the taxable distribution has an inclusion ratio of zero and does not generate any GST tax. The trustee must file IRS Form 706-GS(D-1) (Notification of Distribution From a Generation-Skipping Trust) for each skip person who receives a distribution. A copy of the filed Form 706-GS(D-1) must also be sent to each skip person who received a distribution from the trust. The skip person uses the information on IRS Form 706-GS(D-1) to complete IRS Form 706-GS(D) (Generation-Skipping Transfer Tax For Distributions) and pay any GST tax that may be owing. Treas. Reg. §26.2662-1(b).

§5.6 INCOME TAX DEDUCTION FOR GST TAX PAID

IRC section 164(a)(4) provides for a special income tax deduction for the payment of GST tax on income distributions. IRC section 691(c)(3) provides for a special income tax deduction for the payment of GST tax on income in respect of a decedent with regard to a taxable termination or a direct skip that occurs as a result of the transferor's death.

§5.7 DIRECT SKIP DEFINED

A direct skip (in contrast to an "indirect skip," which is discussed in section 5.29(b), below) is any transfer to a skip person that is subject to federal estate or gift tax. IRC section 2612(c). For example, an inter-vivos taxable gift or a testamentary bequest to a grandchild (who is a skip person) under the transferor's will or a trust included in the transferor's gross estate is a direct skip. A transfer to a trust solely for the benefit of skip persons is also a direct skip. IRC section 2613(a). A direct skip can occur from a probate estate or from a trust (or trust arrangement).

§5.7(a) Amount Of GST Tax Attributable To A Direct Skip

The amount of the direct skip that is subject to GST tax is described in IRC section 2623. If the direct skip occurs at the death of the transferor, the GST tax is in addition to any estate tax that may be owed on property transferred to the skip person.

§5.7(b) Payment Of GST Tax Attributable To A Direct Skip

By definition, a direct skip is always subject to gift tax (which is a tax-exclusive computation) or estate tax (which is a tax-inclusive computation). A direct skip results in the simultaneous imposition of the GST tax and estate or gift tax. The transferor is liable for the GST tax regarding an inter-vivos direct skip (other than a direct skip from a trust). IRC section 2603(a)(3); Treas. Reg. §26.2662-1(c)(1)(iii). The payment of the GST tax by the transferor on an inter-vivos direct skip (other than a direct skip from a trust) causes the GST tax to be calculated on a tax-exclusive basis, similar to the gift tax. This means the GST tax is paid only on the transferred property and not on the dollars used to pay the GST tax. However, the GST tax paid by the transferor on an inter-vivos direct skip is an additional taxable gift. IRC sections 2623 and 2515. The trustee is liable for the GST tax regarding a direct skip from a trust or with respect to property that continues to be held in trust. IRC section 2603(a)(2); Treas. Reg. §26.2662-1(c)(1)(iv). The executor is liable for the GST tax regarding a direct skip (other than a direct skip from a trust or with respect to property that continues to be held in trust) if the transfer is subject to estate tax. Treas. Reg. §26.2662-1(c)(1)(v). The payment of the GST tax by the trustee or the executor also causes the GST tax to be calculated on a tax-exclusive basis. However, a direct skip at death is more expensive than an inter-vivos direct skip. This is because the dollars used to pay the GST tax on the direct skip occurring at death are subject to federal estate tax (but not GST tax).

§5.7(c) Certain Direct Skips Are Not Subject To The GST Tax

Certain direct skips are not subject to the GST tax and are automatically assigned a zero inclusion ratio by the Internal Revenue Code. IRC section 2642(c). Outright gifts to an individual who is a skip person that come within the gift tax annual exclusion amount described in IRC section 2503(b), lifetime gifts that qualify for the special medical or tuition unlimited gift tax exclusion under IRC section 2503(e), and gifts that qualify for the annual gift tax exclusion amount that are made to a trust described in IRC section 2642(c)(2) (i.e., gifts to a trust for a single skip-person-beneficiary that come within the annual gift tax exclusion amount, and the trust is included in that beneficiary's gross estate if he or she dies before the trust terminates, such as an annual exclusion gift to an IRC section 2503(c) minor's trust for the sole benefit of a skip person[9]) are not subject to the GST tax.[10] *See*, Priv. Letter Rul. 200519006.

> **Practice Point:** As previously mentioned, although a *Crummey* withdrawal right over a gift made to a trust results in the gift qualifying for the annual gift tax exclu-

---

[9] A transfer to an IRC section 2503(c) minor's trust may not qualify as a transfer to an IRC section 2642(c) trust if the IRC section 2503(c) trust is not treated as a skip person because of IRC section 2653(c)(3). "Section 2652(c)(3) provides that a person whose support obligation could be discharged with trust property does not have an interest in the trust if such use is discretionary or pursuant to a state Uniform Gifts to Minors Act. However, if the trust instrument requires that trust property be used for a support obligation, then the person is treated as having an interest in the trust. The issue of whether the ability to discharge a support obligation constitutes an interest is important in determining whether there is a direct skip. The occurrence of a direct skip determines when the tax is due, the tax base, and the person liable for the tax. In addition, whether a direct skip has occurred must be determined because the predeceased ancestor exception applies only to direct skips. Example: T transfers $100,000 to a §2503(c) minor's trust for T's grandchild, GC. T must determine whether a direct skip has occurred to know the amount of tax and when the tax would be due. If GC's parent, C, has an obligation to support GC, which obligation could be discharged from the trust, and the ability to do so were treated as an interest in C, the transfer into the trust would not be a direct skip because the trust would not be a skip person as defined in §2613(a)(2). If such were the case, no tax would be due at the time of the original transfer to the trust. However, a taxable termination would occur when C died or the obligation ended. The regulations provide that an individual does not have an interest "merely because a support obligation of that individual may be satisfied by a distribution that is either within the discretion of a fiduciary or pursuant to" a Uniform Gifts or Transfers to Minor's Act. [Treas. Reg. §26.2612-1(e)(2)(i)]. The regulations do not specifically address the issue of discretionary distributions expressed as 'shall pay' or 'as the trustee determines is necessary,' which could be considered mandatory and not discretionary." Section II, D, 7 of Harrington and Acker, 850 T.M., *Generation-Skipping Tax*. *See also*, Section V, D, 5, b of Lischer, 846-2nd T.M., *Gifts to Minors*.

[10] When using a single ILIT with *Crummey* withdrawal powers for skip-person beneficiaries, the ILIT must establish separate trust shares for each skip-person beneficiary. Each separate trust share must comply with the requirements of IRC section 2642(c)(2) in order for the grantor's gift(s) to the ILIT to be GST tax exempt.

sion under IRC section 2503(b), the gift will not be exempt from GST tax if the withdrawal right is held by a skip person and the trust (or trust share) is other than an IRC section 2642(c)(2) trust. Furthermore, the exercise of the withdrawal right by a skip person in a non-IRC section 2642(c)(2) trust will result in a taxable distribution (or possibly a taxable termination). Treas. Reg. §26.2612-1(f), Example 13.

§5.7(d) Multiple Simultaneous Direct Skips

A direct skip is taxed only once, regardless of how many generations are simultaneously skipped. For example, grandparent gifts $50,000 to great-grandchild. Only one direct skip occurs, even though grandparent has skipped his or her grandchildren's generation. Treas. Reg. §26.2612-1(a).

§5.7(e) IRS Reporting Requirements For A Direct Skip

An inter-vivos direct skip that occurs while the transferor is alive is reported on IRS Form 709 (United States Gift [and Generation-Skipping Transfer] Tax Return). Treas. Reg. §26.2662-1(b)(3)(i). A direct skip that occurs at the same time as and as a result of the death of the transferor is reported on IRS Form 706 (United States Estate [and Generation-Skipping Transfer] Tax Return). Treas. Reg. §26.2662-1(b)(3)(ii).

§5.8 SKIP PERSON DEFINED AND GENERATION ASSIGNMENTS

A skip person may be an individual or a trust. Subject to the "transferor move-down rule" discussed in section 5.11, below, a skip person is an individual assigned to a generation that is two or more generations below that of the transferor (such as a grandchild). A trust is a skip person if either (1) all interests in the trust are held by skip persons; or (2) no person holds an interest in the trust and no future trust distributions—other than a distribution the probability of which occurring is so remote as to be negligible (including distributions at the termination of the trust)—can be made, to anyone, other than to a skip person. A non-skip person is any person (or trust) who is not a skip person. IRC section 2613; Treas. Reg. §26.2612-1(d)(2). A transfer to a trust that is a skip person is a GST. IRC section 2612(c)(2). For

GST tax purposes, "trust" includes arrangements analogous to a trust (other than a probate estate). IRC sections 2652(b)(2) and (3). *See,* Treas. Reg. §26.2652-1(b)(2), Example 1, 2, and 3. For GST tax purposes, a beneficiary's "interest" in a trust is described in IRC section 2652(c)(1). An individual who is assigned to more than one generation is assigned to the youngest generation. IRC section 2651(f)(1); Treas. Reg. §26.2651-2 (per T.D. 9214 (7/18/2005)).

§5.8(a) Generation Assignments Summarized

Generation assignments (vis-à-vis the transferor) are determined under IRC section 2651, and are summarized in the following chart.

Generation Assignments	Family Members[11]	Non-Family Members
Transferor's generation (non-skip person)	Transferor, transferor's spouse, transferor's brothers and sisters	Not more than 12½ years younger than the transferor
First generation younger than transferor (non-skip person)	Transferor's children, nieces, nephews and their spouses	More than 12½ but not more than 37½ years younger than the transferor
Second generation younger than transferor (skip person)	Transferor's grandchildren, grandnieces, grandnephews and their spouses	More than 37½ but not more than 62½ years younger than the transferor

[11] Adopted and half-blood individuals are treated as a relationship by full blood. IRC section 2651(b)(3). A legally adopted individual who is under the age of 18 at the time of the adoption, who is not adopted primarily for the purpose of avoiding the GST tax, and who is a descendant of a parent of the adoptive parent (or the spouse or former spouse of the adoptive parent) and who would be assigned to more than one generation per IRC section 2651(f)(1), is now treated as a member of the generation that is one generation below the adoptive parent for GST generation assignment purposes for determining whether a transfer to the adopted individual from the adoptive parent (or the spouse or former spouse of the adoptive parent, or a lineal descendant of a grandparent of the adoptive parent) is subject to the GST tax. Treas. Reg. §26.2651-2(b) (per T.D. 9214 (7/18/2005)). In addition, when the adopted child's generation assignment is adjusted, a corresponding generation assignment adjustment is also made with respect to that transfer, as concerns: (i) the adopted individual's spouse (or former spouse), (ii) the adopted individual's descendants, and (iii) the spouse or former spouse of each descendant of the adopted individual. Treas. Reg. §26.2651-2(c) (per T.D. 9214 (7/18/2005)).

§5.9 PREDECEASED PARENT RULE AND GENERATION ASSIGNMENTS

The predeceased parent rule provides that if a skip person's ancestor, who is a descendant of the transferor (for GST tax purposes), predeceases the transferor, the skip person moves up in generation assignments (vis-à-vis the transferor). Expanded by the Taxpayer Relief Act of 1997 ("TRA 1997"), the "predeceased parent rule" is now applicable to taxable terminations, taxable distributions, and direct skips. The predeceased parent rules also applies to transfers to collateral heirs, such as grand nieces and grand nephews, provided the transferor has no living descendants at the time of the transfer. Treas. Reg. §26.2651-1(b) (per T.D. 9214 (7/18/2005)). Furthermore, if a beneficiary who is a descendant of the transferor (for GST tax purposes) dies within 90 days after the date of a GST transfer that occurs because of the death of the transferor, the beneficiary is treated as having predeceased the transferor, and the deceased beneficiary's child will move up a generation assignment (vis-à-vis the transferor) and be placed in the same generation assignment held by his or her (now deceased) parent vis-à-vis the transferor. IRC section 2651(e); Treas. Reg. §26.2651-1(a)(2)(iii) (per T.D. 9214 (7/18/2005)).

This 90-day survivorship rule expands the "predeceased parent rule" of IRC §2651(e) by allowing a grandchild to move up into his parent's generation for GST tax purposes if the parent dies within 90 days of a transferor.

On July 18, 2005, the IRS issued amendments to the final regulations concerning the predeceased parent rule under IRC section 2651(e). *See,* Treas. Reg. §§26.2612-1, 26.2651-1, 26.2651-2, and 26.2651-3 (per T.D. 9214 [7/18/2005]). The amendments to the final regulations discuss the 90-day survival rule (which is now automatic and does not require an express 90-day survival provision in the governing instrument or a state statute that provides for a 90-day survival period. These amendments change the prior Treasury Regulations concerning how to determine the date of a transfer for purposes of applying the predeceased parent rule and determining when certain adopted individuals and those who come within the predeceased parent rule (and their spouses and descendants) are to be reassigned to a different generation for GST tax purposes.

§5.9(a) Disclaimers And The Predeceased Parent Rule

The predeceased parent rule does not apply to disclaimers, even though under state law the disclaimant is treated as having predeceased the transferor of the disclaimed property. Treas. Reg. §26.2651-1(a)(2)(iv) (per T.D. 9214 (7/18/2005)).

§5.9(b) Additions To A Trust That Is Subject To The Predeceased Parent Rule

If the predeceased parent (i.e., the deceased descendant who is the ancestor of the beneficiary) was dead at the time a transferor's transfer in trust first became subject to estate or gift tax, then the predeceased parent rule will apply to post-1997 taxable distributions and taxable terminations, as well as to direct skips. If a transferor makes an addition to an existing trust after the death of a descendant of the transferor in an intervening generation, the additional property is treated as being held in a separate trust for purposes of the GST tax. Treas. Reg. §26.2651-1(a)(4) (per T.D. 9214 [7/18/2005]). The time of the addition (and not the time of the first transfer to the trust) is the relevant time to determine whether the property attributable to the addition qualifies for the predeceased parent rule.

§5.9(c) Unnatural Order Of Death Rule

A corollary to the predeceased parent rule is the unnatural order of death rule added by the 2001 Tax Act and set forth in IRC section 2632(d). That rule allows a transferor to make a retroactive allocation of the transferor's GST tax exemption to lifetime transfers to an inter-vivos trust if a non-skip beneficiary of the trust, who is a lineal descendant of the transferor's grandparents, dies after December 31, 2000, but before the transferor. The rule does not protect against an unnatural order of death that occurs after the transferor's death. The retroactive allocation of GST tax exemption must be made on the transferor's United States Gift Tax Return for the calendar year in which the non-skip person died.

§5.9(d) Ninety-Day Survival Rule

The ninety (90)-day survivorship rule provides, "*[A]ny individual who dies no later than 90 days after a transfer occurring by reason of the death of the transferor is treated as having predeceased the transferor.*"

Treas. Reg. §26.2651-1(a)(2)(iii) (per T.D. 9214 (7/18/2005)). This survivorship rule expands the "predeceased parent rule" of IRC section 2651(e), by allowing a grandchild to move up into his parent's generation for GST tax purposes if the parent dies within 90 days of a GST event that occurs because of the death of the transferor. The 90-day survival rule is now automatic, thus abrogating the requirement that the ninety (90)-day survival period be expressly provided by applicable local law or the governing instrument.

§5.10 TRANSFEROR DEFINED

Generally, a transferor (for GST tax purposes) means the decedent in the case of property includable in the decedent's gross estate under Chapter 11 of the Internal Revenue Code, and the donor in the case of property subject to gift tax (without regard to exemptions, exclusions, deductions, and credits) under Chapter 12 of the Internal Revenue Code. IRC section 2652(a)(1); Treas. Reg. §26.2652-1(a)(2). Determining the identity of the transferor is important for determining a transferee's generation assignment and whose GST tax exemption may be allocated to the transfer in question. Subject to the special exception concerning property that has been elected for reverse QTIP treatment under IRC 2652(a)(3), the most recent transfer subject to federal estate or gift tax determines the identity of the transferor and whether the transfer is subject to the GST tax. Once a new transferor is determined, any prior allocation of GST tax exemption by a prior transferor is lost. Identifying the transferor is important if the ILIT contains *Crummey* withdrawal rights. The identity of the transferor may change because of a release of a *Crummey* withdrawal right in excess of the five-by-five safe harbor of IRC 2514(e), the waiver of a *Crummey* withdrawal right, or the death of the holder of an unlapsed *Crummey* withdrawal right.

§5.10(a) *Crummey* Powers Can Change The Identity Of The Transferor

A *Crummey* withdrawal right is a general power of appointment. IRC sections 2514 and 2041. Although its lapse during the powerholder's lifetime may not be a taxable release under the five-by-five safe harbor rules of IRC sections 2514(e) and 2041(b)(2), if the powerholder dies before the lapse of the withdrawal right (whether it's a single right of withdrawal or a hanging right of withdrawal) the amount of the unlapsed right of withdrawal at the date of the powerholder's death will be included in the powerholder's estate under IRC section 2041. For GST tax purposes, the deceased powerholder will become the (new) transferor of the amount included in his or her estate. Thus, any GST tax exemption previously allocated by the grantor will be lost and ineffective as to the amount included in the powerholder's estate, and the executor of the deceased powerholder's estate may have to allocate the decedent's GST tax exemption to that amount, to preserve the ILIT's zero (0) inclusion ratio.

Also, if the beneficiary's *Crummey* withdrawal right lapses in an amount greater than five by five and the lapse amount in excess of five by five is a taxable release of a power of appointment under IRC section 2514, the beneficiary will become the new transferor of the lapsed amount in excess of five by five. Thus, any GST tax exemption previously allocated by the grantor will be lost and ineffective as to the amount in excess of five by five. Additionally, if the beneficiary has a retained interest in the ILIT, all or a portion of the value of the ILIT will be included in the beneficiary's gross estate upon his or her death. IRC section 2036(a); Treas. Reg. §20.2041-3(d)(4). The effect of cumulative taxable releases with a retained interest by the beneficiary may result in all (or a significant portion) of the beneficiary's separate trust share being included in his or her gross estate. Treas. Reg. §20.2041-3(d)(5). Furthermore, the beneficiary will become the (new) transferor for GST tax purposes of the trust share that is includable in his or her gross estate, thus wasting any GST tax exemption that was previously allocated to the trust share. IRC section 2652(a)(1); Treas. Reg. §26.2652-1(a)(2). *See*, section 3.11, above.

> **Practice Point:** If an ILIT is designed from the onset to be a GST tax exempt dynasty trust, then it may be prudent to forgo the *Crummey* withdrawal rights—including those limited to five by five, and instead have the grantor make gifts that utilize the grantor's gift tax applicable exclusion amount and GST tax exemption. As mentioned above, there is always a GST tax risk when a beneficiary who holds a *Crummey* withdrawal right dies before the lapse of the withdrawal right—even a withdrawal right that falls within the five-by-five safe harbor rules. This is particularly relevant where the ILIT's beneficiaries are comparable in age to the grantor-insured, or older than the grantor-insured. However, if non-hanging *Crummey* withdrawal

rights are to be used, consider limiting the withdrawal period to 30 or 60 days.

§5.10(b) Gift Splitting By Spouses Creates Two Transferors

If a married couple elects gift splitting under IRC section 2513, each spouse is treated as the transferor (for GST tax purposes only) of one-half of the entire value of the property transferred, regardless of the interest the donor-spouse is actually deemed to have transferred under IRC section 2513. IRC section 2652(a)(2). *See,* Pvt. Letter Rul. 200218001, where the gift-splitting wife was deemed to be the transferor (for GST tax purposes) of one-half of the *entire value* of the property transferred by her husband into a trust for the wife and their children, even though the wife had an ascertainable interest (for purposes of IRC section 2513) in part of the transferred property and thus was not able to gift split (for purposes of Chapter 12 of the Internal Revenue Code) the entire transferred amount.

§5.11 TAXATION OF MULTIPLE SKIPS AND TRANSFEROR MOVE DOWN RULE

A non-GST-tax-exempt trust may be subject to successive taxable distributions, taxable terminations, or direct skips. However, a non-GST-tax-exempt trust will not be subject to double GST taxation when a double skip occurs simultaneously, such as a transfer to a non-GST-tax- exempt trust that is for the sole benefit of a great-grandchild (or more remote descendants), which results in two generations (child and grandchild) being skipped in the same transfer. IRC section 2653. This is because neither the transferor's child nor the grandchild has any interest in the trust. *See,* Treas. Reg. §26.2612-1(a). However, a transfer to a non-GST-tax-exempt trust for the benefit of the transferor's grandchild and great-grandchild is a direct skip (for which a GST tax must be paid) and any distributions to the great-grandchild will also be subject to GST tax. This is because there are two successive skips rather than one double simultaneous skip. As discussed below, any trust distributions to the transferor's grandchild will not be subject to additional GST tax, due to the transferor move-down rule. However, trust distributions to the transferor's great-grandchild will be subject to additional GST tax.

Property held in trust after a GST event has occurred continues to be subject to the GST tax. To determine whether future events constitute GST taxable events, the transferor is treated as occupying one generation above the trust beneficiary (in this instance the grandchild) who has the highest generation assignment vis-à-vis the other trust beneficiaries (in this instance the great-grandchild) in the non-GST-tax-exempt trust. The trust beneficiary who is now just one generation below the transferor (in this instance the grandchild) is no longer a skip person vis-à-vis the transferor. This is known as the "transferor move-down rule." IRC section 2653; Treas. Reg. §26.2653-1(a).

Consequently, any distributions to the grandchild are not taxable distributions (keeping in mind that the transferor has already paid a GST tax on the direct skip into the trust). However, because the great-grandchild occupies a generation that is two generations below the deemed generation of the transferor (as a result of the transferor move-down rule), the great-grandchild remains a skip person vis-à-vis the transferor and any trust distributions to the great-grandchild will be taxable distributions (for which a (second) GST tax must be paid). Treas. Reg. §26.2653-1(b), Example 1.

When the grandchild dies, there will be a taxable termination (for which another GST tax has to be paid). A taxable termination will occur when the grandchild dies (because the only interest in the trust, after the death of the grandchild, is the interest of the great-grandchild, who is a skip person vis-à-vis the transferor). However, because of the taxable termination, the transferor will move down another generation and be deemed to be one generation above that of the great-grandchild. Consequently, any future trust distributions to the great-grandchild will not be taxable distributions (keeping in mind that a GST tax has been paid because of the taxable termination resulting from the grandchild's death).

When the great-grandchild dies and the trust terminates in favor of the great-grandchild's then living children (i.e., the transferor's great-great grandchildren), there will be a taxable termination for which (another) GST tax has to be paid. The multiple skip rule underscores the need for a transferor to allocate his or her GST tax exemption to a GST trust to achieve a zero inclusion ratio and avoid successive GST taxation.

§5.12 INCLUSION RATIO DEFINED

Inclusion ratio is defined under IRC section 2642(a). When allocating GST tax exemption to a trust, the goal is to have a trust with either a zero inclusion ratio (i.e., be 100% GST tax exempt) or an inclusion ratio of one (i.e., be completely subject to GST tax). What is to be avoided is a trust with an inclusion ratio of greater than zero but less than one.

The GST tax is imposed at the "applicable rate," which is the current maximum federal estate tax rate multiplied by the inclusion ratio. IRC section 2641; Treas. Reg. §26.2641-1. Thus, the inclusion ratio is used to determine the rate of GST tax imposed on property that is subject to the GST tax. *See,* Treas. Reg. §26.2642-1. However, to determine the inclusion ratio, you must first determine the applicable fraction.

The applicable fraction is determined as follows: the numerator of the applicable fraction is the amount of GST tax exemption allocated to the trust (or to the property transferred in a direct skip), and the denominator is generally the value of the transferred property (less certain adjustments described in IRC section 2642(a)(2)(B)(ii) for federal estate tax and state death taxes actually recovered (or paid) from the trust (or transferred property) and any charitable deduction allowed under IRC sections 2055 or 2522 with respect to the property). GST tax exemption allocated for the full amount of the transferred property results in an applicable fraction of 1, an inclusion ratio of zero (1-1 = 0), and an "applicable rate" (i.e., GST tax rate) of zero (48% estate tax rate (for 2004) ¥ 0 inclusion ratio = 0 GST tax rate).

Applicable rate = GST tax rate (i.e., maximum federal estate tax rate) × inclusion ratio.

Inclusion ratio = 1- applicable fraction.

$$\text{Applicable fraction} = \frac{\text{GST tax exemption allocated to transfer}}{\text{Value of GST transfer (less certain adjustments)}}$$

Thus, the formula for determining the GST tax liability is:

GST tax liability = value of transferred property subject to GST tax × applicable rate.

§5.12(a) Simple Definition Of Inclusion Ratio

In simpler terms, the inclusion ratio is the percent age of the trust that is subject to GST tax, with an inclusion ratio of zero resulting in zero% of the trust being subject to GST tax,[12] and an inclusion ratio of one resulting in 100% of the trust being subject to GST tax. Thus, an inclusion ratio of .50 would effectively result in 50% of the trust being subject to GST tax. The reason that a trust with an inclusion ratio of greater than zero but less than one should be avoided, is that every distribution, whether to skip persons or non-skip persons, will be only partially exempt from GST tax—an ineffective and wasteful use of the transferor's GST tax exemption.

§5.12(b) Changes To The Inclusion Ratio

A trust maintains its inclusion ratio until (1) a transferor makes an additional transfer of property to the trust; (2) additional GST tax exemption is allocated; (3) there is a new transferor; (4) there is a consolidation or merger of separate trusts; (5) a recapture tax is imposed under IRC section 2032A; or (6) pursuant to IRC section 2653(b), a GST tax is borne by the trust with respect to a transfer of property, if immediately after the transfer, the property remains in the trust (presumably where the inclusion ratio before the payment of the GST tax was greater than zero but less than one). IRC section 2642(d)(1); Treas. Reg. §26.2642-4. In such instances, the applicable fraction (i.e., inclusion ratio) must be re-determined.[13] As discussed below, a trust may be divided, pursuant to a qualified severance, into two separate trusts—one with an inclusion ratio of zero and another with an inclusion ratio of one.

---

[12] Technically speaking no trust is "exempt" from the GST tax (although certain transfers are not GST tax transfers (IRC section 2611(b); Treas. Reg. §26.2601-1(b)) and certain transfers have a zero inclusion ratio (IRC section 2642(c)). A zero inclusion ratio results in a GST tax of $0. Most practitioners refer to a trust with a zero inclusion ratio as a "GST tax exempt trust," even though the term does not technically exist. Similarly, a trust with an inclusion ratio of greater than zero is commonly referred to as a "non-GST tax exempt trust."

[13] The numerator of the recomputed fraction is the sum of the amount of the GST tax exemption allocated to property involved in the new transfer, plus the "nontax portion" of the trust immediately before the new transfer. The denominator of the recomputed fraction is the sum of: (i) the value of the property involved in the new transfer minus any federal estate tax or state death tax actually recovered from the trust attributable to the new property, and minus any charitable deduction allowed under IRC sections 2055 or 2522 with respect to such new property, and (ii) the value of all of the property in the trust (immediately before the new transfer). The "non-tax portion" is the product of the value of all of the property in the trust, and the applicable fraction for the trust before the new transfer. IRC section 2642(d).

Practice Point: If a trust has an inclusion ratio greater than zero, GST tax will always have to paid when the trust makes a taxable distribution or has a taxable termination.

§5.13 RIGHT TO RECOVER GST TAX PAID

Because GST taxes are chargeable to the property generating the tax, a transferor's executor is entitled to recover any GST taxes paid by the transferor's estate, unless that right of recovery is waived in the transferor's governing instrument by specific reference to the GST tax. IRC section 2603(b).

§5.14 THE GST TAX EXEMPTION

Each person is allotted a lifetime exemption from the GST tax. IRC section 2631(a). The exemption was initially $1 million dollars. It was first increased by cost of living adjustments in the Taxpayer Relief Act of 1997 ("TRA 1997"), and subsequently increased, in the 2001 Tax Act, to match the estate tax applicable exclusion amount. The 2001 Tax Act's increase in the GST tax exemption expires on January 1, 2010 (as does the GST tax itself), and on January 1, 2011, the pre-2001 Tax Act GST tax exemption amount is reinstated, as is the GST tax. *See,* section 6.1, below, and Chapter 7, below.

The GST tax exemption amount can be used by the transferor during his or her lifetime; and upon death, any unused exemption can be used by the deceased transferor's executor, and/or it can be automatically allocated pursuant to IRC section 2632(e). The automatic allocation rules are discussed in sections 5.29 and 5.30, below.

Allocation of GST tax exemption can be of a specific amount, or by a formula (that self adjusts in the event of a change in value on audit by the IRS). Treas. Reg. §§26.2632-1(b)(4) and 26.2632-1(d)(1). Some of the most technical and complicated provisions of the GST tax regulations relate to the allocation of GST tax exemption regarding property transferred from a trust or held in trust. This is because if property is held in trust, allocation of GST tax exemption must be made to the entire trust rather than to specific trust assets. Treas. Reg. §26.2632-1(a). Hence, there are special GST tax regulations concerning the treatment of property transferred from a trust or held in trust. These special regulations are discussed in the GST tax separate share rule (section 5.16, below) and in the GST tax qualified severance rule (section 6.3, below). These two rules are designed to treat portions of a trust as separate trusts for GST tax purposes.

Allocation of GST tax exemption is effective as of the date of transfer if made on a timely filed U.S. Gift Tax Return (IRS form 709). Generally, an allocation of GST tax exemption on a late-filed gift tax return is effective on the date the gift tax return is filed. However, special rules exist with regard to certain late allocations, and also with regard to life insurance policies. *See,* section 5.23, below concerning late allocations of GST tax exemption.

> **Practice Point:** Each time a gift is made to an ILIT, a decision has to be made whether or not to allocate GST tax exemption to the trust (or to opt in or opt out of "GST Trust" status, a defined term in IRC section 2632(c)(3)(B)). Reliance on the automatic GST tax exemption allocation rules (discussed in section 5.29, below), may not be sufficient since there is uncertainty as to what constitutes an exception to a "GST Trust."

§5.15 VALUATION OF PROPERTY FOR GST TAX PURPOSES

Generally, the value of property for GST tax purposes is the property's value at the time of the GST, such as the property's date of transfer value (in the case of an inter-vivos gift) or date of distribution value (in the case of a taxable distribution). IRC section 2624(a); Treas. Reg. §26.2642-2. Different rules apply to different types of GST events. In the case of a direct skip of property that is included in the transferor's gross estate, the value of the property is generally its federal estate tax value, as determined under IRC sections 2031 (date of death valuation), 2032 (alternate valuation date value), and 2032A (special use valuation). IRC section 2624(b). However, under certain circumstances, the GST tax regulations require additional conditions to be satisfied if property includable in the transferor's gross estate is to be valued at its federal estate tax value. Treas. Reg. §26.2642-2(b)(2) and (3).[14] If a GST tax is incurred on a taxable termination due to the death

[14] Because these additional conditions apply only to property includable in the transferor's gross estate for federal estate tax purposes where GST tax exemption is to be allocated to a pecuniary bequest or to a residual transfer or residual trust that follows a pecuniary bequest, they will only be applicable to an ILIT where ILIT property is includable in the transferor's gross estate, such as life insurance included under the

of an individual, the property subject to the taxable termination may be valued under IRC section 2032 (alternate valuation date value). IRC section 2624(c).

§5.16 SEPARATE SHARE RULE

The separate share rule is set forth in IRC section 2654(b) and Treas. Reg. §26.2654-1(a). This rule determines when a single trust with multiple beneficiaries will be treated as having substantially separate and independent shares, thus enabling the allocation of GST tax exemption to any of the shares. The separate share rule also determines when certain pecuniary bequests payable from a trust included in the transferor's gross estate will be treated as separate shares for allocating GST tax exemption. And, if there are portions of a single trust that are attributable to transfers from different transferors (such as when gift splitting occurs under IRC section 2513), the separate share rule treats those portions as separate trusts. IRC section 2654(b)(1); Treas. Reg. §2654-1(a)(2).

§5.16(a) Two Requirements For A Single Trust With Multiple Beneficiaries To Be Treated As Having Separate Shares For GST Tax Purposes

The separate share rule provided in Treas. Reg. §26.2654-1(a)(1) states that if a single trust[15] has more than one beneficiary and the ben-

---

three-year rule of IRC section 2035. *See,* Section 13.22 of Sebastian V. Grassi, Jr., *A Practical Guide to Drafting Marital Deduction Trusts (with Sample Forms and Checklists)* (ALI-ABA, Philadelphia, 2004, Supp. 2006) for a detailed discussion of the GST valuation rules.

[15] This rule is limited to trusts or arrangements treated as trusts. Except as otherwise provided in Treas. Reg. §26.2652-1(b) (especially Example 3), the rule does not apply to probate estates. IRC section 2652(b)(1). Thus, trusts that elect under IRC section 645 to be treated as part of the deceased transferor's probate estate are not subject to the separate share rule requirements of Treas. Reg. §26.2654-1(a)(1) and (2) during the period the trust is treated as part of the probate estate. IRC section 2654(b).

> The [separate share] rule should not apply to transfers directly from...[a probate] estate to a separate trust, unless the distributee is not the ultimate recipient of the assets, such as when the residuary [probate] estate is payable to a trustee who is then instructed to distribute a pecuniary amount to an individual or trust....The election to treat a revocable trust as part of a decedent's [probate] estate under Section 645 applies

eficiaries have substantially separate and independent shares vis-à-vis one another (such as a common (pot) trust with distinctly separate interests for the transferor's descendants, with each descendant being entitled to receive income and principal from his or her share), the

---

> for GSTT purposes only with respect to the treatment of a single trust as two or more trusts under Section 2654(b) and does not recharacterize a revocable trust after the grantor's death as...[a probate] estate for other GSTT purposes. Thus, the more lenient separate share rules that apply to [probate] estates would apply to such trusts—at least during that period. It is unclear what happens when the period of [the IRC section 645] election ends and the revocable trust reverts to being treated as a trust again. If the separate share...rules that would have been required in a trust context were not met—because the trust was treated as...[a probate] estate—will these separate trusts be recognized for GSTT purposes once the period of election ends?

Carol A. Harrington, Lloyd Leva Plaine & Howard M. Zaritsky, *Generation-Skipping Transfer Tax Analysis With Forms,* (Warren, Gorham & Lamont, RIA, 2d ed. 2001 & 2006 Supp.)

> [T]he separate share regulations are more lenient for [probate] estates than for trusts. [Probate] [e]states and trusts are, however, subject to the valuation rules of Regulations Section 26.2642-2(b) [discussed in section 13.22, below], the requirements of which, in certain cases, are similar to the separate share requirements.

Id. at ¶2.03[1].

> For GST tax purposes, the definition of a trust in effect prior to TRA '97 included any arrangement (other than...[a probate] estate) which, although not a trust, had substantially the same effect as a trust. TRA '97 added a sentence to Section 2652(b) to provide that, for purposes of the GST tax, a trust does not include any trust during the period that the trust is treated as part of...[a probate] estate under Section 645. [See former Section 2652(b)(1) (second sentence added by TRA '97).] Nevertheless, in a technical correction, the '98 [Tax] Act removed the sentence that had been added by TRA '97. [Pub. L. No. 105-206, section 6013(a)(4)(A).] Instead, the '98 Act added a similar sentence to Section 2654(b), the scope of which is limited to that subsection. [Pub. L. No. 105-206, section 6013(a)(4)(B).] Under Section 2654(b), the portions of a trust attributable to transfers from different transferors and substantially separate and independent shares of different beneficiaries in a trust are treated as separate trusts. Accordingly, with respect to the GST tax, a trust subject to a Section 645 election would be treated as..[a probate] estate only for purposes of the different transferor and separate share rules of Section 2654(b).

Edwin G. Fee, Jr., "Electing to Treat a Revocable Trust as Part of the Estate," 26 *Estate Planning,* 118, 121 (March/April 1999).

share attributable to each beneficiary (or group of beneficiaries) will be treated as a separate share for GST tax purposes only.[16] Treas. Reg. §26.2654-1(a)(1)(i). Two requirements must be met for the rule to apply. If these two requirements are met, GST tax exemption can be allocated to any of the separate shares, and it does not have to be allocated to the whole single trust (which may result in an overuse and waste of the transferor's GST tax exemption). Treas. Reg. §26.2654-1(a)(4). A single trust will be deemed to consist solely of substantially separate and independent shares[17] for different beneficiaries for the purpose of allocating GST tax exemption to some or all of the shares, if both of the following two requirements are met:

---

[16] Treatment of a single trust that has separate shares for GST tax purposes does not permit the separate shares to be treated as separate trusts for purposes of filing separate income tax returns, payment of income taxes, or for purposes of computing any other tax imposed under the Internal Revenue Code. Treas. Reg. §26.2654-1(a)(1)(i).

[17] The term "substantially separate and independent shares" has the meaning as provided in Treas. Reg. §1.663(c)-3 (concerning separate shares for income tax purposes). Under the income tax rules of Treas. Reg. §1.663(c) (and therefore the GST tax rules), separate share treatment is not available under certain circumstances. "Separate share treatment will not be applied to a trust or portion of a trust subject to a [discretionary] power to: (1) Distribute, apportion, or accumulate income, or (2) distribute corpus to or for one or more beneficiaries within a group or class of beneficiaries, *unless* payment of income, accumulated income, or corpus of a share of one beneficiary cannot affect the proportionate share of income, accumulated income, or corpus of any shares of the other beneficiaries, or unless substantially proper adjustment must thereafter be made (under the governing instrument) so that substantially separate and independent shares exist." Treas. Reg. §1.663(c)-3(b) (emphasis added). "Separate share treatment may [nevertheless] be given to a trust or portion of a trust...if the trust or portion of a trust is subject to a power to pay out to a beneficiary of a share (of such trust or portion) an amount of corpus in excess of his proportionate share of the corpus of the trust if the possibility of [the] exercise of the power is remote. For example, if the trust is subject to a power to invade the entire corpus for the health, education, support, or maintenance of A, separate share treatment is applied if [the] exercise of the power requires consideration of A's other income which is so substantial as to make the possibility of [the] exercise of the power remote. If instead it appears that A and B have separate shares in a trust, subject to a power to invade the entire corpus for the comfort, pleasure, desire, or happiness of A, separate share treatment shall not be applied." Treas. Reg. §1.663(c)-3(d). *See*, Treas. Reg. §26.2654-1(a)(5), Example 2 (concerning trustee's ability to make discretionary distributions and separate share treatment not being available).

§5.16(a)(1) Existence Of Shares Requirement

The separate shares must exist from and at all times after the creation of the ILIT (unless the trust is for some reason included in its entirety in the transferor's gross estate for federal estate tax purposes, in which case the separate shares are deemed created at the transferor's date of death). When the ILIT is not included in the transferor's gross estate (which should be the situation for most ILITs, particularly if there is no IRC section 2035 issue), the separate shares must exist at the time of the creation of the ILIT and all times thereafter; otherwise they will not be recognized as separate shares for GST tax purposes. Treas. Reg. §26.2654-1(a)(1)(i). If separate shares do not exist at the onset, a qualified severance of the trust may be required. *See,* section 6.3, below.

§5.16(a)(2) Allocation Requirement

Unless the governing instrument expressly provides otherwise, additions to and distributions from the single trust are allocated pro rata among the separate shares.

§5.16(b) Severance Of A Separate Share From A Single Trust

Separate shares that are part of a single separate trust for GST tax purposes may be severed from the single trust at any time (rather than remaining as separate shares). Treas. Reg. §26.2654-1(a)(3). The severance of a separate share from the single trust and the funding of a severed share must comply with the rules of Treas. Reg. §26.2654-1(b)(1)(ii)(C). Thus, the severance of a separate share from a single trust must be either on a fractional basis, or on a pecuniary basis. However, a pecuniary severance can be made only if it is mandated by the governing instrument. Treas. Reg. §26.2654-1(b)(1)(ii)(C)(2). The requirements for severing a separate share from a single trust are given in the next two sections, immediately below.

§5.16(b)(1) Requirements For A Fractional Severance Of A Separate Share From A Single Trust

If the severance of a separate share from the single trust is made on a fractional basis, the funding of the severed share may be pro-rata or non-pro-rata as to specific assets of the single trust. If non-pro-rata funding is used, the funding of the severed share must be either based on the fair market value of the single trust's assets on the date of funding or provided in a manner that fairly reflects the net appreciation or depreciation in the value of the single trust's assets measured from the valuation date to the date of funding.

§5.16(b)(2) Requirements For A Mandatory Pecuniary Severance Of A Separate Share From A Single Trust

If the severance of a separate share from the single trust is required by the terms of the governing instrument to be made on the basis of a pecuniary amount, the trustee must be required to pay "appropriate interest" on the pecuniary amount; and the pecuniary amount must be funded either (1) entirely with cash; or (2) partly with cash and partly (or solely) with non-cash property (e.g., stocks and bonds) either by using the non-cash assets' date-of-distribution value, or by allocating the trust property in a manner that fairly reflects net appreciation or depreciation in the value of the assets in the fund available to pay the pecuniary amount measured from date of death to date of payment. Treas. Reg. §26.2654-1(a)(1)(ii).

§5.17 ESTATE TAX INCLUSION PERIOD ("ETIP") DEFINED

Allocation of GST tax exemption is not effective until the close of the Estate Tax Inclusion Period ("ETIP"). IRC section 2642(f). An ETIP is the period during which the trust property would be included in the gross estate of the transferor or the transferor's spouse if either were to die.[18] Examples would be transfers to revocable trusts, grantor-retained annuity trusts ("GRATs"), and qualified personal residence trusts ("QPRTs"). Treasury Regulations provide that if any part of a trust is subject to an ETIP, the entire trust is subject to the ETIP.

At the close of the ETIP, the previously allocated GST tax exemption is allocated against the fair market value of the ILIT property. If the amount of GST tax exemption that was initially allocated is less than the fair market value of the ILIT property at the close of

[18] A trust is not considered to be subject to an ETIP if the possibility that the property will be included in the transferor's or transferor spouse's gross estate is so remote as to be negligible. A possibility is so remote as to be negligible if it can be ascertained by actuarial standards that there is less than a 5% probability that the property will be included in the gross estate. Treas. Reg. §26.2632-1(c)(2)(ii)(A).

the ETIP, the ILIT will not be GST tax exempt. *See,* section 3.1, above, for valuation of a life insurance policy. Accordingly it is generally best to wait until the close of the ETIP to allocate GST tax exemption to a trust.[19] An alternative to this approach is to make a formula allocation of GST tax exemption at the beginning of the ETIP; however, the amount of the GST tax exemption being allocated under the formula will not be known until the close of the ETIP. An allocation of GST tax exemption made to a trust during the ETIP cannot be revoked, even though the allocation is not effective until the close of the ETIP. Treas. Regs. §26.2632-1(c)(1).

§5.17(a) Exceptions To ETIP

Treas. Reg. §26.2632-1(c)(2)(ii) provides several exceptions to ETIP, including (1) a reverse QTIP election (typically concerning an inter-vivos QTIP trust established by the donor-spouse for the benefit of the donee-spouse[20]); and (2) a *Crummey* withdrawal right held by the grantor's spouse that is limited to no more than five-by-five ***and*** the withdrawal right terminates no later than sixty (60) days after the transfer to the ILIT—***not*** sixty (60) days after notice of the transfer to the ILIT. This exception concerning spousal *Crummey* withdrawal rights, with its abbreviated period for the *Crummey* withdrawal right to lapse, automatically precludes the use of a hanging right of withdrawal (*See,* section 3.13, above), as concerns the lapse of the spouse's *Crummey* withdrawal right. *See,* Paragraphs 3.1(A)(1) and 3.2(D) of Sample ILIT.

> **Caution:** The most common forms of triggering an ETIP in an ILIT is where these two exceptions are violated.
>
> **Practice Point:** If the ILIT provides the grantor's spouse with a *Crummey* withdrawal right that does lapse within 60 days of the transfer, and the grantor desires to allocate GST tax exemption to the ILIT, consider, modifying the spouse's right of withdrawal. This may be accomplished by judicial modification or reformation, through the exer-

---

[19] Treas. Reg. §26.2632-1(c)(2)(ii)(C).

[20] *See,* section 3.10 of Sebastian V. Grassi, Jr., *A Practical Guide to Drafting Marital Deduction Trusts,* ALI-ABA Philadelphia (2004, Supp 2006), (800) 253-6397, http://www.ali-aba.org/aliaba/BK36/, concerning inter-vivos QTIP trusts and a sample inter-vivos QTIP trust form.

cise of a power to limit (modify) future *Crummey* withdrawal rights reserved by the grantor, or through the power of amendment held by a non-interested trustee. *See,* Paragraphs 3.2(H) and 3.2 (J) of the Sample ILIT.

§5.17(b) Possible Inclusion Of Property Under IRC Section 2035 Is Not An ETIP

Treas. Reg. §26.2632-1(c)(2)(i) provides that possible inclusion of transferred property in the estate of the transferor-grantor because of the three-year inclusion rule of IRC section 2035 is not an ETIP, and GST tax exemption can be effectively allocated to the ILIT during the transferor-grantor's lifetime, even if the transferor-grantor dies within three years of transferring an existing life insurance policy to an ILIT.

§5.17(c) Termination Of ETIP

An ETIP terminates on the first to occur of (i) the death of the transferor; (ii) the time at which no portion of the property is includible in the transferor's gross estate (other than by reason of IRC section 2035) or, in the case of a spouse who has merely consented to gift splitting under IRC section 2513, the time at which no portion would be includible in the gross estate of the consenting spouse (other than by reason of IRC section 2035); (iii) the time of a GST event (such as a taxable distribution or taxable termination) but only with respect to the property involved in the GST event; or (iv) in the case of an ETIP arising by reason of an interest or power held by the transferor's spouse on the first to occur of (a) the death of the spouse or (b) the time at which no portion of the property would be includable in the spouse's gross estate (other than by reason of IRC section 2035). Treas. Regs. §26.2632-1(c)(3). Thus, if the ETIP is created by the spouse holding a *Crummey* withdrawal right that is in excess of five by five and/or lapses more than 60 days after the date of the contribution that gives rise to the Crummey withdrawal right, the ETIP will terminate upon the earlier of the spouse's death or the complete lapse of the *Crummey* withdrawal right (which will lapse annually at the rate of $5,000, or 5% of the value of the trust assets).

§5.18 GIFT SUBJECT TO A *CRUMMEY* WITHDRAWAL RIGHT IS GIFT TO TRUST FOR GST PURPOSES

There is a disconnect between the gift tax annual exclusion rules under IRC section 2503(b) and the GST tax exemption rules concerning transfers to a trust. This disconnect means that although the *Crummey* withdrawal right qualifies for the gift tax annual exclusion, the gift does not automatically qualify for the GST tax exclusion; and if no GST tax exemption is allocated by the insured to the ILIT, the ILIT will not be GST tax exempt. The disconnect exists because, under the GST tax rules, a gift to a trust that has *Crummey* withdrawal rights is not considered a gift to the individual donees; rather, the gift is considered a transfer to the trust itself. Treas. Reg. §26.2642-1(c)(3). *See also*, Treas. Reg. §26.2612-1(d)(2) concerning trusts that are skip persons.

§5.18(a) Special Rule Concerning Skip Person Trusts

An exception to the above-mentioned rule concerns trusts that are skip persons, such as: (i) an IRC section 2642(c)(2) trust for a skip person, and (ii) ***possibly***, an IRC section 2503(c) trust for a minor skip person.[21] However, neither of these two forms of trust is generally suitable for use as an ILIT because they permit only a sole beneficiary, require inclusion of the trust proceeds in the beneficiary's gross estate if the beneficiary dies before the trust terminates, and, in the case of an IRC section 2503(c) trust, the trust is required to terminate when the beneficiary attains age 21.

> **Practice Point:** When funding an ILIT, the insured needs to determine if GST tax exemption should be allocated to the ILIT. Generally, this will require the insured to either "opt in" or "opt out" of the GST tax exemption automatic allocation rules when property is initially transferred to the ILIT. *See*, section 5.29, below.

§5.19 GST TAX CONSEQUENCES OF EXERCISE OF A *CRUMMEY* WITHDRAWAL RIGHT

The exercise of the *Crummey* withdrawal right by a skip person (assuming the trust is **not** a skip person under IRC section 2642(c)(2)

---

[21] *See*, section 5.7(c), above for a discussion of an IRC section 2503(c) trust for a minor skip person.

and no GST tax exemption has been previously allocated by the grantor) is a taxable distribution for GST purposes. Treas. Reg. §26.2612-1(f), Example 13.

§5.20 GST TAX CONSEQUENCES OF LAPSE OF A *CRUMMEY* WITHDRAWAL RIGHT

Transfer of property to an ILIT where a skip person has a *Crummey* withdrawal right is not a direct skip, and does not immediately attract any GST tax provided the ILIT itself is not a "skip person." Treas. Reg. §26.2612-1(f), Example 3. Furthermore (assuming the ILIT itself is not a skip person under IRC section 2642(c)(2)) a skip person's unexercised *Crummey* withdrawal right is not itself a direct skip or a GST tax event if the withdrawal right lapses within the five-by-five safe harbor amount. This means that the grantor remains the original and continuing transferor for GST purposes and any GST tax exemption previously allocated by the transferor will remain intact, assuming the beneficiary does not die while the *Crummey* withdrawal right remains outstanding and/or there is no taxable release of the *Crummey* withdrawal right. IRC sections 2041(a)(2) and 2652(a); Treas. Reg. §§26.2652-1(a)(2) and 26.2601-1(b)(1)(v)(A).

§5.21 GST TAX CONSEQUENCES OF WAIVER OR RELEASE OF A *CRUMMEY* WITHDRAWAL RIGHT

A beneficiary's waiver of a *Crummey* withdrawal right or the lapse of a *Crummey* withdrawal right greater than five by five constitutes a taxable release under IRC section 2514(b). Treas. Reg. §26.2652-1(a)(5), Example 5. A taxable release results in a taxable transfer under Chapter 11 or 12 of the Internal Revenue Code and changes the identity of the transferor for GST tax purposes (with regard to the property subject to Chapter 11 or 12). Treas. Reg. §26.2652-1(a)(2). Any previously allocated GST tax exemption by the original transferor is lost and ineffective when the identity of the transferor changes, thus necessitating allocation of GST tax exemption by the new transferor, if such an allocation is possible, necessary or appropriate. For a typical three-generation ILIT, an allocation of GST tax exemption by a second-generation *Crummey* withdrawal right holder would not be needed, because the third-generation beneficiary would not be a skip person vis-à-vis the second generation beneficiary (who is now the "new" transferor).

A way to avoid a taxable release (and to avoid a change in the identity of the transferor) is to not let a beneficiary waive his or her *Crummey* withdrawal right (in the case of a waiver) or, in the case of a release, to limit a beneficiary's *Crummey* withdrawal right to the lesser of the contribution or five by five. If hanging rights of withdrawal are used (*see,* section 3.13, above), the hanging rights should lapse at the rate of five by five each calendar year.

If a skip person waives his or her *Crummey* withdrawal right or allows a lapse of his or her withdrawal right greater than five by five, a taxable distribution for GST tax purposes is deemed to have occurred to such skip person with respect to the value of the property subject to the taxable release. Treas. Reg. §2612-1(c)(1). Furthermore, the skip person becomes the (new) transferor for GST tax purposes with regard to the amount of the taxable release. Treas. Reg. §§26.2652-1(a)(2) and 26.2652-1(a)(5), Example 5.

§5.22 GST TAX CONSEQUENCES OF GIFT SPLITTING

If a married couple elects gift splitting under IRC section 2513, each spouse is treated as the transferor (for GST tax purposes only) of one-half of the entire value of the property transferred, regardless of the interest the donor-spouse is actually deemed to have transferred under IRC section 2513. IRC section 2652(a)(2). *See,* Pvt. Letter Rul. 200218001, where the gift-splitting wife was deemed to be the transferor (for GST tax purposes) of one-half of the *entire value* of the property transferred by her husband into a trust for the wife and their children, even though the wife had an ascertainable interest (for purposes of IRC section 2513) in part of the transferred property and thus was not able to gift split (for purposes of Chapter 12 of the Internal Revenue Code) the entire transferred amount.

Practice Point: If gift splitting is elected with respect to a life insurance policy that has been transferred to an ILIT and the insured dies within three years of the transfer, the consenting spouse's previously allocated GST tax exemption will be wasted and ineffective. This is because the inclusion of the life insurance proceeds in the gross estate of the insured under IRC section 2035 changes the identity of the transferor for GST purposes to that of the decedent. For this reason, it may be desirable to not elect to gift split for transfers of life insurance policies subject to the three-year inclusion rule of IRC section 2035.

§5.23 LATE ALLOCATION OF GST TAX EXEMPTION TO ILIT

Late allocation of GST tax exemption at the gift tax value of the transferred property is not effective with respect to a life insurance policy or an ILIT if the individual insured has died. Treas. Reg. §26.2642-2(a)(2). However, if the insured has not died, late allocation of GST tax exemption can be made utilizing the value of the life insurance policy or ILIT as of the first day of the calendar month in which the late allocation is filed with the IRS. Treas. Reg. §26.2642-2(a). A late allocation of GST tax exemption is effective on the date the gift tax return is filed with the IRS, and once made is irrevocable. The gift tax return's postmark date will be the deemed filing date for the late allocation of GST tax exemption. Treas. Reg. §26.2632-1(b)(4)(ii). Query whether the addition of IRC section 2642(g)(1) under the 2001 Tax Act, concerning relief from late allocations (*See,* section 6.5, below), will change this result. *See,* Pvt. Letter. Rul. 200227017 concerning late allocation of the deceased-insured's GST tax exemption under second-to-die life insurance policy, where only one of the insureds had died and the policy had not yet matured.

If a GST event occurs on the same date as the filing of the gift tax return, the late allocation of GST tax exemption is deemed to precede the GST event. Treas. Reg. §26.2632-1(b)(4)(ii).

Late allocation of GST exemption is made on IRS Form 709 by attaching a notice of late allocation.[22] Treas. Reg. §26.2642-2(a)(2). The notice of late allocation must state (i) that a late allocation of GST tax exemption is being made to a trust (with the trust being sufficiently identified), (ii) the applicable valuation date for allocating the GST tax exemption to the trust, and (iii) the fair market value of the trust assets on the applicable valuation date. *Id.* A late allocation of GST tax exemption may be made at any time before the due date of the transferor's federal estate tax return, including extensions actually granted. Treas. Reg. §26.2632-1(a). *See also,* section 6.5, below, concerning special procedures for making a late allocation pursuant to IRC section 2642(g).

---

[22] See, Sample form of *"Notice of Late Allocation of GST Tax Exemption to Trust"* in Appendix 4.

Practice Point: Late allocation of GST exemption may be desirable where the trust assets have depreciated in value between the time of the gift and the due date for the gift tax return concerning the gift.

Practice Point: Late allocation of GST exemption may be desirable where a pre-2001 trust is now a GST Trust (because of the 2001 Tax Act's enactment of IRC section 2632(c)(3)(B)) and has been subject to the GST automatic allocation rules. Absent a late allocation, the trust may not have a zero inclusion ratio for GST tax purposes. *See,* section 5.29, below.

Caution: If the insured is seriously or terminally ill at the time of the late allocation, the value of the life insurance policy for GST tax exemption purposes may not be its interpolated terminal reserve value. Instead, the value of the policy may be closer its death benefit amount. *See,* section 3.1(a), above.

§5.24 GST GRANDFATHERED TRUSTS

Three types of trusts are grandfathered for GST tax purposes (and are automatically GST tax exempt): (i) a trust that was irrevocable on 9/25/1985 but only to the extent that a GST transfer is not made out of corpus that was added to the trust after 9/25/1985 or out of income attributable to such corpus (Treas. Reg. §26.2601-1(b)(1)),[23] (ii) any trust (or testamentary trust to be established under a will) executed before 10/22/1986 and not amended thereafter if the decedent died before 1/1/1987 (Treas. Reg. §26.2601-1(b)(2)), and (iii) any trust made by a person who on 10/22/1986, and at all times thereafter, was mentally incompetent and the trust was included in the incompetent person's gross estate. (Treas. Reg. §26.2601-1(b)(3)).

[23] Treas. Reg. Reg. §26.2601-1(b)(1)(ii) states that a trust is not irrevocable as of 9/25/1985 to the extent (i) the property would have been includable in the settlor's gross estate under IRC section 2038 (settlor's power to alter, amend, or revoke) if the settler had died on 9/25/1985, or (ii) the insured under a policy of life insurance treated as a trust under IRC section 2652(b) had an incident of ownership in the policy on 9/25/1985 that would have caused the policy proceeds to be includable in the insured's gross estate under IRC section 2042 if the insured had died on 9/25/1985.

Practice Point: The purchase of an existing life insurance policy for full and adequate consideration by a GST grandfathered trust will not cause the grandfathered trust to lose its GST tax exempt status. Priv. Letter Rul. 200120007

§5.25 MODIFICATIONS TO GST GRANDFATHERED TRUSTS

Treas. Reg. §26.2601-1(b)(4) provides rules for determining when a modification, judicial construction, settlement agreement, or trustee action with respect to a GST grandfathered trust will not cause the trust to lose its GST tax exempt status. Safe harbors are provided for (1) certain distributions of trust principal from a GST grandfathered trust to a new trust or retention of the trust principal in a continuing trust (Treas. Reg. §§26.2601-1(b)(4)(i)(A) and 26.2601-1(b)(4)(i)(E), Examples 1 and 2); (2) certain court-approved settlements of bona fide issues regarding the administration of the GST grandfathered trust or the construction of terms of the trust (Treas. Reg. §26.2601-1(b)(4)(i)(B)); (3) certain judicial constructions of the GST grandfathered trust to resolve ambiguities in the terms of the trust or to correct a scrivener's error (Treas. Reg. §§26.2601-1(b)(4)(i)(C) and 26.2601-1(b)(4)(i)(E), Example 3); and (4) certain modifications of the GST grandfathered trust by judicial reformation or non-judicial reformation (including a trustee distribution, conversion to a unitrust or an equitable adjustment between income and capital gains (Priv. Letter Rul. 200417014; Treas. Reg. §1.643(b)-1; Treas. Reg. §§26.2601-1(b)(4)(i)(D)(2) and 26.2601-1(b)(4)(i)(E), Examples 8, 9, 11 and 12) settlement, or construction that does not satisfy items (1)—(3) immediately preceding) that are valid under applicable state law, provided the modification does not shift a beneficial interest in the trust to any beneficiary who occupies a lower generation (as defined in IRC section 2651) than the person(s) who held the beneficial interest before the modification, and the modification does not extend the time for vesting of any beneficial interest in the trust beyond the period provided for in the original trust (Treas. Reg. §§26.2601-1(b)(4)(i)(D) and 26.2601-1(b)(4)(i)(E), Example 7).[24]

---

[24] *See*, John B. O'Grady and Jennifer Schooley Stringer, "Final Regs. Approve Certain Changes in Grandfathered GST Trusts," 28 *Estate Planning* 526 (November 2001).

The IRS will no longer issue a private letter ruling on whether a trust exempt from GST tax under Treas. Reg. §§26.2601-1(b)(1), (2), or (3) will retain its grandfathered

§5.26 DELAWARE TAX TRAP AND GST GRANDFATHERED TRUSTS[25]

If a non-general power of appointment in a GST grandfathered trust is exercised in a manner that may postpone or suspend the vesting of an interest in trust property beyond the period relating to the rule against perpetuities (i.e., beyond a life in being plus 21 years or beyond 90 years), this will result in the exercise being treated as a constructive addition to the GST grandfathered trust, and will change the identity of the transferor for GST purposes even if the exercise of the power is not treated as a taxable transfer for estate or gift tax purposes (i.e., because the state law has a longer perpetuities period).[26] Treas. Reg. §§26.2601-1(b)(1)(v)(A) and (B). *See also,* IRC sections 2041(a)(3) and 2514(d). Additionally, if the period for vesting is the "*longer* of a life in being plus 21 years *or* 90 years," this too will cause the GST grandfathered trust to lose its GST tax exempt status, except where state law prohibits the use of the longer of the two periods. Treas. Reg. §26.2601-1(b)(1)(v)(D), Examples 6 and 7. *See,* sections 3.16 and 4.7, above concerning the Delaware tax trap.

§5.26(a) Constructive Addition If GST Grandfathered Trust's Liability Is Not Paid By The Trust

Where a GST grandfathered trust is relieved of any liability properly payable out of the assets of such trust, the person who actually satisfies the liability is considered to have made a constructive addition to the GST grandfathered trust in an amount equal to the liabil-

GST exempt status when there is a modification of the grandfathered trust, change in the administration of the grandfathered trust, or a distribution from the grandfathered trust in a factual scenario that is similar to a factual scenario set forth in one or more of the examples contained in Treas. Reg. §26.2601-1(b)(4)(i)(E). Rev. Proc. 2007-3, 2007 -1 I.R.B. 108, section 3.01(58).

[25] *See,* Stephen E. Greer, "The Delaware Tax Trap and the Abolition of the Rule Against Perpetuities," 28 *Estate Planning* 68 (February 2001); and Jesse Dukeminier, "The Uniform Statutory Rule Against Perpetuities And The GST Tax: New Perils For Practitioners And New Opportunities," 30 *Real Property, Probate and Trust Journal* 185 (Summer 1995).

[26] Because Treasury Regulations prohibit the extension of a trust beyond a life in being and 21 years or 90 years (even though local law provides for a longer perpetuities period), the default for the non-exercise of a non-general power of appointment should be a continuation of the trust. The continuation of the trust, whether or not the power is exercised, does not constitute an "extension" of the trust's term.

ity satisfied by that person. The constructive addition occurs when the GST grandfathered trust is relieved of liability (e.g., when the right of recovery is no longer enforceable by the person who paid a tax on behalf of the GST grandfathered trust). Treas. Reg. §26.2601-1(b)-(1)(v)(C). The person satisfying the trust's liability becomes the transferor (for GST tax purposes) of the satisfied amount. Special rules, however, apply with respect to payment of estate taxes on reverse QTIP property. Treas. Reg. §26.2652-1(a)(3). If the surviving spouse's will waives the right to be reimbursed for estate taxes attributable to reverse QTIP property, the waiver (and payment of the estate taxes by the surviving spouse's estate) does not constitute a constructive addition to the reverse QTIP trust. Treas. Reg. §26.2652-1(a)(5), Example 8.

§5.27 PRESERVATION OF ALLOCATION OF GST TAX EXEMPTION TO ILIT PROPERTY INCLUDED IN GRANTOR'S GROSS ESTATE

If the grantor's GST tax exemption is allocated to an ILIT while the ILIT was not subject to an ETIP, and if the life insurance proceeds are included in the grantor's gross estate, the inclusion ratio remains unchanged and the trust property remains exempt from GST tax. Treas. Reg. §26.2642-4(a)(3). No re-calculation of the inclusion ratio will occur so long as the property does not revert to the grantor's estate.

> **Practice Point:** The use of a Reverse QTIP marital deduction trust (where there is a surviving spouse and the deceased grantor is the only insured under the ILIT) to receive the included life insurance proceeds, with the surviving spouse's will waiving any right of reimbursement under IRC section 2207A, will preserve the property's inclusion ratio and minimize its depletion by death taxes. *See,* Paragraph 5.1(A)(8) of Sample ILIT.

> **Practice Point:** Consider the effect of estate tax apportionment against the life insurance proceeds and its impact on trust property with a zero (0) inclusion ratio. Should death taxes be apportioned away from the zero (0) inclusion ratio property?

§5.28 REVERSE QTIP MARITAL DEDUCTION ELECTION

The reverse QTIP election allows the decedent, rather than the surviving spouse, to be treated as the transferor for GST tax purposes of property for which the QTIP marital deduction election is made under IRC section 2056(b)(7). IRC section 2652(a)(3). Since the reverse QTIP election is not available for an IRC section 2056(b)(5) estate tax marital deduction general power of appointment trust, care must be taken to make sure the QTIP trust does not give the surviving spouse any powers that would result in an IRC section 2056(b)(5) general power of appointment trust.

Marital deduction trusts are used in ILITs where (i) the life of only the grantor (and not the grantor's spouse) is insured, (ii) the grantor's surviving spouse is a beneficiary of the ILIT, and (iii) there is a possibility that the transfer of property to the ILIT (such as a life insurance policy) may be included in the grantor's gross estate under the three-year inclusion rule of IRC section 2035.

> **Practice Point:** The reverse QTIP election is important if the grantor has allocated his or her GST tax exemption to the ILIT and wants to preserve the zero (0) inclusion ratio of the ILIT property included in his or her gross estate. In such instance, the ILIT should direct the trustee to allocate any GST tax exempt ILIT property included in the grantor's gross estate that qualifies for the marital deduction to a reverse QTIP trust for the surviving spouse. When the surviving spouse dies, any federal estate tax attributable to the reverse QTIP property should be paid out of either the surviving spouse's own property (provided the beneficiaries of the surviving spouse's estate and the remainder beneficiaries of the reverse QTIP trust are the same) or out of the non-reverse QTIP trust property. Payment of estate taxes by the surviving spouse does not constitute an impermissible constructive addition to the reverse QTIP trust. Treas. Reg. §26.2652-1(a)(5), Example 8. *See,* Paragraph 5.1 of Sample ILIT.

§5.28(a) Partial Reverse QTIP Election Not Permitted

A partial reverse QTIP election is not permitted. Treas. Reg. §26.2652-2(a). It is therefore extremely important for the governing instrument to divide the QTIP marital trust into two separate trusts, one trust equal to the remaining GST tax exemption amount (if any) of the first spouse to die, and one trust for assets in excess of that GST tax exemption amount. *See,* Paragraph 5.1(A)(8) of Sample ILIT. To the extent applicable, it is also important that the QTIP marital trust be divided in a manner that fulfills the requirements of the GST separate trust rule under Treas. Reg. §26.2654-1(b) (or the qualified severance rule under IRC section 2642(a)(3)), and the GST valuation rules under Treas. Reg. §26.2642-2.[27]

§5.29 ALLOCATION OF GST TAX EXEMPTION TO ILIT DURING TRANSFEROR'S LIFETIME[28]

When allocating a transferor's GST tax exemption to a trust, the allocation of GST tax exemption must be made to the entire trust rather than to specific trust assets. If, however, a transfer is a direct skip to a trust (*see* section 5.29(a), below concerning direct skips), the allocation of GST tax exemption to the transferred property is treated as an allocation of GST tax exemption to the trust. Treas. Reg. §26.2632-1(a).

If a direct skip (*see* section 5.7, above) occurs during the transferor's lifetime, the transferor's unused portion[29] of GST tax exemption is automatically allocated to the value of the transferred proper-

---

[27] *See,* Chapter 13 of Sebastian V. Grassi, Jr., *A Practical Guide to Drafting Marital Deduction Trusts (with Sample Forms and Checklists)*, ALI-ABA, Philadelphia, (2004, Supp. 2006) (800) 253-6397, http://www.ali-aba.org/aliaba/bk36/ for a detailed discussion of the GST separate trust rule and the GST valuation rules.

[28] *See,* Diana S. C. Zeydel, "Handling Deemed Allocations of GST Exemption to Lifetime Transfers," 34 *Estate Planning* 3 (March 2007); and Diana S. C. Zeydel, "Handling Affirmative and Deemed Allocations of GST Tax Exemption," 34 *Estate Planning* 12 (February 2007). The March 2007 article discusses the rules governing automatic or deemed allocation of GST tax exemption to direct and indirect skips made during the transferor's lifetime. The February 2007 article discusses the rules on affirmative timely and late allocations of GST tax exemption, the rule permitting retroactive allocation of GST tax exemption in the case of an unnatural order of deaths, and the rules governing automatic allocation of GST tax exemption in the event the transferor has unused GST tax exemption after the due date of the transferor's federal estate tax return. The article also contains numerous sample GST tax exemption notice and allocation forms, and a sample form to terminate a previously filed election out statement.

[29] "For purposes of the deemed allocation to direct skips rule, the unused portion of a transferor's GST exemption is that portion not previously affirmatively allocated by the transferor or deemed allocated under the direct skip rule or the rule applicable to indirect skips to GST trusts discussed in [section 5.29(b), below]....This would mean that a deemed allocation to a direct skip transfer in a particular calendar year will pre-

ty (but not in excess of the fair market value of the property on the date of the transfer, as finally determined for gift tax purposes) to the extent necessary to obtain a zero inclusion ratio. IRC section 2632(b). The transferor may prevent the automatic allocation of his or her GST tax exemption to the direct skip by filing a U.S. Gift Tax Return (IRS Form 709) and attaching a "*Direct Skip GST Allocation Election Out Statement*"[30] concerning the direct skip. IRC section 2632(b)(3). In addition, a timely filed U.S. Gift Tax Return accompanied by payment of the GST tax (as shown on the return with respect to the direct skip) is sufficient to prevent an automatic allocation of GST tax exemption with respect to the transferred property. Treas. Reg. §26.2632-1(b)(1)(i).

> **Practice Point:** There is no deemed allocation of the transferor's unused portion of GST tax exemption to certain direct skip transfers that are non-taxable gifts, which have been statutorily granted a zero inclusion ratio by the Internal Revenue Code. IRC section 2642(c). *See*, section 5.7(C), above. However, if the IRC section 2642(c) gift exceeds the gift tax annual exclusion amount (other than a gift that qualifies for the unlimited annual gift tax exclusion under IRC section 2503(e) regarding the direct payment of medical expenses and tuition), an automatic allocation of the transferor's unused portion of GST tax exemption will be allocated to the value of the direct skip gift tax that exceeds the gift tax annual exclusion amount.

The GST automatic allocation rules for inter-vivos transfers apply to both direct and indirect skips (*see* section 5.29(b), below concerning indirect skips) made during the grantor's lifetime. IRC sections 2632(b) and (c).

The automatic allocation of a transferor's GST tax exemption to a direct skip or indirect skip is effective as of the date of the transfer,

---

cede a deemed allocation to an indirect skip transfer made in the same year, and both will precede any affirmative allocation of GST exemption made to other transfers. Accordingly, to change the order or priority, effective elections out of the deemed allocation rules would be necessary." Diana S. C. Zeydel, "Handling Deemed Allocations of GST Exemption to Lifetime Transfers," 34 *Estate Planning* 3, 4 (March 2007).

[30] *See*, Sample form of "Direct Skip GST Allocation Election Out Statement" in Appendix 4.

and becomes irrevocable on the due date (including extensions actually granted) for filing the U.S. Gift Tax Return for the calendar year in which the transfer is made, whether or not a U.S. Gift Tax Return is actually filed. Treas. Reg. §§26.2632-1(b)(1)(ii) and 26.2632-1(b)-(2)(i).

§5.29(a) ILIT As A Skip Person

A direct skip is a transfer to a skip person that is subject to federal estate or gift tax (*see* section 5.7, above). If property is transferred to an ILIT, the transfer is a direct skip only if the trust itself is a skip person. Treas. Reg. §26.2612-1(a). A trust is a skip person if all the interests in the trust are held by skip persons (which is generally not the case in a traditional ILIT). Treas. Reg. §26.2612-1(d)(2)(i). Thus, if the ILIT is not a skip person it will be necessary for the grantor to allocate his or her GST tax exemption in order for the ILIT to be GST tax exempt. Before the 2001 Tax Act, the grantor had to allocate his or her GST tax exemption to such a trust by filing a timely U.S. Gift Tax Return (IRS Form 709) along with a *"Notice of Allocation of GST Tax Exemption to Trust."*[31] *See*, IRC section 2632(a)(2). As a result of the 2001 Tax Act (discussed in section 5.29(b), below), such notice may not be required. However, as also discussed below, it may be preferable for the grantor to still file a timely U.S. Gift Tax Return along with a *"Notice of Allocation of GST Tax Exemption to Trust"* rather than relying on the new automatic allocation rules of the 2001 Tax Act.

§5.29(b) "Indirect Skip" And "GST Trust" Defined

The 2001 Tax Act provides for automatic allocation of a transferor's unused portion of GST tax exemption to certain lifetime transfers that are (i) subject to gift tax, (ii) not direct skips, and (iii) are made to an inter-vivos trust (such as an ILIT) that could subsequently have a generation-skipping transfer with respect to the transferor ("indirect

---

[31] *See*, Sample form of *"Notice of Allocation of GST Tax Exemption to Trust"* in Appendix 4.

See also, Diana S. C. Zeydel, "Handling Affirmative and Deemed Allocations of GST Tax Exemption," 34 *Estate Planning* 12, 13-14 (February 2007) for a discussion of what is required in a Notice of Allocation of GST Tax Exemption to Trust.

skips"). Such a trust is referred to as a "GST Trust" under IRC section 2632(c)(3)(B). The rule applies to inter-vivos transfers made after December 31, 2000, and to ETIPs ending after December 31, 2000. IRC section 2632(c); Treas. Reg. §26.2632-1(b)(2). This new rule is in addition to the pre-2001 Tax Act automatic GST tax exemption allocation rules concerning lifetime direct skips under IRC section 2632(b) (*see,* the opening paragraphs of section 5.29, above). Thus, as a result of the new law, both lifetime direct skips and lifetime indirect skips are subject to the automatic GST-tax-exemption allocation rules. This new type of lifetime automatic allocation of GST tax exemption to an indirect skip is referred to as an *"inter-vivos automatic GST exemption allocation,"* which is in contrast to the *"testamentary automatic GST exemption allocation"* discussed in section 5.30, below.

In the case of an indirect skip made after December 31, 2000 that is not subject to an ETIP, the transferor's unused portion of GST exemption is automatically allocated to the value of the property transferred in the indirect skip (but not in excess of the fair market value of the property on the date of the transfer, as finally determined for gift tax purposes) to the extent necessary to obtain a zero inclusion ratio. IRC section 2632(c); Treas. Reg. §26.2632-1(b)(2)(i). The automatic allocation of the transferor's GST tax exemption is effective whether or not a U.S. Gift Tax Return is filed, and the automatic allocation is effective as of the date of the transfer to which it relates. The automatic allocation of the transferor's GST tax exemption to the indirect skip is irrevocable after the due date of the U.S. Gift Tax Return for the calendar year in which the indirect skip is made.

In the case of an indirect skip subject to an ETIP, the indirect skip is deemed to be made at the close of the ETIP and the transferor's GST tax exemption is deemed to be allocated at that time against the then fair market value of the trust's property. Treas. Reg. §26.2632-1(b)(2)(i). Special rules apply to electing out of the inter-vivos automatic GST exemption allocation rules concerning transfers that are subject to an ETIP under IRC section 2642(f). Treas. Reg. §§26.2632-1(b)(2)(i), (iii)(A)(1) and (5), (iii)(B), (iii)(C)(1), (iii)(D), and (iii)(E). The election out must be made on before the due date of the gift tax return for the calendar year in which the ETIP closes.

Practice Point: Allocation of GST tax exemption at the close of an ETIP can have disastrous results if the fair market value of the life insurance policy has increased significantly. *See,* section 3.1, above, concerning valuation of life insurance policies.

§5.29(b)(1) Opting In Or Out Of GST Trust Status

The new rule concerning allocation of a transferor's GST tax exemption to indirect skips is overly broad. Trusts that were not initially designed to be GST Trusts may be deemed to be GST Trusts as a result of the uncertainty of the exceptions set forth in IRC section 2632(c)(3)(B)(i)-(vi). Such a result would cause an unintended allocation of the transferor's GST tax exemption. Consequently, the transferor will have to decide whether to opt out of the inter-vivos automatic GST exemption allocation rules, as is permitted under IRC section 2632(c)(5). In this regard, a two-step analysis must be made. First, for those transferors who would like to rely on the new inter-vivos automatic GST exemption allocation rules, they must be certain that the trust at issue meets the definition of a "GST Trust." Second, those transferors who have created "GST Trusts" must make certain that the automatic GST tax exemption allocation is appropriate for such trusts and, if not, elect out of the inter-vivos automatic GST exemption allocation rules. An election out of the rules is accomplished by filing an *"Election Out of Indirect Skip GST Allocation Statement"*[32] on a timely filed U.S. Gift Tax Return (IRS Form 709). *See also,* Priv. Letter Rul. 200535025 where the IRS permitted the taxpayer an extension of time to make a "late" election out of GST Trust status for a "GST Trust" that had been established four years before the enactment of IRC section 2632(c) under the 2001 Tax Act. The IRS held that the taxpayer had acted reasonable and in good faith under IRC Treas. Reg. §301.9100-3.

An election to opt out of the inter-vivos automatic GST exemption allocation rules does not affect the automatic allocation of GST exemption to any transfer not covered by the election out statement. An election out of the inter-vivos automatic GST exemption allocation rules does not apply to any prior-year transfer to a trust, including any transfer subject to an ETIP (even if the ETIP closes after the

---

[32] *See,* Sample form of *"Election Out of Indirect Skip GST Allocation Statement"* in Appendix 4.

election is made). An election out of the inter-vivos automatic GST exemption allocation rules does not prevent the transferor from making a subsequent affirmative allocation of the transferor's available GST exemption to any transfer covered by the prior election out, either on a timely filed Form 709 reporting the transfer, or at a later date in accordance with the provisions of Treas. Reg. §26.2632-1(b)(4). This rule permits a transferor to make a late allocation of GST tax exemption to the previously opted-out trust. An election out of the inter-vivos automatic GST exemption allocation rules with respect to future transfers remains in effect unless and until terminated. Once an election out of the inter-vivos automatic GST exemption allocation rules with respect to future transfers is made, a transferor does not have to file an IRS Form 709 in future years solely to prevent the automatic allocation of the GST exemption to any future transfer covered by the election out. Treas. Reg. §26.2632-1(b)(2)(iii)(D).

GST Trust status is not permanent and could change from year to year depending on the facts and the six situations discussed below in section 5.29(c). Thus, transfers may or may not be subject to the inter-vivos automatic GST exemption allocation, depending on the trust's status that year. Consequently, the transferor may want to consider either permanently opting in or opting out of the inter-vivos automatic GST exemption allocation rules by filing the appropriate notice of election on a timely filed U.S. Gift Tax Return for the first year with respect to which the opting in or opting out is intended to be effective. IRC section 2632(c)(5); Treas. Reg. §26.2632-1(b).

In determining the amount of a transferor's unused GST tax exemption available to be automatically allocated to an indirect skip, allocations are deemed to occur in the following order:

(1) Allocations by the transferor;

(2) Automatic allocations to direct skips occurring during or before the calendar year in which the indirect skip is made; and

(3) Automatic allocations to indirect skips with respect to prior indirect skips.

As noted above, transferors can elect to not have the inter-vivos automatic GST exemption allocation rules apply by affirmatively opting out of the automatic allocation rules on a timely filed U.S. Gift Tax Return. IRC section 2632(c)(5)(A)(i); Treas. Reg. §26.2632-1(b)(2)(iii). Conversely, transferors can elect, on a timely filed U.S. Gift Tax Return, to have the inter-vivos automatic GST exemption allocation rules apply to a non-GST Trust by affirmatively electing to treat the non-GST Trust as if it were a GST Trust. This is accomplished by filing a *"GST Trust Election Statement"*[33] with the U.S. Gift Tax Return. IRC section 2632(c)(5)(A)(ii); Treas. Reg. §26.2632-1(b)(3).

> **Caution:** The election out of the inter-vivos automatic GST exemption allocation rules is not effective to prevent an automatic allocation of GST tax exemption upon the transferor's death. Treas. Reg. §26.2632-1(b)(2)(ii) states that any election out of inter-vivos automatic GST exemption allocation rules has no effect on the application of the testamentary automatic GST exemption allocation rules applicable at the transferor's death under IRC section 2632(e). Thus, to prevent the testamentary automatic allocation of GST tax exemption to a trust that the transferor elected to not have the inter-vivos automatic GST exemption allocation rules apply to (the "inter-vivos GST opt out trust"), the transferor's executor will need to make an affirmative allocation of GST tax exemption on the transferor's federal estate tax return (IRS Form 706) to other transfers (other than to the "inter-vivos GST opt out trust"). *See*, section 5.30, below.

§5.29(c) When The Indirect Skip Automatic Allocation Rules Do Not Apply

There are six situations in which the indirect skip automatic allocation rules do not apply, i.e., the trust will not be deemed a "GST Trust." IRC section 2632(c)(3)(B)(i)-(vi).

§5.29(c)(1) More Than 25% Withdrawable By Non-Skip Persons Of A Certain Age

The first situation in which an inter-vivos trust will not be deemed a "GST Trust" is when the trust instrument provides that *more*

---

[33] *See,* Sample form of *"GST Trust Election Statement"* in Appendix 4.

Note: If the trust was established before January 1, 2001, and the trust is a GST trust (for which the GST automatic allocation rules are applicable), the transferor will also need to file a late allocation of GST tax exemption for all pre-January 1, 2001 transfers to the trust. *See,* section 5.23, above and 6.5, below (concerning late allocation of GST tax exemption).

than 25% of the trust corpus must be distributed to or may be withdrawn by one or more individuals who are non-skip persons: (1) before that individual reaches 46 years of age; or (2) on or before one or more dates specified in the trust instrument that will occur before that individual attains 46 years of age; or (3) before an event that (in accordance with Treasury Regulations, that as of the writing of this book have not yet been issued) may reasonably be expected to occur before the date that individual attains age 46.[34] The rationale for this situation appears to be that a transferor would not want the GST tax exemption allocated to a trust for which more than 25% of the trust corpus (i.e., a substantial portion of the trust corpus) is directed to be distributed to a non-skip person at an age the individual is statistically and most likely expected to attain (in this instance, age 46). IRC section 2632(c)(3)(B)(i).

> **Caution:** This exception will ***not*** apply to ILITs when the trust property is (typically) distributed on the ***later of*** (i) the insured's (or the surviving spouse's) death, or (ii) when the insured's child reaches a specified age. Specifically, this exception does not apply (in most instances) to ILITs because it may not be reasonably expected for the insured (or the surviving spouse) to die before the children (the trust beneficiaries) reach age 46. To avoid the transferor's GST tax exemption being automatically allocated, the transferor will have to timely file a U.S. Gift Tax Return and opt out of the inter-vivos automatic GST exemption allocation rules.[35]

> **Example 1:** Transferor creates a trust for his son that provides that the son will receive discretionary distributions of income and principal until he is 40, at which time the entire balance of the trust corpus will be distributed to him. If the son dies before age 40, the trust corpus will be distributed to the son's then-living descendants, by right of

[34] Relying on the item (3) exception is problematic because of the uncertainty of when regulations will be issued and what circumstances the regulations will consider as "reasonably expected to occur" before a non-skip person reaches age 46.

[35] *See,* Sample form of *"Election Out of Indirect Skip GST Allocation Statement"* in Appendix 4.

representation. This is not a GST Trust because the trust instrument requires that more than 25% of the trust corpus must be distributed to the son before he attains age 46, to wit, age 40.

Example 2: Transferor creates a trust for his son that provides that the son will receive discretionary distributions of income and principal until he is 60, with mandatory principal distributions as follows: one-third at age 40, one-half at 50, and the balance at age 60. If the son dies before reaching age 60, the balance of the trust corpus will be distributed to the son's then-living descendants, by right of representation. This is not a GST Trust even though the trust will not terminate before the son attains age 46 because more than 25% of the trust corpus must be distributed to the son before he attains age 46, to wit, one-third of the corpus will be distributed by age 40.

Example 3: Transferor creates a trust for his son that provides that the son will receive discretionary distributions of income and principal until he is 60, with mandatory principal distributions as follows: 20% at age 45, 25% at age 50, 33% at age 55, and the balance at age 65. If the son dies before reaching age 65, the trust corpus will be distributed to the son's then-living descendants, by right of representation. This is a GST Trust because the trust instrument does not require that more than 25% of the trust corpus be distributed to the son before he attains age 46.

Example 4: Transferor creates a trust for his son that terminates and distributes the corpus to son in 15 years. If the son dies before the trust terminates, the trust corpus will be distributed to the son's then-living descendants, by right of representation. Son is 25 years old at the creation of the trust. This is not a GST Trust because the date of required distribution for the corpus will occur before the son reaches age 46, to wit, age 40.

Example 5: Transferor creates an incentive trust for his son (who is age six at the time) which pays 100% of the trust corpus to the son when he graduates from college. If the son dies before the trust terminates, the trust corpus will be distributed to the son's then-living descendants, by right of representation, or if none, to the transferor's then-living descendants, by right of representation. Until Treasury Regulations are issued, it cannot be determined whether this is a GST Trust because it cannot be determined whether it may reasonably be expected that a child will graduate from college before the child attains age 46.

§5.29(c)(2) More Than 25% Withdrawable By Non-Skip Persons Alive At A Certain Time

The second situation in which an inter-vivos trust will not be deemed a "GST Trust" is when the trust instrument provides that *more than* 25% of the trust corpus must be distributed to or may be withdrawn by one or more individuals who are non-skip persons and who are living on the date of death of another person identified in the instrument (by name or by class) who is more than 10 years older than such individuals. The rationale for this situation appears to be that a transferor would not want the GST tax exemption allocated to a trust that is likely to terminate and be distributed outright to a non-skip person at the death of an individual whom the non-skip person is generally expected to survive. IRC section 2632(c)(3)(B)(ii).

Caution: This exception will ***not*** apply to ILITs when the trust property is (typically) distributed on the ***later of*** (i) the insured's (or the surviving spouse's) death, or (ii) when the insured's child reaches a specified age. Specifically, this exception does not apply (in most instances) because no portion of the ILIT corpus would be distributed outright to the child at the death of the grantor-insured (or the surviving spouse) *unless* the child had already reached a specified age; and in many instances, distributions would be staggered over time. To avoid the transferor's GST tax exemption being automatically allocated, the transferor will have to file IRS Form 709 and opt out of the inter-vivos automatic GST exemption allocation rules.[36] However, once the child (or all the children) reaches the specified age (even though the insured is still alive), if more than 25% of the trust corpus would be distributable to the

---

[36] *See,* Sample form of *"Election Out of Indirect Skip GST Allocation Statement"* in Appendix 4.

child/children (because he or she has attained the specified age and the surviving spouse does not have an intervening life estate (e.g., the surviving spouse is deceased), then at the time the child (or all the children) attains the specified age, the ILIT would no longer be a GST Trust, would come within the second situation described above, and the GST automatic allocation rules would no longer apply.

Example 6: Transferor creates a trust for his mother for her lifetime with discretionary distributions of income and principal to her as determined by the trustee, remainder to transferor's child or, if the transferor's child is not living at the death of the transferor's mother, remainder to the transferor's then-living descendants, by right of representation. At the time of the creation of the trust, the transferor's mother is 70 years old and the transferor's child is 25 years old. This is not a GST Trust because the trust instrument provides that more than 25% of the trust corpus will be distributed to the transferor's child (a non-skip person vis-à-vis the transferor) at the death of the transferor's mother who is (obviously) more than 10 years older than the transferor's child.

Example 7: Transferor creates a trust for the benefit of his spouse and their three children, with discretionary distributions of income and principal to any of them during the spouse's life, and remainder to the transferor's then-living descendants who survive the spouse, by right of representation. This is not a GST Trust because the transferor's children (who are non-skip persons) are eligible to receive more than 25% of the trust corpus at the death of their mother who is more than 10 years older than any of her three children.

Example 8: Transferor creates a trust for the sole benefit of the transferor's second wife for her lifetime. The second wife is the same age as the transferor's youngest child (30). Upon the death of the second wife, the remainder of the trust is to be distributed to the transferor's then-living descendants who survive their stepmother, by right of representation. This is a GST Trust because, although the trust instrument requires that the trust corpus must be distributed to the transferor's children if they are living at the death of their stepmother, the stepmother is not more than 10 years older than the transferor's children. In fact, it is possible the second wife may outlive all of the transferor's children and the trust corpus may pass entirely to the transferor's grandchildren or more-remote descendants.

§5.29(c)(3) Mandatory Distributions Of More Than 25% To Estates Of Certain Non-Skip Persons

The third situation in which an inter-vivos trust will not be deemed a GST Trust is when the trust instrument provides for mandatory distribution of *more than* 25% of the trust corpus to the estate or estates of, or subjects such corpus to a general power of appointment held by, one or more individuals who are non-skip persons if one or more such non-skip persons die on or before a date or event described in IRC section 2632(c)(3)(B)(i) or (ii), which are described in sections 5.29(c)(1) and (2) immediately above.[37] This situation covers trusts that do not meet the literal requirements of the situations described in sections 5.29(c)(1) and (2) above, provided more than 25% of the trust corpus is includable in the non-skip person's estate if he or she were to die prematurely (i.e., before age 46), even if the non-skip person does not otherwise have a right to receive trust distributions or a right to make withdrawals from the trust before the specified events. The rationale assumes that a transferor does not generally intend to allocate the GST tax exemption to a trust that is structured to be includable in a non-skip person's estate (and that will result in the non-skip person becoming the [new] transferor for GST tax purposes). IRC section 2632(c)(3)(B)(iii).

Caution: This exception will ***not*** apply to an ILIT where the child does not hold a testamentary or inter-vivos general power of appointment (other than a *Crummey* withdrawal right) over his or her separate trust share, which share is established at the inception of the ILIT. Nor will this exception apply if the surviving spouse has an intervening life estate in the ILIT, which is typical in single life ILIT for a married couple.

[37] As previously stated above, item (3) noted in section 5.29(c)(1) is problematic and until regulations are issued, should not be relied upon for creating an exception.

Example 9: Transferor creates a discretionary common (pot) trust for his descendants. The pot trust provides that his two children will receive distributions of income and principal for their lives, at the sole discretion of the trustee. At the death of each child, the child has a testamentary general power of appointment over the child's then-existing pro rata share of the trust and if the power of appointment is not exercised, the child's share passes to the child's then-living descendants, by right of representation. This is not a GST Trust because it provides that if a child dies before attaining age 46 (an event described in section 5.29(c)(1) above), more than 25% of the trust corpus is includable in each child's estate as a result of the child's testamentary general power of appointment. In this example, 50% of the trust (or 100% of the child's trust share) would be includable in each child's estate. Presumably the same result would obtain even if the transferor had five children, because the trust provides that the shares of each of them would be includable in their respective estates if they died before attaining age 46.

Example 10: Transferor creates a trust for the sole benefit of the transferor's second wife, income only for her lifetime. The second wife and the transferor's only child are both age 30. Upon the death of the second wife, the remainder of the trust is to be distributed to the transferor's then-living descendants who survive their stepmother, by right of representation. If the child predeceases the stepmother, the child has a testamentary general power of appointment over the child's share of the remainder at the death of the stepmother. This is not a GST Trust because the child's share is includable in the child's estate if the child dies before age 46. Consequently, a trust that was otherwise a GST Trust under section 5.29(c)(2) above is not a GST Trust if it meets the requirements of section 5.29(c)(3) above or section 5.29(c)(4) immediately below.

§5.29(c)(4) Any Portion Of Trust Included In Certain Non-Skip Decedents' Estates

The fourth situation in which an inter-vivos trust will not be deemed a GST Trust is when any portion of the trust would be included in the gross estate of a non-skip person (other than the transferor) if such person died immediately after the transfer. However, there is an exception to this exception, concerning *Crummey* withdrawal rights limited to IRC section 2503(b) amounts. IRC section 2632(c)(3)(B)-(iv). It is possible for a trust described in this situation to periodically switch back and forth between being a GST Trust and not being a GST Trust. This could occur if there were hanging *Crummey* powers held by non-skip beneficiaries at the close of the year. However, once all the non-skip persons' hanging powers lapse, the trust would no longer be a GST Trust. The switching back and forth issue can be dealt with by either affirmatively electing in to GST Trust status,[38] or by affirmatively opting out of GST Trust status.[39]

> **Example 11**: Transferor creates an inter-vivos QTIP trust for his spouse, remainder to their then-living descendants who survive their mother, by right of representation. This is not a GST Trust because it would be includable in the spouse's estate under IRC section 2044 if the spouse died immediately after the transfer. (Note that this fact situation may also qualify under the second situation above.)
>
> **Example 12**: Transferor creates an inter-vivos ILIT for his spouse and descendants (children and grandchildren) that runs for the rule against perpetuities. Immediately after a contribution to the ILIT, each beneficiary has a 30-day *Crummey* withdrawal right over the contribution amount, limited (on a cumulative basis) to the amount specified in IRC section 2503(b) (as adjusted for inflation) as concerns each transferor/contributor to the ILIT. The *Crummey* withdrawal right lapses within the five-by-five safe harbor rules. The *Crummey* withdrawal right is a general power of appointment; and if the transferor's spouse or a child were to die before the exercise or lapse of the withdrawal right, the value of the withdrawal right would be includable in the decedent's gross estate. This is a GST Trust because of the exception for *Crummey* withdrawal rights limited to IRC section 2503(b) amount. IRC sec-

---

[38] *See*, Sample form of *"GST Trust Election Statement"* in Appendix 4.

[39] *See*, Sample form of *"Election Out of Indirect Skip GST Allocation Statement"* in Appendix 4.

tion 2632(c)(3)(B). As discussed later, hanging *Crummey* powers of withdrawal apparently do not fall within the exception to the exception (concerning *Crummey* withdrawal rights limited to IRC section 2503(b) amounts). In other words, if (for the year in question), the cumulative amount of the hanging *Crummey* withdrawal right is greater than the annual gift tax exclusion amount, the trust will not be a GST Trust, and the trust will not be subject to the automatic allocation rules for that tax year. However, in future tax years, the trust may (or may not) be a GST Trust, depending on the amount of the cumulative hanging *Crummey* withdrawal amount. Consequently, the inter-vivos automatic GST exemption allocation rules should not be relied upon, and the transferor should consider filing a one time notice with the IRS to either elect in[40] or elect out [41] of GST Trust status.

Example 13: Transferor creates an ILIT for the benefit of his children. The ILIT contains ***separate trust shares*** for each child. Each child has a *Crummey* withdrawal right with regard to inter-vivos contributions made to his or her trust share. Each child also has a testamentary general power of appointment over his or her trust share. Upon the death of the child, any trust property not otherwise appointed by the child is held in further trust for the deceased child's then living children (i.e., the transferor's grandchildren). This is not a GST Trust since the child's trust share would be includable in his or her estate if the child were to die immediately after the transfer.

§5.29(c)(5) CLATs, CRATs, Or CRUTs

The fifth situation in which an inter-vivos trust will not be deemed a GST Trust is when the trust is a charitable lead annuity trust ("CLAT"), charitable remainder annuity trust ("CRAT"), or a charitable remainder unitrust ("CRUT"). Apparently, the rationale for this

---

[40] See, Sample form of *"GST Trust Election Statement"* in Appendix 4.

[41] *See,* Sample form of *"Election Out of Indirect Skip GST Allocation Statement"* in Appendix 4.

situation is that these forms of trusts have characteristics that would generally not lead a transferor to allocate the GST tax exemption to them. IRC section 2632(c)(3)(B)(v).

§5.29(c)(6) CLUT With A Non-Skip Non-Charitable Remainder Beneficiary

The sixth situation in which an inter-vivos trust will not be deemed a GST Trust is when the trust is a charitable lead unitrust ("CLUT") that is required to pay the principal to a non-skip person if such person is alive when the unitrust interest ends. Given the complexity of this type of planning, apparently Congress felt that if a non-skip person is named as a remainder person, no automatic allocation of GST tax exemption should be made and that inadvertent failures to allocate the GST tax exemption under these circumstances are less likely since the use of a charitable split-interest trust typically involves the transferor's legal and tax counsel. In other words, this type of transferor is deemed to be "sophisticated" and does not need a statutory GST-tax-exemption allocation "safety net". IRC section 2632(c)(3)(B)(vi).

> **Example 14:** Transferor creates a charitable lead unitrust and provides that at the end of the lead interest, the remainder is to be paid to his then-living descendants, by right of representation. At the time of creation of the trust, the transferor has three children. This is not a GST Trust.
>
> **Example 15:** Transferor creates a charitable lead unitrust and provides that at the end of the lead interest, the remainder is to be paid to grandchildren. This, of course, is a GST Trust.

§5.29(d) *Crummey* Withdrawal Right Gifts

For purposes of the six situations described in sections 5.29(c)(1)—(6), above, the value of transferred property is not considered to be includable in the gross estate of a non-skip person or considered to be subject to a right of withdrawal by a non-skip person if the right of withdrawal does not exceed the amount referred to in IRC section 2503(b) with respect to any transferor, i.e., the non-skip person holds a *Crummey* withdrawal right. IRC section 2632(c)(3)(B). It is assumed that powers of appointment held by non-skip persons will not be exercised. IRC section 2632(c)(3)(B).

§5.29(e) Indirect Skips And ETIP

An indirect skip subject to the ETIP rules of IRC section 2642(f) is deemed to have been made at the close of the ETIP, and the automatic allocation of GST exemption occurs at the close of the ETIP based on the fair market value of the trust property at that time. IRC section 2632(c)(4). *See,* section 3.1, above, concerning the valuation of life insurance policies. (It is hoped that the policy has not increased in value and the insured is still insurable at the close of the ETIP.) *See,* Treas. Reg. §26.2632-1(c).

> **Practice Point:** Trusts subject to an ETIP ending after December 31, 2000 may be subject to the new automatic allocation of GST exemption rules unless the transferor elects out. *See,* section 5.29(g) below for how to elect out.

§5.29(f) Filing A Gift Tax Return

IRC section 2503(b) refers to the $10,000 annual gift tax exclusion amount, as adjusted for inflation. Because the above-mentioned exception does *not* refer to the IRC section 2503(b) amount at the time of the transfer, but rather, "with respect to any transferor"—without reference to time—the right of a non-skip beneficiary to withdraw more than the annual gift tax exclusion amount by reason of a cumulative hanging *Crummey* withdrawal right may cause the trust to not be treated as a GST Trust under sections 5.29(c)(1), (3) and (4) above and therefore prevent the inter-vivos automatic GST exemption allocation rules from applying to the trust.

The IRC section 2503(b) exception seems to say that if the withdrawal right is limited to the annual exclusion amount at the time of the transfer, the trust may be a GST Trust (unless it comes within one of the six situations described in IRC section 2632(c)(3)(B)(i)-(vi)). However, if the withdrawal right is a "hanging" power of withdrawal that can accumulate over time, the trust may not be a GST Trust with respect to subsequent gifts, and no inter-vivos automatic GST exemption allocation will occur. This, of course, suggests that it may be desirable to file a timely U.S. Gift Tax Return with a notice of election to either opt in or opt out of the automatic GST-tax-exemption allocation rules. *See,* section 5.29(b)(1), above. By filing a U.S. Gift Tax Return, the transferor can be assured that the desired GST inclusion ratio is achieved and is not dependent on the amount of the beneficiary's right of withdrawal, which could change from year to year and thus affect the trust's classification as a GST Trust or non-GST Trust from year to year.

Regardless of whether the ILIT qualifies as a GST Trust, because all of the provisions of the 2001 Tax Act, including the new automatic inter-vivos automatic GST exemption allocation rules, sunset (expire) on January 1, 2011, it is probably best for the transferor to file a U.S. Gift Tax Return and attach: (1) a *"Notice of Allocation of GST Tax Exemption to Trust"* (and allocate GST tax exemption)[42]; or (2) an IRC section 2632(c)(5) *"Election Out of Indirect Skip GST Allocation Statement"*[43] to opt out of the inter-vivos automatic GST exemption allocation rules of IRC section 2632(c), in which case the transferor will have to either make a one time current and future election to opt out, or make an annual determination whether or not to allocate GST tax exemption to the ILIT contributions; or (3) a *"GST Trust Election Statement"*[44] to treat the ILIT as a GST Trust under IRC section 2632-(c)(5) for current transfers and/or some or all future transfers to the ILIT.

§5.29(g) Final Automatic GST Exemption Allocation Regulations, And Electing In And Out Of "GST Trust" Status

On June 29, 2005, the IRS issued final regulations concerning the electing in and electing out of the inter-vivos automatic GST exemption allocation rules concerning indirect skips and GST Trusts. Treas. Reg. §26.2632-1. (Treasury Decision 9208 [6/29/2005]). The final regulations provide guidance on how to: (1) elect out of the inter-vivos automatic GST exemption allocation rules for current and/or future transfers to a GST Trust, and how to terminate that election (Treas. Reg. §26.2632-1(b)(2)(ii)), and (2) elect to treat a non-GST Trust as a GST Trust and have the inter-vivos automatic GST exemption allocation rules apply to current and/or future transfers to that trust, and how to terminate that election (Treas. Reg. §26.2632-1(b)(3)). The final regulations specifically confirm that an election out of the inter-vivos GST automatic allocation rules for future years is not

---

[42] *See,* Sample form of *"Notice of Allocation of GST Tax Exemption to Trust"* in Appendix 4.

[43] *See,* Sample form of *"Election Out of Indirect Skip GST Allocation Statement"* in Appendix 4.

[44] See, Sample form of *"GST Trust Election Statement"* in Appendix 4.

an election out of the testamentary automatic GST exemption allocation rules under IRC section 2632(e), which are discussed in section 5.30, below. Treas. Reg. §26.2632-1(b)(2)(ii).

Special rules apply to electing out of the inter-vivos automatic GST exemption allocation rules concerning transfers that are subject to an ETIP under IRC section 2642(f). Treas. Reg. §§26.2632-1(b)-(2)(i), (iii)(A)(1) and (5), (iii)(B), (iii)(C)(1), (iii)(D), and (iii)(E); and Treas. Reg. §26.2632-1(c). A *blanket* election out of the inter-vivos automatic GST exemption allocation rules concerning all future indirect skips made by the transferor does not apply to any prior-year transfer to a trust, including any transfer subject to an ETIP (even if the ETIP closes after the election out is made). This is because the timelines of the election out is based on the date of the transfer to the trust, and not on the (future) date of the close of the ETIP. Treas. Reg. §26.2632-1(b)(2)(iii)(D). However, a transferor can affirmatively elect out of the inter-vivos automatic GST exemption allocation rules concerning a prior transfer that is subject to an ETIP if the election out is made on before the due date of the gift tax return for the calendar year in which the ETIP closes and the election out statement specifically describes the ETIP or otherwise identifies the transfer that is subject to the ETIP. Treas. Reg. §26.2632-1(b)(2)(iii)(C).

> **Caution:** An affirmative allocation of GST tax exemption to a transfer that is subject to an ETIP becomes irrevocable after the due date for a timely filed IRS Form 709 reporting the transfer, and the allocation becomes effective at the close of the ETIP. Treas. Reg. §26.2632-1(c)(1)(ii). Consequently, a transferor may want to abstain from making an affirmative election of GST tax exemption to a transfer subject to an ETIP until the ETIP closes. And if the trust is a GST Trust, the transferor should also make a timely election out of the inter-vivos automatic GST exemption allocation rules concerning the ETIP.

A transferor can elect to treat a non-GST Trust as a GST Trust, where the non-GST Trust is subject to an ETIP. Treas. Reg. §§26.2632-1(b)(3)(i).

> **Caution:** The inter-vivos GST automatic allocation rules concerning indirect skips and GST Trusts do not apply to pre-2001 inter-vivos transfers. Advisors may want to consider informing clients who have a pre-2001 ILIT that is

not a GST Trust with regard to post 2000 transfers, that the client may need to make a late allocation of GST tax exemption[45] (or a Rev. Proc 2004-46 election (which is discussed in section 6.5, below) in lieu of a late allocation) ***and*** an election to treat the non-GST Trust as a GST Trust, if the client wants to be assured that the ILIT is GST tax exempt. Similarly, if a pre-2001 ILIT is a GST Trust with regard to post 2000 transfers, but no GST tax exemption was allocated to the pre-2001 transfers, the client should consider: (1) making a late allocation of his or her GST tax exemption (or a Rev. Proc 2004-46 election (which is discussed in section 6.5, below) in lieu of a late allocation) ***and*** an election to treat the ILIT as a GST Trust with regard to all future transfers, or (2) elect out of GST Trust status and the inter-vivos GST automatic allocation rules (and consider a qualified severance of the trust since the ILIT will have an inclusion ratio of greater than zero but less than one as a result of the automatic allocation of GST tax exemption to post December 31, 2000 transfers). Option (1) will result in the ILIT having a zero inclusion ratio and being GST tax exempt. Option (2) will result in the ILIT having an inclusion ratio between one and zero (because of the post 2000 inter-vivos GST automatic allocations), and the ILIT will not be completely exempt from GST tax if a GST event subsequently occurs. *See,* sections 5.23, above and 6.5, below (concerning late allocations of GST tax exemption).

§5.30 ALLOCATION OF GST TAX EXEMPTION TO ILIT UPON DEATH OF TRANSFEROR

If a transferor dies and has not exhausted his or her GST tax exemption through inter-vivos transfers or through allocation by the transferor's executor on the federal estate tax return,[46] the transferor's unused

[45] See, Sample form of *"Notice of Late Allocation of GST Tax Exemption to Trust"* in Appendix 4.

[46] An allocation of a decedent's unused GST tax exemption by the decedent's executor is made on the decedent's federal estate tax return (IRS Form 706). If the estate tax return is filed on or before its due date (including extensions actually granted), the allo-

GST tax exemption is automatically allocated at death.[47] IRC Section 2632(e). This type of automatic allocation is referred to as a *"testamentary automatic GST exemption allocation,"* which is in contrast to the *"inter-vivos automatic GST exemption allocation"* discussed in section 5.29 above and in section 5.32 below. The testamentary automatic GST allocation occurs, first, to direct skips occurring at the transferor's death. Second, to trusts established by the transferor that result in (or may subsequently result in) a taxable distribution or a taxable termination as a result of the transferor's death. IRC section 2632(e). Treas. Reg. §26.2632-1(d)(2) contains provisions that prevent the testamentary automatic GST allocation rule from inadvertently wasting the deceased transferor's unused GST tax exemption. The regulation provides that no testamentary automatic GST allocation will be made to a trust that will have a new transferor with respect to the entire trust before the occurrence of any generation-skipping transfer with respect to the trust (such as a QTIP marital deduction trust for which no reverse QTIP election has been made under IRC section 2652(a)(3)), and no testamentary automatic GST allocation will be made to a trust established by the transferor if, during the nine month period ending immediately after the transferor's death (i) no generation-skipping transfer has occurred with respect to the trust, and (ii) at the end of the nine month period no future generation-skipping transfer can occur with respect to the trust (e.g., a trust beneficiary dies within nine months of the transferor's death which causes the trust to terminate and distribute all of its assets to a person who is not a skip person). If the testamentary automatic GST allocation rules are applicable, then the allocation of GST tax exemption will occur on the due

---

cation of GST tax exemption with respect to property included in the decedent's gross estate is effective as of the decedent's date of death. The executor may allocate the decedent's GST tax exemption by use of a formula. A timely allocation of GST tax exemption by an executor with respect to a lifetime transfer of property that is not included in the transferor's gross estate is made on IRS Form 709. Treas. Reg. §26.2632-1(d)(1).

[47] *See,* Diana S. C. Zeydel, "Handling Affirmative and Deemed Allocations of GST Tax Exemption," 34 *Estate Planning* 12 (February 2007). The article discusses the rules on affirmative timely and late allocations of GST tax exemption, the rule permitting retroactive allocation of GST tax exemption in the case of an unnatural order of deaths, and the rules governing automatic allocation of GST tax exemption in the event the transferor has unused GST tax exemption after the due date of the transferor's federal estate tax return. The article also contains numerous sample GST tax exemption notice and allocation forms, and a sample form to terminate a previously filed election out statement.

date of the filing of the deceased transferor's federal estate tax return, whether or not the return is actually filed. Once GST tax exemption has been allocated under the testamentary automatic GST allocation rules, the allocation is irrevocable and cannot be changed by the deceased transferor's executor.

> **Caution:** The election out of the inter-vivos automatic GST exemption allocation rules (*see*, section 5.29(b)(1), above) is not effective to prevent an automatic allocation of GST tax exemption upon the transferor's death. Treas. Reg. §26.2632-1(b)(2)(ii) states that any election out of inter-vivos automatic GST exemption allocation rules has no effect on the application of the testamentary automatic GST exemption allocation rules applicable at the transferor's death under IRC section 2632(e). Thus, to prevent the testamentary automatic allocation of GST tax exemption to a trust that the transferor elected to not have the inter-vivos automatic GST exemption allocation rules apply to (the "inter-vivos GST opt out trust"), the transferor's executor will need to make an affirmative allocation of GST tax exemption on the transferor's federal estate tax return (IRS Form 706) to other transfers (other to the "inter-vivos GST opt out trust").

§5.31 CERTAIN GST TAX EXEMPTION ALLOCATIONS ARE VOID

Except as provided in Treas. Reg. §26.2642-3 (relating to charitable lead annuity trusts), an allocation of GST tax exemption to a trust is void to the extent the amount allocated exceeds the amount necessary to obtain an inclusion ratio of zero. Allocation of GST tax exemption is also void if the allocation is made to a trust that has no GST potential with respect to the transferor at the time of the allocation, provided, however, a trust is deemed to have GST potential even if the possibility of a GST is so remote as to be negligible. Treas. Reg. §26.2632-1(b)(4)(i).

> **Example:** If GST tax exemption is allocated to a trust in which the transferor's child has an inter-vivos general power of appointment, the allocation is void. Thus, the regulations protect the transferor and the executor from unnecessary waste of the GST tax exemption.

§5.32 U.S. GIFT AND GST TAX RETURN (IRS FORM 709)

In 2004, the IRS revised IRS Form 709 (United States Gift [and Generation-Skipping Transfer] Tax Return) because of the revisions in the GST tax rules promulgated by the 2001 Tax Act, and in particular, the GST automatic allocation rules (discussed in section 5.29, above).[48]

• Transfers to a trust that is a both a non-skip person and is not a "GST Trust" (as defined in IRC section 2632(c)(3)(B)) are reported on Part 1 of **Schedule A**, and a *"Notice of Allocation of GST Tax Exemption to Trust"*[49] must be attached to the 709.

• Direct skips (including transfers to a trust that is a skip person) are reported on Part 2 of **Schedule A**. (Direct skips are gifts that are subject to both gift tax and GST tax. *See*, section 5.7, above.) Allocation of GST tax exemption for direct skips reported on Part 2 of **Schedule A** are made on line 4 of Part 2 of **Schedule C**.

• A new Part 3 ("Indirect Skips") has been added to **Schedule A** of Form 709, which is to be used to report gifts to trusts that are currently subject to only the gift tax, but may later be subject to the GST tax, i.e., a GST Trust (as defined in IRC section 2632(c)(3)(B)). Only those gifts defined as Indirect Skips in IRC section 2632(c)(3)(A) (or those gifts that the donor wants to be treated as Indirect Skips) are to be listed in Part 3 of **Schedule A**. Additionally, if a donor wants to treat gifts to a non-GST Trust as Indirect Skips to a GST Trust (defined in section 5.29(b), above) and ***elect into*** the GST automatic allocation rules of IRC section 2632(c), the donor must check Column C and attach a *"GST Trust Election Statement"*[50] to the Form 709.

• A new line 5 has been added to Part 2 of **Schedule C** of Form 709 for use in reporting the allocation of GST tax exemption to "Indirect Skip" transfers reported on Part 3 of **Schedule A**.

• Column C in Part 2 of **Schedule A** of Form 709 is now used to ***elect out*** of the GST automatic allocation rules of IRC sections 2632(b) con-

---

[48] *See,* David Pratt, "The Anatomy of the New Federal Gift Tax Return, Including a Review of the Gift Tax Statute of Limitations and Gift Splitting Provisions," 31 *ACTEC Journal* 102 (Fall 2005).

[49] *See*, Sample form of *"Notice of Allocation of GST Tax Exemption to Trust"* in Appendix 4.

[50] See, Sample form of *"GST Trust Election Statement"* in Appendix 4.

cerning direct skips, and a "*Direct Skip GST Allocation Election Out Statement*"[51] must be attached to the Form 709. *See,* section 5.29, above.

• Column C in Part 3 of **Schedule A** of Form 709 is now used to ***elect out*** of the GST automatic allocation rules of IRC sections 2632(c) concerning Indirect Skips to a GST Trust, and an *"Election Out of Indirect Skip GST Allocation Statement"*[52] must be attached to the Form 709. *See,* section 5.29(g), above.

• As previously stated, if a donor does not want the inter-vivos GST automatic allocation rules to apply to a current transfer and/or to one or more future transfers, the donor must attach an *"Election Out of Indirect Skip GST Allocation Statement"* to a timely filed Form 709, whether or not a Form 709 otherwise would be required to be filed for that year by the donor. Treas. Reg. §26.2632-1(b)(2)(iii).[53] If, however, the donor wants to treat a non-GST Trust as a GST Trust (defined in section 5.29(b), above) and have current transfers and/or some or all future transfers be subject to the inter-vivos GST automatic allocations rules, the donor must attach a *"GST Trust Election Statement"* to a timely filed Form 709, whether or not a Form 709 otherwise would be required to be filed for that year by the donor. Treas. Reg. §26.2632-1(b)(3).

• Split gifts are now reported on Parts 1, 2, and 3 on page 2 of Form 709, rather than being split out in the Taxable Gift Reconciliation section.[54]

---

[51] *See,* Sample form of "*Direct Skip GST Allocation Election Out Statement*" in Appendix 4.

[52] *See,* Sample form of *"Election Out of Indirect Skip GST Allocation Statement"* in Appendix 4.

[53] On June 29, 2005, the IRS issued final regulations concerning how to elect in and out of the inter-vivos GST automatic allocations rules, and how to terminate those elections. Treas. Reg. §§26.2632-1(b)(2),(3),(4) and 26.2632-1(e). *See,* Treasury Decision 9208 (6/29/2005). The final regulations specifically confirm that an election out of the inter-vivos GST automatic allocation rules for future years is not an election out of the testamentary automatic GST exemption allocation rules under IRC section 2632(e), which are discussed in section 5.30, above. Treas. Reg. §26.2632-1(b)(2)(ii).

[54] A separate Form 709 and a separate *"Election Out of Indirect Skip GST Allocation Statement"* must be filed by each spouse if the gift has been split pursuant to IRC section 2513. Treas. Reg. §26.2632-1(b)(2)(iii). Although not required by the final regulations, a separate Form 709 and a separate *"GST Trust Election Statement"* should be filed by each spouse if the gift has been split pursuant to IRC section 2513. *C.f.,* Treas. Reg. §26.2632-1(b)(2)(iii).

• The instructions for IRS Form 709 also state that IRS Form 709-A, U.S. Short Form Gift Tax Return, is obsolete. All gift tax returns must now be filed on IRS Form 709.

The IRS has issued Form 8892, "Payment of Gift/GST Tax and/or Application for Extension of Time to File Form 709" for a taxpayer to request an extension of time to file IRS Form 709 (and paying any applicable gift or GST taxes). Form 8892 should be used when (i) the taxpayer owes gift or GST tax and has requested an initial extension to file his or her individual income tax return pursuant to IRS Form 4868, (ii) the taxpayer has already obtained an initial four month extension to file Form 709 pursuant to IRS Form 4868 and the taxpayer needs an additional extension of time only for his or her Form 709 (and not for his or her individual income tax return), or (iii) the taxpayer needs an initial extension of time only for his or her Form 709 (and not for his or her individual income tax return).

> **Practice Point:** Consider filing a U.S. Gift Tax Return for the year that the ILIT is created (even if all of the gifts to the ILIT qualify for the gift tax annual exclusion) and make an election to either: (i) treat the ILIT as a GST Trust and have GST tax exemption be automatically allocated to the ILIT, or (ii) elect out of GST Trust status (even if the trust meets one of the exceptions described in IRC section 2632(c)(3)(B)(i)-(vi) (*see,* section 5.29(c), above). This way the grantor (and the practitioner) will be assured of the obtaining the desired GST tax exemption allocation result with regard to the grantor's transfers to the ILIT.

§5.33 CHECKLIST OF 25 RULES FOR GST TAX PLANNING WITH ILITS

The following rules are helpful reminders for dealing with the GST tax and ILITs.

> *Rule 1:* If the ILIT is included in the grantor's gross estate for federal estate tax purposes, be aware of the requirements of the GST tax separate share rule contained in Treas. Reg. §26.2654-1(a)(1)(ii) concerning the payment of a pecuniary bequest from a trust included in the transferor's gross estate. The separate share rule is important if the grantor's executor wants to allocate GST tax exemption to the pecuniary bequest (e.g., a reverse QTIP trust estab-

lished under a pecuniary marital deduction funding formula) or to the residue of the grantor's estate (e.g., the credit shelter trust), rather than to the entire trust (e.g., the decedent's revocable [now irrevocable] living trust). *See,* footnote accompanying section 5.15, above.

Rule 2: If the ILIT is included in the grantor's gross estate for federal estate tax purposes, be aware of the requirements of the GST tax separate trust rule contained in Treas. Reg. §26.2654-1(b)(1) concerning the division of a trust (whether by a formula clause, or otherwise) that is included in the transferor's gross estate, and the requirements of the GST tax qualified severance rule under IRC section 2642(a)(3). The separate trust rule pertains to making a mandatory or discretionary severance of a single trust[55] included in the transferor's gross estate into multiple separate trusts for the purpose of allocating the transferor's GST tax exemption to any of the separate trusts (rather than to the whole [undivided] single trust, which could result in an overutilization and waste of the transferor's GST tax exemption). (Note however, that the GST tax qualified severance rule is meant to replace and supersede the separate trust rule. Preamble to Prop. Treas. Reg. §26.2642-6.) *See also,* footnote accompanying section 5.15, above.

Rule 3: If the ILIT is included in the grantor's gross estate for federal estate tax purposes, be aware of the requirements of the GST tax valuation rules contained in IRC section 2642(b)(2)(A) and Treas. Reg. §26.2642-2(b)(2) and (3). These rules apply to transfers made from a trust included in the transferor's gross estate (and from a transferor's probate estate). If ILIT assets are included in the transferor's gross estate, the goal of the transferor is to have his or her GST tax exemption allocated to those assets based on their federal estate tax value, rather than their value at a later date (such as their date of distribution

---

[55] This rule is limited to trusts or arrangements treated as trusts. Except as otherwise provided in Treas. Reg. §26.2652-1(b) (especially Example 3), the rule is not applicable to probate estates. IRC section 2652(b)(1).

value). If the GST tax valuation rules measure the assets' value other than at their estate tax value, then it may require more GST tax exemption to be allocated, particularly if the assets have appreciated in value during the administration of the transferor's estate. If there is not enough GST tax exemption available to exempt the assets, the trust may not have a zero inclusion ratio. *See,* footnote accompanying section 5.15, above.

Rule 4: If ILIT property that qualifies for the marital deduction (other than an ILIT containing a second to die policy on the life of the grantor and the grantor's spouse) is included in a married grantor's gross estate for federal estate tax purposes, consider using a QTIP marital deduction trust to maintain maximum flexibility for GST tax planning purposes. This will allow for a reverse QTIP election. *See,* sections 5.27 and 5.28, above, and section 11.3, below.

Rule 5: If ILIT property that qualifies for the marital deduction (other than an ILIT containing a second to die policy on the life of the grantor and the grantor's spouse) is included in a married grantor's gross estate for federal estate tax purposes, a reverse QTIP election should not be made to the entire QTIP marital deduction trust if the election and subsequent allocation of GST tax exemption would result in an inclusion ratio greater than zero. Instead, before making the reverse QTIP election and allocation of the grantor's GST tax exemption, the QTIP marital deduction trust should be severed into two trusts, and the governing instrument should provide for the creation of a reverse QTIP trust equal to the amount of the grantor's unused GST tax exemption and a non-GST-tax-exempt QTIP trust to which no GST tax exemption will be allocated. *See,* section 5.28(C), above. *See,* Paragraph 5.1(A)(8) of Sample ILIT.

Rule 6: If ILIT property that qualifies for the marital deduction (other than an ILIT containing a second to die policy on the life of the grantor and the grantor's spouse) is included in a married grantor's gross estate for federal estate tax purposes, and the grantor has not previously allocated GST tax exemption to the ILIT, allocation of GST tax exemption to a reverse QTIP trust may not be the most efficient use of the grantor's GST tax exemption vis-à-vis other GST events because of the QTIP trust's all income to spouse requirement. Therefore, in determining the amount of the grantor's GST tax exemption available for allocation to the reverse QTIP trust by the executor of the grantor's estate, the following allocations should be reviewed: (1) GST tax allocations made on lifetime transfers; (2) automatic GST tax allocations made on lifetime transfers; (3) late GST tax allocations to be made by the grantor's executor concerning lifetime transfers made by the grantor; (4) any GST tax allocations that the executor of the grantor's estate will make concerning direct skips occurring at the grantor's death, transfers in trust to skip persons, or other potential GST transfers, such as taxable distributions or taxable terminations that may occur in the future. After reviewing these allocations, it may be determined that a reverse QTIP election is not desirable. *See,* section 5.3(A), above.

Rule 7: If ILIT property that qualifies for the marital deduction (other than an ILIT containing a second to die policy on the life of the grantor and the grantor's spouse) is included in a married grantor's gross estate for federal estate tax purposes, and the grantor has not previously allocated GST tax exemption to the ILIT, do not make a reverse QTIP election if the unused amount of the deceased transferor's GST tax exemption can instead be allocated to direct skips occurring at the grantor's death and transfers in trust for skip persons that will result in taxable distributions or taxable terminations.

Because the QTIP trust property will be included in the gross estate of the surviving spouse when he or she dies (IRC section 2044), the surviving spouse will become the transferor of the QTIP trust property. Treas. Reg. §26.2652-1(a)(2). Consequently the executor of the surviving spouse's estate can allocate the surviving spouse's GST tax exemption to the QTIP trust property, if necessary.

Rule 8: If ILIT property that qualifies for the marital deduction (other than an ILIT containing a second to die policy on the life of the grantor and the grantor's spouse) is included in a married grantor's gross estate for federal estate tax purposes, consider giving the surviving spouse a testamentary limited power of appointment over the QTIP trust. The class of appointees can be limited to the grantor's descendants. This will permit the surviving spouse to maximize the utility of the reverse QTIP trust election and the predeceased parent rule, because of unforeseen or changed circumstances occurring after the grantor's death. For example, the surviving spouse could appoint the reverse QTIP trust property to a trust for the grantor's grandchildren and more remote descendants who are skip persons, and the surviving spouse could appoint the non-GST-tax-exempt marital trust property to the grantor's children and grandchildren who are non-skip persons (because of the predeceased parent rule). *See,* section 11.8, below. *See,* Paragraph 5.1(A)(3)(a) of Sample ILIT.

Rule 9: If ILIT property that qualifies for the marital deduction (other than an ILIT containing a second to die policy on the life of the grantor and the grantor's spouse) is included in a married grantor's gross estate for federal estate tax purposes, upon the death of the surviving spouse consider having the non-GST-tax-exempt QTIP marital deduction trust property be divided into separate shares for the ultimate benefit of children and for the issue of a deceased child.

This common form of disposition will preserve the predeceased parent rule as to any children who die after the grantor but before the surviving spouse, because the surviving spouse is treated as the transferor of the non-GST-tax-exempt QTIP trust (and any children who die before the surviving spouse's death come under the predeceased parent rule). *See,* section 5.9, above.

Rule 10: If ILIT property that qualifies for the marital deduction ILIT (other than an ILIT containing a second to die policy on the life of the grantor and the grantor's spouse) is included in a married grantor's gross estate for federal estate tax purposes, whenever you are going to allocate GST tax exemption to a pecuniary bequest or to a residual transfer or residual trust that follows a pecuniary bequest (e.g., a pecuniary marital deduction funding formula bequest, a reverse pecuniary funding formula bequest, or a specific bequest of a dollar amount to a devisee), make sure either that the pecuniary bequest is funded within 15 months, or that the pecuniary bequest receives "appropriate interest" under the GST tax valuation rules of IRC section 2642(b)(2)(A) and Treas. Reg. §26.2642-2(b)(2) and (3).[56] Also, if non-cash property (e.g., stock and bonds) is use to satisfy the pecuniary bequest, make sure that the non-cash assets are distributed using either their date of distribution value or in a manner that is fairly representative of the assets' net appreciation and depreciation, as is required under the GST tax valuation rules. A requirement in the governing instrument to pay interest or allocate income to all bequests (including pecuniary bequests from trusts) is recommended to protect the trust in case the funding is not completed within 15 months. *See,* footnote accompanying section 5.15, above. *See,* Paragraph 7.1(B)(3)(a) of Sample ILIT.

Rule 11: If ILIT property that qualifies for the marital deduction (other than an ILIT containing a second to die

---

[56] "Appropriate interest" means interest payable from the transferor's date of death or from the date specified under applicable state law requiring payment of interest on the pecuniary bequest at a rate: (i) at least equal to the statutory rate of interest under state law, or if there is none, 80% of IRC section 7520 interest at the transferor's date of death, *and* (ii) not more than the greater of the statutory rate under state law, or if there is none, 120% of IRC section 7520 interest at the transferor's date of death. Treas. Reg. §26.2642-2(b)(4). If the governing instrument fails to provide for "appropriate interest," it will nevertheless be deemed to do so if: (i) the entire pecuniary bequest is satisfied (or property is irrevocably set aside to satisfy the pecuniary bequest) in full within fifteen (15) months of the transferor's death (as a precaution practitioners should attempt to satisfy all pecuniary bequests within 15 months of the transferor's death); *or* (ii) the governing instrument or applicable local law requires the transferor's fiduciary to allocate to the pecuniary bequest a pro-rata share of the income earned by the estate or trust between the transferor's date of death and the date of payment of the pecuniary bequest. Treas. Reg. §26.2642-2(b)(3)(ii).

policy on the life of the grantor and the grantor's spouse) is included in a married grantor's gross estate for federal estate tax purposes, and the remainder beneficiaries of both the husband's estate plan and the wife's estate plan are the same, make sure both spouses' wills waive the right to reimbursement under IRC section 2207A so as to relieve the reverse QTIP trust from having to reimburse the surviving spouse's estate for the federal estate taxes attributable to that trust, thereby preserving 100% of the GST-tax-exempt property.

However, in a second-marriage situation or when there are different remainder beneficiaries, who should be responsible for the death taxes attributable to the reverse QTIP trust? *See,* sections 4.17 and 5.28, above.

Rule 12: Enable the trustee to distribute the GST tax exempt trust property to skip persons, and the non-GST tax exempt trust property to non-skip persons.

A non-GST tax exempt trust's direct payment of medical expenses and tuition expenses of a skip person does not constitute a GST event. IRC sections 2503(e) and 2611(b)(1). Distributions to skip persons from a trust with a zero inclusion ratio do not generate any GST tax. IRC sections 2602 and 2641; Treas. Reg. §25.2503-6. Similarly, distributions to non-skip persons from a trust with an inclusion ratio greater than zero do not generate any GST tax. *See,* section 5.2, above. *See,* Paragraph 7.1(B)(7) of Sample ILIT.

Rule 13: When creating a GST-tax-exempt ILIT, be careful that the beneficiaries do not possess powers (either as a beneficiary or as a trustee) that constitute general powers of appointment under IRC section 2041. Otherwise, the GST tax-exempt property will be included in the beneficiary's gross estate under IRC section 2041, and that beneficiary will become the "new" transferor for GST tax purposes, thus wasting the grantor's allocation of GST tax exemption. *See,* section 5.10, above. *See also,* Chapter 8 below, and section 1.7, above.

Rule 14: In an ILIT that does not hold a second to die policy on the life of the grantor and the grantor's spouse, consider giving the surviving spouse and children broad testamentary limited powers of appointment over their respective trust shares. These powers can be exercised to reduce or avoid the GST tax. Because the GST tax is scheduled to be repealed in 2010 (for a one-year period), any way to postpone a GST event until then should be considered. *See,* section 11.8, below. *See,* Paragraphs 5.1(A)(3)(a), 5.4(C) (alternate 2) and 5.5(C) of Sample ILIT.

Rule 15: Consider having the GST-tax-exempt ILIT be a discretionary common (pot) trust for the grantor's descendants that runs for the longest period permitted under the rule against perpetuities (if that is consistent with the grantor's desires).

The GST-tax-exempt trust could be established in a jurisdiction that has curtailed or abolished the rule against perpetuities,[57] such as (i) South Dakota (which does not impose a state income tax on trusts, permits trust protectors, domestic asset protection trusts, and is not a creditor-friendly trust jurisdiction); (ii) Delaware—except for real estate (does not impose a state income tax on non-residents, and permits trust protectors and domestic asset protection trusts); (iii) Alaska (which limits powers of appointment to 1,000 years, does not impose a state income tax on trusts, and permits trust protectors and domestic asset protection trusts); (iv) New Hampshire (which imposes a special "income" tax on residents with regard to dividends and interest, and permits trust protectors); (v) Idaho (which imposes a state income tax on all trusts, and permits trust protectors); (vi) Missouri (which imposes a state income

[57] Even though the trust is not subject to the rule against perpetuities, be aware that the exercise of a non-general power of appointment by a trust beneficiary can cause an otherwise GST tax exempt trust to lose its GST-tax-exempt status. The "Delaware Tax Trap" provisions of IRC sections 2041(a)(3) and 2514(d) can cause the exercise of a non-general power of appointment to be subject to estate or gift tax, and thus change the identity of the transferor (or cause a grandfathered GST trust to lose its grandfathered status). Treas. Reg. §§26.2601-1(b)(1)(v)(A) and (B). Because of the Delaware Tax Trap, the default for the non-exercise of a non-general power of appointment should be a continuation of the trust. The continuation of the trust does not constitute an "extension" of the trust's term with regard to the Delaware Tax Trap.

tax on all trusts, and permits domestic asset protection trusts); (vii) Wisconsin (which imposes a state income tax on residents only); and (viii) New Jersey (which imposes a state income tax on all trusts).[58]

Even if the grantor is not a resident of a state that has abolished the rule against perpetuities, the grantor can choose the governing law of that state, provided there is a sufficient connection between the GST-tax-exempt trust and that state, such as having a co-trustee who is a resident of that state. **Caveat**—Professor Ira Mark Bloom of Albany Law School argues that the states, in a blind race to facilitate the exploitation of the GST tax exemption by perpetual dynasty trusts, have overlooked important non-tax societal reasons for the rule against perpetuities, which serves to limit "dead hand control." He asserts that, over time, the administration of such trusts is likely to become unwieldy and very costly, noting that the average grantor will have more than 100 descendants in 150 years, 2,500 beneficiaries in 250 years, and 45,000 beneficiaries in 350 years. *See,* Paragraph 5.3 of Sample Second to Die ILIT contained in Appendix 2.

Even if the trust runs for the longest period permitted under the rule against perpetuities, the grantor can further prolong the insulation of the trust assets from transfer tax by directing or permitting younger generations to share to some degree in the final distribution, rather than following a pure "per stirpes" distribution regime, which inevitably will put the assets in the hands of the oldest descendants, who are closest to the imposition of the estate tax. There-

---

[58] *See,* Daniel G. Worthington, "Perpetual Trust States—The Latest Rankings," 146 *Trust & Estates* 59 (January 2007). Mr. Worthington's top four jurisdictions for establishing a perpetual GST dynasty trust are, South Dakota (first place), Delaware (second place), Alaska and New Hampshire (both tied for third place. Mr. Worthington, does however, express concern that the IRS may not respect Alaska's 1000 year period of vesting for GST tax purposes (in contrast to jurisdictions that have completely repealed the rule against perpetuities and have not just extended the time for vesting). *Id.* at 59 and 61. *See also,* Daniel G. Worthington, "The Problems and Promise Of Perpetual Trust Laws," 143 *Trust & Estates* 15 (December 2004); and Richard W. Nenno, "Choosing and Rechoosing the Jurisdiction for a Trust," 40 *Heckerling Institute on Estate Planning,* Chapter 4 (Matthew Bender/Lexis-Nexis, Newark, NJ, 2006).

fore, consider giving the Independent Trustee (i.e., a trustee who is not related or subordinate [within the meaning of IRC section 672(c) to the grantor or the ILIT beneficiaries and also meets the requirements of IRC section 674(c)] the ability to appoint the trust assets to any of the transferor's then living descendants upon the termination of the trust's term. This will permit trust assets to be distributed to beneficiaries in younger generations. Appointing trust property to younger beneficiaries will permit the trust property to escape estate taxation for another generation, and possibly insulate the trust assets from estate taxes for up to 200 years. Casting the Independent Trustee's power as a limited power of appointment will protect the trustee from a potential abuse of discretion claim.

Rule 16: Minimize distributions to grandchildren from a non-GST-tax-exempt ILIT by having the grantor's children make gifts to the grandchildren from trust distributions. This will avoid a taxable distribution to the grandchildren. If the grantor's intent is to benefit his or her grandchildren, a distribution from a non-GST tax exempt trust can be made to a child followed by a gift from the child to the grandchild. The gift avoids the GST tax, and permits the child to use his or her gift tax annual exclusion amount. Even if the gift is larger than the annual gift tax exclusion amount, the gift tax paid by the child is less costly than a taxable distribution, since the gift tax is calculated on a tax exclusive basis, whereas a taxable distribution is calculated on tax inclusive basis. *See,* section 5.5, above. In this regard make sure the trustee's authority for making discretionary distributions includes "distributions for the purpose of assisting a beneficiary in making gifts to reduce the trust's and my family's overall potential transfer tax liability." *See,* Paragraph 7.11 of Sample ILIT (which will have to be modified to accomplish this purpose).

Rule 17*:* When adding to, combining or merging trusts (which is likely to happen when the surviving spouse's credit shelter trust is merged into the first spouse's credit shelter trust), preserve each trust's GST inclusion ratio. Therefore, do not add or combine trust property that has an inclusion ratio of greater than zero with trust property that has an inclusion ratio of zero. A trust's inclusion ratio will change if there is a consolidation or merger of separate trusts with different inclusion ratios. Treas. Reg. §26.2642-4(a)(2). *See,* section 5.12(B), above. *See,* Paragraphs 7.1(A)(7) and 7.1(B)(5) of Sample ILIT.

Rule 18: Before merging or combining GST-tax-exempt trusts (for example combining the grantor's credit shelter trust and the ILIT), consider the perpetuities period that applies to each trust.

The rule against perpetuities for a credit shelter trust generally starts at the grantor's date of death, whereas the rule against perpetuities for an ILIT generally starts at the inception of the trust. If one grantor survives the creation of the ILIT by 10 to 20 years, an extra generation of descendants may exist, which will extend the perpetuities period of the grantor's credit shelter trust estate for an extra generation. *See,* Paragraphs 7.1(A)(7) and 7.1(B)(5) of Sample ILIT.

Rule 19: When creating a GST tax exempt ILIT for the benefit of skip persons, and the grantor does not want to allocate his or her GST tax exemption to the ILIT (or has exhausted his or her GST tax exemption), make sure that each skip-person-beneficiary's interest in the ILIT is a separate trust share that complies with the requirements of IRC section 2642(c)(2). *See,* section 5.7(C), above.

Rule 20: Do not have a beneficiary waive his or her *Crummey* withdrawal right. A waiver (rather than a lapse) may constitute a taxable release under IRC section 2514(b) and change the identity of the transferor (from the grantor to the beneficiary). Any previously allocated GST exemption by the grantor will be lost and ineffective. *See.* sections 5.10 and 5.21, above.

Rule 21: When establishing an ILIT that is to be GST tax exempt, make sure the grantor's spouse's withdrawal rights are limited to five by five, are non-cumulative (i.e., no hanging *Crummey* withdrawal right for the spouse), and lapse within 60 days of the grantor's contribution to the ILIT (and not 60 days after the notice of the grantor's contribution). Otherwise, there will be an estate tax inclusion period ("ETIP") under IRC section 2642(f), which will prevent the grantor from allocating his or her GST tax exemption until the close of the ETIP. *See,* section 5.17, above.

Rule 22: If possible, do not gift split (IRC section 2513) the transfer of an existing life insurance policy to a GST tax exempt ILIT. If the grantor dies within 3 years of the policy's transfer to the ILIT, the insurance proceeds will be included in the grantor's gross estate under IRC section 2035 and the gift splitting-consenting spouse's previously allocated GST tax exemption will be wasted and ineffective. *See,* section 5.22, above.

Rule 23: If possible, avoid late allocations of GST tax exemption to an ILIT. If the grantor dies before the actual filing date[59] of the late allocation, the GST tax exemption will have to be allocated to the full value of the life insurance proceeds. Treas. Reg. §26.2642-2(a)(2). *See,* section 5.23, above.

Rule 24: Do not rely on the GST tax exemption automatic allocation rules (IRC section 2632(c)) for indirect skips to GST Trusts. Many ILITs that were initially designed to not be GST Trusts (including those where the surviving spouse has a life estate if he or she survives the insured spouse) may, as a result of the GST automatic allocation rules for inter-vivos trusts, be classified as GST Trusts (and have GST tax exemption be automatically allocated to transfers made to such trusts). Consequently, taxpayers should consider making a one time election to permanently opt in or opt out of GST Trust status and the GST automatic allocation rules. IRC section 2632(c)(5). *See,* section 5.29(b)(1), above.

Caution: The filing of an election to opt out of GST Trust status and the GST automatic allocation rules concerning indirect skips to GST Trusts is not effective to prevent an automatic allocation of GST tax exemption to the opted

---

[59] The actual filing date is the date the Form 709 is postmarked to the Internal Revenue Service Center. Treas. Reg. §26.2632-1(b)(4)(ii)(A).

out trust upon the transferor's death. *See*, section 5.30, above.

Rule 25: Annual exclusion gifts to an ILIT are not automatically GST tax exempt, and GST tax exemption may need to be allocated by filing a U.S. Gift Tax Return. Treas. Reg. §26.2642-1(c)(3). *See,* sections 5.18 and 5.32, above.

§5.34 SAMPLE TRUSTEE POWERS FOR GST TAX ISSUES

A sample comprehensive trustee power clause concerning GST tax issues is contained in Paragraph 7.1(B) of Sample ILIT.

As this book was being printed, the IRS issued final GST tax qualified severance regulations (Treasury Decision 9348, issued August 1, 2007) and proposed amendments to Treas. Reg. §§26.2654-1 and 26.2642-6 (Reg. 128843-05, issued August 1, 2007). Practitioners are urged to study the new final regulations and the proposed amendments.

6

2001 Tax Act And Liberalized GST Rules

CHAPTER OVERVIEW

The 2001 Tax Act brought about the one year "repeal" of the federal estate and GST tax in 2010. The 2001 Tax Act also brought about many changes to the GST tax rules. Most of these new rules are designed to avoid the "gotchas" or inflexibility that was the hallmark of the GST rules. Regrettably many, if not most, of these new GST tax rules are automatically repealed when the 2001 Tax Act sunsets on December 31, 2010. Some of these new rules are "taxpayer friendly," although others are less friendly. Nevertheless, the GST tax is a complicated and often overlooked area when drafting and administering ILITs. Of particular importance to the practitioner is the liberalization of the IRS's prior "deadlines" for making GST tax decisions. Many of the 2001 Tax Act provisions concerning the GST tax are remedial, and should be helpful to most practitioners and advisors.

§6.1 INCREASE IN GST-TAX-EXEMPTION AMOUNT AND LOWERING OF GST TAX RATE

Under the 2001 Tax Act, beginning in 2004, the GST tax exemption amount is equal to the estate tax applicable exclusion amount under IRC section 2010(c) for the year in which the generation-skipping transfer is made, and in 2010, the GST tax will be repealed in its entirety (and there will be no GST tax exemption amount). IRC section 2664. In 2011, the GST tax exemption will revert back to the amount it would have been before the 2001 Tax Act. Thus, the GST tax exemption and GST Tax Rate will be as follows:

Year	GST-Tax-Exemption Amounts	GST Tax Rate
2004	$1.5 million (no inflation adjustment)	48%
2005	$1.5 million (no inflation adjustment)	47%
2006	$2 million (no inflation adjustment)	46%
2007	$2 million (no inflation adjustment)	45%
2008	$2 million (no inflation adjustment)	45%
2009	$3.5 million (no inflation adjustment)	45%
2010	Repealed	0%
2011	$1.1 million (plus post-2002 inflation adjustments)	55%

§6.1(a) Distributions And Gifts In 2009 And 2010

In 2009, clients may want to consider making inter-vivos gifts into GST trusts that are not direct skip trusts, paying gift tax, and using their remaining GST tax exemption (because the exemption will disappear in 2010 and will reappear at only $1.1 million, plus post-2002 inflation adjustments, in 2011). An alternative, if direct skips can be made, would be to make direct skips in 2010 when there is no GST tax and the gift tax rate is only 35%. Also, in 2010 when there is no GST, non-GST-tax-exempt trusts should make distributions to skip persons. Consider including a trust protector or special powerholder in the trust instrument who is authorized to appoint the trust property to the grantor's descendants, especially during the no-GST-tax window period of 2010. *See*, Paragraph 8.2(C) of Sample ILIT. Because there will be no GST tax exemption available in 2010 (and thus no ability to create a GST-tax- exempt trust by allocating a person's GST tax exemption), if other irrevocable trusts are established in 2010, it is uncertain if they will be grandfathered from the GST tax when the pre-2001 Tax Act law returns in 2011.[1] If these

---

[1] A testamentary trust (whether established under a will or under a decedent's previously revocable living trust) established by a person who dies in 2010 when there is no federal estate tax or GST tax should be able (theoretically) to make subsequent distributions to skip persons that are not subject to GST tax, since there will be no transferor under section 2652(a)(1) with respect to the testamentary trust. An inter-vivos trust established in 2010 when the GST tax will not be in effect, however, will probably see its subsequent distributions to skip persons be subjected to GST tax, since

trusts are not grandfathered from the GST tax, they will have an inclusion ratio of one.

Also, in 2010 when there is no GST, non-GST-tax-exempt trusts should make distributions to skip persons. Consideration should also be given to including a trust protector or special powerholder in the trust instrument who is authorized to appoint the trust property outright to the grantor's descendants, especially during the no GST-tax-window period of 2010. *See*, Paragraph 8.2(C) of Sample ILIT.

§6.2 RETROACTIVE ALLOCATION OF GST TAX-EXEMPTION FOR NON-SKIP BENEFICIARY'S UNNATURAL ORDER OF DEATH WHILE TRANSFEROR IS ALIVE

The 2001 Tax Act allows a transferor to make a retroactive allocation of the transferor's GST tax exemption to lifetime transfers to an inter-vivos trust if a nonskip beneficiary of the trust dies after December 31, 2000, but before the transferor.[2] IRC section 2632(d). The retroactive allocation does not protect against an unnatural order of death that occurs ***after*** the transferor's death. Nor does the retroactive allocation apply to grantor retained annuity trusts ("GRATs"), qualified personal residence trusts ("QPRTs"), or any inter-vivos trust that is subject to an Estate Tax Inclusion Period ("ETIP") under IRC section 2642(f). The ETIP rules preclude the effective the allocation of the transferor's GST tax exemption during the term of the trust while the trust is subject to possible inclusion in the gross estate of the transferor or transferor's spouse. Any allocation of the GST tax exemption during the ETIP period will not take effect until the expiration of the ETIP and would be applied at the trust's then-fair market value.

---

there will be a transferor when the trust is established, due to the gift tax being in effect in 2010. Query: How does a transferor allocate the GST tax exemption to such a trust? Through a prospective protective election? Will the late allocation rules apply? Will the automatic allocation rules apply? These questions remain unanswered at the moment.

[2] *See*, Diana S. C. Zeydel, "Handling Affirmative and Deemed Allocations of GST Tax Exemption," 34 *Estate Planning* 12 (February 2007). The article discusses the rules on affirmative timely and late allocations of GST tax exemption, the rule permitting retroactive allocation of GST tax exemption in the case of an unnatural order of deaths, and the rules governing automatic allocation of GST tax exemption in the event the transferor has unused GST tax exemption after the due date of the transferor's federal estate tax return. The article also contains numerous sample GST tax exemption notice and allocation forms, and a sample form to terminate a previously filed election out statement.

This retroactive allocation is available only if the predeceasing beneficiary was both a nonskip person and a lineal descendant of the transferor's grandparent or a grandparent of the transferor's spouse, assigned to a generation younger than the generation of the then-living transferor. The value of the property on the date that the property was transferred to the trust is used to determine the applicable fraction and inclusion ratio for the retroactive GST-tax-exemption allocation on a chronological basis (i.e., to earlier transfers first). For example, if a transferor made a transfer of $50,000 to an ILIT in 2002, a transfer of $75,000 to the same ILIT in 2003, and a transfer of $100,000 to the same ILIT in 2004, and the transferor now wants to make a retroactive allocation of GST tax exemption to the ILIT, the transferor must allocate his or her GST tax exemption first to the 2002 transfer of $50,000, then to the 2003 transfer of $75,000 and finally to the 2004 transfer of $100,000, in that order. The retroactive allocation of the GST tax exemption must be made on the transferor's U.S. Gift Tax Return for the calendar year in which the nonskip person died, and the transferor must have unused GST tax exemption available immediately prior to the nonskip person's death. IRC section 2632(d).

Practice Point: If a transfer was gift split under IRC section 2513, each spouse is considered to be a transferor of one-half of the transferred property. Consequently, if a child dies after his father but before his mother, the retroactive allocation of GST tax exemption will be effective only as to his mother's one-half share of the transferred property.

Practice Point: When preparing an annual gift tax return for a client whose ILIT is not GST tax exempt, the tax advisor should inquire if a trust beneficiary has died that year and whether the beneficiary predeceased the transferor. If so, consideration should be given to making a retroactive allocation of the transferor's GST tax exemption to the ILIT. This procedure may also necessitate a qualified severance of the ILIT to separate the skip person's share of the ILIT from the non-GST tax exempt portion of the ILIT.

Caution: The new rule applies for retroactive allocations for non-skip beneficiaries dying after December 31, 2000 and is automatically repealed when the 2001 Tax Act sunsets on December 31, 2010.

§6.3 QUALIFIED TRUST SEVERANCE RULES

The 2001 Tax Act liberalizes the rules for severing a trust. IRC section 2642(a)(3). The Act permits the qualified severance of an existing single trust (inter vivos or testamentary) into multiple trusts, if (1) the severance or division is permitted by applicable local law or is authorized in the governing instrument (*See,* Paragraphs 7.1(A)(8) and 7.1(B)(1) of Sample ILIT); (2) the single trust is divided on a fractional basis (and not on a pecuniary basis)[3]; (3) the terms of the new (divided) trusts provide, in the aggregate, for the same succession of interests of beneficiaries as in the original trust[4]; and (4) if the original trust has an inclusion ratio other than one or zero, the original trust is divided into two trusts, one of which has an inclusion ratio of one and the other of which has an inclusion ratio of zero. This new type of severance is commonly known as a "down stream" severance. Generally speaking, the qualified severance rule is remedial in nature and does not provide the same flexibility as a mandatory severance (discussed in section 5.16(b), above).

The qualified severance may occur at any time. IRC section 2642(a)(3); Priv. Letter Rul. 200223016; Prop. Treas. Reg. § 26.2642-6(c). Also, each of the new (divided) trusts created may be further divided into two or more trusts. IRC section 2642(a)(3)(B)(i). Although the single original trust must be divided on a fractional basis, the new (divided) trusts can be funded on a non-pro-rata (pick and choose) fractional basis, provided the funding is based on date of distribution values and either state statute or the governing instrument permits non-pro-rata funding. Prop. Treas. Reg. §§ 26.2642-6(b)(3)

---

[3] However, any pecuniary amount ($A) can be converted into a fraction, where the numerator is $A, and the denominator is $B, which is also the value of the fund (the multiplicand) against which the fraction is to operate. Thus, (A/B) × B =A. *See, e.g.,* Prop. Treas. Reg. §§ 26.2642-6(b)(3) and 26.2642-6(e), Example 1.

[4] Under the proposed regulations, the beneficiaries of each separate trust resulting from the severance need not be identical to those of the original trust. Where the trustee has the authority to make non-pro-rata discretionary distributions to beneficiaries, the new (divided) trusts are considered to have the same succession of interests of beneficiaries if the terms of the new (divided) trusts are the same as the terms of the original trust, the severance does not shift a beneficial interest in the trust to any beneficiary in a lower generation than the person or persons who held the beneficial interest in the original trust, and the severance does not extend the time for vesting of any beneficial interest in the trust beyond the period provided for in the original trust. Prop. Treas. Reg. §26.2642-6(b)(4) (issued August 24, 2004).

and 1.1001-h(1)(ii); IRC section 2642(a)(3)(B)(ii). However, trusts divided on a pecuniary basis are not recognized as separate trusts. *Id.*

Under pre-2001 Tax Act law, a trustee could not establish inclusion ratios of zero and one by severing a trust that was subject to the GST tax after the trust had been created—the severance had to occur before the creation of the trust, i.e., an "up stream" severance. The qualified severance rule now permits a trust to be divided after its creation and after the allocation of GST tax exemption. A qualified severance also includes any other severance permitted under the Treasury Regulations. IRC section 2642(a)(3)(B)(iii).

§6.3(a) Qualified Severance And GST Grandfathered Trusts

A trust that is grandfathered from the GST tax does not lose its GST-tax-exempt status as a result of a severance, provided the severance complies with the requirements of Treas. Reg. §26.2601-1(b)(4)(i)(D)(1). Under that regulation, a modification (including a severance) of a trust grandfathered from the GST tax will not cause the trust to be subject to the GST tax provisions of Chapter 13 of the Internal Revenue Code if the severance does not (1) shift a beneficial interest in the trust to any beneficiary who occupies a lower generation than the person or persons who held the beneficial interest prior to the modification or (2) extend the time for vesting of any beneficial interest in the trust beyond the period provided for in the original trust. Under the proposed GST-tax-qualified severance regulations, the rules in Treas. Reg. §26.2601-1(b)(4) will continue to apply to severances (and other actions) with respect to trusts grandfathered from the GST tax. Prop. Treas. Reg. § 26.2642-6(d). However, the post-2000 severance of a trust created after September 25, 1985 will be governed by the qualified severance rule of IRC section 2642(a)(3) and the applicable regulations. Prop. Treas. Reg. §§ 26.2642-6(f)(2) and 26.2654-1(c).

§6.3(b) IRS Reporting Requirements For A Qualified Severance

Even if the qualified severance does not result in a taxable termination, the proposed regulations require all qualified severances to be reported to the IRS by (1) filing a Form 706-GS(T) "Generation-Skipping Transfer Tax Return for Terminations" (or such other form prescribed by the IRS) by April 15 of the year that follows the year of the qualified severance (or by the last day of any extension actually granted) and writing "Qualified Severance" in ***red*** ink at the top of the return; and (2) attaching a "Notice of Qualified Severance" to the return that contains a statement identifying the trust that is severed (the "original trust"), the name of the transferor of the original trust, the original trust's date of creation, the original trust's tax identification number, and the original trust's inclusion ratio; and a statement identifying each of the new trusts created as a result of the severance (the "resulting trusts"), the name and tax identification number of each resulting trust, the fraction of trust assets received by each resulting trust, other details explaining the basis for funding each resulting trust (a fraction of the total fair market value of the assets on the date of funding or a fraction of each asset), and the inclusion ratio of each resulting trust. Prop. Treas. Reg. §26.2642-6(c)(6). Taxpayers may rely on the proposed qualified severance regulations before the publication of the final regulations. Prop. Treas. Reg. §§26.2642-6(f)(1) and (2).

§6.3(c) Income Tax Consequences Of A Qualified Severance

A qualified severance will not constitute a taxable exchange of property under IRC section 1001 if (1) state statute or the governing instrument authorizes the qualified severance; (2) the new (divided) trusts are funded on a pro-rata fractional basis; and (3) if the new (divided) trusts are funded on a non-pro-rata fractional basis, state statute or the governing instrument authorizes the trustee to fund the new (divided) trusts on a non-pro-rata basis (using date the assets' of distribution value). Prop. Treas. Reg. §1.1001-1(h)(1). If these conditions are satisfied, the income tax basis of the severed trust assets will be the same as before the severance, and the assets' holding period will be the same. Preamble to the Proposed Regulations. Taxpayers may rely on Prop. Treas. Reg. § 1.1001-1(h)(1) for qualified severances occurring after Aug. 24, 2004 and before the publication of the final regulations. Prop. Treas. Reg. §1.1001-1(h)(2).

§6.3(d) Qualified Severance And Unnatural Order Of Death

The qualified severance rule may be used in conjunction with the unnatural order of death election under IRC section 2632(d), which is discussed in section 6.2, above. For example, an ILIT providing an income interest to the transferor's spouse with the remainder to the transferor's two children may now be divided. This, together with the unnatural order of death election, could allow the ILIT to be divided into two parts, and the transferor's GST tax exemption could be allocated to the part that the deceased child's descendants succeed to, if one of the transferor's children were to predecease the transferor.

§6.3(e) Qualified Severance After Filing Of Federal Estate Tax Return

Another aspect of the qualified severance rule is that a discretionary division may now be made after the filing of the decedent's federal estate tax return. Priv. Letter Rul. 200223016.

Practice Point: Qualified severances would appear to be useful when property with an inclusion ratio of one is to be combined with property that has a zero inclusion ratio. In such a situation, a qualified severance would allow the creation of two trusts, one with an inclusion ratio of one and another trust with an inclusion ratio of zero. A qualified severance can also be helpful at the end of an ETIP where the grantor has previously allocated GST exemption to the trust. In such an instance, the trust may have an inclusion ratio greater than zero (because of the GST tax exemption not being effective until the close of the ETIP), and a qualified severance could create a GST-tax-exempt trust and a non-GST-tax-exempt trust.

Practice Point: Trusts with inclusion ratios between zero and one[5] should be divided in a qualified severance and then GST tax exemption could be allocated—provided the severance itself does not give rise to a GST (e.g., if a severed trust contains only skip beneficiaries after the severance, a GST taxable termination may result). IRC section 2642(a)(3)(B)(ii). That way, the GST-tax-exempt portion (i.e., inclusion ratio of zero) can be distributed primarily for the benefit of skip persons (e.g., grandchildren) and the non-GST-tax-exempt portion (i.e., inclusion ratio of one) can be distributed to non-skip persons (e.g., children) or be

[5] An ILIT could have an inclusion ratio between one and zero because, for example, an insufficient amount of GST tax exemption was allocated to obtain a zero inclusion ratio, or because GST tax exemption was automatically allocated to an indirect skip occurring after December 31, 2000 and the transferor did not allocate GST tax exemption to pre 2001-transfers.

distributed for the benefit of skip persons by the trustee's direct payment of tuition and medical expenses, as is permitted under IRC sections 2503(c) and 2642(c). Otherwise, all distributions to skip persons will trigger GST tax.

Caution: The proposed regulations for a qualified severance retroactively repeal and supersede the GST tax separate trust rule contained in Treas. Reg. § 26.2654-1(b). The proposed regulations are effective for trust severances occurring after December 31, 2000. Needless to say there is much controversy over the IRS's retroactive repeal of the GST tax separate trust rule.

Caution: The qualified severance rule applies for trust severances occurring after December 31, 2000 and is automatically repealed when the 2001 Tax Act sunsets on December 31, 2010. Tax Act sections 564(b)(1) and 901.

§6.4 DETERMINING THE VALUE OF PROPERTY ON A TIMELY GST TAX EXEMPTION ALLOCATION

The 2001 Tax Act provides that the value of property, for purposes of determining the inclusion ratio (and, thereby, the rate of GST tax imposed on taxable events) in connection with timely and automatic allocations of GST tax exemption, is the value as finally determined for gift or estate tax purposes. The value for purposes of an allocation that was made at the end of an ETIP is its estate or gift tax value at the end of the ETIP.[6] IRC sections 2642(b)(1) and (2).

Caution: This new rule is effective for transfers made after December 31, 2000, and is automatically repealed when the 2001 Tax Act sunsets on December 31, 2010.

§6.5 IRS MAY GRANT EXTENSION OF TIME TO MAKE A TIMELY GST TAX EXEMPTION ALLOCATION

Automatic allocations of GST tax exemption are made under IRC section 2632 to certain transfers made during life that are direct skips, so

---

[6] Allocation of GST tax exemption is not effective until the close of the estate tax inclusion period ("ETIP"). IRC section 2642(f). An ETIP is the period during which the trust property would be included in the gross estate of the transferor or the transferor's spouse if either were to die. Treas. Reg. §26.2632-1(c)(2).

that the inclusion ratio for such transfers may be reduced to zero without any affirmative allocation of GST tax exemption on the part of the transferor, i.e., no notice of GST tax exemption has to be filed with a U.S. Gift Tax Return. The 2001 Tax Act expanded the automatic GST-tax-exemption allocation rules concerning certain inter-vivos transfers that are not direct skips, i.e., inter-vivos transfers that are indirect skips. *See,* section 5.29, above. With regard to pre-2001 inter-vivos transfers, however, if a transferor failed to make an affirmative allocation of the GST tax exemption on a timely filed gift tax return, no relief was available, other than to make a late GST tax exemption allocation based on the value of the property as of the filing of the late GST tax exemption allocation. *See,* section 5.23, above. The 2001 Tax Act added IRC section 2642(g) which directs the IRS to grant extensions of time to transferors to allocate their GST tax exemption and to grant exceptions to the filing deadlines, considering all relevant circumstances, including evidence of intent contained in the trust instrument or instrument of transfer to be GST-tax exempt. IRC section 2642(g)(1). If an extension of time is granted to make a GST-tax-exemption allocation, the allocation will not be considered a "late" allocation under Treas. Reg. §26.2642-2(a)(2) but rather a timely allocation under Treas. Reg. §2642-2(a)(1) and, therefore, the applicable fraction and inclusion ratio will be determined as of the date of the transfer, not the date the allocation is actually made. The relief for filing a late but "timely" GST tax exemption will be available to (1) lifetime allocations of GST tax exemption under IRC section 2642(b)(1); (2) death time allocations of GST tax exemptions under IRC section 2642(b)(2); (3) elections out of automatic allocations to direct and indirect skips under IRC sections 2632(b)(3) and (c)(5)(A)(i)[7]; and (4) elections into automatic allocations for non-indirect skips under IRC section 2632(c)(5)(A)(ii).

> **Caution:** This relief is available for requests pending on, or filed after, December 31, 2000, and is automatically repealed when the 2001 Tax Act sunsets on December 31, 2010. 2001 Tax Act sections 564(b)(1) and 901.

§6.5(a) IRS Guidance

The IRS issued preliminary guidance on this relief provision in Notice 2001-50, 2001-34 I.R.B. 189, which is effective for requests

---

[7] *See,* Priv. Letter Rul. 200535025.

for relief pending on or filed after December 31, 2000. The notice states that taxpayers may seek an extension of time to make the above allocations and elections under the rules of Treas. Reg. §301.9100-3. In general, under these rules, relief is granted if it is established to the satisfaction of the IRS that the taxpayer acted reasonably and in good faith, and that the grant of relief will not prejudice the government's interests. Taxpayers requesting relief must follow the procedures for requesting a private letter ruling under Treas. Reg. §301.9100 contained in section 5.02 of Rev. Proc. 2001-1, 2001-1 C.B. 1, 13 (or its successor). Consequently, the taxpayer must pay a user fee to obtain relief.

In Rev. Proc. 2004-46, 2004-2 C.B.142 (Aug. 2, 2004), the IRS issued additional guidance for relief concerning certain inter-vivos gifts to trusts that occurred on or before December 31, 2000 and qualified for the gift tax annual exclusion.[8] This revenue procedure provides a simplified alternate method (and less expensive method—no private letter ruling is required and no user fee is charged for requests filed under the revenue procedure) to obtain an extension of time to make a late allocation of GST tax exemption. As a result of this revenue procedure, there will be no need to obtain a private letter ruling if 15 conditions are satisfied. Relief under the revenue procedure is available if (1) on or before December 31, 2000, the taxpayer made or was deemed to have made a transfer by gift to a trust from which a GST may be made; (2) at the time the taxpayer files the request for relief under the revenue procedure, no taxable distributions have been made and no taxable terminations have occurred; (3) the transfer to the trust qualified for the gift tax annual exclusion under IRC section 2503(b), and the amount of the transfer, when added to the value of all other gifts by the transferor to that donee in the same year, was equal to or less than the amount of the applicable annual exclusion amount under IRC section 2503(b) for the year of the transfer; (4) no GST tax exemption was allocated to the transfer, whether or not a United States Gift Tax Return (IRS Form 709) was filed; (5) at the time the taxpayer files a request for relief under the revenue procedure, the taxpayer has unused GST tax exemption available to allocate to the transfer; (6)

---

[8] See, Lloyd Leva Plaine and Pam H. Schneider, "IRS Simplifies Procedures for Some Late GST Allocations and Reverse QTIP Elections," 101 *Journal of Taxation* 294 (November 2004).

the taxpayer files a United States Gift Tax Return for the year of the transfer to the trust, regardless of whether a Form 709 had been previously filed for that year, and states at the top of the Gift Tax Return that it is being "FILED PURSUANT TO REV. PROC. 2004-46"[9]; (7) the taxpayer reports on the Gift Tax Return the value of the transferred property as of the date of the transfer, (8) the taxpayer allocates GST tax exemption to the trust by attaching a statement to the Gift Tax Return entitled "Notice of Allocation"[10]; and (9) the United States Gift Tax Return for the year of the transfer in question is filed on or before the date prescribed for filing the taxpayer's federal estate tax return for the taxpayer's estate (determined with regard to any extensions actually obtained), regardless of whether an estate tax return is required to be filed. If the IRS grants the relief, the transferor's GST tax exemption will be allocated effective as of the date of the inter-vivos transfer. A grant of relief does not, however, preclude a subsequent determination by the IRS that the transfer is subject to an ETIP under IRC section 2642(f). If relief is denied under this simplified procedure, the taxpayer may still seek relief under Treas. Reg. §301.9100-3, but the private letter ruling request must indicate that relief was denied under Rev. Proc. 2004-46.

§6.5(b) IRS Generous In Granting Relief

The IRS has been quite generous in granting extensions under IRC section 2642(g)(1). For example, in Priv. Letter Rul. 200227017,

---

[9] For example, if the transfer to the trust was in 1999, the taxpayer must file a 1999 IRS Form 709. Some old IRS forms can be downloaded from the IRS' website at www.irs.gov/formspubs/lists/0,,id=97817,00.html.

[10] The Notice of Allocation must contain the following information: (i) a clear identification of the trust, including the trust's taxpayer identification number, as defined in IRC section 6109 and the regulations thereunder, when applicable, (ii) the value of the property transferred as of the date of the transfer (adjusted to account for split gifts, if any), (iii) the amount of taxpayer's unused GST exemption at the time the Notice of Allocation is filed (a taxpayer must have unused GST exemption at the time the Notice of Allocation is filed), (iv) the amount of GST exemption allocated to the transfer, (v) the inclusion ratio of the trust after the allocation, and (vi) a statement that all of the nine requirements (discussed above) of section 3.01 of the Rev. Proc. 2004-46 have been met. The United States Gift Tax Return and its Notice of Allocation, if sent by mail, should be sent to Internal Revenue Service Center, Cincinnati, OH 45999. If the Gift Tax Return is sent by private delivery service, such as FEDEX, it should be sent to Internal Revenue Service Center, 201 W. Rivercenter Blvd., Covington, KY 41012.

the IRS permitted an allocation of GST tax exemption by the deceased insured's executor three years after the funding of an ILIT that held a second-to-die life insurance policy on the lives of the grantor and the grantor's spouse, where one of the spouses had died. The IRS granted the relief because the taxpayers had acted reasonably and in good faith in relying upon their accountant to prepare their U.S. Gift Tax Returns and to allocate their GST tax exemption (which apparently he did not do under the mistaken belief that all annual exclusion gifts under section 2503(b) were automatically GST tax exempt). The IRS was of the opinion that the grant of relief to the taxpayer was not prejudicial to the IRS, a sort of "no harm, no foul" approach (presumably since the life insurance policy had not yet "matured"). *See also*, Priv. Letter Ruls. 200535003, 200229032, 200229033, 200234026, 200235013, 200237021, 200238035, 200238028, 200238018, 200238003, and 200241043.

§6.6 SUBSTANTIAL COMPLIANCE SUFFICES FOR GST-TAX-EXEMPTION ALLOCATIONS

The 2001 Tax Act provides that substantial compliance with the statutory and regulatory requirements for allocating the GST tax exemption under IRC section 2632 is sufficient to establish that the GST tax exemption was allocated to a particular transfer or trust. A taxpayer who demonstrates an intent to have an inclusion ratio of zero with respect to a particular transfer or trust is deemed to have allocated to the transfer or trust sufficient GST tax exemption to produce the lowest possible inclusion ratio. The IRS is directed to consider all relevant circumstances to determine whether there has been substantial compliance, including evidence of intent contained in the trust instrument or instrument of transfer, and such other factors as the Secretary of the Treasury deems appropriate. Drafters may want to consider adding an introductory clause to trusts that are intended to be GST-tax-exempt trusts. In light of the new automatic GST-tax-exemption allocation rules (as to new lifetime transfers under IRC section 2632(c)), the substantial compliance rules or extension of time rules could be best used for GST transfers occurring some time after the transferor's death. IRC section 2642(g)(2). Given the practical difficulty of qualifying for permanent GST Trust status under IRC section 2632(c) without affirmatively electing to have the trust be a GST Trust under the opt in rules of that Code section, the "substantial compliance" rules will be useful until (if) there are clarifying Treasury Regulations for IRC section 2632(c).

> **Caution:** The new rule applies to transfers made after December 31, 2000, and is automatically repealed when the 2001 Tax Act sunsets on December 31, 2010. 2001 Tax Act sections 564(b)(2) and 901.

> **Practice Point:** The "substantial compliance" doctrine may also apply to transfers before January 1, 2001. In Priv. Letter Rul. 200224018 the decedent's estate did not allocate any GST tax exemption on Schedule R of the federal estate tax return. Instead, the executor attached copies of the trusts to the federal estate tax return. The IRS ruled that the trust agreements attached to the federal estate tax return contained sufficient information to constitute substantial compliance with the requirements for making a timely allocation of decedent's GST exemption for federal estate tax purposes. The IRS relied on *Hewlett-Packard Co. v. Commissioner*, 67 T.C. 736 (1977), *acq. in result,* 1979-1 C.B. 1 for the proposition that literal compliance with the procedural instructions to make an election is not always required where the taxpayer complied with the essential requirements of a regulation. Thus, an allocation that does not strictly comply with the instructions on IRS Form 706, or the applicable regulations, will be deemed valid if the information on the estate tax return is sufficient to indicate that the executor intended to make an allocation of GST exemption. By analogy, if a gift tax return has been filed with a copy of the trust attached but no Notice of GST Tax Exemption Allocation was attached, it may, depending on the terms of the trust, be possible to argue that the taxpayer met the requirements of making an election to allocate GST tax exemption to the trust; however, a private letter ruling may have to be requested. *See* Priv. Letter Ruls. 200017013 (failure to file Notice of GST Tax Exemption Allocation with IRS form 709 but sufficient information provided on form 709 to indicate that taxpayers intended the trusts to be GST tax exempt) and 199937026 (failure to file a Schedule R with estate tax return, but sufficient information in trust agreement [that was filed with the estate tax return] to indicate that the

executor intended to make an allocation of GST tax exemption to certain trusts).

§6.7 AUTOMATIC ALLOCATION OF GST TAX EXEMPTION TO INDIRECT SKIPS

The 2001 Tax Act provides for automatic allocation of a transferor's GST tax exemption to certain lifetime transfers that are not direct skips but are made to an inter-vivos trust (such as an ILIT) that subsequently could have a generation-skipping transfer with respect to the transferor ("indirect skips"). IRC section 2632(c). Such a trust is referred to as a "GST Trust" under section 2632(c)(3)(B). The rule applies to inter-vivos transfers made after December 31, 2000, and to ETIP ending after December 31, 2000. §2632(c). This new rule is in addition to the pre-2001 Tax Act automatic GST-tax-exemption allocation rules concerning lifetime direct skips under section 2632(b). Thus, as a result of the new law, both lifetime direct skips and lifetime indirect skips are subject to the automatic GST-tax-exemption allocation rules. (*See* discussion of IRC section 2632(b) and (c), in section 5.29, above.)

> **Caution**: The new automatic allocation rule to indirect skips applies to transfers made after December 31, 2000, and it will be automatically repealed when the 2001 Tax Act sunsets on December 31, 2010. 2001 Tax Act sections 564(b)(2) and 901.

7

Key Changes Affecting Transfer Taxes Under The 2001 Tax Act

§7.1 KEY TRANSFER TAX CHANGES UNDER THE 2001 TAX ACT

Key changes under the 2001 Tax Act to the federal estate, gift, and generation-skipping transfer tax rates and exemption amounts are summarized in the below chart.

Year	Estate And GST Tax Exemption Amount	Estate, Gift, And GST Tax Rates	Gift Tax Exemption Amount	Other
2002	$1,000,000 (Estate) $1,100,000 (GST)	41%-50%	$1,000,000	State Death Tax Credit Reduced 25%.
2003	$1,000,000(Estate) $1,120,000 (GST)	41%-49%	$1,000,000	State Death Tax Credit Reduced 50%.
2004	$1,500,000 (Estate and GST)	45%-48%	$1,000,000	State Death Tax Credit Reduced 75% QFOBI deduction repealed.
2005	$1,500,000 (Estate and GST)	45%-47%	$1,000,000	State Death Tax and GST Credit Repealed. State Death Tax Paid Becomes a Form Deduction on IRS Form 706.

Year	Estate And GST Tax Exemption Amount	Estate, Gift, And GST Tax Rates	Gift Tax Exemption Amount	Other
2006	$2,000,000 (Estate and GST)	Flat 46%	$1,000,000	
2007	$2,000,000 (Estate and GST)	Flat 45%	$1,000,000	
2008	$2,000,000 (Estate and GST)	Flat 45%	$1,000,000	
2009	$3,500,000 (Estate and GST)	Flat 45%	$1,000,000	
2010	Repealed (IRC sections 2210(a) and 2664)	0% (Estate and and GST) 35% (Gift)	$1,000,000	Gift tax rate Carryover basis is instituted.
2011	$1 000,000 (Estate) $1 100,000 *(GST)	37%-55%	$1,000,000	Pre 2001 Tax Act law returns. QFOBI = $300,000 maximum.

* Plus any post 2002 inflation adjustments.

8
Tax-Sensitive Powers Regarding The Beneficiary-Trustee

CHAPTER OVERVIEW

Who serves as a trustee of the ILIT can have profound income and transfer tax consequences for the grantor and for the trustee, especially if the trustee is a beneficiary of the ILIT. This Chapter discusses what the income, estate, and gift tax consequences are of a beneficiary who serves as a trustee of an ILIT.[1] Under no circumstances should an insured ever serve as a trustee of an ILIT!

§8.1 ESTATE TAX ISSUES AND THE BENEFICIARY-TRUSTEE

A beneficiary-trustee's power to make discretionary distributions to *himself or herself* as a trust beneficiary without the limitation of an ascertainable standard constitutes a general power of appointment ("the prohibited power"). IRC sections 2041(b)(1)(A) and 2514(c)(1). Additionally, a beneficiary-trustee's discretionary power over trust property that could be exercised for the benefit of the beneficiary-trustee's creditors or estate also constitutes a prohibited power.

> **Practice Point:** To avoid the prohibited power being included in the beneficiary-trustee's gross estate, the beneficiary-trustee should disclaim the prohibited power in accor-

[1] *See,* Carmen Irizarry-Diaz, "Tax Considerations in the Choice of Trustee," 45 *Tax Management Memorandum* 283 (July 26, 2004); and Georgiana J. Slade, "The Beneficiary as Trustee: A Pandora's Box," 19 *Tax Management Estates, Gifts and Trusts Journal* 197 (November 10, 1994).

dance with IRC section 2518. The beneficiary-trustee may also want to disclaim serving as trustee.[2] Having the beneficiary-trustee merely decline to serve as trustee (and not make a qualified disclaimer of the prohibited power) may result in a "release" or "lapse" of the prohibited power. A "release" or "lapse" of a general power of appointment will result in the beneficiary-trustee making a taxable gift pursuant to per IRC sections 2514(b) and (e), and/or result in the prohibited power being included in the beneficiary-trustee's gross estate pursuant to IRC sections 2041(a)(2) and (b)(2).

§8.1(a) Death Of Beneficiary-Trustee

If the beneficiary-trustee holds the prohibited power and dies, the trust property will be included in his or her gross estate. IRC section 2041; Treas. Reg. §20.2041-1(b).

§8.1(b) Ascertainable Standards[3]

Examples of ascertainable standards include:

- Support;
- Support in reasonable comfort;
- Maintenance;

---

[2] Before accepting the trust, a nominated trustee can disclaim serving as trustee. Uniform Trust Code ("UTC") section 701(b), http://www.law.upenn.edu/bll/ulc/uta/2005final.htm ***or*** http://www.nccusl.org, *Restatement 2d of Trusts* ("Restatement 2d") section 102 and *Restatement 3d of Trusts* ("Restatement 3d") section 35. No particular formality is required for the disclaimer to be effective—it may be written or oral (however, a written disclaimer is the preferred method for tax reasons). Once a nominated trustee has accepted the trust, the trustee cannot disclaim serving as trustee but can resign. UTC section 705, Restatement 2d section 106, and Restatement 3d section 36.

[3] *See*, Trent S. Kiziah, "Four Chosen Words," 145 *Trusts & Estates* 26 (August 2006) concerning the definition of "health, education, support and maintenance." *See also*, section 50 (comments d and e) of the *Restatement (Third) of Trusts* (ALI, Philadelphia 2003) and section 128 (comment e) of *Restatement (Second) of Trusts* (ALI, Philadelphia 1959). It is interesting to note that the comments to the *Restatement (Second) of Trusts* state that a beneficiary is entitled to support out of a trust fund even though the beneficiary has other resources, whereas the comments

- Maintenance in health and reasonable comfort;
- Support in his or her accustomed manner of living;
- Education, including college and professional education;
- Health;
- Health, education, support, and maintenance;
- Medical, dental, hospital, and nursing expenses; and
- Expenses of invalidism. Treas. Reg. §§20.2041-1(c)(2) and 25.2514-1(c)(2).

> **Caution:** Distributions for a beneficiary's "happiness," "welfare," "comfort," or "emergency needs" are not, in and of themselves, ascertainable standards. IRC sections 2041-(b)(1)(A) and 2514(c)(1); Treas. Reg. §§20.2041-1(c)(2) and 25.2514-1(c)(2). Even though state law is determinative in ascertaining the nature and extent of powers held by a decedent,[4] do not deviate from the standards enumerated in the Treasury Regulations. *Morgan v. Commissioner of Internal Revenue Service*, 309 U.S. 78 (1940). *See also*, Rev. Rul. 77-60, 1977-1 C.B. 282, which states that "[a] power to use property to enable the donee to continue an accustomed mode of living, without further limitation, although predictable and measurable on the basis of past expenditures, does not come within the ascertainable standard prescribed in IRC section 2041(b)(1)(A) since the standard of living may include customary travel, entertain-

---

to the *Restatement (Third) of Trusts* state that the trustee is to consider the beneficiary's other resources, but has some discretion in the matter. *Id.* A flexible approach is for the governing instrument to expressly permit the trustee to consider the beneficiary's other resources. *See*, Paragraph 7.11 of Sample ILIT.

> **Caution:** Ascertainable standards for gift tax purposes under IRC section 2511 are ***broader*** than ascertainable standards for power of appointment purposes under IRC sections 2514 and 2041. Thus, an ascertainable standard under IRC section 2511 may not be an ascertainable standard under IRC sections 2514 and 2041. However, an ascertainable standard under IRC sections 2514 and 2041 will be an ascertainable standard under IRC section 2511. *See*, section 8.2(a)(1), below.

[4] In some states, "comfort" is a standard. Illinois, for example, has interpreted "comfort" as if it were "support in reasonable comfort" and accepted it as an ascertainable standard.

ment, luxury items, or other expenditures not required for meeting the donee's 'needs for health, education or support.' Nor does the requirement of a good faith exercise of a power create an ascertainable standard. Good faith exercise of a power is not determinative of its breadth."

§8.1(c) Negation Of Ascertainable Standard

An ascertainable standard is rendered unascertainable for a beneficiary-trustee "if a trust instrument provides that the determination of the trustee shall be conclusive with respect to the exercise or non-exercise of a power...." Treas. Reg. §25.2511-1(g)(2). *Cf,* Treas. Reg. §1.674(b)-1(b)(5)(i). Examples of powers that negate an ascertainable standard include:

• "The trustee's exercise or nonexercise of powers and discretions in good faith shall be conclusive and binding on all interested parties."

• "The trustee shall exercise his or her powers in his or her uncontrolled discretion." *Estate of Friedman*, 94 Cal. App. 3d 667, 156 Cal. Rptr. 597 (1979); *Independence Bank Waukesha (N.A.) v. U.S.*, 761 F.2d 442 (7th Cir. 1985).

It may be desirable to limit the beneficiary-trustee's power.

> **Drafting Example:** *No trustee who is a beneficiary of the trust in question shall possess any power or discretion that is "conclusive," "sole," "absolute," or "uncontrolled" with respect to the exercise or nonexercise of such power or discretion under that trust; and such beneficiary-trustee's power or discretion in that regard shall at all times be exercised or not exercised in a reasonable manner, be limited by a reasonably definite standard, and shall be subject to review and judicial scrutiny.*

§8.1(d) Co-Trustee With Substantial Adverse Interest

The appointment of a co-trustee (including an independent co-trustee) to serve with the beneficiary-trustee does not protect the beneficiary-trustee unless (1) the consent of the co-trustee is required for any discretionary distributions, and (2) the co-trustee has a substantial adverse interest in the trust. IRC section 2041(b)(1)(C)(ii); Treas. Reg. §20.2041-3(c)(2); Priv. Letter Rul. 9030032. *See also*, IRC section 2514(c)(3)(B). Alternatively, the power to make discretionary distributions can be vested exclusively in the independent co-trustee (who need not have a substantial adverse interest). This will prevent attribution of the prohibited power to the beneficiary-trustee.

A person has a "substantial adverse interest" if he or she has a present or future right to obtain a personal benefit from the property that is subject to the power. *Estate of Richard C. Maxant v. Commissioner*, T.C. Memo 1980-414 (1980). A co-holder of a power is considered to have a substantial adverse interest in the exercise of a power over trust property if the co-holder is the remainder beneficiary of the trust.[5] Treas. Reg. §20.2041-3(c)(2), Example 1.

> An interest adverse to the exercise of a power is considered as substantial if its value in relation to the total value of the property subject to the power is not insignificant. For this purpose, the interest is to be valued in accordance with the actuarial principles set forth in §20.2031-7 or, if it is not susceptible to valuation under those provisions, in accordance with the general principles set forth in §20.2031-1.
>
> A taker in default of appointment under a power has an interest which is adverse to an exercise of the power.
>
> A co-holder of the power has no adverse interest merely because of his joint possession of the power nor merely because he is a permissible appointee under a power. However, a coholder of a power is considered as having an adverse interest where he may possess the power after the decedent's death and may exercise it at that time in favor of himself, his estate, his creditors, or the creditors of his estate.

Treas. Reg. §20.2041-3(c)(2).

> **Practice Point:** Having a co-trustee with a substantial adverse interest may still result in the prohibited power being included in the beneficiary-trustee's gross estate if the

---

[5] *See*, Rev. Rul. 79-63, 1979-1 C.B. 302 where the IRS ruled that a joint powerholder did not have a substantial adverse interest in the exercise of an inter-vivos general power of appointment (even though the joint powerholder was a permissible appointee under the inter-vivos general power of appointment) because the joint powerholder was not a taker in default upon the non-exercise of the inter-vivos general power of appointment.

adverse-trustee predeceases the beneficiary-trustee and the beneficiary-trustee is the sole remaining trustee.

Drafting Example:

The power to make discretionary distributions of principal or income to a beneficiary hereunder who is also a trustee, shall be vested exclusively in (and be exercisable only by) the Independent Trustee.[6] *If the incumbent trustee is not an Independent Trustee, the incumbent trustee may appoint an Independent Trustee to serve as co-trustee with the incumbent trustee. The Independent Trustee so appointed shall serve concurrently with the appointing trustee until the appointing trustee resigns, dies, or becomes incapacitated and is succeeded by a successor trustee.*

§8.1(e) Beneficiary-Trustee's Power Of Withdrawal

A beneficiary-trustee, or any beneficiary, can be given a power of withdrawal over trust principal and income without the power of withdrawal being included in his or her gross estate— provided the beneficiary (the "withdrawal right beneficiary") does not die during the time period the power of withdrawal is exercisable and the power has not lapsed. The power of withdrawal must be limited to the safe harbor amounts described in IRC sections 2514(e)(1) and (2) and 2041(b)(2), which is currently $5,000 or 5% of the trust estate (five by five). If the withdrawal right beneficiary dies while the power of withdrawal is exercisable (i.e., has not yet lapsed), the amount of the property subject to the right of withdrawal will be included in the beneficiary's gross estate under IRC section 2041, as a general power of appointment, and the decreased withdrawal right beneficiary will become the "new" transferor of the unlapsed power for GST tax purposes. Any GST tax exemption previously allocated by the grantor will be lost and wasted. Treas. Reg. §26.2652-1(a)(2). Hence, it may not be appropriate to grant a five-by-five withdrawal power to a beneficiary of a trust that comes into existence after the grantor's death, such as the reverse QTIP Marital Trust, Family Trust, Children's Trust or Descendants' Trust, or to the beneficiary of a trust that is designed to be GST tax exempt. However, if such a withdrawal right is granted, consider limiting the withdrawal period to 30 or 60 days to minimize

---

[6] *See*, Paragraph 8.3(I) of Sample ILIT for a comprehensive definition of an Independent Trustee.

the risk of the beneficiary dying during the period the withdrawal right is exercisable.

§8.1(e)(1) Lapse Of Power Of Withdrawal

Use extreme care when granting withdrawal rights in an amount greater than $5,000 or 5% of the value of the trust assets. IRC section 2514(b) indicates that the exercise or release of a general power of appointment will be treated as a transfer by the individual who released the power. Under IRC section 2514(e), a *lapse* of a power of appointment is considered a release. A specific exception to this rule is set forth under IRC section 2514(e)(1) and (2), which states that the *lapse* of a power (in contrast to a *release* or a *waiver* of the power) not exceeding $5,000 or 5% of the value of the assets out of which the power can be satisfied, will not be treated as a transfer. What this means is that a lapse of a withdrawal right in excess of the five-by-five limits will constitute both a taxable release under IRC section 2514(b) and an immediate gift of a future interest to the other trust beneficiaries by the withdrawal right beneficiary. As a result of the gift, the withdrawal right beneficiary will become the "new" transferor of the excess amount for GST tax purposes, and any GST tax exemption previously allocated by the grantor will be wasted. Additionally, because the withdrawal right beneficiary has a retained interest in the trust, all or a portion of the value of the trust will be included in that beneficiary's gross estate upon his or her death. IRC section 2036(a); Treas. Reg. §20.2041-3(d)(4). Furthermore, if the lapse of the excess amount is a completed gift, the withdrawal right beneficiary's retained interest in the excess amount will be valued at $0 for gift tax purposes if the remainder beneficiaries/donees of the excess amount are members of the withdrawal right beneficiary's family. IRC section 2702(a)(2). Priv. Letter Rul. 9804047.

The effect of cumulative taxable releases with a retained interest by the beneficiary may result in all (or a significant portion) of the beneficiary's trust share being included in his or her gross estate. Treas. Reg. §20.2041-3(d)(5). Thus, a power of withdrawal in a trust that comes into existence after the grantor's death, such as the Family Trust, Children's Trust, or Descendants' Trust, should be limited to the five-by-five amount to avoid these disastrous estate and gift tax consequences.

§8.1(f) Beneficiary-Trustee's Ability To Remove A Co-Trustee And Appoint A Successor Co-Trustee

A beneficiary-trustee's ability to remove a co-trustee and appoint a successor co-trustee may constitute a general power of appointment under IRC section 2041. *See*, section 1.3, above, for further discussion on this point.

§8.1(g) Beneficiary-Trustee And Life Insurance

If a beneficiary serves as a trustee of a trust that holds life insurance on that beneficiary's life, the life insurance proceeds will be includable in that beneficiary-trustee's gross estate for estate tax purposes. IRC section 2042. This is because the beneficiary, as trustee, will have incidents of ownership in the life insurance policy. Treas. Reg. §§20.2042-1(c). To avoid this result, a beneficiary-trustee should not serve as a trustee of a trust that holds insurance on his or her life, unless a co-trustee is granted all rights and powers over the policy. Also, the beneficiary-trustee (either as a beneficiary or as a trustee) should not have a power of appointment over the life insurance policy. *See*, Paragraph 7.1(C)(3) of Sample ILIT.

§8.2 GIFT TAX ISSUES AND THE BENEFICIARY-TRUSTEE

The gift tax consequences of a beneficiary-trustee's discretionary distributions of income or principal to another beneficiary of the same trust are as follows.

§8.2(a) Distributions By Beneficiary-Trustee To Other Beneficiaries

If the beneficiary-trustee makes a wholly discretionary distribution of income or principal to another beneficiary of the same trust of which the beneficiary-trustee is also a wholly discretionary beneficiary, the distribution will constitute a taxable gift by the beneficiary-trustee. IRC section 2514. Also, if the beneficiary-trustee (or any beneficiary) is entitled to income and appoints that income to another beneficiary (or another person), the appointment of the income interest is a taxable gift by the beneficiary-trustee to the other beneficiary. Treas. Reg. §§ 25.2514-1(b)(2) and 25.2514-3(e), Example 1.

§8.2(a)(1) Ascertainable Standard

To avoid the gift problem, the beneficiary-trustee's power to distribute property to other beneficiaries of the same trust should be limited to an ascertainable standard.[7] Treas. Reg. §25.2511-1(g)(2). *See*, *Estate of Ruth B. Regester v. Commissioner*, 83 T.C. 1 (1984); Rev. Rul. 79-327, 1979-2 C.B. 342; Treas. Reg. §25.2514-1(b)(2); Priv. Letter Rul. 200243026 (concerning the gift tax consequences of an income beneficiary's exercise of an inter-vivos limited power of appointment over trust principal). Alternatively, the power to make discretionary distributions to any trust beneficiary can be vested exclusively in (and be exercisable only by) an independent trustee. This will prevent a gift being made by the beneficiary-trustee.

Drafting Example:

To the extent a beneficiary-trustee has the authority to make discretionary distributions of income and/or principal to another beneficiary from a trust of which such beneficiary-trustee is then also a current trust beneficiary, the discretionary distributions shall be limited by an ascertainable standard related to the distributee beneficiary's health, education, support, and maintenance in the manner of living to which the distributee beneficiary has been accustomed, considering the resources otherwise available to the distributee beneficiary.

---

[7] **Caution:** Ascertainable standards under IRC section 2511 are ***broader*** than ascertainable standards under IRC sections 2514 and 2041. Thus, an ascertainable standard under IRC section 2511 may not be an ascertainable standard under IRC sections 2514 and 2041. However, an ascertainable standard under IRC sections 2514 and 2041 will be an ascertainable standard under IRC section 2511.

"If a trustee has a beneficial interest in trust property, a transfer of the property by the trustee is not a taxable transfer [for purposes of IRC section 2511] if it is made pursuant to a fiduciary power the exercise or non-exercise of which is limited by a reasonably fixed or ascertainable standard which is set forth in the trust instrument. A clearly measurable standard under which the holder of a power is legally accountable is such a standard for this purpose. For instance, a power to distribute corpus for the education, support, maintenance, or health of the beneficiary; for his reasonable support and ***comfort***; to enable him to maintain his accustomed standard of living; or to ***meet an emergency***, would be such a standard. However, a power to distribute corpus for the pleasure, desire, or happiness of a beneficiary is not such a standard. The entire context of a provision of a trust instrument granting a power must be considered in determining whether the power is limited by a reasonably definite standard." Treas. Reg. §25.2511-1(g)(2). (Emphasis added.)

> **Caution:** If the other beneficiary is a person whom the trustee-beneficiary is legally obligated to support (such as a spouse or a minor child), an ascertainable standard concerning distributions to the other trust beneficiary (whom the beneficiary-trustee is legally obligated to support) will not protect the beneficiary-trustee from estate and gift tax consequences. IRC sections 2041(b)(1)(A) and 2514(c)(1); Treas. Reg. §§20.2041-1(c)(2) and 25.2514-1(c)(2); Rev. Rul. 79-154, 1979-1 C.B. 301.

§8.2(b) Beneficiary-Trustee's Lapse Of Power Of Withdrawal

If a beneficiary-trustee, or any beneficiary, holds a withdrawal right over trust property that is already sheltered from estate tax (due to the application of the deceased grantor's applicable exclusion amount), make sure the right of withdrawal lapses within the five-by-five safe harbor limits of IRC sections 2514(e)(1) and (2). Otherwise, the lapse in excess of five by five may result in a gift of a future interest being made by the powerholder to the other trust beneficiaries for the amount in excess of five by five. *See*, section 8.1(e)(1), above.

§8.3 INCOME TAX ISSUES AND THE BENEFICIARY-TRUSTEE

When a trust is not a grantor trust,[8] the income tax consequences of a beneficiary-trustee's ability to make distributions[9] to him or herself from a trust, even if limited by an ascertainable standard, are as follows.

§8.3(a) Beneficiary-Trustee's Sole Power To Make Distributions

Generally, if a beneficiary-trustee has the sole power to pay trust principal or income to him or herself (or to pay trust income or principal disproportionately among a group of beneficiaries that

[8] A grantor trust is a trust where all of the trust's income and gain is being taxed to the grantor pursuant to IRC sections 671-677. Consequently, IRC section 678(a) should not apply to a beneficiary-trustee where the grantor is being taxed on both the trust's income and corpus. IRC section 678(b). *See*, sections 2.7 - 2.9, above.

[9] "If the trust income or corpus can be distributed to any beneficiary in the discretion of one or more trustees, then two factors must be considered to determine who will pay tax on the trust income: (1) distribution standards, and (2) the relationship of the trustee or trustees to the settlor." Laura H. Peebles, "Tax Aspects of Choice of Trustee," 31 *Estate Planning* 43, 44 (January 2004).

include the beneficiary-trustee), the beneficiary-trustee will be treated as the owner of that portion of the trust property for income tax purposes. IRC section 678(a)(1). *See, Mallinckrodt v. Nunan*, 146 F.2d 1 (8th Cir. 1945), *aff'g* 2 T.C. 1128 (1944), *cert. denied*, 324 U.S. 871 (1945); Rev. Rul. 81-6, 1981-1 C.B. 385; Rev. Rul. 67-241, 1967-2 C.B. 225; Priv. Letter Ruls. 200104005 and 9034004. Such a trust is referred to as a "beneficiary-owned" trust, or a "*Mallinckrodt*" trust. Thus, if there is only one trustee, and that trustee has the unrestricted power to distribute ordinary income to him or herself (or among a group of beneficiaries that include the beneficiary-trustee), that beneficiary-trustee will be taxed on that income, whether or not it is distributed; and the beneficiary-trustee will be taxed on that income if it is paid to someone else (because the beneficiary-trustee could have paid the income to him or herself). Furthermore, if there is only one trustee, and that trustee has the unrestricted power to distribute principal to him or herself (or among a group of beneficiaries that include the beneficiary-trustee), that beneficiary-trustee will be taxed on the trust's capital gains (because the beneficiary-trustee could have paid the principal [which is typically allocable to capital gains under normal fiduciary trust accounting rules] to him or herself). IRC section 678(a)(1). Note that there is no ascertainable standard exception to IRC section 678(a)(1) (concerning a beneficiary-trustee's sole power to distribute income or principal to him or herself pursuant to an ascertainable standard). *But see, U.S. v. Dale King De Bonchamps*, 278 F.2d 127 (9th Cir. 1960). However, if there is an ascertainable standard concerning the right to income or principal, and the standard is not met, then the beneficiary-trustee presumably does not have the right to distribute property to him or herself, and consequently should not be taxed that year on the trust's income or capital gains, as the case may be. However, the law is unclear on this point. Furthermore, there is no five-by-five exception to IRC section 678(a)(1), as there is for IRC sections 2514 and 2041. Thus, a power of withdrawal contained in a marital deduction trust or credit shelter trust, even if limited to the five-by-five safe harbor amount provided in IRC sections 2514(e) and 2041(b)(2), will still result in the beneficiary being taxed on the trust's income and capital gains he or she could have withdrawn, even if the five-by-five power of withdrawal is never exercised. Rev. Rul. 67-241, 1967-2 C.B. 225; Priv. Letter Rul. 200022035.

§8.3(a)(1) Power Of Withdrawal

An unexercised five-by-five withdrawal right produces significant income tax complications by creating partial grantor trust status under IRC section 678(a) with regard to the withdrawal right beneficiary. This should be considered before granting a withdrawal right in the trust that comes into existence after the grantor's death, such as the Family Trust, Children's Trust or Descendants' Trust. Furthermore, if unexercised withdrawal rights accumulate over the years, more of the trust income and corpus will be taxable (for income tax purposes) to the withdrawal right beneficiary. Rev. Rul. 67-241, 1967-2 C.B. 225; Priv. Letter Ruls. 200022035 and 9034004. *See*, Priv. Letter Ruls. 200104005 and 9034004, which refer to the formula for calculating the portion taxable to the withdrawal right beneficiary. *See also*, Treas. Reg. §1.671-3(a)(3).

> **Practice Point:** To avoid the IRC section 678(a) problem associated with a noncumulative five-by-five withdrawal right, require the beneficiary's right of withdrawal over the Marital Trust, Family Trust, Children's Trust, or Descendants' Trust to be exercisable only with the consent of a third party, such as a disinterested trustee who does not have a substantial and adverse interest in the trust or the power of withdrawal.[10]
>
> **Practice Point: Grantor Trumps Beneficiary Under Grantor Trust Rules.** If the grantor holds a power under IRC sections 673 through 677 and the beneficiary holds an IRC section 678 power (such as a *Crummey* withdrawal right) over the same income, the beneficiary's power is disregarded, and the grantor is taxed as the owner of the trust income. IRC section 678(b). Note, however, that it is unclear whether the grantor will be taxed as the owner of the corpus, because IRC section 678(b) refers only to "income," whereas IRC section 678(a)(1) refers to a beneficiary's power to vest "corpus or the income therefrom."
>
> Several commentators are of the opinion that this incongruency is a legislative drafting error, and that the

---

[10] *See*, Paragraph 8.3(K) of Sample ILIT for a comprehensive definition of a disinterested trustee.

grantor trumps the beneficiary as to both income and corpus.[11] In several private letter rulings, the IRS has taken the position that the grantor is treated as the owner of the corpus (whenever possible) despite the existence of an IRC section 678 power (of withdrawal) held by a ben-

---

[11] "Over the years, there have been a number of questions regarding the wording of IRC Section 678, specifically the difference between Section 678(a), which refers to the right 'to the corpus or the income therefrom,' and Section 678(b), which refers to a 'power over income.' This difference matters when the settlor might be taxed on trust income under IRC Section 678(b): Would he be taxed on all of the trust income, or only that taxable income allocable to trust accounting income,...[causing] the *Crummey* powerholder [to be] taxed on the corpus gains and losses? To find out, ...[we refer to] the definitions in IRC Section 643(b), which tells us that the word 'income' in [IRC Subtitle A, Chapter 1,] subchapter J, unless preceded by another adjective, refers to trust accounting income. However, that definition does not apply to subpart E of subchapter J, which is the grantor trust section. In the regulations for subpart E [Treas. Reg. §1.671-2(b)], we are told that 'income' in the subpart E regulations refers to taxable income [i.e., ordinary income and capital gains] rather than trust [accounting] income. Although this reference appears in the regulations rather than in the statute, it is a strong indication that the reference to 'income' in Section 678(b) refers to taxable [income], not trust accounting income. The Section 678 regulations are consistent with this interpretation: Treasury Regulations Section 1.678(a)-1(a) clearly contemplates that the settlor could be taxed on both trust accounting income and corpus transactions [under the IRC section 678(b) tie-breaker rules]." Laura H. Peebles, "*Crummey* Powers Can Increase Your Income Tax," 145 *Trust & Estates* 35, 37 (November 2006).

See, Jonathan E. Gopman, "*Crummey,* The Saga Continues," 25 *Tax Management Estates, Gifts and Trusts Journal* 194, 231 (July 13, 2000); and James C. Davis, "Interaction of the Grantor Trust Rules and Life Insurance," 26 *Estate Planning* 418 (November 1999). "Section 678(b) states that 678(a) does not apply—i.e., the powerholder will not be treated as the grantor 'with respect to a power over income as originally granted or thereafter modified'—if the grantor is otherwise treated as the owner. Does the statute's use of the word 'income,' rather than 'portion,' prevent the grantor from replacing the powerholder as the taxpayer for some types of gains or losses? The author believes the answer is 'no.' Because of the way 'income' is defined in Reg. 1.671-2(b), it is logical to read the phrase 'power over income' as 'power over any portion of a trust.' Several commentators, and perhaps even the IRS, believe this is the proper interpretation, and that the use of the word 'income' was actually a drafting error. The original enactment of Sections 678(a) and 678(b) dates back to 1954, and Congress intended to use the word 'income' because the new Section 678(b) was intended to mirror the language of Section 677(b) , which also used (and still uses) the word 'income.' The use of the word 'income' in Section 677 and its predecessors can be traced back to the beginning in 1924; the word 'portion' does not appear in Section 677 until 1954.

eficiary.[12] Priv. Letter Ruls. 200606006, 200603040, 200011054, 9321050, 9309023, 9226037, 9141027, 8701007, 8308033, 8326074, 8308033, 8142061, 8103074, and 7909031.

An additional incongruence is found in the language of IRC section 678(a)(2) itself, which refers to a beneficiary who has "previously partially *released* or otherwise modified such a power and after the *release* or modification retains such control as would, within the principles of IRC sections 671 to 677, inclusive, subject the grantor of a trust to treatment as the owner thereof." (Emphasis added.) Note that the Code refers to a "release." A release connotes an affirmative act on the part of the power holder. A lapse, on the other hand, requires no action by the power holder. Interestingly, Congress found it necessary to expressly state that a lapse of

---

A good argument can be made that in both Sections 677(b) and 678(b) , the use of the word 'income' is simply an oversight and the statutory language has not been modernized to use the word 'portion.' Reg. 1.677(b)-1 (relating to Section 677(b)) clearly creates the possibility that any type of income of the trust may become taxable to the grantor." *Id.* at 419. (Citations omitted.) *See also*, the articles cited in Jonathan E. Gopman, "The Income Tax Consequences of an Irrevocable Life Insurance Trust," 22 *Tax Management Estates, Gifts and Trusts Journal* 211, 217 n.53 (September - October 1977).

[12]For example, in Priv. Letter Rul. 200606006, the IRS ruled:

> Section 678(b) provides that §678(a) shall not apply with respect to a power over income, as originally granted or thereafter modified, if the grantor of the trust or a transferor (to whom §679 applies) is otherwise treated as the owner under the provisions of subpart E other than §678. Rev. Rul. 85-13, 1985-1 C.B. 184, provides that if a grantor is treated as the owner of the entire trust, the grantor is considered to be the owner of the trust assets for federal income tax purposes. The power granted to Spouse to withdraw amounts contributed to Trust will result in Spouse being treated as the owner of the portion of Trust subject to her withdrawal power, unless as provided in §678(b), Grantor is treated as the owner. Under the terms of Trust, both income and corpus are payable to Spouse during Grantor's life. Accordingly, Grantor is treated as the owner of Trust under §677(a). Because Trust is a grantor trust under §677 with respect to Grantor, it is a grantor trust in its entirety with respect to Grantor notwithstanding the powers of withdrawal held by Spouse that would otherwise make her an owner under §-678. Accordingly, all items of income, deductions, and credits against tax of Trust are included in computing the Grantor's taxable income and credits.

a general power of appointment is a "release" for estate and gift tax purposes. However, the failure of Congress to make a similar statement for income tax purposes appears to be an indication that Congress did not intend to equate a lapse with a release for the grantor trust rules.

Practice Point: If grantor trust status terminates during the grantor's lifetime, the *Crummey* withdrawal right beneficiary may be treated, for income tax purposes, as a grantor of part of the ILIT. *See,* section 2.10(c)(1), above. Also, when the grantor dies, partial grantor trust status may also exist with regard to a *Crummey* withdrawal right beneficiary's unlapsed withdrawal rights. *See,* section 2.11(a), above. It should be noted that the IRS has changed its position on the partial grantor trust status issue at least once. In Priv. Letter Rul. 9026036, the IRS ruled that the withdrawal right holder would be deemed the grantor after the death of the original grantor; however, in Priv. Letter Rul. 9321050 the IRS withdrew the earlier ruling without providing any analysis for its action.[13] Thus, as a result of these rulings, we can conclude that when the original grantor is the owner of the trust under the grantor trust rules, the *Crummey* powerholder is not treated as the owner of the trust under IRC section 678(a), either before or after the grantor's death (assuming the *Crummey* withdrawal right ceases at the grantor's death).

§8.3(b) Distributions Made With Consent Of Co-Trustee

However, if the beneficiary-trustee's power to withdraw or distribute trust property can be exercised only in conjunction with a co-

---

[13]"[I]n PLR 9321050, the IRS reconsidered the issues in PLR 9026036 and revised its ruling to conclude that, after the death of the wife, the husband would not be treated as the owner for federal income tax purposes of the income of the trust. The only change in the IRS's analysis is a deletion of the discussion of legislative history to §678. Thus, it appears that after a trust ceases to be treated as a grantor trust with respect to the grantor, the trust will be treated as a separate taxpayer for income tax purposes and the powerholders will not be treated as the owner of the income of the trust for federal income tax purposes." Georgiana J. Slade, "Life After Execution of an Insurance Trust," 40 *Tax Management Memorandum* 375, 389 (October 25, 1999).

trustee or other third party (who may, but need not be adverse—such as the beneficiary-trustee's beneficiary-sibling or a non-beneficiary sibling[14]), then the beneficiary-trustee will not be treated as the owner of the trust for income tax purposes. IRC section 678(a)(1) applies only to powers exercisable solely by the beneficiary-trustee. It does not apply to jointly exercisable powers. It may be desirable to limit the beneficiary-trustee's power.

Drafting Example:

At any time when there is more than one trustee, no trustee who is also a beneficiary of any trust created under this trust agreement shall exercise any power solely by himself or herself as would cause such beneficiary-trustee to be treated as an owner of any portion of the trust under IRC section 678(a).

§8.3(c) Grantor Trust Status

If the grantor's spouse serves as sole trustee of the ILIT, grantor trust status will be conferred on the grantor. This is because the powers held by the spouse are attributed to the grantor per IRC section 672(3). As trustee, the grantor's spouse would have the ability to control the beneficial enjoyment of the trust property, and grantor trust status would exist with regard to the grantor. IRC section 674.

§8.4 TAX CONSEQUENCES OF DISTRIBUTIONS THAT DISCHARGE A TRUSTEE'S PERSONAL LEGAL OBLIGATIONS

§8.4(a) Estate And Gift Tax Consequences Of A Beneficiary-Trustee's Discharge Of Personal Legal Obligations

Irrespective of the fact that a beneficiary-trustee's power to distribute trust property to him or herself (or to another trust beneficiary) is limited by an ascertainable standard, a trustee's ability to discharge his or her personal legal obligations (including the obligation to support a beneficiary, such as a spouse or minor child) constitutes a general power of appointment to the extent of that obligation (i.e., the ability of the trustee to use the trust property to discharge his or her

---

[14] In order to avoid IRC section 678 treatment, the beneficiary-trustee's spouse should not be the co-trustee or third party because any powers held by the spouse will be attributed to the beneficiary-trustee. IRC section 672(e). *See,* section 2.7(a), above.

personal legal obligations is considered a power of appointment exercisable in favor of the trustee or his or her creditors). Treas. Reg. §§20.2041-1(c)(1) and 25.2514-1(c)(1). *See also,* Priv. Letter Ruls. 199930036 and 9328015. This rule applies to both beneficiary-trustees and non-beneficiary-trustees, i.e., to all individual trustees. The mere existence of the trustee's power or ability to discharge his or her legal obligation is sufficient to constitute a general power of appointment and cause the trust assets to be included in the trustee's gross estate when he or she dies. Priv. Letter Ruls. 9036048 and 8924011. *Cf., Estate of Virgil C. Sullivan v. Commissioner,* T.C. Memo 1993-531.

Furthermore, a distribution by the trustee to or for the benefit of the other beneficiary whom the trustee is legally obligated to support, will constitute the exercise of a power of appointment and result in a gift being made by the trustee to the other beneficiary. IRC section 2514(b).

An ascertainable standard does not protect the trustee from estate or gift tax consequences in this instance because the ascertainable standard exception relates to the health, education, support, and maintenance *of the powerholder.* IRC sections 2041(b)(1)(A) and 2514(c)(1); Treas. Reg. §§20.2041-1(c)(2) and 25.2514-1(c)(2); Rev. Rul. 79-154, 1979-1 C.B. 301. Thus, a beneficiary-trustee should be prohibited from making trust distributions that discharge his or her legal obligations, including the obligation to support a trust beneficiary.

An independent co-trustee can, however, make distributions to any beneficiary the other co-trustee is obligated to support. The independent co-trustee, by definition, will not possess a general power of appointment (concerning the discharge of personal legal obligations) since the distributions will be discharging the legal obligations of the other trustee(s) and not those of the independent co-trustee.

A divorce decree requiring the payment of a child's college expenses should not be considered a support obligation for purposes of IRC section 2041. *See, e.g., Aussie v. Aussie,* 182 Mich. App. 454, 452 N.W.2d 859 (1990).

> **Practice Point:** Prohibit a trustee from making any distributions that would have the effect of discharging the trustee's personal legal obligations, including the obligation of support. A clause that prevents a trustee from using the trust property to discharge his or her personal legal obligations is typically referred to as an "Upjohn" clause,

and is named after the case where the clause was used and discussed by the court. *See*, *William John Upjohn v. United States*, 72-2 U.S.T.C. ¶12,888 (W.D. Mich. 1972).

Drafting Example:

Notwithstanding any provision herein to the contrary, no trustee shall have the power to use or apply trust property (i) for the support and maintenance of anyone the trustee is obligated to support and maintain; or (ii) for the purpose of directly or indirectly discharging the personal legal obligations of the trustee.

§8.4(b) Super Support Exception

The ability of a trustee to use trust property for the "super support" (i.e., beyond the requirements of legal support) should not constitute a general power of appointment. In Priv. Letter Rul. 9030005, the IRS ruled that a beneficiary-trustee's power to distribute corpus to her children for "travel, camping trips, theater, ballet, music lessons, special schooling or instruction to enrich their lives...and college and post-graduate education expenses" did not constitute a general power of appointment.

§8.4(c) Income Tax Consequences Of Discharging A Personal Legal Obligation

The income tax consequences of a trustee's power to distribute trust property to discharge a personal legal obligation are as follows.

Sole power held by a sole trustee (or the sole power held by a co-trustee) to distribute trust property to discharge that trustee's personal legal obligation (other than a personal legal obligation to support or maintain a dependent) causes that trustee to be treated as the owner of the trust property for income tax purposes. Treas. Reg. §1.678(a)-1(b). *Mere possession* by a trustee (as sole trustee or co-trustee) of the power (in a fiduciary capacity)[15] to distribute trust property to discharge the trustee's personal legal obligation to support or maintain a dependent does not in and of itself result in taxable income, except to the extent the income or principal is *actually used or applied* by the trustee. IRC

---

[15] If a beneficiary (other than a beneficiary serving as a trustee or co-trustee) can use trust income to discharge his or her legal obligation of support or maintenance, that beneficiary will be taxed on the trust income, whether or not it is actually used for support or maintenance. Treas. Reg. §1.678(c)-1(b).

section 678(c); Treas. Reg. §1.678(c)-1(a). If such support distributions are actually made, the trustee is taxed under IRC sections 661 and 662 (concerning DNI). Treas. Reg. §§1.678(c)-1(c) and 1.662(a)-4. However, mere possession of the power by the trustee may result in adverse estate tax consequences to the trustee, as discussed above.

A trustee's use of trust property to discharge *another person's* legal obligation will cause the trust property (that is so used) to be income taxed to the person whose legal obligation is discharged (i.e., the person whose legal obligation is discharged is treated as though the trust property were distributed directly to him or her). Treas. Reg. §1.662(a)-4.

§8.5 TAX CONSEQUENCES OF OVERLY-BROAD DISCRETIONARY POWERS OVER INVESTMENTS AND PRINCIPAL-INCOME MATTERS

Although *State Street Trust Co. v. United States*, 263 F.2d 635 (1st Cir. 1959) involved a grantor-trustee of an irrevocable trust, the principles of that case could conceivably apply to a beneficiary-trustee under the appropriate set of facts. The rule to be gleaned from *State Street* is that an overly broad combination of discretion over investments and the allocation of receipts and expenditures could arguably constitute a general power of appointment under IRC section 2041 by enabling the beneficiary-trustee to favor one beneficiary over another by investing in wasting assets or allocating all receipts to income.

§8.5(a) *State Street* Rationale And The Regulations

Although *State Street* has been distinguished by later cases from the First Circuit, the regulations have reserved the right to apply the *State Street* rationale (in seemingly extreme cases). Treas. Reg. §§20.2041-1(b)(1) and 25.2514-1(b)(1) states:

> The mere power of management, investment, custody of assets, or the power to allocate receipts and disbursements as between income and principal, exercisable in a fiduciary capacity, *whereby the holder has no power to enlarge or shift any of the beneficial interests therein except as an incidental consequence of the discharge of such fiduciary duties* is not a power of appointment. Furthermore, the right in a beneficiary of a trust to assent to a periodic accounting, thereby relieving the trustee from further accountability, is not a

power of appointment if the right of assent does not consist of any power or right to enlarge or shift the beneficial interest of any beneficiary therein.

(Emphasis added.)

Practice Point: Make sure that the clause granting trustee powers in the governing instrument states that the trustee must exercise his or her powers in a fiduciary capacity.

Drafting Example:

Trustee must exercise his or her powers solely in a fiduciary capacity and shall possess no powers that would otherwise permit the enlarging or shifting of beneficial interests (except as an incidental consequence of the discharge of such fiduciary duties).

Practice Point: Section 104 of UPIA (1997) permits a trustee to make adjustments to income and principal, and to allocate capital gains to income. This power should not be held by a beneficiary-trustee; rather, the power to adjust should be held by a non-beneficiary trustee, such as an Independent Trustee. *See*, Priv. Letter Rul. 200334025. *See*, Paragraph 7.1(A)(9) of Sample ILIT.

§8.6 TAX CONSEQUENCES OF BENEFICIARY-TRUSTEE'S POWER TO AMEND OR TERMINATE TRUST

An individual beneficiary-trustee's unrestricted power, as a sole trustee or as a co-trustee with another trustee who does not have a substantial and adverse interest in the trust, to amend[16] or terminate a trust of which he or she is a beneficiary, may be a power to affect the beneficial enjoyment of the trust property or its income, and could constitute a general power of appointment for estate and gift tax purposes. Treas. Reg. §§20.2041-1(b)(1) and 25.2514-1(b)(1). *See, Pittsburgh National Bank v. U.S.*, 319 F. Supp. 176 (W.D. Pa. 1970); *Maytag v. U.S.*, 493 F.2d 995 (10th Cir. 1974). *See also*, section 8.1(d), above, concerning "substantial and adverse interest."

---

[16] A beneficiary-trustee's power to amend only the administrative provisions of a trust instrument, which cannot substantially affect the beneficial enjoyment of the trust property or income, is not a power of appointment. Treas. Reg. §§20.2041-1(b)(1) and 25.2514-1(b)(1).

Practice Point: Do not give the beneficiary-trustee, who is an individual, the authority to amend or terminate a trust of which he or she is a beneficiary. Rather, vest the authority exclusively in an independent trustee or a special powerholder, or require judicial approval with objective criteria (that is contained in the trust instrument) as the basis for amendment or termination. *See,* Paragraph 8.2(C) of Sample ILIT.

§8.7 TAX CONSEQUENCES OF DISCLAIMER BY BENEFICIARY-TRUSTEE AND DISCRETIONARY DISTRIBUTIONS

For a disclaimer to be a qualified disclaimer under the Internal Revenue Code, the disclaimed property must pass without any direction on the part of the disclaimant. IRC section 2518(b)(4). If the disclaimant is a beneficiary-trustee and the trust to which the disclaimed property passes gives the disclaiming beneficiary-trustee discretion to distribute the disclaimed property among the trust's other beneficiaries, the disclaimer will not be a qualified disclaimer unless the disclaiming beneficiary-trustee's discretion is limited by an ascertainable standard. Treas. Reg. §25.2518-2(e)(1). *See,* Paragraph 7.1(C)(4) of Sample ILIT.

Practice Point: Before disclaiming the property, the disclaiming beneficiary-trustee could also irrevocably decline (i.e., disclaim[17]) to serve as trustee of the discretionary trust that will hold the disclaimed property. Or, the discretionary trust could contain prophylactic language concerning the effect of such a disclaimer. *See,* Paragraph 8.4 of Sample ILIT.

Practice Point: A disclaiming beneficiary-trustee cannot retain a beneficial interest in the disclaimed property. A special exception exists for qualified disclaimers by a sur-

---

[17] Before accepting the trust, a nominated trustee can disclaim serving as trustee. UTC section 701(b), Restatement 2d section 102, and Restatement 3d section 35. No particular formality is required for the disclaimer to be effective—it may be written or oral (however, a written disclaimer is the preferred method for tax reasons). Once a nominated trustee has accepted the trust, the trustee cannot disclaim serving as trustee but can resign. UTC section 705, Restatement 2d section 106, and Restatement 3d section 36.

viving spouse. A surviving spouse can disclaim an interest in property and still retain a beneficial interest in the disclaimed property, provided the beneficial interest is not discretionary. Treas. Reg. §§25.2518-2(e)(1), (2) and 25.2518-2(e)(5), Examples 4 and 6.[18]

§8.8 TAX CONSEQUENCES OF BENEFICIARY-TRUSTEE'S POWER TO REMOVE AND REPLACE A CO-TRUSTEE

If a beneficiary-trustee has the unrestricted power to remove and replace a co-trustee who holds tax-sensitive powers that, if held by the beneficiary-trustee would constitute a general power of appointment, the beneficiary-trustee will be deemed to hold a general power of appointment. Treas. Reg. §§20.2041-1(b)(1) and 25.2514-1(b)(1). However, the removal and replacement of a co-trustee for reasonable cause by a beneficiary-trustee will not result in the removed co-trustee's tax-sensitive powers being imputed to the beneficiary-trustee. A beneficiary-trustee will also not be deemed to hold a general power of appointment if he or she does not have the unrestricted right to remove a co-trustee and only has the power to remove and replace the co-trustee, under limited conditions which did not exist at the time of the beneficiary-trustee's death. Treas. Reg. §§20.2041-1(b)(3) and 25.2514-1(b)(1). For example, if a beneficiary-trustee can remove and replace a co-trustee (who holds tax sensitive powers) only upon the beneficiary-trustee attaining the age of 50, and the beneficiary-trustee dies before age 50, the beneficiary-trustee is not deemed to hold the tax-sensitive powers of the co-trustee.

A beneficiary-trustee can also safely hold the unrestricted power to remove and replace a co-trustee who holds tax-sensitive powers if the trust instrument restricts the replacement trustee to a person who is not related or subordinate to the beneficiary-trustee, within the meaning of IRC section 672(c), i.e., the replacement trustee is an independent trustee. In Priv. Letter Ruls. 9746007, 9735025, and 9607008, the IRS extended its holding in Rev. Rul. 95-58, 1995-2 C.B. 191 to beneficiaries who were given the unqualified power to remove an existing trustee and appoint a replacement trustee who is

---

[18] *See,* Section 11.4 of Sebastian V. Grassi, Jr., *A Practical Guide to Drafting Marital Deduction Trusts (with Sample Forms and Checklists),* (ALI-ABA, Philadelphia, 2004, Supp. 2006) (800) 253-6397, www.ali-aba.org/aliaba/BK36/.

not related or subordinate to the beneficiaries (within the meaning of IRC section 672(c)). *See*, section 1.7, above.

§8.9 LIMITING A TRUSTEE'S POWER TO AVOID ADVERSE ESTATE, GIFT, AND INCOME TAX TREATMENT

A comprehensive omnibus savings clause that automatically reduces a tax-sensitive power held by a beneficiary-trustee into a safe non-general power and permits a beneficiary-trustee to appoint a special trustee to handle tax-sensitive powers, should be included in the trust agreement. *See*, Priv. Letter Rul. 9036048. *See*, Paragraph 7.1(C)(4) of Sample ILIT.

9

Trustee Selection

CHAPTER OVERVIEW

This chapter examines factors that a grantor should consider in the selecting a trustee for the ILIT, including trustee attributes, duties and liabilities.[1] The chapter also contains a discussion of the non-insured surviving spouse serving as a trustee of the ILIT.

§9.1 SELECTION OF TRUSTEE

In selecting a trustee to administer the ILIT and its subsequent resulting trusts, such as a marital deduction trust and a family (i.e., credit shelter) trust, the grantor needs to consider a myriad of tax and non-tax factors. Because a trust may be in existence for years, if not decades, flexibility concerning successor trustees and co-trustees also needs to be

---

[1] *See,* Sebastian V. Grassi, Jr., "Checklist of Trustee Duties and Common Mistakes Made by Trustees," 31 *Tax Management Estates, Gifts and Trusts Journal* 239 (November 9, 2006); Kimbrough Street, "Growls Or Gratitude? Practical Guidelines For Selection of Individual Trustees and Design of Trustee Succession Plans," 40 *Heckerling Institute on Estate Planning,* Chapter 3 (Matthew Bender/Lexis-Nexis, Newark, NJ 2006); (Roy M. Adams & Charles A. Redd, "How To Select a Trustee—Tax and Non-Tax Considerations," *Cannon Financial Teleconference Series* (Cannon Financial Institute, Inc., Athens, GA January 2004); Laura H. Peebles, "Tax Aspects of Choice of Trustee," 31 *Estate Planning* 43 (January 2004); Julie K. Kwon, "Trustee Succession: Steering The Successor Tide," 9 *ALI-ABA Estate Planning Course Materials* 27 (December 2003); Steve R. Akers, "Twenty-five Things You *Have* to Know About Appointing Trustees," 17 *Probate & Property* 36 (July/August 2003); and Georgiana J. Slade, "The Beneficiary as Trustee: A Pandora's Box," 19 *Tax Management Estates, Gifts and Trusts Journal* 197 (November 10, 1994).

considered. In this regard, the trust instrument should permit an individual trustee to appoint a substitute trustee or co-trustee for property or matters that the individual trustee is unable to handle. *See*, Paragraphs 6.5 and 6.6 of Sample ILIT. Additional flexibility can be achieved by permitting current individual trustees to name their own successors, subject to certain limitations. *See*, Paragraph 6.7 of Sample ILIT. The most significant form of flexibility regarding trustee matters is the ability of the grantor or a beneficiary to remove a trustee and appoint a successor trustee. *See*, Paragraph 6.21 of Sample ILIT.

§9.1(a) Power To Remove And Replace Trustee

If a beneficiary has the unrestricted right to remove a trustee and can appoint himself or herself or a related or subordinate person (within the meaning of IRC section 672(c)) as successor trustee, that beneficiary will be deemed to possess the powers of the trustee, which may result in the beneficiary having a general power of appointment over the trust estate under IRC section 2041. Treas. Reg. §20.2041-1(b). If, however, the beneficiary's power to remove and replace the trustee is limited to appointing someone who is not related or subordinate to the beneficiary, such as an independent trustee or corporate trustee, then the beneficiary is not considered as having a general power of appointment over the trust estate. Rev. Rul. 95-58, 1995-2 C.B. 191; Priv. Letter Rul. 9607008. *See*, Paragraph 8.3(I) of Sample ILIT for a comprehensive definition of an independent trustee. A beneficiary can also be given the power to remove a trustee for reasonable cause, in which case the beneficiary is not bound by the requirements of Rev. Rul. 95-58, and can appoint anyone as the successor trustee. *See*, Paragraph 6.21(A) of Sample ILIT permitting the appointment of a disinterested trustee (as defined in Paragraph 8.3(K) of Sample ILIT). *See* Chapter 8, above, for a discussion of the tax consequences of a beneficiary who serves as trustee.

§9.2 TRUSTEE DUTIES

In selecting a trustee to administer the ILIT and its subsequent resulting trusts, the grantor should be mindful of a trustee's duties.[2] Duties

---

[2] *See*, Charles E. Rounds, Jr., *Loring: A Trustee's Handbook* (2007 Edition) (Aspen Publishers, Inc., New York, NY, 2007), (800) 638-8437, www.aspenpublishers.com;

may be imposed by statute, common law, and the trust instrument. Many, but not all, of the duties imposed by law can be modified by the trust instrument. The paramount duty of a trustee, which underlies all other duties, is his or her fiduciary duty. The trustee stands in a fiduciary relationship with the trust and its beneficiaries. This relationship involves a duty on the part of the trustee to act for the benefit of the trust beneficiaries, and to administer the trust solely in the interest of the trust beneficiaries (and not for the trustee's own benefit).

A corporate fiduciary is familiar and experienced in trust matters; however, few individuals, especially family members, have sufficient experience and expertise to administer a trust on their own. Consequently, the individual trustee will need legal, accounting, investment and tax assistance in fulfilling his or her duties.[3] Thus, there will be additional expenses when an individual serves as the sole trustee. If the individual trustee desires the assistance of a co-trustee, the trust instrument can permit the appointment of a co-trustee, including a corporate trustee, by the individual trustee. *See*, Paragraph 6.5 of Sample ILIT.

The typical duties of a trustee include:

§9.2(a) Duty To Administer The Trust

Once a person has accepted the appointment as a trustee, that person must administer the trust according to its terms as long as that person serves as a trustee—even if that person receives no compensation for serving as a trustee. When the trust contains ambiguous or uncertain terms, the trustee will need professional assistance, and possible judicial interpretation of the trust instrument. A trustee may not

---

Charles E. Rounds, 853 T.M., *Fiduciary Liability of Trustees and Personal Representatives* (BNA Inc., Washington, DC), for a discussion of trustee duties, attributes, and liabilities. *See also,* Uniform Trust Code, http://www.law.upenn.edu/bll/ulc/uta/2005final.htm ***or*** http://www.nccusl.org; *Restatement (Second) of Trusts* (ALI, Philadelphia, 1959); *Restatement (Third) of Trusts (Prudent Investor Rule)* (ALI, Philadelphia, 1992); and *Restatement (Third) of Trusts* (ALI, Philadelphia, 2003); Lauren J. Wolven and Jeffrey A. Zaluda, "Guidance to Help Trustees of Personal Trusts Avoid Liability," 33 *Estate Planning* 27 (October 2006); and Lauren J. Wolven and Jeffrey A. Zaluda, "Practical Strategies for Managing a Trustee's Liability Exposure," 33 *Estate Planning* 31 (September 2006).

[3] *See*, I. Mark Cohen, "Appreciating Individual Trustees," 145 *Trusts & Estates* 32 (December 2006).

resign unless permitted by the terms of the trust, by consent of the beneficiaries, or by a court. *See*, Paragraph 6.3 of Sample ILIT.

§9.2(b) Duty Of Loyalty To The Trust And Its Beneficiaries

The trustee has the duty to administer the trust solely in the interests of the beneficiaries, to be honest, to avoid conflicts of interest and self dealing, and to act in good faith. This is the fundamental fiduciary duty of a trustee.

Common examples of potential self dealing include:

- Sale or lease of property to the trust by the trustee (including the trustee's own securities);
- Purchase of trust property by the trustee at public sale or auction;
- Lease of trust property to the trustee;
- Loan by the trustee to the trust;
- Loan by the trust to the trustee;
- Investment of the trust's assets in the trustee's own securities;
- Employment of agents related to the trustee;
- Personal use of the trust property by the trustee;
- Use of the trust property by the trustee for personal profit; and
- Trustee's engagement in a business that competes with the trust.

These impermissible forms of self dealing and conflict of interest can be waived by the express terms of the trust, by statute, with the consent of the beneficiaries (after full disclosure by the trustee), or by court approval (after full disclosure by the trustee). *See*, Paragraphs 6.19, 7.1(A)(2), 7.1(A)(5), and 7.1(A)(10) of Sample ILIT.

§9.2(c) Duty To Administer The Trust With Reasonable Skill And Care

A trustee must administer the trust with same care, skill, and caution as a prudent person would in dealing with his own property. If the trustee has special skills or is named trustee on the basis of representation of special skills or expertise, the trustee is under a duty to use those skills. *See*, Paragraph 6.18 of Sample ILIT.

§9.2(d) Prudent Investor Rule

The trustee has the duty to prudently invest and reinvest trust assets.[4] This obligation includes the duty to diversify the trust's assets and investments to reduce the risk of loss. This duty may be modified by the grantor.[5] *See*, Paragraph 7.1(A)(1) of Sample ILIT. In the ILIT context, this duty is sometimes referred to as trust owned life insurance ("TOLI") management,[6] and may require the trustee to delegate TOLI management to a life insurance specialist, such as a fee only life insurance advisor.

---

[4] The duty to prudently invest assets also includes the duty to prudently sell assets. *See*, John Jeffrey Pankauski and Robert E. Conner, "Looking for the Exits: A Fiduciary's Sell Strategy Under The Prudent Investor Act," 20 *Probate & Property* 40 (November/December 2006).

[5] *See*, Paul R. Lipton and Susan Fleischner Kornspan, "Expansion of Trustee's Authority May Not Relax the Standard of Care," 29 *Estate Planning* 343 (July 2002), where the authors discuss trust provisions that enlarge the trustee's authority or exonerate the trustee, and conclude that such provisions may or may not change the standard of care owed by the trustee in light of the Prudent Investor Rule and case law.

[6] *See*, Stephan Leimberg, "TOLI Risk Management at Litigation Crossroads," *Steve Leimberg's Estate Planning Newsletter # 1110* (April 12, 2007) at http://www.leimbergservices.com; Stephan Leimberg, "Trust-Owned Life Insurance—Risk Management Guidance for Professional Advisors," *Steve Leimberg's Estate Planning Newsletter # 891* (November 16, 2005) at www.leimbergservices.com ("Leimberg Newsletter #891"). *See, also*, Kathryn A. Ballsun, Patrick J. Collins and Dieter Jurkat, "Trustee Administration of Life Insurance (Part 1 of 4)," 31 *ACTEC Journal* 280 (Spring 2006); E. Randolph Whitelaw and Richard W. Weber, "Trust-Owned Life Insurance: Risk Management Guidance for Fiduciaries," 32 *Estate Planning* 14 (September 2005) ("Whitelaw and Weber"); Mark A. Teitelbaum, "Trust Owned Life Insurance: Is It An Accident Waiting To Happen?," *National Underwriter Life & Health* 38 (May 17, 2004) ("Teitelbaum"); and C. Markham Whitelaw and William C. Ries, "Managing Trust Owned Life Insurance—Revisited," 138 *Trust & Estates* 38 (April 1999) ("Whitelaw & Ries"), where the authors discuss potential TOLI problems, such as: (i) underperforming policies, (ii) policies that are insufficient for the insured's current needs, (iii) newer products that may be more cost efficient, (iv) new products and riders that may offer better options, (v) policies scheduled for a big increase in premiums, (vi) trustee negligence in maintaining the current life insurance policy, (vii) bad trustee investment decisions concerning the retention of a variable life insurance product, (viii) trustee negligence in poor life insurance design or an improper policy, and (ix) trustee negligence in poor selection of a life insurance agent.

"For skilled and unskilled trustee, TOLI management should include policy monitoring, suitability and restructure criteria....Four R's describe the TOLI management process—review, restore, restructure or replace." Whitelaw & Ries at 38.

§9.2(e) Duty To Give Notices, Furnish Information, And Communicate With The Trust Beneficiaries

The trustee has the duty to keep the beneficiaries of a trust reasonably informed of the trust and its administration. This will require the trustee to give notices, furnish information, and communicate with the trust beneficiaries. This duty corresponds with the duty to

---

"A trustee, skilled or unskilled, can accept a guaranteed death benefit policy and transfer all premium adequacy risk to the underwriting carrier, or can retain premium adequacy risk by accepting a non-guaranteed death benefit policy and actively managing policy values. Acceptance of premium adequacy risk implies the grantor's approval to do so, expertise in TOLI risk management, and an affirmative election by the trustee to manage the insurance investment consistent with the trust's objectives. If a trustee does not obtain the grantor's approval, or lacks TOLI risk-based procedures or expertise in policy evaluation, the trustee must recommend restructuring to a guaranteed death benefit policy.... The critical asset management considerations applicable to insurance trusts are product suitability, premium adequacy, and carrier selection. For guaranteed policies, premium adequacy is not a risk, but the carrier's size and ratings must be evaluated. For non-guaranteed policies, premium adequacy is the obvious risk that mandates active management using TOLI-specific risk management procedures and expertise in evaluating premium adequacy. Actuarial evaluation must be used for all determinations regarding premium adequacy, as well as policy acceptance, management and restructuring." Whitelaw and Weber at 16.

Teitelbaum recommends that life insurance agents help trustees in:

• "Setting goals and standards regarding trust owned life insurance. This includes examining life insurance policies and comparing these to alternatives.... Examining client goals and beneficiary needs.

• Examining policy funding and determining if additional funding is necessary. This includes considering whether or not a client's gifting capacity is able to support future premium needs.

• Considering life insurance performance: Will UL [universal life] policies or participating whole life policies perform within a reasonable tolerance of the original illustrations or new client goals? With VL [variable life] insurance, do the subaccounts need to be re-examined based on evolving client needs and subaccount performance?" Teitelbaum at 43.

"The annual performance monitoring questions that should be asked and answered by trust fiduciaries to assure that the trust does not receive too little or pay too much for life insurance coverage include the following:

1. Has the policy inadvertently become a MEC?

2. Should a split-dollar agreement be modified to comply with the most recent split-dollar rules?

3. What is the impact of demutualization on the economic results of trust held coverage?

account. It also corresponds with the duty to monitor a trust beneficiary's need to determine if distributions should be made to that beneficiary, and to determine if a beneficiary's interest in the trust has terminated (e.g., the beneficiary has reached a specified age and is no longer entitled to trust distributions, or the beneficiary has died). *See*, Paragraph 6.20 of Sample ILIT.

§9.2(f) Duty To Collect, Control, And Use Reasonable Care And Skill To Preserve And Protect, Trust Property

This duty corresponds with the duty to prudently invest the trust property.

§9.2(g) Duty To Account To The Beneficiaries

This duty may be modified by the grantor, but not eliminated. *See*, Paragraph 7.9 of Sample ILIT.

§9.2(h) Duty To Keep Accurate Records

A trustee must keep clear and accurate records of the trust's administration. This will be helpful for preparing annual accountings, requesting reimbursements, etc. *See*, Paragraph 7.9(B) of Sample ILIT.

§9.2(i) Duty To Identify And Separate Trust Property

The trustee has the duty to identify trust property, and to not commingle trust property with the trustee's own property, or with the property of other trusts.

---

4. If the policy was issued as other than "preferred risk," has the insured stopped smoking or has there been an improvement in the insured's health?

5. Are there recently issued policies that might provide a better return for the trust's beneficiaries and if so, what are the costs of replacing present coverage?

6. Is there a policy that might lapse and if so, what are the tax and other economic consequences?" ¶5.03 of Howard M. Zaritsky & Stephan R. Leimberg, *Tax Planning With Life Insurance Analysis With Forms—2d Edition*, Warren Gorham & Lamont, Boston, Massachusetts (Supp. 2007).

§9.2(j) Duty To Enforce Trust Claims

The trustee has the duty to enforce claims of the trust (including claims against any predecessor trustee or executor), and to defend the trust against adverse claims that may result in a loss to the trust estate.

§9.2(k) Duty To Make Decisions Concerning Discretionary Distributions

The trustee has a duty to determine whether discretionary distributions should be made, and under what circumstances.[7] This corresponds with the duty to participate in the administration of the trust, and the duty not to delegate.

§9.2(l) Duty To Uphold And Defend The Trust

The trustee has the duty to uphold and defend the trust according to its terms and the grantor's intent.

§9.2(m) Duty To Participate In The Administration Of The Trust

The trustee has the duty to participate in the administration of the trust with the other co-trustees, and to prevent a breach of trust by another co-trustee; and if necessary, to compel a co-trustee to redress a breach of trust.

§9.2(n) Duty Of Impartiality

The trustee has the duty to treat beneficiaries impartially and fairly, both individually and by class, and to balance the competing and conflicting interest of the beneficiaries, such as the income beneficiaries and the remainder beneficiaries, and multiple beneficiaries in the same class.[8] As part of the duty of impartiality, the trustee must con-

---

[7] *See,* J. Stoddard Hayes, Jr. and Bernard T. Wall, "Fiduciary Discretion —Where is the Better Part of Valor?," 132 *Trusts & Estates* 8 (May 1993). *See also, Restatement (Third) of Trusts* section 50 concerning discretionary distributions and what factors a trustee may consider.

[8] *See,* Terry L. Turnipseed, "Tools for Better Balancing the Interests of Income Beneficiaries and Remaindermen," 28 *Tax Management Estates, Gifts and Trusts Journal* 244 (September 11, 2003); and Richard M. Horwood and Jeffrey A. Zaluda, "A Trustee's Balancing Act: Income and Remainder Beneficiaries' Rights," 30 *Estate*

sider the interests and the needs of all the trust beneficiaries when making investment decisions.

§9.2(o) Duty To Make Property Productive

The trustee has the duty to use reasonable care and skill to make the trust property productive. This duty corresponds with the duty to prudently invest the trust property, and may be modified by the grantor.

§9.2(p) Duty Not To Delegate

The trustee has the duty to give personal attention to the trust, and to not delegate to others the performance of any acts the trustee can reasonably be expected to perform personally, such as acts involving the exercise of judgment and discretion.

The Uniform Prudent Investor Act permits a trustee to delegate investment and management functions as is prudent under the circumstances.[9] As previously mentioned, it may be prudent for an ILIT trustee who lacks the expertise to manage TOLI, to delegate that function to a specialist. *See,* section 9.2(d), above.

§9.2(q) Duty To Determine Principal And Income, And To Pay Income

The trustee has the duty to separate income from principal, and to pay income to the income beneficiaries at reasonable intervals. *See,* Paragraphs 7.1(A)(9) and (13) of Sample ILIT.

§9.2(r) Duty Of Confidentiality

The trustee has the duty to keep the affairs of the trust and its beneficiaries confidential, unless otherwise required by law or permitted by the trust instrument. This duty applies to the identity and interests of the beneficiaries, the terms of the trust, and the nature of the trust's assets.

Planning 12 (January 2003) where the authors discuss a trustee's duties to income and remainder beneficiaries, and the trustee's need to consider: (i) the grantor's preference regarding distributions, (ii) relevant law, and (iii) the avoidance of conflicts between the beneficiaries and the trustee.

[9] *See,* Ronald A. Sages, "The Prudent Investor Rule and the Duty Not to Delegate," 134 *Trusts & Estates* 22 (May 1995).

§9.2(s) Duty To Follow Instructions Of Superior Powerholder

The trustee has the duty to act in accordance with the proper exercise of a person's power to control the trustee's actions, such as following the directions of the grantor (as concerns a revocable trust), trust protector, special powerholder, or a beneficiary holding a currently exercisable inter vivos general power of appointment over the trust assets. *See,* Paragraphs 4.2 and 8.2(C) of Sample ILIT.

§9.3 TRUSTEE LIABILITIES

Trustee liability is another factor to be considered by the grantor when selecting a trustee. For example, an individual trustee may be exposed to personal liability for a breach of his or her duty that is owed to the trust beneficiaries. An individual trustee may, however, be judgment proof (or close to it). Corporate trustees, on the other hand, are accountable, regulated, and have liability and fidelity insurance, as well as sufficient assets to satisfy a judgment for a breach of duty.

§9.3(a) Typical Trustee Liabilities

Typical trustee liabilities[10] include the following:

- Environmental matters[11];
- Taxes;
- Tort liability (in the absence of liability insurance and sufficient trust assets);
- Contractual liability (in the absence of an individual trustee disclosing his or her trustee capacity);
- Surcharge for breach of duty, i.e., for failure to perform any of the duties described in section 9.2, above;
- A co-trustee's breach of duty;
- A predecessor trustee's breach of duty;
- An agent's errors and omissions;
- Violation of securities law;

---

[10] *See,* G. Michael Richwine, "How Individual Trustees Can Avoid Liability and Breaches of Trust," 24 *Estate Planning* 481 (December 1997).

[11] *See,* George C. Weir, "Can Fiduciaries Avoid Liability Under Environmental Law?," 19 *Estate Planning* 224 (July/August 1992).

• Violation of consumer protection laws;

• Liability as a title holder; and

• Criminal liability.

§9.4 TRUSTEE ATTRIBUTES

In selecting an individual or corporate trustee, the following factors and characteristics concerning the proposed person should be considered by the grantor:

• The prospective individual trustee's honesty and integrity.

• The prospective individual trustee's impartiality and objectivity.

• The prospective individual trustee's knowledge and experience concerning investments, the prudent investor rule, tax issues, etc., or the ability to recognize when to hire advisers with such knowledge and expertise.

• The prospective individual trustee's administrative capabilities and inclinations, or the ability to recognize when to hire advisers with such knowledge and expertise.

• The prospective trustee's availability, permanence, and continuity. Will the prospective individual trustee be able to devote sufficient time to the affairs of the trust? Will the trustee's location be distant from the trust beneficiaries? Most beneficiaries prefer to deal with a trustee (or trust officer) who is close by. What is the prospective individual trustee's health and age, particularly if the trust term is greater than the prospective individual trustee's life expectancy or period of good health and mental acuity?

• The prospective individual trustee's reliability and ability to handle significant responsibility.

• The prospective trustee's knowledge of the grantor's family, the family's dynamics, the special needs of a disabled or incapacitated beneficiary, the family-owned business, and the ability to remain impartial when resolving family disputes.

• The prospective trustee's ability to not be influenced by an overly aggressive or manipulative beneficiary.

• The prospective trustee's compensation requirements. Corporate trustees generally charge a fee based on a percentage of the trust's assets. In smaller trusts, that can be very expensive, especially when the trustee has a minimum fee charge. Family members often serve without fees or for a modest fee.

• The prospective trustee's citizenship and residence and their potential income tax consequences to the trust.

§9.5 INSURED'S SPOUSE AS BENEFICIARY-TRUSTEE OF THE CONTINGENT MARITAL DEDUCTION TRUST

§9.5(a) General Power Of Appointment Marital Deduction Trust

If the ILIT contains a marital deduction trust that is a general power of appointment trust described in IRC section 2056(b)(5), there should be no adverse transfer tax consequences to the grantor's spouse while serving as sole trustee of that trust after the grantor's death; all of the income is required to be distributed to the spouse and all of the property will be included in the spouse's gross estate under IRC section 2041.

§9.5(b) QTIP Marital Deduction Trust

If the ILIT contains a marital deduction trust that is a QTIP trust, there may be adverse transfer tax consequences to the grantor's spouse if he or she serves as the sole trustee of the QTIP trust.

The potential for adverse tax consequences arises if the grantor's executor elects to make a partial QTIP election as to part of the marital trust. The partial QTIP election may accomplish nothing if the trustee-spouse has the right to discretionary distributions of principal from the non-elected portion of the marital trust. This is because the spouse will hold a general power of appointment (under IRC section 2041) over the non-elected portion and that property will be taxed in the spouse's estate, thus subjecting the non-elected portion of the QTIP trust to double estate taxation.

If the grantor's executor makes a reverse QTIP election under IRC section 2652(a)(3) to use the grantor's GST tax exemption (or to preserve the ILIT's GST inclusion ratio of zero), the trustee-spouse should not possess any powers over the QTIP trust that would be treated as a general power of appointment under IRC section 2041. If the reverse QTIP property is includable in the spouse's gross estate under IRC section 2041 (instead of IRC section 2044(b)(1)(A)), the spouse will be treated as the "new" transferor for GST tax purposes, thus wasting the deceased grantor's GST tax exemption.

> **Practice Point:** A more basic issue is whether the prohibited powers would cause the QTIP trust to be classified as a general power of appointment marital deduction trust under IRC section 2056(b)(5). If so, no reverse QTIP election can be made, thus losing the opportunity to allocate the grantor's unused GST tax exemption (or to preserve the ILIT's GST inclusion ratio of zero by allocating the ILIT property to the reverse QTIP trust). Additionally, a partial QTIP election or *Clayton* contingent QTIP election may not be available, thus losing post-mortem planning opportunities, such as the previously taxed property credit under IRC section 2013 or equalizing the spouses' estates. *But see*, Priv. Letter Rul. 20024015, where the IRS permitted a QTIP election for a trust that gave the surviving spouse a testamentary general power of appointment. In that letter ruling, the IRS stated that "at Taxpayer's death, the value of the qualified share will be includible in Taxpayer's gross estate under section 2041, and Taxpayer will be the transferor of this value for generation-skipping transfer tax purposes."

§9.5(c) Sole Trustee Of Marital Trust

If the grantor's spouse serves as sole trustee of the marital deduction trust, and has the power to withdraw trust principal (even though limited by an ascertainable standard for federal estate tax purposes), nevertheless, the IRS may assert that the spouse holds the power (for income tax purposes only) to vest the corpus in him or herself, and as such, is taxable on any on gain recognized by the trust, under IRC section 678(a). This income tax effect, if desired, could be used to reduce the size of the spouse's estate. The spouse could reduce the estate by using his or her own money to pay the trust's income taxes. *See*, section 8.3, above.

§9.5(d) QDOT Marital Trust

The QDOT rules do not prohibit the noncitizen surviving spouse from serving as a co-trustee of the QDOT marital trust. The only mandatory role of the U.S. trustee is to withhold the QDOT tax imposed on distributions to the surviving spouse. IRC section

2056A(a)(1)(B). However, if the noncitizen surviving spouse is a co-trustee who has the authority to control all substantial decisions of the trust (i.e., control all decisions other than ministerial decisions concerning the trust), and the noncitizen surviving spouse subsequently becomes a non-U.S. resident, the QDOT may be classified as a foreign trust for U.S. income tax purposes. IRC sections 7701(a)(30)(E) and (31)(B); Treas. Reg. §301.7701-7(d).

§9.5(e) Second Marriages

Having the grantor's spouse serve as sole trustee of the marital deduction trust may not be appropriate in second marriages when there are children from the first marriage. Particularly in a second marriage, the interests of the spouse and children may conflict. In this situation, an independent trustee may be better able to carry out the grantor's intent as expressed in the trust.

§9.6 INSURED'S SPOUSE AS BENEFICIARY-TRUSTEE OF THE ILIT OR CREDIT SHELTER TRUST

The issues discussed in Chapter 8 (concerning tax-sensitive powers regarding the beneficiary-trustee) apply to the surviving spouse if he or she serves as a beneficiary-trustee of a non-marital deduction trust, such as the ILIT or resulting credit shelter trust.[12] If the spouse is a grantor of the ILIT, an insured under the ILIT, or a donor of property to the ILIT (other than merely consenting to gift splitting under IRC section 2513), the issues discussed in Chapters 2, 3, and 4 (concerning income, gift, and estate tax) should be reviewed and the spouse should not serve as a trustee of the ILIT. Also, the issues discussed in section 9.5(d), above, concerning foreign trust status, also apply to a non-U.S. citizen surviving spouse and the credit shelter trust. *See*, also, section 1.3, above and section 10.15, below.

Another reason for prohibiting the spouse from serving as a trustee of the ILIT is the lack of flexibility concerning contingent *Crummey* withdrawal right beneficiaries. An independent trustee can be given the power to make discretionary distributions of trust income and principal to the contingent beneficiaries, thereby obviating an IRS

---

[12] *See,* Peter B. Tiernan, "What Powers Over a Credit Shelter Trust Can the Spouse Possess?," 23 *Estate Planning*

attack based on naked *Crummey* withdrawal rights. Depending on the relationship of the beneficiaries to the spouse, the spouse may not be able to hold discretionary distribution powers, and may be limited to holding trust distribution powers limited to an ascertainable standard, which could be more easily enforced by a disgruntled beneficiary.

> **Practice Point:** In no event should the grantor's spouse serve as a trustee of an ILIT that holds a second to die policy that insures the grantor and the spouse.

§9.7 THE INDEPENDENT TRUSTEE

An independent trustee is defined in IRC sections 672(c) and 674(c). *See,* section 2.6, above.

§9.7(a) Using An Independent Trustee

Use of an independent trustee avoids the imputation of the trustee's powers to the beneficiaries and permits greater flexibility for trust distributions. *See*, Paragraph 4.1(A) of Sample ILIT. Also, unlike a beneficiary-trustee (such as the grantor's spouse), an independent trustee can possess tax sensitive powers and make discretionary income and principal distributions to a beneficiary without adverse tax consequences to the independent trustee. The IRS sanctions the unfettered removal and replacement of an incumbent trustee if the replacement trustee is an independent trustee. Thus, the grantor, a beneficiary, or a beneficiary-trustee can be given the power to remove an incumbent trustee for any reason, and replace that trustee with an independent trustee without fear that the IRS will treat the power of removal and replacement as an impermissible power held by the grantor, beneficiary, or beneficiary-trustee (as the case may be). Rev. Rul. 95-58, 1995-2 C.B. 191. Priv. Letter Rul. 9607008. *See*, Paragraph 6.21 of Sample ILIT concerning the removal and replacement of a trustee.

> **Drafting Example:**
>
> *An "Independent Trustee" means a person who is not related or subordinate (within the meaning of IRC section 672 (c)) to me or to any beneficiary with respect to the trust in question.*
>
> **Drafting Example:**
>
> *At any time after Settlor's death, the then surviving adult beneficiaries who are sui juris and not incapacitated, and then eligible to receive current income from the trust, acting by unanimous written consent, may remove the trust's Trustee, for reasonable cause, and*

> *may, in the absence of a nominated successor Trustee then willing or able to serve or continue to serve as Trustee, appoint a successor Trustee(s), who is an Independent Trustee; provided, no person, acting alone, may remove or name a Trustee of a trust that would be included in that person's gross estate solely by reason of this right of removal or appointment.*

§9.7(b) Tax-Sensitive Powers Held By Independent Trustee

As previously mentioned, an independent trustee can possess tax-sensitive powers without adverse tax consequences. *See*, Paragraph 7.1(C)(4) of Sample ILIT regarding the appointment of an independent trustee to exercise certain tax-sensitive powers.

§9.7(c) Second Marriages

An independent trustee is appropriate in second-marriage situations. *See*, section 9.5(e), above.

§9.7(d) QDOTs

An independent trustee is appropriate for marital deduction trusts that are QDOTs (provided the independent trustee is a U.S. trustee).

> **Practice Point:** Within the definition of an "independent trustee," the following individuals are ***not*** related or subordinate parties under IRC section 672(c), as concerns the powerholder: the powerholder's nieces, nephews, grandparents, spouses of children, spouses of grandchildren, spouses of brothers and sisters, and partners of the power holder. However, the following individuals, if they ***are*** a non-adverse party, are treated as a related and subordinate to the powerholder: the powerholder's spouse if living with the powerholder, the powerholder's father, mother, issue, brother or sister, and certain employees of the powerholder or his or her business. Treas. Reg. §1.672(c)-1.

§9.8 INSURED'S SPOUSE AND THE INDEPENDENT TRUSTEE AS CO-TRUSTEES

Having an independent trustee serve as a co-trustee of the marital deduction and credit shelter trusts with the surviving spouse provides flexibility and permits the surviving spouse to have some control, as a co-trustee, over the affairs of the trust. A co-trustee arrangement of this type is always appropriate, if desired by the client; and especially appropriate in second-marriage situations. In such instance, all discretionary powers and all tax-sensitive powers must be exclusively vested in the independent trustee.

Drafting Example:

The power to make discretionary distributions of principal or income not limited by an ascertainable standard shall be vested exclusively in (and exercisable only by) an Independent Trustee. If the incumbent trustee is not an Independent Trustee, the incumbent trustee may appoint an Independent Trustee to serve as co-Trustee with the incumbent trustee. The Independent Trustee so appointed shall serve concurrently with the appointing trustee until the appointing trustee resigns, dies, or becomes incapacitated and is succeeded by a successor trustee (as nominated under this trust agreement).

10

Checklist Of Issues For Drafting An ILIT

CHAPTER OVERVIEW

This book assumes that the practitioner has some experience and knowledge concerning estate planning and trust drafting. This chapter considers, in a checklist format, twenty-five issues that a practitioner should consider when drafting an ILIT.[1] Some drafting issues that are discussed in other chapters are not reiterated here.[2] Nearly half of the checklist items deal with a beneficiary's right to withdraw gifts made to the ILIT. Properly structuring and administering the beneficiary's withdrawal right is crucial if a gift to the ILIT is to be eligible for the gift tax annual exclusion. The Chapter also discusses the easily overlooked tax trap created by reciprocal trusts, reciprocal withdrawal rights, and reciprocal powers of appointment, and provides suggested solutions to deal with these problems. To avoid the three-year rule of IRC section 2035, the ILIT should be drafted and funded prior to the ILIT trustee's submission of an application for life insurance. However, a non-binding test application by the insured (typically showing "an

[1] Additional drafting issues are scattered throughout this book.

[2] For example: (i) the ILIT should be irrevocable *(see,* section 1.1, above), (ii) the beneficiaries should have *Crummey* withdrawal rights (*see,* section 3.5, above), and (iii) the *Crummey* withdrawal rights should lapse in a manner that does not constitute a taxable release (*see,* sections 3.11, 3.12, 3.13, 4.6, and 5.21, above). *See also,* Chapters 11 and 12, below, for additional drafting issues.

ILIT to be drafted" as the potential owner) should avoid an IRC section 2035 issue. *See*, section 4.12, above.

§10.1 AVOID ETIPS AND TAXABLE RELEASES—LIMIT THE SPOUSE'S *CRUMMEY* WITHDRAWAL RIGHT TO FIVE-BY-FIVE AND 60 DAYS AFTER THE CONTRIBUTION

The spouse's withdrawal right should be limited to the five-by-five safe harbor amount of IRC section 2514(e) and the withdrawal right should lapse 60 days after the date of contribution (not 60 days after notice). This will avoid the GST estate tax inclusion period ("ETIP") issue for the spouse. *See*, section 5.17, above. Also, the spouse should not be given a hanging power of withdrawal since it does not come within the ETIP safe harbor rules set forth in Treas. Reg. §26.2632-1(c)(2)(ii). Another concern, as previously mentioned in Chapters 3 and 4, above, is the estate tax problem of the spouse's lapse of a withdrawal right greater than five by five in conjunction with the spouse's retained interest in the trust as a beneficiary. IRC sections 2035, 2036, 2037, and 2038. *See*, Paragraphs 3.1(A) and 3.2(D) of Sample ILIT.

§10.2 AVOID NAKED *CRUMMEY* WITHDRAWAL RIGHTS

The IRS frowns upon beneficiaries who have *Crummey* withdrawal rights and are discretionary beneficiaries or contingent remainder beneficiaries. TAMs 9731004, 9045002, 8727003. Therefore, if possible, draft the ILIT so that there are multiple present-interest beneficiaries, who hold a current income interest, a current right to principal distributions, or a vested remainder interest. Fortunately for taxpayers, the Tax Court disagrees with the IRS concerning contingent remainder beneficiaries who hold *Crummey* withdrawal rights, and the Tax Court has permitted contingent remainder beneficiaries (grandchildren, who would take only if their parents (the current income beneficiaries) predeceased them) to be recognized as valid *Crummey* beneficiaries for whom the gift tax annual exclusion was available to the grantor. *Estate of Maria Cristofani v. Commissioner*, 97 T.C. 74 (1991), *acq. in result only*, 1996-2 C.B. 1. *See*, section 15.4(g), below. The IRS has, however, stated that it will not recognize *Crummey* withdrawal rights granted to persons whose only interest in the ILIT is the *Crummey* withdrawal right itself, i.e., the person has what is commonly referred to as a "naked" Crummey withdrawal right.[3] TAM 9628004. *But see, Estate of Lieselotte Kohlsaat,* T.C. Memo 1997-212 (1997) (gift tax annual exclusion available to 16 contingent remainder beneficiaries who held *Crummey* withdrawal rights and no present interest in the trust itself other than the withdrawal rights); and Priv. Letter Rul. 9030005 (gift tax annual exclu-

---

[3] "A memorandum advising or describing gifts to an irrevocable life insurance trust usually will not require preparation of a covered opinion [under IRS Circular 230], because, although the arrangement may very substantially reduce estate and GST taxes, it does so merely by obtaining the general tax benefits intended by Congress and the Code for lifetime gifts of appreciating assets. Additionally, the IRS has no reasonable basis for opposing the desired tax treatment of such gifts.

There are, however, several situations in which a practitioner may need to prepare a covered opinion [under Circular 230] regarding the creation and funding of an irrevocable life insurance trust. First, although the IRS has approved of the use of *Crummey* withdrawal powers to give a beneficiary a present interest in contributions to a trust so that they qualify for the gift tax annual exclusion, it has repeatedly questioned the efficacy of so-called naked *Crummey* powers, which are held by beneficiaries who lack a significant current interest in the trust. [*See,* Rev. Rul. 73-405, 1973-2 C.B. 321; Rev. Rul. 85-88, 1985-2 C.B. 201; Rev. Rul. 81-7, 1981-1 C.B. 474.] The IRS has lost all of the cases in which this was the principal issue, but they have not acquiesced and there is no reason to believe that they will not continue to challenge the claiming of the exclusion for a gift of a naked *Crummey* power. [*See, Estate of Holland v. Commissioner,* TC Memo. 1997-302; *Estate of Kohlsaat v. Commissioner,* TC Memo. 1997-212; *Estate of Cristofani v. Commissioner,* 97 TC 74 (1991).] Furthermore, the IRS certainly has at least a reasonable basis for asserting that a naked *Crummey* power does not create a present interest. Thus, a covered opinion may be required when recommending the use of a naked *Crummey* power as part of a plan to multiply the available gift tax annual exclusions.[Citation omitted.]

Second, in a 1989 private letter ruling, the IRS ruled against the validity of a so-called hanging *Crummey* power. [*See,* Priv. Letter Rul. 8901004.] While this ruling appears relevant only on the specific documents reviewed in that ruling, it may still be appropriate to provide a covered opinion when advising use of a hanging *Crummey* power. [*See,* section 3.13, above, for a discussion of hanging *Crummey* powers.]

A covered opinion [under Circular 230] may also be required if the insured uses any unusual method to finance the purchase of life insurance by the trust. The income and gift tax treatment of a low-interest or interest-free loan is already well established, as are the treatment of a split-dollar arrangement between the insured (or another person) and the trust. More inventive arrangements, including policy provisions with springing cash values, however, may require a covered opinion to evaluate the relevant legal issues." Howard M. Zaritsky, *Practical Estate Planning Under Circular 230,* ¶3.02[2][b][ii], (Warren, Gorham & Lamont of RIA, Boston, MA, 2005).

See, Form 3-5 in section ¶3.03[4] of *Id.* for a sample covered opinion under Circular 230 regarding an ILIT with a naked hanging *Crummey* withdrawal right.

sion available to grantor's children who were discretionary beneficiaries of "special needs"[4] principal distributions and who held contingent remainder interests that vested only if the grantor's wife (their mother) predeceased the grantor). *See*, section 15.4(j), below. *See*, Paragraph 3.1(A) of Sample ILIT.

> **Practice Point:** A cautious practitioner may want to consider giving the contingent remainder beneficiaries (such as the grandchildren) a certain percentage of the ILIT after the death of the surviving spouse (such as 10% to the grandchildren (or if deceased to the grandchild's estate) and 90% to the children), or a specific devise of $12,000 (the gift tax annual exclusion amount for 2007) to each "unvested" contingent remainder beneficiary who has a *Crummey* withdrawal right. This way the contingent remainder beneficiaries will have a vested interest in the ILIT.[5] Of course any distributions to beneficiaries who are skip persons (such as grandchildren) may attract GST tax if the ILIT is not GST tax exempt, but that may be a small price to pay to give the contingent remainder beneficiaries *Crummey* withdrawal rights and thus provide the donor with more gift tax annual exclusions. Alternatively, make the ILIT a GST trust so that the grandchildren are more than contingent remainder beneficiaries. Another way to avoid the IRS' "naked" power argument is to give all *Crummey* withdrawal right holders a discretionary right to

---

[4] "Special needs" refers to the minor beneficiaries' needs related to travel, camping trips, theater, ballet, music lessons, special schooling, or instruction to enrich their lives. The term does not refer to distributions for the beneficiaries' regular support, health, education, and maintenance while they are minors. Nor does the term refer to distributions that are made to a disabled beneficiary under a so-called "special needs trust."

[5] "If the prospective grantor does not want to grant a current income and principal interest or a vested remainder interest in the trust to a potential powerholder, that powerholder should at least be given a contingent remainder interest in order to fall within the facts of *Cristofani* and *Kohlsaat*. If the grantor is not willing to give the powerholder a contingent remainder interest, then the grantor at least should give the powerholder a discretionary income and principal interest. Although the Service will not allow the annual exclusion in that context, a court might." Donald O. Jansen, "Giving Birth To, Caring For, And Feeding The Irrevocable Life Insurance Trust," 41 *Real Property, Probate and Trust Journal* 571, 606-607 (Fall 2006).

receive income and principal distributions during the grantor's lifetime. *See,* Paragraph 4.1(A) of Sample ILIT.

Caution: If the surviving spouse has an intervening limited power of appointment over the trust corpus (such as a testamentary limited power of appointment over the contingent marital deduction trust or the credit shelter trust), the draftsperson may want to limit that power to prevent the potential divestment of a contingent remainder beneficiary's specific devise.

§10.3 USE TIERED *CRUMMEY* WITHDRAWAL RIGHTS

Consider providing for tiered withdrawal rights by which the spouse may withdraw the gift contribution first (up to five by five), and the children (and grandchildren) second as to the balance of the gift contribution. Tiered withdrawal rights make notice easier, particularly if the annual gift contributions are limited in amount. Tiered *Crummey* withdrawal rights also make it easier to ascertain the consenting spouse's interest for gift splitting under IRC section 2513. Priv. Letter Rul. 200422051. *See,* Paragraph 3.1(A) of Sample ILIT.

Practice Point: If the spouse has a tiered *Crummey* withdrawal right and the grantor's contribution is less than the five-by-five amount, the consenting spouse cannot gift split that contribution amount. The inability to gift split also precludes treating each spouse as a transferor of ½ of that contribution amount for allocation of GST tax exemption. Treas. Reg. §26.2652-1(a)(4).

§10.4 MAKE *CRUMMEY* WITHDRAWAL RIGHTS ASCERTAINABLE

Ensure that the amount subject to the *Crummey* withdrawal right is ascertainable.

§10.4(a) Multiple Beneficiaries With *Crummey* Withdrawal Rights

If there are multiple beneficiaries holding a *Crummey* withdrawal right over the same gift amount, make sure that each donee's right of withdrawal over the gift amount is pro rata, otherwise each donee's power of withdrawal will be unascertainable and the donor's gift to the trust will be a gift of a future interest, i.e., the gift will not be eligible for the gift tax annual exclusion. Rev. Rul. 80-261, 1980-2 C.B. 279. For example, in a tiered *Crummey* withdrawal right where the grantor's spouse can withdraw the first $5,000 of annual gift contribution and any amount above $5,000 the grantor's children can withdraw, the amount withdrawable by the children must be the pro rata amount in excess of the first $5,000 of annual gift contribution. *See*, Paragraph 3.1(A)(2) of Sample ILIT.

§10.4(b) Gift Splitting And *Crummey* Withdrawal Rights

Do not condition the amount of the withdrawal on whether a split-gift election is to be made under IRC section 2513. The IRS has ruled that this constitutes a condition subsequent to the gift and hence makes the gift amount, i.e., the withdrawal amount, unascertainable until the condition subsequent occurs. Priv. Letter Rul. 8022048. Rather, limit the withdrawal right to a single present-interest exclusion or provide that if a donor is married at the time of the contribution, the amount subject to withdrawal is the amount otherwise available under gift splitting, irrespective of whether the gift-splitting election is, in fact, elected. *See*, Paragraph 3.1(A)(3) of Sample ILIT.

§10.4(c) Priority Of *Crummey* Withdrawal Rights

Condition any distribution of principal, termination of trust, trustee discretion, or exercise of any lifetime power of appointment so that such distributions, discretions, terminations, or exercises will not thwart or otherwise defeat an existing *Crummey* withdrawal right that is unexercised and has not yet lapsed. Priv. Letter Ruls. 8213074 and 8121051; TAM 8107009. *See*, Paragraphs 3.2(F), 3.2(J), 4.1(B), 4.2, 7.1(D)(3), 7.2, 7.3, 7.6, 7.10, and 8.2(C) of Sample ILIT.

§10.5 PROVIDE BENEFICIARIES WITH SUFFICIENT TIME TO EXERCISE THEIR *CRUMMEY* WITHDRAWAL RIGHTS

According to the IRS, a beneficiary must have a reasonable amount of time to exercise his or her *Crummey* withdrawal right before it lapses. Rev. Rul. 81-7, 1981-1 C.B. 474.[6] Therefore, a minimum *Crummey*

---

[6] In Rev. Rul. 81-7, 1981-1 C.B. 474, the donor created a trust on December 29, 1979. The trust contained a *Crummey* withdrawal right that lapsed at the end of the

withdrawal period of 15 days is sufficient; although 30 days would be preferable. *Estate of Maria Cristofani v. Commissioner*, 97 T.C. 74 (1991), *acq. in result only*, AOD 1996-010 (15 days sufficient); *Estate of Lieselotte Kohlsaat*, T.C. Memo 1997-212 (1997) (30 days sufficient); Rev. Rul. 83-108, 1983-2 C.B. 167 (45 days sufficient); Priv. Letter Ruls. 8813019, 8134135, 8103074, 8024084, 8006048, and 8004172 (30 days sufficient). Priv. Letter Rul. 8111123 (11 days sufficient if gifts to trust were made on or before December 21). *See*, Paragraph 3.2(D) of Sample ILIT. For GST estate tax inclusion period ("ETIP") purposes, the grantor's spouse's withdrawal right must be limited to no more than 60 days from the date of the contribution to the ILIT. *See*, section 5.17, above. Treas. Reg. §26.2632-1(c)(2)(ii). *See*, Alternate 2 of Paragraph 3.1(A)(1)(a) of Sample ILIT. A withdrawal right granted for only 3 days has been held to be insufficient to create a gift of a present interest. Rev. Rul. 81-7, 1981-1 CB 474; Priv. Letter Rul. 199912016. The IRS has also ruled that a withdrawal right granted for only 4 days is insufficient to create a gift of a present interest. TAM 9628004. In Priv. Letter Rul. 8111123 the IRS declined to express an opinion "with respect to allowance of the [gift tax annual] exclusion where a transfer is made to the trust during the last 10 days of the calendar year."

§10.6 GIVE THE TRUSTEE BROAD DISCRETION TO SATISFY *CRUMMEY* WITHDRAWAL RIGHT NOTICE REQUIREMENTS

Do not require the trustee to give written notice of a beneficiary's withdrawal rights. Rather, give the trustee discretion in how to effectuate reasonable notice to the beneficiaries. *See*, Rev. Rul. 83-108, 1983-2 C.B. 167; Rev. Rul. 81-7, 1981-1 CB 474. *See*, Paragraph 3.2(A) of Sample ILIT.

> **Practice Point:** If the trustee decides to give a one time notice of recurring premium contributions to the guardian or parent of a minor beneficiary, the trustee should also

---

year. The donor did not inform the beneficiary of the existence of the *Crummey* withdrawal right before it lapsed. The ruling stated that, in failing to communicate the existence of the *Crummey* withdrawal right and in narrowly restricting the time for its exercise, the donor did not give the beneficiary a reasonable time to learn of and to exercise the *Crummey* withdrawal right before it lapsed. The donor's conduct made the demand right illusory and effectively deprived the beneficiary of the ability to withdraw the gift contribution. The ruling held that no gift annual exclusion was allowable for the December 29, 1979 gift.

send a one time notice to that beneficiary when he or she reaches the age of majority.

§10.7 GIVE THE TRUSTEE BROAD POWERS TO SATISFY ANY *CRUMMEY* WITHDRAWAL RIGHT

Make sure that any *Crummey* withdrawal right may be satisfied not only against the contribution but also against other trust property, including any insurance policy or fractional interests in the insurance policy. This will provide substance to a *Crummey* withdrawal right, especially as concerns any split-dollar or group term policies held by the trust. *See*, Paragraph 3.2(F) of Sample ILIT.

Fortunately, the IRS has sanctioned the ILIT trustee's ability to distribute fractional interests in the insurance policies as sufficient to satisfy a *Crummey* withdrawal right. Priv. Letter Ruls. 8044080 (whole life policies), 7935091 (term insurance), 8143045, 8138171, 8138170, 8138102, 8134135, 8021058, and 8006109 (group term insurance), and 8051128 (split dollar insurance). *See*, Paragraph 3.2(F) of Sample ILIT.

Practice Point: An insured's direct payment of life insurance premiums life does not constitute an incident of ownership in a life insurance policy owned by a third party (such as an ILIT). In *Estate of Joseph Leder v. Commissioner*, 893 F.2d 237 (10th Cir. 1989), the court held:

> [T]he decedent's payment of premiums is irrelevant in determining whether the decedent retained any "incidents of ownership" in the policy proceeds. See First Nat'l Bank v. United States, 488 F.2d 575, 578 [33 AFTR2d 74-1407] (9th Cir. 1973); Bel v. United States, 452 F.2d 683, 689 [29 AFTR2d 72-1482] (5th Cir. 1971), cert. denied, 406 U.S. 919 (1972); Estate of Headrick v. Commissioner, 93 T.C. 171 [178-79] (1989). Congress intended to eliminate the premium payment test used in the 1939 Code when it adopted section 2042. See First Nat'l Bank, 488 F.2d at 578. Both the House and Senate committee reports stated that section 2042 "revises existing law so that payment of premiums is no

> longer a factor in determining the taxability under this section of insurance proceeds." Id. (emphasis in First Nat'l Bank) (quoting H.R. Rep. No. 1337, 83d Cong., 2d Sess. A316, reprinted in 1954 U.S. Code Cong. & Admin. News 4017, 4459; citing S. Rep. No. 1622, 83d Cong., 2d Sess. 472 (1954)).
>
> The Tax Court examined section 2042 and determined that the decedent never possessed any rights to the insurance policy that would constitute "incidents of ownership." Because the policy proceeds were not includable under section 2042, the Tax Court concluded that the section 2035(d)(2) exception did not apply, and thus under the general rule of section 2035(d)(1) the proceeds from the insurance policy were not includable in the decedent's gross estate.

The IRC section 2042 analysis of *Leder* was followed in *Estate of Eddie L. Headrick v. Commissioner*, 918 F.2d 1263 (6th Cir. 1990), *Estate of Samuel Ard, Jr., v. Commissioner*, T.C. Memo 1990-294 (1990), and *Estate of Frank Martin Perry, Sr., v. Commissioner*, 927 F.2d 209 (5th Cir. 1991). After a series of defeats, the IRS acquiesced in the *Headrick* decision. AOD 1991-012(7/3/1991). *See*, section 1.4(a), above.

§10.8 PERMIT THE TRUSTEE TO APPOINT A GUARDIAN FOR MINOR *CRUMMEY* WITHDRAWAL RIGHT BENEFICIARIES

Because a minor beneficiary is legally incapable of exercising a *Crummey* withdrawal right, a guardian or next friend needs to be able to exercise the right on behalf of the minor beneficiary. A court-appointed guardian is not required if there is a natural guardian, such as a parent (other than the grantor, or the grantor's spouse in the case of a second-to-die policy) or another relative, who can exercise the right of withdrawal on behalf of the minor. *George W. Perkins v. Commissioner*, 27 T.C. 601 (1956); Priv. Letter Ruls. 8229097, 8024084 and 8022048. If there is no natural guardian and the trust instrument or local law does not prevent the appointment of a guardian, the minor's *Crummey* withdrawal right still qualifies as a gift of a present interest under IRC section 2503(b). Rev. Rul. 73-405, 1973-2 C.B. 321; *Mary Hull Naumoff v. Commissioner*, T.C. Memo 1983-435 (1983); Priv. Letter Ruls. 8143045 and 8121069. *See*, Paragraph 3.2(C) of Sample ILIT.

> **Practice Point:** When the minor beneficiary attains the age of majority, notice should be sent directly to the beneficiary (who is now an adult).

§10.9 APPLY FIVE-BY-FIVE SAFE HARBOR *CRUMMEY* WITHDRAWAL RIGHT LAPSE AMOUNT AGAINST THE ENTIRE TRUST ESTATE

The 5% portion of the five-by-five safe harbor lapse amount under IRC section 2514 for *Crummey* withdrawal rights is measured against "the aggregate value of the assets out of which, or the proceeds of which, the exercise of the lapse power could be satisfied." IRC section 2514(e)(2). Thus, to obtain the largest 5% lapse protection amount, the 5% should be measured against the entire trust estate, and not against the amount of the periodic gift contribution. *See*, Paragraphs 3.1(A)(1) and (2) (Alternate 1) of Sample ILIT. *See*, section 3.17, above, concerning the aggregation of multiple *Crummey* withdrawal rights held by a beneficiary.

§10.10 CREATE AN ORDERING RULE OR AGGREGATION RULE FOR A BENEFICIARY'S MULTIPLE *CRUMMEY* WITHDRAWAL RIGHTS

Rev. Rul. 85-88, 1985-2 C.B. 201, holds that only one five-by-five safe harbor lapse is permitted per calendar year per donee for all powers of withdrawal (granted under all trusts) available to that donee during the year. Multiple withdrawal rights held by the same donee over the same or different trusts must be aggregated to determine whether they violate the five-by-five safe harbor amount. *See also*, G.C.M. 39371 (1985). In this regard the ILIT can contain an ordering rule for a donee who holds multiple *Crummey* withdrawal rights. The ILIT can provide that the donee's unexercised withdrawal right in the ILIT property shall lapse after all other unexercised withdrawal rights previously granted to the donee (whether under the ILIT or another instrument) have lapsed. Alternatively, the ILIT can provide that all unexercised withdrawal rights held by the donee shall be aggregated to determine the maximum amount that can lapse within the five-by-five safe harbor provisions of IRC sections 2514(e)(1) and (2). *See,* Paragraph 3.2(L) of Sample ILIT.

§10.11 AVOID THE CREATION OF RECIPROCAL ILITS

In creating ILITs for both a husband and wife, be aware of the dangers of the reciprocal trust doctrine.[7] In *United States v. Estate of Grace*, 395 U.S. 316 (1969), the husband and wife created identical irrevocable trusts for the benefit of the other spouse. The husband's trust for the benefit of his wife was created first, and the wife's trust for the benefit of her husband was created 15 days later. The Supreme Court uncrossed the trusts, and held that each grantor is treated as the putative grantor of another person's trust when the putative grantor is the beneficiary of such other person's trust and the trusts are "interrelated, and...the arrangement, to the extent of mutual value, leaves the settlors in approximately the same economic position as they would have been in had they created trusts naming themselves as life beneficiaries." *Id.*, at 324. In an ILIT context, the reciprocal trust doctrine could cause the wife to be deemed the grantor of her husband's ILIT (concerning insurance on his life) and vice versa. This would cause life insurance proceeds received by the ILIT (irrespective of the three-year rule of IRC section 2035) to be included in each spouse's gross estate under IRC section 2036, thus thwarting the basic objective of the ILIT—the removal of the insurance proceeds from the gross estate of the insured and the insured's spouse. *See,* Rev. Rul. 74-533, 1974-2 C.B. 293 concerning the amount includible in the decedent's estate if the reciprocal trust doctrine applies, and the amount of any gift tax credit for gift taxes paid by the other spouse on the reciprocal gift amount. (If the ILITs are of unequal value, the amount included under IRC section 2036 should be no more than the value of the smaller trust on the applicable valuation date. *Id.*; *Estate of Cole v. Commissioner,* 140 F.2d 636 (8th Cir. 1944).) Additionally, each spouse would be the "new" transferor of the other spouse's ILIT, thus wasting any GST tax exemption previously allocated by the other

---

[7] *See,* Paul E. Van Horn, "Revisiting the Reciprocal Trust Doctrine," 30 *Tax Management Estates, Gift and Trusts Journal* 224 (July 14, 2005). As the author points out, the reciprocal trust doctrine has also been applied in income tax situations. *Krause v. Commissioner*, 57 T.C. 890 (1972), *aff'd*, 497 F.2d 1109 (6th Cir. 1974), *cert. denied*, 419 U.S. 1108 (1975).

spouse (or deemed allocated under the GST tax exemption automatic allocation rules).

Practice Point: In determining whether the reciprocal trust doctrine applies, the following factors will be considered and analyzed: (i) the similarity of the trusts' terms, (ii) the similarity of the trusts' corpus, (iii) the trustees, (iv) the beneficiaries, (v) the proximity of the trusts' execution date, and (vi) the grantors' intent concerning a prearranged plan.

Practice Point: To avoid the reciprocal trust doctrine, consider the following drafting suggestions: (i) give one spouse (but not the other) a broad inter-vivos limited power of appointment, (ii) give each spouse a different form of entitlement under each other's trust—one spouse may be entitled to mandatory distributions of income and distributions of principal for health, education, support and maintenance, while the other spouse may be entitled to receive distributions of income and principal in the sole discretion of an Independent Trustee, (ii) vary the terms of the trust—one trust may be a GST tax exempt dynasty trust, and the other trust may be for a specified length of years, and (iv) execute the trusts on different dates—the farther apart the better.

§10.11(a) Reciprocal Trusts Doctrine Not Applied

In *Estate of Green v. United States,* 68 F.3d 151 (6th Cir. 1995), the Sixth Circuit took a narrow interpretation of *Grace* and refused to follow the Tax Court's broad interpretation of the *Grace* doctrine in *Estate of Bischoff v. Commissioner*, 69 T.C. 32 (1977) and the IRS's position in TAM 8019041. In *Green,* the Sixth Circuit Court of Appeals rejected the reciprocal trust doctrine as it concerned trusts established by grandparents for the benefit of their grandchildren. In *Green,* the grandfather established an inter-vivos irrevocable trust for the benefit of granddaughter 1, naming his wife (the grandmother) as trustee with discretionary trustee powers over investments and distributions of income and principal. Likewise, the grandmother established an inter-vivos irrevocable trust for the benefit of granddaughter 2, naming her husband (the grandfather) as trustee with discretionary trustee powers over investments and distributions of income and principal. Neither the grandfather nor the grandmother was a beneficiary under either trust. The fact that the grandparents had "reciprocal" trustee powers did not give rise to the reciprocal trust doctrine, since neither grandparent was a trust beneficiary and because the trustee powers did not leave them in approximately the same economic position they were in before the trusts were created. In *Estate of Levy v. Commissioner*, T. C. Memo 1983-453 (1983), the Tax Court held that the reciprocal trust doctrine did not apply where one trust gave the spouse a broad inter-vivos limited power of appointment, but the other trust did not.

In Priv. Letter Rul. 9643013, the IRS ruled that the reciprocal trust doctrine was not applicable when husband and wife each established inter-vivos irrevocable trusts and each was the trustee of the other's trust. In the wife's trust both the husband and the children were discretionary income and principal beneficiaries. In the wife's trust the husband held a limited power of appointment over the trust corpus. All discretionary distributions to the beneficiaries of the wife's trust were to be made by an independent trustee, and the independent trustee was prohibited from acquiring life insurance on the life of either the wife or the husband. The husband's trust was identical to the wife's trust except (1) only the children (and not the wife) were trust beneficiaries; and (2) the wife did not possess a limited power of appointment over the corpus of the husband's trust (the power of appointment was instead held by the independent trustee and was limited to the husband's descendants). Regrettably, the IRS did not elaborate on what differences between the trusts were determinative in its ruling. However, one can surmise that the safest way to avoid the reciprocal trust doctrine is to create two trusts that give the spouses distinctly different interests. Although each spouse can serve as trustee of the other's trust, the author believes that an independent trustee should serve as co-trustee with at least one of the spouses. Additionally, the beneficiaries of the trusts should be somewhat different. For example, one trust could give the husband a right to income and principal in the discretion of the independent trustee, while the other trust could give the wife a mandatory right to income and a mandatory right to principal for her health, education, support, and maintenance. *See, also*, Priv. Letter Rul. 200426008 (where the IRS ruled that trusts created by two spouses for each other's benefit were not reciprocal because each trust had materially different terms concerning lifetime distributions).

Practice Point: If spouses have reciprocal ILITs, they should seek judicial modification of the trusts to create the desired distinctions.[8] Alternatively, the spouse with the shortest life expectancy could disclaim his or her interest in the other spouse's ILIT. However, unless the disclaimer is a qualified disclaimer under IRC section 2518 (generally, within 9 months of the creation of the other spouse's ILIT), the trust property is still includible in the disclaiming spouse's gross estate for three years following the non-qualified disclaimer, and the non-qualified disclaimer of the imputed retained interest may have gift tax implications. IRC sections 2035(a) and 2518; Treas. Reg. §§25.2518-1(b) and 25.2511-1(c)(2).

§10.12 AVOID THE CREATION OF RECIPROCAL CRUMMEY WITHDRAWAL RIGHTS

A corollary to the reciprocal trust doctrine is the reciprocal power of withdrawal doctrine, which prohibits annual gift tax exclusions for *Crummey* withdrawal rights "where two or more grantors, acting mutually, each creates a trust for the primary benefit of a child and gives each of the other grantors a corresponding power to withdraw a specified amount from the trust." Rev. Rul. 85-24, 1985-1 C.B. 329.

§10.13 AVOID THE CREATION OF RECIPROCAL GIFTS

Similar to the reciprocal power of withdrawal doctrine is the reciprocal gift doctrine, which prohibits annual gift tax exclusions for gifts made back and forth between donors for the benefit of the other donor's family members. In Priv. Ltr. Rul. 8717003, two brothers and their wives made approximately matching gifts to their own children and to the other brother's children. The IRS uncrossed the gifts made by each aunt and uncle to their nieces and nephews, and treated the donor's gifts to their nieces and nephews as being made to the donor's

[8] Although judicial modification will remove the offending trust provisions and create the desired distinctions, an uncontested modification could be construed as a release or relinquishment of a spouse's interest in the other spouse's ILIT; and if a "relinquishing" spouse dies within 3 years of the uncontested judicial modification, the ILIT property may still be includable in the "relinquishing" spouse's gross estate under IRC section 2035(a).

own children, thereby causing the total gifts to the donor's children to exceed the annual gift tax exclusion amount available to the donor with regard to each child. *See also*, *Sather v. Commissioner*, 251 F. 3d 1168 (8th Cir. 2001); *Estate of Schuler v. Commissioner*, 282 F. 3d 575 (8th Cir. 2002); *John A. Schultz v. United States*, 493 F. 2d 1225 (4th Cir. 1974).

§10.14 AVOID THE CREATION OF RECIPROCAL POWERS OF APPOINTMENT

Another corollary to the reciprocal trust doctrine is the reciprocal power of appointment doctrine, where beneficiaries of different trusts can appoint trust property to one another, unrestricted by an ascertainable standard. In such instance, the IRS will uncross the trusts and will take the position that each beneficiary will be considered to hold a general power of appointment over the trust of which he or she is a beneficiary. Priv. Letter Ruls. 9235025 and 9451049.

§10.15 PROHIBIT THE INSURED FROM POSSESSING OR EXERCISING ANY POWERS OVER THE ILIT

To avoid any potential issues under IRC sections 2036 and 2038, prohibit the insured-grantor from retaining any interests in the property transferred by the insured-grantor to the ILIT. *Estate of Eleanor T.R. Trotter v. Commissioner*, T.C. Memo 2001-250 (2001). In this regard, the ILIT trustee should be prohibited from using the trust assets to discharge the insured's legal obligations, including the obligation of support. *See*, sections 4.2 and 4.3, above. Also, prohibit the insured-grantor (and the insured-grantor's spouse in the case of a second-to-die policy) from exercising *Crummey* withdrawal rights on behalf of the beneficiaries (including the ability to exercise the power pursuant to a power of attorney or as a natural or legal guardian of the beneficiary). This is particularly important since the trustee generally has the ability to transfer the policies insuring the life of the grantor to the beneficiaries. *See*, Rev. Rul. 84-179, 1984-2 C.B. 195. If the insured-grantor has the ability to exercise a withdrawal right and the trustee can satisfy the withdrawal right by distributing the policy to the insured-grantor as guardian, then the insured-grantor will hold incidents of ownership in the policy insuring the grantor's life, albeit in a fiduciary capacity for the benefit of the minor beneficiary (which would probably result in the life insurance proceeds being includable in the insured's gross estate under IRC section 2042). *See*, section 4.10, above. Furthermore, the insured-grantor should not possess any power of appointment over the ILIT. The insured-grantor's retention of a power of limited or general appointment: (i) may result in an incomplete gift being made to the ILIT (and the incomplete gift will not be a gift of a present interest that is eligible for the gift tax annual exclusion), and (ii) will result in the ILIT property being includable in the grantor's gross estate for federal estate tax purposes. IRC sections 2511, 2514, 2041, and Treas. Reg. §20.2042-1(c)(4). *See*, Paragraphs 1.1, 3.2(C), and 4.1(B) of Sample ILIT.

§10.16 PROHIBIT THE INSURED FROM BECOMING A TRUSTEE OF THE ILIT

If the insured-grantor serves as a trustee of the ILIT, the insurance on the grantor's life will be included in his or her gross estate for federal estate tax purposes because of the insured-grantor's incidents of ownership in the policy (since the trustee is the owner of the life insurance policy). Similarly, neither spouse should serve as trustee of an ILIT that holds a second-to-die policy insuring both spouses' lives. IRC section 2042; Treas. Reg. §20.2042-1(c)(4). *See*, Paragraphs 1.1(A) and 6.1(E) of Sample ILIT.

§10.17 NONINSURED SPOUSE AS TRUSTEE

A noninsured spouse who is a beneficiary of an ILIT (when the other spouse is the sole insured under the ILIT) can serve as trustee of the ILIT during the insured-spouse's lifetime, provided: (1) the noninsured spouse holds no powers as trustee that constitute a general power of appointment; (2) the noninsured spouse is prohibited from making distributions that would have the effect of discharging his or her legal obligations, including the obligation of support; and (3) the noninsured spouse does not make gifts to the ILIT (other than merely consenting to gift splitting under IRC section 2513).[9]

Because of the lack of flexibility inherent when a noninsured spouse serves as an ILIT trustee during the insured-spouse's lifetime (especially if the ILIT beneficiaries include minors whom the nonin-

---

[9] *See*, Stuart B. Dorsett, "Having Your Cake and Eating It, Too—Parental Control Over Irrevocable Trusts For Children," 16 Probate & Property 58 (November/December 2002).

sured spouse has a duty to support), it is usually best to name an independent third party to serve as trustee during the insured-spouse's lifetime. After the death of the insured-spouse, the noninsured spouse can serve as trustee of the ILIT, even if he or she is a beneficiary, provided the noninsured spouse holds no powers as trustee that constitute a general power of appointment. (*See*, Chapter 8, above for a discussion of tax-sensitive powers regarding the beneficiary-trustee. *See,* Chapter 9, above for a discussion of the surviving spouse serving as trustee of the ILIT after the insured's death.)

> **Practice Point:** An insured spouse under a second to die policy should not serve as trustee of the ILIT.

§10.18 VEST OWNERSHIP OF THE LIFE INSURANCE EXCLUSIVELY IN THE ILIT TRUSTEE

The ILIT should provide that the grantor relinquish all rights over transferred policies, and that any life insurance policy purchased by the ILIT on the grantor's life is owned exclusively by the trustee. *See*, Paragraphs 1.1(A), 1.2, 7.1(D)(4) of Sample ILIT. *See*, Paragraph 7.1(C)(4) of Sample ILIT. *See,* Priv. Letter Ruls. 200603002 and 9651004, in which the IRS ruled favorably for the taxpayer concerning life insurance policies that were not properly transferred to the ILIT, but where there was sufficient documentary evidence that the insurance company had been instructed to irrevocably transfer the policy to the ILIT and had failed to do so.

§10.19 PROTECT THE TRUSTEE FROM THE LIFE INSURANCE SELECTION PROCESS

In cases where existing life insurance policies are transferred to the ILIT, or where the grantor selects a new policy for the ILIT to acquire, the ILIT trustee will not be significantly involved in the life insurance selection process. What is the trustee's liability should the policy under-perform or, even worse, non-perform? Arguably, the trustee did not exercise the degree of care and diligence required under the circumstances.[10] Oftentimes the trustee during the grantor's lifetime is a

---

[10] *See,* E. Randolph Whitelaw and Richard M. Weber, "Trust-Owned Life Insurance: Risk Management Guidance for Fiduciaries," 32 *Estate Planning* 14 (September 2005) for a discussion of "best practices" trust owned life insurance risk management, especially if there is a non-guaranteed life insurance policy and the ILIT trustee is a corporate trustee.

family member, friend, attorney, or accountant. Therefore, this issue could be a trap for the unwary, and a reason for an individual to refuse to serve as a trustee. A possible solution to the problem is to exculpate and indemnify the trustee with respect to the selection and retention of life insurance. *See*, Paragraphs 7.1(D)(2) and (3) of Sample ILIT.

Also, if the trustee is not sophisticated in life insurance matters, consider the appointment of a life insurance advisor to assist the trustee in the selection, retention, and management of the policy.

Drafting Example:

I hereby designate [Name of Life Insurance Advisor] to serve as the Insurance Advisor to Trustee until such Advisor's death, incapacity or resignation. Notwithstanding anything in this Agreement to the contrary, it is my intention, and I therefore direct, that Trustee shall not purchase, acquire, surrender or otherwise dispose of any insurance or annuity policy except upon the direction of the Insurance Advisor. As to any insurance or annuity policy which Trustee purchases or acquires, Trustee shall have no obligation to determine the suitability of any such policy as an investment of the trust. Prior to the insured's death, the Insurance Advisor shall have sole responsibility for making all decisions regarding retention, sale, surrender, borrowing against cash values, withdrawals, and the exercise of any options available under any policy of life insurance held in the trust. The Insurance Advisor shall have the right to resign at any time which shall be effective thirty (30) days after written notice of the Insurance Advisor's intention to do so is given personally or by registered mail to the then living income beneficiaries or their legal representatives. Upon the occurrence of the death, disability, or resignation of the Insurance Advisor, the then living income beneficiaries, or their legal representatives, shall select a new Insurance Advisor, provided, however, that they shall not select me, a donor or the insured as the Insurance Advisor. The resigning Insurance Advisor shall also have the right to select a new Insurance Advisor if one is not appointed as provided for herein, by the effective date of the Insurance Advisor's resignation.

§10.20 GRANT THE ILIT TRUSTEE BROAD POWERS TO DEAL WITH LIFE INSURANCE MATTERS

In addition to the usual trustee powers, the ILIT trustee should be granted broad powers to deal with life insurance. These powers include:

(1) The acquisition and retention of life insurance (*See*, Paragraphs 7.1(D)(1), (2) and (3) of Sample ILIT);

(2) The ability to request indemnification from a trust beneficiary before making a distribution of the insurance proceeds to that beneficiary (*See*, Paragraph 7.1(D)(7) of Sample ILIT);

(3) The vesting of all incidents of ownership in the trustee (*See*, Paragraph 7.1(D)(4) of Sample ILIT);

(4) The ability to accept an accelerated death benefit or enter into a viatical settlement (*See*, Paragraph 7.1(D)(4) of Sample ILIT);

(5) The ability to sell or transfer the life insurance policy to a person who is exempt from the transfer for value rules under IRC section 101(a)(2), to wit, a grantor trust (with respect to the insured), a partner of the insured, a partnership in which the insured is a (nominal-minority) partner, a corporation in which the insured is an officer or a (nominal-minority) shareholder (*See*, Paragraph 7.1(D)(4) of Sample ILIT);

(6) How the trustee is to pay premiums due on the policies insuring the grantor's life and the options available to the trustee if the grantor stops making gifts to the ILIT (*See*, Paragraph 7.1(D)(5) of Sample ILIT);

(7) The ability to compromise and settle with the life insurance companies (*See*, Paragraph 7.1(D)(6) of Sample ILIT); and

(8) The ability of the trustee to undertake litigation to collect the insurance proceeds and request indemnification from the trust beneficiaries. (*See*, Paragraphs 7.1(D)(6) and (7) of Sample ILIT).

(9) The ability to sell the policy to a life settlement company. (*See*, Paragraph 7.1(D)(4) of Sample ILIT).

§10.21 INCLUDE SPECIAL LANGUAGE FOR GROUP TERM AND SPLIT-DOLLAR INSURANCE

The assignment of a group term policy to an ILIT should include any replacement or renewal insurance and any increase in the amount of coverage. Rev. Rul. 80-289, 1980-2 C.B. 270. Also, the trust should provide that *Crummey* withdrawal rights extend to indirect contributions to the trust, such as deemed gifts arising from a third party's payment of the premium on group term insurance or insurance subject to a split-dollar arrangement. Annual notice of the employer-paid premiums should be sent to the trust beneficiaries along with notice of their right to withdraw the value of the employer-paid premiums. Priv. Letter Ruls. 8143045, 8138170; TAM 9045002. *See,* Paragraphs 1.2, 3.2(G), 7.1(D) and Schedule A of Sample ILIT.

§10.22 INVOKE GRANTOR TRUST STATUS FOR THE ILIT

If the ILIT is a grantor trust under sections 671-677,[11] the income, credits, and deductions of the trust are attributed to the grantor and are included in determining the grantor's income tax liability under IRC section 671.[12] Although the ILIT generally will not hold many income-producing assets, nevertheless it is generally desirable that the trust be a grantor trust since transfers between a grantor (or a grantor trust) and a grantor trust are not recognized for income tax purposes (assuming the same grantor is involved). Rev. Rul. 85-13, 1985-1 C.B. 184; Rev. Rul. 2007-13, 2007-11 I.R.B. 684 (3/12/2007). *See also,* Priv. Letter Ruls. 8718046 and 8636053. Grantor trust status provides potential planning opportunities if the ILIT trustee desires to subsequently sell the life insurance policies for full and adequate consideration to another grantor trust under the transfer for value rule exception of section 101(a)(2). Priv. Letter Rul. 200518061 and 9413045. Grantor trust status also permits the grantor to sell assets to the ILIT without gain being recognized by the grantor. *See,* sections 2.7(h) and 2.8(b)(1), above.

§10.23 ADD DEFINITIONAL FLEXIBILITY BY DESCRIBING BENEFICIARIES RATHER THAN NAMING THEM

Rather than naming individual beneficiaries throughout the ILIT, have a definitional provision in the trust that describes them. This provides

---

[11] The term "defective grantor trust" refers to the grantor being treated as the owner of the trust for income tax purposes, but not for estate tax purposes.

A detailed discussion of the grantor trust rules and how to establish an intentionally defective grantor trust (including a sale to an intentionally defective grantor trust) is beyond the scope of this outline. *See,* Zaritsky, 858-2d T.M., *Grantor Trusts: Sections 671-679,* for a general discussion of the grantor trust rules and the use of inter-vivos trusts (such as ILITs) in estate planning. *See also,* John B. Huffaker and Edward Kessel, "How the Disconnect Between the Income and Estate Tax Rules Created Planning for Grantor Trusts," 100 *Journal of Taxation* 206 (April 2004).

[12] The IRS will not issue a private letter ruling on the grantor trust status of an ILIT. Rev. Proc. 2006-3, 2006-1 IRB 125, section 3.01(37).

greater flexibility in the event of a divorce or after-born or adopted children. *See,* Paragraphs 10.1,10.2, and 8.3(D) of Sample ILIT.

§10.24 STRUCTURE SECOND-TO-DIE ILIT AS A SURVIVORSHIP SPOUSAL ILIT

A survivorship spousal ILIT can provide spouses with access to the cash value of a second-to-die policy owned by an ILIT. *See*, section 14.13, below.

§10.25 PERMIT THE ILIT TRUSTEE TO MAKE LOANS TO AND PURCHASE ASSETS FROM THE INSURED'S ESTATE

Treasury Regulations indicate that life insurance proceeds subject to a legally binding obligation to pay taxes, debts, or other charges of the insured-decedent will be deemed payable to the decedent's estate (to the extent of the obligation) and will be includable in the insured's gross estate for federal estate tax purposes. Treas. Reg. §20.2042-1(b). Therefore, do not direct the ILIT trustee to pay the insured's death taxes, debts or costs of estate administration. Rather, give the trustee the authority to make loans to the insured's estate or to purchase assets from the insured's estate. In this way the ILIT can provide liquidity to the insured's estate without the ILIT assets being subject to inclusion in the insured's gross estate. *See*, section 4.9,above. *See,* Paragraph 5.2 of Sample ILIT.

§10.26 DRAFT THE ILIT IN CONTEMPLATION OF THE UNIFORM TRUST CODE

As of January 2007, the Uniform Trust Code ("UTC")[13] has been adopted in 20 jurisdictions, and is being studied by numerous other states, including Hawaii, Maryland, Michigan, New Jersey, South Dakota, Vermont, and Wisconsin. The UTC is the first national codification of the law of trusts.

Most of the UTC consists of default rules that apply only if the terms of the trust fail to address or insufficiently cover a particular issue, and the scrivener can vary or override most of the UTC's provisions.

According to UTC section 105(b), there are fourteen provisions that cannot be varied or overridden: (1) the requirements for creating a

---

[13] *See*, www.utcproject.org.

valid trust; (2) the duty of a trustee to act in good faith and in accordance with the terms and purposes of the trust and the interests of the beneficiaries; (3) the requirement that a trust and its terms be for the benefit of its beneficiaries, and that the trust have a purpose that is lawful, not contrary to public policy, and possible to achieve; (4) the power of the court to modify or terminate a trust under UTC sections 410 through 416; (5) the effect of a spendthrift provision and the rights of certain creditors and assignees to reach a trust as provided in UTC Article 5; (6) the power of the court under UTC section 702 to require, dispense with, or modify or terminate a trustee's bond; (7) the power of the court under UTC section 708(b) to adjust a trustee's compensation that is ureasonably low or high as specified in the terms of the trust; (8) the duty under UTC sections 813(b)(2) and (3) to notify qualified beneficiaries of an irrevocable trust who have attained 25 years of age of the existence of the trust, of the identity of the trustee, and of their right to request trustee's reports; (9) the duty under UTC section 813(a) to respond to the request of a qualified beneficiary of an irrevocable trust for trustee's reports and other information reasonably related to the administration of a trust; (10) the effect of an exculpatory term under UTC section 1008; (11) the rights under UTC sections 1010 through 1013 of a person other than a trustee or beneficiary; (12) periods of limitation for commencing a judicial proceeding; (13) the power of the court to take such action and exercise such jurisdiction as may be necessary in the interests of justice; and (14) the subject-matter jurisdiction of the court and venue for commencing a proceeding as provided in UTC sections 203 and 204.

Even if an ILIT is created in a state that has not adopted the UTC, it is possible the ILIT may become subject to the UTC. Therefore, when drafting an ILIT, consideration should be given to: (i) the ability of the trustee to move the situs of the trust to a UTC (or a non-UTC) jurisdiction, and (ii) drafting in contemplation of the UTC.[14]

---

[14] "Most of the UTC provisions create default rules that apply unless the governing trust document changes them. The UTC also contains 14 mandatory rules that cannot be varied or changed by the trust document. Default rules create drafting opportunities and choices such as how to override them, whether they should be overridden, and whether they should be relied upon without reference, or actually reinforced in the trust. Mandatory rules create equally important drafting opportunities and compliance requirements, although they cannot be varied." Suzanne Brown Walsh, "Drafting Under The Uniform Trust Code (With Sample Provisions)," 21 *Practical Tax Lawyer* 23, 24 (Winter 2007).

11

Drafting An ILIT For Flexibility And Changing Circumstances

CHAPTER OVERVIEW

An ILIT is irrevocable, and is generally designed to be a long term trust that may last for decades, or in the case of a GST dynasty trust, possibly centuries. When drafting an ILIT, practitioners should resist the temptation to draft to "tightly." Language allowing the trustees and beneficiaries to take into account changed circumstances and changes in the trust and tax laws is extremely important. The more flexible the ILIT is, the more likely it can adapt to changing or unforeseeable circumstances that develop over time.[1] Although an ILIT appears by its

---

[1] *See,* Julius H. Giarmarco, "Drafting A Flexible Irrevocable Life Insurance Trust, Part 2," 26 *Michigan Probate & Estate Planning Journal* 59 (Winter 2006); Julius H. Giarmarco, "Drafting A Flexible Irrevocable Life Insurance Trust," 25 *Michigan Probate & Estate Planning Journal* 20 (Summer 2006); William R. Culp, Jr. and Mark L. Richardson, "Lifetime Special Powers of Appointment Offer Unique Planning Opportunities," 33 *Estate Planning* 34 (October 2006); Domingo P. Such, III, "Fix-Ups Of Estate Plans After They Have become Irrevocable (With Sample Language) (Part 2)," 12 *ALI-ABA Estate Planning Course Materials Journal* 41 (April 2006); Domingo P. Such, III, "Fix-Ups Of Estate Plans After They Have become Irrevocable (With Sample Language) (Part 1)," 12 *ALI-ABA Estate Planning Course Materials Journal* 45 (February 2006); Richard C. Baier, "Drafting Flexibility into an Irrevocable Life Insurance Trust," 19 *Probate & Property* 62 (September/October 2005); Alan S. Aker, "Fixing Broken Irrevocable Trusts," 31 *ACTEC Journal* 221 (Winter 2005); and Ronald D. Aucutt, "Structuring Trust Arrangements for Flexibility," *35th Annual Heckerling Institute on Estate Planning,* Chapter 9 (Matthew Bender/Lexis-Nexis, Newark, NJ 2001); Al W. King, III, "Modern Trusts Are Being Created With More

nature to be an inflexible instrument to most grantors, it is easy to build flexibility into an ILIT from its inception. This chapter provides drafting suggestions for the practitioner that may help the ILIT remain supple, avoid becoming "damaged" over time, and avoid the need for a "judicial fix," such as a trust reformation or modification. Fixing an irrevocable trust is expensive, time consuming, and not always predictable from a tax point of view, especially if a taxable event has already occurred.[2] Generally speaking, under the completed transaction doctrine (which is discussed in section 15.7(c), below), the IRS does not give retroactive effect to a court order that attempts to fix a tax problem that has already occurred. These problems can sometimes be avoided by drafting a flexible ILIT.

§11.1 APPOINT A SPECIAL POWER HOLDER

Appoint a special power holder with the limited power to appoint the trust property (including life insurance policies) during the grantor's lifetime.[3] If the limited power is exercisable by a person who also happens to be serving (or is nominated) as an independent trustee, the power should be exercisable in that person's individual-personal capacity and not in his or her fiduciary capacity. Having the power exercisable in a non-fiduciary capacity: (i) will avoid an argument by the trust beneficiaries (or the potential appointees, i.e., the objects of the power)

Flexibility Resulting In Assets Remaining In Trusts For Longer Periods Of Time," 138 *Trusts & Estates* 28 (January 1999).

[2] *See,* section 15.7(b), below, for a discussion of the IRS' "completed transaction" rule.

[3] *See,* Albert R. Kingan, "Adding Flexibility to Insurance Trusts Funded With Survivorship Life," 26 *Estate Planning* 381 (October 1999); Alan S. Acker, "Every Drafter's Dream: The Flexible Irrevocable Trust," 23 *Tax Management Estates, Gifts and Trusts Journal* 126 (May 14, 1998).

See also, Elizabeth Carrott Minnigh, "Utilizing Trust Protectors in Domestic Estate Planning," 48 *Tax Management Memorandum* 3 (January 8, 2007) ("Minnigh"); Alexander A. Bove, Jr., "Trust Protectors," 144 *Trusts & Estates* 28 (November 2005); and Alexander A. Bove, Jr., "The Trust Protector: Trust(y) Watchdog or Expensive Exotic Pet?," 30 *Estate Planning* 390 (August 2003). "The settlor of an irrevocable trust may appoint a trust protector (i) to oversee the trust administration, (ii) to adjust to changes in circumstances and in the law, and/or (iii) to take appropriate action to ensure that the settlor's objectives and the purposes of the trust are maintained. However, because broad powers potentially may be granted to a trust protector, the settlor should give a great deal of care in selecting a trust protector and in choosing which powers to grant to the trust protector." Minnigh at 3.

that the special power holder-trustee must act in the beneficiaries' (or objects') best interests, (ii) will avoid an argument by the IRS that the power of appointment held by the special power holder-trustee is a fiduciary power,[4] and (iii) will avoid an argument by the IRS that the insured-grantor has reserved a beneficial interest in trust under IRC 2036 because the insured-grantor's creditors can reach the assets, which will also result in gifts to the ILIT being incomplete and the ILIT being includable in the insured-grantor's gross estate for federal estate tax purposes. *See*, section 4.2(d), above (concerning transferred property that is subject to the claims of the grantor's creditors, and IRC section 2036). The trust property can be appointed outright or in further trust. If the terms of the existing ILIT no longer suit the needs of the grantor or the beneficiaries, the special power holder can appoint the policy in further trust, on such terms and conditions, as determined by the special power holder. *See,* Paragraph 8.2(A) of Sample ILIT. Presumably any appointment in further trust would be to a trust that contains provisions desired by the grantor and/or beneficiaries. Granting a special power holder this flexibility will permit the trust property to be distributed in the event of changed circumstances, and possibly provide the grantor with indirect access to the cash value of the policy (assuming the grantor or grantor's spouse is the outright appointee of the ILIT property). However, make sure the limited power of appointment cannot be exercised so as to defeat a *Crummey* withdrawal right which has not been exercised and has not yet lapsed. *See*, Paragraph 4.2 of Sample ILIT.

---

[4] In this regard, *Restatement of The Law Third—Trusts,* §50 (comment a), states in pertinent part:

> A trustee's discretionary power with respect to trust benefits is to be distinguished from a [trustee's] power of appointment. The latter is not subject to fiduciary standards and may be exercised arbitrarily within the scope of the power.... (Tax law generally does not categorize powers in this manner, and even traditional property-law distinctions between fiduciary powers and powers of appointment may be difficult to draw; this is especially so because a true power of appointment can be conferred upon one who is also a trustee, although a power that runs with the office of trustee is strongly presumed to be a fiduciary power.)

Even if the special power holder is not a trustee, the trust instrument should explicitly state that the limited power of appointment is exercisable in a non-fiduciary capacity.

To avoid possible adverse transfer tax consequences to the special power holder, the special power holder should not be the insured, the grantor, or a potential recipient of the appointed trust property. The special power holder should be expressly prohibited from appointing the ILIT property to him or herself, his or her estate, or the creditors of either.

> **Practice Point:** If the special power holder is a beneficiary of the ILIT, the exercise of the special power may have gift tax implications. *See,* section 3.9. However, if the special power holder is the non-insured spouse (who is also trust beneficiary), the appointment of the trust assets by the special power holder-spouse to the insured should qualify for the gift tax marital deduction if the insured is a U.S. citizen. IRC section 2523(b).

> **Practice Point:** Appointment of a special power holder may create grantor trust status under IRC section 674(a) (and possibly under 674(c) if the special power holder can appoint to a new trust with new or different beneficiaries). *See,* section 2.7(c), above.

For the insured to avoid adverse transfer tax consequences under IRC sections 2036,[5] 2037,[6] 2038,[7] or 2042[8] as an object (i.e., potential

---

[5] IRC section 2036(a) does not "apply to a power held *solely by a person other than the decedent.*" Treas. Reg. §20.2036-1(b)(3). (Emphasis added.) *See, Estate of Edward Lathrop Ballard v. Commissioner,* 47 B.T.A. 784 (1942), *aff'd,* 138 F.2d 512 (2d Cir. 1943) where the decedent's wife had the power to alter, amend, or revoke an "irrevocable" inter-vivos trust established by the decedent for the benefit of their children, and upon the wife's death, said power was to revert to the decedent (i.e., the decedent possessed a contingent power to alter, amend, or revoke the trust). However, the decedent predeceased his wife. The court held that the wife's power to alter, amend, or revoke the trust was not to be imputed or attributed to the decedent, and that the gift by the decedent to the trust was a completed gift for gift tax purposes. The fact that the decedent's wife consulted with the decedent concerning the trust "does not mean, however, that the familial relation gave decedent the power to amend or revoke the trust. As a matter of fact, the testimony of decedent's widow presented at the hearing indicates that she gave considerable thought to the problems of the children's trust. She had been taught to handle money and took care of her own financial affairs." 47 B.T.A. 790. The court also held that the decedent did not have a retained interest in the trust (under present day IRC section 2036(a)), a reversionary interest in the trust (under present day IRC section 2037), nor did the decedent have the power at death to control the beneficial enjoyment of the trust property (under present day IRC section 2038). Therefore, none of the trust property was includable in the decedent's

gross estate. *See also, Anna Ball Kneeland v. Commissioner*, 34 B.T.A. 816 (1936) where the decedent established an irrevocable trust for the benefit of his family and gave his wife the power to revoke the trust and have the principal returned to the grantor. The wife never revoked the trust. Quoting the United States Supreme Court in *Helvering v. St. Louis Union Trust Co.,* 296 U. S. 39 (1935), the Tax Court said, "The grantor here, by the trust instrument, left in himself no power to resume ownership, possession or enjoyment except upon a contingency in the nature of a condition subsequent, the occurrence of which was entirely fortuitous so far as any control, design or volition on his part was concerned." The Tax Court also found that the husband's ability to influence his wife did not rise to the level that she was an agent who did his bidding. Said the Tax Court, "We know of no authority for the proposition, that a husband's influence over his wife through her love and affection for him, sufficient to secure a release to him of her legal rights, constitutes a legal power to alter or impair her right of enjoyment of her property." Thus, these cases and the Treasury Regulations support the position that powers held by a spouse or a third party are not attributed to the grantor.

[6] IRC section 2037 does not apply since the potential appointees and the trust beneficiaries do not have to survive the grantor in order to possess or enjoy the trust property.

[7] IRC section 2038 "does not apply...[t]o a power held *solely by a person other than the decedent.*" Treas. Reg. §20.2038-1(a)(3). (Emphasis added.)

[8] IRC section 2042 does not apply since the grantor does not have a "reversionary interest" in the trust property. The special power holder has complete unfettered discretion to appoint the life insurance policy to any of the appointees, which may include the insured as one the *potential* appointees. The insured has no control or veto power over the actions of the independent special power holder. *See, Estate of John Smith v. Commissioner,* 73 T.C. 307 (1979), acq. in result only, AOD 1981-066 (01/12/1981). Said the court, "At his death, Smith could neither have initiated changes in the two [key man life insurance] policies [owned by and payable to the publicly traded company that employed Smith] nor consented to them; the company [in which Smith owned only a few shares of stock and was not a controlling shareholder] alone maintained full control over the policies." The acquiescence implies that the IRS will not consider the right to purchase a life insurance policy owned and made payable to a corporation as an incident of ownership if the corporation ceased paying premiums or wished to surrender and terminate the policy). This case differs from the situation in which a policy is owned by a corporation but made payable to a third party, such as the insured's spouse, as was the case in Rev. Rul 79-46, 1979-1 C.B. 303, in which the IRS ruled that the insured had a reversionary interest in the policy because of his right to purchase the policy owned by his corporate employer, but made payable to the insured's wife.

Also, IRC section 2042 does not apply since there is no reversionary interest greater than 5% that can be attributed to the insured. *See,* Treas. Reg. §20.2042-1(c)(3), which states in pertinent part,

> In order to determine whether or not the value of a reversionary interest immediately before the death of the decedent exceeded 5 percent of the value of the policy, the principles contained in paragraph (c)(3) and

appointee) of the power (*see*, the optional language in Paragraph 4.2 of Sample ILIT (or for the more cautious, consider using the optional 2 language: "the descendants of my mother," as was done in Priv. Letter Rul. 8037116)): (i) the special power holder should be able to exercise the limited power of appointment in his or her sole, absolute and uncontrolled discretion,[9] (ii) the special power holder should prefer-

> (4) of §20.2037-1, insofar as applicable, shall be followed under this subparagraph. In that connection, there must be specifically taken into consideration any incidents of ownership—held by others immediately before the decedent's death which would affect the value of the reversionary interest. For example, the decedent would not be considered to have a reversionary interest in the policy of a value in excess of 5 percent ***if the power to obtain the cash surrender value existed in some other person [such as the ILIT trustee] immediately before the decedent's death and was exercisable by such other person alone and in all events***. (Emphasis added.)

See, Rev. Rul. 79-117, 1979-1 C.B. 305, where "the IRS ruled that a transferor's reversion was without value where his spouse had the power to alter the beneficiaries and defeat the transferor's reversion. True, the ruling arose under §2042(2), where a 5% reversion is considered an 'incident of ownership,' but the regulations under §2042 explicitly refer to the §2037 regulations. And, in *Graham Est. v. Commissioner*, [46 T.C. 415 (1966)] where the decedent's reversion arose only if his daughter affirmatively exercised a power to terminate the trust, the Tax Court held that the value of the reversion could not be ascertained by any recognized valuation principle." Dodge, 50-5th T.M., *Transfers with Retained Interests and Powers,* section III,B,4,b, Bureau of National Affairs, Washington, DC) ("Dodge").

"To generalize, there is no 'retention' under Sections 2036 and 2037 merely because the instrument of transfer expressly allows for the conferring *by a person other than the transferor* of an interest or power on the settlor." Dodge, at section IV,C,2. (Emphasis added). Consequently, there should be no reversionary interest under IRC section 2042 imputed to the insured since the insured has no right to "acquire the policy or force the special powerholder to exercise its power to appoint the policy. Furthermore, merely because the insured is an object of the power held by the special power holder, who is not acting in a fiduciary capacity, is independent, can exercise the power in the power holder's sole, absolute, and uncontrolled discretion, and where there is no pre-arranged understanding between the insured and the special power holder, should not create a 5% reversionary interest in the life insurance policy or its proceeds.

[9] *See, In re Estate of Edgar M. Uhl*, 241 F.2d 867 (7th Cir. 1957), where the grantor, Edgar M. Uhl, created an irrevocable trust and reserved the right to receive $100 of income per month for life. The trust also provided that "the [corporate] Trustee may in his discretion and after consultation with Louis C. Uhl [the grantor's nephew], pay a greater sum than one hundred dollars ($100.00) per month if it shall seem advisable and provided further, that said sum so paid shall not in any event exceed the amount

ably be a person who is not related or subordinate (within the meaning of IRC section 672(c)) to the insured (although it may be possible for a non-insured spouse to be a special power holder[10]), (iii) the special power holder should only be removed for reasonable cause by a court of competent jurisdiction, and (iv) there must be no implied agreement or understanding between the insured and the special power holder that the special power holder will exercise its authority for the benefit of the insured. *See,* Priv. Letter Rul. 9141027 where the trust property was includable in the donor's gross estate under IRC section 2036 because of an implied agreement between the donor and the special power holder (the donor's spouse) that the special power holder would appoint the transferred property to the donor upon the death of the special power holder (and in fact, on the same day the donor transferred the property to the trust, the spouse prepared a codicil to her will appointing the transferred property to the donor). *See,* Priv. Letter Rul. 8037116 where the donor transferred property to an intervivos irrevocable trust for the support and benefit of the descendants

---

of net income received from said property." The Tax Court held that all of the trust corpus was includable in the grantor's gross estate because the state's fraudulent conveyance law would have permitted the grantor's creditors to reach the trust assets, as a fraudulent transfer. The case was reversed in part on appeal. The Seventh Circuit U.S. Court of Appeals found that the fraudulent conveyance statute applied only to the mandatory $100 per month income interest retained by the grantor, and that the fraudulent conveyance statute did not apply to the grantor's discretionary interest in the trust income. Citing *Herzog v. Commissioner,* 116 F.2d 591 (2d Cir. 1941) and *Rheinstrom v. Commissioner*, 105 F.2d 642 (8th Cir. 1939) for the proposition that a grantor's retained interest in a trust that is subject to the sole discretion of a third party is not an interest that is includable in the grantor's gross estate for federal estate tax purposes, the Court held, "that no part of the trust estate, the income from which was not reserved to the grantor, should have been included in the gross estate, in view of the fact that the settlor reserved no right to compel the trustee to pay him any sums other than $100.00 a month, and the trustee was under no duty to pay him more than that." Id. at 1749. In this instance, a state's fraudulent conveyance law should not apply since the insured is not retaining any interest in the trust, but is merely a potential appointee of the policy (and not a beneficiary of the trust). *See,* Paragraph 8.2(D) of Sample ILIT which states that no court can compel the special power holder to exercise the power of appointment. This fact, buttressed by the inability of the insured to remove the special power holder, should effectively insulate the insurance policy from the claims of the insured's creditors.

[10] *See, Estate of Edward Lathrop Ballard,* 47 B.T.A. 784 (1942), *aff'd,* 138 F.2d 512(2d Cir. 1943); *Anna Ball Kneeland v. Commissioner,* 34 B.T.A. 816 (1936), which are discussed in footnote 5, above.

of the donor's mother (i.e., the donor was a potential beneficiary), for the donor's lifetime, remainder in specified percentages to donor's brothers and children of one, or to charity if none of them survive the donor. The IRS ruled that the trust property was not includable in the donor's gross estate since the donor did not retain right to receive income nor the right to designate beneficiaries, even though the donor was within class of beneficiaries to whom trustee could distribute income and principal. The trustee had complete discretion to determine all trust distributions. The IRS also ruled that the donor's retained right to settle accounts and release the trustee from liability and accountability to the beneficiaries was for administrative convenience, and was not equivalent of the right to designate beneficiaries. Furthermore, the trust property was not includable in the donor's gross estate under IRC section 2037 since the trust beneficiaries could receive principal and income during donor's lifetime at trustee's sole discretion and the beneficiaries did not have to survive the donor; accordingly, the donor had no reversionary interest in the trust.

> **Caution:** Be aware of the potential gift tax consequences if the special power holder is also a beneficiary of the ILIT. The lifetime exercise of a special power of appointment over trust corpus by the trust's income beneficiary is a gift equal to the present value of the beneficiary's income interest. The beneficiary's exercise of the power over the corpus does not terminate the income interest. Instead, when trust corpus is transferred, the income generated by the transferred corpus is also (gratuitously) transferred to the transferee of the corpus, thus resulting in a gift of the beneficiary's transferred income interest. *Estate of Ruth B. Regester v. Commissioner*, 83 T.C. 1 (1984). *See,* section 3.9, above.

> **Practice Point:** The special power holder could exercise its power in calendar year 2010, when there is no GST tax, to distribute assets to skip persons. If the trust is not GST tax exempt, (i.e., has an inclusion ratio greater than zero), the special power holder could appoint trust assets to skip persons. Such an appointment would be a direct skip, and if the assets were appointed to a dynasty trust in which all the beneficiaries were skip persons, the trust would be a skip person. Arguably, no post-2010 distributions to skip persons from the dynasty trust should attract GST tax, since

the distributions will not be taxable terminations or taxable distributions. However, this point is not exactly clear and the safer approach may be to make outright distributions to skip beneficiaries in calendar year 2010. *See*, Paragraph 8.2(C) of Sample ILIT.

§11.2 PERMIT DONOR TO VARY ANNUAL *CRUMMEY* WITHDRAWAL RIGHTS

Allow the donor to vary the rights of withdrawal before each year's contribution. Note that the donor cannot change the beneficiaries of the ILIT without running afoul of IRC sections 2036 and 2038, but can change (on an annual basis) which beneficiaries are to be granted *Crummey* withdrawal rights, the amount subject to withdrawal, and/or change the period during which the beneficiary's *Crummey* withdrawal right can be exercised. Priv. Letter Ruls. 9834004, 9030005, 8901004, 8103074, 8103069, and 8003033. *See*, Paragraph 3.2(H) of Sample ILIT.

Because the donor is exercising control over the gift property before the donor's relinquishment of dominion and control over the property and before the donee's receipt of the property, there is no retained interest by the donor in the ILIT, nor in the gifted property. Furthermore, the donor's pre-gift determination of who can have a withdrawal right over the gifted property does not constitute retained control over the beneficial enjoyment of the trust property under IRC sections 2036(a)(2) and 2038. Of course, once the donor completes the gift by transferring the property or cash to the ILIT, the donor can no longer place any conditions on the gift (or on any past gifts); otherwise, the donor would have a retained interest in the gifted property that is includable in his or her gross estate.

A case in which a donor might want to vary the rights of withdrawal concerns a beneficiary who subsequently experiences creditor problems or is going through a divorce.

The Sample ILIT contains default *Crummey* withdrawal rights for the grantor's spouse and descendants. The reason for the default withdrawal rights is to avoid requiring the grantor to specify in the annual gift transmittal letter to the trustee which ILIT beneficiaries are to be granted withdrawal rights, and the conditions of their rights of withdrawal. If the grantor forgets to identify the beneficiaries who are to be given *Crummey* withdrawal rights and the trustee does not give notice to the ILIT beneficiaries (since no beneficiaries are identified in the gift transmittal letter), the IRS will deny the gift tax annual exclusion for the gifted amounts. TAM 9532001. Therefore, the safer approach is to grant a broad right of withdrawal in the ILIT and then have the grantor, in a one time notice to the trustee, identify those beneficiaries who are not to be given withdrawal rights until further notice from the grantor. Sometimes, it is logistically easier (and less expensive) to exclude than to include.

§11.3 INCLUDE CONTINGENT MARITAL DEDUCTION PROVISIONS IN THE ILIT

If the insured is married and the ILIT does not hold a second to die policy on the insured and his or her spouse, consider including a contingent marital deduction trust in the ILIT. If the ILIT proceeds are includable in the insured's gross estate, the contingent marital deduction provisions can eliminate any federal estate tax due upon the insured's death.[11] A marital deduction may be accomplished by requiring the ILIT trustee to distribute the death benefit proceeds to the surviving spouse, either outright or through a marital deduction trust, such as a life estate with a general power of appointment (*see*, section 4.13, above) or a qualified terminable interest ("QTIP") arrangement (*see*, section 4.14, above).

When drafting contingent marital deduction provisions for an ILIT, consider a QTIP arrangement so as to preserve whatever GST inclusion ratio has been established by the insured for the ILIT before the insured's death. Treas. Reg. §26.2642-4(a)(3). Also consider use of a *Clayton* contingent QTIP election rather than a traditional reduce-to-zero marital deduction formula. With the increase in the applicable exclusion amount, the *Clayton* contingent QTIP election provides tremendous post-mortem flexibility to the insured's estate by allowing for a "wait and see" approach to how much of the initial marital bequest should be qualified for the marital deduction and how much

---

[11] For example, the life insurance proceeds can be payable outright to the surviving spouse, be held in a general power of appointment marital deduction trust for the benefit of the surviving spouse, or be held in a QTIP trust for the benefit of the surviving spouse (provided the insured's executor make a QTIP election on IRS Form 706).

should be distributed to the credit shelter or family trust.[12] Treas. Reg. §20.2056(b)-7(d)(3). *See*, section 1.3, above. *See*, Paragraph 5.1 (A)(7) of Sample ILIT.

§11.4 PERMIT TRUSTEE TO TERMINATE THE ILIT

Should estate taxes be permanently repealed or the applicable exclusion amount be significantly increased (in lieu of repeal), trusts that were originally designed to minimize estate taxes may no longer be necessary. If the non-estate tax reasons for an ILIT no longer justify its existence, consider allowing an independent trustee to terminate the trust. *See*, Paragraph 7.6 of Sample ILIT.

The power of a beneficiary-trustee to terminate a trust in his or her sole discretion or as a co-trustee with another trustee who does not have a substantial and adverse interest in the trust may be a power to affect the beneficial enjoyment of the trust property or its income, and could constitute a general power of appointment for estate and gift tax purposes. Treas. Reg. §§20.2041-1(b)(1) and 25.2514-1(b)(1). Therefore, the power to terminate a trust should be held by an independent trustee.

Under common law, a spendthrift clause prevents a trust from being terminated. Therefore, the trust's spendthrift clause should include language that permits the trust's early termination. *See*, Paragraph 7.3 of Sample ILIT.

> **Practice Point:** If the trust contains *Crummey* withdrawal rights, as do most ILITs, be sure to include in the trust termination clause a prohibition of termination while a withdrawal right remains outstanding and has not lapsed; otherwise the IRS may argue that the withdrawal right can be unilaterally cut off by the trustee, and is therefore illusory (i.e., does not qualify as a present interest gift).

> **Caution:** If the ILIT contains a marital deduction trust or a charitable remainder trust, the trustee should be prohibited from exercising its termination power in a manner that would impair the marital or charitable deduction.

---

[12] *See*, Chapter 3 of Sebastian V. Grassi, Jr., *A Practical Guide to Drafting Marital Deduction Trusts (with Sample Forms and Checklists)*, (ALI-ABA, Philadelphia, PA 2004, Supp. 2006) (800) 253-6397, http://www.ali-aba.org/aliaba/BK36/ for a detailed discussion of the *Clayton* contingent QTIP election.

Practice Point: To induce the trustee to exercise its discretion, the trust should provide that the trustee shall be entitled to be held harmless and be indemnified by the trust and the beneficiaries who benefit from the termination of the trust. Such language might read: *"Before terminating a trust hereunder, trustee may request and shall be entitled to be held harmless and receive appropriate indemnification from the trust and the beneficiaries who are going to receive a terminating distribution."*

Because a trustee owes a fiduciary duty to all the trust beneficiaries, including the remainder beneficiaries, the independent trustee may be reluctant to unilaterally exercise its trust termination powers. As a precautionary measure, the independent trustee may seek judicial approval of the contemplated termination. A judge may or may not sanction the proposed termination. Given this possibility, it may be appropriate to also grant the power of termination to a special power holder who owes no fiduciary duty to the trust beneficiaries. Needless to say, this power should only be given to a trusted adviser of the grantor. In addition to holding the power to terminate a trust, the special power holder could also be given the power to appoint the trust's assets to the trust's current beneficiaries in such proportions and manner as the special power holder deems fit. The special power holder should not be the grantor or a beneficiary of the trust, and should meet the definitional requirements of an independent trustee in order to avoid any adverse estate or gift tax consequences as a result of holding these special powers. To induce the special power holder to exercise its power, the trust should provide that the special power holder shall be entitled to be held harmless and be indemnified by the trust and the beneficiaries who benefit from the termination of the trust. Such language might read: *"Before terminating a trust hereunder, the special power holder may request and shall be entitled to be held harmless and receive appropriate indemnification from the trust and the beneficiaries who are going to benefit from the exercise of the special power holder's authority hereunder." See,* Paragraph 8.2 (C) of Sample ILIT.

§11.5 PERMIT TRUSTEE TO AMEND *CRUMMEY* WITHDRAWAL RIGHTS

A trustee who has no beneficial interest in the trust, could be granted the power to amend the *Crummey* withdrawal rights granted in the

ILIT so that gifts will qualify for the annual gift tax exclusion amount if there are future changes in the law. *See,* FSA 199930026. *See,* Paragraph 3.2(J) of Sample ILIT.

§11.6 PERMIT TRUSTEE TO CHANGE THE SITUS OF THE ILIT AND ITS ASSETS

If the ILIT beneficiaries move away from the jurisdiction where the grantor established the ILIT, it may be more convenient for the beneficiaries to deal with a local trustee. Or, another state may have laws which may be more congenial to the purposes and needs of the ILIT than those of the state where the trust was originally established (e.g., South Dakota or Alaska have neither a rule against perpetuities nor a state income tax). Whether or not a trust may be removed from its original jurisdiction is a matter of state law, often times dependent on the grantor's intent. If the grantor's intent is not clear, then the matter becomes one for judicial interpretation. Therefore, provide in the ILIT that the trustee can change the trust's situs.[13] A Trustee may also want to change the situs of a trust to a jurisdiction that provides a greater degree of privacy to the trust's affairs and its beneficiaries, or has more established or favorable trust laws and rules. Possibly the trustee may want to move the trust's assets and situs of administration to a jurisdiction that is less creditor friendly or has (or has not) adopted the Uniform Trust Code or Third Restatement of Trusts. Therefore, provide in the ILIT that the trustee can relocate the trust's assets, and change the trust's situs and governing law. *See,* Paragraph 8.3(A) of Sample ILIT.

> **Caution:** Some states, such as Connecticut, and Washington, D.C., will not respect a change in situs for income tax purposes.
>
> **Practice Point:** When changing a trust's situs, consideration should be given to the effect the new state's law concerning vesting and accumulations (e.g., the rule against per-

---

[13] *See,* ¶406 of Richard W. Nenno, "Choosing and Rechoosing the Jurisdiction for a Trust," 40 *Heckerling Institute on Estate Planning,* Chapter 4, (Matthew Bender/Lexis-Nexis, Newark, NJ 2006); Philip J. Michaels and Laura M. Twomey," How, Why, and When to Transfer the Situs of a Trust," 31 *Estate Planning* 28 (January 2004); and John A. Warnick and Sergio Pareja, "Selecting a Trust Situs in the 21st Century," 16 *Probate & Property* 53 (March/April 2002).

petuities (or the abolishment of the rule against perpetuities)) may have on a trust that is GST tax exempt, and the new state's law's effect on the exercise of a limited power of appointment. Will the new state's law result in a material change to the nature of a beneficial interest, which change constitutes a constructive addition or shift in beneficial interests for GST tax purposes? Will the new state's law cause a Delaware tax trap issue?[14] *See,* Priv. Letter Rul. 199922044 where the IRS ruled that the appointment of a new corporate trustee in a different state from the one in which the trust was currently being administered did not cause a GST grandfathered trust to lose its GST tax exempt status even though the appointment of the new trustee would result in a change in the situs of the trust's administration and a change in the trust's governing law. Similarly, in Priv. Letter Rul. 200543041, the IRS ruled that a change in the situs of nine trusts (which were currently governed under the laws of five different states) to a single state where the law of the new state permitted the trustee to make adjustments between income and principal, would not result in a taxable gift being made by the trust beneficiaries, would not result in a shift of the beneficiaries' interests for GST tax purposes, and would not result in a "material difference" in kind or extent of the legal entitlements enjoyed by the beneficiaries under the taxable exchange rules of IRC section 1001 and the *Cottage Savings* doctrine.[15] *See,* sections 3.4, 4.7, 5.24, 5.25, and 5.26, above.

---

[14] For example, if the trust is GST tax exempt, the GST trust modification rules concerning a trust's change of situs are governed by Treas. Reg. §26.2601-1(b)(4)(i)(E), Example 4, which state there will be a loss of the trust's GST tax exempt status if a change of situs would extend (or abolish) the perpetuity period governing such trust. *See,* Daniel G. Worthington, "Perpetual Trust States—The Latest Rankings," 146 *Trust & Estates* 59 (January 2007); and Daniel G. Worthington, "The Problems and Promise Of Perpetual Trust Laws," 143 *Trust & Estates* 15 (December 2004). *See,* sections 5.24 and 5.25, above, concerning GST grandfathered trusts.

[15] *See,* section 15.7(d), below, for a discussion of IRC section 1001 and the *Cottage Savings* doctrine.

§11.7 PERMIT TRUSTEE TO APPOINT A CO-TRUSTEE

When a corporate trustee is serving as the sole trustee after the grantor's death, it is not uncommon for an adult beneficiary (usually a child) to want to serve as a co-trustee of their trust share. This permits the individual beneficiary to work with the corporate trustee and become part of the decision making process (to the extent such decisions can be made by the beneficiary-co-trustee). Expressly permitting the ILIT trustee to appoint a beneficiary (or a third party) as a co-trustee avoids the delay and cost of obtaining court approval. Similarly, an individual trustee should have the flexibility to appoint a co-trustee (usually a corporate trustee) to assist the individual trustee. *See*, Paragraph 6.5 of Sample ILIT.

§11.8 GIVE THE BENEFICIARIES TESTAMENTARY LIMITED POWERS OF APPOINTMENT

A testamentary limited power of appointment over a beneficiary's trust share permits tremendous post-mortem flexibility upon the beneficiary's death. Because the donee of the power must be prohibited from appointing the trust property to himself or herself, his or her estate, or the creditors of either, the donee's possession of the power will not, in and of itself, result in the power's inclusion in the donee's gross estate. IRC section 2041(b)(1). *See*, Paragraphs 5.1(A)(3)(a), 5.4(C) (alternate 2), 5.5(C), 8.2(A) and 8.2(B) of Sample ILIT.

> **Caution:** Depending on the governing law of the trust, the exercise of a testamentary limited power of appointment may cause a "Delaware tax trap" issue.[16]

§11.9 GIVE THE INSURED, SPOUSE, AND BENEFICIARIES THE ABILITY TO REMOVE AND REPLACE THE ILIT TRUSTEE

An insured-grantor can remove an ILIT trustee at anytime for no cause as long as the insured-grantor cannot name a new replacement trustee (in contrast to a successor trustee already named in the ILIT) who is

---

[16] *See*, Stephen E. Greer, "The Delaware Tax Trap and the Abolition of the Rule Against Perpetuities," 28 *Estate Planning* 68 (February 2001). *See also,* Daniel G. Worthington, "Perpetual Trust States—The Latest Rankings," 146 *Trust & Estates* 59 (January 2007); and Daniel G. Worthington, "The Problems and Promise Of Perpetual Trust Laws," 143 *Trust & Estates* 15 (December 2004).

the grantor, an insured or a person who is "related or subordinate" to the grantor within the meaning of IRC section 672(c). Rev. Rul. 95-58, 1995-2 C.B. 191. Priv. Letter Rul. 9832039 clarifies Rev. Rul. 95-58 by holding that the removal and replacement of a trustee by a grantor does not have to be limited to "cause," as long as the new trustee appointed by the grantor is not related or subordinate to the grantor (within the meaning of IRC section 672(c)). Priv. Letter Rul. 9832039 also clarifies Rev. Rul. 95-58 by holding that the insured's ability to remove a trustee for "cause" and replace that trustee with someone other than the insured does not mean that the insured holds an incident of ownership over the insurance policy held by the ILIT on the insured's life. In Priv. Letter Rul. 9607008, the IRS extended its holding in Rev. Rul. 95-58 to beneficiaries who were given the unqualified power to remove an existing trustee and appoint a replacement trustee who was not related or subordinate to the beneficiaries (within the meaning of IRC section 672(c)).

As a result of these rulings it can be concluded that: (1) the unfettered power to remove an ILIT trustee restricts the removing party (who is an insured, donor, grantor, or beneficiary) in naming a new replacement trustee (in contrast to a successor trustee already named in the ILIT), and the new replacement trustee must be a person who is not related or subordinate to the person who holds the power of removal; and (2) if the power of removal is restricted to reasonable cause, the removing party has greater flexibility in naming a successor or replacement trustee, and is not precluded from naming a new replacement trustee who is related or subordinate to the grantor. However, the person holding the power to remove a trustee should not be able to appoint him or herself, an insured or the grantor as a trustee of the ILIT; and the ILIT should prohibit the appointment of a grantor or an insured as a trustee. *See*, section 1.7, above. *See*, Paragraphs 6.1(E) and 6.21 of Sample ILIT.

§11.10 PERMIT THE TRUSTEE TO EXTEND THE ILIT BEYOND THE RULE AGAINST PERPETUITIES

If the ILIT is GST tax exempt, structure the ILIT as a discretionary common (pot) trust for the grantor's descendants that runs for the longest period permitted under rule against perpetuities, (if that is consistent with the grantor's desires).

Even though the ILIT will run for the longest period permitted under the rule against perpetuities, the grantor can further prolong the insulation of the ILIT assets from transfer tax by directing or permitting younger generations to share to some degree in the final distribution of the trust estate, rather than following a pure "per stirpes" distribution regime which inevitably will put the assets in the hands of the oldest descendants, who are closest to the imposition of the estate tax. Therefore, consider giving an Independent Trustee (i.e., a trustee who is not a beneficiary or a grantor, and who is not related or subordinate to either party, per IRC section 672(c)) the ability to appoint the trust assets outright or to a custodial arrangement (UGMA or UTMA) to any of the grantor's then living descendants upon the termination of the ILIT's term. This will permit trust assets to be distributed to beneficiaries in younger generations. Appointing trust property to younger beneficiaries will permit the trust property to escape estate taxation for another generation, and possibly insulate the ILIT assets from estate taxes for up to 200 years from its inception. Casting the Independent Trustee's power as a limited power of appointment exercisable in a non-fiduciary capacity will also protect the trustee from a potential abuse of discretion claim.[17]

Drafting Example:

> *At any time during the period that is twelve months prior to the expiration of the trust's term, Trustee who is an Independent Trustee, may by written instrument, appoint some, none, or all of the trust property to some, all, or none of my then living descendants, without any requirement of equality among my then living descendants or the appointees of the trust property. Trustee's exercise of the power of appointment shall be in a non-fiduciary capacity. The Independent Trustee may, but need not, consider appointing the trust property to those descendants with a longer life expectancy than to those descendants with a shorter life expectancy. However, two days prior to the expiration of the trust's term, the Independent Trustee's special limited power of appointment contained herein shall cease, and any remaining or non-appointed trust property shall be distributed as follows [etc.].*

---

[17] "A trustee's discretionary power with respect to trust benefits is to be distinguished from a [trustee's] power of appointment. The latter is not subject to fiduciary obligations and may be exercised arbitrarily within the scope of the power." *Restatement of The Law Third—Trusts,* section 50 (comment a).

§11.11 PERMIT THE TRUSTEE TO MAKE DISCRETIONARY DISTRIBUTIONS TO BENEFICIARIES

If the current ILIT contains provisions that the insured no longer desires or does not contain provisions or beneficiaries that the insured desires, have the trustee distribute the life insurance policy to the insured's spouse. If the insured's spouse is a discretionary beneficiary of the ILIT and the trustee has absolute discretion to make a distribution to the spouse for *any* reason (not just for health, education, support, and maintenance), the trustee can distribute the life insurance policy to the spouse who can then transfer the policy to a new ILIT established by the insured or to a new ILIT established by the spouse. *See*, Paragraph 4.1(A) of Sample ILIT. The three-year rule of IRC section 2035 is not applicable since the spouse is not the insured. However, because of the retained interest rule of IRC section 2036(a) concerning gratuitous transfers, the spouse cannot be a beneficiary under the new ILIT.

Discretionary distributions to the insured's spouse also provide a way for the insured to maintain indirect access to the policy's cash value concerning a single life policy that insures the grantor's life. Coupled with a provision authorizing the trustee to borrow, withdraw, or surrender the policy's cash value, the insured's spouse can have access to the policy's cash value during the insured's lifetime. Although this provision does not give the insured direct access to the policy's cash value, it does give the insured indirect access provided the insured remains married. *See,* Paragraphs 4.1(A) and 7.1(D)(4) of Sample ILIT.

Discretionary distributions to trust beneficiaries also provide an opportunity for the insured to create a new ILIT that is more to the liking of the insured, and have the trustee of the existing ILIT transfer the life insurance policies to the new ILIT if it is in the best interests of the existing ILIT beneficiaries. In such instance, the trustee of the existing ILIT must have the authority to distribute the life insurance policy to another trust (i.e., to the new ILIT) for the benefit of the existing ILIT beneficiaries. A trustee-to-trustee transfer of assets should not produce any adverse income, gift, or estate tax results, if the beneficial interests are not materially altered as a result of the transfer. Treas. Reg. § 25.2511-1(g)(1). *See*, section 15.7(d), below concerning the *Cottage Savings* doctrine, which should not apply. However, GST tax exemption issues will need to be closely examined.

When undertaking a trust-to-trust transfer, it is also important that the transfer for value rule not be violated. *See*, section 2.5, above. Generally the transfer for value rule can be complied with by structuring the new ILIT as an intentionally defective grantor trust with regard to the insured, or by having a carryover of the transferor's basis in the policy from one trust to another. *See*, section 2.5(c), above.

Drafting Example:

An Independent Trustee may distribute some or all of the trust property (including life insurance policies) to one or more of the trust beneficiaries or to a trust for the benefit of one or more of the trust beneficiaries, without any requirement of equality among the beneficiaries. The trust receiving the distributed property (which trust may be established by such Trustee) does not need to have the same terms as the original trust. In no event may a Trustee exercise this discretionary power of distribution in a manner that would cause the loss of a marital or charitable estate tax deduction available to my estate, impair an unexercised right of withdrawal that has not yet lapsed, or cause a trust to lose its ability to hold S corporation stock.

A trustee's discretionary distribution power coupled with the ability to distribute/appoint a beneficiary's distributive share to another trust for the benefit of that beneficiary is another way to provide flexibility.[18] For example, if the trust provides for a mandatory distribution of the beneficiary's trust share when the beneficiary attains a specified age, and the trustee determines that it is in the best interests of the beneficiary to have the beneficiary's upcoming distributive share be held in further trust, the trustee could be granted the authority to make a discretionary distribution "to or for the benefit" of the beneficiary, and distribute/appoint the share to another trust. The new trust could be a trust created by the trustee or by the grantor. *See*, Priv. Letter Rul. 9450036, which provides a discussion of the various tax issues that the should be considered when implementing a trust-to-trust

---

[18] *See*, Alan Halperin and Michelle R. Wandler, "Decanting Discretionary Trusts: State Law and Tax Considerations," 29 *Tax Management Estates, Gifts and Trusts Journal* 219 (September 9, 2004). According to the authors, decanting may be used to achieve a variety of goals, including, dealing with change circumstances, modifying trust administrative provisions, modifying trusteeships, extending the trust's termination date (for non-tax reasons), correcting drafting errors, obtaining or terminating grantor trust status, changing the trust's situs and governing law, dividing trust property and establishing separate trust shares or a different dispositive scheme, and reducing potential liability.

transfer. GST tax issues should also be examined to ensure that the new trust does not cause a loss of grandfathered GST tax exempt status[19] or violate the original trust's rule against perpetuities. *See, e.g.,* New York Estates, Powers & Trusts Law section 10-6.6(b), which permits a trustee of a purely discretionary trust to appoint the property in favor of the trustee of another trust. Delaware trust law also provides a trustee with similar authority, as does Alaska and Tennessee. *See,* Delaware Code tit. 12, section 3528; Alaska Statute 13.36.157. Delaware and Alaska also allow decanting where the trustee's authority to make distributions is limited by an ascertainable standard. However, Alaska requires that the ascertainable standard in the new trust be the same as that in the original trust. Alaska's limitation is designed to prevent a trustee-beneficiary from having a general power of appointment.

Drafting Example:

When making a distribution "to or for the benefit" of a beneficiary, an Independent Trustee may distribute or appoint (such appointment being in a non-fiduciary capacity) the trust property to another trust for the benefit of such beneficiary in question. The trust receiving the distribution or appointed property (which trust may be established by such Trustee) may, but need not, have the same terms as the distributing trust. In no event may a Trustee exercise its power hereunder in a manner that would cause the loss of a marital or charitable estate tax deduction available to my estate, impair an unexercised right of withdrawal that has not yet lapsed, or cause a trust to lose its ability to hold S corporation stock.

§11.12 PERMIT THE TRUSTEE TO MERGE THE ILIT WITH ANOTHER ILIT

Give the trustee the power to merge the existing ILIT with another (new) ILIT established by the grantor. After the merger the new ILIT

[19] Treas. Reg. §26.2601-1(b)(4)(i)(A) provides that GST grandfathering is preserved if the trustee has the power, either under the terms of the trust instrument, or under state law, to transfer the assets to a new trust, without having to obtain the consent of the beneficiaries or a court, and the terms of the new trust do not extend (or postpone) the time for vesting of any beneficial interest in the trust beyond the period established in the original trust (i.e., beyond the date the rule against perpetuities applies to the original trust). The Regulation also requires that the power to transfer assets to a new trust must have been available at the time the original trust came irrevocable.

would hold the life insurance policy and the three year rule of IRC section 2035 would not be applicable. State law should be consulted to determine if a merger is permitted; and court approval may be required. Priv. Letter Ruls. 9619047 and 9348029 (where the IRS approved trust mergers where: (i) the mergers were for administrative convenience and consolidation of assets, and (ii) the "new" trusts had substantially identical terms and did not affect the quality, value, or timing of any of the powers, beneficial interests, rights, or expectancies provided for under the terms of the original trusts prior to the merger). *See*, Paragraph 7.1(A)(7) of Sample ILIT.

§11.13 GIVE THE INSURED INDIRECT ACCESS TO ILIT ASSETS

If the insured's spouse is a beneficiary of an ILIT that holds a single life policy that insures only the grantor, the insured can receive "indirect" benefits from the ILIT through his or her spouse. This is accomplished by giving the spouse-trustee the right to invade the trust principal for the spouse's health, education, support, and maintenance without regard to other income or resources available to the spouse. Because the spouse's right to invade the ILIT is limited to an ascertainable standard, the spouse does not possess a general power of appointment. The spouse can use the invaded amounts for his or her benefit and for the benefit of the insured. However, the ILIT trustee cannot make distributions that would have the effect of discharging the insured's legal obligation (if any) to support the spouse, since the discharge of the insured's legal obligation would constitute a retained interest under IRC section 2036. Treas. Reg. §20.2036-1(b)(2). *See,* Paragraph 4.1(B) of Sample ILIT.

As previously mentioned in section 11.11 above, the insured can also have indirect access to the policy's cash value by permitting the trustee borrow or make withdrawals from the policy and then make a discretionary distribution to the insured's spouse. *See,* Paragraphs 4.1(A) and 7.1(D)(4) of Sample ILIT.

Another way for an insured to gain access to the ILIT's assets is through loans from the trustee. The loan should be evidenced by a promissory note bearing a rate of interest that is at least equal to the applicable federal rate under IRC section 1274(d). Although it is possible to accrue interest, it is advisable for the insured to pay interest annually to avoid an IRS challenge that the loan is a sham.

Upon the insured's death, the loan and cumulative interest are paid back to the ILIT from the insured's estate and should be deducible from the grantor's gross estate as a bona fide debt. IRC section 2053(a)(4). An added benefit of the loan technique is that the interest payments are removed from the insured's estate. Moreover, if the ILIT is an intentionally defective grantor trust, the interest payments are not subject to income taxes and are, therefore, a tax-free gift to the beneficiaries of the ILIT. *See,* section 3.18, above. In fact, the insured's power to borrow from the ILIT without adequate security is one of the provisions that creates grantor trust status for income tax purposes. *See,* section 2.7(e), above.

Drafting Example:

Except as otherwise provided in the second sentence, Trustee shall have the authority to lend trust funds to such persons and on such terms, including (but not limited to) interest rates, security, and loan duration, as Trustee deems advisable to protect the trust. However, Trustee may lend to me (or to any insured) trust funds without any security but with an adequate rate of interest.

12

ILIT Administration Checklist

CHAPTER OVERVIEW

Once the ILIT has been drafted, it has to be administered in a manner consistent with its purpose and applicable law.[1] This is especially important with regard to federal tax law matters, particularly as concerns a beneficiary's right to withdraw gifts made to the ILIT. Multiple *Crummey* withdrawal rights held by a beneficiary under different trusts can create unintended tax consequences, and the withdrawal rights need to be coordinated. Community property law issues may also be of significance. Failure to properly administer an ILIT can result in the loss of the gift tax annual exclusion for a grantor who makes gifts to the ILIT, and can also result in the ILIT becoming "damaged." A damaged ILIT can cause adverse tax consequences to the grantor and the trust beneficiaries. Another issue of trust administration is whether the ILIT trustee will have an insurable interest in the grantor's life under applicable state law. The insurable interest rule has become a potential "lightning rod" concerning trust-owned life insurance, and the rule is discussed in length. The discussion also includes possible solutions to deal with the insurable interest rule if the practitioner is establishing a new ILIT, or if an existing ILIT does not have an insurable interest in the grantor-insured.

---

[1] *See,* Georgiana J. Slade, "Life After Execution of an Insurance Trust," 40 *Tax Management Memorandum* 375 (October 25, 1999). In her thirteen point *Checklist For Preparing and Administering an ILIT,* Diana S.C. Zeydel concludes (as point number thirteen): "Maintain your sense of humor. This stuff is absurdly technical for a fairly simple objective." Diana S. C. Zeydel, "A Complete Tax Guide for Irrevocable Life Insurance Trusts," 34 *Estate Planning* 13, 20 (July, 2007).

§12.1 ENSURE THAT REASONABLE NOTICE IS GIVEN TO THE BENEFICIARIES OF THEIR *CRUMMEY* WITHDRAWAL RIGHT

The IRS requires *Crummey* withdrawal right holders to receive reasonable notice of their right of withdrawal (and be given a reasonable amount of time to exercise their withdrawal right before it lapses (*see*, section 10.5, above)); otherwise the IRS deems the withdrawal right illusory and not eligible for the annual gift tax exclusion. *See,* Rev. Rul. 83-108, 1983-2 C.B. 167 (3 days was an insufficient amount of time for beneficiary to have reasonable notice to exercise the beneficiary's *Crummey* withdrawal right); Rev. Rul. 81-7, 1981-1 C.B. 474. In Priv. Letter Rul. 199912016 the IRS determined that a father's contributions to two trusts qualified for the gift tax annual exclusion where the beneficiary had "reasonable" notice of the contribution and the right to withdraw the contribution within 30 days. According to the ruling, the trusts provided "that Child or his custodian will be given reasonable notice of any additions...from any source." Unfortunately, the ruling does not specify what constitutes "reasonable" notice. The IRS also requires that *Crummey* withdrawal right holders be informed when gifts are made to the trust that are subject to their first right of withdrawal. Priv. Letter Rul. 8006048.

Also, do not have the beneficiaries waive notice of their *Crummey* withdrawal rights for future years. TAM 9532001. Rather, each year give notice and obtain a written acknowledgment from the beneficiary that he or she is aware of that year's contributions and is aware of his or her withdrawal rights for the upcoming year. If the policy requires monthly or quarterly premium payments, consider making a single contribution at the beginning of each year, giving notice once, and then using the contribution to pay the premiums as they come due. If the ILIT holds group term insurance, the IRS has approved a form of "one time" notice that identifies the beneficiaries' rights of withdrawal and contains a schedule of future contributions that the employer will make. Priv. Letter Ruls. 8143045, 8138102, 8133070, and 8121069; TAM 9045002. *See*, Paragraph 3.2(A) of Sample ILIT. If an adult beneficiary has actual notice of the ILIT contribution and of the right of withdrawal, no written notice is required. *Estate of Carolyn W. Holland v. Commissioner*, T.C. Memo 1997-302 (1997); Priv. Letter Rul. 8008040. *See*, section 15.4(k), below. If the guardian of a minor *Crummey* withdrawal right beneficiary has actual notice of the contribution and withdrawal right, as would be the case where the guardian is also the trustee, no separate notice is required to the minor *Crummey* withdrawal right beneficiary. Priv. Letter Ruls. 9030005 and 8022048.

> **Practice Point:** Neither the *Crummey* case, nor any revenue rulings or private letter rulings, have required that the trust agreement contain a provision requiring the trustee to give *written* notice to the *Crummey* withdrawal right beneficiaries. In fact, no notice was given to the beneficiaries in the *Crummey* case. However, since the taxpayer has the burden of proof, written notice provides permanent evidence.

§12.2 DO NOT PERMIT A BENEFICIARY TO WAIVE A *CRUMMEY* WITHDRAWAL RIGHT

There is a distinction between a beneficiary waiving his or her right to notice of a contribution to an ILIT that gives rise to a *Crummey* withdrawal right and a beneficiary who waives his or her right to exercise a *Crummey* withdrawal right. They are not the same. In the former situation (waiver of notice) the IRS will attempt to disallow an annual gift tax exclusion for the contribution.[2] TAM 9532001. In the latter situation (waiver of the *Crummey* withdrawal right), the waiver (e.g., "I, Susan Doe, hereby waive my right of withdrawal") constitutes a taxable release under IRC section 2514(b) and will result in the waiving beneficiary making a taxable gift of a future interest to the other ILIT beneficiaries of the value of the waived withdrawal amount. No gift tax annual exclusion will be available for the waiving beneficiary's gift to the other ILIT beneficiaries. Furthermore, the waiving beneficiary will be the (new) transferor of the waived amount for GST tax purposes and the original transferor's allocation of GST tax exemption will be lost and wasted. Treas. Reg. §26.2652-1(a)(2). Additionally, if the waiving beneficiary has retained an interest in the ILIT (such as an income interest for life), a portion of the ILIT will be included in the waiving beneficiary's gross estate. IRC sections 2036(a) and 2041(a)(2). *See also,* Treas. Reg. §§20.2041-3(d)(4) and 3(d)(5). To avoid these adverse tax consequences, a beneficiary should not waive his or her withdrawal right, but should simply permit the withdrawal right to lapse.

---

[2] If a waiver of future notices of contributions is employed, the waiver must be revocable by the beneficiary, and the beneficiary must have the right, at any time, to request notices of future contributions.

§12.3 IF POSSIBLE, HAVE THE ILIT HOLD LIQUID ASSETS

When possible, insure that the ILIT has sufficient funds to satisfy a withdrawal right. This can generally be accomplished by having the grantor make cash gifts to the ILIT that the trustee can then use to satisfy any *Crummey* withdrawal rights and pay life insurance premiums. To give substance to the *Crummey* withdrawal right where an employer pays the premiums directly to the life insurance company, an exceedingly cautious grantor may want to fund an ILIT with some cash (or Series EE U.S. Savings Bonds) if the ILIT holds only group term insurance or split-dollar insurance. *See*, Priv. Letter Ruls. 8103074 (group term policy itself was not subject to a *Crummey* withdrawal right, but premium payments by the employer on the group term policy were subject to right of withdrawal) and 8118051 (cash or assets reducible to cash required). *But see*, Priv. Letter Ruls. 8143045, 8138171, 8138170, 8138102, 8134135, 8021058, and 8006109 (which contain no liquidity seed requirements concerning a group term policy and permit an interest in the group term policy to be distributed). *See also*, Priv. Letter Rul. 8111123 (a contribution qualified for the gift tax annual exclusion where the beneficiaries had withdrawal rights which could be satisfied with "[a]ny trust assets, including any life insurance policies"). *See*, section 10.7, above.

> **Practice Point:** The grantor should generally avoid making premium payments directly to the life insurance company.

§12.4 BE AWARE OF COMMUNITY PROPERTY ISSUES

Generally, when the grantor-insured is a resident of a community or marital property state[3] and the ILIT holds policies insuring just the grantor's life, and the spouse is a beneficiary of the ILIT, the insured-grantor's separate (non-community/non-marital) property should be

---

[3] There are currently ten states that are subject to community, quasi-community or marital property laws: (i) Alaska (elective), (ii) Arizona, (iii) California, (iv) Idaho, (v) Louisiana, (vi) Nevada, (vii) New Mexico, (viii) Texas, (ix) Washington, and (x) Wisconsin. *See, generally*, Section IV, N of Gerald B. Treacy, 802-2nd T.M., *Community Property: General Considerations*, Bureau of National Affairs, Washington, DC; "Incidents of Ownership and Life Insurance Proceeds in a Community Property State," 28 *Tax Management Estates, Gifts and Trusts Journal* 207 (July 10, 2003); and David W. Reinecke and Mark J. Bradley, "Community Property Issues for Noncommunity Property Practitioners," 4 *ALI-ABA Estate Planning Course Materials Journal* 5 (December 1998).

used to fund the ILIT. Furthermore, all policies owned or transferred to the ILIT should be (or changed into) the separate property of the insured-grantor before being transferred to the ILIT. Otherwise the grantor's spouse will be making contributions to a trust for his or her own benefit, resulting in some or all of the value of the ILIT being included in his or her gross estate under IRC section 2036. *See, e.g.,* Rev. Rul. 2003-40, 2003-1 C.B. 813 and Rev. Rul. 94-69, 1994-2 C.B. 241 (concerning Louisiana community property law). For a married couple that has nothing but community property, the couple should enter into an agreement to partition the community property into separate property. Once the property is separately owned, the ILIT should be funded as described above.

Also, it is unclear as to whether funds provided by an insured's employer to pay for group term insurance or split-dollar insurance are community/marital property or the insured's separate property. Therefore, treat carefully any group term life insurance transferred to the ILIT as well as any split-dollar arrangements with the insured-grantor's employer.

If you are dealing with a second-to-die life insurance policy that insures both spouses, the community/marital property issues discussed above should not be an issue, since neither spouse will have an interest in the ILIT.

> **Practice Point:** Many community/marital property states have specific provisions for ownership and payment of premiums on life insurance policies. Since they vary from state to state, the practitioner needs to know his or her relevant state's rules.

§12.5 BE COGNIZANT OF THE GENERATION-SKIPPING TAX RISK AND NEED TO ALLOCATE GST TAX EXEMPTION

Except when the ILIT is an IRC section 2642(c) or an IRC section 2503(c) generation-skipping trust, every ILIT has potential GST tax exposure. Therefore, when an ILIT is established and first funded, the grantor needs to consider whether or not to file a U.S. Gift Tax Return and whether to opt in or out of the inter-vivos automatic GST exemption allocation rules. *See,* section 5.32, above. For reasons previously discussed in section 5.29, above, a grantor should not rely on the inter-vivos automatic GST tax exemption allocation rules of IRC section 2632(c) to ensure that the ILIT is made GST tax exempt.

§12.6 COORDINATE A BENEFICIARY'S MULTIPLE *CRUMMEY* WITHDRAWAL RIGHTS

If a beneficiary has withdrawal rights under other trusts, make sure all the withdrawal rights are coordinated and aggregated for purposes of IRC section 2514(e). As previously mentioned in section 3.17, above, a beneficiary is permitted only one five-by-five safe harbor lapse per calendar year, regardless of how many withdrawal rights have been granted to the beneficiary. This is of particular concern where the beneficiary has withdrawal rights granted under other trusts. *See*, section 10.10, above. *See*, Paragraph 3.2(L) of Sample ILIT.

§12.7 PROHIBIT NONINSURED SPOUSE-BENEFICIARY FROM PAYING LIFE INSURANCE PREMIUMS

A noninsured spouse is considered to be a grantor of an ILIT under IRC section 2036(a)(1) if he or she pays any part of the life insurance premiums (or makes a contribution to the ILIT—other than merely consenting to gift splitting under IRC section 2513). Therefore, do not have a noninsured spouse who is a beneficiary of the ILIT make any contributions to the ILIT. Also, do not permit the grantor-insured to make contributions to the ILIT using community property or the non-insured spouse's separate property.

> **Practice Point:** ILIT contributions made by the insured grantor from a joint bank account in a separate property state (regardless of who funded the account) where, under applicable state law, either the insured-grantor or his or her spouse can withdraw all of the money without the other spouse's consent do not create an IRC section 2036(a) issue for the noninsured spouse-beneficiary. *See, Estate of John Clay v. Commissioner*, 86 T.C. 1266 (1986) where the Tax Court held, "Where parties maintain joint bank accounts, each co-tenant is not necessarily the agent of the other co-tenant. Therefore, premium payments made with funds withdrawn from a joint account are not per se made by the non-withdrawing co-tenant....In the absence of an agency relationship, the mere payment of premiums with funds withdrawn from a joint account does not constitute payment [of the life insurance premium] by the non-withdrawing tenant." *Id.* at 1273 and 1274. This holding is a correct interpretation of the general law of separate prop-

erty states concerning joint bank accounts, since the withdrawal by the insured-grantor severs the joint tenancy and the withdrawn money becomes the separate property of the grantor-insured. Even if the noninsured spouse-beneficiary supplied all of the monies for the joint account, he or she is deemed to have made a gift of a present interest in the amount of the withdrawn funds to the insured-grantor, which qualifies for the unlimited gift tax marital deduction under IRC section 2523(a) or the special increased annual gift tax exclusion amount under IRC section 2523(i)(2) (if the grantor-insured is not a U.S. citizen). Nevertheless, applicable state law should be consulted concerning the rights of joint bank account owners, especially if they are spouses. For the super cautious, consider having the grantor-insured obtain a certified check made payable to the ILIT trustee, or have the bank issue a money order or bank cashier's check made payable to the ILIT trustee; that way there can be no argument from the IRS that the non-withdrawing joint tenant has not made a completed gift to the insured-grantor at the time of the withdrawal.

§12.8 CONSOLIDATE GIFTS TO THE ILIT

When possible, a grantor should minimize the number of gifts made annually to the ILIT. For example, rather than making gifts each quarter as premiums come due, the grantor should make one annual gift each year of an amount sufficient to pay the year's premiums. This will reduce the number of *Crummey* notices that need to be sent out each year, and will help reduce trustee's burden of administration (and trustee fees).

§12.9 DETERMINE IF STATE LAW PERMITS THE ILIT TRUSTEE TO HAVE AN INSURABLE INTEREST IN THE INSURED'S LIFE[4]

§12.9(a) Insurable Interest Requirement

State law (statutory, case law, or common law) governs the ability of a third party (such as an ILIT trustee) to purchase life insurance

---

[4] Parts of this section are excerpted and adapted from *Steve Leimberg's Estate Planning Newsletter* # 990 (July 6, 2006) and *Steve Leimberg's Estate Planning Newsletter* # 941

on the life of another person, such as the grantor of the ILIT.[5] Generally, all states require that one who buys an insurance policy on the life of another must have an insurable interest in the insured's life. (A few states also require that the beneficiary have an insurable interest, too.)[6] A person usually has an insurable interest in the insured's life if that person has a reasonable expectation of benefiting from the insured's continued longevity, or will suffer a loss from the insured's death. Thus, a surety for the insured or a creditor of the insured would have an insurable interest. Similarly, the insured and close family members of the insured are deemed to have an insurable interest in the insured's life.

§12.9(b) Consequences Of Violating The Insurable Interest Rule

The insurable interest requirement must be met when the policy is acquired from the life insurance company. If the insurable inter-

---

(March 9, 2006), http://www.leimbergservices.com. Copyright Leimberg Information Services, Inc. (LISI). Used with permission. All rights reserved. The author gratefully acknowledges the generous contributions of Mary Ann Mancini, Esq. of Bryan Cave, LLP of Washington, D.C., Howard M. Zaritsky, Esq. of Pitcairn Financial group of Vienna Virginia, and Louis S. Harrison, Esq. of Harrison & Held, LLP of Chicago, Illinois in the writing of this section. *See*, Robert B. Barnett, Jr., and Jessica K. Vllasi, "Still Nervous About That Insurable Interest," 146 *Trust & Estates* 52 (May 2007); and Mary Ann Mancini and Howard M. Zaritsky, "Insurable Interests: Après Chawla, le Deluge?," 32 *ACTEC Journal* 194 (Winter 2006).

[5] In states where the insurable interest rule is found in case law, rather than in a statute, the definition of these persons is capable of more subjective interpretation. Without a statute, the determination may be made that in the absence of any case law to the contrary, a person should have an insurable interest in the insured so long as it doesn't violate the public policy behind the rule itself because there was no wagering on a person's life. This analysis is not possible in a state with a statute that clearly sets out who has an insurable interest. In a state with an insurable interest statute, if a person is not listed in the statute, it is presumed the omission was deliberate and such person does not have an insurable interest in the insured. Practitioners trying to establish the existence of an insurable interest in an insurance trust may oftentimes be better off in a state with only a common law insurable interest rule than in a state with an insurable interest statute that does not specifically address trusts, since the public policy behind the insurable interest rules can be argued in a common law insurable interest state. A good argument can be made under the common law that insurance trusts do not wager on an insured's life and therefore there is no public policy preventing a trust from being considered to have an insurable interest in the insured.

[6] *See*, Leimberg Information Services, Inc at http://leimbergservices.com/dt.cfm for a compilation of all the state insurable interest laws.

est rule is met at the time of the policy's acquisition, the policy owner (typically the insured) can then assign the policy to someone who does not have an insurable interest, as long as the insured is not acting as the agent for the assignee when the insured buys the policy. If it is subsequently determined that there was no insurable interest at the time of the policy's acquisition, the life insurance company may be not obligated to pay the death benefit, although it will have to refund any premiums paid (sometimes with interest) less any prior policy withdrawals or borrowing.[7] Worse, if an ILIT does not have an insurable interest in the grantor-insured, the insurance proceeds may be subject to estate tax if the ILIT is located in a state whose insurable interest statute or case law imposes a constructive trust on the proceeds in favor of the decedent's estate, rather than permitting the insurer to void the policy. IRC section 2042. In addition, proceeds paid with respect to a policy issued without an insurable interest may not qualify for exclusion from the beneficiary's gross income as "amounts received under a life insurance contract...paid by reason of the death of the insured." IRC section 101(a). *Atlantic Oil Company v. Patterson*, 331 F.2d 516 (5th Cir. 1964).

§12.9(c) Purpose Of The Insurable Interest Rule

"Under English common law, there was no prohibition against wagering on someone else's life using a contract of insurance. The law changed in 1774 with the adoption of the English Life Assurance Act. The Act was intended to prevent what was perceived to be a social evil—betting on someone else's life for profit."[8] Thus, the purpose of the insurable interest rule is to prevent a person, such as a stranger, from buying life insurance on another person's life where the stranger has no lawful and substantial economic interest in the continuation of the life, health, bodily safety and survival of the insured, and the stranger would not suffer any economic loss if the insured were to die. Without an insurable interest rule, a stranger would actually benefit from the insured's death; and this could encourage wagering or gam-

---

[7] In some states, the life insurance company is obligated to pay the life insurance proceeds to the estate of the insured, and not to the named beneficiary. In other states, such as Michigan, violation of the insurable interest rule voids the policy *ab initio,* and the life insurance company does not have to pay any death benefit—to anyone!

[8] Stephan R. Leimberg and Albert E. Gibbons, "COLI, BOLI, TOLI and Insurable Interests," 28 *Estate Planning* 333 (July 2001).

bling on the insured's life (e.g., "stranger owned life insurance" ("SOLI") aka "investor initiated life insurance" ("IILI") or "investor owned life insurance" (IOLI))[9] or collusion through the use of life insurance, or worse—criminal behavior on the part of the stranger, who has nothing to lose (and everything to gain) if the insured dies. Thus, public policy (and, to a certain extent, criminal law) are the underlying reasons for the insurable interest rule.[10]

---

[9] *See,* Stephan R. Leimberg, "Planners Must Be Aware of the Danger Signals of 'Free' Life Insurance," 34 *Estate Planning* 20 (February 2007); R. Marshall Jones, Stephan R. Leimberg and Lawrence J. Rybka, "'Free' Life Insurance: Risks and Costs of Non-Recourse Premium Financing," 33 *Estate Planning* 3 (July 2006); Stephan R. Leimberg, "Stranger-Owned Life Insurance ('SOLI'): Killing the Goose That Lays Golden Eggs!," 32 *Estate Planning* 43 (January 2005), for a discussion of SOLI, IILI, IOLI, and other forms of "questionable" or unusual life insurance ownership arrangements.

There have been six recent events that "crack down" on the perceived abuses associated with IILI. "These five events are (1) the New York Office of General Counsel Opinion issued in January 2006, (2) the New York Life Insurance Company's suit to rescind a trust-owned policy [and New York Life's firing a number of their agents who were involved in selling IILI arrangements], (3) Utah Insurance Department Bulletin 2006-03 issued in July 2006, (4) Louisiana Insurance Department Bulletin 06-05 issued in September 2006, and (5) the National Association of Insurance Commissioners' five-year ban on a policy financed with the specific intent to be sold to investors." Stephan R. Leimberg, "Planners Must Be Aware of the Danger Signals of 'Free' Life Insurance," 34 *Estate Planning* 20 (February 2007).

As mentioned above, in 2006, the insurance commissioners for New York, Louisiana, and Utah rendered opinions detailing their opposition to IILI and the contention that it violates their respective states' insurable interest laws. On April 2, 2007, the insurance commissioner for Idaho also issued a similar opinion. *Steve Leimberg's Estate Planning Newsletter* #1108 (April 4, 2007) at http://www.leimbergservices.com.

As an indication of Congress' concern about IILI, one need look no further than IRC section 101(j) that was added by the Pension Protection Act of 2006 in response to perceived abuses concerning employers purchasing life insurance (as an investment) on their "rank and file" employees without the employee's knowledge or permission. *See,* section 2.1, above.

[10] The common law of the United States, which has been codified in many states, holds that to allow someone to speculate on a person's life by buying a life insurance policy on such person is against public policy. The possible ramification of allowing such policies would be that any person who is so insured could not feel safe in light of any investor's natural desire to see his or her investment "pay off." In fact, to so endanger someone's life can expose the insurance company to tort liability, as illustrated in *Liberty National Life Ins. Co. v. Weldon*, 267 Ala. 171, 100 So. 2d 696, 61 A.L.R. 2d 1346 (1957).

§12.9(d) Insurable Interest Requirement And Trusts

When a trust is the original purchaser of a policy of insurance on the grantor's life, state law determines if the trust has an insurable interest in the grantor's life.[11] If the state's insurance statute is not explicit about this issue (and many state statutes are not), or if there is no statute, the determination of whether the trust has an insurable interest in the grantor's life instead turns on case law. In this regard the courts will typically either view the trust as a separate legal entity (the "entity view"), or as an aggregation of its beneficiaries (the "aggregation view.") There is little case law on which of these two approaches should be applied to an ILIT. Most of the cases that have considered this issue appear to have adopted the aggregate view, looking at whether the beneficiaries of the trust had insurable interests in the insured.[12] The aggregate view is consistent with black letter trust law that the trustee holds

---

The insurable interest rule also applies to other forms of insurance, such as property and casualty insurance. Without such a rule, the potential for arson, theft and wagering would be a problem. For example, a stranger can not buy a homeowner's insurance policy on another person's house or property.

[11] Most insurable interest statutes will mention certain types of employee trusts, but no other type of trust, as having an insurable interest in the insured under certain circumstances. This leads to the question of whether the omission in the statute of any other type of trust was a deliberate decision by the state legislature to exclude other types of trust arrangements, such as an ILIT. *See, e.g.,* Michigan Compiled Laws Sections 500.2210—500.2212, which permits employee trusts and charities to have an insurable interest in the insured.

[12] *See, McCann v. Metropolitan Life Ins. Co.*, 177 Mass. 280, 58 N.E. 1026 (1901) ; *In re LeBlanc,* 217 BR 365 (Bankr. D. Mass. 1998); *Potter Title & Trust Co. v. Fidelity Trust Co.*, 316 Pa. 316, 175 A. 400 (1934) ; *Empire Life Ins. Co. of Am. v. Moody*, 584 S.W.2d 855 (Tex. 1979); *Volunteer State Life Ins. Co. v. Pioneer Bank*, 46 Tenn. App. 244, 327 S.W.2d 59 (1959).

Many practitioners take comfort in the aggregate view—that a trust is a collection of trust beneficiaries, and the insurable interest rules are applied to those beneficiaries—will protect their insurance trusts from attack because most insurance trust beneficiaries are closely related to the insured. This is also the approach of the proposed Maryland legislation to deal with the *Chawla* decision. But is this really the case? Such a position does not address the present uncertainty under the state statutes of just who is "closely related by blood or by law." Interpreting a trust as a collection of beneficiaries may mean that beneficiaries who are not related to the insured will not be permissible beneficiaries of an insurance trust. Consider, for example, stepchildren, who are beneficiaries of the insurance trust as part of the overall estate plan when there has perhaps been a pooling of assets within the marriage and children of both parents are treated the same under each parent's estate plan.

naked title to the trust property for the benefit of the trust beneficiaries, who, by law, have an equitable interest in the trust property. Thus the trustee is in some ways an "agent" of the beneficiaries, and acts for their benefit.

For example, in *In re LeBlanc*, 217 B.R. 365 (Bankr. D. Mass., 1998), the U.S. Bankruptcy Court for Massachusetts held that a trust for the benefit of those of the insured's children who survive him, or otherwise to his nieces and nephews who survive him, lacked an insurable interest. The insured sought to claim the benefit of a state exemption from creditor claims for a life insurance policy on the life of the debtor, but held by and payable to a person (other than the debtor) who has an insurable interest in the debtor's life. At the time of the bankruptcy suit, the insured was unmarried and he had no children, and the only beneficiaries of the trust were his nieces and nephews. The court stated that the policy was held in favor of the various individuals "through a trust," and analyzed whether or not an insurable interest existed by considering the present beneficiaries of the trust the debtor's nieces and nephews. Thus, the court adopted the "aggregation view" with respect to insurable interests held by a trust.

On the other hand, another case looked at whether a business trust (which is, in reality, more like a partnership than a trust) had an insurable interest when it was listed as the policy owner on the initial application. The policy was, however, initially issued to the insured. The court discussed whether the business trust had a valid claim against the beneficiary (the insured's wife) for the proceeds, because the parties had intended that the trust be the policy owner, in order to finance the purchase of interests in the trust under a buy-sell agreement. The California Appeals Court held that the business trust had an insurable interest only as a creditor of the insured, based on the buy-sell agreement, and that it did not have an insurable interest merely because the insured was a beneficiary. *Caso v. First Colony Life Ins. Co.*, 2003 WL 21019625 (Cal. Ct. App. May 7, 2003). Thus, neither the entity nor aggregation view was dealt with by the court.

Consider, too, unmarried domestic partners who wish to insure each other's lives and want to use an insurance trust because they do not have the advantage of the marital deduction to shield the proceeds from estate tax. Unless these individuals are found to have another type of insurable interest in the insured (such as being in business together, a debtor-creditor relationship, etc.), a trust with such beneficiaries will be unable to obtain insurance on the insured.

§12.9(e) Insurable Interest Requirement And The *Chawla* Trial Court Decision

Prior to 2005 the estate planning community gave little thought to whether an ILIT had an insurable interest in the grantor-insured. It was commonly assumed that if an insured's family members had an insurable interest, then any vehicle that is made up of these family members should also have an insurable interest. Members of an insured's family include the insured, children, grandchildren, and spouses. These people have an insurable interest in one another. A trust for the benefit of these individuals should also have an insurable interest in any one of these individuals.

But then came the bizarre case of *Vera Chawla, Trustee for Harald Giesinger Special Trust v. Transamerica Occidental Life Insurance Company*, 2005 WL 405405 (E.D. Va. Feb. 3, 2005). The case raised an issue to which many estate planners have not given much consideration in the past. Prior to *Chawla*, estate planners generally assumed that an individual could establish an ILIT and then have the trustee acquire life insurance on that individual's life.

In *Chawla* the decedent, Harald Giesinger, applied for a $1 million life insurance policy on May 4, 2000 and listed his close friend and business associate, Vera Chawla, as owner and beneficiary of the policy. The insurer refused to issue the policy because Ms. Chawla did not have an insurable interest in Harald's life. Harald changed the owner and beneficiary of the policy to the Harald Giesinger Special Trust, a pre-existing irrevocable trust. Harald and Vera Chawla were co-trustees of the Special Trust. Harald was the income beneficiary of the Special Trust, and Vera Chawla was the remainder beneficiary of the Special Trust. Harald died on September 23, 2001 (approximately 17 months after the policy was issued), at which point the insurer rescinded the policy, refunded the premiums and alleged that material misrepresentations had been made in the life insurance application and that the Special Trust lacked any insurable interest in the decedent's life. Vera Chawla then sued the life insurance company. Like *Strangi II*,[13] it is another case which illustrates that bad facts make for bad law.

---

[13] *Estate of Albert Strangi v. Commissioner*, T.C. Memo 2003-145 (2003), *aff'd*, 417 F.3d 468 (5th Cir 2005).

The reason for the bad facts in *Chawla*: the insured, Harald Giesinger, lied on the life insurance application and died a little more than a year after applying, apparently from medical causes that should have been disclosed on the application. And this should have been an easy case for the trial court's affirmation of the life insurance company's denial of coverage. The typical governing insurance law is that when there has been a material misrepresentation in the form of an incorrect statement in an insurance application, the insurance policy will be invalidated.[14] So the trial court's opinion continues for a number of pages along this correct line of argument. But then the court's opinion sinks, inexplicably and for no reason. In dicta, the trial court notes:

> Finally, even absent a material misrepresentation, Plaintiff's claim necessarily fails as a matter of law because the trust maintained no insurable interest in the life of the decedent thus rendering the policy void.[15]

The trial court noted that Maryland law states that death benefits may be paid only to the insured, the insured's personal representative, or "a person with an insurable interest" in the insured when the policy is issued.

Maryland law also states that an insurable interest exists in one who is "related closely by blood or law" and that it includes "a substantial economic interest in the continuation of the life, health, bodily safety" of the insured. The law states that an insurable interest expressly does not include "an interest that arises only by, or would be enhanced in value by, the death, disablement, or injury of the individual...."

The trial court noted that the trust "promised to gain more assets upon [Harald's] death...than it would have in the event that [he] had lived" and that the trust "suffered no detriment, pecuniary or otherwise, upon the death of the decedent." Thus, the court held, the trust lacked an insurable interest in Harald. The trial court adopted the entity view of a trust in determining whether the trust held an insurable interest in Harald.

---

[14] *See, e.g. Hofmann v. John Hancock Mutual Life Ins. Co.*, 400 F. Supp. 827 (D. Md. 1975).

[15] 2005 WL 405405, at #6.

In reaching its decision concerning the trust's lack of an insurable interest, the trial court rejected the aggregate view,[16] and instead adopted the entity view based on its reading of the Maryland statute. The court noted that Maryland law defines a "person" as including both an individual and a trustee; and the court construed the Maryland statute as treating the trust as an entity.

§12.9(f) Insurable Interest Requirement And The *Chawla* Appellate Court Decision

Vera Chawla, trustee of the Special Trust, appealed the trial court's decision to the Federal Court of Appeals for the Fourth Circuit, which upheld the trial court's summary judgment award for Transamerica. *Chawla v. Transamerica Occidental Life Ins. Co.*, 440 F.3d 639 (4th Cir. 2006), *aff'g in part, vacating in part,* 2005 WL 405405 (E.D. Va. Feb. 3, 2005). The Fourth Circuit affirmed the trial court's decision based upon the insured's misrepresentations on the life insurance application. The Court of Appeals also recognized that the trial court's insurable interest analysis could be construed as stating that no trust possessed an insurable interest on the life of its grantor. The Fourth Circuit stated that the trial court should not have "addressed an important and novel question of Maryland law" unless there was a real need to do so. Therefore, the Fourth Circuit vacated as unnecessary the trial court's alternative ruling that Harald's Special Trust lacked an insurable interest on the Harald's life. Many practitioners had hoped that the Fourth Circuit would reverse (rather than merely vacate) the district court and hold that a trust had an insurable interest in the life of an insured if the then-current beneficiaries of the trust had insurable interests. The Fourth Circuit's vacating of that part of the district court opinion expressed no view—one way or the other—on the substantive law of a trust having an insurable interest in the life of an insured. *Thus, the Fourth Circuit dodged the insurable interest issue entirely.* As a result, this leaves the insurable interest issue (based upon the applica-

---

[16] Had the trial court adopted the aggregate view, the trust would have had an insurable interest in Harald's life since an insured always has an insurable interest in his or her own life, and Harald was the sole lifetime beneficiary of the trust.

tion of Maryland law) entirely open regarding whether an ILIT has an insurable interest in a policy it buys on the life of the grantor.[17]

§12.9(g) Impact Of The *Chawla* Appellate Court Decision

Many practitioners had hoped that the Fourth Circuit would reverse the trial court's and hold that a trust had an insurable interest in the life of an insured if the then-current beneficiaries of the trust had insurable interests. The mere vacating of the trial court's ruling concerning the insurable interest issue did not resolve the issue. In fact, in some ways, things are now more complex. One arguing against the existence of an insurable interest in an ILIT could still cite the trial court's opinion in *Chawla*, because, even though the discussion of an insurable interest was unnecessary, it still represented the views of the district court judge. The Fourth Circuit's vacating of that part of the trial court's opinion regrettably expresses no view on the substantive law concerning a trust having an insurable interest.

Practitioners evaluating their options after *Chawla* should separate "the law that should be" from "the law that is." Most practitioners would agree that an insured should be able to create an ILIT with an insurable interest, because the insured consents to the acquisition of the policy (either explicitly or implicitly), and because the insured's family members are usually the current beneficiaries. There are a few state court opinions that seem to adopt this view, but none state it

---

[17] *See*, Robert E. Madden, Lisa H. R. Hays, and Frank S. Baldino, "District Court's Holding That Trust Lacks Insurable Interest Vacated on Appeal," 33 *Estate Planning* 46 (July 2006).

Subsequent to the Fourth Circuit's opinion, the Maryland legislature amended section 12-201 of the Insurance Article of the Maryland Code. Maryland law now provides that a trustee of a trust has an insurable interest in the life of an individual insured if, on the date that the policy is issued, the insured is (i) the grantor, (ii) an individual related closely by blood or law to the grantor, or (iii) an individual in whose life the grantor otherwise has an insurable interest, and the life insurance proceeds are primarily for the benefit of trust beneficiaries who have an insurable interest in the insured's life. The amended Maryland law also provides that a partnership, limited partnership or limited liability company has an insurable interest in the lives of its partners or members and those closely related to them by blood or law. Although the amendment applies to all trusts existing before, on, or after June 1, 2006, regardless of the effective date of the trust, only life insurance policies that are in force and for which the insured is alive on or after June 1, 2006 fall into the protection of the revised Maryland statute.

clearly, and both the trial court in *Chawla* and a California Court of Appeals take the contrary view.

Prior to *Chawla*, most practitioners had previously equated insurable interest only with the process of meeting the insurer's underwriting hurdle. *Chawla* makes it obvious that merely convincing an insurer to issue a policy does not mean that there is insurable interest for state law purposes—and that meeting both tests is essential. The *Chawla* case did not cause a problem in the area of insurable interests; it merely brought a problem that already existed, albeit largely ignored, to light.

§12.9(h) Collateral Implications Of *Chawla*

The *Chawla* decision creates several collateral issues that affect practitioners, their clients, life insurance carriers, trust companies, jobs, and a state's tax revenue. Where the client's home state does not have a statute that permits a trust, such as an ILIT, to have an insurable interest, a client may be inclined to establish an ILIT in a state that provides certainty. If, for example, the client chooses Delaware, this will have the following effect: (i) Delaware counsel will have to assist in drafting the ILIT, which will result in additional fees and costs to the client and possible loss of business to the home state attorney, (ii) in order for the ILIT to have a sufficient nexus with Delaware, the ILIT trustee will have to be a Delaware resident (most likely a corporate trustee), which will result in the loss of trust company business in the client's home state, (iii) the client's home state may not be able to tax the ILIT, which will result in a loss of revenue for the client's home state, (iv) the ILIT will purchase the life insurance from a company licensed to do business in Delaware and the policy will be subject to Delaware law, which will result in the loss of a life insurance business in the client's home state, and (v) the client will probably (to play it safe) have to travel to Delaware to execute the trust, to execute the life insurance application, and to take the medical exam, which will result in additional expenses to the client, and a loss of "travel" monies being spent in the client's home state. Thus, the *Chawla* decision has the ability to affect a state's economy in many ways—for the good if state law provides certainty concerning trusts and insurable interests, and for the worse if state law is uncertain.

§12.9(i) Planning With New ILITs After The *Chawla* Appellate Court Decision

The best approach to avoid the insurable interest problem with new ILITs where state law does not recognize a trust having an insurable interest in a grantor is to create the trust and have the ILIT buy the insurance in a state that has enacted a statute giving a trust an insurable interest.[18] Such statutes have been enacted in Delaware,[19]

---

[18] The practitioner will want the insured and the trustees to create as many contacts as possible to a state with a statute that specifically addresses trusts. The agent's location, where the exam is done, where the contract is delivered, where the premiums are paid and the residence of the trustees and the trust are all important contacts.

"In general, carriers require that two of the following three criteria be met in a trust situation in order to issue a policy in a given state: (1) The grantor must be domiciled in the state; (2) The trustee must be domiciled in the state; and (3) The trust instrument must state the trust is to be governed by the laws of the state." Gary R. Lee & Craig Wilkey, 827 T.M., *Life Insurance—A Practical Guide for Evaluating Policies*, section V, A, 4 (Bureau of National Affairs, Washington, DC).

Some state statutes, however, dictate that a policy issued in that state for the benefit of a resident of that state will be controlled by the laws of the state in which it was issued, notwithstanding contrary policy provisions. For example, Texas Insurance Code §21.42 states that Texas law will govern any contract of insurance payable to any citizen or inhabitant of the state by an insurer doing business in Texas, if contracts are made in course of the company's Texas business). See also statutes and cases discussed in L. Russ & T. Segalla, *Couch on Insurance* §24.20 (3d ed.). In such states, practitioners must pay special attention to the contacts that the policy has to the state, to assure that they do not inadvertently abandon the application of the law of the state who has a favorable rule on insurable interests. The general rule is that a policy of insurance is construed, and its validity determined, under the law of the place where the contract was made, absent an express provision in the contract to the contrary. An insurance contract is usually deemed made where the final act necessary to complete the binding contract occurs. Typically, this is the place where the contract is signed by the later of the parties to sign or the place where the first premium check was paid. Therefore, a practitioner who wishes to have the insurable interest of a trust in a policy of life insurance determined under the law of a specific state, should attempt to: (i) have the contract select that state's law as controlling; (ii) have the policy purchased by a trustee who is located in that state; (iii) have the policy delivered to the trustee at its location in that state; and (iv) have the trustee pay the premiums from its location in that state.

[19] Del. Code Ann. Tit. 18, §2704(c)(5) states:

> The trustee of a trust established by an individual has an insurable interest in the life of that individual and the same insurable interest in the life of any other individual as does any person who is treated as the

Virginia,[20] Washington (state),[21] Georgia,[22] Maine,[23] Maryland,[24] and South Dakota,[25] for example, and are being contemplated in other

---

> owner of such trust for federal income tax purposes. The trustee of a trust has the same insurable interest in the life of any individual as does any person with respect to proceeds of insurance on the life of such individual (or any portion of such proceeds) that are allocable to such person's interest in such trust. If multiple beneficiaries of a trust have an insurable interest in the life of the same individual, the trustee of such trust has the same aggregate insurable interest in such life as such beneficiaries with respect to proceeds of insurance on the life of such individual (or any portion of such proceeds) that are allocable in the aggregate to such beneficiaries' interest in the trust.

What Delaware has done is recognize that the trust itself, if created by the insured, has an insurable interest in the insured. In this part of the statute Delaware treats the trust as a separate entity with its own insurable interest in the insured, so long as the insured created the trust. Furthermore, under the Delaware statute, a trust that is not created by the insured but whose beneficiaries have insurable interests in the insured also has an insurable interest in the insured. Delaware treats a trust not created by the insured as an aggregation of its beneficiaries (rather than as a separate entity) and if those beneficiaries have an insurable interest in the insured, then the trust has an insurable interest in the insured, at least to the extent the proceeds are allocable to those beneficiaries with insurable interests.

[20] Va. Code §38.2-301(B)(5) states:

> In the case of a trustee, other than the trustee of a domestic business trust or foreign business trust...the [insurable interest] ...shall be deemed to exist in (i) the individual insured who established the trust, (ii) each individual in whose life the owner of the trust for federal income tax purposes has an insurable interest, and (iii) each individual in whose life a beneficiary of the trust has an insurable interest.

There is no language in the Virginia statute addressing the situation of when some beneficiaries have an insurable interest but not all beneficiaries, as Delaware's statute does.

[21] Wash. Rev. Code Ann. §48.18.030(3)(c) states:

> A guardian, trustee or other fiduciary has an insurable interest in the life of any person for whose benefit the fiduciary holds property, and in the life of any other individual in whose life such person has an insurable interest.

This wording is a little difficult to follow, but under the Washington state statute, a trustee has an insurable interest in any of its beneficiaries and an insurable interest in any person in which a trust beneficiary would have an insurable interest. If a beneficiary is closely related to the insured, then the beneficiary has an insurable interest in the insured, which would result in the trust having an insurable interest in the insured.

[22] Ga. Code §33-24-3(c) states:

> The trustee of a trust established by an individual settlor has an insurable interest in the life of that individual settlor and has the same insur-

states, such as Michigan. If this option is not practical, because the grantor does not want to create a trust or buy the policy in another state, the grantor-insured, rather than the trust, should be the first owner of the life insurance policy.

> able interest in the life of any other individual as does such individual settlor. The trustee of a trust has the same insurable interest in the life of any other individual as does any beneficiary of the trust with respect to proceeds of insurance on the life of such individual or any portion of such proceeds that are allocable to such beneficiary's interest in such trust. If multiple beneficiaries of a trust have an insurable interest in the life of the same individual, the trustee of such trust has the same aggregate insurable interest in such individual's life as such beneficiaries with respect to proceeds of insurance on the life of such individual or any portion of such proceeds that is allocable in the aggregate to such beneficiaries' interest in the trust.

This statute provides all trustees of insurance trusts with an insurable interest in the life of the grantor and the grantor's close family members or other persons in whom the grantor has an insurable interest. It also provides the trustee with an insurable interest in the life of each beneficiary, to the extent that the proceeds of the policy will be allocated to that beneficiary's "interest in such trust." The reference to the "proceeds" payable to a beneficiary's "interest in such trust" produces problems similar to those created by the Delaware statute. A trust for the lifetime benefit of the insured, with provision for the disposition of the proceeds at the insured's death, might not be deemed to have an insurable interest in the insured merely because of the insured's status as a beneficiary, because the proceed could never be allocable to the insured's beneficial interest in the trust.

[23] 24-A Me Rev. Stat. 2404(1).

[24] Md. Ins. Code §12-201(b)(6).

[25] S.D. Code Chapter 58-10-4 states:

> 58-10-4. Insurable interest in personal insurance defined. Insurable interest with reference to personal insurance includes only interests as follows:
>
> (1) Interests in individuals related closely by blood, marriage, or by law, a substantial interest engendered by love and affection;
>
> (2) For other persons, a lawful and substantial economic interest in having the life, health, or bodily safety of the individual insured continue, as distinguished from an interest which would arise only by, or would be enhanced in value by, the death, disablement, or injury of the individual insured;
>
> (3) A person who is a party to a contract or option for the purchase or sale of an interest in a business partnership or firm, or of shares of stock of a closed corporation or of an interest in the shares, has an insurable interest in the life of each individual party to the contract and for the purpose of the contract only, in addition to any insurable interest which may otherwise exist as to the life of the individual;

The grantor-insured should first buy the policy, and then create the trust.[26] After the trust has been created, the grantor-insured can then assign or sell the policy to the trust. Obtaining the policy before the trust is even created will assure that the initial policy owner is the insured, who always has an insurable interest in his or her own life. It will also make it difficult for the insurer (or the IRS) to assert that the insured acted solely as the agent for the trustee in acquiring the policy. Generally, the grantor-insured can assign the policy to anyone the grantor-insured wishes, whether or not the assignee otherwise has an insurable interest.

If the grantor-insured gifts the policy to an ILIT, the grantor-insured will have to live for three years in order to avoid the three year

---

> (4) A charitable organization that meets the requirements of section 501(c)3 of the Internal Revenue Code of 1986, as amended to January 1, 1992, and owns or purchases life insurance on an insured who consents to the ownership or purchase of the insurance has an insurable interest in the life of the insured;
>
> (5) A financial institution, as defined in subdivision 10-43-1(4), to whom a debt is owed has an insurable interest in the life of the insured to the extent of the debt owed by the insured, irrespective of any statute of limitation regarding the enforceability of the debt;
>
> (6) The trustee of a trust established by an individual settlor has an insurable interest in the life of that individual settlor, and has the same insurable interest in the life of any other individual as does such individual settlor. However, the settlor must be the insured or have an insurable interest as required by subdivisions (1) to (5), inclusive, of this section. The trustee of a trust has the same insurable interest in the life of any other individual as does any beneficiary of the trust with respect to proceeds of insurance on the life of such individual or any portion of such proceeds that are allocable to such beneficiary's interest in such trust. If multiple beneficiaries of a trust have an insurable interest in the life of the same individual, the trustee of such trust has the same aggregate insurable interest in such individual's life as such beneficiaries with respect to proceeds of insurance on the life of such individual or any portion of such proceeds that are allocable in the aggregate to such beneficiaries' interest in the trust. A trustee of a business trust has the same insurable interest in the life of any individual as does any beneficial owner in any individual or any beneficial owners in the aggregate in any individual.

Interestingly, the South Dakota statute is "effective retroactively to November 2, ***1889***." S.D. Code Chapter 58-10-16.

[26] A court may view a purchase of the policy and an immediate assignment to a trust as a purchase of the policy by the trust, acting through the insured, as an agent. But if the trust does not exist when the insured buys the policy, it is very difficult to view the insured as the trust's agent.

rule of IRC section 2035.[27] *See,* section 4.1, above. This is certainly a problem, but many insurance policies include (sometimes at a slight additional charge) a rider that doubles the payment if the insured dies within three years of the policy's acquisition. This provides additional liquidity to pay the estate taxes on the life insurance proceeds. A way to avoid IRC section 2035 is for the grantor-insured to sell the policy to the ILIT for full and adequate consideration. *See,* section 3.1, above concerning the valuation of a life insurance policy. Furthermore, if the ILIT is an intentionally defective grantor trust with regard to the insured, there is no transfer for value problem if the policy is gifted or sold to the ILIT. *See,* section 2.5, above.

> **Practice Point:** If the policy is sold to an intentionally defective grantor trust shortly after the insured acquires the policy (with the above mentioned caveat that the ILIT be established after the insured acquires the policy), the cash used to fund the ILIT will come back to the insured. Thus, the sale of the policy will be a non-event for income tax purposes, and the insured will get back the money he or she initially gifts to the ILIT—a winning situation for all involved (assuming the insured can afford both the initial premium and trust funding outlay).

§12.9(j) Planning With Existing ILITs After The *Chawla* Appellate Court Decision

The problem with existing ILITs is potentially more serious, because the defect of the lack of an insurable interest does not disappear with age or length of time that the policy is held. Furthermore, the public policy against allowing a life insurance policy to be acquired by someone who lacks an insurable interest is so strong, that a court may permit the insurer to raise an insurable interest defense even though the life insurance company has accepted the premiums and/or

---

[27] If you run the actuarial odds (with a computer program such as Number Cruncher) of an insured's death within three years of acquiring-transferring the policy to the ILIT, you will discover that even well into a person's 80s, the probability of dying within three years of any given age is very slight. The probability is even smaller—by definition—if the insured was just approved for life insurance. As a backup, the ILIT should include a contingent marital deduction provision if the insured is married and is the sole insured. Do not use a contingent marital deduction where both spouses are insured under a joint policy. *See,* section 11.3, above.

expressly acknowledged the lack of an the insurable interest.[28] Obviously, the law on such issues will vary from state-to-state.

In advising clients, practitioners need to be mindful that they may be allowing their clients to enter into what is essentially a one-sided contract. The policy owner pays the premiums, but there is no certainty that the life insurance company must pay the death benefit to the ILIT. The insurance company can withdraw from the contract at any time by claiming that the policy owner does not have an insurable interest.

There are very few things that can be done to cure the problems of an ILIT that lacks an insurable interest. Of course the existing policy can be cancelled and a new policy obtained by the insured, and then assigned to the trust, as long as the insured remains in good health and the cost of a new policy is not unacceptable. *See,* Chapter 15, below.

Also, the trust situs can be moved to a state with more favorable statutory rules, and the existing policy can then be exchanged for a new one issued under the more favorable state law. The exchange is likely to be tax-free under IRC section 1035. *See,* section 2.14, above. Of course, changing the situs of a trust, and the governing law, is not always easy or inexpensive.

§12.9(k) Possible Need For Clarifying Or Remedial Legislation

As more insureds consider holding life insurance in entities, such as an ILIT, the issue of a trust's lack of an insurable interest may be raised in those states that lack a statute that expressly authorizes a trust to have an insurable interest. Eventually, the determination of whether an ILIT or other type of entity has an insurable interest in the insured

---

[28] Nowhere is it suggested that the trustee request a letter from the insurance company assuring the trustee that the insurance company will not raise the issue of the lack of insurable interest. It is not only the insurance company that can raise the issue and the insurance company may be forced to withhold payment of the death benefit, notwithstanding the letter. If a contractual relationship is found to exist between the parties the letter isn't necessary and if it is determined that no insurance interest existed but the doctrine of estoppel cannot be raised due to the applicable state law, the insurance company will not pay the proceeds, regardless of the letter. If the policy is void but otherwise payable in equity to the insured's estate, the insurance company will pay the proceeds to the estate and not the trust. Therefore, such a letter is useless.

will have to be developed on a state by state basis by the courts, if the issue is not addressed proactively with an appropriate legislative solution that is consistent across the country. Without such consistency, the area of ILITs and other entities holding life insurance policies may turn into a legal quagmire.

A practitioner with a filing cabinet full of old ILITs in which the trustee was the initial purchaser of the policies may also want to consider urging his or her state legislature to enact a clarifying amendment to the state's insurable interest law. Such an amendment might declare that the existence of a trust's insurable interest is determined by whether the trust beneficiaries have an insurable interest (the aggregate view). Such an amendment would not necessarily alter the existing statute, but merely interpret how it was intended to apply to trusts. As such, clarifying legislation would arguably be retroactive in its effect. States should also consider adopting statutory language similar to states that have recently amended their insurable interest laws concerning trusts, such as Delaware, Washington state, Virginia, South Dakota, Georgia, etc.

§12.10 FOLLOW THE PROCEDURES IN APPENDIX 5

Once the ILIT has been drafted and is ready to be funded, the grantor and trustee should also follow the procedures and tax filing rules contained in the "Sample Memorandum to Grantor and Trustee on Operation of ILIT," which is contained in Appendix 5, below.

13

Coordination Of ILIT With Insured's Other Estate Planning Documents

CHAPTER OVERVIEW

An ILIT is an adjunct to the grantor's base estate planning documents.[1] This chapter discusses which key base estate planning documents need to be coordinated with the ILIT to ensure the ILIT's efficacy and survivability, especially if the grantor becomes physically or mentally incapacitated. Sample drafting language for durable powers of attorney is also provided.

§13.1 COORDINATE ILIT WITH INSURED'S REVOCABLE LIVING TRUST AND WILL

If the insured transfers to the ILIT existing life insurance policies that insure only the grantor's life, then not only should a contingent marital trust provision be inserted in the ILIT (if the insured is married), but also the tax apportionment clauses in the insured's will and revocable living trust (if applicable) should be coordinated and should deal

---

[1] Because an ILIT is an adjunct to a person's base estate plan, an ILIT should not be used as a pour-over from a person's estate, will, or other trust. Drafting of coordinated base estate planning documents, such as a revocable living trust, pour-over will, durable power of attorney, and health care declaration is beyond the scope of this book. *See generally*, Sebastian V. Grassi, Jr., *A Practical Guide to Drafting Marital Deduction Trusts (with Sample Forms and Checklists)*, ALI-ABA, Philadelphia, PA (2004, Supp. 2006) (800) 253-6397, http://www.ali-aba.org/aliaba/bk36.asp.

with the contingency concerning the payment of death taxes on the life insurance policy. In the absence of such a provision, IRC section 2206 states that the beneficiaries of the insurance proceeds are to pay their pro rata share of death taxes. Additionally, if a contingent marital trust provision is used, the tax apportionment provisions in the surviving spouse's will must be coordinated to insure consistency with the grantor's overall intent. Even without a surviving spouse, the tax apportionment provisions should be coordinated in the grantor's estate planning documents, since it is unlikely that all of the insured's estate planning documents are going to have identical devisees/beneficiaries and identical dispositive provisions.

For example, what if the life insurance proceeds are includable in a married insured's gross estate and the ILIT has a zero GST tax inclusion ratio? Fortunately, the ILIT proceeds can be paid to a QTIP marital deduction trust and the existing GST tax inclusion ratio can be preserved by having the insured's executor make an IRC section 2652(a)(3) reverse QTIP election as to the whole marital deduction trust (to preserve the insured's previously allocated GST tax exemption). The insured's spouse's will should provide that the right to recover estate taxes under IRC section 2207A (concerning QTIP trust property) is waived and the estate tax is to be apportioned (without the right to recovery or contribution from the QTIP trust property or the recipients of the QTIP trust property) against the residue of the surviving spouse's estate. Be careful with this formulation, however, particularly if the surviving spouse is a second spouse and there are children from different marriages involved.

§13.2 COORDINATE ILIT WITH INSURED'S DURABLE POWER OF ATTORNEY

The insured's durable power of attorney for financial affairs should contain gifting provisions and permit the attorney-in-fact to make irrevocable gifts and transfers directly to beneficiaries and to any irrevocable trust that has been established by the insured. This provision insures that if the insured is incapacitated, the trust can continue to be funded, and thus prevents a potential lapse of the insurance policies. Absent the agent's express authority to make gifts under the durable power of attorney (or applicable state law), the gifts to the ILIT will be challenged by the IRS as being revocable by the insured, and subject to inclusion in the insured's gross estate under IRC section 2038. *See, e.g.*, *Estate of Casey v. Commissioner*, 948 F.2d 895 (4th Cir. 1991); *Estate of Mary Catherine IX Gaynor v. Commissioner*, T.C. Memo 2001-206 (2001); TAMs 9342003 and 9736004.

Drafting Example:

Gifts-Restricted Amount. *My Agent is authorized to make irrevocable gifts that are eligible for exclusion under Internal Revenue Code sections 2503(b) or 2503(e) (concerning direct payment of tuition and/or medical care) as my Agent deems proper, with any of my real estate or personal property, to or for: my spouse (if I am married), any of my descendants (and their spouses), any of my relatives, or any persons who are listed as beneficiaries or devisees (present or contingent) under my will or any trust created by me (and not my Agent), or any charitable organization (including gifts to complete or fulfill a charitable pledge made by me). Any gifts my Agent may make to him or herself as a permissible donee hereunder without the consent of a person who has a substantial adverse interest vis-à-vis my Agent regarding any gifts made from my property shall be limited by an ascertainable standard related to my Agent's health, education, support, and maintenance; provided however, my Agent may make gifts to him or herself not subject to an ascertainable standard (but subject to any other limitations imposed by the provisions of this paragraph) with the prior written consent of a person who has a substantial adverse interest vis-à-vis my Agent regarding any gifts made from my property. My Agent may not make gifts to my Agent's creditors or make gifts that would discharge my Agent's legal obligation of support. Except for qualified transfers under section 2503(e), and gifts to qualified state tuition programs under section 529, no gifts to any individual in a calendar year shall exceed the amount eligible for the annual federal gift tax exclusion under section 2503(b), or twice that amount if I am married and my spouse is a resident or citizen of the United States; provided however, gifts to my spouse (if I am married) shall not be limited to the amount of the annual federal gift tax exclusion, but rather, shall be limited to the amount qualifying for the federal gift tax marital deduction. Gifts to any charitable organization shall be deductible under Internal Revenue Code sections 170 and 2522 in the year in which such gifts are made, and shall not exceed the amount that I can deduct: (i) in the year in which the gift is made and (ii) in any available carry forward years. All such gifts may be made outright, in trust, to a trust (including an irrevocable trust I have created or shall create at any time), or to any legal guardian or custodian under any applicable Uniform Transfers (or Gifts) to Minors Act, as my Agent deems appropriate, even if my Agent is such trustee, guardian, or custodi-*

an. A "substantial adverse interest" refers to an interest in the property subject to the power to make gifts which is adverse to the exercise of the power to make gifts in favor of my Agent, my Agent's estate, or the creditors of either, as such term is defined in Treasury Regulation §§25.2514-3(b)(2) and 20.2041-3(c)(2).

Also, the insured's durable power of attorney for financial affairs should contain HIPAA release authority so that the agent can obtain and disclose medical information about the insured. This information may be necessary if the insured is terminally ill and the ILIT trustee wants to enter into a viatical settlement, or if the ILIT trustee wants to undertake a life settlement.[2] *See*, Chapter 2 concerning viatical settlements and life settlements.

Drafting Example:

HIPAA Release Authority. *This power of attorney authorizes my Agent (or successor Agent) to make various property related decisions on my behalf, some of which relate to my health care. Accordingly, I confirm that in connection therewith, my Agent (or successor Agent) shall be treated as a personal representative for all purposes relating to my personal health information, as provided in 45 C.F.R. section 164.502(g) and other applicable provisions of HIPAA. Therefore, my Agent shall be treated as I would be with respect to my rights regarding the use and disclosure of my individually identifiable health information (aka protected health information) or other medical records. This release authority applies to any information governed by the Health Insurance Portability and Accountability Act of 1996 (aka HIPAA), 42 U.S.C. section 1320d and 45 C.F.R. sections 160-164.*

Regardless of my capacity or ability to make my own health care decisions, I authorize: any physician, health-care professional, dentist, health plan, hospital, clinic, laboratory, pharmacy or other covered health-care provider, any insurance company, and the Medical Information Bureau Inc. or other health-care clearinghouse that has provided treatment or services to me, or that has paid for or is seeking payment from me for such services, or is otherwise a HIPAA-covered entity, to give, disclose, and release to my Agent (or successor Agent), upon request and without restriction, all of my individually identifiable health information and medical records (except psy-

[2] *See*, Section 906.2 of Michael I. Frankel, "Life Settlements: Sale of Life Insurance Policies in the Open Market," *The 39th Annual Heckerling Institute on Estate Planning*, (Matthew Bender/Lexis-Nexis, Newark, NJ 2005); and Michael L. Graham and Jonathan G. Blattmachr, "Planning for the HIPPA Privacy Rule," 29 *ACTEC Journal* 307 (Spring 2004).

chotherapy notes) regarding any past, present, or future medical or mental health condition, including all information relating to the diagnosis and treatment of HIV/AIDS, sexually transmitted diseases, mental illness, and drug or alcohol abuse.

The authority given hereunder to my Agent (or successor Agent) shall supersede any prior agreement that I may have made with my health-care providers to restrict access to or disclosure of my individually identifiable health information.

The authority given my Agent (or successor Agent) concerning HIPAA matters is effective immediately, and shall terminate upon the earlier of: (i) twenty-five years from the date of this instrument, (ii) two years after my death, or (iii) my written revocation received by the HIPAA covered entity. The authority given hereunder to my Agent (or successor Agent) shall not be affected by my disability or incapacity or by the lapse of time. I have the right to revoke this authority, which I may do orally, or in writing, or in any other manner sufficient to evidence my intent to revoke, including the execution of a later signed durable power of attorney with similar provisions and grant of authority. If the HIPAA authority given to my Agent (or successor Agent) is revoked, any person or entity acting in good faith in reliance upon it, and lacking actual knowledge of its revocation, shall be held harmless.

It is understood that my Agent (or successor Agent) has my permission to use and disseminate this information in his or her sole discretion. I understand that once this information is disclosed, it may be re-disclosed by my Agent (or successor Agent), and the information may not be protected by privacy laws or regulations. I acknowledge that my authorization of the use or disclosure of HIPAA protected information is my voluntary act, and I waive any right to privacy that I may have under HIPAA.

My Agent (or successor Agent) shall have the right to bring a legal action in any applicable form against any covered entity that refuses to recognize and accept this authorization for the purposes that I have expressed. Additionally, Agent (or successor Agent) is authorized to sign any documents that he or she deems appropriate to obtain the protected medical information.

I hereby release any covered entity that acts in reliance on this HIPAA authority given to my Agent (or successor Agent) from any liability that may accrue from releasing my protected medical information and for any actions taken by my Agent (or successor Agent).

§13.3 COORDINATE ILIT'S DISPOSITIVE PROVISIONS WITH INSURED'S OTHER DISPOSITIVE PROVISIONS

Coordinate the dispositive provisions of the insured's base estate plan, typically the insured's revocable living trust, with the dispositive provisions of the ILIT. This coordination will permit the two trusts to be merged at a later date. *See,* Paragraph 7.1(A)(7) of Sample ILIT. It is particularly important that the trustee not only have the authority to merge the trusts but also have the ability to keep any shares separate that may have different generation-skipping tax inclusion ratios or have different lengths of time as concerns the rule against perpetuities. The rule against perpetuities starts at the date that an irrevocable trust is established, whereas the rule against perpetuities for a revocable living trust generally starts at the time of the insured's death.

14

Advanced Planning Opportunities And Techniques For ILITs

CHAPTER OVERVIEW

Although no ILIT is "simple," an ILIT can be very "sophisticated" concerning these issues: (i) how the ILIT is to be funded, (ii) the terms of the ILIT, and (iii) its purpose. This chapter[1] discusses several unique ways to fund an ILIT (besides making annual cash gifts to pay the premiums), and also discusses some sophisticated ILIT strategies for the practitioner's consideration.

§14.1 USE ILIT IN CONJUNCTION WITH INSURED'S QUALIFIED PERSONAL RESIDENCE TRUST

An ILIT can be the remainder beneficiary of the insured's qualified personal residence trust ("QPRT") established under IRC section 2702.[2] Upon the expiration of the QPRT term, the personal residence can pass to the ILIT. The insured can then pay fair market rent to the ILIT for the continued use of the personal residence. If the ILIT is structured as an intentionally defective grantor trust, the insured's rental payments to the ILIT will not result in the recognition of any

[1] The author gratefully acknowledges the contribution of Julius H. Giarmarco, Esq., of Giarmarco, Mullins & Horton, P.C. of Troy, Michigan in the writing of this Chapter.

[2] *See,* Albert R. Kingan, "Combining the Benefits of a QPRT With a Life Insurance Trust," 27 *Estate Planning* 486 (December 2000).

taxable income.[3] Moreover, if the residence is the insured's primary residence, the residence will be eligible for IRC section 1033 treatment and the sale of the home by the ILIT will qualify for the IRC section 121 exclusion of gain on the sale of a principal residence. In essence, the insured's payment of the ILIT's income taxes is the equivalent of a tax-free gift to the beneficiaries of the ILIT. The rental income received by the ILIT can then be used by the trustee to purchase insurance on the life of the grantor. This technique can be valuable for clients with taxable estates that exceed the applicable exclusion amount.

Because the donor may die during the QPRT term (in which case the QPRT property will be included in the donor's gross estate), the estate tax inclusion period ("ETIP") rules of IRC section 2642(f) prevent the donor from effectively allocating his or her GST tax exemption at the time the QPRT is established. Under the ETIP rules, the donor's GST tax exemption can be effectively allocated upon the expiration of the QPRT term based upon the then-fair market value of the QPRT property (which hopefully appreciated during the QPRT term). Consequently, naming an ILIT as the remainder beneficiary of a QPRT works best for ILITs that are not generation-skipping trusts.

§14.2 USE ILIT IN CONJUNCTION WITH A BENEFICIARY-CONTROLLED TRUST

A beneficiary-controlled trust provides the primary beneficiary of the trust with the equivalent of outright ownership, tax savings opportunities, and protection from creditors.[4] These benefits are not obtainable with outright ownership of gifted property. In the typical beneficiary-controlled trust, the primary beneficiary is a co-trustee and has the power to remove and replace the other co-trustee. The beneficiary can also have the right to any or all of the trust income and principal

---

[3] Note that Treas. Reg. §25.2702-5(b)(1) prohibits a grantor or the grantor's spouse from purchasing the personal residence from the QPRT or the ILIT while the trust is a grantor trust. The regulations require the governing instrument to expressly preclude such a purchase. Thus the grantor's power to substitute trust assets of an equivalent value under IRC section 675(1) to obtain grantor trust status must be limited to assets other than the personal residence, any life insurance on the life of the grantor, and any IRC section 2036(b) stock. *See,* section 2.7, above, concerning intentionally defective grantor trust status and other methods to obtain grantor trust status.

[4] *See,* Richard A. Oshins and Steven J. Oshins, "Protecting & Preserving Wealth Into The Next Millennium (Part 1)," 137 *Trusts & Estates* 52 (September 1998). *But see,* Charles Harris and Tye J. Klooster, "Beneficiary-Controlled Trusts Can Lose Asset Protection," 145 *Trusts & Estates* 37 (December 2006).

needed for his or her health, education, support, and maintenance, as well as an annual $5,000 or 5% withdrawal right over the trust corpus. The beneficiary is also granted a broad testamentary limited power of appointment over the trust estate. Greater flexibility, tax benefits, and creditor protection can be obtained with two trustees—the beneficiary-trustee and a "friendly" independent trustee. The independent trustee would be vested with all the tax-sensitive powers and all discretionary powers, and the beneficiary-trustee would have all other powers, including managerial rights. The beneficiary-trustee would also have the ability to remove and replace the independent trustee and appoint a successor independent trustee who is not related or subordinate to the beneficiary within the meaning of IRC section 672(c).

A discretionary beneficiary-controlled trust, where all distributions are subject to the absolute discretion of an independent trustee, is an effective tool for creditor and divorce protection. Moreover, the beneficiary-controlled trust can purchase life insurance on the life of the grantor, resulting in significant leveraging of the gifts made to the trust. The life insurance proceeds received by the beneficiary-controlled trust could also be used to promote, advance, or further the beneficiary's interests in a business or other ventures.

§14.3 USE ILIT IN CONJUNCTION WITH A GRANTOR RETAINED ANNUITY TRUST

In a grantor retained annuity trust ("GRAT"), if the grantor dies before the GRAT term ends, the assets in the GRAT revert back to (and are taxable in) the grantor's estate. As such, it would be risky for a GRAT to own a life insurance policy on the grantor's life. However, it is possible to use a GRAT to fund an ILIT (assuming it is not a generation-skipping ILIT—because the estate tax inclusion period ("ETIP") rules of IRC section 2642(f) preclude the effective allocation of the transferor's GST tax exemption until the expiration of the GRAT term). For example, a GRAT could be established that designates an ILIT as the GRAT remainder beneficiary. If the assets transferred to the GRAT appreciate significantly during the GRAT term, the ILIT could receive sufficient capital with which to pay life insurance premiums on the grantor's life. Even greater leverage can be obtained if the assets transferred to the GRAT qualify for valuation discounts, such as an interest in a family limited liability company ("FLLC")[5] or family limited part-

---

[5] *See*, Steven C. Alberty, *Limited Liability Companies: A Planning and Drafting Guide* (ALI-ABA, Philadelphia, 2003, Supp. 2005), for an overview of limited liability companies.

nership ("FLP"). During the GRAT term, the grantor could make low-interest rate loans to the ILIT to pay the life insurance premiums.[6]

§14.4 USE CREDIT SHELTER TRUST AS AN ILIT ON SURVIVING SPOUSE'S LIFE

The marital-family revocable living trust is the cornerstone of many married couples' estate plans. Under the so-called reduce-to-zero marital deduction formula, upon the death of the grantor, an amount equal to grantor's available estate tax applicable exclusion amount is allocated to the family trust (which is also known as a credit shelter trust), and the balance of the grantor's estate is allocated to a trust that qualifies for the marital deduction. The typical family trust provides the surviving spouse (and the grantor's descendants) with income and principal as needed for their health, education, maintenance, and support. Upon the surviving spouse's death, the assets remaining in the family trust pass (estate-tax free) to the grantor's descendants or to a trust for their benefit. *See, e.g.,* Paragraphs 5.4 and 5.5 of Sample ILIT.

For clients who have died and are survived by a spouse, it is possible to use the funds in the family trust to purchase a policy of insurance on the life of the surviving spouse. The life insurance policy could also combine a long term care (nursing home type) benefit for the surviving spouse.[7] However, particular care must be taken when the surviving spouse is also a trustee of the family trust so as to avoid any "incidents of ownership" issues under IRC section 2042. Priv. Letter Rul. 9111028. Accordingly, there should be a co-trustee serving with the surviving spouse, and all rights in the life insurance policy should be held by that co-trustee. *See, e.g.,* Paragraph 7.1(C)(3) of Sample ILIT. Better yet, the surviving spouse should disclaim (pursuant to IRC section 2518) any and all powers over the insurance policy, and disclaim the right to serve as trustee of the credit shelter trust. Rev. Rul. 84-179, 1984-2 C.B. 195; Priv. Letter Rul. 200518005. Furthermore, if the surviving spouse has a limited power of appointment over the credit shelter trust, that power must expressly exclude it from being exercisable over the life insurance policy. *See also,* Priv. Letter Rul. 200617008. In that ruling, the surviving spouse resigned as a co-

---

[6] The loan should be for an adequate rate of interest under IRC section 7872 to avoid an imputed gift as a below market loan. IRC section 7872(a). The $100,000 "exception" in IRC section 7872(d)(1) for gift loans is only applicable for income tax ("subtitle A") purposes, and not for gift tax purposes.

[7] *See,* Howard J. Saks, "Using a Combination Life Insurance-LTC Insurance Policy in The Bypass Trust," 33 *Estate Planning* 28, (September 2006).

trustee of an irrevocable trust that was established and funded by her (now deceased) husband. The surviving spouse resigned prior to the trust's purchase of insurance on her life, none of the consideration for the purchase of the policy was to be supplied by the surviving spouse, and all the consideration for the purchase of the life insurance was to be supplied by the trust. Alternatively, the surviving spouse can disclaim the limited power of appointment.

§14.5 USE INSURED'S GIFT TAX APPLICABLE EXCLUSION AMOUNT TO FUND ILIT

By making a large gift of income-producing property to the ILIT using the insured's $1 million gift tax applicable exclusion amount ($2 million if married and the spouse qualifies for gift splitting under IRC section 2513), the ILIT trustee can use the net after-tax cash flow from the gifted assets to pay the life insurance premiums. In addition, the trustee can also invade trust principal to pay premiums. This technique can be enhanced in two ways. First, by putting the income-producing property in an FLP or FLLC and then gifting nonvoting interests in the FLP or FLLC to the ILIT, valuation discounts (for lack of control and lack of marketability) may be available. As such, the insured's gift tax applicable exclusion amount is leveraged. Second, by designing the ILIT so that it is an intentionally defective grantor trust, the insured will be responsible for paying the ILIT's income taxes. *See*, sections 2.7 and 3.18, above. As a result, the ILIT will have more cash flow available to pay premiums since the ILIT will not be depleted each year by income taxes. In essence, the insured's payment of the ILIT's income taxes is the equivalent of a tax-free gift to the ILIT beneficiaries.

§14.6 OPPORTUNITY SHIFTING TO FUND ILIT[8]

If the grantor has a new venture that requires a small initial investment, but which has great potential for appreciation, the grantor could form a FLP or a FLLC to own the venture. For example, a real estate developer transfers $1 million to a FLP or a FLLC and borrows $4 million to develop a shopping center. After the project is completed in two years, there is projected to be an annual positive cash flow of $150,000 under a triple net lease. The grantor would initially own 1% of the FLP or FLLC (all voting) and the ILIT would own 99% of the FLP

---

[8] *See*, Richard A. Oshins and Steven J. Oshins, "Protecting & Preserving Wealth Into The Next Millennium (Part 2)," 137 *Trusts & Estates* 68 (October 1998) for a general discussion on opportunity shifting.

or FLLC (all nonvoting). The initial gift to the ILIT of the nonvoting interests would be $999,000 (i.e., $1,000,000 x 99%), *less* the applicable valuation discounts for lack of control and lack of marketability. In addition, by making the ILIT an intentionally defective grantor trust, the grantor would pay the income tax on the $150,000, thereby leaving the entire $150,000 in the ILIT to pay life insurance premiums. *See,* sections 2.7 and 3.18, above. Finally, until such time as the FLP or FLLC begins to generate income, the grantor could make low-interest rate loans to the ILIT to pay the life insurance premiums.

§14.7 SALE TO A GRANTOR TRUST TO FUND ILIT

If the ILIT owns a life insurance policy that requires a large annual premium, the grantor could sell appreciated assets to the ILIT on an installment note.[9] The income produced by the appreciated assets (in excess of the note payment) could then be used to pay the life insurance premiums.[10] If the ILIT is an intentionally defective grantor trust, the sale to the ILIT by the grantor will not trigger any capital gain since the grantor is treated as the owner of the ILIT for income tax purposes. *See,* sections 2.7 and 2.8(b)(1), above. Furthermore, by selling assets to the ILIT, the grantor will not be using up his or her gift tax applicable exclusion amount. For purposes of IRC section 2036 (transfers with a retained interest), the ILIT should have some "seed" money equal to at least 10% of the discounted value of the assets that will be sold to the ILIT. The seed money will be a gift to the trust and, therefore, will use up a portion of the grantor's gift tax applicable exclusion amount. Moreover, the grantor will (as a matter of caution) "turn off" any *Crummey* withdrawal rights that might otherwise be available to the ILIT beneficiaries (in order to be 100% certain of obtaining grantor trust status as to the grantor alone). The 10% "seed" money should preempt an IRS attack that IRC section 2036(a)(1) should apply to bring the assets in the ILIT back into the grantor's estate as a transfer with a retained interest. Moreover, consideration should be given to using cash or marketable securities (as opposed to FLP/FLLC

---

[9] *See,* Steven J. Oshins, Al W. King, III and Pierce H. McDowell, III, "Sale To A Defective Trust: A Life Insurance Technique," 137 *Trusts & Estates* 35 (April 1998).

[10] The accumulated income produced by the appreciated assets could also be used to pay for private or commercial premium financing costs if the grantor has taken out a loan to pay for the life insurance. *See,* Rachna D. Balakrishna, "Defective Grantor Trusts: Greater Flexibility and Income Tax Leverage," 32 *Estate Planning* 30 (December 2005); and Lawrence L. Bell, "Grantor Trust/Insurance Trust: Both Income And Estate Tax-Advantaged," 140 *Trusts & Estates* 12 (August 2001).

interests) for the seed money. This will avoid having to "check the box" on the gift tax return, a requirement whenever a valuation discount is taken on a taxable gift. It will also help to avoid the IRC section 2036(a)(1) argument since the ILIT will own some assets other than the assets being sold (i.e., the FLP/FLLC interests).

After the initial gift is made, the ILIT enters into a sales agreement with the grantor to purchase the FLP/FLLC interests. The sale is structured as an interest-only sale with a balloon payment at the end of the stated term. The interest rate used for the sale is the applicable federal rate (AFR) published by the Treasury each month. By selling (as opposed to gifting) the FLP/FLLC interests to an ILIT designed as an intentionally defective grantor trust – in exchange for a promissory note – the gift tax cost can be reduced dramatically. For example, if a married grantor creates an FLP or an FLLC funded with $20 million of assets, and assuming a 35% valuation discount for lack of control and marketability, the grantor (with gift splitting) will be able to gift and sell 99% of the FLP or FLLC interest (all nonvoting) to the ILIT. A gift to the ILIT of 10% of the FLP or FLLC interest would equal $1.3 million (10% × $20,000,000 = $2,000,000, less 35% = $1,300,000). A purchase by the ILIT of 89% of the FLP or FLLC interest would cost $11,570,000 (89% × $20,000,000 = $17,800,000, less 35% = $11,570,000). The grantor would retain the FLP's or FLLC's 1% voting interest. The terms of the installment sale would be a zero down payment and a balloon payment after a term of years, with annual interest payments at the lowest rate necessary to avoid imputed interest under the Internal Revenue Code. Assume that interest rate is 6%. In this example, the interest payment to the grantor would be $694,200 per year (6% x $11,570,000). Since the grantor would be paying tax on all of the ILIT's income, the ILIT's net cash flow (after making the interest payment to the grantor) could be used to pay life insurance premiums. On the death of the grantor-insured, the ILIT applies the insurance proceeds to pay off the note, assuming the note was not paid off during the grantor's life.

Finally, the ILIT could be designed to pass the assets in trust for more than one generation. Using a generation skipping trust, the grantor's GST tax exemption can be allocated to the trust in an amount equal to the initial seed money so that the ILIT is wholly exempt from GST taxes. Thus, there is no need to apply any additional gift or GST tax exemption to the ILIT (except for the annual gifts to pay interest).

This strategy provides two very important wealth transfer opportunities. First, the grantor can sell assets to the ILIT income tax free since transactions between a grantor and a grantor trust are ignored for income tax purposes. Rev. Rul. 85-13, 1985-1 C.B. 184. Second, since the grantor is taxed on all trust income, the payment of income taxes by the grantor is the equivalent of a tax-free gift to the beneficiaries of the trust of the income tax liability each year. Rev. Rul. 2004-64, 2004-2 C.B. 7.

§14.8 ANNUITIES TO FUND ILIT

If the grantor lacks current cash to fund the ILIT premiums, the grantor could use his or her nonqualified tax deferred annuities to fund the ILIT. Grantors who do not anticipate withdrawing funds from their annuities during their lifetime should be forewarned about the tax consequences of passing the tax-deferred annuities on to their children at death. First, the annuities will be taxed as ordinary income to the beneficiaries in their respective income tax brackets. Annuities are considered "income in respect of a decedent" under IRC section 691 and, therefore, do not receive a stepped-up basis when the owner dies. In addition, the annuities are subject to estate taxes. As such, tax-deferred annuities are double taxed, although the beneficiaries do receive an income tax deduction for any estate taxes paid on the annuities under IRC section 691(c).

Instead of double taxation, consider no post-death taxation by having the grantor annuitize the nonqualified tax deferred annuity over the grantor's life expectancy. The grantor could then use the after-tax income from the annuity payments to make annual exclusion gifts to the ILIT. As the annuity income will always be available to pay premiums, the grantor's cash flow problem is solved. Moreover, since the annuity ceases at the grantor's death, there is nothing taxable in his or her estate. Most importantly, the grantor's beneficiaries receive the insurance proceeds in the ILIT both income-tax and estate-tax free. In most instances this technique will leave the grantor's original annuity beneficiaries far better off.

Another annuity ILIT financing technique is the "annuity maximization" technique. Under this technique a deferred annuity is converted (tax-free under IRC section 1035) into a single premium immediate annuity (SPIA), and the after-tax distributions from the SPIA—less any amounts needed by the owner of the annuity to maintain his or her standard of living—are gifted to an ILIT. Alternatively, an individual with a low yield, income-producing asset can sell the investment and use the after-tax sales proceeds to purchase a SPIA. In either case, the gifts to the ILIT can be made via annual exclusion gifts by way of *Crummey* withdrawal powers and/or by using the grantor's $1 million gift tax exemption ($2 million for married couples).

The SPIA provides income to the owner for life, and usually provides a higher income than alternative investments. A portion of the SPIA income is exempt from tax for a period of years (i.e., the exclusion ratio under IRC section 72), depending on the age of the owner at the time of purchase. At the owner's death, the SPIA payments stop and the ILIT collects the life insurance proceeds—income and estate tax-free—for the benefit of the grantor's heirs.

Although it is possible to gift the annuity contract directly to the ILIT (or to gift cash to the ILIT with which to purchase the SPIA) thereby having the payments go directly to the trustee, there are several problems with this approach. First, depending on the face value of the SPIA, a taxable gift may be incurred thereby, needlessly using up a portion of the grantor's $1 million gift tax exemption. Second, an annuity contract held by an entity that is not a "natural person" is not treated for tax purposes as an annuity contract. As such, the inside build-up in the contract would be taxable annually, and if the ILIT is an intentionally defective grantor trust, the grantor would be responsible for paying any income taxes. Although there are several private letter rulings holding that a trust can own an annuity contract as an "agent" for a natural person (i.e., the beneficiary), these rulings cannot be cited as precedents.[11] *See*, Priv. Letter Ruls. 9204014, 9204010, 199905015, 9752035, 9639057, and 199933033.

In summary, using a SPIA in conjunction with an ILIT offers these benefits: (1) the SPIA is likely to generate a higher income than the owner's existing assets; (2) the owner will never outlive the SPIA; (3) if there are sufficient *Crummey* beneficiaries, the gifts to the ILIT will be gift tax-free; and (4) the previous investment is removed from the estate and "replaced" with estate-tax-free life insurance inside the ILIT.

The results of annuity maximization can be more dramatic if the annuity owner is able to obtain an underwriting arbitrage between the annuity company payout and the life insurance policy annual premium amount.[12] The arbitrage occurs ***only if:*** (i) the company issuing the life insurance policy rates the grantor-insured at a favorable rating (i.e., good to great health and a long life expectancy—thus a lower life insurance premium), (ii) the company issuing the annuity rates the

---

[11] *See*, Bruce A. Tannahill, "Handle With Care," 146 *Trust & Estates* 56 (May 2007).

[12] *See*, Timothy P. Malarkey and Stephan R. Leimberg, "Innovative Planning With `No Lapse Guarantee' Life Insurance," 32 Estate Planning 3 (July 2005); and Douglas Moore, "Planning for Third-Party Life Insurance Financing, 31 *Estate Planning* 383 (August 2004).

grantor-insured at a less favorable rating (i.e., poor to bad health and a short life expectancy—thus a higher annuity payout amount), and (iii) the insured lives beyond the period of contestability, which is generally two years from the issuance of the life insurance policy.

> **Practice Point:** Care should be taken when planning the annuity and life insurance purchases to make sure the annuity will generate enough after-tax income to pay the life insurance premiums. This calculation will be especially important in situations where the insured lives beyond his or her life expectancy and all remaining annuity payments become fully taxable as ordinary income. If the ILIT is structured as an intentionally defective grantor, the grantor will be responsible for paying the income tax on the annuity payments, thus permitting the ILIT to use most or all of the annuity payments to pay life insurance premiums.

§14.9 MUNICIPAL BONDS TO FUND ILIT

Municipal bonds, similar to nonqualified tax-deferred annuities, often represent a portion of a grantor's estate that is more likely to be left to children than be spent during the grantor's lifetime. If so, a grantor should consider selling the municipal bonds and purchasing an immediate life annuity on his or her life or on the joint life of the grantor and his or her spouse. In many cases, the after-tax income generated from the immediate annuity will be enough not only to replace the bond income the grantor was previously receiving, but also to make annual exclusion gifts to the ILIT. When the grantor (or the survivor of the grantor and his or her spouse) dies, the annuity ceases and nothing is left in the estate to be taxed. However, the life insurance death benefit received by the ILIT will be free of both income and estate taxes. Contrast this to the municipal bonds that would have been estate-taxed. Similar to the tax-deferred annuity technique described above, this approach is likely to enhance the wealth of the grantor's beneficiaries.

An alternative to selling the municipal bonds is to transfer them to the ILIT. The bonds may be subject to a valuation discount if their interest rate is below the current rate for municipal bonds of similar length and credit worthiness. The tax free interest on the bonds can then be used to pay the life insurance premiums. If the bond interest is not subject to the alternative minimum tax, the trust should not have to pay any income tax on the bond interest. Likewise, the grantor should not have any income tax liability, if the ILIT is a grantor trust, which it should be under IRC section 677(a), since bond interest is used to pay for life insurance premiums on the grantor's life).

§14.10 IRAS TO FUND ILIT

It is often said that qualified retirement plans are the best place to accumulate wealth, but the worst place to distribute it. The reason is that retirement plans, like nonqualified tax-deferred annuities, are double taxed.

If the insured's estate consists primarily of income in respect of a decedent ("IRD"), such as retirement benefits (which is typical for many professionals such as doctors, lawyers, accountants, etc.), the insured can withdraw from the IRA more than his or her annual required minimum distribution amount and use the extra amount to fund an ILIT. When the insured dies, the IRD will be included in the insured's gross estate and will not receive a step up in basis. Thus every dollar of IRD that is inherited by the insured's beneficiaries will be subject to both death taxes and incomes taxes (although IRC section 691(c) provides an income tax deduction for federal taxes paid that are attributable to the IRD). By establishing an ILIT, the insured will: (i) reduce the amount of IRD in his or her estate, and (ii) provide an inheritance that is both income-tax free and death-tax free. An additional benefit of the ILIT is its ability to permit the IRA beneficiaries to possibly stretch out the payment of the IRA proceeds. This stretch-out can be accomplished by having the ILIT loan money to the insured's estate to pay the death taxes attributable to the retirement benefits. *See,* section 10.25, above. If the retirement benefits have to be liquidated to pay death taxes, there will be no stretch out of the benefits, and income taxes will have to be paid on the amounts of the IRA that are withdrawn to pay the death taxes and estate administration expenses—an immediate double taxation! An ILIT can help avoid this type of tax disaster. Thus, in many instances, greater wealth can be created for the next generation by taking early distributions from IRAs and gifting the after-tax amounts to an ILIT. Most financial planners and life insurance professionals have computer programs to analyze and quantify the benefits of this approach.

§14.11 CHARITABLE REMAINDER TRUST TO FUND ILIT

If a grantor has appreciated assets and is charitably inclined, a charitable remainder trust ("CRT") can be used to fund the grantor's ILIT. The grantor can gift the appreciated assets to the CRT, which the CRT trustee can then sell. There is no capital gain on the sale of the appreciated assets because the CRT is tax exempt. During the grantor's lifetime (or the lifetimes of the grantor and his or her spouse), the CRT pays the grantor a fixed percentage of the CRT's value. At the death of the grantor (or at the death of the survivor of the grantor and the grantor's spouse), the assets in the CRT pass (estate-tax free) to the charity. The grantor is entitled to a charitable income tax deduction equal to the present value of the CRT's remainder interest at the time the trust is established. The grantor can use the after-tax income on the CRT distributions (plus the tax savings from the charitable income tax deduction) to make annual exclusion gifts to an ILIT. The net result is that appreciated assets are removed from the grantor's estate, capital gains taxes are avoided, the grantor's favorite charities are benefited, the grantor's heirs are made "whole" because they receive the insurance proceeds in the ILIT both income- and estate-tax free, and the life insurance proceeds can provide liquidity to the grantor's estate.

§14.12 INTRA FAMILY LOANS TO FUND ILIT

An alternative to funding large premium contributions to an ILIT is to have family members make loans to the ILIT.[13] For example, a husband and wife could loan money to their ILIT that owns a second-to-die policy on their lives. The insureds' loans to the ILIT to pay premiums do not constitute a retained interest in the ILIT or an incident of ownership in the underlying life insurance policy, provided the loans are properly documented, provide for an adequate rate of interest required by IRC sections 7872 and 1274 (or, for the more conservative and cautious planners, the IRC 7520 rate), and the loans are not secured by a collateral assignment of the policy on either insured's life.

---

[13] Another alternative is for the ILIT to obtain third party financing through a financial institution. *See*, *Steve Leimberg's Estate Planning Newsletter # 1083* (Feb. 5, 2007) at http://www.leimbergservices.com; Michael Gallop, "Benefits and Risks of Life Insurance Premium Financing," 33 *Estate Planning* 23 (November 2006); R. Marshall Jones, Stephan R. Leimberg and Lawrence J. Rybka, "'Free' Life Insurance: Risks and Costs of Non-Recourse Premium Financing," 33 *Estate Planning* 3 (July 2006); Douglas Moore, "Planning for Third-Party Life Insurance Financing, 31 *Estate Planning* 383 (August 2004); Charles Ratner, "The Post Split Dollar World," *Trusts and Estates*, 181 (December 2003); Jerome M. Hesch and Laura Baek, "The Use of Settlor Guarantees in ILIT Premium Financing," 28 *Tax Management Estates, Gifts and Trusts Journal* 219 (September 11, 2003); and Stephan R. Leimberg and Albert E. Gibbons, "Premium Financing: The Last Choice—Not the First Choice," 28 *Estate Planning* 35 (January 2001). Third party financing through a bank is not subject to the split dollar regulations.

Priv. Letter Ruls. 9809032, 9746004, 9746006, and 9511046.[14] The loans may, however, be subject to the requirements of the split-dollar "loan regime."[15]

---

[14] *But see*, Priv. Letter Rul. 9745019 where the IRS ruled that the insureds' limited collateral assignment in a second-to-die policy owned by their ILIT under a private split-dollar arrangement did not constitute an incident of ownership under IRC section 2042 for federal estate tax purposes, and their payment of premiums under the split-dollar arrangement did not constitute a gift to the ILIT. *See, also*, Priv. Letter Rul. 9636033 where the IRS ruled that there was no gift where the non-insured spouse made premium payments under a private split-dollar arrangement to her husband's ILIT and had a right to be reimbursed by the ILIT for those premium payments. If the only asset of the ILIT is the life insurance policy, at least one commentator is of the opinion that Treas. Reg. § 1.61-22(b)(1)(ii) (concerning the definition of a split-dollar loan arrangement) may require the insured-lender either: (i) to obtain a bare bones limited collateral assignment in the cash surrender value of the policy, or (ii) to obtain a guaranty from the ILIT beneficiaries (and the ILIT beneficiaries may have to be paid by the ILIT for giving their personal guaranty). Donald O. Jansen, "Financed Life Insurance is Back! Premium Loans to ILITS," *30th Annual Notre Dame Tax & Estate Planning Institute* (October 2004); and Donald O. Jansen, "Private/Family Split Dollar Plans," 25 *ACTEC Notes* 68 (Summer 1999). *See, also*, Lawrence Brody and Charles L. Ratner, "Today's Split Dollar," 146 Trusts & Estates 38 (May 2007).

[15] *See*, Treas. Reg. §§1.61-22 (split dollar generally, and the "economic benefit regime" rules); 1.61-22(b) (definition of split-dollar life insurance arrangement); 1.61-22(b)(3) (application of split-dollar loan rules); 1.7872-15(split-dollar loan rules generally, and the "loan regime" rules)); 1.7872-15(a)(2) (definition of split-dollar loan); 1.7872-15(a)(4) (payment of split-dollar loan interest by insured-donor may be disregarded and treated as an additional loan without adequate interest); 1.7872-15(b) (definition of split-dollar life insurance arrangement and split-dollar loan); 1.7872-15(d)(2) and 1.7872-15(j)(2)(ii) (special one time written representation by the insured-donor and the ILIT that must accompany their income tax returns concerning a non-recourse split-dollar loan (to avoid the loan being treated as a "contingent" payment that is subject to unfavorable assumptions when testing the loan for adequate stated interest)). Although IRC section 7872 is generally not applicable to certain loans on which the aggregate indebtedness does not exceed $10,000 (IRC section 7872(c)(2) and (3)), that exception does not apply in the split-dollar context, and the split-dollar loan will be subject to IRC section 7872. Treas. Reg. §1.7872-15(a)(3).

See, also, Lawrence Brody and Charles L. Ratner, "Today's Split Dollar," 146 Trusts & Estates 38 (May 2007); Charles L. Ratner and Stephan R. Leimberg, "A Planner's Guide to Split-Dollar After the Final Regulations," 31 *Estate Planning* 3 (January 2004); Donald O. Jansen, "Taxation of Split Dollar Life Insurance Arrangements Under the Final Regulations, 29 *ACTEC Journal* 285 (Spring 2004), www.actec.org; and Donald O. Jansen, "Financed Life Insurance is Back! Premium Loans to ILITS," *30th Annual Notre Dame Tax & Estate Planning Institute* (October 2004); Charles Ratner, "The Post Split Dollar World," 142 *Trusts & Estates* 18

The intra family loan concept works best where the ILIT owns a policy that can be paid up quickly—over a short period of time (without running afoul of the modified endowment contract rules of IRC section 7702). At the inception of the ILIT each insured would transfer the maximum amount he or she could transfer to the ILIT within the limits of annual gift tax exclusion amount. These annual exclusion gifts would be the "seed" money to service the debt.

If the annual exclusion gift amount is less than 10% of the annual premium amount, the grantors may want to make a taxable gift to the ILIT, up to the amount necessary to fund the trust with the 10% seed amount.

The ILIT beneficiaries would then be granted hanging *Crummey* withdrawal rights up to the annual gift tax exclusion amount. Next, the insureds would loan the ILIT the amount of money necessary to purchase the second-to-die policy, and the ILIT would issue a promissory note payable to the insureds as joint tenants with rights of survivorship.[16] The note would be for a term of years less than the insureds' joint life expectancy with a balloon payment due at the end of the note's term, payable in cash or in kind. Because the ILIT uses the life insurance death benefit proceeds to pay off the note after the death of both of the insureds, any "in kind" repayment of the promissory note must exclude insurance policies on the life of either spouse.

(December 2003); and Gary Lee and Deborah Walker, "A Practical Guide To The Final Regs. Governing Split-Dollar Life Insurance," 99 *Journal of Taxation* 282 (November 2003). According to the Preamble to the final split-dollar regulations, "The final split dollar regulations apply for purposes of Federal income, employment, self-employment, and gift taxes....If a split-dollar loan does not provide for sufficient interest, the loan is a below-market split-dollar loan subject to IRC section 7872 and Treas. Reg. §1.7872-15. If the split-dollar loan provides for sufficient interest, then, except as provided in Treas. Reg. §1.7872-15, the loan is subject to the general rules for debt instruments (including the rules for ...[original issue discount under IRC section 1271 – 1275])....The [final split dollar] regulations apply for gift tax purposes, including private split-dollar life insurance arrangements. Thus, if an irrevocable life insurance trust is the owner of the life insurance contract underlying the split-dollar life insurance arrangement, and a reasonable person would expect that the donor, or the donor's estate, will recover an amount equal to the donor's premium payments, those premium payments are treated as loans made by the donor to the trust and are subject to Treas. Reg. §1.7872-15. In such a case, payment of a premium by the donor is treated as a split-dollar loan to the trust in the amount of the premium payment."

[16] The joint ownership of the notes is the preferred approach to ensure that the ILIT, which is a grantor trust as to both insureds, is able to pay interest in a manner that does not result in any taxable income to either insured, while at least one insured is living.

The note would be pre-payable at any time, without penalty, thus providing flexibility and the potential for discounting the value of the note includable in the insured's gross estate if the prevailing interest rates are less than the note's rate of interest. Each year thereafter, the insureds would continue to make *Crummey* annual exclusion gifts to the ILIT, which the ILIT could use to pay the interest it owes on any loans.[17] Each year the insureds would also loan the ILIT the amount necessary to pay the annual premium on the second-to-die policy, and the ILIT trustee would execute a new promissory note payable to the insureds. (The promissory note would be in the form and manner previously described.)

If the ILIT is structured as an intentionally defective grantor trust as to both of the insureds, the interest paid by the ILIT on the loans should not result in any taxable income to the insureds while both insureds are living. Rev. Rul. 85-13, 1985-1 C.B.184; PLR 200247006. However, when one of the insureds dies, the ILIT will cease to be a grantor trust in its entirety (and will be a partial grantor trust as to the surviving insured) and the last-to-die insured's estate will have to recognize any payment of accrued interest as taxable income in his or her estate. When the first insured dies, one half of the value of the promissory notes would be included in his or her gross estate, but would qualify for the marital deduction. Since the promissory notes would be owned by the insureds as joint tenants with rights of survivorship, the surviving insured would become the sole owner of the ILIT notes by operation of law. The surviving insured could then assign the promissory notes to his or her revocable living trust (to avoid probate) and devise the notes to a charity or to his or her descendants, etc. Alternatively, the surviving spouse could establish a FLP/FLLC and transfer the notes to the FLP/FLLC. Gifts of the FLP/FLLC interests by the surviving spouse should qualify for a discount valuation because of their lack of control and lack of marketability.

As previously mentioned, care must be taken in structuring the FLP/FLLC so as to not run afoul of *Hackl v. Commissioner*, 118 T.C. 279 (2002), *aff'd*, 335 F.3d 664 (7th Cir. 2003) and *Strangi*, T. C. Memo 2003-145 *(2003)*, *aff'd*, 417 F.3d 468 (5th Cir. 2005). If the surviving spouse does not transfer the notes to a FLP/FLLC, the value of the promissory notes, plus any accrued and unpaid interest, would be includable in the surviving spouse's gross estate when he or she dies.

---

[17] To avoid the risk of an IRS "retained interest" argument, the amount of the annual *Crummey* gifts, should, if possible, be greater than the amount of the annual interest payments on the loan amounts.

However, it may be possible to obtain a discount on the value of the ILIT's promissory notes if there is still a lengthy period of time before the notes mature and/or if the interest rates on the notes are less than the current rate of interest for such types of loans.

Depending on how long the insureds live, the ILIT's indebtedness on annual loans used to pay premiums may eventually exceed the policy's death benefit. If this happens, the ILIT trustee may be liable for breach of its fiduciary duty. Also, as previously mentioned, under the final split-dollar regulations issued in 2003, the insureds' lending of money to the ILIT may constitute a private split-dollar funding arrangement that must comply with the regulation's "loan regime" rules where each payment of the premium (or loan of money) by the grantor is treated as a separate loan for federal tax purposes.

> **Caution:** If a grantor intends to forgive or not collect on the note, as part of a prearranged plan, the note will not be considered valuable consideration and the grantor will have made a gift at the time of the loan to the full extent of the loan. *See*, Rev. Rul. 77-299, 1977-2 C.B. 343; *Estate of Lydia G. Maxwell v. Commissioner*, 3 F.3d 591 (2d Cir. 1993); and *Minnie E. Deal v. Commissioner*, 29 T.C. 730 (1958). *See also*, Priv. Letter Rul. 200603002. Also, the insured's guarantee of loans made to the ILIT should be structured to avoid the guarantee being treated by the IRS as a gift to the ILIT.[18]

> **Practice Point:** According to Diana S. C. Zeydel, "The use of notes to fund an ILIT may be viewed as problematic because the ILIT may not be able to satisfy the criteria to support the note as bona fide debt. A number of factors have been identified by the courts as indicative of bona fide debt, which include the ability to pay interest currently and to have assets sufficient to satisfy the debt, perhaps independent of the asset acquired with the proceeds of the loan.[19] However, because an ILIT is typically a grantor

---

[18] *See*, Jerome M. Hesch and Laura Baek, "The Use of Settlor Guarantees in ILIT Premium Financing," 28 *Tax Management Estates, Gifts and Trusts Journal* 219 (September 11, 2003).

[19] *See*, *Miller*, T.C. Memo 1996-3, RIA TC Memo ¶96003, 71 CCH TCM 1674 *aff'd* 113 F.3d 1241, 79 AFTR2d 97-2843 (CA-9, 1997) ("The mere promise to pay a sum of money in the future accompanied by an implied understanding that such promise would not be enforced is not afforded significance for Federal tax purposes, is not deemed to have value, and does not represent adequate and full consideration in

trust, the issue of interest income and the deductibility of the interest expense does not arise.[20] Thus, perhaps an accrual of interest until the policy matures can be justified without raising other tax issues." [21]

§14.13 SURVIVORSPHIP SPOUSAL ILIT

An ILIT that holds a second-to-die policy can be structured to provide one of the spouses with access to the policy's cash value. Priv. Letter Rul. 9748029 demonstrates this planning technique.[22]

The survivorship spousal ILIT must be established by just one of the spouses, preferably the one with the shortest life expectancy. Assuming the husband has the shortest life expectancy, the wife is named as the primary beneficiary of the ILIT, and the trustee can make distributions to her and/or the grantor's children for their health, education, support, and maintenance. The grantor-husband must make all the gifts to the ILIT, but the wife can gift split the annual exclusion gifts made to the other beneficiaries. By gift splitting, the grantor-husband can contribute two times the annual gift tax exclusion per trust beneficiary (other than any gifts to his wife). The wife cannot however be given a *Crummey* withdrawal right over any gifts made to the ILIT.

The net result is that the ILIT trustee can use the survivorship policy's cash values to make discretionary distributions to the wife during her lifetime. These cash values accumulate on a tax-free basis and the trustee can access the cash values through tax-free withdrawals (up

---

money or money's worth. . . . The determination of whether a transfer was made with a real expectation of repayment and an intention to enforce the debt depends on all the facts and circumstances, including whether: (1) There was a promissory note or other evidence of indebtedness, (2) interest was charged, (3) there was any security or collateral, (4) there was a fixed maturity date, (5) a demand for repayment was made, (6) any actual payment was made, (7) the transferee had the ability to repay, (8) records maintained by the transferor and/or the transferee reflected the transaction as a loan, and (9) the manner in which the transaction was reported for Federal tax purposes is consistent with a loan"). *See, also, Santa Monica Pictures, LLC,* T.C. Memo 2005-104, RIA TC Memo ¶2005-104, 89 CCH TCM 1157. *But see, Estate of Rosen*, T.C. Memo 2006-115, RIA TC Memo ¶2006-115, 91 CCH TCM 1220.

[20] Under Rev. Rul. 85-13, 1985-1 CB 184, a loan between a grantor and a grantor trust is not recognized for income tax purposes.

[21] Diana S. C. Zeydel, "How to Create and Administer a Successful Irrevocable Life Insurance Trust," 34 *Estate Planning* 3, 14 (June 2007).

[22] *See,* Albert R. Kingan, "Adding Flexibility to Insurance Trusts Funded With Survivorship Life," 26 *Estate Planning* 381 (October 1999).

to the amount of the policy's basis) and then by policy loans. Thus, the grantor-husband has "indirect" access to the policy's cash value as long as his wife is alive.

To keep the insurance proceeds out of both spouses' estates, neither spouse can be a trustee of the ILIT since both are insured under the policy held by the ILIT. However, the grantor-spouse can name one or more of his adult children as a "friendly" trustee, and can retain the right to remove and replace trustees. *See,* section 11.9, above.

If only one spouse is the grantor, there should be no retained interest by the non-grantor spouse and, therefore, no estate tax inclusion under IRC section 2036. The non-grantor spouse should not make any contributions to the ILIT to avoid estate tax inclusion under IRC sections 2036 and 2038. Finally, the non-grantor spouse's beneficial interest should not include a power of appointment (general or limited), and must be sufficiently restricted so as not to be an incident of ownership under IRC section 2042. The non-grantor spouse can be given the right to receive distributions in the sole and absolute discretion of an independent trustee. Distributions to the non-grantor spouse that are subject to a standard may cause a problem since the non-grantor spouse could enforce the standard and the trustee could (conceivably) be forced to distribute the policy to the spouse as a distribution of trust principal.

Since the non-grantor spouse should not make gifts to the ILIT, what options are available when the grantor-spouse dies to assure that funds are available to continue the premiums due under the survivorship policy? First, the grantor spouse's revocable living trust can leave the grantor's unused estate tax applicable exclusion amount to the ILIT. Second, the ILIT can be protected from the grantor-spouse's early death by owning a single life policy on the grantor's life in an amount sufficient to pay the remaining premiums. Priv. Letter Rul. 9451053. Finally, the ILIT can borrow the necessary funds from the grantor-spouse's estate.

In summary, the survivorship spousal ILIT gives a married couple access to policy cash values through the non-grantor spouse; estate and income tax-free death benefits for their heirs on the surviving spouse's death; and flexibility by naming one or more adult children as trustee.

§14.14 SECOND-TO-DIE LIFE INSURANCE AND THE STANDBY ILIT

An ILIT creates barriers for an insured who desires direct access to the life insurance's cash value, or for an insured who desires flexibility because of the uncertainty surrounding the federal estate tax or because of the possibility of changing family circumstances. Drafting a flexible ILIT helps to alleviate some of these concerns, but even a flexible ILIT cannot permit the insured to have direct access to the policy's cash value without causing the insurance proceeds to be included in the insured's gross estate. For married couples who own a second-to-die life insurance policy, the lack of access to the policy's cash value may cause them to own the policy outright rather than have an ILIT own the policy. Outright ownership of the policy can result in the policy's proceeds being subject to federal estate tax.

Married couples considering a survivorship life insurance policy have an alternative to using an ILIT as the initial owner of the policy. Through the use of disclaimers and a "standby" ILIT, it may be possible for the insured to retain full control of the policy's cash value, avoid making any irrevocable decisions, and reserve the option to eliminate federal estate taxes on the death proceeds.

The strategy works as follows. The spouse with the shortest life expectancy due to advanced age, poor health or gender (let's assume it's the husband) is the initial owner of the survivorship policy, and the wife is named as the first contingent owner upon the husband's death. The wife's contingent ownership interest is fully revocable at any time by the husband. After the husband acquires the policy, he creates an unfunded "standby" ILIT. The unfunded standby ILIT is named as the primary beneficiary of the policy and is also named as the second contingent owner of the policy, i.e., coming after the wife.[23] Should the wife disclaim her ownership interest in the policy within nine months of her husband's death, the policy would pass to the ILIT as the second contingent owner. IRC section 2518. While the husband is alive, he has full access to the policy's cash value through withdrawals and/or loans. The husband can also name a different ILIT as the beneficiary and second contingent owner of the policy if he wishes to change beneficiaries.

[23] A variation of naming a standby ILIT as the primary beneficiary and as the second contingent owner of the policy is to name the husband's credit shelter trust as the primary beneficiary of the policy and as the second contingent owner of the policy. *See*, section 12.1 of Sebastian V. Grassi, Jr., *A Practical Guide to Drafting Marital Deductions Trusts (with Sample Forms and Checklists)*, ALI-ABA, Philadelphia, PA (2004, Supp. 2006) (800) 253-6397, http://www.ali-aba.org/aliaba/BK36/. *See*, Paragraph 7.1(C)(3) of the Sample ILIT for sample language that needs to be included in the husband's credit shelter trust contained in his revocable living trust.

§14.14(a) What Happens If The Husband Dies First?

If the husband dies first, the ownership of the policy passes to the wife as the first contingent owner. The wife then has two options:

First Option. The wife she can keep the ownership of the policy and enjoy unlimited access to the policy's cash value. This would be the logical choice if the couple's estate is not likely to be subject to federal estate tax. If estate taxes become an issue at a later date, the wife can gift the policy to the standby ILIT or to another ILIT, subject to the three-year rule of IRC section 2035. Alternatively, the wife could sell the policy to the standby ILIT (or to another ILIT, such as an ILIT created by her) to avoid the application of the three-year rule, provided the sale is structured to avoid the transfer-for-value rule. Otherwise, the death proceeds will be subject to income taxes. In either case, the wife should not be the sole trustee of the standby ILIT (or the other ILIT) to avoid estate-tax inclusion under IRC section 2042 from incidents of ownership in a fiduciary capacity.

Second Option. Instead of keeping the policy, the wife could execute a qualified disclaimer (pursuant to IRC Sec. 2518) within nine months of her husband's death. As a result of the qualified disclaimer, the policy would pass to the standby ILIT (as the second contingent policy owner) without any transfer tax consequences to the wife. *C.f.*, Priv. Letter Rul. 9707008. Executing a qualified disclaimer would be advisable if the couple has a taxable estate at the time of the husband's death. Even if the wife dies soon after her husband, the life insurance proceeds from the disclaimed policy would not be included in her gross estate under IRC section 2042 because she never possessed any incidents of ownership in the policy. Nor would the three-year rule of IRC section 2035 apply. The reason is that with a qualified disclaimer, the wife is treated as never having owned the policy.

Regardless of which option is selected by the wife, because the husband is the owner of the policy, the policy's value will be included in the husband's gross estate under IRC section 2033. The estate tax value of the policy will be the cost of purchasing another policy of the same value and type on the wife's life. *See*, section 3.1, above, concerning valuation of a life insurance policy.

If the wife retains the policy (i.e., does not make a qualified disclaimer of the policy) and subsequently gifts the policy to an ILIT, the policy's value will be subject to gift taxes under IRC section 2051. If further premiums are payable on the policy, the gift tax value is the policy's interpolated terminal reserve plus the unearned premium. If the policy is paid up, the gift tax value is the single premium the carrier would charge for a comparable contract on the wife's life at the time of the gift. *See*, section 3.1, above concerning the valuation of a life insurance policy.

However, if the wife is uninsurable or highly rated at the time of the gift to the ILIT, the value of the policy is uncertain. *See*, *Estate of Pritchard v. Commissioner*, 4 T.C. 204 (1944) and Treas. Reg. §25.2512-1. In such case, prudence dictates that the wife solicit statements of interest from several life settlement companies. If there are potential purchasers of the policy in the after-market, the after-market value may trump the traditional life insurance valuation rules (which predate the life settlement market) in favor of the willing buyer/willing seller test of Treas. Reg. §25.2512-1.

If properly designed, the standby ILIT created by the husband (as the sole grantor) can include the wife as the beneficiary thereby allowing the wife access to the policy's cash value without estate tax inclusion. Since the wife is not a grantor of the standby ILIT, there is no retained interest in the ILIT under IRC sections 2036 or 2038 causing the death proceeds to be taxed in the wife's estate, provided she does not make any gifts to the ILIT either before or after her husband's death.

For the wife to avoid the life insurance proceeds from being includable in her gross estate under IRC section 2042 (concerning incidents of ownership in a fiduciary capacity), the wife should not be the sole trustee of the standby ILIT. However, the wife can serve as a co-trustee provided she does not possess any powers over the life insurance policy. (For the more cautious, the wife should not be permitted to serve as either a sole trustee or a co-trustee of the standby ILIT.) Also, the wife should not have the unfettered right to remove and replace a trustee unless the power of removal and replacement limits the replacement trustee to a person who is not related or subordinate to the wife. *See*, section 1.7, above. In addition, the wife's beneficial interest in the standby ILIT should not include a power of appointment (general or limited), and the power of appointment must be sufficiently restricted to not be an incident of ownership in the life insurance policy under IRC section 2042.

The wife can receive distributions from the standby ILIT. The distributions can be subject to an ascertainable standard for her health, education, support, and maintenance. Also, an independent trustee can provide the wife with income and principal as needed for the wife's best interests, comfort, and well being.

Since the wife cannot make gifts to the standby ILIT *if she is a beneficiary of the trust*, what options are available to pay policy premiums after the husband's death? First, the husband can leave his remaining (unused) estate tax applicable amount to the standby ILIT. Second, if the standby ILIT was funded during the husband's lifetime with a life insurance policy on the husband's life, the death benefit from that single life policy can pay the remaining premiums on the survivorship policy that the standby ILIT now owns. Third, the standby ILIT can borrow the necessary funds from either the husband's estate and/or from the wife. In either case, the loan should be evidenced by a promissory note bearing interest at the Applicable Federal Rate under IRC section 1274. Finally, the standby ILIT can enter into a third-party premium financing arrangement.

> **Practice Point:** If the wife is not a beneficiary of the standby ILIT, she can make *Crummey* gifts to the standby ILIT that qualify for the gift tax annual exclusion.

§14.14(b) What Happens If The Wife Dies First?

If the wife dies first, the value of the policy will not be includable in her gross estate since no proceeds are payable upon her death and she is not the owner of the policy. Upon the wife's death, the husband is the owner of what has become a single life policy. If the husband decides to retain ownership of the policy, the life insurance proceeds will be includable in his gross estate for federal estate tax purposes pursuant to IRC section 2042. This would be the likely scenario if the husband does not expect to have a taxable estate when he dies. If the husband desires to keep the life insurance proceeds out of his gross estate, he can gift the policy to the an ILIT. In such case, the policy's value will generally be subject to gift tax. *See*, section 3.1, above, concerning the valuation of a life insurance policy. To the extent of the husband's gift tax annual exclusion amount (through *Crummey* withdrawal rights) and the husband's life time gift tax applicable exclusion amount, no gift tax will be payable.

If the husband dies within three years of transferring the policy to an ILIT, the life insurance proceeds will be included in his gross estate pursuant to IRC section 2035. *See*, section 4.1, above. Therefore, it may be advisable to have the ILIT purchase an annual renewable term policy on the husband's life to cover the federal estate tax if should he die within three years of the policy's transfer to an ILIT. After three years, the term policy can be cancelled or, if the husband's health has declined, the term policy can be converted into a permanent policy. Alternatively, if the husband gifts cash to the ILIT, and the ILIT uses the cash to purchase the policy from the husband, the three year rule will not apply since IRC section 2035 only applies to gifts, not sales for "full and adequate consideration." *See*, section 4.1, above.

However, the sale of the policy to the ILIT will trigger the transfer for value rule, thereby causing the death proceeds to be subject to income taxes. *See*, section 2.5, above. But, if the ILIT is a partner of the husband or if the ILIT is an intentionally defective grantor trust the sale of the policy will not invoke the transfer for value rule. *See*, section 2.7, above, concerning the transfer for value rule.

§14.14(c) What If The Husband And Wife Die Simultaneously?

If the husband and wife die simultaneously and it cannot be determined which spouse died first, then under most state's laws each spouse is presumed to have survived the other for purposes of estate distribution.[24] However, the terms of the policy should be examined to determine if a different rule or law may apply. For example, the contract may provide that the owner of the policy (the husband in our example) is deemed to have survived the insured (the husband and wife in our example) if there is a simultaneous death. Assuming the governing state law or the contract presumes the husband survived, the life insurance proceeds would be included in the husband's gross estate for federal estate tax purposes pursuant to IRC section 2042. The life insurance proceeds would not be included in the wife's gross estate since she will be deemed to have predeceased her husband and will not have held any incidents of ownership in the policy prior to her death. However, the survivorship presumption can be reversed in the contingent owner endorsement and in the husband's estate planning documents. If so, then in the event of a simultaneous death the husband will be deemed to have predeceased the wife, and the wife's personal representative (or such other permitted legal representative) will have the option of making the qualified disclaimer on behalf of the wife. Sample wording for a contingent owner endorsement that modifies the survivorship presumption might read as follows:

> *[Name of husband] shall be the owner of the policy during his lifetime. In the event [name of husband] predeceases [name of wife], she shall become the owner of the policy pursuant to this endorsement. If [name of wife], her personal representative or any other person per-*

---

[24] *See,* Section I, J, 3, c of Beverly R. Budin, 826-2nd T.M., *Life Insurance* (Bureau of National Affairs, Washington, D.C.) for a general overview of the simultaneous death of an insured and the policy owner. If the policy insured only one life, most states provide that the insured is presumed to have survived the beneficiary in a simultaneous death. *See,* sections 4 and 5 of the Uniform Simultaneous Death Act. Thus, in a second-to-die policy, the husband and wife would be presumed to have survived the beneficiary if all three individuals died simultaneously.

mitted by law, executes a qualified disclaimer of policy ownership, then the [name of the standby ILIT] shall become the owner of the policy pursuant to this endorsement. In the event [name of husband] and [name of wife] die under circumstances where it cannot be determined who died first, it shall be presumed for purposes of this endorsement that [name of husband] predeceased [name of wife], regardless of any contrary rule or law.

For the wife's disclaimer to be effective under IRC section 2518, the disclaimer must be irrevocable and unqualified, must be in writing and must be delivered to the personal representative of the husband's estate and the life insurance company within nine months of the husband's death. In addition, ownership of the policy and the death benefit proceeds must pass to the standby ILIT without any direction on the part of the wife, and the wife must not have accepted the policy or any of its benefits. Once the qualified disclaimer is made, then for federal estate tax purposes the wife is treated as never having owned the policy.

§14.14(d) Community Property Issues

Additional planning is necessary in community property states to effectively use the standby ILIT technique since each spouse is considered to own a 50% interest in the policy. If the husband predeceases his wife and if she then makes a qualified disclaimer, she will have transferred her 50% interest in the policy to the ILIT. If the wife were to die within three years of making the disclaimer, the full death proceeds will be included in her gross estate for federal estate tax purposes under IRC section 2035. Moreover, if the wife is a beneficiary of the ILIT, some or all of the death proceeds may, depending on applicable state community property law, be taxed in her estate under IRC section 2036 (transfers with a retained interest) regardless of the date of her death. *See, United States v. Martin Wright Gordon*, 406 F.2d 332 (5th Cir 1969) (applying Texas law). However, this result can be easily avoided by having the couple enter into a written agreement treating the policy as the husband's separate property, and having him use his separate property to pay all the policy premiums. Under a separate property agreement the wife would release her community property interest in the policy and in all premiums used to pay for the policy. *See,* section 12.4, above, concerning community property matters.

§14.14(e) Summary

In summary, the standby ILIT technique allows a married couple to have significant flexibility with regard to their survivorship life insurance policy. The technique makes it possible for the insureds to maintain access to the policy's cash value while reserving the right to change the ultimate beneficiaries of the death proceeds. In addition, the strategy offers options that work well whether or not the insureds have a taxable estate in the future.

§14.15 USE ILIT TO FUND BUY-SELL AGREEMENT

One of the problems with a conventional buy-sell agreement is that the surviving owners' estates are significantly larger than the estate of the first owner to die. As each owner dies, the surviving owners' estates increase in value due to their purchase of the deceased owner's interest in the business by the surviving owners (or the corporation's redemption of the deceased owner's interest in the business). Eventually the last surviving owner, who may have started out owning less than a majority interest in the business will end up owning 100% of the business in his or her estate. Assume a corporation has three equal shareholders each owning 100 shares of stock in a closely held corporation, and they enter into a buy-sell redemption agreement funded with life insurance. Assume further that the corporation is valued at $3 million and owns three $1 million life insurance policies on each shareholder's life to fund the buy-sell redemption agreement. The first shareholder to die would receive $1 million from the corporation for his or her shares (which $1 million would be includable in his or her gross estate for federal estate tax purposes), and the corporation would then purchase an additional $500,000 of life insurance on the two surviving shareholders' lives. The estate of the second shareholder to die would then receive $1.5 million from the corporation for his or her shares (which $1.5 million would be includable in his or her gross estate for federal estate tax purposes), and the estate of last surviving shareholder would include a business valued at $4.5 million (i.e., the business at $3 million plus $1.5 million of business owned life insurance on the surviving shareholder's life), and when the surviving shareholder dies, the $4.5 million would be includable in his or her gross estate for federal estate tax purposes.

One possible way to avoid this result is to use ILITs in connection with a cross-purchase buy-sell agreement.[25] For example, the cor-

---

[25] *See,* Robert S. Balter and Alan J. Mittleman, "Using Trusts as Buyers in Shareholders' Agreements," 27 *Tax Management Estates, Gifts and Trusts Journal* 219 (September 12, 2002); and Stephen O. Rothschild, "Uses of the 'BILIT'—Business Irrevocable Life Insurance Trust And Solving Inequities In Business Continuation Agreements," 140 *Trusts & Estates* 22 (July 2001).

poration could be recapitalized into voting and non-voting shares with each shareholder owning 2 voting share and 98 non-voting shares after the recapitalization. Next, each shareholder establishes an ILIT for the benefit of his or her descendants. If desired, the ILIT could be designed as a generation-skipping dynasty trust. The first shareholder's ILIT would own a $500,000 policy on the second shareholder's life and a $500,000 policy on the third shareholder's life; the second shareholder's ILIT would own a $500,000 policy on the first shareholder's life and a $500,000 policy on the third shareholder's life; and the third shareholder's ILIT would own a $500,000 policy on the first and a $500,000 policy on the second shareholder's lives. Thus each shareholder's ILIT would own a total of $1 million of life insurance on the other shareholders' lives. The premiums for the policies owned by each ILIT would typically be paid for by cash gifts made to the ILIT grantor coupled with the beneficiaries having *Crummey* withdrawal rights over the cash gifts. Each shareholder would also gift two share of his or her non-voting stock to his or her ILIT. The three shareholders and their ILITs would then enter into a cross-purchase buy-sell agreement concerning all the shares of stock.

The cross-purchase buy-sell agreement would provide that in the event of the first shareholder's death, the second and third shareholders would personally purchase, in equal portions, the first shareholder's 2 voting shares, and the second and third shareholders' ILITs would be required to purchase, in equal portions, the 96 non-voting shares owned by the first shareholder and also be required to purchase in equal portions, the 2 non-voting shares owned by the first shareholder's ILIT. In addition, pursuant to the terms of the buy-sell agreement, the second shareholder's ILIT would purchase from the first shareholder's ILIT the policy that the first shareholder's ILIT owned on the third shareholder's life, and vice versa. Since these purchases would trigger the transfer-for-value rule for income tax purposes, the ILITs would need to be partners (or members in an LLC) to come within one of the exceptions to the transfer-for-value rule. *See,* section 2.5, above. However, if only two shareholders were involved, and the ILITs were designed as grantor trusts, the transfer-for-value rule would not apply. *See,* section 2.5(c), above.

The purchase price for the life insurance policies would be set forth in the buy-sell agreement and could be based on either the policy's interpolated terminal reserve value or cash surrender value. *See,* section 3.1, above concerning the valuation of life insurance policies.

After the first shareholder dies, the second shareholder's ILIT will need to purchase an additional $500,000 of insurance on the third shareholder's life, and vice versa (since each surviving shareholder's interest in the corporation is now worth approximately $1.5 million). Assuming the second shareholder dies next, the third shareholder's ILIT will use the insurance proceeds received at the second shareholder's death to purchase all of the second shareholder's non-voting shares and the non-voting shares owned by the second shareholder's ILIT, and the third shareholder will personally purchase all of the second shareholder's voting shares. In addition, the third shareholder's ILIT will purchase the policies owned by the second shareholder's ILIT on the third shareholder's life.

By structuring the buy-sell this way, the value of the surviving shareholder's estate is not increased by the purchase of additional shares (except for the voting shares) nor is it increased by the purchase of the life insurance policies on his or her life. Yet the surviving shareholder maintains full control of the corporation as a result of owning all of the voting shares. The surviving shareholder's ILIT will own all the non-voting shares and all the life insurance on the surviving shareholder's life.

If an S corporation is involved, the ILITs will need either Qualified Subchapter S Trust language or Electing Small Business Trust language after the grantor's death. *See,* Paragraph 7.10 of Sample ILIT. If the ILITs are designed as grantor trusts, then during the grantor's lifetime the ILIT would be eligible to hold S corporation stock. *See,* section 2.8(e), above.

Needless to say, this strategy works best when only a few shareholders are owners of a closely held corporation, otherwise the number of life insurance policies that have to be purchased by the ILITs will become "unmanageable."

15

Fixing A Damaged ILIT

CHAPTER OVERVIEW

Because an ILIT is irrevocable[1] and generally designed to last for decades and possibly centuries (in the case of a GST dynasty ILIT), it is impossible for a grantor or a practitioner to contemplate all the permutations of the exigencies of life and those of our ever changing world. No matter how well an ILIT is drafted, and no matter how much flexibility has been built into the ILIT to deal with changing circumstances, at some point, a long term irrevocable trust, such as an ILIT, may need an overhaul or a fix. This chapter[2] discusses how to fix

[1] According to the dictionary, irrevocable means "not able to be revoked, undone, or changed." To the IRS, irrevocable means, "incapable of being recalled or revoked." *Commissioner v. Strong Manufacturing Company*, 124 F.2d 360, 363 (6th Cir. 1941), *rev'd*, 317 U.S. 102 (1942). To the grantor, irrevocable means, "Until I change my mind." To a trust beneficiary, irrevocable means, "Go to court and bust the trust!" To the court, irrevocable means, "What does the *Uniform Trust Code* (*UTC)* or *Restatement (Second/Third) of Trusts* have to say about construing, reforming, modifying, or terminating the trust?" To the wise estate planning attorney, irrevocable means, drafting a trust with sufficient flexibility to deal with changing circumstances, and including provisions in the trust that permit it to be modified and terminated. Thus, "irrevocable" has many different meanings. "'When *I* use a word,' Humpty Dumpty said [to Alice], in rather a scornful tone, 'it means just what I choose it to mean—neither more nor less.'" Lewis Carroll, *Through the Looking Glass*.

[2] The author gratefully acknowledges the generous contributions of Santo ("Sandy") Bisignano, Jr., Esq. of Bisignano & Harrison, LLP of Dallas, Texas, Stephanie E. Donaho, Esq. of Locke Liddell & Sapp, LLP of Houston, Texas, Shari A. Levitan, Esq. of Holland & Knight, LLP of Boston, Massachusetts (in cooperation with The Boston Bar Association, www.bostonbar.org), and Ann Marie Towle, Esq. of Choate, Hall &

an irrevocable trust, which by definition, is incapable of being changed, and therefore cannot be easily or inexpensively changed or fixed.[3] Put another way, there is no perfect and safe—and certainly no inexpensive—way to fix a "damaged" irrevocable trust.

§15.1 OVERVIEW OF A DAMAGED ILIT

Long term irrevocable trusts may need to be fixed at some point because of poor design, sloppy implementation, negligent maintenance, changes in tax laws, changes in the financial and investment environment, changes in beneficiaries, old style "income only" trust provisions, improvements in drafting technique, changes in the grantor's family or financial situation, or changes in a beneficiary's circumstances. In addition to the normal difficulties associated with irrevocable trusts, ILITs have special problems related to the fact that the primary trust asset is life insurance. ILITs are most likely to incur damage and need fixing with regard to: (i) *Crummey* withdrawal rights, (ii) GST matters, (iii) changes in the tax laws, (iv) life insurance policy issues, (v) trust provisions that are no longer necessary, desirable or appropriate under the current circumstances, and (vi) accidental funding of the ILIT with community property. This chap-

---

Stewart, LLP of Boston, Massachusetts (also in cooperation with The Boston Bar Association) in the writing of this Chapter.

See, Charles L. Ratner, "How to Undo An ILIT, If You Really Have To," 145 *Trusts & Estates* 18 (September 2006); Domingo P. Such, III, "Fix-Ups Of Estate Plans After They Have become Irrevocable (With Sample Language) (Part 2)," 12 *ALI-ABA Estate Planning Course Materials Journal* 41(April 2006); Domingo P. Such, III, "Fix-Ups Of Estate Plans After They Have become Irrevocable (With Sample Language) (Part 1)," 12 *ALI-ABA Estate Planning Course Materials Journal* 45 (February 2006); Alan S. Acker, "Fixing Broken Irrevocable Trusts," 31 *ACTEC Journal* 221 (Winter 2005) ("Acker"); and Ronald D. Aucutt, "Restructuring, Refocusing, and Retiring Irrevocable Trusts," 38 *Heckerling Institute on Estate Planning,* Chapter 5 (Matthew Bender/Lexis-Nexis, Newark, NJ 2004) ("Aucutt").

[3] "In assessing situations where clients desire a change to the terms of the trust, consider the following: Do the changes being sought make sense? Are the beneficiaries in agreement? Can the interests of beneficiaries who cannot or who refuse to consent be protected adequately? Can the trustee be protected adequately?....At the risk of stating the obvious, one should consider whether any beneficiary or other person may be considered to have made a gift. At the risk of further stating the obvious, if a beneficiary receives less than the fair market value of his or her interest in the trust, he or she probably has made a gift." Acker at 231.

ter will explore different techniques that an attorney can use to fix some of these ailments.

> **Caution:** All of these techniques must be analyzed for potential income (especially transfer for value issues, potential gain to the policy owner, and the realization of gain or loss under IRC section 1001(a) because of a change in the beneficiaries' legal entitlements, pursuant to *Cottage Savings Association v. Commissioner*, 499 U.S. 554 (1991)[4]), estate, gift and generation skipping transfer tax consequences (especially the effect on a GST grandfathered trust).[5] *See generally,* Chapters 2, 3, 4, 5, and 6 above. And, the employment of these techniques (other than the exercise of a power of appointment) must be done consistent with a trustee's fiduciary duty to the trust beneficiaries. *See,* section 9.2, above.

> **Practice Point:** The attorney for the trustee should advise the trust beneficiaries that the attorney represents the trustee only; and that the beneficiaries have the right to retain independent counsel to review and advise them concerning any proposed reformations or modifications to the trust.

> **Practice Point:** When undertaking a fix, consider the effects of: (i) a spendthrift clause, and (ii) a no contest clause. Will either of these clauses prevent a desired outcome? For example, even if all of the beneficiaries consent to the termination of a trust, they cannot compel termination if it would thwart a material purpose of the trust. *Restatement (Second) of Trusts* section 337(2). A typical spendthrift clause that prevents a beneficiary from alienating his or her interest in the trust is considered a material purpose. *Id.* (comment l). *But see, Restatement (Third) of Trusts* section 65 (comment e) "[S]pendthrift restrictions are not sufficient in and of themselves to establish, or to

---

[4] *See,* section 15.7(d), below, for a discussion of the *Cottage Savings* doctrine.

[5] *See generally,* Donald Tescher and Jordan Klingsberg, "Settlements of Estate and Trust Disputes Must Consider the Tax Impact," 33 *Estate Planning* 32 (December 2006); and Donald Tescher and Jordan Klingsberg, "Tax Consequences of Settlements of Estate and Trust Disputes," 33 *Estate Planning* 29 (Nov. 2006).

create a presumption of, a material purpose that would prevent termination by consent of all the beneficiaries." (Unless otherwise specified, all references in this chapter to the *Restatements* are to the *Restatements of Trusts.)*

§15.1(a) Examples Of A Damaged ILIT

Examples of a damaged ILIT include:

• *Crummey* withdrawal right notice formalities were ignored or neglected. *See,* section 15.5, below.

• The ILIT does not contain *Crummey* withdrawal rights. *See,* section 15.6, below.

• The ILIT's *Crummey* withdrawal rights are ambiguous, inadequate, or out of date. *See,* section 15.7.

• Erroneous GST tax exemption allocation planning, including failure to allocate GST tax exemption, the inadvertent allocation of GST tax exemption, a GST trust that is not 100% GST tax exempt, a non-skip beneficiary predeceases the insured, or the spouse's *Crummey* withdrawal right creates an ETIP. *See,* section 15.8, below.

• Tax problems as a result of poor drafting or changes in the tax law. *See,* section 15.9, below.

• The life insurance policy owned by the ILIT is no longer appropriate under the current circumstances. *See,* section 15.10, below.

• The ILIT does not possess an insurable interest in the life of the insured-grantor. *See,* section 15.11, below.

• Because of the passage of time or a change in circumstances, the ILIT no longer fits the grantor's and/or a beneficiary's needs, or certain provisions of the trust are no longer appropriate or desirable, or after the insured's death the beneficiaries disagree as to the trust's investment policies or to other issues. *See,* section 15.12, below.

• "Pollution" of the ILIT with community property when the ILIT was designed to hold only separate property. *See,* section 15.13, below.

§15.2 *CRUMMEY* WITHDRAWAL RIGHT AILMENTS

A poorly drafted, poorly implemented, or poorly maintained ILIT with *Crummey* withdrawal rights can have many negative consequences, including: (1) inability for a gift to qualify for the gift tax annual exclusion, thereby resulting in the unnecessary use of the grantor's $1 million gift tax applicable exclusion amount, (2) wasting of a beneficiary's lifetime gift tax applicable exclusion amount, (3) inclusion of the life insurance proceeds in the grantor's gross estate for federal estate tax purposes, (4) inclusion of some or all of the life insurance proceeds in a beneficiary's gross estate for federal estate tax purposes, (5) inability to effectively allocate GST tax exemption, and (6) subverting the grantor's objectives.

§15.3 THE *CRUMMEY* CASE

A review of the *Crummey* case and subsequent IRS pronouncements and court rulings is essential in understanding how to salvage a damaged *Crummey* withdrawal right.

In *D. Clifford Crummey v. Commissioner*, 397 F.2d 82 (9th Cir. 1968), the taxpayer-donors established irrevocable trusts for the benefit of each of their four children. Two of the children were minors (under the age of 21). The minor children lived with the taxpayers, and were supported by them. Each time a gift was made to a trust, the beneficiary was given the right to demand at any time, up to December 31st of the year in which the gift was made, the lesser of $4,000 or the amount of the gift. Contributions were made approximately two weeks before the close of the year. If the beneficiary was a minor at the time of the gift, his or her guardian could demand the money on the minor's behalf. If no demand was made by the beneficiary or the guardian, the gift irrevocably became a part of trust corpus. According to the court, "The whole question on this appeal is whether or not a present interest was given by the petitioners to their minor children so as to qualify as an exclusion under §2503(b)." The court held that although demands by the minors were not likely to be made, the gifts, coupled with the demand rights, constituted gifts of a present interest. In *Crummey*, no guardian or agent was ever appointed for the minor children for the years when the gifts under scrutiny were made and, in fact, there could be no demand made by the minors. The court also noted that it was unlikely that the minor beneficiaries knew (or would ever know) about the gifts that were made to the trusts. Said the court:

> Although under our interpretation neither the trust nor the law technically forbid a demand by the minor, the practical difficulties of a child going through the procedures seem substantial. In addition, the surrounding facts indicate the children were well cared for and the obvious

> intention of the trustors was to create a long term trust....As a practical matter, it is likely that some, if not all, of the beneficiaries did not even know that they had any right to demand funds from the trust. They probably did not know when contributions were made to the trust or in what amounts. Even had they known, the substantial contributions were made toward the end of the year so that the time to make a demand was severely limited....We think it unlikely that any demand ever would have been made. *Id.* at 87-88.

§15.3(a) *Crummey* Expands The Holdings In *Kieckhefer* And *Gilmore*

Crummey is not the first time the U.S. Court of Appeals ruled against the Internal Revenue Service concerning demand withdrawal rights held by a minor trust beneficiary. Seventeen years earlier, in *Kieckhefer v. Commissioner*, 189 F.2d 118 (7th Cir. 1951), the court held that where the trust instrument contained no impediments (other than those already imposed by state law) concerning a minor beneficiary's ability to withdraw trust contributions, the trust contributions constituted gifts of a present interest. The court went to great lengths to expose the IRS' fallacy of treating withdrawal rights held by an adult trust beneficiary as gifts of a present interest while treating withdrawal rights held by a minor trust beneficiary as gifts of a future interest. Said the court:

> [T]he conditions and restrictions upon which the Commissioner [of the Internal Revenue Service] relies to convert this gift into one of a future interest are not imposed by the trust instrument but, if they exist, are the result solely of the disability of the beneficiary due to the fact that he is a minor....[T]he fallaciousness of the Commissioner's contention is the failure to distinguish between restrictions and contingencies imposed by the donor (in this case the trust instrument), and such restrictions and contingencies as are due to disabilities always incident to and associated with minors and other incompetents. As to the former [to wit, restrictions and contingencies imposed by the donor (in this case the trust instrument)] it is authoritatively settled that a gift

> upon which the donor imposes such conditions or restrictions is of a future interest. In the latter [to wit, restrictions and contingencies as are due to disabilities always incident to and associated with minors and other incompetents], such restrictions as exist are imposed by state law due to the fact that the beneficiary is incapable of acting on his own. *It is our view, and we so hold, that such restrictions [imposed by law concerning minors] do not transform what otherwise would be a gift of present interest to one of future interest* (emphasis added).

Three years later, in *Gilmore v. Commissioner,* 213 F.2d 520 (6th Cir. 1954),[6] the issue before the Sixth Circuit Court of Appeals was "whether a gift of property [to wit, shares of corporate stock] in trust for the benefit of minors, providing that the trustees pay the principal and income to the beneficiaries upon their demand, with a further provision permitting the trustees to invest the trust funds in income or non-income producing investments, is a gift of a present interest." The court ruled that the gifts of stock were in gifts of a present interest even though the trustees could determine, in their own discretion, whether a beneficiary was incapacitated, and the trustees were empowered to make payments at their sole discretion, among other ways, by using such payments for the benefit of the incapacitated beneficiary.

§15.3(b) The Tests Under *Kieckhefer, Gilmore,* And *Crummey* For A Gift Of A Present Interest

The significance of *Kieckhefer, Gilmore,* and *Crummey* is the ability to structure an irrevocable trust for a beneficiary (minor or adult) that qualifies for the annual gift tax exclusion even if the trustee has absolute discretion over trust distributions. Thus, the test under these three cases is: "Does the donee (or the donee's legal guardian) have the legal right to demand payment of the gift contribution amount, and is the trustee legally obligated to comply with that demand?" If the answer is yes, then the donee (even though a minor

---

[6] Of historical note to tax practitioners, the esteemed Edward H. McDermott, Esq. and John S. Pennell, Esq. of McDermott, Will & Emery of Chicago, Illinois represented the taxpayer in *Gilmore.* No wonder the taxpayer won! (For younger practitioners, John S. Pennell, Esq. is better known as the father of renowned Professor Jeffrey M. Pennell of Emory University Law School.)

and no guardian has been appointed), has a gift of a present interest for gift tax purposes.

§15.4 THE EVOLUTION OF *CRUMMEY*

Through a series of public and private rulings, the IRS has attempted to limit the scope of decisions of *Kieckhefer, Gilmore,* and *Crummey* by adding additional requirements for a gift to a discretionary irrevocable trust to qualify as a gift of a present interest that qualifies for the gift tax annual exclusion. However, as noted below, the courts have resisted many of these changes.

§15.4(a) The IRS Affirms *Kieckhefer, Gilmore, And Crummey* Concerning Minor Beneficiaries Possessing Withdrawal Rights

In light of *Kieckhefer, Gilmore,* and *Crummey*, the IRS issued Rev. Rul. 73-405, 1973-2 C.B. 321, and stated:

> In view of the foregoing decisions, it is now concluded that a gift in trust for the benefit of a minor should not be classified as a future interest merely because no guardian was in fact appointed. Accordingly, if there is no impediment under the trust or local law to the appointment of a guardian and the minor donee has a right to demand distribution, the transfer is a gift of a present interest that qualifies for the annual exclusion allowable under section 2503(b) of the Code.

See also, Mary Hull Naumoff v. Commissioner, T.C. Memo 1983-435 (1983).

Thus, there is no requirement that a guardian be appointed for a gift to a minor beneficiary to be a gift of a present interest that is eligible for the gift tax annual exclusion.

§15.4(b) *Crummey* Withdrawal Rights And Guardians

The IRS has, however, attempted to impose further restrictions on *Kieckhefer, Gilmore,* and *Crummey* by privately ruling that a gift in trust to a minor or incompetent beneficiary should grant the beneficiary sufficient time (30 days in this instance) to exercise his or her withdrawal right for the gift to qualify as a gift of a present interest. (It is presumed that the IRS considers 30 days to be sufficient time for a guardian to be appointed; however, the tax court in *Estate of Maria Cristofani v. Commissioner*, 97 T.C. 74 (1991), *acq. in result only*, AOD 1996-010, permitted just 15 days.) However, under *Kieckhefer*, *Gilmore*, and *Crummey*, the actual appointment of a guardian is not a requirement for a gift in trust to a minor beneficiary to qualify as a gift of a present interest, if the minor beneficiary possesses the right to withdraw the gift amount. Furthermore, *Crummey* dealt with withdrawal rights that lapsed approximately 15 days after the contributions were made to the trusts. *See,* Priv. Letter Ruls. 8813019, 8134135, and 8103074.

§15.4(c) In Certain Instances, A Minor Beneficiary Is Not Required To Have Actual Notice Of A *Crummey* Withdrawal Right

A parent-donor can receive notice of a gift and exercise (or decide not to exercise) a withdrawal right on behalf of a minor-beneficiary. In Priv. Letter Rul. 8008040 the IRS held that such an arrangement resulted in a gift of a present interest. *See also, Estate of Carolyn W. Holland v. Commissioner*, T.C. Memo 1997-302 (1997); Priv. Letter Ruls. 8022048 and 7944019.

§15.4(d) The IRS Requires Adult Beneficiaries To Have Notice Of Their Withdrawal Right And Adequate Opportunity To Exercise Their Withdrawal Right

The IRS has held that after a gift is made to an irrevocable trust, each adult beneficiary must have (i) actual notice of his or her withdrawal right, and (ii) an adequate or reasonable opportunity to exercise the withdrawal right prior to its lapse. Otherwise, the annual gift tax exclusion will not be available with respect to gifts in trust for the benefit of that adult beneficiary. Rev. Rul. 81-7, 1981-1 C.B. 474 (gift tax annual exclusion denied where beneficiary had only 3 days to exercise his/her *Crummey* withdrawal right before it lapsed). *See also,* Priv. Letter Ruls. 8019038, 8121069, 8813019, 9232013, 9532001, and 9625031.

§15.4(e) Notice Of *Crummey* Withdrawal Right Need Not Be In Year Of Gift

However, in Rev. Rul. 83-108, 1983-2 C.B. 167, the IRS held that a gift made on December 29, 1981 to an irrevocable trust which granted the beneficiary a withdrawal right that did not lapse until 1982 constituted a gift of a present interest in 1981. This is because the beneficiary had a reasonable amount of time to exercise the withdrawal right after the gift was made in late December of 1981. Note, in this ruling, the beneficiary did not receive notice of the gift and withdrawal right until January 6, 1982.

§15.4(f) The IRS Attacks Naked *Crummey* Withdrawal Rights

In Priv. Letter Rul. 8727003 the IRS held that a beneficiary must have more than a mere withdrawal right over an irrevocable trust before the gift tax annual exclusion would be allowed for gifts to the trust. The IRS concluded that a "gift coupled with a withdrawal right" would qualify for the gift tax annual exclusion only if the withdrawal right was actually exercised or if the beneficiary had a continuing (i.e., more than a nominal) interest in the trust. *See also*, TAM 9045002 where the IRS held that the contingent trust beneficiaries (the grantor's grandchildren) did not receive a present interest in the trust, nor did the grantor's in-laws who held only *Crummey* withdrawal rights and no further interest in the trust. The IRS ruled that these beneficiaries did not possess a present interest in the trust, because in the IRS' view, adding such beneficiaries with limited rights was nothing more than an attempt to avoid the federal gift tax through a proliferation of annual exclusions.

§15.4(g) *Cristofani* Permits *Crummey* Withdrawal Rights For Contingent Beneficiaries

However, in *Estate of Maria Cristofani v. Commissioner*, 97 T.C. 74 (1991), *acq. in result only*, 1996-2 C.B.1,[7] the Tax Court held that the *Crummey* withdrawal right beneficiaries did not have to have a present vested interest or a vested remainder interest in the trust principal for the gifts to qualify for the gift tax annual exclusion. The court approved *Crummey* withdrawal rights for both the income beneficiaries (Maria's two adult children) and the contingent remainder benefi-

---

[7] The IRS' 1996 acquiescence in *Cristofani* is "in result relating to whether transfers of property to a trust, whose contingent remainder beneficiaries have the right to withdraw an amount not exceeding the section 2503(b) exclusion within 15 days following such transfers, constitute gifts of present interests in property within the meaning of section 2503(b) of the Code."

ciaries (Maria's five minor grandchildren) even though (i) the withdrawal right period was only 15 days, (ii) the two adult children were the natural guardians of their minor children (the grandchildren), and no guardians were ever appointed by the court, and (iii) none of the grandchildren ever received any trust property—the trust terminated 120 days after Maria's death and the trust property was distributed equally to her two adult children.

Said the court, at page 83:

> We do not believe, however, that *Crummey* requires that the beneficiaries of a trust must have a vested present interest or vested remainder interest in the trust corpus or income, in order to qualify for the section 2503(b) exclusion. As discussed in *Crummey,* the likelihood that the beneficiary will actually receive present enjoyment of the property is not the test for determining whether a present interest was received. Rather, we must examine the ability of the beneficiaries, in a legal sense, to exercise their right to withdraw trust corpus, and the trustee's right to legally resist a beneficiary's demand for payment. *Crummey v. Commissioner,* 397 F.2d at 88. Based upon the language of the trust instrument and stipulations of the parties, we believe that each grandchild possessed the legal right to withdraw trust corpus and that the trustees would be unable to legally resist a grandchild's withdrawal demand. We note that there was no agreement or understanding between decedent, the trustees, and the beneficiaries that the grandchildren would not exercise their withdrawal rights following a contribution to the Children's Trust.

See also, Priv. Letter Rul. 9030005 (gift tax annual exclusion available to grantor's children who were discretionary beneficiaries of "super support" principal distributions and who held contingent remainder interests that vested only if the grantor's wife (their mother) predeceased the grantor).

§15.4(h) The IRS Continues To Attack Naked *Crummey* Withdrawal Rights Despite *Cristofani*

Despite the taxpayer victory in *Cristofani*, the IRS continued to attack what it viewed as abusive arrangements designed to improperly expand the availability of annual gift tax exclusions.

In TAM 9141008 the IRS addressed a situation that it felt epitomized "abusive *Crummey* trusts." The decedent, prior to her death, established three irrevocable trusts, one for the benefit of each of her three children. Each trust lasted for a child's lifetime and provided that all income was to be distributed to that child on a quarterly basis. Upon the death of the child, that child was given a limited testamentary power of appointment to appoint the trust to his or her spouse. Any unappointed property was to be held in further trust for the child's then living descendants. Each trust further provided that when the donor made gifts to the trust, each child, his or her spouse, and the child's descendants (i.e., the grantor's grandchildren and great grandchildren) had a *Crummey* withdrawal right as to a pro rata portion of the gift.

At the time that the trusts were established, the decedent had three children and 32 grandchildren and great-grandchildren. From 1984 through 1987, the decedent made gifts of partnership interests having a value of $350,000.00 per year ($10,000 multiplied by 35 beneficiaries). Gift tax returns were filed each year claiming 35 gift tax annual exclusions.

The IRS held that only the gifts to the three children would qualify for the gift tax annual exclusion, and in effect held that unless a beneficiary had more than a contingent interest in the trust, his or her failure to exercise the withdrawal right is, in fact, evidence of a prearranged plan to not exercise his or her withdrawal right despite the fact that the beneficiary has a legal right to do so. With this ruling, the IRS began its onslaught on *Crummey* withdrawal rights under the "prearranged plan" theory.

§15.4(i) The IRS Attacks *Crummey* Withdrawal Rights Based On A "Prearranged Plan" Theory

In the IRS' first action on decision concerning *Cristofani*[8] the IRS announced it would litigate cases "whose facts indicate a greater

[8] AOD 1992-09 (Mar. 23, 1992).

abuse of the Crummey power than those of *Cristofani*, preferably outside the Ninth Circuit."

In the IRS' second action on decision concerning *Cristofani*,[9] the IRS rejected the *Cristofani* decision to the extent it extended *Crummey* withdrawal rights to persons other than holders of income interests or "vested" remainder interests. The IRS said that absent the power holders having "continuing economic interests" in the trust, the *Crummey* doctrine did not apply. The IRS went further by stating it would deny annual gift tax exclusions if the IRS concludes that in substance there was a prearranged understanding that the withdrawal right would not be exercised or that doing so would result in adverse consequences to the beneficiary. Said the IRS,

> [T]he Service disagrees with the Tax Court's sweeping interpretation of *Crummey*. To extend the benefit of the annual exclusion to illusory gifts of present interests would undermine significantly the unified system of estate and gift taxation and invite flagrant abuse of the benefit which Congress intended in enacting section 2503(b). Accordingly, the Service will continue to litigate cases whose facts indicate that the substance of the transfers was merely to obtain annual exclusions and that no bona fide gift of a present interest was intended.

In TAM 9628004, the IRS denied annual exclusions for *Crummey* withdrawal rights with a substance over form argument based on the theory that the donor did not intend to make bona fide gifts.[10] These trusts granted three children, their spouses and seven grandchildren *Crummey* withdrawal rights but under the trust instrument, there was no requirement that the trustee provide notice of gifts to the beneficiaries. Despite the lack of notice requirement in the trust instrument, in most years, notice of the gifts and notice of the beneficiaries' right of withdrawal were made in early December and the withdrawal rights lapsed at the end of December (although gifts were typ-

---

[9] AOD 1996-10 (7/15/1996).

[10] The TAM also mentioned that the *Crummey* withdrawal right beneficiaries only has 4 days to exercise their withdrawal right before it lapse. However, because of the multiplicity of issues discussed in the ruling, it is uncertain that the 4 day withdrawal right period was determinative of the IRS' decision to deny annual gift tax exclusion to the gifts made to the trust.

ically not made to the trust until the last week of December). The IRS completely denied annual gift tax exclusions for all transfers to the trusts. The IRS' position was that many beneficiaries had no genuine interest in the trust other than *Crummey* withdrawal rights. The IRS stated, "[W]here nominal beneficiaries enjoy only discretionary income interests, remote contingent rights to the remainder, or no rights whatsoever in the income or remainder, their non-exercise indicates that there was some kind of prearranged understanding with the donor that these rights were not meant to be exercised or that their exercise would result in undesirable consequences, or both."

> **Practice Point:** The IRS's position in both AOD 1996-010 and Priv. Letter Rul. 9628004 is at odds with the decisions of the Tax Court (*Kohlsatt* and *Holland*, which are discussed below) and the U.S. Court of Appeals for the Ninth Circuit (*Crummey*, which is discussed above). The IRS agrees with the *Crummey* decision, and has cited it in numerous public and private rulings. *See*, Rev. Rul. 85-24, 1985-1 C.B. 329; Rev. Rul. 81-7, 1981-1 C.B. 474; Rev. Rul. 75-415, 1975-2 C.B. 374; Rev. Rul. 73-405, 1973-2 C.B. 321. *See also*, Priv. Letter Ruls. 200341002, 200227017, 200123034, 200011054, 199912016, 9812006, and 9731004 all of which were issued subsequent to AOD 1996-10 and Priv. Letter Rul. 9628004.

§15.4(j) *Estate Of Lieselotte Kohlsaat* Rejects IRS' Prearranged Theory

In *Estate of Lieselotte Kohlsaat*, T.C. Memo 1997-212 (1997),[11] the IRS finally had an opportunity to argue its "prearranged plan" theory in a case that the IRS believed represented the "quintessential abusive *Crummey* trust" situation. In *Kohlsaat*, the taxpayer, before her death, transferred a commercial building worth $155,000 to a trust. No other contributions were made. The trust was for the primary benefit of one of Mrs. Kohlsaat's two adult children (a son and a daughter), who were also the co-trustees of the trust. Each child received a

---

[11] *See*, Jerome A. Deener and Owen G. Fiore, "Kohlsaat Confirms Viability of *Crummey/Cristofani* Trusts-and More," 23 *ACTEC Notes* 174 (Fall 1997); and Jerome A. Deener and Owen G. Fiore, "How to Deal Effectively with Expanded IRS Attacks on *Crummey/Cristofani* Trusts," 22 *ACTEC Notes* 216 (Winter 1996).

50% interest in the trust income and corpus. Each child was also given a special power of appointment to appoint his or her 50% share of the trust property among his or her descendants. Any unappointed property from the daughter's 50% trust share would pass to the daughter's children and minor grandchildren (i.e., to the grantor's grandchildren and minor great-grandchildren). Any unappointed property from the son's 50% trust share would pass to the son's wife and his four sons (i.e., the grantor's daughter in-law and her grandsons). In all, there were 16 contingent remainder beneficiaries, all of whom had *Crummey* withdrawal rights.

Under the trust, each child of the grantor and each contingent remainder beneficiary was given a *Crummey* withdrawal right. Notice of the beneficiary's withdrawal right was sent within six days after the building was contributed to the trust. None of the beneficiaries exercised their withdrawal right and none of the beneficiaries requested notification of future transfers of property to the trust. Eighteen gift tax annual exclusions were claimed. These gifts were disclosed on the decedent's federal estate tax return.

The IRS allowed the gift tax annual exclusion concerning the two children but denied the gift tax annual exclusions with regard to the gifts to the sixteen contingent remainder beneficiaries on the basis that the withdrawal rights were illusory because of a prearranged plan. The IRS argued that a prearranged plan should be found if any one of the following facts existed: (i) the beneficiaries failed to exercise their withdrawal right; (ii) the beneficiaries are led to believe they would be penalized if they exercised their withdrawal right; (iii) the trustees failed to thoroughly explain all aspects of the withdrawal rights to the beneficiaries in a manner sufficient to allow them to make an intelligent and informed decision; or (iv) the beneficiaries are led to believe that the exercise of their withdrawal right would create family disharmony and/or disrupt the donor's estate plan.

The Tax Court rejected the IRS' prearranged plan argument and refused to deny any of the gift tax annual exclusions. In so doing, the court held: (1) there was insufficient evidence to establish that an understanding existed between the donor and contingent beneficiaries that they would not exercise their withdrawal rights; (2) failure to exercise the withdrawal rights, without more, would not give rise to the implication of a prearrangement; and (3) the contingent remainder beneficiaries had actual notice from the trustees regarding their withdrawal rights.

Said the court:

> The evidence [presented by the IRS] does not establish that any understandings existed between decedent and the beneficiaries that the contingent beneficiaries would not exercise those rights following a transfer of property to the trust. At trial, several credible reasons were offered by the trust beneficiaries as to why they did not exercise their rights to demand a distribution of trust property. The fact that none of the beneficiaries exercised their rights or that none of the beneficiaries requested notification of future transfers of property to the trust does not imply to us that the beneficiaries had agreed with decedent not to do so, and we refuse to infer any understanding.
>
> The evidence does not support...[the IRS's] contention that the contingent beneficiaries believed they would be penalized for exercising their rights to demand distributions of trust property or that the trustees purposefully withheld information from the beneficiaries.
>
> Further, the contingent beneficiaries received actual notice from the trustees with regard to their rights. Decedent intended to benefit the contingent beneficiaries by giving them interests in the trust. The contingent beneficiaries were decedent's relatives.
>
> For the reasons stated above, the ***contingent beneficiaries'*** unrestricted rights to demand immediate distributions of trust property are to be treated as present interests in property (emphasis added).

Although the Tax Court did not preclude the possibility of denial of the gift tax annual exclusions under the "prearranged plan" theory, it appears clear that the primary focus of the court was whether the taxpayer, pursuant to the terms of the trust, conferred unrestricted rights of withdrawal on a beneficiary (regardless of the beneficiary's contingent or vested status) and whether the beneficiary had notice of those rights with respect to each gift. Also, the Tax Court's holding affirms that the gift tax annual exclusion is available for *Crummey* withdrawal rights granted to contingent remainder beneficiaries.

§15.4(k) *Estate Of Carolyn W. Holland*—Another Taxpayer Victory

Estate of Carolyn W. Holland v. Commissioner, T.C. Memo 1997-302 (1997), is a Tax Court case dealing with a multiplicity of issues. However, the decision of the court arguably imposes important limits on the scope of the IRS' "prearranged plan" argument.

In *Holland*, the donor established eight trusts, one for each of her eight great-grandchildren. Except for the name of the beneficiary, each trust was identical and gave each beneficiary a sixty day *Crummey* withdrawal right with respect to each gift to the trust. The co-trustees of each trust were two of the donor's grandchildren, Jack and Lewis. Several of the trusts were for Jack's minor children and another trust was for a minor child of Lewis. Each great-grandchild was a vested beneficiary of his or her trust.

The IRS denied the gift tax annual exclusions with respect to gifts to these trusts because (i) written notice of the gift was not provided to the beneficiaries (or their natural guardians) as required under the trust instrument, and (ii) the IRS concluded a prearranged plan existed for the beneficiaries to not to exercise their withdrawal right.

The Tax Court rejected the IRS arguments, and the court held that the gifts to the trusts were gifts of a present interest that qualified for the gift tax annual exclusion. With respect to the failure to give written notice to minor beneficiaries, the court ruled that written notice was not required since the parent of the minor beneficiary was the trustee and therefore did not need to give notice to himself. With respect to the failure to give written notice to the adult beneficiaries, the court stated that such written notice was not required when there was evidence of actual notice. In dealing with the prearranged agreement issue, the court followed its decision in *Cristofani*, and held that the most important factor in determining whether a gift to a *Crummey* type trust was a gift of a present interest is whether or not the beneficiary possessed a legal right to make a demand for payment; not whether it is likely that the minor beneficiary is to receive any enjoyment of that property. In this connection, the court stated, "The sufficiency of the notice given the beneficiaries is a factor in the likelihood that the right of withdrawal will be exercised; it is not a factor in the legal right to demand payment from the trustee. *Crummey v. Commissioner*, 397 F.2d at 88; *Estate of Cristofani v. Commissioner*, at 80 - 81." *Id.* at [72]. The court also found no evidence to support a prearrangement. Said the court, "There is no evidence to support a finding that the ***donees' legal ability to demand payment*** from the trustees was limited by their informal agreement to purchase a CD after the gifts [to the trust] were made. Nor is there any evidence that decedent would not have made the gifts to any donee who did not agree to invest rather than spend the gift." *Id.* at [78]. (Emphasis added.)

§15.5 HOW TO DEAL WITH IGNORED OR NEGLECTED *CRUMMEY* WITHDRAWAL RIGHT NOTICES

Upon discovering that *Crummey* notice requirements have been neglected or ignored, do not assume that nothing can be done and that the gift tax annual exclusion is lost. Instead, consider the following:

§15.5(a) Was *Any* Written Notice Provided?

Determine if some type of written notice of the gifts and corresponding withdrawal right was actually given. This could include copies of the annual notice letters or any written correspondence that puts the beneficiary or his natural or legal guardian on notice when the gifts will be made to the trust and the nature of the withdrawal right with respect to present and future gifts. If a beneficiary received actual notice, have the beneficiary acknowledge in writing that he or she received actual oral notice for the "missing" years. The fact that this is done *prior* to any challenge from the IRS would show that it was in fact done in good faith and not in response to an audit. In addition, in the case of "hanging" *Crummey* powers, a beneficiary might consider withdrawing a small portion of the trust to show that the notice was in fact effective.

§15.5(b) Did The Beneficiary Otherwise Have Actual Notice?

If no proof of written notice can be obtained, determine if the beneficiary, the beneficiary's natural or legal guardian, the beneficiary's legal representative or an agent of the beneficiary had actual notice of the gift. Under both *Kohlsaat* and *Holland, supra,* actual notice of the gift was held to be sufficient. *See also,* Priv. Letter Ruls. 9030005, 8008040, and 8022048. To further document oral notice, consider having the beneficiary sign a written statement confirming the date of each gift, the withdrawal right associated with each gift, and the beneficiary's action with respect to that withdrawal right.

Sample Statement:[12]

> Dear [Name of *Crummey* Withdrawal Right Beneficiary]:
>
> Re: [Name of ILIT] ("Trust")
>
> This letter confirms that you had knowledge of the contribution of $__________ made to the Trust on ______________, 20_______, and that you had the right to withdraw $_________ from the Trust for ____ days as a result of that contribution, and chose to let the power of withdrawal lapse. If this is correct, please sign, date, and return this letter in the enclosed stamped, self-addressed envelope.
>
> Please call if you have any questions.
>
> Sincerely,
>
> [Name of ILIT Trustee]
>
> Dated: ___________, 20__ ______________________
>
> (signature of beneficiary)

§15.5(c) If Written Or Oral Notice Was Not Given, Did The Donee (Or The Donee's Natural Or Legal Guardian) Know Enough About The Gift To Have It Qualify As A Gift Of A Present Interest?

Likewise, if neither written nor oral notice was actually given in connection with a particular gift, the practitioner must determine if the facts and circumstances exist that would put the beneficiary on notice of the circumstances surrounding the gift and the attendant withdrawal rights. For example, did the grantor of the trust discuss the ILIT with his or her children such that each child (or the person who could exercise a power of withdrawal on behalf of a minor or incom-

---

[12] Provided courtesy of Sean Anthony Dunston, Esq. of William L. Babcock, Jr. P.C. of Alexandria, Virginia.

petent beneficiary) has sufficient information regarding the substance and timing of the gifts? Again, *Kohlsaat* and *Holland, supra,* support the position that actual notice is sufficient, and in this context, actual notice could have occurred at the inception of the ILIT or at any time thereafter, even in casual conversation. *See, e.g.,* Priv. Letter Ruls. 8006109, 8111123, 8134135, 8138170, 8138171, and 8143045.

§15.5(d) Can You Provide Notice Now?

Is there sufficient time to still provide some form of notice to the beneficiary?

§15.5(e) Treat The Contributions As A Loan To The Trust

This will require a promissory note to be drawn up between the ILIT and the grantor for the loan amount, and appropriate interest will have to be paid on the loan amount. *See,* IRC section 7872. If the ILIT is a grantor trust, there will be no income tax consequences to the grantor concerning the interest he or she pays or the trust receives. *See,* section 14.3, above.

§15.5(f) Take The Position That No Notice Is Required

The emphasis in *Kieckhefer, Gilmore, and Crummey* was on the possession of the right of withdrawal—not notice. The existence of the withdrawal right was itself sufficient to confer a present interest status on a contribution to an irrevocable trust. The court in *Crummey* never required that written notice, verbal notice, or other notice be given to the beneficiaries. In fact, the court in *Crummey* acknowledged that it was unlikely that certain beneficiaries would ever know of the contributions. Said the court, "it is likely that some, if not all, of the beneficiaries did not even know that they had any right to demand funds from the trust. They probably did not know when contributions were made to the trust or in what amounts." *Crummey, supra,* 397 F.2d at 88. A similar distinction between possession of a right of withdrawal versus notice or knowledge of the right to withdraw is found in *Holland, supra.*

To buttress the position that no notice is required, consider analogizing to IRC sections 2041(a), 2056(b)(5) and 2503(c)(2). IRC section 2041(a) provides for inclusion in a decedent's gross estate of the value of all property with respect to which the decedent possesses a general power of appointment. "General power of appointment" is defined by IRC section 2041(b)(1) as a power *exercisable* in favor of the holder, his estate, his creditors, or the creditors of his estate. It is established that the mere *possession* of a general power of appointment triggers inclusion under IRC section 2041(a) regardless of whether the holder was ever competent to exercise the power. *See, e.g., William R. Boeving v. U.S.*, 650 F.2d 493 (8th Cir. 1981); *Estate of Nancy E. Rosenblatt v. Commissioner*, 633 F.2d 176 (10th Cir. 1980); *Estate of Anna Lora Gilchrist v. Commissioner*, 630 F.2d 340 (5th Cir. 1980); *Estate of Fannie Alperstein v. Commissioner*, 613 F.2d 1213 (2d Cir. 1979), cert. denied, 446 U.S. 918 (1980); *Clarence Blagen Fish v. U.S.*, 432 F.2d 1278 (9th Cir. 1970). IRC section 2056(b) is the general power of appointment marital deduction provision. If the surviving spouse is given the requisite income interest in the property coupled with a general power of appointment, the inability of the surviving spouse to exercise the power of appointment because of incapacity or a lack of knowledge of the power will not disqualify the interest for the marital deduction. *See, Estate of Frank E. Tingley v. Commissioner*, 22 T.C. 402 (1954), *aff'd sub nom. T. Everett Starrett v. Commissioner*, 223 F.2d 163 (1st Cir. 1955); Rev. Rul. 75-350, 1975-2 C.B. 366 (testamentary general power of appointment); Rev. Rul. 55-518, 1955-2 C.B. 384 (inter-vivos general power of appointment). IRC section 2503 provides for a minor trust beneficiary to have a testamentary general power of appointment over the trust property if he or she dies before attaining the age of 21, even though under state law the minor is legally incapable of exercising the power. "[I]f the minor is given a power of appointment exercisable during lifetime or is given a power of appointment exercisable by will, the fact that under the local law a minor is under a disability to exercise an inter vivos power or to execute a will does not cause the transfer to fail to satisfy the conditions of section 2503(c)." Treas. Reg. §25.2503-4(b). *See also*, Rev. Rul. 81-6, 1981-1 C.B. 385.

In short, the theory underlying the above-described treatment of general powers of appointment is analogous to the theory that the *existence* of the legal right to withdraw the contribution, and not the *notice* of such right or the *appointment* of a guardian or conservator for a minor, incompetent or disabled beneficiary, is what creates a present interest and allows the donor to use the gift tax annual exclusion.

§15.5(g) File A Late Gift Tax Return(s) Reflecting The Gifts

If any of the positions contained in sections 15.5(a)-(f), above, apply concerning notice, file a late U.S. Gift Tax Return (assuming a Gift Tax Return was not previously filed for the tax year in question), detailing the reasons that the annual gift tax exclusions are allowable. Under Treas. Reg. §301.6501(c)-1(f),[13] the statute of limitations will close three years after filing of the U.S. Gift Tax Return with respect to the issue if it is adequately disclosed. On the chance that the Gift Tax Return is selected for audit, it is still better to be dealing with the IRS while memories are fresh and the donor is alive, rather than waiting decades until the federal estate tax audit. On the other hand, if none of the positions contained in sections 15.5(a)-(f), above, apply concerning notice, file a U.S. Gift Tax Return showing the ILIT contributions as gifts of a future interest.

§15.6 HOW TO DEAL WITH AN ILIT THAT HAS NO *CRUMMEY* WITHDRAWAL RIGHTS

§15.6(a) Conditional *Crummey* Withdrawal Right Letters

A method of securing a gift tax annual exclusion where the ILIT does not contain *Crummey* withdrawal rights is to create *Crummey* withdrawal rights in the letter of gift transmission to the ILIT trustee. The gift letter would inform the trustee of the gift being made, the terms of the gift, which trust beneficiaries have withdrawal rights, the amount of the withdrawal right, the time period in which a withdrawal right lapses, etc. *See,* Priv. Letter Rul. 8445004 where this technique was used to increase an annual withdrawal right from $3,000 to $10,000.

When using this technique, consider having the donor's gift be in the form of a bank cashier's check or bank money order that cannot be revoked by the donor once the check or money order has been delivered to the trustee. Thus the gift to the trust will be a completed gift since the check or money order is "irrevocable." Otherwise, if the donor dies before a gift check drawn of his or her "standard" checking account clears, the IRS may argue that the gift was not completed

---

[13] *See,* discussion regarding finality of legal issues in T.D. 8845, 1999-2C.B. 683 (December 20, 1999).

before the donor's death and is includable in the donor's gross estate for federal estate tax purposes. *See, John A. Metzger v. Commissioner,* 100 T.C. 204 (1993), *aff'd,* 38 F.3d 118 (4th Cir. 1994) (delivery of a standard check to a non-charitable donee will not be considered a completed gift until the donee deposits the check, regardless of when the check actually clears the donor's bank); *Estate of Elizabeth C. Dillingham v. Commissioner,* 903 F.2d 760 (10th Cir. 1990) (if the donor is terminally ill, the gift will not be considered a completed gift if the donee waits too long to cash the check and donor dies before the check clears the donor's bank).

According to Rev. Rul. 96-56, 1996-2 C.B. 161 (*modifying* Rev. Rul. 67-396, 1967-2 C.B. 351), the delivery of a check to a noncharitable donee will be deemed to be a completed gift for federal gift and estate tax purposes on the earlier of (i) the date on which the donor has so parted with dominion and control under local law as to leave in the donor no power to change its disposition, or (ii) the date on which the donee deposits the check (or cashes the check against available funds of the donee) or presents the check for payment, if it is established that: (1) the check was paid by the drawee bank when first presented to the drawee bank for payment; (2) the donor was alive when the check was paid by the drawee bank; (3) the donor intended to make a gift; (4) delivery of the check by the donor was unconditional; and (5) the check was deposited, cashed, or presented in the calendar year for which completed gift treatment is sought and within a reasonable time of issuance.

> **Practice Point:** There is no requirement that an ILIT contain *Crummey* withdrawal rights. Some practitioners put the *Crummey* withdrawal rights in the annual letter of gift transmission to the trustee. Needless to say it is important that the trustee follow the instructions contained in the letter of gift transmission if the donor wants to be assured of the gift being treated is a gift of a present interest that is eligible for the gift tax annual exclusion. *See,* TAM 9532001 where IRS denied annual gift tax exclusion treatment to gifts made by the donor to her irrevocable trust because the gift transmittal letter failed to inform the trustee which beneficiaries were to have *Crummey* withdrawal rights over the gifted amount.

§15.6(b) Additional Techniques

Additionally, "[t]here may be planning that can reduce the gift tax problems engendered by gifts to a life insurance trust that lacks a *Crummey* power or if the authority for *Crummey* powers were eliminated legislatively. These techniques include:

- Making non-excludible gifts and using up part of the donor's unified credit (applicable exclusion amount);
- Terminating the trust, distributing the policy to the beneficiary, and making gifts of the premium amounts directly to the beneficiaries;
- Converting an existing unfunded ILIT to a funded ILIT by making a large gift to the trustee, who could then use the income from that gift to pay the premiums; and
- Using a private split-dollar arrangement between the donor and the trust [or premium financing] to reduce the trust's premiums."[14]

§15.7 HOW TO DEAL WITH CRUMMEY WITHDRAWAL RIGHTS THAT ARE AMBIGUOUS, INADEQUATE, OR OUT OF DATE

If the ILIT contains *Crummey* withdrawal rights but they are ambiguous, defective or inadequate (possibly because of changes in the tax laws), consider petitioning the court to interpret, reform or modify the terms of the trust.[15]

---

[14] ¶5.03 of Howard M. Zaritsky & Stephan R. Leimberg, *Tax Planning With Life Insurance Analysis With Forms—2d Edition*, Warren, Gorham & Lamont, Boston, Massachusetts (Supp. 2007).

[15] There are obvious problems with going to court, including legal costs, court costs, the potential for uncooperative beneficiaries, and the potential for an uncooperative and/or expensive guardian ad litem.

Likewise, the state's Attorney General may be a necessary party in cases where a charity is named as a contingent beneficiary. In addition, however, the existence of a judicial modification, interpretation, or reformation may actually attract attention by the IRS to a problem that would not otherwise be an "issue." In other words, every practitioner needs to decide whether or not the "fix" will be sufficiently safe in order to offset the fact that it may need to be attached to the decedent's federal estate tax return and may attract attention to an issue which might otherwise have been insignificant or even a non-issue.

Before going to court to fix the trust, consider the following alternatives to judicial assistance: (i) exercise of a power of appointment held by a beneficiary, trustee or other powerholder, (ii) ability to adjust between principal and income under the state's

§15.7(a) Obtain Judicial Interpretation/Construction Of The Trust

A Trustee should seek clarification of ambiguous or uncertain trust terms. When the trust contains ambiguous or uncertain terms, the trustee should seek a judicial interpretation/construction of the trust instrument. *Uniform Probate Code ("UPC")* section 7-201, *Restatement (Second)* section 259 and *Restatement (Third)* section 71 ("Application to Court for Instructions"). When interpreting/construing a settlor's intent, the court must first look to the four corners of the trust instrument, and construe the trust instrument so that each word has meaning, to the extent possible. Extrinsic evidence may be introduced to determine a settlor's intent only when the terms of the trust instrument are internally inconsistent.

When a court interprets/construes a trust instrument, a court is in essence clarifying that the problem never existed because the vague, unclear, or contradictory language in the trust instrument should be interpreted in a manner which produces the correct tax result. While a judgment providing for judicial interpretation/construction is automatically effective from the date of creation of the trust, the interpretation/construction may not be binding on the IRS unless it is consistent with applicable state law as would be determined by the highest court of the state. *Commissioner of Internal Revenue v. Estate of Herman J. Bosch*, 387 U.S. 456 (1967).[16] However, if such a judgment if properly handled with a guardian ad litem, participation by all parties, and an appropriate record, the result may be somewhat influential with the IRS and the federal courts. *See e.g., Estate of Edith V. Henderson v. Commissioner*, T.C. Memo 1989-79 (1989), where the court reiterated the *Bosch* holding that "Federal courts, in the absence of a decision

---

principal and income act, (iii) the ability to convert an offending trust to a unitrust under applicable state, (iv) the ability to restructure the trust's investments pursuant to the state's prudent investor rule, (v) disclaimer, (vi) interpretation by trustee (supported by a memorandum of law prepared by counsel for the trustee), (vii) internal amendment procedures, such as the power of amendment granted to an independent trustee or a trust protector, and (viii) changing the trust situs to a jurisdiction that has more favorable laws.

[16] *See,* Shirley L. Kovar, "Adversity After Bosch," 28 *ACTEC Journal* 88 (2002); Barry F. Spivey "Completed Transactions, Qualified Reformation and *Bosch:* When Does the IRS Care about State Law of Trust Reformation?," 26 *ACTEC Notes* 345 (2001) ("Spivey") concerning how the *Bosch* decision and its progeny affect the ability of taxpayers to settle controversies as to the meaning of wills and trusts and to correct mistakes in such documents without adverse tax consequences.

by a state's highest court, must apply the appropriate state law after giving due regard to the rulings of other courts in that state." *Id. See also, American Nurseryman Publishing Co. v. Commissioner,* 75 T.C. 271 (1980) concerning the Tax Court's rejection (for tax purposes) of a state court order that declared a transaction null and void a year after the tax event had occurred. If, however, the state court's order interpreting/construing the trust is accepted by the IRS, the court's order will avoid any IRC section 2035 three-year rule problems or any problems with the release of a general power of appointment under IRC sections 2514 and 2041.

If the trust is GST tax exempt, the GST tax rules governing the modification of a trust grandfathered from the GST tax should be considered. *See,* Treas. Reg. §26.2601-1(b)(4).[17] For example, the GST trust modification rules concerning judicial construction to correct an ambiguity or a scrivener's error are set forth in Treas. Reg. §§26.2601-1(b)(4)(i)(C) and 26.2601-1(b)(4)(i)(E), Example 3. For example, a judicial interpretation/construction of ambiguous trust provisions will not affect the trust's GST tax exempt status since the construction does not change the trust but only clarifies the original terms of the trust instrument. *See,* Priv. Letter Ruls. 9522032 and 9528012.

§15.7(b) Reform The ILIT

A court can reform the terms of a trust, even if unambiguous, to conform the terms of the trust to the settlor's intention if it is proved by clear and convincing evidence that both the settlor's intent and the terms of the trust were affected by a mistake of fact or law, whether in expression or inducement.[18] *UTC* section 415, *Restatement (Second)* section 333 (comment e), *Restatement (Third)* section 62 (comment b); *In Re Estate of Duncan,* 232 A.2d 717 (Pa. 1967); *Roos v. Roos,* 203

---

[17] *See,* John B. O'Grady and Jennifer Schooley Stringer, "Final Regs. Approve Certain Changes in Grandfathered GST Trusts," 28 *Estate Planning* 526 (November 2001) ("O'Grady & Schooley").

[18] A settlor's intent can generally be proven by: (i) the nature of the trust (e.g., a qualified personal residence trust, which is a creature of the Internal Revenue Code and is designed to minimize estate and gift tax consequences), (ii) the terms of the trust (e.g., marital deduction provisions), or (iii) extrinsic evidence (e.g., the grantor's letter of intent (often used in conjunction with a special needs trust), the drafting attorney's notes, an affidavit of the grantor, etc.).

A.2d 140 (Del. Ch. 1964); *Robinson v. Robinson,* 720 So.2d 540 (Fla. App. 1998). According to the comments of *UTC* section 415:

> A mistake of expression occurs when the terms of the trust misstate the settlor's intention, fail to include a term that was intended to be included, or include a term that was not intended to be included. A mistake in the inducement occurs when the terms of the trust accurately reflect what the settlor intended to be included or excluded but this intention was based on a mistake of fact or law. *See, Restatement (Third) of Property: Donative Transfers* section 12.1(comment i). Tentative Draft No. 1, approved 1995. Mistakes of expression are frequently caused by scriveners' errors while mistakes of inducement often trace to errors of the settlor.
>
> Reformation is different from resolving an ambiguity. Resolving an ambiguity involves the interpretation [/construction] of language already in the instrument. Reformation, on the other hand, may involve the addition of language not originally in the instrument, or the deletion of language originally included by mistake, if necessary to conform the instrument to the settlor's intent. Because reformation may involve the addition of language to the instrument, or the deletion of language that may appear clear on its face, reliance on extrinsic evidence is essential.

Unlike judicial modification (which is a substantive change caused by change of circumstances) or judicial interpretation/construction (which is a judgment interpreting vague, ambiguous or contradictory provisions in a trust instrument), judicial reformation is a "correction" of the trust *ab initio*. The IRS may respect a judicial reformation when the evidence is appropriate that a *scrivener's error* occurred which is contradictory to the intention of the settlor and the settlor's overall instructions to the scrivener. *See, Lake Shore National Bank v. Coyle,* 296 F. Supp. 412 (N.D. Ill. 1968), *rev'd on other grounds,* 419 F.2d 958 (7th Cir. 1969) (where the federal district court applied state (Illinois) law to permit a retroactive reformation due to a scrivener's error); *Estate of Arthur S. Kraus v. Commissioner,* 875 F.2d 597 (7th Cir. 1989) (rejection of retroactive reformation correcting scrivener's error, but case remanded to Tax Court because of newly discovered evidence that may change the Tax Court's findings and ruling). Absent a qualified reformation contained in a federal statute (to wit, IRC section 2055(e)(3) concerning charitable split interest trusts) or a federal regulation (to wit, Treas. Reg. §25.2702-5(a)(2) concerning qualified personal residence trusts, and Treas. Reg. §20.2056A-4(a)(2) concerning qualified domestic trusts) that permits a reformation to be effective retroactively, the IRS rarely recognizes retroactive reformations for tax purposes when the taxable event has already occurred (the "completed transaction rule"[19]). Quoting its opinion in *M.T. Straight Trust v. Commissioner,* 24 T.C. 69 (1955), *aff'd,* 245 F.2d 327 (8th Cir. 1957), the Tax Court in *American Nurseryman Publishing Co. v. Commissioner,* 75 T.C. 271 (1980), said that it recognized that "[t]here are numerous cases in which the construction or interpretation of an instrument by a decision of a State court involving the taxpayer and rendered subsequent to the taxable period involved has been relied upon to determine the tax consequences of the document," but the court stated that "In the instant case, however, the reformation decree is not a determination of the legal effect of the original trust instrument under local law, nor does it purport to be such a determination. On the contrary, it alters and modifies the instrument." *Id.* at 275. The Tax Court went on to observe that "as a general rule a reformation of an instrument has retroactive effect as between the parties to the instrument, but not as to third parties who previously acquired rights under the instrument. On that basis, we held that for Federal tax purposes, the reformation was effective only from the date thereof [i.e., from the date of the state court's order of reformation]." *Id.* at 276. *See, also,* Rev. Rul 93-79, 1993-2 C.B. 269; Priv. Letter Rul. 199922045 ("Retroactive changes to the legal effects of a transaction through judicial nullification of a transfer or judicial reformation of a document are not accorded retro-

---

[19] "Under the 'completed transaction' rule which is adhered to by the federal courts, once a tax event occurs that gives the government a right to tax revenue, a later state court reformation of a trust that would change the tax result will be ignored even though the reformation proceeding is in strict accordance with state law. Each statutory qualified reformation is an exception to the completed transaction rule that is intended to permit modifications to particular trusts that will have retroactive tax effects. Conversely, if a tax event has not yet occurred, the Service will honor the prospective tax effects of a reformed trust if the reformation is binding on all interested parties—even if the reformation is contrary to state law [Rev. Rul. 73-142, 1973-1 C.B. 405]." Spivey at 345.

active effect for Federal tax purposes if the Federal tax consequences have attached to the transaction. *M. T. Straight Trust v. Commissioner*, 245 F.2d 327 (8th Cir. 1957); *Sinopoulo v. Jones*, 154 F.2d 648 (10th Cir. 1946); *American Nurseryman Publishing Co. v. Commissioner*, 75 T.C. 271, 276- 277 (1980), *aff'd* without published opinion, 673 F.2d 1333 (7th Cir. 1981); Rev. Rul. 93-79, 1993-2 C.B. 269; Rev. Rul. 73-142, 1973-1 C.B. 405."[20])

The IRS may also recognize a reformation where the trustees inadvertently fail to carry out the terms of the trust and the court reforms the existing trust to carry out the terms set forth in the trust. Priv. Letter Rul. 200550015. This is analogous to the scrivener's error—a unilateral mistake made by another person, through no fault of the grantor.

However, if the IRS recognizes a retroactive reformation, the benefit of a judicial reformation is that it avoids the IRC section 2035 three year rule concerning the insured (if that is a problem) and avoids a powerholder being tainted by IRC sections 2514 and 2041 general power of appointment problems, because the reformation is presumably effective as of the creation of the trust. *See e.g.,* Priv. Letter Rul. 200311020 (state court order reforming trust based on a scrivener's error was determined by the IRS to be consistent with applicable state law and was given retroactive effect by the IRS, and accordingly, the decedent's surviving spouse did not have general power of appointment over assets of her deceased husband's trust, and upon the surviving spouse's death, assets of decedent's trust would not be includable in surviving spouse's gross estate under IRC section 2041); Priv. Letter Rul. 200314009 (where scrivener's error permitted grantor to be a successor trustee of her ILIT, the IRS approved the state court's retroac-

---

[20] "Unlike the situation in *Bosch*, the decree in this case was handed down [by a state's lower court] before the time of the event giving rise to the [federal estate] tax (that is, the date of the grantor's death). Thus, while the [lower court's] decree would not be binding on the Government as to questions relating to the grantor's power to appoint himself as trustee prior to the date of the decree, it is controlling after such date since the decree, in and of itself, effectively extinguished the power [of the grantor to appoint himself as a successor trustee of an intervivos irrevocable trust that he established for the benefit of his wife and children]. In other words, while there may have been a question whether the grantor had such power [to appoint himself as trustee] prior to the [lower court's] decree, there is no question that he did not have the power [to appoint himself as trustee] thereafter." *Id.*

tive reformation to correct the error, and accordingly, the IRS ruled that the reformation was not considered a release or transfer of any retained interest or power that would subject the ILIT assets to inclusion in the grantor's gross estate under IRC section 2035, nor would the grantor possess any incidents of ownership in the life insurance policy owned by the trust, as reformed, under IRC section 2042); Priv. Letter Rul. 200615025 (where scrivener's error resulted in life insurance policy proceeds from the insured's ILIT to be distributed to the insured's revocable living trust, the IRS gave retroactive effect to the reformation to correct the ILIT drafting error (which error constituted a mistake in fact (in contrast to a mistake in law)) and have the life insurance proceeds be distributed to the family (i.e., credit shelter) trust contained in the ILIT since the insured had not (yet) died and was able to supply documentary evidence of his intention to exclude the life insurance proceeds from his estate; the IRS also ruled that the insured did not posses incidents of ownership over the life insurance policy owned by the ILIT and therefore the 3 year rule of IRC section 2035 would not apply when the insured died); Priv. Letter Rul. 200127042 (use of disclaimers and a state court order reforming ILIT based on a scrivener's error was given effect as of date of order where the ILIT held a second to die policy and the ILIT was reformed after the death of the husband but more than 3 years before the death of the surviving spouse, because of disclaimer, the spouse held no incidents of ownership in the policy under IRC section 2042, and because the court's order of reformation was more than 3 years old, IRC sections 2035, 2036 and 2038 would not be applicable upon the spouse's death as concerns the second to die policy); Priv. Letter Rul. 200033015 (trust reformation to correct a scrivener's error to allow adopted minor children to share in trust did not create income or gift tax liability for any party since the reformation did not change any of the beneficial interests but merely clarified the settlor's original intent that adopted minors (and not adopted adults) should be included in the class of trust beneficiaries); Priv. Letter Ruls. 9847025 and 9832039 (retroactive trust reformation allowed and accepted by IRS to correct scrivener's error concerning ability of insured to be appointed successor trustee of their ILIT, and as a result of the reformation, IRC sections 2035 and 2042 would not apply when the insured die).

> **Practice Point:** Because a judicial reformation may not always be recognized by the IRS, consider obtaining a judicial interpretation/construction of the trust instrument.

> **Practice Point:** The IRS has recognized reformations to correct errors made by a life insurance carrier concerning the policy's legal owner and beneficiary. Typically, the insured has transferred an existing life insurance policy to a third party (such as an ILIT) more than 3 years before death but the insurance carrier has failed to properly document or complete the paperwork concerning the transfer. Applying the "intent facts" doctrine (rather than the "policy facts" doctrine[21]), the IRS has ruled that the insured will not be subject to the three year rule of IRC section 2035 and that the insured will not have incidents of ownership in the policy under IRC section 2042. *See,* Priv. Letter Rul. 200603002; TAM 9651004. *See also,* section 4.1, above.

If the trust is GST tax exempt, the GST tax rules governing the modification of a trust grandfathered from the GST tax should be considered. *See,* Treas. Reg. §26.2601-1(b)(4). For example, the GST trust modification rules concerning judicial and non-judicial trust reformation and modification are governed by Treas. Reg. §§26.2601-1(b)-(4)(i)(D) and 26.2601-1(b)(4)(i)(E), Example 7.

§15.7(c) Modify The ILIT To Achieve Favorable Tax Objectives

A court can also modify a trust to achieve a settlor's tax objectives. The modification must be in a manner that is not contrary to the settlor's probable intention. The modification can be retroactive.[22] *UTC* section 416.

---

[21] *See,* section I,C,4 of Beverly R. Budin, 826-2nd T.M., *Life Insurance,* Bureau of National Affairs, Washington, DC for a discussion of the "policy facts" doctrine and its exceptions.

[22] As previously mentioned, IRS is not bound by trust modifications concerning tax events that have already occurred i.e., are "completed transactions." Absent specific statutory or regulatory authority (e.g., IRC section 2055(e)(3) (concerning charitable split interest trusts); Treas. Reg. §§25.2702-5(a)(2) (concerning qualified personal residence trusts), 20.2056A-4(a)(2) (concerning qualified domestic trusts)), binding recognition is normally given only to modifications made prior to the event that gives rise to the tax liability. Thus, the modification of a trust will not cure an adverse tax consequence resulting from a taxable release of a general power of appointment since the event giving rise to the tax liability has already occurred and is a "completed transaction." *See,* Rev. Rul. 73-142, 1973-1 C.B. 405; *Arnold Van Den Wymelenberg v. U.S.*, 397 F.2d 443 (7th Cir. 1968), *cert. denied* 393 U.S. 953 (1969) ("not even judicial ref-

Modification is different from reformation. Reformation is available when the terms of a trust fail to reflect the settlor's original, particularized intent. The mistaken terms are then reformed to conform to this specific intent. Modification, however, allows the terms of the trust to be changed to meet the settlor's tax-saving objective as long as the resulting terms, particularly the dispositive provisions, are not inconsistent with the settlor's probable intent. Modification is similar to the cy pres doctrine for charitable trusts, and is similar to the equitable doctrine of deviation for unanticipated circumstances.

---

ormation can operate to change the federal tax consequences of a completed transaction"); *Estate of Arthur S. Kraus*, T.C. Memo 1988-154 (1988), *aff'd in part and rev'd in part* 875 F.2d 597 (7th Cir. 1989), on remand, 60 T.C. Memo 312 (1990). *See also, Commissioner of Internal Revenue v. Estate of Herman J. Bosch*, 387 US 456 (1967), where the Court considered whether a state trial court's characterization of property rights conclusively binds a federal court or agency in a federal tax controversy. The Court concluded that the decision of a state trial court as to an underlying issue of state law should not be controlling when applied to a federal statute. Rather, the highest court of the state is the best authority on the underlying substantive rule of state law to be applied in the federal matter. If there is no decision by that court, then the federal authority must apply what it finds to be state law after giving "proper regard" to the state trial court's determination and to relevant rulings of other courts of the state. In this respect, the federal agency may be said, in effect, to be sitting as a state court. Thus, where federal tax liability turns upon the character of a property interest held and transferred under state law, federal authorities are not bound by a state trial court's determination concerning the property interest unless the state trial court's decision is consistent with an existing decision of the state's highest court; and in the absence of a decision from the state's highest court concerning the property interest, the federal court must apply what it finds state law to be, after giving proper regard to decisions of other courts of that state. **Caution:** Even though the IRS may not be bound by a state trial court's decision, the *Bosch* case does not mean that the parties to the state court action are not bound by the state trial court's decision.

"Taxpayers will generally find themselves in the position of having to convince the Internal Revenue Service, the U.S. Tax Court, or a federal district court of the applicable state law because of the near-impossibility of making the United States a party to a state court proceeding. The government will be dismissed as a party in a state court action unless Congress has specifically waived sovereign immunity, which it has done in very limited instances in the tax arena (none of which involve trust reformation). The net effect of Bosch and the doctrine of sovereign immunity seems to be that when property rights are in issue the federal tax liability must be litigated exclusively in the federal courts with proper regard to state law. Tax refund and deficiency proceedings are intended to be the only means of judicially determining federal tax liabilities. Spivey at 346.

If the trust is GST tax exempt, the GST tax rules governing the modification of a trust grandfathered from the GST tax should be considered. *See,* Treas. Reg. §26.2601-1(b)(4).[23] For example, the GST trust modification rules concerning judicial and non-judicial trust reformation and modification are governed by Treas. Reg. §§26.2601-1(b)(4)(i)(D) and 26.2601-1(b)(4)(i)(E), Example 7.

§15.7(d) Modify The ILIT Due To Changed Circumstances

If a change in circumstances not known to the settlor and not anticipated by the settlor would result in impairing the purpose of the trust, a court can modify the trust if modification will further the purposes of the trust. To the extent practicable, the modification must be consistent with the settlor's intent. The court may also modify the administrative terms of a trust if continuation of the trust on its existing terms would be impracticable or wasteful or impair the trust's administration. *UTC* section 412, *Restatement (Second)* section 167 and *Restatement (Third)* section 66. If changed circumstances exist, the trustee is under a duty to petition the court for modification of the trust or for a deviation from the terms of the trust. *Restatement (Second)* section 167 and *Restatement (Third)* section 66. Given the unanticipated tax law changes and uncertainty concerning the permanency/repeal of the federal estate tax, it would appear that such a modification should be easily obtained.

A division or reformation of a trust may result in realization of gain on the distribution of appreciated assets to the new trusts; therefore, care needs to be taken not to trigger the realization of gain or loss as a taxable exchange under IRC section 1001(a) pursuant to *Cottage Savings Association v. Commissioner*, 499 U.S. 554 (1991).[24] Fortunate-

---

[23] *See*, O'Grady & Schooley, supra.

[24] Treas. Reg. §1.1001-1(a) provides in pertinent part, that the gain or loss realized from the sale or exchange of property for other property differing materially either in kind or in extent, is treated as income or loss sustained. According to *Cottage Savings*, Treas. Reg. §1.1001-1 reasonably interprets IRC section 1001(a), and an exchange of property gives rise to a realization event under IRC section 1001(a) if the properties exchanged are "materially different." According to the Court, properties are viewed as "different" in a sense that is "material" to the Internal Revenue Code when their possessors enjoy legal entitlements, different in kind or extent from the properties given up. Thus, if an action by a trust constitutes an exchange of property and the property

ly there are may instances where the IRS has ruled that the transactions did not result in the beneficiaries' trust interests differing materially as a result of the transaction and therefore there was no taxable exchange. *See, e.g.,* Priv. Letter Rul. (partition of beneficiaries' interest in a GST grandfathered trust with a non-pro-rata distribution of assets (permitted by state law) to two new trusts for the benefit of the beneficiaries); Priv. Letter Rul. 200624003 (division of grandfathered GST exempt trust into two separate GST tax exempt trusts to be funded in kind on a non-pro-rata basis with regard to assets not capable of being divided pro rata, where trust instrument was silent concerning non-pro-rata distributions but state statute permitted the trustee to allocate particular assets in proportionate or disproportionate shares when distributing trust property or dividing or terminating a trust); Priv. Letter Ruls. 200617001(court ordered trust modification to require trustee to allocated capital gains to corpus for trust to obtain charitable set aside income tax deduction, where prior to the modification trustee only had discretionary authority under trust instrument to determine income and principal), 200513005 (merger pursuant to state statutory trust law of 3 trusts into 1 trust to facilitate the trust's ownership of S corporation stock), 200449020 (merger pursuant to state statutory trust law and court order of nearly identical trusts into 1 trust), 200121023 (court reformation and modification of trust), 200121024 (court reformation and modification of trust), 200103049 (court ordered

---

received as a result of the exchange is materially different form the property given up, a taxable exchange has occurred, and gain or loss is realized. *See, also,* Rev. Rul. 69-486, 1969-2 C.B. 159 (taxable exchange occurred where trustee made non-pro-rata distributions of trust property to beneficiaries and neither state law nor the trust instrument authorized non-pro-rata distributions). *But see,* Aucutt at section 503.2, where the author states, "The estate planning community is solidly of one mind that the *Cottage Savings* doctrine has no place in the tax treatment of trust reformations, in which there are no exchanges and in which the beneficiaries' receipt of trust corpus is governed by [IRC] section 102, not [IRC] section 1001. The argument under [IRC] section 102(a), which is not always self-evident, runs like this: Gifts and bequests are excluded from gross income. This includes gifts and bequests made through the use of trusts. In choosing to benefit donees through the use of a trust, a donor chooses to subject that gift or bequest not only to the terms of the governing instrument, but to the governing local law and to the explicit or inherent power of the courts. A reformation pursuant to the governing local law and/or approval of the appropriate court is merely a part of the process of determining what form the gift or bequest will take. It does not change [IRC] section 102(a), which mandates that that gift or bequest be free of income tax."

division of single trust into two separate independent trusts) and 199912034 (partition pursuant to state statutory trust law of a GST grandfathered trust into separate sub-trusts for the benefit of each beneficiary). *See also,* Priv. Letter Ruls. 200543041 (no taxable exchange where the situs of the trust was changed to a jurisdiction that authorized the trustee to make adjustments between income and principal), 200207018 (no taxable exchange where the trust instrument authorizes trustee's actions), 200118038 (no taxable exchange on the partition/division of a trust), 200303027 (no taxable exchange on consolidation of multiple trusts), 200112038 (no taxable exchange where the trust events results from a beneficiary's actions that are authorized in the trust instrument), 200135007 (no taxable exchange where state law authorizes the trust action, with or without court approval), 200119047 (no taxable exchange where the trust event arises from a court approved settlement of a bonafide dispute). *But see,* Priv. Letter Rul. 200231011 where the IRS did apply the *Cottage Savings* interpretation of IRC section 1001(a) to trust interests, and required the realization of gain as the result of the modification of a trust which changed a beneficiary's current income interest (that was subject to a floor and a ceiling) into annual payments of 7% of the fair market value of the trust property, with the trustee having some discretion to make additional payments under certain circumstances.[25] The IRS cited *Gladys Cheesman Evans v. Commissioner,* 30 T.C. 798 (1958) as authority for the taxpayer's realization of gain under the *Cottage Savings* doctrine. In *Evans,* "the taxpayer exchanged her income interest in a trust for an annuity, and the court concluded that this was a realization event. Taxpayer's income interest had entitled her to dividends paid by a corporation, the stock of which was owned by the trust. She transferred the income interest to her husband, who agreed in exchange to pay her fixed sums annually until her death."

> **Practice Point:** Judicial reformation or modification will not cure an IRC section 2041 problem, if it is deemed to cause a "release" of the power of appointment in such a

---

[25] *See,* Barbara A. Sloan, "Consequence of PLR 200231011: *Cottage Savings* or Cottage Industry?," 29 *ACTEC Journal* 102 (Fall 2003). According to the article, "The [*Cottage Savings*] issue [of 'materially different' interests] for income tax purposes [under IRC section 1001(a)] is not the equivalency of the values of the interests involved, but rather the nature of the legal entitlements under the rights involved." *Id.* at 106.

way that the powerholder who was tainted is deemed to have made a gift. IRC section 2514(b).

Practice Point: A taxable exchange may occur under the *Cottage Savings* doctrine where trust action is taken outside of applicable state law or outside of the terms of the trust instrument. When in doubt, obtain a private letter ruling.

If the trust is GST tax exempt, the GST tax rules governing the modification of a trust grandfathered from the GST tax should be considered. *See,* Treas. Reg. §26.2601-1(b)(4).[26] For example, the GST trust modification rules concerning judicial and non-judicial trust reformation and modification are governed by Treas. Reg. §§26.2601-1(b)(4)(i)(D) and 26.2601-1(b)(4)(i)(E), Example 7. In relevant part Treas. Reg. §26.2601-1(b)(4)(i)(D)(1) provides that a judicial modification of an otherwise GST tax exempt trust will not cause the trust to lose its exempt status if the judicial modification does not shift beneficial enjoyment of the trust assets to any beneficiary who occupies a lower generation than the person or persons who held beneficial interests before the modification. Further, "a shift in beneficial interest to a lower generation will be deemed to have occurred if the modification can result in...an increase in the amount of a GST transfer...." Treas. Reg. §26.2601-1(b)(4)(i)(D)(2). If the judicial modification or reformation will allow for more property to be transferred to the ILIT gift tax free, will this necessarily be considered an increase in the amount of a GST transfer to younger generation beneficiaries? Obtaining a favorable private letter ruling may be the most prudent course of action. *See,* sections 5.24 and 5.25, above.

§15.7(e) Sell The Life Insurance Policy To A New ILIT

As an alternative to judicial assistance, consider having the existing ILIT (which has the inadequate or out of date *Crummey* withdrawal rights) sell the life insurance policy to a new ILIT that contains the appropriate *Crummey* withdrawal provisions. The new ILIT should be an intentionally defective grantor trust with regard to the insured, and care should be taken to ensure that the sale of the life insurance policy from the existing ILIT to the new ILIT does not trigger the transfer for value rule under IRC section 101(a)(2). *See,* sec-

---

[26] *See,* O'Grady & Schooley, supra.

tions 2.5 and 2.7, above. Consider obtaining the consent and indemnification by the grantor(s) and beneficiaries of the existing ILIT. Also consider the ethical requirements and whether the existing ILIT trustee (or the new ILIT trustee) requires separate legal representation, particularly if the existing or new ILIT trustee is a family member and not a corporate trustee. Consider whether the existing ILIT, if it is no longer holding assets and has been terminated, will need to be disclosed on the grantor's federal and state estate tax returns. Finally, consider how to value the policy to be sold, particularly when the insured is in poor health. *See,* section 3.1, above.

§15.8 HOW TO DEAL WITH GST TAX EXEMPTION ALLOCATION AILMENTS

Allocation of GST tax exemption to an ILIT has become more complicated as a result of the enactment of the indirect skip rules of IRC section 2632(c) under the 2001 Tax Act. Consequently, an ILIT that was not supposed to have any GST tax exemption allocated to it may now be classified as a GST trust, and the grantor's GST tax exemption is being automatically (and unnecessarily) allocated to the ILIT under the new indirect skip rules. Conversely, an ILIT that was designed to be GST tax exempt may not be 100% GST tax exempt due to a failure to properly allocate GST tax exemption. Another GST issue is where the ILIT is subject to an estate tax inclusion period ("ETIP"). After ascertaining the grantor's intent concerning the GST tax exemption issue, consider the following:

§15.8(a) Inadvertent Allocation Of GST Tax Exemption To ILIT

If the ILIT was not supposed to have any GST tax exemption allocated to it but GST tax exemption has been allocated under the new indirect skip rules of IRC section 2632(c), the grantor can file a late allocation of GST tax exemption (*see,* section 5.23, above), or file a U.S. Gift Tax Return under Rev. Proc. 2004-46, 2004-31 I.R.B. 141 (7/29/2004) (*see,* section 6.5, above), or elect into "GST trust" status by filing a one time election with a current U.S. Gift Tax Return (*see,* section 5.29(b)(1), above), or elect out of "GST trust status" by filing a one time election with a current U.S. Gift Tax Return (*see,* section 5.29(b)(1), above). *See also,* section 5.29(g), above. Electing out of GST trust status may result in the ILIT having an inclusion ratio greater than zero but less than one. A qualified severance of the ILIT may be appropriate if the grantor is concerned that the ILIT may make distributions to skip persons. *See,* section 6.3, above. Another option is for the grantor to obtain from the IRS an extension of time to elect out of the automatic GST tax exemption allocation rules. *See,* section 6.5, above.

> **Practice Point:** Many of these options, especially filing for the relief under Treas. Reg. §301-9100-1 to obtain an extension of time from the IRS to elect out of the automatic GST tax exemption allocation rules, are expensive. Sometimes, the best alternative is to live with the partially exempt trust, especially if the amount of "wasted" GST tax exemption is relatively small.

§15.8(b) Failure To Allocate GST Tax Exemption To ILIT

If the ILIT was supposed to be exempt from GST tax and no GST tax exemption has been allocated, the grantor can file a late allocation of GST tax exemption (*see,* section 5.23, above), or file a U.S. Gift Tax Return under Rev. Proc. 2004-46, 2004-31 I.R.B. 141 (7/29/2004) (*see,* section 6.5, above), and/or elect into "GST trust" status by filing a one time election with a current U.S. Gift Tax Return (*see,* section 5.29(b)(1), above). The grantor may also be able to obtain from the IRS an extension of time to make a timely allocation of GST tax exemption. *See,* section 6.5, above.

> **Practice Point:** Certain trust distributions for the benefit of skip persons are not subject to GST tax, even if the trust is not GST tax exempt. *See,* section 5.2, above. Also, certain trusts are grandfathered from the GST tax. *See,* sections 5.24 and 5.27, above.

§15.8(c) GST Trust Is Not 100% GST Tax Exempt

If the insured has died and the ILIT is a dynasty trust or has skip person beneficiaries and the ILIT is not 100% GST tax exempt, consider the following:

(1) If possible, have the deceased insured's executor allocate GST tax exemption to the ILIT on the decedent's Federal Estate Tax Return. *See,* section 5.30, above.

(2) Obtain from the IRS an extension of time to make a timely allocation of GST tax exemption to the ILIT. *See,* section 6.5, above.

(3) Have the ILIT trustee undertake a qualified severance of the trust. *See,* section 6.3, above.

(4) If possible, have ILIT beneficiaries exercise their limited powers of appointment so as to postpone a GST event, such as a taxable termination. *See,* sections 4.7, 5.3 and 11.8, above.

(5) If possible, have the ILIT trustee make non-GST distributions to skip-person beneficiaries, as is permitted under IRC section 2503(e) (concerning direct payment of medical expenses and tuition).

§15.8(d) Non-Skip Beneficiary With Descendants Predeceases The Insured

If a child of the insured dies after the ILIT has been funded but while the insured is alive, and the ILIT is not a GST trust (i.e., at the time of the child's death no GST tax exemption has been allocated to the ILIT), and the ILIT provides for a per stirpes distribution, the insured will need to allocate GST tax exemption to the ILIT. Although the children of the predeceased child will move up in generation assignment vis-à-vis the transferor under the predeceased parent rule (*see,* section 5.9, above) with regard to future transfers to the ILIT, prior transfers to the ILIT will not be GST tax exempt, and the ILIT will have an inclusion ratio greater than zero. Thus any distributions to the children of the predeceased child will be subject to GST tax. A way to avoid the GST tax is for the insured-transferor to make a retroactive allocation (rather than a late allocation) of GST tax exemption to the ILIT. *See,* section 6.2, above.

§15.8(e) Spouse's *Crummey* Withdrawal Right Creates An ETIP

Allocation of GST tax exemption is not effective until the close of the Estate Tax Inclusion Period ("ETIP"). IRC section 2642(f). An ETIP is the period during which the trust property would be included in the gross estate of the transferor or the transferor's spouse if either were to die. Treasury Regulations provide that if any part of an ILIT is subject to an ETIP, the entire ILIT is subject to the ETIP. At the close of the ETIP, the transferor can allocate GST tax exemption to the then fair market value of the ILIT (not to the fair market value of the transfer that gave rise to the ETIP). An ETIP is of particular concern if the insured has died or been diagnosed with a terminal illness during the period of time between the transfer to the ILIT and the close of the ETIP, in which case the transferor's GST tax exemption must be allocated to the fair market value of the ILIT. *See,* section 3.1, above for valuation of a life insurance policy.

Fortunately Treas. Reg. §26.2632-1(c)(2)(ii) provides several exceptions to ETIP, including if the grantor's spouse's *Crummey* withdrawal right is limited to no more than five-by-five ***and*** the withdrawal right terminates no later than sixty (60) days after the transfer to the ILIT—***not*** sixty (60) days after notice of the transfer to the ILIT. This exception with its abbreviated period for the *Crummey* withdrawal right to lapse, automatically precludes the use of a hanging right of withdrawal as concerns the lapse of the spouse's *Crummey* withdrawal right.

If the ILIT provides the grantor's spouse with a *Crummey* withdrawal right that does lapse within 60 days of the transfer, and the grantor desires to allocate GST tax exemption to the ILIT, consider modifying the spouse's right of withdrawal. This may be accomplished by judicial modification or reformation, through the exercise of a power to limit (modify) future *Crummey* withdrawal rights reserved by the grantor, or through the power of amendment held by a non-interested trustee. *See* Priv. Letter Rul. 200127042 where, because of a scrivener's error, the court reformed an ILIT to exclude the spouse from having a Crummey withdrawal right. *See,* Paragraphs 3.2(H) and 3.2 (J) of the Sample ILIT. *See,* section 5.17, above for a discussion of the ETIP rules.

> **Practice Point:** If the spouse's *Crummey* withdrawal right is no longer necessary due to the increase in the gift tax annual exclusion amount, so the premium payments can be funded with only the *Crummey* amounts available to the other beneficiaries, consider having the donor exclude the spouse from having a *Crummey* withdrawal right with regard to future trust contributions. However, be careful about having the spouse waive his or her *future Crummey* withdrawal rights. If the waiver is not a qualified disclaimer under IRC section 2518, the spouse's waiver of his or her future *Crummey* withdrawal right may be a taxable gift.[27]

---

[27] Most ILITs have a provision that permits a donor to restrict or eliminate the withdrawal rights of a particular beneficiary. So even if there is an expectation, even a guarantee, of future contributions to the ILIT by the donor, there is no guarantee that there will be *Crummey* withdrawal rights for any particular person. Furthermore,

> **Caution:** A beneficiary's waiver of a *current* unlapsed (or hanging) *Crummey* withdrawal right will result in a taxable release of a general power of appointment under IRC sections 2514 and 2041. *See,* section 12.2, above.

§15.9 HOW TO DEAL WITH AN ILIT THAT HAS PROBLEMS AS A RESULT OF POOR DRAFTING OR CHANGES IN THE TAX LAW

§15.9(a) Modify The ILIT To Achieve Favorable Tax Objectives

A court can modify a trust to achieve a settlor's tax objectives. *See,* section 15.7(c), above.

§15.9 (b) Reform The ILIT To Conform With The Grantor's Intent

A court can reform the terms of a trust, even if unambiguous, to conform the terms of the trust to the settlor's intention. *See,* section 15.7 (b), above.

§15.9(c) Modify The ILIT Due To Changed Circumstances

If a change in circumstances not known to the settlor and not anticipated by the settlor would result in impairing the purpose of the trust, a court can modify the trust if modification will further the purposes of the trust. *See,* section 15.7(d), above.

§15.9(d) Have The Trustee Adjust Between Income And Principal

If permitted by state statute, have the ILIT trustee adjust between income and principal (or convert to a unitrust) if the ILIT contains old style "income only" trust provisions. An adjustment to

---

there is no guarantee that there would be any other gift contributions made by the donor or withdrawal rights in the future. So unlike *Estate of Ruth B. Regester v. Commissioner*, 83 T.C. 1 (1984), where the donee had a vested income interest and an inter-vivos limited power of appointment over the trust property, here the spouse would be relinquishing rights over no (vested) property currently in existence. *See,* section 3.9, above. Consequently, there should be no gift tax consequences as a result of the spouse's waiver of a future right of withdrawal, or if there is, the value should be zero or minimal. *But see,* Priv. Letter Rul. 200127042 (where the IRS expressed no opinion concerning the gift tax consequences of a trust reformation due to a scrivener's error, in which the spouse disclaimed her *Crummey* withdrawal right and her future beneficial interests in the ILIT).

increase income will provide a larger annual payout to the income beneficiaries and may satisfy their needs.[28] *See,* section 104 of The Uniform Principal and Income Act of 1997.

If the trust is GST tax exempt, the GST tax rules governing the modification of a trust grandfathered from the GST tax should be considered. *See,* Treas. Reg. §26.2601-1(b)(4). For example, the GST trust modification rules concerning the conversion of a GST tax exempt trust into a unitrust or making an equitable adjustment between income and principal are set forth in Treas. Reg. §§1.643(b)-1 and 26.2601-1(b)(4)(i)(E), Examples 8, 9, 11, and 12.[29]

§15.9(e) Terminate The ILIT If No Purpose Of The Grantor Remains To Be Achieved

A court can terminate a trust if no purpose of the trust remains to be achieved or the purposes of the trust have become impossible to achieve. *UTC* section 410(a), *Restatement (Second)* section 334 (comment b) and *Restatement (Third)* section 61.

§15.9(f) Terminate The ILIT Upon The Consent Of The Interested Parties

A court can terminate or modify a non-charitable irrevocable trust if all the beneficiaries consent and (i) the continuance of the trust is not necessary to achieve any material purpose of the trust, or (ii) the termination or modification would not be inconsistent with a material purpose of the trust. *UTC* section 411(b), *Restatement (Second)* section 337 and *Restatement (Third)* section 65. *See also, Restatement (Second)* sections 338 and 340. However, while the settlor is alive, the beneficiaries must obtain the settlor's consent to modify or terminate a non-charitable irrevocable trust where the modification or termination would be inconsistent with a material purpose of the trust. *UTC* section 411(a) and *Restatement (Third)* section 65(2). *See also, Restate-*

---

[28] *See,* section 6.2 of Grassi, *A Practical Guide to Drafting Marital Deduction Trusts (with Sample Forms and Checklists)* (ALI-ABA, Philadelphia 2004, Supp. 2006), www.ali-aba.org/aliaba/BK36/ for further discussion of a trustee's power to adjust between income and principal, and the corresponding income tax consequences.

[29] *See,* O'Grady & Schooley, supra.

ment (Second) section 338(1). Generally speaking, obtaining the settlor's consent should not create an IRC section 2038 issue. Treas. Reg. §20.2038-1(a)(2), states that "[i]f the decedent's power [to terminate the trust] could be exercised only with the consent of all parties having an interest (vested or contingent) in the transferred property, and if the power [to terminate the trust] adds nothing to the rights of the parties under local law" then IRC section 2038 does not apply.[30]

§15.9(g) Terminate The ILIT With Beneficiary's Consent

If the settler is deceased, the trustee can distribute all the trust assets to the beneficiaries. If the beneficiaries consent to the trustee's actions, this will cause the trust to terminate, notwithstanding that the material purposes of the trust have not been fully accomplished. *UTC* section 1009 and *Restatement (Second)* section 342.

> **Caution:** To avoid the argument that the beneficiaries have made gifts to one another by consenting to a termination and distribution of the trust property, the distribution should be made in accordance with the terms of the trust (if any) or in proportion to each beneficiary's respective interest in the trust.

---

[30] However, in Rev. Rul. 70-513, 1970-2 C.B. 194, the IRS ruled that IRC section 2038 applied where the grantor had to acquiesce in a trustee's decision to terminate an inter-vivos irrevocable trust established by the grantor for the benefit of his son. The IRS deemed the grantor's power of acquiescence akin to the power to "veto" a trustee's decision concerning the beneficial enjoyment of the trust property with regard to the disposition of the terminated trust property, i.e., the disposition of the trust's remainder interest. Said the IRS, "The fact that the [grantor's] power [to acquiesce to the trust's termination during the grantor's lifetime] could be exercised only after the trustees had taken action [i.e., decided to terminate the trust] does not alter its basic nature as a joint power exercisable by the decedent in conjunction with other persons within the meaning of section 2038 of the Code. In disposing of a similar issue, the court in *Estate of Carrie Grossman v. Commissioner*, 27 T.C. 707 (1957), noted 'it is irrelevant whether the decedent's participation initiates the termination, or, as here, is in the nature of a consent after others have set the machinery in motion, it being sufficient under the statute merely that she act 'in conjunction' with the others....' citing *Thorp's Estate v. Commissioner*, 164 F. 2d 966 (1947), *certiorari denied* 333 U.S. 843; and *Du Charme's Estate v. Commissioner*, 164 F. 2d 959 (1947)."

§15.10 HOW TO DEAL WITH A LIFE INSURANCE POLICY THAT IS NO LONGER ADEQUATE OR APPROPRIATE

If the current life insurance policy is no longer adequate or appropriate or is too costly, or if a newer type of life insurance product would better suit the needs of the grantor, consider:

§15.10(a) Tax Deferred Exchange Of Life Insurance Policy

Have the ILIT trustee enter into an IRC section 1035 exchange of the policy. *See,* section 2.15, above. An exchange of a policy within the same life insurance company may be advantageous. The existing carrier may not require a full medical underwriting, may reduce or eliminate the sales loads and other policy expenses. A newly designed product, such as another life insurance policy or an annuity that better suits the needs of the insured may be needed. It may also be prudent to obtain the assistance of a fee only life insurance advisor to analyze and recommend appropriate products. *See generally,* Chapter 16, below.

§15.10(b) Cancel A Term Policy Or Convert It Into A Permanent Policy

The trustee can cancel a term life insurance policy. Since a term policy has no cash or investment component, there will be no adverse income tax consequences to the policy owner. Alternatively, have the ILIT trustee convert a term policy (if possible) into a permanent life insurance product.

§15.10(c) Pay Up The Policy

Have the ILIT trustee convert the policy into a paid up policy with reduced coverage or convert the policy into to a policy of extended term insurance. The grantor can then use the "freed up" premium amount to obtain new life insurance coverage, if that is possible.

§15.10(d) Use Cash Dividends

If possible, use the policy's cash dividends to purchase new life insurance coverage.

§15.10(e) Surrender The Policy

Have the ILIT trustee surrender the policy for its existing cash value less any surrender charges (although there may be recognition of gain on the part of the ILIT or grantor, depending on how the trust is taxed for income tax purposes), and purchase a new policy. *See,* section 2.18, above. Also, consider a viatical or life settlement as an alternative to surrendering the policy. *See,* sections 2.2 and 2.4, above. The life settlement proceeds could be used to purchase a new life insurance policy.[31] If the insured is terminally ill, accelerated death benefits may be available. *See,* section 2.2, above.

§15.10(f) Prepare A New ILIT And Obtain A New Life Insurance Policy

Sometimes, the existing ILIT is woefully inadequate either for tax purposes or because of changed circumstances, and the policy owned by the ILIT has little or no value (an increasingly common event in our low interest rate/depressed stock market environment). If the grantor is insurable at reasonable rates, the grantor can stop funding the existing ILIT, establish a new ILIT, fund the new ILIT, and then have the new ILIT purchase a life insurance policy that is better suited to the grantor's current situation. Obviously, this solution has the benefit of being "clean" for tax purposes; however, it is not viable where insurance is no longer available on the life of the grantor at a reasonable cost or where the grantor is terminally ill. Once the new ILIT is operational, the old ILIT can continue as an investment vehicle, be terminated through discretionary distributions, or be terminated because it is no longer economical to continue the trust.

> **Caution:** If the old policy lapses and there are outstanding policy loans, the policy owner may recognize income. *See,* section 2.18, above.

§15.11 HOW TO DEAL WITH AN ILIT THAT LACKS AN INSURABLE INTEREST

There are very few things that can be done to cure the problems of an ILIT that lacks an insurable interest. Of course the existing policy can be cancelled and a new policy obtained by the insured, and then transferred to the trust, as long as the insured remains in good health and the cost of a new policy is not unacceptable. If the policy is gifted to the trust, the insured will be subject to the 3 year rule of IRC section

---

[31] *See,* Charles Ratner, "Cash Out or Cash In?," 144 *Trusts and Estates* 49 (May 2005).

2035. *See,* section 4.1, above. If the policy is sold for its fair market value to the trust, then the 3 year rule of IRC section 2035 will not be applicable. Another alternative is for the trust situs to be moved to a state with more favorable statutory rules concerning insurable interests (such as Delaware, Virginia and Washington state), and the existing policy can then be exchanged for a new one issued under the more favorable state law. The exchange is likely to be tax-free under IRC section 1035. *See,* section 2.15, above. Of course, changing the situs of a trust, and the governing law, is not always easy or inexpensive. *See,* section 12.9, above.

§15.12 HOW TO DEAL WITH AN ILIT THAT IS NO LONGER APPROPRIATE OR DESIRABLE

If the ILIT is no longer appropriate or desirable, or if the ILIT no longer fits the needs of the grantor and/or a beneficiary and the ILIT needs to be terminated, or if the policy needs to be removed from the ILIT, or if a new trust needs to be established to deal with a beneficiary's changed circumstances (such as creditor problems, divorce, tax or other issues), consider:

§15.12(a) Sell The Life Insurance Policy To A New ILIT

The old ILIT can sell the policy for its fair market value to a new ILIT that contains provisions better suited to the current situation and circumstances. If the new ILIT is a grantor trust under IRC sections 671—677 with regard to the insured, there should be no transfer for value problem since the transfer of the policy to the grantor trust is disregarded for income tax purposes, and is therefore not considered a transfer for valuable consideration.[32] *See,* section 2.5, above. If, the old

---

[32] "One commentator has correctly suggested that a trustee-to-trustee transfer of life insurance is most appropriate if (1) the old trust has shortcomings that make it undesirable for tax or other reasons (e.g., the trust is not set up to handle cash gifts large enough to permit the payment of the premiums required to keep both old and new policies in force when coverage is increased or the trust will not qualify under S corporation rules to hold such stock); (2) the old trust's terms do not adequately address the special needs or situation of a particular beneficiary; or (3) the old trust does not adequately address changes in the grantor objectives (e.g., the grantor wants to eliminate or cut down or increase the interest of a beneficiary or class of beneficiaries or wants to change the shares of beneficiaries or the timing of when they receive their money). [Citation omitted.] This same commentator also wisely suggests that the

ILIT sells the policy for full and adequate consideration in money or money's worth to the new ILIT, IRC section 2035 will not be not applicable; nor should there be any potential gift tax issues with regard to the new ILIT (especially if the new ILIT contains different dispositive provisions or different beneficiaries than the old ILIT) since the old ILIT is receiving full and adequate consideration for the transfer of the policy. *See,* section 3.1, above concerning the valuation of life insurance policies.

> **Practice Point:** The fair market value of the policy can be reduced by having the old ILIT borrow some or all of the policy's cash surrender value (but not in excess of the old ILIT's income tax basis in the policy). The cash surrender

---

trustee of the old trust obtain releases from the beneficiaries (both of current and future interests), and allow them to review the new trust or examine a summary of its terms. The beneficiaries also should be given a fair comparison of what the terms of the new trust will mean to them, distinguishing the terms of the new trust from those of the old trust. Obviously, this procedure may render the trustee-to-trustee approach impractical for some trusts, but such disclosure and release are probably essential to protect the trustee from possible future liability." ¶5.03 of Howard M. Zaritsky & Stephan R. Leimberg, *Tax Planning With Life Insurance Analysis With Forms—2d Edition*, Warren Gorham & Lamont, Boston, Massachusetts (Supp. 2007).

When an existing ILIT sells a life insurance policy to a new ILIT, the following factors must be considered. First, does the existing ILIT permit the trustee to sell the policy? Second, if the beneficiaries of the new ILIT are different than the existing ILIT, will the trustee of the existing ILIT face some challenge for selling the policy? If so, this challenge can be minimized if the grantor informs the trustee in writing that he or she will no longer be making gifts to the existing ILIT (with which to pay premiums). Third, in determining the fair market value of the policy being sold, the trustee of the existing ILIT should take into account the insured's age and health. In fact, the trustee might be well advised to shop the policy with two or three life settlement companies before agreeing to a sales price. Fourth, the grantor must be willing to fund the new ILIT with sufficient cash to purchase the policy from the existing ILIT. Moreover, this gift will use up some of the grantor's gift tax applicable exclusion amount (or will be subject to gift tax if there is no applicable exclusion amount available). For the more cautious practitioner who wants to be assured of complete grantor trust status, it is generally advisable to not grant *Crummey* withdrawal rights when the new ILIT is initially funded. However, if it is clear that the "tie-breaker" rule of IRC section 678(b) will clearly create grantor status with respect to the insured (*see*, section 2.13, above), then *Crummey* withdrawal rights can be granted, and the insured will be treated as the grantor of the trust. Finally, the grantor must understand that the existing ILIT will continue after it sells the policy; however, the existing ILIT's only asset will (presumably) be the cash it received from the sale of the life insurance policy to the new ILIT.

value could then be loaned by the old ILIT to the new ILIT, and if both ILITs are grantor trusts, the interest paid by the new ILIT to the old ILIT under the promissory note (and the interest received by the old ILIT) will be ignored for income tax purposes. Rev. Rul. 85-13, 1985-1 C.B. 184

§15.12(b) Distribute The Life Insurance Policy To A New ILIT

If state law or the trust instrument permits, have the ILIT trustee distribute (appoint) the policy in (further) trust for the benefit of the current beneficiaries where the new (further) trust contains provisions that are better suited to the grantor's and/or beneficiaries' current situation.[33] *See*, Priv. Letter Rul. 9450036, which provides a discussion of the various tax issues that should be considered when implementing a trust to trust transfer. If the original ILIT is GST tax exempt, the rule against perpetuities for the new ILIT should be limited to the period for the original ILIT. Treas. Reg. §26.2601-1(b)(1)(V)(D), Examples 4 and 5. Also, if the original ILIT is GST tax exempt, Treas. Reg. §26.2601-1(b)(1)(v)(B) requires there be no postponement of vesting

---

[33] *See, e.g.*, section 10-6.6(b) of New York Estates, Powers & Trusts Law, which permits a trustee of a purely discretionary trust to appoint the property in favor of the trustee of another trust. Delaware, Alaska, and Tennessee trust law also provides a trustee with similar authority. *See*, Delaware Code tit. 12, section 3528. If state law does not grant a trustee this power, consider moving the situs of the trust's administration to a jurisdiction that provides this power to the trustee. When changing the situs and governing law of a trust, the trustee should consider the state income tax ramifications and GST tax implications. For example, if the trust is GST tax exempt, the GST trust modification rules concerning a trust's change of situs are governed by Treas. Reg. §26.2601-1(b)(4)(i)(E), Example 4, which state there will be a loss of the trust's GST tax exempt status if a change of situs would extend (or abolish) the perpetuity period governing such trust (such as a GST tax exempt trust governed by the common law rule against perpetuities that is moved to Alaska, which has a 1000 year perpetuity period). *See*, Alan Halperin and Michelle R. Wandler, "Decanting Discretionary Trusts: State Law and Tax Consequences," 29 *Tax Management Estates, Gifts and Trusts Journal* 219 (September 9, 2004) ("Halperin & Wandler") for an in depth discussion of the GST tax, gift tax, income tax, and distributable net income ("DNI") issues when a trustee appoints or distributes trust property to a new trust. *See also*, David G. Shaftel and Jonathan G. Blattmachr, "Alaska's 2006 Amendments to Its Trust and Estates Statute," 34 *Estate Planning* 10, 12-13 (January 2007) concerning Alaska's decanting statute, which permits decanting even if the trust contains ascertainable distribution standards (provided the new trust also contains the same standards).

beyond lives in being at the creation of the original ILIT plus 21 years, or 90 years from the creation of the original ILIT, or else the trust could lose its GST tax exempt status.

If the trust is GST tax exempt, the GST tax rules governing the modification of a trust grandfathered from the GST tax should also be considered. *See,* Treas. Reg. §26.2601-1(b)(4).[34] For example, the GST trust modification rules permit a trustee to distribute principal from a GST tax exempt trust to a new trust without causing a loss of the GST tax exemption, if: (i) the terms of the original trust permit such a distribution without the consent or approval of the beneficiary or court, or if, when the original trust became grandfathered from the GST tax, state law authorized distributions to a new trust without the consent or approval of any beneficiary or court, and (ii) the new trust does not suspend the vesting, ownership or alienation of property beyond the common law rule against perpetuities (or 90 years) measured from the date the original trust became irrevocable. Treas. Reg. §§26.2601-1(b)(4)(i)(A) and 26.2601-1(b)(4)(i)(E), Examples 1 and 2.

To limit the involvement of the grantor of the existing ILIT, consider having the new trust be created as a declaration of trust by the trustee of the existing ILIT, rather than as an agreement of trust. Ideally, the bill for legal services should be rendered to the trustee of the existing ILIT, who may require additional funds to pay the bill.

If the existing ILIT does not contain express language permitting the trustee to make trust distributions in further trust, is the typical distribution language of "to or for the benefit of" the beneficiary sufficient authority? A trustee relying solely on this language may require judicial interpretation/construction of the existing ILIT before acting.[35] Query: Can the IRS challenge the authority of the trustee that

---

[34] *See*, O'Grady & Schooley, supra.

[35] "The power to decant may exist at common law, *see, e.g., Phipps v. Palm Beach Trust Co.*, 142 Fla. 782, 196 So. 299 (1940). The argument is that a trustee's power to invade principal for a beneficiary is a special power of appointment. If a power of appointment can be exercised by outright distribution to one or more beneficiaries currently, it also can be exercised to create trust interests for one or more of those same beneficiaries. The new trusts can grant a beneficiary a power of appointment the beneficiary did not have under the old trust, but it probably cannot include remaindermen who were not current beneficiaries or remaindermen of the old trust." Steven M. Fast and Steven G. Margolin, "Whose Trust Is It Anyway? (With Sample Trust

has made a transfer to a new ILIT, or is that challenge solely the purview of the beneficiaries of the existing ILIT?

"In early rulings following *Cottage Savings*, the IRS suggested that a distribution in further trust might constitute a taxable exchange of an interest by each beneficiary of the original trust for an interest in a new trust if the beneficiary's new interest was 'materially different' from its old interest. [Citation omitted.] However, in recent years, the IRS appears to recognize that a distribution in further trust does not constitute a recognition event for a beneficiary if the distribution is authorized either by the trust document [*see*, Priv. Letter Ruls. 200207018 and 200010037] by local law [*see*, Priv. Letter Ruls. 200135007 and 200423006]. This new approach makes sense. In the context of a trust decanting (at the sole discretion of the trustee), the beneficiaries are not exchanging any interests."[36]

Drafting Example:

"After the death of the survivor of the Settlor and the Settlor's spouse, an Independent Trustee may appoint any part or all of the trust property to the trustee of any other trust having a perpetuities period not exceeding the perpetuities period of the trust hereunder, whenever and by whomsoever made, including any other trust or trusts made by the Independent Trustee hereunder, and wherever the trustee of such other trust may reside or be incorporated. The beneficiaries shall include exclusively all or any one or more of the beneficiaries of the trust hereunder. An 'Independent Trustee' is a Trustee

---

Provisions) 12 *ALI-ABA Estate Planning Course Materials Journal* 25, 57 (December 2006). However, *Restatement Third, Property (Wills and Other Donative Transfers)* §17.1 Comment g refutes the notion that a trustee's discretionary authority to distribute trust property confers upon the trustee the common law power to decant (appoint) the existing trust property to a new trust. This is a reversal of the position taken in the *Restatement Second, Property (Donative Transfers)* §11.1 Comment d (which did permit decanting of trust property under a power of appointment theory). Thus, under the *Restatement Third, Property (Wills and Other Donative Transfers)*, a trustee's fiduciary distributive power over trust property is not the equivalent of a power to appoint, and in order for a trustee to decant (appoint) the trust property to a new trust, the trustee must have express authority (statutory or in the governing instrument) to decant or appoint the trust property to another trust. *In accord*, *Restatement (Third) of Trusts* (ALI, Philadelphia 2003) §50, Comment a, which states: "A trustee's discretionary power with respect to trust benefits is to be distinguished from a power of appointment. The latter [i.e., a power of appointment] is not subject to fiduciary obligations and may be exercised arbitrarily within the scope of the power."

[36] Halperin & Wandler at 227.

who is not a beneficiary of that trust and is not a related or subordinate party to any such beneficiary, as defined in Section 672(c) of the Internal Revenue Code, applied as though the beneficiary were the 'grantor' under that Section. For purposes of this definition, a 'beneficiary' shall mean (i) any individual to whom the income or principal of the trust may be paid currently and (ii) any individual to whom a future payment may be made other than an individual who may receive a payment from the trust only in the event of the exercise of a power of appointment in favor of that individual." [37]

§15.12(c) Merge The ILIT

Have the ILIT trustee merge (if permitted under state law) the existing ILIT into a new ILIT established by the grantor. If the new ILIT contains substantially the same dispositive provisions, the same governing law, the same beneficiaries, and the same standards for distributions, the merger should be permissible, and there should be no gift tax. If the new ILIT will receive the original transferor's basis in the policy, or come within another exception to the transfer for value rule of IRC section 101(a)(2), there should be no transfer for value problems. *See,* section 2.5, above. The GST tax inclusion ratio of the new ILIT should be the same as the GST tax inclusion ratio of the old ILIT, and care should be taken to make sure that the merger does not cause a trust that is grandfathered from the GST tax to lose its GST tax exempt status. Treas. Reg. §26.2601-1(b)(4)(i)(E), Example 6. *See,* sections 5.24 and 5.25, above. Also, the new ILIT's rule against perpetuities period should speak from the same time period (and lives in being, if applicable) as contained in the old ILIT. *See,* Paragraph 5.1(A)(7) of Sample ILIT.

> **Practice Point:** If the old trust is not a grantor trust and the new trust is a grantor trust, consider the effect that an income tax reimbursement provision may have. Will the income tax reimbursement provision be in the best interests of the trust beneficiaries? Should the trustees obtain a court order authorizing the merger? Will an income tax reimbursement provision cause a GST grandfathered trust

---

[37] This sample language is adapted from Steven M. Fast and Steven G. Margolin, "Whose Trust Is It Anyway? (With Sample Trust Provisions) 12 *ALI-ABA Estate Planning Course Materials Journal* 25, 57 (December 2006).

to lose its GST tax exempt status? Conversely, will the lack of an income tax reimbursement clause cause a GST grandfathered trust to lose its GST tax exempt status because of a constructive addition due to the grantor's payment of the trust's income tax? Is there a *Cottage Savings* taxable exchange issue?

§15.12(d) Distribute The Policy To The Insured's Spouse

If the terms of the trust permit, have the ILIT trustee distribute the life insurance policy to the non-insured spouse, who is a beneficiary of the ILIT (assuming there is no transfer for value issue). *See,* section 2.5, above. The non-insured spouse can then contribute the life insurance policy to an ILIT that the spouse or grantor has created. Although IRC section 2035 will not apply to the transfer by the non-insured spouse to the new ILIT (since IRC section 2035 applies to an insured), IRC sections 2036, 2038 and 2041 may apply to the non-insured spouse if he or she is a beneficiary of the new ILIT. *See,* sections 2.5(b)(5), 4.1, 4.2, and 4.3, above. If the value of the policy is large, the non-insured spouse may not have sufficient gift tax exemption (currently $1 million), or may not wish to use gift tax exemption, to make the transfer to the new ILIT. Accordingly, this technique is most useful for term insurance, or with a policy that has a low value but a high death benefit amount.

§15.12(e) Sell The Policy To One Of The Protected Party Exceptions Under The Transfer For Value Rule

If the insured is a bonafide partner in a partnership, or is a bonafide member of a limited liability company that is taxed as a partnership ("LLC"), or is an officer or shareholder in a corporation, consider transferring the policy from the ILIT to the partnership, or to a partner of the insured, or to the LLC, or to a member of the LLC, or to the corporation. *See,* section 2.5(c), above.

15.12(f) Modify The ILIT Due To Changed Circumstances

If a change in circumstances not known to the settlor and not anticipated by the settlor would result in impairing the purpose of the trust, a court can modify the trust if modification will further the purposes of the trust. *See,* section 15.7(d), above.

15.12(g) Modify Or Terminate The ILIT By Consent

A court can modify or terminate a trust upon the consent of the settlor and all the beneficiaries, even if the modification or termination is inconsistent with a material purpose of the trust. Also, a court can terminate a trust if all the beneficiaries consent and the court concludes that the continuance of the trust is not necessary to achieve a material purpose of the trust. Furthermore, a court can modify a trust if all the beneficiaries consent and the court concludes that modification is not inconsistent with a material purpose of the trust. *UTC* section 411, *Restatement (Second)* section 338(2) and *Restatement (Third)* section 65. *See, also,* section 15.9(g), above.

15.12(h) Terminate An Uneconomical ILIT

A trustee or court can terminate an ILIT if the trustee or court concludes that the value of the trust property is insufficient to justify the costs of administration. A court may also modify or terminate a trust (or remove the trustee and appoint a different (presumably less expensive) trustee) if the court determines that the value of the trust property is insufficient to justify the cost of administration. *UTC* section 414. *See also, Restatement (Second)* sections 335-338 and *Restatement (Third)* sections 61, 64, and 65.

15.12(i) Split The ILIT

If after the death of the insured the some of the trust beneficiaries are in disagreement over the investment policies of the trustee or have different ideas about how the trust should be administered, consider splitting the trust into separate shares for the beneficiaries. *See,* Priv. Letter Ruls. 9851006 and 9851007 where the IRS recognized a divorcing couple's split of an inter-vivos charitable remainder unitrust into two separate trusts—one for each spouse. *Cf.* IRC section 2642(a)(3) concerning qualified severances or GST purposes. A trust split where the beneficiary's property interests are not affected (even though the trusts may hold different assets), should not constitute a sale or exchange under the *Cottage Savings* doctrine. *See,* Priv. Letter Rul. 200602031. The GST trust modification rules concerning the division of a GST tax exempt trust are set forth in Treas. Reg. §26.2601-1-(b)(4)(i)(E), Example 5.[38]

---

[38] *See,* O'Grady & Schooley, supra.

§15.13 HOW TO DEAL WITH COMMUNITY PROPERTY AILMENTS

ILITs can be damaged when the ILIT is accidentally funded with community property (instead of being funded solely with the insured-grantor's separate property) and the non-insured spouse is a beneficiary and/or trustee of the ILIT.[39] One solution to such a tainted trust is to terminate the ILIT by distributing the policy to the trust beneficiaries, and starting all over again. Another way to deal with the problem is for the tainted policy to be purchased for its fair market value by a new ILIT that has been established by the insured-grantor and funded solely with his or her separate property.

Other creative approaches to this problem include: (i) a partition and exchange of funds with an effective date prior to the transfers (it is uncertain that this would work), (ii) treatment of the transfers as loans (this may work, especially in a situation where the client has also neglected to issue *Crummey* withdrawal right notices and therefore there has been no inconsistent treatment of the transfers as a gift), and (iii) use of any of the distribution/sale to new trust, etc. techniques discussed above. In addition, of course, there is a significant chance that if the problem is nominal in amount, is corrected, and a substantial amount of period lapses, the problem will never arise. A creative drafting approach is to include a provision in the governing instrument (this is a drafting solution and not a post facto solution) that prohibits a trustee from accepting community property, and if the trustee inadvertently accepts community property, that property is treated as a demand loan to the ILIT (with interest payable at the appropriate IRC section 7520 rate for a demand loan) to be satisfied at a later date, so that the community property would never be treated as a gift or contribution to the ILIT.

---

[39] *See, generally,* Section IV, N of Gerald B. Treacy, 802-2nd T.M.,, Bureau of National Affairs, Washington, D.C.

16

General Overview Of Life Insurance Policies

CHAPTER OVERVIEW

Because the primary asset of an ILIT is life insurance (which can be a very sophisticated financial product), the more an attorney knows about life insurance, the more value the attorney will add to the estate planning process since he or she will be better able to work with the client's life insurance agent and structure an appropriate estate plan for the client.

This chapter[1] provides an overview of the general types of life insurance policies an attorney may encounter when assisting a client in

[1] The author gratefully acknowledges the contributions of Jon J. Gallo, Esq. of Greenberg Glusker Fields Claman Machtinger & Kinsella, LLP, Los Angles, California; Gary R. Lee, Esq. LLM (Tax), CPA, CFP of Deloitte & Touche, LLP of Boston, Massachusetts; Charles L. Ratner, Esq., CLU, ChFC of Ernst & Young, LLP of Cleveland, Ohio; Jane A. Hays, Esq., CLU of The Downey Group, Inc., of Champaign, Illinois; Craig A. Wilkey, MBA, CLU, ChFC of Financial Architects Partners of Boston, Massachusetts; Leslie C. Giordani, Esq. of Giordani, Schurig, Beckett & Tackett, LLP of Austin, Texas; Douglas W. Stein, Esq. of Barris, Sott, Denn & Driker, PLLC of Detroit, Michigan; and Stephan R. Leimberg, Esq. of Bryn Mawr, Pennsylvania in the writing of this Chapter. *See*, Jon J. Gallo, "Life Insurance Due Diligence for Dummies: What the Attorney Preparing a Life Insurance Trust Ought to Know," 44 *The Practical Lawyer*, 75 (September 1998), portions of which have been reproduced, edited and modified with the permission of Jon. J. Gallo, Esq. and ALI-ABA; Jonathan C. Blattmachr, "Some Fundamental and Fine Points in Uses of Life Insurance in Estate and Financial Planning," 37 *Heckerling Institute on Estate Planning*, Chapter 2 (Matthew Bender/Lexis-Nexis, Newark, NJ 2003); Harold L. Wilshinsky,

the establishment of an ILIT, and discusses the major risk factors/elements that affect a life insurance policy. The chapter contains a chart that summarizes the important features, advantages, and disadvantages of term life insurance, traditional whole life, universal life, and variable universal life. The chapter also discusses the management of trust owned life insurance ("TOLI") and provides suggested "best management practices" for TOLI.

The discussion that follows is not, however, a substitute for the policy owner obtaining proper and competent advice from a licensed life insurance agent[2]; and, if appropriate, from a fee-only life insurance advisor.

§16.1 SELECTING THE RIGHT LIFE INSURANCE POLICY

§16.1(a) Selecting The Correct Policy[3]

Life insurance policies may be divided into two fundamental cat-

---

"Life Insurance Products For The High-Net-Worth Client," 135 *Trusts & Estates* 56 (October 1996) ("Wilshinsky"); Malarkey and Leimberg, "Innovative Planning With 'No Lapse Guarantee' Life Insurance," 32 *Estate Planning* 3 (July 2005) ("Malarkey and Leimberg"); Leimberg and Doyle, *Tools & Techniques of Life Insurance Planning—3rd Edition*, The National Underwriter Company, Cincinnati, Ohio (2004), www.nuco.com ("Leimberg & Doyle"); Chapter 1 of Zaritsky and Leimberg, *Tax Planning With Life Insurance Analysis With Forms -2d Edition*, Warren Gorham & Lamont, Boston, Massachusetts (Supp. 2007) ("Zaritsky and Leimberg"); Lee and Wilkey, 827 T.M., *Life Insurance—A Practical Guide for Evaluating Policies*, Bureau of National Affairs, Washington, DC ("Lee and Wilkey"); Chapters 1, 8, 9, 10, and 11 of Ben G. Baldwin, *The Lawyer's Guide to Insurance (Personal Insurance Coverage for Professionals and Their Clients)*, American Bar Association, Chicago, Illinois (1999) ("Baldwin"); and ¶4.04 of Jonathan D. Pond, *Personal Financial Planning Handbook: With Forms & Checklists* (Warren, Gorham & Lamont, Boston, Massachusetts) for more detailed information about the different types of life insurance products that are available. *See also*, Stephan R. Leimberg and Albert E. Gibbons, "Performing Due Diligence With Respect to Life Insurance Trusts Is Crucial," 30 *Estate Planning* 248 (May 2003); and Brody, Richey, and Baier, 828 T.M., *Compensating Employees with Insurance* (Bureau of National Affairs, Washington, DC) ("Brody, Richey and Baier").

[2] *See*, Worksheet 5, "Broker Questionnaire," of Lee and Wilkey for questions to ask when vetting a life insurance agent.

[3] "Today, there is no absolutely 'right' life insurance product. There are four basic policy types [term, whole life, universal life, and variable life] and an infinite number of variations. Where diversification is warranted, certainly each type should be seriously considered. Where diversification is not appropriate, the agent and other advisors must

egories: term and permanent.[4] In reality, all life insurance may be viewed as term insurance, with various forms of permanent insurance

---

take into account the client's personal investment philosophy, his or her gift tax status, cash flow capabilities and health condition in determining policy suitability." Wilshinsky at 70.

See, Worksheets 1 and 2 from Lee and Wilkey for a flowchart on client risk tolerance and life insurance policy selection, respectively. *See also,* "Life Insurance Policy Suitability and Selection Questionnaire" at page 197 of Baldwin; and Chapter 4 of Leimberg & Doyle. Worksheet 2 of Lee and Wilkey is reproduced in Table 1.

In general, Lee and Wilkey suggest the following:

(1) Consider whole life insurance if the owner desires maximum product guarantees and the life insurance company has a strong dividend crediting history; but, do not purchase whole life insurance if premium flexibility is desired or unbundled product disclosure is desired.

(2) Consider whole life/term blend if the owner desires to maximize the product performance and the life insurance company has a strong dividend crediting history; but, do not purchase whole life/term blend if the owner desires: (i) maximum product guarantees, (ii) premium payment flexibility, or (iii) unbundled product disclosure.

(3) Consider universal life if the owner desires premium flexibility and unbundled product disclosure; but, do not purchase universal life if the owner desires: (i) maximum product guarantees, and (ii) lower volatility associated with a whole life policy.

(4) Consider secondary guarantee universal life if the owner desires a guaranteed death benefit and unbundled product disclosure; but, do not purchase secondary guarantee universal life if the owner desires: (i) growth of the cash value, or (ii) access to the cash value.

(5) Consider variable life (whole life product structure vs. universal life structure) if the owner desires a guaranteed death benefit; but, do not purchase variable life if the owner desires premium flexibility.

(6) Consider variable universal life if the owner desires premium flexibility and unbundled product disclosure; but, do not purchase universal life if the owner desires: (i) maximum product guarantees, and (ii) lower volatility associated with a whole life policy.

Lee and Wilkey at section III, D.

[4] "Permanent" insurance is a misnomer since some "permanent" policies can (and are designed to) last for a finite period of time. Steve Leimberg and Timothy Malarkey suggest that the correct nomenclature is "cash value" insurance (for what has been traditionally referred to as "permanent" insurance). Malarkey and Leimberg at 4. Term insurance deals with the "***If I die*** situation." Permanent insurance, on the other hand deals with the "***When I die*** situation." Typical cash value life insurance policies include, whole life, universal life, variable life and variable universal life, all of which are discussed in section 16.3, below.

Term insurance has been compared to renting a house—the policy owner can never build up any equity in the policy. Permanent insurance has been compared to owning a house—the policy owner can usually build up equity in the policy.

combining term insurance protection with a cash value (or investment) account as a means of pre-funding a portion of the cost of the term protection and building equity in the policy. Within each category are numerous variations as a result of product design and/or add-on riders. In reviewing what follows, it is helpful to note how the various moving parts or risk factors (which are discussed in section 16.4 below), operate in the various types of policies.

§16.1(a)(1) Using Tax Free Dollars To Pay Life Insurance Premiums

As previously mentioned, all life insurance is term insurance (since all life insurance includes the cost of term insurance, which, from the life insurance company's perspective is its "net amount at risk," or the company's "risk element" under the policy). According to Ben G. Baldwin, CLU, CFP, ChFC, MSFS, and MSM, the question to be asked and answered is not "What type of life insurance should the client purchase?" Rather, the question to be asked and answered is: "What is the best way to pay for the life insurance coverage that the client desires and can afford?" Pure term insurance, which is the "lowest outlay" form of life insurance coverage requires premium payments to be made from after tax dollars. Hence pure term insurance premiums are the most "tax expensive" form of premium payment. On the other hand, variable universal life insurance, which requires a larger premium payment than pure term insurance, in the earlier years, can be a less "tax expensive" form of life insurance coverage. This is accomplished by using the variable universal life policy's annual earnings on its cash value component to pay part of the life insurance premium costs.[5] Generally speaking, the accumulation of earnings in an equity-building life insurance policy's cash value component is "income tax deferred." Thus, the use of the "tax deferred" earnings to pay some or all of the annual premiums is a less "tax expensive' form of premium payment. If the owner of the equity-building life insurance policy holds the policy until his or her death, the investment income earned by the policy's cash value component escapes income taxation totally, and the life insurance proceeds are received income tax free by the beneficiary. If the policy is owned by an ILIT, the life insurance proceeds

[5] *See*, Burke A. Christensen, "Life Insurance: The Under -appreciated Tax Shelter," 135 *Trusts & Estates* 57 (November 1996). Additional federal income tax advantages of cash value life insurance include: (1) income tax free death benefit; (2) tax deferred growth of cash values; (3) payment of premiums with pre-tax dollars; (4) tax free withdrawals; (5) tax free loans; and (6) tax free repayment of loans at death. *Id.* at 58.

can also avoid federal estate taxes—a triple tax benefit! And, if the ILIT has been structured as a GST tax exempt trust, the life insurance proceeds can be used to benefit future generations of beneficiaries free of the confiscatory GST tax—a fourth benefit!

§16.1(b) Different Life Insurance Companies Offer Different Products

Even though a life insurance company may be highly rated, the quality and pricing of products offered by that life insurance company may vary. For example, one company may offer a very high quality, competitively priced term product, but may not have high quality, competitively priced permanent products. Also, ratings of life insurance companies and their products change over time. This can make shopping for the "right policy with the right company" a challenge.

It is vital to select a knowledgeable, sophisticated life insurance agent, both to design the most desirable policy and also to provide long term, quality policy service, independent of the life insurance carrier. Life insurance acquired for ILIT ownership may be a very long term investment. It may also be appropriate to hire an independent fee-only life insurance advisor to assist in the analysis and make appropriate recommendations. Also, consider reviewing illustrations from more than one life insurance company.

Determine whether it is practical to obtain layers of coverage from more than one company for diversification. Likewise, determine whether the husband and wife should obtain insurance from different companies.

§16.1(c) Basic Rules Of Thumb In Selecting A Life Insurance Policy

In his easy to read and understand book, *The Lawyer's Guide to Insurance (Personal Insurance Coverage for Professionals and Their Clients)*, Ben G. Baldwin, provides eight basic "rules of thumb" for a prospective insured who is considering life insurance coverage:

(1) Know the costs of the product, especially in the early years of coverage.

(2) Establish long-term relationships with quality insurance companies and quality intermediaries [such as a life insurance agent or a fee-only life insurance advisor].

(3) Choose control [over the policy] over no control.

(4) Choose flexibility [over the policy such as the death benefit amount, the premium amount, investment decisions, etc.] over inflexibility.

(5) Choose quality over current or future interest rate promises.

(6) Choose a survivor among insurance companies and intermediaries [rather than a "here today, gone bankrupt (or become insolvent) tomorrow" insurance company].[6]

(7) Accept the fact that assets within insurance contracts require management just as every other asset on a balance sheet does.

(8) Demand [**written**] disclosure of the intermediary's compensation before purchasing.[7]

§16.2 LIFE INSURANCE POLICY SELECTION DUE CARE

Life insurance policy selection due care[8] should always consist of four interdependent elements: (1) the policy must be suitable, (2) the life insurance company must be strong, (3) the policy must be competitive and well designed, and (4) the whole story must be credible.

> **Caution:** "There is no simple way to compare or analyze life insurance policies. If there were, fee-only consultants would have written a short article explaining how to do it and then moved on to other occupations."[9]

§16.2(a) Policy Suitability

The policy must be suitable. Much like investments, certain types of insurance products have dominant features and benefits that will align themselves with certain characteristics the policy owner desires for the coverage. The parameters for determining suitability, which are discussed below, include: (i) premium amount, (ii) death benefit amount, (iii) policy flexibility, (iv) ability to select investments

---

[6] "Independent academic research, however, suggests that it is not possible to construct reliable models for prediction of carrier insolvency...." Kathryn A. Ballsun, Patrick J. Collins, and Dieter Jurkat, "Evidencing Care, Skill and Caution in The Management of ILITs (Part 3 of 4)," 32 *ACTEC Journal* 145 (Fall 2006).

[7] Baldwin at 22-23. *See,* Worksheet 5 of Lee and Wilkey for a sample life insurance broker questionnaire.

[8] *See, e.g.,* James D. Schwartz, Gordon W. Netzorg, and Susan Bernhardt, "Due Diligence in Life Insurance Selection," 8 *Probate & Property* 39 (March/April 1994).

[9] Glenn S. Daily, "Danger: Fiduciary Liability Ahead," (May 10, 2004), http://www.glenndaily.com/fiduciaries.htm.

and influence the return, (v) tax considerations, (vi) risks, (vii) appropriateness of the arrangement, and (viii) cash value buildup.

§16.2(a)(1) Premium

Is there a maximum annual premium the policy owner is willing to pay for the coverage? If the underwriters want to charge the policy owner more for the insurance, will the policy owner raise his premium tolerance or compromise on other aspects of the policy design? Does the policy owner want to pay the premium for a particular number of years?

§16.2(a)(2) Death Benefit

The policy owner's estate plan may call for either a level or increasing death benefit. For example, a growing estate may require an increasing death benefit to pay estate or inheritance taxes. On the other hand, if the policy owner is willing to implement estate tax reduction strategies sooner rather than later, a level death benefit may be adequate. In a compensation-related case, the parties may want the death benefit to track increases in compensation. Or, the death benefit may be entirely incidental to the overall purpose of the insurance, i.e., where the insurance is to be used for asset accumulation and retirement income. In these cases, the death benefit will be minimized vis-à-vis the premium paid.

§16.2(a)(3) Flexibility

The policy owner may want the flexibility to skip or change the premium amount. For example, if the policy owner has varying demands on his or her cash flow or the policy owner's business is cyclical, the ability to skip or reduce the premium for a year or two may be an important element of policy design. The policy owner may also want to be able to increase the premium without increasing the death benefit. This is an efficient way to use the policy as a tax deferred (and possibly tax free) savings or investment vehicle. The policy owner may want to be able to reduce the death benefit from time to time. The flexibility to reduce the death benefit enables the policy owner to modify the policy as the policy owner's need for life insurance decreases over the years. This flexibility also enables the policy owner to maximize the policy's cash value or reduce the premium commitment in the policy's later years.

§16.2(a)(4) Ability To Influence Investment Return

If the policy owner wants to be able to direct the investment of the policy's cash value component, then a variable life product may be the appropriate type of policy. If the policy owner does not want to worry about asset allocation decisions with respect to the life insurance policy, and is willing to permanently forgo that potential control, then a variable life product is not appropriate.

§16.2(a)(5) Tax Considerations

The level of premium, duration of the premium payments, and policy flexibility may need to be coordinated with income, gift or GST tax considerations. Predictability of policy performance, policy flexibility, and cash value maximization may be desirable in certain tax-oriented designs such as generation-skipping or split dollar.

§16.2(a)(6) Risks[10]

The policy owner may (or may not) want to be certain that the planned premium will always be adequate to support the death benefit. The policy owner may (or may not) need to be certain that he or she will pay premiums for the number of years he or she planned to pay them. The certainty described here is typically (and mistakenly) associated with a particular type of policy, to wit, whole life. Actually, certainty as to outlay or result is more truly associated with the level of funding (premium) than the type of policy. If the policy owner seeks protection from creditor claims against the insurer's general fund, then a variable life product may be appropriate. In addition to the foregoing, there is the risk that the recommended product will not be suitable for the policy owner's circumstances, the planning strategy, or the premium payment technique. Additionally, there is the risk that the advisors' risk tolerance or interests may differ from the policy owner's, and those differences may eclipse the appropriate selection and product design process for the policy owner.

---

[10] Risk also includes the policy's inability to adapt to the policy owner's changing circumstances. A guaranteed life insurance product where the company assumes "all" or most of the risks, such as a traditional whole life policy, may be riskier than a non-guaranteed product due to the guaranteed product's lack of flexibility and inability to adapt to the policy owner's changing needs, such as premium amount, face amount, etc. However, to control the level of risk when using a non-guaranteed product, the product's performance and appropriateness must be monitored.

§16.2(a)(7) Appropriateness For The Arrangement

Certain arrangements such as split dollar and premium financing call for careful selection, design, and funding of the life insurance product. Too often, the insurance product and premium level are selected first and then split dollar is recommended as a payment mechanism. The only guarantee in this arrangement is trouble.

§16.2(a)(8) Cash Value Buildup

Will the policy be a source of income in the future? If so, when? How much? Will it potentially be important to rely on the policy value to sustain the death benefit, with no or reduced ongoing cash premium payments? Anticipated cash surrender values may be one of the most important aspects to consider in life insurance due care.

§16.2(b) The Life Insurance Company Must Be Strong

There is no question that the policy owner will not want to do business with a life insurance company that he or she might outlive. Thus, the financial strength of any life insurance company submitted by the agent must be verified by the major life insurance company rating services.[11]

---

[11] Major life insurance company rating services are: A.M. Best Company (www.ambest.com), Moodys (www.Moodys.com), Standard & Poor's (www.standardandpoors.com), Fitch (www.fitchreatings.com) and Weiss Research (www.weissratings.com). Many of these companies' ratings are published annually in *The Insurance Forum* (www.theinsuranceforum.com). Generally, Moody and Weiss are the toughest raters.

"Superior track records in the insurance industry are as ephemeral as those in the money management industry. This should not be surprising because insurance carriers invest in the same capital markets as other institutional money managers; and, it is rare in even moderately efficient markets to find investments that offer more than zero net present value when properly adjusted for their risk. Just as the persistence of abnormal returns generated by top ranked money managers into future periods is often no better than chance, so also, the predictability of investment results from insurance carriers is low. Indeed, modern portfolio theory suggests that the best track record may merely reflect the fact that the winner assumed the highest amount of risk (and was fortunate enough to have the bets pay off during the period under evaluation)." Kathryn A. Ballsun, Patrick J. Collins, and Dieter Jurkat, "Standards of Prudence and Management of the Insurance Portfolio (Part 2 of 4)," 32 *ACTEC Journal* 66, 84 (Summer 2006). (Citation omitted.)

§16.2(b)(1) Rating Services

However, ratings themselves are primarily indicative of the ability of the life insurance company to meet its obligations, i.e., to pay the claim. By no means do high ratings from the major rating services assure the policy owner that: (i) the company is in a position to achieve the projections made in the policy illustration; (ii) the company's products are competitive and well designed; (iii) the company's products are appropriate for the policy owner's needs (as discussed above); and (iv) the company has treated its policyholders well in the past (or will continue to do so in the future). Unfortunately, these four critical points are often overlooked in the rush to limit selection to life insurance companies with the highest ratings.

When an insurance company is highly rated it is important to find out which agency rated the company and to understand how that agency rates insurance companies. The four major rating agencies that use information beyond what is found in the company's annual reports are A.M. Best, Standard & Poor's, Moody's and Duff and Phelps. Weiss Research, generally a less used rating source, tends to limit its information to the insurance company's annual reports. A.M. Best uses a rating range from A++ to D. Standard & Poor's uses a range from AAA to CCC. Moody's uses a range from Aaa to DD. Duff and Phelps uses a range from AAA to DD. As result, a B rating can mean that the company is a second tier company under Weis or a fourth tier company under Duff and Phelps.

Each rating agency looks for different information. A.M. Best rates most insurance companies based on their relative strength. Standard & Poor's only rates companies that request a rating, and issue a rating based on the insurance company's claims paying ability. Moody's rates insurance companies based on their financial strength, as indicated by the company's ability to pay senior policyholder obligations. Lastly, Duff and Phelps rates insurance companies on their claims paying ability. However, Duff and Phelps does so with an analytical and statistical bent based on the insurance company's liquidity and solvency.

§16.2(c) Competitive And Well-Designed Policy

The life insurance product must be competitive and well designed. Some products of similar stripe are better packaged for the policy owner's situation than others. They may be more flexible, for example, or allow more premium to be paid in vis-à-vis the death benefit. Some products enable the policy owner, rather than the life insurance company, to control the level of risk the policy owner assumes. Some products enable the policy owner to control the level of compensation paid to the agent, thereby increasing the efficiency of the product at the same premium. Some life insurance companies may have significantly more flexible and generous underwriting, which can make a dramatic difference in required policy premiums, death benefit and in cash value, for a particular premium amount. Finally, some products are simply more competitive, meaning legitimately competitive, than others.

§16.2(d) Credibility

The last element is policy/illustration credibility. This is as crucial an area of modern life insurance practice as there is, and the policy owner should expect valuable insight (and empirical data) from the life insurance agent on these points:

(1) Does a close examination of the non-guaranteed elements of policy performance suggest credibility?

(2) Is the life insurance company well positioned by virtue of current strength and past performance to deliver on the projected illustration? Does the company's record, in terms of dividend history and results in mortality, interest crediting rate, lapses, and expenses suggest it has delivered in the past and will continue to do so in the future? Does a company with current outstanding pricing give fair pricing treatment to old policies too, so that the policy owner will share in the "good times" too?

(3) Does the life insurance company support the market in which the policy owner is buying, i.e., if the policy owner is going to buy split dollar insurance, does the company do in-force illustrations (also known as in-force ledgers) for split dollar cases? Has the company been a consistent presence in the particular market? Has the company passed along mortality and expense improvements to all policyholders? These are the questions that the agent should be prepared to address.

§16.3 UNDERSTANDING COMMON LIFE INSURANCE POLICIES[12]

§16.3(a) Term Insurance

Term insurance[13] is the simplest form of life insurance. Term insurance is temporary insurance that provides coverage for a limited

---

[12] *See*, Table 2, below, for a chart that compares and contrasts the general features of term life, whole life, universal life, and variable universal life insurance. *See also*, "Menu of Life Insurance Products" at page 183 of Baldwin; and Figures 1.3, 18.3, and 18.4 of Leimberg and Doyle at 13-14, 283 and 284.

[13] *See*, Chapter 16 of Leimberg & Doyle; and ¶1.02 of Zaritsky and Leimberg.

duration (i.e., for a term of years). Term insurance provides a death benefit and nothing more; at the end of the term, the coverage expires. Since most term policies expire before the insured dies, many term policies never pay a death benefit. Nearly all of the premium for a term policy is for the cost of the insurance ("COI")[14] or the "net amount at risk" ("NAR"),[15] (i.e., the mortality expense), plus the life

---

[14] "Cost of insurance charges (COIs) are deductions from...life insurance [premiums]...to cover the insurer's anticipated payments for death claims. They are the largest single cost of any policy, typically accounting for about 75% of total premiums. (Indeed, if claims are not the largest single cost factor, then the product probably isn't really insurance against the risk of death.) These deductions are much like term life insurance premiums in that they are predominantly for claims paid during a given period (typically 1 year). For this reason, COIs are frequently referred to as the pure 'risk' portion of the premium, reimbursing the insurance company for the risk associated with paying the death benefit. Because the risk of death increases with age, so does the COI. COI is calculated each year using two factors: the net 'at-risk' amount [i.e., the NAR] of the policy death benefit and a COI rate provided by the insurance company for each age corresponding to each policy year for each product. The net at risk amount is multiplied by the rate to determine the COI; the higher the death benefit or the rate, the greater the COI and therefore the higher the premium. For example, assume an insurance company provides permanent life insurance for a group of 1,000 policyholders whom all are insured for $100,000 and three (3) insureds out of the group of 1,000 die in a given year. The insurance company pays $300,000 to the beneficiaries of those three insureds. The insurance company must therefore collect $300 from each policy owner over the course of the period in order to pay this $300,000. The COI Rate would equal $3.00 per $1,000 of death benefit (i.e. each insured paid $3.00 multiplied times 100 for each $1,000 of death benefit). Of course, as the average age of the population increases, the risk of more deaths increases and so does the COI and therefore the premium." Christopher P. Cline and Barry D. Flagg, "Fiduciary Pitfalls with Trust-Owned Life Insurance," *American Bankers Association Teleconference Meeting* 8 (August 24, 2006).

"The medical underwriting and the proposed insured's rating will affect the COI." Douglas Moore and Mitchell K. Higgins, "Planning and Investing With Private Placement Life Insurance" 30 *Estate Planning* 336, 340 (July 2003).

[15] "The NAR is, of course, not the entire death benefit, but only the amount of the insurance company's money your beneficiary gets if you die while the policy is in force. Death benefit amounts in excess of the NAR are either: (i) money the policy owner has paid into the policy or (ii) money earned by the policy owner's money. A term insurance policy is nearly all NAR because it has no cash value. A cash-value life insurance policy with a $100,000 death benefit and a $60,000 cash value has only $40,000 of NAR...." Burke A. Christensen, "Life Insurance: The Under-appreciated Tax Shelter," 135 *Trusts & Estates* 57 (November 1996). Thus, NAR = policy death benefit amount - policy cash value.

insurance company's load/expense. Collectively the NAR and load/expense charges are oftentimes referred to as the mortality and expense charges ("M&E").[16] *See,* section 16.4, below. Thus, term insurance is pure life insurance protection without any build up of cash value, i.e., there is no cash savings or investment component.[17]

---

[16] "In addition to COI and M&E, there are two separate taxes associated with obtaining a domestic life insurance policy. First, the federal deferred acquisition cost (DAC) tax is applied to each premium payment. Each carrier calculates the DAC tax and may pass through different levels of DAC tax charge to the policy owner. This tax cannot be avoided. The second tax is a state premium tax. Each state imposes its own premium tax. This tax varies considerably from state to state. Some carriers charge 'state specific' taxes, while other carriers charge a level amount for all states. This can have a dramatic effect on premium tax costs. Hence, the state in which the policy is issued may be an important factor. States such as Delaware, South Dakota, and Alaska have premium tax rates that tend to be more favorable than those of many other states. The return on the investments of the policy is then reduced by traditional investment management fees and administration expenses of the fund managers that would ordinarily apply. The better the investment performance, the less significant the COI and M&E are to the overall return." Douglas Moore and Mitchell K. Higgins, "Planning and Investing With Private Placement Life Insurance" 30 *Estate Planning* 336, 340 (July 2003).

[17] The notion of "buy term insurance and invest the difference" can be accomplished in two ways. The first way is to buy term insurance and invest the premium savings in the financial markets, and hope for the best. The second way is to buy permanent insurance. The second way is the preferred method for long term life insurance coverage since the permanent product is doing exactly what the insured desires—the insured is buying term insurance (the risk portion) and investing the difference (the cash value component). Some of the key differences between the first and second method is: (i) the first method is a voluntary saving method, whereas the second method is a forced method of savings (assuming the policy owner refrains from borrowing against or withdrawing cash from the policy), (ii) under the first method the insured assumes all the risk with regard to the investment, whereas under the second method, the investment risk can, depending on the policy, be shifted to the life insurance company, (iii) under the first method the insured is always using after tax dollars to purchase term insurance coverage, whereas under the second method the insured can use "tax free" dollars to purchase term coverage, (iv) under the first method the investment may be subject to capital gains or income tax if the insured liquidates some of his or her investments before death (or after death under a carry over income tax basis regime), whereas under the second method the insured may be able to make "tax free" withdrawals (up to basis), and the insured's beneficiaries can receive the death proceeds income tax free (and death tax free if the policy is owned by an ILIT), and (v) under the first method, if the insured dies after the term insurance coverage ends, there will be no death benefit—only the investment monies (if any).

Because there is no cash value (or investment) component in term insurance, the owner of the policy can not take out a loan or make a withdrawal from a term policy. Term insurance is the lowest outlay form of insurance—in the early years. However, term insurance becomes more expensive with every renewal since it is age based and as the insured becomes older, the probability of death becomes greater.[18] The higher the actuarial probability of death in a given year, the greater the COI and higher the premium.

Most term policies are sold based on a current or illustrated rate schedule and a higher guaranteed schedule of maximum premiums that may be charged if the policy is renewed and the illustrated premium is no longer in effect. Since there is no cash value build up in the policy to help offset increased costs upon renewal of the policy, annual renewable term life insurance tends to be most sensitive of all life insurance products to fluctuations in risk factors, such as the interest/investment return and mortality experience of the life insurance company. *See,* section 16.4, below. The maximum guaranteed premium that the life insurance company may charge on renewal of a term policy is generally substantially higher than the premium illustrated by the insurance company. If the life insurance company's underwriting practices are poor and the company insures many bad risks (i.e., has a higher than expected mortality experience), or the reinsurance company used by the life insurance company has too many bad risks, there is a substantial risk that premiums for an annual renewable term policy will be increased, up to (but not in excess of) the maximum guaranteed premium.

---

[18] Term life insurance is an inexpensive way to replace lost income due to the premature death of a wage earner (such as a working spouse-parent), or as an inexpensive way to provide income to pay for the cost of a replacement caregiver if the primary caregiver (such as a non-working spouse-parent) dies prematurely. Because term life insurance is designed for a specified term of years—it is not designed to provide an inheritance. Permanent life insurance that provides a cash surrender value, such as whole life, universal life, or variable universal life is, however, designed to replace lost income ***and*** to provide an inheritance.

"Term insurance is indicated when the need for life insurance is temporary, when the largest possible amount of coverage is desired for a given amount of annual cash outlay, when the need is intermediate or long-term but the buyer's cash flow is currently insufficient to purchase the needed coverage under a higher premium permanent policy, when the policy owner has better investment opportunities outside the insurance policy than inside it, and as a 'rider' when additional death benefits are desired in conjunction with cash value life insurance or 'packages' of policies." Malarkey and Leimberg at 4.

Term insurance is either renewable or nonrenewable. Renewable term is more expensive, but the extra cost is often offset by the increased flexibility and security of being able to maintain coverage if the insured becomes uninsurable for any reason. Many renewable term policies permit the insured to maintain coverage past the age of 65 without evidence of insurability. Most renewable term policies offer a conversion feature permitting the policy to be converted to a permanent policy without evidence of insurability.[19] This is particularly advantageous to an insured who wants permanent coverage and whose health has declined while holding the term policy. Some term policies renew to age 90, but become so expensive that they are impractical for long term estate planning solutions. As a general rule, term insurance maintained for more than 20 years is not competitive with permanent insurance. However, 30 year level term insurance has recently become much more competitive. *See,* Table 1.

From an ILIT trustee's "best practices" perspective, term insurance, because of its simplicity, requires the least amount of annual trust owned life insurance ("TOLI") management.[20]

---

[19] A prospective purchaser should always determine: (1) Whether the policy is convertible to all of the life insurance company's cash value products (whole life, variable life, universal life, and variable universal life) or just certain of those products, and are those products attractively priced? If not, the conversion rider will be of limited value. (2) How long is the conversion feature is valid? This can be a trap for the unwary, particularly the younger insured who may ordinarily decide to convert at an age that is well beyond the policy year mandated by the contract. (3) Will the conversion be done at the same underwriting classification as the term policy for the entire amount of the new policy, or will evidence of insurability be required at the time of the conversion? (4) What credits, if any, will the life insurance company offer for converting to a cash value policy? (5) Will the life insurance company permit a conversion when a disability waiver of premium is in effect and will it apply the waiver to the new policy?

[20] *See,* Christopher P. Cline and Barry D. Flagg, "The Prudent Investor and Trust-Owned Life Insurance (TOLI)—Part 1," 115 *American Bankers Association Trust & Investments* 38 (January/February 2007) (ftp://theinsuranceadvisor.com/documents/ABA_TOLI.pdf); Christopher P. Cline and Barry D. Flagg, "The Prudent Investor and Trust-Owned Life Insurance (TOLI)—Part 2," 116 *American Bankers Association Trust & Investments* 34 (March/April 2007) (ftp://theinsuranceadvisor.com/documents/ABA_TOLI_PartII.pdf); Christopher P. Cline and Barry D. Flagg, "The Prudent Investor and Trust-Owned Life Insurance (TOLI)—Part 3," 117 *American Bankers Association Trust & Investments* 42 (May/June 2007) (ftp://theinsuranceadvisor.com/documents/ABA_TOLI_PartIII.pdf) ("Suitability of TOLI holdings is largely determined by two criteria: investment performance and policy expenses."); Stephan Leimberg, "TOLI Risk Management at Litigation Crossroads," *Steve Leim-*

§16.3(a)(1) Popular Types Of Term Life Insurance

The more popular variations of term insurance are:

---

berg's Estate Planning Newsletter # 1110 (April 12, 2007) at http://www.leimbergservices.com; Stephan Leimberg, "Trust-Owned Life Insurance—Risk Management Guidance for Professional Advisors," *Steve Leimberg's Estate Planning Newsletter # 891* (November 16, 2005) at www.leimbergservices.com ("Leimberg Newsletter #891"). *See, also,* Kathryn A. Ballsun, Patrick J. Collins and Dieter Jurkat, "Trustee Administration of Life Insurance (Part 1 of 4)," 31 *ACTEC Journal* 280 (Spring 2006); E. Randolph Whitelaw and Richard W. Weber, "Trust-Owned Life Insurance: Risk Management Guidance for Fiduciaries," 32 *Estate Planning* 14 (September 2005) ("Whitelaw and Weber"); Mark A. Teitelbaum, "Trust Owned Life Insurance: Is It An Accident Waiting To Happen?," *National Underwriter Life & Health* 38 (May 17, 2004) ("Teitelbaum"); and C. Markham Whitelaw and William C. Ries, "Managing Trust Owned Life Insurance—Revisited," 138 *Trust & Estates* 38 (April 1999) ("Whitelaw & Ries"), where the authors discuss potential TOLI problems, such as: (1) underperforming policies, (2) policies that are insufficient for the insured's current needs, (3) newer products that may be more cost efficient, (4) new products and riders that may offer better options, (5) policies scheduled for a big increase in premiums, (6) trustee negligence in maintaining the current life insurance policy, (7) bad trustee investment decisions concerning the retention of a variable life insurance product, (8) trustee negligence in poor life insurance design or an improper policy, and (9) trustee negligence in poor selection of a life insurance agent.

"For skilled and unskilled trustee, TOLI management should include policy monitoring, suitability and restructure criteria....Four R's describe the TOLI management process—review, restore, restructure or replace." Whitelaw & Ries at 38.

"A trustee, skilled or unskilled, can accept a guaranteed death benefit policy and transfer all premium adequacy risk to the underwriting carrier, or can retain premium adequacy risk by accepting a non-guaranteed death benefit policy and actively managing policy values. Acceptance of premium adequacy risk implies the grantor's approval to do so, expertise in TOLI risk management, and an affirmative election by the trustee to manage the insurance investment consistent with the trust's objectives. If a trustee does not obtain the grantor's approval, or lacks TOLI risk-based procedures or expertise in policy evaluation, the trustee must recommend restructuring to a guaranteed death benefit policy.... The critical asset management considerations applicable to insurance trusts are product suitability, premium adequacy, and carrier selection. For guaranteed policies, premium adequacy is not a risk, but the carrier's size and ratings must be evaluated. For non-guaranteed policies, premium adequacy is the obvious risk that mandates active management using TOLI-specific risk management procedures and expertise in evaluating premium adequacy. Actuarial evaluation must be used for all determinations regarding premium adequacy, as well as policy acceptance, management and restructuring." Whitelaw and Weber at 16.

Teitelbaum recommends that life insurance agents help trustees in: (1) "Setting goals and standards regarding trust owned life insurance. This includes examining life insurance policies and comparing these to alternatives.... Examining client goals and beneficiary needs. (2) Examining policy funding and determining if additional fund-

• **Annual Renewable Term.** Annual renewable term life insurance provides a death benefit for the present year and guarantees the right to renew for the following year at a specified rate. Consequently, the

---

ing is necessary. This includes considering whether or not a client's gifting capacity is able to support future premium needs. (3) Considering life insurance performance: Will UL [universal life] policies or participating whole life policies perform within a reasonable tolerance of the original illustrations or new client goals? With VL [variable life] insurance, do the subaccounts need to be re-examined based on evolving client needs and subaccount performance?" Teitelbaum at 43.

"The annual performance monitoring questions that should be asked and answered by trust fiduciaries to assure that the trust does not receive too little or pay too much for life insurance coverage include the following: (1) Has the policy inadvertently become a MEC? (2) Should a split-dollar agreement be modified to comply with the most recent split-dollar rules? (3) What is the impact of demutualization on the economic results of trust held coverage? (4) If the policy was issued as other than 'preferred risk,' has the insured stopped smoking or has there been an improvement in the insured's health? (5) Are there recently issued policies that might provide a better return for the trust's beneficiaries and if so, what are the costs of replacing present coverage? (6) Is there a policy that might lapse and if so, what are the tax and other economic consequences?" ¶5.03 of Zaritsky and Leimberg.

Lee and Wilkey recommend that the following factors be examined when evaluating a policy on an ongoing basis: (1) obtain an in-force illustration of the existing policy; (2) review the current premium payment amount and determine if the insured may qualify for a premium reduction due to improvement in health, cessation of smoking, etc.; (3) review the policy's beneficiary designation to see if it is are up to date and reflects the policy owner's current desires; (4) ascertain the amount of current loans or withdrawals against the policy, and determine their effect on the policy's future performance and death benefit payout; and (5) consider all the possible "exit" strategies if the policy owner no longer desires or can no longer afford to retain the policy, such as a surrender of the policy, purchasing extended term coverage, electing reduced paid up coverage, an IRC section 1035 exchange to an annuity, or a life settlement. *Id.* at section VII.

"An in-force illustration is an updated projection of an existing policy. By incorporating known historical performance data from purchase to the date the in-force illustration is run, and then projecting policy performance forward based on assumptions, an up-to-date projection can be obtained showing how the policy actually performed in the past and how, using actual past performance as a base, the policy is likely to perform in the future. A policy owner has a right to obtain an in-force illustration without cost from his agent or broker on an annual basis. By reviewing in-force illustrations, the policy can be monitored to see if it is performing as expected. It is an invaluable tool for gauging required premium payments, accumulations of cash values, and the effect of loans on policy performance. By monitoring a policy through review of in-force illustrations, under performance can be discovered and appropriate adjustments made to insure the policy stays in force without fear of lapsing." Lee and Wilkey at section VII, A.

death benefit stays level but the premium increases every year. Annual renewable term is most appropriate for short term coverage, typically five years or less. If coverage for a longer period is desired, it may be less expensive to purchase level term. Because of the increasing premium costs and lack of cash value, annual renewable term is generally not suitable for an ILIT.

• **Level Term.** Level term life insurance is written for a fixed death benefit with a guaranteed level annual premium for a period of years (5, 10, 20, or 30 years). Popular types include ten year convertible and renewable term, twenty year convertible and renewable term, and term to age 65. At the end of the term, the insured must apply for new insurance if needed, or may be able to continue coverage on a year to year basis under the existing policy by paying an annual term rate premium (which can be cost prohibitive depending on the insured's age).

• **Decreasing Term.** Decreasing term life insurance is also known as "declining balance term" and is frequently sold by life insurance companies as "mortgage insurance" to pay off an insured's mortgage if he or she dies during the term of the loan. Premiums remain constant over the period of coverage, but the amount of life insurance coverage decreases annually. In addition to providing mortgage pay off protection, these policies are generally used to provide a surviving spouse with a fixed monthly income for a specified period of time and are often used to assure college education for children.

• **Modified Term.** Modified term life insurance is usually set up to function as term insurance for five to ten years and then to automatically convert to permanent insurance.

§16.3(b) Whole Life Insurance[21]

Whole life insurance is the oldest form of "permanent"[22] (or cash value) insurance and features premiums that are level (rather than

[21] "*Advantages Of Whole Life Insurance:* (1) It guarantees a level premium, minimum cash value and minimum death benefit. (2) The quasi-compulsory nature of whole life (pay the premiums when due or else the policy lapses) removes the temptation to skip premium payments, which can result in future funding problems. (3) Because a whole life premium is fixed, policy owners can be more certain about cash flow planning. (4) Policy owners are not involved with the personal management of the underlying investment assets. The insurer's bond and mortgage portfolio of assets held in the general account is managed by investment professionals and is intended to provide relatively stable results. (5) Because it is a relatively simple product to administer, whole life may tend to have somewhat lower long-term expenses than variable life, although its initial charges are often higher.

increasing with age) and a guaranteed cash value and a guaranteed death benefit. As a general rule, premiums are payable for the "whole life" of the insured or until the policy endows, usually at age 100.[23] Thus, whole life has a much higher initial premium than term insurance; however, as the insured ages, the premiums for term insurance increase and eventu-

---

Disadvantages Of Whole Life Insurance: (1) Because conservative assumptions are used with a whole life policy, its premium level, while guaranteed, is high compared to the potential cost of a universal life or variable universal life policy. Blending term with whole life can bring the initial premium more in-line. However, as more term insurance is used, the guarantees of whole life weaken. Furthermore, few insurance companies guarantee their term rates on this rider and the paid-up additions that are intended to replace the term insurance are based on dividends that are also not guaranteed. (2) There is much less premium flexibility with whole life than with universal life or variable universal. (3) Whole life does not have the capability for face amount increases or decreases. If additional coverage is needed, a new policy has to be bought, generally resulting in duplicative charges. (4) The whole life contract is a bundled product using a black-box approach. The policy components are not clearly defined which makes it more difficult for the policy owner to analyze the reasonableness of the underlying policy design assumptions in the sales illustration. (5) Since it has no investment options, whole life provides no investment flexibility to policy owners." Wilshinsky at 57. (Citations omitted.)

[22] All permanent insurance has two components: (1) a term (i.e., the net amount at risk ("NAR")) component, and (2) and a cash value (i.e., the investment) component. Thus, all permanent life insurance is term insurance coupled with an investment component.

[23] A whole life insurance policy "endows" when its cash value equals the policy's original face amount. When this occurs, the policy owner receives the face amount in cash. The amount of the endowment proceeds that exceed the owner's basis in the policy will be taxed as ordinary income, which can create a significant income tax liability. Assuming all policy payments have been made, endowment of a whole life insurance policy is structured to occur when the insured attains age 100, since mortality tables generally assume that all insured have died by age 100. The life insurance company can offer the assurance that the whole life policy will endow since the life insurance company is assured of receiving each year's premium in order to endow. Universal life policies endow at a given age (usually 85, 90, or 95) at the policy's then existing cash value amount; and depending on premium payments and policy performance, a universal policy's cash value amount can be substantially less than the original face amount of the policy. *See,* section 16.3(c), below, for a discussion of universal life.

Many life insurance companies now offer policies that "endow" at age 115, thus avoiding the income tax problem when an insured "out lives" his or her policy. *See,* Howard J. Saks, "Life Insurance Policies With Contractual Maturity Beyond Age 100 More Widely Available," 24 *Estate Planning* 186 (May 1997); Howard J. Saks, "True 'Whole of Life' Coverage Is Recognized as New Insurance Policy Is Introduced," 21 *Estate Planning* 371 (November/December 1994).

ally become "prohibitive" if the insured has a long life span. In a traditional whole life policy (also referred to as an "ordinary whole life policy"), the premiums are structured so that the combination of the premium payments and the guaranteed minimum crediting rate will result in the policy reserves equaling the original face amount of the policy at age 100. The assumptions used by life insurance companies in pricing traditional whole life products are generally more conservative than, for example, the (more aggressive) assumptions currently used to price no-lapse/secondary guarantee universal life.

The level premium system results in the life insurance company collecting more in a policy's early years than the company needs to pay claims in those years. In the policy's later years, increased mortality results in less being collected than needed to pay claims, but the shortfall is covered by the earnings on the excess premiums collected in the earlier years.

Premium payments are divided between risk protection (mortality charges) and a savings or investment account. The savings or investment account is typically composed of long term bonds and mortgages selected by the life insurance company, and the investments are part of the life insurance company's general investment account that is available to its creditors if the life insurance company should experience financial problems. The risk protection (mortality charges) represents pure term insurance and the investment portion acts as a savings account inside the policy, commonly known as cash value.[24] Premium payments also are applied to the life insurance company's load/expenses. *See,* section 16.4, below. Each year the policy is in force the amount at risk (the pure term insurance component)

---

[24] "In many ways, cash value is the measure of product stability and an indicator of the viability of the product in terms of being able to deliver long term performance. Although it may be tempting to structure a policy with a minimum of cash to maximize the internal rate of return on the death benefit, unless there is a premature death, contracts funded at lower premium levels generally provide lower future values and are more prone to lapse. In most policies cash value growth serves a dual role of enhancing policy performance by reducing the net amount at risk in a policy—the pure death benefit amount against which insurance charges are applied. The one exception is for increasing death benefit universal life products (option B) where the net amount at risk remains level throughout the life of the product. Finally, the cash value represents the policy asset value that can be exchanged for a new policy if the policyholder becomes dissatisfied with the current carrier. A policy can be terminated for the cash surrender value or the cash surrender value can be used in a §1035 exchange to obtain another life insurance policy or an annuity product." Lee and Wilkey at section V, B, 3, a.

decreases and the cash value (investment component) increases. Each year the increase in the policy's cash value component offsets the amount of pure term insurance coverage that is needed to provide the death benefit. Together, the pure term insurance component and the (increasing) cash value component provide the death benefit. The cash value is a liquid asset available to the owner of the policy through borrowing or surrendering the policy. *See*, sections 2.16 and 2.18, above. The year by year build-up of cash value through dividends or interest credited to the policy is usually free from current income taxes because of tax favored treatment. *See*, section 2.15, above. When the policy is surrendered for its cash value, income taxes are due only on the amount that exceeds the total premium paid less tax free dividends received, if any. *See*, section 2.18, above.

In traditional whole life[25] the premiums remains level, and the company cannot increase the premiums to reflect actual mortality experience.[26] *See*, section 16.4, below. However, the illustrated premium structure which forms the basis on which many whole life policies are sold assumes that the company will credit the cash value of the policy with annual dividends[27] or interest in excess of the guaranteed rate. Such excess dividends or interest may be used to offset the premiums, thereby decreasing the number of years that premiums must be paid

---

[25] *See*, Chapter 13 of Leimberg & Doyle; and ¶1.03 of Zaritsky and Leimberg.

[26] Some whole life policies have a modified premium format, whereby the premium increases by 50% or 100% in the 11th or 16th policy years, respectively.

[27] A participating whole life policy may pay dividends. Dividends reflect better investment, mortality and expense results than are used in determining the premium. *See*, section 16.2(a), below. Dividends are considered a tax free return of premium to the extent they do not exceed the premiums paid unto the policy. *See*, section 2.15, above. Dividends are not guaranteed. The dividends can generally be applied in several ways: (1) be paid in cash to the policy owner; (2) be used to reduce the next premium payment; (3) purchase paid-up (single premium) additional insurance coverage; (4) be held by the carrier in an interest bearing account for the benefit of the policy owner; (5) be used to purchase units of one year term insurance (typically equal to the cash value amount in the policy), and (6) be used to reduce policy loans. Dividends are most commonly used, however, to purchase paid-up additional insurance coverage that will increase the death benefit or to reduce the premiums with the death benefit remaining level. It is the paid-up additions that generate values and death benefits in excess of those guaranteed by the policy.

by the policy owner before the premiums "vanish."[28] However, the vanish date is not guaranteed. The company may reduce the amount of dividends or interest credited to the policy to a minimum guaranteed level if it is unable to attain the illustrated investment yield, or if expenses increase, or if it experiences increased mortality. As a result, the number of years that the premium must be paid can increase substantially over that illustrated if the policy is to be kept in force for the insured's lifetime. Moreover, if the product is current assumption (interest sensitive) whole life, premiums can be adjusted up to a guaranteed maximum.

Whole life is well suited for a policy owner who wants permanent protection, fixed premium payments, and guarantees with respect to the cash value account and the death benefit amount. Thus an extremely "conservative" policy owner will generally find the whole life to be within the policy owner's accepted level of (no or low) risk tolerance.

§16.3(b)(1) Popular Types Of Whole Life Insurance

The major variations of whole life insurance are discussed below.

• **Limited-Pay Whole Life.**[29] Traditional whole life insurance features a level premium payable for the insured's lifetime or until the policy endows. In limited-pay whole life, the level premium is designed to be

---

[28] A great virtue of whole life is that once the dividends comfortably exceed the (fixed) premium, they can be used to reduce the premium and then buy paid-up additions. The insured can be fairly certain that while no further premiums will be required, the values and benefits will continue to grow. Cash payment of premiums can actually become unnecessary earlier than just mentioned if policy values and dividends can meet the required premiums without the policy's death benefit ever dropping below the initial face amount. This technique is known as "vanishing premium." The premiums do not really vanish; they simply are paid by the policy and not by the policy owner. Some mistakenly assume that the policy is fully "paid-up" at that point; i.e., that the company has guaranteed that it has received all of the premium it needs to maintain the death benefit. This assumption is not valid. Technically and contractually, the premiums do not vanish. The "vanish" depicted in an illustration is merely the company's projection that as of a certain time, the policy's cash values and dividends/excess credits will be sufficient to pay the premiums internally and still maintain the death benefit. Again, these are only projections, which are exquisitely sensitive to assumptions about mortality, interest, lapses and expenses. It is pure conjecture as to when cash premiums will no longer be required and whether premiums, once vanished, might subsequently reappear.

[29] *See*, Chapter 12 of Leimberg & Doyle; and ¶1.04 of Zaritsky and Leimberg.

payable over a period shorter than the insured's lifetime. Since the life insurance company must collect the same actuarial amount under either type of policy in order to create the required reserves but has a much shorter period of time, the premiums payable for the same protection under a limited-pay whole life policy are greater than those payable under a traditional whole life policy providing the same protection. In a true limited pay policy, the number of premiums payments is guaranteed. This is in contrast to a "vanishing" premium, where the number of premium payments is not guaranteed.

• **Single Premium Whole Life.**[30] Single premium whole life insurance is a form of limited-pay whole life insurance that requires only a one-time premium payment. Once that payment is made, no further premium payments are required to keep the policy in force for the insured's entire life. All single premium life insurance policies purchased on or after June 20, 1988 are likely to be classified as a modified endowment contract ("MEC") under IRC section 7702A, and are subject to special income tax rules. *See,* sections 2.15 to 2.18, above.

• **Current Assumption Whole Life.**[31] Current assumption whole life, also known as "interest sensitive whole life," features a level premium that remains fixed for only a specified period of time, usually three to five years. At the end of the three to five year period, the amount of the premium, and possibly the amount of the death benefit, will be redetermined based on the actual cash value of the policy, which is a function of the crediting rate declared by the insurance company during that fixed period. Since the crediting rate is a function of the investment return of the insurance company on its interest-sensitive block of policies, as well as expenses and mortality experience, an interest-sensitive policy is actually sensitive not only to investment performance but to all risk factors, including expense and mortality experience. *See,* section 16.4, below. If investment performance, expenses and mortality experiences are poor, the insurance company may increase the premium up to a guaranteed maximum, represented by the minimum interest guarantee and the maximum mortality charges set forth in the policy.

If the insurance company *increases* the premium, the policy owner has the option to:

---

[30] *See,* Chapter 14 of Leimberg & Doyle; and ¶1.10 of Zaritsky and Leimberg.

[31] *See,* Chapter 9 of Leimberg & Doyle; and ¶1.08 of Zaritsky and Leimberg. Current assumption whole life is essentially the same as a participating whole life policy, except that the better results are reflected in excess interest credits rather than dividends.

(1) Continue paying premiums at the old level and receive a reduced death benefit;

(2) Pay the increased premium and keep the death benefit level; or,

(3) If there is sufficient cash surrender value, pay premiums at the old level and augment those payments through use of the policy's cash values.

If the life insurance company *reduces* the premium, the owner has the option to:

(1) Continue paying premiums at the old level and increase the death benefit, subject to proof of insurability;

(2) Continue paying premiums at the old level, keep the death benefit level, and increase the cash value of the policy, effectively creating a "vanishing" premium once cash values increase to the requisite level; or,

(3) Pay a lower premium and keep the death benefit level.

• **Blended Whole Life/Term Insurance.**[32] Blended whole life/term insurance is a combination of whole life insurance (often referred to as the "base") and term insurance. Blending is used to reduce the total premiums required to maintain a desired amount of death benefit, permanently.[33]

The whole life portion of the blend offers the guarantees associated with that product. The term element offers low-cost coverage, but the term rates can be subject to marked increases up to a very costly guaranteed maximum under the policy. In a blended policy, the total death benefit is comprised of the guaranteed death benefit from the whole life, paid-up additions, and the term insurance. Thus, the blended product is designed so that dividends or interest paid on the whole life base will be used to buy paid up additions (additional blocks or units of paid up whole life insurance) that will ultimately replace the

---

[32] *See*, Chapter 16 of Leimberg & Doyle; and Glenn S. Daily, "The Basics of Blending," *NAPFA Advisor* (August 1997), http://www.glenndaily.com/fiduciaries.htm.

[33] "An alternative to a whole life/term blend product where a permanent product is desired but budget constraints exist, is to purchase a universal life policy funded at a minimum premium level that approximates a term policy. So long as the cash value remains at a sufficient level to pay mortality costs and administrative expenses, the coverage will remain in force. Premiums can be increased to make the product more stable in later years when budget constraints no longer exist." Lee and Wilkey at Section III C 4.

term insurance component.[34] Consequently, dividend/interest performance on the whole life base is extremely important.

While it is a common misconception that because of the term element, a blended contract carries more risk than an "all base" contract, a blended contract is in fact subject to less risk of underperformance, at the same premium outlay and face amount, than a non-blended contract. Assuming equal premium outlays and death benefits, a blended policy will have greater cash value than a non-blended contract, because blending reduces internal policy loads and commissions, and potential surrender charges. Blending will enhance cash value and minimize surrender charges, as quickly as possible.[35]

With both a base contract and a blended contract, the policy owner is subject to risks associated with poor mortality or interest/investment experience. There have not, historically, been increases in COI (cost of insurance) charges for mortality. If there were, such increases could occur in the base contract too. Theoretically, a life insurance company might be able to increase term rider premiums because of poor mortality experience, without also increasing the base COI in the same way, but life insurance companies have not done so.

---

[34] The caveat with the blend is that if the dividends or crediting rate drops and/or term charges rise, the replacement of the term component will take longer, perhaps much longer. In some cases, additional premium would be required to maintain the death benefit if dividends or the crediting rate fall far enough and fast enough. So, to cushion the policy for adequate performance under lower dividends or crediting rates, it is common to add a "paid-up additions rider" or add additional premium that buys paid-up additional insurance at virtually net rates. These riders or additional premium can be a very cost-effective way for the policyholder to create a strong policy.

[35] The use of a term rider with base whole life, universal life, or variable life coverage can significantly reduce total out of pocket outlay and the level of annual premiums. The use of a term rider can significantly enhance early cash values, reduce policy loads and commissions, and alternatively enhance the death benefit and help the policy owner fund the policy with lower total outlays. *See,* Charles L. Ratner, "Life Insurance Policy Replacements: Real Peanuts or Just a Shell Game?," 139 *Trust and Estate* 12 (April 2000). The safest plan may be to use a policy with a substantial term/base blend but fund it aggressively, especially in the early years, with outlays based on all-base design, and on a conservative dividend, interest, or return rate.

§16.3(c) Universal Life[36]

Universal life was developed in the late 1970s in response to rising interest rates in the money market. Universal life classically illustrates the separate term component and cash value component of permanent insurance.

Universal life allows the insured to literally buy term insurance and invest the rest within the same policy. The hallmark of universal life is its flexibility; the flexibility to design the policy at the outset to

---

[36] *See*, Chapter 17 of Leimberg & Doyle; and ¶1.06 of Zaritsky and Leimberg; and Howard J. Saks, "Comparing Universal Life and Whole Life Policies for Both Individual and Survivorship Insurance Needs," 21 *Estate Planning* 312 (September/October 1994).

"*Advantages Of Universal Life:* (1) Universal life has premium flexibility, which can be easily tailored to the policy owner's cash flow needs. (2) Universal life offers a relatively low initial premium. Because it uses current assumptions and not guarantees in establishing a premium level, the going-in costs may be much lower than those for whole life. (3) Universal life has death benefit flexibility. There are definite cost savings if the policy face amount is increased rather than having to purchase a brand new policy for additional coverage. Should projected, future estate settlement costs warrant lower taxes, the face amount can be easily decreased and the premium adjusted downwards without the expense of surrendering a portion of the policy. (4) Universal life is more explicit and transparent in its charges than whole life, wherein sales illustrations and the actual policy will explicitly state the current and guaranteed maximum charges. Annual universal life policy statements show the amount of credited interest and the actual expense and mortality charges deducted during the policy year. (5) Universal life has no investment options, so its expenses may be somewhat less than those associated with a variable universal life product. (6) As an interest-sensitive product with a guaranteed minimum interest rate, universal life has cash value build-ups that will always increase (at least the 4 - 5 percent guaranteed rate). Since there are no investment choices, management of the investment aspects of the product is left with the insurance company and not the policy owner.

Disadvantages Of Universal Life: (1) Universal life offers fewer guarantees than whole life. (2) Universal life often requires closer monitoring than whole life. Its premium flexibility can often tempt policy owners to skip payments or pay less than was initially determined to be prudent relying upon higher interest earnings higher future payments being made, if needed. (3) When features like the guaranteed minimum death benefit are used, the potential lower cost of universal life versus whole life often disappears or becomes less significant. (4) Since the interest rate credited to universal life is based on the company's general account, a portfolio of primarily short-term and intermediate-term bonds, the policy's cash value performance is limited. (5) Because there are no investment options, there is no investment flexibility for policy owners." Wilshinsky at 58.

meet a certain objective and then to reshape the policy to suit changing circumstances. The premium payments for a universal life policy are not fixed. In all other forms of permanent insurance, premiums are payable for the insured's life (or for a shorter fixed period when limited-pay whole life is involved) in fixed amounts and on a fixed schedule. Thus, while the insured is young, the policy owner can pay "less" premium in order to maintain the term insurance component. As the insured ages and the term insurance component costs increase, the policy owner will (presumably) have more income available to pay premiums in excess of the term insurance cost. This flexibility demonstrates one of the key differences between universal life and traditional whole life (which requires a constant level premium).

Another aspect of a universal policy's flexibility is that the policy owner can raise or lower the death benefit without getting a new policy. However, increases in death benefit coverage usually require new evidence of insurability. Thus, a universal life policy owner can adjust the amount of savings and death benefits as he or she determines (within prescribed limits).

Universal life, which is often referred to as "flexible premium adjustable life,"[37] features premiums in which both the frequency and

---

[37] "Universal life ('UL') is a 'flexible-premium' 'current assumption' 'adjustable death benefit' type of ...[permanent insurance]. These contracts are also referred to as flexible premium adjustable life....UL is indicated in long-term coverage needs where maximum flexibility of premium cash flow is desired, and where the insured's financial needs and cash flow are likely to change. This makes UL suitable in the business, retirement planning, and employee benefits fields to finance salary continuation and nonqualified deferred compensation plans, death benefit only plans, key person coverage, buy-sell agreements, and insurance inside qualified retirement plans." Malarkey and Leimberg at 8 and 9.

"[A]s the term 'flexible premium adjustable life' suggests, the policy owner can pay whatever premium he or she chooses to pay, within certain limits. The amount of premium paid can be changed at any time, and premium payments can even be skipped if there is enough cash value to pay for the equivalent of the term coverage provided under the contract. Skipping premiums is not treated as the creation of a policy loan....[A]s the term 'current assumption' suggests, current interest rates, as well as current mortality and expense charges, are directly and immediately reflected in the policy cash values....[A]s the term 'adjustable death benefit' suggests, the policy death benefits can be increased or decreased at the policy owner's demand. Increases typically require evidence of continued insurability." Zaritsky and Leimberg at ¶1.06[1].

Note: Adjustable life is a flexible premium life insurance product that is a hybrid of traditional whole life and universal life. With the introduction of universal life, the popularity of adjustable life has waned over the years. *See,* Chapter 7 of Leimberg & Doyle; and ¶1.09 of Zaritsky and Leimberg.

amount of premium payments are flexible within prescribed limits.[38] As typically structured, the planned universal life premium for a given death benefit is set considerably lower than the traditional whole life premium. Universal life, like whole life, may be designed with a blended policy design, combining a term rider and a base amount of coverage. The premium for a universal life policy is first applied to a sales load and then deposited into a "side fund" where it is credited interest at the insurer's current crediting rate. Monthly charges for administrative expenses and the cost of insurance on the amount at risk are then withdrawn from the side fund. There is a minimum guarantee (floor) on the crediting rate and a maximum guarantee (ceiling) on the cost-of-insurance.

Because universal life premiums are not fixed, the policy owner may skip making one or more premium payments as long as the cash value of the universal policy is sufficient to cover that month's mortality and expense charges.[39] Under a whole life policy, a skipped premium would be treated as a policy loan which would reduce the death benefit and result in an interest charge. Within certain limitations, the policy owner can also increase the universal life premiums through so-called "dump-ins" at sharply reduced loads, without evidence of insurability.

An unattended universal policy can create problems. For example, if the cash value of a universal life policy is allowed to drop to a low level, the future contributions that will be required to keep the policy in effect will be substantially similar to the cost of annually increasing term insurance, and the cost of maintaining the policy may become prohibitive. Moreover, if the cash value is allowed to drop below the level necessary to keep a universal life policy in force, the policy will terminate and a new policy will have to be purchased, with the premiums based on the current age and health of the insured. Thus, universal life does not guarantee any given death benefit beyond the first month or year of the policy unless sufficient premiums are

---

[38] By increasing premium payments the policy owner can increase his or her investment in the contract and the policy's cash value account. If the Option B/Option 2 payout is chosen, the cash value account and its earnings will be paid income tax free to the beneficiary as part of the death benefit.

[39] The universal life policy can be cushioned against an increase in mortality charges or a decrease in interest rates by paying a premium designed to endow the policy at an assumed interest rate lower than the life insurance company's current crediting rate. The result will be a policy that appears to the policy owner (and more particularly to his or her checkbook) like a whole life policy.

paid to maintain the cash value (known as the "accumulation account") at an adequate level to pay mortality and expense charges, which are deducted each month and can change over time.

In a universal policy, the policy owner can usually select between two death benefit payouts: (i) Option A/Option 1 (which is for the policy's face amount), or (ii) Option B/Option 2 (which is for the policy's face amount plus the balance of the policy's cash value account, thus providing a larger payout amount).[40] Such an option does not exist for the traditional whole life policy, which typically pays only the face amount.

The cash value account of a universal life policy is invested by the life insurance company, and is part of the company's general account. The policy owner does not control the investment of the policy's cash value. The cash value account is typically invested in short term fixed income investments, such as short term bonds (which in the 1980's were paying very high rates of interest and consequently policy owners were abandoning lower yielding policies, such as traditional whole life, for higher yielding universal life policies).[41] The policy owner has access to the policy's cash value via loans or withdrawals. In traditional whole life, the policy owner only has access to the policy's cash value via loans.

---

[40] With Option A/Option 1, the policyholder only pays cost-of-insurance charges (i.e., the net amount at risk) for the ever-decreasing difference between the initial face amount and the cash value. Option B/Option 2 is more expensive than an Option A/Option 1 payout because the policy owner must always pay the net amount at risk or cost-of-insurance to maintain the initial face amount of coverage without the cash value account being used as an offset to reduce the net amount at risk. The policyholder can change the death benefit option. For example, the policyholder may select an increasing death benefit for the first 16 years of the policy (i.e., an Option B/Option 2 payout) and then change to a level death benefit (i.e., an Option A/Option 1 payout). This approach allows the policyholder to pay more premium into the policy in the funding years. Option B/Option 2 is not available for a no lapse guarantee universal life policy.

[41] Some universal life ("UL") products, such as Equity Index Universal Life ("EIUL") have crediting rates that are based in part on the positive performance of an equity index, such as the S&P 500® (excluding dividends) with a guarantee that the crediting rate can never fall below a minimum percentage (such as 1%) in any given year when the index posts negative returns. As such, EIUL has a cap on the policy's upside performance (usually capped at 10% or 11%) and a floor (usually at 0% or 1%) on the downside performance, but does so with extra load/costs to the policy owner. EIUL is considered a market hedged product somewhere between traditional UL and secondary guarantee VUL.

Some universal life policies now combine long term care coverage as part of the insurance product. These policies provide both a death benefit and long term care coverage, in the event that the insured needs home care, nursing home care, etc. However, this type of combination policy is not suitable for an ILIT if the policy would pay long term care benefits to an insured. If the policy were to pay long term benefits (or make them available) to or for the benefit of the insured, the IRS may assert that the policy proceeds are includable in the insured's gross estate under IRC sections 2036 and 2042. [42]

In some universal products, back end loads result in cash values building more rapidly than in traditional whole life products. Most whole life policies recover initial policy costs (commissions, underwriting, etc.) from the initial premiums, a practice known as front-end

---

[42] One alternative for a surviving spouse desiring to purchase a combination universal life-long term care policy (a "combo policy") is to have a credit shelter (bypass) trust own the policy. Although, most credit shelter trusts allow distributions of income and principal to the surviving spouse, many affluent widows or widowers do not need the money from the credit shelter trust to maintain their standard of living. The ability to "leverage" the credit shelter trust with a combo policy is enhanced because no gift taxes are incurred as the credit shelter trust pays premiums for the combo policy. In addition, upon the surviving spouse's death, the insurance proceeds received by the credit shelter trust are both income and estate tax free. While this idea can conserve assets, offset future liquidity needs, and leverage more money for heirs, there are a few pitfalls to be avoided. First, the trust agreement must give the trustee the authority to purchase such a policy. Second, care must be taken so that the surviving spouse does not have an incident of ownership over the combo policy. If so, the insurance proceeds will be included in the surviving spouse's gross estate. If the surviving spouse is not the trustee, then IRC section 2042 would not be applicable provided the surviving spouse never owned the combo policy, did not transfer the combo policy to the trust, and did not transfer any of the consideration for the purchase or maintenance of the combo policy. If it is desirable for the surviving spouse to serve as trustee, then a co-trustee should also be named and all powers over the combo policy should be vested exclusively in the co-trustee. *See*, Rev. Rul. 84-179, 1984-2 C.B. 195. Third, if the credit shelter trust gives the surviving spouse a limited power of appointment, then the power should be drafted so that the power does not include any powers over the combo policy. *See*, Priv. Letter Ruls. 9111028 and 9602010. Finally, the fact that the surviving spouse is a beneficiary of the credit-shelter trust should not cause the proceeds of the policy on the surviving spouse's life to be included in his or her estate. *See*, Priv. Letter Rul. 9602010. In the case of a credit shelter trust desiring to acquire a combo policy, if the drafting techniques discussed above are not already in place, steps can be taken to eliminate the potential problems through modification of the insured's position or powers as trustee and/or full or partial release of his or her limited power of appointment.

loading or "heaped" commission structures. Some universal life policies defer recovery of initial policy costs until the later years of the policy (known as "back-end loading"), thereby permitting cash values to increase more rapidly. Universal life products typically have surrender charges that apply to reduce the policy's cash value if the policy is terminated within the first ten to fifteen years. As a practical matter, whole life policies have charges essentially equivalent to surrender charges, but they are not separately identified.

A universal life policy (the "base") can also be blended with term insurance. The universal life's death benefit may be comprised of a relatively low amount of base and a large amount of term rider. These policy designs can make universal products even more competitive than they otherwise might be.

A unique feature of universal life (and of variable universal life, discussed in section 16.3(e), below) is the transparency of the policy as a result of unbundled product disclosure. In a traditional whole life policy, the insured sees only the "end result" without a breakdown of what is occurring within the policy. In a universal life policy (including variable universal life policy), the various "working" elements (or risks, which are discussed in section 16.4, below) are disclosed and the policy owner sees the interaction of mortality charges/costs, expense loads, crediting rates, premium payments, etc. Transparency helps the policy owner understand how a thinly funded universal (including a variable universal) life policy can fail.

Since a universal policy permits the policy owner to minimize premium payments and to adjust the amount of payments, a universal policy is sensitive to the various risk factors discussed in section 16.4, below. Thus, the policy owner is subject to certain investment risks and mortality risks. Because of these risks and the policy's flexibility, from an ILIT trustee's "best practices" perspective, universal life insurance typically requires annual TOLI management.[43]

---

[43] *See,* Leimberg Newsletter #891. *See also,* Randolph Whitelaw and Richard M. Weber, "Trust-Owned Life Insurance: Risk Management Guidance for Fiduciaries," 32 *Estate Planning* 14 (September 2005), where the authors discuss the risk of liability for trustees who handle TOLI (especially non-guaranteed policies), and suggest a "best practices" standard of care with respect to TOLI risk management. According to the authors, a trustee's conduct of prudent investing is evaluated against a *process* standard – not a *performance* standpoint. Consequently, the prudent investor rule places great importance on the establishment, documentation and implementation of prudent decision-making procedures.

§16.3(c)(1) No Lapse Guarantee Universal Life

Many life insurance companies offer a no lapse guarantee rider that provides a lifetime (until death or a certain age selected by the insured, such as age 100) benefit even if the "traditional" universal life policy has no cash value, so long as a specified premium is paid when due and other conditions are met.[44] The no lapse guarantee rider is typ-

---

Of the many pitfalls that lay in wait for unsuspecting ILIT trustees are "flexible premium" non-guaranteed death benefit policies, such as universal life, variable universal life, and adjustable life. To be a flexible premium policy means that the policy owner has a contractual right to basically pay whatever premium he or she wants whenever he or she wants to maintain a positive account balance. Flexible premium policies have a guaranteed schedule of insurance charges, but allow the life insurance company to charge less than the guarantees when appropriate. The problem with these types of policies is that many ILIT trustees do not have the ability to actually calculate the needed premium schedule in order to maintain a 100% premium adequacy at the time of policy acceptance, as well as in subsequent years. Many ILIT trustees are less than diligent in their review of premium adequacy. Additionally, many trustees mistakenly rely upon the policy illustration in their file for this premium adequacy calculation. The mistake is that illustrations assume constant interest rates and the current scale of insurance charges, while in reality, market conditions and actual interest returns, among other factors, dictate the future cost of insurance charges. A common result of the ILIT trustee's faulty reliance upon policy illustrations is a situation where the grantor has to make larger than expected gifts (or loans) to the ILIT in order to sustain the flexible premium policy. Failure to pay the increased premium can either cause the policy to lapse in the near future or to substantially shorten its guarantees. Some of the steps that ILIT trustees can take in order to reduce criticism of their acquisition of a flexible premium life insurance product are:

(1) Be involved in the policy selection. Focus on the product suitability, particularly the premium adequacy for the life of the grantor.

(2) Ignore in-force illustrations as accurate determinations for future premium adequacy.

(3) Prior to the ILIT's receipt or acquisition of a flexible premium non-guaranteed policy, receive confirmation from the grantor of the policy's suitability as well as current and future premium adequacy issues.

(4) Confirm annually that: (a) the scheduled premiums are adequate to sustain the policy to the insured's life expectancy; (b) the policy is performing up to the expectations of the insured; and (c) the insurance carrier's third-party financial ratings are stable.

(5) With regard to policies with investment options, such as variable policies (including variable universal life), the trustee should always be aware of the asset allocation strategy to ensure that it meets the insured's objectives and the prudent investor rule.

[44] A no lapse guarantee rider is typically attached to a traditional universal life policy, and modifies the policy.

ically available up to ages 100 through 120, as selected by the policy owner. Regardless of the policy owner's cash flow situation, the specified premiums must be paid in "good" times and in "bad" times—there is no flexibility. These no lapse guarantee riders offer relatively inexpensive permanent death benefit guarantees, coupled with significantly lower (or no) cash value increases.[45] No lapse guarantee life insurance functions like owning term insurance to whatever age the guarantee has been established by the insured (typically between ages 100 - 120). In addition, many life insurance companies are now offer-

---

[45] *See,* Malarkey and Leimberg concerning no lapse guarantee universal life insurance ("NLGUL").

"In the opinion of many, the NLGUL asset class is unique. It features (relatively inexpensive) permanent death benefit guarantees at the expense of cash value performance. Analytically, NLGUL policies typically offer very attractive guaranteed death benefit internal rates of return ("IRR") up to, and a bit past, life expectancy. (It is not uncommon to see these death benefit IRRs approach, and exceed, an after-tax rate of 7% even beyond life expectancy.) WL [whole life] and UL death benefit returns may be (or may not be, depending on the case) projected to be as favorable, but the illustrated WL and UL death benefit returns will assuredly carry the assumption of performance risk by the policy owner....Some argue that it is prudent to think of NLGUL policies as largely illiquid. The reason is that it is unlikely that these contracts will have a cash value that is attractive for any other possible uses in the future—due to the projected underperformance of the cash value. The lack of a significant cash value is clearly a disadvantage if a cash value that can be rolled over to another new product innovation is desired in the future. Nevertheless, most who use NLGUL are not uncomfortable with the illiquidity, given the relatively certain shifting of permanent death benefit risk to the insurance carrier. Further, proponents argue that, in many cases of trust-owned insurance, the existence of a notable cash value is, at best, a secondary bonus to a family, given that the cash is likely to have been tied up in trust anyway....Finally, the last potential disadvantage of NLGUL is that, while the death benefit is likely to have relatively little downside, NLGUL is also less likely than alternative contracts to have a notable performance upside in the event of rising interest rates, or bull equity markets (which could positively drive the WL/UL and VUL [variable universal life] markets, respectively). Those who favor NLGUL would counter that the lack of upside is a fair trade-off for the very attractive "locked-in" IRR at death. Obviously, an NLGUL contract is most appealing and appropriate for clients seeking to assure the financial security of future generations through the most cost-and tax-effective and economically certain wealth transfer mechanism possible....But because of NLG's illiquidity and consequent lack of flexibility, in most cases clients will be best served by using NLG as a relatively modest portion of an insurance portfolio that is carefully diversified across carriers, products, and cash value/death benefit performance projections." Malarkey and Leimberg at 13-14.

ing "secondary guarantee"[46] universal life products that are pure no lapse UL policies from their inception (i.e., there is no rider concerning the no lapse guarantee) that are similarly designed to maintain the death benefit even if the policy's cash value is zero so long as premium payment requirements continue to be met, in essence, providing a "term to age 100 or beyond" type of product. Currently, these products are favorably priced, however, pressure for the life insurance company to maintain an appropriate reserve level may cause no lapse/secondary guarantee universal life policies to come more in line with traditional universal life product pricing in the future.[47]

No lapse/secondary guarantee[48] universal life policies are attractive to policy owners who: (1) are typically 75 years or older, i.e., they are less likely to be concerned about changes that would affect the desirability of holding on to a policy with a low cash value, (2) have sufficient liquidity and capital outside of the no guarantee lapse policy, i.e., they are not dependent on the policy's cash value for their future living expenses, (3) are not overly concerned with the life insurance company's claims paying ability ratings, i.e., they are risk takers, (4) understand the inflexibility of the policy and the potential losses involved in a lapse of the policy, (5) are committed to funding the policy for its specified duration, (6) expect to die sooner than the expiration of the no lapse guarantee period, which is typically between ages 100 through 120, (7) do not want premium increases, i.e., they want to pay a certain fixed premium amount, (8) are concerned about the low (or decreasing) interest rates in the fixed income market, (9) are concerned about premiums that were/are supposed to "vanish" but have (or will) not, (10) are concerned about the lackluster/underperformance of variable life and variable universal life products, (11) plan to hold the policy until their death and are (presumably) not concerned with the policy's cash value amount, i.e., they do not plan to

---

[46] This guaranty is in addition to the life insurance company's guarantee with regard to its minimum crediting rate, maximum mortality costs, and maximum load expenses; hence the name "secondary guarantee." Some life insurance companies also offer a secondary guarantee VUL product, but in doing so may limit the type of sub-account investments available to the policy owner. These secondary guarantee VUL policies are referred to a "Guaranteed Variable Universal Life."

[47] However, life insurance companies domiciled or doing business in New York are now required to hold higher reserves for no-lapse/secondary guarantee universal policies.

[48] The term "no lapse/secondary guarantee," refers collectively to both a "traditional" UL policy with a no lapse guarantee rider, and to a secondary guarantee UL policy.

withdraw or borrow from the policy, and (12) are an ILIT trustee who understands the risks inherent in a no-lapse guarantee policy and has received appropriate exculpatory language in the ILIT.[49]

Some commentators[50] have recommended caution in purchasing no lapse/secondary guarantee universal life policies for several reasons,

---

[49] *See*, John T. Bannen, "No Lapse/Secondary Guarantee Life Insurance Policies: What Are They, And Are They Appropriate For Estate Planning?," 12 *ALI-ABA Estate Planning Course Materials Journal* 5 (June 2006). *See*, Paragraph 7.1(D)(2) of Sample ILIT for sample exculpatory language.

[50] *See, e.g.,* Peter Katt, "The Potential Problems with No-Lapse Premium Guarantees," XXV *AAII Journal* 33 (July 2003), http://www.peterkatt.com/articles/AAII_jul2003.html. In his article, Mr. Katt opines that no lapse premium guarantee ("NLPG") universal policies "should not be used: (i) in place of term insurance; (ii) for designs that require large cash values; (iii) when increasing death benefits are needed; or (iv) when there is much of a chance that future premium payments will be missed." According to Mr. Katt, "It is liquidity for estate taxes that puts NLPGs on its natural turf. Compared to market-priced policies with a defined-benefit design [such as participating whole life and traditional universal life policies], NLPGs have one potential advantage, two potential disadvantages and one potential disaster, [as follows]:

- The static-pricing [i.e., fixed premium amount] of NLPGs provide premium certainty. Future pricing factors (primarily fixed-income yields), in retrospect, may cause market-priced policies' premiums to be consistently higher than NLPG guaranteed premiums. **Advantage NLPG**.
- If fixed-income yields increase, market-priced policies [such as participating whole life and traditional universal life] may turn out to be a much better value. **Advantage market-priced policies.**
- Market-priced policies have much higher cash values that can be withdrawn, borrowed, or available upon termination. **Advantage market-priced policies.**
- NLPG policies can become such a good deal that the [life insurance] company becomes insolvent and is seized. **NLPG disaster.** " *Id.* (Emphasis added.)

"If the cash surrender value must be accessed for lifetime needs by policy loans or withdrawals, the guarantee may be forfeited or reduced. A guaranteed policy is relatively inflexible and involves a greater solvency bet on the carrier than exists with a variable policy. Some observers question whether the carriers can financially support the aggressive guarantees they are making in certain blocks of business. The terms of the guarantee are generally complex. The policy will be relatively rigid with regard to the amount and timing of premium payments. The carriers do not typically notify a policyholder of a change in or loss of the guarantee. Such policies, therefore, require careful monitoring. If the Code §1035 exchange amount paid to the policy at the outset varies from the amount originally estimated, the guarantee may be shortened or ineffective. Illustrations need to be examined after the policy is issued. In-force illustrations need to be reviewed to confirm continuing guarantees. Underwriting may also

including: (1) the additional premium cost of the no-lapse or second guarantee rider, (2) the policy's lower or non-existent cash value (a possible concern if the policy lapses due to the non-payment of premiums, or if the policy owner wants to restructure or exchange the policy for an different type of life insurance policy), (3) the lack of premium payment flexibility (however, the required minimum premium will not increase and is lower than in a non-guaranteed universal life policy), (4) the policy's low crediting rate will prevent it from sharing in any meaningful increase (upside) if the carrier's crediting rate or dividend rate increases with regard to its other products, and (5) the possible danger identified by Moody's in a Special Comment issued in July, 2004, in which the rating service expressed its concern over the effect that "aggressively priced" no lapse guarantees create significant losses that impact the company's profitability and ability to pay claims. Shortly thereafter, Fitch Ratings downgraded two of Pacific Life Corp's insurance subsidiaries, citing among other reasons potential risks from being a market leader in universal life policies with no lapse riders.[51]

---

be more variable between carriers than is the case with non-guaranteed policies. In short, there are a multitude of questions that should be analyzed carefully in advance of purchase having to do with the definition and mechanics of the guarantee, such as: (1) What happens to the guarantee at age 100? (2) What happens to the guarantee with post-issue policy changes? (3) Can the guarantee be restored, and if so how? (4) What are the restrictions on the guarantee? (5) What is the effect of the guarantee on current assumption performance? In many cases, after review a client may decide that he or she is better off with a well-designed, flexible premium policy that is monitored appropriately and is well funded." Jane A. Hays, "What Every Estate Planner Needs To Know About Life Insurance," *Estate Planning for Illinois Attorneys: The Basics and Beyond 2005 Edition,* Section 12.22 (Illinois Institute For Continuing Legal Education, Springfield, IL, 2005).

[51] *See,* John T. Bannen, "No Lapse Guarantee Life Insurance Policies: The Answer to an Insured's Payer or a Fiduciary Nightmare?," 30 *ACTEC Journal* 246 (Spring 2005). However, in August 2006, Pacific Life raised its premiums for its no lapse guarantee universal life products.

"Clients and their advisors who are contemplating policy restructuring should consider contemporary policy options, which in turn often depend on the age and health of the insured. For example, it may be more effective from the standpoint of ongoing premiums/gifts to consider exchanging account values (assuming the insured is insurable on a favorable basis) into a 'no-lapse' guarantee universal life policy. At best, no-lapse guarantee policies provide the advantage of an attractively low, guaranteed premium, and seemingly offer the best features of whole life (guaranteed premiums) and universal life (lower premium outlay). While such [no-lapse guarantee] policies may well resolve the crisis of a failing policy, it's critical that the trustee understand what the [no-lapse guarantee] policy is and *is not.* It *is* equivalent to a level premium

These concerns underscore the importance of buying no lapse/secondary guarantee universal life insurance policy from a strong, highly rated life insurance company. In addition, borrowing from or making late premium payments to a no lapse/secondary guaranty policy will result in an increase in future premiums, which increase can far exceed the amount borrowed or paid late.

> **Caution:** When no lapse riders first became available, it was not uncommon for the rider to contain very strict requirements for the no lapse guarantee to remain in effect. Paying the rider premium just one day past the due date (but within the policy's premium payment grace period) would, in some instances, be sufficient for the rider to lapse and cause the policy owner to lose the no lapse/secondary guarantee. A policy loan or withdrawal could also affect the no lapse/secondary guarantee. Read the no lapse guarantee rider carefully and understand its requirements, restrictions, and premium payment timeliness requirements. Also, if possible, try to purchase the no-lapse insurance product from the parent life insurance company, rather than from a subsidiary, which may not be as financially secure as the parent company, or obtain a statement from the parent company that it stands behind the subsidiary's obligations.

> **Practice Point:** An ILIT trustee who owns a no lapse/secondary guarantee universal life policy must be careful to make sure premiums are paid on time in order to avoid triggering a "penalty" provision in a no-lapse/secondary guarantee policy. A late premium payment could reduce or terminate the no lapse/secondary guarantee, as well as reduce the death benefit amount. Therefore, the grantor should consider making *Crummey* contributions well in advance of the policy's anniversary date in order to provide the ILIT trustee with sufficient time to deposit the gift amount, send out the *Crummey* notices, and pay the premium prior to its due date. An especially cautious ILIT trustee may want to consider having the grantor gift an

---

term insurance policy with little or no cash value. It is *not* likely to develop any more death benefit than the stipulated death benefit, long-term cash values will be minimal or non-existent, and because these "secondary guarantees" may produce a strain on the carrier's reserves, only insurers with very strong financial strength ratings should be considered. These trade-offs require confirmation of current trust objectives and product suitability by the trust beneficiaries." Whitelaw and Weber at 24.

extra year of premium into the ILIT. The extra premium would act as a "reserve" fund (or "buffer") to be used if the grantor is late in making a *Crummey* contribution in subsequent years.

Practice Point: If split dollar funding may be used to reduce the insured's anticipated gifting (and gift tax consequences) then a policy with low or no cash value will be inflexible. A policy with a no lapse guarantee structure (as opposed to a policy with significant cash value) may therefore become seriously problematic, if any change becomes necessary in the split dollar funding plan. If it becomes desirable to temporarily suspend, reduce, or reallocate premium payments between the parties, then having as much policy cash value, as possible, becomes critically important to the successful management of the policy and the maintenance of the full death benefit.

§16.3(d) Variable Life Insurance[52]

All of the permanent insurance products discussed above (to wit, whole life and universal life) are general account policies, i.e., the

[52] *See*, Chapter 18 of Leimberg & Doyle; and ¶1.05 of Zaritsky and Leimberg.

"*Primary Advantages Of Variable Life*: (1) Variable universal life offers a relatively low initial premium to policy owners, compared to whole life. (2) Variable life provides the most growth potential of any type of life insurance so the opportunity exists for either the lowest cost or the most death benefit for the same premium level. Ibbotson Associates, Inc., has documented the relative historical performance of common stocks and bonds in a study of financial instruments over the past 70 years from December 31, 1925 to December 31, 1995. For most time periods, stocks, as represented by Standard and Poor's 500 Index, generally produced higher returns than bonds (the primary asset backing whole life and universal life policies) by 2 percent to 3 percent a year. In fact, the results of investing $1000 and letting it grow over this 70-year period clearly favored stocks, though they have also been more volatile in the short-term than bonds. (3) Variable universal life allows policy owners to determine the amount and timing of premiums within broad limits as well as increasing or decreasing the face amount. (4) Policy owners choose how their money is invested, so they have more investment flexibility compared with whole life or universal life. (5) Variable life also provides that amounts not in the guaranteed interest account are protected from the claims of the insurer's general creditors in the event of a company insolvency. (6) Like universal life, variable universal life clearly discloses the charges in the policy. Since variable life insurance is considered to be a security, prospective buyers get a prospectus that describes policy charges in some detail. The annual policy statement shows the investment component (customarily referred to the cash value) of the policies is represented by assets which are part of the life insurance company's general fund and the investments are controlled by the life insurance company. Variable life insurance, which was first introduced in 1976, is a form of permanent insurance, and is often viewed as a sort of mutual fund that is used to purchase life insurance coverage. The cash value of a variable policy may be allocated to legally separated investment accounts that are invested and administered by the life insurance company but the investments are selected (and monitored) by the owner of the policy from a group of funds made available within the product design.[53] The owner has the option to allocate cash value among a guaranteed fixed account (which is not a security) as well as to various mutual fund-like investments (known as "sub-accounts"), such as:

- Stocks (aggressive, conservative, and blend);
- Bonds (short term, mid term, and long term);
- Government securities;
- Total Return Accounts (stocks, bonds, cash, and so on);
- Money market accounts;
- International accounts; and
- Real estate accounts.

---

actual expenses charged during the policy year as well as the investment performance of any options with money allocated to them.

Primary Disadvantages Of Variable Life: (1) The biggest disadvantage of variable universal life is investment risk. Some policy owners will not have the risk tolerance for variable life because they fear coverage may lapse or higher premiums will be necessary if investment performance is poor (less than originally illustrated). (2) The age and/or health of some insureds will suggest that the long-term growth potential of stocks may not have adequate time to work to their advantage. (3) Because of the potential for negative investment returns and the fact that premiums can be easily skipped, there is a greater need to monitor the policy's investment performance than with whole life. (4) Variable life policies tend to have somewhat higher expenses over the long-term than do whole life and universal life. This—explained by variable life's more expensive administrative systems and its security status—demands that it comply with certain regulatory requirements (like providing a prospectus to potential buyers)." Wilshinsky at 60-61. (Citations omitted.)

[53] Variable life designed on a *whole* life chassis (as opposed to a variable *universal* life product) is basically a whole life policy where the policy owner invests the cash values in mutual fund type investments. Consequently the policy owner has to monitor the performance of the selected investments.

As previously noted, the investment accounts underlying variable life insurance are legally separate from the life insurance company's general account and are not subject to the claims of the life insurance company's creditors. Except to the extent that cash value is allocated to the guaranteed interest account, the investment risk is shifted entirely to the policy owner, and the life insurance company provides no guarantees with respect to the policy's cash value account. However, unlike a general account policy where the amount credited to the cash value is determined periodically by the life insurance company, the actual performance of the investment account in a variable policy passes through to the policy owner, less a fixed administrative charge. The typical variable life prospectus illustrates the policy based on hypothetical gross annual rates of investment return of 0%, 6%, and 12%.[54] Good investment performance will result in a larger cash value, while poor investment performance will result in a smaller cash value. Poor investment performance may require the policy owner to pay additional premiums in order to maintain the (full) face amount of coverage. Furthermore, poor investment performance could actually produce a negative rate of investment return which could cause the policy to lapse earlier than illustrated in the 0% illustration.

A variable life insurance policy may be structured with fixed premiums (or with flexible premiums, in the case of a variable universal life policy). Premium payment plans include, a single premium payment, payment for a limited number of years, or payment for the life of the insured.

Some variable life insurance policies have higher administrative costs than general account policies. In theory, the extra cost may be offset by the pass through of the increased earnings of the policy's investment account.

---

[54] However, any rate of return can be illustrated. It is suggested that several illustrations be run so the client can better understand the risk and the reward inherent in a variable policy. Until recently, the Securities and Exchange Commission ("SEC") prohibited the use of a Monte Carlo simulation for variable policies. However, this rule changed in 2205 when the SEC approved NASD rule 22 rule 2210 (IM-2210-6) which allowed the use of Monte Carlo simulations for variable life insurance policies after February 2005. A Monte Carlo simulation generates a number of mathematical possible outcomes by generating a random investment return for each period. The more simulations run the more accurate one can expect the result to be. Since the SEC now permits the use of a Monte Carlo simulation an advisor should ensure that one is run and that the number of simulations is sufficient to allow the client to make an informed decision.

§16.3(d)(1) Similarities Of Variable Life And Variable Universal Life

Variable life ("VL") and variable universal life ("VUL") (*see*, section 16.3(e), below) are similar in the following ways: (1) the policy owner can select how the premiums are invested; (2) except to the extent that cash value is allocated to the policy's fixed or guaranteed interest account, neither policy is guaranteed a minimum interest rate on its cash value account—the policy owner assumes all the risk; (3) each policy's cash value fluctuates depending on the performance of the investments selected by the policy owner; (4) each policy's cash value account grows income tax deferred; and (5) both policies are considered a security that requires the selling agent to hold a special license.[55]

§16.3(d)(2) Differences Between Variable Life And Variable Universal Life

The key differences between VL and VUL are: (1) the premium amounts in a VUL policy are flexible, but the premium amounts in a VL are not flexible; (2) a VUL policy owner can vary the frequency or amount of premiums, a VL policy owner can not; (3) a VUL policy owner can increase or decrease the death benefit amount and can select an Option A/Option 1 or Option B/Option 2 payout, a VL policy owner can not; (4) a VUL policy owner can make withdrawals from the policy's cash value, a VL policy owner can not (but a VL owner can, however, access the cash value through policy loans); and (5) a VUL policy owner receives "unbundled product disclosure" from the life insurance company, a VL policy owner does not.[56]

§16.3(d)(3) Appropriateness Of Variable Life

Variable insurance is appropriate only if the owner is able to monitor the investments, has a tolerance for investment risk, and intends to hold the policy for at least 10 years (in order to ride out market fluctuations). The appeal of variable life is the ability to tap into the potential upside of the stock market (when it rallies),[57] and to be

---

[55] Adapted from Figures 1.3 and 18.3 of Leimberg & Doyle.

[56] Adapted from Figures 1.3 and 18.3 of Leimberg & Doyle.

[57] Another potentially appealing aspect of variable life insurance is that if the insurance company becomes insolvent, the policy owner's investment account is not subject to the insurance company's general creditors.

assured that the cash value of the policy is not subject to the claims of the life insurance company's creditors (assuming the owner of the policy has not chosen to invest in the life insurance company's own general account). Since the death benefit may be structured to increase proportionately to the increase in the cash value of the policy, variable insurance may also be seen as providing a hedge against inflation.

§16.3(d)(4) Special License Required To Sell Variable Life Insurance

Because of the sub-account investment options available to the policy owner, a life insurance agent selling variable life insurance must have a variable life license, and all policy illustrations must be accompanied by a current prospectus. Not all life insurance agents are licensed to sell variable insurance, and therefore may not recommend the product.

§16.3(d)(5) TOLI Best Practices And Variable Life Insurance

From an ILIT trustee's "best practices" perspective, variable life insurance requires more annual TOLI management than does traditional whole life insurance.[58]

§16.3(e) Variable Universal Life[59]

Variable universal life ("VUL") insurance is a hybrid type of permanent insurance that combines the investment flexibility of variable

---

[58] *See,* footnotes 20 and 42, above, concerning TOLI management issues.

[59] *See*, Chapter 18 of Leimberg & Doyle; and ¶1.07 of Zaritsky and Leimberg. *See also,* Peter Katt, "The Do's and Don'ts of Buying Variable Life Insurance Policies," *XXI AAII Journal* 37 (July 1999), http://www.peterkatt.com/articles/AAII_jul1999.html; Peter Katt, "Variable Life Insurance: Be Wary of Policy 'Delusions'," XXV *AAII Journal* 34 (November 2003), http://www.peterkatt.com/articles/AAII_nov2003.html; and Charles L. Ratner, "Private Placement Life Products: Domestic, Offshore or Atoll? The Reality Check Please," 140 *Trusts & Estates* 48 (July 2001) which discusses the tax and investment aspects of variable universal life insurance in the context of a domestic "off-the-shelf" product, and as a domestic and offshore private placement product.

"Variable life products are most suitable for those individuals who want control over their cash values and need or desire increasing life insurance protection. VUL offers greater certainty of death benefit levels than VL as long as premiums continue to be paid at the level necessary to maintain the death benefit. Under option B, death benefit levels are more certain to increase. VUL also permits the policy owner to life with the premium and face amount flexibility of universal life. VUL is sometimes referred to as "flexible premium variable life" or "universal life II." A VUL policy owner has control over the policy's face amount, investments, premiums, and premium payments. In many VUL policies the policy owner can select the accounts from which the policy's expenses and mortality charges are deducted. The policy owner can usually select between two death benefit payouts: (i) Option A/Option 1 (which is for the policy's face amount), or (ii) Option B/Option 2 (which is for the policy's face amount plus the balance of the policy's cash value account).

A VUL policy (the "base") can be blended with term insurance. The term component can make the policy more efficient for the owner because it can have lower COI than the base and/or the premium attributable to the term component will not be part of the life insurance agent's commission. The term component may also cause other policy charges, such as the M&E charge to be lower. In a well designed term component that creates savings for the owner, the base should be minimized, the term component should be maximized and the owner should fund the policy aggressively, especially in the early years, with premium outlays being made on an all base design and on a conservative investment rate of return on the base's investment sub-account.[60]

---

increase the face amount of coverage with evidence of insurability. Given the risks and uncertainties associated with both cash values and death benefit levels, variable life products can be attractive supplements to an existing life insurance plan that assures a minimum required base level of coverage. It is less suitable as the means of providing the minimum basic level of coverage. VL and, more particularly, VUL are especially suitable for many business insurance needs where flexibility and growth of cash values and death benefits are necessary or attractive features. It can be used to provide potentially higher tax-deferred cash value accumulations in nonqualified deferred compensation plans than traditional policies or UL. With successful investment of cash values, the death benefit levels of variable products are more likely than those of traditional products to keep pace with increases in the values of closely-held business interests when a variable product funds a buy-sell agreement. VL and VUL may be equally attractive for key person insurance and other business applications or in insured pension plans." Leimberg & Doyle at 270-271.

Ben Baldwin does not recommend VUL unless the prospective insured can commit to annually funding the policy such that the (tax free) earnings on the policy's cash value account pay the mortality and expense charges. If a prospective insured cannot commit to that level of funding, Baldwin recommends that the prospect consider renewable and convertible term life insurance as an alternative to VUL. Baldwin at 227-228.

[60] *See*, footnote 35, above concerning term blending.

§16.3(e)(1) Similarities Of Universal Life And Variable Universal Life Insurance

Universal life ("UL") and VUL are similar in the following ways: (1) they both allow "blending," that is, the insured may buy term insurance and invest the rest within the same policy; (2) they both provide a guaranteed death benefit while the policy is in force; (3) the premium amounts are flexible (however, the policy owner should be careful to not under-fund the policy); (4) the policy owner can vary the frequency and amount of premium payments; (5) the policy owner can decrease or increase (subject to proof of insurability) the amount of the policy's death benefit; (6) the policy owner can choose the Option A/Option1 or Option B/Option 2 death benefit; (7) partial withdrawals of cash from the policy are permitted; (8) policy loans are permitted[61]; (9) the cash value account grows income tax deferred; (10) mortality and expense charges are deducted monthly; and (11) the life insurance company provides "unbundled product disclosure."[62]

§16.3(e)(2) Differences Between Universal Life And Variable Universal Life Insurance

The key differences between UL and VUL are: (1) a VUL policy owner can select how the premiums are invested, such as equity funds, bond funds, money market funds, etc., but a UL owner can not select how premiums are invested—they are invested in the life insurance company's general investment account and are subject to minimum and maximum crediting rates, whereas in a VUL policy the policy owner is not subject to minimum or maximum crediting rates; (2) the cash value account in a VUL policy will fluctuate based on the performance of the investment portfolio selected by the policy owner, but a UL's cash value account will not fluctuate in value based on fluctuations in the company's general portfolio; (3) there are no interest rate guarantees on a VUL's cash value account that is allocated other than to the guaranteed interest account; but there is a guaranteed interest rate on a UL's cash value account; (4) the cash value account in a UL is represented by assets which are part of the life insurance company's general fund that is subject to the claims of the life insurance compa-

---

[61] Because of the administration expenses and taxes assessed against new money coming into a VUL, it is generally less expensive for the policy owner to borrow from the policy than to make a withdrawal that the policy owner plans to repay. *See,* Baldwin at 220 for further discussion on VUL policy loans versus withdrawals.

[62] Adapted from Figures 1.3 and 18.3 of Leimberg & Doyle.

ny's creditors, whereas, the cash value account in a VUL that is allocated other than to the guaranteed interest account is represented by a separate investment account that is not subject to the claims of the life insurance company's creditors; (5) VUL is a security that requires a special license to be sold, but a UL is not a security; and (6) because VUL is a security, its expense loading is limited by the Securities Act of 1940, but a UL's expense loading is not limited and may be higher than that of a VUL.[63]

16.3(e)(3) Variable Universal Life Insurance Fees And Expenses

VUL policy fee structures are an important basis of comparison between registered and private placement products and domestic and offshore private placement products. First, there are the charges and fees assessed against the VUL premium before it is deposited into the separate investment account. These include the sales load to cover expenses associated with putting the policy in force, paying commissions, etc. The sales load might range from 4% to 6% of the premium, with a cap of 9% of all premiums paid within the lesser of 20 years or life expectancy. In addition, the life insurance company is reimbursed for the tax it has to pay to the state in which the policy is sold. This charge is usually about 2% of the premium. There is also the DAC tax of approximately 1% of the premium, which is to reimburse the life insurance company for the tax it pays to the federal government for putting the business in force.[64] There is also a state premium tax. After the deductions for those loads and taxes, the VUL premiums are deposited into the separate investment account and allocated among the funds in accordance with the policy owner's designated allocation. The policy owner can periodically change the fund account to which the premium is to be allocated. Each month the life insurance compa-

---

[63] Adapted from Figures 1.3 and 18.3 of Leimberg & Doyle.

[64] "The DAC tax is actually not an additional tax paid to the Treasury but rather a charge—typically passed on to contract holders by domestic carriers—approximating the present value of the increased cost resulting from the insurance carrier's being required to amortize certain policy acquisition expenses over ten years rather than immediately deducting such expenses. Carriers typically charge approximately from 30 basis points [i.e., 0.30%] to 1.50% [i.e., 150 basis points] of contributed premiums to recover this cost. Many carriers offer the contract holder an option to amortize this cost over an extended period. Other carriers may not explicitly add a DAC tax as a separate expense but rather will recover this cost through an increased M&E charge." Robert D. Colvin, "Planning for International Private Placement Insurance: The U.S. Perspective," 96 *Journal of Taxation* 94, 100 (February 2002).

ny charges the separate account with the cost of the insurance ("COI") for the amount at risk. The life insurance company can increase the cost of insurance ("COI") costs up to a contractual maximum. The life insurance company also deducts a mortality and expense ("M&E") risk charge. The M&E charge is supposed to compensate the life insurance company for certain risks it assumes under variable life insurance policies. The M&E charge is generally limited to 90 basis points (0.9%) on the cash value on an annual basis. Life insurance companies differ widely in the way they impose the M&E charge, ranging from the full 90 basis points for the life of the policy, to perhaps 65 basis points for the life of the policy, to a tiered approach of perhaps 30 basis points for 15 years and 10 basis points thereafter. Another approach to tiering is to charge a certain M&E risk for the first $X million of cash value and a lower charge for additional cash value. There are additional expenses for the management and administration of the separate account investments. Any investment returns are earned net of these expenses. Finally, surrender charges help a life insurance company recoup un-recovered sales commissions and other expenses. These charges are generally imposed during the first 10, 15, or 20 policy years. The charges decline over the years the policy is in force.

Unfortunately, VUL illustrations usually show a constant return on the cash value, rather than the fluctuating returns that are much more likely to occur. The danger here is that in prolonged bear markets, as the cash value dips, the amount at risk increases. It is possible for the investment sub-accounts, to experience a negative return (i.e., below 0% return), which could affect the policy's viability. Unless internal charges are taken from a guaranteed interest account, the policy will have to sell-off fund investment units at depressed values to cover COI deductions. These kinds of fluctuations can wreak havoc on a VUL policy that is not sufficiently funded to weather a down (or bear) market. Thus, it is fair to say that the keys to success with VUL are: (1) adequate funding, (2) sound investment management, and (3) where permitted, managing the policy in a way that minimizes the impact of market downturns on policy performance. One such technique is paying the COI from the guaranteed interest account or a money market fund, and heavily funding the policy (i.e., paying more than the annual minimum premium).

A VUL policy that is heavily funded in the early years and whose policy owner has the cash flow to sustain the policy in a bear market, can produce tremendous income tax benefits to the policy owner or, greatly reduce the aggregate long term cash premium outlays necessary to sustain the death benefit. This is because the earnings on the sub-accounts accumulate income tax free and are use to pay for the cost of the net amount at risk (i.e., the tax free earnings are used to pay for the term insurance component of the VUL policy), and if the policy owner has selected an Option B/Option 2 payout, all of the accumulated earnings (which were never taxed) are received income tax free by the beneficiaries. When held in an ILIT, the insured's beneficiaries can also receive the death benefits free of death taxes.

As a general rule, policy loans on universal, variable, and variable universal life insurance are not subject to income taxation.[65] However, if an insurance policy is allowed to lapse prior to death and the owner has borrowed against the policy in an amount in excess of his or her basis in the policy, the amount of such excess will be taxable income. *See,* section 2.18, above.

> **Example:** Assume a male age 35 purchases a variable policy with a death benefit of $300,000 and a $4,000 annual premium. Assume also that the policy produces a gross annual rate of investment return of 9%. The policyholder pays premiums until age 65 or a total of $120,000. Starting at age 65 the policyholder begins to borrow $40,000 a year from the policy at 5% loan interest. At age 72, the cash value will be $360,000 and the loan account will be $342,000. If the policy is then surrendered and the cash value is used to pay off the loan, the policyholder will have taxable income of $240,000, which is the amount by which the cash value exceeds total premium payments ($360,000 - $120,000 = $240,000). If the policyholder did not wish to incur such phantom income, it would then be necessary to begin to pay premiums again in an amount necessary to keep the policy in force (i.e., not surrender the policy), as well as forgoing further borrowing. It is possible for the policyholder to find himself in what Joseph M. Belth refers to as a "surrender squeeze" in which it is expensive to either keep the policy in effect or surrender it!

---

[65] "Loans or withdrawals will reduce a [VUL] policy's cash value and death benefit. By borrowing or withdrawing funds from a policy, funds are no longer available to earn returns available from the underlying investment options where they previously resided, which will have a permanent effect on policy performance....All or part of the amounts withdrawn may be included in gross income depending upon the investment [i.e., basis] in the contract. Withdrawals in excess of cost basis are taxable as ordinary income." Baldwin at 219. *See,* sections 2.16 and 2.17, above.

16.3(e)(4) TOLI Best Practices And Variable Universal Life Insurance

Because of the policy's tremendous flexibility and the risks associated with the separate account investments selected by the policy owner, from an ILIT trustee's "best practices" perspective, variable universal life insurance requires more annual TOLI management.[66]

§16.3(f) Joint Lives Life Insurance[67]

Joint lives insurance provides "second to die" or "first to die" coverage. A second to die policy is intended to pay a death benefit only when the last insured dies. Thus, second to die policies are frequently used by a husband and wife to pay estate and inheritance taxes upon the death of the second spouse (especially where estate taxes have been deferred because of the use of the unlimited marital deduction, which was enacted in 1981). *See,* section 1.11, above. Second to die policies are also used in ILITs and in conjunction with wealth replacement trusts. *See,* section 1.12, above. Some life insurance companies will issue policies up to the combined insureds' net worth to accommodate the funding of the ILIT or wealth replacement trust.

A second to die policy is usually less expensive than two separate policies and is appropriate when the insureds want to receive the proceeds at the survivor's death, such as when the surviving spouse dies and there is a need to pay estate taxes and administration expenses. Second to die life insurance is not appropriate when insurance proceeds are needed for income replacement, such as to provide funds for the proper care and support of the insured's surviving spouse and/or children.

Many second to die life insurance policies involve a combination of permanent (base) and term insurance in order to lower the premium. The policies can be paid up at the first death or premiums can continue until the second death. Premiums can be paid for life or can be structured to "vanish." Most joint life policies are traditional whole life, current assumption whole life or universal life. Some life insurance companies offer the second to die feature as a rider to a primary single insured.

Because second to die life insurance does not pay a death benefit until the last of the two insured dies, a life insurance company may

---

[66] *See,* footnotes 20 and 42, above, concerning TOLI management issues

[67] *See,* Chapters 11 and 15 of Leimberg & Doyle; and ¶¶1.11 and 1.12 of Zaritsky and Leimberg.

be willing to insure a person who is in poor health and would not otherwise be able to obtain life insurance coverage (provided the other insured is in "good" health).

Since a second to die life insurance policy insures two lives, the obligation to pay premiums continues after the death of the first insured. After the death of the first insured, the probability of the surviving insured's death is greater and, in some policy structures, the premiums increase. Riders can reduce or eliminate the payment of premiums after the death of the first insured.

> **Practice Point:** In the absence of a rider, it may be prudent for a surviving spouse to be left enough money (either outright or through trust distributions) to be able to pay the continuing premiums on the second to die policy.

Because the life insurance company will receive the use of the premiums for a longer period of time (for two lives instead of for one life), the premiums on a second to die policy are usually relatively low (but are paid over a longer period of time).

First to die contracts also insure joint lives but proceeds are payable at the first death. Total premium cost is usually substantially less than separate policies on both lives since only one death benefit is payable.

§16.3(g) Private Placement Life Insurance

Private placement life insurance ("PPLI") is a custom designed, institutionally priced life insurance policy that is offered only to qualified persons.[68] PPLI policies are always structured as separate account

[68] "[M]any offering memoranda for offshore PPVUL [a.k.a. PPLI] policies reference 'qualified purchaser' or 'accredited investor' standards, as used in U.S. securities law, to describe suitable investors. In the offshore context, this should be considered merely a guideline and not a strict requirement because offshore policies are not actually subject to SEC regulations [i.e., the private placement product is not registered with the SEC]. However, if the premiums of an offshore PPVUL policy are to be invested in funds that do require investors to be 'qualified purchasers,' then the policy owner must be a 'qualified purchaser' for that purpose. In the domestic context, because private placement products in the United States are subject to SEC regulations, each purchaser must be a 'qualified purchaser' under section 2(a)(51) of the Investment Company Act of 1940, 15 U.S.C. §80a-2(a)(51) and an 'accredited investor' under section 501(a) of Regulation D of the 1933 Act, 17 C.F.R. 230.501(a)." Leslie C. Giordani and Michael H. Ripp, Jr., "Private Placement Life Insurance Planning (Part 1)," 12 *ALI-ABA Estate Planning Course Materials Journal* 43, 46 (June 2006).

policies (i.e., as VUL policies) and have the greatest degree of investment alternatives available. PPLI policies are security-based policies, which means that the policy itself is an investment security because the lifetime value (which typically affects the death benefit) is determined by the investment choices made by the policy owner. Like any other variable product, there are investment diversification requirements that have to be met.[69] Because a PPLI policy can typically only be offered to qualified purchasers, the cost of the policy and agent commissions tend to be dramatically lower than an "off-the-shelf" VUL policy since there are no marketing fees or registration fees for PPLI. Moreover, the qualified purchaser market expects "institutional pricing" and does not, therefore, tolerate the presence of high retail commissions when paying the significant premiums typical to PPLI (i.e., at least $4-5 million). The lower agent commissions and policy fees allow the investment in a PPLI policy to perform better than a comparable "off-the-shelf" VUL policy. However, some life insurance companies are designing "off-the-shelf" PPLI products that compete with the traditional custom designed PPLI policy.[70]

---

[69] IRC section 817(h) references IRC section 851(b)(3) which requires that no one investment may represent more than 55% of the value of the separate account. No two investments can represent more than 70% of the value of the separate account, no three investments can represent more than 80% of the value of the separate account, and no four investments can represent more than 90% of the value of the separate account. In addition, to meet the IRC section 817(h) safe harbor, no more than 55% of the value of a segregated account can be attributable to cash, cash items, government securities, and securities of other regulated investment companies.

[70] "The recent popularity of private placement has caused several insurance carriers to develop a shelf product with a more flexible investment array that is offered as a private placement product. These products are constructed with an extremely broad range of investment options, including hedge funds, which are all created to satisfy the appetite of the vast majority of investors. Unlike a negotiated private placement offering, these products are sold through the carrier's normal distribution channel with traditional, although sometimes reduced, sales commissions." Lee and Wildy at section VI, B. Such companies include American International Group, Inc., Sun Life Financial, Massachusetts Mutual, and New York Life, among others.

"For those individuals who need life insurance coverage in excess of $10 million, substantial cost savings can be incurred by using a PPLI contract over a traditional retail ["off-the-shelf"] contract. This is not to say that some clients will not be well served by retail contracts. For those who seek simplicity, don't desire flexible investment options and don't mind paying a little bit more, retail contracts will fit the bill. However, for the sophisticated client who earned his money the hard way, and has a tendency to be a tough negotiator on fees, PPLI offers a comfortable home." Grant R. Markuson, "The Lure of Private Placement," 142 *Trusts & Estates* 58, 61 (May 2003).

A PPLI policy owner may direct that policy assets be invested in a wide array of investments, including mutual funds, real estate stocks, bonds, derivatives, timber, REITs, or hedge funds.[71] Using PPLI to achieve income tax free growth of such investments is a compelling benefit for the high net worth investor. Accordingly, PPLI is more of a tax driven investment product than a life insurance protection product.[72]

PPLI policies are structured as VUL products. Typically, the policy owner will have at least $1 million of cash to invest in the policy, either initially or over several years, although some life insurance companies require a commitment of $5 million to $10 million in total premiums.[73] As a general rule, a commitment of at least $5 million of premium over the first five years is usually necessary to allow the policy owner to choose certain types of investments, such as hedge funds or discretionary managed accounts. In all cases, the ability of the policy owner to control the underlying investments is usually carefully circumscribed to ensure compliance with the investor control rules set

---

[71] *See,* James R. Cohen and Jeffrey S. Bortnick, "PPLI Invested In Hedge Funds," 145 *Trusts & Estates* 52 (May 2006).

[72] *See,* Leslie C. Giordani and Michael H. Ripp, Jr., "Private Placement Life Insurance Planning (Part 2)," 12 *ALI-ABA Estate Planning Course Materials Journal* 25 (August 2006); Leslie C. Giordani and Michael H. Ripp, Jr., "Private Placement Life Insurance Planning (Part 1)," 12 *ALI-ABA Estate Planning Course Materials Journal* 43 (June 2006); Charles L. Ratner, "PPLI Primer," 144 *Trusts & Estates* 32 (September 2005); Douglas Moore and Mitchell K. Higgins, "Planning and Investing with Private Placement Life Insurance," 30 *Estate Planning* 336 (July 2003); Grant R. Markuson, "The Lure of Private Placement," 142 *Trusts & Estates* 58 (May 2003); Grant R. Markuson, "Private Placement Life Insurance: New Insights for an Enduring Technique," a special supplement to 141 *Trusts & Estates* (December 2002); Lewis D. Solomon and Lewis J. Saret, "Reaping the Benefits of Offshore Private Placement Life Insurance," 29 *Estate Planning* 435 (September 2002); Jeffrey A. Zaluda and Lauren J. Wolven, "The Use of Private Placement Life Insurance in Tax and Estate Planning," 43 *Tax Management Memorandum* 187 (May 20, 2002); and Robert D. Colvin, "Planning for International Private Placement Insurance: The U.S. Perspective," 96 *Journal of Taxation* 94 (February 2002). *See also,* Charles L. Ratner, "Private Placement Life Products: Domestic, Offshore or Atoll? The Reality Check Please," 140 *Trusts & Estates* 48 (July 2001) which discusses the tax and investment aspects of variable universal life insurance in the context of a domestic "off-the-shelf" product, and as a private placement product – both domestically and offshore.

[73] *See,* Lee and Wilkey at section VI, B; and Richard L. Harris, "The Problems With PPLI," 143 *Trusts & Estates* 40 (May 2004).

forth by the IRS.[74] Furthermore, to optimize investment return, many investors choose to create a MEC contract by heavier funding up front that maximizes the benefit of tax-free compounding. [75]

§16.3(g)(1) Domestic Vs. Offshore PPLI

PPLI policies can be purchased both domestically and offshore.[76] Offshore PPLI products have enhanced tax advantages because the state premium tax should not be payable.[77] However, to secure the offshore benefits, it is important that all aspects of the policy including application, medical exam, initial premium payment and delivery of the policy are conducted offshore.[78] The avoidance of state premium

---

[74] *See,* discussion of PPLI and Investor Control in section 16.3(g)(4), below.

[75] Because more funds are invested earlier in a MEC policy, a MEC policy will generally have a larger initial cash value account than a non-MEC policy. Consequently, a MEC policy will also have lower COI and M&E charges than a non-MEC policy since there is less NAR for the insurance company concerning the MEC policy. MEC status will not create any adverse income tax issues if the policy owner does not plan on withdrawing money from the PPLI policy during his or her lifetime. *See,* section 2.17, above.

[76] *See,* ¶1.16 of Zaritsky and Leimberg for a discussion of offshore life insurance companies. *See also,* Craig Douglas Hampton "International Life Insurance Presents Unique Planning Opportunities," 24 *Tax Management Estates, Gifts and Trusts Journal* 175 (July 8, 1999).

[77] "Policies issued in a U.S. state are generally subject to a state premium tax ranging between 8 basis points and 3% on life insurance and annuity contributions. Since contracts issued by offshore insurance companies [including Section 953(d) electing carriers] are typically issued exclusively to non-U.S. persons or entities, those policies generally are not subject to U.S. state premium taxes. Nevertheless, this is a state-by-state issue and the rules for avoiding imposition of this tax in a particular state can vary considerably depending on the applicable statutes as well as the attitude of the relevant state regulators. Certain states claim that if the insured is resident in that state, a sufficient nexus exists for taxation in that state regardless of any other factors. Some states may impose a procurement tax on contracts purchased by residents of that state from carriers not registered in that state. The legitimacy of such procurement taxes is subject to certain debate depending on the particular facts and circumstances." Robert D. Colvin, "Planning for International Private Placement Insurance: The U.S. Perspective," 96 *Journal of Taxation* 94, 100 (February 2002).

[78] Although an offshore PPLI policy should not be subject to SEC regulations and may be offered to non-accredited investors, the conservative practitioner should follow the SEC regulations to avoid any uncertainty. Moreover, virtually all offshore carriers require it.

tax can result in savings of 2-3%. In addition, an offshore policy can effectively avoid the DAC tax if the policy owner does not make an IRC section 953(d) election.[79] However, if the issuer does not make an IRC section 953(d) election, the policy owner must pay a 1% U.S. federal excise tax on the premium payments for the policies on the life of U.S. citizens.[80] In spite of the federal excise tax, the reduced DAC tax and avoidance of the state premium tax can have a significant positive impact on the policy's performance.

When purchasing an offshore PPLI policy, consideration should be given to both the jurisdiction and the life insurance company. Countries that recognize separate accounts and afford creditor protection to a PPLI policy are more desirable than countries that do not.[81] The amount of regulatory oversight, economic and political stability, and availability of qualified legal professionals are also important factors to be considered when selecting an offshore jurisdiction.

§16.3(g)(2) PPLI Costs

In addition to the state premium tax and the DAC tax paid by domestic PPLI policies, there are other costs associated with the operation and acquisition of a domestic or offshore PPLI policy. As dis-

---

Additional tax savings can also be accomplished by using an offshore ILIT to own the PPLI policy, if estate tax planning is an issue. In addition to the classic estate planning issues associated with life insurance, there are significant income tax issues that must be carefully considered when using an offshore ILIT. For example, there are special tax issues associated with outbound transfers (IRC sections 679 and 684), inbound transfers (IRC section 672), income taxes on distributions of accumulated earnings (IRC section 668), the throwback rules (IRC sections 665-668), and the interaction of U.S. and foreign tax systems. In effect, the interplay and cumulative effect of the specialized rules applicable to foreign trusts makes the tax treatment of an offshore ILIT significantly more complex. In addition to the income tax issues, the additional reporting requirements may also prove to be quite onerous. *See*, Elizabeth M. Schurig and Carolyn M. Beckett, "Foreign Reporting: Get it Right," 145 *Trusts & Estates* 32 (July 2006) for an excellent overview of the tax compliance issues, forms that have to be filed with the IRS, and the consequence of non-compliance. In addition to the complexities of the tax law, a careful review of the foreign jurisdiction's trust law and the retention of competent local counsel usually complicates matters further.

[79] The IRC section 953(d) election allows a foreign life insurance company to be treated as a domestic corporation for tax purposes. Most offshore subsidiaries of U.S. insurers make an IRC section 953(d) election.

[80] IRC section 4371.

[81] For example, Bermuda, Bahamas, Cayman Island, and Guernsey are but a few of the jurisdictions that have separate account legislation.

cussed above, every PPLI policy is subject to M&E charges. The M&E charges generally range between 0.5% and 1.1%, and are typically lower than most commercially available policies. Small offshore life insurance companies tend to have higher M&E charges.

Because PPLI policies are primarily sold as an income tax free wrapper for investments,[82] brokerage costs will be incurred. Brokerage costs depend on the type of asset being held by the policy and the broker. In addition to the brokerage costs, there will be an investment manager's fee.[83] This fee will vary depending on the investment manager, the size of the assets, and the nature of the investment. For example, and index fund may cost significantly less than an actively traded portfolio.

The last significant fee in a PPLI policy is the cost of the insurance ("COI"). The COI varies based on the age, sex, and health status of the insured, the amount of life insurance being purchased, the reinsurance cost, retention limits, and the life insurance company's experience. If there is a significant spread between the cash value and death benefit, and the policy is large enough, consideration should be given to the identity and credit worthiness of the direct insurer and its reinsurance companies.

Due to the inherent costs of a PPLI policy (primarily the COI and M&E charges), a PPLI policy is approximately 1 to 1.5% more expensive then a similarly situated brokerage account. However, the increased cost is a small price to pay to avoid income taxes on the underlying PPLI investments.

§16.3(g)(3) PPLI Design Issues

Because PPLI is a custom designed policy, design issues that are otherwise moot in other types of life insurance policies, need to be

---

[82] "PPLI takes maximum advantage of the income tax efficiencies of life insurance. PPLI enables an investor to purchase the least income tax efficient investment, such as hedge funds, and turn them into tax-free investments. It also allows the avoidance of recognition of short-term capital gain in actively managed funds. These benefits are compounded in that income tax liabilities generated by hedge funds and other actively managed accounts are usually paid out of an investor's other assets, meaning that investors may need to sell assets to raise cash, which may trigger additional taxable gain. Investments held through PPLI can avoid these issues." Jeffrey A. Zaluda and Lauren J. Wolven, "The Use of Private Placement Life Insurance in Tax and Estate Planning." 43 *Tax Management Memorandum* 187 (May 20, 2002).

[83] Richard H. Mayer, Donald R. Levy, *Planning for the Affluent,* page 12-9, (Aspen Publishers, New York, NY 2003).

carefully addressed. A policy should always meet the definition of life insurance under IRC section 7702. Prior to purchasing a PPLI policy, the terms of the policy should be carefully reviewed by an actuary to ensure the policy qualifies as life insurance under U.S. tax law. While this is a minor concern for domestic policies, it is a significant concern for offshore policies issued by very small carriers. If the policy does not qualify as life insurance for U.S. tax purposes, then all gains recognized during the year will be taxed to the policy owner.

Once the PPLI policy is purchased, continued diligence by a servicing agent is recommended. The policy should be reviewed annually to ensure that the diversification requirements of IRC section 817(h) (concerning variable products) are scrupulously followed. The failure to meet the diversification requirements will result in the policy owner recognizing all of the income from the investments during the year.

§16.3(g)(4) PPLI And Investor Control

Although a full discussion of investor control is beyond the scope of this Chapter, rudimentary understanding of the investor control rules is helpful. To retain the income tax benefits of a life insurance policy, it is vital that no investor control exist. If the investor control rules are violated, the PPLI policy will be ignored and the policy owner will be presumed to own the policy's underlying investments.

The investor control rules have emerged through a series of revenue rulings and private letter rulings.[84] The essence of the doctrine is that while a PPLI policy owner is free to choose an investment manager to manage the policy's separate account, the owner should have not control over the actual selection of investments.

The investor control rules are important in the PPLI environment, particularly in the context of hedge funds, which are frequently chosen as separate account investments. In Rev. Rul. 81-225, 1981-2 C.B. 12, the IRS ruled that when the sole asset of a PPLI policy was a publicly traded mutual fund and the owner's position within the contract was "substantially identical" to the position that the owner would have had outside the contract, investor control was presumed. Consequently, the owner of the PPLI policy was treated as the owner

---

[84] Rev. Ruls. 77-85, 1977-1 C.B. 12; 80-274, 1980-2 C.B. 271; 81-225, 1981-2 C.B. 12; 82-54, 1982-1 C.B. 11; 2003-91, 2 C.B. 347; and 2003-92, 2003-2 C.B. 350. *See also*, Richard L. Harris, "The Problems With PPLI," 143 *Trusts & Estates* 40 (May 2004).

of the mutual fund investments and would be taxed on all income from the investments. However, if the investment fund is not publicly available or if the investment is an insurance dedicated fund, there is no investor control even if the position is "substantially identical" to the position that the owner would have had outside the contract. It is for this reason that many hedge funds now have insurance dedicated funds. Treas. Reg. § 1.817-5(f)(2)(i).

In Priv. Letter Rul. 20024401,[85] the IRS set forth rules that must be followed for hedge funds and other investment funds owned by PPLI policies. The taxpayer argued that the mere fact that the hedge fund was not an insurance dedicated fund was not sufficient to treat the PPLI policy owner as the owner of the investments since the hedge fund was available only to a limited number of investors. The taxpayer also argued that Treasury Regulations specifically permit variable separate accounts to invest in non-registered (i.e., private) partnerships that are not insurance dedicated funds. *See,* Example (3) of Treas. Reg. §1.817-5(g). The IRS ruled that there was investor control and that the PPLI policy owner was required to recognize all income from the underlying investments.

In Rev. Rul. 2003-91, 2003-2 C.B. 347, the IRS focused on the amount of control an investor can have over the investments and strategies of a given sub-account, and over the selection of an investment advisor for a given sub-account within a variable life insurance contract. The IRS confirmed the generally accepted principle that owners of PPLI contracts are permitted to allocate investments among a limited menu of "insurance dedicated funds" without constituting investor control. However, the IRS implied that if the investor exercises any authority or influence in the selection or replacement of an investment advisor, such exercise would violate the investor control rules.

The same day, the IRS released Rev. Rul. 2003-92, 2003-33 I.R.B. 350, in which it ruled that policy owners cannot direct separate account funds to be invested in non-insurance dedicated partnerships (i.e., hedge funds). The IRS essentially ruled that in order for a hedge fund to be a permissible investment in a variable life insurance contract, the hedge fund must only be offered to insurance companies and not to individual investors. The validity of Rev. Ruls. 2003-91 and

---

[85] This Private Letter Ruling is also referred to as the "Keyport Ruling." *See,* David S. Neufeld, "The 'Keyport Ruling' and the Investor Control Rule: Might Makes Right?," 102 *Tax Notes* 403 (January 20, 2003).

2003-92 were highly questionable in light of Treas. Reg. §§1.817-5(f)(2)(i) and (g). The Treasury Regulations appeared to directly contradict the reasoning of the Revenue Rulings and called their validity into question.[86] Interestingly, one week later the IRS issued Proposed Treasury Regulations changing the diversification Regulations and removing the conflicting non-registered partnership exception.[87] These Regulations were made final on February 28, 2005, per Treasury Decision 9185 (2/28/2005).

To summarize, the IRS's position highlights the fact that the underlying investment funds in a PPLI policy must be insurance dedicated funds or separate managed accounts over which the policy owner has no discretion or other forms of control. If the policy owner attempts to exercise too much investor control over investment manager activities, the policy will lose the tax protection afforded to life insurance. Priv. Letter Rul. 200420017.

§16.3(g)(5) PPLI And Loan Spread Provisions

An often overlooked but vital design feature of any PPLI policy is the loan spread provisions. For increased flexibility, it is important that the PPLI policy provide the policy owner with the ability to access cash values on a cost advantageous basis. Some life insurance companies have very advantageous rates for cash build-up but charge high interest rates for policy loans. In a MEC contract, the use of policy loans is critical, since a cash withdrawal is taxed at ordinary income rates. Consequently, careful consideration should be given to the policy loan provisions.

§16.3(g)(6) PPLI And Force-Outs

"One of the most important non-tax design issues relates to whether a life insurance company will warrant against 'force-outs' of cash value when the cash value grows more quickly than expected, thereby pushing up the required net amount at risk beyond the initially specified amount [thereby violating the guideline premium test under IRC section 7702]. Policy holders must pay tax at ordinary income tax rates on force-outs of cash. Accordingly, the optimal result is for the life insurance company to negotiate with the reinsurance

---

[86] *See,* Ralph Carter, Jr., "Crackdown Requires Review of Variable Insurance and Annuity Set-Ups," 72 *Practical Tax Strategies 298* (May 2004).

[87] REG-163974-02 (7/29/03).

company to guarantee that the 'at risk' portion of the PPLI policy will always remain sufficiently ahead of the cash value, without the need to force cash out of the policy. If this is not possible, [and it rarely will be possible to negotiate with the reinsurance company,] the PPLI policy servicing agent must pay careful attention to policy performance each year and pre-plan against this result."[88]

§16.4 UNDERSTANDING LIFE INSURANCE RISK FACTORS[89]

What follows is somewhat of an oversimplification. However, present day life insurance policies are so complex and there are so many variations that some simplification is necessary.

§16.4(a) The Four Risk Factors

The goal of the life insurance company is to keep the premium dollars received invested for a period of time and at a rate of return sufficient to permit it to make a profit, while maintaining adequate reserves to provide the promised death benefit when the insured dies. This is accomplished by pricing the policy to take into account four primary risk factors that impact company profitability:

(1) Mortality or claims experience (based on mortality tables that usually assume all of the insured have died by age 100);

(2) Interest/investment experience (e.g., return on the policy's savings component, and the return on the insurance company's general account investments);

(3) Lapse rates; and

---

[88] Leslie C. Giordani and Michael H. Ripp, Jr., "Private Placement Life Insurance Planning (Part 1)," 12 *ALI-ABA Estate Planning Course Materials Journal* 43, 64 (June 2006).

See, section 2.17, above concerning the income taxation of policy withdrawals that occur within the first fifteen years of the policy's issuance.

[89] *See*, Table 2, below, for a chart that compares and contrasts the general features of term life, whole life, universal life, and variable universal life insurance. *See also,* Burke A. Christensen, "Insurance Sales Illustrations To Avoid," 137 *Trusts & Estates* 96 (October 1998); Ben G. Baldwin, Jr., "Risk & Return Potential in Life Insurance Products," 137 *Trusts & Estates* 42 (April 1998); "Menu of Life Insurance Products" at page 183 of Baldwin; and Figures 1.3, 18.3 and 18.4 of Leimberg and Doyle at 13-14, 283 and 284.

(4) Loading/expenses (insurance company business expenses such as actuarial design, marketing expenses, sales commissions, costs of underwriting, administrative expenses, etc.).[90]

Since each risk factor affects the pricing of the policy and the amount of premium needed to sustain the policy, it may be helpful to think of each risk factor as a moving part of the insurance contract.[91] Prior to the 1980s, life insurance companies absorbed the risk factors and sold policies with fixed guarantees as to cost, cash values, and death benefit; e.g., the policies guaranteed a specified death benefit and cash value in exchange for payment of a fixed, lifetime premium. In the last thirty years, increased competition in the financial services industry has resulted in available policies evolving into financial products whose death benefit and cash values parallel other contemporary financial instruments, e.g., universal life, variable life, and variable universal life. In large measure, contemporary life insurance policies differ from one another in how the risk factors interact and the extent to which these policies result in the risks being retained by the life insurance company, shared with the policy owner or passed along to the policy owner.[92] In many products, the insured assumes risk in return

---

[90] "While different insurers use different names for these expenses, they all fall into one of three categories: fixed administration expenses, cash-wrap fees, and premium loads." Christopher P. Cline and Barry D. Flagg, "The Prudent Investor and Trust-Owned Life Insurance (TOLI)—Part 2," 116 *American Bankers Association Trust & Investments* 34, 39 (March/April 2007).

[91] "[I]nsurance pricing is always based on three (3) components:

(1) Claims paid for death benefits, or cost of insurance [charges] (COI);

(2) Expenses associated with policy design and administration (E); and

(3) [Policy] investment earnings (i%).

In other words, premiums are always based on this formula: Premiums = COI + E - i%." Barry D. Flagg, CFP, CLU and ChFC, *The Insurance Advisor.com* (http://www.theinsuranceadvisor.com/index.asp?id=68).

[92] A contract is merely an agreement concerning the allocation of risk between the parties regarding the subject matter. In the life insurance context, risks are allocated between the insurance company and the policy owner, depending on the type of policy, its terms, and guarantees.

"The sharing of risk between the carrier and the policy owner is depicted in the life insurance illustration through the display of two projected performance calculations—'guaranteed values' and 'current values.' The guaranteed values reflect the total amount of risk the carrier is willing to assume. The current values are hypothetical projections of what product performance would be based on current pricing and performance assumptions. The difference between the guaranteed values and the projected values is the amount of risk assumed by the policy owner in relying on the illustrated numbers." Lee and Wilkey at section III,B,1.

for potential investment reward. Unfortunately, the insured all-too often is either unaware of the risks, fails to realize the full extent of his or her exposure, or, the insured and ILIT trustee do not adequately monitor the risk and policy performance, over time.

§16.4(b) Mortality Risk

Mortality[93] risk is the risk that the insured will die in a particular year. Statisticians are unable to determine individual mortality but can predict mortality with great accuracy for large groups of individuals. (For example, the probability that a 40 year old male non-smoker in good health will die within 20 years is 10%, while the probability that a 60 year old male non-smoker in good health will die within 20 years is 50%.) Such statistics are often referred to as mortality or life expectancy tables. Insurance companies refer to such statistics as mortality experience or claims experience.

If the majority of persons insured by a company survive to the age indicated in the life expectancy tables, the life insurance company has an average mortality or claims experience. If the majority of insured survive longer than indicated in the tables, the life insurance company has a better than average mortality or claims experience, i.e., a lower mortality experience. A life insurance company that has average or better than average mortality experience should theoretically be more profitable than a company that has below average mortality experience. If the majority of the insured die sooner than indicated in the life expectancy tables, the insurance company has a below average mortality or claims experience, i.e., a bad or worse mortality or claims experience, and is paying death claims sooner than anticipated, and the company may be less profitable.

§16.4(b)(1) Do The Mortality Assumptions Reflect The Life Insurance Company's Actual Experience?

It is important to determine if the mortality assumptions in the illustration represent the actual mortality experience of the life insur-

---

[93] "Mortality represents the insurer's ability to match risk with premiums, i.e., how carefully the insurer underwrites policies and how closely the experience (rate of deaths) that actually occurs parallels what was projected by the insurer in setting its rates. If more deaths occur in a given period than expected, [policy] dividends will be adversely affected. If fewer deaths occur than projected, [policy] dividends will be positively affected." Leimberg & Doyle at 94.

ance company; and if not, inquire as to why. (Additionally, you may also want to ask for a copy of industry standard tables as a method of comparison). Some insurance illustration software includes an annual decline in mortality experience, based on assumed improvements in medical care. Ask if the illustrations assume future mortality improvements. If so, obtain an alternative illustration that does not incorporate such ongoing mortality improvements so that the effect of such assumptions on the premium will be clearly identified. If two life insurance companies provide illustrations and there is a substantial spread in the mortality assumptions, what facts—such as stricter underwriting—justify the assumption that one company will have lower mortality experience than the other? If the life insurance company claims that strict underwriting is responsible for lower than average mortality experience, does actual experience match the assumed mortality rate?

If mortality or claims experience is worse than illustrated, the life insurance company's increased costs can be passed along to the policy owner. In a term life insurance policy, adverse mortality or claims experience can be passed along by adjusting the illustrated premium up to, but not in excess of, the higher guaranteed premium. In most permanent products (other than variable products), the life insurance company is able to pass along adverse mortality experience through a decrease in the crediting rate or dividend rate (but not below the guaranteed rate). The life insurance company can also pass along its adverse mortality or claims experience through increased mortality charges ("cost of insurance" or "COI" charges) up to the guaranteed maximum charges as stated in the policy.

§16.4(b)(2) Who Bears The Mortality Risk Depends On The Contract[94]

• **Traditional Whole Life.** The policy owner bears the mortality risk (through reduced dividends or a reduced crediting rate), but only up

---

[94] Adapted from Lee and Wilkey.

"The risk for the policy owner with regard to mortality pricing is that the actuary may have been too optimistic in making mortality projections. For example, if the actuary projects an annual improvement in the mortality rate of two percent, but the annual improvement proves to be less than the projection, the actual cost of the policy will be higher than originally illustrated. For term policies, this means that a higher than scheduled premium increase will occur. For participating policies from a mutual insurer, the mortality shortfall may result in a lower dividend. For whole life policies

to the maximum amount specified in the contract. The insurance company bears any excess mortality risk.

• **Universal Life.** The policy owner bears the mortality risk (through increased charges), but only up to the maximum amount specified in the contract. The insurance company bears any excess mortality risk.

• **Variable and Variable Universal Life.** The policy owner bears the mortality risk (through increased charges), but only up to the maximum amount specified in the contract. The insurance company bears any excess mortality risk.

§16.4(c) Interest/Investment Risk

Interest/investment risk is the risk that the life insurance company's general investment account or the policy's cash value will earn less than initially projected. The life insurance company's investment experience directly affects the interest or dividends credited to cash value policies. Whether the life insurance company's investment experience is a major risk factor depends on the type of policy. At one extreme, the typical term policy, which has no cash value, is not dependent on the life insurance company's investment experience, except to the extent that investment performance affects the continued viability of the life insurance company or cause the company to increase premiums to the maximum allowed in the contract. At the other extreme, variable policies, such as variable life and variable universal life, pass the entire investment risk to the policy owner if the cash value component is invested in a non-guaranteed investment subaccount. In between are general account cash value policies, such as whole life and universal life. For these policies, the life insurance company guarantees a minimum crediting rate, usually between 2% - 3%. On the other hand, higher crediting rates are almost always used to illustrate projected policy performance, particularly in "vanishing" premium illustrations. The life insurance company bears the risk involved in meeting the guaranteed crediting rates. Most or all of the risk in meeting the higher illustrated rates are shifted to the policy owner.

---

issued by a stock company, it will result in lower cash values. The bottom line of an overly optimistic projected mortality rate is that the policy owner will end up with less than projected unless the shortfall is made up in one of the other risk areas. The advisor should be especially aware that companies who make optimistic mortality assumptions in pricing their products will produce illustrations that look consistently better than their competition. The best way to compare policies is to become informed and to consult a reputable consulting actuary or life underwriter." Brody, Richey, and Baier at section II,A,3,a.

Investment risk affects not only the crediting rate of the policy's cash value account but also the safety of the underlying principal. Accordingly, it is necessary to determine the degree of market risk the insurance company is assuming with invested assets.

§16.4(c)(1) Who Bears The Interest/Investment Risk Depends On The Contract[95]

• **Traditional Whole Life.** The life insurance company bears the interest/investment risk up to the guaranteed cash value of the policy.

---

[95] Adapted from Lee and Wilkey.

Ben Baldwin offers this warning concerning interest/investment risks: "All life insurance containing investment capital, be it whole life, universal life, variable life, or variable universal life, runs on the investment returns earned on the investment capital. Earnings on the investment capital are limited by the amount the policy owner chooses to invest within the contract (little investment means little returns), and what the government and the marketplace permit the investment to earn. When policy earnings are less than policy costs, policy owners must pay more into the policy to cover costs or the policy will use [i.e., consume] the capital in the policy to cover costs. When capital has been completely used up [i.e., entirely consumed] to cover costs, policies terminate, unless policy owners can make substantial payments to cover ongoing policy costs. Policy owners must evaluate *all* the risks and potential investment earnings on the investment alternatives offered by insurance companies, both general and separate accounts." Baldwin at 207.

"In a one-year term policy with no dividends or cash values, all investment risk is borne by the company. However, in variable life products without guarantees, the investment risk, including loss of principal, belongs to the policy owner. Investment risk in other policies is shared, in varying degrees, between the company and policy owners. The effect of a company's failure to meet its projected investment return or interest rate assumptions is generally a reduction in cash values, dividends or death benefit. In such cases, a policy owner must make additional premium contributions to the policy to maintain the values originally illustrated. In evaluating a policy illustration shown to a client, the advisor should make certain that interest rate assumptions made in the illustration are reasonable in light of current interest rates and investment returns. Even if an insurance company's general portfolio is higher than average current interest rates and investment returns, those market forces, if sustained, will exert a downward pressure on the company's portfolio. Thus, even though current company rates are illustrated, to be conservative, the product illustration should also provide a projection based on an interest rate that is one percent or two percent lower than current company rates. Another way to protect the client is to recommend variable policies that provide a guarantee against loss of principal, especially if the client is an individual to whom the death benefit is important. Large companies may be willing to assume greater risk and buy a variable policy that does not have a guarantee against loss of principal." Brody, Richey and Baier at section II,A,3,b.

• **Universal Life.** The life insurance company bears the interest/investment risk up to the policy's minimum crediting rate guarantee.

• **Variable and Variable Universal Life.** The policy owner bears all the interest/investment risk, except on cash value allocated to the guaranteed interest account.

§16.4(d) Lapse Risk

Lapse risk is the risk that the policy owner will surrender or cancel the policy before the life insurance company has recouped its initial costs of placing the life insurance coverage. Thus, lapse risk deals with the number and timing of policy surrenders and cancellations. Low lapse rates[96] tend to increase an insurer's profitability.[97] Insurance companies charge underwriting costs, commissions and establish first year cash values in the year the policy is issued rather than amortizing those costs over future years. This results in the life insurance company losing money in the first year. Thus, if a policy lapses before the life insurance company recovers its policy acquisition costs (commissions, underwriting, allocable share of administration expenses, etc.) the company will incur a loss. Life insurance companies with low lapse rates are able to recover first year costs over the lifetime of the policy. Moreover, most lapses in early policy years are by persons who are confident of their ability to obtain new insurance; few persons who are uninsurable or suspect future health problems permit policies to lapse. So a high early lapse rate is a warning sign that the insurance company may be incurring a higher than normal rate of loss. Companies with low lapse rates, on the other hand, retain a higher proportion of insured, and the company should, theoretically, be more profitable.

§16.4(d)(1) Who Bears The Lapse Risk Depends On The Contract[98]

• **Traditional Whole Life.** The life insurance company bears the lapse risk, and hedges that risk by providing a low initial cash value in the policy.

---

[96] Lapse rates are also known as "persistency experience." A high persistency means a low lapse rate, and usually greater profits for the life insurance company.

[97] Generally a life insurance company makes a profit on whole life policies that have been in existence for at least seven years.

[98] Adapted from Lee and Wilkey.

• **Universal Life.** The policy owner bears the lapse risk up to the amount of the policy's surrender charges.

• **Variable and Variable Universal Life.** The policy owner bears the lapse risk up to the amount of the policy's surrender charges.

§16.4(e) Expense Risk

Expense[99] risk is the risk that costs of administering the life insurance product will be greater than initially anticipated by the life insurance company. Expense risks are borne similarly to mortality risks. All policies have maximum expense charges as a contractual provision. The policy owner bears the expense risk up to the maximum amount specified in the contract; the life insurance company bears the expense risk in excess of that amount. The life insurance company's overhead is the least important of the four risk factors enumerated in section 16.4(a), above. Mortality and investment performance have a greater impact on a life insurance policy's performance. However, poor management practices can result in a decreased crediting rate on the policy's cash value account. The life insurance company's expenses are reflected in the discussion of earnings in most life insurance company rating reports.

§16.4(e)(1) Who Bears The Expense Risk Depends On The Contract[100]

• **Traditional Whole Life.** The policy owner bears the expense risk (through reduced dividends or a reduced crediting rate), but only up to the maximum amount specified in the contract. The insurance company bears any excess expense risk.

"Lapse risk is the risk that a policy will terminate or the policy owner will surrender the policy before the company can recoup its costs of selling and issuing the insurance. A surrender or lapse in the early years will generally result in a significant loss to the insurance company. On the whole, a company with lower lapse ratios can price its products lower than a company with higher lapse ratios because it has a greater chance of recouping its initial investment and making money. A low lapse ratio also indicates the stability of the risk class being underwritten. This often goes hand-in-hand with lower mortality risk." Brody, Richey and Baier at section II,A,3,c.

[99] Expenses are also referred to as "loading," which is a "term that encompasses all the insurer's business expenses in marketing, issuing, administering, and paying claims on policies. If the insurer's cost of doing business is greater than projected, [policy] dividends will be adversely affected. If the insurer is able to contain costs and keep them below projected amounts, [policy] dividends will be positively affected." Leimberg & Doyle at 94.

[100] Adapted from Lee and Wilkey.

• **Universal Life.** The policy owner bears the expense risk (through increased charges), but only up to the maximum amount specified in the contract. The insurance company bears any excess expense risk.

• **Variable and Variable Universal Life.** The policy owner bears the expense risk (through increased charges), but only up to the maximum amount specified in the contract. The insurance company bears any excess expense risk.

§16.5 UNDERSTANDING LIFE INSURANCE POLICY ILLUSTRATIONS

After a life insurance company has been selected, "illustrations" are presented for various policies. What do these illustrations mean and how do you make sense out of them? [101]

§16.5(a) How Illustrations Work

A life insurance illustration is a scenario based on a specific set of assumptions involving the company's anticipated mortality experience, lapse rate, investment performance, and expenses. However, the assumptions are usually not guaranteed by the insurance company and the risk of non-performance is borne by the policy owner, as discussed above. For example, an illustration showing the performance of a policy based on a 9% crediting rate illustrates the cost and performance of that policy—***if*** the company's expenses and earnings meet a specified goal each year ***and*** the company's mortality or claims experience is at least as good as projected. However, the insurance company does

---

"Compared to the other risks, expense risk is of less concern. Many insurance products guarantee expense levels. In those policies, the company bears this risk. Even when the level of expenses is not guaranteed on a particular product, the impact of this item on the policy owner's overall risk is minimal." Brody, Richey and Baier at section II,A,3,d.

[101] *See,* Lee and Wilkey at section V, B; and Chapter 4 of Leimberg & Doyle. *See also,* Neil Alexander, "Understanding Life Insurance Illustrations," *Journal of Accountancy* (February 2003) Online issues, www.aicpa.org/pubs/jofa/feb2003/alexand.htm. When obtaining an illustration, make sure it contains the full (legal) name of the life insurance company and its state of domicile, a current date, the name and type of product that is illustrated, and the state for which the illustration is being prepared (typically the insured's domicile).

not guarantee that claims, expenses, and investment experience in the future will be as shown in the illustration.[102]

> **Practice Point:** The insured and trustee should be certain to carefully review the entire illustration, not just an excerpt of it (and, for variable policies, the prospectus). The illustration will state, usually in the lower margin, its total number of pages. Review or reliance on only selected portions of the illustration may lead to serious misconceptions. An illustration is not a substitute for the actual policy. For the more cautious policy owner, a specimen life insurance policy (and its applicable riders) should be reviewed before making a final purchase decision. The life insurance policy is the contract between the parties and it is the document that the policy owner should rely on for a clear statement concerning what premiums, death benefits and cash values are guaranteed.

§16.5(b) What Happens If The Assumptions In Illustrations Are Not Realized?

If the company's claims, expense and investment experience in the future are worse than illustrated, one of two possible scenarios will generally result:

(1) Either the company reserves the right to increase the premium it will charge for the policy, up to a guaranteed maximum; or,

(2) The premium will remain level, but the number of years that the premium must be paid will increase.

---

[102] "However, the actual assumptions that underlie policy illustrations are proprietary information; and, without knowing the underlying assumptions, it is difficult to determine how single variable changes illuminate actual policy risks. Actuaries, in part, focus on the risk that the assumptions underlying product development and pricing are misspecified or incorrectly determined. Actuaries term the risk that a pricing model's flaws preclude corporate profitability objectives 'pricing risk.' If there is a high degree of pricing risk (*e.g., each* relevant variable can be at the upper bound of 'reasonableness' at some time but the assumption that *all* variables exhibit favorable interaction for most or all of the time may be unreasonable), then there is a high probability that the insurance contract will fail to deliver adequate return on equity to the carrier; or will fail to deliver projected values to the policyholder absent additional premiums." Kathryn A. Ballsun, Patrick J. Collins and Dieter Jurkat, "Standards of Prudence and Management of the Insurance Portfolio (Part 2 of 4)," 32 *ACTEC Journal* 66, 89 (Summer 2006).

§16.5(c) Look For A Guaranteed Maximum Period

Most insurance illustrations contain footnotes or other annotations that should divulge whether the premium being illustrated is the guaranteed maximum. If the illustrated premium is not the guaranteed maximum, or if the illustration does not permit you to determine the guaranteed maximum, a new illustration should be prepared that sets forth this information.

§16.5(d) Look Out For Excessive Optimism

When reviewing an illustration, bear in mind that the illustration assumes that the life insurance company will attain a specific profit goal and will credit a general account policy with a certain dividend level or percentage rate of return for the life of the policy. Always ask for an alternative illustration with reductions of 100 basis points (i.e., 1%) drop in the crediting rate or dividend rate and 200 basis points (i.e., a 2%) drop in the crediting rate or dividend rate. Using the Best's report for the insurance company in question, determine the company's current net return. If the illustration for a general account policy is projecting a higher crediting rate or dividend rate than what the life insurance company is currently earning, request a written explanation for this optimistic forecast.

§16.5(d)(1) New Money Or Portfolio Basis

Determine whether the rate of return that the life insurance company is earning is being computed using a portfolio or a new money basis. The portfolio approach takes into consideration all assets, while the new money approach looks to the rate at which the carrier can currently invest assets. If interest rates are declining, the portfolio approach tends to overstate probable future earnings since older assets that are producing a higher rate of return tend to average out the declining interest rates on new investments. If the market is rising, the new money approach tends to exaggerate the company's earnings since new investments will not be burdened with the lower overall return of the company's older assets that are producing a lower rate of return. You must accordingly ask some questions, especially if the policy being illustrated appears much less expensive than competing policies and other factors, such as blending, are equal.

§16.5(e) Questions For Term Insurance Illustrations

Here are some questions to ask about the illustrations for term life insurance policies:

• For what period is the illustrated premium guaranteed? Some term policies (known as annual renewable term) guarantee the illustrated premium for only the first year. Other term policies (known as level term policies) guarantee the illustrated premium for the first five, ten, fifteen, twenty, or thirty years. Once the illustrated premium is no longer guaranteed, the company is free to raise the premium to reflect actual claims, expense and investment experience, but not in excess of the guaranteed maximum premium amount.

• What is the maximum premium that may be charged and how often may the premium be adjusted? Some term policies permit the carrier to increase premiums on each anniversary. Adjustments are less frequent for other policies.

• Can the term policy be converted to permanent coverage and up to what age?[103] Does conversion require proof of insurability?

• Does the term policy provide for waiver of premiums in the event of disability? If so, does life insurance coverage continue for life or does life insurance terminate at the end of a stated term?

§16.5(f) Questions For Permanent Life Insurance Illustrations

Here are some questions to ask about the illustrations for permanent life insurance policies:

• If a blended product is illustrated, is the illustrated premium the guaranteed maximum? If it is not, what is the guaranteed maximum? What percentage of the initial death benefit is whole life, and what percentage is term?

• If current assumption (interest-sensitive) whole life is illustrated, is the illustrated premium the guaranteed maximum? If it is not, what is the guaranteed maximum?

• What interest or dividend crediting rate is being assumed in the illustration? What is the guaranteed minimum crediting rate?

• What are the surrender charges?

• What differences are shown between accumulated values and cash surrender values?

• What differences are shown between early premiums paid and cash surrender values?

---

[103] *See,* footnote 19, above, concerning questions to ask regarding convertibility of a term policy.

• Is the life insurance company currently meeting the illustrated interest or dividend crediting rate, and has it met it in prior years? For how many prior years? Based on your assumptions as to the state of the economy, is it reasonable to assume that the life insurance company will be able to meet that interest or dividend crediting rate assumption in future years?

• Is the yield assumption credible? If two life insurance companies provide illustrations and one illustration is based on a substantially higher yield or crediting rate assumption than the other, what facts justify the assumption that the company will permanently be more profitable than the other?

• What will be the result if the life insurance company is unable to credit the policy with the illustrated yield? If the product is "pure" whole life and the illustration shows that the premium will "vanish" after a specified number of years, the effect of the company's failure to meet the illustrated interest or dividend crediting rate will result in increasing the number of years premiums must be paid before they "vanish," if ever. If the product is blended whole life-term and the illustrated premium is not the guaranteed maximum for the term component, the failure of the company to meet the illustrated crediting rate will result in increasing the number of years premiums must be paid, increasing the annual premium up to the guaranteed maximum, or both. Have new illustrations prepared showing the effect of decreasing the crediting rate in 1% (i.e., 100 basis points) increments to the guaranteed minimum crediting rate.

• Is the current illustrated crediting rate being paid to existing policies? Some life insurance companies credit new policies with a higher interest or dividend rate than existing policies. If so, find out why. Do differences in product types justify different crediting rates or may the life insurance company be illustrating unreasonably high crediting rates during the policy's first year in order to attract new business, or treating existing policyholders less well, than new ones?

§16.5(g) Questions For Blended Insurance Illustrations

With respect to blended insurance products, ask the term questions about the term component and the permanent life questions about the whole life component.

§16.5(h) Questions For Second To Die Insurance Illustrations

Illustrations for second to die insurance by some life insurance companies tend to be more aggressive in their mortality, yield and bonus assumptions than similar illustrations of the same life insurance companies for single life insurance. In addition to the questions outlined above, second to die insurance raises some special questions.

• Are non-guaranteed bonus credits or termination dividends included in the illustration?

• To induce high persistency (i.e., to induce policy owners to not let their policies lapse), some life insurance companies offer "bonus" credits (extra interest being credited after the policy has been in effect for a specified number of years) or "termination dividends" (a dividend payable at surrender or death) on second to die policies. As a general rule, termination dividends are not guaranteed. Some bonus credits may be guaranteed. If the credits or dividends are not guaranteed, the illustration should be resubmitted without the credits and dividends.

• If the first spouse to die passes away substantially before his or her actuarial life expectancy, will otherwise "vanished" premiums reappear?

§16.5(i) Questions For Variable Insurance Illustrations

Here are some questions to ask about the illustrations for variable life insurance:

• What investment funds are available, what has been their performance, and what is the size of their asset base?[104] There is substantial diversity in the investment funds made available by different life insurance companies. What has been the fund's past performance? How long has the fund been in existence? Who manages the fund and what is his or her track record? What are the expense levels associated with different funds?

• What are the hypothetical gross and net annual return assumptions? Are the hypothetical gross and net annual returns reasonable? If the net return varies in different illustrated variable products, determine the reason for the difference. The illustration will show investment advisory fees and fund operating expenses deducted from the gross yield to

---

[104] Selection of product should reflect a policy owner's investment philosophy. If the policy owner is a passive investor and believes that index funds will optimize performance over time, the illustration should project a policy with index funds selections (in addition to non-index fund selections).

arrive at the net yield. Are the net fees based on an average of fund sub-accounts or are they based on specific fund accounts?[105]

• Request an illustration showing a gross return of 0% per annum (flat return), 4% per annum (conservative return), 6% per annum (moderate return), and 8% per annum (aggressive return), and then see how long that return will support the policy. Will the gross return adequately fund the policy for the insured's life expectancy or until age 100?

• Are the correct investment funds illustrated? The advisory fees and other costs may differ significantly between funds.

• Is the death benefit guaranteed? Will the death benefit be payable even though the investment funds perform significantly below the illustration? Some, but not all variable policies guarantee payment of the stated death benefit if a specified minimum level of premiums have been paid or if a separate rider is purchased at additional cost.

• Any cash value withdrawals or planned policy loans should be illustrated prior to purchasing the policy to make certain the policy can remain in force after the cash value reductions have occurred. Like with any other permanent life insurance policy, if the policy is allowed to lapse, any gain in excess of premium payments will be taxed as ordinary income. *See,* section 2.18, above.

§16.5(j) Questions For Universal Insurance Illustrations

Here are some questions to ask about the illustrations for universal life insurance:

• What interest rate is being assumed? Is a "bonus" crediting rate that kicks in after several years being assumed?

• Request an illustration showing the guaranteed crediting rate, 4% per annum (conservative return), 6% per annum (moderate return), and

[105] If specific fund allocations are used to model "net returns," make sure that they reflect the actual funds the policy owner intends to use for investing the cash value. Illustration performance can look better when "low-cost" funds (generally stock index funds) are used. However, if the policy owner intends on making allocations to funds with heavier management fees (actively managed funds, international fund or specialty funds) then the illustration will understate the actual costs embedded in the insurance contract.

8% per annum (aggressive return), and then see how long that return will support the policy. Will the return adequately fund the policy for the insured's life expectancy or until age 100?

• Ask the applicable permanent life questions discussed in section 16.5(f), above.

• Ask the applicable variable life questions discussed in section 16.5(i), above, if the policy is a variable universal life policy.

§16.5(k) Obtaining The Information

The American Society of CLU and ChFC, a national organization of insurance and financial service professionals (800-927-2427, www.financialpro.org), has developed the Life Insurance Illustration Questionnaire ("IQ") as an educational tool to help professionals and consumers understand the different non-guaranteed performance assumptions use by insurance companies in the design of policies and the creation of illustrations. It consists of 25 questions directed to the insurance company on a number of non-guaranteed policy elements, such as mortality, interest or crediting rates, policy lapse rates, and company expenses. It has been developed primarily for non-SEC regulated products.[106] It is recommended that the IQ be submitted for each company on whose behalf an illustration is presented.

---

[106] To quote from the Introduction to the IQ:

"The purpose of the IQ is to help the student of life insurance understand the different non-guaranteed performance assumptions which insurance companies use to design and create sales illustrations. It has been developed primarily for non-SEC regulated products. Students should understand that sales illustrations are useful in developing the best combination of policy specifications to achieve the buyer's objective. However, illustrations have little value in predicting actual performance or in comparing products and companies.

Most life insurance products sold today have adjustable pricing. This can be accomplished either as a traditional "participating" product or as a product with "non-guaranteed pricing elements" such as changeable interest crediting rates, mortality charges, expense charges, etc. All adjustable pricing products incorporate some guarantees. However, the ***sales illustrations are usually designed to present potential benefits and costs under a set of non-guaranteed assumptions more optimistic than the guarantees.*** The insurance company generally limits its responsibility to the guarantees. So ***the risks associated with the inability of a product to achieve the higher illustrated benefits, or lower illustrated costs, than those generated by the guarantees are borne by the policy holder.*** A study of the responses to the IQ should help the student better understand those risks." (Emphasis added.)

Table 1
Flowchart of General Criteria for Selection of a Life Insurance Policy[107]

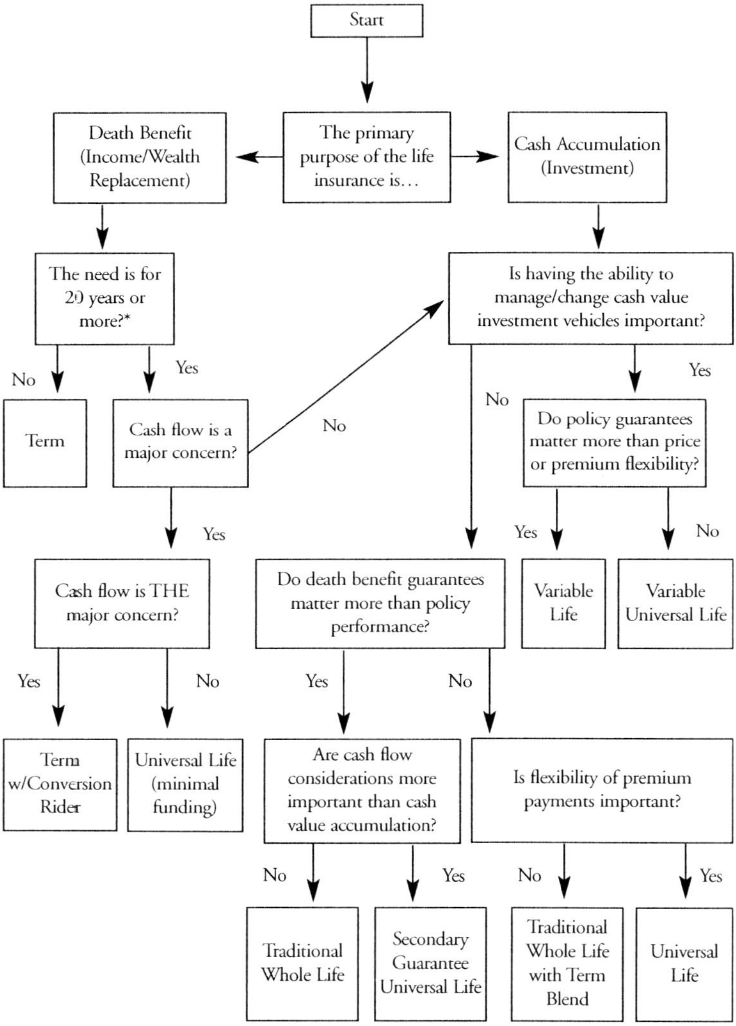

*15-20 years is the general rule—actual comparative calculations of term vs. permanent coverage should be done to assess the break point where the tax benefits of a permanent policy exceed a "buy term and invest the rest" strategy.

---

[107] Adapted from Worksheet 2 from Lee and Wilkey. Reproduced with the permission of Gary R. Lee, Esq. and Tax Management, Inc., a subsidiary of The Bureau of National Affairs, Inc., Washington, DC. All rights reserved.

Table 2
Checklist Of Features, Advantages, And Disadvantages Of Typical Life Insurance Policies[108]

Term Life	Traditional Whole Life	Universal Life	Variable Universal Life
Important Features Annual or fixed term coverage. Affordable, low cost coverage designed to meet temporary needs. May be convertible to permanent coverage. No cash value. Offered with level premiums for a fixed term of years. Death benefit is fixed and level. **Advantages** Lowest premium cost for short-term needs. Fixed level premium during coverage term. No investment risk. Less trustee management required of the policy.	**Important Features** Lifetime coverage. Premiums are fixed and level. Minimum crediting rate (or cash value increase) is guaranteed. Cash values invested in life insurance carrier's general account. Dividends are paid annually. Dividends may be paid to policy owner, reduce or "offset" future premiums or buy additional coverage. Term riders may reduce premiums. Death benefit is fixed and level. Guaranteed to endow at age 100. **Advantages** Fixed annual premium. Conservative portfolio backing (bonds and mortgages.)	**Important Features** Lifetime coverage. Flexible premiums, and adjustable death benefit amount. Cash values invested in life insurance carrier's general account (typically short term liquid investments). Guaranteed minimum crediting rate. Crediting rates paid monthly. Mortality and expense charges deducted monthly. Performance riders reduce premium. Guaranteed death benefit option. Death benefit can be face value only (Option A), or death benefit can be face value plus cash value (Option B). "No lapse guarantee" available. Unbundled (transparent) product disclosure.	**Important Features** Lifetime coverage. Flexible premiums, and adjustable death benefit. Policy owner chooses how cash values are invested (typically through mutual fund like investments). Mortality and expense charges deducted monthly. Performance riders reduce premium. Unbundled (transparent) product disclosure. **Advantages** Complete premium flexibility. Possible superior long-term returns in diversified investment options. Cash value held separately from carrier's general account and

[108]Prepared by Eugene F. Lovasco, Esq., CPA, CLU and John Marshall, CLU, ChFC of ALCOS, Sterling Heights, Michigan. www.alcos.com. Used with permission. All rights reserved. *See also,* "Menu of Life Insurance Products" at page 183 of Baldwin; Figures 1.3, 18.3 and 18.4 of Leimberg and Doyle at 13-14, 283 and 284; and http://www.axa-equitable.com/poducts/life_types.html.

Term Life	Traditional Whole Life	Universal Life	Variable Universal Life
Disadvantages Fixed level term premium period expires. Insurance need may outlast coverage term. Premiums increase each year for annual renewable term. Premiums rise sharply after fixed level term period expires. No equity build up in the policy. No policy loans or withdrawals.	Strong long-term guarantees. Tax deferred equity build up in the policy. Can borrow (but not withdraw) policy's cash value. Less trustee management required of the policy than Universal Life or Variable Universal Life. **Disadvantages** Premium is inflexible. Cash values subject to life insurance carrier's financial strength and not protected from the carrier's insolvency. Carrier chooses how premiums are invested (typically long term bonds and mortgages). Costly to policy owner if policy lapses early. Must pay interest on cash borrowed from the policy. Can not withdraw policy's cash value. No unbundled (transparent) product disclosure. More trustee management required of the policy.	**Advantages** Lowest annual premium costs. Policy's investment return more predictable than the investment return of a variable universal life policy. Complete premium flexibility. Tax deferred equity build up in the policy. Can borrow or withdraw policy's cash value. **Disadvantages** Inadequate early funding may create large premiums later. Mortality charges can increase. Cash values subject to life insurance carrier's financial strength and not protected from the carrier's insolvency. Carrier chooses how premiums are invested. Must pay interest on cash borrowed from the policy. Not guaranteed to endow at age 100. More trustee management required of the policy.	protected from carrier's insolvency. Tax deferred equity build up in the policy. Can borrow or withdraw policy's cash value. Length of coverage determined by policy owner. **Disadvantages** Inadequate early funding may create large premiums later. No guaranteed minimum crediting rate (unless investment chosen by policy owner provides a guarantee). Mortality charges can increase. Policy owner assumes cash value investment risk. Possible market loss on cash value investments. Asset management charges depend on investment options chosen. Must pay interest on cash borrowed from the policy. Not guaranteed to endow at age 100. More trustee management required of the policy and its investments.

17

Sample Irrevocable Life Insurance Trust Forms (And Other Related Items)

§17.1 SAMPLE ILIT FORM[1]

Appendix 1 contains a sample form of irrevocable trust designed to hold life insurance on the life of one person, who is married. This form is the sample ILIT that is referenced throughout this book. The trust is drafted on the assumption that the grantor alone will be making contributions to the trust. The sample form contains a contingent Marital Trust that is intended to qualify for the QTIP marital deduction. The Family Trust (also known as a credit shelter trust) contains ascertainable standards, and thus allows the surviving spouse to serve as sole trustee of that trust, upon the insured's death, without adverse estate tax consequences. The Family Trust contains provisions permitting it to be divided into a marital deduction trust for state death tax purposes. Such provisions permit the full use of the deceased grantor's federal estate tax applicable exclusion amount when there is a state

[1] This form is designed to be a supplement to (and not a substitution for) the grantor's primary estate planning document, such as a revocable living trust. This form is not meant to be a pour-over recipient of the grantor's probate estate or the grantor's revocable living trust. Michigan practitioners should note that the form complies with Michigan's Estates and Protected Individuals Code that went into effect on April 1, 2000.

death tax that has decoupled from the federal applicable exclusion amount or is different from the federal transfer tax regime, and state death tax law permits a marital deduction for the surviving spouse. The ILIT is *not* designed to be GST tax exempt. If the transferor wants to be assured that none of the transferor's GST tax exemption is automatically allocated to the ILIT (because, for example, the ILIT does not come within one of the limited exceptions to a "GST Trust"), the transferor should "opt-out" of the GST automatic allocation rules by filing a notice with the IRS.[2]

As this is a sample form, practitioners must be careful when using the form to adapt it to comply with new developments in federal and state estate, gift, and generation-skipping transfer tax law and to modify it to comply with applicable state law and the particular requirements and needs of their client; accordingly, the author makes no representations or warranties as to the efficacy of the form.

§17.2 SAMPLE SECOND-TO-DIE ILIT FORM[3]

Appendix 2 contains a sample form of irrevocable trust designed to hold life insurance on the last to die of a married couple. The ILIT is designed to be GST tax exempt, but because of the hanging *Crummey* withdrawal rights, it may *not* qualify as a GST Trust (to which the grantor's GST tax exemption will be automatically allocated). Therefore, the transferor will need to annually allocate his or her GST tax exemption to contributions[4] or to file a notice with the IRS requesting that the trust be deemed a GST Trust.[5] As this is a sample form, practitioners must be careful when using the form to adapt it to comply with new developments in federal and state estate, gift, and generation-skipping transfer tax law and to modify it to comply with applicable state law and the particular requirements and needs of their client; accordingly, the author makes no representations or warranties as to the efficacy of the form.

---

[2] *See,* Sample form of *"Election Out of Indirect Skip GST Allocation Statement"* in Appendix 4.

[3] *See,* Footnote 1, above.

[4] *See*, Sample form of *"Notice of GST Exemption Allocation to Trust"* in Appendix 4.

[5] See, Sample form of *"GST Trust Election Statement"* in Appendix 4.

§17.3 SAMPLE ILIT FORM FOR AN UNMARRIED PERSON[6]

Appendix 3 contains a sample form of irrevocable trust designed to hold life insurance on an unmarried person with descendants. The ILIT is designed to be GST tax exempt, but because of the hanging *Crummey* withdrawal rights, it may *not* qualify as a GST Trust (to which the grantor's GST tax exemption will be automatically allocated). Therefore, the transferor will need to annually allocate his or her GST tax exemption to contributions[7] or to file a notice with the IRS requesting that the trust be deemed a GST Trust.[8] As this is a sample form, practitioners must be careful when using the form to adapt it to comply with new developments in federal and state estate, gift, and generation-skipping transfer tax law and to modify it to comply with applicable state law and the particular requirements and needs of their client; accordingly, the author makes no representations or warranties as to the efficacy of the form.

§17.4 ATTACHMENTS TO U.S. GIFT TAX RETURNS

Appendix 4 contains a sample notice of allocating GST tax exemption to a trust, a sample notice of opt-out of the GST automatic allocation rules of IRC section 2632(b) concerning direct skips, a sample notice of opt-out of the GST automatic allocation rules of IRC section 2632(c) concerning indirect skips, a sample notice of treatment of an irrevocable trust as a GST trust for purposes of IRC section 2632, and a sample notice of late allocation of GST tax exemption to a trust pursuant to Treas. Reg. §26.2642-2(a).

§17.5 SAMPLE DOCUMENTS TO GRANTORS, TRUSTEES, AND BENEFICIARIES

Appendix 5 contains a memorandum to the grantor and trustee on the operation of an ILIT, a sample letter from the grantor to the ILIT trustee concerning which ILIT beneficiaries are ***excluded*** from having a *Crummey* withdrawal right, and a sample *Crummey* withdrawal right notice-letter from the ILIT trustee to the ILIT beneficiaries.

---

[6] *See,* Footnote 1, above.

[7] *See,* Sample form of "*Notice of GST Exemption Allocation to Trust*" in Appendix 4.

[8] *See,* Sample form of *"GST Trust Election Statement"* in Appendix 4.

If you have any questions, suggestions, or comments concerning these forms, please do not hesitate to write, or contact me at (248) 269-2020, svgjr@aol.com or at www.grassiandtoering.com. If you contact me by e-mail, please supply your name, your firm's name, your address, and your phone number. Thank you.

Appendix 1

SAMPLE IRREVOCABLE LIFE INSURANCE TRUST

Note: This form is a sample irrevocable life insurance trust that is designed to hold a single life policy on a married grantor. The trust is **not** designed to hold a second to die life insurance policy, **nor** is the trust designed to be GST tax exempt. If the transferor wants to be assured that none of the transferor's GST tax exemption is automatically allocated to the ILIT (because, for example, the ILIT does not come within one of the limited exceptions to a "GST Trust,") the transferor should "opt-out" of the GST automatic allocation rules by filing a notice with the IRS (*see,* "Election Out Statement" in Appendix 4).The trust is drafted on the assumption that the grantor alone will be making contributions to the trust. The trust contains two alternate forms of *Crummey* withdrawal rights. Optional and alternate language is contained in brackets { }.

This form is designed to be an adjunct to (and not a substitution for) the grantor's base estate plan, such as a revocable living trust. This form should not be used as a pour-over from a person's probate estate, will, or other trust.

The sample form contains a contingent Marital Trust that is intended to qualify for the QTIP marital deduction. Such a trust may be useful if ILIT property is includable in the grantor's gross estate, and the grantor is married. The fiduciary of the grantor's estate has the authority to elect all or a portion of the Marital Trust for QTIP treatment through a *Clayton* contingent QTIP election. The portion of the Marital Trust property not elected for QTIP treatment is held in the Family Trust (i.e., the credit shelter trust) for the benefit of the surviving spouse and the deceased grantor's children. The Family Trust contains provisions permitting it to be divided into a marital deduction trust for state death tax purposes. Such provisions permit the full use of the deceased grantor's federal estate tax applicable exclusion amount when there is a state death tax that has decoupled from the federal applicable exclusion amount or is different from the federal transfer tax regime, and state death tax law permits a marital deduction for the surviving spouse.

Practice note: Michigan practitioners should note that the sample trust form complies with Michigan's Estates and Protected Individuals Code, which went into effect April 1, 2000.

As this is a sample form, practitioners must be careful when using the form to adapt it to comply with new developments in federal and state estate, gift and generation-skipping transfer tax law and to modify it to comply with applicable state law and the particular requirements and needs of their client; accordingly, the author makes no representations or warranties as to the efficacy of the form.

TABLE OF CONTENTS
for
THE «SETTLORFULLNAME» IRREVOCABLE TRUST

ARTICLE 1
CREATION AND FUNDING THE TRUST

ARTICLE 2
IRREVOCABILITY

ARTICLE 3
WITHDRAWAL RIGHTS

ARTICLE 4
DISTRIBUTION DURING LIFETIME

4.1 Distribution of Principal and Income During Lifetime

4.2 Limited Power of Appointment by Special Power Holder

4.3 Distribution In Satisfaction of Unlapsed Withdrawal Right

ARTICLE 5
DISTRIBUTION AFTER DEATH

5.1 Distributions of Amounts Included in My Estate If I am Survived by My Spouse

5.2 Purchase of Assets and Loans

5.3 Administration of the Balance of the Trust Property

5.4 Family Trust

5.5 Children's Trust

5.6 Absence of Beneficiaries

ARTICLE 6
TRUSTEES

6.1 Initial and Successor Trustees

6.2 Incapacity of Trustee

6.3 Resignation by Trustee

6.4 Trustee May Delegate to Co-Trustee

6.5 Trustee May Appoint a Co-Trustee

6.6 Trustee May Appoint a Substitute Trustee

6.7 Individual Trustee May Nominate Successor Trustee

6.8 Sole Beneficiary—Trustee Authorized

6.9 Action by One Trustee

6.10 Multiple Trustees

6.11 Trustee's Fees

6.12 Qualifying as Trustee

6.13 Title and Powers

6.14 Other Trustee's Acts and Accounts, and Delivery of Trust Records

6.15 Corporate Successor

6.16 Proceeds Application

6.17 Notice

6.18 Trustee Liability

6.19 Conflict of Interest

6.20 Initial Notice of Trustee Status

6.21 Removal of Trustee

ARTICLE 7
TRUSTEE POWERS AND TRUST ADMINISTRATION

7.1 Trustee Powers

7.2 Beneficiary Under Disability

7.3 Spendthrift Provisions

7.4 Certificate of Trust Existence and Authority

7.5 Multiple Copies

7.6 Termination of Trust

7.7 Accrued Income

7.8 Right of Representation

7.9 Accountings and Information to Beneficiaries

7.10 S Corporation Stock

7.11 Guidelines for Discretionary Distributions

ARTICLE 8
GENERAL PROVISIONS

8.1 Rule Against Perpetuities

8.2 Power of Appointment Matters

8.3 Law, Definitions, Captions, and Severability

8.4 Disclaimer by Beneficiary

8.5 Actions by Incapacitated or Minor Beneficiaries

8.6 Virtual Representation

8.7 Arbitration

ARTICLE 9
SURVIVAL AND ANTI-LAPSE

9.1 Survival of Beneficiary

9.2 Negation of Anti-Lapse Statute

ARTICLE 10
MY FAMILY

10.1 Spouse

10.2 Children

SCHEDULE A

Property Transferred to The «SettlorFullName» Irrevocable Trust, dated «DateofExecution»

[Revised thru 06252007]

THE «SETTLORFULLNAME» IRREVOCABLE TRUST

Name of Trust:	The «SettlorFullName» Irrevocable Trust, dated «DateofExecution»
Initial Trustee:	«InitialTrustee»
Successor Trustees:	«AltTrustee1» «AltTrustee2» «AltTrustee3» «AltTrustee4»
Date of Execution:	«DateofExecution»

I, «SettlorFullName», on «DateofExecution», sign this Trust Agreement ("Agreement") with «InitialTrustee» as trustee (who, and any successor trustee, substitute trustee, or co-trustee, will be called "Trustee" in this Agreement and referred to in singular neuter pronouns), on the following terms and conditions. The original trust established hereunder by me is hereinafter sometimes referred to as the "initial trust."

ARTICLE 1
CREATION AND FUNDING THE TRUST

1.1 Creation of Trust. I create this trust as a means by which assets, which may include one (1) or more policies of insurance on my life, the life of any other person, or the joint lives of two or more persons, directly or indirectly in any arrangement deemed appropriate by Trustee, may be held for the benefit of my beneficiaries, on the terms and conditions set forth in this Agreement. It is my intent in creating this trust that all gifts made to this trust by me (directly or indirectly) be both complete and generally gifts of present interests for federal gift tax purposes. All provisions of this trust shall be construed in such a manner as best to affect these intents. Accordingly, no power enumerated herein or accorded to trustees, or granted pursuant to law, whether singularly, jointly or as a whole, shall be construed:

(A) To enable me: (i) to become a Trustee hereunder (or to possess or exercise any powers of such office), (ii) to vote any stock described in IRC section 2036(b) which may at any time be directly or indirectly given to any trust hereunder, (iii) to possess or exercise any power of appointment (including a right of withdrawal) with respect to any such trust, (iv) to possess, exercise or retain any power or interest described in IRC sections 2036, 2037 and 2038, (v) if I am the insured under any policy of insurance held by any trust hereunder, to exercise any incident of ownership within the meaning of IRC section 2042 with respect to that policy held by the trust, (vi) to receive any distributions on behalf of a beneficiary (regardless of my relationship to the beneficiary), or (vii) to possess or exercise any rights or discretion granted to a beneficiary hereunder; and

(B) To permit any trust distribution which would have the effect of discharging any legal obligation of mine (including any obligation that I may have at any time relating to the support and/or education of any beneficiary hereunder).

1.2 Transfer of Property to Trust. I hereby irrevocably transfer and assign to Trustee the property listed in **SCHEDULE A**, to be held and administered according to the terms of this trust. In connection with the transfer of any life insurance policies to Trustee, I agree to execute, in addition to an appropriate assignment of ownership form, any and all other instruments necessary or appropriate to permit Trustee to exercise all rights, powers, options, privileges or incidents of ownership that I may have had as the owner of such policies. With regard to any group term policies assigned to Trustee, the transfer of such policies also includes any future policies to be issued, or policies in supplementation thereof, or in succession, substitution, replacement or renewal thereof, and any increase in the amount of coverage.

Any person may transfer property acceptable to Trustee at any time. Trustee may accept a transfer of property that is subject to one or more conditions imposed by the donor (including giving a particular beneficiary (or a group of beneficiaries) a right to withdraw a contribution and the conditions for the lapse of a beneficiary's right of withdrawal) if Trustee deems it to be in the best interests of the trust and the beneficiaries. No condition imposed on a transfer of property and accepted by Trustee may in any way alter, amend, or change the rights of a beneficiary with respect to any prior transfers of property to the trust. Trustee may also refuse to accept any transfer of property if Trustee deems the refusal to be in the best interests of the trust and its beneficiaries.

1.3 Restrictions on Donors. Any individual (other than a donor's spouse who merely consents to gift splitting under IRC section 2513 concerning the donor's contribution to the trust) who makes a "contribution" (as defined in the Paragraph entitled, "**Contribution Defined**") to a trust in the first instance (in contrast to a beneficiary's exercise or lapse of a power of withdrawal or power of appointment) (such individual hereinafter sometimes being referred to as a "donor") shall, with respect to the contribution to the trust in question, be subject to the same limitations, restrictions, exceptions, and exclusions that I am subject to under this Agreement (but only insofar as they relate to the contributed property or to the trust in question (and any trusts derived therefrom)).

1.4 Restriction on My Spouse. If the trust holds a policy of life insurance on the joint, first or last to die of myself and my Spouse as the insureds, then and in that event, my Spouse shall be subject to the same restrictive terms, conditions, limitations and overall restrictions that I am subject to under this Agreement. Furthermore, if my Spouse is a donor to the trust, my Spouse shall be subject to the same restrictive terms, conditions, limitations and overall restrictions that I am subject to under this Agreement. In these regards, my Spouse shall be treated as though my Spouse were a grantor of the trust in question, and the words referring to me in the singular, such as "me," "I," "my" or "mine," shall where the context requires, refer to "us", "we", or "ours" instead.

1.5 Construction of Agreement. The Rule In Shelley's case and the Doctrine of Worthier Title (or any similar rule, doctrine or statute) shall not apply to this Agreement, nor shall this Agreement be construed under any such rule, doctrine or statute.

{Start Optional Paragraph 1.6}

1.6 Intent and Material Purpose of Trust. Without limiting, restricting or compelling the exercise of a Trustee's (or a Special Power Holder's) discretionary authority set forth in this Agreement, some of the material purposes of this Agreement are: (i) to retain assets in trust for the benefit of the trust's beneficiary, (ii) to provide creditor and asset protection to the trust's beneficiary, (iii) to provide spendthrift protection for the trust's beneficiary, (iv) to provide for the orderly and professional management and investment of trust assets, (v) to protect the trust's beneficiary from the trust's beneficiary's inabilities, disabilities, in-laws, ex-spouses, creditors, and predators, both now and in the future, (vi) to provide a financial "safety-net" for the trust's beneficiary, (vii) to provide potential resources that may be available to deal with the uncertainties of the economy, emergencies, and other vicissitudes and exigencies of daily life, and (viii) to minimize transfer, death and generation skipping transfer taxes. **{End Optional Paragraph 1.6}**

ARTICLE 2
IRREVOCABILITY

2.1 Irrevocable Trust. This trust is irrevocable. Applicable state law notwithstanding, I have no power, whether alone or in conjunction with others, and in whatever capacity, to control and direct payments or to alter, amend, modify, revoke, or terminate this Agreement or any trust provision or interest, in whole or in part, or to designate who shall possess or enjoy the trust property or trust income, whether under this trust or any statute or other rule of law. I retain no right, title, interest, or incident of ownership in any trust property.

ARTICLE 3
WITHDRAWAL RIGHTS

{Begin Alternate 1 to Paragraph 3.1—For single life policy on Settlor. 5x5 Tiered Withdrawal Rights—First to Spouse, Then to Descendants. To be used with Alternate 1 to Paragraph 3.2 (D).}

3.1 Withdrawal Rights. Unless otherwise provided pursuant to the paragraph item entitled, "**Restriction of a Withdrawal Right,"**

the following withdrawal rights shall exist with respect to contributions to the trust:

(A) Immediately following any contribution to the trust, my Spouse, my descendants, (individually a "donee," collectively the "donees") who are living on the date of the contribution (and have not been excluded from exercising their withdrawal right with respect to the contribution in question), shall have the right to withdraw from the trust the following amount:

(1) **First, to My Spouse.** In the case of my Spouse, the withdrawal rights with respect to any contribution amount (excluding however any amount of the contribution which is attributable to my Spouse as a deemed gift maker under the gift splitting rules of IRC section 2513) shall take priority and be satisfied fully before the withdrawal rights authorized in paragraph item (2) immediately below are satisfied. My Spouse's withdrawal rights shall not exceed whichever is **less**: (i) an amount equal to the value of the contribution, or (ii) the greater of five thousand ($5,000) dollars or five (5%) percent of the trust estate out of which, or the proceeds of which, the exercise of this withdrawal right could be satisfied (or such greater dollar amount or percentage as may be specified in IRC section 2514(e)); and

(2) **Second, to My Descendants.** In the case of a descendant of mine, the withdrawal rights with respect to any contribution shall not exceed whichever is **less**: (i) an amount equal to the value of the contribution after subtracting the amount, if any, subject to withdrawal by my Spouse under paragraph item (1) immediately above and dividing the remainder by the number of my descendants living at the time of the contribution, who have not been excluded from exercising their withdrawal right with respect to the contribution in question, or (ii) the greater of five thousand ($5,000) dollars or five (5%) percent of the trust estate out of which, or the proceeds of which, the exercise of this withdrawal right could be satisfied (or such greater dollar amount or percentage as may be specified in IRC section 2514(e)).

(3) **Additional Limitation on Amount Subject to Withdrawal.** To the extent a donee is also the donor of a contribution, or is treated as donor of one-half (1/2) of a contribution for federal gift tax purposes, that donee shall have no right of withdrawal with respect to such contribution to which they are the donor (or treated as the donor), and shall never thereafter be considered to have had a right of withdrawal with respect to such contribution. Furthermore, in no event may the amount subject to withdrawal by a donee under this Paragraph exceed in any calendar year the amount of the federal gift tax exclusion under IRC section 2503(b) available to the donor with respect to gifts to such donee, provided however, if requested by a married donor at the time of a contribution, the alternative limitation based on the gift tax annual exclusion shall be two (2) times the amount of the gift tax annual exclusion. In determining the amount of this withdrawal limitation, there shall be taken into consideration all previous gifts made to such donee from (or attributable to) such donor (and the donor's spouse, to the extent relevant) during the same calendar year, which gifts were eligible for the federal gift tax annual exclusion (and, in the case of my Spouse, were not eligible for the federal gift tax marital deduction).

(B) **Return of Excess Distribution.** If any donee receives a distribution in excess of the amount he or she is authorized to withdraw under this Paragraph, Trustee shall immediately notify such donee in writing, requiring the prompt repayment of such excess amount.

These withdrawal rights take precedence over any other power or discretion granted Trustee or any other person. **{End of Alternate 1 to Paragraph 3.1.}**

{Begin Alternate 2 to Paragraph 3.1 – For single life policy on Settlor. Tiered Withdrawal Rights—First to Spouse First with 30

Day Lapse of 5x5 Withdrawal Right to avoid ETIP, then to Descendants prorata with Hanging *Crummey* Power. Permits large (premium) gifts to Descendants. No Hanging *Crummey* Power to Spouse. To be used with Alternate 2 to Paragraph 3.2 (D).}

3.1 Withdrawal Rights. Unless otherwise provided pursuant to the paragraph item entitled, "**Restriction of a Withdrawal Right,**" the following withdrawal rights shall exist with respect to contributions to the trust:

(A) Immediately following any contribution to the trust, my Spouse and my descendants (individually a "donee," collectively the "donees") who are living on the date of the contribution (and have not been excluded from exercising their withdrawal right with respect to the contribution in question), shall have the right to withdraw from the trust the following amount:

(1) First, to My Spouse. In the case of my Spouse, the withdrawal rights with respect to any contribution amount (excluding however any amount of the contribution which is attributable to my Spouse as a deemed gift maker under the gift splitting rules of IRC section 2513) shall take priority and be satisfied fully before the withdrawal rights authorized in paragraph item (2) immediately below are satisfied. My Spouse's withdrawal rights shall not exceed whichever is **less**: (i) an amount equal to the value of the contribution, or (ii) the greater of five thousand ($5,000) dollars or five (5%) percent of the trust estate out of which, or the proceeds of which, the exercise of this withdrawal right could be satisfied (or such greater dollar amount or percentage as may be specified in IRC section 2514(e)).

(a) Lapse of Spouse's Withdrawal Right. The withdrawal rights granted my Spouse under this paragraph item (1) are all non-cumulative and shall lapse, if not exercised, on the earlier of: (i) thirty (30) calendar days following the date of the contribution to which such withdrawal rights relate, or (ii) the day preceding the my Spouse's date of death (provided the date of death occurs more than fifteen (15) days following the date of the contribution to which such withdrawal rights relate). No payment may be made in a subsequent year on account of my Spouse's failure to exercise a withdrawal right in a prior year. The lapse of my Spouse's withdrawal rights shall not be considered a contribution or gift to the trust estate. My Spouse's withdrawal right shall not terminate merely because of the termination of the initial trust, but shall continue with respect to all trusts under this Agreement, in which my Spouse is an interested trust beneficiary, until the withdrawal right lapses as described above. My Spouse's withdrawal right shall, upon termination of the initial trust, be exercisable first out of that portion of the trust fund that is deducted/elected for the federal estate tax marital deduction (as described in the sub-paragraph entitled, **"Continuation of Withdrawal Right After My Death"**).

(2) **Second, to My Descendants.** In the case of a descendant of mine, the withdrawal rights with respect to any contribution shall not exceed an amount equal to the value of the contribution after subtracting the amount, if any, subject to withdrawal by my Spouse under paragraph item (1) immediately above and dividing the remainder by the number of my descendants living at the time of the contribution, who have not been excluded from exercising their withdrawal right with respect to the contribution in question.

(3) **Additional Limitation on Amount Subject to Withdrawal.** To the extent a donee is also the donor of a contribution, or is treated as donor of one-half (1/2) of a contribution for federal gift tax purposes, that donee shall have no right of withdrawal with respect to such contribution to which they are the donor (or treated as the donor), and shall never thereafter be considered to have had a right of with-

drawal with respect to such contribution. Furthermore, in no event may the amount subject to withdrawal by a donee under this Paragraph exceed in any calendar year the amount of the federal gift tax exclusion under IRC section 2503(b) available to the donor with respect to gifts to such donee, provided however, if requested by a married donor at the time of a contribution, the alternative limitation based on the gift tax annual exclusion shall be two (2) times the amount of the gift tax annual exclusion. In determining the amount of this withdrawal limitation, there shall be taken into consideration all previous gifts made to such donee from (or attributable to) such donor (and the donor's spouse, to the extent relevant) during the same calendar year, which gifts were eligible for the federal gift tax annual exclusion (and, in the case of my Spouse, were not eligible for the federal gift tax marital deduction).

(B) Return of Excess Distribution. If any donee receives a distribution in excess of the amount he or she is authorized to withdraw under this Paragraph, Trustee shall immediately notify such donee in writing, requiring the prompt repayment of such excess amount.

These withdrawal rights take precedence over any other power or discretion granted Trustee or any other person. **{End of Alternate 2 to Paragraph 3.1}**

3.2 Rules Concerning Withdrawal Rights. With respect to the withdrawal rights created under this Article, unless otherwise provided pursuant to the paragraph item entitled, **"Restriction of a Withdrawal Right,"** the following rules shall apply:

(A) Notification of Withdrawal Right. Each eligible donee (or the person who would exercise an eligible donee's withdrawal right) shall be kept reasonably informed of all withdrawable contributions to the trust which are made or are anticipated to be made. Notification may be made orally or in writing, and such efforts may include, by way of example (and without limitation), annually apprising each donee of his or her withdrawal rights, by providing the donee with a single notice sufficient to apprise him or her of his or her current and expected future withdrawal rights, or any other means to provide each eligible donee (or the person who would exercise an eligible donee's withdrawal right) with reasonable or actual notice. In no event shall the failure of any donee to receive such notice be deemed to abrogate his or her withdrawal rights in accordance with the provisions of this Article. A donee's right of withdrawal is not contingent upon such notice; and unless otherwise expressly limited (as is permitted pursuant to the sub-paragraph entitled, **"Restriction of a Withdrawal Right,"**) a donee's withdrawal right shall become effective upon Trustee's receipt (actual, constructive or imputed) of the withdrawable contribution (whether such contribution is a direct or indirect contribution to the trust). Upon written request by a donee, Trustee shall furnish full, detailed information with respect to any contributions subject to withdrawal by the donee.

(B) Withdrawal Right to be Exercised by Written Request. Each eligible donee can exercise a withdrawal right by a written request timely delivered to Trustee indicating the amount the donee desires to withdraw. The withdrawal right shall be a privilege that may be exercised only voluntarily and not under compulsion. As of the date a request for withdrawal is made pursuant to the provisions of this Article, the donee's right to receive the permitted amount requested shall be vested and shall not be terminated by the subsequent death or disability of the donee or any administrative delay resulting from actions taken by Trustee to effect distribution hereunder to the donee. Any property distributed by Trustee pursuant to an exercised withdrawal right shall be for the sole benefit of the donee who has exercised such withdrawal right. Trustee shall promptly comply with every demand under a withdrawal right that is exercised.

(C) Incapacity or Disability of Donee. If any eligible donee is unable to exercise a withdrawal right because of incapacity or disability (including minority), his or her authorized representative (to the extent such authorized representative is not prohibited from acting on behalf of the donee), including (but not limited to) a legal or natural guardian, committee, conservator, agent, next friend, or attorney-in-fact under a durable power of attorney, may make the withdrawal on the donee's behalf, and if there be no such authorized representative, Trustee will designate an appropriate adult individual (who may be Trustee, a trust officer, the donee's parent, the donee's sibling, a relative of the donee, or any other person) who may make the withdrawal on the donee's behalf. However, in no event can I, the donor of the contribution, or a person whose life is insured under a life insurance policy owned by the trust, make the withdrawal for any donee regardless of such individual's relationship to the donee. Any property received pursuant to the withdrawal right shall be held for the use and benefit of the donee and shall not be used by the person who exercised the withdrawal right on behalf of the donee to discharge that person's legal obligation of support for that donee.

{Begin Alternate 1 to sub-paragraph (D)—Lapse limited to amount of contribution, with lapse occurring 30 days after contribution. To be used with Alternate 1 of Paragraph 3.1}

(D) **Lapse of Withdrawal Right**. The withdrawal rights created under this Article are all non-cumulative and shall lapse, if not exercised, on the earlier of: (i) thirty (30) calendar days following the date of the contribution to which such withdrawal rights relate (or such minimal additional amount of time as may be necessary for a legal guardian/conservator to be appointed on behalf of the incapacitated or disabled donee, if such an appointment is in fact necessary), or (ii) the day preceding the donee's date of death (provided the date of death occurs more than fifteen (15) days following the date of the contribution to which such withdrawal rights relate). No payment may be made in a subsequent year on account of the donee's failure to exercise a withdrawal right in a prior year. The lapse of a donee's withdrawal rights shall not be considered a contribution or gift to the trust estate. **{End of Alternate 1 to sub-paragraph (D)}**

{Begin Alternate 2 to sub-paragraph (D)—Hanging *Crummey* withdrawal right. Creates ETIP problems with spouse (unless

spouse's withdrawal amount is limited to 5x5, with lapse of spouse's right of withdrawal occurring within 60 days after the contribution is made to the trust (not 60 days after the spouse receives notice of the contribution)). Amount of withdrawal right for other beneficiaries is limited to 5 x 5 amount, with lapse occurring 30 days after the contribution and any amount of contribution greater than 5x5 is subject to a continuing right of withdrawal until the amount in excess of 5x5 eventually lapses within the safe harbor amounts of 5x5. To be used with Alternate 2 of Paragraph 3.1}

(D) **Structured Lapse of Withdrawal Right**. The withdrawal rights created under this Article (other than withdrawal rights granted to my Spouse, if any) shall be cumulative, and each eligible donee's unexercised right to withdraw a contribution shall lapse on December 31 of each year (whether or not a contribution was made in that year), or, if earlier, thirty (30) days after the contribution to which it relates (or such minimal additional amount of time as may be necessary for a legal guardian/conservator to be appointed on behalf of the incapacitated or disabled donee, if such an appointment is in fact necessary), in an amount equal to the greater of five thousand ($5,000.00) dollars or five percent (5%) of the value of the trust estate out of which, or the proceeds of which, the exercise of the withdrawal right could be satisfied (or such greater dollar amount or percentage as may be specified in IRC section 2514(e)) (the "Lapse Protection Amount"); provided, however, the Lapse Protection Amount shall be measured and determined after first ascertaining all other powers (if any) held by such donee that must, under IRC section 2514(e), be aggregated to determine the largest lapse that can occur concerning the withdrawal right under this subparagraph without it being considered a release of a general power of appointment. To the extent that a withdrawal right exceeds the Lapse Protection Amount, the donee's withdrawal right with respect to such excess shall continue in all later years (even after a donor's death) subject to the same lapse provisions, but such continuing withdrawal right over the excess may only be exercised by the donee with the consent of an Independent or Disinterested

Trustee. Withdrawal rights for contributions made during the period of December 3 through December 31 shall not lapse in the calendar year when the contribution was made, but shall continue to be exercisable in the following year or years. (For example, if a contribution allocable to a donee is $12,000 in a calendar year and the applicable Lapse Protection Amount is $5,000, then if the withdrawal right is not exercised, it shall lapse as to $5,000 of the contribution, but shall continue to the next calendar year as to $7,000. If there is no contribution allocable to that donee in the next two subsequent calendar years, and the allocable amounts are not withdrawn, that donee's right of withdrawal shall lapse by $5,000 and $2,000 in the first and second subsequent years, respectively.) Nothing in this provision shall have the effect of a condition subsequent, nor a retroactive recharacterization of the amount of a donor's gifts or the amount subject to any donee's power to withdraw. Neither the amount of a donor's gifts nor any amount subject to any donee's power to withdraw are to be reduced, modified or recharacterized as a result of any action or determination by any court or other governmental or administrative agency. The lapse of a donee's withdrawal rights shall not be considered a contribution or gift to the trust estate. The provisions of this sub-paragraph concerning the lapse of withdrawal rights do **not** pertain to withdrawal rights granted to my Spouse.

{End of Alternate 2 to sub-paragraph (D).}

(E) Continuation of Withdrawal Right After My Death. Each withdrawal right which is in effect at my death shall continue in effect after my death as to the Marital Trust (as concerns only the withdrawal rights of my Spouse), the Family Trust or Children's Trust until it lapses as described in sub-paragraph (D) above**;** provided however, my Spouse's withdrawal right shall be exercisable first out of that portion of the Martial Trust that has been elected/deducted for the federal estate tax marital deduction, provided further, that if an IRC 2652(a)(3) reverse QTIP election has been made, my Spouse's withdrawal rights shall first be satisfied out of the Marital Trust property so elected/deducted for the marital deduction for which no reverse

QTIP election has been made. If all of the initial trust principal is otherwise distributable to the Marital Trust or if only part of the initial trust principal is distributable to the Marital Trust (but the remaining amount of the initial trust to be distributed to the Family Trust or Children's Trust is otherwise insufficient to satisfy the then outstanding withdrawal rights), a Disinterested Trustee may instead, as a matter of administrative convenience, first pay over and distribute to the donee from the principal of the initial trust the amount that is still subject to the eligible donee's right of withdrawal, before distributing any trust principal to the Marital Trust. Trustee, may in its discretion, delay the funding of the Family Trust or Children's Trust for a reasonable period of time, in order to permit sufficient time for withdrawal rights to be exercised or lapse (as the case may be). On the day preceding the date of the donee's death, all withdrawal rights that have not previously lapsed, shall lapse with respect to that donee (provided the date of death occurs more than fifteen (15) days following the date of the contribution to which such withdrawal rights relate). Any distribution of income or principal made to or for the benefit of a donee during the period after my death while there is a continuation of the donee's withdrawal right hereunder shall be considered as a distribution in full or partial satisfaction of such donee's unlapsed right of withdrawal.

(F) Satisfying a Withdrawal Right. Trustee shall promptly comply with every demand under a withdrawal right that is exercised. Trustee may satisfy any withdrawal rights under this Article by distributing cash, other trust property, fractional interests in trust property, or split dollar interest in a life insurance policy, as Trustee deems appropriate. Trustee is specifically authorized to borrow money from any source, including but not limited to the cash surrender values of any life insurance policies transferred to or held by the trust, to sell trust property, to surrender or otherwise dispose of any life insurance policies or other property transferred to or held by the trust, and to take any other action that may be necessary and appropriate to assure that withdrawal rights will be satisfied in a timely and expedient manner. Without limiting Trustee's broad discretionary power to select trust property to satisfy a withdrawal right, I prefer that cash or tangible property be distributed to donees before distributing life insurance policies and other intangible property to donees (especially as concerns donees who are skip persons), unless Trustee decides that another selection is warranted. While any withdrawal right is outstanding Trustee shall not exercise any discretion or authority that would impede or thwart the withdrawal right.

(G) "Contribution" Defined. "Contribution" means a non-testamentary transfer (direct or indirect, actual or imputed to the donor) to Trustee of any cash or other property (or interest therein) (including, for the year of the trust's creation, the property creating the trust) to be held as part of the trust funds, which would be treated under Chapter 12 of the Internal Revenue Code as a taxable gift of the donor or the donor's spouse (before taking into account the exclusion allowed by IRC section 2503(b)), and shall also include any premiums on policies of life insurance (or any interests therein) owned by the trust which premiums are paid, by me or any other person or entity (including my employer or former employer), directly to any insurance company issuing the policies rather than first being paid to Trustee. In the case of any premium which is paid directly to an insurance company, the date of the contribution to the trust shall be deemed to be the date on which the premium payment is transmitted to the insurance company issuing the policy. The amount of any contribution is its federal gift tax value, as determined by Trustee at the time of the transfer. Contributions made by a donor's attorney-in-fact under a durable power of attorney shall be considered as made by the donor.

(H) Restriction of a Withdrawal Right. Any person (or that person's duly authorized agent acting under a power of attorney or other proper legal representative) who makes a contribution to any trust created under this Agreement may inform Trustee at the time of such contribution and with respect solely to the new contribution then being made (and with respect to future contributions to be made by that person), do one (1) or more of the following: (i) exclude any beneficiary who would otherwise have a withdrawal right from exercising that withdrawal right as to such new or future contribution; (ii) increase or decrease the amount subject to a beneficiary's withdrawal right as to such new or future contribution, except that the amount subject to the withdrawal right shall not exceed the amount of the contribution; (iii) change the period during which any beneficiary's withdrawal right as to such new or future contribution may be exercised; and (iv) change the manner and period during which any beneficiary's withdrawal right as to such new or future contribution shall lapse. No such direction may in any way alter, amend or change any beneficiary's withdrawal right with respect to any prior contributions.

(I) **Forfeiture of Withdrawal Right.** Except with respect to an outstanding withdrawal right which has been outstanding for fewer than fifteen (15) days from the date of such contribution, any donee having a withdrawal right shall immediately forfeit such right upon making an assignment for the benefit of his or her creditors, filing a voluntary petition in bankruptcy, being adjudicated a bankrupt or an insolvent, or consenting to or acquiescing in the appointment of a trustee in bankruptcy or a receiver in bankruptcy for all or any substantial part of his or her assets or properties, which forfeiture shall continue during the pendency of any such proceeding and end upon the termination thereof.

(J) **Power to Amend.** Trustee, other than an Interested Trustee, may by a written instrument filed with the trust records, amend this Article to the minimum extent necessary to assure that contributions to the initial trust and its beneficiaries quality for the gift tax annual exclusion for federal gift tax purposes, and/or are not subject to an estate tax inclusion period for generation skipping transfer tax purposes. Such Trustee may not amend the initial trust in any manner that would cause any portion of the trust funds to be included in a donor's gross estate, my gross estate, that of my spouse (if I am married), or that of any of my descendants and their spouses, to a greater extent than before such amendment. An amendment made in good faith shall be conclusive on all persons interested in the trust and such Trustee shall not be liable for the consequences of any amendment or for not having amended the trust. No amendment shall limit or alter the rights of a beneficiary in any trust funds held by Trustee before the amendment.

(K) Determination of Donor's Prior Gifts to Donee. Trustee may without liability assume that no prior gifts to any donee under this Article were made by a donor or a donor's spouse other than contributions to the initial trust, unless Trustee shall have actual written notice to the contrary. In determining the amount of prior gifts to or for a donee not made under this Agreement, Trustee may rely on a written statement signed or duly authorized by the donor setting forth the nature, date, and amount of such prior gifts; and in the absence of such written statement Trustee shall be under no obligation to ascertain the same.

(L) Special Rule for Multiple Withdrawal Rights. The amounts involved in a withdrawal right described as " the greater of five thousand ($5,000) dollars or five (5%) percent of the trust estate out of which, or the proceeds of which, the exercise of this withdrawal right could be satisfied (or such greater dollar amount or percentage as may be specified in IRC section 2514(e))" or language of similar import with reference to IRC section 2514(e), shall be measured after subtracting all other amounts that the same person could have withdrawn during the same calendar year from this or any other fund, to the extent that such powers must, under applicable federal gift tax law, be aggregated in determining whether the lapse of the right of withdrawal under this Article is a release of a general power of appointment; provided however, a person making a contribution may, at the time of the contribution, specify the order in which multiple withdrawal rights are to lapse (as concerns the contribution).

(M) Satisfaction of a Withdrawal Right Constitutes an Advancement. The satisfaction of a donee's right of withdrawal under this Article shall constitute and be treated as an advancement, and shall be charged (without interest) against the ultimate share (if any) provided for the donee and his or her descendants; provided however, the foregoing shall not apply to the satisfaction of a withdrawal right granted to my donee-Spouse.

ARTICLE 4
DISTRIBUTION DURING LIFETIME

4.1 Distribution of Principal and Income During Lifetime. During my life, Trustee shall hold and administer the trust estate, as follows:

(A) Income and Principal. Trustee may use some or all of the trust's net income and principal to pay premiums on policies of life insurance owned by the trust. In addition, an Independent or a Disinterested Trustee may distribute to and among my Spouse (who shall be the preferred beneficiary hereunder) and my descendants, in whatever proportions such Trustee deems appropriate, so much of the trust principal and income (including all or none) as such Trustee in its sole, absolute and uncontrolled discretion, shall determine (with no requirement as to equality or any pro rata scheme of distribution). An Interested Trustee may, in its discretion, distribute income and principal among the aforementioned beneficiaries for their health, education, support and maintenance considering all other resources available to each such beneficiary (including any legal obligation of support that another person may owe to such beneficiary). Any undistributed income shall be added to principal.

(B) Restrictions on Distributions. No distribution of trust income or principal shall be made by Trustee if it would impair a withdrawal right granted under the Article entitled, "**Withdrawal Rights**," and no Trustee may make any distribution to or for his or her own benefit, nor may Trustee make any distribution to or for the benefit of any individual which distribution would discharge or satisfy Trustee's legal obligation to support such individual. Furthermore, Trustee shall not use any trust income or principal in a manner that would give me any pecuniary benefit or would discharge or satisfy my legal obligations, including any legal obligation of support.

4.2 Limited Power of Appointment by Special Power Holder. I hereby name as a special power holder the first of the following who is from time to time willing and able to act:

(1) **Name and address of Special Power Holder 1;**

(2) **Name and address of Special Power Holder 2; and**

(3) **Name and address of Special Power Holder 3.**

During my life, the special power holder, may in its sole, absolute and uncontrolled discretion appoint (by a written instrument delivered to Trustee prior to my death), some, all or none of the trust estate (excluding: (i) life insurance on the special power holder's life, and (ii) any amount still subject to withdrawal by a person) as the special power holder (acting in his, her or its individual-personal capacity and not in a fiduciary capacity (even though the special power holder may also be serving (or is nominated to serve) as a Trustee)) as the special power holder determines, to any one or more of {**Optional 1:** myself, or **Optional 2:** my mother's descendants,}[1] my Spouse, my descendants or to another trust for any such person's benefit, (but not to the special power holder, the special power holder's estate, or the creditors of either), without regard to equality among the objects or the appointees, and without the appointed property being chargeable against the proportionate share of corpus held in trust for the payment of income to the beneficiary as if the corpus constituted a separate trust; and Trustee shall not make any compensating adjustments to trust beneficiaries who are not the appointees or to trust beneficiaries who receive unequal shares/amounts of the appointed property.

Provided, however, (i) in no event can I exercise the power granted hereunder, regardless of my relationship to the special power holder, (ii) that no such distribution may be applied or distributed such that it would give the special power holder any pecuniary benefit or would discharge or satisfy my legal obligations, my Spouse's legal obligations, or the power holder's legal obligations, and (iii) no such distribution may be made if it

---

[1] *See,* Section 11.1 of main text concerning use of the optional language.

would impair an unexercised or unlapsed withdrawal right granted under the Article entitled, "**Withdrawal Rights**."

Once appointed, a special power holder may only be removed for reasonable cause by a court of competent jurisdiction.

In the event a special power holder resigns, is removed by a court of competent jurisdiction, becomes incapacitated, or is deceased, I and/or my Spouse may appoint a successor to such special power holder, by delivering a written instrument to Trustee. Any special power holder nominated or appointed hereunder must meet the definitional requirements of an Independent Trustee.

4.3 Distribution In Satisfaction of Unlapsed Withdrawal Right. Any distribution of income or principal to a beneficiary under this Article shall be considered as a distribution in full or partial satisfaction of such beneficiary-donee's unlapsed right of withdrawal under the Article entitled, **" Withdrawal Rights."**

ARTICLE 5
DISTRIBUTION AFTER DEATH

5.1 Distributions of Amounts Included in My Estate If I am Survived by My Spouse. Upon my death, if I am survived by my Spouse, and if without reference to any provisions of this Paragraph any portion of the initial trust estate shall be includible in my gross estate for federal estate tax purposes, then such portion of the trust estate (but such portion only) shall be distributed to the Marital Trust established hereunder; provided, however, that the amount to be distributed to the Marital Trust shall be reduced by the excess of the aggregate amount of property still then subject to withdrawal by all persons (other than my Spouse) pursuant to the Article entitled, **"Withdrawal Rights"** over the amount of the initial trust property that would otherwise not be distributed to the Marital Trust. Trustee is authorized to obtain and act in reliance upon the opinion of tax counsel in making any determination concerning the includability of all or any portion of the trust property in my gross estate, and Trustee shall be exonerated from all liability to any interested party for Trustee's good faith determination. If generation skipping transfer tax exemption has been previously allocated to the initial trust so that at the time of my death the initial trust (and any life insurance proceeds received or to be received by that trust or any other trusts to be established hereunder) have a generation skipping transfer tax inclusion ratio of zero (0), then and in that event, Trustee and my personal representative shall attempt to preserve the zero (0) inclusion ratio under an IRC section 2652(a)(3) reverse QTIP election as concerns the Marital Trust.

(A) Marital Trust. Trustee shall hold and administer the Marital Trust for the following purposes:

(1) Income. Trustee shall pay all the net income to my Spouse until death, at least annually, or on a more frequent basis if my Spouse so reasonably requests.

(2) Principal. Trustee may use that portion of principal necessary for my Spouse's health, education, support and maintenance in my Spouse's accustomed manner of living at the time of my death, considering my Spouse's current income and other assets reasonably and readily available to my Spouse. Furthermore, a Disinterested Trustee may, in its sole, absolute and uncontrolled discretion, distribute such amounts of principal to or for the benefit of my Spouse as the Disinterested Trustee shall determine. If an IRC section 2652(a)(3) reverse QTIP election has been made, Trustee shall make principal distributions first from the Non-Exempt Marital Trust before making principal distributions from the Exempt Reverse QTIP Marital Trust. In making distributions of principal, Trustee shall consider the needs of my Spouse as more important than the needs of the remainder beneficiaries.

(a) Spousal Power of Withdrawal. If my Spouse is living on December 31 of each year, and with the consent of a Disinterested Trustee so requests, Trustee shall distribute to my Spouse the greater of that amount referred to in IRC section 2514(e)(1) (currently, Five Thousand Dollars ($5,000)) or that percentage referred to in IRC section 2514(e)(2) (currently, Five Percent (5%)) of the trust on that date; provided however: (i) if a partial QTIP election has been made and the Marital Trust has been divided into the two (2) separate trusts, my Spouse's withdrawal right shall be limited to the principal of the Qualified Marital Trust; and/or (ii) if an IRC section 2652(a)(3) reverse QTIP election has been made, the right of withdrawal shall be limited to only the Non-Exempt Marital Trust. This right of withdrawal may be disclaimed in whole or in part by my Spouse, or my Spouse's agent under a power of attorney, or my Spouse's conservator, or the personal representative of my Spouse's estate, or, if my Spouse has no probate estate, the trustee of any trust created by my Spouse containing one-third or more in value of my Spouse's assets, or any other person permitted by law. A disclaimer shall become effective upon the first to occur: (i) as provided by law; or (ii) upon written notice to Trustee. A disclaimer of this right of withdrawal shall result in the irrevocable extinguishment of the right of withdrawal as to the portion disclaimed. This right shall not accumulate from year to year, and if not exercised shall lapse. The limitation determined with reference to IRC sections 2514(e)(1) and (2) shall be reduced to any smaller limit that would result from first taking into account all other powers held by my Spouse that must, under IRC section 2514(e), be aggregated to determine the largest lapse that can occur without being treated as a release.

(3) **Residue.** At my Spouse's death, Trustee shall (except to the extent my Spouse's will contains a waiver of the right to recovery or a different direction for the payment of such taxes) pay from that portion of the Marital Trust (other than any amount of the Marital Trust that qualifies for a federal estate tax charitable deduction) that is includible in my Spouse's gross estate, the approximate amount of death taxes (computed on a marginal basis) payable as a result of

inclusion of any portion of the Marital Trust in my Spouse's gross estate (provided, however, such amount shall be in lieu of any contribution for taxes to which the personal representative of my Spouse's estate may otherwise be entitled); provided, however, if an IRC section 2652(a)(3) reverse QTIP election has been made, Trustee shall make all such payments first from the Non-Exempt Marital Trust before making any payments from the Exempt Marital Trust. If any Marital Trust property hereunder is elected and deducted from my Spouse's gross estate under IRC section 2057 (concerning qualified family owned businesses) then no such death tax shall be apportioned against or be payable from such elected and deducted property if to do so would otherwise prohibit or disqualify the property from qualifying for a deduction under IRC section 2057. Additionally, upon the request of the fiduciary of my Spouse's estate, Trustee is authorized to pay (or reimburse my Spouse's estate) for all reasonable legal and other fees, costs and expenses attributable to the valuation of the Marital Trust that is includible in my Spouse's gross estate; provided, however, no payments (or reimbursements) shall be made from the Exempt Marital Trust or the Non-Qualified Marital Trust. Trustee may rely upon the written statement by my Spouse's personal representative of the amounts payable pursuant to this provision.

(a) **Testamentary Limited Power of Appointment.** The remaining property in the Marital Trust shall then be distributed to my mother's and/or my father's descendants and their spouses and charitable organizations, as my Spouse appoints, except that this limited power of appointment may not be exercised in favor of my Spouse, my Spouse's estate, or the creditors of either. If the Marital Trust has been divided or established as separate trusts (e.g., a partial QTIP election has been made, a reverse QTIP election has been made, etc.), my

Spouse may exercise the limited power of appointment differently with respect to each of the separate trusts (even otherwise identical trusts) derived from the divided trust. To the extent my Spouse does not effectively exercise this limited power of appointment, the remaining property in the Marital Trust shall be distributed to and be administered under the provisions of the Paragraph entitled, "**Children's Trust**."

(4) **Qualifying Assets**. Only property (or its proceeds) that is eligible for the marital deduction (to the extent applicable) shall be distributed to and be held by the Marital Trust, and such property (or proceeds) shall be undiminished by death taxes. Any property (or proceeds) that do not qualify for the marital deduction shall be distributed to the Family Trust, to be administered, distributed and disposed of under the terms of that trust.

(5) **GST Tax Separate Trust Rule.** The Marital Trust shall be deemed to be a separate and independent trust for generation-skipping transfer tax purposes; and Trustee shall comply with the separate trust rule of Treas. Reg. section 26.2654-1(b), to the extent applicable.

(6) **QTIP Election**. My fiduciary shall have the power to make any election required to qualify the Marital Trust for the marital deduction, including the authority to elect under IRC section 2056(b)(7) (concerning qualified terminable interest property) to qualify all or none or any fractional or percentage share of the Marital Trust for the federal estate tax marital deduction. In determining the fraction or percentage interest, the assets, values, deductions, exclusions, credits, prior taxable gifts, etc. as finally determined for federal estate tax purposes shall control. My fiduciary, in exercising its discretion with respect to IRC section 2056(b)(7), shall attempt, if possible, to minimize, or eliminate the federal estate

tax payable by my estate at the time of my death, taking account of all relevant factors pertinent to this estate planning objective (including the permanent repeal of the federal estate tax, the size of my Spouse's estate, etc.), unless the anticipated incremental estate taxes occasioned by my Spouse's death or the anticipated length of survival of my Spouse (due to state of health, age, etc.) make a lesser election or no election more appropriate. My fiduciary shall not be liable to any interested party for any decision made in good faith and with reasonable diligence with respect to the IRC section 2056(b)(7) election.

(7) **Overriding Trust Provisions Concerning "Clayton" Contingent QTIP Election**. If an election is made to qualify a fractional or percentage portion (but not all) of the Marital Trust for the federal estate tax marital deduction under IRC section 2056(b)(7), I give to the Marital Trust only that fractional or percentage share of the Marital Trust as to which my fiduciary shall make the QTIP election under IRC section 2056(b)(7). That portion of the Marital Trust as to which my fiduciary shall not make the IRC section 2056(b)(7) QTIP marital deduction election shall be distributed to the Family Trust, to be administered, distributed and disposed of under the terms of that trust. In allocating assets between the Marital Trust and the Family Trust, Trustee may use cash or non-cash property (including undivided interests in property) or a combination of each, and may distribute assets ratably or non-ratably.

(8) **Reverse QTIP Election**. If an IRC section 2652(a)(3) reverse QTIP election is to be made, then prior to the election and the allocation of my generation-skipping tax exemption, the Marital Trust so qualified for the marital deduction, shall, if and as necessary, be divided on a fractional basis and established as two (2) separate trusts rather than one in order to permit the IRC section 2652(a)(3) election to be made with respect to one of these trusts (the "Exempt Reverse QTIP Marital Trust", of which I

(rather than my Spouse) will be the transferor for generation-skipping tax purposes and which will have an inclusion ratio of zero (0) for generation-skipping tax purposes) but not with respect to the other (the "Non-Exempt Marital Trust" which will have an inclusion ratio of one (1) for generation-skipping tax purposes); and in the event of such a division, the Non-Exempt Marital Trust shall receive the minimum fractional share necessary to leave the Exempt Reverse QTIP Marital Trust with a corpus of the desired value and an inclusion ratio of zero (0), so as to be entirely exempt from generation skipping tax. Unless the context requires otherwise, the term "Marital Trust" also includes both the Exempt Reverse QTIP Marital Trust and the Non-Exempt Marital Trust. The Exempt Reverse QTIP Trust shall be deemed to be a separate and independent trust under Treas. Reg. section 26.2654-(1)(b) for generation-skipping transfer tax purposes, to the extent applicable. In allocating assets between the Exempt Reverse QTIP Marital Trust and the Non-Exempt Marital Trust, Trustee may use cash or non-cash property (including undivided interests in property) or a combination of each, and may distribute assets ratably or non-ratably.

(9) Disclaimer. My Spouse, or my Spouse's agent under a power of attorney, or my Spouse's conservator, or the personal representative of my Spouse's estate, or, if my Spouse has no probate estate, the trustee of any self settled revocable living trust created by my Spouse containing one-third or more in value of my Spouse's liquid assets, or any other person permitted by law, shall have the right to disclaim all or any part of the marital bequest and any property or rights comprising the Marital Trust, the Family Trust or the Disclaimer Trust (or assets otherwise allocable to those trusts).

Any part or property of the Marital Trust (or assets to be allocated to the Marital Trust) that is disclaimed shall become part of the Family Trust (and my Spouse shall not be treated as having predeceased me), and any part or property of the Family Trust or Disclaimer Trust (or assets to be allocated to such Trusts) that is disclaimed shall be distributed to the trust described in, and be administered under the provisions of the Paragraph entitled, **"Children's Trust,"** as if my Spouse had predeceased me.

If the Family Trust contains a power of appointment, exercisable by my Spouse, either as a beneficiary or as a Trustee over the disclaimed property (other than an inter vivos "5x5" withdrawal right limited to the dollar and percentage amounts set forth in IRC sections 2041(b)(2)(A) and (B) and 2514(e)(1) and (2)) (as is permitted by Treas. Reg. section 25.2518-2(e)(5), Example 7) and powers limited by an ascertainable standard (as is permitted by Treas. Reg. section 25.2518-2(e)(2)), then and in that event, any interest in the marital bequest that is disclaimed and otherwise allocable to the Family Trust, shall not be allocated to the Family Trust, but shall instead be allocated to a new, separate trust to be known as the "Disclaimer Trust," the provisions of which are identical to those of the Family Trust, including trusteeship, except that my Spouse shall neither possess nor exercise any general power of appointment (or any power prohibited by IRC section 2518 or applicable Treasury Regulations), either as beneficiary or as a Trustee over the Disclaimer Trust, either during lifetime or on death.

To the extent permitted by law (and not prohibited by local or federal law), disclaimers under this subparagraph may be either "qualified" disclaimers or nonqualified disclaimers under federal tax law; provided, however, if the disclaimer is not a qualified disclaimer under federal tax law, then and in that event, any property (or interest therein) disclaimed by my Spouse in the first instance shall instead be distributed to and be administered under the provisions of the Paragraph entitled, **"Children's Trust,"** as if my Spouse had predeceased me. A disclaimer shall become effective upon the first to occur: (i) as provided by law; or (ii) upon written notice to Trustee.

(10) Restriction on Spouse's Powers Concerning Marital Deduction Trust. It is my intent that the marital deduction gift to my Spouse and the property comprising the trust estate of the Marital Trust shall qualify for the federal estate tax marital deduction applicable to my estate, to the extent such property is so elected/deducted for the marital deduction. To this end, all powers and discretions granted to my Spouse over the Marital Trust shall not be exercised or exercisable except in a manner consistent with this intent. Therefore, my Spouse shall neither possess nor exercise any powers or discretions over the Marital Trust (that is so elected/deducted for the marital deduction) to the extent such powers or discretions are prohibited by or inconsistent with applicable federal tax law (as concerns the marital deduction).

(11) Restriction on Trustee Power Concerning Marital Deduction Trust. It is my intent that the marital deduction gift to my Spouse and the property comprising the trust estate of the Marital Trust shall qualify for the federal estate tax marital deduction applicable to my estate, to the extent such property is so elected/deducted for the marital deduction. To this end, all Trustee powers and discretions with respect to the administration of the Marital Trust shall not be exercised or exercisable except in a manner consistent with this intent. All doubtful questions regarding the allocation or apportionment of Marital Trust receipts and disbursements to or between principal and income shall be resolved in favor of the income beneficiary, it being intended that, at the very least, my Spouse be given substantially that degree of beneficial enjoyment of the Marital Trust property during the remainder of my Spouse's lifetime which the principles of the law of trusts accord to a person who is unqualifiedly designated as the life beneficiary of a trust. Furthermore, if the Marital Trust consists of any property that is not productive of a reasonable rate of income, my Spouse may require Trustee either to make the property productive or convert it within a reasonable time to income-producing property or to provide out of other assets of the Marital Trust the equivalent of the income such property would produce if it were productive of a reasonable rate of income.

5.2 Purchase of Assets and Loans. At any time after my death, including the period during the administration of my probate estate (including the post-mortem administration of any inter-vivos revocable trusts created by me) (collectively "my estate") Trustee may, after first making provision for any distributions required by the Paragraph entitled, "**Distributions of Amounts Included in My Estate If I am Survived by My Spouse**," use the trust funds, in Trustee's discretion, to lend money to and buy assets from my estate, my Spouse's estate, the estates of any of my descendants, or from the trustee of any other trust created by me, my Spouse or my descendants (collectively "our estates"), on such terms and conditions as Trustee deems to be in the best interests of the beneficiaries of the trusts established under this Agreement, provided, however, Trustee may not buy assets from our estates other than at their fair market value, nor may Trustee lend money to our estates without receiving adequate security and an adequate rate of interest. In addition to the foregoing, Trustee may also purchase, otherwise acquire, and hold for an indefinite term any business or business interest, as shareholder, creditor, partner, proprietor or otherwise, even though of a character, proportion, or amount other than prescribed by law for trust investments; to exercise, or delegate to others discretionary power to exercise complete control and management of any business, and in connection therewith to enter and perform contracts, commitments, orders, and engagements, to incur, pay, compromise, settle and discharge expenses and debts, to elect, employ and compensate directors, officers, employees, or agents (who may include Trustee or any employee or agent thereof), and to deal with and act for such business in any capacity (including any banking or trust capacity and the lending of money out of Trustee's own funds) and to be compensated therefor; to rely upon the reports of accountants and others as to the operations and financial condition of any business, without independent investigation and without obligation to file with any court; to take any action reasonably necessary to carry out any agreement for the transfer of any business interest upon an individual's death or upon cessation of an individual's active participation in the conduct of the business; to participate in any buy-sell, restrictive purchase or retirement agreement relating to any business interest; and to join in partnership, membership and joint venture agreements, to participate in any incorporation, reorganization, merger, consolidation, recapitalization, liquidation or dissolution of any business or any change in its nature, and to invest additional capital in, subscribe to or buy additional stock or securities of or make new or increased secured, unsecured or subordinated loans to any business.

Trustee may not, however, make grants to our estates or otherwise distribute funds except through bona fide loans or purchases, it not being my intention to make any persons who are not specifically so identified in this Agreement, the beneficiaries of any trust created hereunder. However, as concerns trust assets includible in my gross estate, and if I am survived by my Spouse, no Trustee shall exercise any power under this Agreement to the extent that such exercise would prevent those trust assets from qualifying for the federal estate tax marital deduction. If no personal representative is appointed with respect to an estate under applicable state law, the "administration" of an estate will include the settlement of debts, claims, and taxes in respect of an estate by the trustee of any revocable trust or by any other person in actual possession of assets in which the individual had a legal or equitable interest. Trustee shall not be liable for any loss suffered by the trust as a result of the existence of the powers granted in this provision.

To facilitate the possible exercise of these discretionary powers, Trustee is authorized to defer any division of the initial trust estate for a reasonable period of time sufficient to accomplish the forgoing; however, as concerns trust assets includible in my gross estate, and if I am survived by my Spouse, no Trustee shall exercise any power under this Agreement to the extent that such exercise would prevent those trust assets from qualifying for the federal estate tax marital deduction.

Notwithstanding anything in this Agreement to the contrary although it is my intent and purpose under this Paragraph to make trust assets available to provide the possibility that the assets of the initial trust can be made available to provide liquid assets (through loans and purchases) for the payment of taxes and other obligations of our estates, if that becomes necessary or appropriate in the opinion of the personal representative of such estate, Trustee shall not have the power to use any trust property for the benefit of our estates as defined in Treas. Reg. section 20.2042-1(b) unless such property is already included in our gross estates for federal estate tax purposes.

5.3 Administration of the Balance of the Trust Property. The balance of the trust property not disposed of under the prior provisions of this Article shall be administered and disposed of as follows:

(A) Residue to Family Trust. If I am survived by my Spouse, the remaining trust property shall be administered and disposed of as provided in the Paragraph entitled, "**Family Trust**."

(1) Disclaimer. My Spouse, or my Spouse's agent under a power of attorney, or my Spouse's conservator, or the personal representative of my Spouse's estate, or, if my Spouse has no probate estate, the trustee of any trust created by my Spouse containing one-third or more in value of my Spouse's assets, or any other person permitted by law, shall have the right to disclaim all or any part of my Spouse's benefits under the Paragraph entitled "**Family Trust**." Any part of the Family Trust that is disclaimed shall be distributed to and administered under the provisions of the Paragraph entitled, "**Children's Trust**" as if my Spouse had predeceased me. Disclaimers under this provision may, but need not, be "qualified disclaimers" under federal tax law. A disclaimer shall become effective upon the first to occur: (i) as provided by law, or (ii) upon written notice to Trustee.

(B) Residue to Children's Trust. If I am not survived by my Spouse, the remaining trust property shall be administered and disposed of as provided in the Paragraph entitled, "**Children's Trust.**"

{Begin Alternate 1 to Paragraph 5.4 ("Family Trust")—To be used if there may be a need to establish a state death tax marital deduction trust due to state decoupling from the federal estate tax.}

5.4 Family Trust. Trustee shall hold the Family Trust for the following purposes:

(A) Income. Trustee shall pay all the net income to my Spouse until death, at least annually, or on a more frequent basis if my Spouse so reasonably requests.

(B) Principal. If the trust's net income and other assets reasonably and readily available to my Spouse are insufficient to maintain the health, education, support and maintenance of my Spouse in my Spouse's accustomed manner of living at the time of my death, Trustee shall use that portion of principal necessary to enable my Spouse to maintain that standard of living as concerns my Spouse's health, education, support and maintenance. Without limiting Trustee's discretion, I suggest that no principal of the Family Trust be distributed to my Spouse until the readily marketable assets of any Marital Trust and any State Death Tax Marital Deduction Trust (defined below) are exhausted (other than my Spouse's principal residence) unless there is a compelling reason to do so. Furthermore, a Disinterested Trustee may, in its sole, absolute and uncontrolled discretion, distribute such amounts of principal to or for the benefit of my Spouse and my then living descendants, in such amounts and proportions (with no requirement as to equality or any pro rata scheme of distribution) as the Disinterested Trustee shall determine (including the terms and conditions thereof), after giving due consideration to the needs of my Spouse, who is the primary and preferred beneficiary of the Family Trust. If possible, the Disinterested Trustee shall consult with my Spouse concerning any proposed distributions.

(C) Residue. At my Spouse's death, the remaining Family Trust property, together with any income of the Family Trust not distributed during my Spouse's lifetime, shall be distributed to the trust described in, and be administered under the provisions of, Paragraph 5.5 entitled, "**Children's Trust**."

(D) State Death Tax Marital Deduction Election. My fiduciary shall have the power to make any election required to qualify the Family Trust for a state death tax marital deduction, including the authority to elect to qualify all or none or any fractional or percentage share of the Family Trust for a state death tax marital deduction. In general, that fractional or percentage interest of the Family Trust that exceeds the amount or portion that can be transferred to the Family Trust free of state death taxes at my death shall be elected for the state death tax marital deduction available to my estate. In determining the fraction or percentage interest, the assets, values, deductions, exclusions, credits, prior taxable gifts, etc. as finally determined for applicable death tax purposes shall control. My fiduciary, in exercising its discretion to qualify all or a portion of the Family Trust for a state death tax marital deduction, shall attempt, if possible, to minimize, or eliminate the state death tax payable by my estate at the time of my death, taking account of all relevant factors pertinent to this estate planning objective (including the permanent repeal of the federal and state death tax, the size of my Spouse's estate, etc.), unless the anticipated incremental death taxes occasioned by my Spouse's death or the anticipated length of survival of my Spouse (due to state of health, age, etc.) make a lesser election or no election more appropriate. My fiduciary shall not be liable to any interested party for any decision made in good faith and with reasonable diligence with respect to a state death tax marital deduction. I HEREBY ACKNOWLEDGE THAT IF ALL OF THE FAMILY TRUST IS ELECTED FOR THE STATE DEATH TAX MARITAL DEDUCTION, THAT UNDER CERTAIN CIRCUMSTANCES THERE MAY BE NO ASSETS REMAINING IN THE FAMILY TRUST.

(1) Overriding Provisions Concerning State Death Tax Marital Deduction Trust. If any portion of the Family Trust is elected and deducted for a state death tax marital deduction, that portion so elected and deducted shall be held in a separate trust for the benefit of my Spouse; and such trust shall be referred to as the "State Death Tax Marital Deduction Trust." The terms, conditions and provisions of State Death Tax Marital Deduction Trust shall be as similar as possible to the terms, conditions and provisions of the Family Trust. However, the State Death Tax Marital Deduction Trust's terms, conditions, provisions, Trustee powers, and powers granted my Spouse, shall comply with all requirements (and limitations) of the applicable state death tax marital deduction rules and requirements. In this regard, unless the applicable state death tax marital deduction rules and requirements permit otherwise, no Trustee of the State Death Tax Marital Deduction Trust shall distribute income or principal to or for the benefit of anyone, other than to or for the benefit of my Spouse during my Spouse's lifetime, which income shall be distributed at least annually to or for the benefit of my Spouse or on a more frequent basis if my Spouse so reasonably requests.

If the State Death Tax Marital Deduction Trust contains any property that has been disclaimed under IRC section 2518 by my Spouse, my Spouse shall neither possess nor exercise any general power of appointment (or any power prohibited by IRC section 2518 or applicable Treasury Regulations), either as beneficiary or as a Trustee over such disclaimed property, either during lifetime or on death.

When my Spouse dies, state death taxes attributable to the State Death Tax Marital Deduction Trust that is includable in my Spouse's estate for state death tax purposes, shall (in the absence of a different method specified under my Spouse's will) be paid {**Drafting Note:** Choose either Option 1 or Option 2. **Option 1:** by my Spouse's estate. **Option 2:** from the State Death Tax Marital Deduction Trust.}

(2) **Funding State Death Tax Marital Deduction Trust.** In funding the State Death Tax Marital De-

duction Trust, Trustee shall use only assets that qualify for the state death tax marital deduction; provided, however, Trustee shall not fund the State Death Tax Marital Deduction Trust with assets that are exempt in the first instance from such state death tax or are excluded from inclusion in my gross estate for such state death tax purposes. In funding the State Death Tax Marital Deduction Trust, Trustee may use cash or non-cash property (including undivided interests in property) or a combination of each, and may distribute assets ratable or non-ratably.

(3) **Restriction on Spouse's Powers Concerning State Death Tax Marital Deduction Trust**. It is my intent that the state death tax marital deduction gift to my Spouse and the property comprising the trust estate of the State Death Tax Marital Deduction Trust shall qualify for the applicable state death tax marital deduction applicable to my estate, to the extent such property is so elected/deducted for the state death tax marital deduction. To this end, all powers and discretions granted to my Spouse over the State Death Tax Marital Deduction Trust shall not be exercised or exercisable except in a manner consistent with this intent. Therefore, my Spouse shall neither possess nor exercise any powers or discretions over the State Death Tax Marital Deduction Trust (that is so elected/deducted for the state death tax marital deduction) to the extent such powers or discretions are prohibited by or inconsistent with applicable state tax law (as concerns the state death tax marital deduction).

(4) **Restriction on Trustee Power Concerning State Death Tax Marital Deduction Trust.** It is my intent that the state death tax marital deduction gift to my Spouse and the property comprising the trust estate of the State Death Tax Marital Deduction Trust shall qualify for the applicable state death tax marital deduction applicable to my estate, to the extent such property is so elected/deducted for the state death tax marital deduction. To this end, all

Trustee powers and discretions with respect to the administration of the State Death Tax Marital Deduction Trust shall not be exercised or exercisable except in a manner consistent with this intent. All doubtful questions regarding the allocation or apportionment of State Death Tax Marital Deduction Trust receipts and disbursements to or between principal and income shall be resolved in favor of the income beneficiary, it being intended that, at the very least, my Spouse be given substantially that degree of beneficial enjoyment of the State Death Tax Marital Deduction Trust property during the remainder of my Spouse's lifetime which the principles of the law of trusts accord to a person who is unqualifiedly designated as the life beneficiary of a trust. Furthermore, if the State Death Tax Marital Deduction Trust consists of any property that is not productive of a reasonable rate of income, my Spouse may require Trustee either to make the property productive or convert it within a reasonable time to income-producing property or to provide out of other assets of the State Death Tax Marital Deduction Trust the equivalent of the income such property would produce if it were productive of a reasonable rate of income. **{End of Alternate 1 to Paragraph 5.4 ("Family Trust").}**

{Begin Alternate 2 to Paragraph 5.4 ("Family Trust") – "Traditional" Family/Credit Shelter Trust with no state death tax marital deduction trust provisions.}

5.4 Family Trust. Trustee shall hold the Family Trust for the following purposes:

(A) Income. Trustee in its discretion (a) may pay net income (i) to or for the benefit of my Spouse until death and/or (ii) to or for the benefit of one or more of my descendants, or (b) may accumulate all or any part of net income.

Trustee shall distribute or accumulate net income using the following ascertainable standard: first, my Spouse, for my Spouse's health, education, support and maintenance in my Spouse's accustomed manner of living at the time of my death; second, my descendants, for their health, education, support, and maintenance. Furthermore, a Disinterested Trustee may, in its sole, absolute and uncontrolled discretion, distribute such amounts of income to or for the benefit of my Spouse and my then living descendants, in such amounts and proportions as the Disinterested Trustee shall determine, after giving due consideration to the needs of my Spouse, who is the primary and preferred beneficiary of the Family Trust. If possible, the Disinterested Trustee shall consult with my Spouse concerning any proposed income distributions.

(B) **Principal.** If the trust's net income and other assets reasonably and readily available to my Spouse are insufficient to maintain the health, education, support and maintenance of my Spouse in my Spouse's accustomed manner of living at the time of my death, Trustee shall use that portion of principal necessary to enable my Spouse to maintain that standard of living as concerns my Spouse's health, education, support and maintenance, considering all other resources readily available to my spouse. Without limiting Trustee's discretion, I suggest that no principal of the Family Trust be distributed to my Spouse until the readily marketable assets of the Marital Trust are exhausted (other than my Spouse's principal residence) unless there is a compelling reason to do so. Furthermore, a Disinterested Trustee may, in its sole, absolute and uncontrolled discretion, distribute such amounts of principal to or for the benefit of my Spouse and my then living descendants, in such amounts and proportions (with no requirement as to equality or any pro rata scheme of distribution) as the Disinterested Trustee shall determine (including the terms and conditions thereof), after giving due consideration to the needs of my Spouse, who is the primary and preferred beneficiary of the Family Trust. If possible, the Disinterested Trustee shall consult with my Spouse concerning any proposed distributions.

(C) **Testamentary Limited Power of Appointment.** At my Spouse's death, Trustee shall distribute the remaining assets in the Family Trust to my descendants and their spouses, and charitable organizations, as my Spouse appoints, except that this limited power of appointment may not be exercised in favor of my Spouse, my Spouse's estate, or the creditors of either. To the extent my Spouse does not effectively exercise this limited power of appointment, upon my Spouse's death the remaining assets in the Family Trust shall be distributed to and be administered under the provisions of the Paragraph entitled, "**Children's Trust**." **{End of Alternate 2 to Paragraph 5.4 ("Family Trust").}**

5.5 Children's Trust. Trustee shall divide the remaining trust property, including additions from any sources, into separate shares, equal in value, one for each child of mine who survives me and my Spouse and one for each child of mine who does not survive me and my Spouse but is survived by then living descendants. Each share set aside for a child of mine who does not survive me and my Spouse but is survived by then living descendants, shall be further divided by Trustee into separate shares for the descendants, such descendants to take by right of representation. Each share shall then be held in trust and be administered by Trustee, as follows:

(A) Income and Principal. Trustee may pay to or for the benefit of the beneficiary those portions of income and principal that Trustee in its discretion determines necessary for the reasonable health care, education, support and maintenance of the beneficiary and the beneficiary's immediate family (reasonable support and maintenance includes, but is not limited to, obtaining and maintaining a primary residence, purchasing and maintaining a suitable motor vehicle, paying for all the expenses of a first wedding and honeymoon (including pre-marital counseling and planning), or becoming established or remaining in a business or profession for which the beneficiary seems suited). Trustee may retain title to any residence so purchased. Trustee shall add undistributed income to principal, at Trustee's discretion. Furthermore, a Disinterested Trustee may, in its sole, absolute and uncontrolled discretion, distribute such amounts of income and principal to or for the benefit of the beneficiary, as the Disinterested Trustee shall determine.

(B) **Residue.** When the beneficiary attains the age of thirty (30) years, Trustee shall distribute all remaining assets to the beneficiary.

(C) **Death of Beneficiary and Testamentary Limited Power of Appointment.** If the beneficiary dies before being entitled to distribution of the remaining trust property, Trustee shall distribute the remaining trust property to such charitable organizations, the deceased beneficiary's spouse, my descendants and my descendants' spouses (other than the deceased beneficiary, the deceased beneficiary's estate, or the creditors of either), as the deceased beneficiary appoints; provided, however, that any property appointed to the deceased beneficiary's spouse shall be held in trust and that trust must provide that (i) only income, but not principal, may be distributed to the spouse, (ii) the spouse shall not be trustee, (iii) the trust will terminate no later than the spouse's death (and the trust may terminate earlier on events such as the spouse's remarriage or cohabitation with an unrelated person), and (iv) upon termination, the trust property shall be allocated or distributed (in a manner designated by the deceased beneficiary) among my descendants (other than the deceased beneficiary, the deceased beneficiary's estate, or the creditors of either), and their spouses, subject to the above limitations. To the extent this limited power of appointment is not exercised effectively, Trustee shall distribute the then remaining trust property to the deceased beneficiary's then living descendants, by right of representation (or if there are none, to the then living descendants, by right of representation, of the individual who is next in line of lineal ascent from the deceased beneficiary to me (including me in such line of ascent), who has descendants then living). The share of any ultimate beneficiary in default of appointment for whose primary benefit another trust then is held or is to be held under this Agreement shall be added to the other trust and held, or partly held and partly distributed, as if it had been an original part of the other trust.

5.6 Absence of Beneficiaries. If all of the beneficiaries of any trust created under this Agreement should die before the trust assets have vested in them, Trustee shall distribute all remaining assets of each such trust as follows:

(A) **One-Half to My Heirs**. One-half (1/2) (or all, if there are no persons to take under paragraph item (B) below) to my heirs (other than to any state or governmental entity) who would have taken my estate and such shares as they would have taken it, had I died unmarried and intestate in the state which I was domiciled at the time of my death, determined on the later of my death or the death of the last of such beneficiaries to die; and

(B) **One-Half to My Spouse's Heirs**. One-half (1/2) (or all, if there are no persons to take under paragraph item (A) above) to the heirs (other than to any state or governmental entity) of the person to whom I am legally married at the time of my death who would have taken said person's estate and in such shares as they would have taken it, had said person died unmarried and intestate in the state which I was domiciled at the time of my death, determined on the later of said person's death or the death of the last of such beneficiaries to die.

(C) **Balance to Charity.** If there are no persons to take under either paragraph items (A) or (B) above, then all remaining trust assets shall be distributed free of trust to a charitable organization(s) selected by Trustee, in memory of me and the person to whom I am legally married at the time of my death. Until such time as the events described in the preceding sentence occur, no charity shall have any right or interest in the trust or be entitled to receive information concerning the trust or be joined in any action pertaining to the trust, nor shall any governmental agency (such as the state's attorney general's office) be entitled to receive any information concerning the trust (as a result of such potential charitable donation) or be joined in any action concerning the trust (as a result of such potential charitable donation) and no consent, approval or other action shall be necessary, required or authorized by or from such charity or the governmental agency (as a result of such potential charitable donation). In other words, until the events in the first sentence of this sub-paragraph occur, the charity and the governmental agency shall not be interested trust beneficiaries (in any sense of the meaning), and shall have no standing, whether by rule, statute or common law. Trustee is directed to review our prior charitable giving records (if any) to assist Trustee in selecting the charitable organization(s) and the percentage amount for each charity (if Trustee has selected more than one charitable organization).

If, after six (6) months of reasonable search following the occurrence of an event that requires the determination of heirs hereunder, Trustee is unable to identify and locate any such heirs, it shall be presumed that the person described above has no heirs and the property shall be distributed as if there are "no persons to take" under the relevant paragraph item.

ARTICLE 6
TRUSTEES

6.1 Initial and Successor Trustees.

(A) Subject to the provisions of the Paragraphs entitled, **"Removal of Trustee"** (and any other pertinent provisions of this Agreement), the following persons shall serve (to the extent not prohibited from serving as a trustee), in priority of the order listed, as Trustee of the initial trust:

- «InitialTrustee», «InitialTrtAddr»
- «AltTrustee1», «AltTrst1Address»
- «AltTrustee2», «AltTrst2Address»
- «AltTrustee3», «AltTrst3Address»
- «AltTrustee4», «AltTrst4Address»

(B) Subject to the provisions of the Paragraphs entitled, **"Removal of Trustee"** (and any other pertinent provisions of this Agreement), the following persons shall serve (to the extent not prohibited from serving as a trustee), in priority of the order listed, as Trustee of the Marital Trust, Family Trust and any trust under the provisions of the Paragraph entitled, **"Children's Trust**."

- my Spouse—as concerns the Marital Trust and Family Trust—(but only as a Co-Trustee with a person nominated herein or appointed pursuant to this Agreement)

- «InitialTrustee», «InitialTrtAddr»
- «AltTrustee1», «AltTrst1Address»
- «AltTrustee2», «AltTrst2Address»
- «AltTrustee3», «AltTrst3Address»
- «AltTrustee4», «AltTrst4Address»

(C) If a Trustee (or a person nominated as a trustee) is dead, incapacitated, resigns from a trusteeship, is prohibited from serving as a trustee, or declines to serve as a trustee of any trust created under this Agreement, then unless otherwise prohibited, a remaining Co-Trustee (or in the absence thereof, the successor Trustee), who is not prohibited from serving as a trustee, shall serve as sole Trustee of such trust, without need of court approval.

(D) Except as otherwise provided in the Paragraph entitled, "**Removal of Trustee**," in the absence of a nominated successor Trustee then able to act, a successor Trustee shall be appointed by a majority of the current income beneficiaries of the trust in question who are sui juris and not incapacitated. If a majority of such current income beneficiaries cannot agree on a successor Trustee, any current income beneficiary or outgoing Trustee can petition a court of competent jurisdiction, ex parte, to designate an appropriate person as successor Trustee. The court shall not acquire any jurisdiction over the trust, except to the extent necessary to appoint a successor Trustee.

(E) I shall not be eligible to serve as a Trustee of any trust established under this Agreement, nor may any Trustee delegate its powers or duties to me.

(F) A person who has made an *irrevocable* beneficiary designation naming this Agreement (or its Trustee) as an irrevocable beneficiary of the asset can not serve as a Trustee under this Agreement.

(G) A person who is prohibited from serving as a Trustee of a particular trust or its property shall not serve as a Trustee of the trust in question or as a Trustee of that trust's property, nor may any Trustee delegate its powers or duties to such person.

(H) Unless otherwise consented to by the current income beneficiaries of the trust in question, no person shall serve as a trustee if to do so would result in the trust being: (i) classified as a "foreign trust" under the Code, and (ii) subjected to greater or additional taxation as a result of such classification, or the loss of the trust's ability to legally hold S corporation stock; provided however, such person may in the absence of the aforesaid consent, serve as a Co-Trustee if the trust would (continue to) be classified as a United States person under IRC section 7701(a)(30).

6.2 Incapacity of Trustee. If a Trustee is incapacitated, then he or she will be deemed to have automatically resigned as Trustee.

6.3 Resignation by Trustee. Trustee may resign as trustee of any or all trusts under this Agreement at any time by giving written notice, specifying the effective date of resignation, to the then acting Co-Trustee(s) of the trust in question, or if none, then to the designated successor Trustee nominated (or appointed) herein. If no successor Trustee is designated, the resigning Trustee shall give notice to all the current income beneficiaries of the trust in question who are sui juris.

6.4 Trustee May Delegate to Co-Trustee. Any Trustee may, from time to time, delegate to any other Trustee by a dated written instrument any or all of such Trustee's powers (except those, if any, not exercisable by such other Trustee, or which are not reasonable or prudent to delegate to such other Trustee). Consistent with the delegating Trustee's tenure, such delegation may be temporary or permanent, and if temporary, may be for any duration of time or until any event specified by the delegating Trustee. Any person dealing in good faith with any Trustee may rely without inquiry upon the Trustee's certificate with respect to any delegation.

6.5 Trustee May Appoint a Co-Trustee. A Trustee may by a dated written instrument filed with the trust records, designate, appoint and compensate any person (not prohibited from serving as a trustee) as a Co-Trustee. The Co-Trustee may be an Interested Trustee, Disinterested Trustee or an Independent Trustee. The Co-Trustee shall not possess or exercise any power or authority that it is otherwise prohibited from possessing or exercising. Any Co-Trustee so appointed may, without liability, accept without examination or review the accounts rendered, the actions taken, and the property delivered by or for any appointing Trustee or any Co-Trustee of the appointing Trustee. A Co-Trustee so appointed may be removed at any time, with or without cause, by the appointing Trustee(s), other than an Interested Trustee. A Co-Trustee appointed solely by an Interested Trustee may be removed for reasonable cause by the appointing Interested Trustee. Except as otherwise provided herein, a Co-Trustee so appointed shall serve only as long as the Trustee who appointed such Co-Trustee (or, if such Co-Trustee was named by more than one (1) Trustee acting together, by the last to serve of such Trustees), and such Co-Trustee shall not become the successor Trustee or a successor Co-Trustee, unless: (i) such Co-Trustee has been nominated by me as the successor Trustee hereunder, (ii) such Co-Trustee is elected or appointed as the successor Trustee of the trust in question, (iii) such Co-Trustee is appointed as a Co-Trustee by the successor Trustee of the trust in question, (iv) a majority of the current income beneficiaries of the trust in question who are sui juris and not incapacitated, consent in writing to the continuation of the appointed Co-Trustee as the successor Trustee, (v) all of the specifically named successor Trustees of the trust in question consent, in writing, to the continuation of the appointed Co-Trustee as the successor Trustee, or (vi) a court of competent jurisdiction consents to the appointment of such Co-Trustee as the successor Trustee.

6.6 Trustee May Appoint a Substitute Trustee. If Trustee is unable or unwilling to exercise a fiduciary power with regard to a specific trust matter or assets, Trustee may by a dated written instrument filed with the trust records, designate, appoint and compensate any person (not prohibited from serving as a trustee) as a substitute Trustee for any trust matters or assets that the appointing Trustee is unwilling or unable to act as Trustee, or for trust assets in another jurisdiction, with any trust powers set out in this Agreement or provided by law (except those, if any, not exercisable by such substitute Trustee) that the appointing Trustee delegates to the substitute Trustee, and to specify which jurisdiction's law is to govern questions relating to the administration of such matters and assets. Any substitute Trustee so appointed, may, without liability, accept without examination or review the accounts rendered, the actions taken, and the property delivered by or for the appointing Trustee or any Co-Trustee of an appointing Trustee. A substitute Trustee may be removed at any time, with or without cause, by the appointing Trustee(s), other than an Interested Trustee. A substitute Trustee appointed solely by an Interested Trustee may be removed for reasonable cause by the appointing Interested Trustee. A substitute Trustee may be removed at any time, with or without cause, by any successor Trustee. If Trustee chooses to not appoint a substitute Trustee with respect to the exercise of a fiduciary power, Trustee may petition a court of competent jurisdiction to request the appointment of a special trustee to exercise the fiduciary power on a temporary or permanent basis, or may request that the court exercise the fiduciary power on a temporary or permanent basis. A special trustee appointed by the court shall be treated as a "substitute Trustee."

6.7 **Individual Trustee May Nominate Successor Trustee.** Each individual Trustee (including successors) shall have the right to nominate a successor Trustee(s) (who is not prohibited from serving as a trustee) by a dated written instrument filed with the trust records and delivered to all the current income beneficiaries of the trust in question who are sui juris. A nomination may be changed or revoked until it takes effect. Except as otherwise provided in the next sentence, the appointment of a nominated successor under this provision shall take effect only if and when all Trustees that have been previously nominated or appointed by me fail or decline to qualify or cease to act with respect to the trust in question, and a majority of the current income beneficiaries of the trust in question who are sui juris (other than the appointing beneficiary-trustee) do not object in writing to the appointment of such nominated successor Trustee by the appointing Trustee. The restrictions of the preceding sentence shall not, however, apply if: (i) all of the then nominated successor Trustees of the trust in question consent, in writing, to the appointment of the nominated successor(s) as the next successor Trustee(s) to the appointing Trustee, (ii) a majority of the current income beneficiaries of the trust in question (except the appointing beneficiary-trustee) who are sui juris and not incapacitated, consent in writing, to the appointment of the nominated successor(s) as the next successor Trustee(s) to the appointing Trustee, or (iii) a court of competent jurisdiction consents to the appointment of the nominated successor(s) as the next successor Trustee(s) to the appointing Trustee. A Trustee nominated pursuant to the provisions of this Paragraph shall be deemed to be a Trustee that has been nominated in the Paragraph entitled, **"Initial and Successor Trustees."**

6.8 Sole Beneficiary—Trustee Authorized. Except as otherwise expressly provided in this Agreement, if the sole Trustee of a trust is a beneficiary of the trust, Trustee may appoint but shall not be required to appoint a Co-Trustee. A beneficiary's interest may not be merged or converted into a legal life estate or estate for years because the beneficiary is the sole Trustee. If this would still happen under applicable law, then a Co-Trustee shall be appointed in preference to such merger or conversion.

6.9 Action by One Trustee. Unless a Co-Trustee elects otherwise in writing, when more than one person is serving as Trustee, any one of them (who is not prohibited from acting), may, acting alone, exercise any power and authority of Trustee, and may sign any checks, agreements or other documents on behalf of the trust, and the signature of any one such Trustee shall be sufficient to bind the trust in the same manner as though said check, agreement or other document had been signed by all the Co-Trustees (who are not prohibited from acting), and no person dealing with the signing Trustee shall be obliged to inquire as to the other Co-Trustee's acquiescence to such action.

6.10 Multiple Trustees. While two (2) or more Trustees are then acting, the following provisions shall apply where the context permits:

(A) When more than one person is serving as Trustee and at least one of them is a Disinterested or Independent Trustee, the Trustee who is not a Disinterested or Independent Trustee shall not participate in the exercise or non-exercise of any discretionary authority granted by this Agreement;

(B) When more than two (2) Trustees are then acting, the decision of a majority of the Trustees (who are eligible to participate in the action or decision) shall control in all matters pertaining to the administration of any trust created under this Agreement, and if there are an even number of eligible Trustees and a majority decision can not be achieved, then the disputed matter shall be submitted to binding arbitration;

(C) If only two (2) Trustees are then acting and both are eligible to participate in the action or decision, the concurrence and joinder of both shall be required, and if they both cannot mutually agree on the action or decision, the matter in dispute shall be submitted to binding arbitration;

(D) A Trustee who is eligible to participate in an action or decision shall be presumed to have approved a proposed act or decision to refrain from acting if that Trustee fails to indicate approval or disapproval thereof within fifteen (15) days after a written request for approval, and a Trustee shall not be required to continue to make a proposal which has been disapproved on at least two (2) occasions if that Trustee has informed a disapproving Co-Trustee (who is eligible to participate in the action or decision) that continued disapproval will be assumed until notice to the contrary has been received;

(E) When more than two (2) Trustees are then acting, any disapproving Trustee (who is eligible to participate in the action or decision) may be absolved from personal liability by registering a written disapproval with the records of the trust, and the disapproving Trustee shall thereafter act with the other Trustees in any manner necessary or appropriate to effectuate the decision of the majority, if any;

(F) Any Trustee who is not eligible to participate in an action or decision shall not be liable therefor; and

(G) The Trustees may execute documents by jointly signing one document or separately signing concurrent counterpart documents.

6.11 Trustee's Fees. Trustee shall be entitled to fair and reasonable compensation for services performed, and to reimbursement for expenses (even though Trustee may also be my personal representative and/or an accountant, attorney, investment advisor or other agent retained by my personal representative or Trustee, and Trustee's fees shall be in addition to (and not in diminution of) any other compensation otherwise payable to such persons concerning their services to my estate or the trusts established under this Agreement). The fairness and reasonableness of

Trustee's fees shall not be determined on the basis of only the time spent, but may be computed by the method which Trustee and those professionals hired by it customarily utilize in determining the compensation it will receive from clients or customers for its services. If Trustee is a professional person charging clients by the hour, then said person's hourly rate charged clients shall be a major factor in determining said person's compensation as Trustee. Trustee may, without prior approval by any court or any beneficiary, pay from and charge the trust estate with such fees, compensation, reimbursements, and expenses at such times and intervals as may be established by Trustee.

6.12 Qualifying as Trustee. A substitute Trustee, successor Trustee or Co-Trustee shall qualify upon signing an acceptance of trust and delivering it to the appointing Trustee(s) (if any); and in the case of a successor Trustee, the acceptance of trust shall be delivered to all the current income beneficiaries of the trust in question who are sui juris and not incapacitated and to all the other then acting Trustees of the trust in question. Unless a bond is otherwise requested by a majority of the trust's current trust beneficiaries, no bond shall be required of a Trustee (to the extent such requirement can be waived). If a person becomes eligible to serve as a Trustee because of a death, resignation, removal, or appointment, the notice of acceptance of trust must be given within thirty (30) days of eligibility. If eligibility to serve occurs because of the attainment of a specified age, the notice of acceptance may be given at any time.

6.13 Title and Powers. Except as otherwise provided or expressly limited, any successor Trustee, Co-Trustee or substitute Trustee shall have all the title, powers, and discretion of the Trustee succeeded, the other Co-Trustee(s), or the appointing Trustee(s) (as the case may be), without the necessity of any conveyance or transfer.

6.14 Other Trustee's Acts and Accounts, and Delivery of Trust Records. A successor Trustee is under no obligation to review the acts or to examine the accounts of a predecessor or any Co-Trustee of a predecessor. In no event is a successor Trustee liable for acts, omissions, or failures to account properly prior to the successor's qualification. A substitute Trustee or a Co-Trustee appointed by another Trustee is under no obligation to review the acts or to examine the accounts of an appointing Trustee or any Co-Trustee of an appointing Trustee. In no event is a substitute Trustee or a Co-Trustee appointed by another Trustee liable for acts, omissions, or failures to account properly prior to such substitute Trustee's qualification or such Co-Trustee's qualification. A Trustee is under no obligation to inquire into or examine the acts or accounts of a personal representative who is transferring property to Trustee. If any Trustee is removed, resigns or otherwise ceases to act as Trustee of any trust hereunder, that Trustee shall immediately surrender all records with respect to such trust to the then acting Trustee(s) of the trust in question or, if no other Trustee is then acting with respect to such trust, to the successor Trustee upon receipt of written notice of the acceptance of the trusteeship by the successor Trustee.

6.15 Corporate Successor. Any corporate successor to the trust business of any corporate Trustee acting under this Agreement shall become Trustee in place of its predecessor, without the necessity of any conveyance or transfer.

6.16 Proceeds Application. No person paying money or delivering any property to Trustee need see to its application.

6.17 Notice. Any notice or other communication that is required to be in writing shall be delivered personally, telegraphed, telexed, or telecopied, or sent by first class, certified, registered, or express delivery, postage prepaid, to the last known address of the party in question, or by any other means reasonably intended to effect actual delivery. Any such notice or communication shall be deemed given when so delivered personally, telegraphed, telexed, telecopied; or if mailed, or delivered by express delivery (such as FEDEX), on the earlier of the date of receipt or two (2) days after the date of mailing or the sender's delivery to the express delivery courier. Unless otherwise specifically provided in this Agreement, Trustee may rely on any information, telephone conversation, e-mail, notice, certificate, affidavit, letter, telegram, or other document or communication reasonably believed by it to be genuine, or on any evidence reasonably deemed by it to be sufficient. Trustee shall incur no liability for any payment or distribution made in good faith without actual knowledge of a changed condition affecting any person's interest in the trust.

6.18 Trustee Liability. Trustee shall act in a fiduciary manner, and exercise good faith, ordinary prudence, and reasonable care in the discharge of its duties and the exercise of its powers under the terms of this Agreement. Trustee, however, shall not be liable for the acts, omissions, or defaults of any agent hired with reasonable care and in good faith.

6.19 Conflict of Interest. No Trustee shall be per se disqualified by reason of owning an interest in real or personal property, or in a corporation or other business venture or entity, or by reason of being an officer, director, member or employee of any corporation or other business venture or entity, an interest in which is also a part of the trust in question.

6.20 Initial Notice of Trustee Status. For a revocable trust, within twenty-eight (28) days after Trustee's acceptance of trust or my death, whichever is later, and for all other trusts, within twenty-eight (28) days after acceptance of the trust, Trustee shall, to the extent required by law, inform in writing each interested trust beneficiary of the trust's existence, of the court in which the trust is registered, if it is registered, of Trustee's name and address, and of the interested trust beneficiary's right to request and receive both a copy of the trust's terms that describe or affect the interested trust beneficiary's interest and relevant information about the trust property. In addition, upon reasonable request, Trustee shall, to the extent required by law, provide an interested trust beneficiary with a copy of the trust's terms that describe or affect the interested trust beneficiary's interest and with relevant information about the trust property.

6.21 Removal of Trustee. I may remove a Trustee then serving or nominated to serve, for reasonable cause, and I may appoint a successor (other than a person who is prohibited from serving as a Trustee or a person whose life is insured by the trust in question) to replace the Trustee (or nominated Trustee) that I remove for reasonable cause. I may also (but not more than once in a twenty-four (24) month period) remove a Trustee then serving or nominated to serve for no cause, and I may appoint a successor to replace the Trustee (or nominated Trustee) that I remove for no cause, provided the replacement Trustee I appoint pursuant to this sentence is not me, not a person whose life is insured by the trust in question, not a person who is prohibited from serving as a Trustee, and is not related or subordinate (within the meaning of IRC section 672 (c)) to me. Any replacement Trustee appointed as aforesaid shall serve as Trustee prior to any other person who has been nominated as a Trustee. My Spouse may remove a Trustee then serving or nominated to serve, for reasonable cause. Subject to the foregoing, a majority of the current income beneficiaries of the trust in question who are sui juris and not incapacitated, may remove a Trustee for reasonable cause.

A Co-Trustee or nominated successor Trustee may remove an incumbent Trustee for reasonable cause at any time, and if successful in the removal of the incumbent Trustee, the Trustee who sought the removal shall be reimbursed from the trust estate for its reasonable expenses (including attorney fees) incurred in obtaining the removal of the incumbent Trustee. If a Co-Trustee or a nominated successor Trustee is not successful in its good faith attempt to remove the incumbent Trustee, a court of competent jurisdiction shall decide whether the reasonable expenses incurred by a Co-Trustee or nominated successor Trustee seeking the removal should be paid by the trust estate and/or trust beneficiaries personally (or a combination of both).

In applying these powers, the following rules apply (subject to the conditions and limitations imposed upon me concerning the removal and replacement of a Trustee):

(A) In the absence of a nominated successor Trustee (as set forth in the Paragraph entitled, "**Initial and Successor Trustees"**) then willing or able to serve or continue to serve as Trustee, a majority of the current income beneficiaries of the trust in question who are sui juris and not incapacitated may appoint in writing, a successor Trustee who is a Disinterested or Independent Trustee, located in or outside the United States; provided, however, no beneficiary, acting alone, may remove or name a Trustee of a trust that would be included in that person's estate solely by reason of this right of removal or appointment. In selecting a non-U.S. Trustee, the beneficiaries are reminded to consider the potential (adverse) tax consequences of such an appointment.

(B) A power to remove a Trustee shall be exercised by a writing delivered to the then-serving Trustee, indicating the removal's effective date, the name of the successor Trustee, and the successor Trustee's agreement to serve.

(C) "Reasonable cause" for removal of a Trustee shall mean any one of the following:

(1) The incapacity or disability of Trustee.

(2) The willful or negligent mismanagement by Trustee of the trust's assets.

(3) The abuse or abandonment of, or inattention to, the trust or its assets by Trustee.

(4) A federal or state charge against Trustee involving the commission of a felony or serious misdemeanor.

(5) An act of stealing, dishonesty, fraud, embezzlement, moral turpitude, or moral degeneration by Trustee.

(6) The use of narcotics or excessive use of alcohol by Trustee.

(7) Trustee's poor physical, mental or emotional health which causes Trustee to be unable to devote sufficient time to administer the trust.

(8) Trustee's failure to comply with a written fee agreement or other legally enforceable written agreement affecting the operation of the trust.

(9) The failure of a corporate Trustee to appoint a senior officer with at least five (5) years of experience in the administration of trusts to handle the trust account.

(10) Changes by a corporate Trustee in the account officer responsible for the handling of the trust account more frequently than every five (5) years (unless such change is made at the request of or with the acquiescence of a Co-Trustee or the trust beneficiaries).

(11) The relocation by Trustee away from the location where the trust operates so as to interfere with the convenient administration of the trust.

(12) The removal of all current income beneficiaries from the State where the corporate Trustee is licensed to conduct business as a corporate Trustee.

(13) A demand from Trustee for unreasonable compensation for such Trustee's service.

(14) Unreasonably poor investment performance (as compared to appropriate investment benchmark indices).

(15) Unreasonable lack of communication between Trustee and the trust's current income beneficiaries.

(16) Unreasonably inaccurate or unclear transaction statements or statements of account.

(17) Unreasonable conflicts between Trustee and the trust's beneficiaries caused by Trustee.

(18) Merger, acquisition or deteriorating financial condition of a corporate Trustee.

(19) Where it would appear to be in the best interests of the current trust beneficiaries to have an Independent Trustee serve as sole Trustee.

(20) Any other reason for which a state court of competent jurisdiction would remove a trustee.

ARTICLE 7
TRUSTEE POWERS AND TRUST ADMINISTRATION

7.1 **Trustee Powers.** Subject to the provisions entitled, "**Limitations on Powers**," and any other pertinent provisions or limitations specified elsewhere in this Agreement, every Trustee may exercise, in a fiduciary manner, without court order, any of the following powers, and any others that are granted by law—to the extent not inconsistent with the powers granted in this Agreement. Except as expressly otherwise permitted, no powers shall be possessed or exercised by Trustee, or interpreted, in any manner that would prevent an existing bequest from qualifying for the marital or charitable deduction or would prevent an increase in basis (if applicable) under the Code; provided, however, such prohibition shall not be construed as a direction by me to my fiduciary to exercise any election or option that may be available under any tax or other law in such a manner as will result in a larger amount passing to the marital or charitable deduction bequest in the first instance, than if a contrary election were made. Such powers include:

(A) Additional Powers.

(1) Invest and reinvest the trust assets (or leave them temporarily un-invested) in any type of property and every kind of investment, in the same manner as a prudent investor would invest his or her own assets. Trustee may take title to any securities in the name of any custodian or nominee, without disclosing this relationship, and such securities may be held in "street name" by a brokerage firm or other custodian. Trustee may vote proxies. Irrespective of the prudent investor rule, Trustee may acquire and/or retain life insurance policies on the life of any beneficiary or person whom Trustee has an insurable interest. Furthermore, I prefer that my interest in any Closely Held Business Entity (defined below) in which I am an owner at the time of my death (or that is owned by the initial trust at the time of my death (or which the initial trust has the right to receive as a result of my death)) be retained by Trustee, unless, in the reasonable judgment of Trustee, there are persuasive or compelling reasons to dispose of any such interest. I understand that retention of any such business interest is inherently risky, but I believe in the fundamental soundness of each such interest and that the risk assumed by retaining any such business interest is justified. I further believe that each such business interest is and will continue to be capable of superior economic performance (production of greater net income, attaining a greater capital value, or both) than could be achieved from the sale of such business interest and reinvestment of the proceeds of such sale. As used herein, the term "Closely Held Business Entity" shall include a corporation, partnership (general or limited), limited liability company, joint venture, sole proprietorship or other entity under the laws of any state or other jurisdiction, but does not include any interests that are regularly traded on an established exchange or over-the-counter.

(2) Lease, buy, sell, exchange, or option any real or personal property, for cash or credit, at public or private sale, and with such warranties or indemnifications as Trustee may deem advisable. Trustee may borrow money for any proper purpose from itself or from unrelated parties. Trustee may mortgage, encumber, grant security interests or pledge any trust property, including purchasing securities on margin.

(3) On behalf of itself and/or all future Trustees, disclaim, release, or restrict the scope of any power held in connection with any trust (even if a power is not presently exercisable or is exercisable in a fiduciary capacity that requires the exercise of the power), including any administrative or management power, whether such power is expressly granted in this Agreement or implied by law. Trustee shall make such disclaimer, release, or restriction, if any, by a written instrument specifying the power to be disclaimed, released, or restricted and the nature of any such restriction. Any power disclaimed or released by Trustee shall be extinguished, as concerns that Trustee only, but if Trustee also expressly disclaims, releases or restricts the power on behalf of all future Trustees then the power shall be extinguished as to all future Trustees as well. Trustee may also disclaim any disclaimable interest, in whole or in part, including property, interests in property, and benefits of any kind receivable by any trust (including but not limited to, insurance contracts, qualified plan proceeds, deferred compensation proceeds, stock options, tax sheltered annuity proceeds, retirement account proceeds, etc.) in any manner permitted by law or by a "transfer" within the requirements of IRC section 2518(c)(3) (concerning certain transfers treated as disclaimers).

(4) Trustee may hold any qualified family-owned business (as that term is defined in IRC section 2057) ("QFOBI") for which a QFOBI election is made, in a separate trust for the benefit of the beneficiaries, with the QFOBI being the sole asset of the trust. If for any reason a trust established under this Agreement that contains a QFOBI fails to qualify as a qualified heir (as that term is defined in IRC section 2057), Trustee may appoint the QFOBI interest to one or more persons who do qualify as qualified heirs in the estates, interests, and proportions, including an appointment to a trustee in trust for a beneficiary (but only if the trust is a qualified heir), as Trustee, in its discretion, may determine.

(5) Purchase or otherwise acquire, for cash, credit or installments, form, create, organize, invest in, reinvest in, retain or continue for an indefinite term, any "Business Entity" (as defined below) located within or without the United States, regardless of the form of participation or ownership and even though it may be closely or privately held or may constitute all or a large portion of the trust property of a trust; have and exercise all the powers necessary and incidental to ownership in such Business Entity, including making tax elections, and authorizing or voting to authorize the making of charitable contributions by such Business Entity; comply with the provisions of any agreement restricting the disposition of an interest in the Business Entity; participate in the conduct of such Business Entity or rely upon others to do so, and take or delegate to others discretionary power to take any action with respect to its management and affairs that a person could take as owner of such Business Entity, including the voting of securities, and the determination of all questions of policy; take possession of the assets of such Business Entity and exercise complete control and management of such Business Entity, and in connection therewith, enter into and perform contracts, commitments, orders, and engagements; incur expenses and debts in connection with the conduct and operation of such Business Entity, and pay and discharge such expenses and debts; join in and execute legal documents and agreements, operating agreements, partnership agreements and amendments thereto; participate in any incorporation, reorganization, merger, consolidation, recapitalization, liquidation or dissolution of such Business Entity or any change in its nature and retain and continue such changed or successor Business Entity; enter into buy-sell agreements or similar types of agreements; invest additional capital in, subscribe to or buy additional stock or securities of or make or guarantee new or increased secured, subordinated loans to any Business Entity with trust funds; rely upon the reports of certified public accountants, appraisers, consultants and other professional advisors, without independent investigation and without obligation to file any report with any court in any jurisdiction; elect, employ and compensate directors, officers, employees or agents of any Business Entity, who may include Trustee or a director, officer or agent of Trustee; show in summary form in Trustee's accountings, if any, only the financial position of a Business Entity and not include in detail all the business transactions; deal with and act for such Business Entity in any capacity, including any banking or trust capacity and the loaning of money out of a trustee's own funds, and be compensated therefor; sell, pledge or liquidate any interest in such Business Entity; provided, however, that notwithstanding the provisions of this sub-paragraph, Trustee shall not purchase or otherwise acquire, form, create, organize, invest or reinvest in any Business Entity by which Trustee is employed or in which Trustee (or Trustee's family) directly or indirectly owns an interest, unless (i) Trustee is a descendant of my grandparents or a spouse of such a descendant; (ii) a current trust beneficiary, a descendant of such beneficiary's grandparents, a descendant of my grandparents or a spouse of any of such persons is employed by or owns (directly or indirectly) an interest in such Business Entity; or (iii) a current trust beneficiary consents to such action in a duly acknowledged instrument filed with the trust records; provided, further, that Trustee may continue to hold interests in any Business Entity held by the trust at the time Trustee began serving as such. As used herein, the term "Business Entity" shall include a corporation, partnership (general or limited), limited liability company, joint venture, sole proprietorship or other entity under the laws of any state or other jurisdiction, but does not include any interests that are regularly traded on an established exchange or over-the-counter. Trustee may make or terminate elections with respect to S corporation stock; and during the term of any trust under this Agreement, (i) if Trustee sells any interest in a corporation or if the assets of any entity constituting a corporation in which the trust has an ownership interest are sold, and (ii) if the corporation has made an election to be taxed under Subchapter S of the Code, Trustee may distribute to the income beneficiary such amounts of income and/or principal as shall be necessary to pay any income tax caused by such sale, if the income or gain attributable to such sale is taxed directly to the income beneficiary under applicable federal tax law. If the personal representative of my estate makes an election under IRC section 6324A (concerning the special lien for estate tax deferred under IRC section 6166), or a corresponding state statute, to create a special lien for the payment of any deferred death tax (including tax attributable to property not passing under this Agreement), Trustee may subject trust property to such lien. If Trustee is my Spouse or a descendant of mine, I hereby waive any conflict of interest occasioned thereby, especially if that individual also personally holds an interest in the Business Entity. Any contractual and tort liabilities arising from the Business Entity or its operation shall be satisfied first from its assets and only secondarily from other assets of the trust, if practicable.

(6) Establish any educational savings plans pursuant to IRC sections 529 or 530 (or their successors), or any similar plans; to remove and/or add beneficiary(s) to such plans; and to add and/or remove successor owners of any such plans, all as Trustee may deem proper and expedient; and to exercise all other powers and options involving such plans.

(7) Merge or consolidate any trust created hereunder together with any other trusts (regardless by whom created) having the same beneficiaries, substantially the same dispositive provisions and, to the extent applicable, the same generation-skipping tax inclusion ratios. After the merger or consolidation, Trustee shall inform the current trust beneficiaries which of the constituent trusts is the surviving trust. If the applicable rules limiting the maximum duration of trusts (such as any rules governing perpetuities, vesting, accumulations or the suspension of alienation) start from different dates with reference to the trusts or additions to trusts, or if the trusts have different tax attributes, or if the trust assets are of a different nature, of if there are other significant differences in their provisions, merger or consolidation may still take place; but the assets of the trusts may be maintained in segregated accounts, or records of undivided shares of assets may be maintained. In considering the merger or consolidation of any trusts, Trustee shall give consideration to the potential for adverse tax consequences, including the revocation of Subchapter S status for stock held in trust. Trustee may administer such merged and consolidated trusts as a single trust or unit. If, however, such a merger or consolidation does not appear feasible, as determined in the discretion of Trustee, Trustee may consolidate the assets of such trusts for purposes of investment and trust administration while retaining separate records and accounts for the respective trusts.

(8) Sever any trust or divide any trust into multiple separate trusts; establish separate trusts; establish subtrusts; and make qualified severances. Without the consent of any beneficiary, Trustee may allocate, divide or distribute trust property in cash or in kind or partly in each, including undivided interests, and without making pro rata distribution of specific assets and without regard to the income tax basis of any asset. Non-pro rata distributions or allocations of property may be made based on the property's date of distribution value, in a manner fairly representative of the properties' net appreciation and depreciation, or in any other manner permitted (or required) by law. As to any property incapable of exact division, it shall not be necessary for Trustee to divide the same physically into parts to which each trust shall be entitled, but individual parts thereof may, by appropriate book entries, be allocated among the trusts. In any case where exact division of property or allocation of undivided interests therein between or among the trusts hereunder is not practical or expedient, Trustee may select assets to be appropriated in whole or in part to any of said trusts. Furthermore, Trustee may allot different kinds or disproportionate portions or undivided interests in property among beneficiaries; and determine the value of any allotted property without compensating adjustment, even if the basis for federal income tax purposes of property allotted to any beneficiary is not fairly representative of all property available for distribution.

(9) Except as may be otherwise provided in this Agreement, allocate an item of income or expense to either trust income or principal, as permitted or provided by applicable local law. With respect to any item not established clearly by such law, Trustee shall have discretion to determine whether items should be reasonably charged or credited to income or principal or allocated between income and principal. Except as may be otherwise provided in this Agreement, Trustee shall generally resolve any question about the allocation or apportionment of receipts and disbursement, to or between income and principal, in favor of the trust's current income beneficiary. If the power to adjust between principal and income is otherwise permitted by applicable local law (and is not expressly prohibited under this Agreement), that power shall be vested exclusively in an Independent

Trustee. Absent a written request from a current trust beneficiary, an Independent Trustee who is an individual shall not be required to determine if the power to adjust should be exercised.

(10) Employ and compensate such lawyers, accountants, agents, nurses, professional care managers, caregivers, professionals, and other persons as Trustee may deem useful and appropriate for the proper administration of the trust and for the care of a current trust beneficiary; provided however, the foregoing authority shall not restrict a Trustee's sole, absolute and uncontrolled discretion (if any) concerning distributions to or for the benefit of such beneficiary, nor shall the foregoing be construed to mandate such distributions to or for the benefit of such beneficiary. Trustee may employ an investment adviser in managing the investments of the trust (including any investments in mutual funds, investment trusts, or managed accounts), delegate to this adviser any discretionary investment authorities, and rely on the adviser's investment recommendations.

(11) Institute and defend litigation, and compromise and adjust claims against or on behalf of the trust on such terms as Trustee may deem appropriate.

(12) Amend the provisions of any trust so as to qualify that trust as a "qualified domestic trust" within the meaning of IRC sections 2056(d)(2) and 2056A when, in Trustee's sole judgment, such an amendment is deemed advisable, but only in the event my Spouse is not a citizen of the United States.

(13) Distribute net income accrued or earned during the period from the date of my death to the date of complete funding of all trusts to be established under this Agreement as of the date of my death, and to make preliminary distributions of principal during such period, to the trustee of any one or more of such trusts or to any one or more of the beneficiaries of such trust in such amounts and at such times as Trustee considers appropriate. Despite the preceding sentence, such distributions of income and principal shall be made in a manner which is consistent with applicable administrative and dispositive provisions in this Agreement. In making distributions of net income to beneficiaries, Trustee may disburse the net income in monthly or other convenient installments based upon its estimate of the amount thereof, and shall annually adjust any difference between estimated and realized net income. If on the death of any beneficiary there is a deficiency of income thus occasioned, the same may be charged to the principal account from which the income was paid.

(14) Make (or refrain from making) any tax elections and allocations Trustee may consider appropriate; however, Trustee's authority hereunder is to be exercised only in a fiduciary capacity and may not be used to enlarge or shift any beneficial interest except as an incidental consequence of the discharge of fiduciary duties. All tax elections and allocations made by Trustee in good faith shall not require equitable adjustments. Trustee shall not incur any liability for tax elections or allocations made in good faith.

(15) In Trustee's sole, absolute and uncontrolled discretion, permit a current trust beneficiary to use trust owned real property and personal property free of rent or expense.

(16) Make commitments extending beyond the term of any trust.

(17) Hold trust property of several trusts under this Agreement in common ownership or in a common fund, each trust having an undivided interest in the property or fund, dividing the income proportionately and accounting for them separately, until actual division becomes necessary or desirable.

(18) Defer distribution of trust property after the termination of any trust until all matters involving such trust have been settled.

(19) Purchase liability, casualty, and other appropriate insurance for the protection of the trust estate.

(20) Perform all other acts necessary for the proper management, investment, and distribution of the trust property.

(B) Generation-Skipping Tax Matters. In order to minimize the impact of any generation-skipping transfer tax that may be applied to any of the trusts created by this Agreement or their beneficiaries, Trustee shall take the following actions, where and to the extent applicable; and Trustee may take such other appropriate action as is required or permitted by law (or applicable Treasury Regulations) concerning generation skipping transfer tax matters:

(1) If any trust under this Agreement would, otherwise by reason of an allocation of generation-skipping transfer tax exemption to it, have an inclusion ratio, as defined in IRC section 2642(a) of neither one (1) nor zero (0), then prior to such allocation Trustee shall divide, on a fractional basis, the total trust assets into two (2) separate trusts of equal or unequal value, to permit allocation of the exemption solely to one trust (the "exempt trust") so that the exempt trust will have an inclusion ratio of zero (0); any such division shall be accomplished by allocating to the other trust (the "non-exempt trust" which will have an inclusion ratio of one (1)) the minimum fractional share necessary to leave the exempt trust with a corpus of the desired value and an inclusion ratio of zero (0), so as to be entirely exempt from generation-skipping tax. In the event an existing trust has an inclusion ratio other than zero (0) or one (1), then such trust shall be divided on a fractional basis so that two (2) trusts will be created from the one, one of which will have an inclusion ratio of zero (0), and one of which will have an inclusion ratio of one (1). Trustee is also authorized to sever or divide a single trust into multiple trusts under the "qualified severance" rule of IRC section 2642(a)(3) and to fund the severed trusts in any manner permitted or required by law (including the funding of the severed or divided trusts on a non-pro-rata basis). References hereunder to "trust" or "trusts" refer also to arrangements that are treated as trusts for generation-skipping purposes and to separate shares of a trust, when appropriate to the context, if the shares are, as "substantially separate and independent shares of different beneficiaries" or otherwise, entitled to be treated as separate trusts for generation-skipping tax purposes.

(2) If Trustee divides a trust into two (2) trusts, one which has an inclusion ratio of one (1) and the other which has inclusion ratio of zero (0), I direct Trustee to make the division in a manner that permits the trusts to be treated as separate trusts in accordance with applicable Treasury Regulations (e.g., Treas. Reg. sections 26.2654-1(a) and (b)). Unless applicable Treasury Regulations (e.g., Treas. Reg. section 26.2654-1(b)(1)) require or permit otherwise, if the new trusts are severed on a fractional basis, the separate trusts need not be funded on a pro rata fractional basis; provided, however, if funding is on a non-pro-rata fractional basis, Trustee shall fund the trusts based on the fair market value of the assets on the date of funding, in a manner that fairly reflects the net appreciation or depreciation in the value of the assets measured from the valuation date to the date of funding, or in any other manner required or permitted by law. In funding the severed trusts, it is my desire that Trustee first distribute to the non-exempt Trust, property (or its proceeds) that constitutes Income in Respect of a Decedent, before distributing other property. Where applicable (and unless applicable Treasury Regulations require or permit otherwise), if the severance is required (by the terms of this Agreement) to be made on the basis of a pecuniary amount, the payment of the pecuniary amount shall, to the extent required, be satisfied in a manner that complies with Treas. Reg. sections 26.2654-1(a)(1)(ii) (A) **and** (B) (which concerns the payment of appropriate interest and the method of funding the pecuniary amount).

(3) Where applicable, Trustee is directed to comply with the valuation rules of Treas. Reg. section 26.2642-2 and the separate share rules of Treas. Reg. section 26.2654-1, to wit:

(a) Unless applicable Treasury Regulations require or permit otherwise, Trustee shall, to the extent applicable, satisfy the "appropriate interest" requirement: (i) by paying or irrevocably setting aside property in satisfaction of a pecuniary amount within fifteen (15) months of the date of death of the transferor, (ii) by paying appropriate interest as defined in Treas. Reg. section 26.2642-2(b)(4) on a pecuniary amount, or (iii) by allocating to a pecuniary amount a pro rata share of trust income from the transferor's date of death to the payment date.

(b) Unless applicable Treasury Regulations require or permit otherwise, Trustee shall, to the extent applicable, pay such pecuniary amount: (i) in cash, (ii) solely or partly in kind, using date of distribution values, or (iii) solely or partly in kind, in a manner that fairly reflects net appreciation and depreciation in the value of the assets in the fund available to pay the pecuniary amount, measured from the date of valuation to the date of distribution.

(c) Unless applicable Treasury Regulations require or permit otherwise, in instances where a generation-skipping tax exemption is to be allocated to a residual transfer that follows a pecuniary payment, I direct that: (i) the pecuniary payment receive "appropriate interest" as described in item (a) above, and (ii) if the pecuniary payment is to be satisfied solely or partly in kind, that the funding of such in kind distribution be in a manner described in items (b)(ii) and (iii) above.

(d) In determining the denominator for the "applicable fraction" used in calculating the inclusion ratio for any trust, it is my intent that where this Agreement (or Trustee) creates separate trusts, one with an inclusion ratio of one (1) and one with an inclusion ratio of zero (0), that the "applicable fraction" be calculated under the Treasury Regulations in effect at such time to accomplish the intended result.

(e) In determining how to satisfy the appropriate interest and funding requirements and how to obtain the desired "applicable fraction" described above, Trustee shall have complete discretion, and shall not be held liable for any consequence of the exercise of this discretion, made in good faith. I recognize that Trustee's decision as to how to satisfy these requirements may affect the amounts ultimately allocated to the various trusts hereunder; nevertheless, I intend this provision to apply.

(4) Except as may otherwise be provided in this Agreement (or be provided by applicable law), when a trust (the "original trust") is divided into exempt and non-exempt trusts or otherwise into separate trusts, references in this Agreement to the original trust shall collectively refer to the separate trusts derived from it. Trustee may make different tax elections (including the allocation of generation skipping transfer tax exemption), exercise investment, administrative and distributive discretion, and donees of powers of appointment may exercise their powers, differently with respect to each of the separate trusts (even otherwise identical trusts) derived from the original trust.

(5) If a trust under this Agreement, whether created under this provision or not, is entirely exempt or non-exempt from generation-skipping tax and adding property to it would partially subject the trust to generation-skipping tax, or change its inclusion ratio, Trustee shall hold that property in a separate trust in lieu of making the addition.

(6) Trustee is authorized to divide property in a trust into separate trusts with different transferors; such a trust may have more than one transferor. Trustee shall make any payment to, or for the benefit of, a beneficiary from any trust that has more than one transferor for generation-skipping transfer tax purposes (i) pro rata, from the separate portions attributable to transferors relative to whom the beneficiary is a non-skip person for generation-skipping tax purposes, and, to the extent of any balance, (ii) in ascending order of inclusion ratios of the portions for generation-skipping tax purposes, from the separate portions attributable to transferors relative to whom the beneficiary is a skip person for generation-skipping tax purposes, and such distributions need not be ratable among trusts or trust shares with the same inclusion ratios.

(7) If exempt and non-exempt trusts are established under this Agreement, Trustee shall have the power to make distributions (including distributions resulting from a partial or complete termination of a trust) to beneficiaries who are "non-skip persons" first from non-exempt trusts established for them and then from exempt trusts established for them; in addition, distributions to beneficiaries who are "skip persons" may be made first from exempt trusts established for them and only thereafter from non-exempt trusts established for them. Distributions need not be ratable among trusts or trust shares with the same inclusion ratios. In making distributions from a non-exempt trust, Trustee is authorized to make generation-skipping tax exempt distributions to beneficiaries who are skip persons, as permitted by IRC section 2611(b)(1) (concerning direct payments for tuition and medical expenses). "Skip persons" and "non-skip persons" shall be defined for purposes of this Agreement in accordance with IRC section 2613.

(8) Upon division, or distribution or termination of an exempt trust and a non-exempt trust, Trustee may allocate property from the exempt trust first to a share or trust from which a generation-skipping transfer is more likely to occur.

(9) A Disinterested Trustee in its sole, absolute and uncontrolled discretion may at any time prior to the death of the beneficiary, by an instrument in writing: (i) confer upon the beneficiary (other than me or my Spouse (if I am married)) a power exercisable, by and only by will, which specifically refers to the power created hereunder, to appoint all or part of the beneficiary's trust share to the creditors of the beneficiary's estate, and the instrument conferring the power and its terms and conditions may require consent of a Disinterested Trustee who is not the creator of the power and who does not have a substantial interest in the property subject to the power, which interest is adverse to the exercise of the power within the meaning of IRC sections 2514(c) and 2041(b) and Treas. Reg. sections 25.2514-3(b)(2) and 20.2041-(3)(c)(2); (ii) revoke or modify any such instrument previously executed, with or without executing a replacement instrument; and/or (iii) irrevocably relinquish the powers conferred under Paragraphs 7.1(B)(9)(i) and/or (ii) above. For purposes of the preceding sentence, the term "creditors" does not include the Trustee who confers the power or whose consent is required to exercise the power. Without limiting Trustee's discretion, Trustee may use the authority conferred by this provision to subject the trust property to federal estate tax instead of the federal generation-skipping transfer tax when it appears that it may reduce overall taxes to do so. The power granted may be by a formula or limited by a formula, in the discretion of the Disinterested Trustee. The beneficiary's power conferred by Trustee pursuant to this provision shall not be exercisable in any manner so as to postpone the vesting of any estate or interest in the appointed property or to suspend the absolute ownership or power of alienation of the appointed property for a period ascertainable without regard to applicable rules limiting the maximum duration of trusts (such as any rules governing perpetuities, vesting, accumulations or the suspension of alienation), and the validity of any exercise shall be measured with respect to such rules, to the extent applicable.

(C) Limitation on Powers.

(1) When more than one person is serving as Trustee and at least one of them is not beneficially interested in the exercise or non-exercise of a power or election, the beneficially interested Trustee shall not participate in the exercise or non-exercise of the power or election.

(2) If a bequest has been elected/deducted for the marital deduction and is to be held in trust, it is my intent that the marital deduction gift to my Spouse and the property of such trust shall qualify for the federal estate tax marital deduction applicable to my estate. To this end, all Trustee powers and discretions (whether granted under this Article or elsewhere) with respect to allocations of property to the trust and with respect to the administration of the trust shall not be exercised or exercisable except in a manner consistent with this intent. All doubtful questions regarding the allocation or apportionment of trust receipts and disbursements to or between principal and income shall be resolved in favor of the income beneficiary, it being intended that, at the very least, my Spouse be given substantially that degree of beneficial enjoyment of the trust property during the remainder of my Spouse's lifetime which the principles of the law of trusts accord to a person who is unqualifiedly designated as the life beneficiary of a trust. Furthermore, if the trust consists of any property that is not productive of a reasonable rate of income, my Spouse may require Trustee either to make the property productive or convert it within a reasonable time to income-producing property or to provide out of other assets of the trust the equivalent of the income such property would produce if it were productive of a reasonable rate of income.

(3) No beneficiary or Trustee (either alone or in conjunction with other Trustees or persons) shall possess or exercise any power, discretion or incidents of ownership with respect to any insurance owned by the trust on his or her life; nor shall such beneficiary or Trustee hold or possess any power of appointment over such life insurance, unless such life insurance policies or proceeds would otherwise be includible in the beneficiary's or Trustee's gross estate (for federal estate tax purposes) at the beneficiary's or Trustee's death without regard to such power of appointment. If a Trustee holds (or is to receive) any such policy or policies as a part of the trust estate, then and in that event: (i) the powers conferred on the owner of such policy shall be exercised only by the other then acting Trustee, who is not an insured under the policy; (ii) the life insurance policy or policies shall be received, held and administered in and as a separate sub-trust of the original trust from which it is derived, segregated from the original trust properties, and the insured beneficiary shall be excluded as a beneficiary of the sub-trust (i.e., not eligible to receive or control any distributions of income or principal from the sub-trust); (iii) the insured (including an insured Trustee) shall not serve as a Trustee of such sub-trust; (iv) the sub-trust Trustee (who shall also serve as a Co-Trustee of the original trust) may pay from the original trust (other than a trust qualified and elected for the marital or charitable deduction) any premiums, costs or charges associated with the insurance policies held by the sub-trust (and in no event shall such premiums, costs or charges be paid from any trust assets that are (or have been) contributed by the insured, and the insured shall not be entitled to contribute or transfer property to the original trust or to the sub-trust); and (v) in all other respects the terms of the newly created sub-trust shall be as consistent with the original trust from which it is derived. If the insured Trustee is the only then acting Trustee of the original trust, then such powers over the life insurance policy or policies shall instead be exercised by a substitute Trustee designated pursuant to the provisions of this Agreement dealing with the trusteeship; provided however, if any rule of law or court decision construes the ability of the insured Trustee to name a substitute Trustee as an incident of ownership, the designation of a substitute Trustee shall be implemented either by: (i) a majority of the current income beneficiaries, or (ii) by a court of competent jurisdiction.

(4) No Trustee shall have the power to use or apply trust property (i) for the support and maintenance of anyone the Trustee is obligated to support and maintain, or (ii) for the purpose of directly or indirectly discharging the personal legal obligations of the Trustee. No beneficiary-trustee who is an individual shall have the power to terminate a trust early of which he or she is a beneficiary. At any time when there is more than one Trustee, no Trustee who is also a beneficiary of any trust created under this Agreement shall exercise any power solely by himself or herself as would cause such beneficiary-Trustee to be treated as an owner of any portion of the trust under IRC section 678 (a). No Trustee who is also a beneficiary of any trust created under this Agreement shall have the power, as a then acting Trustee of such trust, to make discretionary distributions to him or herself except: (i) to the extent necessary for such beneficiary—Trustee's health, education, support and maintenance as described in IRC sections 2041 and 2514 (concerning powers of appointment and ascertainable standards) in his or her accustomed manner of living (considering the resources reasonably available to him or her), or (ii) with the consent of a person who has a substantial interest in the trust property adverse to the exercise of the power in favor of such beneficiary—Trustee or such beneficiary—Trustee's estate or the creditors of either (as the case may be), within the meaning of IRC sections 2514 (c) and 2041(b) and Treas. Reg. sections 25.2514-3(b)(2) and 20.2041-(3)(c)(2); and such beneficiary-Trustee shall exercise its Trustee powers solely in a fiduciary capacity and shall not possess or exercise any powers that would otherwise permit that beneficiary-Trustee to enlarge or shift any of the beneficial interests under that trust (except as an incidental consequence of the discharge of such fiduciary duties); and to the extent such beneficiary-Trustee has the authority to make discretionary distributions of income and/or principal to another beneficiary from a trust of which beneficiary-Trustee is then also a then current trust beneficiary, the discretionary distributions shall be limited by an ascertainable standard related to the distributee beneficiary's health, education, support and maintenance in the manner of living to which the distributee beneficiary has been accustomed, and except as may otherwise be provided elsewhere in this Agreement, the beneficiary-Trustee shall consider the resources otherwise reasonably available to the distributee beneficiary, when making such distributions. No beneficiary-Trustee who is an individual shall make discretionary distributions to or for the benefit of any beneficiary of a trust holding assets as a result of a disclaimer by or on behalf of such individual beneficiary-Trustee, except distributions limited to an ascertainable standard concerning the other beneficiary's health, education, support and maintenance. Furthermore, no beneficiary-Trustee who is a beneficiary of the trust in question shall possess any power or discretion that is "conclusive," "sole," "absolute" or "uncontrolled" with respect to the exercise or non-exercise of such power or discretion under that trust; and such beneficiary-Trustee's power or discretion in that regard shall at all times be exercised or not exercised in a reasonable manner, be limited by a reasonably definite standard, and shall be subject to review and judicial scrutiny. Trustee's discretionary power to allot and/or to pay or apply the income and/or principal of any trust established under this Agreement ("*such trust*") to or for the use or benefit of any beneficiary of *such trust* shall be exercisable solely by Trustee(s) other than any Trustee who is a permissible beneficiary of the income and/or principal of any other trust ("*such other trust*"), if any Trustee of *such other trust* is a permissible beneficiary of *such trust.* If at any time there is no Trustee qualified and acting for the purpose of exercising such discretionary powers other than a Trustee described in the preceding sentence, such discretionary powers shall be exercisable by an Independent Trustee. If the provisions of this sub-paragraph preclude all of the then-serving Trustees from exercising a discretion or power otherwise granted them, an Independent Trustee may be appointed by Trustee as an additional Trustee, with the sole authority to exercise the discretion or power, and such additional Trustee may only be removed for reasonable cause.

(D) Life Insurance Matters.

(1) A primary purpose of this Agreement after my death is to enable Trustee, in Trustee's discretion, to help provide liquidity to meet the demands that may confront my estate and family at such time. The liquidity demands that may arise as a result of my death are impossible to predict because of uncertainties as to the other assets that may then be available, the debts and taxes that may then be due, and the cash needs that may remain outstanding for the support of individuals dependent upon me or to maintain business enterprises in which I may have invested. I believe that the best technique to meet these uncertain liquidity demands is for Trustee to invest all or a substantial portion of the trust assets in life insurance during my lifetime, even though such life insurance policies may constitute a disproportionate part, or all, of the trust estate. I recognize that, in the long run, life insurance may not yield as high a rate of return as other available investments, or that it may even experience a negative rate of return (a loss of principal); however, I believe that the benefits of life insurance investments, including the larger payment (compared to other investments) if an insured should die short of his or her normal life expectancy, outweigh the possibility of a lower yield in the long run.

(2) I recognize that the selection and continued ownership of life insurance policies raises questions of prudence and due diligence, whether such policies are acquired by Trustee or transferred to Trustee. Therefore, I expressly authorize (but do not obligate) Trustee, in its discretion, and acting upon the recommendation and representations of any person selling, or in any way associated with the marketing, promotion or sale of life insurance, to purchase any life insurance (including a no lapse/secondary guarantee life insurance policy) from one or more insurers. Trustee may (but shall not be required): (i) to verify that any particular life insurance policy satisfies the requirements for a "life insurance contract" under IRC section 7702; (ii) to compare the performance or pricing or the projected performance or pricing of a particular life insurance policy with the performance or pricing or the projected performance or pricing of any other life insurance policy that then may be available from any source; (iii) to assess the appropriateness of purchasing or retaining any life insurance policy as an investment for the trust as compared to other then available investment vehicles that are not life insurance policies; and (iv) to investigate the strength or solvency of the company that issued or is offering a given life insurance policy. I acknowledge that Trustee is not a guarantor of any life insurance policy held in the trust or payable to the trust, whether purchased by, transferred to, or payable to Trustee. By this Paragraph I do not intend to reserve any right to control or direct Trustee, and the decision on trust investments is expressly reserved exclusively to Trustee.

(3) Trustee, who is an individual and is not a professional trustee, shall not be liable to me or to any beneficiary for any loss or damage suffered in connection with performance or lack of performance of any insurance policy owned by the trust (or payable to the trust) or as a result of the financial condition, including insolvency, of any insurer. The fact that Trustee may have made inquiry regarding any such matter prior to acquisition or transfer of a policy or after the acquisition or transfer of such policy shall place no duty upon Trustee to make any further inquiry, but shall be considered activity beyond the scope of Trustee's normal duties (however, the forgoing shall not prevent Trustee from delegating such duties to an agent, such as a fee only life insurance advisor, if appropriate). Trustee shall not be liable to me or to any trust beneficiary for any loss or damage suffered in connection with the performance, or failure to perform, of any life insurance policy or the insolvency of any life insurance company. On behalf of myself and my successors, heirs, and assigns, I hereby indemnify and hold harmless Trustee from and against any and all claims, liabilities, penalties, and costs, including attorneys' fees, arising from any claim, demand, order or other action related in any way to investing in and/or retaining any life insurance policies and exercising or failing to exercise any incident of ownership therein concerning any life insurance policies that were selected or approved by me, and any judgment against Trustee in this regard shall be satisfied from the trust fund, and to the extent the trust fund is insufficient, against my personal assets, including assets acquired directly or indirectly by transferees by reason of my death. For purposes of this Paragraph, a "professional trustee" is a person who derives a significant portion of his or her work revenue from serving as a trustee of inter-vivos or testamentary trusts.

(4) With respect to any insurance policies that are purchased or transferred to Trustee, I claim no right, title, interest, or incidents of ownership therein at this time, nor shall I have any incidents of ownership therein, presently or in the future, nor shall I be the beneficiary of any such policies, nor shall I exercise any right, power, option, election, privilege or incident of ownership under any such policies; and furthermore, I shall have no duty to pay premiums, assessments or other charges necessary to keep any policy in force and shall incur no liability to the beneficiaries of this Agreement or to any other person if any policy lapses for non-payment of premiums, assessments or charges, or otherwise becomes uncollectible. Trustee shall have all of the rights of the owner of such policies and, without the consent or approval of me or any other person, may, in its sole discretion, exercise or decline to exercise, any election, option, right or privilege available to Trustee, as owner of the policy. Such powers include, by way of example, and without limitation: (i) to reduce the amount of any policy or convert or exchange any policy into other forms of insurance; (ii) to enter into non-taxable and taxable exchanges, transfers and/or sales of trust property; (iii) to make withdrawals from any policy, or to surrender any policy for its cash surrender value; (iv) to borrow upon and pledge any policy in connection with a loan; (v) to take paid-up insurance; (vi) to elect extended term insurance; (vii) to collect dividends, death or other benefits (including disability benefits or an accelerated death benefit), surrender payments, and any other payment which may be due or collectible; (viii) to enter into a split-dollar or other premium sharing or financing arrangement with any person or entity; (ix) to split any policy into two or more policies; (x) to allow dividends to remain with the insurance company or to use them to reduce premiums or to purchase additional insurance; (xi) to use cash values to pay premiums; (xii) direct the manner in which the policy account of any variable life insurance policy shall be allocated among the various investment options from time to time available under such policy, and to change such allocation from time to time, as provided in such policy; (xiii) make any and all elections with respect to any death benefit options provided under any life insurance policy, and change such election from time to time; (xiv) determine how much, if any, of each year's target or similar premium amount of any flexible premium life insurance policy to pay, taking into consideration such tax and financial considerations each year as Trustee deems relevant; (xv) to exercise any options of settlement that may be available under the terms of said policies; (xvi) to determine and modify the current amount of life insurance coverage under an existing policy; (xvii) to accept an accelerated death benefit or enter into a viatical or life settlement concerning any policy; (xviii) to sell or transfer a life insurance policy; and (xix) to enter into premium financing arrangements.

(5) Trustee may, in Trustee's discretion, pay any premiums or other charges from the trust estate or by application of dividends on the policy. If the trust funds are inadequate to pay such premiums or charges, or if Trustee shall deem it inadvisable to pay such premiums or charges, Trustee may, in Trustee's discretion, do one or more of the following: (i) sell a sufficient portion of the property of the trust estate or borrow on the collateral of the property of the trust estate (including borrowing from a beneficiary, Trustee or an affiliate of Trustee), to obtain funds necessary to pay the premiums or charges; (ii) convert a policy into a paid up policy in whatever amount may be provided by the terms of such policy, or convert any such policy to a policy of extended term insurance in whatever amount may be provided by the terms of such policy; (iii) use any automatic premium loan feature; (iv) borrow against any policy cash reserves (whether or not on the policy for which premium or charges will be paid); (v) elect any automatic non-forfeiture feature; (vi) surrender any policy to obtain its cash surrender value; (vii) sell any policy; (viii) reduce the amount of the death benefit; (ix) exercise any other right, option, power, election or privilege under any policy held in trust by Trustee; (x) if I am married, assign and deliver the policy to my Spouse if he or she is an interested trust beneficiary (and not a donor or an insured under the policy); (xi) distribute the policy pursuant to any authority or discretion exercisable by the Trustee concerning distributions of trust principal; (xii) terminate the trust and distribute the policy pursuant to the provisions of this Agreement concerning termination of trusts (to the extent applicable); (xiii) assign the policy to the then current income beneficiaries (other than me or any donor) in equal shares and deliver such policies to them; or (xiv) distribute or liquidate the policy and deliver the policy or liquidation proceeds in such manner, amount, proportions and to such beneficiaries as may be determined or directed by a court of competent jurisdiction. Trustee shall not be responsible for the non-payment of premiums if the trust lacks the ability to pay them, and Trustee shall not be liable to anyone if the policies shall lapse (in whole or in part) or be otherwise uncollectible because the trust lacks the ability to pay the premiums. If Trustee has knowledge of an impending lapse or insufficiency of trust assets to pay premiums and other charges, Trustee shall make reasonable efforts to promptly notify in writing: (a) me (if I am not incapacitated or otherwise unavailable), and (b) at least one adult current trust beneficiary, who is sui juris, in order to advise us of the situation so that appropriate steps can be considered and, if need be, appropriate steps can be undertaken to provide sufficient funds to the trust estate in order to preserve the life insurance policy.

(6) Upon the death of an insured hereunder: (i) Trustee shall furnish the necessary proofs of death to the insurance company or companies which issued any policies of insurance, the proceeds of which are payable to Trustee; (ii) Trustee shall collect the proceeds of all such policies of insurance, and (iii)

Trustee shall collect and receive any other property which may be made payable to Trustee. For such purpose, Trustee shall have full power and authority to execute and deliver any receipt or other voucher for such proceeds or property, to institute any suit or suits at law or in equity to enforce the payment of the proceeds of any such policies or to collect any such other property, and, in case of controversy or litigation over the collection of the same, to adjust, compromise or otherwise settle any controversy or contest concerning said policies of insurance or other property, or the collection thereof. Trustee shall be responsible for the proceeds of the insurance only when, as and if collected or paid to it.

(7) Trustee may, in Trustee's discretion, refuse to enter into or maintain any litigation, endorse policy payments, or take other action respecting any trust insurance policies, until Trustee has been indemnified against all expenses and liabilities which, in Trustee's judgment, may be involved in such action.

(8) Trustee need not inquire whether or not Trustee or the trust has been designated the beneficiary of any insurance policy or other death benefit, and Trustee need act with respect to such policies only after receipt of written notice that Trustee or the trust is a beneficiary.

(9) For trust accounting purposes, policy dividends and increases in value before the death of the insured under any life insurance policy or policies held by the trust shall be treated as principal, and not income.

(10) Any additional insurance policies, no matter how acquired (including, but not limited to acquisition by gift, conversion, reissue, consolidation), may be listed on **Schedule A**, but failure to do so does not affect the trust's policy ownership.

I SPECIFICALLY ACKNOWLEDGE THAT TRUSTEE WOULD NOT ACCEPT THE POSITION OF TRUSTEE UNLESS ITS DUTIES AND RESPONSIBILITIES WERE LIMITED AS SET FORTH ABOVE; AND TRUSTEE, WHO IS AN

INDIVIDUAL AND IS NOT A PROFESSIONAL TRUSTEE, IS INDEMNIFIED.

7.2 Beneficiary Under Disability. Irrespective of whether a trust makes explicit reference to this Paragraph, if a beneficiary is under the age of thirty (30) years, legally disabled, incapacitated, or, in Trustee's opinion, incapable of managing a trust distribution, Trustee (i) may hold or distribute the income and principal in such manner as provided by law or as is otherwise permitted by authority granted Trustee in this Paragraph or elsewhere in this Agreement; (ii) may expend directly any income or principal that it is authorized to use for the beneficiary; or (iii) may pay it over to or for the benefit of the beneficiary, or to the beneficiary's legal representative, if any, or to any near relative or friend, or to any adult with whom the beneficiary is residing, for expenditure on the beneficiary's behalf, without any further responsibility for its application. If Trustee is directed to distribute any portion of trust principal to that beneficiary (including trust principal distributable pursuant to a beneficiary's right of withdrawal), the trust principal shall vest in interest in the beneficiary indefeasibly, but Trustee, in its discretion, may distribute the portion to a custodian for the beneficiary as selected by Trustee (who may be the Trustee) under a Uniform Transfers (Gifts) to Minors Act or similar act, or hold the portion as a separate and distinct trust until the later of (i) the beneficiary reaches the age of thirty (30) years; or (ii) after the removal of the legal disability; or (iii) after the recovery from the incapacity; or (iv) after the time Trustee deems the beneficiary is capable of managing a trust distribution. If Trustee holds the portion as a separate trust, Trustee may pay to or for the benefit of the beneficiary so much of the income and principal as Trustee deems advisable for the reasonable health care, education, support and maintenance of the beneficiary and the beneficiary's spouse and descendants; and, if the beneficiary dies before receiving all of his or her portion, Trustee shall distribute the remaining portion to the beneficiary's estate. Trustee shall not exercise its discretion hereunder in a manner that would impair a beneficiary's unexercised right of withdrawal that has not yet lapsed, or prevent an existing bequest from qualifying for the marital or charitable deduction, or would prevent an increase in basis (if applicable) under the Code, or would impair the status or qualification of a trust that holds shares of stock in a Subchapter S corporation, or would otherwise impair or prevent a qualified family-owned business interest deduction taken under IRC section 2057, or would otherwise impair or prevent special use valuation under IRC section 2032A.

7.3 **Spendthrift Provisions.** To the fullest extent permitted by law, a beneficiary's interest in the trust (including income and principal) shall not be subject to the beneficiary's liabilities or creditor claims or an encumbrance, sale, voluntary or involuntary transfer or assignment, anticipation or legal process, or claims for alimony or child support; nor shall the trust be liable for any beneficiary's debt to any agency, public office or department of the State of ________________ or any other state, or of the United States, or to any other creditor of the beneficiary, nor shall the trust be subject to the process of seizure of any court. Moreover, no power of appointment or power of withdrawal shall be subject to involuntary exercise. Furthermore, no part of the trust estate shall be subject to the claims of any creditor for the provision of support, maintenance, care, or services, including residential care, by any public entity, office, department or agency of the State of Michigan, or of any other state, or the United States, or any other governmental agency. However, this spendthrift provision shall not restrict the voluntary exercise of a power of appointment or the voluntary exercise of a withdrawal right granted by this Agreement. This spendthrift provision shall not prevent or prohibit the complete or partial termination of a trust, the amendment, modification or reformation of a trust, or the acceleration of the payment of principal to or for the benefit of a beneficiary. This spendthrift provision shall not prevent the voluntary: (i) sale, (ii) gift or (iii) transfer of a beneficiary's interest in the trust, to: (a) charity, or (b) between family members and/or other trust beneficiaries, if, but only if, such voluntary sale, voluntary gift or voluntary transfer to the charity, family members/and or other trust beneficiaries is pre-approved by Trustee in writing. If Trustee believes that a beneficiary shall not benefit as greatly from any outright distribution of trust income or principal because of the availability of such distribution to the beneficiary's creditors, Trustee shall instead expend those amounts for the benefit of the beneficiary as Trustee in its sole, absolute and uncontrolled discretion determines. However,

Trustee may, but need not, without liability or accountability, pay on the order of the beneficiary, any distribution to which the beneficiary may otherwise be entitled to, to those persons the beneficiary directs. It is my intention to insulate all trust funds from the claims of the creditors of the beneficiary and especially involuntary transfers of the trust asset or interests in the trust, to the greatest extent possible under applicable law, while enabling Trustee to give the beneficiary the maximum possible benefit and enjoyment of all of the trust income and principal to which the beneficiary is entitled. The foregoing provisions of this Paragraph 7.3 not withstanding, Trustee shall not exercise its discretion hereunder in a manner that would impair a beneficiary's unexercised right of withdrawal that has not yet lapsed, or would prevent an existing bequest from qualifying for the marital or charitable deduction, or would prevent an increase in basis (if applicable) under the Code, or would impair the status or qualification of a trust that holds shares of stock in a Subchapter S corporation, or would impair or prevent a qualified family owned business interest deduction taken under IRC section 2057, or would impair or prevent special use valuation under IRC section 2032A.

7.4 **Certificate of Trust Existence and Authority.** Trustee may, at any time, record, file, or deliver a Certificate of Trust Existence and Authority ("Certificate") with or to any clerk, register of deeds, transfer agent, or other similar agency or office or to any person dealing with Trustee. The Certificate shall contain a verbatim synopsis of certain provisions of this Agreement and shall be signed and acknowledged by me, Trustee, or an attorney for me or Trustee, and shall be in the form of an affidavit. Any purchaser or person dealing with Trustee shall be entitled to rely on the Certificate as a full statement of the provisions of this Agreement that are pertinent to the particular transaction. Photocopies of the executed Certificate shall have the same effect and authority as the executed Certificate.

7.5 **Multiple Copies.** There is only one (1) signed original of this Agreement. Anyone may rely on a copy of said document as certified by a notary public or similar official to be a true copy of the signed original (and of the amendments or other writings, if any, endorsed on or attached thereto) to the same effect as if such copy were the signed original. Anyone may rely upon any statement of fact certified by anyone who appears from the original document or a certified copy thereof to be a Trustee hereunder.

7.6 Termination of Trust. If at any time the size of any trust created under this Agreement is so small that the trust is uneconomical to administer, or if for any other reason in the opinion of Trustee (who is not an Interested Trustee), the trust is no longer necessary, or is impractical, or inappropriate to continue for any reason under the current circumstances, including changes in economic and factual circumstances or changes in federal, state or local rules of law (tax or otherwise), including permanent repeal of the federal estate tax and/or the federal generation skipping transfer tax, or it would not be in the best interests of some or all of the beneficiaries for the trust to continue, such Trustee may, with or without prior or subsequent court approval, terminate part or all of the trust and distribute part or all of the trust funds, as the case may be: (i) to or for the benefit of the primary (or preferred) beneficiary for whom the trust was established, if there is such a beneficiary, or in the absence thereof, to or for the benefit of the person(s) to whom Trustee then must or may pay the trust's current income, in proportion to their interest(s) in trust income; however, if there is more than one beneficiary to whom current income could be paid but the interests are indefinite, Trustee shall distribute the trust assets to or for the benefit of the beneficiaries who are my descendants, by right of representation, or if no descendant of mine is a beneficiary, to all then living income and then living residuary beneficiaries of the trust equally, or (ii) in such other manner or amount(s) as a court of competent jurisdiction may direct, in order to carry out my intentions. Upon such termination, the rights of all other persons who might otherwise have an interest as succeeding life tenant or in a remainder, shall cease. In exercising its authority hereunder, the Disinterested Trustee may distribute all or less than all of the trust assets, while retaining some trust assets in a continuing trust when it appears it may be advantageous or beneficial to the beneficiary (or beneficiaries) to continue to hold such assets in trust. Before terminating a trust hereunder, Trustee may request and shall be entitled to be held harmless and receive appropriate indemnification from the beneficiaries who are going to receive a terminating distribution. Trustee shall not terminate a trust if it would impair a beneficiary's unexercised right of withdrawal that has not yet lapsed, or prevent an existing bequest from qualifying for the marital or charitable deduction, or would prevent an increase in basis (if applicable) under the Code, or would impair the status or qualification of a trust that holds shares of stock in a Subchapter S corporation, or would otherwise impair or prevent a qualified family owned business interest deduction taken under IRC section 2057, or would otherwise impair or prevent special use valuation under IRC section 2032A. Trustee shall not be liable for either exercising or failing to exercise its discretion to terminate a trust.

7.7 **Accrued Income.** Except as otherwise expressly provided to the contrary, upon the death of a beneficiary, any accrued or undistributed income shall be held and accounted for, or distributed, in the same manner as if it had been received and accrued after the beneficiary's death.

7.8 **Right of Representation.** Whenever a distribution or division of property is to be made to a person's descendants or issue by "right of representation," or if the manner of distribution or division is not specified, the property shall be divided into as many equal shares as there are (i) then-living descendants in the generation nearest to the designated person that contains one or more then-living descendants and (ii) deceased descendants in the same generation who left then-living descendants, if any. Each then-living descendant in the nearest generation is to be allocated one share. The remaining shares, if any, are to be combined and then divided in the same manner among the then-living descendants of the deceased descendants as if the then-living descendants who were allocated a share and their then-living descendants had predeceased the designated person.

7.9 **Accountings and Information to Beneficiaries.** Trustee's duty to inform and account to the beneficiaries shall be governed by the following rules.

(A) **Recipients of Information and Accountings.** While a trust holds, at year end, either (i) unmatured life insurance policies, or (ii) unmatured life insurance policies and cash, marketable securities or other liquid assets with a combined liquid value (excluding any life insurance cash surrender value(s)) of less than fifty thousand ($50,000) dollars, adjusted for the cost-of-living, Trustee shall not be required to prepare or file an annual accounting either with the court or with any beneficiary unless such an accounting is either ordered by a court of competent jurisdiction or is specifically requested in writing by a then living current trust beneficiary who is twenty-five (25) years of age or older, is sui juris, not incapacitated and who is actually then receiving trust distributions (other than distributions of tangible personal property) in which case Trustee shall furnish an accounting to the court or beneficiary consistent with the court's order or the beneficiary's reasonable requirements. Subject to the foregoing, upon the earlier of: (i) life insurance proceeds being received by the trust, or (ii) when the trust holds, at year end, more than fifty thousand ($50,000) dollars of combined value of cash, marketable securities, or other liquid assets (excluding any life insurance cash surrender value(s)), adjusted for the cost-of-living, Trustee shall inform and account to: (i) the current trust beneficiaries who are sui juris, and (ii) to such other persons as may be ordered by a court of competent jurisdiction.

(B) **Statement of Account.** Trustee shall keep a true account of the affairs of the trust. At least annually and upon termination of the trust or a change of Trustee, Trustee shall (subject to the above provision entitled, "**Recipients of Information and Accountings**"), render a statement of account. The statement of account shall, at a minimum, list the trust assets, if feasible giving their market values, the trust liabilities, receipts, and disbursements, state the source and amount of the trustee's compensation, and inform the beneficiary that of the time allowed (to wit, 1 year after the date the beneficiary or a representative of the beneficiary is sent a report that adequately discloses the existence of a potential claim for breach of trust) for commencing a proceeding against a Trustee for breach of trust. The statement of account, if any, shall be delivered as soon as practicable after the close of the accounting period or upon the termination of the trust, or change of Trustee.

(C) **Inspection of Records.** The books and records of Trustee relating to this Agreement shall be open at all reasonable times to inspection only by the current trust beneficiary or the current trust beneficiary's accredited representatives, unless otherwise ordered by a court having jurisdiction; provided however, during my lifetime, only I (or my designated agent, if I am incapacitated) shall have this right of inspection. The foregoing sentence notwithstanding, upon good cause shown, a court having jurisdiction may order Trustee to keep other beneficiaries reasonably informed of the trust and its administration.

(D) **Settlement of the Account.** A receipt in full or a release by the beneficiaries or by the conservator or other legal representatives of those beneficiaries who are disabled shall be binding, as to those beneficiaries and as to all matters and transactions stated in the account or shown by it.

(E) **Court Approval of Account.** Trustee is entitled at any time to have a judicial settlement of its account, and attorney fees, expenses, guardian ad litem fees, and other charges incident to the judicial proceeding may be charged against the trust fund.

(F) **Delivery of Accountings.** If the current trust beneficiary is another trust, the statement of account shall be delivered to the trustee of the other trust. If any current trust beneficiary is a minor or otherwise disabled, delivery shall be made to the conservator of his or her estate or, if none, then to his or her parent, legal guardian, or nearest of kin or an adult with whom he or she is living. Trustee may deliver the statement of account to other trust beneficiaries in its discretion.

7.10 S Corporation Stock. If any stock of a corporation that then operates or that Trustee shall deem likely to operate in the near future as an S corporation (as defined in IRC section 1361(a)) is held by a trust or becomes distributable to a trust created under this Agreement, and such trust is not eligible or is no longer eligible, or may not be eligible or qualified to hold S corporation stock (for whatever the reason—including because of discretionary authority granted Trustee), Trustee may implement any of the following alternatives with respect to the S corporation stock:

(A) Where the original trust is for a sole beneficiary, Trustee may create for that beneficiary (provided the beneficiary meets the requisite qualifications under IRC section 1361) a separate trust (or sub-trust) that qualifies as a Qualified Subchapter S Trust under IRC section 1361(d) ("QSST"), and then distribute such stock to the newly created trust.

(B) Where the original trust is for multiple beneficiaries, Trustee may create for each beneficiary (provided the beneficiary meets the requisite qualifications under IRC section 1361): (i) a separate trust, (ii) a separate sub-trust, or (iii) substantially separate and independent shares for each beneficiary (as is permitted under IRC section 1361(d)(3)), and allocate the S corporation stock among the newly created trusts or shares based on each beneficiary's current interest in the income of the original trust, and if no beneficiary is entitled to current income from the original trust, Trustee may allocate the S corporation stock among the newly created trusts or shares in a manner that Trustee deems fair and appropriate. Each newly created trust or share shall hold that beneficiary's appropriate share of the S corporation stock, and shall qualify as a QSST.

(C) Trustee may, in its discretion: (i) create for a beneficiary (or group of beneficiaries) a separate trust (or sub-trust) that qualifies as an Electing Small Business Trust under IRC section 1361 (e) (provided the beneficiary or group of beneficiaries meet the requisite qualifications thereunder) ("ESBT") and distribute such stock to the newly created trust(s), provided however, no distribution from the newly created trust(s) shall be made to any person (whether a current beneficiary or future or contingent beneficiary) other than to a person who is eligible to be an ESBT beneficiary (as determined under the Code), and the number of "potential current beneficiaries" of the ESBT shall not exceed the number of shareholders permitted under IRC section 1361(b); furthermore, any currently exercisable inter-vivos power of appointment held by a beneficiary concerning the S corporation stock to be held by the ESBT (other than a beneficiary's inter-vivos power of withdrawal) is hereby automatically modified and limited concerning the number and class of appointees eligible to receive the S corporation stock so that the number of actual appointees shall not shall not exceed the number of shareholders permitted under IRC section 1361(b) and the class of appointees shall not include those persons who are ineligible to hold the S corporation stock (as determined under the Code), (ii) elect to qualify any trust as any form of eligible stockholder of an S corporation under current or future legislation, or (iii) distribute such stock to the beneficiaries (provided the beneficiaries are eligible S corporation shareholders) as if the trust had terminated, while continuing to hold any other non-S corporation property in trust.

Each newly created QSST shall have mandatory distributions of income (as defined in IRC section 643(b)) and no one shall have any power to appoint or distribute any portion of the QSST property to anyone other than to the beneficiary of the trust. In all other respects the newly created trusts shall be as consistent as possible with the original trusts and still qualify as QSSTs or ESBTs (as the case may be). Trustee may take any action necessary with regard to S corporations, including making any elections required to qualify stock as S corporation stock, qualify a trust as an S corporation shareholder, and sign all necessary tax returns and forms.

It is my intent that any S corporation stock comprising a portion of the trust estate be eligible to be held pursuant to the terms of this Agreement, either as an ESBT, a QSST, or in any other manner permitted by the Internal Revenue Code or the Regulations or rulings thereunder. Accordingly, Trustee is granted the power to amend, modify or reform this Agreement to the minimum extent necessary to permit this Agreement and its trusts to hold S corporation stock during the continuance of this Agreement in accordance with the Internal Revenue Code, Regulations and rulings thereunder; but in no event shall Trustee amend, modify or reform this Agreement or any trust in a manner that would impair a beneficiary's unexercised right of withdrawal that has not yet lapsed or prevent an existing bequest from qualifying for the marital or charitable deduction or would prevent an increase in basis (if applicable) under the Code, or would impair the status or qualification of a trust that holds shares of stock in a Subchapter S corporation, or would otherwise impair or prevent a qualified family owned business interest deduction taken under IRC section 2057, or would otherwise impair or prevent special use valuation under IRC section 2032A, or prevent a disclaimer from being a qualified disclaimer under IRC section. As a cautionary note, Trustee is reminded that it should determine the effect the exercise of its authority hereunder may have on any disabled or handicapped beneficiary (particularly with regard to the beneficiary's eligibility to receive (or continue to receive) public or private benefits or assistance related to the beneficiary's disability/handicap). I realize that the decision to exercise the discretion granted under this Paragraph is extremely difficult, and, in consideration of Trustee agreeing to serve as a trustee under this Agreement, I specifically exonerate Trustee from any liability to any person with respect to the exercise or non-exercise of the discretion granted under this Paragraph.

Trustee shall not make a distribution of the S corporation stock to any person whose ownership of the stock would reasonably be expected to cause the corporation's Subchapter S election to be terminated. Trustee may (and is encouraged to) request a written opinion from tax counsel if Trustee is uncertain about the effect a contemplated distribution of the S corporation stock may have on the corporation's Subchapter S election.

7.11 Guidelines for Discretionary Distributions. Except as may be otherwise provided elsewhere in this Agreement, when exercising discretion relating to a distribution of income or principal, Trustee (other than an Interested Trustee) may, but need not, consider all other reasonably available income and liquid assets of the beneficiary known upon reasonable inquiry by that Trustee, as well any legal obligation of support owed to the beneficiary by another person. A beneficiary who receives discretionary distributions of income or principal need not deplete income and liquid assets below an amount Trustee deems reasonable.

ARTICLE 8
GENERAL PROVISIONS

8.1 Rule Against Perpetuities.

(A) Measuring Period. Upon the expiration of twenty-one (21) years after the death of the last survivor of a class consisting of me, my descendants, the beneficiaries and contingent beneficiaries under this Agreement, the lineal descendants of such beneficiaries, and the spouses of any of the aforesaid, who are living (or in gestation) on the date on which the interest or trust or power of appointment was created for purposes of the applicable Rule Against Perpetuities, every trust created under this Agreement, by the exercise of a power of appointment or otherwise, every power of appointment granted by this Agreement, and every interest, trust or power of appointment that may be created by the exercise of a power of appointment granted herein, shall terminate, if it has not then vested indefeasibly (as provided in paragraph item (B) below) or previously terminated; provided however, this provision shall not apply to any interest established by the exercise of a general power of appointment conferred by this Agreement if the exercise is valid both under this Agreement and under the applicable Rule Against Perpetuities, and under the applicable Rule Against Perpetuities such interest is allowed a new perpetuities period, in which case, the interest established by the general power of appointment shall terminate as provided in the instrument in which such power is exercised, subject to the Rule Against Perpetuities (if any) that may be applicable to such newly established interest. The exercise of any non-general power of appointment granted under this Agreement shall be subject to the perpetuities period of this Agreement and shall not be extended by the exercise of such power.

(B) Vesting of Trust Interests Prior to Expiration of Perpetuities Period. If on the day preceding the expiration of the applicable rules limiting the maximum duration of trusts (such as any rules governing perpetuities, vesting, accumulations or the suspension of alienation), any property is held in trust (except any trust all of the assets of which are then unqualifiedly withdrawable by its primary beneficiary), such property shall immediately vest indefeasibly in (i) the primary beneficiary for whom the trust was established, if there is such a beneficiary, or in the absence of a primary beneficiary to the person(s) to whom Trustee then must or may pay the trust's current income, in proportion to their interest(s) in trust income; however, if there is more than one beneficiary to whom current income could be paid but the interests are indefinite, the trust property shall vest indefeasibly in the beneficiaries who are my descendants, by right of representation, or if no descendant of mine is a beneficiary, then the trust property shall vest indefeasibly in all of the then living income and then living residuary beneficiaries of the trust equally, or (ii) in such other persons or amount(s) as a court of competent jurisdiction may direct, in order to carry out my intentions. For purposes of this Paragraph, to "vest indefeasibly" means that the interest shall continue in trust but be subject to a general power of appointment held by the beneficiary and exercisable by will or by deed at any time in favor of any person (including the beneficiary, the beneficiary's estate or the creditors of either), and if the interest continues in trust until its termination, the interest, in default of appointment, shall be paid to the beneficiary, if living or, if not living to the beneficiary's estate.

8.2 Power of Appointment Matters.

(A) Scope of Appointment. Except as otherwise limited, any trust principal or income as to which a power of appointment is exercised shall be distributed to one or more members of the permissible class of appointees upon such conditions and estates, in such manner (in trust, to an existing trust, to a trust to be created, or otherwise), with such powers, in such amounts or proportions (equal or unequal), and at such time or times as the holder of the power (donee) may specify in the instrument exercising the power (but not beyond the period permitted by any applicable rules limiting the maximum duration of trusts (such as any rules governing perpetuities, vesting, accumulations or the suspension of alienation)). Unless the instrument exercising a power of appointment explicitly states that if an appointee is deceased that the appointment is in favor of the appointee's descendants (or explicit words of similar import and intent), any power of appointment exercised in favor of a deceased appointee shall lapse and a surviving descendant of the deceased appointee shall not be substituted for the deceased appointee. The donee may appoint a different trustee to administer a trust created by the exercise of the power and may change the situs of the trust administration and direct that the trust shall be governed by the law of the new situs or any other jurisdiction. The trustee under an appointment in further trust may be any person not prohibited from serving as Trustee under this Agreement and may be given fiduciary powers (including discretionary powers over distributions), exercisable, however, only in favor of permissible objects of the exercised power. If the donee does not direct otherwise, a trust created by the exercise of the power shall be administered by the trustee hereof subject to the same management powers conferred on the trustee. With respect to any sub-trusts or trusts that have been divided, the donee may exercise his or her power differently with respect to each sub-trust or separate trusts (even otherwise identical trusts) derived from the original or divided trust. No power of appointment may be exercised by any individual under this Agreement with respect to policies of insurance on the life of such individual, or the proceeds thereof, unless such policies or proceeds would be includible in the individual's gross estate (for federal estate tax purposes) at such individual's death without regard to such power of appointment.

(B) **Manner of Exercise and Determination of Effective Appointment.** Except as may be explicitly required otherwise in this Agreement, any power, including a power of appointment, granted to a person under this Agreement may be exercised either by (i) such individual by his or her last will and testament or (ii) a written direction other than a will executed by such person or such person's duly authorized and empowered legal representative and delivered to Trustee during the person's lifetime (or such other period required by the power) (hereinafter referred to as a "written direction"), which will or written direction makes specific reference to the power of appointment sought to be exercised so that Trustee is able to sufficiently and correctly identify which power under this Agreement is in fact being exercised by the donee. Except as provided otherwise in this Agreement, a power of appointment may be effectively exercised: (i) even if the donee is a minor, incapacitated or under disability, (ii) all of the assets constituting the trust with respect to which the power is granted have not been received by Trustee, or (iii) whether the instrument exercising the power is executed before or after the date on which any trust for the donee is created (including a trust in which the donee is granted the power). Any instrument exercising the power may be revoked or amended at any time before it becomes effective. Trustee may rely upon any instrument that is admitted to probate in any jurisdiction as the last will of the donee; and may distribute the property as provided herein in default of an effective appointment by will if, within six (6) months after the date of the donee's death, Trustee has not received a certified copy of the donee's will that has been admitted to probate and that purports to exercise the power; but the Trustee shall not be required to make any distribution to those who take in default of an effective appointment if Trustee is reasonably in doubt about whether there has been an effective exercise of the power. The provisions in the preceding sentence are for the protection of the Trustee and shall not affect any right or recourse that an appointee or beneficiary in default of appointment may have against any recipient(s) of the distributed property. Admission of a will to probate within six (6) months after the donee's death shall not be a condition to the effective exercise of a power.

(C) Trust Termination and Limited Power of Appointment by Special Power Holder. Each trust may, from time to time, have a special power holder. A special power holder may be appointed: (i) by me, in a writing delivered to the Trustee of the trust in question, (ii) by a majority in interest of the current trust beneficiaries of the trust in question, with one (1) vote being cast by each such beneficiary who is sui juris, one (1) vote being cast for each such minor beneficiary by his or her custodial parent, and one (1) vote being cast by the legal guardian for any such beneficiary having a legal guardian, (iii) by the Trustee then serving of the trust in question, or (iv) by a court of competent jurisdiction. Once appointed, a special power holder may not be removed except by a court of competent jurisdiction and then only for reasonable cause. A special power holder appointed by me shall serve prior to a special power holder appointed hereunder by any other person. In the event that two or more instruments of appointment concerning a special power holder exist and are inconsistent, the latest by date shall control, consistent with the priority of appointment specified above, and any inconsistencies in appointment maybe resolved by the unanimous decision of the existing Trustees and then nominated successor Trustees of the trust in question.

After my death, the special power holder may terminate a trust, in whole or in part, pursuant to the criteria set forth in the Paragraph entitled, **"Termination of Trust."** Furthermore, after my death, Trustee shall distribute all or any part of the trust estate (other than life insurance on the special power holder's life) as the special power holder (in a non-fiduciary capacity) from time to time appoints in a writing that is delivered to Trustee, to any one or more of the trust's beneficiaries, including contingent remainder beneficiaries (but not to the special power holder, the special power holder's estate, or the creditors of either) and in such proportions (equal or unequal) and in such manner (whether out right or in trust) as the special power holder specifies. Provided, however, that no such distribution may be applied or distributed that would give the special power holder any pecuniary benefit or would discharge or satisfy the special power holder's legal obligations. Any person serving or appointed to serve as a special power holder must not be related or subordinate (within the meaning of IRC section 672 (c)) to me or to any beneficiary of the trust in question. A special power holder (then acting or nominated) may resign at any time by giving written notice, specifying the effective date of resignation to Trustee of the trust in question or to any current income beneficiary of the trust in question. If the special power holder is incapacitated, then he or she will be deemed to have automatically resigned as special power holder.

Notwithstanding any other provision of this Agreement, the special power holder shall not exercise any power or discretion conferred under this Agreement: (i) for the direct or indirect benefit of the special power holder, the special power holder's estate, or the creditors of either, (ii) that would cause the special power holder to possess a general power of appointment within the meaning of IRC sections 2041 and 2514, (iii) that would impair a beneficiary's outstanding withdrawal right that has not yet lapsed, (iv) that would prevent an existing bequest from qualifying (or continuing to qualify) for the marital or charitable deduction or would prevent an increase in basis (if applicable) under the Internal Revenue Code, (v) that would impair the status or qualification of a trust that holds shares of stock in a Subchapter S corporation, (vi) that would otherwise impair or prevent a qualified family owned business interest deduction taken under IRC section 2057, (vii) would otherwise impair or prevent special use valuation under IRC section 2032A, or (viii) would prevent a disclaimer from being a qualified disclaimer under IRC section 2518. The special power holder, acting in its capacity hereunder, shall have no fiduciary duty to any trust beneficiary and shall be indemnified and held harmless by the trust and the beneficiaries who are going to be benefited by the exercise of the special power holder's authority hereunder.

(D) Compelled Exercise of Power of Appointment Not Effective. The purported exercise of a power of appointment (including a power of withdrawal) granted under this Agreement shall be of no force or effect if such purported exercise was the result of compulsion. If such purported exercise is the result of compulsion, Trustee shall administer the property subject to such power of appointment as if said purported exercise had not occurred. The purported exercise of a power of appointment shall be deemed to be the result of compulsion if such purported exercise is in response to or by reason of any order or other direction of any court having jurisdiction over the donee, Trustee, the property subject to said power or the trust containing such property. A donee's legal representative may not exercise a power given to the donee under this Agreement if such purported exercise is in response to or by reason of any such order or other direction of any court having jurisdiction over the legal representative unless such order or other direction was obtained by the legal representative in a proceeding in which the legal representative was the petitioner or voluntarily acquiesced and was not otherwise under compulsion.

8.3 Law, Definitions, Captions, and Severability.

(A) Governing Law. Except as otherwise provided in this Paragraph 8.3(A), the validity, administration, meaning and effect, and all rights of beneficiaries under this Agreement and its provisions (and any other instrument related to this Agreement) shall be governed by the laws of the State of ____________________. The administration, meaning and effect, and rights of beneficiaries under a trust established by the exercise of a power of appointment granted hereunder shall be governed by the laws of whatever jurisdiction may be designated either in such instrument of appointment or in the resulting trust (or, absent such designation, by the laws of the State of ___________). This Paragraph 8.3(A) shall apply regardless of any change of residence of any Trustee or any beneficiary, or the appointment or substitution of a Trustee residing in another jurisdiction. Trustee may, with the prior written consent of a majority of the trust's current beneficiaries who are sui juris and not incapacitated, change the situs of such trust and/or its assets and elect to have the validity, administration, meaning and effect or rights of beneficiaries of such trust and/or its assets be governed by the laws of another jurisdiction, in or outside the United States (including that jurisdiction's law concerning the maximum duration of trusts). Trustee may not change the situs of a trust, the trust's assets or the trust's governing law in order to: (i) thwart the purpose of the trust, or (ii) limit Trustee's liability to a beneficiary due to an existing breach of duty. The jurisdiction whose laws govern the validity, meaning and effect, and rights of beneficiaries of any trust may, but need not, be the same as the situs of the trust's assets or the situs of the administration of such trust. This Agreement shall be exempt from mandatory registration (although Trustee may, in its discretion register any trust). Absent a written request from a current trust beneficiary who is sui juris and not incapacitated, Trustee who is an individual shall not be required to determine if the situs of a trust or its assets should be moved from its current jurisdiction to a different jurisdiction or if the governing law of the trust or its assets should be changed.

(B) **Gender.** Whenever necessary in this Agreement and where the context permits, the singular term and the related pronoun shall include the plural (particularly as concerns my Spouse, if my Spouse is a donor), the masculine, and the feminine, and, as to Trustee, the neuter.

(C) **Charity**. The term "charity" or "charitable organization" means an organization so constituted that gratuitous transfers to such organization are deductible, in the first instance, as charitable transfers for federal income, estate (if the Federal estate tax is applicable), or gift tax purposes (as the case may be).

(D) **Child, Issue, and Descendants.** For purposes of determining who is a child, grandchild or descendant of any person (including myself):

(1) The term "issue" or "descendants" means all individuals who are descended from the individual referred to in the first, second, or any other degree, provided the individual in each degree in the line of descent is a child, as defined below, of the individual in the prior degree.

(2) The term "child" means a descendant in the first degree of the parent designated; but such term does not include a stepchild, a foster child, a grandchild or any more remote descendant, unless that individual is adopted as a child (as set forth below).

(3) Subject to the above provisions:

(a) Any adoption begun before the adopting parent's death (i.e., the child has been "placed" with the adopting parent), if the adoption is legally completed by the (deceased) person's spouse within two (2) years after such death (provided the adopted child is under the age of eighteen (18) at the date of adoption) shall be deemed accomplished prior to death.

(b) Posthumous children are to be considered living at the death of their parent.

(E) Current Trust Beneficiary. "Current trust beneficiary" means a beneficiary about which either items (i) or (ii) below, is true: (i) the beneficiary has a current right to receive all or a portion of a mandatory distribution of income, or the beneficiary is currently eligible to receive a discretionary distribution of all or a portion of income; or (ii) the beneficiary is currently eligible to receive all or a portion of a mandatory or discretionary distribution of principal. A "current income beneficiary" is a beneficiary described in item (i), above. If an action under this Agreement must be (or is permitted to be) taken, exercised, affirmed or is referenced by the trust's "current income beneficiaries" and there are no current income beneficiaries of the trust in question (or there are no current income beneficiaries of the trust in question who are eligible to act), then and in that event, the current trust beneficiaries shall act in place of the "current income beneficiaries," and the current trust beneficiaries shall be subject to the same qualifications and limitations that are imposed upon the current income beneficiaries, such as "majority, "sui juris," "not incapacitated," "of the trust in question," etc. In no event may I act on behalf of a current trust beneficiary, regardless of my relationship to the beneficiary.

(F) Death Taxes. "Death taxes" means all estate, inheritance, succession, legacy, transfer or similar duties or taxes and any income or similar taxes on appreciation incurred solely as the result of my death, as well as any and all interest and penalties relating to such duties or taxes which are properly imposed by any federal, state, domestic or foreign taxing authority. "Death taxes" do not include any generation-skipping transfer tax.

(G) Health, Education, Support and Maintenance. "Health, education, support, and maintenance" shall be construed in such a manner as to be an ascertainable standard for federal estate and gift tax purposes, such that the exercise, release, or lapse of a power which is limited by this standard will not be taxable for federal estate and gift tax purposes. If Trustee has discretionary authority to make distributions for a beneficiary's health, education, support and maintenance, those standards shall constitute a ceiling on

Trustee's discretionary authority, and shall not be interpreted as a floor that mandates distribution, i.e., Trustee's discretion is to be limited to matters pertaining to the beneficiary's health, education, support and maintenance. In determining "support" for a beneficiary, Trustee may take into account the obligations of support that the beneficiary owes to other individuals. "Health" shall include (but not be limited to) medical, mental, dental, hospital, and nursing expenses and expenses of invalidism.

(H) **Incapacity**. In the event that any Trustee or any beneficiary hereunder comes into possession of any of the following: (i) a court order, which such Trustee or beneficiary deems to be jurisdictionally proper and still currently applicable, holding a person to be legally incapacitated to act in his or her own behalf or appointing a guardian or conservator of the person or property (or similar fiduciary) to act for him or her, or (ii) a written report of a licensed psychologist, a licensed medical or osteopathic physician stating that he or she has examined a person and has concluded that such person is unable to give prompt and intelligent consideration to financial matters because of excessive use of drugs or alcohol, accident, physical or mental illness, progressive or intermittent physical or mental deterioration, or other similar cause, or (iii) evidence which such Trustee deems to be credible and still currently applicable that a person has disappeared, is unaccountably absent, is incarcerated, or is being detained under duress where he or she is unable to effectively manage his or her property or financial affairs; then and in that event and under those circumstances: (a) such person shall be deemed to have thereupon become "incapacitated", as that term is used in and for all of the purposes of this Agreement, and (b) such incapacity shall be deemed to continue until such court order, written reports, and/or circumstances have become inapplicable or have been revoked.

(1) Any psychologist's or physician's aforesaid report may be revoked by a similar report to the effect that such person is no longer thus incapacitated executed either (i) by the originally certifying psychologist or physician or (ii) by another licensed, unrelated psychologist or physician.

(2) No Trustee shall be under any duty to institute any inquiry into a person's possible incapacity, but the expense of any such inquiry reasonably instituted may be paid from trust assets.

(3) Each person who signs this instrument or an acceptance of Trusteeship or Trust Protector hereunder (a "Consenting Person"), by so signing: (i) consents to and agrees to cooperate in any medical examination necessary to carry out the terms of this provision; (ii) waives all provisions of law relating to disclosure of confidential medical information insofar as that disclosure would be pertinent to any inquiry under this provision, and directs all health care providers to complete the certification required by this provision; (iii) agrees that all individually identifiable health information and medical records (except psychotherapy notes) of the Consenting Person, including any written opinion relating to the Consenting Person's capacity/incapacity or ability to serve as a Trustee (or Trust Protector) that the requesting party has requested, may be released to the following people (a "Requesting Party"), whom the Consenting party hereby appoints as their personal representative in that regard, to wit, a then acting Co-Trustee hereunder, a nominated successor Trustee hereunder, a then acting Trust Protector hereunder, or a nominated successor Trust Protector hereunder. This release authority applies to any information governed by the Health Insurance Portability and Accountability Act of 1996 (aka HIPAA), 42 U.S.C. §1320d et seq. and 45 C.F.R. 160-164, and applies even if the Requesting Party has not yet been appointed as a successor Trustee or successor Trust Protector, as the case may be; and (iv) agrees that the obligations under this provision shall be specifically enforceable. The Requesting Party need not describe the purpose of each request made, but may simply note it is made at his or her request, as allowed under the HIPAA rules.

This HIPAA authorization is effective immediately, shall not expire (except upon the death of the Consenting Party), but may be revoked by a written instrument executed by the Consenting Party. If this HIPAA authorization is revoked, any person or entity acting in good faith in reliance upon it, and lacking actual knowledge of its revocation, shall be held harmless by the Consenting Party. The Consenting Party understands that once the above information is disclosed, it may be re-disclosed by the Requesting Party, and that the information may not be protected by privacy laws or regulations. The Consenting Party acknowledges that authorizing the use or disclosure of this information is their voluntary act. The Consenting Party understands and acknowledges that a health care provider may not condition the Consenting Party's receipt of health care or medical treatment upon his or her authorization (or lack thereof) under the terms of this provision. If a Consenting Party fails within a reasonable time to cooperate hereunder (including having a medical examination and disclosing its results to a Requesting Party), then such Consenting Party shall be deemed to have resigned as a Trustee or Trust Protector (as the case may be), provided at the time the request was made by the Requesting Party there was a reasonable basis to request such medical examination, and provided further that no such request (in which the Consenting Party cooperated) may be made more than once every twenty-four (24) months. To the extent the cost of the medical examination is not paid for by the Consenting Party's health insurance (including Medicare, Medicaid, or other third party provider), the trust shall pay such costs (and may pay all the costs of the medical examination).

(I) Independent Trustee. An "Independent Trustee" means a person: (i) who is not related or subordinate (within the meaning of IRC section 672 (c)) to any beneficiary, power holder (including a person who holds the power to remove a Trustee), or transferor (as defined below) (as the case may be regarding the identity of the appropriate "power holder") with respect to the trust in question; (ii) who cannot be benefited by the exercise or non-exercise of any power given Trustee by this Agreement or by law; (iii) who is not a beneficiary of the trust in question, not an insured under a policy of life insurance owned by the trust, not a person who is prohibited from serving as a trustee of the trust in question, and is not an individual who has gratuitously transferred or joined in the gratuitous transfer of property to the trust in question (a "transferor"); and (iv) if a general power of appointment is held by a beneficiary that may only be exercised with the consent of an Independent Trustee, the term "Independent Trustee" also means a person who is not the creator of the power and who does not have a substantial interest in the property subject to the power which is otherwise adverse to the exercise of the power in favor of the beneficiary, the beneficiary's estate, or the creditors of either (as the case may be) within the meaning of IRC sections 2514 (c) and 2041(b) and Treas. Reg. sections 25.2514-3(b)(2) and 20.2041-(3)(c)(2). A transferor's spouse who merely consents to gift splitting under IRC section 2513 concerning the transferor's transfer of property to the trust shall not be deemed to have "joined in the transfer of property."

(J) Interested Trust Beneficiary. "Interested trust beneficiary" means a person that has one (1) or more of the following interests in the trust: (i) life estate, (ii) eligible recipient of a mandatory or discretionary distribution by the Trustee of income or principal, (iii) eligible recipient of a mandatory or discretionary distribution by the Trustee of income or principal upon termination of an interest of a person described in items (i) or (ii) above, or (iv) presently exercisable or current testamentary general or special power of appointment.

(K) Interested Trustee and Disinterested Trustee. "Interested Trustee" means for any trust a Trustee who is (i) a transferor of property to the trust, including a person whose disclaimer resulted in property passing to the trust; or (ii) a person who is, or in the future may be, eligible to receive income or principal pursuant to the terms of the trust. A

Trustee described in item (i) above is an Interested Trustee only with respect to the transferred property (including income and gain on, and reinvestment of, such property). A person is included in item (ii) above if he or she has a remote contingent remainder, but a person is not included in item (ii) above if the person's only interest is as a potential appointee under a power of appointment held by another individual in his or her non-fiduciary capacity, the exercise of which will take effect only in the future, such as a testamentary power of appointment held by a living individual or the person's only interest is as a potential distributee under the Paragraph entitled, "**Absence of Beneficiaries**." A trustee who is not an Interested Trustee is a "Disinterested Trustee." An Independent Trustee is a "Disinterested Trustee." If a general power of appointment held by a beneficiary may only be exercised with the consent of a Disinterested Trustee, the term "Disinterested Trustee" also means a person who is not the creator of the power and who does not have a substantial interest in the property subject to the power which is adverse to the exercise of the power in favor of the beneficiary, the beneficiary's estate, or the creditors of either (as the case may be) within the meaning of IRC sections 2514 (c) and 2041(b) and Treas. Reg. sections 25.2514-3(b)(2) and 20.2041-(3)(c)(2).

(L) **Internal Revenue Code**. References to "Code," "Internal Revenue Code," "IRC" (or similar abbreviations) or to provisions thereof are to the Internal Revenue Code of 1986, as amended at the time in question. References to the "Regulations" or "Treas. Reg." are to the Treasury Regulations under the Code. If, by the time in question, a particular provision of the Code has been renumbered or the Code has been superseded by a subsequent federal tax law, the reference shall be deemed to be to the renumbered provision or the corresponding provision of the subsequent law, unless to do so would clearly be contrary to my intent as expressed in this Agreement, and a similar rule shall apply to references to the Regulations. All tax-related terms shall have the same meaning that they have in the Code.

(M) **May, Must and Shall.** Unless expressly provided otherwise in this Agreement concerning distributions to the beneficiary in question (or class of beneficiaries), Trustee shall exercise its authority (and discretion) to make distributions of trust income or principal in accordance with the terms and purposes of the trust, subject to the following:

(1) "May" is discretionary; and unless the discretion is made "sole," "absolute" or "uncontrolled," Trustee must act reasonably and in good faith. If the discretion is made "sole," "absolute" or "uncontrolled," Trustee must act honestly, in good faith, and not recklessly or capriciously.

(2) Unless expressly provided otherwise in this Agreement concerning distributions to the beneficiary in question (or class of beneficiaries), when making discretionary distributions where Trustee's discretion is "sole," absolute," or "uncontrolled," Trustee may, but need not, consider any other income or resources readily available to that beneficiary.

(3) Unless expressly provided otherwise in this Agreement concerning distributions to the beneficiary in question (or class of beneficiaries), when making distributions (including discretionary distributions) limited to a beneficiary's health, education, support or maintenance (or similar ascertainable standard), Trustee shall consider any other income or resources readily available to that beneficiary for such purposes and take into consideration the standard of living of the beneficiary.

(4) Except as otherwise qualified or restricted, "must" is mandatory, and "shall" is mandatory.

(N) **Sui Juris.** An individual who has the legal capacity to mange his or her own affairs and is not under a legal disability to act for one's self (such as minority, a guardianship, committee or conservatorship, etc.) is an individual who is sui juris.

(O) **Then Living.** The term "then living," when used in any provision in this Agreement, refers to the time when the event necessitating reference to such provision occurred rather than to the subsequent time when the directions of such provision may actually be implemented.

(P) **Trust.** "Trust," without further qualification or specification, shall refer to all trusts under this Agreement, and to the assets of any such trust or trusts.

(Q) **Captions.** Captions in this Agreement are used for convenience and shall not limit, broaden, or qualify the text.

(R) **Provisions Severable.** The provisions of this Agreement are severable. If any provision is determined to be invalid, all other provisions shall remain valid. Trustee may modify any provision determined to be invalid, illegal or unenforceable to the minimum extent necessary to remedy such provision.

(S) **Counterparts.** This Agreement may be executed in any number of counterpart signature pages, all of which together will constitute the entire, original document.

8.4 Disclaimer by Beneficiary. Any beneficiary may disclaim any property, interests in property, proceeds of property, disclaimable interest, or power of appointment (whether presently exercisable or not). A beneficiary who disclaims any property, interests in property, proceeds of property, disclaimable interest, or power of appointment (whether presently exercisable or not) shall not retain, possess, or exercise any interest in or power over the disclaimed property, either during lifetime or upon death (whether as a beneficiary or as a trustee), which interest or power is prohibited by law (such as interests or powers prohibited by IRC section 2518 (as concerns qualified disclaimers)). For example, if the disclaim property devolves to a foundation and the disclaimant is an officer, director, trustee or "control person" of the foundation, then and in that event, the disclaimed property shall be held in a separate fund by the foundation and the disclaimant shall only serve as an Administrative Director/Trustee with respect to the fund. An Administrative Director/Trustee is only authorized to take such actions as are necessary to preserve and maintain the property within the meaning of Treas. Reg. section 25.2518-2(d)(2), and, accordingly, is prohibited from participating in the exercise, or decision not to exercise, any discretion over payments, distributions, applications or accumulations of income or principal by the foundation's directors/trustees, including the selection of the ultimate charitable beneficiaries of the separate fund.

8.5 Actions by Incapacitated or Minor Beneficiaries. Except as may otherwise be provided elsewhere in this Agreement, a minor beneficiary, or a beneficiary who is legally incapacitated, or a beneficiary who is under a under a disability, may act through his or her authorized representative (to the extent such authorized representative is not prohibited from acting on behalf of the beneficiary), including (but not limited to) a natural or legal guardian, committee, conservator, agent, next friend, or attorney-in-fact under a durable power of attorney (as the case may be). If there is no such authorized representative, Trustee may designate an appropriate adult individual (who may be Trustee, a trust officer, a relative of the beneficiary, or any other person) who (to the extent not prohibited from acting on behalf of the beneficiary) may act on behalf of the beneficiary. In no event may I act on behalf of such beneficiary, regardless of my relationship to the beneficiary.

8.6 Virtual Representation. I direct that, in any proceeding relating to a trust hereunder, service upon any person under a legal disability need not be made when another person not under a disability is a party to the proceeding and has the same interest as the person under the disability. The person under the disability shall nevertheless be bound by the results of the proceeding. The same rule shall apply to non-judicial settlements, releases, exonerations and indemnities.

8.7 Arbitration. Whenever a matter is required under this Agreement to be submitted to arbitration, the following rules shall apply. The arbitration shall be held, except as may otherwise be provided herein, in accordance with the Uniform Arbitration Act (or such similar act) as adopted by the State of ____________ (or the state whose law is then governing the administration of the trust, as described in the sub-paragraph entitled, **"Governing Law"**). The rules of arbitration shall be decided by the arbitrator. The parties shall select a single arbitrator for this purpose. To be qualified to be selected as an arbitrator: (i) a person must be well versed and knowledgeable in the area of trust law, or (ii) a person with expertise in the subject matter of the dispute (e.g., a professional appraiser if the dispute involves valuation). If the parties cannot agree on an arbitrator, a party can petition the probate court having jurisdiction over the trust and request the probate court to appoint a qualified arbitrator (who need not reside in the same county as the probate court). If the place of arbitration can not be agreed upon by the parties, then the place of arbitration shall be in the metropolitan [Name of City and State] area as decided by the arbitrator. If at the time of the dispute the trust's governing law is the State of ______________, the rules of discovery as set forth in that State's rules of civil procedure shall be available in connection with the arbitration, and the law of the State of ______________ law will govern the rights and obligations of the parties with respect to the matters in controversy. The award of the arbitrator shall be accompanied by a written statement of the basis for such award and may be enforced by any court having proper jurisdiction.

ARTICLE 9
SURVIVAL AND ANTI-LAPSE

9.1 Survival of Beneficiary. Except as provided in sub-paragraph (A) below, no person shall be considered to have survived another or considered to be living upon the death of another if he or she shall die within 120 hours after the death of such other.

(A) Exceptions.

(1) Where Treas. Reg. section 26.2651-1(a)(2)(iii) applies.

(2) As to any gift that will qualify for the marital deduction, my Spouse shall be deemed to have **[Note:** chose either "**survived**" or "**predeceased**"**]** me if we die under circumstances where it is not clear who survived.

9.2 Negation of Anti-Lapse Statute. A gift fails if an individual beneficiary does not satisfy a condition of survival and there is no substitute beneficiary indicated in this Agreement who satisfies the conditions for taking. The provisions of an anti-lapse statute shall not apply to preserve a gift for an individual or individuals who are not identified as a substitute or substitutes in this Agreement.

ARTICLE 10
MY FAMILY

10.1 Spouse. I am married to «SpouseFullName» at the time this Agreement is executed. For purposes of this Agreement, "my

Spouse" refers to «SpouseFullName», provided that such individual and I have not become subject to a "divorce or separation instrument" (as that term is defined under IRC section 71(b)(2)), and further provided that no action for annulment, separation, separate maintenance, dissolution of marriage or similar proceeding has been filed with or is pending before a court or other such tribunal, in which case such individual and their heirs (had such individual died intestate), but not my heirs, shall be deemed to have died for all purposes under this Agreement (and thus to have predeceased me) regardless of the legal relationship between us and (i) this Agreement shall be held, administered and distributed as if such individual(s) had in fact died, (ii) such individual(s) shall cease to act as a Trustee (and any successor Trustees nominated or appointed by such individual(s) shall be deemed to have automatically resigned as a Trustee or shall not take office as a Trustee (as the case may be)), (iii) such individual(s) shall have no rights or powers under this Agreement, (iv) such individual(s) shall not be (or continue to be) a beneficiary of this Agreement or be (or continue to be) a donee/holder of a testamentary power of appointment or be a permissible appointee or recipient of trust property under a power of appointment, and (v) such individual(s) shall be treated for all purposes under this Agreement (other than for purposes of the Paragraph entitled, **"Rule Against Perpetuities"**) as having predeceased me without surviving issue; provided however, the foregoing items (i) - (v) shall not thwart or impair any beneficiary's unexercised withdrawal right that has not yet lapsed.

10.2 Children. My children as of the date of this Agreement are:

- «Child1» (DOB: «Child1DOB»)
- «Child2» (DOB: «Child2DOB»)

I have no other children or any deceased children with descendants surviving.

This Agreement is executed, delivered, and the trust accepted, on «DateofExecution».

WITNESSES:

____________________________ ____________________________

«ExecutingWitness» «SettlorFullName», Settlor

________________________ ________________________

«ExecutingWitness» «InitialTrustee», Trustee

ACKNOWLEDGMENT BY SPOUSE

I, «SpouseFullName», understand that this trust may hold policies that insure my life, and if that should occur, or if I am a donor, I acknowledge that I will be subject to the provisions of Paragraph 1.4, entitled, **"Restriction on My Spouse."**

I also acknowledge that if there is marital disharmony between me and «SettlorFullName» in the future, I will be subject to the provisions of and Paragraph 10.1, entitled, **"Spouse."** ***I acknowledge that at this time there is no marital disharmony between me and «SettlorFullName».***

____

«SpouseFullName»

STATE OF)

)**ss.**

COUNTY OF)

Subscribed and sworn to before me on «DateofExecution» by «SettlorFullName», «SpouseFullName» and «InitialTrustee», who personally appeared before me. «SettlorFullName», «SpouseFullName» and «InitialTrustee»are personally known to me (or have produced ________________________ as identification).

____

Notary Public

________________County, __________

Acting in the County of ________________

My Commission expires: ________________

SCHEDULE A

Property Transferred to The «SettlorFullName» Irrevocable Trust, dated «DateofExecution»

With regard to any group term policies listed herein, the transfer of such policies also includes any future policies to be issued, or policies in sup-

plementation thereof, or in succession, substitution, replacement or renewed thereof, and any increase in the amount of coverage.

(This Schedule A is included only for the convenience of Trustee and beneficiaries, and any failure to list trust assets on Schedule A will in no way alter the trust's ownership of those assets.)

DATE	ITEM	VALUE	TAX BASIS

Appendix 2

SAMPLE SECOND-TO-DIE IRREVOCABLE LIFE INSURANCE TRUST

Note: This form is a sample irrevocable life insurance trust that is designed to hold a second to die life insurance policy on a married couple. The trust is designed to be GST tax exempt, but because of the hanging *Crummey* withdrawal rights may **not** qualify as a GST Trust (to which the grantor's GST tax exemption will be automatically allocated). Therefore, the transferor will need to annually allocate his or her GST tax exemption to contributions or will need to make a one time election on IRS Form 709 to have the trust be treated as a GST Trust (*see*, "GST Trust Election Statement" in Appendix 4). The trust contains a hanging *Crummey* right of withdrawal, and permits a donor to make gift contributions to the beneficiaries up to the annual exclusion amount. Optional and alternate language is contained in brackets { }.

This form is designed to be an adjunct to (and not a substitution for) the grantor's base estate plan, such as a revocable living trust. This form should not be used as a pour-over from a person's probate estate, will, or other trust.

Practice Note: Michigan practitioners should note that the sample forms complies with Michigan's Estates and Protected Individuals Code, which went into effect April 1, 2000.

As this is a sample form, practitioners must be careful when using the form to adapt it to comply with new developments in federal and state estate, gift and generation-skipping transfer tax law and to modify it to comply with applicable state law and the particular requirements and needs of their client; accordingly, the author makes no representations or warranties as to the efficacy of the form.

[Revised thru 06292007]

THE «SETTLORFULLNAME» IRREVOCABLE TRUST

Name of Trust: The «SettlorFullName» Irrevocable Trust, dated «DateofExecution»

Initial Trustee: «InitialTrustee»

Successor Trustees: «AltTrustee1»

«AltTrustee2»

«AltTrustee3»

«AltTrustee4»

Date of Execution: «DateofExecution»

I, «SettlorFullName», on «DateofExecution», sign this Trust Agreement ("Agreement") with «InitialTrustee» as trustee (who, and any successor trustee, substitute trustee, or co-trustee, will be called "Trustee" in this Agreement and referred to in singular neuter pronouns), on the following terms and conditions. The original trust established hereunder by me is hereinafter sometimes referred to as the "initial trust."

ARTICLE 1
CREATION AND FUNDING THE TRUST

1.1 Creation of Trust. I create this trust as a means by which assets, which may include one (1) or more policies of insurance on my life, the life of any other person, or the joint lives of two or more persons, directly or indirectly in any arrangement deemed appropriate by Trustee, may be held for the benefit of my beneficiaries, on the terms and conditions set forth in this Agreement. It is my intent in creating this trust that all gifts made to this trust by me (directly or indirectly) be both complete and generally gifts of present interests for federal gift tax purposes. All provisions of this trust shall be construed in such a manner as best to affect these intents. Accordingly, no power enumerated herein or accorded to trustees, or granted pursuant to law, whether singularly, jointly or as a whole, shall be construed:

(A) To enable me: (i) to become a Trustee hereunder (or to possess or exercise any powers of such office), (ii) to vote any stock described in IRC section 2036(b) which may at any time be directly or indirectly given to any trust hereunder, (iii) to possess or exercise any power of appointment (including a right of withdrawal) with respect to any such trust, (iv) to possess, exercise or retain any power or interest described in IRC sections 2036, 2037 and 2038, (v) if I am the insured under any policy of insurance held by any trust hereunder, to exercise any incident of ownership within the meaning of IRC section 2042 with respect to that policy held by the trust, (vi) to receive any distributions on behalf of a beneficiary (regardless of my relationship to the beneficiary), or (vii) to possess or exercise any rights or discretion granted to a beneficiary hereunder; and

(B) To permit any trust distribution which would have the effect of discharging any legal obligation of mine (including any obligation that I may have at any time relating to the support and/or education of any beneficiary hereunder).

1.2 Transfer of Property to Trust. I hereby irrevocably transfer and assign to Trustee the property listed in **SCHEDULE A**, to be held and administered according to the terms of this trust. In connection with the transfer of any life insurance policies to Trustee, I agree to execute, in addition to an appropriate assignment of ownership form, any and all other instruments necessary or appropriate to permit Trustee to exercise all rights, powers, options, privileges or incidents of ownership that I may have had as the owner of such policies. With regard to any group term policies assigned to Trustee, the transfer of such policies also includes any future policies to be issued, or policies in supplementation thereof, or in succession, substitution, replacement or renewal thereof, and any increase in the amount of coverage.

Any person may transfer property acceptable to Trustee at any time. Trustee may accept a transfer of property that is subject to one or more conditions imposed by the donor (including giving a particular beneficiary (or a group of beneficiaries) a right to withdraw a contribution and the conditions for the lapse of a beneficiary's right of withdrawal) if Trustee deems it to be in the best interests of the trust and the beneficiaries. No condition imposed on a transfer of property and accepted by Trustee may in any way alter, amend, or change the rights of a beneficiary with respect to any prior transfers of property to the trust. Trustee may also refuse to accept any transfer of property if

Trustee deems the refusal to be in the best interests of the trust and its beneficiaries.

1.3 Restrictions on Donors. Any individual (other than a donor's spouse who merely consents to gift splitting under IRC section 2513 concerning the donor's contribution to the trust) who makes a "contribution" (as defined in the Paragraph entitled, "**Contribution Defined**") to a trust in the first instance (in contrast to a beneficiary's exercise or lapse of a power of withdrawal or power of appointment) (such individual hereinafter sometimes being referred to as a "donor") shall, with respect to the contribution to the trust in question, be subject to the same limitations, restrictions, exceptions, and exclusions that I am subject to under this Agreement (but only insofar as they relate to the contributed property or to the trust in question (and any trusts derived therefrom)).

1.4 Restriction on My Spouse. If the trust holds a policy on the life of my Spouse or a life insurance policy covering first or last to die, or joint deaths, of myself and my Spouse as the insureds, then and in that event, my Spouse shall be subject to the same restrictive terms, conditions, limitations, and overall restrictions that I am subject to under this Agreement. Furthermore, if my Spouse is a donor to the trust, my Spouse shall be subject to the same restrictive terms, conditions, limitations, and overall restrictions that I am subject to under this Agreement. In these regards, my Spouse shall be treated as though my Spouse were a grantor of the trust in question, and the words referring to me in the singular, such as "me," "I," "my" or "mine," shall, where the context requires, refer to "us", "we", or "ours" instead.

1.5 Construction of Agreement. The Rule In Shelley's case and the Doctrine of Worthier Title (or any similar rule, doctrine or statute) shall not apply to this Agreement, nor shall this Agreement be construed under any such rule, doctrine or statute.

{Start Optional Paragraph 1.6}

1.6 Intent and Material Purpose of Trust. Without limiting, restricting or compelling the exercise of a Trustee's (or a Trust Protector's or a Special Power Holder's) discretionary authority set forth in this Agreement, some of the material purposes of this Agreement are: (i) to retain assets in trust for the benefit of the trust's beneficiary, (ii) to provide creditor and asset protection to the trust's beneficiary, (iii) to provide spendthrift protection for the trust's beneficiary, (iv) to provide for the orderly and professional management and investment of trust assets, (v) to protect the trust's beneficiary from the trust's beneficiary's inabilities, disabilities, in-laws, ex-spouses, creditors, and predators, both now and in the future, (vi) to provide a financial "safety-net" for the trust's beneficiary, (vii) to provide potential resources that may be available to deal with the uncertainties of the economy, emergencies, and other vicissitudes and exigencies of daily life, and (viii) to minimize transfer, death and generation skipping transfer taxes. **{End Optional Paragraph 1.6}**

ARTICLE 2
IRREVOCABILITY

2.1 Irrevocable Trust. This trust is irrevocable. Applicable state law notwithstanding, I have no power, whether alone or in conjunction with others, and in whatever capacity, to control and direct payments or to alter, amend, modify, revoke, or terminate this Agreement or any trust provision or interest, in whole or in part, or to designate who shall possess or enjoy the trust property or trust income, whether under this trust or any statute or other rule of law. I retain no right, title, interest, or incident of ownership in any trust property.

ARTICLE 3
WITHDRAWAL RIGHTS

3.1 Withdrawal Rights. Unless otherwise provided pursuant to the paragraph item entitled, "**Restriction of a Withdrawal Right,"** the following withdrawal rights shall exist with respect to contributions to the trust:

(A) Immediately following any contribution to the trust, each of [my children] [my descendants] (individually a "donee," collectively the "donees") who are living on the date of the contribution (and have not been excluded from exercising their withdrawal right with respect to the contribution in question), shall have the right to withdraw an amount equal to a proportionate share of the value of the contribution. Such proportionate share will be the value of the contribution, divided by the number of donees living at the time of the contribution, who have not been excluded from exercising their withdrawal right with respect to the contribution in question; provided, however, that the maximum amount that a donee may withdraw with respect to all contributions made by the same donor during a single calendar year shall be the **lesser** of: (i) the total amount of such contributions, or (ii) the amount of the federal gift tax exclusion under IRC section 2503(b) available to the donor with respect to gifts to such donee, provided however, if requested by a married donor at the time of a contribution, the alternative limitation based on the gift tax annual exclusion shall be two (2) times the amount of the gift tax annual exclusion. In determining the amount of this withdrawal limitation, there shall be taken into consideration all previous gifts made to such donee from (or attributable to) such donor (and the donor's spouse, to the extent relevant) during the same calendar year, which gifts were eligible for the federal gift tax annual exclusion. To the extent a donee is also the donor of a contribution, or is treated as donor of one-half (1/2) of a contribution for federal gift tax purposes, that donee shall have no right of withdrawal with respect to such contribution to which they are the donor (or treated as the donor), and shall never thereafter be considered to have had a right of withdrawal with respect to such contribution.

(B) Return of Excess Distribution. If any donee receives a distribution in excess of the amount he or she is authorized to withdraw under this Paragraph, Trustee shall immediately notify such donee in writing, requiring the prompt repayment of such excess amount.

These withdrawal rights take precedence over any other power or discretion granted Trustee or any other person.

3.2 Rules Concerning Withdrawal Rights. With respect to the withdrawal rights created under this Article, unless otherwise provided pursuant to the paragraph item entitled, **"Restriction of a Withdrawal Right,"** the following rules shall apply:

(A) Notification of Withdrawal Right. Each eligible donee (or the person who would exercise an eligible donee's withdrawal right) shall be kept reasonably informed of all withdrawable contributions to the trust which are made or are anticipated to be made. Notification may be made orally or in writing, and such efforts may include, by way of example (and without limitation), annually apprising each donee of his or her withdrawal rights, by providing the donee with a single notice sufficient to apprise him or her of his or her current and expected future withdrawal rights, or any other means to provide each eligible donee (or the person who would exercise an eligible donee's withdrawal right) with reasonable or actual notice. In no event shall the failure of any donee to receive such notice be deemed to abrogate his or her withdrawal rights in accordance with the provisions of this Article. A donee's right of withdrawal is not contingent upon such notice; and unless otherwise expressly limited (as is permitted pursuant to the sub-paragraph entitled, **"Restriction of a Withdrawal Right,"**) a donee's withdrawal right shall become effective upon Trustee's receipt (actual, constructive or imputed) of the withdrawable contribution (whether such contribution is a direct or indirect contribution to the trust). Upon written request by a donee, Trustee shall furnish full, detailed information with respect to any contributions subject to withdrawal by the donee.

(B) Withdrawal Right to be Exercised by Written Request. Each eligible donee can exercise a withdrawal right by a written request timely delivered to Trustee indicating the amount the donee desires to withdraw. The withdrawal right shall be a privilege that may be exercised only voluntarily and not under compulsion. As of the date a request for withdrawal is made pursuant to the provisions of this Article, the donee's right to receive the permitted amount requested shall be vested and shall not be terminated by the subsequent death or disability of the donee or any administrative delay resulting from actions taken by Trustee to effect distribution hereunder to the donee. Any property distributed by Trustee pursuant to an exercised withdrawal right shall be for the sole benefit of the donee who has exercised such withdrawal right. Trustee shall promptly comply with every demand under a withdrawal right that is exercised.

(C) Incapacity or Disability of Donee. If any eligible donee is unable to exercise a withdrawal right because of incapacity or disability (including minority), his or her authorized representative (to the extent such authorized representative is not prohibited from acting on behalf of the donee), including (but not limited to) a legal or natural guardian, committee, conservator, agent, next friend, or attorney-in-fact under a durable power of attorney, may make the withdrawal on the donee's behalf, and if there be no such authorized representative, Trustee will designate an appropriate adult individual (who may be Trustee, a trust officer, the donee's parent, the donee's sibling, a relative of the donee, or any other person) who may make the withdrawal on the donee's behalf. However, in no event can I, the donor of the contribution, or a person whose life is insured under a life insurance policy owned by the trust, make the withdrawal for any donee regardless of such individual's relationship to the donee. Any property received pursuant to the withdrawal right shall be held for the use and benefit of the donee and shall not be used by the person who exercised the withdrawal right on behalf of the donee to discharge that person's legal obligation of support for that donee.

(D) Structured Lapse of Withdrawal Right. The withdrawal rights created under this Article shall be cumulative, and each eligible donee's unexercised right to withdraw a contribution shall lapse on December 31 of each year (whether or not a contribution was made in that year), or, if earlier, thirty (30) days after the contribution to which it relates (or such minimal additional amount of time as may be necessary for a legal guardian/conservator to be appointed on behalf of the incapacitated or disabled donee, if such an appointment is in fact necessary), in an amount equal to the greater of five thousand ($5,000.00) dollars or five percent (5%) of the value of the trust estate out of which, or the proceeds of which, the exercise of the withdrawal right could be satisfied (or such greater dollar amount or percentage as may be specified in IRC section

2514(e)) (the "Lapse Protection Amount"); provided, however, the Lapse Protection Amount shall be measured and determined after first ascertaining all other powers (if any) held by such donee that must, under IRC section 2514(e), be aggregated to determine the largest lapse that can occur concerning the withdrawal right under this subparagraph without it being considered a release of a general power of appointment. To the extent that a withdrawal right exceeds the Lapse Protection Amount, the donee's withdrawal right with respect to such excess shall continue in all later years (even after a donor's death) subject to the same lapse provisions, but such continuing withdrawal right over the excess may only be exercised by the donee with the consent of an Independent or Disinterested Trustee. Withdrawal rights for contributions made during the period of December 3 through December 31 shall not lapse in the calendar year when the contribution was made, but shall continue to be exercisable in the following year or years. (For example, if a contribution allocable to a donee is $12,000 in a calendar year and the applicable Lapse Protection Amount is $5,000, then if the withdrawal right is not exercised, it shall lapse as to $5,000 of the contribution, but shall continue to the next calendar year as to $7,000. If there is no contribution allocable to that donee in the next two subsequent calendar years, and the allocable amounts are not withdrawn, that donee's right of withdrawal shall lapse by $5,000 and $2,000 in the first and second subsequent years, respectively.) Nothing in this provision shall have the effect of a condition subsequent, nor a retroactive recharacterization of the amount of a donor's gifts or the amount subject to any donee's power to withdraw. Neither the amount of a donor's gifts nor any amount subject to any donee's power to withdraw are to be reduced, modified or recharacterized as a result of any action or determination by any court or other governmental or administrative agency. The lapse of a donee's withdrawal rights shall not be considered a contribution or gift to the trust estate.

(E) Continuation of Withdrawal Right After My Death. Each withdrawal right which is in effect at my death shall continue in effect after my death as to Descendants' Trust until it lapses as described in sub-paragraph (D) above. Trustee, may in its discretion, delay the funding of the Descendants' Trust for a reasonable period of time, in order to permit sufficient time for withdrawal rights to be exercised or lapse (as the case may be). On the day preceding the date of the donee's death, all withdrawal rights that have not previously lapsed, shall lapse with respect to that donee (provided the date of death occurs more than fifteen (15) days following the date of the contribution to which such withdrawal rights relate). Any distribution of income or principal made to or for the benefit of a donee during the period after my death while there is a continuation of the donee's withdrawal right hereunder shall be considered as a distribution in full or partial satisfaction of such donee's unlapsed right of withdrawal.

(F) **Satisfying a Withdrawal Right**. Trustee shall promptly comply with every demand under a withdrawal right that is exercised. Trustee may satisfy any withdrawal rights under this Article by distributing cash, other trust property, fractional interests in trust property, or split dollar interest in a life insurance policy, as Trustee deems appropriate. Trustee is specifically authorized to borrow money from any source, including but not limited to the cash surrender values of any life insurance policies transferred to or held by the trust, to sell trust property, to surrender or otherwise dispose of any life insurance policies or other property transferred to or held by the trust, and to take any other action that may be necessary and appropriate to assure that withdrawal rights will be satisfied in a timely and expedient manner. Without limiting Trustee's broad discretionary power to select trust property to satisfy a withdrawal right, I prefer that cash or tangible property be distributed to donees before distributing life insurance policies and other intangible property to donees (especially as concerns donees who are skip persons), unless Trustee decides that another selection is warranted. While any withdrawal right is outstanding Trustee shall not exercise any discretion or authority that would impede or thwart the withdrawal right.

(G) "Contribution" Defined. "Contribution" means a nontestamentary transfer (direct or indirect, actual or imputed to the donor) to Trustee of any cash or other property (or interest therein) (including, for the year of the trust's creation, the property creating the trust) to be held as part of the trust funds, which would be treated under Chapter 12 of the Internal Revenue Code as a taxable gift of the donor or the donor's spouse (before taking into account the exclusion allowed by IRC section 2503(b)), and shall also include any premiums on policies of life insurance (or any interests therein) owned by the trust which premiums are paid, by me or any other person or entity (including my employer or former employer), directly to any insurance company issuing the policies rather than first being paid to Trustee. In the case of any premium which is paid directly to an insurance company, the date of the contribution to the trust shall be deemed to be the date on which the premium payment is transmitted to the insurance company issuing the policy. The amount of any contribution is its federal gift tax value, as determined by Trustee at the time of the transfer. Contributions made by a donor's attorney-in-fact under a durable power of attorney shall be considered as made by the donor.

(H) Restriction of a Withdrawal Right. Any person (or that person's duly authorized agent acting under a power of attorney or other proper legal representative) who makes a contribution to any trust created under this Agreement may inform Trustee at the time of such contribution and with respect solely to the new contribution then being made (and with respect to future contributions to be made by that person), do one (1) or more of the following: (i) exclude any beneficiary who would otherwise have a withdrawal right from exercising that withdrawal right as to such new or future contribution; (ii) increase or decrease the amount subject to a beneficiary's withdrawal right as to such new or future contribution, except that the amount subject to the withdrawal right shall not exceed the amount of the contribution; (iii) change the period during which any beneficiary's withdrawal right as to such new or future contribution may be exercised; and (iv) change the manner and period during which any beneficiary's withdrawal right as to such new or future contribution shall lapse. No such direction may in any way alter, amend or change any beneficiary's withdrawal right with respect to any prior contributions.

(I) Forfeiture of Withdrawal Right. Except with respect to an outstanding withdrawal right which has been outstanding for fewer than fifteen (15) days from the date of such contribution, any donee having a withdrawal right shall immediately forfeit such right upon making an assignment for the benefit of his or her creditors, filing a voluntary petition in bankruptcy, being adjudicated a bankrupt or an insolvent, or consenting to or acquiescing in the appointment of a trustee in bankruptcy or a receiver in bankruptcy for all or any substantial part of his or her assets or properties, which forfeiture shall continue during the pendency of any such proceeding and end upon the termination thereof.

(J) Power to Amend. Trustee, other than an Interested Trustee, may by a written instrument filed with the trust records, amend this Article to the minimum extent necessary to assure that contributions to the initial trust and its beneficiaries quality for the gift tax annual exclusion for federal gift tax purposes, and/or are not subject to an estate tax inclusion period for generation skipping transfer tax purposes. Such Trustee may not amend the initial trust in any manner that would cause any portion of the trust funds to be included in a donor's gross estate, my gross estate, that of my spouse (if I am married), or that of any of my descendants and their spouses, to a greater extent than before such amendment. An amendment made in good faith shall be conclusive on all persons interested in the trust and such Trustee shall not be liable for the consequences of any amendment or for not having amended the trust. No amendment shall limit or alter the rights of a beneficiary in any trust funds held by Trustee before the amendment.

(K) Determination of Donor's Prior Gifts to Donee. Trustee may without liability assume that no prior gifts to any donee under this Article were made by a donor or a donor's spouse other than contributions to the initial trust, unless Trustee shall have actual written notice to the contrary. In determining the amount of prior gifts to or for a donee not made under this Agreement, Trustee may rely on a written statement signed or duly authorized by the donor setting forth the nature, date, and amount of such prior gifts; and in the absence of such written statement Trustee shall be under no obligation to ascertain the same.

(L) **Special Rule for Multiple Withdrawal Rights.** The amounts involved in a withdrawal right described as " the greater of five thousand ($5,000) dollars or five (5%) percent of the trust estate out of which, or the proceeds of which, the exercise of this withdrawal right could be satisfied (or such greater dollar amount or percentage as may be specified in IRC section 2514(e))" or language of similar import with reference to IRC section 2514(e), shall be measured after subtracting all other amounts that the same person could have withdrawn during the same calendar year from this or any other fund, to the extent that such powers must, under applicable federal gift tax law, be aggregated in determining whether the lapse of the right of withdrawal under this Article is a release of a general power of appointment; provided however, a person making a contribution may, at the time of the contribution, specify the order in which multiple withdrawal rights are to lapse (as concerns the contribution).

(M) **Satisfaction of a Withdrawal Right Constitutes an Advancement.** The satisfaction of a donee's right of withdrawal under this Article shall constitute and be treated as an advancement, and shall be charged (without interest) against the ultimate share (if any) provided for the donee and his or her descendants.

ARTICLE 4
DISTRIBUTION DURING LIFETIME

4.1 Distribution of Principal and Income During Lifetime. Until the death of the last to die of myself and my Spouse, Trustee shall hold and administer the trust estate, as follows:

(A) **Income and Principal**. Trustee may use some or all of the trust's net income and principal to pay premiums on policies of life insurance owned by the trust. In addition, a Disinterested Trustee may distribute to and among my descendants, in whatever proportions the Disinterested Trustee deems appropriate, so much of the trust principal and income (including all or none) as the Disinterested Trustee in its sole, absolute and uncontrolled discretion, shall determine. An Interested Trustee may, in its discretion, distribute income and principal among the aforementioned beneficiaries for their health, education, support and maintenance considering all other resources available to each such beneficiary (including any legal obligation of support that another person may owe to such beneficiary). Any undistributed income shall be added to principal.

(B) **Restrictions on Distributions**. No distribution of trust income or principal shall be made by Trustee if it would impair a withdrawal right granted under the Article entitled, "**Withdrawal Rights**," and no Trustee may make any distribution to or for his or her own benefit, nor may Trustee make any distribution to or for the benefit of any individual which distribution would discharge or satisfy Trustee's legal obligation to support such individual. Furthermore, Trustee shall not use any trust income or principal in a manner that would give me or my Spouse any pecuniary benefit or would discharge or satisfy our legal obligations, including any legal obligation of support.

4.2 **Limited Power of Appointment by Special Power Holder.** I hereby name as a special power holder the first of the following who is from time to time willing and able to act:

(1) **Name and address of Special Power Holder 1;**

(2) **Name and address of Special Power Holder 2; and**

(3) **Name and address of Special Power Holder 3.**

Until the death of the last to die of myself and my Spouse, the special power holder, may in its sole, absolute and uncontrolled discretion appoint (by a written instrument delivered to Trustee prior to death of the last to die of my Spouse and me), some, all or none of the trust estate (excluding: (i) life insurance on the special power holder's life, and (ii) any amount still subject to withdrawal by a person) as the special power holder (acting in his, her or its individual-personal capacity and not in a fiduciary capacity (even though the special power holder may also be serving (or is nominated to serve) as a Trustee)) as the special power holder determines, to any one or more of {**Optional 1:** myself, my Spouse, or **Optional 2:** my mother's descendants, the descendants of my Spouse's mother,}[1] my descendants or to another trust for any such person's benefit, (but not to the special power holder, the special power holder's estate, or the creditors of either), without regard to equality among the objects or the appointees, and without the appointed property being chargeable against the proportionate share of corpus held in trust for the payment of income to the beneficiary as if the corpus constituted a separate trust; and Trustee shall not make any compensating adjustments to trust beneficiaries who are not the appointees or to trust beneficiaries who receive unequal shares/ amounts of the appointed property.

Provided, however, (i) in no event can I or my Spouse exercise the power granted hereunder, regardless of our relationship to the special power holder, (ii) that no such distribution may be applied or distributed such that it would give the special power holder any pecuniary benefit or would discharge or satisfy my legal obligations, my Spouse's legal obligations, or the power holder's legal obligations, and (iii) no such distribution may be made if it would impair an unexercised or unlapsed withdrawal right granted under the Article entitled, "**Withdrawal Rights**."

Once appointed, a special power holder may only be removed for reasonable cause by a court of competent jurisdiction.

In the event a special power holder resigns, is removed by a court of competent jurisdiction, becomes incapacitated, or is deceased, I and/or my Spouse may appoint a successor to such special power holder, by delivering a written instrument to Trustee. Any special power holder nominated or appointed hereunder must meet the definitional requirements of an Independent Trustee.

---

[1] *See,* Section 11.1 of main text concerning use of the optional language.

4.3 Distribution In Satisfaction of Unlapsed Withdrawal Right. Any distribution of income or principal to a beneficiary under this Article shall be considered as a distribution in full or partial satisfaction of such beneficiary-donee's unlapsed right of withdrawal under the Article entitled, "**Withdrawal Rights.**"

ARTICLE 5
DISTRIBUTION AFTER DEATH

5.1 Purchase of Assets and Loans. At any time after the death of the last to die of myself and my Spouse, including the period during the administration of my and my Spouse's probate estates (including the post-mortem administration of any inter-vivos revocable trusts created by either of us) Trustee may use the trust funds, in Trustee's discretion, to lend money to and buy assets from my estate, my Spouse's estate, the estates of any of our descendants, or from the trustee of any other trust created by me, my Spouse or our descendants (collectively "our estates"), on such terms and conditions as Trustee deems to be in the best interests of the beneficiaries of the trusts established under this Agreement, provided, however, Trustee may not buy assets from our estates other than at their fair market value, nor may Trustee lend money to our estates without receiving adequate security and an adequate rate of interest. In addition to the foregoing, Trustee may also purchase, otherwise acquire, and hold for an indefinite term any business or business interest, as shareholder, creditor, partner, proprietor or otherwise, even though of a character, proportion, or amount other than prescribed by law for trust investments; to exercise, or delegate to others discretionary power to exercise complete control and management of any business, and in connection therewith to enter and perform contracts, commitments, orders, and engagements, to incur, pay, compromise, settle and discharge expenses and debts, to elect, employ and compensate directors, officers, employees, or agents (who may include Trustee or any employee or agent thereof), and to deal with and act for such business in any capacity (including any banking or trust capacity and the lending of money out of Trustee's own funds) and to be compensated therefor; to rely upon the reports of accountants and others as to the operations and financial condition of any business, without independent investigation and without obligation to file with any court; to take any action reasonably necessary to carry out any agreement for the transfer of any business interest upon an individual's death or upon cessation of an individual's active participation in the conduct of the business; to participate in any buy-sell, restrictive purchase or retirement agreement relating to any business interest; and to join in partnership, membership and joint venture agreements, to participate in any incorporation, reorganization, merger, consolidation, recapitalization, liquidation or dissolution of any business or any change in its nature, and to invest additional capital in, subscribe to or buy additional stock or securities of or make new or increased secured, unsecured or subordinated loans to any business.

Trustee may not, however, make grants to our estates or otherwise distribute funds except through bona fide loans or purchases, it not being my intention to make any persons who are not specifically so identified in this Agreement, the beneficiaries of any trust created hereunder. If no personal representative is appointed with respect to an estate under applicable state law, the "administration" of an estate will include the settlement of debts, claims, and taxes in respect of an estate by the trustee of any revocable trust or by any other person in actual possession of assets in which the individual had a legal or equitable interest. Trustee shall not be liable for any loss suffered by the trust as a result of the existence of the powers granted in this provision.

To facilitate the possible exercise of these discretionary powers, Trustee is authorized to defer any division of the initial trust estate for a reasonable period of time sufficient to accomplish the forgoing.

Notwithstanding anything in this Agreement to the contrary although it is my intent and purpose under this Paragraph to make trust assets available to provide the possibility that the assets of the initial trust can be made available to provide liquid assets (through loans and purchases) for the payment of taxes and other obligations of our estates, if that becomes necessary or appropriate in the opinion of the personal representative of such estate, Trustee shall not have the power to use any trust property for the benefit of our estates as defined in Treas. Reg. section 20.2042-1(b) unless such property is already included in our gross estates for federal estate tax purposes.

5.2 Administration of the Balance of the Trust Property. After the last to die of myself and my Spouse, and after making provision for the purchase of any estate assets or loans (as specified in the Paragraph entitled **"Purchase of Assets and Loans"**), the balance of the trust property shall be administered and disposed of as provided in the Paragraph entitled, **"Descendants' Trust**."

{Begin Alternate 1 to Paragraph 5.3—Separate Dynasty Trust Shares Created for Grantor's Children}

5.3 Descendants' Trust. Trustee shall divide the remaining trust property, including additions from any sources, into separate shares, equal in value, one for each child of mine who survives me and one for each child of mine who does not survive me but is survived by then living descendants. Each share set aside for a child of mine who does not survive me but is survived by then living descendants, shall be further divided by Trustee into separate shares for the descendants, such descendants to take by right of representation. Each share shall then be held in trust and be administered by Trustee for the benefit of the child and/or his or her descendants for whom the trust share was established, as follows:

(A) A Disinterested Trustee may distribute to or the benefit of my child (if living) and/or his or her descendants then living (from time to time), in whatever proportions the Disinterested Trustee deems appropriate, so much of the trust principal and income (including all or none) as the Disinterested Trustee in its sole, absolute and uncontrolled discretion, shall determine. An Interested Trustee may, in its discretion, distribute to or for the benefit of my child (if living) and/or his or her descendants then living (from time to time), in whatever proportions the Interested Trustee deems appropriate, so much of the trust principal and income as the Interested Trustee shall determine for my child and/ or his or her descendants' reasonable health, education, support and maintenance; and in making such distributions, the Interested Trustee may (but need not) take into consideration other income and resources known upon reasonable inquiry by the Interested Trustee to be reasonably available to the beneficiary. Any undistributed income shall be added to principal.

(1) Without limiting Trustee's discretion, I encourage Trustee to consider making loans and buying assets while retaining title in the trust, including real and tangible personal property, for the benefit and rent-free use by a beneficiary or beneficiaries, whenever Trustee determines that such loans or assets would be beneficial for such beneficiary or beneficiaries.

(B) Without limiting Trustee's discretion, Trustee may consider the needs of a child of mine as more important than the needs of my grandchildren or other remote descendants.

(C) At any time during the period that is twelve months prior to the expiration of the trust's term, Trustee who is an Independent Trustee, may by written instrument, appoint some, none or all of the trust property to my child (if living) and/or to some, all or none of my child's then living descendants, without any requirement of equality among my child or his or her then living descendants or the appointees of the trust property. Trustee's exercise of the power of appointment shall be in a non-fiduciary capacity. The Independent Trustee may, but need not, consider appointing the trust property to those descendants with a longer life expectancy than to those descendants with a shorter life expectancy. However, two days prior to the expiration of the trust's term, the Independent Trustee's special limited power of appointment contained herein shall cease, and any remaining or non-appointed trust property shall be distributed as provided below.

(D) Upon the expiration of the trust's term, Trustee shall distribute the remaining and/or non-appointed trust property to my child's living descendants, by right of representation; and if my child has no then living descendants, Trustee shall instead distribute the remaining and/or non-appointed trust property to the then living descendants, by right of representation, of the individual who is next in line of lineal ascent from the deceased beneficiary to me (including me in such line of ascent), who has descendants then living.

(E) The trust's term shall run for the longest period of time permitted by the rule against perpetuities (or other applicable law governing the maximum duration of trusts), as provided in Paragraph 8.1, entitled, **"Rule Against Perpetuities."**

(F) If prior to the expiration of the trust's term, neither my child nor any of his or her descendants are then living, then and in that event, Trustee shall divide the trust property, into separate shares, equal in value, one for each child of mine who is then living and one for each child of mine who is deceased but is survived by then living descendants. Each share set aside for a child of mine who is deceased but is survived by then living descendants, shall be further divided by Trustee into separate shares for the descendants, such descendants to take by right of representation. Each share shall then be held in trust and be administered by Trustee for the benefit of the child and/or his or her descendants for whom the trust share was established, as set forth in the preceding provisions of this Paragraph 5.3. In this regard, Trustee may, for administrative convenience, combine a trust share established hereunder with an existing trust share that Trustee is currently administering for the benefit of the same beneficiary (or beneficiaries). **{End of Alternate 1 to Paragraph 5.3}**

{Begin Alternate 2 to Paragraph 5.3—Common Pot Dynasty Trust For All of the Grantor's Descendants}

5.3 Descendants' Trust. All property distributed to or receivable by the Descendants' Trust shall be held and administered by Trustee as follows:

(A) A Disinterested Trustee may distribute to or for the benefit of my descendants then living (from time to time), in whatever proportions the Disinterested Trustee deems appropriate, so much of the trust principal and income (including all or none) as the Disinterested Trustee in its sole, absolute and uncontrolled discretion, shall determine. An Interested Trustee may, in its discretion, distribute to or for the benefit of my descendants then living (from time to time), in whatever proportions the Interested Trustee deems appropriate, so much of the trust principal and income as the Interested Trustee shall determine for my descendants' reasonable health, education, support and maintenance; and in making such distributions, the

Interested Trustee may (but need not) take into consideration other income and resources known upon reasonable inquiry by the Interested Trustee to be reasonably available to the beneficiary. Any undistributed income shall be added to principal.

(1) Without limiting Trustee's discretion, I encourage Trustee to consider making loans and buying assets while retaining title in the trust, including real and tangible personal property, for the benefit and rent-free use by a beneficiary or beneficiaries, whenever Trustee determines that such loans or assets would be beneficial for such beneficiary or beneficiaries.

(B) Without limiting Trustee's discretion, Trustee may consider the needs of a child of mine as more important than the needs of my grandchildren or other remote descendants.

(C) At any time during the period that is twelve months prior to the expiration of the trust's term, Trustee who is an Independent Trustee, may by written instrument, appoint some, none or all of the trust property to some, all or none of my then living descendants, without any requirement of equality among my then living descendants or the appointees of the trust property. Trustee's exercise of the power of appointment shall be in a non-fiduciary capacity. The Independent Trustee may, but need not, consider appointing the trust property to those descendants with a longer life expectancy than to those descendants with a shorter life expectancy. However, two days prior to the expiration of the trust's term, the Independent Trustee's special limited power of appointment contained herein shall cease, and any remaining or non-appointed trust property shall be distributed as provided below.

(D) Upon the expiration of the trust's term, Trustee shall distribute the remaining and/or non-appointed trust property to my then living descendants, by right of representation.

(E) The trust's term shall run for the longest period of time permitted by the rule against perpetuities (or other applicable law governing the maximum duration of trusts), as provided in Paragraph 8.1, entitled, **"Rule Against Perpetuities." {End of Alternate 2 to Paragraph 5.3}**

5.4 Absence of Beneficiaries. If all of the beneficiaries of any trust created under this Agreement should die before the trust assets have vested in them, Trustee shall distribute all remaining assets of each such trust as follows:

(A) One-Half to My Heirs. One-half (1/2) (or all, if there are no persons to take under paragraph item (B) below) to my heirs (other than to any state or governmental entity) who would have taken my estate and such shares as they would have taken it, had I died unmarried and intestate in the state which I was domiciled at the time of my death, determined on the later of my death or the death of the last of such beneficiaries to die; and

(B) One-Half to My Spouse's Heirs. One-half (1/2) (or all, if there are no persons to take under paragraph item (A) above) to the heirs (other than to any state or governmental entity) of the person to whom I am legally married at the time of my death who would have taken said person's estate and in such shares as they would have taken it, had said person died unmarried and intestate in the state which I was domiciled at the time of my death, determined on the later of said person's death or the death of the last of such beneficiaries to die.

(C) Balance to Charity. If there are no persons to take under either paragraph items (A) or (B) above, then all remaining trust assets shall be distributed free of trust to a charitable organization(s) selected by Trustee, in memory of me and the person to whom I am legally married at the time of my death. Until such time as the events described in the preceding sentence occur, no charity shall have any right or interest in the trust or be entitled to receive information concerning the trust or be joined in any action pertaining to the trust, nor shall any governmental agency (such as the state's attorney general's office) be entitled to receive any information concerning the trust (as a result of such potential charitable donation) or be joined in any action concerning the trust (as a result of such potential charitable donation) and no consent, approval or other action shall be necessary, required or authorized by or from such charity or the governmental agency (as a result of such potential charitable donation). In other words, until the events in the first sentence of this sub-paragraph occur, the charity and the governmental agency shall not be interested trust beneficiaries (in any sense of the meaning), and shall have no standing, whether by rule, statute or common law. Trustee is directed to review our prior charitable giving records (if any) to assist Trustee in selecting the charitable organization(s) and the percentage amount for each charity (if Trustee has selected more than one charitable organization).

If, after six (6) months of reasonable search following the occurrence of an event that requires the determination of heirs hereunder, Trustee is unable to identify and locate any such heirs, it shall be presumed that the person described above has no heirs and the property shall be distributed as if there are "no persons to take" under the relevant paragraph item.

ARTICLE 6
TRUSTEES

6.1 Initial and Successor Trustees.

(A) Subject to the provisions of the Paragraphs entitled, **"Removal of Trustee"** (and any other pertinent provisions of this Agreement), the following persons shall serve (to the extent not prohibited from serving as a trustee), in priority of the order listed, as Trustee of the initial trust:

- «InitialTrustee», «InitialTrtAddr»
- «AltTrustee1», «AltTrst1Address»
- «AltTrustee2», «AltTrst2Address»
- «AltTrustee3», «AltTrst3Address»
- «AltTrustee4», «AltTrst4Address»

(B) Subject to the provisions of the Paragraphs entitled, **"Removal of Trustee"** (and any other pertinent provisions of this Agreement), the following persons shall serve (to the extent not prohibited from serving as a trustee), in priority of the order listed, as Trustee of the Descendants' Trust.

- «InitialTrustee», «InitialTrtAddr»
- «AltTrustee1», «AltTrst1Address»

- «AltTrustee2», «AltTrst2Address»
- «AltTrustee3», «AltTrst3Address»
- «AltTrustee4», «AltTrst4Address»

(C) If a Trustee (or a person nominated as a trustee) is dead, incapacitated, resigns from a trusteeship, is prohibited from serving as a trustee, or declines to serve as a trustee of any trust created under this Agreement, then unless otherwise prohibited, a remaining Co-Trustee (or in the absence thereof, the successor Trustee), who is not prohibited from serving as a trustee, shall serve as sole Trustee of such trust, without need of court approval.

(D) Except as otherwise provided in the Paragraph entitled, "**Removal of Trustee**," in the absence of a nominated successor Trustee then able to act, a successor Trustee shall be appointed by a majority of the current income beneficiaries of the trust in question who are sui juris and not incapacitated. If a majority of such current income beneficiaries cannot agree on a successor Trustee, any current income beneficiary or outgoing Trustee can petition a court of competent jurisdiction, ex parte, to designate an appropriate person as successor Trustee. The court shall not acquire any jurisdiction over the trust, except to the extent necessary to appoint a successor Trustee.

(E) I shall not be eligible to serve as a Trustee of any trust established under this Agreement, nor may any Trustee delegate its powers or duties to me.

(F) A person who has made an *irrevocable* beneficiary designation naming this Agreement (or its Trustee) as an irrevocable beneficiary of the asset can not serve as a Trustee under this Agreement.

(G) A person who is prohibited from serving as a Trustee of a particular trust or its property shall not serve as a Trustee of the trust in question or as a Trustee of that trust's property, nor may any Trustee delegate its powers or duties to such person.

(H) Unless otherwise consented to by the current income beneficiaries of the trust in question, no person shall serve as a trustee if to do so would result in the trust being: (i) classified as a "foreign trust" under the Code, and (ii) subjected to greater or additional taxation as a result of such classification, or the loss of the trust's ability to legally hold S corporation stock; provided however, such person may in the absence of the aforesaid consent, serve as a Co-Trustee if the trust would (continue to) be classified as a United States person under IRC section 7701(a)(30).

6.2 **Resignation by Trustee.** Trustee may resign as trustee of any or all trusts under this Agreement at any time by giving written notice, specifying the effective date of resignation, to the then acting Co-Trustee(s) of the trust in question, or if none, then to the designated successor Trustee nominated (or appointed) herein. If no successor Trustee is designated, the resigning Trustee shall give notice to all the current income beneficiaries of the trust in question who are sui juris.

6.3 **Resignation by Trustee.** Trustee may resign as trustee of any or all trusts under this Agreement at any time by giving written notice, specifying the effective date of resignation to any beneficiary who is eligible to receive current income from the trust in question.

6.4 **Trustee May Delegate to Co-Trustee.** Any Trustee may, from time to time, delegate to any other Trustee by a dated written instrument any or all of such Trustee's powers (except those, if any, not exercisable by such other Trustee, or which are not reasonable or prudent to delegate to such other Trustee). Consistent with the delegating Trustee's tenure, such delegation may be temporary or permanent, and if temporary, may be for any duration of time or until any event specified by the delegating Trustee. Any person dealing in good faith with any Trustee may rely without inquiry upon the Trustee's certificate with respect to any delegation.

6.5 **Trustee May Appoint a Co-Trustee.** A Trustee may by a dated written instrument filed with the trust records, designate, appoint and compensate any person (not prohibited from serving as a trustee) as a Co-Trustee. The Co-Trustee may be an Interested Trustee, Disinterested Trustee or an Independent Trustee. The Co-Trustee shall not possess or exercise any power or authority that it is otherwise prohibited from possessing or exercising. Any Co-Trustee so appointed may, without liability, accept without examination or review the accounts rendered, the actions taken, and the property delivered by or for any appointing Trustee or any Co-Trustee of the appointing Trustee. A Co-Trustee so appointed may be removed at any time, with or without cause, by the appointing Trustee(s), other than an Interested Trustee. A Co-Trustee appointed solely by an Interested Trustee may be removed for reasonable cause by the appointing Interested Trustee. Except as otherwise provided herein, a Co-Trustee so appointed shall serve only as long as the Trustee who appointed such Co-Trustee (or, if such Co-Trustee was named by more than one (1) Trustee acting together, by the last to serve of such Trustees), and such Co-Trustee shall not become the successor Trustee or a successor Co-Trustee, unless: (i) such Co-Trustee has been nominated by me as the successor Trustee hereunder, (ii) such Co-Trustee is elected or appointed as the successor Trustee of the trust in question, (iii) such Co-Trustee is appointed as a Co-Trustee by the successor Trustee of the trust in question, (iv) a majority of the current income beneficiaries of the trust in question who are sui juris and not incapacitated, consent in writing to the continuation of the appointed Co-Trustee as the successor Trustee, (v) all of the specifically named successor Trustees of the trust in question consent, in writing, to the continuation of the appointed Co-Trustee as the successor Trustee, or (vi) a court of competent jurisdiction consents to the appointment of such Co-Trustee as the successor Trustee.

6.6 Trustee May Appoint a Substitute Trustee. If Trustee is unable or unwilling to exercise a fiduciary power with regard to a specific trust matter or assets, Trustee may by a dated written instrument filed with the trust records, designate, appoint and compensate any person (not prohibited from serving as a trustee) as a substitute Trustee for any trust matters or assets that the appointing Trustee is unwilling or unable to act as Trustee, or for trust assets in another jurisdiction, with any trust powers set out in this Agreement or provided by law (except those, if any, not exercisable by such substitute Trustee) that the appointing Trustee delegates to the substitute Trustee, and to specify which jurisdiction's law is to govern questions relating to the administration of such matters and assets. Any substitute Trustee so appointed, may, without liability, accept without examination or review the accounts rendered, the actions taken, and the property delivered by or for the appointing Trustee or any Co-Trustee of an appointing Trustee. A substitute Trustee may be removed at any time, with or without cause, by the appointing Trustee(s), other than an Interested Trustee. A substitute Trustee appointed solely by an Interested Trustee may be removed for reasonable cause by the appointing Interested Trustee. A substitute Trustee may be removed at any time, with or without cause, by any successor Trustee. If Trustee chooses to not appoint a substitute Trustee with respect to the exercise of a fiduciary power, Trustee may petition a court of competent jurisdiction to request the appointment of a special trustee to exercise the fiduciary power on a temporary or permanent basis, or may request that the court exercise the fiduciary power on a temporary or permanent basis. A special trustee appointed by the court shall be treated as a "substitute Trustee."

6.7 Individual Trustee May Nominate Successor Trustee. Each individual Trustee (including successors) shall have the right to nominate a successor Trustee(s) (who is not prohibited from serving as a trustee) by a dated written instrument filed with the trust records and delivered to all the current income beneficiaries of the trust in question who are sui juris. A nomination may be changed or revoked until it takes effect. Except as otherwise provided in the next sentence, the appointment of a nominated successor under this provision shall take effect only if and when all Trustees that have been previously nominated or appointed by me or my Spouse fail or decline to qualify or cease to act with respect to the trust in question, and a majority of the current income beneficiaries of the trust in question who are sui juris (other than the appointing beneficiary-trustee) do not object in writing to the appointment of such nominated successor Trustee by the appointing Trustee. The restrictions of the preceding sentence shall not, however, apply if: (i) all of the then nominated successor Trustees of the trust in question consent, in writing, to the appointment of the nominated successor(s) as the next successor Trustee(s) to the appointing Trustee, (ii) a majority of the current income beneficiaries of the trust (excluding the appointing beneficiary-trustee) who are sui juris and not incapacitated consent, in writing, to the appointment of the nominated successor(s) as the next successor Trustee(s) to the appointing Trustee, or (iii) a court of competent jurisdiction consents to the appointment of the nominated successor(s) as the next successor Trustee(s) to the appointing Trustee. A Trustee nominated pursuant to the provisions of this Paragraph shall be deemed to be a Trustee that has been nominated in the Paragraph entitled, **"Initial and Successor Trustees."**

6.8 Sole Beneficiary—Trustee Authorized. Except as otherwise expressly provided in this Agreement, if the sole Trustee of a trust is a beneficiary of the trust, Trustee may appoint but shall not be required to appoint a Co-Trustee. A beneficiary's interest may not be merged or converted into a legal life estate or estate for years because the beneficiary is the sole Trustee. If this would still happen under applicable law, then a Co-Trustee shall be appointed in preference to such merger or conversion.

6.9 Action by One Trustee. Unless a Co-Trustee elects otherwise in writing, when more than one person is serving as Trustee, any one of them (who is not prohibited from acting), may, acting alone, exercise any power and authority of Trustee, and may sign any checks, agreements or other documents on behalf of the trust, and the signature of any one such Trustee shall be sufficient to bind the trust in the same manner as though said check, agreement or other document had been signed by all the Co-Trustees (who are not prohibited from acting), and no person dealing with the signing Trustee shall be obliged to inquire as to the other Co-Trustee's acquiescence to such action.

6.10 Multiple Trustees. While two (2) or more Trustees are then acting, the following provisions shall apply where the context permits:

(A) When more than one person is serving as Trustee and at least one of them is a Disinterested or Independent Trustee, the Trustee who is not a Disinterested or Independent Trustee shall not participate in the exercise or non-exercise of any discretionary authority granted by this Agreement;

(B) When more than two (2) Trustees are then acting, the decision of a majority of the Trustees (who are eligible to participate in the action or decision) shall control in all matters pertaining to the administration of any trust created under this Agreement, and if there are an even number of eligible Trustees and a majority decision can not be achieved, then the disputed matter shall be submitted to binding arbitration;

(C) If only two (2) Trustees are then acting and both are eligible to participate in the action or decision, the concurrence and joinder of both shall be required, and if they both cannot mutually agree on the action or decision, the matter in dispute shall be submitted to binding arbitration;

(D) A Trustee who is eligible to participate in an action or decision shall be presumed to have approved a proposed act or decision to refrain from acting if that Trustee fails to indicate approval or disapproval thereof within fifteen (15) days after a written request for approval, and a Trustee shall not be required to continue to make a proposal which has been disapproved on at least two (2) occasions if that Trustee has informed a disapproving Co-Trustee (who is eligible to participate in the action or decision) that continued disapproval will be assumed until notice to the contrary has been received;

(E) When more than two (2) Trustees are then acting, any disapproving Trustee (who is eligible to participate in the action or decision) may be absolved from personal liability by registering a written disapproval with the records of the trust, and the disapproving Trustee shall thereafter act with the other Trustees in any manner necessary or appropriate to effectuate the decision of the majority, if any;

(F) Any Trustee who is not eligible to participate in an action or decision shall not be liable therefor; and

(G) The Trustees may execute documents by jointly signing one document or separately signing concurrent counterpart documents.

6.11 Trustee's Fees. Trustee shall be entitled to fair and reasonable compensation for services performed, and to reimbursement for expenses (even though Trustee may also be my personal representative and/or an accountant, attorney, investment advisor or other agent retained by my personal representative or Trustee, and Trustee's fees shall be in addition to (and not in diminution of) any other compensation otherwise payable to such persons concerning their services to my estate or the trusts established under this Agreement). The fairness and reasonableness of

Trustee's fees shall not be determined on the basis of only the time spent, but may be computed by the method which Trustee and those professionals hired by it customarily utilize in determining the compensation it will receive from clients or customers for its services. If Trustee is a professional person charging clients by the hour, then said person's hourly rate charged clients shall be a major factor in determining said person's compensation as Trustee. Trustee may, without prior approval by any court or any beneficiary, pay from and charge the trust estate with such fees, compensation, reimbursements, and expenses at such times and intervals as may be established by Trustee.

6.12 Qualifying as Trustee. A substitute Trustee, successor Trustee or Co-Trustee shall qualify upon signing an acceptance of trust and delivering it to the appointing Trustee(s) (if any); and in the case of a successor Trustee, the acceptance of trust shall be delivered to all the current income beneficiaries of the trust in question who are sui juris and not incapacitated and to all the other then acting Trustees of the trust in question. Unless a bond is otherwise requested by a majority of the trust's current trust beneficiaries, no bond shall be required of a Trustee (to the extent such requirement can be waived). If a person becomes eligible to serve as a Trustee because of a death, resignation, removal, or appointment, the notice of acceptance of trust must be given within thirty (30) days of eligibility. If eligibility to serve occurs because of the attainment of a specified age, the notice of acceptance may be given at any time.

6.13 Title and Powers. Except as otherwise provided or expressly limited, any successor Trustee, Co-Trustee or substitute Trustee shall have all the title, powers, and discretion of the Trustee succeeded, the other Co-Trustee(s), or the appointing Trustee(s) (as the case may be), without the necessity of any conveyance or transfer.

6.14 Other Trustee's Acts and Accounts, and Delivery of Trust Records. A successor Trustee is under no obligation to review the acts or to examine the accounts of a predecessor or any Co-Trustee of a predecessor. In no event is a successor Trustee liable for acts, omissions, or failures to account properly prior to the successor's qualification. A substitute Trustee or a Co-Trustee appointed by another Trustee is under no obligation to review the acts or to examine the accounts of an appointing Trustee or any Co-Trustee of an appointing Trustee. In no event is a substitute Trustee or a Co-Trustee appointed by another Trustee liable for acts, omissions, or failures to account properly prior to such substitute Trustee's qualification or such Co-Trustee's qualification. A Trustee is under no obligation to inquire into or examine the acts or accounts of a personal representative who is transferring property to Trustee. If any Trustee is removed, resigns or otherwise ceases to act as Trustee of any trust hereunder, that Trustee shall immediately surrender all records with respect to such trust to the then acting Trustee(s) of the trust in question or, if no other Trustee is then acting with respect to such trust, to the successor Trustee upon receipt of written notice of the acceptance of the trusteeship by the successor Trustee.

6.15 Corporate Successor. Any corporate successor to the trust business of any corporate Trustee acting under this Agreement shall become Trustee in place of its predecessor, without the necessity of any conveyance or transfer.

6.16 Proceeds Application. No person paying money or delivering any property to Trustee need see to its application.

6.17 Notice. Any notice or other communication that is required to be in writing shall be delivered personally, telegraphed, telexed, or telecopied, or sent by first class, certified, registered, or express delivery, postage prepaid, to the last known address of the party in question, or by any other means reasonably intended to effect actual delivery. Any such notice or communication shall be deemed given when so delivered personally, telegraphed, telexed, telecopied; or if mailed, or delivered by express delivery (such as FEDEX), on the earlier of the date of receipt or two (2) days after the date of mailing or the sender's delivery to the express delivery courier. Unless otherwise specifically provided in this Agreement, Trustee may rely on any information, telephone conversation, e-mail, notice, certificate, affidavit, letter, telegram, or other document or communication reasonably believed by it to be genuine, or on any evidence reasonably deemed by it to be sufficient. Trustee shall incur no liability for any payment or distribution made in good faith without actual knowledge of a changed condition affecting any person's interest in the trust.

6.18 Trustee Liability. Trustee shall act in a fiduciary manner, and exercise good faith, ordinary prudence, and reasonable care in the discharge of its duties and the exercise of its powers under the terms of this Agreement. Trustee, however, shall not be liable for the acts, omissions, or defaults of any agent hired with reasonable care and in good faith.

6.19 Conflict of Interest. No Trustee shall be per se disqualified by reason of owning an interest in real or personal property, or in a corporation or other business venture or entity, or by reason of being an officer, director, member or employee of any corporation or other business venture or entity, an interest in which is also a part of the trust in question.

6.20 Initial Notice of Trustee Status. For a revocable trust, within twenty-eight (28) days after Trustee's acceptance of trust or my death, whichever is later, and for all other trusts, within twenty-eight (28) days after acceptance of the trust, Trustee shall, to the extent required by law, inform in writing each interested trust beneficiary of the trust's existence, of the court in which the trust is registered, if it is registered, of Trustee's name and address, and of the interested trust beneficiary's right to request and receive both a copy of the trust's terms that describe or affect the interested trust beneficiary's interest and relevant information about the trust property. In addition, upon reasonable request, Trustee shall, to the extent required by law, provide an interested trust beneficiary with a copy of the trust's terms that describe or affect the interested trust beneficiary's interest and with relevant information about the trust property.

6.21 Removal of Trustee. My Spouse or I may at any time remove a Trustee or a nominated Trustee, for reasonable cause, and my Spouse or I may appoint a successor (other than a person who is prohibited from serving as a Trustee or a person whose life is insured by the trust in question) to replace the Trustee (or nominated Trustee) that my Spouse or I remove for reasonable cause. My Spouse or I may (but not more than once in a twenty-four (24) month period), remove a Trustee or a nominated Trustee, for no cause, and my Spouse or I may appoint a successor Trustee to replace the Trustee (or nominated Trustee) that was removed for no cause, provided the replacement Trustee is not me or my Spouse, not a person whose life is insured by the trust in question, not a person who is prohibited from serving as a Trustee, and is not related or subordinate (within the meaning of IRC section 672(c)) to either me or my Spouse. Any replacement Trustee appointed as aforesaid shall serve as Trustee prior to any other person who has been nominated as a Trustee. Subject to the foregoing, a majority of the current income beneficiaries of the trust in question who are sui juris and not incapacitated, may remove a Trustee for reasonable cause.

A Co-Trustee or nominated successor Trustee may remove an incumbent Trustee for reasonable cause at any time, and if successful in the removal of the incumbent Trustee, the Trustee who sought the removal shall be reimbursed from the trust estate for its reasonable expenses (including attorney fees) incurred in obtaining the removal of the incumbent Trustee. If a Co-Trustee or a nominated successor Trustee is not successful in its good faith attempt to remove the incumbent Trustee, a court of competent jurisdiction shall decide whether the reasonable expenses incurred by a Co-Trustee or nominated successor Trustee seeking the removal should be paid by the trust estate and/or trust beneficiaries personally (or a combination of both).

In applying these powers, the following rules apply (subject to the conditions and limitations imposed upon me and my Spouse concerning the removal and replacement of a Trustee):

(A) In the absence of a nominated successor Trustee (as set forth in the Paragraph entitled, "**Initial and Successor Trustees")** then willing or able to serve or continue to serve as Trustee, a majority of the current income beneficiaries of the trust in question who are sui juris and not incapacitated may appoint in writing, a successor Trustee who is a Disinterested or Independent Trustee, located in or outside the United States; provided, however, no beneficiary, acting alone, may remove or name a Trustee of a trust that would be included in that person's estate solely by reason of this right of removal or appointment. In selecting a non-U.S. Trustee, the beneficiaries are reminded to consider the potential (adverse) tax consequences of such an appointment.

(B) A power to remove a Trustee shall be exercised by a writing delivered to the then-serving Trustee, indicating the removal's effective date, the name of the successor Trustee, and the successor Trustee's agreement to serve.

(C) "Reasonable cause" for removal of a Trustee shall mean any one of the following:

(1) The incapacity or disability of Trustee.

(2) The willful or negligent mismanagement by Trustee of the trust's assets.

(3) The abuse or abandonment of, or inattention to, the trust or its assets by Trustee.

(4) A federal or state charge against Trustee involving the commission of a felony or serious misdemeanor.

(5) An act of stealing, dishonesty, fraud, embezzlement, moral turpitude, or moral degeneration by Trustee.

(6) The use of narcotics or excessive use of alcohol by Trustee.

(7) Trustee's poor physical, mental or emotional health which causes Trustee to be unable to devote sufficient time to administer the trust.

(8) Trustee's failure to comply with a written fee agreement or other legally enforceable written agreement affecting the operation of the trust.

(9) The failure of a corporate Trustee to appoint a senior officer with at least five (5) years of experience in the administration of trusts to handle the trust account.

(10) Changes by a corporate Trustee in the account officer responsible for the handling of the trust account more frequently than every five (5) years (unless such change is made at the request of or with the acquiescence of a Co-Trustee or the trust beneficiaries).

(11) The relocation by Trustee away from the location where the trust operates so as to interfere with the convenient administration of the trust.

(12) The removal of all current income beneficiaries from the State where the corporate Trustee is licensed to conduct business as a corporate Trustee.

(13) A demand from Trustee for unreasonable compensation for such Trustee's service.

(14) Unreasonably poor investment performance (as compared to appropriate investment benchmark indices).

(15) Unreasonable lack of communication between Trustee and the trust's current income beneficiaries.

(16) Unreasonably inaccurate or unclear transaction statements or statements of account.

(17) Unreasonable conflicts between Trustee and the trust's beneficiaries caused by Trustee.

(18) Merger, acquisition or deteriorating financial condition of a corporate Trustee.

(19) Where it would appear to be in the best interests of the current trust beneficiaries to have an Independent Trustee serve as sole Trustee.

(20) Any other reason for which a state court of competent jurisdiction would remove a trustee.

ARTICLE 7
TRUSTEE POWERS AND TRUST ADMINISTRATION

7.1 **Trustee Powers.** Subject to the provisions entitled, "**Limitations on Powers**," and any other pertinent provisions or limitations specified elsewhere in this Agreement, every Trustee may exercise, in a fiduciary manner, without court order, any of the following powers, and any others that are granted by law—to the extent not inconsistent with the powers granted in this Agreement. Except as expressly otherwise permitted, no powers shall be possessed or exercised by Trustee, or interpreted, in any manner that would prevent an existing bequest from qualifying for the marital or charitable deduction or would prevent an increase in basis (if applicable) under the Code; provided, however, such prohibition shall not be construed as a direction by me to my fiduciary to exercise any election or option that may be available under any tax or other law in such a manner as will result in a larger amount passing to the marital or charitable deduction bequest in the first instance, than if a contrary election were made. Such powers include:

(A) Additional Powers.

(1) Invest and reinvest the trust assets (or leave them temporarily un-invested) in any type of property and every kind of investment, in the same manner as a prudent investor would invest his or her own assets. Trustee may take title to any securities in the name of any custodian or nominee, without disclosing this relationship, and such securities may be held in "street name" by a brokerage firm or other custodian. Trustee may vote proxies. Irrespective of the prudent investor rule, Trustee may acquire and/or retain life insurance policies on the life of any beneficiary or person whom Trustee has an insurable interest. Furthermore, I prefer that my interest in any Closely Held Business Entity (defined below) in which I am an owner at the time of my death (or that is owned by the initial trust at the time of my death (or which the initial trust has the right to receive as a result of my death)) be retained by Trustee, unless, in the reasonable judgment of Trustee, there are persuasive or compelling reasons to dispose of any such interest. I understand that retention of any such business interest is inherently risky, but I believe in the fundamental soundness of each such interest and that the risk assumed by retaining any such business interest is justified. I further believe that each such business interest is and will continue to be capable of superior economic performance (production of greater net income, attaining a greater capital value, or both) than could be achieved from the sale of such business interest and reinvestment of the proceeds of such sale. As used herein, the term "Closely Held Business Entity" shall include a corporation, partnership (general or limited), limited liability company, joint venture, sole proprietorship or other entity under the laws of any state or other jurisdiction, but does not include any interests that are regularly traded on an established exchange or over-the-counter.

(2) Lease, buy, sell, exchange, or option any real or personal property, for cash or credit, at public or private sale, and with such warranties or indemnifications as Trustee may deem advisable. Trustee may borrow money for any proper purpose from itself or from unrelated parties. Trustee may mortgage, encumber, grant security interests or pledge any trust property, including purchasing securities on margin.

(3) On behalf of itself and/or all future Trustees, disclaim, release, or restrict the scope of any power held in connection with any trust (even if a power is not presently exercisable or is exercisable in a fiduciary capacity that requires the exercise of the power), including any administrative or management power, whether such power is expressly granted in this Agreement or implied by law. Trustee shall make such disclaimer, release, or restriction, if any, by a written instrument specifying the power to be disclaimed, released, or restricted and the nature of any such restriction. Any power disclaimed or released by Trustee shall be extinguished, as concerns that Trustee only, but if Trustee also expressly disclaims, releases or restricts the power on behalf of all future Trustees then the power shall be extinguished as to all future Trustees as well. Trustee may also disclaim any disclaimable interest, in whole or in part, including property, interests in property, and benefits of any kind receivable by any trust (including but not limited to, insurance contracts, qualified plan proceeds, deferred compensation proceeds, stock options, tax sheltered annuity proceeds, retirement account proceeds, etc.) in any manner permitted by law or by a "transfer" within the requirements of IRC section 2518(c)(3) (concerning certain transfers treated as disclaimers).

(4) Trustee may hold any qualified family-owned business (as that term is defined in IRC section 2057) ("QFOBI") for which a QFOBI election is made, in a separate trust for the benefit of the beneficiaries, with the QFOBI being the sole asset of the trust. If for any reason a trust established under this Agreement that contains a QFOBI fails to qualify as a qualified heir (as that term is defined in IRC section 2057), Trustee may appoint the QFOBI interest to one or more persons who do qualify as qualified heirs in the estates, interests, and proportions, including an appointment to a trustee in trust for a beneficiary (but only if the trust is a qualified heir), as Trustee, in its discretion, may determine.

(5) Purchase or otherwise acquire, for cash, credit or installments, form, create, organize, invest in, reinvest in, retain or continue for an indefinite term, any "Business Entity" (as defined below) located within or without the United States, regardless of the form of participation or ownership and even though it may be closely or privately held or may constitute all or a large portion of the trust property of a trust; have and exercise all the powers necessary and incidental to ownership in such Business Entity, including making tax elections, and authorizing or voting to authorize the making of charitable contributions by such Business Entity; comply with the provisions of any agreement restricting the disposition of an interest in the Business Entity; participate in the conduct of such Business Entity or rely upon others to do so, and take or delegate to others discretionary power to take any action with respect to its management and affairs that a person could take as owner of such Business Entity, including the voting of securities, and the determination of all questions of policy; take possession of the assets of such Business Entity and exercise complete control and management of such Business Entity, and in connection therewith, enter into and perform contracts, commitments, orders, and engagements; incur expenses and debts in connection with the conduct and operation of such Business Entity, and pay and discharge such expenses and debts; join in and execute legal documents and agreements, operating agreements, partnership agreements and amendments thereto; participate in any incorporation, reorganization, merger, consolidation, recapitalization, liquidation or dissolution of such Business Entity or any change in its nature and retain and continue such changed or successor Business Entity; enter into buy-sell agreements or similar types of agreements; invest additional capital in, subscribe to or buy additional stock or securities of or make or guarantee new or increased secured, subordinated loans to any Business Entity with trust funds; rely upon the reports of certified public accountants, appraisers, consultants and other professional advisors, without independent investigation and without obligation to file any report with any court in any jurisdiction; elect, employ and compensate directors, officers, employees or agents of any Business Entity, who may include Trustee or a director, officer or agent of Trustee; show in summary form in Trustee's accountings, if any, only the financial position of a Business Entity and not include in detail all the business transactions; deal with and act for such Business Entity in any capacity, including any banking or trust capacity and the loaning of money out of a trustee's own funds, and be compensated therefor; sell, pledge or liquidate any interest in such Business Entity; provided, however, that notwithstanding the provisions of this sub-paragraph, Trustee shall not purchase or otherwise acquire, form, create, organize, invest or reinvest in any Business Entity by which Trustee is employed or in which Trustee (or Trustee's family) directly or indirectly owns an interest, unless (i) Trustee is a descendant of my grandparents or a spouse of such a descendant; (ii) a current trust beneficiary, a descendant of such beneficiary's grandparents, a descendant of my grandparents or a spouse of any of such persons is employed by or owns (directly or indirectly) an interest in such Business Entity; or (iii) a current trust beneficiary consents to such action in a duly acknowledged instrument filed with the trust records; provided, further, that Trustee may continue to hold interests in any Business Entity held by the trust at the time Trustee began serving as such. As used herein, the term "Business Entity" shall include a corporation, partnership (general or limited), limited liability company, joint venture, sole proprietorship or other entity under the laws of any state or other jurisdiction, but does not include any interests that are regularly traded on an established exchange or over-the-counter. Trustee may make or terminate elections with respect to S corporation stock; and during the term of any trust under this Agreement, (i) if Trustee sells any interest in a corporation or if the assets of any entity constituting a corporation in which the trust has an ownership interest are sold, and (ii) if the corporation has made an election to be taxed under Subchapter S of the Code, Trustee may distribute to the income beneficiary such amounts of income and/or principal as shall be necessary to pay any income tax caused by such sale, if the income or gain attributable to such sale is taxed directly to the income beneficiary under applicable federal tax law. If the personal representative of my estate makes an election under IRC section 6324A (concerning the special lien for estate tax deferred under IRC section 6166), or a corresponding state statute, to create a special lien for the payment of any deferred death tax (including tax attributable to property not passing under this Agreement), Trustee may subject trust property to such lien. If Trustee is my Spouse or a descendant of mine, I hereby waive any conflict of interest occasioned thereby, especially if that individual also personally holds an interest in the Business Entity. Any contractual and tort liabilities arising from the Business Entity or its operation shall be satisfied first from its assets and only secondarily from other assets of the trust, if practicable.

(6) Establish any educational savings plans pursuant to IRC sections 529 or 530 (or their successors), or any similar plans; to remove and/or add beneficiary(s) to such plans; and to add and/or remove successor owners of any such plans, all as Trustee may deem proper and expedient; and to exercise all other powers and options involving such plans.

(7) Merge or consolidate any trust created hereunder together with any other trusts (regardless by whom created) having the same beneficiaries, substantially the same dispositive provisions and, to the extent applicable, the same generation-skipping tax inclusion ratios. After the merger or consolidation, Trustee shall inform the current trust beneficiaries which of the constituent trusts is the surviving trust. If the applicable rules limiting the maximum duration of trusts (such as any rules governing perpetuities, vesting, accumulations or the suspension of alienation) start from different dates with reference to the trusts or additions to trusts, or if the trusts have different tax attributes, or if the trust assets are of a different nature, of if there are other significant differences in their provisions, merger or consolidation may still take place; but the assets of the trusts may be maintained in segregated accounts, or records of undivided shares of assets may be maintained. In considering the merger or consolidation of any trusts, Trustee shall give consideration to the potential for adverse tax consequences, including the revocation of Subchapter S status for stock held in trust. Trustee may administer such merged and consolidated trusts as a single trust or unit. If, however, such a merger or consolidation does not appear feasible, as determined in the discretion of Trustee, Trustee may consolidate the assets of such trusts for purposes of investment and trust administration while retaining separate records and accounts for the respective trusts.

(8) Sever any trust or divide any trust into multiple separate trusts; establish separate trusts; establish sub-trusts; and make qualified severances. Without the consent of any beneficiary, Trustee may allocate, divide or distribute trust property in cash or in kind or partly in each, including undivided interests, and without making pro rata distribution of specific assets and without regard to the income tax basis of any asset. Non-pro rata distributions or allocations of property may be made based on the property's date of distribution value, in a manner fairly representative of the properties' net appreciation and depreciation, or in any other manner permitted (or required) by law. As to any property incapable of exact division, it shall not be necessary for Trustee to divide the same physically into parts to which each trust shall be entitled, but individual parts thereof may, by appropriate book entries, be allocated among the trusts. In any case where exact division of property or allocation of undivided interests therein between or among the trusts hereunder is not practical or expedient, Trustee may select assets to be appropriated in whole or in part to any of said trusts. Furthermore, Trustee may allot different kinds or disproportionate portions or undivided interests in property among beneficiaries; and determine the value of any allotted property without compensating adjustment, even if the basis for federal income tax purposes of property allotted to any beneficiary is not fairly representative of all property available for distribution.

(9) Except as may be otherwise provided in this Agreement, allocate an item of income or expense to either trust income or principal, as permitted or provided by applicable local law. With respect to any item not established clearly by such law, Trustee shall have discretion to determine whether items should be reasonably charged or credited to income or principal or allocated between income and principal. Except as may be otherwise provided in this Agreement, Trustee shall generally resolve any question about the allocation or apportionment of receipts and disbursement, to or between income and principal, in favor of the trust's current income beneficiary. If the power to adjust between principal and income is otherwise permitted by applicable local law (and is not expressly prohibited under this Agreement), that power shall be vested exclusively in an Independent

Trustee. Absent a written request from a current trust beneficiary, an Independent Trustee who is an individual shall not be required to determine if the power to adjust should be exercised.

(10) Employ and compensate such lawyers, accountants, agents, nurses, professional care managers, caregivers, professionals, and other persons as Trustee may deem useful and appropriate for the proper administration of the trust and for the care of a current trust beneficiary; provided however, the foregoing authority shall not restrict a Trustee's sole, absolute and uncontrolled discretion (if any) concerning distributions to or for the benefit of such beneficiary, nor shall the foregoing be construed to mandate such distributions to or for the benefit of such beneficiary. Trustee may employ an investment adviser in managing the investments of the trust (including any investments in mutual funds, investment trusts, or managed accounts), delegate to this adviser any discretionary investment authorities, and rely on the adviser's investment recommendations.

(11) Institute and defend litigation, and compromise and adjust claims against or on behalf of the trust on such terms as Trustee may deem appropriate.

(12) Make (or refrain from making) any tax elections and allocations Trustee may consider appropriate; however, Trustee's authority hereunder is to be exercised only in a fiduciary capacity and may not be used to enlarge or shift any beneficial interest except as an incidental consequence of the discharge of fiduciary duties. All tax elections and allocations made by Trustee in good faith shall not require equitable adjustments. Trustee shall not incur any liability for tax elections or allocations made in good faith.

(13) In Trustee's sole, absolute and uncontrolled discretion, permit a current trust beneficiary to use trust owned real property and personal property free of rent or expense.

(14) Make commitments extending beyond the term of any trust.

(15) Hold trust property of several trusts under this Agreement in common ownership or in a common fund, each trust having an undivided interest in the property or fund, dividing the income proportionately and accounting for them separately, until actual division becomes necessary or desirable.

(16) Defer distribution of trust property after the termination of any trust until all matters involving such trust have been settled.

(17) Purchase liability, casualty, and other appropriate insurance for the protection of the trust estate.

(18) Perform all other acts necessary for the proper management, investment, and distribution of the trust property.

(B) **Generation-Skipping Tax Matters.** In order to minimize the impact of any generation-skipping transfer tax that may be applied to any of the trusts created by this Agreement or their beneficiaries, Trustee shall take the following actions, where applicable; and Trustee may also take such other actions as are required (or permitted) by law (or applicable Treasury Regulations) concerning generation skipping transfer tax matters:

(1) If any trust under this Agreement would, otherwise by reason of an allocation of generation-skipping transfer tax exemption to it, have an inclusion ratio, as defined in IRC section 2642(a) of neither one (1) nor zero (0), then prior to such allocation Trustee shall divide, on a fractional basis, the total trust assets into two (2) separate trusts of equal or unequal value, to permit allocation of the exemption solely to one trust (the "exempt trust") so that the exempt trust will have an inclusion ratio of zero (0); any such division shall be accomplished by allocating to the other trust (the "non-exempt trust" which will have an inclusion ratio of one (1)) the minimum fractional share necessary to leave the exempt trust with a corpus of the desired value and an inclusion ratio of zero

(0), so as to be entirely exempt from generation-skipping tax. In the event an existing trust has an inclusion ratio other than zero (0) or one (1), then such trust shall be divided on a fractional basis so that two (2) trusts will be created from the one, one of which will have an inclusion ratio of zero (0), and one of which will have an inclusion ratio of one (1). Trustee is also authorized to sever or divide a single trust into multiple trusts under the "qualified severance" rule of IRC section 2642(a)(3) and to fund the severed trusts in any manner permitted or required by law (including the funding of the severed or divided trusts on a non-pro-rata basis). References hereunder to "trust" or "trusts" refer also to arrangements that are treated as trusts for generation-skipping purposes and to separate shares of a trust, when appropriate to the context, if the shares are, as "substantially separate and independent shares of different beneficiaries" or otherwise, entitled to be treated as separate trusts for generation-skipping tax purposes.

(2) If Trustee does in fact divide a trust into two (2) trusts, one which has an inclusion ratio of one (1) and the other which has inclusion ratio of zero (0), I direct Trustee to make the division in a manner that permits the trusts to be treated as separate trusts in accordance with applicable Treasury Regulations (e.g., Treas. Reg. sections 26.2654-1(a) and (b)). Unless applicable Treasury Regulations (e.g., Treas. Reg. section 26.2654-1(b)(1)) require (or permit) otherwise, if the new trusts are severed on a fractional basis, the separate trusts need not be funded on a pro rata fractional basis; provided, however, if funding is on a non-pro rata fractional basis, Trustee shall fund the trusts based on either the fair market value of the assets on the date of funding or in a manner that fairly reflects the net appreciation or depreciation in the value of the assets measured from the valuation date to the date of funding. In funding the severed trusts, it is my desire that Trustee first distribute to the non-exempt Trust, property (or its proceeds) that constitutes Income in Respect of a Decedent, before distributing other property. Where applicable (and unless applicable Treasury Regulations require (or permit) otherwise), if the severance is required (by the terms of this Agreement) to be made on the basis of a pecuniary amount, the payment of the pecuniary amount shall, to the extent required, be satisfied in a manner that complies with Treas. Reg. sections 26.2654-1(a)(1)(ii) (A) **and** (B) (which concerns the payment of appropriate interest and the method of funding the pecuniary amount).

(3) Where applicable, Trustee is directed to comply with the valuation rules of Treas. Reg. section 26.2642-2 and the separate share rules of Treas. Reg. section 26.2654-1, to wit:

(a) Unless applicable Treasury Regulations require (or permit) otherwise, Trustee shall, to the extent applicable, satisfy the "appropriate interest" requirement: (i) by paying or irrevocably setting aside property in satisfaction of a pecuniary amount within fifteen (15) months of the date of death of the transferor, (ii) by paying appropriate interest as defined in Treas. Reg. section 26.2642-2(b)(4) on a pecuniary amount, or (iii) by allocating to a pecuniary amount a pro rata share of trust income from the transferor's date of death to the payment date.

(b) Unless applicable Treasury Regulations require (or permit) otherwise, Trustee shall, to the extent applicable, pay such pecuniary amount: (i) in cash, (ii) solely or partly in kind, using date of distribution values, or (iii) solely or partly in kind, in a manner that fairly reflects net appreciation and depreciation in the value of the assets in the fund available to pay the pecuniary amount, measured from the date of valuation to the date of distribution.

(c) Unless applicable Treasury Regulations require (or permit) otherwise, in instances where a generation-skipping tax exemption is to be allocated to a residual transfer that follows a pecuniary payment, I direct that: (i) the pecuniary payment receive "appropriate interest" as described in item (a) above, and (ii) if the pecuniary payment is to be satisfied solely or partly in kind, that the funding of such in kind distribution be in a manner described in items (b)(ii) and (iii) above.

(d) In determining the denominator for the "applicable fraction" used in calculating the inclusion ratio for any trust, it is my intent that where this Agreement (or Trustee) creates separate trusts, one with an inclusion ratio of one (1) and one with an inclusion ratio of zero (0), that the "applicable fraction" be calculated under the Treasury Regulations in effect at such time to accomplish the intended result.

(e) In determining how to satisfy the appropriate interest and funding requirements and how to obtain the desired "applicable fraction" described above, Trustee shall have complete discretion, and shall not be held liable for any consequence of the exercise of this discretion, made in good faith. I recognize that Trustee's decision as to how to satisfy these requirements may affect the amounts ultimately allocated to the various trusts hereunder; nevertheless, I intend this provision to apply.

(4) Except as may otherwise be provided in this Agreement (or be provided by applicable law), when a trust (the "original trust") is divided into exempt and non-exempt trusts or otherwise into separate trusts, references in this Agreement to the original trust shall collectively refer to the separate trusts derived from it. Trustee may make different tax elections (including the allocation of generation skipping transfer tax exemption), exercise investment, administrative and distributive discretion, and donees of powers of appointment may exercise their powers, differently with respect to each of the separate trusts (even otherwise identical trusts) derived from the original trust.

(5) If a trust under this Agreement, whether created under this provision or not, is entirely exempt or non-exempt from generation-skipping tax and adding property to it would partially subject the trust to generation-skipping tax, or change its inclusion ratio, Trustee shall hold that property in a separate trust in lieu of making the addition.

(6) Trustee is authorized to divide property in a trust into separate trusts with different transferors; such a trust may have more than one transferor. Trustee shall make any payment to, or for the benefit of, a beneficiary from any trust that has more than one transferor for generation-skipping transfer tax purposes (i) pro rata, from the separate portions attributable to transferors relative to whom the beneficiary is a non-skip person for generation-skipping tax purposes, and, to the extent of any balance, (ii) in ascending order of inclusion ratios of the portions for generation-skipping tax purposes, from the separate portions attributable to transferors relative to whom the beneficiary is a skip person for generation-skipping tax purposes, and such distributions need not be ratable among trusts or trust shares with the same inclusion ratios.

(7) If exempt and non-exempt trusts are established under this Agreement, Trustee shall have the power to make distributions (including distributions resulting from a partial or complete termination of a trust) to beneficiaries who are "non-skip persons" first from non-exempt trusts established for them and then from exempt trusts established for them; in addition, distributions to beneficiaries who are "skip persons" may be made first from exempt trusts established for them and only thereafter from non-exempt trusts established for them. Distributions need not be ratable among trusts or trust shares with the same inclusion ratios. In making distributions from a non-exempt trust, Trustee is authorized to make generation-skipping tax exempt distributions to beneficiaries who are skip persons, as permitted by IRC section 2611(b)(1) (concerning direct payments for tuition and medical expenses). "Skip persons" and "non-skip persons" shall be defined for purposes of this Agreement in accordance with IRC section 2613.

(8) Upon division, or distribution or termination of an exempt trust and a non-exempt trust, Trustee may allocate property from the exempt trust first to a share or trust from which a generation-skipping transfer is more likely to occur.

(9) A Disinterested Trustee in its sole, absolute and uncontrolled discretion may at any time prior to the death of the beneficiary, by an instrument in writing: (i) confer upon the beneficiary (other than me or my Spouse (if I am married)) a power exercisable, by and only by will, which specifically refers to the power created hereunder, to appoint all or part of the beneficiary's trust share to the creditors of the beneficiary's estate, and the instrument conferring the power and its terms and conditions may require consent of a Disinterested Trustee who is not the creator of the power and who does not have a substantial interest in the property subject to the power, which interest is adverse to the exercise of the power within the meaning of IRC sections 2514(c) and 2041(b) and Treas. Reg. sections 25.2514-3(b)(2) and 20.2041-(3)(c)(2); (ii) revoke or modify any such instrument previously executed, with or without executing a replacement instrument; and/or (iii) irrevocably relinquish the powers conferred under Paragraphs 7.1(b)(9)(i) and/or (ii) above. For purposes of the preceding sentence, the term "creditors" does not include the Trustee who confers the power or whose consent is required to exercise the power. Without limiting Trustee's discretion, Trustee may use the authority conferred by this provision to subject the trust property to federal estate tax instead of the federal generation-skipping transfer tax when it appears that it may reduce overall taxes to do so. The power granted may be by a formula or limited by a formula, in the discretion of the Disinterested Trustee. The beneficiary's power conferred by Trustee pursuant to this provision shall not be exercisable in any manner so as to postpone the vesting of any estate or interest in the appointed property or to suspend the absolute ownership or power of alienation of the appointed property for a period ascertainable without regard to applicable rules limiting the maximum duration of trusts (such as any rules governing perpetuities, vesting, accumulations or the suspension of alienation), and the validity of any exercise shall be measured with respect to such rules, to the extent applicable.

(C) Limitation on Powers.

(1) When more than one person is serving as Trustee and at least one of them is not beneficially interested in the exercise or non-exercise of a power or election, the beneficially interested Trustee shall not participate in the exercise or non-exercise of the power or election.

(2) No beneficiary or Trustee (either alone or in conjunction with other Trustees or persons) shall possess or exercise any power, discretion or incidents of ownership with respect to any insurance owned by the trust on his or her life; nor shall such beneficiary or Trustee hold or possess any power of appointment over such life insurance, unless such life insurance policies or proceeds would otherwise be includible in the beneficiary's or Trustee's gross estate (for federal estate tax purposes) at the beneficiary's or Trustee's death without regard to such power of appointment. If a Trustee holds (or is to receive) any such policy or policies as a part of the trust estate, then and in that event: (i) the powers conferred on the owner of such policy shall be exercised only by the other then acting Trustee, who is not an insured under the policy; (ii) the life insurance policy or policies shall be received, held and administered in and as a separate sub-trust of the original trust from which it is derived, segregated from the original trust properties, and the insured beneficiary shall be excluded as a beneficiary of the sub-trust (i.e., not eligible to receive or control any distributions of income or principal from the sub-trust); (iii) the insured (including an insured Trustee) shall not serve as a Trustee of such sub-trust; (iv) the sub-trust Trustee (who shall also serve as a Co-Trustee of the original trust) may pay from the original trust (other than a trust qualified and elected for the marital or charitable deduction) any premiums, costs or charges associated with the insurance policies held by the sub-trust (and in no event shall such premiums, costs or charges be paid from any trust assets that are (or have been) contributed by the insured, and the insured shall not be entitled to contribute or transfer property to the original trust or to the sub-trust); and (v) in all other respects the terms of the newly created sub-trust shall be as consistent with the original trust from which it is derived. If the insured Trustee is the only then acting Trustee of the original trust, then such powers over the life insurance policy or policies shall instead be exercised by a substitute Trustee designated pursuant to the provisions of this Agreement dealing with the trusteeship; provided however, if any rule of law or court decision construes the ability of the insured Trustee to name a substitute Trustee as an incident of ownership, the designation of a substitute Trustee shall be implemented either by: (i) a majority of the current income beneficiaries, or (ii) by a court of competent jurisdiction.

(3) No Trustee shall have the power to use or apply trust property (i) for the support and maintenance of anyone the Trustee is obligated to support and maintain, or (ii) for the purpose of directly or indirectly discharging the personal legal obligations of the Trustee. No beneficiary-trustee who is an individual shall have the power to terminate a trust early of which he or she is a beneficiary. At any time when there is more than one Trustee, no Trustee who is also a beneficiary of any trust created under this Agreement shall exercise any power solely by himself or herself as would cause such beneficiary-Trustee to be treated as an owner of any portion of the trust under IRC section 678(a). No Trustee who is also a beneficiary of any trust created under this Agreement shall have the power, as a then acting Trustee of such trust, to make discretionary distributions to him or herself except: (i) to the extent necessary for such beneficiary—Trustee's health, education, support and maintenance as described in IRC sections 2041 and 2514 (concerning powers of appointment and ascertainable standards) in his or her accustomed manner of living (considering the resources reasonably available to him or her), or (ii) with the consent of a person who has a substantial interest in the trust property adverse to the exercise of the power in favor of such beneficiary—Trustee or such beneficiary—Trustee's estate or the creditors of either (as the case may be), within the meaning of IRC sections 2514(c) and 2041(b) and Treas. Reg. sections 25.2514-3(b)(2) and 20.2041-(3)(c)(2); and such beneficiary-Trustee shall exercise its Trustee powers solely in a fiduciary capacity and shall not possess or exercise any powers that would otherwise permit that beneficiary-Trustee to enlarge or shift any of the beneficial interests under that trust (except as an incidental consequence of the discharge of such fiduciary duties); and to the extent such beneficiary-Trustee has the authority to make discretionary distributions of income and/or principal to another beneficiary from a trust of which beneficiary-Trustee is then also a then current trust beneficiary, the discretionary distributions shall be limited by an ascertainable standard related to the distributee beneficiary's health, education, support and maintenance in the manner of living to which the distributee beneficiary has been accustomed, and except as may otherwise be provided elsewhere in this Agreement, the beneficiary-Trustee shall consider the resources otherwise reasonably available to the distributee beneficiary, when making such distributions. No beneficiary-Trustee who is an individual shall make discretionary distributions to or for the benefit of any beneficiary of a trust holding assets as a result of a disclaimer by or on behalf of such individual beneficiary-Trustee, except distributions limited to an ascertainable standard concerning the other beneficiary's health, education, support and maintenance. Furthermore, no beneficiary-Trustee who is a beneficiary of the trust in question shall possess any power or discretion that is "conclusive," "sole," "absolute" or "uncontrolled" with respect to the exercise or non-exercise of such power or discretion under that trust; and such beneficiary-Trustee's power or discretion in that regard shall at all times be exercised or not exercised in a reasonable manner, be limited by a reasonably definite standard, and shall be subject to review and judicial scrutiny. Trustee's discretionary power to allot and/or to pay or apply the income and/or principal of any trust established under this Agreement ("*such trust*") to or for the use or benefit of any beneficiary of *such trust* shall be exercisable solely by Trustee(s) other than any Trustee who is a permissible beneficiary of the income and/or principal of any other trust ("*such other trust*"), if any Trustee of *such other trust* is a permissible beneficiary of *such trust*. If at any time there is no Trustee qualified and acting for the purpose of exercising such discretionary powers other than a Trustee described in the preceding sentence, such discretionary powers shall be exercisable by an Independent Trustee. If the provisions of this sub-paragraph preclude all of the then-serving Trustees from exercising a discretion or power otherwise granted them, an Independent Trustee may be appointed by Trustee as an additional Trustee, with the sole authority to exercise the discretion or power, and such additional Trustee may only be removed for reasonable cause.

(D) Life Insurance Matters.

(1) A primary purpose of this Agreement after my death is to enable Trustee, in Trustee's discretion, to help provide liquidity to meet the demands that may confront my estate and family at such time. The liquidity demands that may arise as a result of my death are impossible to predict because of uncertainties as to the other assets that may then be available, the debts and taxes that may then be due, and the cash needs that may remain outstanding for the support of individuals dependent upon me or to maintain business enterprises in which I may have invested. I believe that the best technique to meet these uncertain liquidity demands is for Trustee to invest all or a substantial portion of the trust assets in life insurance during my lifetime, even though such life insurance policies may constitute a disproportionate part, or all, of the trust estate. I recognize that, in the long run, life insurance may not yield as high a rate of return as other available investments, or that it may even experience a negative rate of return (a loss of principal); however, I believe that the benefits of life insurance investments, including the larger payment (compared to other investments) if an insured should die short of his or her normal life expectancy, outweigh the possibility of a lower yield in the long run.

(2) I recognize that the selection and continued ownership of life insurance policies raises questions of prudence and due diligence, whether such policies are acquired by Trustee or transferred to Trustee. Therefore, I expressly authorize (but do not obligate) Trustee, in its discretion, and acting upon the recommendation and representations of any person selling, or in any way associated with the marketing, promotion or sale of life insurance, to purchase any life insurance (including a no lapse/secondary guarantee life insurance policy) from one or more insurers. Trustee may (but shall not be required): (i) to verify that any particular life insurance policy satisfies the requirements for a "life insurance contract" under IRC section 7702; (ii) to compare the performance or pricing or the projected performance or pricing of a particular life insurance policy with the performance or pricing or the projected performance or pricing of any other life insurance policy that then may be available from any source; (iii) to assess the appropriateness of purchasing or retaining any life insurance policy as an investment for the trust as compared to other then available investment vehicles that are not life insurance policies; and (iv) to investigate the strength or solvency of the company that issued or is offering a given life insurance policy. I acknowledge that Trustee is not a guarantor of any life insurance policy held in the trust or payable to the trust, whether purchased by, transferred to, or payable to Trustee. By this Paragraph I do not intend to reserve any right to control or direct Trustee, and the decision on trust investments is expressly reserved exclusively to Trustee.

(3) Trustee, who is an individual and is not a professional trustee, shall not be liable to me or to any beneficiary for any loss or damage suffered in connection with performance or lack of performance of any insurance policy owned by the trust (or payable to the trust) or as a result of the financial condition, including insolvency, of any insurer. The fact that Trustee may have made inquiry regarding any such matter prior to acquisition or transfer of a policy or after the acquisition or transfer of such policy shall place no duty upon Trustee to make any further inquiry, but shall be considered activity beyond the scope of Trustee's normal duties (however, the forgoing shall not prevent Trustee from delegating such duties to an agent, such as a fee only life insurance advisor, if appropriate). Trustee shall not be liable to me or to any trust beneficiary for any loss or damage suffered in connection with the performance, or failure to perform, of any life insurance policy or the insolvency of any life insurance company. On behalf of myself and my successors, heirs, and assigns, I hereby indemnify and hold harmless Trustee from and against any and all claims, liabilities, penalties, and costs, including attorneys' fees, arising from any claim, demand, order or other action related in any way to investing in and/or retaining any life insurance policies and exercising or failing to exercise any incident of ownership therein concerning any life insurance policies that were selected or approved by me, and any judgment against Trustee in this regard shall be satisfied from the trust fund, and to the extent the trust fund is insufficient, against my personal assets, including assets acquired directly or indirectly by transferees by reason of my death. For purposes of this Paragraph, a "professional trustee" is a person who derives a significant portion of his or her work revenue from serving as a trustee of intervivos or testamentary trusts.

(4) With respect to any insurance policies that are purchased or transferred to Trustee, I claim no right, title, interest, or incidents of ownership therein at this time, nor shall I have any incidents of ownership therein, presently or in the future, nor shall I be the beneficiary of any such policies, nor shall I exercise any right, power, option, election, privilege or incident of ownership under any such policies; and furthermore, I shall have no duty to pay premiums, assessments or other charges necessary to keep any policy in force and shall incur no liability to the beneficiaries of this Agreement or to any other person if any policy lapses for non-payment of premiums, assessments or charges, or otherwise becomes uncollectible. Trustee shall have all of the rights of the owner of such policies and, without the consent or approval of me or any other person, may, in its sole discretion, exercise or decline to exercise, any election, option, right or privilege available to Trustee, as owner of the policy. Such powers include, by way of example, and without limitation: (i) to reduce the amount of any policy or convert or exchange any policy into other forms of insurance; (ii) to enter into non-taxable and taxable exchanges, transfers and/or sales of trust property; (iii) to make withdrawals from any policy, or to surrender any policy for its cash surrender value; (iv) to borrow upon and pledge any policy in connection with a loan; (v) to take paid-up insurance; (vi) to elect extended term insurance; (vii) to collect dividends, death or other benefits (including disability benefits or an accelerated death benefit), surrender payments, and any other payment which may be due or collectible; (viii) to enter into a split-dollar or other premium sharing or financing arrangement with any person or entity; (ix) to split any policy into two or more policies; (x) to allow dividends to remain with the insurance company or to use them to reduce premiums or to purchase additional insurance; (xi) to use cash values to pay premiums; (xii) direct the manner in which the policy account of any variable life insurance policy shall be allocated among the various investment options from time to time available under such policy, and to change such allocation from time to time, as provided in such policy; (xiii) make any and all elections with respect to any death benefit options provided under any life insurance policy, and change such election from time to time; (xiv) determine how much, if any, of each year's target or similar premium amount of any flexible premium life insurance policy to pay, taking into consideration such tax and financial considerations each year as Trustee deems relevant; (xv) to exercise any options of settlement that may be available under the terms of said policies; (xvi) to determine and modify the current amount of life insurance coverage under an existing policy; (xvii) to accept an accelerated death benefit or enter into a viatical or life settlement concerning any policy; (xviii) to sell or transfer a life insurance policy; and (xix) to enter into premium financing arrangements.

(5) Trustee may, in Trustee's discretion, pay any premiums or other charges from the trust estate or by application of dividends on the policy. If the trust funds are inadequate to pay such premiums or charges, or if Trustee shall deem it inadvisable to pay such premiums or charges, Trustee may, in Trustee's discretion, do one or more of the following: (i) sell a sufficient portion of the property of the trust estate or borrow on the collateral of the property of the trust estate (including borrowing from a beneficiary, Trustee or an affiliate of Trustee), to obtain funds necessary to pay the premiums or charges; (ii) convert a policy into a paid up policy in whatever amount may be provided by the terms of such policy, or convert any such policy to a policy of extended term insurance in whatever amount may be provided by the terms of such policy; (iii) use any automatic premium loan feature; (iv) borrow against any policy cash reserves (whether or not on the policy for which premium or charges will be paid); (v) elect any automatic non-forfeiture feature; (vi) surrender any policy to obtain its cash surrender value; (vii) sell any policy; (viii) reduce the amount of the death benefit; (ix) exercise any other right, option, power, election or privilege under any policy held in trust by Trustee; (x) if I am married, assign and deliver the policy to my Spouse if he or she is an interested trust beneficiary (and not a donor or an insured under the policy); (xi) distribute the policy pursuant to any authority or discretion exercisable by the Trustee concerning distributions of trust principal; (xii) terminate the trust and distribute the policy pursuant to the provisions of this Agreement concerning termination of trusts (to the extent applicable); (xiii) assign the policy to the then current income beneficiaries (other than me or any donor) in equal shares and deliver such policies to them; or (xiv) distribute or liquidate the policy and deliver the policy or liquidation proceeds in such manner, amount, proportions and to such beneficiaries as may be determined or directed by a court of competent jurisdiction. Trustee shall not be responsible for the non-payment of premiums if the trust lacks the ability to pay them, and Trustee shall not be liable to anyone if the policies shall lapse (in whole or in part) or be otherwise uncollectible because the trust lacks the ability to pay the premiums. If Trustee has knowledge of an impending lapse or insufficiency of trust assets to pay premiums and other charges, Trustee shall make reasonable efforts to promptly notify in writing: (a) me (if I am not incapacitated or otherwise unavailable), and (b) at least one adult current trust beneficiary, who is sui juris, in order to advise us of the situation so that appropriate steps can be considered and, if need be, appropriate steps can be undertaken to provide sufficient funds to the trust estate in order to preserve the life insurance policy.

(6) Upon the death of an insured hereunder: (i) Trustee shall furnish the necessary proofs of death to the insurance company or companies which issued any policies of insurance, the proceeds of which are payable to Trustee; (ii) Trustee shall collect the proceeds of all such policies of insurance, and (iii) Trustee shall collect and receive any other property which may be made payable to Trustee. For such purpose, Trustee shall have full power and authority to execute and deliver any receipt or other voucher for such proceeds or property, to institute any suit or suits at law or in equity to enforce the payment of the proceeds of any such policies or to collect any such other property, and, in case of controversy or litigation over the collection of the same, to adjust, compromise or otherwise settle any controversy or contest concerning said policies of insurance or other property, or the collection thereof. Trustee shall be responsible for the proceeds of the insurance only when, as and if collected or paid to it.

(7) Trustee may, in Trustee's discretion, refuse to enter into or maintain any litigation, endorse policy payments, or take other action respecting any trust insurance policies, until Trustee has been indemnified against all expenses and liabilities which, in Trustee's judgment, may be involved in such action.

(8) Trustee need not inquire whether or not Trustee or the trust has been designated the beneficiary of any insurance policy or other death benefit, and Trustee need act with respect to such policies only after receipt of written notice that Trustee or the trust is a beneficiary.

(9) For trust accounting purposes, policy dividends and increases in value before the death of the insured under any life insurance policy or policies held by the trust shall be treated as principal, and not income.

(10) Any additional insurance policies, no matter how acquired (including, but not limited to acquisition by gift, conversion, reissue, consolidation), may be listed on **Schedule A**, but failure to do so does not affect the trust's policy ownership.

I SPECIFICALLY ACKNOWLEDGE THAT TRUSTEE WOULD NOT ACCEPT THE POSITION OF TRUSTEE UNLESS ITS DUTIES AND RESPONSIBILITIES WERE LIMITED AS SET FORTH ABOVE; AND TRUSTEE, WHO IS AN INDIVIDUAL AND IS NOT A PROFESSIONAL TRUSTEE, IS INDEMNIFIED.

7.2 Beneficiary Under Disability. Irrespective of whether a trust makes explicit reference to this Paragraph, if a beneficiary is under the age of thirty (30) years, legally disabled, incapacitated, or, in Trustee's opinion, incapable of managing a trust distribution, Trustee (i) may hold or distribute the income and principal in such manner as provided by law or as is otherwise permitted by authority granted Trustee in this Paragraph or elsewhere in this Agreement; (ii) may expend directly any income or principal that it is authorized to use for the beneficiary; or (iii) may pay it over to or for the benefit of the beneficiary, or to the beneficiary's legal representative, if any, or to any near relative or friend, or to any adult with whom the beneficiary is residing, for expenditure on the beneficiary's behalf, without any further responsibility for its application. If Trustee is directed to distribute any portion of trust principal to that beneficiary (including trust principal distributable pursuant to a beneficiary's right of withdrawal), the trust principal shall vest in interest in the beneficiary indefeasibly, but Trustee, in its discretion, may distribute the portion to a custodian for the beneficiary as selected by Trustee (who may be the Trustee) under a Uniform Transfers (Gifts) to Minors Act or similar act, or hold the portion as a separate and distinct trust until the later of (i) the beneficiary reaches the age of thirty (30) years; or (ii) after the removal of the legal disability; or (iii) after the recovery from the incapacity; or (iv) after the time Trustee deems the beneficiary is capable of managing a trust distribution. If Trustee holds the portion as a separate trust, Trustee may pay to or for the benefit of the beneficiary so much of the income and principal as Trustee deems advisable for the reasonable health care, education, support and maintenance of the beneficiary and the beneficiary's spouse and descendants; and, if the beneficiary dies before receiving all of his or her portion, Trustee shall distribute the remaining portion to the beneficiary's estate. Trustee shall not exercise its discretion hereunder in a manner that would impair a beneficiary's unexercised right of withdrawal that has not yet lapsed, or prevent an existing bequest from qualifying for the marital or charitable deduction, or would prevent an increase in basis (if applicable) under the Code, or would impair the status or qualification of a trust that holds shares of stock in a Subchapter S corporation, or would otherwise impair or prevent a qualified family-owned business interest deduction taken under IRC section 2057, or would otherwise impair or prevent special use valuation under IRC section 2032A.

7.3 Spendthrift Provisions. To the fullest extent permitted by law, a beneficiary's interest in the trust (including income and principal) shall not be subject to the beneficiary's liabilities or creditor claims or an encumbrance, sale, voluntary or involuntary transfer or assignment, anticipation or legal process, or claims for alimony or child support; nor shall the trust be liable for any beneficiary's debt to any agency, public office or department of the State of ________________ or any other state, or of the United States, or to any other creditor of the beneficiary, nor shall the trust be subject to the process of seizure of any court. Moreover, no power of appointment or power of withdrawal shall be subject to involuntary exercise. Furthermore, no part of the trust estate shall be subject to the claims of any creditor for the provision of support, maintenance, care, or services, including residential care, by any public entity, office, department or agency of the State of Michigan, or of any other state, or the United States, or any other governmental agency. However, this spendthrift provision shall not restrict the voluntary exercise of a power of appointment or the voluntary exercise of a withdrawal right granted by this Agreement. This spendthrift provision shall not prevent or prohibit the complete or partial termination of a trust, the amendment, modification or reformation of a trust, or the acceleration of the payment of principal to or for the benefit of a beneficiary. This spendthrift provision shall not prevent the voluntary: (i) sale, (ii) gift or (iii) transfer of a beneficiary's interest in the trust, to: (a) charity, or (b) between family members and/or other trust beneficiaries, if, but only if, such voluntary sale, voluntary gift or voluntary transfer to the charity, family members/and or other trust beneficiaries is pre-approved by Trustee in writing. If Trustee believes that a beneficiary shall not benefit as greatly from any outright distribution of trust income or principal because of the availability of such distribution to the beneficiary's creditors, Trustee shall instead expend those amounts for the benefit of the beneficiary as Trustee in its sole, absolute and uncontrolled discretion determines. However, Trustee may, but need not, without liability or accountability, pay on the order of the beneficiary, any distribution to which the beneficiary may otherwise be entitled to, to those persons the beneficiary directs. It is my intention to insulate all trust funds from the claims of the creditors of the beneficiary and especially involuntary transfers of the trust asset or interests in the trust, to the greatest extent possible under applicable law, while enabling Trustee to give the beneficiary the maximum possible benefit and enjoyment of all of the trust income and principal to which the beneficiary is entitled. The foregoing provisions of this Paragraph 7.3 not withstanding, Trustee shall not exercise its discretion hereunder in a manner that would impair a beneficiary's unexercised right of withdrawal that has not yet lapsed, or would prevent an existing bequest from qualifying for the marital or charitable deduction, or would prevent an increase in basis (if applicable) under the Code, or would impair the status or qualification of a trust that holds shares of stock in a Subchapter S corporation, or would impair or prevent a qualified family owned business interest deduction taken under IRC section 2057, or would impair or prevent special use valuation under IRC section 2032A.

7.4 **Certificate of Trust Existence and Authority.** Trustee may, at any time, record, file, or deliver a Certificate of Trust Existence and Authority ("Certificate") with or to any clerk, register of deeds, transfer agent, or other similar agency or office or to any person dealing with Trustee. The Certificate shall contain a verbatim synopsis of certain provisions of this Agreement and shall be signed and acknowledged by me, Trustee, or an attorney for me or Trustee, and shall be in the form of an affidavit. Any purchaser or person dealing with Trustee shall be entitled to rely on the Certificate as a full statement of the provisions of this Agreement that are pertinent to the particular transaction. Photocopies of the executed Certificate shall have the same effect and authority as the executed Certificate.

7.5 **Multiple Copies.** There is only one (1) signed original of this Agreement. Anyone may rely on a copy of said document as certified by a notary public or similar official to be a true copy of the signed original (and of the amendments or other writings, if any, endorsed on or attached thereto) to the same effect as if such copy were the signed original. Anyone may rely upon any statement of fact certified by anyone who appears from the original document or a certified copy thereof to be a Trustee hereunder.

7.6 **Termination of Trust.** If at any time the size of any trust created under this Agreement is so small that the trust is uneconomical to administer, or if for any other reason in the opinion of Trustee (who is not an Interested Trustee), the trust is no longer necessary, or is impractical, or inappropriate to continue for any reason under the current circumstances, including changes in economic and factual circumstances or changes in federal, state or local rules of law (tax or otherwise), including permanent repeal of the federal estate tax and/or the federal generation skipping transfer tax, or it would not be in the best interests of some or all of the beneficiaries for the trust to continue, such Trustee may, with or without prior or subsequent court approval, terminate part or all of the trust and distribute part or all of the trust funds, as the case may be: (i) to or for the benefit of the primary (or preferred) beneficiary for whom the trust was established, if there is such a beneficiary, or in the absence thereof, to or for the benefit of the person(s) to whom Trustee then must or may pay the trust's current income, in proportion to their interest(s) in trust income; however, if there is more than one beneficiary to whom current income could be paid but the interests are indefinite, Trustee shall distribute the trust assets to or for the benefit of the beneficiaries who are my descendants, by right of representation, or if no descendant of mine is a beneficiary, to all then living income and then living residuary beneficiaries of the trust equally, or (ii) in such other manner or amount(s) as a court of competent jurisdiction may direct, in order to carry out my intentions. Upon such termination, the rights of all other persons who might otherwise have an interest as succeeding life tenant or in a remainder, shall cease. In exercising its authority hereunder, the Disinterested Trustee may distribute all or less than all of the trust assets, while retaining some trust assets in a continuing trust when it appears it may be advantageous or beneficial to the beneficiary (or beneficiaries) to continue to hold such assets in trust. Before terminating a trust hereunder, Trustee may request and shall be entitled to be held harmless and receive appropriate indemnification from the beneficiaries who are going to receive a terminating distribution. Trustee shall not terminate a trust if it would impair a beneficiary's unexercised right of withdrawal that has not yet lapsed, or prevent an existing bequest from qualifying for the marital or charitable deduction, or would prevent an increase in basis (if applicable) under the Code, or would impair the status or qualification of a trust that holds shares of stock in a Subchapter S corporation, or would otherwise impair or prevent a qualified family owned business interest deduction taken under IRC section 2057, or would otherwise impair or prevent special use valuation under IRC section 2032A. Trustee shall not be liable for either exercising or failing to exercise its discretion to terminate a trust.

7.7 Accrued Income. Except as otherwise expressly provided to the contrary, upon the death of a beneficiary, any accrued or undistributed income shall be held and accounted for, or distributed, in the same manner as if it had been received and accrued after the beneficiary's death.

7.8 Right of Representation. Whenever a distribution or division of property is to be made to a person's descendants or issue by "right of representation," or if the manner of distribution or division is not specified, the property shall be divided into as many equal shares as there are (i) then-living descendants in the generation nearest to the designated person that contains one or more then-living descendants and (ii) deceased descendants in the same generation who left then-living descendants, if any. Each then-living descendant in the nearest generation is to be allocated one share. The remaining shares, if any, are to be combined and then divided in the same manner among the then-living descendants of the deceased descendants as if the then-living descendants who were allocated a share and their then-living descendants had predeceased the designated person.

7.9 Accountings and Information to Beneficiaries. Trustee's duty to inform and account to the beneficiaries shall be governed by the following rules.

(A) Recipients of Information and Accountings. While a trust holds, at year end, either (i) unmatured life insurance policies, or (ii) unmatured life insurance policies and cash, marketable securities or other liquid assets with a combined liquid value (excluding any life insurance cash surrender value(s)) of less than fifty thousand ($50,000) dollars, adjusted for the cost-of-living, Trustee shall not be required to prepare or file an annual accounting either with the court or with any beneficiary unless such an accounting is either ordered by a court of competent jurisdiction or is specifically requested in writing by a then living current trust beneficiary who is twenty-five (25) years of age or older, is sui juris, not incapacitated and who is actually then receiving trust distributions (other than distributions of tangible personal property) in which case Trustee shall furnish an accounting to the court or beneficiary consistent with the court's order or the beneficiary's reasonable requirements. Subject to the foregoing, upon the earlier of: (i) life insurance proceeds being received by the trust, or (ii) when the trust holds, at year end, more than fifty thousand ($50,000) dollars of combined value of cash, marketable securities, or other liquid assets (excluding any life insurance cash surrender value(s)), adjusted for the cost-of-living, Trustee shall inform and account to: (i) the current trust beneficiaries who are sui juris, and (ii) to such other persons as may be ordered by a court of competent jurisdiction.

(B) Statement of Account. Trustee shall keep a true account of the affairs of the trust. At least annually and upon termination of the trust or a change of Trustee, Trustee shall (subject to the above provision entitled, "**Recipients of Information and Accountings**"), render a statement of account. The statement of account shall, at a minimum, list the trust assets, if feasible giving their market values, the trust liabilities, receipts, and disbursements, state the source and amount of the trustee's compensation, and inform the beneficiary of the time allowed (to wit, 1 year after the date the beneficiary or a representative of the beneficiary is sent a report that adequately discloses the existence of a potential claim for breach of trust) for commencing a proceeding against a Trustee for breach of trust. The statement of account, if any, shall be delivered as soon as practicable after the close of the accounting period or upon the termination of the trust, or change of Trustee.

(C) Inspection of Records. The books and records of Trustee relating to this Agreement shall be open at all reasonable times to inspection only by the current trust beneficiary or the current trust beneficiary's accredited representatives, unless otherwise ordered by a court having jurisdiction; provided however, during my lifetime, only I (or my designated agent, if I am incapacitated) shall have this right of inspection. The foregoing sentence notwithstanding, upon good cause shown, a court having jurisdiction may order Trustee to keep other beneficiaries reasonably informed of the trust and its administration.

(D) Settlement of the Account. A receipt in full or a release by the beneficiaries or by the conservator or other legal representatives of those beneficiaries who are disabled shall be binding, as to those beneficiaries and as to all matters and transactions stated in the account or shown by it.

(E) Court Approval of Account. Trustee is entitled at any time to have a judicial settlement of its account, and attorney fees, expenses, guardian ad litem fees, and other charges incident to the judicial proceeding may be charged against the trust fund.

(F) Delivery of Accountings. If the current trust beneficiary is another trust, the statement of account shall be delivered to the trustee of the other trust. If any current trust beneficiary is a minor or otherwise disabled, delivery shall be made to the conservator of his or her estate or, if none, then to his or her parent, legal guardian, or nearest of kin or an adult with whom he or she is living. Trustee may deliver the statement of account to other trust beneficiaries in its discretion.

7.10 S Corporation Stock. If any stock of a corporation that then operates or that Trustee shall deem likely to operate in the near future as an S corporation (as defined in IRC section 1361(a)) is held by a trust or becomes distributable to a trust created under this Agreement, and such trust is not eligible or is no longer eligible, or may not be eligible or qualified to hold S corporation stock (for whatever the reason—including because of discretionary authority granted Trustee), Trustee may implement any of the following alternatives with respect to the S corporation stock:

(A) Where the original trust is for a sole beneficiary, Trustee may create for that beneficiary (provided the beneficiary meets the requisite qualifications under IRC section 1361) a separate trust (or sub-trust) that qualifies as a Qualified Subchapter S Trust under IRC section 1361 (d) ("QSST"), and then distribute such stock to the newly created trust.

(B) Where the original trust is for multiple beneficiaries, Trustee may create for each beneficiary (provided the beneficiary meets the requisite qualifications under IRC section 1361): (i) a separate trust, (ii) a separate sub-trust, or

(iii) substantially separate and independent shares for each beneficiary (as is permitted under IRC section 1361(d)(3)), and allocate the S corporation stock among the newly created trusts or shares based on each beneficiary's current interest in the income of the original trust, and if no beneficiary is entitled to current income from the original trust, Trustee may allocate the S corporation stock among the newly created trusts or shares in a manner that Trustee deems fair and appropriate. Each newly created trust or share shall hold that beneficiary's appropriate share of the S corporation stock, and shall qualify as a QSST.

(C) Trustee may, in its discretion: (i) create for a beneficiary (or group of beneficiaries) a separate trust (or sub-trust) that qualifies as an Electing Small Business Trust under IRC section 1361 (e) (provided the beneficiary or group of beneficiaries meet the requisite qualifications thereunder) ("ESBT") and distribute such stock to the newly created trust(s), provided however, no distribution from the newly created trust(s) shall be made to any person (whether a current beneficiary or future or contingent beneficiary) other than to a person who is eligible to be an ESBT beneficiary (as determined under the Code), and the number of "potential current beneficiaries" of the ESBT shall not exceed the number of shareholders permitted under IRC section 1361(b); furthermore, any currently exercisable inter-vivos power of appointment held by a beneficiary concerning the S corporation stock to be held by the ESBT (other than a beneficiary's inter-vivos power of withdrawal) is hereby automatically modified and limited concerning the number and class of appointees eligible to receive the S corporation stock so that the number of actual appointees shall not shall not exceed the number of shareholders permitted under IRC section 1361(b) and the class of appointees shall not include those persons who are ineligible to hold the S corporation stock (as determined under the Code), (ii) elect to qualify any trust as any form of eligible stockholder of an S corporation under current or future legislation, or (iii) distribute such stock to the beneficiaries (provided the beneficiaries are eligible S corporation shareholders) as if the trust had terminated, while continuing to hold any other non-S corporation property in trust.

Each newly created QSST shall have mandatory distributions of income (as defined in IRC section 643(b)) and no one shall have any power to appoint or distribute any portion of the QSST property to anyone other than to the beneficiary of the trust. In all other respects the newly created trusts shall be as consistent as possible with the original trusts and still qualify as QSSTs or ESBTs (as the case may be). Trustee may take any action necessary with regard to S corporations, including making any elections required to qualify stock as S corporation stock, qualify a trust as an S corporation shareholder, and sign all necessary tax returns and forms.

It is my intent that any S corporation stock comprising a portion of the trust estate be eligible to be held pursuant to the terms of this Agreement, either as an ESBT, a QSST, or in any other manner permitted by the Internal Revenue Code or the Regulations or rulings thereunder. Accordingly, Trustee is granted the power to amend, modify or reform this Agreement to the minimum extent necessary to permit this Agreement and its trusts to hold S corporation stock during the continuance of this Agreement in accordance with the Internal Revenue Code, Regulations and rulings thereunder; but in no event shall Trustee amend, modify or reform this Agreement or any trust in a manner that would impair a beneficiary's unexercised right of withdrawal that has not yet lapsed or prevent an existing bequest from qualifying for the marital or charitable deduction or would prevent an increase in basis (if applicable) under the Code, or would impair the status or qualification of a trust that holds shares of stock in a Subchapter S corporation, or would otherwise impair or prevent a qualified family owned business interest deduction taken under IRC section 2057, or would otherwise impair or prevent special use valuation under IRC section 2032A, or prevent a disclaimer from being a qualified disclaimer under IRC section. As a cautionary note, Trustee is reminded that it should determine the effect the exercise of its authority hereunder may have on any disabled or handicapped beneficiary (particularly with regard to the beneficiary's eligibility to receive (or continue to receive) public or private benefits or assistance related to the beneficiary's disability/handicap). I realize that the decision to exercise the discretion granted under this Paragraph is extremely difficult, and, in consideration of Trustee agreeing to serve as a trustee under this Agreement, I specifically exonerate Trustee from any liability to any person with respect to the exercise or non-exercise of the discretion granted under this Paragraph.

Trustee shall not make a distribution of the S corporation stock to any person whose ownership of the stock would reasonably be expected to cause the corporation's Subchapter S election to be terminated. Trustee may (and is encouraged to) request a written opinion from tax counsel if Trustee is uncertain about the effect a contemplated distribution of the S corporation stock may have on the corporation's Subchapter S election.

7.11 Guidelines for Discretionary Distributions. Except as may be otherwise provided elsewhere in this Agreement, when exercising discretion relating to a distribution of income or principal, Trustee (other than an Interested Trustee) may, but need not, consider all other reasonably available income and liquid assets of the beneficiary known upon reasonable inquiry by that Trustee, as well any legal obligation of support owed to the beneficiary by another person. A beneficiary who receives discretionary distributions of income or principal need not deplete income and liquid assets below an amount Trustee deems reasonable.

ARTICLE 8
GENERAL PROVISIONS

8.1 Rule Against Perpetuities.

(A) Measuring Period. Upon the expiration of twenty-one (21) years after the death of the last survivor of a class consisting of me, my descendants, the beneficiaries and contingent beneficiaries under this Agreement, the lineal descendants of such beneficiaries, and the spouses of any of the aforesaid, who are living (or in gestation) on the date on which the interest or trust or power of appointment was created for purposes of the applicable Rule Against Perpetuities, every trust created under this Agreement, by the exercise of a power of appointment or otherwise, every power of appointment granted by this Agreement, and every interest, trust or power of appointment that may be created by the exercise of a power of appointment granted herein, shall terminate, if it has not then vested indefeasibly (as provided in paragraph item (B) below) or previously terminated; provided however, this provision shall not apply to any interest established by the exercise of a general power of appointment conferred by this Agreement if the exercise is valid both under this Agreement and under the applicable Rule Against Perpetuities, and under the applicable Rule Against Perpetuities such interest is allowed a new perpetuities period, in which case, the interest established by the general power of appointment shall terminate as provided in the instrument in which such power is exercised, subject to the Rule Against Perpetuities (if any) that may be applicable to such newly established interest. The exercise of any non-general power of appointment granted under this Agreement shall be subject to the perpetuities period of this Agreement and shall not be extended by the exercise of such power.

(B) Vesting of Trust Interests Prior to Expiration of Perpetuities Period. If on the day preceding the expiration of the applicable rules limiting the maximum duration of trusts (such as any rules governing perpetuities, vesting, accumulations or the suspension of alienation), any property is held in trust (except any trust all of the assets of which are then unqualifiedly withdrawable by its primary beneficiary), such property shall immediately vest indefeasibly in (i) the primary beneficiary for whom the trust was established, if there is such a beneficiary, or in the absence of a primary beneficiary to the person(s) to whom Trustee then must or may pay the trust's current income, in proportion to their interest(s) in trust income; however, if there is more than one beneficiary to whom current income could be paid but the interests are indefinite, the trust property shall vest indefeasibly in the beneficiaries who are my descendants, by right of representation, or if no descendant of mine is a beneficiary, then the trust property shall vest indefeasibly in all of the then living income and then living residuary beneficiaries of the trust equally, or (ii) in such other persons or amount(s) as a court of competent jurisdiction may direct, in order to carry out my intentions. For purposes of this Paragraph, to "vest indefeasibly" means that the interest shall continue in trust but be subject to a general power of appointment held by the beneficiary and exercisable by will or by deed at any time in favor of any person (including the beneficiary, the beneficiary's estate or the creditors of either), and if the interest continues in trust until its termination, the interest, in default of appointment, shall be paid to the beneficiary, if living or, if not living to the beneficiary's estate.

8.2 Power of Appointment Matters.

(A) Scope of Appointment. Except as otherwise limited, any trust principal or income as to which a power of appointment is exercised shall be distributed to one or more members of the permissible class of appointees upon such conditions and estates, in such manner (in trust, to an existing trust, to a trust to be created, or otherwise), with such powers, in such amounts or proportions (equal or unequal), and at such time or times as the holder of the power (donee) may specify in the instrument exercising the power (but not beyond the period permitted by any applicable rules limiting the maximum duration of trusts (such as any rules governing perpetuities, vesting, accumulations or the suspension of alienation)). Unless the instrument exercising a power of appointment explicitly states that if an appointee is deceased that the appointment is in favor of the appointee's descendants (or explicit words of similar import and intent), any power of appointment exercised in favor of a deceased appointee shall lapse and a surviving descendant of the deceased appointee shall not be substituted for the deceased appointee. The donee may appoint a different trustee to administer a trust created by the exercise of the power and may change the situs of the trust administration and direct that the trust shall be governed by the law of the new situs or any other jurisdiction. The trustee under an appointment in further trust may be any person not prohibited from serving as Trustee under this Agreement and may be given fiduciary powers (including discretionary powers over distributions), exercisable, however, only in favor of permissible objects of the exercised power. If the donee does not direct otherwise, a trust created by the exercise of the power shall be administered by the trustee hereof subject to the same management powers conferred on the trustee. With respect to any sub-trusts or trusts that have been divided, the donee may exercise his or her power differently with respect to each sub-trust or separate trusts (even otherwise identical trusts) derived from the original or divided trust. No power of appointment may be exercised by any individual under this Agreement with respect to policies of insurance on the life of such individual, or the proceeds thereof, unless such policies or proceeds would be includible in the individual's gross estate (for federal estate tax purposes) at such individual's death without regard to such power of appointment.

(B) Manner of Exercise and Determination of Effective Appointment. Except as may be explicitly required otherwise in this Agreement, any power, including a power of appointment, granted to a person under this Agreement may be exercised either by (i) such individual by his or her last will and testament or (ii) a written direction other than a will executed by such person or such person's duly authorized and empowered legal representative and delivered to Trustee during the person's lifetime (or such other period required by the power) (hereinafter referred to as a "written direction"), which will or written direction makes specific reference to the power of appointment sought to be exercised so that Trustee is able to sufficiently and correctly identify which power under this Agreement is in fact being exercised by the donee. Except as provided otherwise in this Agreement, a power of appointment may be effectively exercised: (i) even if the donee is a minor, incapacitated or under disability, (ii) all of the assets constituting the trust with respect to which the power is granted have not been received by Trustee, or (iii) whether the instrument exercising the power is executed before or after the date on which any trust for the donee is created (including a trust in which the donee is granted the power). Any instrument exercising the power may be revoked or amended at any time before it becomes effective. Trustee may rely upon any instrument that is admitted to probate in any jurisdiction as the last will of the donee; and may distribute the property as provided herein in default of an effective appointment by will if, within six (6) months after the date of the donee's death, Trustee has not received a certified copy of the donee's will that has been admitted to probate and that purports to exercise the power; but the Trustee shall not be required to make any distribution to those who take in default of an effective appointment if Trustee is reasonably in doubt about whether there has been an effective exercise of the power. The provisions in the preceding sentence are for the protection of the Trustee and shall not affect any right or recourse that an appointee or beneficiary in default of appointment may have against any recipient(s) of the distributed property. Admission of a will to probate within six (6) months after the donee's death shall not be a condition to the effective exercise of a power.

(C) **Trust Termination and Limited Power of Appointment by Special Power Holder.** Each trust may, from time to time, have a special power holder. A special power holder may be appointed: (i) by me, in a writing delivered to the Trustee of the trust in question, (ii) by a majority in interest of the current trust beneficiaries of the trust in question, with one (1) vote being cast by each such beneficiary who is sui juris, one (1) vote being cast for each such minor beneficiary by his or her custodial parent, and one (1) vote being cast by the legal guardian for any such beneficiary having a legal guardian, (iii) by the Trustee then serving of the trust in question, or (iv) by a court of competent jurisdiction. Once appointed, a special power holder may not be removed except by a court of competent jurisdiction and then only for reasonable cause. A special power holder appointed by me shall serve prior to a special power holder appointed hereunder by any other person. In the event that two or more instruments of appointment concerning a special power holder exist and are inconsistent, the latest by date shall control, consistent with the priority of appointment specified above, and any inconsistencies in appointment maybe resolved by the unanimous decision of the existing Trustees and then nominated successor Trustees of the trust in question.

After my death, the special power holder may terminate a trust, in whole or in part, pursuant to the criteria set forth in the Paragraph entitled, **"Termination of Trust."** Furthermore, after my death, Trustee shall distribute all or any part of the trust estate (other than life insurance on the special power holder's life) as the special power holder (in a non-fiduciary capacity) from time to time appoints in a writing that is delivered to Trustee, to any one or more of the trust's beneficiaries, including contingent remainder beneficiaries (but not to the special power holder, the special power holder's estate, or the creditors of either) and in such proportions (equal or unequal) and in such manner (whether out right or in trust) as the special power holder specifies. Provided, however, that no such distribution may be applied or distributed that would give the special power holder any pecuniary benefit or would discharge or satisfy the special power holder's legal obligations. Any person serving or appointed to serve as a special power holder must not be related or subordinate (within the meaning of IRC section 672 (c)) to me or to any beneficiary of the trust in question. A special power holder (then acting or nominated) may resign at any time by giving written notice, specifying the effective date of resignation to Trustee of the trust in question or to any current income beneficiary of the trust in question. If the special power holder is incapacitated, then he or she will be deemed to have automatically resigned as special power holder.

Notwithstanding any other provision of this Agreement, the special power holder shall not exercise any power or discretion conferred under this Agreement: (i) for the direct or indirect benefit of the special power holder, the special power holder's estate, or the creditors of either, (ii) that would cause the special power holder to possess a general power of appointment within the meaning of IRC sections 2041 and 2514, (iii) that would impair a beneficiary's outstanding withdrawal right that has not yet lapsed, (iv) that would prevent an existing bequest from qualifying (or continuing to qualify) for the marital or charitable deduction or would prevent an increase in basis (if applicable) under the Internal Revenue Code, (v) that would impair the status or qualification of a trust that holds shares of stock in a Subchapter S corporation, (vi) that would otherwise impair or prevent a qualified family owned business interest deduction taken under IRC section 2057, (vii) would otherwise impair or prevent special use valuation under IRC section 2032A, or (viii) would prevent a disclaimer from being a qualified disclaimer under IRC section 2518. The special power holder, acting in its capacity hereunder, shall have no fiduciary duty to any trust beneficiary and shall be indemnified and held harmless by the trust and the beneficiaries who are going to be benefited by the exercise of the special power holder's authority hereunder.

(D) Compelled Exercise of Power of Appointment Not Effective. The purported exercise of a power of appointment (including a power of withdrawal) granted under this Agreement shall be of no force or effect if such purported exercise was the result of compulsion. If such purported exercise is the result of compulsion, Trustee shall administer the property subject to such power of appointment as if said purported exercise had not occurred. The purported exercise of a power of appointment shall be deemed to be the result of compulsion if such purported exercise is in response to or by reason of any order or other direction of any court having jurisdiction over the donee, Trustee, the property subject to said power or the trust containing such property. A donee's legal representative may not exercise a power given to the donee under this Agreement if such purported exercise is in response to or by reason of any such order or other direction of any court having jurisdiction over the legal representative unless such order or other direction was obtained by the legal representative in a proceeding in which the legal representative was the petitioner or voluntarily acquiesced and was not otherwise under compulsion.

8.3 Law, Definitions, Captions, and Severability.

(A) Governing Law. Except as otherwise provided in this Paragraph 8.3(A), the validity, administration, meaning and effect, and all rights of beneficiaries under this

Agreement and its provisions (and any other instrument related to this Agreement) shall be governed by the laws of the State of ________________. The administration, meaning and effect, and rights of beneficiaries under a trust established by the exercise of a power of appointment granted hereunder shall be governed by the laws of whatever jurisdiction may be designated either in such instrument of appointment or in the resulting trust (or, absent such designation, by the laws of the State of__________). This Paragraph 8.3(A) shall apply regardless of any change of residence of any Trustee or any beneficiary, or the appointment or substitution of a Trustee residing in another jurisdiction. Trustee may, with the prior written consent of a majority of the trust's current beneficiaries who are sui juris and not incapacitated, change the situs of such trust and/or its assets and elect to have the validity, administration, meaning and effect or rights of beneficiaries of such trust and/or its assets be governed by the laws of another jurisdiction, in or outside the United States (including that jurisdiction's law concerning the maximum duration of trusts). Trustee may not change the situs of a trust, the trust's assets or the trust's governing law in order to: (i) thwart the purpose of the trust, or (ii) limit Trustee's liability to a beneficiary due to an existing breach of duty. The jurisdiction whose laws govern the validity, meaning and effect, and rights of beneficiaries of any trust may, but need not, be the same as the situs of the trust's assets or the situs of the administration of such trust. This Agreement shall be exempt from mandatory registration (although Trustee may, in its discretion register any trust). Absent a written request from a current trust beneficiary who is sui juris and not incapacitated, Trustee who is an individual shall not be required to determine if the situs of a trust or its assets should be moved from its current jurisdiction to a different jurisdiction or if the governing law of the trust or its assets should be changed.

(B) Gender. Whenever necessary in this Agreement and where the context permits, the singular term and the related pronoun shall include the plural (particularly as concerns my

Spouse, if my Spouse is a donor), the masculine, and the feminine, and, as to Trustee, the neuter.

(C) Charity. The term "charity" or "charitable organization" means an organization so constituted that gratuitous transfers to such organization are deductible, in the first instance, as charitable transfers for federal income, estate (if the Federal estate tax is applicable), or gift tax purposes (as the case may be).

(D) Child, Issue, and Descendants. For purposes of determining who is a child, grandchild or descendant of any person (including myself):

(1) The term "issue" or "descendants" means all individuals who are descended from the individual referred to in the first, second, or any other degree, provided the individual in each degree in the line of descent is a child, as defined below, of the individual in the prior degree.

(2) The term "child" means a descendant in the first degree of the parent designated; but such term does not include a stepchild, a foster child, a grandchild or any more remote descendant, unless that individual is adopted as a child (as set forth below).

(3) Subject to the above provisions:

(a) Any adoption begun before the adopting parent's death (i.e., the child has been "placed" with the adopting parent), if the adoption is legally completed by the (deceased) person's spouse within two (2) years after such death (provided the adopted child is under the age of eighteen (18) at the date of adoption) shall be deemed accomplished prior to death.

(b) Posthumous children are to be considered living at the death of their parent.

(E) Current Trust Beneficiary. "Current trust beneficiary" means a beneficiary about which either items (i) or (ii) below, is true: (i) the beneficiary has a current right to receive all or a portion of a mandatory distribution of income, or the beneficiary is currently eligible to receive a discretionary distribution of all or a portion of income; or (ii) the beneficiary is currently eligible to receive all or a portion of a mandatory or discretionary distribution of principal. A "current income beneficiary" is a beneficiary described in item (i), above. If an action under this Agreement must be (or is permitted to be) taken, exercised, affirmed or is referenced by the trust's "current income beneficiaries" and there are no current income beneficiaries of the trust in question (or there are no current income beneficiaries of the trust in question who are eligible to act), then and in that event, the current trust beneficiaries shall act in place of the "current income beneficiaries," and the current trust beneficiaries shall be subject to the same qualifications and limitations that are imposed upon the current income beneficiaries, such as "majority, "sui juris," "not incapacitated," "of the trust in question," etc. In no event may I act on behalf of a current trust beneficiary, regardless of my relationship to the beneficiary.

(F) **Death Taxes**. "Death taxes" means all estate, inheritance, succession, legacy, transfer or similar duties or taxes and any income or similar taxes on appreciation incurred solely as the result of my death, as well as any and all interest and penalties relating to such duties or taxes which are properly imposed by any federal, state, domestic or foreign taxing authority. "Death taxes" do not include any generation-skipping transfer tax.

(G) **Health, Education, Support and Maintenance.** "Health, education, support, and maintenance" shall be construed in such a manner as to be an ascertainable standard for federal estate and gift tax purposes, such that the exercise, release, or lapse of a power which is limited by this standard will not be taxable for federal estate and gift tax purposes. If Trustee has discretionary authority to make distributions for a beneficiary's health, education, support and maintenance, those standards shall constitute a ceiling on Trustee's discretionary authority, and shall not be interpreted as a floor that mandates distribution, i.e., Trustee's discretion is to be limited to matters pertaining to the beneficiary's health, education, support and maintenance. In determining "support" for a beneficiary, Trustee may take into account the obligations of support that the beneficiary owes to other individuals. "Health" shall include (but not be limited to) medical, mental, dental, hospital, and nursing expenses and expenses of invalidism.

(H) **Incapacity**. In the event that any Trustee or any beneficiary hereunder comes into possession of any of the following: (i) a court order, which such Trustee or beneficiary deems to be jurisdictionally proper and still currently applicable, holding a person to be legally incapacitated to act in his or her own behalf or appointing a guardian or conservator of the person or property (or similar fiduciary) to act for him or her, or (ii) a written report of a licensed psychologist, a licensed medical or osteopathic physician stating that he or she has examined a person and has concluded that such person is unable to give prompt and intelligent consideration to financial matters because of excessive use of drugs or alcohol, accident, physical or mental illness, progressive or intermittent physical or mental deterioration, or other similar cause, or (iii) evidence which such Trustee deems to be credible and still currently applicable that a person has disappeared, is unaccountably absent, is incarcerated, or is being detained under duress where he or she is unable to effectively manage his or her property or financial affairs; then and in that event and under those circumstances: (a) such person shall be deemed to have thereupon become "incapacitated", as that term is used in and for all of the purposes of this Agreement, and (b) such incapacity shall be deemed to continue until such court order, written reports, and/or circumstances have become inapplicable or have been revoked.

(1) Any psychologist's or physician's aforesaid report may be revoked by a similar report to the effect that such person is no longer thus incapacitated executed either (i) by the originally certifying psychologist or physician or (ii) by another licensed, unrelated psychologist or physician.

(2) No Trustee shall be under any duty to institute any inquiry into a person's possible incapacity, but the expense of any such inquiry reasonably instituted may be paid from trust assets.

(3) Each person who signs this instrument or an acceptance of Trusteeship or Trust Protector hereunder (a "Consenting Person"), by so signing: (i) consents to and agrees to cooperate in any medical examination necessary to carry out the terms of this provision; (ii) waives all provisions of law relating to disclosure of confidential medical information insofar as that disclosure would be pertinent to any inquiry under this provision, and directs all health care providers to complete the certification required by this provision; (iii) agrees that all individually identifiable health information and medical records (except psychotherapy notes) of the Consenting Person, including any written opinion relating to the Consenting Person's capacity/incapacity or ability to serve as a Trustee (or Trust Protector) that the requesting party has requested, may be released to the following people (a "Requesting Party"), whom the Consenting party hereby appoints as their personal representative in that regard, to wit, a then acting Co-Trustee hereunder, a nominated successor Trustee hereunder, a then acting Trust Protector hereunder, or a nominated successor Trust Protector hereunder. This release authority applies to any information governed by the Health Insurance Portability and Accountability Act of 1996 (aka HIPAA), 42 U.S.C. §1320d et seq. and 45 C.F.R. 160-164, and applies even if the Requesting Party has not yet been appointed as a successor Trustee or successor Trust Protector, as the case may be; and (iv) agrees that the obligations under this provision shall be specifically enforceable. The Requesting Party need not describe the purpose of each request made, but may simply note it is made at his or her request, as allowed under the HIPAA rules. This HIPAA authorization is effective immediately, shall not expire (except upon the death of the Consenting

Party), but may be revoked by a written instrument executed by the Consenting Party. If this HIPAA authorization is revoked, any person or entity acting in good faith in reliance upon it, and lacking actual knowledge of its revocation, shall be held harmless by the Consenting Party. The Consenting Party understands that once the above information is disclosed, it may be re-disclosed by the Requesting Party, and that the information may not be protected by privacy laws or regulations. The Consenting Party acknowledges that authorizing the use or disclosure of this information is their voluntary act. The Consenting Party understands and acknowledges that a health care provider may not condition the Consenting Party's receipt of health care or medical treatment upon his or her authorization (or lack thereof) under the terms of this provision. If a Consenting Party fails within a reasonable time to cooperate hereunder (including having a medical examination and disclosing its results to a Requesting Party), then such Consenting Party shall be deemed to have resigned as a Trustee or Trust Protector (as the case may be), provided at the time the request was made by the Requesting Party there was a reasonable basis to request such medical examination, and provided further that no such request (in which the Consenting Party cooperated) may be made more than once every twenty-four (24) months. To the extent the cost of the medical examination is not paid for by the Consenting Party's health insurance (including Medicare, Medicaid, or other third party provider), the trust shall pay such costs (and may pay all the costs of the medical examination).

(I) Independent Trustee. An "Independent Trustee" means a person: (i) who is not related or subordinate (within the meaning of IRC section 672 (c)) to any beneficiary, power holder (including a person who holds the power to remove a Trustee), or transferor (as defined below) (as the case may be regarding the identity of the appropriate "power holder") with respect to the trust in question; (ii) who cannot be benefited by the exercise or non-exercise of any power given Trustee by this Agreement or by law; (iii) who is not a beneficiary of the trust in question, not an insured under a policy of life insurance owned by the trust, not a person who is prohibited from serving as a trustee of the trust in question, and is not an individual who has gratuitously transferred or joined in the gratuitous transfer of property to the trust in question (a "transferor"); and (iv) if a general power of appointment is held by a beneficiary that may only be exercised with the consent of an Independent Trustee, the term "Independent Trustee" also means a person who is not the creator of the power and who does not have a substantial interest in the property subject to the power which is otherwise adverse to the exercise of the power in favor of the beneficiary, the beneficiary's estate, or the creditors of either (as the case may be) within the meaning of IRC sections 2514(c) and 2041(b) and Treas. Reg. sections 25.2514-3(b)(2) and 20.2041-(3)(c)(2). A transferor's spouse who merely consents to gift splitting under IRC section 2513 concerning the transferor's transfer of property to the trust shall not be deemed to have "joined in the transfer of property."

(J) Interested Trust Beneficiary. "Interested trust beneficiary" means a person that has one (1) or more of the following interests in the trust: (i) life estate, (ii) eligible recipient of a mandatory or discretionary distribution by the Trustee of income or principal, (iii) eligible recipient of a mandatory or discretionary distribution by the Trustee of income or principal upon termination of an interest of a person described in items (i) or (ii) above, or (iv) presently exercisable or current testamentary general or special power of appointment.

(K) Interested Trustee and Disinterested Trustee. "Interested Trustee" means for any trust a Trustee who is (i) a transferor of property to the trust, including a person whose disclaimer resulted in property passing to the trust; or (ii) a person who is, or in the future may be, eligible to receive income or principal pursuant to the terms of the trust. A Trustee described in item (i) above is an Interested

Trustee only with respect to the transferred property (including income and gain on, and reinvestment of, such property). A person is included in item (ii) above if he or she has a remote contingent remainder, but a person is not included in item (ii) above if the person's only interest is as a potential appointee under a power of appointment held by another individual in his or her non-fiduciary capacity, the exercise of which will take effect only in the future, such as a testamentary power of appointment held by a living individual or the person's only interest is as a potential distributee under the Paragraph entitled, "**Absence of Beneficiaries**." A trustee who is not an Interested Trustee is a "Disinterested Trustee." An Independent Trustee is a "Disinterested Trustee." If a general power of appointment held by a beneficiary may only be exercised with the consent of a Disinterested Trustee, the term "Disinterested Trustee" also means a person who is not the creator of the power and who does not have a substantial interest in the property subject to the power which is adverse to the exercise of the power in favor of the beneficiary, the beneficiary's estate, or the creditors of either (as the case may be) within the meaning of IRC sections 2514 (c) and 2041(b) and Treas. Reg. sections 25.2514-3(b)(2) and 20.2041-(3)(c)(2).

(L) Internal Revenue Code. References to "Code," "Internal Revenue Code," "IRC" (or similar abbreviations) or to provisions thereof are to the Internal Revenue Code of 1986, as amended at the time in question. References to the "Regulations" or "Treas. Treas. Reg. " are to the Treasury Regulations under the Code. If, by the time in question, a particular provision of the Code has been renumbered or the Code has been superseded by a subsequent federal tax law, the reference shall be deemed to be to the renumbered provision or the corresponding provision of the subsequent law, unless to do so would clearly be contrary to my intent as expressed in this Agreement, and a similar rule shall apply to references to the Regulations. All tax-related terms shall have the same meaning that they have in the Code.

(M) May, Must and Shall. Unless expressly provided otherwise in this Agreement concerning distributions to the beneficiary in question (or class of beneficiaries), Trustee shall exercise its authority (and discretion) to make distributions of trust income or principal in accordance with the terms and purposes of the trust, subject to the following:

(1) "May" is discretionary; and unless the discretion is made "sole," "absolute" or "uncontrolled," Trustee must act reasonably and in good faith. If the discretion is made "sole," "absolute" or "uncontrolled," Trustee must act honestly, in good faith, and not recklessly or capriciously.

(2) Unless expressly provided otherwise in this Agreement concerning distributions to the beneficiary in question (or class of beneficiaries), when making discretionary distributions where Trustee's discretion is "sole," absolute," or "uncontrolled," Trustee may, but need not, consider any other income or resources readily available to that beneficiary.

(3) Unless expressly provided otherwise in this Agreement concerning distributions to the beneficiary in question (or class of beneficiaries), when making distributions (including discretionary distributions) limited to a beneficiary's health, education, support or maintenance (or similar ascertainable standard), Trustee shall consider any other income or resources readily available to that beneficiary for such purposes and take into consideration the standard of living of the beneficiary.

(4) Except as otherwise qualified or restricted, "must" is mandatory, and "shall" is mandatory.

(N) Sui Juris. An individual who has the legal capacity to mange his or her own affairs and is not under a legal disability to act for one's self (such as minority, a guardianship, committee or conservatorship, etc.) is an individual who is sui juris.

(O) Then Living. The term "then living," when used in any provision in this Agreement, refers to the time when the event necessitating reference to such provision occurred rather than to the subsequent time when the directions of such provision may actually be implemented.

(P) **Trust.** "Trust," without further qualification or specification, shall refer to all trusts under this Agreement, and to the assets of any such trust or trusts.

(Q) **Captions.** Captions in this Agreement are used for convenience and shall not limit, broaden, or qualify the text.

(R) **Provisions Severable.** The provisions of this Agreement are severable. If any provision is determined to be invalid, all other provisions shall remain valid. Trustee may modify any provision determined to be invalid, illegal or unenforceable to the minimum extent necessary to remedy such provision.

(S) **Counterparts.** This Agreement may be executed in any number of counterpart signature pages, all of which together will constitute the entire, original document.

8.4 Disclaimer by Beneficiary. Any beneficiary may disclaim any property, interests in property, proceeds of property, disclaimable interest, or power of appointment (whether presently exercisable or not). A beneficiary who disclaims any property, interests in property, proceeds of property, disclaimable interest, or power of appointment (whether presently exercisable or not) shall not retain, possess, or exercise any interest in or power over the disclaimed property, either during lifetime or upon death (whether as a beneficiary or as a trustee), which interest or power is prohibited by law (such as interests or powers prohibited by IRC section 2518 (as concerns qualified disclaimers)). For example, if the disclaim property devolves to a foundation and the disclaimant is an officer, director, trustee or "control person" of the foundation, then and in that event, the disclaimed property shall be held in a separate fund by the foundation and the disclaimant shall only serve as an Administrative Director/Trustee with respect to the fund. An Administrative Director/Trustee is only authorized to take such actions as are necessary to preserve and maintain the property within the meaning of Treas. Reg. section 25.2518-2(d)(2), and, accordingly, is prohibited from participating in the exercise, or decision not to exercise, any discretion over payments, distributions, applications or accumulations of income or principal by the foundation's directors/trustees, including the selection of the ultimate charitable beneficiaries of the separate fund.

8.5 Actions by Incapacitated or Minor Beneficiaries. Except as may otherwise be provided elsewhere in this Agreement, a minor beneficiary, or a beneficiary who is legally incapacitated, or a beneficiary who is under a under a disability, may act through his or her authorized representative (to the extent such authorized representative is not prohibited from acting on behalf of the beneficiary), including (but not limited to) a natural or legal guardian, committee, conservator, agent, next friend, or attorney-in-fact under a durable power of attorney (as the case may be). If there is no such authorized representative, Trustee may designate an appropriate adult individual (who may be Trustee, a trust officer, a relative of the beneficiary, or any other person) who (to the extent not prohibited from acting on behalf of the beneficiary) may act on behalf of the beneficiary. In no event may I act on behalf of such beneficiary, regardless of my relationship to the beneficiary.

8.6 Virtual Representation. I direct that, in any proceeding relating to a trust hereunder, service upon any person under a legal disability need not be made when another person not under a disability is a party to the proceeding and has the same interest as the person under the disability. The person under the disability shall nevertheless be bound by the results of the proceeding. The same rule shall apply to non-judicial settlements, releases, exonerations and indemnities.

8.7 Arbitration. Whenever a matter is required under this Agreement to be submitted to arbitration, the following rules shall apply. The arbitration shall be held, except as may otherwise be provided herein, in accordance with the Uniform Arbitration Act (or such similar act) as adopted by the State of ____________ (or the state whose law is then governing the administration of the trust, as described in the sub-paragraph entitled, **"Governing Law"**). The rules of arbitration shall be decided by the arbitrator. The parties shall select a single arbitrator for this purpose. To be qualified to be selected as an arbitrator: (i) a person must be well versed and knowledgeable in the area of trust law, or (ii) a person with expertise in the subject matter of the dispute (e.g., a professional appraiser if the dispute involves valuation). If the parties cannot agree on an arbitrator, a party can petition the probate court having jurisdiction over the trust and request the probate court to appoint a qualified arbitrator (who need not reside in the same county as the probate court). If the place of arbitration can not be agreed upon by the parties, then the place of arbitration shall be in the metropolitan [Name of City and State] area as decided by the arbitrator. If at the time of the dispute the trust's governing law is the State of ______________, the rules of discovery as set forth in that State's rules of civil procedure shall be available in connection with the arbitration, and the law of the State of ______________law will govern the rights and obligations of the parties with respect to the matters in controversy. The award of the arbitrator shall be accompanied by a written statement of the basis for such award and may be enforced by any court having proper jurisdiction.

ARTICLE 9
SURVIVAL AND ANTI-LAPSE

9.1 Survival of Beneficiary. Except as provided in sub-paragraph (A) below, no person shall be considered to have survived another or considered to be living upon the death of another if he or she shall die within 120 hours after the death of such other.

(A) Exceptions. Where Treas. Reg. section 26.2651-1(a)(2)(iii) applies.

9.2 Negation of Anti-Lapse Statute. A gift fails if an individual beneficiary does not satisfy a condition of survival and there is no substitute beneficiary indicated in this Agreement who satisfies the conditions for taking. The provisions of an anti-lapse statute shall not apply to preserve a gift for an individual or individuals who are not identified as a substitute or substitutes in this Agreement.

ARTICLE 10
MY FAMILY

10.1 Spouse. I am married to «SpouseFullName» at the time this Agreement is executed. For purposes of this Agreement, "my Spouse" refers to «SpouseFullName».

10.2 Children. My children as of the date of this Agreement are:

- «Child1» (DOB: «Child1DOB»)
- «Child2» (DOB: «Child2DOB»)

I have no other children or any deceased children with descendants surviving.

This Agreement is executed, delivered, and the trust accepted, on «DateofExecution».

WITNESSES:

______________________________	______________________________
«ExecutingWitness»	«SettlorFullName», Settlor
______________________________	______________________________
«ExecutingWitness»	«InitialTrustee», Trustee

ACKNOWLEDGMENT BY SPOUSE

I, «SpouseFullName», understand that this trust may hold policies that insure my life, and if that should occur, or if I am a donor, I acknowledge that I will be subject to the provisions of Paragraph 1.4, entitled, **"Restriction on My Spouse."**

____

«SpouseFullName»

STATE OF)
)ss.
COUNTY OF)

Subscribed and sworn to before me on «DateofExecution» by «SettlorFullName», «SpouseFullName» and «InitialTrustee», who personally appeared before me. «SettlorFullName», «SpouseFullName» and «InitialTrustee» are personally known to me (or have produced ____ as identification).

____

Notary Public

__________________________County, ____________

Acting in the County of _________________________

My Commission expires: _______________________

SCHEDULE A

Property Transferred to The «SettlorFullName» Irrevocable Trust, dated «DateofExecution»

With regard to any group term policies listed herein, the transfer of such policies also includes any future policies to be issued, or policies in supplementation thereof, or in succession, substitution, replacement or renewed thereof, and any increase in the amount of coverage.

(This Schedule A is included only for the convenience of Trustee and beneficiaries, and any failure to list trust assets on Schedule A will in no way alter the trust's ownership of those assets.)

DATE	ITEM	VALUE	TAX BASIS

Appendix 3

SAMPLE IRREVOCABLE LIFE INSURANCE TRUST FOR AN UNMARRIED PERSON WITH DESCENDANTS

Note: This form is a sample irrevocable life insurance trust that is designed to hold policy on the life of an unmarried person with descendants. The trust is designed to be GST tax exempt, but because of the hanging *Crummey* withdrawal rights may **not** qualify as a GST Trust (to which the grantor's GST tax exemption will be automatically allocated). Therefore, the transferor will need to annually allocate his or her GST tax exemption to contributions or will need to make a one time election on IRS Form 709 to have the trust be treated as a GST Trust (*see*, "GST Trust Election Statement" in Appendix 4). The trust contains a hanging *Crummey* right of withdrawal, and permits a donor to make gift contributions to the beneficiaries up to the annual exclusion amount. Optional and alternate language is contained in brackets { }.

This form is designed to be an adjunct to (and not a substitution for) the grantor's base estate plan, such as a revocable living trust. This form should not be used as a pour-over from a person's probate estate, will, or other trust.

Practice Note: Michigan practitioners should note that the sample forms complies with Michigan's Estates and Protected Individuals Code, which went into effect April 1, 2000.

As this is a sample form, practitioners must be careful when using the form to adapt it to comply with new developments in federal and state estate, gift and generation-skipping transfer tax law and to modify it to comply with applicable state law and the particular requirements and needs of their client; accordingly, the author makes no representations or warranties as to the efficacy of the form.

THE «SETTLORFULLNAME» IRREVOCABLE TRUST

ARTICLE 1
CREATION AND FUNDING THE TRUST

ARTICLE 2
IRREVOCABILITY

ARTICLE 3
WITHDRAWAL RIGHTS

ARTICLE 4
DISTRIBUTION DURING LIFETIME

ARTICLE 5
DISTRIBUTION AFTER DEATH

ARTICLE 6
TRUSTEES

ARTICLE 7
TRUSTEE POWERS AND TRUST ADMINISTRATION

7.10 S Corporation Stock

7.11 Guidelines for Discretionary Distributions

ARTICLE 8
GENERAL PROVISIONS

8.1 Rule Against Perpetuities

8.2 Power of Appointment Matters

8.3 Law, Definitions, Captions, and Severability

8.4 Disclaimer by Beneficiary

8.5 Actions by Incapacitated or Minor Beneficiaries

8.6 Virtual Representation

8.7 Arbitration

ARTICLE 9
SURVIVAL AND ANTI-LAPSE

9.1 Survival of Beneficiary

9.2 Negation of Anti-Lapse Statute

ARTICLE 10
MY FAMILY

10.1 Single Person

10.2 Children

[Revised thru 06182007]

THE «SETTLORFULLNAME» IRREVOCABLE TRUST

Name of Trust: The «SettlorFullName» Irrevocable Trust, dated «DateofExecution»

Initial Trustee: «InitialTrustee»

Successor Trustees: «AltTrustee1»

«AltTrustee2»

«AltTrustee3»

«AltTrustee4»

Date of Execution: «DateofExecution»

I, «SettlorFullName», on «DateofExecution», sign this Trust Agreement ("Agreement") with «InitialTrustee» as trustee (who, and any successor trustee, substitute trustee, or co-trustee, will be called "Trustee" in this Agreement and referred to in singular neuter pronouns), on the following terms and conditions. The original trust established hereunder by me is hereinafter sometimes referred to as the "initial trust."

ARTICLE 1
CREATION AND FUNDING THE TRUST

1.1 Creation of Trust. I create this trust as a means by which assets, which may include one (1) or more policies of insurance on my life, the life of any other person, or the joint lives of two or more persons, directly or indirectly in any arrangement deemed appropriate by Trustee, may be held for the benefit of my beneficiaries, on the terms and conditions set forth in this Agreement. It is my intent in creating this trust that all gifts made to this trust by me (directly or indirectly) be both complete and generally gifts of present interests for federal gift tax purposes. All provisions of this trust shall be construed in such a manner as best to affect these intents. Accordingly, no power enumerated herein or accorded to trustees, or granted pursuant to law, whether singularly, jointly or as a whole, shall be construed:

(A) To enable me: (i) to become a Trustee hereunder (or to possess or exercise any powers of such office), (ii) to vote any stock described in IRC section 2036(b) which may at any time be directly or indirectly given to any trust hereunder, (iii) to possess or exercise any power of appointment (including a right of withdrawal) with respect to any such trust, (iv) to possess, exercise or retain any power or interest described in IRC sections 2036, 2037 and 2038, (v) if I am the insured under any policy of insurance held by any trust hereunder, to exercise any incident of ownership within the meaning of IRC section 2042 with respect to that policy held by the trust, (vi) to receive any distributions on behalf of a beneficiary (regardless of my relationship to the beneficiary), or (vii) to possess or exercise any rights or discretion granted to a beneficiary hereunder; and

(B) To permit any trust distribution which would have the effect of discharging any legal obligation of mine (including any obligation that I may have at any time relating to the support and/or education of any beneficiary hereunder).

1.2 Transfer of Property to Trust. I hereby irrevocably transfer and assign to Trustee the property listed in **SCHEDULE A**, to be held and administered according to the terms of this trust. In connection with the transfer of any life insurance policies to Trustee, I agree to execute, in addition to an appropriate assignment of ownership form, any and all other instruments necessary or appropriate to permit Trustee to exercise all rights, powers, options, privileges or incidents of ownership that I may have had as the owner of such policies. With regard to any group term policies assigned to Trustee, the transfer of such policies also includes any future policies to be issued, or policies in supplementation thereof, or in succession, substitution, replacement or renewal thereof, and any increase in the amount of coverage.

Any person may transfer property acceptable to Trustee at any time. Trustee may accept a transfer of property that is subject to one or more conditions imposed by the donor (including giving a particular beneficiary (or a group of beneficiaries) a right to withdraw a contribution and the conditions for the lapse of a beneficiary's right of withdrawal) if Trustee deems it to be in the best interests of the trust and the beneficiaries. No condition imposed on a transfer of property and accepted by Trustee may in any way alter, amend, or change the rights of a beneficiary with respect to any prior transfers of property to the trust. Trustee may also refuse to accept any transfer of property if Trustee deems the refusal to be in the best interests of the trust and its beneficiaries.

1.3 Restrictions on Donors. Any individual (other than a donor's spouse who merely consents to gift splitting under IRC section 2513 concerning the donor's contribution to the trust) who makes a "contribution" (as defined in the Paragraph entitled, "**Contribution Defined**") to a trust in the first instance (in contrast to a beneficiary's exercise or lapse of a power of withdrawal or power of appointment) (such individual hereinafter sometimes being referred to as a "donor") shall, with respect to the contribution to the trust in question, be subject to the same limitations, restrictions, exceptions, and exclusions that I am subject to under this Agreement (but only insofar as they relate to the contributed property or to the trust in question (and any trusts derived therefrom)).

1.4 Construction of Agreement. The Rule In Shelley's case and the Doctrine of Worthier Title (or any similar rule, doctrine or statute) shall not apply to this Agreement, nor shall this Agreement be construed under any such rule, doctrine or statute.

{Start Optional Paragraph 1.5}

1.5 Intent and Material Purpose of Trust. Without limiting, restricting or compelling the exercise of a Trustee's (or a Trust Protector's or a Special Power Holder's) discretionary authority set forth in this Agreement, some of the material purposes of this Agreement are: (i) to retain assets in trust for the benefit of the trust's beneficiary, (ii) to provide creditor and asset protection to the trust's beneficiary, (iii) to provide spendthrift protection for the trust's beneficiary, (iv) to provide for the orderly and professional management and investment of trust assets, (v) to protect the trust's beneficiary from the trust's beneficiary's inabilities, disabilities, in-laws, ex-spouses, creditors, and predators, both now and in the future, (vi) to provide a financial "safety-net" for the trust's beneficiary, (vii) to provide potential resources that may be available to deal with the uncertainties of the economy, emergencies, and other vicissitudes and exigencies of daily life, and (viii) to minimize transfer, death and generation skipping transfer taxes. **{End Optional Paragraph 1.5}**

ARTICLE 2
IRREVOCABILITY

2.1 Irrevocable Trust. This trust is irrevocable. Applicable state law notwithstanding, I have no power, whether alone or in conjunction with others, and in whatever capacity, to control and direct payments or to alter, amend, modify, revoke, or terminate this Agreement or any trust provision or interest, in whole or in part, or to designate who shall possess or enjoy the trust property or trust income, whether under this trust or any statute or other rule of law. I retain no right, title, interest, or incident of ownership in any trust property.

ARTICLE 3
WITHDRAWAL RIGHTS

3.1 Withdrawal Rights. Unless otherwise provided pursuant to the paragraph item entitled, "**Restriction of a Withdrawal Right,**" the following withdrawal rights shall exist with respect to contributions to the trust:

(A) Immediately following any contribution to the trust, each of [my children] [my descendants] (individually a "donee," collectively the "donees") who are living on the date of the contribution (and have not been excluded from exercising their withdrawal right with respect to the contribution in question), shall have the right to withdraw an amount equal to a proportionate share of the value of the contribution. Such proportionate share will be the value of the contribution, divided by the number of donees living at the time of the contribution, who have not been excluded from exercising their withdrawal right with respect to the contribution in question; provided, however, that the maximum amount that a donee may withdraw with respect to all contributions made by the same donor during a single calendar year shall be the **lesser** of: (i) the total amount of such contributions, or (ii) the amount of the federal gift tax exclusion under IRC section 2503(b) available to the donor with respect to gifts to such donee, provided however, if requested by a married donor at the time of a contribution, the alternative limitation based on the gift tax annual exclusion shall be two (2) times the amount of the gift tax annual exclusion. In determining the amount of this withdrawal limitation, there shall be taken into consideration all previous gifts made to such donee from (or attributable to) such donor (and the donor's spouse, to the extent relevant) during the same calendar year, which gifts were eligible for the federal gift tax annual exclusion. To the extent a donee is also the donor of a contribution, or is treated as donor of one-half (1/2) of a contribution for federal gift tax purposes, that donee shall have no right of withdrawal with respect to such contribution to which they are the donor (or treated as the donor), and shall never thereafter be considered to have had a right of withdrawal with respect to such contribution.

(B) Return of Excess Distribution. If any donee receives a distribution in excess of the amount he or she is authorized to withdraw under this Paragraph, Trustee shall immediately notify such donee in writing, requiring the prompt repayment of such excess amount.

These withdrawal rights take precedence over any other power or discretion granted Trustee or any other person.

3.2 Rules Concerning Withdrawal Rights. With respect to the withdrawal rights created under this Article, unless otherwise provided pursuant to the paragraph item entitled, **"Restriction of a Withdrawal Right,"** the following rules shall apply:

(A) Notification of Withdrawal Right. Each eligible donee (or the person who would exercise an eligible donee's withdrawal right) shall be kept reasonably informed of all withdrawable contributions to the trust which are made or are anticipated to be made. Notification may be made orally or in writing, and such efforts may include, by way of example (and without limitation), annually apprising each donee of his or her withdrawal rights, by providing the donee with a single notice sufficient to apprise him or her of his or her current and expected future withdrawal rights, or any other means to provide each eligible donee (or the person who would exercise an eligible donee's withdrawal right) with reasonable or actual notice. In no event shall the failure of any donee to receive such notice be deemed to abrogate his or her withdrawal rights in accordance with the provisions of this Article. A donee's right of withdrawal is not contingent upon such notice; and unless otherwise expressly limited (as is permitted pursuant to the sub-paragraph entitled, **"Restriction of a Withdrawal Right,"**) a donee's withdrawal right shall become effective upon Trustee's receipt (actual, constructive or imputed) of the withdrawable contribution (whether such contribution is a direct or indirect contribution to the trust). Upon written request by a donee, Trustee shall furnish full, detailed information with respect to any contributions subject to withdrawal by the donee.

(B) **Withdrawal Right to be Exercised by Written Request**. Each eligible donee can exercise a withdrawal right by a written request timely delivered to Trustee indicating the amount the donee desires to withdraw. The withdrawal right shall be a privilege that may be exercised only voluntarily and not under compulsion. As of the date a request for withdrawal is made pursuant to the provisions of this Article, the donee's right to receive the permitted amount requested shall be vested and shall not be terminated by the subsequent death or disability of the donee or any administrative delay resulting from actions taken by Trustee to effect distribution hereunder to the donee. Any property distributed by Trustee pursuant to an exercised withdrawal right shall be for the sole benefit of the donee who has exercised such withdrawal right. Trustee shall promptly comply with every demand under a withdrawal right that is exercised.

(C) **Incapacity or Disability of Donee**. If any eligible donee is unable to exercise a withdrawal right because of incapacity or disability (including minority), his or her authorized representative (to the extent such authorized representative is not prohibited from acting on behalf of the donee), including (but not limited to) a legal or natural guardian, committee, conservator, agent, next friend, or attorney-in-fact under a durable power of attorney, may make the withdrawal on the donee's behalf, and if there be no such authorized representative, Trustee will designate an appropriate adult individual (who may be Trustee, a trust officer, the donee's parent, the donee's sibling, a relative of the donee, or any other person) who may make the withdrawal on the donee's behalf. However, in no event can I, the donor of the contribution, or a person whose life is insured under a life insurance policy owned by the trust, make the withdrawal for any donee regardless of such individual's relationship to the donee. Any property received pursuant to the withdrawal right shall be held for the use and benefit of the donee and shall not be used by the person who exercised the withdrawal right on behalf of the donee to discharge that person's legal obligation of support for that donee.

(D) Structured Lapse of Withdrawal Right. The withdrawal rights created under this Article shall be cumulative, and each eligible donee's unexercised right to withdraw a contribution shall lapse on December 31 of each year (whether or not a contribution was made in that year), or, if earlier, thirty (30) days after the contribution to which it relates (or such minimal additional amount of time as may be necessary for a legal guardian/conservator to be appointed on behalf of the incapacitated or disabled donee, if such an appointment is in fact necessary), in an amount equal to the greater of five thousand ($5,000.00) dollars or five percent (5%) of the value of the trust estate out of which, or the proceeds of which, the exercise of the withdrawal right could be satisfied (or such greater dollar amount or percentage as may be specified in IRC section 2514(e)) (the "Lapse Protection Amount"); provided, however, the Lapse Protection Amount shall be measured and determined after first ascertaining all other powers (if any) held by such donee that must, under IRC section 2514(e), be aggregated to determine the largest lapse that can occur concerning the withdrawal right under this subparagraph without it being considered a release of a general power of appointment. To the extent that a withdrawal right exceeds the Lapse Protection Amount, the donee's withdrawal right with respect to such excess shall continue in all later years (even after a donor's death) subject to the same lapse provisions, but such continuing withdrawal right over the excess may only be exercised by the donee with the consent of an Independent or Disinterested Trustee. Withdrawal rights for contributions made during the period of December 3 through December 31 shall not lapse in the calendar year when the contribution was made, but shall continue to be exercisable in the following year or years. (For example, if a contribution allocable to a donee is $12,000 in a calendar year and the applicable Lapse Protection Amount is $5,000, then if the withdrawal right is not exercised, it shall lapse as to $5,000 of the contribution, but shall continue to the next calendar year as to $7,000. If there is no contribution allocable to that donee in the next two subsequent calendar years, and the allocable amounts are not withdrawn, that donee's right of withdrawal shall lapse by $5,000 and $2,000 in the first and second subsequent years, respectively.) Nothing in this provision shall have the effect of a condition subsequent, nor a retroactive recharacterization of the amount of a donor's gifts or the amount subject to any donee's power to withdraw. Neither the amount of a donor's gifts nor any amount subject to any donee's power to withdraw are to be reduced, modified or recharacterized as a result of any action or determination by any court or other governmental or administrative agency. The lapse of a donee's withdrawal rights shall not be considered a contribution or gift to the trust estate.

(E) Continuation of Withdrawal Right After My Death. Each withdrawal right which is in effect at my death shall continue in effect after my death as to Descendants' Trust until it lapses as described in sub-paragraph (D), above. Trustee, may in its discretion, delay the funding of the Descendants' Trust for a reasonable period of time, in order to permit sufficient time for withdrawal rights to be exercised or lapse (as the case may be). On the day preceding the date of the donee's death, all withdrawal rights that have not previously lapsed, shall lapse with respect to that donee (provided the date of death occurs more than fifteen (15) days following the date of the contribution to which such withdrawal rights relate). Any distribution of income or principal made to or for the benefit of a donee during the period after my death while there is a continuation of the donee's withdrawal right hereunder shall be considered as a distribution in full or partial satisfaction of such donee's unlapsed right of withdrawal.

(F) Satisfying a Withdrawal Right. Trustee shall promptly comply with every demand under a withdrawal right that is exercised. Trustee may satisfy any withdrawal rights under this Article by distributing cash, other trust property, fractional interests in trust property, or split dollar interest in a life insurance policy, as Trustee deems appropriate. Trustee is specifically authorized to borrow money from any source, including but not limited to the cash surrender values of any life insurance policies transferred to or held by the trust, to sell trust property, to surrender or otherwise dispose of any life insurance policies or other property transferred to or held by the trust, and to take any other action that may be necessary and appropriate to assure that withdrawal rights will be satisfied in a timely and expedient manner. Without limiting Trustee's broad discretionary power to select trust property to satisfy a withdrawal right, I prefer that cash or tangible property be distributed to donees before distributing life insurance policies and other intangible property to donees (especially as concerns donees who are skip persons), unless Trustee decides that another selection is warranted. While any withdrawal right is outstanding Trustee shall not exercise any discretion or authority that would impede or thwart the withdrawal right.

(G) "Contribution" Defined. "Contribution" means a non-testamentary transfer (direct or indirect, actual or imputed to the donor) to Trustee of any cash or other property (or interest therein) (including, for the year of the trust's creation, the property creating the trust) to be held as part of the trust funds, which would be treated under Chapter 12 of the Internal Revenue Code as a taxable gift of the donor or the donor's spouse (before taking into account the exclusion allowed by IRC section 2503(b)), and shall also include any premiums on policies of life insurance (or any interests therein) owned by the trust which premiums are paid, by me or any other person or entity (including my employer or former employer), directly to any insurance company issuing the policies rather than first being paid to Trustee. In the case of any premium which is paid directly to an insurance company, the date of the contribution to the trust shall be deemed to be the date on which the premium payment is transmitted to the insurance company issuing the policy. The amount of any contribution is its federal gift tax value, as determined by Trustee at the time of the transfer. Contributions made by a donor's attorney-in-fact under a durable power of attorney shall be considered as made by the donor.

(H) Restriction of a Withdrawal Right. Any person (or that person's duly authorized agent acting under a power of attorney or other proper legal representative) who makes a contribution to any trust created under this Agreement may inform Trustee at the time of such contribution and with respect solely to the new contribution then being made (and with respect to future contributions to be made by that person), do one (1) or more of the following: (i) exclude any beneficiary who would otherwise have a withdrawal right from exercising that withdrawal right as to such new or future contribution; (ii) increase or decrease the amount subject to a beneficiary's withdrawal right as to such new or future contribution, except that the amount subject to the withdrawal right shall not exceed the amount of the contribution; (iii) change the period during which any beneficiary's withdrawal right as to such new or future contribution may be exercised; and (iv) change the manner and period during which any beneficiary's withdrawal right as to such new or future contribution shall lapse. No such direction may in any way alter, amend or change any beneficiary's withdrawal right with respect to any prior contributions.

(I) **Forfeiture of Withdrawal Right.** Except with respect to an outstanding withdrawal right which has been outstanding for fewer than fifteen (15) days from the date of such contribution, any donee having a withdrawal right shall immediately forfeit such right upon making an assignment for the benefit of his or her creditors, filing a voluntary petition in bankruptcy, being adjudicated a bankrupt or an insolvent, or consenting to or acquiescing in the appointment of a trustee in bankruptcy or a receiver in bankruptcy for all or any substantial part of his or her assets or properties, which forfeiture shall continue during the pendency of any such proceeding and end upon the termination thereof.

(J) **Power to Amend.** Trustee, other than an Interested Trustee, may by a written instrument filed with the trust records, amend this Article to the minimum extent necessary to assure that contributions to the initial trust and its beneficiaries quality for the gift tax annual exclusion for federal gift tax purposes, and/or are not subject to an estate tax inclusion period for generation skipping transfer tax purposes. Such Trustee may not amend the initial trust in any manner that would cause any portion of the trust funds to be included in a donor's gross estate, my gross estate, that of my spouse (if I am married), or that of any of my descendants and their spouses, to a greater extent than before such amendment. An amendment made in good faith shall be conclusive on all persons interested in the trust and such Trustee shall not be liable for the consequences of any amendment or for not having amended the trust. No amendment shall limit or alter the rights of a beneficiary in any trust funds held by Trustee before the amendment.

(K) Determination of Donor's Prior Gifts to Donee. Trustee may without liability assume that no prior gifts to any donee under this Article were made by a donor or a donor's spouse other than contributions to the initial trust, unless Trustee shall have actual written notice to the contrary. In determining the amount of prior gifts to or for a donee not made under this Agreement, Trustee may rely on a written statement signed or duly authorized by the donor setting forth the nature, date, and amount of such prior gifts; and in the absence of such written statement Trustee shall be under no obligation to ascertain the same.

(L) Special Rule for Multiple Withdrawal Rights. The amounts involved in a withdrawal right described as " the greater of five thousand ($5,000) dollars or five (5%) percent of the trust estate out of which, or the proceeds of which, the exercise of this withdrawal right could be satisfied (or such greater dollar amount or percentage as may be specified in IRC section 2514(e))" or language of similar import with reference to IRC section 2514(e), shall be measured after subtracting all other amounts that the same person could have withdrawn during the same calendar year from this or any other fund, to the extent that such powers must, under applicable federal gift tax law, be aggregated in determining whether the lapse of the right of withdrawal under this Article is a release of a general power of appointment; provided however, a person making a contribution may, at the time of the contribution, specify the order in which multiple withdrawal rights are to lapse (as concerns the contribution).

(M) Satisfaction of a Withdrawal Right Constitutes an Advancement. The satisfaction of a donee's right of withdrawal under this Article shall constitute and be treated as an advancement, and shall be charged (without interest) against the ultimate share (if any) provided for the donee and his or her descendants.

ARTICLE 4
DISTRIBUTION DURING LIFETIME

4.1 Distribution of Principal and Income During Lifetime. During my lifetime, Trustee shall hold and administer the trust estate, as follows:

(A) Income and Principal. Trustee may use some or all of the trust's net income and principal to pay premiums on policies of life insurance owned by the trust. In addition, a Disinterested Trustee may distribute to and among my descendants, in whatever proportions the Disinterested Trustee deems appropriate, so much of the trust principal and income (including all or none) as the Disinterested Trustee in its sole, absolute and uncontrolled discretion, shall determine. An Interested Trustee may, in its discretion, distribute income and principal among the aforementioned beneficiaries for their health, education, support and maintenance considering all other resources available to each such beneficiary (including any legal obligation of support that another person may owe to such beneficiary). Any undistributed income shall be added to principal.

(B) Restrictions on Distributions. No distribution of trust income or principal shall be made by Trustee if it would impair a withdrawal right granted under the Article entitled, "**Withdrawal Rights**," and no Trustee may make any distribution to or for his or her own benefit, nor may Trustee make any distribution to or for the benefit of any individual which distribution would discharge or satisfy Trustee's legal obligation to support such individual. Furthermore, Trustee shall not use any trust income or principal in a manner that would give me or my spouse (if

I am married) any pecuniary benefit or would discharge or satisfy our legal obligations, including any legal obligation of support.

4.2 Limited Power of Appointment by Special Power Holder. I hereby name as a special power holder the first of the following who is from time to time willing and able to act:

(1) Name and address of Special Power Holder 1;

(2) Name and address of Special Power Holder 2; and

(3) Name and address of Special Power Holder 3.

During my life, the special power holder, may in its sole, absolute and uncontrolled discretion appoint (by a written instrument delivered to Trustee prior to my death), some, all or none of the trust estate (excluding: (i) life insurance on the special power holder's life, and (ii) any amount still subject to withdrawal by a person) as the special power holder (acting in his, her or its individual-personal capacity and not in a fiduciary capacity (even though the special power holder may also be serving (or is nominated to serve) as a Trustee)) as the special power holder determines, to any one or more of {**Optional 1:** myself, or **Optional 2:** my mother's descendants,}[1] my descendants or to another trust for any such person's benefit, (but not to the special power holder, the special power holder's estate, or the creditors of either), without regard to equality among the objects or the appointees, and without the appointed property being chargeable against the proportionate share of corpus held in trust for the payment of income to the beneficiary as if the corpus constituted a separate trust; and Trustee shall not make any compensating adjustments to trust beneficiaries who are not the appointees or to trust beneficiaries who receive unequal shares/amounts of the appointed property.

Provided, however, (i) in no event can I exercise the power granted hereunder, regardless of my relationship to the special power holder, (ii) that no such distribution may be applied or distributed such that it would give the special power holder any pecuniary benefit or would discharge or satisfy my legal obliga-

---

[1] *See,* Section 11.1 of main text concerning use of the optional language.

tions, or the power holder's legal obligations, and (iii) no such distribution may be made if it would impair an unexercised or unlapsed withdrawal right granted under the Article entitled, "**Withdrawal Rights**."

Once appointed, a special power holder may only be removed for reasonable cause by a court of competent jurisdiction.

In the event a special power holder resigns, is removed by a court of competent jurisdiction, becomes incapacitated, or is deceased, I may appoint a successor to such special power holder, by delivering a written instrument to Trustee. Any special power holder nominated or appointed hereunder must meet the definitional requirements of an Independent Trustee.

4.3 Distribution In Satisfaction of Unlapsed Withdrawal Right. Any distribution of income or principal to a beneficiary under this Article shall be considered as a distribution in full or partial satisfaction of such beneficiary-donee's unlapsed right of withdrawal under the Article entitled, **"Withdrawal Rights."**

ARTICLE 5
DISTRIBUTION AFTER DEATH

5.1 Purchase of Assets and Loans. At any time after my death, including the period during the administration of my probate estate (including the post-mortem administration of any inter-vivos revocable trusts created by me) Trustee may use the trust funds, in Trustee's discretion, to lend money to and buy assets from my estate, the estates of any of my descendants, or from the trustee of any other trust created by me, or my descendants (collectively "our estates"), on such terms and conditions as Trustee deems to be in the best interests of the beneficiaries of the trusts established under this Agreement, provided, however, Trustee may not buy assets from our estates other than at their fair market value, nor may Trustee lend money to our estates without receiving adequate security and an adequate rate of interest. In addition to the foregoing, Trustee may also purchase, otherwise acquire, and hold for an indefinite term any business or business interest, as shareholder, creditor, partner, proprietor or otherwise, even though of a character, proportion, or amount other than prescribed by law for trust investments; to exercise, or delegate to others discretionary power to exercise complete control and management of any business, and in connection therewith to enter and perform contracts, commitments, orders, and engagements, to incur, pay, compromise, settle and discharge expenses and debts, to elect, employ and compensate directors, officers, employees, or agents (who may include Trustee or any employee or agent thereof), and to deal with and act for such business in any capacity (including any banking or trust capacity and the lending of money out of Trustee's own funds) and to be compensated therefor; to rely upon the reports of accountants and others as to the operations and financial condition of any business, without independent investigation and without obligation to file with any court; to take any action reasonably necessary to carry out any agreement for the transfer of any business interest upon an individual's death or upon cessation of an individual's active participation in the conduct of the business; to participate in any buy-sell, restrictive purchase or retirement agreement relating to any business interest; and to join in partnership, membership and joint venture agreements, to participate in any incorporation, reorganization, merger, consolidation, recapitalization, liquidation or dissolution of any business or any change in its nature, and to invest additional capital in, subscribe to or buy additional stock or securities of or make new or increased secured, unsecured or subordinated loans to any business.

Trustee may not, however, make grants to our estates or otherwise distribute funds except through bona fide loans or purchases, it not being my intention to make any persons who are not specifically so identified in this Agreement, the beneficiaries of any trust created hereunder. If no personal representative is appointed with respect to an estate under applicable state law, the "administration" of an estate will include the settlement of debts, claims, and taxes in respect of an estate by the trustee of any revocable trust or by any other person in actual possession of assets in which the individual had a legal or equitable interest. Trustee shall not be liable for any loss suffered by the trust as a result of the existence of the powers granted in this provision.

To facilitate the possible exercise of these discretionary powers, Trustee is authorized to defer any division of the initial trust estate for a reasonable period of time sufficient to accomplish the forgoing.

Notwithstanding anything in this Agreement to the contrary although it is my intent and purpose under this Paragraph to make trust assets available to provide the possibility that the assets of the initial trust can be made available to provide liquid assets (through loans and purchases) for the payment of taxes and other obligations of our estates, if that becomes necessary or appropriate in the opinion of the personal representative of such estate, Trustee shall not have the power to use any trust property for the benefit of our estates as defined in Treas. Reg. section 20.2042-1(b) unless such property is already included in our gross estates for federal estate tax purposes.

5.2 Administration of the Balance of the Trust Property. After my death, and after making provision for the purchase of any estate assets or loans (as specified in the Paragraph entitled **"Purchase of Assets and Loans"**), the balance of the trust property shall be administered and disposed of as provided in the Paragraph entitled, **"Descendants' Trust**."

5.3 Descendants' Trust. All property distributed to or receivable by the Descendants' Trust shall be held and administered by Trustee as follows:

(A) A Disinterested Trustee may distribute to or for the benefit of my descendants then living (from time to time), in whatever proportions the Disinterested Trustee deems appropriate, so much of the trust principal and income (including all or none) as the Disinterested Trustee in its sole, absolute and uncontrolled discretion, shall determine. An Interested Trustee may, in its discretion, distribute to or for the benefit of my descendants then living (from time to time), in whatever proportions the Interested Trustee deems appropriate, so much of the trust principal and income as the Interested Trustee shall determine for my descendants' reasonable health, education, support and maintenance; and in making such distributions, the Interested Trustee may (but need not) take into consideration other income and resources known upon reasonable inquiry by the Interested Trustee to be reasonably available to the beneficiary. Any undistributed income shall be added to principal.

(1) Without limiting Trustee's discretion, I encourage Trustee to consider making loans and buying assets while retaining title in the trust, including real and tangible personal property, for the benefit and rent-free use by a beneficiary or beneficiaries, whenever Trustee determines that such loans or assets would be beneficial for such beneficiary or beneficiaries.

(B) Without limiting Trustee's discretion, Trustee may consider the needs of a child of mine as more important than the needs of my grandchildren or other remote descendants.

(C) At any time during the period that is twelve months prior to the expiration of the trust's term, Trustee who is an Independent Trustee, may by written instrument, appoint some, none or all of the trust property to some, all or none of my then living descendants, without any requirement of equality among my then living descendants or the appointees of the trust property. The Independent Trustee may, but need not, consider appointing the trust property to those descendants with a longer life expectancy than to those descendants with a shorter life expectancy. However, two days prior to the expiration of the trust's term, the Independent Trustee's special limited power of appointment contained herein shall cease, and any remaining or non-appointed trust property shall be distributed as provided below.

(D) Upon the expiration of the trust's term, Trustee shall distribute the remaining and/or non-appointed trust property to my then living descendants, by right of representation.

(E) The trust's term shall run for the longest period of time permitted by the rule against perpetuities (or other applicable law governing the maximum duration of trusts), as provided in Paragraph 8.1, entitled, **"Rule Against Perpetuities."**

5.4 Absence of Beneficiaries. If all of the beneficiaries of any trust created under this Agreement should die before the trust assets have vested in them, Trustee shall distribute all remaining assets of each such trust as follows:

(A) All to My Heirs. All to my heirs (other than to any state or governmental entity) who would have taken my estate and such shares as they would have taken it, had I died unmarried and intestate in the state which I was domiciled at the time of my death, determined on the later of my death or the death of the last of such beneficiaries to die; and

(B) Balance to Charity. If there are no persons to take under paragraph items (A) above, then all remaining trust assets shall be distributed free of trust to a charitable organization(s) selected by Trustee, in memory of me and the person to whom I am legally married at the time of my death. Until such time as the events described in the preceding sentence occur, no charity shall have any right or interest in the trust or be entitled to receive information concerning the trust or be joined in any action pertaining to the trust, nor shall any governmental agency (such as the state's attorney general's office) be entitled to receive any information concerning the trust (as a result of such potential charitable donation) or be joined in any action concerning the trust (as a result of such potential charitable donation) and no consent, approval or other action shall be necessary, required or authorized by or from such charity or the governmental agency (as a result of such potential charitable donation). In other words, until the events in the first sentence of this sub-paragraph occur, the charity and the governmental agency shall not be interested trust beneficiaries (in any sense of the meaning), and shall have no standing, whether by rule, statute or common law. Trustee is directed to review our prior charitable giving records (if any) to assist Trustee in selecting the charitable organization(s) and the percentage amount for each charity (if Trustee has selected more than one charitable organization).

If, after six (6) months of reasonable search following the occurrence of an event that requires the determination of heirs hereunder, Trustee is unable to identify and locate any such heirs, it shall be presumed that the person described above has no heirs and the property shall be distributed as if there are "no persons to take" under the relevant paragraph item.

ARTICLE 6
TRUSTEES

6.1 Initial and Successor Trustees.

(A) Subject to the provisions of the Paragraphs entitled, **"Removal of Trustee"** (and any other pertinent provisions of this Agreement), the following persons shall serve (to the extent not prohibited from serving as a trustee), in priority of the order listed, as Trustee of the initial trust:

- «InitialTrustee», «InitialTrtAddr»
- «AltTrustee1», «AltTrst1Address»
- «AltTrustee2», «AltTrst2Address»
- «AltTrustee3», «AltTrst3Address»
- «AltTrustee4», «AltTrst4Address»

(B) Subject to the provisions of the Paragraphs entitled, **"Removal of Trustee"** (and any other pertinent provisions of this Agreement), the following persons shall serve (to the extent not prohibited from serving as a trustee), in priority of the order listed, as Trustee of the Descendants' Trust.

- «InitialTrustee», «InitialTrtAddr»
- «AltTrustee1», «AltTrst1Address»
- «AltTrustee2», «AltTrst2Address»
- «AltTrustee3», «AltTrst3Address»
- «AltTrustee4», «AltTrst4Address»

(C) If a Trustee (or a person nominated as a trustee) is dead, incapacitated, resigns from a trusteeship, is prohibited from serving as a trustee, or declines to serve as a trustee of any trust created under this Agreement, then unless otherwise prohibited, a remaining Co-Trustee (or in the absence thereof, the successor Trustee), who is not prohibited from serving as a trustee, shall serve as sole Trustee of such trust, without need of court approval.

(D) Except as otherwise provided in the Paragraph entitled, "**Removal of Trustee**," in the absence of a nominated successor Trustee then able to act, a successor Trustee shall be appointed by a majority of the current income beneficiaries of the trust in question who are sui juris and not incapacitated. If a majority of such current income beneficiaries cannot agree on a successor Trustee, any current income beneficiary or outgoing Trustee can petition a court of competent jurisdiction, ex parte, to designate an appropriate person as successor Trustee. The court shall not acquire any jurisdiction over the trust, except to the extent necessary to appoint a successor Trustee.

(E) I shall not be eligible to serve as a Trustee of any trust established under this Agreement, nor may any Trustee delegate its powers or duties to me.

(F) A person who has made an *irrevocable* beneficiary designation naming this Agreement (or its Trustee) as an irrevocable beneficiary of the asset can not serve as a Trustee under this Agreement.

(G) A person who is prohibited from serving as a Trustee of a particular trust or its property shall not serve as a Trustee of the trust in question or as a Trustee of that trust's property, nor may any Trustee delegate its powers or duties to such person.

(H) Unless otherwise consented to by the current income beneficiaries of the trust in question, no person shall serve as a trustee if to do so would result in the trust being: (i) classified as a "foreign trust" under the Code, and (ii) subjected to greater or additional taxation as a result of such classification, or the loss of the trust's ability to legally hold S corporation stock; provided however, such person may in the absence of the aforesaid consent, serve as a Co-Trustee if the trust would (continue to) be classified as a United States person under IRC section 7701(a)(30).

6.2 Resignation by Trustee. Trustee may resign as trustee of any or all trusts under this Agreement at any time by giving written notice, specifying the effective date of resignation, to the then acting Co-Trustee(s) of the trust in question, or if none, then to the designated successor Trustee nominated (or appointed) herein. If no successor Trustee is designated, the resigning Trustee shall give notice to all the current income beneficiaries of the trust in question who are sui juris.

6.3 Resignation by Trustee. Trustee may resign as trustee of any or all trusts under this Agreement at any time by giving written notice, specifying the effective date of resignation to any beneficiary who is eligible to receive current income from the trust in question.

6.4 Trustee May Delegate to Co-Trustee. Any Trustee may, from time to time, delegate to any other Trustee by a dated written instrument any or all of such Trustee's powers (except those, if any, not exercisable by such other Trustee, or which are not reasonable or prudent to delegate to such other Trustee). Consistent with the delegating Trustee's tenure, such delegation may be temporary or permanent, and if temporary, may be for any duration of time or until any event specified by the delegating Trustee. Any person dealing in good faith with any Trustee may rely without inquiry upon the Trustee's certificate with respect to any delegation.

6.5 Trustee May Appoint a Co-Trustee. A Trustee may by a dated written instrument filed with the trust records, designate, appoint and compensate any person (not prohibited from serving as a trustee) as a Co-Trustee. The Co-Trustee may be an Interested Trustee, Disinterested Trustee or an Independent Trustee. The Co-Trustee shall not possess or exercise any power or authority that it is otherwise prohibited from possessing or exercising. Any Co-Trustee so appointed may, without liability, accept without examination or review the accounts rendered, the actions taken, and the property delivered by or for any appointing Trustee or any Co-Trustee of the appointing Trustee. A Co-Trustee so appointed may be removed at any time, with or without cause, by the appointing Trustee(s), other than an Interested Trustee. A Co-Trustee appointed solely by an Interested Trustee may be removed for reasonable cause by the appointing Interested Trustee. Except as otherwise provided herein, a Co-Trustee so appointed shall serve only as long as the Trustee who appointed such Co-Trustee (or, if such Co-Trustee was named by more than one (1) Trustee acting together, by the last to serve of such Trustees), and such Co-Trustee shall not become the successor Trustee or a successor Co-Trustee, unless: (i) such Co-Trustee has been nominated by me as the successor Trustee hereunder, (ii) such Co-Trustee is elected or appointed as the successor Trustee of the trust in question, (iii) such Co-Trustee is appointed as a Co-Trustee by the successor Trustee of the trust in question, (iv) a majority of the current income beneficiaries of the trust in question who are sui juris and not incapacitated, consent in writing to the continuation of the appointed Co-Trustee as the successor Trustee, (v) all of the specifically named successor Trustees of the trust in question consent, in writing, to the continuation of the appointed Co-Trustee as the successor Trustee, or (vi) a court of competent jurisdiction consents to the appointment of such Co-Trustee as the successor Trustee.

6.6 **Trustee May Appoint a Substitute Trustee.** If Trustee is unable or unwilling to exercise a fiduciary power with regard to a specific trust matter or assets, Trustee may by a dated written instrument filed with the trust records, designate, appoint and compensate any person (not prohibited from serving as a trustee) as a substitute Trustee for any trust matters or assets that the appointing Trustee is unwilling or unable to act as Trustee, or for trust assets in another jurisdiction, with any trust powers set out in this Agreement or provided by law (except those, if any, not exercisable by such substitute Trustee) that the appointing Trustee delegates to the substitute Trustee, and to specify which jurisdiction's law is to govern questions relating to the administration of such matters and assets. Any substitute Trustee so appointed, may, without liability, accept without examination or review the accounts rendered, the actions taken, and the property delivered by or for the appointing Trustee or any Co-Trustee of an appointing Trustee. A substitute Trustee may be removed at any time, with or without cause, by the appointing Trustee(s), other than an Interested Trustee. A substitute Trustee appointed solely by an Interested Trustee may be removed for reasonable cause by the appointing Interested Trustee. A substitute Trustee may be removed at any time, with or without cause, by any successor Trustee. If Trustee chooses to not appoint a substitute Trustee with respect to the exercise of a fiduciary power, Trustee may petition a court of competent jurisdiction to request the appointment of a special trustee to exercise the fiduciary power on a temporary or permanent basis, or may request that the court exercise the fiduciary power on a temporary or permanent basis. A special trustee appointed by the court shall be treated as a "substitute Trustee."

6.7 **Individual Trustee May Nominate Successor Trustee.** Each individual Trustee (including successors) shall have the right to nominate a successor Trustee(s) (who is not prohibited from serving as a trustee) by a dated written instrument filed with the trust records and delivered to all the current income beneficiaries of the trust in question who are sui juris. A nomination may be changed or revoked until it takes effect. Except as otherwise provided in the next sentence, the appointment of a nominated successor under this provision shall take effect only if and when all Trustees that have been previously nominated or appointed by me fail or decline to qualify or cease to act with respect to the trust in question, and a majority of the current income beneficiaries of the trust in question who are sui juris (other than the appointing beneficiary-trustee) do not object in writing to the appointment of such nominated successor Trustee by the appointing Trustee. The restrictions of the preceding sentence shall not, however, apply if: (i) all of the then nominated successor Trustees of the trust in question consent, in writing, to the appointment of the nominated successor(s) as the next successor Trustee(s) to the appointing Trustee, (ii) a majority of the current income beneficiaries of the trust (excluding the appointing beneficiary-trustee) who are sui juris and not incapacitated consent, in writing, to the appointment of the nominated successor(s) as the next successor Trustee(s) to the appointing Trustee, or (iii) a court of competent jurisdiction consents to the appointment of the nominated successor(s) as the next successor Trustee(s) to the appointing Trustee. A Trustee nominated pursuant to the provisions of this Paragraph shall be deemed to be a Trustee that has been nominated in the Paragraph entitled, **"Initial and Successor Trustees."**

6.8 Sole Beneficiary—Trustee Authorized. Except as otherwise expressly provided in this Agreement, if the sole Trustee of a trust is a beneficiary of the trust, Trustee may appoint but shall not be required to appoint a Co-Trustee. A beneficiary's interest may not be merged or converted into a legal life estate or estate for years because the beneficiary is the sole Trustee. If this would still happen under applicable law, then a Co-Trustee shall be appointed in preference to such merger or conversion.

6.9 Action by One Trustee. Unless a Co-Trustee elects otherwise in writing, when more than one person is serving as Trustee, any one of them (who is not prohibited from acting), may, acting alone, exercise any power and authority of Trustee, and may sign any checks, agreements or other documents on behalf of the trust, and the signature of any one such Trustee shall be sufficient to bind the trust in the same manner as though said check, agreement or other document had been signed by all the Co-Trustees (who are not prohibited from acting), and no person dealing with the signing Trustee shall be obliged to inquire as to the other Co-Trustee's acquiescence to such action.

6.10 Multiple Trustees. While two (2) or more Trustees are then acting, the following provisions shall apply where the context permits:

(A) When more than one person is serving as Trustee and at least one of them is a Disinterested or Independent Trustee, the Trustee who is not a Disinterested or Independent Trustee shall not participate in the exercise or non-exercise of any discretionary authority granted by this Agreement;

(B) When more than two (2) Trustees are then acting, the decision of a majority of the Trustees (who are eligible to participate in the action or decision) shall control in all matters pertaining to the administration of any trust created under this Agreement, and if there are an even number of eligible Trustees and a majority decision can not be achieved, then the disputed matter shall be submitted to binding arbitration;

(C) If only two (2) Trustees are then acting and both are eligible to participate in the action or decision, the concurrence and joinder of both shall be required, and if they both cannot mutually agree on the action or decision, the matter in dispute shall be submitted to binding arbitration;

(D) A Trustee who is eligible to participate in an action or decision shall be presumed to have approved a proposed act or decision to refrain from acting if that Trustee fails to indicate approval or disapproval thereof within fifteen (15) days after a written request for approval, and a Trustee shall not be required to continue to make a proposal which has been disapproved on at least two (2) occasions if that Trustee has informed a disapproving Co-Trustee (who is eligible to participate in the action or decision) that continued disapproval will be assumed until notice to the contrary has been received;

(E) When more than two (2) Trustees are then acting, any disapproving Trustee (who is eligible to participate in the action or decision) may be absolved from personal liability by registering a written disapproval with the records of the trust, and the disapproving Trustee shall thereafter act with the other Trustees in any manner necessary or appropriate to effectuate the decision of the majority, if any;

(F) Any Trustee who is not eligible to participate in an action or decision shall not be liable therefor; and

(G) The Trustees may execute documents by jointly signing one document or separately signing concurrent counterpart documents.

6.11 Trustee's Fees. Trustee shall be entitled to fair and reasonable compensation for services performed, and to reimbursement for expenses (even though Trustee may also be my personal representative and/or an accountant, attorney, investment advisor or other agent retained by my personal representative or Trustee, and Trustee's fees shall be in addition to (and not in diminution of) any other compensation otherwise payable to such persons concerning their services to my estate or the trusts established under this Agreement). The fairness and reasonableness of Trustee's fees shall not be determined on the basis of only the time spent, but may be computed by the method which Trustee and those professionals hired by it customarily utilize in determining the compensation it will receive from clients or customers for its services. If Trustee is a professional person charging clients by the hour, then said person's hourly rate charged clients shall be a major factor in determining said person's compensation as Trustee. Trustee may, without prior approval by any court or any beneficiary, pay from and charge the trust estate with such fees, compensation, reimbursements, and expenses at such times and intervals as may be established by Trustee.

6.12 Qualifying as Trustee. A substitute Trustee, successor Trustee or Co-Trustee shall qualify upon signing an acceptance of trust and delivering it to the appointing Trustee(s) (if any); and in the case of a successor Trustee, the acceptance of trust shall be delivered to all the current income beneficiaries of the trust in question who are sui juris and not incapacitated and to all the other then acting Trustees of the trust in question. Unless a bond is otherwise requested by a majority of the trust's current trust beneficiaries, no bond shall be required of a Trustee (to the extent such requirement can be waived). If a person becomes eligible to serve as a Trustee because of a death, resignation, removal, or appointment, the notice of acceptance of trust must be given within thirty (30) days of eligibility. If eligibility to serve occurs because of the attainment of a specified age, the notice of acceptance may be given at any time.

6.13 Title and Powers. Except as otherwise provided or expressly limited, any successor Trustee, Co-Trustee or substitute Trustee shall have all the title, powers, and discretion of the Trustee succeeded, the other Co-Trustee(s), or the appointing Trustee(s) (as the case may be), without the necessity of any conveyance or transfer.

6.14 Other Trustee's Acts and Accounts, and Delivery of Trust Records. A successor Trustee is under no obligation to review the acts or to examine the accounts of a predecessor or any Co-Trustee of a predecessor. In no event is a successor Trustee liable for acts, omissions, or failures to account properly prior to the successor's qualification. A substitute Trustee or a Co-Trustee appointed by another Trustee is under no obligation to review the acts or to examine the accounts of an appointing Trustee or any Co-Trustee of an appointing Trustee. In no event is a substitute Trustee or a Co-Trustee appointed by another Trustee liable for acts, omissions, or failures to account properly prior to such substitute Trustee's qualification or such Co-Trustee's qualification. A Trustee is under no obligation to inquire into or examine the acts or accounts of a personal representative who is transferring property to Trustee. If any Trustee is removed, resigns or otherwise ceases to act as Trustee of any trust hereunder, that Trustee shall immediately surrender all records with respect to such trust to the then acting Trustee(s) of the trust in question or, if no other Trustee is then acting with respect to such trust, to the successor Trustee upon receipt of written notice of the acceptance of the trusteeship by the successor Trustee.

6.15 Corporate Successor. Any corporate successor to the trust business of any corporate Trustee acting under this Agreement shall become Trustee in place of its predecessor, without the necessity of any conveyance or transfer.

6.16 Proceeds Application. No person paying money or delivering any property to Trustee need see to its application.

6.17 Notice. Any notice or other communication that is required to be in writing shall be delivered personally, telegraphed, telexed, or telecopied, or sent by first class, certified, registered, or express delivery, postage prepaid, to the last known address of the party in question, or by any other means reasonably intended to effect actual delivery. Any such notice or communication shall be deemed given when so delivered personally, telegraphed, telexed, telecopied; or if mailed, or delivered by express delivery (such as FEDEX), on the earlier of the date of receipt or two (2) days after the date of mailing or the sender's delivery to the express delivery courier. Unless otherwise specifically provided in this Agreement, Trustee may rely on any information, telephone conversation, e-mail, notice, certificate, affidavit, letter, telegram, or other document or communication reasonably believed by it to be genuine, or on any evidence reasonably deemed by it to be sufficient. Trustee shall incur no liability for any payment or distribution made in good faith without actual knowledge of a changed condition affecting any person's interest in the trust.

6.18 Trustee Liability. Trustee shall act in a fiduciary manner, and exercise good faith, ordinary prudence, and reasonable care in the discharge of its duties and the exercise of its powers under the terms of this Agreement. Trustee, however, shall not be liable for the acts, omissions, or defaults of any agent hired with reasonable care and in good faith.

6.19 Conflict of Interest. No Trustee shall be per se disqualified by reason of owning an interest in real or personal property, or in a corporation or other business venture or entity, or by reason of being an officer, director, member or employee of any corporation or other business venture or entity, an interest in which is also a part of the trust in question.

6.20 Initial Notice of Trustee Status. For a revocable trust, within twenty-eight (28) days after Trustee's acceptance of trust or my death, whichever is later, and for all other trusts, within twenty-eight (28) days after acceptance of the trust, Trustee shall, to the extent required by law, inform in writing each interested trust beneficiary of the trust's existence, of the court in which the trust is registered, if it is registered, of Trustee's name and address, and of the interested trust beneficiary's right to request and receive both a copy of the trust's terms that describe or affect the interested trust beneficiary's interest and relevant information about the trust property. In addition, upon reasonable request, Trustee shall, to the extent required by law, provide an interested trust beneficiary with a copy of the trust's terms that describe or affect the interested trust beneficiary's interest and with relevant information about the trust property.

6.21 Removal of Trustee. I may remove a Trustee then serving or nominated to serve, for reasonable cause, and I may appoint a successor (other than a person who is prohibited from serving as a Trustee or a person whose life is insured by the trust in question) to replace the Trustee (or nominated Trustee) that I remove for reasonable cause. I may also (but not more than once in a twenty-four (24) month period) remove a Trustee then serving or nominated to serve for no cause, and I may appoint a successor to replace the Trustee (or nominated Trustee) that I remove for no cause, provided the replacement Trustee I appoint pursuant to this sentence is not me, not a person whose life is insured by the trust in question, not a person who is prohibited from serving as a Trustee, and is not related or subordinate (within the meaning of IRC section 672 (c)) to me. Any replacement Trustee appointed as aforesaid shall serve as Trustee prior to any other person who has been nominated as a Trustee. Subject to the foregoing, a majority of the current income beneficiaries of the trust in question who are sui juris and not incapacitated, may remove a Trustee for reasonable cause.

A Co-Trustee or nominated successor Trustee may remove an incumbent Trustee for reasonable cause at any time, and if successful in the removal of the incumbent Trustee, the Trustee who sought the removal shall be reimbursed from the trust estate for its reasonable expenses (including attorney fees) incurred in obtaining the removal of the incumbent Trustee. If a Co-Trustee or a nominated successor Trustee is not successful in its good faith attempt to remove the incumbent Trustee, a court of competent jurisdiction shall decide whether the reasonable expenses incurred by a Co-Trustee or nominated successor Trustee seeking the removal should be paid by the trust estate and/or trust beneficiaries personally (or a combination of both).

In applying these powers, the following rules apply (subject to the conditions and limitations imposed upon me concerning the removal and replacement of a Trustee):

(A) In the absence of a nominated successor Trustee (as set forth in the Paragraph entitled, "**Initial and Successor Trustees**") then willing or able to serve or continue to serve as Trustee, a majority of the current income beneficiaries of the trust in question who are sui juris and not incapacitated may appoint in writing, a successor Trustee who is a Disinterested or Independent Trustee, located in or outside the United States; provided, however, no beneficiary, acting alone, may remove or name a Trustee of a trust that would be included in that person's estate solely by reason of this right of removal or appointment. In selecting a non-U.S. Trustee, the beneficiaries are reminded to consider the potential (adverse) tax consequences of such an appointment.

(B) A power to remove a Trustee shall be exercised by a writing delivered to the then-serving Trustee, indicating the removal's effective date, the name of the successor Trustee, and the successor Trustee's agreement to serve.

(C) "Reasonable cause" for removal of a Trustee shall mean any one of the following:

(1) The incapacity or disability of Trustee.

(2) The willful or negligent mismanagement by Trustee of the trust's assets.

(3) The abuse or abandonment of, or inattention to, the trust or its assets by Trustee.

(4) A federal or state charge against Trustee involving the commission of a felony or serious misdemeanor.

(5) An act of stealing, dishonesty, fraud, embezzlement, moral turpitude, or moral degeneration by Trustee.

(6) The use of narcotics or excessive use of alcohol by Trustee.

(7) Trustee's poor physical, mental or emotional health which causes Trustee to be unable to devote sufficient time to administer the trust.

(8) Trustee's failure to comply with a written fee agreement or other legally enforceable written agreement affecting the operation of the trust.

(9) The failure of a corporate Trustee to appoint a senior officer with at least five (5) years of experience in the administration of trusts to handle the trust account.

(10) Changes by a corporate Trustee in the account officer responsible for the handling of the trust account more frequently than every five (5) years (unless such change is made at the request of or with the acquiescence of a Co-Trustee or the trust beneficiaries).

(11) The relocation by Trustee away from the location where the trust operates so as to interfere with the convenient administration of the trust.

(12) The removal of all current income beneficiaries from the State where the corporate Trustee is licensed to conduct business as a corporate Trustee.

(13) A demand from Trustee for unreasonable compensation for such Trustee's service.

(14) Unreasonably poor investment performance (as compared to appropriate investment benchmark indices).

(15) Unreasonable lack of communication between Trustee and the trust's current income beneficiaries.

(16) Unreasonably inaccurate or unclear transaction statements or statements of account.

(17) Unreasonable conflicts between Trustee and the trust's beneficiaries caused by Trustee.

(18) Merger, acquisition or deteriorating financial condition of a corporate Trustee.

(19) Where it would appear to be in the best interests of the current trust beneficiaries to have an Independent Trustee serve as sole Trustee.

(20) Any other reason for which a state court of competent jurisdiction would remove a trustee.

ARTICLE 7
TRUSTEE POWERS AND TRUST ADMINISTRATION

7.1 Trustee Powers. Subject to the provisions entitled, "**Limitations on Powers**," and any other pertinent provisions or limitations specified elsewhere in this Agreement, every Trustee may exercise, in a fiduciary manner, without court order, any of the following powers, and any others that are granted by law—to the extent not inconsistent with the powers granted in this Agreement. Except as expressly otherwise permitted, no powers shall be possessed or exercised by Trustee, or interpreted, in any manner that would prevent an existing bequest from qualifying for the marital or charitable deduction or would prevent an increase in basis (if applicable) under the Code; provided, however, such prohibition shall not be construed as a direction by me to my fiduciary to exercise any election or option that may be available under any tax or other law in such a manner as will result in a larger amount passing to the marital or charitable deduction bequest in the first instance, than if a contrary election were made. Such powers include:

(A) Additional Powers.

(1) Invest and reinvest the trust assets (or leave them temporarily un-invested) in any type of property and every kind of investment, in the same manner as a prudent investor would invest his or her own assets. Trustee may take title to any securities in the name of any custodian or nominee, without disclosing this relationship, and such securities may be held in "street name" by a brokerage firm or other custodian. Trustee may vote proxies. Irrespective of the prudent investor rule, Trustee may acquire and/or retain life insurance policies on the life of any beneficiary or person whom Trustee has an insurable interest. Furthermore, I prefer that my interest in any Closely Held Business Entity (defined below) in which I am an owner at the time of my death (or that is owned by the initial trust at the time of my death (or which the initial trust has the right to receive as a result of my death)) be retained by Trustee, unless, in the reasonable judgment of Trustee, there are persuasive or compelling reasons to dispose of any such interest. I understand that retention of any such business interest is inherently risky, but I believe in the fundamental soundness of each such interest and that the risk assumed by retaining any such business interest is justified. I further believe that each such business interest is and will continue to be capable of superior economic performance (production of greater net income, attaining a greater capital value, or both) than could be achieved from the sale of such business interest and reinvestment of the proceeds of such sale. As used herein, the term "Closely Held Business Entity" shall include a corporation, partnership (general or limited), limited liability company, joint venture, sole proprietorship or other entity under the laws of any state or other jurisdiction, but does not include any interests that are regularly traded on an established exchange or over-the-counter.

(2) Lease, buy, sell, exchange, or option any real or personal property, for cash or credit, at public or private sale, and with such warranties or indemnifications as Trustee may deem advisable. Trustee may borrow money for any proper purpose from itself or from unrelated parties. Trustee may mortgage, encumber, grant security interests or pledge any trust property, including purchasing securities on margin.

(3) On behalf of itself and/or all future Trustees, disclaim, release, or restrict the scope of any power held in connection with any trust (even if a power is not presently exercisable or is exercisable in a fiduciary capacity that requires the exercise of the power), including any administrative or management power, whether such power is expressly granted in this Agreement or implied by law. Trustee shall make such disclaimer, release, or restriction, if any, by a written instrument specifying the power to be disclaimed, released, or restricted and the nature of any such restriction. Any power disclaimed or released by Trustee shall be extinguished, as concerns that Trustee only, but if Trustee also expressly disclaims, releases or restricts the power on behalf of all future Trustees then the power shall be extinguished as to all future Trustees as well. Trustee may also disclaim any disclaimable interest, in whole or in part, including property, interests in property, and benefits of any kind receivable by any trust (including but not limited to, insurance contracts, qualified plan proceeds, deferred compensation proceeds, stock options, tax sheltered annuity proceeds, retirement account proceeds, etc.) in any manner permitted by law or by a "transfer" within the requirements of IRC section 2518(c)(3) (concerning certain transfers treated as disclaimers).

(4) Trustee may hold any qualified family-owned business (as that term is defined in IRC section 2057) ("QFOBI") for which a QFOBI election is made, in a separate trust for the benefit of the beneficiaries, with the QFOBI being the sole asset of the trust. If for any reason a trust established under this Agreement that contains a QFOBI fails to qualify as a qualified heir (as that term is defined in IRC section 2057), Trustee may appoint the QFOBI interest to one or more persons who do qualify as qualified heirs in the estates, interests, and proportions, including an appointment to a trustee in trust for a beneficiary (but only if the trust is a qualified heir), as Trustee, in its discretion, may determine.

(5) Purchase or otherwise acquire, for cash, credit or installments, form, create, organize, invest in, reinvest in, retain or continue for an indefinite term, any "Business Entity" (as defined below) located within or without the United States, regardless of the form of participation or ownership and even though it may be closely or privately held or may constitute all or a large portion of the trust property of a trust; have and exercise all the powers necessary and incidental to ownership in such Business Entity, including making tax elections, and authorizing or voting to authorize the making of charitable contributions by such Business Entity; comply with the provisions of any agreement restricting the disposition of an interest in the Business Entity; participate in the conduct of such Business Entity or rely upon others to do so, and take or delegate to others discretionary power to take any action with respect to its management and affairs that a person could take as owner of such Business Entity, including the voting of securities, and the determination of all questions of policy; take possession of the assets of such Business Entity and exercise complete control and management of such Business Entity, and in connection therewith, enter into and perform contracts, commitments, orders, and engagements; incur expenses and debts in connection with the conduct and operation of such Business Entity, and pay and discharge such expenses and debts; join in and execute legal documents and agreements, operating agreements, partnership agreements and amendments thereto; participate in any incorporation, reorganization, merger, consolidation, recapitalization, liquidation or dissolution of such Business Entity or any change in its nature and retain and continue such changed or successor Business Entity; enter into buy-sell agreements or similar types of agreements; invest additional capital in, subscribe to or buy additional stock or securities of or make or guarantee new or increased secured, subordinated loans to any Business Entity with trust funds; rely upon the reports of certified public accountants, appraisers, consultants and other professional advisors, without independent investigation and without obligation to file any report with any court in any jurisdiction; elect, employ and compensate directors, officers, employees or agents of any Business Entity, who may include Trustee or a director, officer or agent of Trustee; show in summary form in Trustee's accountings, if any, only the financial position of a Business Entity and not include in detail all the business transactions; deal with and act for such Business Entity in any capacity, including any banking or trust capacity and the loaning of money out of a trustee's own funds, and be compensated therefor; sell, pledge or liquidate any interest in such Business Entity; provided, however, that notwithstanding the provisions of this sub-paragraph, Trustee shall not purchase or otherwise acquire, form, create, organize, invest or reinvest in any Business Entity by which Trustee is employed or in which Trustee (or Trustee's family) directly or indirectly owns an interest, unless (i) Trustee is a descendant of my grandparents or a spouse of such a descendant; (ii) a current trust beneficiary, a descendant of such beneficiary's grandparents, a descendant of my grandparents or a spouse of any of such persons is employed by or owns (directly or indirectly) an interest in such Business Entity; or (iii) a current trust beneficiary consents to such action in a duly acknowledged instrument filed with the trust records; provided, further, that Trustee may continue to hold interests in any Business Entity held by the trust at the time Trustee began serving as such. As used herein, the term "Business Entity" shall include a corporation, partnership (general or limited), limited liability company, joint venture, sole proprietorship or other entity under the laws of any state or other jurisdiction, but does not include any interests that are regularly traded on an established exchange or over-the-counter. Trustee may make or terminate elections with respect to S corporation stock; and during the term of any trust under this Agreement, (i) if Trustee sells any interest in a corporation or if the assets of any entity constituting a corporation in which the trust has an ownership interest are sold, and (ii) if the corporation has made an election to be taxed under Subchapter S of the Code, Trustee may distribute to the income beneficiary such amounts of income and/or principal as shall be necessary to pay any income tax caused by such sale, if the income or gain attributable to such sale is taxed directly to the income beneficiary under applicable federal tax law. If the personal representative of my estate makes an election under IRC section 6324A (concerning the special lien for estate tax deferred under IRC section 6166), or a corresponding state statute, to create a special lien for the payment of any deferred death tax (including tax attributable to property not passing under this Agreement), Trustee may subject trust property to such lien. If Trustee is my spouse (if I am married) or a descendant of mine, I hereby waive any conflict of interest occasioned thereby, especially if that individual also personally holds an interest in the Business Entity. Any contractual and tort liabilities arising from the Business Entity or its operation shall be satisfied first from its assets and only secondarily from other assets of the trust, if practicable.

(6) Establish any educational savings plans pursuant to IRC sections 529 or 530 (or their successors), or any similar plans; to remove and/or add beneficiary(s) to such plans; and to add and/or remove successor owners of any such plans, all as Trustee may deem proper and expedient; and to exercise all other powers and options involving such plans.

(7) Merge or consolidate any trust created hereunder together with any other trusts (regardless by whom created) having the same beneficiaries, substantially the same dispositive provisions and, to the extent applicable, the same generation-skipping tax inclusion ratios. After the merger or consolidation, Trustee shall inform the current trust beneficiaries which of the constituent trusts is the surviving trust. If the applicable rules limiting the maximum duration of trusts (such as any rules governing perpetuities, vesting, accumulations or the suspension of alienation) start from different dates with reference to the trusts or additions to trusts, or if the trusts have different tax attributes, or if the trust assets are of a different nature, of if there are other significant differences in their provisions, merger or consolidation may still take place; but the assets of the trusts may be maintained in segregated accounts, or records of undivided shares of assets may be maintained. In considering the merger or consolidation of any trusts, Trustee shall give consideration to the potential for adverse tax consequences, including the revocation of Subchapter S status for stock held in trust. Trustee may administer such merged and consolidated trusts as a single trust or unit. If, however, such a merger or consolidation does not appear feasible, as determined in the discretion of Trustee, Trustee may consolidate the assets of such trusts for purposes of investment and trust administration while retaining separate records and accounts for the respective trusts.

(8) Sever any trust or divide any trust into multiple separate trusts; establish separate trusts; establish subtrusts; and make qualified severances. Without the consent of any beneficiary, Trustee may allocate, divide or distribute trust property in cash or in kind or partly in each, including undivided interests, and without making pro rata distribution of specific assets and without regard to the income tax basis of any asset. Non-pro rata distributions or allocations of property may be made based on the property's date of distribution value, in a manner fairly representative of the properties' net appreciation and depreciation, or in any other manner permitted (or required) by law. As to any property incapable of exact division, it shall not be necessary for Trustee to divide the same physically into parts to which each trust shall be entitled, but individual parts thereof may, by appropriate book entries, be allocated among the trusts. In any case where exact division of property or allocation of undivided interests therein between or among the trusts hereunder is not practical or expedient, Trustee may select assets to be appropriated in whole or in part to any of said trusts. Furthermore, Trustee may allot different kinds or disproportionate portions or undivided interests in property among beneficiaries; and determine the value of any allotted property without compensating adjustment, even if the basis for federal income tax purposes of property allotted to any beneficiary is not fairly representative of all property available for distribution.

(9) Except as may be otherwise provided in this Agreement, allocate an item of income or expense to either trust income or principal, as permitted or provided by applicable local law. With respect to any item not established clearly by such law, Trustee shall have discretion to determine whether items should be reasonably charged or credited to income or principal or allocated between income and principal. Except as may be otherwise provided in this Agreement, Trustee shall generally resolve any question about the allocation or apportionment of receipts and disbursement, to or between income and principal, in favor of the trust's current income beneficiary. If the power to adjust between principal and income is otherwise permitted by applicable local law (and is not expressly prohibited under this Agreement), that power shall be vested exclusively in an Independent Trustee. Absent a written request from a current trust beneficiary, an Independent Trustee who is an individual shall not be required to determine if the power to adjust should be exercised.

(10) Employ and compensate such lawyers, accountants, agents, nurses, professional care managers, caregivers, professionals, and other persons as Trustee may deem useful and appropriate for the proper administration of the trust and for the care of a current trust beneficiary; provided however, the foregoing authority shall not restrict a Trustee's sole, absolute and uncontrolled discretion (if any) concerning distributions to or for the benefit of such beneficiary, nor shall the foregoing be construed to mandate such distributions to or for the benefit of such beneficiary. Trustee may employ an investment adviser in managing the investments of the trust (including any investments in mutual funds, investment trusts, or managed accounts), delegate to this adviser any discretionary investment authorities, and rely on the adviser's investment recommendations.

(11) Institute and defend litigation, and compromise and adjust claims against or on behalf of the trust on such terms as Trustee may deem appropriate.

(12) Make (or refrain from making) any tax elections and allocations Trustee may consider appropriate; however, Trustee's authority hereunder is to be exercised only in a fiduciary capacity and may not be used to enlarge or shift any beneficial interest except as an incidental consequence of the discharge of fiduciary duties. All tax elections and allocations made by Trustee in good faith shall not require equitable adjustments. Trustee shall not incur any liability for tax elections or allocations made in good faith.

(13) Make commitments extending beyond the term of any trust.

(14) Hold trust property of several trusts under this Agreement in common ownership or in a common fund, each trust having an undivided interest in the property or fund, dividing the income proportionately and accounting for them separately, until actual division becomes necessary or desirable.

(15) In Trustee's sole, absolute and uncontrolled discretion, permit a current trust beneficiary to use trust owned real property and personal property free of rent or expense.

(16) Defer distribution of trust property after the termination of any trust until all matters involving such trust have been settled.

(17) Purchase liability, casualty, and other appropriate insurance for the protection of the trust estate.

(18) Perform all other acts necessary for the proper management, investment, and distribution of the trust property.

(B) **Generation-Skipping Tax Matters.** In order to minimize the impact of any generation-skipping transfer tax that may be applied to any of the trusts created by this

Agreement or their beneficiaries, Trustee shall take the following actions, where applicable; and Trustee may also take such other actions as are required (or permitted) by law (or applicable Treasury Regulations) concerning generation skipping transfer tax matters:

(1) If any trust under this Agreement would, otherwise by reason of an allocation of generation-skipping transfer tax exemption to it, have an inclusion ratio, as defined in IRC section 2642(a) of neither one (1) nor zero (0), then prior to such allocation Trustee shall divide, on a fractional basis, the total trust assets into two (2) separate trusts of equal or unequal value, to permit allocation of the exemption solely to one trust (the "exempt trust") so that the exempt trust will have an inclusion ratio of zero (0); any such division shall be accomplished by allocating to the other trust (the "non-exempt trust" which will have an inclusion ratio of one (1)) the minimum fractional share necessary to leave the exempt trust with a corpus of the desired value and an inclusion ratio of zero (0), so as to be entirely exempt from generation-skipping tax. In the event an existing trust has an inclusion ratio other than zero (0) or one (1), then such trust shall be divided on a fractional basis so that two (2) trusts will be created from the one, one of which will have an inclusion ratio of zero (0), and one of which will have an inclusion ratio of one (1). Trustee is also authorized to sever or divide a single trust into multiple trusts under the "qualified severance" rule of IRC section 2642(a)(3) and to fund the severed trusts in any manner permitted or required by law (including the funding of the severed or divided trusts on a non-pro-rata basis). References hereunder to "trust" or "trusts" refer also to arrangements that are treated as trusts for generation-skipping purposes and to separate shares of a trust, when appropriate to the context, if the shares are, as "substantially separate and independent shares of different beneficiaries" or otherwise, entitled to be treated as separate trusts for generation-skipping tax purposes.

(2) If Trustee does in fact divide a trust into two (2) trusts, one which has an inclusion ratio of one (1) and the other which has inclusion ratio of zero (0), I direct Trustee to make the division in a manner that permits the trusts to be treated as separate trusts in accordance with applicable Treasury Regulations (e.g., Treas. Reg. sections 26.2654-1(a) and (b)). Unless applicable Treasury Regulations (e.g., Treas. Reg. section 26.2654-1(b)(1)) require (or permit) otherwise, if the new trusts are severed on a fractional basis, the separate trusts need not be funded on a pro rata fractional basis; provided, however, if funding is on a non-pro rata fractional basis, Trustee shall fund the trusts based on either the fair market value of the assets on the date of funding or in a manner that fairly reflects the net appreciation or depreciation in the value of the assets measured from the valuation date to the date of funding. In funding the severed trusts, it is my desire that Trustee first distribute to the non-exempt Trust, property (or its proceeds) that constitutes Income in Respect of a Decedent, before distributing other property. Where applicable (and unless applicable Treasury Regulations require (or permit) otherwise), if the severance is required (by the terms of this Agreement) to be made on the basis of a pecuniary amount, the payment of the pecuniary amount shall, to the extent required, be satisfied in a manner that complies with Treas. Reg. sections 26.2654-1(a)(1)(ii) (A) **and** (B) (which concerns the payment of appropriate interest and the method of funding the pecuniary amount).

(3) Where applicable, Trustee is directed to comply with the valuation rules of Treas. Reg. section 26.2642-2 and the separate share rules of Treas. Reg. section 26.2654-1, to wit:

(a) Unless applicable Treasury Regulations require (or permit) otherwise, Trustee shall, to the extent applicable, satisfy the "appropriate interest" requirement: (i) by paying or irrevocably setting aside property in satisfaction of a pecuniary amount within fifteen (15) months of the date of death of the transferor, (ii) by paying appropriate interest as defined in Treas. Reg. section 26.2642-2(b)(4) on a pecuniary amount, or (iii) by allocating to a pecuniary amount a pro rata share of trust income from the transferor's date of death to the payment date.

(b) Unless applicable Treasury Regulations require (or permit) otherwise, Trustee shall, to the extent applicable, pay such pecuniary amount: (i) in cash, (ii) solely or partly in kind, using date of distribution values, or (iii) solely or partly in kind, in a manner that fairly reflects net appreciation and depreciation in the value of the assets in the fund available to pay the pecuniary amount, measured from the date of valuation to the date of distribution.

(c) Unless applicable Treasury Regulations require (or permit) otherwise, in instances where a generation-skipping tax exemption is to be allocated to a residual transfer that follows a pecuniary payment, I direct that: (i) the pecuniary payment receive "appropriate interest" as described in item (a) above, and (ii) if the pecuniary payment is to be satisfied solely or partly in kind, that the funding of such in kind distribution be in a manner described in items (b)(ii) and (iii) above.

(d) In determining the denominator for the "applicable fraction" used in calculating the inclusion ratio for any trust, it is my intent that where this Agreement (or Trustee) creates separate trusts, one with an inclusion ratio of one (1) and one with an inclusion ratio of zero (0), that the "applicable fraction" be calculated under the Treasury Regulations in effect at such time to accomplish the intended result.

(e) In determining how to satisfy the appropriate interest and funding requirements and how to obtain the desired "applicable fraction" described above, Trustee shall have complete discretion, and shall not be held liable for any consequence of the exercise of this discretion, made in good faith. I recognize that Trustee's decision as to how to satisfy these requirements may affect the amounts ultimately allocated to the various trusts hereunder; nevertheless, I intend this provision to apply.

(4) Except as may otherwise be provided in this Agreement (or be provided by applicable law), when a trust (the "original trust") is divided into exempt and non-exempt trusts or otherwise into separate trusts, references in this Agreement to the original trust shall collectively refer to the separate trusts derived from it. Trustee may make different tax elections (including the allocation of generation skipping transfer tax exemption), exercise investment, administrative and distributive discretion, and donees of powers of appointment may exercise their powers, differently with respect to each of the separate trusts (even otherwise identical trusts) derived from the original trust.

(5) If a trust under this Agreement, whether created under this provision or not, is entirely exempt or non-exempt from generation-skipping tax and adding property to it would partially subject the trust to generation-skipping tax, or change its inclusion ratio, Trustee shall hold that property in a separate trust in lieu of making the addition.

(6) Trustee is authorized to divide property in a trust into separate trusts with different transferors; such a trust may have more than one transferor. Trustee shall make any payment to, or for the benefit of, a beneficiary from any trust that has more than one transferor for generation-skipping transfer tax purposes (i) pro rata, from the separate portions attributable to transferors relative to whom the beneficiary is a non-skip person for generation-skipping tax purposes, and, to the extent of any balance, (ii) in ascending order of inclusion ratios of the portions for generation-skipping tax purposes, from the separate portions attributable to transferors relative to whom the beneficiary is a skip person for generation-skipping tax purposes, and such distributions need not be ratable among trusts or trust shares with the same inclusion ratios.

(7) If exempt and non-exempt trusts are established under this Agreement, Trustee shall have the power to make distributions (including distributions resulting from a partial or complete termination of a trust) to beneficiaries who are "non-skip persons" first from non-exempt trusts established for them and then from exempt trusts established for them; in addition, distributions to beneficiaries who are "skip persons" may be made first from exempt trusts established for them and only thereafter from non-exempt trusts established for them. Distributions need not be ratable among trusts or trust shares with the same inclusion ratios. In making distributions from a non-exempt trust, Trustee is authorized to make generation-skipping tax exempt distributions to beneficiaries who are skip persons, as permitted by IRC section 2611(b)(1) (concerning direct payments for tuition and medical expenses). "Skip persons" and "non-skip persons" shall be defined for purposes of this Agreement in accordance with IRC section 2613.

(8) Upon division, or distribution or termination of an exempt trust and a non-exempt trust, Trustee may allocate property from the exempt trust first to a share or trust from which a generation-skipping transfer is more likely to occur.

(9) A Disinterested Trustee in its sole, absolute and uncontrolled discretion may at any time prior to the death of the beneficiary, by an instrument in writing: (i) confer upon the beneficiary (other than me or my spouse (if I am married)) a power exercisable, by and only by will, which specifically refers to the power created hereunder, to appoint all or part of the beneficiary's trust share to the creditors of the beneficiary's estate, and the instrument conferring the power and its terms and conditions may require consent of a Disinterested Trustee who is not the creator of the power and who does not have a substantial interest in the property subject to the power, which interest is adverse to the exercise of the power within the meaning of IRC sections 2514(c) and 2041(b) and Treas. Reg. sections 25.2514-3(b)(2) and 20.2041-(3)(c)(2); (ii) revoke or modify any such instrument previously executed, with or without executing a replacement instrument; and/or (iii) irrevocably relinquish the powers conferred under Paragraphs 7.1(b)(9)(i) and/or (ii) above. For purposes of the preceding sentence, the term "creditors" does not include the Trustee who confers the power or whose consent is required to exercise the power. Without limiting Trustee's discretion, Trustee may use the authority conferred by this provision to subject the trust property to federal estate tax instead of the federal generation-skipping transfer tax when it appears that it may reduce overall taxes to do so. The power granted may be by a formula or limited by a formula, in the discretion of the Disinterested Trustee. The beneficiary's power conferred by Trustee pursuant to this provision shall not be exercisable in any manner so as to postpone the vesting of any estate or interest in the appointed property or to suspend the absolute ownership or power of alienation of the appointed property for a period ascertainable without regard to applicable rules limiting the maximum duration of trusts (such as any rules governing perpetuities, vesting, accumulations or the suspension of alienation), and the validity of any exercise shall be measured with respect to such rules, to the extent applicable.

(C) Limitation on Powers.

(1) When more than one person is serving as Trustee and at least one of them is not beneficially interested in the exercise or non-exercise of a power or election, the beneficially interested Trustee shall not participate in the exercise or non-exercise of the power or election.

(2) No beneficiary or Trustee (either alone or in conjunction with other Trustees or persons) shall possess or exercise any power, discretion or incidents of ownership with respect to any insurance owned by the trust on his or her life; nor shall such beneficiary or Trustee hold or possess any power of appointment over such life insurance, unless such life insurance policies or proceeds would otherwise be includible in the beneficiary's or Trustee's gross estate (for federal estate tax purposes) at the beneficiary's or Trustee's death without regard to such power of appointment. If a Trustee holds (or is to receive) any such policy or policies as a part of the trust estate, then and in that event: (i) the powers conferred on the owner of such policy shall be exercised only by the other then acting Trustee, who is not an insured under the policy; (ii) the life insurance policy or policies shall be received, held and administered in and as a separate sub-trust of the original trust from which it is derived, segregated from the original trust properties, and the insured beneficiary shall be excluded as a beneficiary of the sub-trust (i.e., not eligible to receive or control any distributions of income or principal from the sub-trust); (iii) the insured (including an insured Trustee) shall not serve as a Trustee of such sub-trust; (iv) the sub-trust Trustee (who shall also serve as a Co-Trustee of the original trust) may pay from the original trust (other than a trust qualified and elected for the marital or charitable deduction) any premiums, costs or charges associated with the insurance policies held by the sub-trust (and in no event shall such premiums, costs or charges be paid from any trust assets that are (or have been) contributed by the insured, and the insured shall not be entitled to contribute or transfer property to the original trust or to the sub-trust); and (v) in all other respects the terms of the newly created sub-trust shall be as consistent with the original trust from which it is derived. If the insured Trustee is the only then acting Trustee of the original trust, then such powers over the life insurance policy or policies shall instead be exercised by a substitute Trustee designated pursuant to the provisions of this Agreement dealing with the trusteeship; provided however, if any rule of law or court decision construes the ability of the insured Trustee to name a substitute Trustee as an incident of ownership, the designation of a substitute Trustee shall be implemented either by: (i) a majority of the current income beneficiaries, or (ii) by a court of competent jurisdiction.

(3) No Trustee shall have the power to use or apply trust property (i) for the support and maintenance of anyone the Trustee is obligated to support and maintain, or (ii) for the purpose of directly or indirectly discharging the personal legal obligations of the Trustee. No beneficiary-trustee who is an individual shall have the power to terminate a trust early of which he or she is a beneficiary. At any time when there is more than one Trustee, no Trustee who is also a beneficiary of any trust created under this Agreement shall exercise any power solely by himself or herself as would cause such beneficiary-Trustee to be treated as an owner of any portion of the trust under IRC section 678(a). No Trustee who is also a beneficiary of any trust created under this Agreement shall have the power, as a then acting Trustee of such trust, to make discretionary distributions to him or herself except: (i) to the extent necessary for such beneficiary-Trustee's health, education, support and maintenance as described in IRC sections 2041 and 2514 (concerning powers of appointment and ascertainable standards) in his or her accustomed manner of living (considering the resources reasonably available to him or her), or (ii) with the consent of a person who has a substantial interest in the trust property adverse to the exercise of the power in favor of such beneficiary-Trustee or such beneficiary-Trustee's estate or the creditors of either (as the case may be), within the meaning of IRC sections 2514(c) and 2041(b) and Treas. Reg. sections 25.2514-3(b)(2) and 20.2041-(3)(c)(2); and such beneficiary-Trustee shall exercise its Trustee powers solely in a fiduciary capacity and shall not possess or exercise any powers that would otherwise permit that beneficiary-Trustee to enlarge or shift any of the beneficial interests under that trust (except as an incidental consequence of the discharge of such fiduciary duties); and to the extent such beneficiary-Trustee has the authority to make discretionary distributions of income and/or principal to another beneficiary from a trust of which beneficiary-Trustee is then also a then current trust beneficiary, the discretionary distributions shall be limited by an ascertainable standard related to the distributee beneficiary's health, education, support and maintenance in the manner of living to which the distributee beneficiary has been accustomed, and except as may otherwise be provided elsewhere in this Agreement, the beneficiary-Trustee shall consider the resources otherwise reasonably available to the distributee beneficiary, when making such distributions. No beneficiary-Trustee who is an individual shall make discretionary distributions to or for the benefit of any beneficiary of a trust holding assets as a result of a disclaimer by or on behalf of such individual beneficiary-Trustee, except distributions limited to an ascertainable standard concerning the other beneficiary's health, education, support and maintenance. Furthermore, no beneficiary-Trustee who is a beneficiary of the trust in question shall possess any power or discretion that is "conclusive," "sole," "absolute" or "uncontrolled" with respect to the exercise or non-exercise of such power or discretion under that trust; and such beneficiary-Trustee's power or discretion in that regard shall at all times be exercised or not exercised in a reasonable manner, be limited by a reasonably definite standard, and shall be subject to review and judicial scrutiny. Trustee's discretionary power to allot and/or to pay or apply the income and/or principal of any trust established under this Agreement ("*such trust*") to or for the use or benefit of any beneficiary of *such trust* shall be exercisable solely by Trustee(s) other than any Trustee who is a permissible beneficiary of the income and/or principal of any other trust ("*such other trust*"), if any Trustee of *such other trust* is a permissible beneficiary of *such trust*. If at any time there is no Trustee qualified and acting for the purpose of exercising such discretionary powers other than a Trustee described in the preceding sentence, such discretionary powers shall be exercisable by an Independent Trustee. If the provisions of this sub-paragraph preclude all of the then-serving Trustees from exercising a discretion or power otherwise granted them, an Independent Trustee may be appointed by Trustee as an additional Trustee, with the sole authority to exercise the discretion or power, and such additional Trustee may only be removed for reasonable cause.

(D) Life Insurance Matters.

(1) A primary purpose of this Agreement after my death is to enable Trustee, in Trustee's discretion, to help provide liquidity to meet the demands that may confront my estate and family at such time. The liquidity demands that may arise as a result of my death are impossible to predict because of uncertainties as to the other assets that may then be available, the debts and taxes that may then be due, and the cash needs that may remain outstanding for the support of individuals dependent upon me or to maintain business enterprises in which I may have invested. I believe that the best technique to meet these uncertain liquidity demands is for Trustee to invest all or a substantial portion of the trust assets in life insurance during my lifetime, even though such life insurance policies may constitute a disproportionate part, or all, of the trust estate. I recognize that, in the long run, life insurance may not yield as high a rate of return as other available investments, or that it may even experience a negative rate of return (a loss of principal); however, I believe that the benefits of life insurance investments, including the larger payment (compared to other investments) if an insured should die short of his or her normal life expectancy, outweigh the possibility of a lower yield in the long run.

(2) I recognize that the selection and continued ownership of life insurance policies raises questions of prudence and due diligence, whether such policies are acquired by Trustee or transferred to Trustee. Therefore, I expressly authorize (but do not obligate) Trustee, in its discretion, and acting upon the recommendation and representations of any person selling, or in any way associated with the marketing, promotion or sale of life insurance, to purchase any life insurance (including a no lapse/secondary guarantee life insurance policy) from one or more insurers. Trustee may (but shall not be required): (i) to verify that any particular life insurance policy satisfies the requirements for a "life insurance contract" under IRC section 7702; (ii) to compare the performance or pricing or the projected performance or pricing of a particular life insurance policy with the performance or pricing or the projected performance or pricing of any other life insurance policy that then may be available from any source; (iii) to assess the appropriateness of purchasing or retaining any life insurance policy as an investment for the trust as compared to other then available investment vehicles that are not life insurance policies; and (iv) to investigate the strength or solvency of the company that issued or is offering a given life insurance policy. I acknowledge that Trustee is not a guarantor of any life insurance policy held in the trust or payable to the trust, whether purchased by, transferred to, or payable to Trustee. By this Paragraph I do not intend to reserve any right to control or direct Trustee, and the decision on trust investments is expressly reserved exclusively to Trustee.

(3) Trustee, who is an individual and is not a professional trustee, shall not be liable to me or to any beneficiary for any loss or damage suffered in connection with performance or lack of performance of any insurance policy owned by the trust (or payable to the trust) or as a result of the financial condition, including insolvency, of any insurer. The fact that Trustee may have made inquiry regarding any such matter prior to acquisition or transfer of a policy or after the acquisition or transfer of such policy shall place no duty upon Trustee to make any further inquiry, but shall be considered activity beyond the scope of Trustee's normal duties (however, the forgoing shall not prevent Trustee from delegating such duties to an agent, such as a fee only life insurance advisor, if appropriate). Trustee shall not be liable to me or to any trust beneficiary for any loss or damage suffered in connection with the performance, or failure to perform, of any life insurance policy or the insolvency of any life insurance company. On behalf of myself and my successors, heirs, and assigns, I hereby indemnify and hold harmless Trustee from and against any and all claims, liabilities, penalties, and costs, including attorneys' fees, arising from any claim, demand, order or other action related in any way to investing in and/or retaining any life insurance policies and exercising or failing to exercise any incident of ownership therein concerning any life insurance policies that were selected or approved by me, and any judgment against Trustee in this regard shall be satisfied from the trust fund, and to the extent the trust fund is insufficient, against my personal assets, including assets acquired directly or indirectly by transferees by reason of my death. For purposes of this Paragraph, a "professional trustee" is a person who derives a significant portion of his or her work revenue from serving as a trustee of inter-vivos or testamentary trusts.

(4) With respect to any insurance policies that are purchased or transferred to Trustee, I claim no right, title, interest, or incidents of ownership therein at this time, nor shall I have any incidents of ownership therein, presently or in the future, nor shall I be the beneficiary of any such policies, nor shall I exercise any right, power, option, election, privilege or incident of ownership under any such policies; and furthermore, I shall have no duty to pay premiums, assessments or other charges necessary to keep any policy in force and shall incur no liability to the beneficiaries of this Agreement or to any other person if any policy lapses for non-payment of premiums, assessments or charges, or otherwise becomes uncollectible. Trustee shall have all of the rights of the owner of such policies and, without the consent or approval of me or any other person, may, in its sole discretion, exercise or decline to exercise, any election, option, right or privilege available to Trustee, as owner of the policy. Such powers include, by way of example, and without limitation: (i) to reduce the amount of any policy or convert or exchange any policy into other forms of insurance; (ii) to enter into non-taxable and taxable exchanges, transfers and/or sales of trust property; (iii) to make withdrawals from any policy, or to surrender any policy for its cash surrender value; (iv) to borrow upon and pledge any policy in connection with a loan; (v) to take paid-up insurance; (vi) to elect extended term insurance; (vii) to collect dividends, death or other benefits (including disability benefits or an accelerated death benefit), surrender payments, and any other payment which may be due or collectible; (viii) to enter into a split-dollar or other premium sharing or financing arrangement with any person or entity; (ix) to split any policy into two or more policies; (x) to allow dividends to remain with the insurance company or to use them to reduce premiums or to purchase additional insurance; (xi) to use cash values to pay premiums; (xii) direct the manner in which the policy account of any variable life insurance policy shall be allocated among the various investment options from time to time available under such policy, and to change such allocation from time to time, as provided in such policy; (xiii) make any and all elections with respect to any death benefit options provided under any life insurance policy, and change such election from time to time; (xiv) determine how much, if any, of each year's target or similar premium amount of any flexible premium life insurance policy to pay, taking into consideration such tax and financial considerations each year as Trustee deems relevant; (xv) to exercise any options of settlement that may be available under the terms of said policies; (xvi) to determine and modify the current amount of life insurance coverage under an existing policy; (xvii) to accept an accelerated death benefit or enter into a viatical or life settlement concerning any policy; (xviii) to sell or transfer a life insurance policy; and (xix) to enter into premium financing arrangements.

(5) Trustee may, in Trustee's discretion, pay any premiums or other charges from the trust estate or by application of dividends on the policy. If the trust funds are inadequate to pay such premiums or charges, or if Trustee shall deem it inadvisable to pay such premiums or charges, Trustee may, in Trustee's discretion, do one or more of the following: (i) sell a sufficient portion of the property of the trust estate or borrow on the collateral of the property of the trust estate (including borrowing from a beneficiary, Trustee or an affiliate of Trustee), to obtain funds necessary to pay the premiums or charges; (ii) convert a policy into a paid up policy in whatever amount may be provided by the terms of such policy, or convert any such policy to a policy of extended term insurance in whatever amount may be provided by the terms of such policy; (iii) use any automatic premium loan feature; (iv) borrow against any policy cash reserves (whether or not on the policy for which premium or charges will be paid); (v) elect any automatic non-forfeiture feature; (vi) surrender any policy to obtain its cash surrender value; (vii) sell any policy; (viii) reduce the amount of the death benefit; (ix) exercise any other right, option, power, election or privilege under any policy held in trust by Trustee; (x) if I am married, assign and deliver the policy to my Spouse if he or she is an interested trust beneficiary (and not a donor or an insured under the policy); (xi) distribute the policy pursuant to any authority or discretion exercisable by the Trustee concerning distributions of trust principal; (xii) terminate the trust and distribute the policy pursuant to the provisions of this Agreement concerning termination of trusts (to the extent applicable); (xiii) assign the policy to the then current income beneficiaries (other than me or any donor) in equal shares and deliver such policies to them; or (xiv) distribute or liquidate the policy and deliver the policy or liquidation proceeds in such manner, amount, proportions and to such beneficiaries as may be determined or directed by a court of competent jurisdiction. Trustee shall not be responsible for the non-payment of premiums if the trust lacks the ability to pay them, and Trustee shall not be liable to anyone if the policies shall lapse (in whole or in part) or be otherwise uncollectible because the trust lacks the ability to pay the premiums. If Trustee has knowledge of an impending lapse or insufficiency of trust assets to pay premiums and other charges, Trustee shall make reasonable efforts to promptly notify in writing: (a) me (if I am not incapacitated or otherwise unavailable), and (b) at least one adult current trust beneficiary, who is sui juris, in order to advise us of the situation so that appropriate steps can be considered and, if need be, appropriate steps can be undertaken to provide sufficient funds to the trust estate in order to preserve the life insurance policy.

(6) Upon the death of an insured hereunder: (i) Trustee shall furnish the necessary proofs of death to the insurance company or companies which issued any policies of insurance, the proceeds of which are payable to Trustee; (ii) Trustee shall collect the proceeds of all such policies of insurance, and (iii) Trustee shall collect and receive any other property which may be made payable to Trustee. For such purpose, Trustee shall have full power and authority to execute and deliver any receipt or other voucher for such proceeds or property, to institute any suit or suits at law or in equity to enforce the payment of the proceeds of any such policies or to collect any such other property, and, in case of controversy or litigation over the collection of the same, to adjust, compromise or otherwise settle any controversy or contest concerning said policies of insurance or other property, or the collection thereof. Trustee shall be responsible for the proceeds of the insurance only when, as and if collected or paid to it.

(7) Trustee may, in Trustee's discretion, refuse to enter into or maintain any litigation, endorse policy payments, or take other action respecting any trust insurance policies, until Trustee has been indemnified against all expenses and liabilities which, in Trustee's judgment, may be involved in such action.

(8) Trustee need not inquire whether or not Trustee or the trust has been designated the beneficiary of any insurance policy or other death benefit, and Trustee need act with respect to such policies only after receipt of written notice that Trustee or the trust is a beneficiary.

(9) For trust accounting purposes, policy dividends and increases in value before the death of the insured under any life insurance policy or policies held by the trust shall be treated as principal, and not income.

(10) Any additional insurance policies, no matter how acquired (including, but not limited to acquisition by gift, conversion, reissue, consolidation), may be listed on **Schedule A**, but failure to do so does not affect the trust's policy ownership.

I SPECIFICALLY ACKNOWLEDGE THAT TRUSTEE WOULD NOT ACCEPT THE POSITION OF TRUSTEE UNLESS ITS DUTIES AND RESPONSIBILITIES WERE LIMITED AS SET FORTH ABOVE; AND TRUSTEE, WHO IS AN INDIVIDUAL AND IS NOT A PROFESSIONAL TRUSTEE, IS INDEMNIFIED.

7.2 Beneficiary Under Disability. Irrespective of whether a trust makes explicit reference to this Paragraph, if a beneficiary is under the age of thirty (30) years, legally disabled, incapacitated, or, in Trustee's opinion, incapable of managing a trust distribution, Trustee (i) may hold or distribute the income and principal in such manner as provided by law or as is otherwise permitted by authority granted Trustee in this Paragraph or elsewhere in this Agreement; (ii) may expend directly any income or principal that it is authorized to use for the beneficiary; or (iii) may pay it over to or for the benefit of the beneficiary, or to the beneficiary's legal representative, if any, or to any near relative or friend, or to any adult with whom the beneficiary is residing, for expenditure on the beneficiary's behalf, without any further responsibility for its application. If Trustee is directed to distribute any portion of trust principal to that beneficiary (including trust principal distributable pursuant to a beneficiary's right of withdrawal), the trust principal shall vest in interest in the beneficiary indefeasibly, but Trustee, in its discretion, may distribute the portion to a custodian for the beneficiary as selected by Trustee (who may be the Trustee) under a Uniform Transfers (Gifts) to Minors Act or similar act, or hold the portion as a separate and distinct trust until the later of (i) the beneficiary reaches the age of thirty (30) years; or (ii) after the removal of the legal disability; or (iii) after the recovery from the incapacity; or (iv) after the time Trustee deems the beneficiary is capable of managing a trust distribution. If Trustee holds the portion as a separate trust, Trustee may pay to or for the benefit of the beneficiary so much of the income and principal as Trustee deems advisable for the reasonable health care, education, support and maintenance of the beneficiary and the beneficiary's spouse and descendants; and, if the beneficiary dies before receiving all of his or her portion, Trustee shall distribute the remaining portion to the beneficiary's estate. Trustee shall not exercise its discretion hereunder in a manner that would impair a beneficiary's unexercised right of withdrawal that has not yet lapsed, or prevent an existing bequest from qualifying for the marital or charitable deduction, or would prevent an increase in basis (if applicable) under the Code, or would impair the status or qualification of a trust that holds shares of stock in a Subchapter S corporation, or would otherwise impair or prevent a qualified family-owned business interest deduction taken under IRC section 2057, or would otherwise impair or prevent special use valuation under IRC section 2032A.

7.3 Spendthrift Provisions. To the fullest extent permitted by law, a beneficiary's interest in the trust (including income and principal) shall not be subject to the beneficiary's liabilities or creditor claims or an encumbrance, sale, voluntary or involuntary transfer or assignment, anticipation or legal process, or claims for alimony or child support; nor shall the trust be liable for any beneficiary's debt to any agency, public office or department of the State of ________________ or any other state, or of the United States, or to any other creditor of the beneficiary, nor shall the trust be subject to the process of seizure of any court. Moreover, no power of appointment or power of withdrawal shall be subject to involuntary exercise. Furthermore, no part of the trust estate shall be subject to the claims of any creditor for the provision of support, maintenance, care, or services, including residential care, by any public entity, office, department or agency of the State of Michigan, or of any other state, or the United States, or any other governmental agency. However, this spendthrift provision shall not restrict the voluntary exercise of a power of appointment or the voluntary exercise of a withdrawal right granted by this Agreement. This spendthrift provision shall not prevent or prohibit the complete or partial termination of a trust, the amendment, modification or reformation of a trust, or the acceleration of the payment of principal to or for the benefit of a beneficiary. This spendthrift provision shall not prevent the voluntary: (i) sale, (ii) gift or (iii) transfer of a beneficiary's interest in the trust, to: (a) charity, or (b) between family members and/or other trust beneficiaries, if, but only if, such voluntary sale, voluntary gift or voluntary transfer to the charity, family members/and or other trust beneficiaries is pre-approved by Trustee in writing. If Trustee believes that a beneficiary shall not benefit as greatly from any outright distribution of trust income or principal because of the availability of such distribution to the beneficiary's creditors, Trustee shall instead expend those amounts for the benefit of the beneficiary as Trustee in its sole, absolute and uncontrolled discretion determines. However, Trustee may, but need not, without liability or accountability, pay on the order of the beneficiary, any distribution to which the beneficiary may otherwise be entitled to, to those persons the beneficiary directs. It is my intention to insulate all trust funds from the claims of the creditors of the beneficiary and especially involuntary transfers of the trust asset or interests in the trust, to the greatest extent possible under applicable law, while enabling Trustee to give the beneficiary the maximum possible benefit and enjoyment of all of the trust income and principal to which the beneficiary is entitled. The foregoing provisions of this Paragraph 7.3 not withstanding, Trustee shall not exercise its discretion hereunder in a manner that would impair a beneficiary's unexercised right of withdrawal that has not yet lapsed, or would prevent an existing bequest from qualifying for the marital or charitable deduction, or would prevent an increase in basis (if applicable) under the Code, or would impair the status or qualification of a trust that holds shares of stock in a Subchapter S corporation, or would impair or prevent a qualified family owned business interest deduction taken under IRC section 2057, or would impair or prevent special use valuation under IRC section 2032A.

7.4 **Certificate of Trust Existence and Authority.** Trustee may, at any time, record, file, or deliver a Certificate of Trust Existence and Authority ("Certificate") with or to any clerk, register of deeds, transfer agent, or other similar agency or office or to any person dealing with Trustee. The Certificate shall contain a verbatim synopsis of certain provisions of this Agreement and shall be signed and acknowledged by me, Trustee, or an attorney for me or Trustee, and shall be in the form of an affidavit. Any purchaser or person dealing with Trustee shall be entitled to rely on the Certificate as a full statement of the provisions of this Agreement that are pertinent to the particular transaction. Photocopies of the executed Certificate shall have the same effect and authority as the executed Certificate.

7.5 Multiple Copies. There is only one (1) signed original of this Agreement. Anyone may rely on a copy of said document as certified by a notary public or similar official to be a true copy of the signed original (and of the amendments or other writings, if any, endorsed on or attached thereto) to the same effect as if such copy were the signed original. Anyone may rely upon any statement of fact certified by anyone who appears from the original document or a certified copy thereof to be a Trustee hereunder.

7.6 Termination of Trust. If at any time the size of any trust created under this Agreement is so small that the trust is uneconomical to administer, or if for any other reason in the opinion of Trustee (who is not an Interested Trustee), the trust is no longer necessary, or is impractical, or inappropriate to continue for any reason under the current circumstances, including changes in economic and factual circumstances or changes in federal, state or local rules of law (tax or otherwise), including permanent repeal of the federal estate tax and/or the federal generation skipping transfer tax, or it would not be in the best interests of some or all of the beneficiaries for the trust to continue, such Trustee may, with or without prior or subsequent court approval, terminate part or all of the trust and distribute part or all of the trust funds, as the case may be: (i) to or for the benefit of the primary (or preferred) beneficiary for whom the trust was established, if there is such a beneficiary, or in the absence thereof, to or for the benefit of the person(s) to whom Trustee then must or may pay the trust's current income, in proportion to their interest(s) in trust income; however, if there is more than one beneficiary to whom current income could be paid but the interests are indefinite, Trustee shall distribute the trust assets to or for the benefit of the beneficiaries who are my descendants, by right of representation, or if no descendant of mine is a beneficiary, to all then living income and then living residuary beneficiaries of the trust equally, or (ii) in such other manner or amount(s) as a court of competent jurisdiction may direct, in order to carry out my intentions. Upon such termination, the rights of all other persons who might otherwise have an interest as succeeding life tenant or in a remainder, shall cease. In exercising its authority hereunder, the Disinterested Trustee may distribute all or less than all of the trust assets, while retaining some trust assets in a continuing trust when it appears it may be advantageous or beneficial to the beneficiary (or beneficiaries) to continue to hold such assets in trust. Before terminating a trust hereunder, Trustee may request and shall be entitled to be held harmless and receive appropriate indemnification from the beneficiaries who are going to receive a terminating distribution. Trustee shall not terminate a trust if it would impair a beneficiary's unexercised right of withdrawal that has not yet lapsed, or prevent an existing bequest from qualifying for the marital or charitable deduction, or would prevent an increase in basis (if applicable) under the Code, or would impair the status or qualification of a trust that holds shares of stock in a Subchapter S corporation, or would otherwise impair or prevent a qualified family owned business interest deduction taken under IRC section 2057, or would otherwise impair or prevent special use valuation under IRC section 2032A. Trustee shall not be liable for either exercising or failing to exercise its discretion to terminate a trust.

7.7 **Accrued Income.** Except as otherwise expressly provided to the contrary, upon the death of a beneficiary, any accrued or undistributed income shall be held and accounted for, or distributed, in the same manner as if it had been received and accrued after the beneficiary's death.

7.8 **Right of Representation.** Whenever a distribution or division of property is to be made to a person's descendants or issue by "right of representation," or if the manner of distribution or division is not specified, the property shall be divided into as many equal shares as there are (i) then-living descendants in the generation nearest to the designated person that contains one or more then-living descendants and (ii) deceased descendants in the same generation who left then-living descendants, if any. Each then-living descendant in the nearest generation is to be allocated one share. The remaining shares, if any, are to be combined and then divided in the same manner among the then-living descendants of the deceased descendants as if the then-living descendants who were allocated a share and their then-living descendants had predeceased the designated person.

7.9 Accountings and Information to Beneficiaries. Trustee's duty to inform and account to the beneficiaries shall be governed by the following rules.

(A) Recipients of Information and Accountings. While a trust holds, at year end, either (i) unmatured life insurance policies, or (ii) unmatured life insurance policies and cash, marketable securities or other liquid assets with a combined liquid value (excluding any life insurance cash surrender value(s)) of less than fifty thousand ($50,000) dollars, adjusted for the cost-of-living, Trustee shall not be required to prepare or file an annual accounting either with the court or with any beneficiary unless such an accounting is either ordered by a court of competent jurisdiction or is specifically requested in writing by a then living current trust beneficiary who is twenty-five (25) years of age or older, is sui juris, not incapacitated and who is actually then receiving trust distributions (other than distributions of tangible personal property) in which case Trustee shall furnish an accounting to the court or beneficiary consistent with the court's order or the beneficiary's reasonable requirements. Subject to the foregoing, upon the earlier of: (i) life insurance proceeds being received by the trust, or (ii) when the trust holds, at year end, more than fifty thousand ($50,000) dollars of combined value of cash, marketable securities, or other liquid assets (excluding any life insurance cash surrender value(s)), adjusted for the cost-of-living, Trustee shall inform and account to: (i) the current trust beneficiaries who are sui juris, and (ii) to such other persons as may be ordered by a court of competent jurisdiction.

(B) Statement of Account. Trustee shall keep a true account of the affairs of the trust. At least annually and upon termination of the trust or a change of Trustee, Trustee shall (subject to the above provision entitled, "**Recipients of Information and Accountings**"), render a statement of account. The statement of account shall, at a minimum, list the trust assets, if feasible giving their market values, the trust liabilities, receipts, and disbursements, state the source and amount of the trustee's compensation, and inform the beneficiary of the time allowed (to wit, 1 year after the date the beneficiary or a representative of the beneficiary is sent a report that adequately discloses the existence of a potential claim for breach of trust) for commencing a proceeding against a Trustee for breach of trust. The statement of account, if any, shall be delivered as soon as practicable after the close of the accounting period or upon the termination of the trust, or change of Trustee.

(C) **Inspection of Records.** The books and records of Trustee relating to this Agreement shall be open at all reasonable times to inspection only by the current trust beneficiary or the current trust beneficiary's accredited representatives, unless otherwise ordered by a court having jurisdiction; provided however, during my lifetime, only I (or my designated agent, if I am incapacitated) shall have this right of inspection. The foregoing sentence notwithstanding, upon good cause shown, a court having jurisdiction may order Trustee to keep other beneficiaries reasonably informed of the trust and its administration.

(D) **Settlement of the Account.** A receipt in full or a release by the beneficiaries or by the conservator or other legal representatives of those beneficiaries who are disabled shall be binding, as to those beneficiaries and as to all matters and transactions stated in the account or shown by it.

(E) **Court Approval of Account.** Trustee is entitled at any time to have a judicial settlement of its account, and attorney fees, expenses, guardian ad litem fees, and other charges incident to the judicial proceeding may be charged against the trust fund.

(F) **Delivery of Accountings.** If the current trust beneficiary is another trust, the statement of account shall be delivered to the trustee of the other trust. If any current trust beneficiary is a minor or otherwise disabled, delivery shall be made to the conservator of his or her estate or, if none, then to his or her parent, legal guardian, or nearest of kin or an adult with whom he or she is living. Trustee may deliver the statement of account to other trust beneficiaries in its discretion.

7.10 S Corporation Stock. If any stock of a corporation that then operates or that Trustee shall deem likely to operate in the near future as an S corporation (as defined in IRC section 1361(a)) is held by a trust or becomes distributable to a trust created under this Agreement, and such trust is not eligible or is no longer eligible, or may not be eligible or qualified to hold S corporation stock (for whatever the reason—including because of discretionary authority granted Trustee), Trustee may implement any of the following alternatives with respect to the S corporation stock:

(A) Where the original trust is for a sole beneficiary, Trustee may create for that beneficiary (provided the beneficiary meets the requisite qualifications under IRC section 1361) a separate trust (or sub-trust) that qualifies as a Qualified Subchapter S Trust under IRC section 1361 (d) ("QSST"), and then distribute such stock to the newly created trust.

(B) Where the original trust is for multiple beneficiaries, Trustee may create for each beneficiary (provided the beneficiary meets the requisite qualifications under IRC section 1361): (i) a separate trust, (ii) a separate sub-trust, or (iii) substantially separate and independent shares for each beneficiary (as is permitted under IRC section 1361(d)(3)), and allocate the S corporation stock among the newly created trusts or shares based on each beneficiary's current interest in the income of the original trust, and if no beneficiary is entitled to current income from the original trust, Trustee may allocate the S corporation stock among the newly created trusts or shares in a manner that Trustee deems fair and appropriate. Each newly created trust or share shall hold that beneficiary's appropriate share of the S corporation stock, and shall qualify as a QSST.

(C) Trustee may, in its discretion: (i) create for a beneficiary (or group of beneficiaries) a separate trust (or sub-trust) that qualifies as an Electing Small Business Trust under IRC section 1361 (e) (provided the beneficiary or group of beneficiaries meet the requisite qualifications thereunder) ("ESBT") and distribute such stock to the newly created trust(s), provided however, no distribution from the newly created trust(s) shall be made to any person (whether a current beneficiary or future or contingent beneficiary) other than to a person who is eligible to be an ESBT beneficiary (as determined under the Code), and the number of "potential current beneficiaries" of the ESBT shall not exceed the number of shareholders permitted under IRC section 1361(b); furthermore, any currently exercisable inter-vivos power of appointment held by a beneficiary concerning the S corporation stock to be held by the ESBT (other than a beneficiary's inter-vivos power of withdrawal) is hereby automatically modified and limited concerning the number and class of appointees eligible to receive the S corporation stock so that the number of actual appointees shall not shall not exceed the number of shareholders permitted under IRC section 1361(b) and the class of appointees shall not include those persons who are ineligible to hold the S corporation stock (as determined under the Code), (ii) elect to qualify any trust as any form of eligible stockholder of an S corporation under current or future legislation, or (iii) distribute such stock to the beneficiaries (provided the beneficiaries are eligible S corporation shareholders) as if the trust had terminated, while continuing to hold any other non-S corporation property in trust.

Each newly created QSST shall have mandatory distributions of income (as defined in IRC section 643(b)) and no one shall have any power to appoint or distribute any portion of the QSST property to anyone other than to the beneficiary of the trust. In all other respects the newly created trusts shall be as consistent as possible with the original trusts and still qualify as QSSTs or ESBTs (as the case may be). Trustee may take any action necessary with regard to S corporations, including making any elections required to qualify stock as S corporation stock, qualify a trust as an S corporation shareholder, and sign all necessary tax returns and forms.

It is my intent that any S corporation stock comprising a portion of the trust estate be eligible to be held pursuant to the terms of this Agreement, either as an ESBT, a QSST, or in any other manner permitted by the Internal Revenue Code or the Regulations or rulings thereunder. Accordingly, Trustee is granted the power to amend, modify or reform this Agreement to the minimum extent necessary to permit this Agreement and its trusts to hold S corporation stock during the continuance of this Agreement in accordance with the Internal Revenue Code, Regulations and rulings thereunder; but in no event shall Trustee amend, modify or reform this Agreement or any trust in a manner that would impair a beneficiary's unexercised right of withdrawal that has not yet lapsed or prevent an existing bequest from qualifying for the marital or charitable deduction or would prevent an increase in basis (if applicable) under the Code, or would impair the status or qualification of a trust that holds shares of stock in a Subchapter S corporation, or would otherwise impair or prevent a qualified family owned business interest deduction taken under IRC section 2057, or would otherwise impair or prevent special use valuation under IRC section 2032A, or prevent a disclaimer from being a qualified disclaimer under IRC section. As a cautionary note, Trustee is reminded that it should determine the effect the exercise of its authority hereunder may have on any disabled or handicapped beneficiary (particularly with regard to the beneficiary's eligibility to receive (or continue to receive) public or private benefits or assistance related to the beneficiary's disability/handicap). I realize that the decision to exercise the discretion granted under this Paragraph is extremely difficult, and, in consideration of Trustee agreeing to serve as a trustee under this Agreement, I specifically exonerate Trustee from any liability to any person with respect to the exercise or non-exercise of the discretion granted under this Paragraph.

Trustee shall not make a distribution of the S corporation stock to any person whose ownership of the stock would reasonably be expected to cause the corporation's Subchapter S election to be terminated. Trustee may (and is encouraged to) request a written opinion from tax counsel if Trustee is uncertain about the effect a contemplated distribution of the S corporation stock may have on the corporation's Subchapter S election.

7.11 Guidelines for Discretionary Distributions. Except as may be otherwise provided elsewhere in this Agreement, when exercising discretion relating to a distribution of income or principal, Trustee (other than an Interested Trustee) may, but need not, consider all other reasonably available income and liquid assets of the beneficiary known upon reasonable inquiry by that Trustee, as well any legal obligation of support owed to the beneficiary by another person. A beneficiary who receives discretionary distributions of income or principal need not deplete income and liquid assets below an amount Trustee deems reasonable.

ARTICLE 8
GENERAL PROVISIONS

8.1 Rule Against Perpetuities.

(A) Measuring Period. Upon the expiration of twenty-one (21) years after the death of the last survivor of a class consisting of me, my descendants, the beneficiaries and contingent beneficiaries under this Agreement, the lineal descendants of such beneficiaries, and the spouses of any of the aforesaid, who are living (or in gestation) on the date on which the interest or trust or power of appointment was created for purposes of the applicable Rule Against Perpetuities, every trust created under this Agreement, by the exercise of a power of appointment or otherwise, every power of appointment granted by this Agreement, and every interest, trust or power of appointment that may be created by the exercise of a power of appointment granted herein, shall terminate, if it has not then vested indefeasibly (as provided in paragraph item (B) below) or previously terminated; provided however, this provision shall not apply to any interest established by the exercise of a general power of appointment conferred by this Agreement if the exercise is valid both under this Agreement and under the applicable Rule Against Perpetuities, and under the applicable Rule Against Perpetuities such interest is allowed a new perpetuities period, in which case, the interest established by the general power of appointment shall terminate as provided in the instrument in which such power is exercised, subject to the Rule Against Perpetuities (if any) that may be applicable to such newly established interest. The exercise of any non-general power of appointment granted under this Agreement shall be subject to the perpetuities period of this Agreement and shall not be extended by the exercise of such power.

(B) Vesting of Trust Interests Prior to Expiration of Perpetuities Period. If on the day preceding the expiration of the applicable rules limiting the maximum duration of trusts (such as any rules governing perpetuities, vesting, accumulations or the suspension of alienation), any property is held in trust (except any trust all of the assets of which are then unqualifiedly withdrawable by its primary beneficiary), such property shall immediately vest indefeasibly in (i) the primary beneficiary for whom the trust was established, if there is such a beneficiary, or in the absence of a primary beneficiary to the person(s) to whom Trustee then must or may pay the trust's current income, in proportion to their interest(s) in trust income; however, if there is more than one beneficiary to whom current income could be paid but the interests are indefinite, the trust property shall vest indefeasibly in the beneficiaries who are my descendants, by right of representation, or if no descendant of mine is a beneficiary, then the trust property shall vest indefeasibly in all of the then living income and then living residuary beneficiaries of the trust equally, or (ii) in such other persons or amount(s) as a court of competent jurisdiction may direct, in order to carry out my intentions. For purposes of this Paragraph, to "vest indefeasibly" means that the interest shall continue in trust but be subject to a general power of appointment held by the beneficiary and exercisable by will or by deed at any time in favor of any person (including the beneficiary, the beneficiary's estate or the creditors of either), and if the interest continues in trust until its termination, the interest, in default of appointment, shall be paid to the beneficiary, if living or, if not living to the beneficiary's estate.

8.2 Power of Appointment Matters.

(A) Scope of Appointment. Except as otherwise limited, any trust principal or income as to which a power of appointment is exercised shall be distributed to one or more members of the permissible class of appointees upon such conditions and estates, in such manner (in trust, to an existing trust, to a trust to be created, or otherwise), with such powers, in such amounts or proportions (equal or unequal), and at such time or times as the holder of the power (donee) may specify in the instrument exercising the power (but not beyond the period permitted by any applicable rules limiting the maximum duration of trusts (such as any rules governing perpetuities, vesting, accumulations or the suspension of alienation)).

Unless the instrument exercising a power of appointment explicitly states that if an appointee is deceased that the appointment is in favor of the appointee's descendants (or explicit words of similar import and intent), any power of appointment exercised in favor of a deceased appointee shall lapse and a surviving descendant of the deceased appointee shall not be substituted for the deceased appointee. The donee may appoint a different trustee to administer a trust created by the exercise of the power and may change the situs of the trust administration and direct that the trust shall be governed by the law of the new situs or any other jurisdiction. The trustee under an appointment in further trust may be any person not prohibited from serving as Trustee under this Agreement and may be given fiduciary powers (including discretionary powers over distributions), exercisable, however, only in favor of permissible objects of the exercised power. If the donee does not direct otherwise, a trust created by the exercise of the power shall be administered by the trustee hereof subject to the same management powers conferred on the trustee. With respect to any sub-trusts or trusts that have been divided, the donee may exercise his or her power differently with respect to each sub-trust or separate trusts (even otherwise identical trusts) derived from the original or divided trust. No power of appointment may be exercised by any individual under this Agreement with respect to policies of insurance on the life of such individual, or the proceeds thereof, unless such policies or proceeds would be includible in the individual's gross estate (for federal estate tax purposes) at such individual's death without regard to such power of appointment.

(B) Manner of Exercise and Determination of Effective Appointment. Except as may be explicitly required otherwise in this Agreement, any power, including a power of appointment, granted to a person under this Agreement may be exercised either by (i) such individual by his or her last will and testament or (ii) a written direction other than a will executed by such person or such person's duly authorized and empowered legal representative and delivered to Trustee during the person's lifetime (or such other period required by the power) (hereinafter referred to as a "written direction"), which will or written direction makes specific reference to the power of appointment sought to be exercised so that Trustee is able to sufficiently and correctly identify which power under this Agreement is in fact being exercised by the donee. Except as provided otherwise in this Agreement, a power of appointment may be effectively exercised: (i) even if the donee is a minor, incapacitated or under disability, (ii) all of the assets constituting the trust with respect to which the power is granted have not been received by Trustee, or (iii) whether the instrument exercising the power is executed before or after the date on which any trust for the donee is created (including a trust in which the donee is granted the power). Any instrument exercising the power may be revoked or amended at any time before it becomes effective. Trustee may rely upon any instrument that is admitted to probate in any jurisdiction as the last will of the donee; and may distribute the property as provided herein in default of an effective appointment by will if, within six (6) months after the date of the donee's death, Trustee has not received a certified copy of the donee's will that has been admitted to probate and that purports to exercise the power; but the Trustee shall not be required to make any distribution to those who take in default of an effective appointment if Trustee is reasonably in doubt about whether there has been an effective exercise of the power. The provisions in the preceding sentence are for the protection of the Trustee and shall not affect any right or recourse that an appointee or beneficiary in default of appointment may have against any recipient(s) of the distributed property. Admission of a will to probate within six (6) months after the donee's death shall not be a condition to the effective exercise of a power.

(C) Trust Termination and Limited Power of Appointment by Special Power Holder. Each trust may, from time to time, have a special power holder. A special power holder may be appointed: (i) by me, in a writing delivered to the Trustee of the trust in question, (ii) by a majority in interest of the current trust beneficiaries of the trust in question, with one (1) vote being cast by each such beneficiary who is sui juris, one (1) vote being cast for each such minor beneficiary by his or her custodial parent, and one (1) vote being cast by the legal guardian for any such beneficiary having a legal guardian, (iii) by the Trustee then serving of the trust in question, or (iv) by a court of competent jurisdiction. Once appointed, a special power holder may not be removed except by a court of competent jurisdiction and then only for reasonable cause. A special power holder appointed by me shall serve prior to a special power holder appointed hereunder by any other person. In the event that two or more instruments of appointment concerning a special power holder exist and are inconsistent, the latest by date shall control, consistent with the priority of appointment specified above, and any inconsistencies in appointment maybe resolved by the unanimous decision of the existing Trustees and then nominated successor Trustees of the trust in question.

After my death, the special power holder may terminate a trust, in whole or in part, pursuant to the criteria set forth in the Paragraph entitled, **"Termination of Trust."** Furthermore, after my death, Trustee shall distribute all or any part of the trust estate (other than life insurance on the special power holder's life) as the special power holder (in a non-fiduciary capacity) from time to time appoints in a writing that is delivered to Trustee, to any one or more of the trust's beneficiaries, including contingent remainder beneficiaries (but not to the special power holder, the special power holder's estate, or the creditors of either) and in such proportions (equal or unequal) and in such manner (whether out right or in trust) as the special power holder specifies. Provided, however, that no such distribution may be applied or distributed that would give the special power holder any pecuniary benefit or would discharge or satisfy the special power holder's legal obligations. Any person serving or appointed to serve as a special power holder must not be related or subordinate (within the meaning of

IRC section 672 (c)) to me or to any beneficiary of the trust in question. A special power holder (then acting or nominated) may resign at any time by giving written notice, specifying the effective date of resignation to Trustee of the trust in question or to any current income beneficiary of the trust in question. If the special power holder is incapacitated, then he or she will be deemed to have automatically resigned as special power holder.

Notwithstanding any other provision of this Agreement, the special power holder shall not exercise any power or discretion conferred under this Agreement: (i) for the direct or indirect benefit of the special power holder, the special power holder's estate, or the creditors of either, (ii) that would cause the special power holder to possess a general power of appointment within the meaning of IRC sections 2041 and 2514, (iii) that would impair a beneficiary's outstanding withdrawal right that has not yet lapsed, (iv) that would prevent an existing bequest from qualifying (or continuing to qualify) for the marital or charitable deduction or would prevent an increase in basis (if applicable) under the Internal Revenue Code, (v) that would impair the status or qualification of a trust that holds shares of stock in a Subchapter S corporation, (vi) that would otherwise impair or prevent a qualified family owned business interest deduction taken under IRC section 2057, (vii) would otherwise impair or prevent special use valuation under IRC section 2032A, or (viii) would prevent a disclaimer from being a qualified disclaimer under IRC section 2518. The special power holder, acting in its capacity hereunder, shall have no fiduciary duty to any trust beneficiary and shall be indemnified and held harmless by the trust and the beneficiaries who are going to be benefited by the exercise of the special power holder's authority hereunder.

(D) Compelled Exercise of Power of Appointment Not Effective. The purported exercise of a power of appointment (including a power of withdrawal) granted under this Agreement shall be of no force or effect if such purported exercise was the result of compulsion. If such purported exercise is the result of compulsion, Trustee shall administer the property subject to such power of appointment as if said purported exercise had not occurred. The purported exercise of a power of appointment shall be deemed to be the result of compulsion if such purported exercise is in response to or by reason of any order or other direction of any court having jurisdiction over the donee, Trustee, the property subject to said power or the trust containing such property. A donee's legal representative may not exercise a power given to the donee under this Agreement if such purported exercise is in response to or by reason of any such order or other direction of any court having jurisdiction over the legal representative unless such order or other direction was obtained by the legal representative in a proceeding in which the legal representative was the petitioner or voluntarily acquiesced and was not otherwise under compulsion.

8.3 Law, Definitions, Captions, and Severability.

(A) Governing Law. Except as otherwise provided in this Paragraph 8.3(A), the validity, administration, meaning and effect, and all rights of beneficiaries under this Agreement and its provisions (and any other instrument related to this Agreement) shall be governed by the laws of the State of ________________. The administration, meaning and effect, and rights of beneficiaries under a trust established by the exercise of a power of appointment granted hereunder shall be governed by the laws of whatever jurisdiction may be designated either in such instrument of appointment or in the resulting trust (or, absent such designation, by the laws of the State of __________). This Paragraph 8.3(A) shall apply regardless of any change of residence of any Trustee or any beneficiary, or the appointment or substitution of a Trustee residing in another jurisdiction. Trustee may, with the prior written consent of a majority of the trust's current beneficiaries who are sui juris and not incapacitated, change the situs of such trust and/or its assets and elect to have the validity, administration, meaning and effect or rights of beneficiaries of such trust and/or its assets be governed by the laws of another jurisdiction, in or outside the United States (including that jurisdiction's law concerning the maximum duration of trusts). Trustee may not change the situs of a trust, the trust's assets or the trust's governing law in order to: (i) thwart the purpose of the trust, or (ii) limit Trustee's liability to a beneficiary due to an existing breach of duty. The jurisdiction whose laws govern the validity, meaning and effect, and rights of beneficiaries of any trust may, but need not, be the same as the situs of the trust's assets or the situs of the administration of such trust. This Agreement shall be exempt from mandatory registration (although Trustee may, in its discretion register any trust). Absent a written request from a current trust beneficiary who is sui juris and not incapacitated, Trustee who is an individual shall not be required to determine if the situs of a trust or its assets should be moved from its current jurisdiction to a different jurisdiction or if the governing law of the trust or its assets should be changed.

(B) Gender. Whenever necessary in this Agreement and where the context permits, the singular term and the related pronoun shall include the plural, the masculine, and the feminine, and, as to Trustee, the neuter.

(C) Charity. The term "charity" or "charitable organization" means an organization so constituted that gratuitous transfers to such organization are deductible, in the first instance, as charitable transfers for federal income, estate (if the Federal estate tax is applicable), or gift tax purposes (as the case may be).

(D) Child, Issue, and Descendants. For purposes of determining who is a child, grandchild or descendant of any person (including myself):

(1) The term "issue" or "descendants" means all individuals who are descended from the individual referred to in the first, second, or any other degree, provided the individual in each degree in the line of descent is a child, as defined below, of the individual in the prior degree.

(2) The term "child" means a descendant in the first degree of the parent designated; but such term does not include a stepchild, a foster child, a grandchild or any more remote descendant, unless that individual is adopted as a child (as set forth below).

(3) Subject to the above provisions:

(a) Any adoption begun before the adopting parent's death (i.e., the child has been "placed" with the adopting parent), if the adoption is legally completed by the (deceased) person's spouse within two (2) years after such death (provided the adopted child is under the age of eighteen (18) at the date of adoption) shall be deemed accomplished prior to death.

(b) Posthumous children are to be considered living at the death of their parent.

(E) **Current Trust Beneficiary.** "Current trust beneficiary" means a beneficiary about which either items (i) or (ii) below, is true: (i) the beneficiary has a current right to receive all or a portion of a mandatory distribution of income, or the beneficiary is currently eligible to receive a discretionary distribution of all or a portion of income; or (ii) the beneficiary is currently eligible to receive all or a portion of a mandatory or discretionary distribution of principal. A "current income beneficiary" is a beneficiary described in item (i), above. If an action under this Agreement must be (or is permitted to be) taken, exercised, affirmed or is referenced by the trust's "current income beneficiaries" and there are no current income beneficiaries of the trust in question (or there are no current income beneficiaries of the trust in question who are eligible to act), then and in that event, the current trust beneficiaries shall act in place of the "current income beneficiaries," and the current trust beneficiaries shall be subject to the same qualifications and limitations that are imposed upon the "current income beneficiaries," such as "majority, "sui juris," "not incapacitated," "of the trust in question," etc. In no event may I act on behalf of a current income beneficiary, regardless of my relationship to the beneficiary.

(F) **Death Taxes**. "Death taxes" means all estate, inheritance, succession, legacy, transfer or similar duties or taxes and any income or similar taxes on appreciation incurred solely as the result of my death, as well as any and all interest and penalties relating to such duties or taxes which are properly imposed by any federal, state, domestic or foreign taxing authority. "Death taxes" do not include any generation-skipping transfer tax.

(G) **Health, Education, Support and Maintenance.** "Health, education, support, and maintenance" shall be construed in such a manner as to be an ascertainable standard for federal estate and gift tax purposes, such that the exercise, release, or lapse of a power which is limited by this standard will not be taxable for federal estate and gift tax purposes. If Trustee has discretionary authority to make distributions for a beneficiary's health, education, support and maintenance, those standards shall constitute a ceiling on Trustee's discretionary authority, and shall not be interpreted as a floor that mandates distribution, i.e., Trustee's discretion is to be limited to matters pertaining to the beneficiary's health, education, support and maintenance. In determining "support" for a beneficiary, Trustee may take into account the obligations of support that the beneficiary owes to other individuals. "Health" shall include (but not be limited to) medical, mental, dental, hospital, and nursing expenses and expenses of invalidism.

(H) **Incapacity**. In the event that any Trustee or any beneficiary hereunder comes into possession of any of the following: (i) a court order, which such Trustee or beneficiary deems to be jurisdictionally proper and still currently applicable, holding a person to be legally incapacitated to act in his or her own behalf or appointing a guardian or conservator of the person or property (or similar fiduciary) to act for him or her, or (ii) a written report of a licensed psychologist, a licensed medical or osteopathic physician stating that he or she has examined a person and has concluded that such person is unable to give prompt and intelligent consideration to financial matters because of excessive use of drugs or alcohol, accident, physical or mental illness, progressive or intermittent physical or mental deterioration, or other similar cause, or (iii) evidence which such Trustee deems to be credible and still currently applicable that a person has disappeared, is unaccountably absent, is incarcerated, or is being detained under duress where he or she is unable to effectively manage his or her property or financial affairs; then and in that event and under those circumstances: (a) such person shall be deemed to have thereupon become "incapacitated", as that term is used in and for all of the purposes of this Agreement, and (b) such incapacity shall be deemed to continue until such court order, written reports, and/or circumstances have become inapplicable or have been revoked.

(1) Any psychologist's or physician's aforesaid report may be revoked by a similar report to the effect that such person is no longer thus incapacitated executed either (i) by the originally certifying psychologist or physician or (ii) by another licensed, unrelated psychologist or physician.

(2) No Trustee shall be under any duty to institute any inquiry into a person's possible incapacity, but the expense of any such inquiry reasonably instituted may be paid from trust assets.

(3) Each person who signs this instrument or an acceptance of Trusteeship or Trust Protector hereunder (a "Consenting Person"), by so signing: (i) consents to and agrees to cooperate in any medical examination necessary to carry out the terms of this provision; (ii) waives all provisions of law relating to disclosure of confidential medical information insofar as that disclosure would be pertinent to any inquiry under this provision, and directs all health care providers to complete the certification required by this provision; (iii) agrees that all individually identifiable health information and medical records (except psychotherapy notes) of the Consenting Person, including any written opinion relating to the Consenting Person's capacity/incapacity or ability to serve as a Trustee (or Trust Protector) that the requesting party has requested, may be released to the following people (a "Requesting Party"), whom the Consenting party hereby appoints as their personal representative in that regard, to wit, a then acting Co-Trustee hereunder, a nominated successor Trustee hereunder, a then acting Trust Protector hereunder, or a nominated successor Trust Protector hereunder. This release authority applies to any information governed by the Health Insurance Portability and Accountability Act of 1996 (aka HIPAA), 42 U.S.C. §1320d et seq. and 45 C.F.R. 160-164, and applies even if the Requesting Party has not yet been appointed as a successor Trustee or successor Trust Protector, as the case may be; and (iv) agrees that the obligations under this provision shall be specifically enforceable. The Requesting Party need not describe the purpose of each request made, but may simply note it is made at his or her request, as allowed under the HIPAA rules. This HIPAA authorization is effective immediately, shall not expire (except upon the death of the Consenting Party), but may be revoked by a written instrument executed by the Consenting Party. If this HIPAA authorization is revoked, any person or entity acting in good faith in reliance upon it, and lacking actual knowledge of its revocation, shall be held harmless by the Consenting Party. The Consenting Party understands that once the above information is disclosed, it may be re-disclosed by the Requesting Party, and that the information may not be protected by privacy laws or regulations. The Consenting Party acknowledges that authorizing the use or disclosure of this information is their voluntary act. The Consenting Party understands and acknowledges that a health care provider may not condition the Consenting Party's receipt of health care or medical treatment upon his or her authorization (or lack thereof) under the terms of this provision. If a Consenting Party fails within a reasonable time to cooperate hereunder (including having a medical examination and disclosing its results to a Requesting Party), then such Consenting Party shall be deemed to have resigned as a Trustee or Trust Protector (as the case may be), provided at the time the request was made by the Requesting Party there was a reasonable basis to request such medical examination, and provided further that no such request (in which the Consenting Party cooperated) may be made more than once every twenty-four (24) months. To the extent the cost of the medical examination is not paid for by the Consenting Party's health insurance (including Medicare, Medicaid, or other third party provider), the trust shall pay such costs (and may pay all the costs of the medical examination).

(I) **Independent Trustee.** An "Independent Trustee" means a person: (i) who is not related or subordinate (within the meaning of IRC section 672 (c)) to any beneficiary, power holder (including a person who holds the power to remove a Trustee), or transferor (as defined below) (as the case may be regarding the identity of the appropriate "power holder") with respect to the trust in question; (ii) who cannot be benefited by the exercise or non-exercise of any power given Trustee by this Agreement or by law; (iii) who is not a beneficiary of the trust in question, not an insured under a policy of life insurance owned by the trust, not a person who is prohibited from serving as a trustee of the trust in question, and is not an individual who has gratuitously transferred or joined in the gratuitous transfer of property to the trust in question (a "transferor"); and (iv) if a general power of appointment is held by a beneficiary that may only be exercised with the consent of an Independent Trustee, the term "Independent Trustee" also means a person who is not the creator of the power and who does not have a substantial interest in the property subject to the power which is otherwise adverse to the exercise of the power in favor of the beneficiary, the beneficiary's estate, or the creditors of either (as the case may be) within the meaning of IRC sections 2514 (c) and 2041(b) and Treas. Reg. sections 25.2514-3(b)(2) and 20.2041-(3)(c)(2). A transferor's spouse who merely consents to gift splitting under IRC section 2513 concerning the transferor's transfer of property to the trust shall not be deemed to have "joined in the transfer of property."

(J) Interested Trust Beneficiary. "Interested trust beneficiary" means a person that has one (1) or more of the following interests in the trust: (i) life estate, (ii) eligible recipient of a mandatory or discretionary distribution by the Trustee of income or principal, (iii) eligible recipient of a mandatory or discretionary distribution by the Trustee of income or principal upon termination of an interest of a person described in items (i) or (ii) above, or (iv) presently exercisable or current testamentary general or special power of appointment.

(K) Interested Trustee and Disinterested Trustee. "Interested Trustee" means for any trust a Trustee who is (i) a transferor of property to the trust, including a person whose disclaimer resulted in property passing to the trust; or (ii) a person who is, or in the future may be, eligible to receive income or principal pursuant to the terms of the trust. A Trustee described in item (i) above is an Interested Trustee only with respect to the transferred property (including income and gain on, and reinvestment of, such property). A person is included in item (ii) above if he or she has a remote contingent remainder, but a person is not included in item (ii) above if the person's only interest is as a potential appointee under a power of appointment held by another individual in his or her non-fiduciary capacity, the exercise of which will take effect only in the future, such as a testamentary power of appointment held by a living individual or the person's only interest is as a potential distributee under the Paragraph entitled, "**Absence of Beneficiaries**." A trustee who is not an Interested Trustee is a "Disinterested Trustee." An Independent Trustee is a "Disinterested Trustee." If a general power of appointment held by a beneficiary may only be exercised with the consent of a Disinterested Trustee, the term "Disinterested Trustee" also means a person who is not the creator of the power and who does not have a substantial interest in the property subject to the power which is adverse to the exercise of the power in favor of the beneficiary, the beneficiary's estate, or the creditors of either (as the case may be) within the meaning of IRC sections 2514 (c) and 2041(b) and Treas. Reg. sections 25.2514-3(b)(2) and 20.2041-

(3)(c)(2). Unless otherwise and explicitly provided to the contrary, any power or discretion conferred on an Interested Trustee or Disinterested Trustee may be exercised by an Independent Trustee or by a court of competent jurisdiction.

(L) **Internal Revenue Code**. References to "Code," "Internal Revenue Code," "IRC" (or similar abbreviations) or to provisions thereof are to the Internal Revenue Code of 1986, as amended at the time in question. References to the "Regulations" or "Treas. Treas. Reg. " are to the Treasury Regulations under the Code. If, by the time in question, a particular provision of the Code has been renumbered or the Code has been superseded by a subsequent federal tax law, the reference shall be deemed to be to the renumbered provision or the corresponding provision of the subsequent law, unless to do so would clearly be contrary to my intent as expressed in this Agreement, and a similar rule shall apply to references to the Regulations. All tax-related terms shall have the same meaning that they have in the Code.

(M) **May, Must and Shall.** Unless expressly provided otherwise in this Agreement concerning distributions to the beneficiary in question (or class of beneficiaries), Trustee shall exercise its authority (and discretion) to make distributions of trust income or principal in accordance with the terms and purposes of the trust, subject to the following:

(1) "May" is discretionary; and unless the discretion is made "sole," "absolute" or "uncontrolled," Trustee must act reasonably and in good faith. If the discretion is made "sole," "absolute" or "uncontrolled," Trustee must act honestly, in good faith, and not recklessly or capriciously.

(2) Unless expressly provided otherwise in this Agreement concerning distributions to the beneficiary in question (or class of beneficiaries), when making discretionary distributions where Trustee's discretion is "sole," absolute," or "uncontrolled," Trustee may, but need not, consider any other income or resources readily available to that beneficiary.

(3) Unless expressly provided otherwise in this Agreement concerning distributions to the beneficiary in question (or class of beneficiaries), when making distributions (including discretionary distributions) limited to a beneficiary's health, education, support or maintenance (or similar ascertainable standard), Trustee shall consider any other income or resources readily available to that beneficiary for such purposes and take into consideration the standard of living of the beneficiary.

(4) Except as otherwise qualified or restricted, "must" is mandatory, and "shall" is mandatory.

(N) **Sui Juris.** An individual who has the legal capacity to mange his or her own affairs and is not under a legal disability to act for one's self (such as minority, a guardianship, committee or conservatorship, etc.) is an individual who is sui juris.

(O) **Then Living.** The term "then living," when used in any provision in this Agreement, refers to the time when the event necessitating reference to such provision occurred rather than to the subsequent time when the directions of such provision may actually be implemented.

(P) **Trust.** "Trust," without further qualification or specification, shall refer to all trusts under this Agreement, and to the assets of any such trust or trusts.

(Q) **Captions.** Captions in this Agreement are used for convenience and shall not limit, broaden, or qualify the text.

(R) **Provisions Severable.** The provisions of this Agreement are severable. If any provision is determined to be invalid, all other provisions shall remain valid. Trustee may modify any provision determined to be invalid, illegal or unenforceable to the minimum extent necessary to remedy such provision.

(S) **Counterparts.** This Agreement may be executed in any number of counterpart signature pages, all of which together will constitute the entire, original document.

8.4 Disclaimer by Beneficiary. Any beneficiary may disclaim any property, interests in property, proceeds of property, disclaimable interest, or power of appointment (whether presently exercisable or not). A beneficiary who disclaims any property, interests in property, proceeds of property, disclaimable interest, or power of appointment (whether presently exercisable or not) shall not retain, possess, or exercise any interest in or power over the disclaimed property, either during lifetime or upon death (whether as a beneficiary or as a trustee), which interest or power is prohibited by law (such as interests or powers prohibited by IRC section 2518 (as concerns qualified disclaimers)). For example, if the disclaim property devolves to a foundation and the disclaimant is an officer, director, trustee or "control person" of the foundation, then and in that event, the disclaimed property shall be held in a separate fund by the foundation and the disclaimant shall only serve as an Administrative Director/Trustee with respect to the fund. An Administrative Director/Trustee is only authorized to take such actions as are necessary to preserve and maintain the property within the meaning of Treas. Reg. section 25.2518-2(d)(2), and, accordingly, is prohibited from participating in the exercise, or decision not to exercise, any discretion over payments, distributions, applications or accumulations of income or principal by the foundation's directors/trustees, including the selection of the ultimate charitable beneficiaries of the separate fund.

8.5 Actions by Incapacitated or Minor Beneficiaries. Except as may otherwise be provided elsewhere in this Agreement, a minor beneficiary, or a beneficiary who is legally incapacitated, or a beneficiary who is under a under a disability, may act through his or her authorized representative (to the extent such authorized representative is not prohibited from acting on behalf of the beneficiary), including (but not limited to) a natural or legal guardian, committee, conservator, agent, next friend, or attorney-in-fact under a durable power of attorney (as the case may be). If there is no such authorized representative, Trustee may designate an appropriate adult individual (who may be Trustee, a trust officer, a relative of the beneficiary, or any other person) who (to the extent not prohibited from acting on behalf of the beneficiary) may act on behalf of the beneficiary. In no event may I act on behalf of such beneficiary, regardless of my relationship to the beneficiary.

8.6 Virtual Representation. I direct that, in any proceeding relating to a trust hereunder, service upon any person under a legal disability need not be made when another person not under a disability is a party to the proceeding and has the same interest as the person under the disability. The person under the disability shall nevertheless be bound by the results of the proceeding. The same rule shall apply to non-judicial settlements, releases, exonerations and indemnities.

8.7 Arbitration. Whenever a matter is required under this Agreement to be submitted to arbitration, the following rules shall apply. The arbitration shall be held, except as may otherwise be provided herein, in accordance with the Uniform Arbitration Act (or such similar act) as adopted by the State of ___________ (or the state whose law is then governing the administration of the trust, as described in the sub-paragraph entitled, **"Governing Law"**). The rules of arbitration shall be decided by the arbitrator. The parties shall select a single arbitrator for this purpose. To be qualified to be selected as an arbitrator: (i) a person must be well versed and knowledgeable in the area of trust law, or (ii) a person with expertise in the subject matter of the dispute (e.g., a professional appraiser if the dispute involves valuation). If the parties cannot agree on an arbitrator, a party can petition the probate court having jurisdiction over the trust and request the probate court to appoint a qualified arbitrator (who need not reside in the same county as the probate court). If the place of arbitration can not be agreed upon by the parties, then the place of arbitration shall be in the metropolitan [Name of City and State] area as decided by the arbitrator. If at the time of the dispute the trust's governing law is the State of ______________, the rules of discovery as set forth in that State's rules of civil procedure shall be available in connection with the arbitration, and the law of the State of ______________law will govern the rights and obligations of the parties with respect to the matters in controversy. The award of the arbitrator shall be accompanied by a written statement of the basis for such award and may be enforced by any court having proper jurisdiction.

ARTICLE 9
SURVIVAL AND ANTI-LAPSE

9.1 Survival of Beneficiary. Except as provided in sub-paragraph (A) below, no person shall be considered to have survived another or considered to be living upon the death of another if he or she shall die within 120 hours after the death of such other.

(A) Exceptions. Where Treas. Reg. section 26.2651-1(a)(2)(iii) applies.

9.2 Negation of Anti-Lapse Statute. A gift fails if an individual beneficiary does not satisfy a condition of survival and there is no substitute beneficiary indicated in this Agreement who satisfies the conditions for taking. The provisions of an anti-lapse statute shall not apply to preserve a gift for an individual or individuals who are not identified as a substitute or substitutes in this Agreement.

ARTICLE 10
MY FAMILY

10.1 Single Person. I am a single person.

10.2 Children. My children as of the date of this Agreement are:

- «Child1» (DOB: «Child1DOB»)
- «Child2» (DOB: «Child2DOB»)

I have no other children or any deceased children with descendants surviving.

This Agreement is executed, delivered, and the trust accepted, on «DateofExecution».

WITNESSES:

______________________	______________________
«ExecutingWitness»	«SettlorFullName», Settlor
______________________	______________________
«ExecutingWitness»	«InitialTrustee», Trustee

STATE OF)

)**ss.**

COUNTY OF)

Subscribed and sworn to before me on «DateofExecution» by «SettlorFullName», and «InitialTrustee», who personally appeared before me. «SettlorFullName», and «InitialTrustee» are personally known to me (or have produced ______________________________ as identification).

____

Notary Public

______________________County, ___________

Acting in the County of ____________________

My Commission expires: ____________________

SCHEDULE A

Property Transferred to The «SettlorFullName» Irrevocable Trust, dated «DateofExecution»

With regard to any group term policies listed herein, the transfer of such policies also includes any future policies to be issued, or policies in supplementation thereof, or in succession, substitution, replacement or renewed thereof, and any increase in the amount of coverage.

(This Schedule A is included only for the convenience of Trustee and beneficiaries, and any failure to list trust assets on Schedule A will in no way alter the trust's ownership of those assets.)

DATE	ITEM	VALUE	TAX BASIS

Appendix 4

Attachments To U.S. Gift Tax Return 709 For Tax Year 2007[1]

Notice Of Allocation Of GST Tax Exemption To Trust[2]

Taxpayer, John Q. Doe, SS# 111-22-3333, expressly allocates to The John Q. Doe Irrevocable Trust, dated January 1, 2007; Large National Bank, 123 Main Street, Detroit, Michigan 48001, Trustee; (EIN 12-3456789) ("Trust"), the smallest amount of the taxpayer's unused generation-skipping transfer tax exemption necessary to produce an inclusion ratio (as defined in IRC section 2642(a)) which is equal to zero (0), based on the value of the gift as finally determined for federal gift tax purposes, as concerns the transfer/valuation date. This is a formula allocation that will change if values are changed on audit.

Accordingly, the Trust has an inclusion ratio of zero (0) for generation-skipping transfer tax purposes, after this allocation.

A gift of cash was made to the Trust on January 1, 2007. The fair market value of the cash gift to the Trust on January 1, 2007, was $13,565.

The above gift was transferred into a Trust that does not qualify for the direct skip exclusion or GST Trust exclusion for generation-skipping transfer tax purposes. Therefore, the donor is allocating generation-skipping transfer tax exemption, per above.

---

[1] These sample Notices are for illustration purposes only and should not be relied on by a taxpayer. All taxpayers should seek independent legal advice, and all tax practitioners should make an independent determination of the appropriateness of using any sample form, and modify the sample form accordingly.

[2] This is an annual notice that will have to be filed each year property is transferred (or a gift is made) to the trust.

Direct Skip GST Allocation Election Out Statement[3]

NOTICE TO ELECT OUT OF *DIRECT* SKIP GST AUTOMATIC ALLOCATION RULES OF IRC SECTION 2632(b) CONCERNING THE JOHN Q. DOE IRREVOCABLE TRUST, DATED JANUARY 1, 2007

Pursuant to Treas. Reg. §26.2632-1(b)(1)(i), Taxpayer, John Q. Doe, SS# 111-22-3333, hereby elects that the GST automatic allocation rules will not apply to any transfers to The John Q. Doe Irrevocable Trust, dated January 1, 2007; Large National Bank, 123 Main Street, Detroit, Michigan 48001, Trustee; (EIN 12-3456789) ("Trust"), made by the taxpayer in 2007 or to any additional transfers the taxpayer may make to the Trust in subsequent years. In 2007 the taxpayer transferred $100,000 cash to the Trust. As a result of this election to opt-out of the automatic GST allocation rules concerning direct skips, the Trust will have an inclusion ratio (as defined in IRC section 2642(a)) of one (1) for generation-skipping transfer tax purposes.

Election Out Of Indirect Skip GST Allocation Statement[4]

NOTICE TO ELECT OUT OF *INDIRECT* SKIP GST AUTOMATIC ALLOCATION RULES OF IRC SECTION 2632(c) CONCERNING THE JOHN Q. DOE IRREVOCABLE TRUST, DATED JANUARY 1, 2007

Pursuant to Treas. Reg. §26.2632-1(b)(2)(iii), Taxpayer, John Q. Doe, SS# 111-22-3333, hereby elects that the GST automatic allocation rules will not apply to any transfers to The John Q. Doe Irrevocable Trust, dated January 1, 2007; Large National Bank, 123 Main Street, Detroit, Michigan 48001, Trustee; (EIN 12-3456789) ("Trust"), made by the taxpayer in 2007 or to any additional transfers the taxpayer may make to the Trust in subsequent years. As a result of this election to opt-out of the automatic GST allocation rules concerning direct skips, the Trust will have an inclusion ratio (as defined in IRC section 2642(a)) of one (1) for generation-skipping transfer tax purposes.

---

[3] A separate Form 709 and a separate "*Direct Skip GST Allocation Election Out Statement*" must be filed by each spouse if the gift has been split pursuant to IRC section 2513. Treas. Reg. §26.2632-1(b)(2)(iii)(A).

[4] A separate Form 709 and a separate "*Election Out of Indirect Skip GST Allocation Statement*" must be filed by each spouse if the gift has been split pursuant to IRC section 2513. Treas. Reg. §26.2632-1(b)(2)(iii).

GST Trust Election Statement[5]

NOTICE OF TREATMENT OF THE JOHN Q. DOE IRREVOCABLE TRUST, DATED JANUARY 1, 2007, AS A GST TRUST FOR PURPOSE OF IRC SECTION 2632(c)

Pursuant to Treas. Reg. §26.2632-1(b)(3), Taxpayer, John Q. Doe, SS# 111-22-3333, hereby elects to have the GST automatic allocation rules apply to any transfers to The John Q. Doe Irrevocable Trust, dated January 1, 2007; Large National Bank, 123 Main Street, Detroit, Michigan 48001, Trustee; (EIN 12-3456789) ("Trust"), made by the taxpayer in 2007 or to any additional transfers the taxpayer may make to the Trust in subsequent years. It is the taxpayer's intention that the taxpayer's unused generation-skipping tax exemption be allocated to transfers made by the taxpayer to the Trust from January 1, 2007 onward so as to produce an inclusion ratio (as defined in IRC section 2642(a)) of zero (0) for the Trust for generation-skipping transfer tax purposes.

Notice Of Late Allocation Of GST Tax Exemption To Trust[6]

Taxpayer: John Q. Doe, SS# 111-22-3333.

Trust: The John Q. Doe Irrevocable Trust, dated January 1, 1999; Large National Bank, 123 Main Street, Detroit, Michigan 48001, Trustee; (EIN 34-5678912) ("Trust").

Year Transfer of Assets Reported: 1999.

Applicable Valuation Date (per Treas. Reg. §26.2642-2(a)(2)) for Allocating the GST Tax Exemption To the Trust: March 1, 2007.

---

[5] Although not required by the final regulations, a separate Form 709 and a separate *"GST Trust Election Statement"* should be filed by each spouse if the gift has been split pursuant to IRC section 2513. *Cf.*, Treas. Reg. §26.2632-1(b)(2)(iii).

Note: If the trust was established before January 1, 2001, and the trust is a GST trust (for which the GST automatic allocation rules are applicable), the transferor will also need to file a late allocation of GST tax exemption for all pre-January 1, 2001 transfers to the trust. *See,* section 5.23, above (concerning late allocations of GST tax exemption).

[6] *See,* section 5.23, above concerning a late allocation of GST tax exemption. *See also,* section 6.5, above, concerning special relief from the IRS to make a "retroactive" late allocation.

If a U.S. Gift Tax Return was not filed when the gift was originally made in 1999, a late return for the year of the gift (IRS Form 709 for 1999) will need to be filed, and the notice of late allocation of GST tax exemption will need to be attached to the 1999 late return.

Fair Market Value of The Trust Assets on The Applicable Valuation Date: (1) Cash held by Trust in bank account: $__________; and (2) Trust owned life insurance policy issued by First Mutual Life Insurance Company, Policy # 001110001 (*see* attached IRS Form 712): $__________. The insured is alive, is not in danger of imminent death, and is not aware of any medical problems that would unexpectedly shorten the insured's life expectancy.

Election To Value Assets On First Day of the Month: For purposes of the late allocation of GST exemption hereby made to the Trust, the taxpayer elects under the Treasury Regulations to value the assets of the Trust as of the first day of the month on which this U.S. Gift Tax Return for the calendar year 2007 is filed.

Formula Allocation of GST Tax Exemption: The taxpayer hereby allocates to the Trust the smallest amount of the taxpayer's unused generation-skipping transfer tax exemption necessary to produce an inclusion ratio (as defined in IRC section 2642(a)) for the Trust that is closest to or, if possible, equal to zero (0) for generation-skipping transfer tax purposes. This is a formula allocation that will change if values are changed on audit. Accordingly, the Trust has an inclusion ratio of zero (0) for generation-skipping transfer tax purposes, after this allocation.

/s/______________________________
John Q. Doe, taxpayer and the insured

Appendix 5

Sample Documents To Grantors, Trustees, And Beneficiaries

SAMPLE MEMORANDUM TO GRANTOR AND TRUSTEE ON OPERATION OF ILIT

To: Settlor and Initial Trustee

From: [Name of Attorney]

Date: «DateofExecution»

Re: Instructions for The «SettlorFullName» Irrevocable Trust, dated «DateofExecution» ("Trust")

U.S. TREASURY CIRCULAR 230 NOTICE

This memorandum and any opinions expressed herein are not intended or written to constitute either a "covered opinion" or a "reliance opinion" under applicable U. S. Treasury Regulations or U.S. Treasury Circular 230 governing practice before the IRS. Any opinions expressed herein are not intended or written to be used, and may not be used or relied upon by the recipient, for the purpose of avoiding penalties that may be imposed by the Internal Revenue Service.

This memorandum will explain some of the tax implications of the Trust, as well as the procedures for funding the Trust and for paying premiums on life insurance policies owned by the Trust.

It is my understanding that none of the beneficiaries of the Trust who have withdrawal rights have lapsing powers of withdrawal under other trust instruments [other than {insert name of other trusts where there are lapsing powers of withdrawal}].[1] If my understanding is incorrect and there are other trusts under which any of the beneficiaries have such powers, I would appreciate your so advising me and sending me a copy of such trust agreement. The IRS requires all lapsing powers of withdrawal to be aggregated for the calendar year in question in order to determine the maximum amount that a trust beneficiary can permit to safely lapse under the so-called "five-by-five" non-taxable lapse rule.

[Please note that the Trust is not designed to be automatically exempt from the Generation-Skipping Transfer Tax ("GST tax"). To be exempt from the GST tax, it will be necessary for you to allocate part of your GST tax exemption to the Trust via a properly prepared and filed United States Gift Tax Return each year a contribution is made to the Trust.[2] If you want the Trust to be exempt from the GST tax, you may also want to consider having your tax adviser file a one-time notice of election to have the Trust be treated as a "GST Trust" under IRC section 2632(c)(5)(A)(ii).[3] If you want to be assured that your GST tax exemption will not automatically allocated to the Trust during your lifetime, you may want to consider having your tax adviser file a one-time notice to "opt-out" of the GST tax automatic allocation rules under IRC section 2632(c)(5)(A)(i).[4]]

[**Alternative 1—For Single Life Policy**] Please also note that the Trust is ***not*** designed to hold a second-to-die life insurance policy.

[**Alternative 2—For Second-To-Die Policy**] Please also note that the Trust is designed to hold a second-to-die life insurance policy on your life and the life of your spouse. Therefore, your spouse is subject to the same limitations and restrictions that you are under the Trust.

---

[1] Note: Language contained in brackets [ ] is either alternative language or optional language, depending on the circumstances. Because this is a sample memorandum, it will need to be adapted to the client's particular situation and the terms of the ILIT.

[2] *See*, sample form of "*Notice of GST Exemption Allocation to Trust*" in Appendix 4.

[3] See, Sample form of *"GST Trust Election Statement"* in Appendix 4.

[4] *See*, Sample form of "*Election Out Statement*" in Appendix 4.

SECTION 1
YOUR IRREVOCABLE TRUST

The primary reason for assigning life insurance policies to the Trust is to keep the policy proceeds outside of your estate [and that of your spouse] for federal estate tax purposes. By doing so, the estate tax savings can be significant. However, the proceeds from any existing policy that is transferred to the Trust are still included in your gross estate (for estate tax purposes) if you die within three (3) years of the transfer.

As we have discussed, the Trust:

• Is irrevocable and cannot be changed once it has been signed.

• Is administered by the initial Trustee and the successor Trustees you have named.

• Can own life insurance policies or any other assets that the Trustee chooses to invest in.

• Gives your lifetime beneficiaries a withdrawal right in order to qualify gifts to the Trust for the federal gift tax annual exclusion.

• May need to have its own federal taxpayer identification number, and may have to file income tax returns depending upon the amount of income and the Trustee's method of reporting.

Please remember that you cannot administer the Trust after you sign it. It must be administered totally by the Trustee in accordance with the instructions in the Trust.

If you and the Trustee diligently follow the guidelines I have set forth, the Trust should accomplish its planning goals and objectives.

SECTION 2
INSTRUCTIONS

For the Trust to meet your planning goals, it is important that you and the Trustee understand the irrevocable trust basics that are explained in this section. It is critical that you and the Trustee adhere strictly to the following chronological guidelines.

Your Trust's Chronology

An irrevocable trust's chronology can be described as a progression of steps. The following steps are critical in maintaining the effectiveness of the Trust:

• You execute the Trust.

• If applicable, the Trust applies for and obtains a tax identification number for the Trust from the Internal Revenue Service, which is used as the tax ID number for the Trust's bank and investment accounts. The insurance companies will also ask for this number.

• You [(and not your spouse)] make a gift of cash to the Trust. [If you are a resident of a community property state, the gift should be drawn on an account in your name alone that contains your separate property.] If the gift is a check drawn on a joint bank account with your spouse and your spouse is a beneficiary of your Trust, I urge you to obtain a certified check, bank money order or bank cashier's check made payable to your Trustee. If possible, the gift should be an amount that is more than the anticipated insurance premium. The gift should be made at least forty-five (45) days before the life insurance premium due date (to provide sufficient time for the beneficiaries to consider whether they should exercise their withdrawal right) as follows:

> ☐ A check for $_____________ payable to «InitialTrustee» (with the notation in the memorandum section of the check "«SettlorFullName» Irrevocable Trust, dated «DateofExecution»"). (You should not pay premiums on Trust-owned policies directly to the insurer.)
>
> **Caution:** If you are ***excluding*** any Trust beneficiary from having a right of withdrawal concerning your contribution to the Trust (see, Paragraph 3.2(H) of your Trust, entitled, *"Restriction of a Withdrawal Right"*), you must provide written notification of this fact to the Trustee at the same time that you make a contribution to the Trust (e.g., you must provide the written notification when you deliver a gift check to the Trustee). See the attached sample letter in ***Exhibit 2.***
>
> ☐ The Trustee opens and funds a bank account (such as a checking, savings, or money market account) in the name of the Trust with the Trustee as the only signatory. This account should be opened in the following name: "«InitialTrustee», Trustee, or any Successor Trustee of The «SettlorFullName» Irrevocable Trust, dated «DateofExecution»."

• After you make the gift to the Trust, the Trustee immediately sends a written notice, by certified mail (return receipt requested), to all of the Trust's beneficiaries telling them of the date and amount of the gift. The Trustee also informs the beneficiaries that they have the right to immediately withdraw their appropriate share of the gift and that their right to do so will stay open for a specified period of time, as established by the terms of the Trust or notice of gift contribution, as the case may be.

• If the beneficiaries do not withdraw their share of the gift contribution, the Trustee is free to invest the gift, purchase life insurance on your life, or pay the premiums on existing life insurance policies held by the Trust. When the beneficiary does not withdraw his or her share of the gift contribution amount, the right of withdrawal "lapses" for gift tax purposes. It is very important that the nonwithdrawal be treated as a nontaxable "lapse" rather than a taxable "release." The Trust has been prepared and designed on the premise that the beneficiaries do [***not***] have rights of withdrawal over other trusts. If any beneficiary should die holding a power of withdrawal that has not lapsed, the value of the property subject to that power would be includable in his or her gross estate and may be subject to death taxes.

• The Trustee applies for the (new) life insurance as the **owner** and **beneficiary** of the policy.

• The Trustee can apply for the life insurance either before or after you make the gift to the Trust, as long as Trustee is the one who applies for it as the **owner** and **beneficiary**.

• The Trustee should not submit the application before the Trust is in existence (although you may submit a nonbinding test application before the existence of the Trust).

• After the withdrawal period expires, the Trustee pays insurance premiums from the Trust's checking or money market account.

• The Trust provides that the Trustee can loan money to or purchase assets from your estate or living trust. This is how the Trustee gets the Trust's life insurance proceeds into your estate or living trust to pay death taxes and estate administration expenses.

Funding Your Trust

To assign an existing life insurance policy to the Trust, you should first change the beneficiary of the policy to the following:

"«InitialTrustee», Trustee, or any Successor Trustee of The «SettlorFullName» Irrevocable Trust, dated «DateofExecution»."

Immediately after the beneficiary designation has been changed, you should then change the ownership of the existing policy to the following:

"«InitialTrustee», Trustee, or any Successor Trustee of The «SettlorFullName» Irrevocable Trust, dated «DateofExecution»."

The Trustee should be in possession of all Trust property, including any life insurance policies transferred to the Trust.

Please note that to avoid the application of the three-year rule described below, the Trustee should be the initial applicant, owner, and beneficiary of any new life insurance policies insuring your life.

You should not transfer an existing insurance policy to the Trust if the total premiums paid for such policy are less than the total loans taken against the policy. In such event, please contact me for further instructions.

When transferring an existing life insurance policy to the Trust, a gift is made equal to the value of the policy. If you are not terminally ill, the gift tax value of the policy is normally the policy's "interpolated terminal reserve" on the date of transfer to the Trust. You should request this figure from your insurance agent. The insurance company will provide you this information on IRS Form 712. Your tax adviser will also need a copy of Form 712 to complete your gift tax return (see below).

An Analysis Of The Trust's Chronological Components

An understanding of the Trust's chronological components is helpful.

• Your Trust is no different from any other kind of irrevocable trust, with one exception, and that is the withdrawal right given to the beneficiaries which allows them to withdraw gifts made on their account from the Trust for a limited amount of time.

• In the absence of a withdrawal right, gifts that you make to the Trust will not qualify for the annual gift tax exclusion. For a gift to qualify for the annual gift tax exclusion, it must be a gift of a present interest, which is the present right of the recipient to use and enjoy the gift, thus the need for the right of withdrawal.

• You may wish to know if you can transfer an existing policy into the Trust. The answer is a qualified "yes." The qualification has to do with a waiting period imposed by the Internal Revenue Code. Under the tax law, you cannot transfer an existing policy to an irrevocable trust and avoid federal estate tax on the proceeds without waiting for three (3) years to pass. This three-year rule is a remnant from prior law with respect to "gifts in contemplation of death." Given the three-year rule, you may wish to acquire a new policy. As previously mentioned, the Internal Revenue Code assesses a gift tax on the value of the policies transferred to the Trust, and a United States Gift Tax Return may have to be filed by you.

Keep in mind these additional important points:

• Your Trust is [***not***] a grantor trust.

• Your Trust needs to have its own taxpayer identification number if it is not a grantor trust.

• Your Trust may need to obtain a taxpayer identification number, even if it is a grantor trust.

• Your Trust needs to be closely monitored to make sure that proper contributions are made, that proper withdrawal letters are sent out, and that all proper procedures are followed.

• The Trustee must set up investment accounts and keep accurate books and records on behalf of the Trust.

SECTION 3
WITHDRAWAL RIGHT NOTIFICATIONS

Existing law and the terms of the Trust require the Trustee to make a reasonable effort to notify the Trust's lifetime beneficiaries of any gifts that are made to the Trust and their right to withdraw their appropriate share of the gift amount, as described above.

Attached as ***Exhibit 3*** to this memorandum is a sample letter that we suggest the Trustee use to properly notify the Trust's lifetime beneficiaries of those gifts. Two copies of this letter should be hand delivered or sent via ***certified mail, return receipt.*** One copy of the letter should be signed (acknowledged) by the beneficiary and returned to the Trustee without delay. If the beneficiary does not exercise the withdrawal right, then the gift will lapse as provided in the Trust. ***Please note that the very last sentence at the very end of the sample letter wherein the beneficiary waives the right to future notices is only intended as a "fail-safe" in case written notice is inadvertently not given by the Trustee.***

Once all withdrawal right notification letters have been returned to the Trustee, or have lapsed, any insurance premiums that are due may be paid by the Trustee from the funds held in the name of the Trust.

If a beneficiary is a minor, the legal guardian or other legal representative of the minor beneficiary may sign on the minor's behalf. However, you (and any other insured under the Trust) may not act in that capacity.

Caution: If you are ***excluding*** any Trust beneficiary from having a right of withdrawal concerning your contribution to the Trust (see, Paragraph 3.2(H) of your Trust, entitled, *"Restriction of a Withdrawal Right"*), you must provide written notification of this fact to the Trustee at the same time that you make a contribution to the Trust (e.g., you must provide the written notification when you deliver a gift check to the Trustee). See the attached sample letter in ***Exhibit 2.***

I encourage you to call me if you have any questions with regard to the notification process.

SECTION 4
CORRESPONDENCE

All correspondence pertaining to the Trust should be saved by you and the Trustee. This correspondence should include:

• Copies of all ***Withdrawal Right Notification Letters*** that are sent to beneficiaries, and copies of these letters, if any, after they have been signed by the Trust beneficiaries. The signed certified mail return receipts should also be attached to these letters. These signed (acknowledged) letters may be needed in the event of a gift tax audit, or in the event of an estate tax audit at the time of your death.

• Copies of any correspondence with the IRS, including Form SS-4 that the Trustee uses to file for the Trust's taxpayer identification number (if applicable).

• Copies of any other correspondence from my office, the Trustee, or any other source that pertains to the administration of the Trust.

The Trustee has to be very meticulous in maintaining the records of the Trust; and whenever necessary, should seek our advice and counsel, that of your tax adviser, life insurance professional, and financial planner.

I strongly recommend that the Trustee send copies of all correspondence that is mentioned in this section to your tax adviser.

SECTION 5
GIFT TAX RETURNS, GIFT SPLITTING, AND GENERATION-SKIPPING TRANSFER TAX MATTERS

If your combined annual gifts to the Trust (or to a beneficiary of the Trust) exceed the annual gift tax exclusion amount, or if you do not grant a right of withdrawal to a Trust beneficiary, your tax adviser will have to file a gift tax return (Form 709) with the IRS to report these gifts. However, generally no gift tax will have to be paid until these gifts exceed the amount of the gift tax "exemption" amount that is available to you.

Irrespective of the amount of your annual gifts to the Trust, it may be necessary for you to file an annual U.S. Gift Tax Return and allocate part of your GST tax exemption to the gifts. By allocating your GST tax exemption on a timely filed U.S. Gift Tax Return (or by filing a one time election to treat the Trust as a "GST Trust," whereby your GST tax exemption is automatically allocated to each year's contributions (if you are gift splitting with your spouse, each of you will have to file this election)), you will be ensuring that distributions from the Trust will not be subject to the confiscatory GST tax (concerning distributions to grandchildren or other more remote descendants). The GST tax (and the allocation of your GST tax exemption) is a very complicated area, and should be handled by my office.

[It is my understanding that you do ***not*** intend to allocate your GST tax exemption to the Trust and the Trust has been drafted based on that understanding. Nevertheless, please let me know if there are any deaths in the family so that I may determine if there is a GST tax issue as a result of the death. In any event, the IRS may treat the Trust as being a "GST Trust" and automatically allocate your GST tax exemption. If you want to avoid an automatic allocation of your GST tax exemption, you will need to file a one time election to opt out of the IRS's automatic GST tax allocation rules (if you are gift splitting with your spouse, each of you will have to file this election).]

SECTION 6
ANNUAL TRUST ACCOUNTINGS

Both [state] law and the terms of the Trust require the Trustee to prepare an annual accounting of the affairs of the Trust, under certain conditions. A copy of the accounting must be sent to the "current" Trust beneficiaries. Please see the Trust's paragraph entitled,

"Accountings and Information to Beneficiaries," (in Article 7), which sets forth the particulars concerning the content and format of the annual accounting. I suggest that an accountant experienced in trust accounting issues and trust accounting law assist the Trustee in the preparation of the Trust's annual accounting, if it is required.

SECTION 7
INCOME TAX

If the only asset owned by the Trust is one or more life insurance policies, then the Trust will not have any reportable income. In such case, your tax adviser could file an income return (Form 1041) for the Trust showing zero income, but it is not recommended. If the Trust does have income, then pursuant to Internal Revenue Code section 677(a)(3), such income is taxable to you to the extent it is used to pay the life insurance premiums. In such case, the Trustee may be required to file a federal (IRS Form 1041) and state informational income tax return for the Trust if it has taxable income. Please see the attached ***Exhibit 1*** for additional information and the reporting-filing options that are available to the Trustee.

If you or your tax adviser should have any questions regarding the above, please do not hesitate to contact me.

EXHIBIT 1 TO SAMPLE MEMORANDUM
Reporting-Filing Options Available to the Trustee

IRS regulations pertaining to the filing requirements of trustees of a "grantor" trust, such as your irrevocable trust, are contained in Treas. Reg. §1.671-4. These regulations set forth certain optional filing methods, which expand the exceptions to the requirement of filing IRS Form 1041.

Treas. Reg. §1.671-4 provides alternative optional reporting methods that may be adopted by the trustee. In general, the alternative methods cannot be used by: (i) a common trust fund as defined in IRC section 584(a); (ii) a trust that has its situs or any of its assets located outside the United States; (iii) a trust that is a qualified subchapter S trust as defined in IRC section 1361(d)(3) ("QSST"); (iv) a trust all of which is treated as owned by one grantor or one other person whose taxable year is a fiscal year; (v) a trust all of which is treated as owned by one grantor or one other person who is not a United States person; (vi) a trust all of which is treated as owned by two or more grantors or other persons, one of whom is not a United States person; or (vii) a trust all of which is treated as owned by one grantor or one other person, if the grantor or other person is an exempt recipient for information reporting purposes. However, if at least one grantor does not fall in the categories above, the alternative methods may be used for the other grantor who is an exempt recipient or a fiscal year taxpayer. A "grantor" is the person(s) who is treated as the "owner" for income tax purposes under the grantor trust rules set forth in IRC sections 671-679.

If the trustee of a grantor trust (where a portion of the trust (or the entire trust) is deemed to be owned by one or more grantors) does not use one of the applicable alternative methods discussed below, the trustee must obtain a taxpayer identification number for the trust ("TIN"), and furnish the trust's name, the trust's TIN, and the trust's address to all payors. Each year a payor will deliver a 1099 to the trustee, showing the trust as the payee. Those items of trust income, deductions and credit that are deemed to be owned entirely (or partially) by one or more grantors are disclosed on a separate statement attached to IRS form 1041 (and are not reported on IRS form 1041). A copy of the separate statement must be given to each grantor showing the trust's income, deductions and credits that are deemed to be owned by that grantor, who must then report the income, deductions and credits on the grantor's personal income tax return (IRS form 1040). *See*, Treas. Reg. §1.671-4(a).

If The Trust Is A Grantor Trust In Its Entirety And There Is Only One Grantor

If the trust is considered to be a grantor trust in its entirety with respect to one person only (**note:** a husband and wife who file a joint income tax return are treated as one person per Treas. Reg. §1.671-4(b)(8)), the trustee has three officially sanctioned alternative reporting methods, which are discussed in Alternatives 1-3, below. The trustee may change reporting methods by following the notice requirements set forth in Treas. Reg. §1.671-4(9).

Alternative 1. Under the first alternative (the Grantor TIN alternative), the trustee must obtain an IRS Form W-9 (or an acceptable substitute) from the grantor, and then furnish the grantor's name, the grantor's taxpayer identification number ("TIN") (e.g., the grantor's social security number per Treas. Reg. §301.6109-1(a)(1)(ii)), and the trust's address to all payors during the year. Because the W-9 shows the grantor's address (and not the trust's address), the trustee should not furnish the W-9 to a payor. A "payor" is any person who is required to make any type of information return (including Form 1099 or Schedule K-1) with respect to the trust for the taxable year. Each year a payor will deliver a 1099 to the trustee, and the trustee will then deliver the 1099 to the grantor who will attach the 1099 to the grantor's income tax return and report the income. If the grantor is not a trustee or co-trustee (which would be the case with respect to your Trust), the trustee must also furnish an annual statement to the grantor: (i) showing the items of income, deduction, and credit of the trust for the taxable year; (ii) showing the identification of the payor of each item of income; (iii) showing such other information needed by the grantor to prepare his or her income tax return; and (iv) informing the grantor that he or she is treated as the owner of the trust's income, deductions and credits for the taxable years and that the grantor must include such information in his or her income tax return for that year. *See,* Treas. Reg. §§1.671-4(b)(1), 1.671-4(b)(2)(i)(A) and 1.671-4(b)(2)(ii). Under the Grantor TIN alternative, the trustee is not required to file any income tax return or other information with the IRS per Treas. Reg. §1.671-4(b)(2)(ii)(B).

When your Trust is no longer a "grantor trust", the trustee will need to obtain a TIN for the trust per Treas. Reg. §§1.671-4(h) and 301.6109-1(a)(3).

Note: If the grantor's W-9 indicates that the grantor is subject to backup withholding, the trustee must notify all payors of the grantor's backup withholding requirement. *See,* Treas. Reg. §1.671-4(e).

[While you are living and the trust qualifies as a "grantor trust" under the Internal Revenue Code, I recommend that the trustee use the Grantor TIN alternative method of reporting for your Trust.]

Alternative 2. Under the second alternative (the Trust TIN alternative), the trustee provides the trust's name, the trust's taxpayer identification number ("TIN") (*see,* Treas. Reg. §301.6109-1(a)(1)(ii)), and the trust's address to all payors. Each year a payor will deliver a 1099 to the trustee, showing the trust as the payee. The trustee must categorize and aggregate all the 1099 income and then issue its own 1099 showing the trust as the payor and the grantor as the payee of the 1099 income. This extra step will require a commitment of time and expense that most grantors prefer to avoid, if possible. If the grantor is not a trustee or co-trustee (which would be the case with respect to your Trust), the trustee must also furnish an annual statement to the grantor: (i) showing the items of income, deduction, and credit of the trust for the taxable year; (ii) showing the identification of the payor of each item of income; (iii) showing such other information needed by the grantor to prepare his or her income tax return; and (iv) informing the grantor that he or she is treated as the owner of the trust's income, deductions and credits for the taxable years and that the grantor must include such information in his or her income tax return for that year. *See*, Treas. Reg. §§1.671-4(b)(2)(i)(B) and 1.671-4(b)(iii). Under the Trust TIN alternative, the trustee is not required to file any income tax return or other information with the IRS (other than the 1099 that it issues to the grantor).

Alternative 3. Under the third alternative (the Notice alternative), the trustee provides the trust's name, the trust's taxpayer identification number ("TIN") and the trust's address to all payors. Each year a payor will deliver a 1099 to the trustee, showing the trust as the payee. Each year the trustee files an IRS form 1041 on behalf of the trust but does not report the trust's income, credits or deductions on the trust's IRS Form 1041. *See*, Treas. Reg. §1.671-4(a) and the instructions to IRS Form 1041. Instead, the trust's income, credits and deductions are reported on the grantor's personal income tax return (IRS Form 1040). Each year the trustee attaches a statement to the trust's IRS Form 1041, similar to the following:

"The trust in question is a grantor trust in its entirety under the grantor trust rules of sections 671-679 of the Internal Revenue Code. Therefore, all of the trust's income, capital gains, deductions and credits for the calendar year in question are reportable by the grantor of the trust, «SettlorFullName», *[Settlor's Social Security Number], and will be shown on that individual's income tax return (IRS Form 1040), to the extent that such individual is required to file an income tax return for the year in question."*

This third alternative method is merely a variation of the Trust TIN alternative, which is discussed in Alternative 2, above. This third alternative requires the trust to have its own TIN and requires the trustee to file an "informational" IRS Form 1041 each year on behalf of the trust. Treasury Regulations permit a trustee to change to the Grantor TIN alternative, which is discussed in Alternative 1, above. This is accomplished by filing a final IRS Form 1041 for the trust for the tax year immediately preceding the year that the trustee wishes to begin using the IRS Form 1099 alternative. On the front of the final IRS Form 1041, the trustee must write "Pursuant to Treasury Regulation §1.671-4(g), this is the final Form 1041 for this grantor trust." *See*, Treas. Reg. §1.6714(g)(1).

If The Trust Is A Grantor Trust In Its Entirety And There Are Multiple Grantors

If the trust is considered to be a grantor trust in its entirety with respect to two or more persons (other than a husband and wife, who, as previously mentioned, are treated as one person under Treasury Regulations if they file a joint income tax return), the trustee has one alternative reporting method. Under this alternative reporting method, the trustee must provide the trust's name, the trust's TIN (*See*, Treas. Reg. §301.6109-1(a)(1)(ii)), and the trust's address to all payors. Each year a payor will deliver a 1099 to the trustee, showing the trustee as the payee. The trustee must categorize, aggregate and allocate all the 1099 income between the multiple grantors and then issue its own 1099 to each grantor showing the trust as the payor and the grantors as the payees of the 1099 income. The trustee must also furnish an annual statement to each grantor: (i) showing the items of income, deduction, and credit of the trust for the taxable year; (ii) showing the identification of the payor of each item of income; (iii) showing such other information needed by the grantor to prepare his or her income tax return; and (iv) informing the grantor that he or she is treated as the owner of the trust's income, deductions and credits for the taxable years and that the grantor must include such information in his or her income tax return for that year. *See*, Treas. Reg. §1.671-4(b)(3). The trustee is not required to file any income tax return or other information with the IRS (other than the 1099s that it issues to each grantor). Treas. Reg. §1.671-4(b)(3)(iii).

If The Trust Is Not A Grantor Trust In Its Entirety

If the trust is not a grantor trust in its ***entirety*** with respect to one or more grantors, the trustee must obtain a taxpayer identification number for the trust ("TIN"), and furnish the trust's name, the trust's TIN, and the trust's address to all payors. Each year a payor will deliver a 1099 to the trustee, showing the trust as the payee. The trustee must then report the trust's income, deductions and credits on IRS form

1041. The trustee may also be required to issue IRS form K-1 to the trust beneficiaries (concerning trust distributions that occurred for the tax year in question). *See*, Treas. Reg. §1.641(a)-1.

If a ***portion*** of the trust is a grantor trust with respect to one or more grantors, those items considered owned by the grantor(s) are not reported by the trustee on IRS form 1041, and are instead disclosed on a separate statement attached to IRS form 1041. A copy of the separate statement must be given to each grantor showing the trust's income, deductions and credits that are deemed to be owned by that grantor. All items of trust income, deductions and credits that are not deemed to be owned by a grantor are reported by the trustee on IRS form 1041. *See*, Treas. Reg. §1.671-4(a).

EXHIBIT 2 TO SAMPLE MEMORANDUM

Sample Letter To Trustee Of Exclusion Of Trust Beneficiary From Having A Withdrawal Right

«SettlorFullName»

[Settlor Address]

Date:______________________________

«InitialTrustee»

«InitialTrtAddr»

Re: The «SettlorFullName» Irrevocable Trust, dated «DateofExecution» ("Trust")

Dear Trustee:

Enclosed please find the following, which are gifts to the Trust:

1) Gift check(s) totaling: $______________________________.

Pursuant to Paragraph 3.2(H) of the Trust, entitled, *"Restriction of a Withdrawal Right,"* I hereby **exclude** the below described Trust beneficiary/beneficiaries from having a right to withdraw the gift contribution, and such person(s) shall not be notified of the gift contribution to the Trust.

The following beneficiary/beneficiaries are excluded from having a right of withdrawal:

> *[Insert name of trust beneficiary (or describe class of trust beneficiaries (such as "my grandchildren and great grandchildren")) to be excluded from having a right of withdrawal].*

Unless I inform you otherwise in a subsequent writing signed and dated by me (or by a duly authorized agent under a power of attorney), withdrawal rights as to any future gifts by me to the Trust shall be exclude the above beneficiary/beneficiaries.

Very truly yours,

«SettlorFullName»

EXHIBIT 3 TO SAMPLE MEMORANDUM

Sample *Crummey* Withdrawal Right Notice To ILIT Beneficiaries

«InitialTrustee»

«InitialTrtAddr»

[phone and fax]

Date ______________________________

Certified Mail, Return Receipt Requested

To: __________________________________

[Name of Beneficiary]

[Beneficiary Address]

Re: Notice of Withdrawal Rights Concerning The «SettlorFullName» Irrevocable Trust, dated «DateofExecution» ("Trust")

Dear __________________________________:

[Name of Beneficiary]

Enclosed is a copy of this letter. The original is for your records, the copy is to be returned to me as an acknowledgment of your receipt of this original letter.

You are a beneficiary of the Trust and have been granted certain beneficial rights concerning contributions made to the Trust.

You are encouraged to consult the terms of the Trust as to your rights under the Trust, including your rights of withdrawal. This letter is merely a summary of certain rights you possess or have been granted. If there is an inconsistency between this letter and the terms of the Trust, the terms of the Trust control, including the amount(s) you have been granted a right to withdraw.

The Trust is designed to hold certain life insurance policies on the life of «SettlorFullName» [and Settlor's spouse], and after the death of «SettlorFullName» [and Settlor's spouse], to hold the proceeds of those policies. It is anticipated that during the course of each calendar year «SettlorFullName» [and/or Settlor's spouse] will make gifts to the Trust, which if not withdrawn by you (or the other beneficiaries) may be used to pay the premiums on those life insurance policies.

Please be advised that «SettlorFullName» [and/or Settlor's spouse] recently made a contribution to the Trust on [date contribution received by Trustee].

[***Begin Alternative 1—five-by-five*** **Crummey** ***Withdrawal Right to All Beneficiaries***] Generally, under the terms of the Trust, the contributions are withdrawable on a prorata basis by the non-excluded beneficiaries. However, in no event may you withdraw more than [the greater of] five thousand ($5,000) dollars worth of Trust property [or 5 percent of the value of the Trust] per calendar year, subject to the Internal Revenue Code's limitation on the amount that can be given to you as an annual exclusion gift (i.e., gift-tax free) by the donor. Each Trust beneficiary's right of withdrawal is for a limited duration, and if not exercised, generally expires (lapses) upon the earlier of (i) the day before his or her death; (ii) December 31st; (iii) thirty (30) days from the date of the contribution to the Trust. If a beneficiary fails to exercise his or her withdrawal right and it expires (lapses), the beneficiary cannot exercise it at a later date. [***End of Alternative 1***]

[***Begin Alternative 2—Group Term Insurance with five-by-five*** **Crummey** ***Withdrawal Rights to All Beneficiaries***] Generally, under the terms of the Trust, the contributions are withdrawable on a prorata basis by the non-excluded beneficiaries. Under the terms of the Trust you have the immediate right to withdraw the amount of the contribution, and the right to withdraw from the Trust property (each time a premium is paid by the employer of «SettlorFullName»), the federal gift tax value of the premium contributions made by that employer as concerns the group term insurance coverage provided by that employer. The employer pays the group term insurance premium on a monthly basis. The amount of the monthly premiums subject to withdrawal each month is anticipated to be $________________. However, in no event may you withdraw from the Trust (including the value of the group term policy premium contributions) more than five thousand ($5,000) dollars [or 5 percent of the value of the Trust] per calendar year, subject to the Internal Revenue Code's limitation on the amount that can be given to you as an annual exclusion gift (i.e., gift-tax free) by the donor. Each Trust beneficiary's right of withdrawal is for a limited duration, and if not exercised, generally expires (lapses) upon the earlier of (i) the day prior to their death, (ii) December 31st, (iii) thirty (30) days from the date of the contribution to the Trust. If a beneficiary fails to exercise his or her withdrawal right and it expires (lapses), the beneficiary cannot exercise it at a later date. [***End of Alternative 2***]

[***Begin Alternative 3—Tiered five-by-five Withdrawal Right to Spouse with Hanging* Crummey *Withdrawal Rights to All Other Beneficiaries***] Generally, under the terms of the Trust, [Settlor's spouse] has the right to withdraw the greater of $5,000 worth of Trust property or 5 percent of the Trust property (as concerns the contributions) each calendar year, and the balance of the contributions are withdrawable on a pro rata basis by the nonexcluded beneficiaries subject to the Internal Revenue Code's limitation on the amount that can be given to the beneficiaries as an annual exclusion gift (i.e., gift-tax free) by the donor. Each Trust beneficiary's right of withdrawal is for a limited duration, and if not exercised, generally expires upon the earlier of (i) the day before their death; (ii) December 31st; (iii) thirty (30) days from the date of the contribution to the Trust, except as provided in Paragraph 3.2(D) of the Trust, entitled, "Structured Lapse of Withdrawal Right," which provides that in certain circumstances part or all of the withdrawal right will automatically continue or "hang," but will then terminate in future years. If a beneficiary fails to exercise his or her withdrawal right and it expires, the beneficiary cannot exercise it at a later date. [***End of Alternative 3***]

[***Begin Alternative 4—Hanging* Crummey *Withdrawal Rights to All Beneficiaries***] Generally, under the terms of the Trust, the contributions are withdrawable on a pro rata basis by the nonexcluded beneficiaries subject to the Internal Revenue Code's limitation on the amount that can be given to the beneficiaries as an annual exclusion gift (i.e., gift-tax free) by the donor. Each Trust beneficiary's right of withdrawal is for a limited duration, and if not exercised, generally expires upon the earlier of (i) the day before his or her death; (ii) December 31st; (iii) thirty (30) days from the date of the contribution to the Trust, except as provided in Paragraph 3.2(D) of the Trust, entitled, "Structured Lapse of Withdrawal Right," which provides that in certain circumstances part or all of the withdrawal right will automatically continue or "hang," but will then terminate (lapse) in future years. If a beneficiary fails to exercise his or her withdrawal right and it expires, the beneficiary cannot exercise it at a later date. [***End of Alternative 4***]

Subject to the foregoing (which is a brief summary of the withdrawal rights set forth in the Trust), the dollar value of your right of withdrawal with respect to the recent contribution is *estimated* to be approximately: $_____________________. If you desire to know the *actual* amount of your withdrawal right, please contact me, and I will calculate the amount.

If you desire to exercise your right of withdrawal, please inform me immediately, in writing.

You may call me at any time concerning the status of any contributions and the amount that is subject to withdrawal by you.

The IRS requests that you (or if you are a minor or a person under a legal disability, your guardian or legal representative) acknowledge your receipt of this letter, therefore I would appreciate your signing, dating, and returning to me immediately a copy of this letter for my records. You may fax your response to me.

If you have any questions, please do not hesitate to contact me.

Sincerely,

____

«InitialTrustee» Trustee of the Trust

Acknowledgment of Receipt of Withdrawal Notice

I hereby acknowledge receipt of notification of my right of withdrawal under the Trust and the contribution(s) made to the Trust. Further, I understand that additional contributions will be made to the Trust in future years, and I may be given a right of withdrawal with respect to such contributions. Unless I notify you to the contrary, you do not need to notify me regarding future contributions to the Trust when I am given a right of withdrawal.

Date:_________________________

____

[Signature of beneficiary or
his/her guardian/legal representative
(or parent) if beneficiary is a minor
or under a legal disability]

Table Of Cases

(References are to sections)

A

B

Cristofani, Maria, Estate of v. Commissioner, 97 T.C. 74 (1991), *acq. in result only*, 1996-2 C.B. 1, 10.2, 10.2 n5, 10.5

Crummey v. Commissioner, 397 F.2d 82 (9th Cir. 1968), 3.5, 3.5 n14, 15.3, 15.3(b), 15.4, 15.4(k), 15.5(f)

D

Deal, Minnie E. v. Commissioner, 29 T.C. 730 (1958), 14.12

Detroit Bank and Trust Co. v. United States, 467 F.2d 964 (6th Cir. 1972), *cert. denied*, 410 U.S. 929 (1973), 1.4(a) n10

DeWitt, Helen Ward, Estate of, T.C. Memo 1994-552 (1994), 4.1

Dillingham, Elizabeth C., Estate of v. Commissioner, 903 F.2d 760 (10th Cir. 1990), 15.6(a)

Du Charme's Estate v. Commissioner, 164 F.2d 959 (6th Cir. 1947), 4.3(b) n28, 15.9(f) n30

Duncan, In Re Estate of, 232 A.2d 717 (Pa. 1967), 15.7(b)

Duncan, John A. v. United States, 368 F.2d 98 (5th Cir. 1996), 3.8

E

Empire Life Ins. Co. of Am. v. Moody, 584 S.W.2d 855 (Tex. 1979), 12.9(d) n12

Evans, Gladys Cheesman v. Commissioner, 30 T.C. 798 (1958), 15.7(d)

F

Falk, Sands G. v. Commissioner, T.C. Memo 1965-22 (1965), 3.10

First National Bank of Oregon v. United States, 488 F.2d 575 (9th Cir. 1973), 1.4(a) n10, 10.7

Fish, Clarence Blagen v. United States, 432 F.2d 1278 (9th Cir. 1970), 15.5(f)

Fondren v. Commissioner, 324 U.S. 18 (1945), 3.4 n9

Frew, Walter E., Estate of v. Commissioner, 8 T.C. 1240 (1947), *acq.* 1947-2 C.B., 4.2(f), 4.3(d)

Friedberg, Sidney M., Estate of v. Commissioner, T.C. Memo 1992-310, 4.1 n6

Friedman, Estate of, 94 Cal. App.3d 667, 156 Cal. Rptr. 597 (1979), 8.1(c)

Fruehauf, Harry R., Estate of v. Commissioner, 427 F.2d 80 (6th Cir. 1970), 4.11

Fuchs, Bert L., Estate of v. Commissioner, 47 T.C. 199 (1966), *acq.*, 1967-1 C.B. 2, 4.10(b), 4.10(b) n36

G

H

I

J

K

L

M

N

O

P

R

S

T

U

V

W

Table Of Statutes, Rules, And Regulations

(References are to sections)

S

T

U

V

W

Index Of Subjects

(*References are to sections*)

E

J

O

P

T

U

V

W